Personal Financial Planning

sixth edition

Personal Financial Planning

sixth edition

Lawrence J. Gitman
San Diego State University

Michael D. Joehnk
Arizona State University

End-of-Chapter Feature, *"Getting a Handle on Your Financial Future,"*
contributed by Robert W. McLeod, CFP, CFA, *University of Alabama*
and Saliba, Reinhart, McLeod & Company

Williams Integrated Case contributed by Vickie Hampton, *University of Texas, Austin*

THE DRYDEN PRESS
HARCOURT BRACE COLLEGE PUBLISHERS

Fort Worth Philadelphia San Diego New York Orlando Austin San Antonio
Toronto Montreal London Sydney Tokyo

Editor in Chief	*Robert A. Pawlik*
Acquisitions Editor	*Michael Roche*
Developmental Editor	*Millicent Treloar*
Project Editor	*Jennifer Johnson*
Production Manager	*Alison Howell*
Book Designer	*Nick Welch*
Permissions Editors	*Van Strength*
	and Mark Brelsford

Address for Editorial Correspondence
The Dryden Press, 301 Commerce Street, Suite 3700, Fort Worth, TX 76102

Address for Orders
The Dryden Press, 6277 Sea Harbor Drive, Orlando, FL 32887
1-800-782-4479, or 1-800-433-0001 (in Florida)

Printed in the United States of America

Library of Congress Catalog Number: 92-081936

ISBN: 0-03-075481-X

4 5 6 7 8 9 0 1 2   0 6 9   9 8 7 6 5 4 3

THE DRYDEN PRESS
HARCOURT BRACE COLLEGE PUBLISHERS

THE DRYDEN PRESS SERIES IN FINANCE

THE HBJ COLLEGE OUTLINE SERIES

Lawrence J. Gitman is a professor of finance at San Diego State University. He received his bachelor's degree from Purdue University, his M.B.A. from the University of Dayton, and his Ph.D. from the University of Cincinnati. Professor Gitman is a prolific textbook author and has over thirty-five articles appearing in *Financial Management*, the *Financial Review*, the *Journal of Financial Planning*, the *Journal of Risk and Insurance*, the *Journal of Financial Research, Financial Practice and Education*, the *Journal of Financial Education*, and other publications. His major textbooks include *Principles of Managerial Finance*, Sixth Edition, *Basic Managerial Finance*, Third Edition, *The World of Business*, which is coauthored with Carl McDaniel, and *Fundamentals of Investing*, Fifth Edition, which is coauthored with Michael D. Joehnk. Gitman and Joehnk also wrote *Investment Fundamentals: A Guide to Becoming a Knowledgeable Investor*, which was selected as one of 1988's ten best personal finance books by *Money* magazine.

An active member of numerous professional organizations, Professor Gitman is past president of the Academy of Financial Services, the Midwest Finance Association, and the FMA National Honor Society. In addition, he is a Certified Financial Planner (CFP). Gitman also serves as a member of the Board of Directors, F & C International Corporation (NASDAQ–FCIN), Cincinnati, Ohio. He lives with his wife and two children in La Jolla, California, where he is an avid bicyclist.

Michael D. Joehnk is a professor of finance at Arizona State University. He received his bachelor's and Ph.D. degrees from the University of Arizona and his M.B.A. from Arizona State University. A Chartered Financial Analyst (CFA), he has served as a member of the Candidate Curriculum Committee and the Council of Examiners of the Institute of Chartered Financial Analysts. He has also served as a Director of the Phoenix Society of Financial Analysts, a vice-president of the Financial Management Association, and secretary-treasurer of the Western Finance Association.

Professor Joehnk is active in research and is the author (or coauthor) of some 50 articles, five books, and numerous monographs. His articles have appeared in *Financial Management*, the *Journal of Finance*, the *Journal of Bank Research*, the *Journal of Portfolio Management*, the *Journal of Consumer Affairs*, the *Journal of Financial and Quantitative Analysis*, the *AAII Journal*, the *Journal of Financial Research*, the *Bell Journal of Economics*, the *Daily Bond Buyer, Financial Planner*, and other publications. In addition to coauthoring several books with Lawrence J. Gitman, Professor Joehnk is the author of a highly successful paperback trade book, *Investing for Safety's Sake*; he was the editor of *Institutional Asset Allocation*, which was sponsored by the Institute of Chartered Financial Analysts and is published by Dow Jones-Irwin. He also is a contributor to the *Handbook for Fixed Income Securities*. In addition, he has held a variety of editorial positions and is currently serving as Executive Co-Editor of the *Journal of Financial Research*. He and his wife live in Scottsdale, Arizona, where they enjoy collecting Southwestern art.

PREFACE

The financial services revolution continues to usher in exciting changes in the institutions, instruments, and techniques of personal financial planning. The widespread use of personal computers, along with tax and regulatory reforms, major changes in financial institutions, new methods of borrowing, expanded insurance products, and new investment vehicles have dramatically changed the field of personal finance. It has evolved into a well-structured, fully integrated discipline that we now call personal financial planning.

The sixth edition of this book reflects feedback from past users as well as nonusers, practicing financial planners, students, and our own research. It provides helpful new approaches, expanded coverage in selected areas, and special pedagogical features while retaining the basic organizational structure, topical coverage, superior readability and useful instructional aids that marked the success of the first five editions. As with the preceding edition, this one continues to emphasize comprehensive personal financial planning. The most notable addition in this regard has been the introduction of end-of-chapter financial advisory sections, captioned "Getting a Handle on Your Financial Future." These discussions include checklists and provide specific suggestions for use by students in applying the material presented in the chapter to their personal financial circumstances.

MAJOR CHANGES IN THE SIXTH EDITION

The sixth edition has been thoroughly updated to reflect the cutting edge of contemporary personal financial planning. The most notable changes will be described first as general changes and then as specific chapter-by-chapter changes.

GENERAL CHANGES

- A greater emphasis is given throughout the text to *real-life* financial planning and decision making.

- New to the end of each chapter is "Getting a Handle on Your Financial Future." These sections, prepared by a practicing financial planner, provide advice and checklists that give students — both those just starting out and those who are "thirtysomething" — help in immediately applying the concepts presented in the chapter.

- Both new and expanded discussions of the interpersonal and emotional issues involved in each stage of the financial planning process are included in order to strengthen the behavioral dimension of the text.

- By taking an action-oriented perspective, the text continues to emphasize and illustrate personal financial decision-making *procedures*. This emphasis continues to be enhanced by the inclusion of the updated and revised *Mark and Ana Williams continuous case*, which provides personal and financial information about a real-life family in order to allow students to develop a specific comprehensive financial plan.

- To facilitate the decision-making process, the book's *worksheets* have been greatly expanded as well as refined, and are now produced in a standardized format. Each provides a step-by-step framework for making a particular financial decision.

- The *computer-based problem-solver disk*, described inside the back cover of this book, has been completely rewritten and refined by Professor James B. Pettijohn, a recognized expert in the development of financial software. *FP/PC: Financial Planning on the Personal Computer* is a fully interactive teaching device that affords students a practical look at the role of the computer in the personal financial planning process.

SPECIFIC CHAPTER-BY-CHAPTER CHANGES

- A discussion of interpersonal and emotional dimensions of the personal financial planning process was added to Chapter 1. The discussion of the economy was expanded to include monetary and fiscal policy, gross domestic product (GDP), and the consumer price index (CPI). Career coverage was expanded to give attention to gender and race, making career decisions, and career strategies for the 1990s. In addition, the revised *Mark and Ana Williams continuous case* is introduced at this point, along with relevant personal and financial data.

- In Chapter 2, the format of the balance sheet now lists assets in order of relative liquidity and classifies liabilities as current or long-term. Recommended procedures for preparing balance sheets and income statements have also been added.

- The discussion of financial goals in Chapter 3 includes a new section on the special planning concerns of managing two incomes and adapting to changes in marital status. Also included is a major discussion and demonstration of time value of money concepts — both future value and present value for both lump sums and annuities.

- Chapter 4 contains a complete up-to-date discussion of recent interpretations and technical refinements in the tax law. In addition, coverage of filing status has been expanded and relocated and the preparation of Form 1040EZ is discussed and demonstrated.

- The discussion of the new financial marketplace in Chapter 5 now includes a section on the banking industry crisis — both the S&L crisis and the problems in commercial banking. In addition, the discussion of checking accounts now describes ways to arrange overdraft protection.

- Ways to cover the down payment and closing costs when the buyers' savings are inadequate are now covered in Chapter 6, along with the procedure for estimating the size of mortgage one can afford. In addition, behavioral factors to consider when making either rent-or-buy or homebuying decisions are now discussed. Also included are discussions of using a mortgage broker, pre-qualifying for a mortgage loan, choosing an adjustable-rate mortgage index, monitoring mortgage payments, and the motives and analytical procedures (including a new worksheet) for deciding whether to refinance a mortgage. The expanded discussion of buying an automobile now includes detailed purchase consideration information, more on price negotiation, and specifics on closing the deal.

- Chapter 7 continues to emphasize the positive aspects of what it takes to build a strong credit history; in addition, the material on credit bureaus, credit bureau reports, and bankruptcy has been greatly expanded, and coverage of *secured credit cards* and *credit card fraud* has been added. Also new to this chapter is a discussion of how to find the credit card that is right for you.

- Chapter 8 contains a whole new section on *student loans* — the various types of federally-sponsored educational loan programs (including Stafford and Perkins loans) are fully discussed in terms of student qualifications, loan limits, application procedures, and repayment terms. Also new to this chapter is a box on home equity installment loans. In addition, the Buy-on-Time-or-Pay-Cash worksheet has been revised to reflect the latest tax treatment of interest expense on consumer loans.

- Chapter 9 has been carefully reworked to reflect the latest standards in the fields of risk management and life insurance. Several new types of insurance products are discussed, including *low-load* whole life policies, *joint life insurance, survivorship (last to die) insurance*, and *living benefits*. Also, in light of some of the financial difficulties that the life insurance industry has experienced, the material on life insurance ratings has been greatly expanded.

- Chapter 10 has been reorganized to focus on four major categories of health insurance — medical expense, long-term care, special coverages, and disability income — and the specific policy provisions and costs of each is discussed individually. In addition, cost containment provisions in medical expense insurance plans and expanded detailed discussions of both long-term care and disability income insurance policies are now included.

- The discussion of coinsurance in Chapter 11 has been revised in several places in order to make this potentially confusing concept more understandable, and material has been added on inflation protection riders.

- A number of changes have been made to Chapter 12 on investing in stocks and bonds, including a whole new section on the growing trend toward *market globalization* and different ways of investing in foreign securities. Also added was some discussion on how to go about selecting stocks for investment purposes. In the area of bonds, a new box was added on buying U.S. Treasury Securities at the auctions; also added is material on

U.S. Treasury zero-coupon bonds and mortgage-backed securities.

- In Chapter 13, the coverage of the various securities markets and market indexes has been updated and expanded, and new material has been added on *pink sheet stocks* and market regulations.
- The most obvious change to Chapter 14 is that commodities and options are now presented and discussed as *derivative securities*, in keeping with the way they are actually treated and viewed in the market. But there are other changes as well, including a new section on how mutual funds are organized and run; in addition, the discussion of mutual funds has been expanded to include *socially responsible* funds and *international* funds.
- The discussion of retirement planning in Chapter 15 has been expanded and updated, as necessary. One of the most noteworthy additions to this chapter is the new material on the three biggest pitfalls to sound retirement planning; material has also been added to this chapter on insurance company ratings as they apply to annuity products and *guaranteed investment contracts* (or GICs for short).
- The impact of recent tax legislation on estate planning and the effects of the latest legislative developments on trusts and estates are covered in Chapter 16. In addition, the discussion of the common features of wills and the sample clauses were revised and clarified. The discussion of co-ownership that focuses on ways people can take title to property was revised to include community property.

ORGANIZATION OF THE BOOK

Personal Financial Planning addresses all of the major personal financial planning problems that individuals and families encounter. It presents a model of the major elements of effective money management. All of the latest financial planning tools and techniques are discussed. Most of the widely used examples involve young people so that the student reader may more easily identify with each situation.

This comprehensive text is written in a low-key, personal style and uses state-of-the-art pedagogy to present the key concepts and procedures used in sound financial planning and effective money management. The roles of various financial decisions in the overall personal financial planning process are clearly delineated.

The book is divided into six parts. Part One presents the basic principles of personal financial planning and then covers personal financial statements, cash budgets, and taxes. Part Two concerns the management of assets, including cash and savings instruments, housing, and other major assets. Part Three covers debt management, including the various types of open account borrowing and consumer loans. Part Four deals with insurance planning and considers life insurance, health care plans, and property and liability insurance. Part Five concerns investments, including stocks, bonds, mutual funds, real estate, and other investment vehicles, and how to make transactions in securities markets. Part Six is devoted to retirement and estate planning. All these parts are tied together via the *Mark and Ana Williams continuous case*, which begins at the end of Chapter 1 with an extensive inventory of personal and financial data. Additional elements of the Williamses' financial plans are then introduced at the ends of Parts One through Five, and Chapters 15 and 16 so that the students can deal with the unfolding elements of a complete financial plan.

PEDAGOGY

Each chapter opens with an element called *Financial Facts or Fantasies*, a series of six true-false questions concerning the material covered, for which answers and brief explanations are appropriately placed throughout the chapter. In addition, each major section of the chapter begins with a critical thinking question designed to stimulate interest in the material that follows by challenging the student to relate it to his or her personal life. Each chapter contains two boxes set off from the text material and containing brief discussions of relevant personal financial planning material that serve to enrich the topical coverage. Numerous exhibits, each containing descriptive captions, are used throughout to more fully illustrate key points in the text.

Many chapters contain discussions and illustrations of how the personal computer can be used in various phases of financial planning and, where appropriate, brief descriptions of some of the more popular computer software are included. A running glossary provides brief definitions of key terms. End-of-chapter material includes roughly 20 review questions and problems that students can use to test their grasp of the material. Two case problems highlighting the important analytical topics and concepts are also supplied.

Following the case is a listing of about ten information sources, including general information articles from popular personal finance publications such as *Kiplinger's Personal Finance Magazine, Money*, and *Consumers Digest*, and a separate listing of relevant government documents and other publications.

The final item in each chapter is the new financial advisory section, "Getting a Handle on Your Financial Future." And, of course, as noted before, each part of the book ends with the Williamses continuous case.

ANCILLARY MATERIALS

Recognizing the importance of outstanding support materials to the instructor and the student, we have continued to improve and expand our ancillary package.

Worksheets

A file folder containing *blank worksheets* identical to those presented and used in the text is included free of charge with each new copy of the book. Each worksheet provides a logical format for dealing with some aspect of personal financial planning such as preparation of a cash budget, home affordability analysis, or automobile lease versus purchase analysis.

Instructor's Manual and Test Bank

A comprehensive *Instructor's Manual and Test Bank* has been prepared to assist the teacher. For each chapter, the manual includes

- An outline
- Discussion of major topics
- A list of key concepts
- Solutions to all end-of-chapter questions, problems, and cases
- *Outside projects* that can be assigned to students so that they can apply major concepts and techniques presented in the chapter (instructions for outside projects are printed on separate sheets to make duplication for classroom distribution a simple task)
- Solutions to all questions on the text continuous case
- Two additional integrative cases, each with a detailed solution. One of the cases deals with a young couple, and the other addresses the financial concerns faced by single parents.
- A complete test bank that has been revised, updated, and expanded by Carlene Creviston of Ball State University includes true-false and multiple-choice questions, as well as four to six short problems for nearly every chapter.

Computerized Test Bank

A computerized version of the printed test bank is available on either a 5¼″ or 3½″ IBM-compatible diskette. It comes in either the regular computerized test bank format or in a WordPerfect file that can be easily edited.

Workbook

Carlene Creviston of Ball State University has updated the *Workbook* to assist students in mastering the information and techniques presented in the text and to serve as a resource manual as they develop personal financial plans. Specific components for each chapter include

- A thorough outline of concepts discussed
- Completion exercises that stress vocabulary
- Comprehensive case problems (with solutions) that demonstrate the application of chapter concepts

Most chapters include both problem-solving exercises (with solutions) and comprehensive cases.

Personal Financial Planning Disk

The computer-based problem-solver—*FP/PC: Financial Planning on the Personal Computer*—was revised for this edition of the book by its author, Professor James B. Pettijohn of Southwest Missouri State University. The disk performs like any of the widely used commercially available software packages and is completely interactive; best of all, being very user-friendly, it streamlines the recordkeeping and problem-solving activities presented in the text. A computer logo is used in the margin to identify sections of the book to which the disk is applicable. End-of-chapter problems and cases that can be solved with the disk are keyed with the same logo. Some worksheets used in the text are formatted on the disk to provide assistance in applying some of the more complex procedures, ranging from financial statement and budget preparation to tax estimation, investment management, and retirement planning. The software has been extensively tested to ensure its accuracy and ease of use. *FP/PC* is made available to users of *Personal Financial Planning*, Sixth Edition. The software will operate on IBM PC's or true compatible machines with at least 512K of memory and is available in both 5¼ and 3½ inch diskette sizes.

ACKNOWLEDGMENTS

In addition to the many individuals who made significant contributions to this book by their expertise, classroom experience, guidance, general advice, and reassurance, we also appreciate the students and faculty who used the book and provided valuable feedback on it, confirming our conviction that a truly teachable personal financial planning text could be developed.

Of course, we are indebted to all the academicians and practitioners who have created the body of knowledge contained in this text. We particularly wish to thank several people who gave the most significant help in developing and revising it. The first is Robert W. McLeod, CFP, CFA, of the University of Alabama and Saliba, Reinhart, McLeod & Company, for developing the end-of-chapter financial advisory sections, "Getting a Handle on Your Financial Future." In addition, we want to thank Vickie Hampton of the University of Texas at Austin for her intensive review of the entire manuscript and for her work on the continuous cases. Also, we want to thank Jim Pettijohn for developing the state-of-the-art software. Larry A. Cox, CFP of the University of Georgia deserves thanks for his advice and work on the insurance chapters, particularly those on life and health insurance. Thanks is also due Robert J. Wright of Wright & Wright, CPAs, for his assistance in the chapter on taxes; and John C. Bost, Esq., of San Diego State University for his help in revising and updating the estate planning chapter.

The Dryden Press, which shared our objective of producing a truly teachable text, relied on the experience and advice of numerous excellent reviewers. We appreciate their many suggestions that have had a significant impact on the various editions of this book. Our thanks go to the following: Linda Afdahl, Michael J. Ahern III, Robert J. Angell, H. Kent Baker, Catherine L. Bertelson, Steve Blank, Dan Casey, P. R. Chandy, Maurice L. Crawford, David Durst, Mary Ellen Edmundson, Ronald Ehresman, Jim Farris, Sharon Hatten Garrison, Carol Zirnheld Green, C. R. Griffen, John L. Grimm, Chris Hajdas, Forrest Harlow, Kendall P. Hill, Darrell D. Hilliker, Arlene Holyoak, Frank Inciardi, Kenneth Jacques, Dixie Porter Johnson, Peggy Keck, Karol Kitt, George Klander, Xymena S. Kulsrud, Carole J. Makela, Charles E. Maxwell, George Muscal, Robert Nash, Albert Pender, Franklin Potts, Fred Power, Arnold M. Rieger, Vivian Rippentrop, Gayle M. Ross, Rosemary Walker, Gary Watts, Grant J. Wells, Betty Wright, and R. R. Zilkowski.

Because of the wide variety of topics covered in this book, we called upon many experts for whose insight on recent developments we are deeply grateful. We would like to thank them and their firms for allowing us to draw on their knowledge and resources, particularly Scott Knudten, State Farm Insurance; Pat Rupp, CFP, IDS, Inc; Stephen Roman, Len Lovin, and Rich Wilburn, from Valley National Bank of Arizona; Robin Gitman, McKusick & Associates Real Estate; Mark Nussbaum, Western Federal

Savings; John Rains, Wells Fargo Bank; Fred Weaver, Great Western Bank; Flora Weston, Coldwell Banker Realtors; and Bill Shaffer, Waysys, Inc.

We would like to thank our colleagues at San Diego State University and Arizona State University for their expertise, encouragement, and support. Also, we want to thank Marlene G. Bellamy of Writeline Communication Associates for her assistance in research, writing, proofing, and preparing the *Instructor's Manual*, Jamey Stephenson of A.S.U. for his research assistance throughout much of this book and his invaluable help in preparing the material on student loans (in Chapter 8), and Beth Baugh, managing editor of the *Journal of Financial Research* (at Arizona State), for her research assistance and editorial help. We would also like to express our appreciation to Carlene Creviston for her review and assistance in revising the *Test Bank* and *Workbook*. Special mention is due to Pam Hively, Frances Grieshaber, Sheryl McMaster, and Jade Pearce for their outstanding assistance, particularly in keyboarding the manuscript.

The editorial staff of The Dryden Press has been most cooperative. We wish to thank Alison Howell, production manager, Nick Welch, designer, Van Strength, permissions editor, Robert Watrous, copy editor, and Shirley Kessel, indexer. Special thanks go to Mike Roche, acquisitions editor, and Millicent Treloar, developmental editor, without whose support this revision would not have been as lively and contemporary in approach as we believe it is and whose expert management of the writing and reviewing of the text proved invaluable. We are also grateful to Jennifer Johnson, project editor, who ably assured the book's timely and accurate production.

Finally, our wives, Robin and Charlene, have provided needed support and understanding during the writing of this book. We are forever grateful to them.

Lawrence J. Gitman
La Jolla, California

Michael D. Joehnk
Scottsdale, Arizona

November 1992

CONTENTS

Personal Financial Planning

sixth edition

PART one

Foundations of Financial Planning

CHAPTER 1

Understanding the
Financial Planning Process

Would you believe that as a college graduate, you can expect to earn, on average, $2 million or more over your lifetime — and perhaps double that if you are part of a dual-income family and/or have an advanced degree? Managing that amount of money wisely is a challenging task. Consider, for example, Susan and Michael McKinney. College educated and in their late 20s, together they earn $71,000 a year — he is a sales representative for an electronics firm, and she is a systems analyst for a major manufacturing firm. While the McKinneys have the money to enjoy a comfortable lifestyle now, they also recognize the importance of controlling their financial future. They analyzed their current financial situation and set both short- and long-term goals, such as buying a new car next year, purchasing a condominium in three years, and starting an investment program. They realize that they may have to forego some luxuries today to reach these future goals. Susan and Michael are smart: They're planning for their financial future. Unfortunately, many people treat personal financial decisions as a series of unorganized, uncoordinated events. Consequently, their quest for financial security is less likely to be successful. Achieving financial security requires identifying reasonable goals, developing organized plans, implementing these plans, and revising them as personal circumstances change.

FINANCIAL *facts* OR *fantasies*

Are the following statements financial facts (true) or fantasies (false)?

An improved standard of living is one of the payoffs of sound money management. *T*

A savings account is an example of a ~~real~~ *FINANCIAL* asset, as it represents something on deposit at a bank or S&L. *F*

Personal financial planning involves the restatement of personal financial goals into specific plans and, ultimately, into financial arrangements that put those plans into action. *T*

Over the long run, gaining an extra percent or two on an investment makes little *A LOT OF* difference in the amount of earnings generated. *F*

Generally speaking, inflation has little *A GREAT* effect on personal financial planning. *F*

A high salary is the most important factor in choosing a particular job or career. *F*

1. BENEFITS
2. WKING CONDITIONS
3. PERSONAL GOALS
4. SKILLS
5. VALVES
6. DESIRED LIFESTYLE
7. GEOGRAPHY PREFERENCES

5

THE REWARDS OF SOUND FINANCIAL PLANNING

A person's standard of living and patterns of consumption are related and can profoundly affect the accumulation of wealth. If your primary financial goal is to achieve maximum wealth accumulation, what kind of standard of living and consumption patterns would you exhibit? Before reading on, take a few moments to consider the tradeoffs among standard of living, consumption, and wealth accumulation.

We live in a complex, fast-paced world with rapidly changing social, economic, political, and technological environments. Developing personal strategies to improve our lifestyles becomes increasingly difficult, and we are faced with a bewildering array of choices — where to live, what career to follow, what car to buy, when to change jobs, how much to save or invest, to name just a few. Before we can evaluate our options and make informed decisions, we all need to set goals to give direction to our lives. As we move through the 1990s, many of the financial goals our parents took for granted — home ownership, a college education, job security, building a substantial nest egg for retirement — are becoming harder to obtain. As a result, two incomes may be required to maintain an acceptable standard of living, and it may take longer to be able to afford a home.

Setting goals is extremely important in personal money management. Most of us worry about our personal finances. Even if we're managing pretty well today, we are concerned about the future. We want to maintain and improve our current quality of life, be able to afford a nice car, live in a well-furnished home, and take expensive vacations. We also want to prepare for the future so that we can send our children to college and have funds for retirement.

The most effective way to achieve these and other financial objectives is through *personal financial planning*. It helps individuals and families to define their short- and long-term financial goals and de-velop appropriate financial strategies for reaching them. However, many of us are intimidated by today's complex financial environment and wonder how best to manage our finances in light of the volatile national economy. Although we know that financial planning is even more important now than ever before, we're unsure of where to start. The goal of this book is to take the mystery out of the personal financial planning process and to provide the tools that you can use to take charge of your personal finances.

Because needs and goals change as personal circumstances change, personal financial planning is a lifelong activity. As you will learn, creating flexible plans and revising them on a regular basis is the key to building a sound financial future. Of course, planning alone does not guarantee success, but if used effectively and consistently, it can help you control your life and use your resources wisely. As a result, it will make a profound effect on your standard of living, consumption patterns, and ultimately, the amount of your accumulated wealth.

STANDARD OF LIVING

One of the major benefits of personal financial planning is that it helps us to acquire, use, and control our financial resources more efficiently. In essence, it allows us to gain more enjoyment from our income and thus improve our **standard of living** — the necessities, comforts, and luxuries we have or desire. The quality of our lives is, for most of us, closely tied to our standard of living. The presence or absence of certain material items — such as a home, cars, and jewelry — are commonly associated with quality of life. Large, expensive, or "fancy" items, for example, are viewed as components of a high standard of living. The availability of money for entertainment, health, education, art, music, and travel also contributes to the quality of life. Although many other factors — geographical location, public facilities, local cost of living, pollution, traffic, and population density — also affect the quality of an individual's life, wealth is commonly viewed as its primary determinant. Of course, many so-called wealthy people live "plain" lives, choosing to save or invest their money rather than spend it on luxuries and frills. Even so, their quality of life is probably no lower than that of a more flamboyant consumer.

One trend that has had a profound effect on our standard of living is the *two-income family*. What was relatively rare in the early 1970s has become commonplace today, and, in the process, the incomes of millions of families have risen sharply. Granted, two incomes increase the things we can afford to buy, but they also carry with them greater responsibilities for managing money wisely. This is where personal financial planning comes in: By carefully planning future purchases and financial activities, people can set goals consistent with their desired quality of life.

An improved standard of living is one of the payoffs of sound money management.

Fact: The very heart of sound financial planning and effective money management is the ability to gain a greater level of enjoyment from the money one makes and thus improve one's standard of living.

CONSUMPTION PATTERNS

Spending money more wisely is another payoff of financial planning. Basically, such planning gives you a better idea of what you should do with the money you make. Given a certain level of income, you can either spend it now or save a portion of it for future consumption. Determining both your current and future **consumption** patterns is an important part of the personal money management process. The goal, of course, is to plan how to spend your money to get the most satisfaction from your income dollar.

Current Consumption Your current level of consumption is based on the necessities of life and your average propensity to consume. A minimum level of consumption would allow you to obtain only the **necessities of life:** food, clothing, and shelter. Although the quantity and types of food, clothing, and shelter purchased may differ among individuals depending on their wealth, some amount of these items is essential for survival. **Average propensity to consume** refers to the percentage of each dollar of income that is spent, on average, for current consumption rather than saved. People exhibiting high average propensities to con-

sume may do so because their income is low and they must spend a large portion of it just for basic necessities. On the other hand, there are many "ultra consumers" who choose to splurge on a few items and scrimp elsewhere. Clearly these people also exhibit high average propensities to consume. Conversely, individuals earning large amounts quite often have low average propensities to consume, since the cost of necessities represents only a small proportion of their income. Still, it is not unusual to find two people with significantly different incomes but the same average propensity to consume due to differences in standard of living. The person making more money may believe it is essential to buy better-quality and/or more items and thus on average spend the same percentage of each dollar of income as the person making far less.

Future Consumption. In any carefully developed financial plan, a portion of current income will be set aside for deferred, or future, consumption. For example, we may want to put money aside to build up a retirement fund so that we can maintain a desirable standard of living in our later years. In this case, we fully intend to spend the money put aside, but not until we retire. Thus, we are deferring actual consumption to some time in the future. Other examples of deferred consumption include saving for a child's education, a primary residence or vacation home, a major acquisition (like a car or home entertainment center), or even a vacation. The money put

---

standard of living
The necessities, comforts, and luxuries enjoyed or aspired to by an individual or group.

consumption
The using up of goods or services in the satisfaction of wants.

necessities of life
Items that are needed for survival—food, clothing, and shelter.

average propensity to consume
The percentage of each dollar of income that a person spends, on average, for current consumption.

aside for such deferred consumption is placed in various savings and/or investment vehicles to generate a return over the time it is held. The portion of our current income committed to future consumption will be a function of the amount of money we earn on the one hand and our level of current spending on the other. The more we earn and/or the less we devote to current consumption, the more we can commit to meeting future consumption needs. In any case, *some* portion of current income should be set aside *regularly* for future consumption purposes—this creates good saving habits.

ACCUMULATION OF WEALTH

A certain portion of current income is used to meet the everyday *expenses* of living: Food, clothing, insurance, utilities, entertainment, and so on. Another part is used to acquire *assets*, such as cars, a home, or stocks and bonds. For the most part, it is our assets that determine how wealthy we are. Personal financial planning plays a critical role in the accumulation of wealth, as it helps us direct our financial resources to the most productive areas. As a rule, a person's **wealth** at any point in time is a function of the total value of all the items he or she owns. Wealth consists of financial and real assets. **Financial assets** are intangible, paper assets, such as savings accounts and securities (stocks, bonds, mutual funds, and so forth). They are earning assets that are held for the returns they promise. **Real assets**, in contrast, are tangible, physical assets, such as real estate, that can be held for either consumption (like the home you live in) or investment purposes (like the duplex you bought for rental purposes). In general, the goal of most people is to accumulate as much wealth as possible while maintaining current consumption at a level that provides a desired standard of living.

A savings account is an example of a real asset, as it represents something on deposit at a bank or S&L. *Fantasy:* A savings account, like stocks, bonds, and mutual funds, is an example of a *financial asset*—an intangible, "paper" asset. Real assets, in contrast, refer to *tangibles*—long-lived, physical items like houses, cars, and appliances.

Assume that you have decided to take charge of your financial future through personal financial planning. Once you establish your financial goals, in what specific areas will you need to develop plans? Try to answer this question before reading on.

Personal financial planning is the key to achieving financial goals. No one is exempt from the need to develop personal financial plans—neither new college graduates, nor the growing number of single, mobile, urban professionals, nor single parents, midcareer married breadwinners, nor senior-level corporate executives. Knowing what you hope to accomplish financially and how you intend to do it clearly gives you an edge over someone who merely reacts to financial events as they unfold. For example, purchasing a new car immediately after graduation may be important to you, but evaluating and possibly arranging financing before your shopping trip—as opposed to simply accepting the financing arrangement offered by an auto dealer—might save you a considerable amount of money. Moreover, since some dealers advertise low-interest loans but then charge higher prices for their cars, knowing all your costs in advance can help you identify the best deal. For most people, buying a car represents a major expenditure that warrants careful consideration and planning. It not only involves a substantial outflow of cash up front but also usually results in an increased level of consumer debt that must be repaid over time.

DEFINING YOUR FINANCIAL GOALS

What are your **financial goals?** Have you spelled them out, at least over the short run? The fact is, without financial goals it is difficult, if not impossible, to effectively manage your financial resources. We all need to know where we are going, in a financial sense, in order to direct the major financial events in our lives. Perhaps achieving financial independence at a relatively early age is important to you. If so, then things like saving, investing, and retirement planning will become an important part of your life. Whatever your financial goals or preferences, they must be stated in monetary terms, since money, and the *utility* (defined later) it buys, is an integral part of financial planning.

The Role of Money. **Money** is the common denominator by which all financial transactions are gauged. It is the medium of exchange used as a measure of value in our economy. Without the standard unit of exchange provided by the dollar, it would be difficult to set specific personal financial goals and to measure progress in achieving them. Money, as we know it today, is therefore the key consideration in establishing *financial* goals. Yet it is not money as such that most people want. Rather, it is the utility that money makes possible. **Utility** refers to the amount of satisfaction a person receives from purchasing certain types or quantities of goods and services. Often the utility or satisfaction provided, rather than the cost, is the overriding factor in the choice between two items of differing price. A special feature may provide additional utility in one item, causing it to be the preferred one. For example, many people prefer to pay more to buy a car with a CD player rather than buy one with a "standard" cassette player. The added utility may result from the actual usefulness of the special feature, from the "status" it is expected to provide, or both. Regardless, different people receive varying levels of satisfaction from similar items that are not necessarily related to the cost of the items. When evaluating alternative qualities of life, consumption patterns, and forms of wealth accumulation, it is clear, therefore, that utility should be considered along with cost.

The Psychology of Money. Money and its utility are not only economic concepts, but are also closely linked to the psychological concepts of values, emotion, and personality. Your personal value system — the ideals and beliefs you hold important and use to guide your life — will also shape your attitudes toward money and wealth accumulation. If status and image are important to you, you may spend a high proportion of your current income to acquire luxu-

ries. If you place a high value on family life, you may choose a career that offers regular hours and less stress or an employer with "flextime" rather than a higher-paying position requiring travel and lots of overtime. Clearly, your financial goals and decisions should be consistent with your values. Identifying your values allows you to formulate financial plans that provide greater personal satisfaction and quality of life.

People will react differently to similar situations involving money. Depending upon timing and circumstances, emotional responses to money may be positive — such as love, happiness, and security — or negative — such as fear, greed, and insecurity. For example, some people, upon receipt of a paycheck,

---

wealth
The total value of all items owned by an individual, such as bank accounts, stocks, bonds, home, and automobiles.

financial assets
Intangible assets, such as savings accounts and securities, that are acquired for some promised future return.

real assets
Tangible physical assets, such as real estate and automobiles, that can be held for either consumption or investment purposes.

personal financial planning
Planning that covers the key elements of an individual's financial affairs and is aimed at achievement of his or her financial goals.

financial goals
Short- and long-range results that an individual wants to attain, such as controlling living expenses, managing one's tax burden, establishing savings and investment programs, and meeting retirement needs.

money
The medium of exchange used as a measure of value in financial transactions.

utility
The amount of satisfaction an individual receives from purchasing certain types or quantities of goods and services.

Money Attitudes Can Make or Break a Marriage

Kathleen Gurney is convinced that the real fatal attraction in America today is between a man and a woman who look at money differently.

Forget whether the other person's face or body sets your heart to pounding. Ignore such trivialities as common tastes and interests, personalities and attitudes toward kids and pets. If a couple is out of sync in its financial goals, she believes, the health and wealth of its marriage may be headed for trouble.

Gurney, an author and former University of Southern California psychology professor who heads Cincinnati's Financial Psychology Corporation, says her research shows unmistakably that money is "our last social

taboo" and "our last frontier of self-disclosure — particularly for women."

Why should that be true in 1991? Because, she says, too many women still are being raised in the tradition of the 19th century American novelist Edith Wharton, who advised: "Never talk about money, and think about it as little as possible."

While opposite characteristics can initially seem attractive, in money as in other areas, in the end trouble is brewing in a match between, say, what Gurney calls "a power/control baron" (an extreme achiever who needs to be in charge) and "a compromiser" (one used to delegating and deferring responsibility, but eager all the

same to feel more self-confident).

As gender differences blur, what are thought of as traditionally male attitudes toward money show up increasingly among women, and vice versa. So what's truly important, Gurney believes, is that both members of the partnership "must have the same goals."

How do you find out whether you and your mate — current or potential — are a financial couple made in heaven? Gurney's "Moneymax Questionnaires" normally employ at least 28 questions, but she provided six specially devised, previously unpublished queries that may give you an initial insight.

Do you agree or disagree with each of the following statements?:

---

feel satisfaction in their work. Others feel relief in knowing they can pay past-due bills. Still others experience anxiety over what to do with the money. Also, for some people saving and accumulating money to provide financial security is a high priority, while others place greater emphasis on spending money on material goods in order to reduce anxiety and enhance feelings of self-worth.

Money is a primary motivator of personal behavior. It has a strong affect on one's self-image. Therefore, each individual's unique personality and emotional makeup determine the importance and role of money in her or his life. You should become aware of your own attitudes toward money because they are the basis of your "money personality" and

management style. Some questions to ask yourself are: How important is money to you? Why? What types of spending give you satisfaction? Are you a risk taker? Do you need to have large financial reserves to feel secure? Such an understanding is a prerequisite to the development of realistic and effective financial goals and plans. For example, if you are a person who prefers immediate satisfaction, you will find it more difficult to achieve long-term net worth or savings goals than if you are highly disciplined and primarily concerned with achieving a comfortable retirement at an early age. Clearly, tradeoffs between current and future benefits are strongly affected by values, emotion, and personality.

1. I am concerned that the financial and investment decisions I make are right for me.
2. I can't resist spending money whenever I have some.
3. I feel better if I am in charge of the money management.
4. I wish I were more confident in managing money and investments.
5. I wish I were more rational and less emotional in my use of money.
6. I prefer staying in charge of money and investments.

Gurney's scoring:

If you agreed with both questions 1 and 4, you feel anxious when making financial decisions; if you disagreed with both, you feel confident with your financial decision-making skills; if your answers were split, you only feel somewhat confident of your money management skills.

If you agreed with both questions 2 and 5, you're feeling emotional in your use of your money; if you disagreed with both, you tend to handle money rationally; if your answers were split, you're only somewhat emotional.

If you agreed with both questions 3 and 6, you desire and need a sense of control and integral involvement with your money; if you disagreed with both, you don't want or need to be in control; if your answers were split, you only somewhat need to be in control and could feel comfortable sharing the management of your money or deferring to another.

"Life is much easier if the partners share the same attitude toward money," Gurney says, adding that money — not sex or in-laws or children — is now the number 1 cause of divorce in America.

The bottom line for lovers? Couples who want to avoid the most common conflicts of modern marriage should make sure they're compatible in the economics and finance class — and not just in chemistry.

Source: Louis Rukeyser, Tribune Media Services, Inc.

While this textbook emphasizes a rational, unemotional approach to personal financial planning, it is important to recognize that universally applicable financial plans do not exist. Every financial plan must not only consider the individual's wants, needs, and financial resources, but must also *realistically reflect* his or her personality and emotional reactions to money. Conflicts between personality, goals, and values must be resolved early in the planning process. Obviously, plans requiring high levels of annual savings to achieve future consumption goals will be inconsistent with a highly indulgent personality that is fueled by a need to consume. In such a case, goals will have to be moderated in order to achieve an acceptable balance between current and future consumption. In all cases, a key to effective personal financial planning is a *realistic* understanding of the role of money and its utility in the individual's life. Effective financial plans are both economically and psychologically sound.

Money and Relationships. Money is one of the most emotional issues in any relationship. It is also one of the hardest subjects to discuss. Most people are uncomfortable and therefore avoid talking about money matters, even with their partners. However, differing opinions of how a family's money should be spent can threaten the stability of a marriage or cause many arguments between parents and children. Learning to communicate about

EXHIBIT 1.1

A Summary of Personal Financial Goals

It is important to set financial objectives carefully. They must be realistically attainable, since they are the basis for financial planning.

PERSONAL FINANCIAL GOALS				
Name(s) _____			**Date** _____	
Type of Financial Goal	**Brief Description**	**Degree of Priority (High, Medium, or Low)**	**Target Date**	**Cost**
Increase income				
Gain control over living expenses				
Have more money left over for discretionary/ entertainment purchases				
Set up an education fund for yourself, your spouse, and/or your children				
Establish an emergency fund to meet unexpected expenses				
Implement procedures to keep your tax burden to a minimum				
Put money aside for a home, car, and/or other major expenditures				
Pay off/reduce personal debt; bring monthly debt service requirements down to a more manageable level				
Provide adequate protection against personal risks — life, disability, health, property, and liability insurance				
Start a general savings and investment program to accumulate capital and achieve financial security				
Start your own business				
Set up a retirement fund to supplement social security and employer-sponsored retirement programs				
Maximize the disposition/transfer of estate to heirs				
Other personal financial objectives and goals				

money with your partner and/or children is, therefore, a critical step in developing effective financial plans.

As we noted earlier, there are many distinct money personality types. One person may be very analytic and see money as a means of control, another may view it as a way to express affection, and yet another may use it to boost her or his power and self-esteem. It's not always easy to discover whether your partner's financial style is compatible with your own. The quiz in the *Issues in Money Management* box provides some insight into your money attitudes and how they compare to your partner's.

When couples have very different attitudes toward money—for example, if one person likes to prepare detailed budgets but the other is an impulse shopper—conflicts are bound to arise. The increase in two-income households has also shifted the way men and women deal with money. No longer is the man the sole wage earner who controls the family's finances. Typically, the more income the woman contributes, the more say she may want in their financial decision making.

The best way to resolve money disputes is to be aware of your partner's financial style, keep the lines of communication open, and be willing to compromise. It's highly unlikely that you can change your partner's style—or your own, for that matter—but you can work out your differences. Financial planning is an especially important part of the process of resolving conflict. You will gain a better understanding of your differences by working together to establish a set of financial goals that take into account each person's needs and values. For instance, you may be a risk taker who likes to speculate in the stock market, while your cautious partner believes that all your money should go into a savings account in case one of you loses your job. If you can agree on the amount of money you should have readily available in low-risk investments and savings accounts, you can then allocate a specific portion of your funds to riskier investments.

Types of Financial Goals. Financial goals cover a wide range of financial desires—from controlling living expenses to meeting retirement needs, from setting up a savings and investment program to minimizing the amount of taxes you pay. Your financial goals should be defined as *specifically* as possible and focus on the *results* you want to at-

tain. Simply saying you want to save money next year is not a specific goal. How much do you want to save, and for what purpose? Formulating a goal such as "save 10 percent of my take-home pay each month to start an investment program" clearly states what you want to do and why.

Equally important, as mentioned earlier, your goals should be *realistically attainable*, since they form the basis on which your financial plans are established. If you set your savings goals too high—for example, 25 percent when your basic living expenses already account for 85 percent of your take-home pay—the goal becomes unattainable. If set too low, you may not accumulate enough funds for a meaningful investment program. Clearly, if the goals are little more than "pipe dreams," the integrity of the financial plans may be suspect as well (not to mention a possible source of frustration). Finally, financial goals should be ranked in order of priority and set with a definite time frame in mind—are they short-range goals, such as saving for a vacation, to be attained within the next year or long-range goals, such as purchasing a vacation home, not to be realized for many more years?

Exhibit 1.1 provides a worksheet that lists many different types of financial goals. It is not intended to be an exhaustive inventory of each and every kind of personal financial objective. Rather it represents some of the more common and important types of financial goals. Some individuals certainly could have other, more personal or more detailed goals in addition to those listed. Also, it is highly unlikely that anyone at any given point in time would be pursuing all of the listed goals at once. Instead, as we go through life, we'll find that some financial goals become more important than others. You will want to develop a set of personal financial goals that is meaningful to you at this particular stage of your life.

A LIFETIME OF PLANNING

How will you achieve the financial goals you set for yourself? The answer, of course, lies in the financial plans that you establish. Financial plans provide the direction necessary for achieving your financial objectives. Once in place, they can be put into action through various types of financial strategies.

The financial planning process involves a number of steps and a number of different yet interrelated types of plans. All financial planning begins with

EXHIBIT 1.2

The Personal Financial Planning Life Cycle

As people go through different stages in their lives, their income patterns change as well as the types of financial plans they pursue.

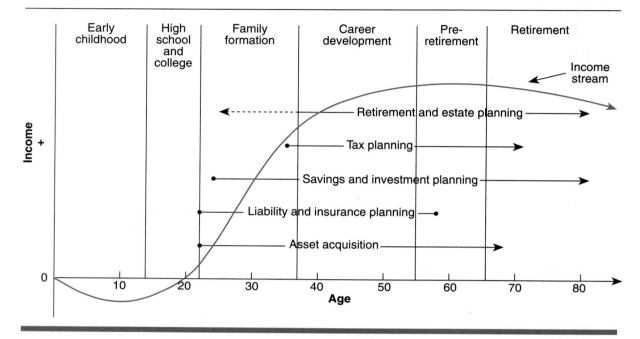

identifying your personal needs and wants and establishing your realistic goals. It requires a basic understanding of personal financial statements, budgets, and taxes (presented in Chapters 2, 3, and 4, respectively).

Financial plans cover the most important financial dimensions of your life. Some plans deal with the more immediate aspects of money management, such as preparing budgets for use in managing spending. Others focus on acquiring major assets, such as a car or a home. Liability plans control borrowing, insurance plans reduce financial risks, savings and investment plans provide for emergency funds and future wealth accumulation, and tax plans minimize tax payments. You also need retirement plans that provide financial security when you stop working and estate plans to ensure the orderly and cost-effective transfer of assets to your heirs.

Personal financial planning involves the restatement of personal financial goals into specific plans and, ultimately, into financial arrangements that put those plans into action.

Fact: Personal financial plans are based on the various financial goals that individuals set for themselves. Once in place, the plans are put into action through various types of financial strategies.

The Life Cycle of Financial Plans. As we move from childhood to retirement age, we go through different life stages. Exhibit 1.2 illustrates the various components of a typical *financial planning life cycle* as it compares to these different life stages. It shows that as we pass from one state of maturation to the next, our patterns of income change simultaneously. From our early childhood days, when we relied on our parents for support, to

EXHIBIT 1.3
Life Cycle Financial Data

The finances of those in different stages of the life cycle vary. Income tends to increase, then decline over the life cycle, while home ownership and other assets tend to increase. Debts tend to increase and then taper off over the life cycle.

Age of Family Head	Average Household Income	Percent Who Own Home	Median Equity in Home	Median Value of Other Major Assets[1]	Median Debt Level[2]
Under 35	$26,400	36.8%	$21,000	$131,500	$48,700
35–44	44,200	65.9	40,000	163,300	67,100
45–54	52,800	76.6	59,000	199,200	57,200
55–64	38,500	82.2	54,000	275,900	56,800
65–74	27,600	80.2	47,000	290,400	52,600
75 and over	20,900	72.8	50,500	240,900	24,000

[1]Includes financial assets (bank accounts, CDs, and investment portfolios) plus other personal assets such as cars, business ownership, investment real estate.

[2]Excluding mortgage debt on principal residence.

Source: Arthur Kennickell and Janice Shack-Marquez, "Changes in Family Finances from 1983 to 1989: Evidence from the Survey of Consumer Finances," *Federal Reserve Bulletin*, Board of Governors of the Federal Reserve System, Washington, D.C., January 1992, pp. 1–16.

our early adulthood, when we started our families and, very likely, held our first "real" jobs, we can see a noticeable change in income pattern. First, the negative income—in the form of reliance on our parents for money—is eventually replaced with a rapidly increasing positive stream of earnings as we embark on our chosen careers. Then, as we move from career development to preretirement years, our income becomes more stable. Finally, our income begins to trail off (ideally, only a bit) as we enter our retirement years. Thus, as our emphasis in life changes, so do the kinds of financial plans we pursue—that is, at various points in our lives, different types of financial goals and plans become more important than others.

Obviously, not everyone follows this "typical" pattern, and each life situation needs its own financial goals and plans. Today, many people in their 20s are postponing marriage, while career development may take precedence over marriage and starting a family. Controlling expenses, managing credit, or saving for a new car may be goals when you are 25 and single. New career strategies—more job changing, several different careers over a lifetime, for example—are common. Some women interrupt their careers to stay at home with their children, whether for six months or six years, and then reenter the

work force. Their families need to plan for periods of reduced income. A divorce or the death of a spouse can drastically change one's financial circumstances. Remarriage often involves a special type of financial plan, the prenuptial agreement, that spells out the disposition of assets each person brings into the marriage in the event of divorce or death. In times of economic difficulties, loss of a job or being forced to take early retirement means learning to cope with reduced income. Because life expectancies are increasing, many of us may need extra financial resources to care for elderly parents at the same time we are raising children.

These and other changing life situations make sound financial planning more important than ever in the 1990s. Careful planning makes it possible to get through tough times and prosper in good times. While certain financial goals are important regardless of age—having extra resources to fall back on in an economic downturn should be a priority whether you are 25, 45, or 65—your goals and plans at each stage of life will be based on your particular circumstances.

Exhibit 1.3 summarizes data that demonstrate life cycle differences in the finances of various age groups. Income tends to increase, then decline over the life cycle; home ownership and other assets tend to increase; debts tend to increase and then decline. Clearly those in midlife (ages 35 to 55) tend to have more income and debts than those persons below age 35 and above age 55.

Asset Acquisition Planning.

One of the first categories of financial planning we typically encounter is asset acquisition. We accumulate *assets*—things we own—throughout our lives. These include *liquid assets* (cash, savings accounts, and money market funds) used for everyday expenses, *personal property* (furniture, appliances, clothing, jewelry, home electronics, and similar items) and *real property* (homes, automobiles, and other major asset purchases). Chapters 5 and 6 focus on important considerations with regard to the acquisitions of savings, other liquid assets, and major assets such as housing and automobiles.

Liability and Insurance Planning.

Another category of financial planning is liability planning. A *liability* is something we owe and is represented by the amount of debt we have incurred. We create liabilities by borrowing money. By the time most of us graduate from college, we have debts of some sort—education loans, car loans, credit card balances, and so on. Our borrowing needs typically increase as we acquire other assets—a home, furnishings, and appliances. Regardless of the source of credit, such transactions have one thing in common: *The debt must be repaid at some future time*. Using credit effectively requires careful planning and is the topic of Chapters 7 and 8. As we will see, how we manage our debt burden is just as important as how we manage our assets.

Obtaining adequate *insurance coverage* is also essential. Like borrowing money, it is generally something that is introduced at a relatively early point in our life cycle (usually early in the family foundation stage). Insurance provides a means of reducing financial risk and protecting both income (life, health insurance, and disability) and assets (property and liability insurance). Most consumers regard insurance as absolutely essential—and for good reason. One serious illness or accident can wipe out everything that one has accumulated over years of hard work. However, overinsuring or misinsuring can be costly too. The appropriate types and amounts of insurance coverage are examined in Chapters 9, 10, and 11.

Planning Your Savings and Investment Programs.

As your income begins to increase, so does the importance of savings and investment planning. People *save* initially in order to establish an emergency fund for meeting unexpected expenses. Eventually, however, they devote greater attention to *investing* excess income as a means of accumulating wealth, either for retirement or for major expenditures such as a child's college education. Wealth may be acquired through savings and subsequent investing of funds in various investment media—common or preferred stocks, government or corporate bonds, real estate, and so on. Success is determined by how profitably excess funds are invested.

The impact of alternative rates of return on accumulated wealth is illustrated in Exhibit 1.4. It shows that if you had $1,000 today and could keep it invested at 10 percent, you would accumulate a considerable sum of money over time. For example, at the end of 40 years you would have $45,259 from your original $1,000. Earning a higher rate of return has even greater rewards. Some might assume that earning, say, two percentage points more—that is, 12 rather than 10 percent—would not matter a great deal. But it certainly would! Note that if you could earn 12 percent over the 40 years, you would accumulate $93,051, or *more than twice as much* as what you would accumulate at 10 percent. Note also that *how long you invest* is just as important as *how much you earn* on your investments. As shown in Exhibit 1.4 with either rate of return, investing for 40 rather than 30 years results in about three times as much accumulated capital! This is the magic of compound interest, which explains why it's so important to start creating strong savings and investment habits early in life. We will more fully examine savings in Chapter 5 and investments in Chapters 12, 13, and 14.

Over the long run, gaining an extra percent or two on an investment makes little difference in the amount of earnings generated.

Fantasy: Gaining an extra percent or two on an investment can make a *tremendous* difference—often thousands of dollars—that increases the longer the investment is held.

Tax Planning.

In spite of all the talk about tax reform, and even after the sweeping tax revision of 1986 and subsequent changes, the fact is that our tax

EXHIBIT 1.4

How a $1,000 Investment Can Grow over Time

Differences in the rates of return earned on investments can have a dramatic impact on the amount of money you make from your investments, especially as the length of the investment period increases.

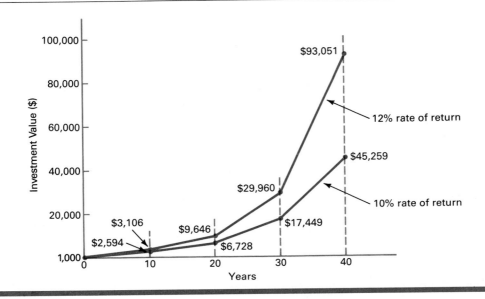

code continues to be highly complex. Some income is taxed as ordinary income, some is treated as portfolio (investment) income, some is treated as passive income, some is tax free, and some is tax deferred. Then there are tax shelters, which use various aspects of the tax code (such as depreciation expenses) to legitimately reduce an investor's tax liability. *Tax planning* considers all these dimensions and more. It involves looking at an individual's current and projected earnings and developing strategies that will *defer* and/or *minimize taxes*. Tax plans should reflect the desired form in which returns are to be received — active income, portfolio income, passive income, capital gains, or tax-sheltered income. These plans are closely tied to investment plans and will often specify certain investment strategies. Although the use of tax planning is most common among individuals with high incomes, sizable

savings can also result for people with lower levels of income. We will examine taxes and tax planning in Chapter 4.

Retirement and Estate Planning. While you are still working, you should be managing your finances to attain those goals you feel are important in old age. These might include extensive travel, plans for visiting children, dining out frequently at better restaurants, and perhaps a vacation home or boat. It is important to see that *retirement planning* begins long before you actually retire. As a rule, most people do not start thinking about retirement until well into their 40s or 50s. This is unfortunate, since it usually results in a *substantially reduced* level of retirement income. The sooner you start, the better off you will be. Take, for instance, the IRA (individual retirement account), in which certain wage earners

Using the PC in Personal Financial Planning

Make no mistake about it—personal financial planning is made a lot easier through the use of a personal computer. Within a matter of minutes, a PC can compute and analyze enormous amounts of data and then project the results on a screen in the form of charts, tables, or graphs. A well-programmed personal computer can readily accomplish all of the following tasks and more:

- Prepare detailed financial budgets, complete with monthly comparisons of actual and budgeted figures
- Prepare tax returns and perform complicated tax planning
- Evaluate the financial benefits and costs of major purchases

- Keep a full inventory of all types of insurance coverage
- Analyze the merits of all sorts of securities and investment vehicles
- Monitor the risk-and-return performance of a fully diversified investment portfolio
- Evaluate alternative retirement plans and identify actions necessary to achieve a desired level of income at retirement

Of course, the computer won't do all the work by itself—*you* have to provide the necessary data and operate the unit (which generally involves responding to questions or sets of instructions). What it will do is dramatically reduce the amount of time and effort necessary for

you to set up your financial plans and to manage your money effectively.

It is relatively easy to learn how to operate a PC and use it for financial planning. One or two short courses in computers, which are readily available from most computer stores, community colleges, and universities, should provide the basic skills you need. (Learning how to *program* a computer is another matter altogether and takes considerably more time.) When purchasing a computer system (which includes hardware and software), a critical question about hardware is the amount of memory the unit has—clearly, it must be enough to permit the financial planning applications you have in mind.

are allowed to invest up to $2,000 per year. If you can earn 12 percent and put $2,000 per year in an IRA for 25 years (that is, start investing for retirement at age 40), your account will grow to $267,000. However, if you start your retirement program ten years earlier (at age 30), your IRA will grow to a whopping $865,000—even though you are investing a total of only $20,000 more ($2,000 per year for an extra ten years), your IRA will *triple* in size. We will look at IRAs and other aspects of retirement planning in Chapter 15.

Accumulating assets to enjoy in retirement is only part of the long-run planning process. As people grow older, they eventually must start considering how they can most effectively pass on their wealth to

heirs—an activity called *estate planning*. We will examine this complex subject, which deals with such topics as wills, trusts, and the effects of gift, estate, and inheritance taxes, in Chapter 16.

THE PERSONAL COMPUTER IN FINANCIAL PLANNING

As it has in so many other aspects of our lives, the personal computer (PC) has found its way into financial planning. Indeed, financial planning is a natural application of the PC—what better way to handle all the number crunching involved in budgeting, tax planning, and investment management? These

Perhaps most important, *before* buying any PC, be sure you have a good idea of the memory requirements of the different software programs you plan to use, both immediately and in the future.

The prices of computers have dropped substantially in recent years, and many discounts and package prices are available. In early 1992, you could buy a reasonably sophisticated computer (processor, hard disk, keyboard, monitor) for $1,000 to $1,500, depending on the amount of internal memory, hard disk storage, operating speed, and whether it has a color or monochrome monitor. Printers range from about $250 for a good-quality dot-matrix model to $1,500 for a personal laser printer. A modem, which provides access to many types of information services through a telephone line, adds another $100. It is useful in investment management, because it provides access to financial databases that contain information on thousands of companies.

You will also need software — the programs that tell the computer which functions to perform. With the right software, you should be able to do just about anything you want in the way of computer-based financial planning. There are hundreds of reasonably priced, "user-friendly" programs available for personal financial planning and money management, and the list grows almost daily. (See Chapter 3 for descriptions of some popular financial planning software.) The cost of most of the consumer-oriented programs (as opposed to those tailored for professional money managers) runs from as low as $50 to $500 or more. Since it usually takes at least two or three programs to effectively implement a complete computer-based financial planning and money management system, you can expect to spend around $500 or more just for the software. Clearly, computer systems — even for home use — aren't cheap, but, if properly used, they can be worth the money.

and other tasks include a good deal of time-consuming, analytical work and mathematical computations, all of which can be aided considerably by the personal computer.

Rapidly changing PC technology has made available very sophisticated **hardware** (the physical parts of a computer system, such as the processor, disk drive, monitor, and printer) and **software** (the programs that tell the computer which functions to perform). While PCs have been getting more powerful and sophisticated, their prices continue to drop. Today their cost is very reasonable. For the serious financial planner who wants to do a lot of her or his own work, they can well be worth an investment of about $1,250 to $2,000. The accompanying *Smart Money* box reviews the benefits and costs of computer-based financial planning.

We feel that just as the PC is widely used in the everyday world of financial planning, it should be used in the teaching of personal finance. Accordingly, we

hardware
The physical parts of a computer system, such as processor, disk drives, monitor, and printer.

software
Programs that tell a computer which functions to perform.

will introduce the personal computer repeatedly throughout this book. In addition, a simple, menu-driven computer program has been developed for use with many of the analytical and computational procedures addressed in the text. Known as the *Personal Financial Planning Disk*, this program is written for IBM and IBM-compatible computers and is keyed to various sections of the textbook for use in performing many of the routine financial calculations and procedures presented. To help you recognize these sections, we have keyed the major text headings and selected end-of-chapter problems with the following symbol: 🔒

THE PLANNING ENVIRONMENT

The financial planning environment is made up of a number of players and is affected by economic conditions and consumer prices. What effect do you think government, business, consumers, economic conditions, and consumer prices will have on your financial plans? Spend a few moments answering this question before reading on.

Financial planning is not carried out in isolation but in an economic environment created by the actions of business, government, and consumers. Your purchase, saving, investment, and retirement plans and decisions are influenced by both the present and future state of the economy. An understanding of the economic environment will thereby allow you to make better financial plans and decisions.

As an example, a strong economy can lead to big profits in the stock market, which can positively affect your investment and/or retirement programs. The economy can also affect the interest rates you pay on your mortgage and credit cards and those you earn on saving accounts and bonds. Periods of high inflation can lead to price increases that come so fast it is hard to make ends meet. It is important, therefore, to understand the environment in which you will carry out your financial plans and strategies. This section briefly looks at two key aspects of the planning environment: the major players in the environment and the economy.

THE PLAYERS

The financial planning environment contains various interrelated groups of players, each attempting to fulfill certain goals (see Exhibit 1.5). Although their objectives are not necessarily incompatible, they do impose some constraints on one another. There are three vital groups: the government, business, and consumers.

Government. The federal, state, and local governments provide us with many essential public goods and services, such as police and fire protection, national defense, highways, and health care. Government also plays a major role in establishing special policies that regulate business and consumers. The federal government plays a major role in regulating the level of economic activity, as discussed later in this chapter. In addition, government is a customer of business and an employer of consumers. As a result, it is a source of revenue for business and wages for consumers. The relationship between government and businesses and consumers is depicted in Exhibit 1.5. The two principal constraints from the perspective of personal financial planning are taxes and government regulations.

Taxation. The federal government levies taxes on income, state governments levy taxes on sales and income, and local governments levy taxes primarily on real estate and personal property. The largest tax bite for consumers is federal income taxes, which may take as much as 31 percent of earnings. These taxes are somewhat progressive, because (up to a point) the greater the taxable income, the higher the tax rate. Change in tax rates and regulations will increase or decrease the amount of income consumers have to spend. Therefore, careful consideration should be given to the effects of taxes on personal money management activities. Due to the constraints of the tax structure and the potential magnitude of taxes, *financial decisions should be evaluated on an "after-tax" basis.* (Taxes are discussed in Chapter 4.)

EXHIBIT 1.5

The Financial Planning Environment

Business, government, and consumers are the major participants in our economic system. They all interact with one another to produce the environment in which we carry out our financial plans.

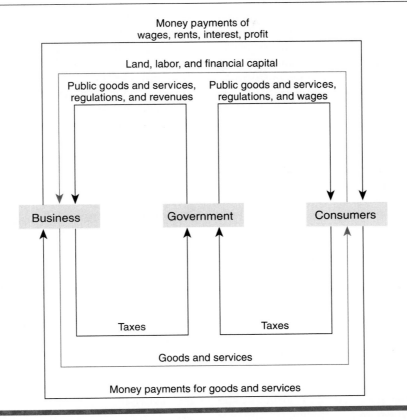

Regulation.   Federal, state, and local governments place many regulations on consumer- and citizen-related activities. Aimed at protecting the consumer from fraudulent and undesirable actions by sellers and lenders, these regulations require certain types of businesses to have licenses, maintain certain hygienic standards, adequately disclose financial charges, and warrant their goods and services. Other laws protect sellers from adverse activities by consumers, for example, shoplifting and nonpayment of services rendered. Certainly, any decisions relating to achieving personal financial goals should take into consideration both the legal requirements that protect consumers and those that constrain their activities.

Business.   As shown in Exhibit 1.5, business provides consumers with goods and services and in return receives payment in the form of money. In order to produce these goods and services, firms must hire labor and use land and capital (what economists refer to as *factors of production*). In return, firms pay out wages, rents, interest, and profits to the various factors of production. Thus, businesses are a key part of the circular flow of income that sustains our free enterprise system. In general, their presence creates a competitive environment in which consumers may select from an array of goods and services. There are, of course, certain industries, such as public utilities, in which the degree of competition or choice offered the consumer is limited, for economic reasons, by various regulatory bodies. As indicated in the preceding section, all businesses are limited in some way by federal, state, and/or local laws. An understanding of various business activities should permit consumers to make better purchases and help them determine with which firms to deal.

Consumers. The consumer is the central player in the financial planning environment. Consumer choices ultimately determine the kinds of goods and services businesses will provide. In addition, the consumer's choice of whether to spend or save has a direct impact on the present and future circular flows of income. A cutback in spending is usually associated with a decline in economic activity, while an increase helps the economy recover. Although consumers are often thought to have free choices in the marketplace, they must operate within an environment that interacts with government and business. While they can affect these parties through their elected officials and by their purchase actions, lobbyists and consumer groups are necessary for any real impact. The individual consumer should not expect to change government or business independently. As an *individual* consumer, you are best off accepting the existing environment and planning your transactions within it.

THE ECONOMY

Our economy is the result of interaction among government, business, and consumers, as well as the economic conditions in other nations. The government's goal is to regulate the economy and provide economic stability and high levels of employment through specific policy decisions. These government decisions have a major impact on the economic and financial planning environment. The federal government's *monetary policy*, programs for controlling the amount of money in circulation (the money supply), is used to stimulate or contract economic growth. For example, increases in the money supply tend to lower interest rates. This typically leads to a higher level of consumer and business borrowing—and spending—that increases overall economic activity. The reverse is also true. Reducing the money supply raises interest rates, thereby reducing consumer and business borrowing—and spending—and slowing economic activity.

The government's other principal tool for managing the economy is *fiscal policy*, its programs of taxation and spending. Increased spending for social services, education, defense, and other programs stimulates the economy while decreased spending slows economic activity. Increasing taxes, on the other hand, gives businesses and individuals less to spend and, as a result, negatively affects economic activity. Conversely, decreasing taxes stimulates the economy.

Economic Cycles. Although the government uses monetary and fiscal policy to regulate the economy and provide economic stability, the level of economic activity changes constantly. The upward and downward movement creates economic cycles (also called business cycles.) These cycles vary in length and in how high or low the economy moves. An economic cycle typically contains four stages: **expansion, recession, depression**, and **recovery**. Exhibit 1.6 shows how each of these stages relates to employment and production levels, two key indicators of economic activity. The stronger the economy, the higher the levels of employment and production. Eventually a period of economic expansion will peak and begin to move downward, becoming a recession when the decline lasts more than six months. A depression occurs when a recession worsens to the point where economic activity is almost at a standstill. The recovery phase, with increasing levels of employment and production, follows either a recession or a depression. For more than 45 years, the government has been reasonably successful in keeping the economy out of a depression, although we have experienced periods of rapid expansion and high inflation followed by periods of deep recession.

Economic growth is measured by changes in the **gross domestic product (GDP)**, the total of all goods and services produced by workers located within the country. The broadest measure of economic activity, it is reported quarterly and is used to compare trends in national output. A rising GDP means the economy is growing. The *rate* of GDP growth is also important. Although actual GDP rose steadily from 1982 to 1990, the percentage increase varied widely from year to year.

Another important yardstick of economic health is the unemployment rate. The swings in unemployment from one phase of the cycle to the next can be substantial. For example, during the Great Depression of the 1930s, U.S. unemployment reached a staggering 25 percent of the work force. In contrast, during the expansion in 1968, unemployment dropped to slightly less than 4 percent. More recently, the 1981–1982 recession–in which unemployment rose to over 10 percent — was the worst experienced in this country since the Great Depression. During the expansion that followed and lasted until late 1990, unemployment fell to 5.3 percent before rising to more than 7.1 percent during the recessionary period of the early 1990s.

Unemployment, inflation, interest rates, bank failures, corporate profits, taxes, and government deficits are all examples of economic conditions that can have a direct and profound impact on our financial well-being, since they affect the very heart of our financial plans — our level of income, investment returns, interest earned and paid, taxes paid, and, in general, prices paid for goods and services consumed.

Inflation, Prices, and Planning. As we just saw, our economy is based on the exchange of goods and services between businesses and their customers — consumers, government, and other businesses — for a medium of exchange called money. The mechanism that facilitates this exchange is a system of *prices*. Technically speaking, the price of something is *the amount of money the seller is willing to accept in exchange for a given quantity of some good or service* — for instance, $3 for a pound of meat or $10 for an hour of work. When the general level of prices *increases* over time, the economy is said to be experiencing a period of **inflation**. The most common measure of inflation is the **consumer price index (CPI)**, an index based on the changes in the cost of a market basket of consumer goods and services. The United States has experienced a general rise in the level of prices for the past

35 years or so. And at times the rate of inflation has been fairly substantial — in 1980, for instance, prices went up by 13.5 percent. Fortunately, inflation has dropped dramatically in this country and the annual rate of inflation has remained below 5 percent in every year since 1983, except 1990 when it was 5.4 percent. Indeed, there is considerable hope that inflation is finally under control and will remain in the range of 3 to 5 percent for the foreseeable future.

Inflation is of vital concern to financial planning. It affects not only what we pay for the various goods and services we consume but also what we earn in

expansion
The phase of the economic cycle during which the levels of employment and economic activity/growth are both high; generally accompanied by rising prices for goods and services.

recession
The phase of the economic cycle during which the levels of employment and economic activity/growth are both slowing down.

depression
The phase of the economic cycle during which the employment level is low and economic activity and growth are at a virtual standstill.

recovery
The phase of the economic cycle during which the employment level is improving and the economy is experiencing increased activity and growth.

gross domestic product (GDP)
The total of all goods and services produced by workers located in a country; used to monitor economic growth.

inflation
A state of the economy in which the general price level is rising due to excessive demand or rapidly rising production costs; usually occurs during the recovery and expansion phases of the economic cycle.

consumer price index (CPI)
A measure of cost of living and inflation based on the changes in the cost of a market basket of consumer goods and services.

EXHIBIT 1.6

The Economic Cycle

The economy goes through various stages over time, though real depressions are extremely rare. These stages tend to be cyclical and directly affect the levels of employment and production.

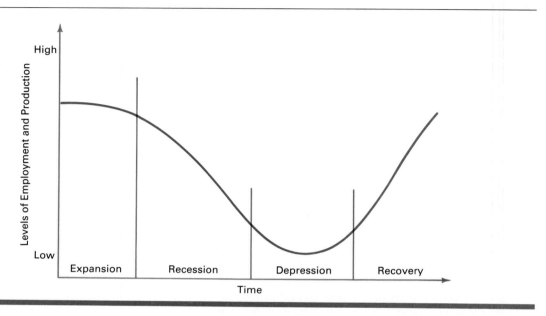

our jobs. Inflation tends to give an illusion of something that does not exist. That is, while we seem to be making more money, we really aren't. As prices rise, we need more income because our **purchasing power** — the amount of goods and services we can buy with our dollars — declines. For example, assume that you earned $24,500 in 1990 and received annual raises so that your salary was $28,000 by 1993. That represents an annual growth rate of 4.6 percent. If inflation averaged 5 percent per year, however, your purchasing power would have decreased, even though your income rose. You would require $28,362 just to keep pace with inflation. It is, therefore, important to look at what you can earn in terms of its purchasing power, not just in absolute dollars.

Inflation also directly affects interest rates. High rates of inflation drive up the cost of borrowing money, ultimately leading to higher mortgage payments, higher monthly car payments, and so on. High inflation rates also have a detrimental effect on stock prices, generally causing them to go down. Finally, sustained high rates of inflation can have devastating effects on retirement plans and other long-range financial goals — indeed, for many people it can put such goals out of reach. Clearly, low inflation is good for the economy, for interest rates and stock prices, and, in general, for financial planning.

Generally speaking, inflation has little effect on personal financial planning.

Fantasy: Inflation is a vital concern to financial planning, as it affects not only the prices we pay for the goods and services we consume, but also the amount of money we make. Clearly, if ignored, inflation can wreak havoc on our budgets and financial plans.

WHAT DETERMINES YOUR PERSONAL INCOME?

The amount of money you make is a function of many factors, including your age, your level of education, and your career. What combination of age, educational level, and career do you think will provide you with the best opportunity to make a lot of money? Take a moment to answer this question before reading on.

An obvious and important factor in determining how well we live is the amount of income we earn. In the absence of any inheritance or similar financial windfall, your income will depend in large part on demographic factors such as your age, gender, race, and marital status. Your education and choice of a career also influence your earning power. Making a lot of money is not easy. But it can be done! A high level of income—whether derived from your job, your own business, or your investments—is within your reach if you are willing to provide the necessary dedication and hard work, along with a well thought-out set of financial plans. Exhibit 1.7 presents data relative to the effect of age, education, and career on annual income. Looking at the median income shown in the far right column you can see that, as a rule, the closer you are to middle age, the more education you have, and the more professionally or managerially oriented your career, the greater your income will be.

YOUR AGE, GENDER, RACE, AND MARITAL STATUS

Although age, gender, and race are variables over which you have no control, it is interesting to look at their relationship to income. Typically, people with low incomes fall into the very young or very old age groups, while the period of highest earnings generally occurs between the ages of 35 and 55. This distribution results because those below age 35 are just developing their trades or beginning to move up in their jobs, while many over 55 are working only part-time or are completely retired. In the 25–34 age group, the median income of the heads of household is about $30,000; this jumps to about $41,500 for those in the 45–54 age group and then falls sharply in the 65-and-over group to about $16,000. It is very likely that your own income will vary over time; therefore, when setting financial goals and making financial plans, you should consider expected changes in earnings.

Gender and race also affect earning potential. Although the gap between the earnings of men and women has been narrowing, women still earn only 70 to 75 percent as much as men. Until recently women tended to choose or be limited to jobs in lower-paying "traditional" fields—sales clerks, teaching, clerical work, for example. Women's salaries are also negatively affected when they take time off to raise their children. They lose seniority, miss out on training opportunities, and are generally unable to regain lost ground, regardless of the amount of time off they take. Salaries of minority workers are below those of whites. On average, African-Americans earn only about 60 percent as much as white workers, and Hispanics, about 72 percent as much. The outlook is promising for both women and minorities, however, with the elimination of many barriers that prevented them from acquiring the education and skills necessary for higher-paying careers. Pay differences should decrease further as women and minorities are better represented among the ranks of corporate executives and other professions.

Your income also depends on whether you are married or single. The median income of married-couple families was about $40,000 in 1990, compared to about $18,000 for single people. While single individuals may be supporting only themselves, many do have children or others they must also support.

> **purchasing power**
> The amount of goods and services each dollar buys at a given point in time.

EXHIBIT 1.7

How Age, Education, Gender, and Career Are Related to Annual Income

The amount of money you earn is closely tied to your age, education, gender, and career. Generally, the closer you are to middle age (35–55), the more education you have, and the more professionally or managerially oriented your career, the greater your income will be.

	Annual Income (Head of Household)				
	Under $25,000	$25,000 –$34,999	$35,000 –$49,999	Over $50,000	Median Income
Age	Percent in Each Income Bracket by Age				
15 – 24	65.8%	17.6%	11.2%	5.3%	$18,663
25 – 34	40.0	16.9	21.0	19.1	29,823
35 – 44	28.5	16.7	22.3	32.6	37,635
45 – 54	26.6	14.0	19.9	39.6	41,423
55 – 64	40.4	15.5	16.9	27.2	30,819
65 and over	69.8	12.2	8.6	9.5	15,771
Education (highest level)	Percent in Each Income Bracket by Education				
Elementary					
8 years or less	77.3%	10.5%	7.3%	4.9%	$12,696
High School					
1–3 years	64.5	14.7	11.7	9.1	17,767
4 years	43.7	18.6	19.2	18.5	28,060
College					
1–3 years	32.1	17.7	22.3	27.8	35,083
4 or more years	17.4	13.3	20.3	49.0	49,180

	Median Income by Gender	
Career (full-time)	Women	Men
Executive, administrators, and managerial	$24,589	$40,103
Professional specialty	27,933	39,449
Technical and related support	21,768	31,371
Sales	16,057	29,676
Admin. support (incl. clerical)	17,517	25,138
Precision production, craft and repair	17,457	26,499
Machine operators, assemblers, and inspectors	14,463	22,343
Transportation and material moving	16,288	23,612
Handlers, equipment cleaners, helpers, and laborers	14,095	18,046
Service workers	11,669	18,903
Farming, forestry, and fishing	11,305	13,885

Source: U.S. Bureau of the Census, *Statistical Abstract of the United States: 1991* (111th edition) Washington, D.C., 1991, Tables No. 680 (page 417) and No. 723 (page 450).

YOUR EDUCATION

Your level of formal education is a controllable factor that has a considerable effect on your income. This is not to say that all people with equivalent formal educations will earn similar incomes. Rather, formal education is simply a tool that, when properly applied, can lead to higher earnings. As Exhibit 1.7 illustrates, heads of household who have more formal education earn higher annual incomes than those with lesser degrees. According to a survey published in *Money* magazine in October 1991, the average high school graduate earns about $13,620, compared to $25,308 for someone with a bachelor's degree. And a Ph.D. and other professional degrees can double the earnings of a college graduate. Over a lifetime, these differences really add up! Although education alone cannot guarantee a high income,

EXHIBIT 1.8
Average Salaries for Selected Professions

Professional and managerial workers tend to earn higher salaries than those in occupations requiring less formal education. Specialists within an occupation also tend to have higher incomes. Salaries also depend on the demand for a particular type of expertise and the region of the country.[a]

	Salary		
Occupation	**Entry-level**	**Senior**	**Manager**
Architect, health care	$24,000	$43,000	$71,000
Auditor	26,650	40,150	63,220
Community health nurse	21,000 (LPN)	32,000 (RN)	42,000
Compensation and benefits administrator	26,440	39,500	56,420
Computer programmer	25,820	40,360	57,880
Corporate attorney	40,360	66,240	73,240
Credit and collections representative	22,740	33,900	50,040
Electronic engineer	32,000	44,000	70,000
Financial analyst	28,060	41,500	59,260
Industrial engineer	30,420	46,420	59,060
Marketing product manager	NA	53,000	58,000
Market research analyst	24,900	39,660	49,340
Medical technologist	22,500	29,300	43,480
Public relations representative	24,040	40,380	56,880
Quality control expert	30,600	46,640	59,340
Software engineer	31,060	50,520	62,875
Systems analyst	30,000	40,500	57,500
Tax accountant	28,560	40,840	59,940

[a]The salary ranges for the careers listed represent an average of ranges reported in the articles.

Source: Margaret Mannix, David Bowermaster, and Sarah Burke, "Regional Salary Survey" and "Hot Tracks in 20 Professions," *U.S. News & World Report*, November 11, 1991, pp. 92–102.

these statistics suggest that your earning potential is greatly enhanced when you start with a good formal education.

YOUR CAREER

How much you earn over your lifetime depends also on your career. Your choice of a career is closely related to your level of education and determined by your particular skills, interests, lifestyle preferences, and personal values. In addition, social, demographic, economic, and technological trends may affect your decision as to what fields offer the best opportunities for the future. While not a prerequisite for many types of careers, such as sales, service, and certain types of manufacturing and clerical work, formal education generally leads to greater decision-making responsibilities—and increased

income potential—within a career. Exhibit 1.8 presents an alphabetical list of average salaries from entry level, senior, and managerial positions for a variety of careers, compiled from *U.S. News and World Report's* "1992 Career Guide." As shown in Exhibits 1.7 and 1.8, professional and managerial workers, who typically have a college degree, tend to earn the highest salaries. Clearly those careers requiring greater formal education or specialized skills typically result in higher incomes.

Making Career Decisions. Salary is not the only factor to consider in career and job decisions. Employee benefits can increase your total compensation package by 30 percent or more. Benefits may include tuition-reimbursement programs for continuing education, life and health insurance, disability insurance, pension and profit-sharing plans, and

401(k) retirement plans. Some companies and industries are known for their generous benefit packages, while others offer far less attractive packages. The size of the company typically affects its benefits because, in general, small firms can't afford to offer as many benefits as larger ones. You should consider both salary and benefits when comparing employment opportunities.

Finally, you must take into account personal values relating to work and lifestyle. What types of work situations do you prefer — independent, team, high pressure, stable, physically or intellectually challenging, public contact? Why do you want to work — for monetary gain, to help others, to change society, for personal achievement, to gain expertise? Lifestyle values — where you want to live, the importance of cultural or athletic activities, your desire for travel, family considerations — may help you narrow your career options. For example, because of the great personal satisfaction you gain from helping children learn, you may accept limited salary potential in order to teach pre-school children in a Head Start program. If you prefer living and working in a rural area rather than in a big city, you may have to accept a lower salary for your chosen career.

Like financial planning, career planning is a lifelong process that includes short-term and long-term goals. No longer do most people stay in one field or remain with one company for their lifetimes. Most educational institutions have placement offices that can teach you how to make career decisions, and there are many good books about careers and the job search process. Magazines such as *Business Week, Money, Kiplinger's Personal Finance, Newsweek, Time,* and *U.S. News & World Report* often feature articles on the best job opportunities for the future. Government publications, particularly the *Occupational Outlook Handbook*, which is revised biannually, also provide excellent career information.

Career Strategies for the 1990s. Today's workplace is considerably different than that of our parents. The average American starting his or her career in the 1990s can expect to have at least ten jobs for five or more employers, and many of us will have two, three, or even more careers over our life-

times. Some of these changes will be based on personal decisions, but others may be the result of layoffs from corporate downsizings, as occurred during the early 1990s. Many of us have family friends who suddenly found themselves unemployed and found it necessary to switch careers. For instance, a production manager for an automobile manufacturer who feels that her prospects for another job in the auto industry are slim may buy a quick-print franchise and become her own boss. Job security is practically a thing of the past, and corporate loyalty has given way to a more self-centered career approach requiring new career strategies.

To protect your earning power during economic downturns and to develop it to its fullest potential during prosperous times, you should develop a personal portfolio of skills, both general and technical. Know your strengths, develop them through on-the-job training programs and continuing education courses, and add new skills. These will allow you to branch out from your first job into new directions and to new companies. Don't be afraid to take new assignments that will give you a broader base of experience and skills, whether within the same field or company or to transfer your skills to new areas. Computer skills, knowledge of a foreign language, problem-solving abilities, and managerial skills will enhance your value as an employee. The more diverse your background (within reason!), the better off you will be in terms of both promotability and employability. Keep up with changes in the marketplace, broaden your contacts within your industry and among your professional colleagues, know which industries have potential and which are in trouble, and know what skills are in demand in your field.

Don't limit yourself by getting locked into one industry. Defining what you do in terms of your skills or profession allows you to uncover new opportunities. Suppose, for instance, you are a human resources manager laid off by a financial services firm. Because financial services jobs have declined substantially in recent years, you need to find fields with job growth. Your research might lead you to health care, a field that has added several hundred thousand new jobs per year.

Clearly, the establishment of educational and career goals is closely related to personal financial

EXHIBIT 1.9

Organizational Model

This text emphasizes making financial decisions relative to assets, credit, insurance, investments, and retirement and estates in a fashion consistent with financial plans developed to achieve desired financial results.

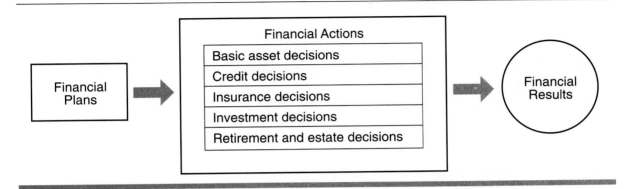

planning. Only after such goals are identified can you develop realistic personal financial goals and plans.

A high salary is the most important factor in choosing a particular job or career.

Fantasy: Salary is only one of many considerations in selecting a job or career. Employee benefit packages, working conditions, personal goals, skills, values, desired lifestyle, geographic preferences, and similar factors must be evaluated when making these important decisions.

AN OVERVIEW OF THE TEXT

This text is divided into six parts, each devoted to the explanation of a different aspect of personal financial planning:

- **Part One:** Foundations of Financial Planning
- **Part Two:** Managing Basic Assets
- **Part Three:** Managing Credit
- **Part Four:** Managing Insurance Needs
- **Part Five:** Managing Investments
- **Part Six:** Retirement and Estate Planning

The book is developed around the organizational model shown in Exhibit 1.9.

Our organizational scheme revolves around financial decision making that is firmly established on an operational set of financial plans. We believe that through sound financial plans, individuals can make financial decisions that will lead to desired financial results. Therefore, starting with Part One, where we look at personal accounting, budgeting and financial planning, and taxes, we move successively through the various types of decisions that individuals make when implementing their financial plans.

In order to allow you to gain some hands-on financial planning experience, a continuous case is developed and presented at the end of various chapters and parts of the text. The case begins at the end of this chapter with an inventory of personal and financial data for the Mark and Ana Williams family. With this data, opportunities to develop various components of the Williamses' financial plan appear at the end of Parts One through Five, Chapter 15, and Chapter 16. At each of these points, any additional data is presented, if needed, along with statements and questions aimed at directing the development of the aspect of the Williamses' financial plan related to the material presented in that part or chapter of the text. Completion of all of these components will result in a comprehensive financial plan for the Williamses. Of course, depending on course objectives and time constraints, the preparation of the Williamses' financial plan may or may not be required by your instructor.

SUMMARY

- One of the major benefits of personal financial planning is that it helps you to more effectively marshal and control your financial resources and thus gain an improved standard of living.
- In order to effectively manage your financial resources, you must *realistically* spell out your financial goals. Goals are essential to sound financial planning and should be set in terms of the desired results. They should reflect your values and change as personal circumstances dictate.
- A fully integrated set of financial plans includes financial budgets (covering living expenses and major asset acquisitions), liability and insurance planning, savings and investment planning, tax planning, and retirement and estate planning. Though these plans change over time, they provide the direction necessary for achieving your financial goals.
- The practice of financial planning is ideally suited to using the personal computer because of all the number crunching involved.

- Financial planning is conducted in an environment in which the government, business, and consumers are all influential participants, and financial decisions are affected by economic cycles and the impact of inflation on prices.
- Demographics, education, and chosen career are all important factors influencing your level of income. As a rule, people in the 35–55 age group tend to earn more than others, as do those in the more professional or managerial positions. Equally important, statistics show a strong, direct relationship between level of education and amount of income. Gender, race, and marital status also appear to affect earning potential.
- When making career decisions, in addition to salary, you must consider employee benefits, personal values, and your own lifestyle. Career plans should provide for flexibility through continuing on- and off-job education, job and employer changes, and protection of earning power in economic downturns.

QUESTIONS AND PROBLEMS

1. What is a standard of living? What are the factors that affect quality of life?
2. Are consumption patterns related to quality of life? Explain.
3. What is average propensity to consume? Is it possible for two people with very different incomes to have the same average propensity to consume?
4. Discuss the various forms in which wealth can be accumulated.
5. What is the role of money in setting financial plans? What is the relationship of money to utility?
6. Explain why financial plans must be psychologically as well as economically sound. What is the best way to resolve money disputes in a relationship?
7. Identify at least five financial goals that are important to you. Use a worksheet like the one in Exhibit 1.1 to describe your goals. Generally

speaking, why is it important to set realistically attainable financial goals?

8. What are the various components normally found in a complete set of financial plans?

9. Mark Potter's investments over the past several years have not lived up to his full expectations. He is not really concerned, though, since the difference is only about two percentage points. Do you have any advice for Mark?

10. Describe tax planning. How does it fit into the financial planning framework?

11. There's no sense in worrying about retirement until you reach "middle age." Discuss this point of view.

12. What role can a personal computer play in personal financial planning?

13. Discuss the following statement: "It is the interaction among government, business, and consumers that determines the environment in which personal financial plans must be made."

14. What are the stages of an economic cycle? Explain their significance for one's personal finances.

15. What is inflation, and why should it be a concern in financial planning?

16. "All people having equivalent formal education earn similar incomes." Do you agree or disagree with this statement? Explain your position.

17. Discuss the need for career planning throughout the life cycle and its relationship to financial planning. What are some of your personal career goals?

CONTEMPORARY CASE APPLICATIONS

1.1 Neil's Need to Know: Personal Finance or Tennis?

During the Christmas break of his final year at Mountain View College, Neil Stone planned to put together his résumé in preparation for his actively seeking full-time employment as a medical technician during the spring semester. To help Neil prepare for the job interview process, his older brother arranged for him to meet with a friend, Marilyn Nave, who has been a practicing medical technician since her graduation from Mountain View two years earlier. Neil and Marilyn met for lunch, and Marilyn provided him with numerous pointers on résumé preparation, the interview process, job opportunities, and so on.

After answering Neil's many questions, Marilyn asked Neil to bring her up to date on a variety of topics related to Mountain View College. Of special interest to Marilyn were the many changes that had taken place in the faculty and curriculum of the medical technology department since her graduation. As they discussed courses, Marilyn indicated that of all the electives she had taken, she had found the course in personal financial planning most useful. Neil said that he still had one elective to take and had been giving some thought to personal financial planning, although he was currently leaning toward a beginning tennis course. Neil felt that since a number of his friends would be taking tennis, it would be a lot of fun. He pointed out that since he never expected to get rich and already knew how to balance his checkbook, the personal financial planning course did not seem well suited to his needs. Marilyn said that there is certainly much more to personal financial planning than balancing a checkbook and that the course was highly relevant regardless of income level. She strongly believed that the personal financial planning course would be more beneficial to Neil than beginning tennis — a course that she herself had taken while at Mountain View College.

Questions

1. Describe to Neil the goals and rewards of the personal financial planning process.

2. Explain to Neil what is meant by financial planning and why it is important regardless of income.

3. Describe the financial planning environment to Neil. Explain the role of the consumer in, and the impact of economic conditions on, this environment.

4. What arguments would you present in order to convince Neil that the personal financial planning course would be more beneficial for him than beginning tennis?

1.2 Sid's Dilemma: Finding a New Job

Sid Como, a 47-year-old retail store manager earning $45,000 a year, had worked for the same company during his entire 28-year career. Then came a major recession that resulted in massive layoffs throughout the retail industry. He was among the unlucky people who lost their jobs. Now, ten months later, he is still unemployed. Sid's ten-months' severance pay and six months' unemployment compensation have run out. However, when he first became a store manager he had taken a personal financial planning course offered at the local university. Because he then adopted careful financial planning practices, he now has sufficient savings and investments to carry him through several more months of unemployment. Currently, his greatest financial need is to find a job.

Sid has actively sought work but finds himself overqualified for lower-paying jobs that are available and underqualified for higher-paying, more desirable positions. There have been no new openings for positions equivalent to the manager's job he lost. Although Sid attended college for two years after high school, he did not earn a degree. Sid is divorced and close to his two grown children who live in the same city.

The options facing Sid are:

- wait out the recession until another, equivalent retail store manager position opens up.
- move to another area of the country where store manager positions are still available.
- accept a lower-paying job for two or three years and go back to school evenings to finish his college degree and qualify for a better position.
- consider other types of jobs that could benefit from his managerial skills.

Questions

1. What important career factors should Sid consider when evaluating his options?
2. What important personal factors should Sid consider when deciding among his career options?
3. What recommendations would you give Sid in light of both the career and personal dimensions of his options noted in Questions 1 and 2 above?
4. What career strategies should today's workers employ in order to avoid Sid's dilemma?

FOR MORE INFORMATION

General Information Articles

Bernstein, Aaron. "What Happened to the American Dream." *Business Week*, August 19, 1991, pp. 80–85.

Bodnar, Janet. "How to Fight Fair about Money." *Kiplinger's Personal Finance Magazine*, July 1991, pp. 65–68.

Dumaine, Brian. "Investing for a New Future." *Fortune*, January 27, 1992, pp. 68–71.

Giese, William. "Your Inflation Rate: Staying Afloat." *Kiplinger's Personal Finance Magazine*, January 1992, pp. 45–46.

Harris, Diane. "How You Can Live Better." *Money*, October 1991, pp. 132–146.

Kosnett, Jeff. "What to Do in '92." *Kiplinger's Personal Finance Magazine*, January 1992, pp. 36–39. (Similar articles in each January issue.)

Luciano, Lani. "Where to Find the Best Jobs." *Money*, March 1991, pp. 142–150.

"Money Guide." *U.S. News & World Report*, published annually in July.

Nussbaum, Bruce. "A Career Survival Kit." *Business Week*, October 7, 1991, pp. 98–104.

————. "I'm Worried about My Job!" *Business Week*, October 7, 1991, pp. 94–97.

O'Reilly, Brian. "Preparing for Leaner Times." *Fortune*, January 27, 1992, pp. 40–47.

Young, Maria C., and Barbara M. O'Neill. "Mind Over Money: The Emotional Aspects of Financial Decisions." *Journal of Financial Planning*, January 1992, pp. 32–38.

Government Documents and Other Publications

Bolles, Richard. *What Color Is Your Parachute? A Practical Manual for Job Hunters and Career Changers*. Berkeley, CA: Ten Speed Press, 1991. (Revised annually.)

Financial Planning Bibliography. (Denver, CO: College for Financial Planning); 9725 E. Hampden Avenue, Denver, CO 80231; 303-755-7101.

Gurney, Kathleen. *Your Money Personality: What It Is and How You Can Profit from It.* New York: Doubleday, 1988.

Matthews, Arlene Modica. *If I Think about MONEY So Much, Why Can't I Figure It Out?* New York: Summit Books, 1991.

Occupational Outlook Handbook. Washington, DC: U.S. Department of Labor, 1990. (Revised every two years.)

Quinn, Jane Bryant. *Making the Most of Your Money.* New York: Simon & Schuster, 1991.

Most of use have expressed financial goals in one form or another. While in school, your goal may be to have enough money to purchase a new automobile or to have additional spending money. Upon graduation you may have a goal of owning your own home. Your parents may have a goal of helping you pay for your education, while your grandparents may be concerned with financing their retirement and managing their estate. While there are as many different financial goals as there are people, the major financial goals are summarized in Exhibit 1.1. Notice that the goals are characterized by the priority, time frame, and the target date for achieving the goal.

In order to achieve your financial goals you must establish financial plans that provide the direction required to achieve your objectives. The major type of financial plans include (1) liability and insurance, (2) savings and investments, (3) tax, and (4) retirement and estate plans.

As you might expect, people go through different stages in their lives and, therefore, their income pattern and the financial goals that they express may change. This personal financial planning life cycle as described in Exhibit 1.2 points out the fact that setting financial goals and implementing plans to achieve them continues throughout your life.

The amount that you will earn over your lifetime is normally a function of your education and career choice. However, the fact that you may be well educated and/or have a high income does not guarantee financial security. In order for you to effectively manage your finances, you must realistically set your financial goals from which you will develop your financial plans.

The process of financial planning can best be described through the use of an organizational model, as shown in Exhibit 1.9. Sound financial plans must be established before financial actions can be taken to achieve the intended results. Such plans are

If You Are Just Starting Out

In order to develop a workable personal financial plan, you must be able to set financial goals that are realistically attainable. Rank them in order of priority, and assign a definite time frame for realizing the goal. For someone just starting a career, the first task that must be performed is a financial inventory of assets and liabilities and a review of income and expenses. It is essential to keep good records to assist you in setting your financial goals and to monitor your performance toward achieving these goals.

Initially your financial goals may appear to be somewhat simplistic in that they may not include all of the areas of financial planning. In general, the financial goals for someone just starting out revolve around four main areas. These are record keeping, liability and insurance, savings, and investments.

Record Keeping:

1. Develop a good system of record keeping in order to monitor your progress. There are many software packages that can assist you in this process or you may create your own spreadsheets.

2. Generate balance sheets on a periodic basis.

3. Make an analysis of your current income and expenditures in order to gain control over this area.

4. Create a statement of projected income and expenses and analyze to look for problems and opportunities.

Liability and Insurance:

1. You might want to borrow money for some worthwhile purpose in order to establish your credit record.

2. In order to manage your debt more efficiently, you might want to consolidate your outstanding obligations to reduce monthly payments and to free funds for other goals.

3. If you are single with no dependents, you should have adequate long-term disability, health, property, and liability coverage because they are most important at this stage in the financial planning life cycle.

4. If you are married and/or have dependents, you should also have additional life insurance to cover your dependent's needs in the event of your death.

Savings and Investments:

1. Set aside an emergency fund to meet unexpected expenses. This is usually equal to three months' income.

2. Establish a regular savings program.

3. Decide on a proper mix of assets (cash, stocks, bonds, and so on) in your investment portfolio and allocate funds accordingly.

4. Review you investments and savings periodically to monitor performance.

based upon an analysis of your current financial condition that includes your personal income statement and balance sheet. These statements will assist you in setting realistic financial goals and monitoring your progress toward achieving them. Based upon the financial plans that you develop, you will take certain financial actions. The decisions that have to be made to achieve the desired results include basic asset decisions, as well as decisions involving credit, insurance, investments, retirement and estate planning.

Remember, financial planning is a lifelong process, but the sooner you get started and the more effort that you put into it, the better off you will be. So let's get started!

If You Are Thirtysomething

Once you have become established in your career, your income should continue to rise. As your income increases, you will hopefully have more excess funds that can be used to meet your financial goals, and you probably have a greater ability to accept risks in return for higher expected returns. Establishing a good record-keeping system in early years will assist you in monitoring your performance toward achieving your initial financial goals. However, as you get older additional goals come into play. Among the areas that should be reviewed as you mature are insurance, real estate and other goals, investments, tax planning, and retirement and estate planning.

Insurance:

1. Evaluate all of your personal insurance plans to see if there are any gaps in coverage.

2. Adjust coverage levels to reflect changes in your income and net worth.

3. Consider professional liability insurance.

Real Estate and Other Goals:

1. Soon after you are established in your career, you may wish to purchase a home. You should set aside funds to provide for the downpayment and possibly the closing costs.

2. If you have or are contemplating having children, establish an education fund.

3. If you have or plan to have children, project your income and expenses to accommodate the additional cost of raising a child.

Investments:

1. Review your investments to consider any changes in your attitude towards risk and your time horizon for achieving your financial goals.

2. Be sure the amount going into your investment portfolio is consistent with your ability to achieve your goals in the allotted time frame and at your risk level.

Tax Planning:

1. Always maintain adequate tax records. As your income increases, so does your tax bill without adequate planning.

2. Plan for the tax implications of increased income and be aware of potential changes in the tax laws.

3. Evalute your investments to see if they are achieving the best after-tax rate of return.

4. Review your income tax returns with your accountant to determine that you are taking advantage of all applicable tax-savings techniques and to ensure that you understand the ways in which you might save on your taxes in the future.

Retirement and Estate Planning:

1. Review your employer's retirement options to ensure that you have made proper elections.

2. Estimate expected retirement benefits and compare them to estimated expenditures.

3. Make plans to correct any deficiency in retirement income as soon as possible.

4. Maintain an up-to-date will and powers of attorney.

5. Estimate the value of your estate and establish trusts where applicable.

6. Make sure that guardians have been appointed for dependent children.

Mark and Ana Williams are a young couple in their mid-20s. They are married and both working at jobs they enjoy. Not only do they like their employment, but they are earning good salaries for recent college graduates. Together they make over $55,000 a year. Mark comes from an affluent family and is accustomed to having this kind of money, but Ana's family is not as well off financially. Because of her father's temporary job loss while she was growing up and then his death when she was 16, Ana is much more concerned about financial security than is Mark.

Mark and Ana have always been very open with each other when it comes to money. They had many discussions on how they felt about money and what they wanted to accomplish financially even before they were married. However, in the past few months both of them have started to realize that if they really want to accomplish their financial goals they need to establish a financial plan. While watching one of the many New Year's Day college football games, they saw an advertisement for a financial planning firm. Later that evening Mark and Ana decided to get some professional financial planning advice.

After talking with several financial planners, Mark and Ana selected a professional, Lisa DelaRosa, CFP, to work with. During their first conference with Ms. DelaRosa, they discussed many things that would influence their financial plan. It was reaffirmed that Ana is more security oriented and less willing to take risk than is Mark. Mark, on the other hand, really enjoys spending more than saving. Both of them agreed, however, that they would like to purchase a condominium just as soon as they can.

Ms. DelaRosa made a point to emphasize the sizable income they have for such a young couple. She also noted the fact that Ana currently earns more than Mark. Mark was clear that this disparity in their incomes was not a problem in their relationship for either him or Ana. Ana agreed, adding that, as with most pharmacists, she started out at a relatively high income but her income would peak by the time she was in her 30s unless she wanted to go into business for herself. At this time she does not plan on starting her own business. She is more interested in having a family and being able to spend time with Mark and the children (after they arrive).

Mark feels that his income will continue to increase more than Ana's. He is quite ambitious and is considering returning to college for his MBA after working a few years. If Mark is still with his current employer, First Federal Savings will pay for his continuing education.

In their conversation, Mark and Ana brought up the concern that they had not been able to save as much money since their marriage as they would have liked. Most of their current assets are from gifts given to Mark before they were married and to both of them as wedding presents. They are concerned that they will not be able to build up an adequate emergency fund and meet their other goals if they don't find some way to start saving more regularly. Ana also noted that they had started using credit more than she would like. Mark agreed, but he isn't as concerned about this as is Ana.

Mark wants to be sure that Ana would be able to live comfortably in case of his premature death. Ana feels she can get by on her salary, but Ms. DelaRosa assured both of them that life insurance evaluation would be included in their financial plan. She also pointed out that all types of personal insurance and their employee benefit plans would be evaluated.

At the end of their first conference, Ms. DelaRosa gave Mark and Ana some forms to fill out and mail to her before their next meeting. These forms are presented on the following pages. Read over the information Mark and Ana provided so that you can "get acquainted" with them. As you first read the case, you will probably not understand all the vocabulary or why certain information is even included on the forms. But remember, this is just Chapter 1 of the text. By the time you reach Chapter 16, Mark and Ana, as well as their financial data, will be old friends, and you will feel very comfortable with what all of this means!

WILLIAMS *Background*

PERSONAL FINANCIAL INFORMATION

CLIENT INFORMATION

Name _____ Mark Allen Williams _____

Birth Date _____ 6/7/68 _____

Social Security No. _____ 263-55-4312 _____

Business Phone _____ 512/555-2842 _____

Residence Address _____ 12608 Hallow Trail _____

City, State & Zip _____ Milford, USA 61703 _____

Residence Phone _____ 512/555-8163 _____

Wedding Date _____ 10/28/91 _____

SPOUSE INFORMATION

Name _____ Ana Marie Williams _____

Birth Date _____ 7/28/69 _____

Social Security No. _____ 103-76-8667 _____

Business Phone _____ 512/555-6287 _____

CHILDREN

Name	Birth Date	Grade
None		

EDUCATION

	School	Degree	Year Received
Mark	State University	B.S. Economics	5/90
Ana	State University	B.S. Pharmacy	5/91

OCCUPATION

	Employer	Position	Years From To
Mark	First Federal Savings	Loan Officer	6/90–present
Ana	Consumers' Drug Emporium	Staff Pharmacist	9/91–present

CONSULTANTS FOR FINANCIAL PLANNING

	Name	Address	Phone
Attorney	Stanley Madison	112 Park Tower Road Mildord, USA 61703	555-4168
Accountant	None		
Bank Officer	Sandra Ortega	First Federal Savings Milford, USA 61704	555-2842
Insurance Agent	William Brown	3562 Main Street Milford, USA 61704	555-5221
Securities Broker	Robert McDonald	Riverview Towers, Suite 805 Milford, USA 61704	555-1151

LOCATION OF DOCUMENTS	
Wills/Trusts	None
<u>Insurance:</u> Life	Group policies through 1st Federal Savings & Consumer's Drug Emporium Information booklets on file at apartment
Health	Group policy through 1st Federal Savings & Consumer's Drug Emporium Information booklets on file at apartment
Disability	Group policy through Consumer's Drug Emporium Information booklet on file at apartment
Auto	File at apartment
Deeds: Title to cars	File at apartment
Birth/Marriage/Other Cert.	File at apartment

ASSETS – January 1, 1993

	Location	Balance	Rate of Interest	Maturity
Checking:	First Federal Savings (opened 10/15/91)	$1,385	4.0%	N/A
Money Market Accounts/Funds:	Milford National Bank (opened 6/5/87)	$4,025	5.5%	N/A
CDs	First Federal Savings	$2,000	6.8%	6/13/93
	First Federal Savings	$1,500	7.0%	6/5/93
Cash on Hand		$185		

Security Investments:

Number of Shares	Security	Cost or Basis			Current Value	
		Date Acquired	Per Share	Total	Per Share	Total
100	Apple Computer stock (Mark's property)	3/5/85	24-3/4	$2,475	59-1/8	$5,913
100	General Motors stock (wedding present)	10/22/91	37-7/8	$3,788	33-1/4	$3,325
244.70	Fidelity Puritan Fund	12/31/91	$12.26	$3,000	$14.12	$3,455

	Year	Make	Model	Cost	Current Value
Current Automobiles:	1989	Mazda	626	$13,800	$8,500
	1991	Ford	Explorer	$15,100	$11,000

Personal Property:		Market Value
	Clothing	$4,200
	Furniture and appliances	$5,600
	Stereo & T.V.	$1,500
	Jewelry	$2,900
	(Other) computer equipment	$2,500

LIABILITIES – January 1, 1993

To Whom Owed	Original Amount of Account	Property or Service Purchased	Interest Rate	Current Balance
Ford Credit Corp.	$11,100	Ford Explorer	10.5%	$7,687
First Federal Savings	$3,500	Computer Equipment	13.0%	$1,524
Milford National Bank	$4,000	Education (Mark)	6.0%	$2,606
Milford National Bank	$6,000	Education (Ana)	6.0%	$5,030

	Payment Amount	How Often Paid	Total Number of Payments	Date of First Payment
Ford Credit Corp.	$284	monthly	48	7/10/91
First Federal Savings	$118	monthly	36	2/07/91
Milford National Bank	$77	monthly	60	1/20/91
Milford National Bank	$116	monthly	60	1/20/92

CREDIT CARDS – all joint accounts

Company	Number	Annual Fee	Interest Rate	Maximum Line of Credit	Outstanding Balance
Texaco	33 231 17718 61991	$ 0	18%	—	$ 0
Visa	4310 4516 3100 3259	$ 0	19%	$3,000	$1,250
MasterCard	3529 0317 2432 0917	$20	14%	$6,000	$2,830
American Express	2782 163539 62005	$45	—	—	$ 0
Neiman-Marcus	1626 55127	$ 0	18%	—	$285
Sears	0 50186 96182 0	$ 0	21%	$2,000	$1,650
Dominique's Boutique	361 05891	$ 0	18%	—	$260

Company	Minimum Monthly Payment	Grace Period	Calculation Method
Texaco	10% of balance or $20, whichever is greater	yes	Av. Daily Bal.
Visa	5% of balance or $25, whichever is greater	no	Av. Daily Bal.
MasterCard	5% of balance or $20, whichever is greater	yes	Adjusted Bal.
American Express	Total balance	—	—
Neiman-Marcus	10% of balance or $50, whichever is greater	yes	Av. Daily Bal.
Sears	3% of balance or $15, whichever is greater	yes	Av. Daily Bal.
Dominique's Boutique	10% of balance or $50, whichever is greater	yes	Past Due Bal.

1992 INCOME

	Current Year
Salary (Mark's)	$25,000
Bonuses	
Salary (Ana's)	$30,000
Bonuses (received in December)	$2,000
Interest[1]	516
Dividends[2]	346
Capital gains distributions[3]	126
Sale of Securities	
Maximum Global Mutual Funds[4]	4,943

[1]Checking ($55 a year, paid monthly), money market accounts/funds ($220 a year, paid monthly), CDs ($241 paid in June).

[2]Apple Computer ($48 a year), General Motors ($160 a year), Fidelity Puritan Fund ($138 a year). All dividends paid quarterly in March, June, September, and December.

[3]All distributions paid quarterly in March, June, September, and December.

[4]150 shares purchased January 5, 1985, at $57.13/share and sold January 5, 1992 at $32.95/share.

Income after tax deductions but before insurance deductions (take-home pay):

Mark	$1,549 per month
Ana	$1,859 per month
Bonus	$1,487 (December only)

1992 EXPENSES

	Cash Flow Monthly[1]	Cash Flow Annually
Medical/Dental Expenses (not covered by insurance)	$ 50	$ 600
Rent	600	7,200
Charitable contributions	75	900
Food/Groceries, etc.	400	4,800
Food away from home	175	2,100
Clothing	140	1,680
Utilities (electricity and water)	185	2,220
Telephone	45	540
Appliance and furniture purchases	84	1,008
Auto maintenance – gas, tires, etc.	180	2,160
Auto loan payments	284	3,408
Entertainment	175	2,100
Vacation (taken in August)		1,500
Gifts, birthdays, etc. ($500 in December, $35/month for all other months)		885
Disability insurance	25	300
Life insurance	15	180
Auto insurance (paid semiannually in January and June)		884
Personal care	55	660
Income taxes withheld ($360 extra withheld in December)	825	10,260
Social Security taxes withheld ($153 extra withheld in December)	351	4,365
Education loan payments	193	2,316
Computer loan payments	118	1,416
Revolving credit minimum payments	354	4,248
Miscellaneous	75	900

[1]Regular monthly expenditures

INSURANCE INFORMATION

LIFE INSURANCE

Insured:	Mark	Ana
Type of L.I.	Group Term	Group Term
Face Amount	$25,000 (1 times salary)	$50,000
Beneficiary	Ana	Mark
Owner	Mark	Ana
Annual Premium	Employer paid	$15/month (payroll deduction)

DISABILITY INSURANCE

Insured:		Ana
Policy number		Employer group policy
Definition of Disability		Own job for 2 years, any job educationally suited for after 2 years
Mo. Benefit		65% of gross monthly salary
Waiting Period	Sick	90 days
	Acc.	90 days
Benefit Period	Sick	to age 65
	Acc.	to age 65
Premiums		$25/month (payroll deduction)

MEDICAL INSURANCE

INSURED

	Mark	Ana
Company	American Health & Life	US Health (HMO)
Policy Number	Group #063-111	Group #168521 AGC

HOSPITALIZATION

Room Rate	80% of semiprivate rate	100% of semiprivate rate
Number of Days	unlimited	unlimited

MAJOR MEDICAL

Maximum	$500,000/year	unlimited
Deductible	$500/person/year	$10 copayment per doctor's visit $ 5 copayment per prescription
% Participation	80/20	—
Cap on Participation	$1,000/year	—
Maternity	covered	covered
Dental	no	no
Annual Premiums	employer paid for employee	employer paid for employee

COMMENTS

Mark's Policy:	Spouse could be covered for $60/month. Coordination of benefits provision is included in policy.
Ana's Policy:	Must use HMO facilities and selected hospitals. Spouse could be covered for $90/month. Coordination of benefits provision is included in policy.

AUTO INSURANCE

Auto Covered	(1) 1989 Mazda 626	(2) 1991 Ford Explorer
Company	U.S. Casualty	U.S. Casualty
Policy Number	156-88876-AOB6	same
Liability	40,000 or 20/40/15	40,000 or 20/40/15
Medical Payments	$2,500/person	$2,500/person
Uninsured Motorists	40,000 or 20/40/15	40,000 or 20/40/15
Collision	(Actual Cash Value)	(Actual Cash Value)
Deductible	$200	$200
Comprehensive	(Actual Cash Value)	(Actual Cash Value)
Deductible	$ 50	$50
Annual Premium	$399	$485
Comments	Paid semiannually in January and June	same

RETIREMENT INFORMATION

Person Covered	Mark	Ana
Type of Pension Plan	Qualified, noncontributory, defined benefits	No pension plan offered
Vesting	5-year vesting, nothing currently vested	—
Beneficiary	Ana	—
Other Plans Available	401(k)—no employer contribution. 8% average return over the past 6 years	401(k)—employer contributes 50¢ for each $1.00 of employee contribution. 9% average return over the past 3 years
Vesting	Immediate	Immediate
Current Value	$0	$0

ESTATE PLANNING INFORMATION

Mark and Ana would each like to leave all of their assets to each other in case of death. They would also like to reduce estate transfer costs as much as possible.

Mark would like his secondary beneficiaries to be his mother and his father. Ana would like her mother to be her secondary beneficiary.

FINANCIAL GOALS

Short range (1 year):

> To start a regular savings plan, to have an adequate emergency fund, to buy a condominium.

Intermediate range (1–5 years):

> To pay off all revolving credit debt, to buy a house, to have a child. They plan to keep the condo as rental property.

Long term (over 5 years):

> To have a second child, to be able to retire when Mark is 60 and live at least as well as they are now.

What is your single most important financial objective at this time:

> To buy a condominium

FINANCIAL PRIORITIES

		Mark	Ana
a.	LIVING: paying monthly bills	1	1
b.	PLEASURE: spending money	2	5
c.	RETIREMENT: invest in future	8	6
d.	DISABILITY: protect against	7	3
e.	DEATH: take care of family	3	8
f.	REDUCE TAXES: spend to save	4	7
g.	INVESTING: accumulate assets	5	2
h.	CHILDREN: future needs	6	4

Prioritized with 1 being most important and 8 being least important

OTHER INFORMATION

1. Are you able to save regularly?   No

2. How much are you able to save annually? $1,300   Where?   Money market account

3. Do you invest regularly?   No   Current assets were gifts from parents

4. Do you feel that you are financially organized?   Yes—somewhat

5. Do you budget your money?   No written budget

6. If you were to die, could your spouse handle the finances?

    Mark: yes
    Ana: yes

7. How do you feel about saving for retirement?   It's important, but have other goals that are more important right now.

8. If you had an extra $5,000 what would you do with it?

    Mark: buy a condominium
    Ana: pay off the revolving credit debt

9. How do you feel about taking investment risks?

    Mark: moderate risk taker
    Ana: risk adverse

10. How is your health?

    Mark: Excellent
    Ana: Excellent

CHAPTER 2

Measuring Your Financial Standing

In order to develop sound financial plans and effectively manage your money, you must be able to keep track of your current financial condition and periodically assess the progress you're making toward your financial goals. Such are the functions of personal financial statements. There are two types of personal financial statements, the balance sheet and the income and expenditures statement, both of which are essential to developing and monitoring personal financial plans. In fact, trying to manage money without the aid of personal financial statements is a lot like being left aboard a drifting ship. Not knowing where you are within the ocean's vast expanse, you would first need to determine your location. Then, with the assistance of certain navigational aids, you could plot your course to safety. Think of financial statements as navigational aids. You use them to gauge your financial position at various points in time and to judge the progress you're making toward your financial goals. Understanding how to prepare and interpret personal financial statements is one of the cornerstones of personal financial planning. Without some standards by which to measure your financial condition, establishing financial goals and evaluating your progress toward those goals is difficult, if not impossible.

FINANCIAL *facts* OR *fantasies*

Are the following statements financial facts (true) or fantasies (false)?

Since financial statements are used to record actual results, they're really not that important in personal financial planning.

You would list a leased car as an asset on your personal balance sheet.

Only the principal portion of a loan should be recorded on the liability side of a balance sheet.

Whereas the balance sheet summarizes your financial condition at a given point in time, the income and expenditures statement reports on your financial performance over time.

Generating a cash surplus is desirable, since it adds to your net worth.

When evaluating your income and expenditures statement, primary attention should be given to the top line: income received.

THE ROLE OF FINANCIAL STATEMENTS IN FINANCIAL PLANNING

Personal financial statements contain important information used in the financial planning process. What kind of personal financial information would you need in order to assess your financial position at various points in time and monitor the progress you're making toward your financial goals? Try to answer this question before reading on.

As we saw in Chapter 1, personal financial planning involves the establishment of an integrated set of financial plans and the development of corresponding financial strategies for putting them into action. Clearly, in order to set realistic plans and strategies, we must know where we stand financially. Once the plans and strategies are in place, we then need a system for monitoring our progress. Personal financial statements can help in both stages by defining your current financial condition and enabling you to track changes in your financial position over time.

To begin with, the *balance sheet* provides a statement of your financial condition by describing the assets you hold, debts you owe, and your net worth at a given point in time. Then it helps you keep track of the progress you're making toward your goals, in building up your assets and/or reducing your debt. Thus, it is indispensable in setting, monitoring, and revising financial plans. Also, by revealing the kinds of changes that are taking place in your financial position, it helps you know when it is time to alter your financial plans.

In contrast, the *income and expenditures statement* provides a measure of financial performance over time. It keeps track of income earned, as well as expenditures made, over a given period of time (usually a year). A key ingredient in financial planning is gaining budgetary control over expenses and purchases. Without such control, you could well find yourself without the funds necessary for carrying out your financial plans. A statement of income and expenditures is helpful in this regard as it provides a way to check actual expenses and purchases against the amounts budgeted. Corrective action can then be taken when discrepancies exist between the actual and budgeted amounts.

The primary function of financial statements, therefore, is to summarize your financial position as it *actually* exists and report on various financial transactions that have *really* occurred. On the other hand, financial plans deal with mapping out the *future* and, at first glance, may appear to be incompatible with financial statements because of their different time references. Yet the whole planning system would indeed collapse without statements to provide feedback on your financial progress. Somewhere along the line, you must look at how actual results compare with your plans. Fortunately, there are many good computer programs that simplify the job of preparing personal financial statements and performing other personal financial planning tasks. The *Smart Money* box describes some popular personal finance software.

Think of financial statements as *planning tools* that provide an up-to-date evaluation of your financial well-being, help you identify potential financial problems, and in general help you make better-informed financial decisions. The following sections take a detailed look at the basic personal financial statements, starting with the balance sheet.

Since financial statements are used to record actual results, they're really not that important in personal financial planning.

Fantasy: Personal financial statements let you know where you stand financially. As such, they not only help you set up realistic financial plans and strategies but also provide a system for monitoring the amount of progress you're making toward the financial goals you've set.

THE BALANCE SHEET: A STATEMENT OF YOUR FINANCIAL CONDITION 🔲

A balance sheet reports the things you own, on the one hand, relative to the money you owe and your financial worth, on the other. What do you currently own and owe? List and evaluate all items you own and owe, noting their current dollar value, before reading on.

The **balance sheet** — or *statement of financial position* — summarizes a person's (or family's) financial condition at a certain point in time. Think of a balance sheet as a snapshot taken of a person's financial position on one day out of the year. Technically, you could have a (slightly) different balance sheet each day of the year. A balance sheet represents a summary of what you own — your *assets* — balanced against what you owe — your *liabilities*, or debts — and what you are worth — your *net worth*. The accounting relationship between these three categories is called the *balance sheet equation* and is expressed as follows:

Total assets = Total liabilities + Net worth

ASSETS: THE THINGS YOU OWN

Assets are the items you own. They are mostly tangible, although in certain instances they may also be intangible. An item is classified as an asset regardless of whether it was purchased for cash or financed with debt. In other words, even if an asset has not been fully paid for, it is considered owned by the individual and should be listed on the balance sheet. An item that is leased, in contrast, is not shown as an asset, since it is actually owned by someone else.

Assets can be grouped in a variety of ways. One useful procedure is to group them on the basis of their underlying characteristics and uses, as shown in Exhibit 2.1. This results in four broad categories: Liquid assets, investments, real property, and personal property. **Liquid assets** are the cash and near-cash holdings of individuals that are used to meet living expenses, make purchases, pay bills and loans, and provide for emergencies and unexpected opportunities. **Investments** include those (mostly intangible) assets that are acquired in order to earn a return. These assets may consist of either real property or financial assets. Although usually held for future rather than current consumption, they can be converted into cash and are therefore more liquid than real or personal property. **Real property** is represented by tangible assets that generally have

fairly long life spans and are used for shelter, transportation, and recreation: these assets also carry relatively high price tags. **Personal property** is also tangible but generally is less costly than real property. Such assets provide the general creature comforts of life. During 1990 the assets of the average American household consisted of about 16.1 percent liquid assets, 35.7 percent investments (including pensions), 32.8 percent real property (including housing), and 15.4 percent personal property.

Regardless of their type, all assets are recorded on the balance sheet at their current **fair market value**, which may differ considerably from their original purchase price. Fair market value is either the actual value of the asset (such as money in a checking account) or the price that the asset can reasonably be expected to sell for in the open market (like a used car or a home).

---

balance sheet
A key financial statement that summarizes a person's assets, liabilities, and net worth is measured at a specified point in time.

assets
Items that one owns.

liquid assets
Assets that are held in the form of cash or can be readily converted to cash with minimal or no loss in value; used to meet living expenses, make purchases, pay bills and loans, and provide for emergencies and unexpected opportunities.

investments
Assets like stocks, bonds, and mutual funds that are acquired for the purpose of earning a return rather than providing a service.

real property
Tangible assets that are held to fill basic shelter, transportation, and recreation needs; usually have relatively long lives and high costs.

personal property
Tangible assets that are held to provide the general comforts of life; includes things like clothing, house furnishings, and jewelry.

fair market value
The price that an asset can reasonably be expected to sell for in the open market.

Using Personal Financial Planning Software

Managing your personal finances used to be a tedious, time-consuming job. Now, however, you can streamline the financial planning process by using one of the many affordable, easy-to-use personal finance software programs. The computer can track expenses, write checks, pay bills electronically, prepare financial statements and budgets, help with tax planning, set up savings programs to reach certain goals, monitor and/or recommend investments, analyze loans, and/or prepare a comprehensive financial plan. Because programs vary considerably in capabilities, sophistication, and price, you must evaluate your particular needs before choosing the program(s) appropriate for you. The following brief descriptions of some popular general money management software will help you decide if you can benefit from computerized financial planning. (Prices are list prices

as of early 1992, but substantial discounts are often available from large software retailers.)

Quicken (Intuit; IBM and Macintosh; $70) and *Andrew Tobias's Managing Your Money* (MECA; IBM and Macintosh; $220) are the most popular general money management programs. *Quicken* is one of the easiest personal finance programs to learn because it is based on electronic versions of the familiar checkbook and check register. It includes check writing, budgeting, and investment features. (At the present time, only the IBM version can handle investments.) As transactions are entered, they are automatically added to the appropriate expense categories, making it easy to monitor and control expenses. You can also keep track of your stock, bond, and mutual fund investments and calculate rates of return on your investments. *Quicken* updates portfolio values each time

you enter a new securities transaction or update price quotes. It will also access price quotes from *Prodigy*, an on-line information service.

Managing Your Money (MYM) is also easy to use, but this more comprehensive program offers more versatility and flexibility— at a higher price. In addition to tracking expenses, preparing budgets, and monitoring investments, it calculates net worth, projects taxes, and analyzes cash flow. It is based on a series of interrelated modules called "chapters." When you enter an item in the checkbook module, any other modules that may be affected, such as net worth, taxes, or securities, will change automatically. With *MYM*, you can also perform more complex financial planning analysis, such as calculating life insurance needs, analyzing loan options, and developing retirement savings plans. It has greater investment tracking and analysis

---

You would list a leased car as an asset on your personal balance sheet.

Fantasy: You are only "using" the leased car; you do not own it. Accordingly, it should not be included as an asset on the balance sheet.

Liquid Assets.   Liquid assets are those low-risk financial assets that are held in the form of cash or can readily be converted to cash with little or no loss

in value. These assets are held to meet the everyday needs of life. Cash can be held either in the form of cash on hand or in a *demand deposit* (checking account). Savings are also part of one's liquid assets and can be held in such financial instruments as *time deposits* (savings accounts), certificates of deposit that mature within one year, money market deposit accounts, or money market mutual funds.

capabilities than *Quicken* and, with a supplementary program called *Managing the Market* (IBM only; $150), can access quotes from the *Dow Jones News/Retrieval* service as well as perform other investment management tasks. (The Macintosh version is more limited to its investment and financial planning options.)

WealthBuilder (Reality Technologies and *Money* Magazine; IBM and Macintosh, $170) is a more sophisticated planning program—it won't handle the day-to-day tasks like check writing—best suited for those who already have some wealth. It takes more time to learn the program and must be tailored to your personal situation. You start by developing a monthly budget and a balance sheet (you can transfer data to prepare these from *Quicken* or *MYM*). Then you establish financial goals, including a timetable, the amount required, and how

much is already saved. The program calculates the monthly savings and level of return required to reach the goal. You can ask what-if questions and change rates of return to reflect current market conditions. *WealthBuilder* will recommend how to divide investments among various alternatives based on your personal risk preferences. It includes a database of mutual funds, stocks, and bonds so you can look for suitable investments. Future updates of the database can be purchased. The main attraction of this program is its ability to give you a comprehensive plan that is tied to your goals. By changing assumptions you can see the effect of different strategies on your overall financial plans.

Several other programs provide quick answers to specific planning questions but don't provide an integrated plan. *MoneyPlans* (Parsons Technol-

ogy; IBM; $49) has a series of separate worksheets to help you calculate life insurance needs, perform an automobile lease versus purchase analysis, choose whether to use cash or borrow to make a major purchase, and compare various mortgage or other loan alternatives. *Andrew Tobias's Financial Advisor* (MECA; IBM; $45) is actually one *MYM* module. It allows you to calculate the cost of specific goals, such as what your child's college education will cost or how much your savings or investments will be worth at a future date. It also has loan analysis capabilities, so you can see the effect of changing your payment amount or refinancing a loan, and it has a retirement planning section.

Sources: Robert Cullen, "Smiling Interfaces," *Personal Investor*, November 1991, pp. 54–57; Kristin Davis, "Money Management Made Easy," *Kiplinger's Personal Finance Magazine*, January 1992, pp. 65–69; and "Financial Planning Software: The Long and Short Answers," *Changing Times*, January 1991, pp. 80–81.

Investments. Investments are assets that are acquired in order to earn a return rather than provide a service. These assets, which typically consist largely of intangible *financial assets* (stocks, bonds, and other types of securities), tend to be held for the anticipated future benefit they offer. Popular investments assets include common and preferred stocks and corporate, government, and municipal bonds. Certificates of deposit with maturities of greater than one year, shares in investment companies—especially mutual funds—and real estate are also popular. Business ownership, the cash values of life insurance, retirement funds such as IRAs and 401(k) plans, and other investment vehicles such as commodities and financial futures, and options represent still other forms of investment assets. (With regard to retirement fund accounts, only those balances that are eligible to be withdrawn should be

EXHIBIT 2.1

Commonly Held Personal Assets

The specific types and amounts of personal assets held will vary from one person or family to another. Most households will likely hold some liquid assets, possibly even some investments, and real and personal property.

Liquid Assets

Cash
  On hand
  In checking account

Savings accounts
  At banks, S&Ls
  At other thrift institutions
  Money market funds and deposits
  Certificates of Deposit
  (< 1 year maturity)

Investments

Stocks and bonds
  Common stock
  Preferred stock
  Corporate bonds
  Government and Municipal bonds

Certificates of Deposit
  (> 1 year maturity)

Investment companies
  Closed-end funds
  Mutual funds

Real Estate
Business ownership
Cash values of life insurance
Cash value of pensions
Other investment vehicles
  Commodities and financial futures
  Options
  Precious minerals
  Collectibles
  Annuities and limited partnerships

Retirement fund, investments
  IRA, 401(k) plans

Real Property

Housing
Automobiles
Recreational equipment

Personal Property

Furniture
Stereos, TVs, and appliances
Clothing
Jewelry
Artwork

shown as an asset on the balance sheet.) Investment assets tend to be acquired in order to achieve long-run personal financial goals. They vary in marketability (the ability to sell quickly) from high (stocks and bonds) to low (real estate and business ownership investments).

Real and Personal Property.   Real and personal property are tangible assets that can be lived in, sat on, driven, or worn. They are used in our everyday lives and, in essence, provide support for our daily activities. Examples of real and personal property include homes, cars, recreational vehicles, second homes (mountain cabins or lakeside cottages), tractors, lawn mowers and other yard equipment, tools, furniture and appliances, VCRs and home entertainment centers, clothing and jewelry, and artworks. Some families spend a lot of money on such things, while others get by with far less. Except for real estate, some kinds of (older) cars, and perhaps jewelry and artwork, most types of real and personal property rapidly decline in value shortly after being put into use. In fact, the resale value of some of these assets, such as clothing and furniture, may quickly drop to only a small fraction of their original cost.

LIABILITIES: THE MONEY YOU OWE

Liabilities represent an individual's or family's debts. They could result from department store charges, bank credit card charges, installment loans, or mortgages on housing and other real estate. A given liability, regardless of its source, is something that is owed and must be repaid in the future. Liabilities are generally classified as either current or long term. A **current**, or **short-term liability** is any debt due within one year of the date of the balance sheet. A **long-term liability** is a debt due one year or more from the date of the balance sheet. Exhibit 2.2 lists some common types of liabilities that may appear on a personal balance sheet. The level and status of an individual's liabilities are given careful consideration by potential lenders because very high levels of debt and overdue debts are both viewed with a great deal of disfavor.

Current Liabilities.   One type of current liability arises from charges for the purchase of consumable

goods and services. Utility bills, rent, insurance premiums, taxes, medical bills, repair bills, and all similar debts fall into this category. Typically, these bills are due to be paid in full upon receipt or by a specified date, usually within one month of the billing date. Include these bills as liabilities only if you owe the funds now (an unpaid bill). Do not include something you may owe in the future, such as next month's utility bill.

A second type of current liability is **open account credit obligations** — the balances outstanding against preestablished credit lines, which are used to purchase various types of goods and services. For most people, such credit means the use of "plastic" — that is, a credit card. The balances on some credit cards (like bank and department store credit cards) can be paid off over time with small "minimum payments"; however, others, like gas or most travel and entertainment cards (American Express, for example), require payment in full upon receipt of the monthly statement. Another type of open account credit is the line of credit offered by most banks and S&Ls. A *line of credit* also provides a preauthorized amount of credit. Rather than use a credit card, you access the line of credit by writing a check against either your regular checking account or a special credit line set up at your bank or financial institution. The amount of the liability on open account credit obligations is the total balance outstanding, not the monthly payment; the outstanding balance will be printed on your monthly statement.

---

liabilities

Debts, such as credit card charges, installment loan balances, and real estate mortgages.

current (short-term) liability

Any debt due within one year of the date of the balance sheet.

long-term liability

Any debt due in one year or more from the date of the balance sheet.

open account credit obligations

Current liabilities that represent the balances outstanding against preestablished credit lines, which are used to purchase various types of goods and services.

EXHIBIT 2.2

Common Types of Personal Liabilities

The type of debt you have can include everything from current liabilities such as unpaid utility bills and credit card balances to long-term liabilities such as mortgages and consumer loans. Regardless of the type, they all have one thing in common—they are obligations that must be paid off in the future.

Current Liabilities	*Long-Term Liabilities*
Utility bills	Home (primary residence) mortgage
Rent	Other residence (second home) mortgages
Insurance premiums	Real estate investment mortgages
Taxes	Automobile loans
Medical/dental bills	Appliance and furniture loans
Repair bills	Home improvement loans
Bank credit card balances	Single-payment bank loans
Department store credit card balances	Education loans
Travel and entertainment card balances	Margin loans (on securities)
Gas and other credit card balances	Other loans
Bank line of credit balances	
Other current liabilities	

Long-Term Liabilities. Debt obligations with final repayment dates more than one year from the date of the balance sheet are classified as *long-term liabilities.* They typically include real estate mortgages, most consumer installment loans, education loans, and margin loans used to purchase securities. **Real estate mortgages** are loans associated with housing and other real estate purchases; they normally have lives of 15 years or more. They most commonly result from the purchase of a home but sometimes from real estate investments such as apartments or office buildings. Real estate mortgages are normally paid on an installment basis. **Consumer installment loans** include all debts (other than mortgages) for which a series of payments are required over a specified period of time. Installment loans are generally used to finance such purchases as automobiles, appliances, furniture, and boats. Other types of long-term liabilities include single-payment bank loans, education loans, and margin loans on securities.

All types of loans must be shown on the balance sheet. Although most loans will fall into the category of long-term liabilities, *any loans that come due within a year should be shown as current liabilities.* Examples of such short-term loans include a six-month, single-payment bank loan or a nine-month consumer installment loan for a refrigerator. Regardless of the type of loan, *only the latest outstand-*

ing loan balance should be shown as a liability on the balance sheet since at any given point in time it is the *latest* balance still due—not the initial loan balance—that matters. Another important and closely related point is that *only the principal portion of a loan or mortgage* should be listed as a liability on the balance sheet. In other words, you should not include the interest portion of your payments as part of your balance sheet debt. The principal actually defines the amount of debt you owe at a given point in time and does not include any future interest payments. You may have to contact the lender or refer to a *loan amortization table* for the loan in order to determine the amount of this liability.

Only the principal portion of a loan should be recorded on the liability side of the balance sheet. *Fact:* The principal portion of a loan represents the unpaid balance and is the amount of money you owe; interest, in contrast, is a charge that will be levied over time for the use of the money.

NET WORTH: A MEASURE OF YOUR FINANCIAL WORTH

Net worth is the amount of actual wealth or **equity** an individual or family has in owned assets. It can be viewed as the amount of money that would remain after selling all owned assets at their estimated fair market values and paying off all liabilities (assuming there are no transaction costs). As noted earlier, every balance sheet must "balance" so that total assets equals total liabilities and net worth. Rearranging this equation, we get net worth equals total assets minus total liabilities. Once the fair market value of assets and the level of liabilities have been established, net worth is easily calculated by subtracting total liabilities from total assets. If net worth is less than zero, the family is technically insolvent. While this form of **insolvency** does not mean that the family will end up in bankruptcy proceedings, it does reflect the absence of adequate financial planning.

Net worth typically increases over the life cycle of an individual or family. For example, the balance sheet of a college student will probably be fairly simple. Assets would include modest liquid assets (cash, checking and savings accounts) and personal property, plus maybe a car. Liabilities might include utility bills, perhaps some revolving credit obligations, and automobile and education loans. At this point in life, net worth would typically be very low, because assets are small in comparison to liabilities. A 29-year-old, single financial analyst would have more liquid assets and personal property, may have started an investment program, and may have purchased a condominium. Net worth would be rising but may still be low due to the increased liabilities associated with real and personal property purchases. The higher net worth of a two-career couple in their late 30s with children would reflect a greater proportion of assets relative to liabilities as they save for college expenses and retirement.

In the long-run financial planning process, the level of net worth is important. Once a family has established a goal of accumulating a certain level or type of wealth, progress toward that goal is best analyzed by monitoring net worth.

BALANCE SHEET FORMAT AND PREPARATION

Exhibit 2.3 presents a hypothetical balance sheet prepared for Fred and Denise Weaver on December 31, 1992. Assets are listed on the left side and liabilities on the right. The net worth entry is shown on the right side of the statement just below the liabilities. The subheadings included in Exhibits 2.1

and 2.2 may be used to break the statement into various categories. The totals for these categories are shown as subtotals in the statement. Regardless of how the various assets and liabilities are categorized, the statement should *balance*. Total assets equal the sum of total liabilities and net worth, as shown in the balance sheet equation.

You should prepare your personal balance sheet at least once a year, preferably every three to six months. Begin by listing your assets at their fair market value as of the date you are preparing the balance sheet, using the categories in Exhibit 2.1 as a guide. To determine the fair market value of assets, use checking and savings account records, bills of sale, investment account statements, and similar sources of information to get their original costs. For most personal property, values are then adjusted for the age of the item. The values of investments, a home, and a car are easier to estimate, because there are published sources of information such as stock and bond quotations, advertisements for comparable homes, and the *Blue Book* for used car values. Certain items — for example, homes, jewelry, and artwork — may appreciate, or increase, in value over time. The values of other assets — cars and most other types of personal property — depreciate, or decrease in value, over time.

---

real estate mortgages
Loans associated with housing and other real estate purchases; they normally have lives of 15 years or more.

consumer installment loans
Loans (other than mortgages) that are repaid in a series of fixed, scheduled payments.

net worth
An individual's or family's actual wealth; determined by subtracting total liabilities from total assets.

equity
The actual ownership interest in a specific asset or group of assets.

insolvency
The financial state in which net worth is less than zero.

EXHIBIT 2.3

The Weavers' Balance Sheet

A balance sheet is set up to show what you own on one side (your assets) and how you paid for them on the other (debt or equity).

BALANCE SHEET					
Name(s) Fred and Denise Weaver			Dated December 31, 1992		

ASSETS			LIABILITIES AND NET WORTH		
Liquid Assets			**Current Liabilities**		
Cash on hand	$ 90		Utilities	$ 120	
In checking	375		Rent		
Savings accounts	760		Insurance premiums		
Money market funds and deposits	800		Taxes		
Certificates of deposit (<1 yr. to maturity)			Medical/dental bills	75	
			Repair bills		
Total Liquid Assets		$2,025	Bank credit card balances	395	
			Dept. store credit card balances	145	
Investments			Travel and entertainment card balances	125	
Stocks	$1,250		Gas and other credit card balances		
Bonds Corp.	1,000		Bank line of credit balances		
Certificates of deposit (>1 yr. to maturity)			Other current liabilities	45	
Mutual funds	1,500		**Total Current Liabilities**		$905
Real estate			**Long-Term Liabilities**		
Retirement funds, IRA	2,000		Primary residence mortgage	$62,000	
Other			Second home mortgage		
Total Investments		$5,750	Real estate investment mortgage		
			Auto loans	2,740	
Real Property			Appliance/furniture loans	800	
Primary residence	$70,000		Home improvement loans		
Second home			Single-payment loans		
Car(s): '89 Toyota Camry	7,000		Education loans	3,800	
Car(s): '86 Ford Escort	2,000		Other long-term loans from parents	4,000	
Recreation equipment	400				
Other			**Total Long-Term Liabilities**		$73,340
Total Real Property		$79,400			
Personal Property					
Furniture and appliances	$2,250				
Stereos, TVs, etc.	1,450				
Clothing	1,200		**(II) Total Liabilities**	$ 74,245	
Jewelry	1,500				
Other			**Net Worth [(I)–(II)]**	$ 19,330	
Total Personal Property		$6,400			
(I) Total Assets		$93,575	**Total Liabilities and Net Worth**	$ 93,575	

Next, list all current and long-term liabilities, using the categories in Exhibit 2.2 as a starting point. *You should show all outstanding charges — even if you have not received the bill — as current liabilities on the balance sheet.* For example, assume that on June 23 you used your Visa card to charge $240 for a set of tires. You typically receive your Visa bill around the tenth of the following month. If you were preparing a balance sheet dated June 30, the $240 should be shown on it as a current liability — even though the bill won't arrive until July 10. Remember to list only the principal balance of any loan obligation.

The final step in the preparation of your balance sheet is to calculate net worth. Subtracting your total liabilities from your assets results in your net worth, which reflects the equity you have in your assets.

A BALANCE SHEET FOR FRED AND DENISE WEAVER

The relationship between assets, liabilities, and net worth and the general format of the balance sheet is perhaps best illustrated with an example. Toward that end, we will now examine the financial statements of Fred and Denise Weaver, a young couple whose balance sheet as of December 31, 1992, appears in Exhibit 2.3.

Fred and Denise live in a midwestern suburb, were married in 1989, and currently have no children. Fred is 28 years old and has just completed his fifth year as a marketing representative for a large soap manufacturer. He is quite satisfied with his job and expects to continue his career in the sales and marketing area. Fred's boss recently assured him that the company is pleased with his performance and has "big plans" for him. Denise is 26 and holds a bachelor's degree in primary education. After teaching one year, she realized that a career in education was not for her, so she went back to school full-time and earned a master's degree in business administration (M.B.A.). In June 1992 she began working at a local advertising firm. The Weavers live in their own condominium, which they purchased in October 1990. Fred and Denise love to travel, and snow skiing is one of their favorite pastimes. They plan to have children in a few years, but for now they want to devote their efforts toward developing some degree of financial stability and independence.

The Weavers' Assets. Given their ages, the Weavers' asset position looks quite good. Their dominant asset is their condo. In addition, they have a total of $3,750 spread among investments in common stock, corporate bonds, and government securities, plus retirement funds of $2,000. The Weavers' cash and checking balances of $465 and savings of $1,560 are liquid assets that should allow them to meet their bill payments and cover small, unexpected expenditures. But the real strength of their financial position cannot be evaluated without examining their debts, which may be high as a result of their borrowing to purchase certain of their assets, especially their home.

The Weavers' Liabilities. Looking at the Weavers' liabilities, we can see that their primary liability is the $62,000 mortgage on their condo. As might be expected, since they purchased their condo just over two years ago, the mortgage is still quite large relative to the condo's market value of $70,000. The Weavers' *equity*, or actual ownership interest in the condo, is approximately $8,000 ($70,000 market value minus the $62,000 outstanding mortgage loan). Their current liabilities total $905. It is likely that these liabilities must be paid, at least partially, within the next month, since monthly billing cycles are the most common. Other debts shown on the balance sheet include a $2,740 balance on an installment loan for one of their cars, an $800 balance on an installment loan used to purchase furniture, a $3,800 balance on an education loan for Denise's M.B.A., and a $4,000 balance on a personal loan from their parents to partly finance the down payment on their condo. Contrasting the Weavers' total liabilities of $74,245 to their total assets of $93,575 provides a more realistic view of their current wealth position.

The Weavers' Net Worth. The Weavers' balance sheet in Exhibit 2.3 shows their net worth as $19,330. Actually, considering their ages, Fred and Denise are not doing too badly. The $19,330 figure is the amount Fred and Denise would have if they sold their assets for the $93,575 (at which they are valued on the balance sheet) and used the proceeds to repay their debts of $74,245 (assuming there are no transaction costs). Of course, they are not expected to take such actions, but, by calculating their net worth at specified points in time, they can measure the results of their financial plans and decisions on their wealth position. As you might expect, a large or increasing wealth position is preferred to a low or declining one.

THE INCOME AND EXPENDITURES STATEMENT: A MEASURE OF YOUR FINANCIAL PERFORMANCE

An income and expenditures statement provides a summary of the income you received and the money you spent over a given period of time, usually one year. Do you know how much you received and spent during the last year? Before reading on, make a list of each item and amount of your income and expenditures during the most recent year.

While the balance sheet describes a person's or family's financial position at a given point in time, the **income and expenditures statement** captures the various financial activities that have occurred over time—normally over the course of a year, although it technically can cover any time period (monthly, quarterly, and so on). Think of this statement as a motion picture that not only shows actual results over time but allows for their comparison to budgeted financial goals as well. Equally important, the statement evaluates the amount of saving and investing that has taken place during the time period covered.

The income and expenditures statement is made up of three major parts: *income, expenditures*, and *cash surpluses (or deficits)*. As we will see a bit later, a cash surplus (or deficit) is merely the difference between income and expenditures. The statement is prepared on a **cash basis**, which means that *the only transactions recorded are those involving actual cash receipts or actual cash outlays*. In effect, the statement describes a person's or family's financial activities in terms of the cash inflows and out-

flows. (As a point of clarification, the term *cash* is used in this case to include not only coin and currency but also checks drawn against demand deposits and certain types of savings accounts.)

Income and expenditure patterns change depending on where an individual or family is in the life cycle. Both income and spending levels rise steadily to a peak in the 45–54 age bracket. On average, persons in this age group, whose children are typically in college or no longer at home, generally have the highest level of income; they also spend more than other age groups on entertainment, dining out, transportation, education, insurance, and charitable contributions. Families in the 35–44 age bracket have slightly lower average levels of income and expenditures but very different spending patterns. Because they tend to have school-age children, they spend more on food at home, housing, clothing, and other personal needs. The average percentage of income spent, however, is about the same—85 to 87 percent—for all age brackets through age 55, when it drops slightly to 82 percent. It rises sharply to 98 percent, however, for persons 65 and over.

Whereas the balance sheet summarizes your financial condition at a given point in time, the income and expenditures statement reports on your financial performance over time.
Fact: A balance sheet is like a photograph of your financial condition (covering just one day out of the year), while an income and expenditures statement is like a motion picture (covering the full year or some other time period).

INCOME: THE AMOUNT OF CASH IN

Items shown as **income** on the income and expenditures statement include earnings received as wages, salaries, self-employment income, bonuses, and commissions; interest and dividends received from savings and investments; and proceeds from the sale of assets, such as stocks and bonds or a car. Other income items include pension or annuity income, rent received from leased assets, alimony and child support, scholarships, grants, social security received, tax refunds, and other miscellaneous types of income. As noted above, only income that has ac-

EXHIBIT 2.4
Sources of Income

For most gainfully employed people, the vast majority of total income is made up of wages and salaries.

> Wages and salaries
> Self-employment income
> Bonuses and commissions
> Pensions and annuities
> Investment income:
>   Interest received
>   Dividends received
>   Proceeds from sale of securities
>   Rents received from leased assets
> Alimony and child support received
> Scholarships and grants received
> Social security received
> Other income:
>   Proceeds from sale of assets
>   Tax refunds
>   Miscellaneous (gifts, royalties, and so on)

tually been received should be shown. This approach forces an honest representation of the way things were during the year, not the way they were expected to be. Note also that the proper figure to use is *gross* wages, salaries, and commissions, which constitute the amount of income you receive from your employer *before* taxes and other payroll deductions are taken out. You should not use *take-home* pay, since that will understate your income by the amount of these deductions. Common sources of income which should be shown on the income and expenditures are listed in Exhibit 2.4.

EXPENDITURES: THE AMOUNT OF CASH OUT

Items shown as *expenditures* on the income and expenditures statement represent money used for outlays. Due to the many different kinds of expenditures, it is perhaps easiest to categorize them by the types of benefits they provide, as shown in Exhibit 2.5. A quick review of the exhibit reveals that expenditures consist of several different types of transactions: (1) *living expenses* (such as rent, food, medical expenses, repairs, insurance, and utilities), (2) *purchases of various kinds of assets* (like cars, stereos, furniture, appliances, and clothing), (3) *tax payments*, and (4) *debt payments* (on mortgages, installment loans, credit cards, and so on). Thus, ex-

penditures involve the outflow of cash for living expenses, and to purchase or acquire assets, pay taxes, and/or reduce debt. Some are **fixed expenditures** that usually are contractual, predetermined, and involve equal payments each period (typically each

income and expenditures statement
A key financial statement that presents one's income, expenditures, and cash surpluses or deficits over a designated time period.

cash basis
A method of preparing financial statements in which only cash income and cash expenditure items are recorded.

income
Earnings received as wages, salaries, bonuses and commissions, interest and dividends received from savings and investments, and proceeds from the sale of assets.

expenditures
Money spent on living expenses, to purchase assets, pay taxes, and/or repay debt.

fixed expenditures
Expenditures involving equal payments each period (typically each month).

EXHIBIT 2.5
Common Types of Household Expenditures

Classifying expenses into major categories, such as those shown below, simplifies record-keeping and statement preparation. The percentages shown in parentheses represent the estimated average annual expenditures by major categories as a percentage of average before-tax household income, based on a government survey of consumer expenditures.

Housing (18%)
Mortgage payments
Rent
Repairs and additions
Household services

Utilities (6%)
Gas and electric
Garbage service
Telephone
Water
Cable TV

Food (13%)
Groceries
Dining out

Transportation (16%)
Purchase or loan payments
Gas and oil
License fees
Repairs
Lease payments
Other transportation

Health Care (5%)
Doctor bills
Dental bills
Hospital bills
Health insurance

Clothing, Shoes, and Accessories (5%)

Personal Insurance and Pensions (9%)
Life insurance
Disability income insurance
Pensions and Social Security

Taxes (9%)
Income
Property

Appliances, Furniture, or Other Assets (3%)
Purchases
Installment payments
Repairs and maintenance

Personal Care (1%)
Laundry and dry cleaning
Cosmetics
Hairdresser

Recreation, Entertainment, and Vacation (6%)
Admissions
Alcoholic beverages
Hobby supplies
Cigarettes and tobacco
Sports equipment
Records and tapes
Vacation and travel

Other Items (18%)
Postage and stationery
Personal allowance
Books and magazines
Tuition
Legal fees
Interest expenses
Dues and club memberships
Gifts
Church and charity
Pets
Child care
Miscellaneous unclassified expenditures

Source: "Consumer Expenditures Survey in 1990," *News Release 91–607*, Washington, D.C., Bureau of Labor Statistics, November 22, 1991.

month)—examples include mortgage and install-ment loan payments, insurance premiums, profes-sional or union dues, club dues, monthly savings or investment programs, and cable television fees. Others (such as food, clothing, utilities, entertain-ment, and medical expenses) are **variable expen-ditures**, since their amounts are always changing.

Just as only the amounts of cash actually received are shown as income, only the amounts of money actually paid out in cash are listed as expenditures. If an item—particularly an asset—is acquired through borrowing, only the net or actual dollar amount of money paid out (that is, purchase price minus amount borrowed) is included as an expenditure. In effect, the financed portion of such an outlay is not viewed as an expenditure until debt payments are actually made. Instead, credit purchases of this type are shown as an asset and corresponding liability *on the balance sheet*. Payments against these loans are shown on the income and expenditures statement in the period they are actually made: In other words, cash expenditures include actual *payments* against loans but not the amounts of the loans themselves. For example, assume you purchase a new car for $10,000 in September. You make a down payment of $2,000 and finance the remaining $8,000 with a three-year, 10.5 percent installment loan. Your September 30 income statement would show a cash expenditure of $2,000, and each subsequent monthly income statement would include your monthly loan payment of $260. Your September 30 balance sheet would show the car as an asset valued at $10,000 and loan balance as an $8,000 long-term liability. The market value of the car and the loan balance would be adjusted on future balance sheets.

Finally, when developing your list of expenditures for the year, remember to include the amount of income and social security taxes withheld from your paycheck as well as any other payroll deductions taken out, such as for health insurance, savings plans, retirement and pension contributions, and professional/union dues. These deductions (from *gross* wages, salaries, and commissions) represent personal expenditures even if they do not involve the *direct* payment of cash.

CASH SURPLUS (OR DEFICIT)

The third component of the income and expenditures statement captures the net result of the period's financial activities. The cash surplus (or deficit) for the period is obtained by subtracting total expenditures from total income and allows you to determine at a glance how you did financially over the period. The figure can be zero, positive, or negative. A value of zero indicates that expenditures were exactly equal to income for the period. A positive figure indicates that the expenditures were less than income and therefore a **cash surplus** resulted. A negative value indicates that the period's expenditures exceeded income, thereby resulting in a **cash deficit**.

When a cash surplus exists, it can be used for savings or investment purposes, to acquire assets, or reduce (that is, make payments on) debt. Additions to savings or investments (it is hoped) will result in increased future income, while payments on debt will have a favorable effect on cash flow by reducing future expenditures. In contrast, when a cash deficit occurs, the shortfall must be covered by either drawing your savings or investments down, reducing assets, or borrowing. Either strategy will have undesirable effects on your financial future. One final point: The cash surplus (or deficit) figure does not necessarily indicate that funds are simply lying around waiting to be used. Because the income and expenditures statement reflects what has actually occurred, the disposition of the surplus (or deficit) is reflected in the asset, liability, and net worth accounts on the balance sheet. For example, if the surplus were used to make investments, it would be represented by an increase in the asset account. If it were used to pay off a loan, it would be represented by a reduction in that liability account. Of course, if the surplus were used to increase cash balances, the funds would be available for use.

Balance Sheet Effects of a Cash Surplus.
The effect of a cash surplus on the income and expenditures statement is to *increase* the net worth account on the balance sheet. This increase results because an asset account increases without a corresponding increase in any liability. Note that this could be *any* asset, from a savings or investment account to a new car or room addition. In order for the balance sheet equation to balance, an increase in assets without any increase in liabilities must result in an increase in net worth. Even if the cash surplus is used to reduce a liability, *an increase in net worth will still result*. To illustrate, assume that Balance Sheet A in Exhibit 2.6 represents a family's balance sheet at December 31, 1991. If the family's income and expenditures statement for the *following* year, 1992, showed a cash surplus of $1,500 and these funds were used to *increase assets*, Balance Sheet B would represent the family's financial position at December 31, 1992. If the $1,500 surplus were used instead to repay a debt, Balance Sheet C would reflect the family's financial position at December 31,

---

variable expenditures
Expenditures that involve payments of varying amounts from one time period to the next.

cash surplus
An excess amount of income over expenditures that can be used for savings or investments and to acquire assets or reduce debt. Results in increased net worth.

cash deficit
An excess amount of expenditures over income resulting in insufficient funds that must be made up either by drawing down savings or investments, reducing assets, or through borrowing. Results in decreased net worth.

EXHIBIT 2.6
Impact of a Cash Surplus on the Balance Sheet

A cash surplus on the income and expenditures statement will lead to an increase in net worth on the balance sheet and can be used to either acquire assets or reduce debts.

Balance Sheet A
December 31, 1991

Assets		*Liabilities and Net Worth*	
Total assets	$30,000	Total liabilities	$22,000
Total	$30,000	Net worth	8,000
		Total	$30,000

Balance Sheet B
December 31, 1992 ($1,500 surplus used to increase assets)

Assets		*Liabilities and Net Worth*	
Total assets	$31,500	Total liabilities	$22,000
Total	$31,500	Net worth	9,500
		Total	$31,500

Balance Sheet C
December 31, 1992 ($1,500 surplus used to repay debts [decrease liabilities])

Assets		*Liabilities and Net Worth*	
Total assets	$30,000	Total liabilities	$20,500
Total	$30,000	Net worth	9,500
		Total	$30,000

1992. Regardless of what is done with the surplus, the family's net worth increases by the amount of the surplus ($1,500) from its level of $8,000 at the end of 1991 to $9,500 at the end of 1992.

Generating a cash surplus is desirable, since it adds to your net worth.
Fact: A cash surplus on the income and expenditures statement will increase your net worth on the balance sheet.

Balance Sheet Effects of a Cash Deficit.
While surpluses add to net worth, deficits *reduce* it. Again, in order for the balance sheet equation to balance, this has to be the case. If the shortfall (deficit) is financed by reducing an asset (for example, by drawing down a savings account), a reduction in net worth will result. If it is financed by borrowing, the net worth will still be reduced, as the example in Exhibit 2.7 indicates. Again, Balance Sheet A represents a family's financial position at December 31, 1991. Assume that the family's income and expendi-

tures statement for the *following* year, 1992, shows a cash deficit of $1,500. Balance sheets B and C show the two alternatives for meeting the deficit: in B by reducing assets and in C by borrowing. Regardless of the method used, the family's net worth decreased by $1,500 in 1992.

In summary, cash surpluses, regardless of how used, result in increases in net worth and cash deficits, regardless of how covered, result in decreases. Increases in net worth are associated with *growing* financial strength; obviously, cash deficits indicate *declining* financial strength.

PREPARING THE INCOME AND EXPENDITURES STATEMENT

As shown in Exhibit 2.8, the income and expenditures statement is dated to define the period covered. The first set of entries includes all income items and a total income figure. Next, the expenditures are listed and totaled. Although not essential, the statement's readability is greatly enhanced by including various income and expenditure category

EXHIBIT 2.7
Impact of a Cash Deficit on the Balance Sheet

A cash deficit on the income and expenditures statement is undesirable, since it leads to a decrease in the balance sheet's net worth. This shortfall has to be covered by either reducing assets (selling some investments) or taking on more debt.

Balance Sheet A
December 31, 1991

Assets		Liabilities and Net Worth	
Total assets	$30,000	Total liabilities	$22,000
Total	$30,000	Net worth	8,000
		Total	$30,000

Balance Sheet B
December 31, 1992 ($1,500 deficit financed by a reduction in assets)

Assets		Liabilities and Net Worth	
Total assets	$28,500	Total liabilities	$22,000
Total	$28,500	Net worth	6,500
		Total	$28,500

Balance Sheet C
December 31, 1992 ($1,500 deficit financed by borrowing [increase liabilities])

Assets		Liabilities and Net Worth	
Total assets	$30,000	Total liabilities	$23,500
Total	$30,000	Net worth	6,500
		Total	$30,000

headings. These not only permit a better understanding of the general nature of the income and expenditure items but also greatly simplify the budget control process (described in Chapter 3). The final entry, representing the cash surplus (or deficit), is shown as the result obtained by subtracting total expenditures from total income. This entry constitutes the *bottom line* of the statement and basically is a summary of the *net cash flow* that resulted from the financial activities during the designated period.

Preparing an income and expenditures statement is really not as difficult as it may appear. Although this statement should be prepared at least annually, you may find it useful to prepare quarterly or semi-annual statements. The first step is to determine your income from all sources for your chosen time period. If you are like most people, you probably have a very good idea of how much you make at work. But if you are unsure, you can always look at your check stubs for the amount of your *gross* pay. Regardless of the procedure you use, you should not overlook bonuses, commission checks, and overtime pay. Bank statements provide information on interest earned on savings accounts, and statements from brokerage houses, mutual funds, and so on provide information on securities bought and sold, dividends received, and other investment matters. You should also keep a running list of other income sources such as rents, tax refunds, and sales of assets.

Next, establish meaningful expenses categories, such as those listed in Exhibit 2.5. It is probably best to break out the fixed and variable expenses. Information on monthly house (or rent) payments, loan payments, and other fixed payments (such as for insurance premiums and cable TV), is readily available from either the payment book often provided or your checkbook (or, in the case of payroll deductions, your check stubs). (Note: Be careful with so-called *adjustable-rate loans*, since the amount of monthly loan payments will change along with the changes in the interest rates.) Variable expenses are undoubtedly the toughest expenditures to keep

EXHIBIT 2.8

The Weavers' Income and Expenditures Statement

The income and expenditures statement essentially shows what you earned, how you spent your money, and how much you were left with (or, if you spent more than you took in, how much you went "in the hole").

INCOME AND EXPENDITURES STATEMENT			
Name(s) _____ Fred and Denise Weaver _____			
For the _____ Year _____ Ending _____ December 31, 1992 _____			
INCOME			
Wages and salaries	Name: Fred Weaver	$	35,000
	Name: Denise Weaver		15,450
	Name:		
Self-employment income			
Bonuses and commissions	Fred—sales commissions		2,275
Pensions and annuities			
Investment income	Interest received		195
	Dividends received		120
	Rents received		
	Sale of securities		
	Other		
Other income			
	(I) Total Income	$	53,040
EXPENDITURES			
Housing	Rent/mortgage payment (include insurance and taxes, if applicable)		6,864
	Repairs, maintenance, improvements		1,050
Utilities	Gas, electric, water		1,750
	Phone		480
	Cable TV and other		240
Food	Groceries		2,425
	Dining out		3,400
Autos	Loan payments		2,520
	License plates, fees, etc.		250
	Gas, oil, repairs, tires, maintenance		2,015
Medical	Health, major medical, disability insurance (payroll deductions or not provided by employer)		1,200
	Doctor, dentist, hospital, medicines		305
Clothing	Clothes, shoes, and accessories		1,700
Insurance	Homeowner's (if not covered by mortgage payment)		425
	Life (not provided by employer)		260
	Auto		695
Taxes	Income and social security		15,430
	Property (if not included in mortgage)		1,000
Appliances, furniture, and other major purchases	Loan payments		800
	Purchases and repairs		450
Personal care	Laundry, cosmetics, hair care		700
Recreation and entertainment	Vacations		2,000
	Other Recreation and entertainment		2,630
Other items	Tuition and books: Denise		1,400
	Gifts		215
	Loan payments: Education loans		900
	Loan payments: Parents		600
	(II) Total Expenditures	$	51,704
	CASH SURPLUS (OR DEFICIT) [(I)–(II)]	$	1,336

track of. Since trying to keep receipts for each and every transaction usually does not work too well, most people tend to rely on their check registers and credit card statements for information on these items. In many cases, the figures that show up on the income and expenditures statement amount to little more than educated "guesstimates" of the amount of money spent on the various categories of expenses, such as entertainment, clothing, and so on. While some of this is obviously necessary and appropriate, too much guesswork can lead to unreliable numbers that will greatly reduce the usefulness of these statements.

Fortunately, there are a number of good computer software packages available that take much of the work out of financial reporting and other personal financial planning tasks. Such programs are designed specifically for personal computers and will print out not only personalized income and expenditure statements but also up-to-date balance sheets. However, you still have to keep track of your expenditures and input the data.

The final step is to subtract total expenditures from total income. This gives the cash surplus (a positive number) or deficit (a negative number).

AN INCOME AND EXPENDITURES STATEMENT FOR FRED AND DENISE WEAVER

Fred and Denise Weaver's income and expenditures statement for the year ended December 31, 1992, is provided in Exhibit 2.8 and illustrates the relationship among total income, total expenditures, and cash surplus (or deficit). This statement, which was prepared using the background material presented earlier, along with the Weavers' balance sheet (Exhibit 2.3), is best evaluated by separately analyzing their income, expenditures, and cash surplus (or deficit).

The Weavers' Income. Fred's wages clearly represent the family's chief source of income, although Denise has finished her M.B.A. and will now be making a major contribution. Other sources of income include $195 in interest received on their savings accounts and bond investments and $120 in dividends received on their common stock holdings. The Weavers' total income for the year ended December 31, 1992, amounts to a very respectable $53,040.

The Weavers' Expenditures. The Weavers' major expenditures, as shown in Exhibit 2.8, can be traced to their home mortgage, food, and income and social security taxes. Other sizable expenditures during the year included home repairs and additions, gas and electricity, auto loan payments, gas and oil for cars, clothing, shoes, insurance, furniture loan payments, personal care, recreation, books and tuition, and education loan payments. Total expenditures for the year amounted to $51,704. Note that the expenditure categories in the Weavers' income and expenditures statement are similar to those given in Exhibit 2.5. Ideally these categories should be set up in a manner most suitable to the individual's — or family's — data requirements. Note, too, that the expenditure items represent actual cash outlays made by the Weavers during the year ended December 31, 1992.

The Weavers' Cash Surplus. The Weavers' cash surplus of $1,336 for the year is found by subtracting the total expenditures of $51,704 from the total income of $53,040. They end up with a cash surplus, since they took in more money than they spent. This surplus could be used to increase savings; invest in stocks, bonds, or other vehicles; or make payments on some outstanding debts. The correct strategy depends on their financial goals. If a cash deficit had resulted, the Weavers would have had to withdraw savings, liquidate investments, or borrow an amount equal to the deficit in order to meet their financial commitments (that is, "make ends meet"). With their *surplus* of $1,336, the Weavers have made a positive contribution to their net worth.

USING YOUR PERSONAL FINANCIAL STATEMENTS ▪

Personal financial statements can be used to assess your progress toward achievement of long-term financial goals. How would you use your personal financial statements to do this? Take a few moments to answer this question before reading on.

ISSUES IN MONEY MANAGEMENT

Keeping Good Records of Your Financial Affairs

An up-to-date file of your financial records should contain not only assets, liabilities, sources of income, and expenditure items, but also other records that are important for tax purposes or would be relevant in the event of disability or death. Most of these records can be kept at home. A shoebox may be sufficient for some people, but you are probably better off paying about $50 for a sturdy, fireproof box that can typically hold at least six years' worth of documents. Hard-to-replace records such as stock certificates, a divorce decree, or a power of attorney should be stored in a safe-deposit box. Banks charge about $25 to $50 a year for a box 3″ × 5″ × 24″, sufficient for most families.

The records you must safeguard at home or at your bank can be divided into the following two groups, depending on how long you must keep them (see the accompanying table for suggestions):

FOR SIX OR MORE YEARS.

If the IRS hasn't begun an audit of your tax return six years after you file it, you can reward yourself by tossing out copies of the return and of the records that prove your income, deductions, and other entries for the year. (Only if you are suspected of filing a fraudulent return is there no statute of limitations on an IRS audit.)

Similarly, investment records such as annual mutual fund accountings and partnership K-1

statements must be kept until six years after you have sold the asset. That same holding period applies to receipts and canceled checks for improvements to your home and to documents identifying nondeductible contributions to an individual retirement account. Without verification of the amount and date of the nondeductible contribution, you could be hit with a stiff tax bill when you make withdrawals from your IRA.

FOR LIFE.

A copy of your will can be stored in a safe-deposit box, but keep the original at home or with your lawyer. In many states your safe-deposit box will be sealed when you die, thus making it hard for relatives to take

Your financial statements—the balance sheet and the income and expenditures statement—should provide the information you need to examine your financial position, monitor your financial activities, and track the progress you're making toward your financial goals. Very likely, your financial statements are like those of most other people—not a lot of substance at present perhaps, but certainly no shortage of potential. Regardless of the particulars surrounding your case, it should be clear that a thorough understanding of your current financial status will enable you to better direct your financial plans and activities toward your personal financial goals.

THE NEED FOR ADEQUATE RECORDS

Financial statements should be prepared at least once each year, ideally in conjunction with preparing a budget. Many people prefer to update their financial statements every three or six months. In order to simplify the preparation process, a **ledger**, or financial record book, should be set up. The ledger should contain a separate section for assets, liabilities, sources of income, and expenditure items. Separate accounts can be established for each item within each section. The ledger should be updated continuously throughout the year. Whenever a

from it your will and funeral instructions. Moreover, planners generally suggest you keep up-to-date photos and fingerprints of your children in case of emergency.

Finally, make a list of all your records, as well as of the names, addresses and phone numbers of advisers such as you accountant, broker, financial planner, insurance agents and lawyer. Copies of the lists should be kept in the safe-deposit box and with your lawyer or planner.

Above all, don't lose control of your paper trail. "Once you get a handle on your records, don't let go," says financial planner Victoria Ross. "It's important to be organized—for you and your relatives."

How Long and Where to Keep Your Records

RECORDS TO KEEP SIX OR MORE YEARS

At home:
Accident reports
Brokerage and fund transactions
Insurance policies
Keogh statements
Loan records
Major purchase receipts
Stock-option agreements
Tax records, including alimony payments, charitable contributions, copies of tax returns, medical bills, partnership agreements, property tax records, 1099s

In your safe-deposit box:
Certificates of deposit
House records, including deed, title insurance policy, receipts, and canceled checks for capital improvements
Nondeductible IRA records
Partnership statements (K-1s)

RECORDS TO KEEP ALL YOUR LIFE

At home:
Birth certificates
Death certificates
List of bank accounts
List of financial assets
List of financial advisers
Medical records
Powers of attorney
Trust agreements
Wills
W–2 statements

In your safe-deposit box:
Alimony agreement
Custody agreement
Divorce decree
Military papers
Naturalization papers
Prenuptial agreement
Videotape or photos of valuables

Source: Carla A. Fried, "Records: Most of Us Squirrel More Paper Than Is Necessary," *Money*, September 1988, pp. 157–158. Used with permission.

---

transaction or change in any of these accounts occurs, an appropriate entry should be made in the ledger. For example, if you make a $300 cash purchase of a VCR, the item should be recorded both as an asset and an expenditure of $300. When you later prepare your financial statements, the VCR would be shown as an asset valued at its fair market value on the balance sheet and as a $300 expenditure on the income and expenditures statement. Of course, had you borrowed to pay for the VCR, the amount borrowed would be recorded and shown as a liability on the balance sheet rather than as an expenditure on the income and expenditures statement. Any

loan payments made during the period would be shown on the income statement. Similar records must be maintained for asset sales, loan repayment, sources of income, and so on.

The ledger provides a summary of all your financial transactions. You also need to set up a record-

> **ledger**
> A financial record book containing sections for assets, liabilities, sources of income, and expenditure items.

keeping system for all back-up documents. These would include paycheck stubs, checkbook registers and canceled checks, receipts for major purchases, credit card receipts and statements, other major bills (home and automobile repair, for example), receipts for tax-deductible expenses, other information required to prepare tax returns, records of securities transactions, and similar items. Of course, this system should also include major documents such as legal documents (loan agreements, mortgages, wills, divorce papers, and so on), insurance policies, original securities certificates, copies of tax returns, and automobile ownership records.

Clearly, a good record-keeping system that provides up-to-date data for use in preparing financial statements is a cornerstone of effective financial planning. Without current data, the likelihood of omitting some of these items from the financial statements or the planning process is much greater. Regardless of the system used, some type of records should be maintained to provide accurate information for use in preparing the balance sheet and the income and expenditures statement. Good records will make the preparation of financial statements a lot easier. Toward that end, the *Issues in Money Management* box provides helpful advice for keeping good records of your financial affairs.

TRACKING FINANCIAL PROGRESS: RATIO ANALYSIS

Each time you prepare your financial statements, you should analyze them in order to assess how well you are doing in light of your financial goals. For example, with an income and expenditures statement, you can compare actual financial results to budgeted figures to make sure you have your spending under control. Likewise, comparing a set of financial plans to a balance sheet will reveal how you are doing in meeting your savings and investment goals, reducing your debt, or building up a retirement reserve. In addition to assessing your future, financial statements help you track your progress over time — that is, you can compare current to historical performance.

In effect, you want to find out if things are improving or getting worse. You can usually do this by ex-

amining certain financial ratios. These ratios can be compared over time to evaluate your financial performance. Moreover, if you need to apply for a loan, there is a good chance that the lending agency will also look at these ratios to judge your ability to carry additional debt. Four of the most important money management ratios are (1) solvency ratio, (2) liquidity ratio, (3) savings ratio, and (4) debt service ratio. The first two are associated primarily with the balance sheet, while the last two relate primarily to the income and expenditures statement.

Balance Sheet Ratios. When evaluating your balance sheet, you should be most concerned with the net worth figure, since it indicates your financial worth at a given point in time. As explained earlier in this chapter, you are technically insolvent when your total liabilities exceed your total assets — that is, when you have a negative net worth. The **solvency ratio** shows, in percentages, the extent to which you are exposed to insolvency, or how much "cushion" you have as a protection against insolvency. It is calculated as follows:

$$\text{Solvency ratio} = \frac{\text{Total net worth}}{\text{Total assets}}$$

The Weavers' solvency ratio in 1992 is

$$\frac{\$19,330}{\$93,575} = 0.21, \text{ or } 21 \text{ percent}$$

This tells us that Fred and Denise could withstand only about a 21 percent decline in the market value of their assets before they would be insolvent. The low value for this ratio suggests they should consider improving it in the future.

While the solvency ratio gives an indication of potential financial problems, it does not deal directly with the ability to pay current debts. This issue is addressed more appropriately with the **liquidity ratio**. This important ratio shows how long you could continue to pay current liability expenditures with existing liquid assets in the event of a loss of income. It is calculated by dividing liquid assets by total current debts; "current" in this case means any bills or charges that must be paid within one year. The ratio is computed as follows:

$$\text{Liquidity ratio} = \frac{\text{Liquid assets}}{\text{Total current debts}}$$

The Weavers' liquid assets (see Exhibit 2.3) are made up of cash on hand and in their checking account, savings, and the money market mutual fund balance. These total $2,025 ($90 + $375 + $760 + 800). Their current liabilities of bills and open account credit balances total $905 ($120 + $75 + $395 + $145 + $125 + $45). The portions of their mortgage, installment, and personal loan payments that are due within one year total $11,684 ($6,864 in mortgage payments + $2,520 in auto loan payments + $800 in furniture loan payments + $900 in education loan payments + $600 in loan payment to parents—all found on the income and expenditures statement in Exhibit 2.8. Adding their total current liabilities ($905) to the current portion of their loans ($11,684) yields total current debts of $12,589. Thus, the Weavers' have a liquidity ratio of:

$$\frac{\$2,025}{\$12,589} = 0.16, \text{ or 16 percent}$$

This ratio indicates that the Weavers can cover only about 16 percent of their existing one-year debt obligations with their current liquid assets. In other words, they have about two months (one month is 1/12, or 8 percent) of coverage. If an unexpected event occurred that curtailed their income, their liquid reserves would be exhausted very quickly. While there is no hard and fast rule as to what this ratio should be, it seems low for the Weavers. They should consider strengthening it along with their effort to improve their solvency ratio. They should be able to do so now that Denise is working full-time. They can hold any added cash surpluses in the form of liquid assets, ideally through additions to their money market fund.

The amount of liquid reserves will vary with your personal circumstances and "comfort level." Another useful liquidity guideline is to have a reserve fund equal to three to six months of after-tax income available to cover living expenses. The Weavers' after-tax income for 1992 was $3,134 per month ([$53,040 − $15,430] ÷ 12). Therefore, this guideline suggests they should have between $9,402 and

$18,804 in liquid assets—considerably more than the $2,025 on their latest balance sheet. If you feel that your job is secure and/or you have other potential sources of income, you may be comfortable with three or four months in reserve. If you tend to be very cautious financially, you may want to build a larger fund. In troubled economic times, you may want to keep six months or more of income in this fund as protection should you lose your job.

Income and Expenditures Statement Ratios. When evaluating your income and expenditures statement, you should be concerned with the *bottom line*, which shows the amount of the cash surplus (or deficit) resulting from the period's activities. This figure indicates how well you have done during the period. You can relate it to income by calculating a **savings ratio**, which is done most effectively with after-tax income, as follows:

$$\text{Savings ratio} = \frac{\text{Cash surplus}}{\text{Income after taxes}}$$

For the Weavers, the savings ratio is

$$\frac{\$1,336}{\$53,040 - \$15,430} = \frac{\$1,336}{\$37,610} = \begin{array}{l} 0.035, \text{ or} \\ 3.5 \text{ percent} \end{array}$$

Fred and Denise saved about 3.5 percent of their after-tax income, which is a bit on the low side (American families, on average, normally save about 5 to 8 percent). How much to save is a personal choice. Some families would plan much higher

---

solvency ratio
Total net worth divided by total assets; measures solvency.

liquidity ratio
Liquid assets divided by total current debts; measures ability to pay current debts.

savings ratio
Cash surplus divided by after-tax income; indicates relative amount of cash surplus achieved.

levels, particularly if they are saving to achieve an important goal, such as buying a home.

While maintaining an adequate level of savings is obviously important to personal financial planning, so is the ability to pay debts promptly. In fact, debt payments have a *higher* priority: The **debt service ratio** allows you to make sure you're carrying a reasonable debt load. It is calculated as follows:

$$\text{Debt service ratio} = \frac{\text{Total monthly loan payments}}{\text{Monthly gross (before-tax) income}}$$

This ratio excludes current liabilities such as outstanding bills and open account credit balances and therefore considers only mortgage, installment, and personal loan obligations. Reviewing the Weavers' income and expenditures statement in Exhibit 2.8, you can see that on an *annual* basis these obligations total $11,684 ($6,854 in mortgage payments plus $2,520 in auto loan payments plus $800 in furniture loan payments plus $900 in education loan payments plus $600 in loan payments to parents). Dividing this total by 12 results in an estimate of the Weavers' total *monthly* loan payments of $974. The Weavers' *annual* gross income, also found in Exhibit 2.8, totals $53,040, which equals $4,420 monthly ($53,040/12). Substituting the Weavers' $974 total monthly loan payment and their monthly *gross* income of $4,420 into the formula yields a debt service ratio of

$$\frac{\$974}{\$4,420} = 0.22, \text{ or } 22 \text{ percent}$$

Monthly loan payments account for about 22 percent of Fred and Denise's gross income. This relatively low debt service ratio indicates that the Weavers should have little, if any, difficulty in meeting their monthly loan payments. From a financial planning perspective, you should try to keep your debt service margin somewhere under 35 percent or so, since that's generally viewed as a manageable level of debt—and, of course, the lower the debt service ratio, the easier it is to meet loan payments as they come due.

When evaluating your income and expenditures statement, primary attention should be given to the top line: income received.

Fantasy: You should give most of your attention to the *bottom* line (the amount of the cash surplus or deficit), since it indicates how well you have controlled your expenditures relative to the amount of income available and, in turn, how you contributed to your net worth position.

GETTING A WINDOW ON THE FUTURE

So far, we have looked at financial statements in terms of helping us evaluate what has happened in the past. However, they can also be used to assist us in achieving future financial goals. They serve best in that capacity when they are tied to the annual budgeting process, described in detail in the next chapter. For the moment, let's suppose that Fred and Denise have set a goal to increase their net worth by at least $7,000 in 1993. They feel that this is a reasonable goal because Denise is now working full-time. Such an increase can take place in two different ways. On one hand, the Weavers can prepare a 1993 cash budget (using procedures described in the next chapter) that will specifically provide for an increase in net worth by controlling their income and expenditures. Alternatively, they can rely on increases in the market value of some of their assets—particularly their stocks and bonds and, possibly, their house. They must be concerned, though, that some of their assets could also *decline* in market value, causing their net worth to decrease. Clearly, this is a certainty with their automobiles, recreational equipment, and personal property items.

Exhibit 2.9 details how the Weavers expect their net worth to increase in 1993. Part A shows a budgeted increase of $6,554, and part B shows the Weavers' estimates of increases and decreases in the market values of their assets (the net increase from this source in 1993 is expected to be $1,400). Line B is only an estimate, of course, and Fred and Denise certainly are not relying on it alone to achieve their net worth goal. They expect that in the long run many of their assets will increase in value—that is

---

EXHIBIT 2.9

Forecasted Changes in the Weaver Net Worth Position (as of December 31, 1993)

Increases in net worth do not have to happen by chance; rather, they can be planned out in advance.

net worth = total assets – total liabilities

A.   Increases in Net Worth Planned with the 1993 Budget:

(1)	Make $6,864 in monthly payments on home mortgage; $6,200 is interest, leaving payments to reduce the loan by	$ 684
(2)	Make payments on an auto loan of $2,520 and furniture loan of $800; combined interest on both is $350, leaving payments to reduce the loan by	2,970
(3)	Reduce loan to parents	800
(4)	Make education loan payment of $900; $300 is interest, reducing the loan by	600
(5)	Increase savings (and invest in money market fund)	1,500
	(a) Budgeted increase in net worth	$6,554

B.   Expected Increases (Decreases) in Market Value of Assets:

(1)	House (3% increase)	$2,100
(2)	Automobiles (10% decrease)	(900)
(3)	Recreational equipment (50% decrease)	(200)
(4)	Personal property (jewelry will increase, but furniture and clothing will decrease; assume they offset)	0
(5)	Investments (7% increase)	400
	(b) Expected net increase in market value of assets	$1,400
Total expected increase in net worth in 1993 = (a) + (b)		$7,945

---

one of the reasons they purchased them—but they are less sure of these increases on a year-to-year basis. If everything does work out as planned, the Weavers' net worth at December 31, 1993, will be about $27,284—which is found by adding the total expected increase to their net worth of $7,954 (found in Exhibit 2.9) to their latest net worth of $19,330 (from Exhibit 2.3).

SUMMARY

- The preparation and use of personal financial statements is important to financial planning, because they enable you not only to keep track of your current financial position but to monitor the amount of progress being made toward your financial goals.

- A balance sheet reports on your financial condition at a given point in time by providing a summary of the things you own (assets), the money you owe (liabilities), and your financial worth (net worth).

- The asset side (left side) of the balance sheet reflects the things you own and is made up of liquid assets, investments, and real and personal property. The other side (right side) of the balance sheet shows how you used debt and net worth to finance your assets and is made up of current liabilities (unpaid bills and open account credit obligations), long-term liabilities (real estate mortgages, consumer installment loans, education loans, and margin loans), and net worth.

> **debt service ratio**
> Total monthly loan payments divided by monthly gross (before tax) income; provides a measure of ability to service monthly loan payments in a prompt and timely fashion.

■ The income and expenditures statement provides a summary of the income you received and the money you spent over a given period of time. It is prepared on a cash basis and, as such, reflects your actual cash flow. Expenditures consist of the outflow of cash to (1) meet living expenses, (2) purchase various kinds of assets, (3) pay taxes, and (4) reduce debt.

■ An important element of the income and expenditures statement is the size of the cash surplus (or deficit). A cash surplus can be used to increase assets and/or reduce debts and will have a direct positive effect on the net worth account in the balance sheet. A cash deficit, in contrast, reduces assets and/or increases debts and acts as a drain on net worth.

■ In addition to tracking your progress toward your financial goals, personal financial statements are also useful in assessing how well you are doing relative to your past performance (that is, are things getting better or worse?). Such insight can usually be obtained through the use of financial ratios like the solvency, liquidity, savings, and debt service ratios.

■ Financial statements can also be used to assist you in achieving your financial goals by providing a vehicle for planning and forecasting future net worth.

QUESTIONS AND PROBLEMS

1. Match each lettered item below with the most appropriate description:
   a. Balance sheet
   b. Time deposits
   c. Liquid assets
   d. Cash surplus/deficit
   e. Income and expenditures statement
   f. Liabilities
   g. Demand deposits
   h. Expenditures greater than income
   i. Income
   j. Assets
   ___ Money owed
   ___ Checking account
   ___ Earnings
   ___ Financial position
   ___ Items owned
   ___ Savings or money market account
   ___ Demand and time deposits
   ___ Financial performance
   ___ Increase/decrease in assets or investments
   ___ Deficit

2. Explain the role the personal computer can play in the personal financial planning process. Briefly discuss the capabilities of some of the popular personal financial planning programs.

3. Distinguish investments from real and personal property. Categorize the following as investments, real property, or personal property:
   a. Clothing and shoes
   b. Promissory notes
   c. Gold bars
   d. Priceless paintings
   e. Automobiles

4. Chris Jones is preparing his balance sheet as of June 30, 1992. He is having difficulty classifying three items and asks for your help. Which, if any, of the following transactions are assets or liabilities?
   a. He rents a house for $400 a month.
   b. On June 21, 1992, he bought a diamond ring for his wife and charged it to his VISA card. The ring cost $600, but he has not yet received the bill.
   c. He makes monthly payments of $120 on an installment loan. about half of which is interest and the balance repayment of principal. He has 20 payments left totaling $2,400.

5. What is the balance sheet equation? Explain when a family may be viewed as technically insolvent.

6. Put yourself ten years into the future. Construct a fairly detailed and realistic balance sheet and income and expenditures statement reflecting what you would like to achieve by that time.

7. Deborah Lee bought a new house with a fair market value of $105,000. She has an outstanding mortgage loan of $94,500. How much is her equity in the house?

8. What is an income and expenditures statement? What role does it serve in personal financial planning? What are its three components?

9. Name some of the major sources of income. What are the four basic types of expenditures?

10. Chris Jones is preparing his income and expenditures statement for the year ending June 30, 1992. He is having difficulty classifying some items and asks for your help. Which, if any, of the following transactions are income or expenditure items.
    a. He borrowed $2,000 from his parents last fall but so far has made no payments.
    b. He paid $1,200 in taxes during the year and is due a tax refund of $450, which he has not yet received.
    c. He invested $1,800 in some common stock.

11. Explain what *cash basis* means in the following statement: "An income and expenditures statement should be prepared on a cash basis." How and where are credit purchases shown when statements are prepared on a cash basis?

12. Is it possible to have a cash deficit on an income and expenditures statement?

13. Describe some of the areas or items you would consider when evaluating your balance sheet. Cite several ratios that could help in this effort.

14. Explain why primary emphasis in the evaluation of an income and expenditures statement is placed on the "bottom line." Discuss how you might go about analyzing your own income and expenditures statement. What ratio would be useful here?

15. Jessica Alvarez has monthly gross income of $1,750 and total monthly loan payments of $780. How would you characterize Jessica's ability to meet her loan payments? What if her monthly gross income were the same, but her monthly loan payments were only $500?

16. Bill and Nancy Ballinger are about to construct their balance sheet and income and expendi-

tures statement for the year ending December 31, 1992. They have put together the following information:

Rent received on mountain cabin	$ 1,250
Other debts	19,350
Bill from State Farm Insurance	120
Amount spent on groceries	4,750
Income tax paid in 1992	18,190
Other expenses incurred in 1992	9,200
Certificates of deposit	20,000
Cash	60
Car loan	2,900
Bill's salary	55,200
Balance due on J. C. Penney credit card	450
Phone bills paid in 1992	640
Gas and electric bills paid in 1992	1,990
Principal amount of home loan	148,500
Property taxes paid in 1992	3,180
Estimated value of home	185,000
1987 Nissan	2,700
Other assets	15,000
Amount invested in mutual funds	58,000
Principal amount of cabin loan	30,000
Nancy's pay	28,750
1991 tax refund received	1,560
Doctor bill	60
Gas, oil, and car repairs	1,800
Mortgage payments on house	19,500
Life insurance premiums paid	850
Laundry and hair care expenses	1,230
Checking account	1,520
Savings accounts	7,250
Bill from gas and electric companies	140
Income received from interest, dividends, etc.	7,000
Other entertainment	3,650
Balance due on Visa card	1,550
Market value of mountain cabin	47,000
Home entertainment center	1,800
Amount outstanding on MasterCard	900
Loan payments made on car	2,150
Shoes, clothing, etc. purchased in 1992	2,600
Money spent on Arizona vacation	3,400
1990 Chevrolet	7,500
Estimated value of clothes and other personal effects	6,500
Value of home furnishings	15,200
Loan payments made on cabin	6,250
Doctor and dentist bills paid in 1992	980

Based on this information, construct the Ballingers' December 31, 1992, balance sheet *and* income and expenditures statement for the year ending December 31, 1992; use forms like the ones in Exhibits 2.3 and 2.8.

17. Why might you be interested in forecasting a balance sheet, an income and expenditures statement, or a segment of either one, such as net worth?

18. Explain two ways in which net worth could increase (or decrease) from the one period to the next. Which way would make the change in net worth more likely to occur? Why?

CONTEMPORARY CASE APPLICATIONS

■ 2.1 Elizabeth Walker Prepares a Balance Sheet for Her Banker

Elizabeth Walker has been asked by her banker to submit a personal balance sheet as of June 30, 1992, in support of an application for a $3,000 home improvement loan. She has come to you for help in preparing it. So far, she has prepared a list of her assets and liabilities as follows:

Cash on hand		$ 70
Balance in checking account		180
Balance in money market deposit account with Mid-American Savings		650
Bills outstanding:		
Telephone	$ 20	
Electricity	70	
Charge account balance	190	
Visa	180	
MasterCard	220	
Taxes	400	
Insurance	220	1,300
Home and property		68,000
Home mortgage loan		52,000
Automobile:		
1989 Honda Accord		6,000
Installment loan balances:		
Auto loans	$3,000	
Furniture loan	500	3,500
Personal property:		
Furniture	$1,050	
Clothing	900	1,950
Investments:		
U.S. government savings bonds	$ 500	
Stock of WIMCO Corporation	3,000	3,500

Questions

1. From the data given, prepare Elizabeth Walker's balance sheet, dated June 30, 1992 (follow the balance sheet form shown in Exhibit 2.3).

2. Evaluate her balance sheet relative to the following factors: (a) solvency, (b) equity in her dominant asset, (c) liquidity, and (d) debt serviceability.

3. If you were her banker, how would you feel about giving Ms. Walker the loan if you had to base your decision solely on her balance sheet? Explain.

■ 2.2 Chuck Takes a Look at the Schwartzes' Finances

Chuck and Judy Schwartz recently have become a bit concerned about their finances. Judy is an engineer for a large petroleum company while Chuck is a full-time student majoring in industrial design at Generic State University. Chuck also tends to the housekeeping chores and maintains the financial records. In order to find out how well he managed their finances last year, Chuck has amassed the following data for the year ending December 31, 1992:

Judy's salary	$37,000
Reimbursement for travel expenditures	1,950
Interest on:	
Savings account	110
Bonds of Alpha Corporation	70
Groceries	4,150
Rent	9,600
Utilities	960
Gas and auto expenditures	650
Chuck's tuition, books, and supplies	3,300
Books, magazines, and periodicals	280
Clothing and other miscellaneous expenditures	2,700
Cost of photographic equipment purchased with charge card	2,200
Amount paid to date	1,600
Judy's travel expenditures	1,950
Purchase of a new car (cost)	9,750
Outstanding loan balance on car	7,300
Purchase of bonds in Alpha Corporation	4,900

Questions

1. Using the information provided, prepare an income and expenditures statement for the Schwartzes for the year ending December 31, 1992 (follow the form shown in Exhibit 2.8).

2. Based on the statement you prepared, assess the Schwartzes' financial performance last year, commenting on the following: (a) their total income, (b) their total expenditures, (c) their cash surplus (or deficit), and (d) the resulting increase or decrease in their net worth.

3. Forecast their net worth a year from now (at December 31, 1993) assuming their total income increases by 10 percent, their total expenses increase by 7 percent, and the market value of their total assets increases by 8 percent. (Their December 31, 1992, total assets were $21,500 and net worth was $3,110.) Discuss your findings.

FOR MORE INFORMATION

General Articles

Cullen, Robert. "Smiling Interfaces." *Personal Investor*, November 1991, pp. 54–57.

Davis, Kirstin. "Money Management Made Easy." *Kiplinger's Personal Finance Magazine*, January 1992, pp. 65–69.

Fenner, Elizabeth. "14 Terrific Moves that Can Save Plenty." *Money*, December 1991, pp. 76–82.

Henderson, Nancy. "Weeding Out Your Home Files." *Changing Times*, January 1991, pp. 41–43.

"How Are You Doing?" *U.S. News & World Report*, July 30, 1990, pp. 71–79.

Hughes, James W. "Understanding the Squeezed Consumer." *American Demographics*, July 1991, pp. 44–49.

Kobliner, Beth. "Tight Times for Twentysomethings." *Money*, August 1991, pp. 54–59.

Luciano, Lani. "How to Cut Your Expenses 20%." *Money*, December 1991, pp. 70–75.

Mahar, Maggie. "Last of the Big Spenders? A New Style Consumer Will Scale Down, Save More." *Barrons*, March 11, 1991, pp. 10–11, 34–40.

GETTING A HANDLE ON YOUR FINANCIAL FUTURE

Accurate and timely personal financial statements are essential to the financial planning process. In order to see where you are going, you have to know where you are. Personal financial statements fill this role.

The two major financial statements used in personal financial planning are the balance sheet and the income statement. The balance sheet presents a picture of your assets, liabilities, and net worth at a point in time, while the income statement shows what happened over a period of time. Each of the statements requires accurate and timely information. You should begin the lifelong process of monitoring your financial progress with the development of a good record-keeping system. This can be accomplished by the purchase of a ledger book or computer software providing this capability. Once this is done and records of your income and expenses and your assets and liabilities are gathered, you are ready to construct your financial statements.

If You Are Just Starting Out

The first thing that you need to do is to gather all of the information necessary to construct your personal financial statements. For your balance sheet you need to itemize your assets according to their fair market value and your liabilities according to the current outstanding balance. In the case of real and personal property, you may have to just estimate the values. Remember, you need to be as realistic as possible with the values you place on your assets so as not to overstate your financial position.

A good source of information on your income and expenditures is your tax return. However, this only considers taxable income and expenditures. You would need to adjust the information on the tax return for nontaxable income (gifts, social security, and so on) and cash expenses (such as rent, utilities, food, clothing, principal repayment on notes, and so on) to construct your income and expenditure statement. If you did not file a tax return last year, you will probably need to refer to your checkbook register or receipts for the necessary information to construct this statement.

The following checklists will help you construct your statements:

Balance Sheet:

1. Where possible the balance sheet should conform with the ending period for the statement of income and expenditures.

2. Classify as liquid assets any that are held in cash or can be readily converted into cash with little or no loss of value.

3. Determine as best you can the fair market value of your real and personal assets.

4. List your assets that are held for investment purposes — in other words, those held for future rather than present consumption.

5. Don't forget to include assets held under uniform gifts or transfers to minors acts, in trusts, or cash value of life insurance policies.

6. Some of your liabilities can be classified as unpaid bills, which might include rent and utilities, repair bills, insurance premiums due, and medical and dental expenses.

7. Your credit card balances are included in the section on revolving credit.

8. Consumer installment loans would include automobile, furniture, and appliance loans. You would probably not have any mortgage loans at this stage in your financial life cycle.

9. Other loans would include your student loans and loans from friends and family.

Income and Expenditure Statement:

1. Choose an appropriate time period for the analysis, usually the most recent year.

2. Only list income that has actually been received, as this statement is on a cash basis.

3. Use gross wages before taxes are removed, because taxes are later treated as expenditures.

4. Don't forget to include tax refunds as a source of income.

5. Categorize your expenditures by the types of benefits provided, such as living expenses, asset purchases, tax payments, and/or debt payments.

6. Where possible determine if the expenditures are fixed or variable. In other words, identify which are controllable.

7. Remember to include your social security and income taxes as an expenditure. Also include any other items withheld from your pay, such as health insurance, pension contribution, and so on.

8. Calculate your cash surplus or deficit.

9. Project your income and expenditures for the next year and calculate the cash surplus or deficit.

In order to construct the balance sheet you must classify your assets and liabilities. Exhibit 2.3 gives an illustration of the major classifications. For example, your assets could be classified as liquid assets, real property, personal property, and investments, while your liabilities are unpaid bills, revolving credit balances, consumer installment loans, mortgage loans, and other loans. The difference between your total assets and total liabilities is your net worth. The change in net worth is often used to monitor progress toward wealth accumulation.

An example of an income and expenditures statement is shown in Exhibit 2.8. You should classify your income according to the source: wages and salaries, bonuses and commissions, pensions and annuities, investment income, and other income. Your cash expenses can be classified as living expenses, asset purchases, tax payments, and/or debt payments. In addition you might want to classify your expenditures as fixed or variable. The difference in total income and total cash expenditures is the cash surplus or deficit. If you have a deficit, it must be financed from savings in previous periods or by borrowing.

In order to assess how well you are doing, you would want to compare your personal financial statements over time. In addition, you might want to calculate some key ratios to evaluate your performance and to determine your ability to carry additional debt. Among the ratios are the solvency ratio, liquidity ratio, savings ratio, and debt service ratio shown on pages 72–74.

If You Are Thirtysomething

Once your have established your record-keeping system and have constructed your income and expenditure statements and balance sheets over a couple of years, your attention should focus on monitoring the changes in the statements and analyzing the effects of the changes. This is necessary to alert you to situations that would require a change in strategy to achieve a particular financial goal.

The financial statements that you have constructed give you the ability to track your performance over time. What you are interested in determining is whether or not your financial position is improving. One approach is to calculate financial ratios such as the solvency, liquidity, savings, and debt service ratios and compare them over time as well as monitor the growth in your personal net worth.

As you grow older, you will notice a number of changes in your financial statements. For one, they will become more complicated as you add assets and liabilities to your statements, your sources of income expand, and your expenditures increase. You should look for the following changes to items on your statements:

Balance Sheet:

1. As you accumulate more assets it is relatively easy to add them to your balance sheet at cost, which represents the "fair market value." However, with the passage of time you may fail to adjust your older assets to their true market value, which overstates your assets and net worth.

2. The investment portfolio becomes larger and more complicated as you diversify your holdings.

3. Your liabilities become more complicated with the addition of mortgage loans and home equity lines of credit.

4. Your net worth should be increasing as long as your income exceeds your expenditures or the value of your assets is growing at a faster rate than your liabilities.

Income and Expenditure Statement:

1. Your sources of income should show an increase in investment income as surplus cash is put into real and financial investments.

2. As you get older, your real growth in earnings may level off or decline, but this should be offset by investment income.

3. In retirement your income will come from your annuities, pensions, social security, and investments. Some of these are fixed while others will adjust with inflation.

4. As your marital and family situation changes, you will need to be prepared for changes in your expenditures. This will require careful planning in order to accommodate change.

CHAPTER

Planning Your Financial Future

Go ahead, fantasize for a moment. Picture yourself a few years from now—out of school (at last!), married, and with a good-paying job that holds promise for the future. Then one day, you receive a registered letter with a cashier's check for $100,000, informing you that a great-uncle you didn't even know died and left you that part of his estate. Clearly, your financial future has taken a big turn for the better. Now you will have to do some financial planning to decide what to do with all that money: Your financial future depends on it. Many people erroneously believe that financial planning is only for the wealthy. Nothing could be further from the truth! Whether you have a lot of money or a little money, personal financial planning is still necessary. If the fantasy of a big monetary windfall never materializes in your life, if indeed your income seems inadequate, you can nevertheless take steps to control and improve your financial situation. And taking the right steps is basically what personal financial planning is all about: a conscientious and systematic climb toward achievement of preset financial goals. In order to reap the full benefits of personal financial planning, though, you need a well-defined set of financial goals, a fully developed set of financial plans, and a carefully prepared series of cash budgets.

FINANCIAL *facts* OR *fantasies*

Are the following statements financial facts (true) or fantasies (false)?

Financial plans are set up after the annual budget is prepared.

Most professional financial planners earn their income from the commissions they receive on the financial products they sell.

Defining financial goals is the first step in the personal financial planning process.

A cash budget is a report that shows the amount of money you will be spending from month to month.

If a budget shows a cash deficit for the year, then you have no choice but to borrow enough money to make up the shortfall.

One of the final steps in the cash budgeting process is to compare actual results to budgeted amounts.

83

FINANCIAL PLANNING AND BUDGETING: MAPPING OUT YOUR FINANCIAL FUTURE

Budgeting provides not only direction for future financial activities but also a way of keeping financial transactions on track. How might a budget prove useful in helping your achieve your financial goals? Take a few moments to answer the question before reading on.

Financial planning and budgeting enable families to achieve greater wealth and financial security by means of well-defined plans and carefully developed and implemented strategies and controls. On the one hand, they provide *direction* by helping us work toward specific financial goals; on the other, they provide *control* by bringing the various dimensions of our personal financial affairs into focus. Financial planning and budgeting are a lot like road maps: Once we know where we want to go, they show us how to reach our destination. Both are essential to sound personal money management and to the attainment of personal financial goals.

WHICH COMES FIRST— THE BUDGET OR THE PLAN?

Taking a closer look at financial planning, you see that it is a process by which personal financial goals are translated first into specific financial plans and then into financial strategies through which the plans can be implemented. In contrast, a **budget** is a detailed short-term financial forecast that is used to monitor and control expenditures and purchases. *Budgets exist as a way to help us achieve the financial goals we set in our financial plans.* They provide the mechanism through which the financial plans are carried out. Developed in line with established financial plans, budgets provide a detailed statement of estimated income versus estimated expenditures, purchases, and investments.

Exhibit 3.1 gives a schematic overview of various financial statements and reports, and their relation-

ship to one another. Note that whereas financial plans provide direction to annual budgets, the success (or lack thereof) in carrying out the budget will directly affect our balance sheet and income and expenditures statement. As we move from plans to budgets to actual statements, we see the critical role that financial statements play in providing *feedback* to the financial plans and budgets — that is, they let us know what kind of progress we are making toward our financial goals and whether or not we are staying within our budget.

Financial plans are set up after the annual budget is prepared.
Fantasy: The financial plans come first, then the budget. The budget is part of our financial plans and exists as a way to help us carry them out.

THE FINANCIAL PLANNING PROCESS

The financial planning process generally involves the following steps:

1. Define financial goals.
2. Develop financial plans and strategies for achieving goals.
3. Implement financial plans and strategies.
4. Periodically develop and implement budgets for use in monitoring and controlling progress toward goal achievement.
5. Evaluate results relative to plans and budgets on a regular basis and, when necessary, take corrective action.
6. Revise and replace goals as personal circumstances change.

The first step in financial planning is to define your financial goals. The next step is to develop financial plans and strategies that will be compatible with your goals. Once these have been defined, it is time to put them to work, that is, to implement them. But you cannot just turn the switch on and walk away. Rather, you must periodically develop and implement budgets for monitoring and controlling outcomes, and, when necessary, you must alter your financial objectives. In effect, the financial planning process runs full circle as you come back to defining revised goals and making corresponding revisions in your financial plans.

EXHIBIT 3.1

The Interlocking Network of Financial Plans and Statements

Personal financial planning involves a whole network of financial reports that link future goals and plans with actual results. Such a network provides direction, control, and feedback.

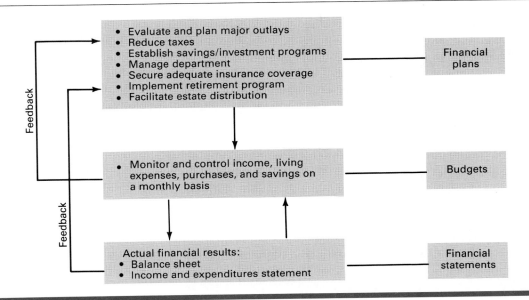

As discussed earlier, communicating with your partner about financial goals and learning about each other's "money personality" are important to successful personal financial planning. In addition to setting goals, you will need to decide how to divide the responsibility for money management tasks and decision making. Many couples divide up the responsibility for routine financial decisions, often on the basis of expertise and interest, and jointly make major decisions. Each family needs to consider its members' interests, skills, and spending styles when developing a money management system consistent with its goals. Allowing children to participate in the personal financial planning process encourages the formation of good money management skills. Such involvement will allow them to learn how to set and implement their own financial goals, and to understand where the household's money goes. Some families schedule regular "financial meetings," while others involve family members in a less formal manner.

A Comprehensive Financial Plan. To get an idea of what is involved in a **comprehensive per-** sonal financial plan, let's use a professionally prepared plan as a basis. Essentially, what a comprehensive plan should do is provide an individual or family with a whole set of detailed plans and recommendations to follow in order to achieve a variety of specific financial goals. A well-defined financial plan is based on a complete inventory of a family's personal and financial circumstances. This includes a family profile (health status, number and ages of

budget
A detailed financial forecast used to monitor and control expenditures and purchases; it provides a mechanism for carrying out financial plans to achieve short-run financial goals.

comprehensive personal financial plan
A set of detailed plans and recommendations for achieving specific financial goals, as compiled from a family profile; information on current income, expenses, and financial condition; tax returns; insurance coverages; retirement programs; and estate plans.

EXHIBIT 3.2

Summary of the Recommendations from a Comprehensive, Professionally Prepared Financial Plan

Professionally prepared, comprehensive financial plans are custom-tailored to provide detailed recommendations aimed at the achievement of specific personal financial goals. However, to be effective, the financial plans and recommendations must be implemented—they should be viewed as a launching pad, not a landing strip! The following recommendations are given for a dual-career couple in their 40s with two children.

Education of Children

■ Recommendation:	Engage in a systematic program of prefunding the children's education by putting $60,000 in a custodial account or by setting aside $9,500 annually for the next nine years.
■ Desired result:	Savings of $200,000 in a custodial account at the end of nine years.

Income for Disability

■ Recommendation:	Make no change to present disability program.
■ Desired result:	Adequate income provided in the event of long-term disability.

Medical Insurance

■ Recommendation:	Increase major medical insurance to at least $500,000.
■ Desired result:	Adequate insurance coverage in the event of serious illness.

Property and Casualty Insurance

■ Recommendation 1:	Reduce liability coverage under present insurance to the suggested minimum and purchase an excess liability policy in the amount of $2 million.
■ Recommendation 2:	Confirm that the dwelling coverage is at least 80 percent of its replacement value.
■ Desired result:	Adequate overall insurance protection.

Proper Disposition of Estate

■ Recommendation 1:	Purchase $250,000 of universal life insurance on husband's life at an annual cost of approximately $3,000 to provide both insurance and tax-free accumulation.
■ Desired result:	Provide capital for projected survivor income shortages.
■ Recommendation 2:	New wills should first place the unified credit amount in trust for the surviving spouse; the balance of each spouse's estate should qualify for the unlimited marital deduction.
■ Desired result:	Estate tax savings of $80,000 and $45,000, respectively.
■ Recommendation 3:	Consider the use of a testamentary trust in their wills for the benefit of their children.
■ Desired result:	Protection and management of assets until minor children have completed school.

Retirement Income

■ Recommendation:	Follow systematic investment program (described in detail).
■ Desired result:	Monthly income in first year of retirement will be $10,500.

Investment Program

■ Recommendation:	Over a period of time to be determined by tax advice, couple should:
	Place $20,000 in commercial real estate
	Place $12,000 in a cash reserve account
	Place $16,000 in a tax-deferred annuity
	Place $10,000 in municipal bonds
	Place $15,000 in growth stock
	Place $12,500 in an exploratory oil and gas partnership
	Invest excess cash flow annually
■ Desired results:	Write-offs will save $10,500 in income taxes; capital at retirement will be $725,000.

children, education status, and any special considerations); information on current income, expenses, and financial condition (assets, investments, and debts); tax returns; insurance coverages; retirement programs; and estate plans. In addition, information about personal and family expectations, motivations, risk tolerances, and objectives must be obtained. A professional financial planner would gather such information using an extensive, multipage questionnaire and personal interviews.

Once this inventory is complete, the first step in the financial planning process can be taken: to define and prioritize personal financial goals. These goals would pertain to such general activities as (1) capital accumulation for specific needs and goals (like the purchase of a house or vacation home, children's education, or retirement); (2) reduction of income taxes; (3) protection against personal risk (insurance coverage); (4) investment and property management; and/or (5) maximizing the distribution of an estate to the heirs. A written plan would then be prepared that included all of the family's major financial goals, along with detailed strategies and recommendations for each. Such a professionally prepared plan could well be a 25-to-50 page (or longer) document that explained, summarized, and recorded the recommendations as well as the results expected from their implementation.

A summary of the recommendations from a real-life comprehensive, professionally prepared financial plan is shown in Exhibit 3.2. This particular financial plan covered 77 pages, plus an appendix, and cost $1,500. It was prepared for a couple in their early 40s with two children; the husband is a bank executive earning nearly $70,000 a year, and the wife earns $35,000 a year as an accountant for a regional department store chain. Note the recommendations covering children's education, insurance planning, estate planning, retirement plans, and investment programs. This couple is now at the point where they can implement the recommendations and begin working toward their established goals. They now have something specific to shoot for and can set up their annual budget accordingly.

PROFESSIONAL FINANCIAL PLANNERS

The number of people turning to financial planning as a way of gaining control over their financial affairs is increasing almost as rapidly as the variety and complexity of the financial products being offered to them. This environment, not surprisingly, has led to one of the fastest-growing fields in finance — **professional financial planners**. These are the people to whom others turn for professional help in setting up and carrying out fully developed financial plans. In 1979 there were about 25,000 financial planners plying their trade; it is estimated that in 1991 their ranks had grown to more than 300,000 nationwide.

Types of Planners. All financial planners work for some sort of fee. Most are compensated from the commissions they earn on the financial products they sell, while others charge only a fee based on the complexity of the plan they prepare. Some financial planners are simply converted insurance salespeople or securities dealers who do little more than continue to sell the same financial products they always have (life insurance, stocks, bonds, mutual funds, and annuities), except now they do it under the guise of being a "financial planner." On the other hand, many large, established financial institutions, recognizing the enormous potential, are getting into this field in a big way and stand ready to compete with the best financial planners. There are also a number of independent financial planners who offer nothing but sound, high-quality service. Regardless of whether they are independent or affiliated operations, full-service financial planners help their clients to articulate their long- and short-run financial goals and alert them to the importance of systematically planning for their financial needs.

In addition to this type of personal financial planning service, there is a growing list of institutions offering **computerized financial plans**. For $0 to

---

professional financial planner
An individual or firm that assists clients in establishing long- and short-run financial goals and in developing and implementing financial plans aimed at their achievement.

computerized financial plans
Computer-generated financial plans that offer simple advice on major areas of personal money management; while they are relatively inexpensive, they are also somewhat impersonal.

EXHIBIT 3.3

Tips for Picking a Competent Financial Planner

The following tips offered by Price Waterhouse's Consumer Financial Institute and others should prove useful in choosing a competent personal financial planner.

1. Shop around. Get recommendations and interview several candidates.
2. Scrutinize backgrounds. Look for degrees in economics, accounting, business, or finance. Are their previous occupations (bookkeeper, tollbooth operator) germane to planning? How long have they been in business?
3. Check for participation in continuing education programs. Someone whose last class was five years ago may be poorly informed today.
4. Insist on proof of registration or certification. Firms that offer securities advice must register with the Securities and Exchange Commission or the National Association of Securities Dealers. CFPs must be registered with the International Board of Certified Financial Planners (Denver, CO; (303) 850-0333), and ChFCs must be registered with the American Society (Bryn Mawr, PA; (215) 526-2500).
5. Ask to see plans your candidates prepared for other clients. Make sure the plans are thorough and individualized.
6. Get client references, and check them.
7. Find out with whom the planners consult to prepare their plans. Who are their lawyers and accountants? If they have no reputable backup, beware.
8. If a planner is affiliated with a larger firm, check its reputation with state regulators, the SEC, and industry associates.
9. Perhaps most important, find out how your candidates are compensated. Are they paid through fees, commissions, or both? Many believe that fee-based financial planners are generally more objective, since their income is not tied directly to selling financial products.

Source: Excerpted from David Morrow, "A Checklist for Picking a Planner," *FORTUNE 1989 Investors' Guide*, page 202. Copyright © 1989 *Time Inc.* All rights reserved.

$500, these computerized services — available from Paine Webber, Merrill Lynch, Prudential-Bache, IDS/American Express, and other investment firms — provide basic advice on how to keep up with current bills, save for college or retirement, reduce taxes, or restructure investment portfolios. These professional planners may be the most appropriate course of action for those who have neither the time, inclination, nor expertise to do the planning on their own. The costs may well be worth the benefits, especially when you consider that for some people the alternative is not to plan at all.

Most professional financial planners earn their income from the commissions they receive on the financial products they sell.

Fact: The vast majority of professional financial planners make their living by selling financial products (life insurance, mutual funds, annuities, and so on) to you — in fact, some merely use the "financial plan" as a tool for selling these products.

Choosing a Financial Planner. Planners who have completed the required course of study and earned the Certified Financial Planner (CFP) or Chartered Financial Consultant (ChFC) designation are often a better choice than the many self-proclaimed financial planners. Of course, CPAs, attorneys, investment managers, and other professionals without such certifications in many instances do provide sound financial planning advice. Unfortunately, though, the field is still largely unregulated, and almost anyone can call himself or herself a financial planner. Most financial planners are honest and reputable, but there have been cases of fraudulent practices. It is therefore critical to thoroughly check out a potential financial advisor — and preferably interview two or three. Choosing the wrong one could wipe out your hard-earned savings. Use the questions in Exhibit 3.3 to find out as much as possible about the planner's experience and compensation.

The way a planner is paid — fees, commissions, or both — should be one of your major concerns. Obviously, you need to be aware of potential conflicts of interest when using a planner with ties to a brokerage firm, insurance company, or bank. Many planners are now providing clients with disclosure forms outlining fees and/or commissions for various transactions. In addition to asking questions, you should check with your state securities department (for those planners registered to sell securities) and the Securities and Exchange Commission to see if there are any pending lawsuits, complaints by state or federal regulators, personal bankruptcies, or convictions for investment-related crimes. However, even these agencies may not have accurate or current information; simply being properly registered and without a record of disciplinary actions provides no guarantee that the planner's track record is good. You may also want to do some additional checking about the planner within the local financial community. Clearly, you should do your homework before engaging the services of a professional financial planner.

SPECIAL PLANNING CONCERNS

Several situations require special attention during the personal financial planning process. For example, employee benefit plans have become increasingly complex, and many companies offer a variety of insurance coverage and retirement benefit choices. Understanding your options allows you to select the best coverage, at the best price, for your situation. Because some benefits are tax-deferred or can be purchased with pretax dollars, careful benefit planning may allow you to reduce taxes and increase your take-home pay. Employee benefits are covered in greater detail in later chapters. As discussed in the *Issues in Money Management* box, there are times when it's a good idea *not* to make important financial decisions. Two other special planning concerns are managing money in a two-income family and adapting to changes in marital status.

Managing Two Incomes. More and more families are joining the ranks of dual-income households. Until recently, many couples viewed the second income as a source of financial security and a way to afford "extras." Today, many people depend on a second income to make ends meet. Often, however, a second income does not increase a couple's bottom line as much as expected. With it may come higher expenses. Child care, taxes, clothing, dry cleaning, transportation, lunches, and similar expenses can consume a very large portion of a second paycheck. The worksheet in Exhibit 3.4 provides a way to assess the net monthly income of a second paycheck, both without and with the impact of employer-paid benefits. When using the worksheet be sure to include only those expenses that are directly related to the second job; some personal expenses would exist in the absence of a second job. In addition, couples should coordinate their employee benefits in order to obtain the needed coverage at a minimum cost.

When analyzing the benefits of a second income, you must also consider the intangible costs (additional demands on your life, less time with family, and higher stress) and benefits (career development, job satisfaction, and sense of worth). For instance, if the nonworking spouse takes a part-time job while the children are young, not much may be added to household income, but it could keep the spouse on a career track and ease the transition to full-time work later. Clearly, it is important to consider personal circumstances and goals when you are assessing the costs and benefits of a second income.

For this reason, two-income families should develop financial plans that consider the possibility of the loss of one income for any reason, including a spouse's staying at home with young children, going back to school, or losing a job. In some cases, couples use the second income to meet the basic expenditures associated with their luxurious lifestyles. They should analyze past income and expenditure statements to study spending patterns and identify areas where expense reductions are possible. Such reductions would then be incorporated into the budgeting process (described later in this chapter).

The dual-income situation often complicates the establishment of a money management system. Spouses need to decide how to allocate income to household expenditures, family financial goals, and personal spending goals. Some options include placing all income into a single joint account; having each spouse contribute equal amounts into a joint

ISSUES IN MONEY MANAGEMENT

When Not to Make Important Financial Decisions

On the day of her twin sister's funeral, Karen Kopelman was inundated with calls and cards from real estate brokers eager to sell her sister's apartment. "It was just shocking," says the Houston teacher, "Money brings out the evil in people."

Ms. Kopelman's experience isn't unusual. A death in the family, the birth of a child, and similar turning points in life represent great opportunities for financial professionals eager to sell investments, insurance, and other products.

But they're among the worst times for individuals to make major financial decisions.

"People usually aren't in the best frame of mind," says Mary Calhoun, a consultant to securities lawyers, in Watertown, Mass. Most securities arbitration cases she says, originate from situations in which people suddenly had large lump sums to invest, from an inheritance, divorce, or retirement.

David Shellenberger, a Boston attorney who concentrates in securities arbitration, says it's important to avoid making quick or radical decisions. "People will tend to lose large lump sums they receive suddenly, simply because they don't know how to handle money," he says.

Here are some of life's cradle-to-grave events that attract financial salespeople, and what they try to sell.

MOVING OR BUYING A HOME.

Doing either identifies a person as a good candidate for life insurance, homeowner's insurance, and banking services. And it's easy for salespeople to find out whom to call.

The Postal Service sells lists of people who fill out national change of address forms. Insur-

ance companies, banks, and credit-card companies are among the buyers.

Insurance agents, financial planners, banks, and others also purchase information from filings on home closings to spot prospects for a variety of products and services, including life insurance, financial planning, and credit cards.

BIRTH OF A CHILD.

Marketers can get this information from several sources—including hospitals. Financial planners and stockbrokers often try to interest parents and grandparents in buying annuities, mutual funds, zero-coupon bonds, and other investments as college-funding vehicles. Insurance agents try to sell life insurance policies.

The only financial-planning consideration new parents really need to worry about

account that is used to make expenditures consistent with achievement of their joint goals, while retaining individual discretion over each spouse's remaining income; or contributing a proportional share of each income to finance joint expenditures and goals. Couples may experiment with different strategies until they find one that works best for them. Consideration, of course, must be given to the amount each spouse earns and various emotional and behavioral factors in their relationship. Regard-

less of the money management system, each spouse needs to have some money of his or her own that he or she can spend without accountability.

Adapting to Changes in Marital Status. Any change in marital status results in a need to review personal financial plans and money management procedures. Marriage may create a two-income household, raising the special planning concerns discussed above. In the event of divorce, income

immediately is whether they have enough life insurance to take care of the newborn if they die. And even if they don't have enough coverage, they shouldn't allow themselves to be pressured into making an expensive decision quickly. Instead, they can purchase low-cost term-life insurance.

LOSE OR CHANGE JOB.

Brokers often scan the newspapers for information about layoffs and cutbacks in an effort to capture the severance packages and lump-sum payouts of former employees.

People who have recently left a job should be aware that financial professionals who approach them may have a conflict of interest. Those who earn commissions from sales of financial products may be more interested in selling than in providing the kind of guidance the individual needs.

"Other than jump at the first call they get, they may want to do a little more investigating," says Barbara Roper of the Consumer Federation of America. The only deadline people may have is if they have received a lump-sum distribution of tax-deferred retirement savings. They must roll that money into an individual retirement account or other retirement plan within 60 days of receiving it, to avoid paying income taxes on the earnings, and a 10% penalty if they are under age 59½.

DEATH IN THE FAMILY.

This is a time when individuals are the most vulnerable — especially if they have received money from insurance policies, an inheritance or the sale of a home. Sometimes the bereaved are approached by strangers. Ms. Kopelman says that the real estate brokers who contacted her after her sister's death read the death notice in the newspaper.

* * *

In general, the recently bereaved shouldn't rush into any financial decision. One source of help for those who have lost a spouse: the Widowed Persons Service at the American Association of Retired Persons. The service, which has programs across the country, "gets a lot of calls from widows under siege," by brokers and other financial salespeople says an AARP spokeswoman. For information on the program in your community, write to 601 E Street, N.W., Washington, D.C. 20049.

Source: Adapted from Ellen E. Schultz, "When It's the Wrong Time for Big Financial Decisions," *The Wall Street Journal*, October 29, 1991, pp. C1, C12.

may decrease because alimony and/or child support payments cause one salary to be divided between two households. Single parents may have to stretch limited financial resources further in order to meet added expenses such as child care. Remarriage brings additional financial considerations, including decisions involving children from prior marriages and managing the assets each spouse brings to the marriage. Some couples find it helpful to develop a prenuptial contract that sets forth their agreement on financial matters, such as the control of assets, their disposition in the event of death or divorce, and other important money issues.

Death of a spouse is another change that greatly affects financial planning. The surviving spouse is typically faced with decisions on how to receive and invest life insurance proceeds and manage other assets. In families where the deceased made most of the financial decisions with little or no involvement of the surviving spouse, the survivor may be over-

EXHIBIT 3.4

Analyzing the Benefit of a Second Income

This worksheet can be used to estimate the net monthly income of a second paycheck. Your employer should be able to estimate your noncash benefits. Calculating the bottom line twice, first using only money income and then employer-paid benefits, can be an eye-opener. The values shown for the Diaz's indicate that without the employer-paid benefits of $816 (line 2) they would realize net monthly income of $854 (line 1 − line 3) and with them their net monthly income would be $1,670 (line 4). Note that even though the social security tax shows up as a job-related expense, it is buying future benefits.

SECOND INCOME ANALYSIS

Name(s) ___Areala and Marcos Diaz___   Date: ___December 31, 1993___

MONTHLY CASH INCOME

Gross pay	$ 2,500
Pretax contributions (401(k) plans, dependent-care-reimbursement accounts)	200
Additional job-related income (bonuses, overtime, commissions)	0
(1) Total Cash Income	$ 2,700

EMPLOYER-PAID BENEFITS

Health insurance	$ 275
Life insurance	50
Pension contributions	300
Thrift-plan contributions	0
Social security	191
Profit sharing	0
Other deferred compensation	0
(2) Total Benefits	$ 816

EXHIBIT 3.4 (continued)

MONTHLY JOB-RELATED EXPENSES

Federal income tax	$ 750
Social security tax	191
State income tax	125
Child care	320
Clothing and personal care	150
Dry cleaning	100
Meals away from home	100
Public transportation	0
Gasoline	60
Auto-related expenses (parking, maintenance)	50
Other	0
(3) Total Expenses	$ 1,846
(4) Net Income (Deficit) [(1)+(2)−(3)]	$ 1,670

Source: Adapted from Kevin McManus, "How to Get the Most from Two Incomes," *Changing Times*, July 1989, p. 24.

whelmed by the need to take on financial responsibilities. Advance planning can minimize many of these problems. Couples should, on a regular basis, review all aspects of their finances. Each spouse should understand what is owned and owed, participate in formulating financial goals and investment strategies, and fully understand estate plans (covered in detail in Chapter 16).

DEFINING YOUR FINANCIAL GOALS

The financial planning process begins with the definition of both long-run and short-run financial goals, which in turn provide direction for financial plans and budgets. Do you have long-run and short-run financial goals? Before reading on, spend a few moments formulating and listing them.

As noted earlier, setting financial goals is the first step in the personal financial planning process. Once set, these goals provide direction for your financial plans. But just as you cannot prepare plans for attaining goals that are not yet formulated, you cannot begin the financial planning process without a knowledge of your current financial position. (Methods for evaluating current financial position via personal financial statements were described in Chapter 2.)

After your current financial position has been evaluated, both long-run and short-run financial goals can be established. Your goals will, of course, depend on your personal situation and where you are in the life cycle. Some long-term goals, such as saving for retirement, may not change as you move through life, while others will vary. Short-term goals, by their nature, will change frequently. Exhibit 3.5 presents some typical short- and long-term goals of persons in different life situations.

As noted earlier, it is important to involve your immediate family in the goal-setting process in order to eliminate potential future conflicts. By having each family member effectively "buy into" these plans, a cooperative team effort should result, thereby improving the family's chances of achieving its goals. Once your goals have been defined and approved, appropriate cash budgets can be prepared. Normally, long-run financial goals are set first, followed by a series of corresponding short-run goals.

Defining financial goals is the first step in the personal financial planning process.
Fact: Once you've specified your financial goals, you can develop financial plans, strategies, and budgets consistent with achieving them.

SETTING LONG-RUN FINANCIAL GOALS

Long-run financial goals should indicate the individual's or family's wants and desires for the next 2 to 5 years on out to the next 30 or 40 years. Of course, many people find it difficult to pinpoint exactly what they will want 30 or so years from now; however, if they at least give some thought to the matter, they should be able to establish some tentative long-run financial goals. Recognize, though, that many long-run goals will change over time. For example, an individual might set a goal of retiring at age 55 with a net worth of $400,000. At age 50, this same person might decide to purchase a condominium in Florida and retire at age 62 with a net worth of $500,000. Although this individual's long-run goal is changed, note that his short-run goals will remain pretty much the same: to make substantial, regular contributions to savings or investments in order to accumulate the desired net worth.

Putting a Dollar Value on Financial Goals.
Some financial goals can be defined in rather general terms. Others should be defined more precisely, perhaps even to the extent of assigning fairly specific dollar values. Consider, for example, the goal of buying your first home in six years. The first question you must answer is how much to spend. Let's say that you have done some "window shopping" and feel that, *taking future inflation into consideration*, you will have to spend about $90,000 to get the kind of house you like. Of course, you will not need the full amount, but given a 20 percent down payment ($90,000 × .20 = $18,000) plus closing costs, you estimate that you will need around $20,000. You now have a fairly well-defined long-run financial goal: *to accumulate $20,000 in six years in order to buy a home that will cost about $90,000.*

The next question is how to get all that money. If you are like many people, you will probably accumulate it by saving or investing a set amount each month or year. You can easily figure what you will have to save or invest each year if you know what your goal is and how much you think you can earn on your savings or investments. In this case, if you have to start from scratch (that is, have nothing saved today) and if you estimate that you can earn about 10 percent on your money, you will have to save or invest about $2,600 per year for each of the next six years to accumulate $20,000 over that time period. Now you have another vital piece of information: *You know what you must do over the next six years in order to reach your financial goal.*

The Time Value of Money.   To correctly compare dollar values occurring at different points in time, you need to understand the **time value of money**, the idea that a dollar today is worth more than a dollar received in the future. As long as you can earn a positive rate of return on your investments (ignoring taxes and other behavioral factors), in a strict financial sense you should always prefer to receive equal amounts of money sooner rather than later. The two key time value concepts, *future value* and *present value* are discussed separately below. (*Note:* Although the following time value discussions and demonstrations rely on the use of financial tables, many inexpensive business calculators have these tables built into them and therefore

EXHIBIT 3.5

How Financial Goals Change over the Life Cycle

Financial goals are not static but change continually over an individual's or family's lifetime. Here are listed some typical short-term and long-term goals for a number of different personal situations.

Personal Situation	Short-Term Goals	Long-Term Goals
College senior	Find a job Rent an apartment Get a bank credit card Buy a car	Repay college loans Begin an investment program Buy a condominium
Single, mid-20s	Prepare a budget Buy a new television and VCR Get additional job training Build an emergency fund Take a Caribbean vacation Reduce expenses 10%	Begin law school Build an investment portfolio Start a retirement fund
Married couple with children, late 30s	Trade in car Repaint house Get braces for children Increase second income: from part-time to full-time job Review life and disability insurance	Buy a second car Increase college fund contributions Buy a larger home Diversify investment portfolio
Married couple with grown children, mid-50s	Buy new furniture Shift investment portfolio into income- producing securities Review skills Take cruise vacation	Decide whether to relocate upon retirement Retire at age 62 Sell house and buy smaller residence Travel to Europe and the Orient

can be conveniently used to make time value calculations.)

Future Value. The **future value** is the value to which an amount today will grow if it earns a specific rate of interest over a given period of time. Assume, for example, that you make annual deposits of $2,000 into a savings account that pays 5 percent interest per year. At the end of 20 years, you would have made deposits totaling $40,000 (20 × $2,000). If you made no withdrawals, your account balance would have increased to $66,132! This growth in value occurs not only as a result of earning interest, but because of **compounding**—the interest earned each year is left in the account and becomes part of the balance (or principal) on which interest is paid in subsequent years.

To demonstrate future value, let's return to the goal of accumulating $20,000, for a down payment on a home to be purchased six years from now. You might be tempted to solve this problem by simply

long-run financial goals
Goals that are set well into the future, typically to retirement and sometimes beyond.

time value of money
The concept that a dollar today is worth more than a dollar received in the future; it exists as long as one can earn a positive rate of return (interest rate) on investments.

future value
The value to which an amount today will grow if it earns a specific rate of interest over a given period of time. It can be used to find the yearly savings needed to accumulate a given future amount of money.

compounding
When interest earned each year is left in the account and becomes part of the balance (or principal) on which interest is paid in subsequent years.

dividing the $20,000 goal by the six-year period: $20,000/6 = $3,333. Unfortunately, this procedure would be incorrect, since it would fail to take into account the *time value of money*. The correct way to approach this problem is to use the future value concept. For instance, if you can invest $100 today at 10 percent, you will have $110 in a year: You will earn $10 on your investment ($100 × .10 = $10), plus get your original $100 back. Once you know the length of time *and* rate of return involved, you can find the future value of any investment by using the following simple formula:

Future value = Amount invested × Future value factor.

Tables of future value factors are available to facilitate and simplify the computations in this formula (see Appendix A). The table is very easy to use: Simply find the factor that corresponds to a given year *and* interest rate. Referring to Appendix A, you will find the future value factor for a six-year investment earning 10 percent to be 1.772 (the factor that lies at the intersection of six years and 10 percent).

Returning to the problem at hand, let's say you already have accumulated $5,000 toward the purchase of a new home. To find the future value of that investment in six years earning 10 percent, you can use the above formula as follows:

Future value = $5,000 × 1.772 = $8,860.

The $8,860 is how much you will have in six years if you invest the $5,000 at 10 percent. Because you feel you are going to need $20,000, you are still $11,140 short of your goal. How are you going to accumulate an additional $11,140?

Again you can utilize the future value concept, but this time you will employ an annuity factor. An **annuity** is an equal cash flow that occurs annually — for example, $1,000 per year for each of the next five years with payment to be made at the end of each year. You can find out how much you will have to save each year to accumulate a given amount by using the following equation:

$$\text{Yearly savings} = \frac{\text{Amount of money desired}}{\text{Future value annuity factor}}$$

When dealing with an annuity you will have to use a different table of factors, such as that in Appendix B.

Note that it is very much like the table of future value factors and, in fact, is used in exactly the same way: The proper future value annuity factor is the one that corresponds to a given year *and* interest rate. As an example, you'll find in Appendix B that the future value annuity factor for six years and 10 percent is 7.716. Using this factor in the above equation, you can find out how much to save each year to accumulate $11,140 in six years given a 10 percent rate of return, as follows:

$$\text{Yearly savings} = \frac{\$11,140}{7.716} = \underline{\$1,443.75}.$$

You will have to save about $1,445 a year to reach your goal. Note in the example that you must add $1,445 a year to the $5,000 you already have in order to build up a pool of $20,000 in six years. At a 10 percent rate of return, the $1,445 per year will grow to $11,140 and the $5,000 will grow to $8,860 so that in six years you will have $11,140 + $8,860 = $20,000.

How much, you may ask, would you have to save each year if you did not have the $5,000 to start with? In this case, your goal would still be the same (to accumulate $20,000 in six years), but, since you would be starting from scratch, the full $20,000 would have to come from yearly savings. Assuming you can still earn 10 percent over the six-year period, you can use the same future value annuity factor (7.716) and compute the amount of yearly savings as follows:

$$\text{Yearly savings} = \frac{\$20,000}{7.716} = \underline{\$2,592.02}.$$

or approximately $2,600. Note that this amount corresponds to the $2,600 figure cited earlier.

Using the future value concept, you can readily find either the future value to which an investment will grow over time or the amount that you must save each year to accumulate a given amount of money by a specified future date. In either case, the procedures will enable you to put monetary values on long-run financial goals.

Present Value. The **present value**, on the other hand, is the value *today* of an amount to be received in the future. It is the amount you would have to invest today at a given interest rate over the specified time period in order to accumulate the future amount. The process of finding present value is called **discounting**. It is the inverse of *compounding* to find future value. For instance, assume that you are 35 years old and wish to accumulate a retirement fund of $300,000 by the time you are age 60 (25 years from now). You estimate that you can earn 7 percent annually on your investments during the next 25 years. Assuming you wish to create the retirement fund (future value) by making a single lump-sum deposit today, you can use the following formula:

Present value = Future value × Present value factor.

Tables of present value factors (see Appendix C) make this calculation easy. First, find the present value factor for a 25-year investment at a 7 percent discount rate (the factor that lies at the intersection of 25 years and 7 percent) in Appendix C; it is .184. Then, substitute the future value of $300,000 and the present value factor of .184 into the formula as follows:

Present value = $300,000 × .184 = $55,200.

The $55,200 represents the amount you would have to deposit today into an account paying 7 percent annual interest in order to accumulate $300,000 at the end of 25 years.

Present value techniques can also be used to determine how much you can withdraw from your retirement fund each year over a specified time horizon. Assume that at age 55 you wish to begin making equal annual withdrawals over the next 30 years from your $300,000 retirement fund. At first, you might think you could withdraw $10,000 per year ($300,000/30 years). However, any unwithdrawn funds still on deposit would continue to earn 7 percent annual interest. To find the amount of the equal annual withdrawal, you again need to consider the time value of money. Specifically, you would use the following formula:

$$\text{Annual withdrawal} = \frac{\text{Initial deposit}}{\text{Present value annuity factor}}.$$

The present value annuity factors for various numbers of years and rates are given in Appendix D. To find the annual withdrawal (or payment), which is an *annuity*, substitute the $300,000 initial deposit and the present value annuity factor for 30 years and

7 percent of 12.409 (from Appendix D) into the equation above to get:

$$\text{Annual withdrawal} = \frac{\$300,000}{12.409} = \underline{\underline{\$24,176}}.$$

The result indicates that you can withdraw $24,176 each year for 30 years. This value is clearly much larger than the $10,000 annual withdrawal mentioned earlier.

Furthermore, present value techniques can be used to analyze investments. Suppose you have an opportunity to purchase an annuity investment that promises to pay you $700 per year for five years. You know that you will receive a total of $3,500 ($700 × 5 years) over the five-year period. However, you wish to earn a minimum annual return of 8 percent on your investments. What is the most you should pay for this annuity today? You can answer this question by rearranging the terms in the equation above to get:

Initial deposit = Annual withdrawal
    × Present value annuity factor.

In terms of the equation, the "initial deposit" would represent the maximum price to pay for the annuity; "annual withdrawal" would represent the maximum price for the annuity; the "annual withdrawal" would represent the annual annuity payment of $700. The present value annuity factor for five years and 8 percent (found in Appendix D) is 3.993. Substituting this into the equation, you get:

Initial deposit = $700 × 3.993 = $2,795.10.

---

annuity
An equal cash flow that occurs annually.

present value
The value today of an amount to be received in the future; it is the amount that would have to be invested today at a given interest rate over a specified time period in order to accumulate the future amount.

discounting
The process of finding present value; the inverse of compounding to find future value.

What's a Bird in the Hand Really Worth?

A dream come true: You make it to the bonus round on *Wheel of Fortune*. Vanna White strolls among the prizes. Like everybody else, you're drawn to the $25,000 in cash. But you're also intrigued by the $50,000 annuity. Isn't that twice as much as $25,000? Why has nearly every previous contestant shunned the annuity? What's the catch?

The solution to that puzzle begins with understanding this one:

T*E T*ME V***E *F M**EY

The time value of money isn't an incomprehensible concept like quantum mechanics or the NFL wild-card formula—quite the contrary. "It's the bird in the hand versus two in the bush," explains Eileen Sharkey, a Denver financial planner and president of the Institute of Certified Financial Planners. It's no

surprise that getting $10,000 today is worth more than getting that exact sum a year from now. In addition to the way inflation erodes the buying power of the dollar, you have to consider what that money would have earned over time. That's the time value of money.

So is the $50,000 annuity a better deal than $25,000 cash? If the 50 grand comes as a lump sum 20 years from now, forget it. The annuity is worth less than $10,000 today. If the money is paid out in monthly installments over the next two decades, the present value is higher, but still not $25,000.

But the *Wheel* deal is much better. The full $50,000 is awarded right away to buy two separate annuities. Here's how it worked for one winner: Just over $22,500 was used to buy an

annuity paying $341 each month for seven years; the other $27,500 bought a deferred annuity that guarantees a $50,000 lump-sum payment after seven years. The time value of money works for the winner, who will receive payments totaling almost $80,000.

You don't have to win the *Wheel* to run smack into the time value of money. Consider these examples:

PAYING FOR COLLEGE.

It's not outlandish to think today's newborn will need $100,000 to cover the cost of four years at a public university. Since freshman year is 18 years away, the time value of money can do a lot for you in the meantime. The higher the assumed time value of money—think of it as the interest rate

---

The most you should pay for the $700, five-year annuity given your 8 percent annual return is $2,795.10. Paying this price would allow you to earn exactly 8 percent on the investment.

By using the present value concept, you can easily determine the present value of a sum to be received in the future, equal annual future withdrawals available from an initial deposit, and the initial deposit that would generate a given stream of equal annual withdrawals. These procedures, like future value concepts, allow you to place monetary values on long-run financial goals. The accompanying *Smart Money* box provides some additional practical insights into the importances and power of time value of money.

Putting Target Dates on Financial Goals.

Financial goals are most effective when set in reference to certain goal dates. *Goal dates* are target points in the future at which time certain financial activities are expected to be concluded; they may serve as checkpoints in the progress toward some financial goals or as deadlines for the achievement of others. For example, one goal may be to purchase a boat in 1994 (the goal date) and another to accumulate a net worth of $200,000 by 2011, with goal dates of 1997 and 2002 set as checkpoints for the attainment of net worth of $10,000 and $110,000, respectively. It is usually helpful to set goal dates at intervals of two to five years for the first ten years or so and at five- to ten-year intervals thereafter. As time

the money can earn—and the longer it will work for you, the less money you will need now. Assuming an annual yield of 9%, you need just over $21,000 today to cover that $100,000 expense in 18 years.

SAVING A ZILLION.

How many times have you heard you can save big bucks by paying off your mortgage fast? Someone with a 15-year, $100,000 mortgage at 11% will pay almost $140,000 less in interest than a buyer who stretches the same loan over 30 years. Even ignoring the fact that few homeowners stay in the same place for 15 years, the savings are wildly exaggerated because that example ignores the time value of money. The 15-year buyer parts with the money earlier—via bigger monthly

payments—and therefore forfeits what it could earn.

HITTING THE JACKPOT.

In the spring of 1989, 14 ticketholders shared the winnings of Pennsylvania's $115 million lottery jackpot. Each will receive $8,255,641, to be paid in annual installments of $317,524. When the fact that the prize is doled out over 26 years is taken into account, however, the value of the winners' take drops by more than 50%. It cost Pennsylvania just slightly over $45 million to fund the $115 million prize.

There's no magic involved in figuring how the time value of money fits into your financial decisions. Present value/future value computations are easy with a financial calculator. Texas Instruments and Hewlett

Packard offer good ones for less than $50.

At least keep in mind the Rule of 72, the formula for estimating how long it takes for an amount of money to double. Dividing 72 by the assumed interest rate tells you about how many years is required. Ten dollars today will be worth $20 in eight years, for example, if you assume a 9% interest rate. Similarly, waiting eight years to get $10 is the same as getting only $5 today.

Although this formula won't produce precise answers to your questions, it should remind you to crank the time value of money into your calculations.

Source: Adapted from Kevin McCormally, "The Saying That a Bird in the Hand Is Worth Two in the Bush Applies to Money, Too," *Changing Times*, August 1989, p. 16.

passes, adjustments to the financial plans may have to be made; or, as desired financial outcomes are realized, goals may also have to be changed. In other words, the person or family may recognize that the goals were set either too high or too low. If the goals appear to be too high, they must be revised and made more realistic. If they are too low, they should be evaluated and set at a level that will force the individual or family to make financially responsible decisions rather than squandering surplus funds.

GOALS FOR THE SHORT-RUN

Short-run financial goals are set each year; they cover a 12-month period and should be consistent

with established long-run goals. These short-run goals become the key input for the *cash budget*—a tool used to plan for short-run income and expenditures. The individual's or family's immediate goals, expected income for the year, and long-run financial goals must all be taken into account when defining short-run goals. In addition, consideration must be given to the latest financial position, as reflected by

> **short-run financial goals**
> Goals that are set each year and cover a 12-month period; they should be consistent with established long-run goals.

EXHIBIT 3.6

The Weavers' Summary of Long-Run and Short-Run Personal Financial Goals

It is important to establish long-run financial goals in order to lend a general sense of direction to the financial decisions and activities we undertake. Short-run financial goals support the long-run goals by specifying what we hope to achieve in the next year or so; they specify the dollar outlay required for their achievement as well as relative priority.

PERSONAL FINANCIAL GOALS

Name(s) **Fred and Denise Weaver**   Date **December 27, 1992**

LONG-RUN GOALS

Goal Date	Goal Description
1995	Pay off all loans other than mortgage.
	Save money for new home.
	Increase investment portfolio.
	Start family.
	Buy new car (trade Camry).
2000	Begin college fund.
	Save money for new home.
	Buy minivan (trade every 4 years).
	Diversify and increase investments.
	Review life and disability insurance.
2005	Buy new $185,000 home.
	Purchase new furniture.
	Increase annual contribution to college funds.
2010	Increase investments, retirement funds.
	Purchase sailboat.
	Take European vacation.
	Accumulate net worth of $80,000.
2015	Children in college.
	Buy third car for children.
	Remodel home.
	Accumulate net worth of $110,000.
	Take Australian vacation.
2020	Children finish college.
	Build retirement funds.
	Investigate where to live upon retirement.
	Accumulate net worth of $175,000.
2025	Retire from jobs.
	Sell home, buy condominium.
	Travel to Orient.
	Accumulate net worth of $275,000.

SHORT-RUN GOALS (for the coming year)

Priority	Goal Description	Dollar Outlay
1	Buy new tires, brakes for Escort.	$425
2	Buy career clothes for Denise.	1,500
3	Buy suit & sport jacket for Fred.	650
4	Accumulate net worth of $25,000.	—
5	Buy electric garage door opener.	350
6	Take two-week vacation to Hawaii.	4,000
7	Buy workshop equipment.	1,500
8	Take ski trip to Colorado.	1,800
9	Replace stereo system components.	1,450
10		

the current balance sheet, and spending in the year immediately preceding, as reflected in the income and expenditures statement for that period. Short-run planning should also include the establishment of an emergency fund containing three to six months' worth of income. This special savings account serves as a safety valve that can be used in case of financial emergencies — for example, a temporary loss of income.

The degree of effectiveness in reaching short-run goals significantly affects the ability to achieve long-run goals. If short-run goals are not attained, the likelihood of achieving long-run goals is greatly reduced. In setting short-run goals, current desires must not be allowed to override the requirements for achieving long-run goals. The general tendency to prefer current consumption over consumption in the distant future may be the greatest challenge when setting short-run goals. Short-run sacrifices may be necessary in order to provide for a comfortable future; realizing this fact 10 or 20 years too late may make some important financial goals unattainable.

THE FINANCIAL GOALS OF FRED AND DENISE WEAVER

In Chapter 2, we were introduced to Fred and Denise Weaver, whose financial data were used to develop their financial statements. We will use the Weavers' financial data throughout this chapter to illustrate various aspects of financial planning and budgeting. The Weavers' long- and short-run financial goals, which they set in December of 1992, are described in the following sections.

The Weavers' Long-Run Financial Goals.

Since Fred and Denise are 28 and 26 years old, respectively, they have set their most distant long-run financial goal 33 years from now — a point in time at which they would like to retire. The top portion of Exhibit 3.6 presents a summary of the Weavers' long-run financial goals. They have set their goal dates arbitrarily at 1995, 2000, 2005, 2010, 2015, 2020, and 2025. As time passes, they will probably adjust both the goals and the dates. Although most of their goals do not have dollar amounts attached, Fred and Denise can still use them to lend general direction

to their short-run financial plans. In the planning process, the Weavers have made estimates of the costs of achieving their various long-run goals and then set the short-run goals necessary for attaining them.

The Weavers' Short-Run Financial Goals.

In the final week of December 1992, Fred and Denise set their short-run financial goals for the coming year. They considered three factors: (1) their current financial condition as reflected in their balance sheet (Exhibit 2.3); (2) their latest income and expenditures statement (Exhibit 2.8), from which they were able to evaluate their past spending patterns in order to estimate their spending requirements for 1993; and (3) their *long-run* financial goals (top of Exhibit 3.6), which provided the framework for the Weavers' short-run goals. The Weavers short-run financial goals for the coming year, along with the dollar outlay required to achieve each of them, are given in the bottom portion of Exhibit 3.6.

In order to simplify the process of eliminating expenditures in the event that sufficient funds are not available, the Weavers have assigned priorities to their short-run goals. The first three items are considered necessities, and the fourth is associated with their long-run net worth goal. (Note that because of the many interactions affecting it, the dollar outlay required to achieve the net worth goal cannot be clearly specified.) The remaining items are extras, or luxuries, that the Weavers would like to acquire during the year but probably can do without. Once they have prepared their budget, the Weavers will be able to determine which of their short-run goals they can afford during the coming year.

SETTING UP A CASH BUDGET

Cash budgets are prepared from schedules of estimated income and expenditures for the coming year and provide a system of disciplined spending. How would you go about estimating your income and expenditures for the coming year? Before reading on, spend a few moments answering this question.

Once you have established your short-run financial goals, you can prepare a cash budget for the coming year. Recall that a budget is a short-term financial planning device designed to allow you to achieve your short-run financial goals. As such, it also makes a positive contribution toward the achievement of your *long-run* financial goals.

By taking the time to evaluate your current financial situation, spending patterns, and goals, you can develop a realistic budget that is consistent with your personal lifestyle, family situation, and values. As you go through the budgeting process, you will have to decide how to allocate your income to reach your financial objectives. The resulting budget will be a valuable money management tool that provides the necessary information to monitor and control your finances in a fashion consistent with goal achievement. If carefully followed, your budget will enable you to accomplish two very important objectives. First, it will help you implement a system of *disciplined spending* as opposed to just existing from one paycheck to the next. Second, it will assist you in reducing the amount of money wasted on *needless spending* and, in so doing, increase the amount of funds allocated to savings and investments.

Just as your goals change over your lifetime, so will your budget. Typically, the number of income and expense categories increases as your life becomes more complex, you accumulate more assets and debts, and you have more family responsibilities. For example, the budget of a college student would be quite simple, with limited income from part-time jobs, parental contributions, and/or scholarships and grants. Expenses might include basic living expenses, clothes, books, car expenses, and entertainment. Once the student graduates and goes to work full-time, he or she will have to develop a budget that covers additional expenses such as rent, insurance, work clothes, and commuting costs. Clearly, as you move through the life cycle your financial situation will become increasingly more complex, thereby further increasing the importance of financial planning activities such as budgeting. Not until retirement can you expect this process to begin to simplify.

Like the income and expenditures statement, a *budget should be prepared on a cash basis*; thus, we refer to this document as a **cash budget**. In es-

sence, a cash budget deals with cash receipts and cash expenditures that are expected to occur in the coming year. For budgeting purposes, it makes no difference whether money is being spent on living expenses or on loan payments; in either case, an outflow of cash is involved, and therefore the amounts would be included in the cash budget. On the other hand, an asset purchased on credit would not be included, at least not until payments were made on the loan. Basically, a cash budget contains estimates of income and expenditures, including savings and investments, that are expected to occur in the coming year. It is usually divided into monthly intervals, although in some cases other time intervals may be more convenient.

The cash budget preparation process has three stages: estimating income, estimating expenditures, and finalizing the budget. When estimating income and expenditures, you should take into account any anticipated changes in the cost of living and their impact on your budget components. If your income is fixed — not expected to change over the budgetary period — increases in various items of expenditure will probably cause the purchasing power of your income to deteriorate.

A cash budget is a report that shows the amount of money you will be spending from month to month. *Fantasy:* A cash budget is a projection of *both* income and expenditures and is usually prepared on a monthly basis.

ESTIMATING INCOME

The first step in the cash budget preparation process is to prepare a **schedule of estimated income** for the coming year. Since bills are most commonly rendered and paid monthly, it is best to estimate income as well as expenditures using monthly intervals. The income forecast takes into consideration all income expected for the year — for example, the take-home pay of both spouses, expected bonuses or commissions, pension or annuity income, and interest, dividend, rental and security sale income. Many families find it useful to use a schedule like the one in Exhibit 3.7 to project their income.

When estimating income, keep in mind that *any*

item expected to be received for which repayment is required is not considered income. For instance, a loan is treated not as a source of income but as a *liability* for which scheduled repayments are required. Note also that unlike the income and expenditures statement, it is *take-home pay* that generally should be used on the cash budget rather than gross income before deductions and withholdings. This makes sense, since in a cash budget you want to direct your attention to those areas over which you have some control — and most people certainly have little, if any, control over things like taxes withheld, contributions to company insurance and pension plans, and the like. In effect, take-home pay represents the amount of *disposable income* you receive from your employer.

ESTIMATING EXPENDITURES

The second step in the cash budgeting process is by far the most difficult: It involves preparing a **schedule of estimated expenditures** for the coming year. This is usually done by using the actual expenditures from previous years (as found on income and expenditures statements and in supporting information for those periods), along with predetermined short-run financial goals. Good financial records, as discussed in Chapter 2, make it easier to develop realistic expense estimates. If you do not have past expenditure data, you could reexamine old checkbook registers and credit card statements to approximate expenditures. Families without past expenditure data could also use a "needs approach" to develop spending forecasts; that is, needs are projected and dollar values attached to them in order to make estimates of future expenditures. Careful attention should be given to expenditures associated with medical disabilities, divorce and child support, and similar special circumstances.

Regardless of whether historical information is available, it is important that you *become aware of your expenditure patterns and how your money is being spent*. In the absence of spending data, you can develop useful information by keeping track of your expenses over several months. Carefully study your spending habits to see if you are doing things that should be eliminated (like writing too many small, frivolous checks or using credit cards too

freely). In addition, you will probably find it easier to budget expenditures if you group them into several general categories, rather than trying to estimate each and every item. An example of one such grouping scheme — patterned after the categories used with the income and expenditures statement in Chapter 2 — is provided in Exhibit 3.8. Included on the budget expenditures form are suggested spending guidelines for each major category. The percentage that you allocate will depend on your age, lifestyle, and where you live. For instance, housing costs will vary depending on location; it costs considerably more to buy a home in San Diego than in Indianapolis. Dining out generally is more expensive in metropolitan areas than in rural areas; if you live in the suburbs, your commuting expenses may be higher than those for city-dwellers.

Initially, achievement of all short-run goals should be built into your expenditure estimates. To do this effectively, the cost of achieving the goals as well as the timing of the expenditures should be estimated. Any current or short-run contributions toward achievement of long-run goals should also be quantified and appropriately scheduled into the budget. Equally important are scheduled additions to savings and investments, since *planned savings* should be high on everyone's list of goals. If the inclusion of all these items will not allow the budget to balance, some of them may have to be removed from the final budget. Estimates of expenditures should be based on current price levels and then increased by a percentage that reflects the anticipated rate of

---

cash budget
A budget that takes into account estimated monthly cash receipts and expenditures for the coming year.

schedule of estimated income
A part of the cash budget that shows an item-by-item breakdown of the estimated income for each month of the coming year.

schedule of estimated expenditures
A part of the cash budget that shows an item-by-item breakdown of the estimated expenditures for the coming year.

EXHIBIT 3.7

The Weavers' Schedule of Estimated Income for 1993

The Weavers' income will increase substantially now that Denise is working full-time and they are a two-career, two-income family.

CASH BUDGET: ESTIMATED INCOME

Name(s) __Fred and Denise Weaver__

For the __Year__   Ending __December 31, 1993__

SOURCES OF INCOME		Jan.	Feb.	Mar.	April.	May	June	July	Aug.	Sep.	Oct.	Nov.	Dec.	Total for the Year
Take-home pay	Name: Fred	$2,250	$2,250	$2,250	$2,440	$2,440	$2,440	$2,440	$2,440	$2,440	$2,440	$2,440	$2,440	$28,710
	Name: Denise	1,525	1,525	1,525	1,525	1,525	1,700	1,700	1,700	1,700	1,700	1,700	1,700	19,525
	Name:													
Bonuses and commissions														
Pensions and annuities							1,350						1,300	2,650
Investment income	Interest			55			55			55			55	220
	Dividends			35			35			35			35	140
	Rents													
	Sale of securities													
	Other													
Other income														
TOTAL INCOME		$3,775	$3,775	$3,865	$3,965	$3,965	$5,580	$4,140	$4,140	$4,230	$4,140	$4,140	$5,530	$51,245

EXHIBIT 3.8

The Weavers' Initial Schedule of Estimated Annual Expenditures for 1993

The initial schedule of estimated expenditures is usually prepared on an annual basis, since some of the numbers are probably going to have to be changed anyway; preparing the schedule this way saves a lot of time if the budget does not balance. (Note: the parenthetical numbers provide suggested guidelines of how much of the average family's income is spent in each major category.)

CASH BUDGET: ESTIMATED EXPENDITURES		
Name(s) Fred and Denise Weaver		
For the Year	Ending December 31, 1993	

	EXPENDITURE CATEGORIES	Annual Amounts
Housing (12–30%)	Rent/mortgage payment (include insurance and taxes, if applicable)	$ 6,864
	Repairs, maint., improvements	1,550
Utilities (4–8%)	Gas, electric, water	1,850
	Phone	500
	Cable TV and other	300
Food (15–25%)	Groceries	3,000
	Dining out	3,900
Autos (5–18%)	Loan payments	2,520
	License plates, fees, etc.	250
	Gas, oil, repairs, tires, maintenance	2,375
Medical (2–10%)	Health, major medical, disability insurance (payroll deductions or not provided by employer)	
	Doctor, dentist, hospital, medicine	375
Clothing (3–8%)	Clothes, shoes and accessories	3,500
Insurance (4–8%)	Homeowner's (if not covered by mortgage payment)	450
	Life (not provided by employer)	300
	Auto	740
Taxes (N/A)	Income and social security	
	Property (if not included in mortgage)	1,100
Appliances, furniture and other major purchases (2-8%)	Loan payments	150
	Purchases and repairs Workshop equipment	1,500
	Other: New stereo equipment	1,450
Personal care (1–3%)	Laundry, cosmetics, hair care	1,200
Recreation and entertainment (2–8%)	Vacations Hawaii & Colorado	5,800
	Other recreation and entertainment	2,750
Savings and investments (3–10%)	Savings, stocks, bonds, etc.	4,500
Other expenditures (1–10%)	Charitable contributions	450
	Gifts	500
	Education Loan	900
	Subscriptions, magazines, books	185
	Other: Loan payment—parents	900
	Other: Misc.	600
Fun money (1–5%)		3,000
	TOTAL EXPENDITURES	$ 53,459

inflation. For example, if the monthly food bill is estimated at $350 and 4 percent inflation is expected in food prices, the estimated monthly food expenditure should be budgeted at $364—or $350 + $14 ($350 × 4 percent). An expenditure category of **fun money** should also be included. This money, which family members use as they wish without reporting how they spent it, gives each one some degree of financial independence and thus helps provide for a healthy family budget relationship.

FINALIZING AND PREPARING THE CASH BUDGET

Once income and expenditures estimates have been made, the budget can be *finalized*. This involves comparing projected income and expenditures on month-to-month and annual bases. A **balanced budget** results when the total income for the year *equals or exceeds* total expenditures.

The Budget Format. The **budget summary** basically summarizes and combines projections from the schedules of estimated income and expenditures. It is broken into three sections: income, expenditures, and the difference between them, which may be either a surplus or a deficit. Within the first two sections, the individual items of income and expenditure are shown separately. Usually the budget shows monthly figures as well as an annual total for each income and expenditure item. In many situations, the number of budget entries dictates whether it is better to break the budget into separate schedules, as we have illustrated—one for estimated income, one for estimated expenditures (including savings and investments), and one summarizing the total monthly cash budget. The income and expenditures schedules can be prepared separately and the budget summary then used to bring these components together to determine the amount of any surpluses or deficits. Admittedly, there is a lot of "number crunching" in personal cash budgeting. As discussed in Chapter 2, use of one of the personal financial planning software programs available for your personal computer can greatly streamline the budgeting process.

What to Do with Monthly Deficits. Even though the budget for the year may balance, expenditures in certain months may exceed income, causing a monthly **budget deficit**. Likewise, income in some months may exceed expenditures, causing a monthly **budget surplus**. Two remedies exist: (1) Expenditures might be transferred from months in which budget deficits occur to months in which budget surpluses exist or, conversely, income might be transferred from months with surpluses to months with deficits. (2) Savings, investments, or borrowing may be used to cover temporary deficits. Since the budget for the year is balanced, the need for funds to cover these shortages is only temporary. When a month having a budget surplus is reached, funds used to cover deficits can be returned to savings and investments, or loans can be repaid. Either of the preceding remedies for a monthly budget deficit in a balanced annual budget is possible, but the second is probably more practical.

What to Do If You End the Year in the Red. It is more difficult to resolve the problem of an annual budget deficit. Three approaches exist. One is either *liquidate enough savings and investments* or *borrow enough* to meet the total budget shortfall for the year. This action is not recommended, because it violates the objective of budgeting—to set expenditures at a level that will provide for a reasonable standard of living while allowing positive contributions toward the achievement of long-run goals. Drawing down savings and investments or borrowing in order to make the budget balance tends to reduce net worth. People who use this approach are *not* living within their means.

A second—and preferred—approach is to *cut low priority expenditure items* out of the budget in order to bring the total budget into balance. This approach forces the budget to balance without using external sources of funds. Low-priority expenditures are those items associated with the short-run financial goals believed to be least important. Some people who use this technique to bring their budgets into balance divide their expenditures into two groups—inflexible and flexible. *Inflexible expenditures* are those that must be made on the basis of either contracts or necessity; mortgage payments, loan payments, and utility bills are examples. *Flex-*

ible expenditures are for noncontractual, non-necessity items, such as recreation, entertainment, and certain clothing purchases. These flexible expenditures can be cut from the budget in order to bring it into balance.

A third approach is to *increase income* by assuming a second, perhaps part-time job or finding an alternative job that pays more. This is probably the most difficult approach, for it is likely to result in a significant change in leisure activities and lifestyle. Individuals who have no savings or investments to liquidate, cannot borrow funds to meet a shortfall, and are unable to meet expenditures for necessity items may find that taking a second job or changing jobs provides the only feasible course of action for balancing their budgets.

The budget is complete once all monthly deficits have been considered, and the total annual budget is balanced. As a result, the income for the year should equal or exceed the year's expenditures, and no monthly deficits should exist.

If a budget shows a cash deficit for the year, then you have no choice but to borrow enough money to make up the shortfall.
Fantasy: While borrowing is one way to cover a budget shortfall, there are other alternatives; liquidating some of your savings or investments or reducing your spending are two of them.

A CASH BUDGET FOR FRED AND DENISE WEAVER

Using their short-run financial goals (bottom of Exhibit 3.6) and their past financial statements (Exhibits 2.3 and 2.8), Fred and Denise Weaver have prepared their cash budget for the 1993 calendar year. They have done this by using separate schedules of estimated income and expenditures along with a budget summary.

Schedule of Estimated Income. The Weavers' schedule of estimated income for the year ended December 31, 1993, is shown in Exhibit 3.7 and provides an item-by-item breakdown for each month in that year. Their total annual income is expected to

be $51,245. Using the amount of take-home pay, as the Weavers did, eliminates the need to show taxes, social security payments, and other payroll deductions in the expenditure portion of the budget. Note also that both Fred and Denise anticipate salary increases—Fred in April and Denise in June.

Schedule of Estimated Expenditures. The Weavers' initial schedule of estimated *annual* expenditures, for the year ended December 31, 1993, is presented in Exhibit 3.8. Note that Fred and Denise have built $3,000 (or $250 a month) into their budget as fun money. They will divide the fun money equally between them and will not report on its disposition. Another significant aspect of their schedule of estimated expenditures is the $4,500 included under savings and investments. In light of scheduled debt repayment, Fred and Denise estimate that putting that amount aside will enable them to easily exceed their net worth goal of $25,000 (discussed at length in Chapter 2). Note also that the Weavers are anticipating only a slight amount of inflation and have considered the effects on their budget by adjusting certain expenditures upward for anticipated price increases. Aside from this, the schedule of estimated expenditures shown in Exhibit 3.8 is self-explanatory. Of course, it represents

---

fun money
Money that is allocated to family members to use as they wish without reporting how they spend it.

balanced budget
A budget in which total income for the year equals or exceeds total expenditures.

budget summary
A statement that summarizes and combines projections of estimated income, estimated expenditures, and the difference between them, which may be either a surplus or a deficit.

budget deficit
A situation that occurs when the expenditures exceed the income in a cash budget.

budget surplus
A situation that occurs when the income exceeds the expenditures in a cash budget.

only the Weavers' first estimate of their expenditures, aimed at the achievement of *all* of the short-run goals listed in the bottom portion of Exhibit 3.6.

Finalizing the Weavers' Cash Budget.

Reviewing the Weavers' initial schedule of expenditures (Exhibit 3.8), we can see that the initial estimate results in total expenditures of $53,459. Given their estimated income of $51,425 (Exhibit 3.7), it is clear that their budget is not balanced: a budget deficit of $2,214 exists. In order to bring the budget into balance, Fred and Denise are going to have to cut certain low-priority goals from their budget, reschedule some of their loan payments, and/or reduce their fun money allocation. After some deliberation, they decide to make the following adjustments:

1. Replace only part of stereo system, reducing the outlay by $700
2. Reduce purchase of workshop equipment by $600
3. Shorten trip to Hawaii, saving $1,000
4. Reschedule $200 of loan repayment to parents
5. Reduce allocation of fun money by $240 for the year ($20 per month)

These expenditure reductions of $2,740 have lowered the total scheduled expenditures for the year to $50,719, which now falls within the total income estimate of $51,245. Since expenditures are now at desired levels, the schedule of estimated expenditures can now be prepared on a monthly basis, as is done in Exhibit 3.9. The expenditure totals, as adjusted, are given in the final column of the schedule. Once these adjustments are made, estimated annual expenditures no longer exceed estimated annual income, and the budget is now balanced. Of course, the Weavers may decide that the budget surplus of $526 ($51,245 − $50,719) is not large enough to allow for unexpected expenditures. Therefore, they may want to further reduce other discretionary expenditures.

The Weavers' final step in the budgeting process is to analyze monthly surpluses and deficits in order to estimate whether or not savings, investments, or borrowing should be used to meet any monthly deficits. To do this, they have prepared the budget summary that appears in Exhibit 3.10. Estimated income figures are derived from Exhibit 3.7 and estimated expenditures, as adjusted, from Exhibit 3.9. The summary shows monthly cash surpluses and deficits that total $526 in the black for the year. This surplus can be used to add to the Weavers' savings and investments or to repay a portion of one of their loans. The bottom line of the budget summary lists the cumulative, or running, totals of the cash surpluses and deficits.

Note that although monthly deficits occur on and off throughout the year, their magnitude and timing result in a cumulative deficit for the months of February through August. This is due primarily to the costs of their Hawaiian vacation in March. In order to cover these deficits, Fred and Denise have arranged an interest-free loan from their parents. Had they been required to use their savings to finance these temporary deficits, they would have had to forego some of their interest earnings, included as part of their estimated income. If they wished to reduce the deficits more quickly, they could postpone the stereo purchase until later in the year and delay some clothing and entertainment expenditures. Were the Weavers completely unable to obtain funds to cover these deficits, they would have had to reschedule their planned expenditures or income.

COMPARING ACTUAL RESULTS TO BUDGETED FIGURES

In the final analysis, a cash budget will have value only if (1) it is put into use and (2) careful records are kept of actual income and expenditures. Keeping such records tells you whether you are staying within budget limits. Record income and expenditures often enough to ensure that nothing of any significance is overlooked, yet not so often that it becomes a nuisance. You can then use this information each month to compare actual income and spending to budgeted figures. This way it will be easy to identify the major budget categories in which income is falling far short (by 5 to 10 percent or more) or where spending is far exceeding desired levels (that is, actuals 5 to 10 percent or more above budget). Once you have identified these areas, you can take corrective action to ensure that the budget will stay on course.

A **budget record book** facilitates such record-keeping. Looseleaf binders with separate pages for each of the various income and expenditure categories serve this purpose quite well. At the beginning of each month, the amount budgeted for each category should be recorded. Then, as income is received and money spent, entries should be made in the appropriate categories. Instead of making these entries each day in the book, many people prefer to record them first on a **master income and expenditure sheet**, from which the appropriate entries are posted to the record book at specified intervals, such as every five to seven days. In either case, entries are rounded to the nearest dollar—that is accurate enough for budget purposes and it makes the arithmetic a lot easier.

At the end of each month, the income and expenditure category accounts in the budget record book should be totaled. Each of these monthly totals should then be compared to the amounts budgeted for the month and any surplus or deficit determined. In theory, there should be zero variances in each budget category, but this normally occurs only for income accounts, like take-home pay, or for single, fixed-payment accounts, like mortgages, loan payments, and insurance premiums. More often than not, the other categories will end each month with positive or negative variances, indicating that a cash surplus or shortfall has occurred. It is not enough to simply determine the size of the monthly variances; they should be subjected to some analysis, particularly the larger ones. The presence of a surplus, of course, is no cause for concern; however, a deficit—which indicates either that the income did not materialize as expected or spending exceeded projections—does require attention.

An account deficit that occurs in only one period is less of a problem than one that occurs in a series of periods. If recurring deficits indicate that an account may have been underbudgeted, the budget may need to be adjusted to a level sufficient to cover the outlays. Budget adjustments of this type are usually accomplished by reducing the amount budgeted for accounts that may be either overbudgeted or nonessential. Only in exceptional situations should budget adjustments be financed by drawing down savings and investments or by borrowing.

Control is important not only in individual categories or accounts but also in the total budget for the month. By examining end-of-month totals for all accounts, it is possible to determine whether a net budget surplus or deficit exists. Based on this find-

ing, you can take appropriate action to maintain a balanced budget for the remainder of the year. The existence of total budget surpluses is advantageous, since the excess funds can be used for savings, investments, or debt repayment. Total period deficits, however, signal the need for corrective action, which normally consists of adjusting spending in subsequent months in order to end the year with a balanced budget.

An example of a budget control schedule for the Weaver budget is shown in Exhibit 3.11. The **budget control schedule** provides a summary of how actual income and expenditures compare to the various budget categories and where budget variances exist. Surpluses and deficits are recorded for each account category as well as for the total budget for the month. This kind of periodic feedback is essential for budgetary control and to make sure that actual income and expenditures are staying within the amounts budgeted. A budget control schedule enables the user to identify problem areas and take the actions necessary to bring individual accounts and/or the whole budget into balance. As far as the Weavers' budget is concerned, we can see that the actual income and expenditure levels are reasonably close to their targets. The Weavers were off by only $118 in January, $56 in February, and $245 in March. In each of these months there was a positive cash surplus variance—the amount of cash surplus (deficit) realized was in excess of the amount that had been budgeted. No single income or expenditure item was responsible for these excess cash surpluses. The biggest variances occurred in *food* and

---

budget record book
A document, usually a looseleaf binder, that has separate pages for each of the various income and expenditure categories.

master income and expenditure sheet
A record of income and expenditure items from which appropriate entries are posted to the budget record book at specified intervals.

budget control schedule
A summary that shows how actual income and expenditures compare to the various budget categories and where surpluses or deficits exist.

EXHIBIT 3.9

The Weavers' Final Schedule of Estimated Monthly Expenditures for 1993

When put on a monthly basis, the schedule of estimated expenditures shows in detail projected month-by-month spending patterns; you can tell at a glance where most of your money is going each month.

CASH BUDGET: ESTIMATED EXPENDITURES

Name(s)   Fred and Denise Weaver

For the   Year _____   Ending _____ December 31, 1993

EXPENDITURE CATEGORIES		Jan.	Feb.	Mar.	Apr.	May	June	July	Aug.	Sep.	Oct.	Nov.	Dec.	Total for the Year
Housing	Rent/mortgage payment (include insurance and taxes, if applicable)	$572	$572	$572	$572	$572	$572	$572	$572	$572	$572	$572	$572	$6,864
	Repairs, maint., improvements	100	450	100	100	100	100	100	100	100	150	160	100	1,550
Utilities	Gas, electric, water	180	180	180	110	110	135	165	180	140	130	160	180	1,850
	Phone	40	40	40	40	45	45	40	40	40	40	45	45	500
	Cable TV and other	25	25	25	25	25	25	25	25	25	25	25	25	300
Food	Groceries	250	250	250	250	250	250	250	250	250	250	250	250	3,000
	Dining out	325	325	325	325	325	325	325	325	325	325	325	325	3,900
Autos	Loan payments	210	210	210	210	210	210	210	210	210	210	210	210	2,520
	License plates, fees, etc.				170						80			250
	Gas, oil, repairs, tires, maintenance	160	410	160	160	160	160	365	160	160	160	160	160	2,375
Medical	Health, major medical, disability insurance (not provided by employer)	paid by employers and payroll deductions												
	Doctor, dentist, hospital, medicines	30	30	30	30	30	45	30	30	30	30	30	30	375
Clothing	Clothes, shoes, and accessories	150	150	500	400	200	200	300	500	200	300	300	300	3,500
Insurance	Homeowners (if not covered by mortgage payment)				225						225			450
	Life (if not provided by employer)							300						300
	Auto					370						370		740
Taxes	Income and social security	assumed equal to amounts withheld from paycheck												
	Property (if not included in mortgage)		550						550					1,100
Appliances, furniture, and other	Loan payments	60	60	30										150
	Purchases and repairs						750			300	300	300		1,650
Personal care	Laundry, cosmetics, hair care	100	100	100	100	100	100	100	100	100	100	100	100	1,200
Recreation and entertainment	Vacations Hawaii, Colorado			3,000									1,800	4,800
	Other recreation and entertainment	250	250	200	200	200	300	300	200	200	200	200	250	2,750
Savings and investments	Savings, stocks, bonds, etc.	375	375	375	375	375	375	375	375	375	375	375	375	4,500
Other expenditures	Charitable contributions		100			100			150	100		100		450
	Gifts			100		25	25			100			250	500
	Education loan payment	75	75	75	75	75	75	75	75	75	75	75	75	900
	Subscriptions, magazines, books	10	25	10	10	10	50	10	10	20	10	30	10	185
	Other: Loan payment—parents					350						350		700
	Other: Misc.	50	50	50	50	50	50	50	50	50	50	50	50	600
Fun Money		230	230	230	230	230	230	230	230	230	230	230	230	2,760
TOTAL EXPENDITURES		$3,102	$4,457	$6,650	$3,657	$3,912	$4,002	$3,822	$4,182	$3,502	$3,747	$4,357	$5,357	$50,719

EXHIBIT 3.10

The Weavers' Monthly Cash Budget Summary

The Weavers' cash budget summary shows several months in which substantial cash deficits are expected to occur; they can use this information to develop plans for covering these monthly shortfalls.

CASH BUDGET: MONTHLY SUMMARY

Name(s): Fred and Denise Weaver

For the ____ Year ____   Ending _December 31, 1993_

INCOME	Jan.	Feb.	Mar.	Apr.	May	June	July	Aug.	Sep.	Oct.	Nov.	Dec.	Total for the Year
Take-home pay	$3,775	$3,775	$3,775	$3,965	$3,965	$4,140	$4,140	$4,140	$4,140	$4,140	$4,140	$4,140	$48,235
Bonuses and commissions						1,350						1,300	2,650
Pensions and annuities													
Investment income			90			90			90			90	360
Other income													
(I) Total Income	$3,775	$3,775	$3,865	$3,965	$3,965	$5,580	$4,140	$4,140	$4,230	$4,140	$4,140	$5,530	$51,245
EXPENDITURES													
Housing	$672	$1,022	$672	$672	$672	$672	$672	$672	$672	$672	$672	$672	$8,414
Utilities	245	245	245	175	180	205	230	245	205	195	230	250	2,650
Food	575	575	575	575	575	575	575	575	575	575	575	575	6,900
Autos	370	620	370	540	370	370	575	370	370	450	370	370	5,145
Medical	30	30	30	30	30	45	30	30	30	30	30	30	375
Clothing	150	150	500	400	200	200	300	500	200	300	300	300	3,500
Insurance				225	370		300			225	370		1,490
Taxes		550						550					1,100
Appliances, furniture, and other	60	60	30			750			300	300	300		1,800
Personal care	100	100	100	100	100	100	100	100	100	100	100	100	1,200
Recreation and entertainment	250	250	3,200	200	200	300	300	200	200	200	200	2,050	7,550
Savings and investments	375	375	375	375	375	375	375	375	375	375	375	375	4,500
Other expenditures	135	250	235	135	610	180	135	285	245	135	605	385	3,335
Fun Money	230	230	230	230	230	230	230	230	230	230	230	230	2,760
(II) Total Expenditures	$3,192	$4,457	$6,562	$3,657	$3,912	$4,002	$3,822	$4,132	$3,502	$3,787	$4,357	$5,337	$50,719
CASH SURPLUS (OR DEFICIT) [(I) – (II)]	$583	$(682)	$(2,697)	$308	$53	$1,578	$318	$8	$728	$353	$(217)	$193	$526
CUMULATIVE CASH SURPLUS (OR DEFICIT)	$583	$(99)	$(2,796)	$(2,488)	$(2,435)	$(857)	$(539)	$(531)	$197	$550	$333	$526	$526

EXHIBIT 3.11

The Weavers' Budget Control Schedule for January, February, and March 1993

The budget control schedule provides important feedback on how the actual cash flow is stacking up to the forecasted cash budget. If the variances are significant enough and/or continue month after month, that is perhaps a signal that either spending habits or the cash budget should be altered.

BUDGET CONTROL SCHEDULE

Name(s): Fred and Denise Weaver

For the 3 Months Ending March 31, 1993

	Month: January				Month: February				Month: March			
	Budgeted Amount (1)	Actual (2)	Monthly Variance (3)	Year-to-Date Variance (4)	Budgeted Amount (5)	Actual (6)	Monthly Variance (7)	Year-to-Date Variance (8)	Budgeted Amount (9)	Actual (10)	Monthly Variance (11)	Year-to-Date Variance (12)
INCOME												
Take-home pay	$3,775	$3,792	$ 17	$ 17	$3,775	$3,792	$ 17	$ 34	$ 3,775	$3,792	$ 17	$ 51
Bonuses and commissions												
Pensions and annuities												
Investment income									90	86	(4)	(4)
Other income												
(I) Total Income	$3,775	$3,792	$ 17	$ 17	$3,775	$3,792	$ 17	$ 34	$3,865	$3,878	$ 15	$ 47
EXPENDITURES												
Housing	$ 672	$ 672	$ 0	$ 0	$1,022	$1,022	$ 0	$ 0	$ 672	$ 672	$ 0	$ 0
Utilities	245	257	(8)	(8)	245	252	7	(1)	245	228	(17)	(18)
Food	575	559	(16)	(16)	575	548	(27)	(43)	575	450	(125)	(168)
Autos	370	385	15	15	620	601	(19)	(4)	370	310	(60)	(64)
Medical	30	0	(30)	(30)	30	45	15	(15)	30	0	(30)	(45)
Clothing	150	190	40	40	150	135	(15)	25	500	475	(25)	0
Insurance												
Taxes					550	550	0	0			0	0
Appliances, furniture, and other	60	60	0	0	60	60	0	0	30	30	0	0
Personal care	100	85	(15)	(15)	100	120	20	5	100	75	(25)	(20)
Recreation and entertainment	250	210	(40)	(40)	250	240	(10)	(50)	3,200	3,285	85	35
Savings and investments	575	575	0	0	575	575	0	0	575	575	0	0
Other expenditures	135	118	(17)	(17)	250	245	(5)	(22)	235	200	(35)	(57)
Fun Money	230	200	(30)	(30)	230	225	(5)	(35)	230	230	0	(35)
(II) Total Expenditures	$ 3,192	$ 3,091	$(101)	$(101)	$4,457	$ 4,418	$ (39)	$(140)	$ 6,562	$6,330	$(232)	$(372)
CASH SURPLUS (OR DEFICIT) [(I) − (II)]	$ 583	$ 701	$ 118	$ 118	$ (682)	$ (626)	$ 56	$ 174	$(2,697)	$(2,452)	$(372)	$ 419
CUMULATIVE CASH SURPLUS (OR DEFICIT)	$ 583	$ 701			$ (99)	$ 75			$(2,796)	$(2,377)		

Key: Col. (3) = Col. (2) − Col. (1); Col. (7) = Col. (6) − Col. (5); Col. (11) = Col. (10) − Col. (9)

auto expenses, but neither was far off the mark. Thus, for the first three months of the year, the Weavers seem to be doing a good job of controlling their income and expenditures. They have, in fact, been able to achieve a cumulative cash deficit that is $419 (actual of − $2,377 versus budgeted of − $2,796) less than the amount budgeted as a result of cutting discretionary expenditures. If, in contrast, there had been substantial variances in one (or more) of the accounts, they would have been able to look more closely at that account (or accounts) to learn the cause of any variances and then initiate corrective action.

One of the final steps in the cash budgeting process is to compare actual results to budgeted amounts. *Fact:* Comparing actual results to budgeted amounts is essential to sound budgetary control, and provides a mechanism for isolating areas in need of corrective actions.

S U M M A R Y

- Personal financial planning provides a logical framework for making financial decisions that are consistent with your long- and short-run financial goals. Sound financial planning involves not only defining financial goals and objectives, but developing, implementing, and controlling plans and strategies for putting goals into action.
- During the financial planning process, special attention should be given to employee benefits planning and timing of financial decisions — especially during periods of personal stress or major life changes, managing two incomes, and adapting to changes in marital status.
- Long-run financial goals should provide general directon for the long haul, while short-run goals should be more specific in nature. Of course, short-run goals should be consistent with established long-run goals. Both long-run and short-run financial goals will change depending on personal circumstances and stage in the life cycle.
- When putting a dollar value on your financial goals, be sure to consider the *time value of money* and, if appropriate, use the notion of *future value* or *present value* when preparing your estimates. These techniques explicitly recognize that a dollar today is worth more than a dollar in the future.
- One of the major benefits of a cash budget is that it will help you to implement a system of disciplined spending. In addition, by curbing the amount of money wasted on needless spending, it can increase the amount of funds allocated to savings and investments.
- Household budgets should be set up on a cash basis and should identify the planned monthly cash receipts and cash expenditures for the coming year. The objective is to take in more money than you spend, so that you'll be able to save money and thereby add to your net worth over time.
- The final step in the cash budgeting process is to compare actual receipts and expenditures to budgeted figures to learn if, in fact, you are living within your budget and if not, to initiate appropriate corrective actions.

Q U E S T I O N S   A N D   P R O B L E M S

1. What is the difference between a budget and a financial plan? Does a budget play any role in a financial plan?
2. Identify the six key steps involved in the financial planning process. What role should partners and/or families play in this process?
3. Describe a comprehensive financial plan. How are such plans constructed, and what kind of information do they contain?
4. What is a professional financial planner? Does it make any difference whether the financial planner earns money from commissions made on products sold, or on the fees he or she charges?

5. Discuss briefly how the following situations affect personal financial planning:
   a. major life changes such as the birth of a child or loss of a job
   b. being part of a dual-income couple
   c. changes in marital status
6. Distinguish between long-run and short-run financial goals. Be sure to mention:
   a. personal situation and state of life cycle
   b. flexibility
   c. inflation considerations
   d. goal dates
   e. the key input to the cash budget
7. Over the past several years, Helen Chang has been able to put aside money on a regular basis; as a result, today she has $14,188 in savings and investments. She wants to establish her own business in five years and feels she will need $50,000 to do so.
   a. If she can earn 12 percent on her money, how much will her $14,188 savings/investments be worth in five years?
   b. Given your answer to part a, will Helen have the $50,000 she needs? If not, how much more money will she need?
   c. Given your answer to part b, how much will Helen have to save each year over the next five years to accumulate the additional money assuming she can earn interest at a rate of 12 percent?
   d. If Helen feels she can afford to save only $2,000 a year, given your answer to part a, will she have the $50,000 she needs to start her own business in five years?
8. Bill Shaffer wishes to have $200,000 in a retirement fund 20 years from now. He can create the retirement fund by making a single lump-sum deposit today.
   a. If he can earn 10 percent on his investments, how much must Bill deposit today in order to create the retirement fund?
   b. How much must Bill deposit today if at maximum he can only earn 8 percent on his investments? Compare and discuss this result in light of your finding in part a.
   c. If upon retirement in 20 years Bill plans to invest the $200,000 in a fund that earns 12 percent, what is the maximum annual with-

drawal he can make over the following 15 years?
   d. How much would Bill need to have on deposit at retirement in order to annually withdraw $35,000 over the 15 years assuming that the retirement fund earns 12 percent?
   e. In order to achieve his annual withdrawal goal of $35,000 calculated in part d, how much more than the amount calculated in part a must Bill deposit today in an investment earning 10 percent annual interest in order to create the retirement fund in 20 years?
9. Use future or present value techniques to solve the following problems:
   a. Starting with $10,000, how much will you have in 10 years if you can earn 15 percent on your money? If you can earn only 8 percent?
   b. If you inherited $25,000 today and invested all of it in a security that paid a 10 percent rate of return, how much would you have in 25 years?
   c. If the average new home costs $125,000 today, how much will it cost in 10 years if the price increases by 5 percent each year?
   d. You feel that in 15 years it will cost $60,000 to give your child a college education. Will you have enough if you take $20,000 *today* and invest it for the next 15 years at 8 percent? If you must start *from scratch*, how much will you have to save each year to have $60,000 in 15 years if you can earn an 8 percent rate of return on your investments?
   e. If you can earn 12 percent, how much will you have to save each year if you want to retire in 35 years with $1 million?
   f. You plan to have $750,000 in savings and investments when you retire at age 60. Assuming you can earn an average of 9 percent on this portfolio, how much is the maximum annual withdrawal you can make over a 25-year period?
10. Describe the cash budget and its income and expense schedules. What is a budget deficit? How does it differ from a budget surplus?
11. The Smith family has prepared their annual

budget for 1993. They have divided it into 12 monthly budgets. Although only one monthly budget balances, they have managed to balance the overall budget for the year. What remedies are available to the Smith family for meeting the monthly budget deficits?

12. Below is a portion of Jeffrey Cook's budget record for April 1993. Fill in the blanks in columns 6 and 7.

13. Why is it important to analyze actual budget surpluses or deficits at the end of each month?

14. How can accurate records and control procedures be utilized to ensure effectiveness in the financial planning process?

15. Dave and Betty Williamson are preparing their budget for 1993. Help the Williamsons reconcile the following differences, giving reasons to support your answers:

    a. Their only source of income is Dave's salary, which amounts to $2,000 a month before taxes. Betty wants to show the $2,000 as their monthly income, whereas Dave argues that his take-home pay of $1,650 is the correct value to show.

    b. Betty wants to make a provision for fun money, an idea that Dave cannot understand. He asks, "Why do we need fun money when everything is provided for in the budget?"

▶ 16. Prepare a record of your income and expenditures for the last 30 days; then prepare a personal budget for the next month (using a schedule of estimated expenditures like the one in Exhibit 3.8). Use the budget to control and regulate your expenditures during the month. Discuss the impact of the budget on your spending behavior as well as any differences between your expected and actual spending patterns.

Item Number (1)	Item (2)	Amount Budgeted (3)	Amount Expended (4)	Beginning Balance (5)	Monthly Surplus (Deficit) (6)	Cumulative Surplus (Deficit) (7)
1	Rent	$350	$360	$20	$_____	$_____
2	Utilities	150	145	15	_____	_____
3	Food	310	275	−15	_____	_____
4	Auto	25	38	−5	_____	_____
5	Recreation and entertainment	50	60	−50	_____	_____

C O N T E M P O R A R Y   C A S E   A P P L I C A T I O N S

3.1 The Sullivans' Version of Financial Planning

John and Irene Sullivan are a married couple in their mid 20s. John is a computer analyst and earns $22,350 per year after taxes. Irene works as a sales rep and takes home $18,750 per year. Since their marriage four years ago, John and Irene have been living comfortably. Their income has exceeded their expenditures, and they have accumulated a net worth of nearly $25,000 — $15,000 represents equity in their home, cars, furniture, and other personal belongings, and the other $10,000 is held in the form of savings accounts and common stock investments. Because their income has always been more than adequate to allow them to live in the fashion they desire, the Sullivans have done no financial planning.

Irene has just learned that she is two months pregnant and is concerned about how they will make ends meet if she quits work after their child is born. Each time she and John discuss the matter, John tells her not to worry since "we have always managed to pay our bills on time." Irene cannot understand this, as her income will be completely eliminated. In order to convince Irene that there is no need for concern, John has prepared the following income statement for the past year.

Income Statement for John and Irene Sullivan (Past Year)

Income

John's take-home pay	$22,350
Irene's take-home pay	18,750
Total income	$41,100

Expenditures

Necessities:

Food	$4,200	
Clothing	2,300	
Housing	9,000	
Utilities and telephone	2,900	
Medical (nonreimbursed)	600	
Insurance	800	
Transportation	2,800	
Total necessities		$22,600

Luxuries and investments:

Trip to Europe	$5,000	
Recreation and entertainment	4,000	
Purchase of common stock	7,500	
Addition to money market account	500	
Total luxuries		17,000
Total expenditures		$39,600

He points out that their expenditures for necessities last year were $22,600, which just about equaled his take-home pay, and with an anticipated 10 percent pay raise, his income next year should exceed this amount. John also points out that they can always draw down their savings or sell some of their stock if they get in a bind. When asked about the long-run implications of their finances, John replies that there will be "no problems" since his boss has assured him of a bright future with the company. John also emphasizes that in a few years Irene can go back to work if necessary. In spite of John's somewhat convincing arguments, Irene still feels uncomfortable with their rather matter-of-fact approach to financial planning — she knows there has to be a better way.

Questions

1. If the Sullivans continue to manage their finances as described, what do you expect the long-run consequences to be? Discuss.

2. Critically evaluate the Sullivans' approach to financial planning. Point out any fallacies in John's arguments, and be sure to mention (a) implications for the long run, (b) the potential impact of inflation, and (c) the impact on their net worth.

3. Describe to John and Irene the procedures they should use to get their financial house in order. Be sure to discuss the role that long- and short-run financial plans and budgets might play.

▌ 3.2 Joe Garcia Learns to Budget

Joe Garcia graduated from college in 1991 and moved to Atlanta to take a job as a market research analyst. He was pleased to be financially independent and was sure that, with his $25,000 salary, he could cover his living expenses and also have plenty of money left over to furnish his studio apartment and enjoy the wide variety of social and recreational activities available in Atlanta. He opened several department store charge accounts and also obtained a bank credit card.

For a while Joe managed pretty well on his monthly take-home pay of $1,450, but by the end of 1992 he was having trouble fully paying all his credit card charges each month. Concerned that his spending had gotten out of control and that he was barely making it from paycheck to paycheck, he decided to compile a list of his expenses for the past calendar year and develop a budget. He hoped not only to reduce his credit card debts but also to begin a regular savings program.

He prepared the following summary of expenses for 1992:

Item	Annual Expenditure
Rent	$6,000
Auto insurance	520
Car loan payments	2,340
Clothing	1,200
Installment loan for stereo	540
Personal care	240
Phone	300
Cable TV	240
Gas and electricity	720
Medical care	120
Dentist	70
Groceries	1,500
Dining out	1,200
Car expenses (gas, repairs, fees, and so on)	780
Furniture purchases	900
Recreation and entertainment	1,020
Other expenses	600

After reviewing his 1992 expenses, he made the following assumptions about his expenses for 1993:

1. All expenses remain at the same levels, with the following exceptions:

a. Auto insurance, car expenses, gas and electricity, and groceries will increase 5 percent.

b. Clothing purchases will decrease to $1,000.

c. Phone and cable TV will increase $5 per month.

d. Furniture purchases will decrease to $660, most of which is for a new television.

e. He will take a one-week vacation to Lake Tahoe in July at a cost of $1,100.

2. All expenses will be budgeted in equal monthly installments except for the vacation and the following:

a. Car insurance is paid in two installments due in June and December.

b. He plans to replace the brakes on his car in February at a cost of $120.

c. Visits to the dentist will be made in March and September.

3. He will eliminate his bank credit card balance by making extra monthly payments of $75 during each of the first six months.

With regard to his income, he has just received a raise so that his take-home pay will be $1,575 per month.

Questions

1. a. Prepare an estimated annual expense schedule for Joe for the year ending December 31, 1993, using the format shown in Exhibit 3.8.

b. Compare Joe's estimated expenses to his expected income and make recommendations that will help him balance his budget.

2. After making any necessary adjustments, prepare Joe's monthly estimated expenditures and cash budget summary for the year ending December 31, 1993, using the format shown in Exhibits 3.9 and 3.10.

3. Analyze the budget and advise Joe on his financial situation. Suggest some long- and short-term financial goals for Joe and discuss some steps he can take to reach them.

FOR MORE INFORMATION

General Information Articles

Dumaine, Brian, et al. "Strategies for the Stages of Life." *Fortune 1992 Investor's Guide*, Fall 1991, pp. 123–140.

Giese, William. "Do Your Investments Fit Your Goals?" *Changing Times*, February 1991, pp. 51–55.

McManus, Kevin. "How to Get the Most from Two Incomes." *Changing Times*, July 1989, pp. 22–28.

Luciano, Lani. "Getting the Most from Your Company Benefits." *Money*, May 1991, pp. 109–120.

"Money Mistakes that Waylay Young Families." *Changing Times*, June 1991, p. 76.

O'Reilly, Brian. "Picking the Right Financial Planner," *Fortune*, February 25, 1991, pp. 144–147.

Rowland, Mary. "Finances Can Be Trickier the Second Time Around." *Business Week*, July 22, 1991, pp. 86–87.

———. "The Best Ways to Teach Your Kids about Money." *Money*, March 1990, pp. 126–135.

Schultz, Ellen E. "Detective Work: Checking Out a Financial Advisor." *The Wall Street Journal*, September 13, 1990, pp. C1, 19.

———. "Is a Financial Planner Really Necessary?" *The Wall Street Journal*, May 13, 1991, pp. C1, 19.

Simon, Ruth. "How to Talk with Your Parents about Money." *Money*, December 1991, pp. 145–153.

Government Documents and Other Publications

Consumer Guide to Financial Independence. Atlanta, GA: Foundation for Financial Planning; Two Concourse Parkway, Suite 800, Atlanta, GA 30328; (800) 945-4237.

Felton-Collins, Victoria. *Couples and Money* (New York: Bantam Books, 1990).

Financial Planning: A Career Profile. Denver, CO: International Board of Standards and Practices for Certified Financial Planners, Inc.; 1660 Lincoln Street, Suite 3050, Denver, CO 80264.

Lewin, Elizabeth S., CFP. *Your Personal Fitness Program, 1991–1992 Edition*. New York: Facts on File, 1991.

Lawrence, Judy. *Common Cents: The Complete Money Management Workbook*. Albuquerque, NM: Lawrence & Co., 1989.

GETTING A HANDLE ON YOUR FINANCIAL FUTURE

In order to be successful in your personal financial planning you must understand the steps in the process. The first step is to define your financial goals. These can be either short-term goals of less than one year or long-term goals that are projected well into the future. Where possible you should put a monetary value on these goals and you should set a goal date. For long-term goals you should establish checkpoints to monitor your performance toward achieving a goal. Exhibit 3.6 shows an illustration of short-term and long-term goals.

The next step is to formulate plans and strategies that are compatible with your goals. This should include the recommendations from a professional financial planner or your own determination of the amounts of money to be saved and/or the types of investment vehicles to use. The third step is probably the most important. This is the implementation of the plan. If no action is taken, then the desired results will not be obtained. In order to achieve this you must establish a system of monitoring and controlling the process and, if necessary, revise and replace goals. This evaluation phase involves the development and use of cash budgets.

Cash budgets are short-term financial planning devices that are constructed from the schedules of

If You Are Just Starting Out

Once you have evaluated your current financial position as explained in Chapter 2, you are ready to set your financial goals in terms of the money required and the goal date. While short-term goals such as taking a vacation or buying a new CD player may not seem difficult to establish in monetary terms, long-term goals such as the amount of funds to acquire for retirement require much analysis.

Once your goals are established, you need to see if they are achievable given your expected income and expenses, as developed in the form of a cash budget. If the goals that you have set are not achievable in the time allotted, you need to either increase the funds allocated to this goal, earn a higher rate of return on the funds, or change the goal either as to the time or amount needed. The use of your personal financial statements and cash budgets will help you monitor your progress toward achieving your goals.

The following suggestions and recommendations will help you get started.

Financial Goals:

1. Set goals in monetary terms along with anticipated dates for achievement.

2. Where possible, prioritize your goals.

3. Set your short-term goals each year and make sure they are consistent with long-term goals.

4. Be careful not to let short-term desires override the requirements for achieving long-term goals.

5. For long-term goals set not only a goal date, but also checkpoints to monitor progress towards the goal.

Cash Budgets:

1. Be sure to use net or take-home pay as income.

2. Any item for which repayment is required is not considered income. Therefore, a loan would be a liability for which scheduled expenditures must be made to repay.

3. If you do not have a record of actual expenditures in the previous year to aid you in estimating your next year's expenditures, project your needs and assign a dollar value to them.

4. Base all expenditures on current price levels and then adjust for inflation.

5. Don't forget to include planned savings in your expenditures.

estimated income and expenditures. If followed carefully, the cash budget will help you establish a system of disciplined spending and avoid unnecessary expenditures or impulse purchases. In order to construct a cash budget, you must first estimate your income for the coming year, usually on a monthly basis as shown in Exhibit 3.7. Then you must prepare an initial estimate of your expenditures. This is usually the most difficult part of the process as it includes not only expenditures but funding of your goals as well. An example is found in Exhibit 3.8.

The next step in this process is to finalize and prepare the cash budget. This involves a reconciliation of projected income and expenditures for the year. If expenditures exceed income, then adjustments must be made to expenditures in order to balance the budget. This is illustrated in Exhibit 3.9. This is combined with the income projection to construct the cash budget summary, as shown in Exhibit 3.10.

The final step is to compare actual results to budgeted amounts. This is essential to the planning process, as it provides a mechanism for identifying problem areas that need corrective action. This is illustrated in Exhibit 3.11.

If You Are Thirtysomething

Although the financial planning process does not change with the passage of time, your ability to achieve your financial goals does. When you were just starting out it appeared that most of your goals were short-term in nature and such goals as funding your retirement seemed unimportant due to the fact that this was 40–45 years away. If you have a long period of time to achieve a financial goal, the less money you currently have to put aside regardless of the rate of return.

As you get older and your worklife expectancy gets shorter, financial planning becomes even more important. If you make a mistake, you have less time to recover from it. As a result of this problem you need to monitor your progress more closely and be willing to make changes more quickly as time is of the essence. The following suggestions and recommendations may help you in this process.

Financial Goals:

1. Once you are established in your career and your family, your goals may emphasize capital accumulation to fund goals such as the purchase of a house or vacation home, children's education, or retirement.

2. Management of your tax liability becomes more important.

3. You may adjust your investments more frequently to achieve your goals.

4. The goal of protecting your assets becomes more important as you accumulate more wealth.

5. Finally the goal of maximizing the distribution of your estate to your heirs moves into prominence.

Cash Budget:

1. As you get older your earned income may become more predictable but may decline in importance when compared to your investment income.

2. Your pattern of expenditures should be set. This would aid in planning.

3. You should be running a surplus in your budget that could be reallocated to help achieve your financial goals.

4. If long-term goals are in jeopardy, take immediate action with your expenditures because of the shorter time frame.

5. Pay closer attention to deviations in actual versus budgeted expenditures.

CHAPTER 4

Managing Your Taxes

A typical American family—two wage earners with two dependent children—currently pays federal income and social security taxes of almost $13,000 a year on annual income of $46,000. In addition, it must pay state and local income taxes, sales taxes, and property taxes. When all these taxes are totaled, *the average American family pays somewhere between 25 and 40 percent of its income in taxes.* It is, therefore, no surprise that tax planning is an important aspect of personal financial planning. It is a year-round activity; tax consequences must be considered both when making major financial decisions and when developing and revising your financial plans. The overriding objective of tax planning is very simple: to *maximize* the amount of money you keep by *minimizing* the amount of taxes you pay. As long as it is done honestly and within the tax codes, there is nothing immoral, illegal, or unethical about trying to minimize your tax bite. Most tax planning centers on ways to minimize income and estate taxes. Chapter 16 considers estate taxes. This chapter concentrates on income taxes, particularly on the federal income tax, which is the largest and most important tax for the individual or family. In addition, it is concerned only with those provisions that apply to us as individual taxpayers (there's another whole body of tax laws and tax rates that apply to corporations and businesses—which we do not consider in this book).

FINANCIAL *facts* OR *fantasies*

Are the following statements financial facts (true) or fantasies (false)?

Every individual or married couple is required to file a federal income tax return regardless of the amount of income earned.

The amount of federal income tax withheld depends on both your level of earnings and the number of withholding allowances claimed.

Federal income taxes are levied against the *total* amount of money earned.

A tax credit is like a deduction or exemption in that it reduces your taxable income.

Tax avoidance is an illegal practice that could result in financial penalties and even prison sentences.

An easy way to earn tax-deferred income is to invest in Series EE savings bonds.

PRINCIPLES OF FEDERAL INCOME TAXES

The amount of income you report for tax purposes and the way you file your returns both have significant bearing on the amount of taxes you must pay. Why must we pay federal income taxes, and what procedures must we follow when preparing and filing federal income tax returns? Before reading on, spend a few moments answering these questions.

Taxes are dues we pay for membership in our society; they are the cost of living in this country. Federal, state, and local tax receipts fund government activities and a wide variety of public services, from national defense to local libraries. We cannot directly control the tax laws because they are established by the legislators we elect. However, incorporating effective tax planning in the personal financial planning process should help you minimize taxes. With good tax planning, you will have more money to spend and invest. Most tax planning focuses on federal income taxes, generally the largest component of your taxes.

The federal income tax law was outlined in the *Internal Revenue Code of 1939*. In 1954 this code was revised to further clarify and more precisely state its provisions. Since then, a number of amendments have been added to the code that have attempted to simplify it, eliminate infrequently used provisions, and repeal and modify other provisions. The code's various sections and amendments deal with the tax effects of practically all personal and business transactions. The administration and enforcement of federal tax laws is the responsibility of the *Internal Revenue Service (IRS)*, which is part of the U.S. Department of the Treasury. The IRS is responsible for making sure that people pay their taxes as required by the various tax codes.

Without a doubt, the biggest and perhaps most controversial piece of tax legislation to come out of Congress in the last 50 years was the *Tax Reform Act of 1986*. (The *Technical and Miscellaneous Revenue Act of 1988* later refined and clarified a number of

the 1986 act's provisions.) The purpose of this act was threefold: (1) to simplify the tax code for individual taxpayers; (2) to reduce taxpayer abuses by closing many existing loopholes; and (3) to shift a significant amount of the tax burden from individuals to corporations. The net result of this legislation was far-reaching, as it removed millions of low-income families from the tax rolls, reduced the number of tax brackets from fifteen down to just three, eliminated some popular tax deductions, did away with the preferential treatment of capital gains, and sharply curbed the ability of individual taxpayers to generate tax-sheltered income. Unfortunately, in spite of all the political rhetoric to the contrary, the U.S. tax code remains so complex that taxpayers who itemize their deductions often require costly professional help just to file a return.

The provisions of the tax code may change annually with regard to tax rates, amounts and types of deductions and personal exemptions, and similar items. Often these changes are not finalized until late in the year. The tax tables and calculations presented in this chapter are based on the tax laws applicable to calendar 1991—those in effect at the time this book went to press. Any known changes for 1992 are shown parenthetically. Although tax rates and other provisions will change, the basic procedures will remain the same. Before preparing your tax returns be sure to review the current regulations; IRS publications and other tax preparation guides (see end-of-chapter references) should be helpful in this regard.

THE ECONOMICS OF INCOME TAXES

It should come as little surprise to learn that most people simply do not like to pay taxes! Some of this feeling undoubtedly stems from the widely held perception that a lot of government spending amounts to little more than bureaucratic waste. But a good deal of it is probably also due to the fact that taxpayers really get nothing tangible in return for their money. After all, paying taxes is not like spending $7,000 on a car, boat, or European vacation. The fact is, we too often tend to overlook or take for granted the many services that are provided by the taxes we pay—public schools and state colleges, roads and highways, and parks and recreational facilities, not to mention police and fire protection, retirement benefits, and many other health and social services.

Income taxes provide the major source of revenue for the federal government. Personal income taxes are scaled on progressive rates. To illustrate how this **progressive tax structure** works, we will use the following data for single taxpayers filing 1991 returns:

Taxable Income	Tax Rate
$0 to $20,350	15%
$20,351 to $49,300	28%
Over $49,301	31%

Now consider three possible taxable incomes: (1) $15,000, (2) $30,000, and (3) $60,000. The tax liability on these incomes would be:

(1) $ 2,250 — i.e., $15,000 × .15
(2) $ 5,755 — i.e., [($30,000 − $20,350) × .28]
              + [$20,350 × .15]
(3) $14,476 — i.e., [($60,000 − $49,300) × .31]
              + [($49,300 − $20,350) × .28]
              + [$20,350 × .15]

Notice that as income moves from a lower to a higher bracket, the higher rate applies *only to the additional income in that bracket* and not to the entire income. For example, you pay the 28 percent rate only on that portion of the $30,000 in income that exceeds $20,350. As a result of this kind of progressive scale, the more money you make, the progressively more you pay in taxes. Note also that the progressive tax structure actually results in total taxes that are lower than implied by the stated tax rates; when you relate the amount of taxes paid to the level of income earned, the tax rate drops considerably.

Returning to the three income levels illustrated above, we can see what happens to the **average tax rate**:

Taxable Income	Tax Liability	Stated Tax Rate	Average Tax Rate
(1) $15,000	$2,250	15%	15% ($2,250/$15,000)
(2) $30,000	$5,755	28%	19.2% ($5,755/$30,000)
(3) $60,000	$14,476	31%	24.1% ($14,476/$60,000)

Clearly, taxes are still progressive, but the size of the bite is not as bad as the stated tax rate might suggest.

The Economic Recovery Tax Act (ERTA) of 1981 attempted to mitigate the impact of inflation on our income taxes, often referred to as **bracket creep**. Here, even when the rate of increase in your income matches the rate of inflation, you may still wind up losing to inflation if your additional income is taxed at higher rates. If this occurs, the growth in your after-tax income will fall short of the inflation rate. The progressive nature of taxes is at the core of bracket creep and, when combined with inflation, can have a cruel effect on family income. Inflation leads to a higher level of income, which pushes you into a higher tax bracket and causes you to pay even more taxes, resulting in your take-home pay going up at a slower rate than inflation. In an attempt to keep bracket creep in check, one of the provisions of ERTA was to *index* the tax brackets, standard deductions, and personal exemptions to the consumer price index. In this way, as inflation increased, so, too, would both the income-level steps in each tax bracket and the personal exemption amounts. The Tax Reform Act of 1986 further curtailed the effects of bracket creep by sharply *reducing* the number of tax brackets and *widening* the income levels within each bracket. Thus, a jump to a higher tax bracket occurs far less often today than it did in the past, and it takes a much larger increase in income to trigger a jump to a new bracket.

income taxes
A type of tax levied on taxable income by the federal government as well as many state and local governments.

progressive tax structure
A tax structure in which the larger the amount of taxable income, the higher the rate at which it is taxed.

average tax rate
The rate at which each dollar of taxable income is taxed on average; calculated by dividing tax liability by taxable income.

bracket creep
A situation in which increases in income are taxed at higher rates, causing the growth in after-tax income to fall short of the inflation rate.

YOUR FILING STATUS

The taxes you pay depend in part on your *filing status*, the category that identifies you based on your marital status and family situation. Filing status is an important factor in determining whether you are required to file an income tax return, the amount of your standard deduction, and your tax rate. Your filing status is based on your status on the last day of your tax year (usually December 31). If you have a choice of filing status, you should calculate taxes both ways and choose the status that results in the lower tax liability. There are five different filing status categories.

Single taxpayers are unmarried or legally separated from their spouses by either a separation or final divorce decree. *Married filing jointly* refers to married couples who combine their income and allowable deductions and file one tax return. *Married filing separately*, the next category, occurs when each spouse files his or her own return, reporting only his or her income, exemptions, and deductions. *Head of household* refers to a taxpayer who is unmarried or considered unmarried and pays more than half of the cost of keeping up a home for himself or herself and an eligible dependent child or relative. The final category is *qualifying widow or widower with dependent child*, which applies to persons whose spouses died within two years of the tax year (for example, in 1989 or 1990 for the 1991 tax year) and support a dependent child. They may use joint return tax rates and are eligible for the highest standard deduction. (After the two-year period, they may file under the head of household status if they qualify.)

In general, married taxpayers who file jointly have a lower tax liability than if they file separately. However, sometimes these married couples pay more in total taxes than if they were single taxpayers. Combining the two incomes results in *bracket creep* — it pushes the couple into a higher tax bracket resulting in a "marriage tax." The amount of the extra tax depends on the level of each spouse's earnings and usually occurs when the smaller of the two partner's taxable income is equal to at least 30 percent of the couple's total taxable income. As an example, compare the taxes owed by a married couple *filing jointly* with total taxable income of $90,000 to those owed by *two single taxpayers* with taxable incomes of $45,000 each:

Filing Status	Total Tax Due
Married couple filing jointly	$21,016
Two *single* taxpayers: taxes of $9,955 each	− 19,910
"Marriage tax" (See Exhibit 4.5)	$ 1,106

Combining their incomes pushes the married couple into the 31 percent tax bracket and results in a tax liability that is $1,106 higher than the amount paid by the two *single* taxpayers, who fall into the 28 percent tax bracket. It is illegal, however, for married individuals to use the single filing status. But a couple planning a December wedding may reap considerable tax savings by postponing their wedded until January of the next year.

The tax brackets (rates) for married couples filing separately are higher than for joint filers and generally result in higher tax payments. In some cases, however, it may be advantageous for spouses to file separate returns. For instance, if one spouse has a moderate income and substantial medical expenses and the other has a low income and no medical expenses, filing separately may provide a tax savings.

Every individual or married couple who earns a specified level of income is required to file a tax return. Exhibit 4.1 provides a list of some of the more common filing requirements that existed in 1991. Like the personal tax rates, these minimums are adjusted annually in keeping with the annual rate of inflation. Note that if your income falls below the prevailing minimum levels, you are not required to file a tax return. However, if you had any tax withheld during the year, you must file a tax return — even if your income falls *below* minimum filing amounts — in order to receive a refund of these taxes.

Every individual or married couple is required to file a federal income tax return regardless of the amount of income earned.
Fantasy: Only those individuals or married couples who earn a specified minimum level of income or wish to receive a refund of withheld taxes are required to file a tax return.

YOUR TAKE-HOME PAY

Income taxes are usually collected on a **pay-as-you-go** basis, under which your employer withholds (deducts) a portion of your income every pay

EXHIBIT 4.1

Income Tax Filing Requirements (1991)

Individuals and married couples are required to file tax returns only if their incomes meet or exceed minimum levels. These minimums vary depending upon the taxpayer's filing status.

Filing Status	Minimum Income
Single individual, under 65	$ 5,550[a]
Single individual, 65 or older	6,400
Married couple, joint return, both under 65	10,000
Married couple, joint return, one spouse 65 or older	10,650
Married couple, joint return, both 65 or older	11,300
Married couple, separate return, any age	2,150
Head of household, under 65	7,150
Head of household, 65 or older	8,000
Qualifying widow(er) with dependent child, under 65	7,850
Qualifying widow(er) with dependent child, 65 or older	8,500

[a]Anyone who is claimed as a dependent on someone else's return (such as a student or elderly parent) must file a return if his or her gross income exceeds $550 in unearned income (such as interest and dividends) or $3,400 in earned income (such as wages and salary).

period and periodically sends it to the Internal Revenue Service on a scheduled basis. Self-employed persons must likewise deduct and forward a portion of their income to the Internal Revenue Service each quarter. After the close of the taxable year, you calculate the taxes you owe and file your tax return. At the time of filing, you receive full credit for the amount of taxes withheld from your income during the year. Depending on whether the amount of taxes withheld is larger or smaller than the actual taxes you incurred, you will either (1) receive a refund from the Internal Revenue Service (if too much tax was withheld from your paycheck) or (2) have to pay additional taxes (when the amount withheld was not enough to cover your tax liability). Withholdings are normally made not only for federal income taxes, but also for FICA (or social security) taxes and if applicable, state and local income taxes. In addition to taxes, you may have other deductions for items such as life and health insurance, savings plans, retirement programs, professional or union dues, and/or charitable contributions—all of which lower your take-home pay. Your *take-home pay* is what you are left with after subtracting the amount withheld from your *gross earnings*.

Federal Withholding Taxes. The amount of **federal withholding** taxes deducted from your gross earnings each pay period depends on both the level of your earnings and the number of withholding allowances you have claimed on a form called a W-4, that you must complete for your employer(s). Obviously, given the progressive nature of federal income taxes, the more you make, the more you can expect to have withheld from your paycheck. Withholding allowances are based, for the most part, on the number of people your income supports and act to reduce the amount of taxes withheld from your income. A taxpayer is entitled to one for himself or herself, one for the spouse (if filing jointly), and one for each dependent claimed. In addition, a *special*

pay-as-you-go basis
A method of paying income taxes in which the employer (or self-employed person) deducts a portion of income every pay period (or quarter) and sends it to the IRS.

federal withholding taxes
Taxes—based on the level of earnings and the number of withholding allowances claimed—that are deducted by an employer from the employee's gross earnings each pay period.

allowance can be taken by those (1) who are single and have one job; (2) who are married, have only one job, and have a nonworking spouse; or (3) whose wages from a second job or whose spouse's wages (or the total of both) are $1,000 or less. *Additional withholding allowances* can be claimed by (1) heads of households, (2) those with at least $1,500 of child or dependent-care expenses for which they plan to claim to credit, and (3) those with an unusually large amount of deductions. Of course, you can elect to have your employer withhold amounts greater than those prescribed by the withholding tables.

FICA (or Social Security Taxes). All employed workers (except certain federal employees) have to pay a combined old-age, survivor's, disability, and hospital insurance tax under provisions of the **Federal Insurance Contributions Act (FICA).** Known more commonly as the **social security tax**, it is applied to a stipulated amount of every employee's wages as mandated by Congress. This tax is paid equally by employer and employee. In 1991, the total social security tax rate was 15.3 percent, which was levied against the first $53,400 of an employee's earnings. Therefore, in 1991 7.65 percent would have been deducted from your paycheck until you earned more than $53,400 ($55,500 in 1992, with a 1.45 percent Medicare surcharge on amounts between $55,500 and $130,200). Self-employed persons pay the full tax — 15.3 percent in 1991 — and can deduct 50 percent of it on their tax returns.

The social security tax rate changes (that is, rises) over time, as does the tax base, which is linked to the cost of living. As with income taxes, your employer is required by law to withhold social security taxes from your paycheck. However, unlike income taxes, you have to pay social security only up to a stipulated maximum amount. In 1991, as noted above, once your salary went over $53,400, you stopped paying social security taxes for the balance of that year (the 1.45 percent Medicare surcharge was paid on earned income between $53,400 and $125,000). Finally, while the number of withholding allowances you claim has a bearing on the amount of income taxes withheld, it has absolutely no effect on the amount of social security taxes you pay. Everybody pays the same rate on the same amount of earnings, regardless of the number of dependents claimed.

The amount of federal income tax withheld depends on both your level of earnings and the number of withholding allowances claimed.

Fact: The more you make and the fewer withholding allowances you claim, the more will be withheld from your paycheck.

State and Local Income Taxes. Unlike federal income taxes, state and local income taxes differ from state to state. If levied, these taxes are generally tied to the individual's level of earnings. While state and local income taxes that have been withheld (or paid) are deductible on federal returns, federal taxes may or may not be deductible on the state or local return, depending on state and local laws. Especially in large cities, local income taxes can amount to as much as 2 percent of income — and in some states, the state income tax can be 15 percent or more.

IT'S TAXABLE INCOME THAT MATTERS

Various sections of the Internal Revenue Code define the key component of **taxable income**. Unfortunately, because of the numerous conditions and exceptions surrounding the tax treatment and or deductibility of certain income and expense items, the actual amount of taxable income is often difficult to determine. In its simplest form, taxable income can be found according to the following procedure:

	Gross income
Less:	Adjustments to (Gross) Income
Equals:	Adjusted gross income (AGI)
Less:	Larger of standard or itemized deductions
Less:	Exemptions
Equals:	Taxable income

The above looks simple enough — just subtract certain adjustments, deductions, and exemptions from your gross income, and you will get taxable income. As we will see, however, there are a number of problems that arise in defining what is included in these items.

Gross Income. Basically, **gross income** includes any and all income that is subject to federal taxes. Some of the more common forms of gross income include:

EXHIBIT 4.2

Common Types of Tax-Exempt Income

On some forms of income, you do not have to pay any taxes at all, since they can be totally or partially excluded from gross income.

Child support payments
Compensation from accident, health, and life insurance policies
Disability payments (limited in some cases)
Employee fringe benefits (limited to certain items)
Federal income tax refunds
Gifts
Inheritances
Interest on state or local government obligations
Military allowances
Return of original investment capital
Scholarships and fellowships (limited as to amount and time)
Social security benefits (amount exempted depends on total income)
Stock rights and stock dividends
Veterans' benefits
Welfare and other public assistance benefits
Workers' compensation payments

- Wages and salaries
- Bonuses, commissions, and tips
- Interest and dividends received
- Alimony received
- Business and farm income
- Gains from the sale of assets
- Income from pensions and annuities
- Income from rents and partnerships
- Prizes, lottery, and gambling winnings

In addition to these sources of income, there are other types that are considered to be *tax exempt* and as such are excluded—totally or partially—from gross income. Tax-exempt income does not even have to be listed on the tax return. A partial list of different types of tax-exempt income is shown in Exhibit 4.2.

Federal income taxes are levied against the *total amount of money earned*.

Fantasy: Federal income taxes are levied against your *taxable income*, which is the amount remaining after adjustments, deductions, and exemptions have been subtracted from gross income.

Three Kinds of Income. One of the major provisions of the 1986 Tax Reform Act was the cre-

ation of three basic categories of income, devised as a way to limit write-offs from tax-sheltered investments: (1) active (ordinary "earned") income, (2) portfolio (investment) income, and (3) passive income. *Active income* is the broadest category and consists of everything from wages and salaries to bonuses, tips, pension income, and alimony. It is made

Federal Insurance Contributions Act (FICA); social security tax

The law establishing the combined old-age, survivor's, disability, and hospital insurance tax levied on both employer and employee, also called the *social security tax.*

taxable income

The amount of income that is subject to taxes; calculated by subtracting adjustments, the larger of standard or itemized deductions, and exemptions from gross income.

gross income

The total of all income (before any adjustments, deductions, and/or exemptions) generated by a taxpayer; it includes active, portfolio, and passive income.

up of income earned on the job, as well as most other forms of *noninvestment* income. *Portfolio income*, in contrast, is comprised of the earnings generated from various types of investment holdings — in fact, this category of income covers most (but not all) types of investments, from stocks, bonds, savings accounts, and mutual funds to stock options and commodities. For the most part, portfolio income consists of interest, dividends, and capital gains (that is, the profit on the sale of an investment). Finally, there is *passive income*, a special category of income that is comprised chiefly of income derived from real estate, limited partnerships, and other forms of tax shelters.

The key feature of these categories is that they limit the amount of deductions and write-offs that can be taken, particularly with regard to portfolio and passive income. Specifically, the amount of allowable, deductible expenses associated with portfolio and passive income *is limited to the amount of income derived from these two sources.* For example, if you had a total of $380 in portfolio income for the year, you could write off no more than $380 in portfolio-related interest expense. Note, however, that if you have more portfolio expenses than income, you can "accumulate" the difference and write it off in later years (when you have sufficient portfolio income) or when you finally sell the investment. Likewise, the same rules generally apply to passive income and related expenses (with a few notable exceptions, which will be discussed later in this chapter). Thus, if you own limited partnerships that generate no income, you cannot write off the losses from those partnerships (at least not in the year in which they occur — as with investment expenses, you can "accumulate" these losses and write them off later).

It is important to understand that for deduction purposes, the portfolio and passive income categories cannot be mixed and/or combined with each other or with active income. *Investment-related expenses can be used only with portfolio income*, and with a few exceptions, *passive investment expenses can be used only to offset the income from passive investments.* As it turns out, therefore, all the other allowances and deductions (as described below) are written off against the total amount of *active* income generated by the taxpayer. In essence, the tax-

payer's income from wages, salaries, bonuses, tips, pensions, alimony, and so on is all added up, and it is against this amount that the various deductions are subtracted to arrive at adjusted gross income and, ultimately, the amount of taxable income.

Adjustments to (Gross) Income. Adjustments to income are allowable deductions from gross income that include certain types of employee and personal retirement, insurance, and support expenses. Most of these deductions are nonbusiness in nature. The following list, though not exhaustive, includes items that can be treated as adjustments to income:

- IRA deductions (limited)
- Self-employment tax deduction (limited to 50 percent of amount paid)
- Self-employed health insurance deduction (limited to 25 percent of amount paid)
- Keogh retirement plan and self-employed SEP deduction (limited)
- Penalty on early withdrawal of savings
- Alimony paid

There are some important restrictions that were placed on IRA deductions by the 1986 Tax Reform Act that taxpayers should be aware of. In particular, contributions to IRA accounts (of up to $2,000 for a wage earner and $250 for a nonworking spouse) are tax deductible *only* if the taxpayer is not covered by a qualified company-sponsored retirement program, or if the taxpayer's annual income is below a specified minimum: *$40,000 for married couples, $25,000 for single individuals.* (Note that if one spouse is covered by an employer plan, then *both* individuals' IRA contributions are restricted as a tax deduction depending on their income.) In essence, a taxpayer can be covered by an employer pension plan and also deduct contributions to his or her own IRA account so long as the income constraints are met. Note that allowable tax deductible IRA contributions are phased out between $40,000 and $50,000 for married couples (and $25,000–$35,000 for individuals) so that a married worker earning, say, $45,000 a year would be able to deduct an IRA contribution of only $1,000 (plus $125 for a nonworking spouse); workers earning more than $50,000 (or $35,000 if single) who are covered by a company pension plan would not be allowed any deduction. (The income limitations apply only to workers who are covered by employer-provided retirement plans; there is no income limitation on workers who are not covered by company programs.) When the total of any IRA contributions and any other allowable adjustments to income are subtracted from gross income, you are left with **adjusted gross income (AGI)**, which in itself is an important calculation, since certain itemized deductions are limited by its amount.

Deductions: Itemized or Standard? The next step in calculating your taxes is to subtract allowable deductions from your adjusted gross income to determine taxable income. This is perhaps the most complex part of the tax preparation process. You have two options: list your *itemized deductions* (specified tax-deductible personal expenses) or take the *standard deduction*, a blanket deduction that depends on your filing status. Obviously, you should use the method that results in larger allowable deductions.

Itemized Deductions. Deducting **itemized expenses** allows taxpayers to reduce their AGI by the amount of their allowable personal expenditures. The Internal Revenue Code defines the types of nonbusiness items that can be deducted from adjusted gross income. Some of the more common ones are as follows:

- Medical and dental expenses (in excess of 7.5 percent of AGI)
- State, local, and foreign income and property taxes; and state and local personal property taxes
- Residential mortgage interest and investment interest (limited)
- Charitable contributions (limited to 50 percent, 30 percent, or 20 percent of AGI depending on certain factors)
- Casualty and theft losses (in excess of 10 percent of AGI)
- Moving expenses (some limits)
- Job and other expenses (in excess of 2 percent of AGI)

Beginning in 1991, taxpayers with AGI in excess of $100,000 ($50,000 for marrieds filing separately) lost part of their itemized deductions. (In 1992 the base level of AGI rose to $105,250; $52,625 for marrieds filing separately.) This phaseout applies to certain categories of deductions, including taxes, home mortgage interest, charitable contributions, moving expenses, unreimbursed employee expenses, and other miscellaneous deductions subject to the 2 percent limit. Medical expenses, casualty and theft losses, and investment interest are exempt from this phaseout, and the amount of the total reduction in itemized deductions cannot be more than 80 percent of the total deductions to which the phaseout applies. These total itemized deductions are reduced by 3 percent of AGI over $100,000 (or $50,000 for married taxpayers filing separately). As an example, assume your AGI is $150,000, deductions (in excess of any specified percentages of AGI) affected by the income limitation total $45,000, and other deductions total $10,000. You must reduce deductions by $1,500 [($150,000 AGI − $100,000) × .03 = $1,500]. Therefore, you would subtract $1,500 from your $55,000 total itemized deductions, for an allowed deduction of $53,500. This loss of itemized deductions has the effect of raising your tax rate to 31.93 percent [31.00% + (3% × 31%)]. Married taxpayers with combined income over $100,000 and high itemized deductions that can be allocated to one spouse (such as medical expenses) may find that filing separately will allow them to avoid this phaseout.

A deduction is allowed for medical and dental expenses paid during the taxable year; however, it is limited to the amount by which such expenditures *exceed*, not equal, 7.5 percent of adjusted gross income. Medical insurance premiums and any expenses incurred in the diagnosis, cure, mitigation,

---

adjustments to (gross) income
Allowable deductions from gross income that include certain types of employee and personal retirement, insurance, and support expenses.

adjusted gross income (AGI)
The amount of income remaining after subtracting adjustments to income from gross income.

itemized expenses
Personal expenditures that can be deducted from adjusted gross income when determining taxable income.

EXHIBIT 4.3

Some Interest Is Deductible, Some Is Not

Because interest paid on first and second mortgages on a principal residence and a second home is the only form of noninvestment interest that can be deducted for tax purposes, borrowing against home equity has become popular in recent years. To be deductible, these loans must conform to rather rigid ground rules, which are illustrated in the following example.

Here's a hypothetical example of how the new rules on deductibility of *mortgage interest expense* would affect the tax return of a married couple who want to borrow against the value of their home, which is now worth $350,000:

Original first mortgage loan, taken out in 1985	$220,000
Current balance owed on first mortgage loan	193,000

The couple took out a home equity loan of $120,000 and used $75,000 to renovate their house and $45,000 for other purposes. They can deduct all of the interest on both mortgages:

- The first mortgage was taken out before October 13, 1987.
- Even though the home equity line (second mortgage) was over $100,000, all of the interest is deductible because:
  1. The total of the proceeds used for home improvements ($75,000) plus the current balance on the first mortgage ($193,000) are $268,000, below the $1 million limit.
  2. The portion *not* used for home improvement ($45,000) is below the $100,000 limit.

Their remaining unrestricted borrowing power for tax purposes is:

- Up to $37,000 for any purpose ($82,000 limit [$350,000 home value − $268,000 mortgage balance used to buy, build, or improve home] less $45,000 from existing home equity line *not* used for home improvements).
- Up to $82,000 for tuition and/or medical expenses ($350,000 home value − $268,000 mortgage balance).
- Whatever it costs (up to the $1 million limit) to make any home improvements and/or buy a second home.

and treatment of disease and injury or in the prevention of disease may be counted as medical and dental expenses. Specifically, they include costs related to doctors, dentists, hospitals, corrective devices such as eyeglasses, transportation, medicine and drugs, education for the physically or mentally handicapped, and the cost of medical insurance. Surgery for purely cosmetic reasons is not deductible. Of course, you cannot deduct any item for which you are reimbursed by medical insurance. The Internal Revenue Code also allows taxpayers to deduct certain taxes from AGI, including state, local, and foreign income taxes; state, local, and foreign real property taxes; and state and local personal property taxes.

Another deduction is permitted for interest paid on first and second mortgages. These mortgages must be on the taxpayer's principal residence or second home such as a summer cabin or vacation condo. In most cases, you can deduct all of your home mortgage interest. There are some limitations, however, depending on the date of the mortgage, the amount of the mortgage, and how you used the proceeds. Interest on mortgages of any amount acquired before October 13, 1987, is fully deductible. After October 13, 1987, mortgages taken out in order to buy, build, or improve your home are fully deductible if these mortgages, together with any mortgages taken out before October 13, 1987, total $1 million or less. Interest on mortgages taken out for uses other than to buy, build, or improve your home (called *home equity loans* and described more fully in Chapter 7) is deductible on loans up to $100,000. (These items are halved for married taxpayers filing separately.) If a home equity loan exceeds $100,000, interest on the portion used for home improvements or for educational or medical purposes is tax deductible up to the $1 million total mortgage interest limit. Exhibit 4.3 employs a simple illustration to summarize and clarify the treatment of interest expense on home equity loans.

As explained in the preceding material on *gross income*, interest may also be deductible when incurred for investment purposes as long as such interest expense does not exceed the amount of *portfolio income* reported by the taxpayer. The deduction for interest paid on consumer loans, allowed for decades, was eliminated in 1991.

To encourage charitable giving, a deduction is allowed for the amount of such contributions up to a maximum of 50 percent of adjusted gross income. (*Note*: A maximum contribution limit of 30 percent or 20 percent may apply in certain cases.) Contributions must be made to qualified organizations outlined by the IRS. They include contributions of money and property, but contributions of labor are not deductible. Another deduction that can be taken is for any personal casualty or theft losses, such as those suffered from fire, storms, vandalism, or robbery. These deductions are limited to the amount of each loss above $100 and then only to that portion in excess of 10 percent of adjusted gross income. Job-related moving expenses are also treated as itemized deductions. In essence, as long as the move meets certain IRS restrictions, some or all of the expenses associated with the move can be written off against income.

The final category of allowable deductions is for job and other expenses. This catchall category includes everything from unreimbursed employee expenses such as job travel, union dues, and job education to safe deposit box rental and tax preparation fees. (The amount of allowable deductions for business-related meals and entertainment is limited to 80 percent of the amount actually spent on them). The total of all these job and other expenses is deductible *only to the extent that it exceeds 2 percent of adjusted gross income*. Thus, if you have an AGI of $25,000, your total job and other expense deductions would have to exceed $500 (which is 2 percent of the AGI, or .02 × $25,000 = $500); if expenses amounted to $800, for instance, you would write off $300 in these deductions: $800 − $500 = $300. The accompanying *Smart Money* box provides useful suggestions for documenting not only your itemized expenses and deductions, but your income as well. Records like those suggested are important both for preparing your return and justifying your return under audit.

Standard Deductions.   Instead of itemizing personal deductions, a taxpayer can take the **stan-**dard deduction**, which is a type of blanket deduction that is meant to capture the various deductible expenses that taxpayers normally incur. People who don't want to itemize their deductions take the stipulated standard deduction, which varies depending on the taxpayer's filing status (single, married filing jointly, and so on), age (65 or older), and vision (blind). In 1991 the standard deduction varied from $3,400 to $8,300. Exhibit 4.4 includes the 1991 standard deduction table that can be used to calculate your standard deduction. Each year the standard deduction amounts are adjusted in response to changes in the cost of living. For instance, the standard deduction for a single taxpayer increased from $3,400 in 1991 to $3,600 in 1992; for married couples filing joint returns, it increased from $5,700 in 1991 to $6,000 in 1992.

The decision to itemize deductions or take the standard deduction may be changed from year to year, or even in the same year: taxpayers who find they have chosen the wrong option and paid too much may recompute their tax using the other method and claim a refund for the difference. As an example, suppose you computed and paid your taxes, which amounted to $2,450, using the standard deduction. A few months later you find that had you itemized your deductions, your taxes would have been only $1,950. Using the appropriate forms, you can file an *amended return (Form 1040X)* showing a $500 refund ($2,450 − $1,950). In order to avoid having to file an amended return as a result of using the wrong deduction technique, you should estimate your deductions using both the itemized and standard deduction amounts and then choose the alternative that results in lower taxes. As a matter of interest, most taxpayers use the standard deduction; generally homeowners who pay home mortgage interest and property taxes itemize, however, since those expenses alone typically exceed the allowable standard deduction.

---

standard deduction
A blanket deduction that depends on the taxpayer's filing status, age, and vision and can be taken by a taxpayer instead of itemizing deductions.

Documenting Your Income, Deductions, and Expenses

It's not enough that you have to pay taxes. In figuring out how much, you may practically suffocate under a blanket of paper, especially if you itemize (as a third of all taxpayers do). In this case, each deduction, from babysitting expenses to gambling losses, must be substantiated with standard forms, receipts, statements, diaries and canceled checks. And, of course, all taxpayers must document earnings, from wages to tips to dividends.

The job must be done not only to figure out what you owe — or, glory be, what Uncle Sam owes you — but also to justify the return in case of an audit.

Even if you plan to hire a preparer to do your return, you should identify your deductions yourself. Otherwise, one might be overlooked. After all, only you can know what each chit of paper represents. Furthermore, if you hand the paper pile to your accountant, he will bill you perhaps hundreds of dollars to do the sorting.

Once the papers are organized by income and deduction category, you are ready to add up your totals. These lump sums are all your tax preparer wants to see; leave the receipts at home. "I'm not your auditor," says Alan Westheimer, a tax partner with Pannell Kerr Forster in Houston. "What I need is numbers you can back up if you have to." If you do give papers to your tax preparer, be sure to make copies for your own files.

Here is what you will generally need to assemble, depending on your sources of income, deductions, and expenses:

INCOME AND LOSSES

The W-2 form (showing salary, wages, and taxes withheld) and the W-2P (for monthly distribution from a pension) must be attached to your return. Most other income, such as self-employment income, interest, royalty income, dividends, lump-sum payments from pensions and annuities, state and local tax refunds, and mutual fund earnings and gains, is documented on 1099 forms. Capital gains and losses are also reported on 1099s: one form is mailed to you, one to the Internal Revenue Service. The IRS uses a computer matching system that spots discrepancies between income statements on your return and the 1099s they have received. A 1099 needs to be attached to the return only in the event that tax has been withheld.

Income from tips should be backed up with Forms 4070-A, 4070 and 4137. Income (and losses) from partnerships, estates and trusts, and S corporations is documented on Schedule K-1.

The IRS requires that both W-2 forms and 1099s be sent to taxpayers by January 31. The law does not require, however, that K-1 schedules be available by April 15. If the party responsible — such as a brokerage, bank, or even the company you work for — does not mail your schedules on time, you should call them. If you do not receive the schedules by the April 15 deadline, tax experts recommend that you file for an automatic extension and complete your return when you have the required information.

EXPENSES

■ **Mortgage interest.** Form 1098, which the lender

sends you, covers this.

- **Dependent-care payments.** Canceled checks and statements from caretakers, babysitters, or child-care organizations will document your expenses.
- **Charitable contributions.** Any charitable deduction for items worth $500 or more must be supported by statements from receiving organizations verifying the fair market value of the property. For items over $5,000, you need a professional appraisal. Old clothes should be valued at what a buyer might reasonably pay in a thrift shop or secondhand outlet. You should have a log for out-of-pocket costs on service done for a charity, such as the use of your car.
- **Medical expenses not reimbursed by insurance.** To be deductible, expenses must exceed 7.5 percent of your adjusted gross income. One exception is the cost of premiums paid by self-employed taxpayers for medical- and dental-care coverage. Twenty-five percent of those expenses are deductible from

your self-employment income. The 75 percent balance is subject to the 7.5 percent floor. Pull together receipts for prescription medicine or special health equipment authorized by your doctor and bills from doctors, clinics and the like for treatment. If travel was necessary for medical treatment, you will want lodging (up to $50 a night) and meal receipts.

- **Miscellaneous expenses.** Document these with receipts for expenditures such as union dues, safe deposit box rental, investment advice, membership dues for a professional organization, and business publications. A comprehensive listing is included in the 1040 instruction booklet. Generally, they must be more than 2 percent of your adjusted gross income.
- **Employee business expenses that are not reimbursed are treated as miscellaneous expenses.** You may deduct 80 percent of the amount spent on business meals and entertainment. Collect receipts showing the date, cost, place of meal or

entertainment, names of those involved, and purpose of the event. Travel expenses are fully deductible if substantiated by receipts. A log will document business car trips and mileage on which you may deduct a per-mile charge ($.275 in 1991) or actual operating expenses (gas, oil, insurance, repairs, depreciation, lease payments, tolls, parking, and so on).

- **Rental-property expenses.** Collect your real estate tax bill and itemized receipts for repairs and maintenance. Back up the depreciation deduction with the closing statement from your purchase of the property. If you plan to deduct expenses connected with a vacation house that you rent out for a minimum of 15 days, you must have a log showing the number of days you rented the property and how many days you used it yourself.

Source: Holly Wheelright, "Checklist: What You Need to Collect," *Money*, January 1989, pp. 75–78. (Updated for 1991 tax code changes.) Used with permission.

EXHIBIT 4.4

Calculating Standard Deduction Amounts under Various Filing Alternatives (1991)

The standard deduction for taxpayers depends on filing status, age, and vision. The following IRS forms can be used to estimate your allowable standard deduction.

STEP 1.   Check the correct number of boxes below.

| You | 65 or older_____ | Blind_____ |
| Your spouse | 65 or older_____ | Blind_____ |

Total number of boxes you checked .... _____

STEP 2.   Find your standard deduction.

If your filing status is:	and number of boxes checked in Step 1 above are:	your standard deduction is:
Single	0	$3,400
	1	4,250
	2	5,100
Married filing jointly or Qualifying widow(er) with dependent child	0	$5,700
	1	6,350
	2	7,000
	3	7,650
	4	8,300
Married filing separately[a]	0	$2,850
	1	3,500
	2	4,150
	3	4,800
	4	5,450
Head of household	0	$5,000
	1	5,850
	2	6,700

[a]If your spouse itemizes deductions on a separate return, you must also itemize deductions rather than take the standard deduction.

Exemptions. Deductions based on the number of persons supported by the taxpayer's income are called **exemptions**. A taxpayer can claim an exemption for himself or herself, his or her spouse, and any *dependents*—which include children or other relatives earning less than a stipulated minimum level of income ($2,150 in 1991) and for whom the taxpayer provides at least half of their total support. This income limitation is waived for children under the age of 24 who are full-time students. Therefore, a college student, for example, could earn $8,000 and still be claimed as an exemption by his or her parents as long as all other dependency requirements are met. In 1991 each exemption claimed was worth $2,150 ($2,300 in 1992). The personal exemption amount is tied to the cost of living and will change annually in line with the prevailing rates on inflation.

Exemptions are phased out and eliminated altogether for taxpayers with high levels of AGI. The phaseout provision introduced in 1991 applies to single taxpayers with AGI over $100,000 and married couples filing jointly with AGI over $150,000 ($105,250 and $157,900, respectively, in 1992). This phaseout, together with the itemized deduction phaseout, raises the effective tax rate for a single taxpayer with AGI over $100,000 and one exemption to about 33 percent and for a married couple with two children, to more than 34 percent.

Moreover, a personal exemption can be claimed only once. If a child is *eligible* to be claimed as an exemption by his or her parents, then the child does not have the choice of using a personal exemption on his or her own tax return regardless of whether or not the parents use the child's exemption.

In 1991 a family of four could take total exemptions of $8,600—that is, 4 × $2,150. Subtracting the amount claimed for itemized deductions (or the standard deduction) and exemptions from AGI results in the amount of your *taxable income*, which is the basis on which your taxes are figured. A taxpayer who makes $40,000 a year may have only, say, $25,000 in taxable income after deductions and exemptions. It is the *lower*, taxable income figure that determines how much tax an individual must pay.

Tax Credits. Once taxable income has been determined, the *tax liability*, or amount of taxes owed, must be calculated. This is done either with the help of a table or by applying certain specified formulas, depending on the amount of one's taxable income. Taxpayers, however, are allowed to make certain deductions, known as **tax credits**, directly from their tax liability.

A tax credit is much more valuable than a deduction or an exemption, since it directly reduces, dollar for dollar, the amount of *taxes due*, whereas a deduction or an exemption merely reduces the amount of *taxable income*. For example, assume that a single taxpayer in the 28 percent tax bracket has $1,000 in deductions and another in the same bracket has a $1,000 tax credit. Look at what happens to the amount of taxes paid:

		$1,000 Deduction	$1,000 Tax Credit
	Gross income	$38,000	$38,000
Less:	Other deductions/ exemptions	6,000	6,000
Less:	$1,000 deduction	1,000	–
	Taxable income	$31,000	$32,000
	Tax liability*	6,035	6,315
Less:	$1,000 tax credit	–	1,000
	Taxes paid	$ 6,035	$ 5,315

*Note: tax liability figured as follows: the first $20,350 of taxable income taxed at 15%, the balance at 28%.

In effect, the tax credit in this example has reduced taxes (and therefore *increased* after-tax income) by over $700!

A frequently used tax credit is for child- and dependent-care expenses. This credit is based on the amount spent for dependent care while a taxpayer (and spouse, if married) works or goes to school. The qualifying dependent must be less than 13 years old, except in the case of a disabled dependent or spouse. The base amount of the credit is limited to $2,400 for one dependent and $4,800 for two or more dependents. The actual amount of the credit is a percentage of the amount spent or of the limit, whichever is less. The percentages range from 20 to 30 percent, depending on the taxpayer's AGI. For example, a couple with AGI of $30,000 who spent $3,000 on child care expenses for their two young children would receive a dependent care credit of $600 (.20 × $3,000).

Another important credit is the earned income credit, a special credit for lower-income workers who have dependent children. It consists of three different credits: the basic credit, the health insurance credit, and the extra credit for a child born during the tax year. To be eligible for the earned income credit, taxpayers must have earned income (from wages) and AGI of less than $21,250 ($22,370 for 1992) and have a qualifying child living with them in their home in the United States. Taxpayers must file a return to receive the credit, even if their earnings fall below the minimum levels shown in Exhibit 4.1. The maximum credit was $2,020 in 1991 ($2,211 in 1992). Other common tax credits include:

- Credit for the elderly or the disabled
- Foreign tax credit
- Credit for prior year minimum tax
- Mortgage interest credit
- Credit for fuel from a nonconventional source
- General business credit

---

exemptions
Deductions from adjusted gross income based on the number of persons supported by the taxpayer's income.

tax credits
Deductions from a taxpayer's tax liability that directly reduce his or her taxes due rather than taxable income.

In order to receive one of these credits, the taxpayer usually must file along with his or her return a separate schedule in support of the tax credit claimed.

A tax credit is like a deduction for exemptions in that it reduces your taxable income.
Fantasy: A tax credit is far more valuable than a deduction or exemption, since it directly reduces, dollar for dollar, the amount of taxes due.

THERE'S NOTHING OUT OF THE ORDINARY ABOUT CAPITAL GAINS

Prior to the Tax Reform Act of 1986, capital gains were taxed at highly preferential rates — that is, such gains were taxed at much lower rates than active earned income. Technically, a capital gain occurs whenever an asset (such as a stock, bond, or real estate) is sold for more than its original cost. Thus, if you purchased stock for $50 per share and sold it for $60, you'd have a capital gain of $10 per share. As of early 1992, capital gains are taxed at a maximum rate of 28 percent. Therefore, only taxpayers in the 31 percent bracket (in 1991, single filers with taxable income over $49,300 and married couples filing jointly with taxable income over $82,150) benefit from a lower tax rate on capital gains. To qualify for the 28 percent rate, taxpayers in the 31 percent bracket must have long-term capital gains (gains on assets held more than one year) in excess of any short-term *capital losses*. (In contrast to a capital gain, a *capital loss* occurs when an asset is sold for less than its original cost.) The reinstatement of more attractive (lower) capital gains tax rates is being considered by Congress.

As a rule, most capital gains will probably be included as part of the taxpayer's *portfolio income*, by adding any capital gains (actually realized) to the amount of dividends, interest, and rents generated by the taxpayer to arrive at total investment income. While there are no limits on the amount of capital gains taxpayers can generate, there are some IRS-imposed restrictions on the amount of capital losses that can be taken in a given year. Specifically, a taxpayer can write off capital losses, dollar for dollar, against any capital gains. For example, if a taxpayer has $10,000 in capital gains, she can write off up to $10,000 in capital losses. After that, no more than $3,000 in additional capital losses can be written off against other (active, earned) income. Thus, in our example, if the taxpayer had $18,000 in capital losses, she could only write off $13,000 of it in the current year; $10,000 against the capital gains she generated in that year and another $3,000 against her active income. Anything left ($5,000 in this case) would have to be written off in later years in the same order as indicated above: first against any capital gains and then up to $3,000 against active income. (Note: to qualify as a deductible item, the capital loss *must result from the sale of some income-producing asset*, such as stocks and bonds. The capital loss on a nonincome-producing asset, such as a car or TV set, does *not* qualify for tax relief.)

The Special Case of Selling Your Home.

Homeowners, for a variety of reasons, are given special treatment in the tax codes, and the way capital gains are taxed on the sale of a home is no exception. Essentially, the tax on any gain you make from the sale of your home can be *deferred* almost indefinitely as long as you buy another home of equal or greater value within a stipulated time period. Note that this provision applies only to your *principal residence* and not to any other homes or real estate you may own. Here is how it works: If you sell your home and purchase and use a new one within 24 months, any gain made on the sale of the old home will not be taxable as long as the amount paid for the new home is equal to or greater than the sale proceeds from the old home. (Note that the home you purchase need not be a new home in order to qualify for this special tax treatment; it only need be "new" to you and, as such, can be a previously occupied, older house.) If a new home is not purchased within 24 months from the date of the sale of the old home, taxes must be paid on all capital gains realized from the sale of this *and any previous homes*.

If the price of the new home is lower than the sale price of the old home, the amount by which the price of the old residence exceeds that of the new one is subject to tax. For instance, assume that you sell your first home, which you purchased for $70,000 three years ago, for $83,000. In this case you will have a capital gain of $13,000 ($83,000 − $70,000). Further, suppose that within 24 months of the sale of your old home you purchase and use a new one costing $80,000. As a result, you have to pay taxes on the $3,000 in profits that you pocketed. In contrast, if the new home cost $90,000, no taxes will be due in the current year, since the $90,000 purchase price exceeds the $83,000 for which the old home was sold.

While you can sell and buy homes over and over again and defer the taxes on all profits literally to the day you die, there is a provision in the tax code that allows people 55 or older to take a one-time exclusion of $125,000 in capital gains earned from the sale of principal residences. For married couples filing joint returns, it requires merely that one of the spouses be 55 or older and that the couple have owned and lived in the house as their principal residence for three years out of the five-year period ending in the date of sale. This feature provides a real break for homeowners, since it allows them a one-time chance to earn up to $125,000 of tax-free income.

To illustrate, consider the case of Homer and Lucile Greenman, who are both 58 years old and have decided to retire in sunny Arizona. They purchased their first house 30 years ago for $25,000 and have since owned three other homes, each higher priced than the last. They have been offered $250,000 for their present home, for which they paid $100,000 in the late 1970s. Their records show that they realized $40,000 in profits from their first three houses. When this is added to the $150,000 gain they will realize on their present home, they will have to declare $190,000 in capital gains if they decide to retire into a rental unit. However, because of their ages, they are eligible for the $125,000 tax-free exclusion. Thus, they will have to pay taxes on only $65,000 of their gain (that is, $190,000 − $125,000). On the other hand, if the Greenmans decide to buy another home when they retire, all they have to do is buy one for $125,000 (the $250,000 sale price of their current home less the one-time exclusion of $125,000) and they can keep $125,000 — *tax-free* — and avoid any taxes altogether.

OTHER FILING CONSIDERATIONS

There are several other factors to consider when filing your tax return. If you have income that is not subject to withholding, you may be required to file a declaration of *estimated taxes* with your return and

to pay taxes on a quarterly basis. The regular filing deadline is April 15, but, if necessary, taxpayers can seek an extension of this deadline. In addition, you can file an *amended return* to correct an already-filed return.

Estimated Taxes.   Because federal withholding taxes are taken only from income earned on a regular basis, such as that paid in the form of wages, the Internal Revenue Service requires certain people to pay **estimated taxes** on income earned from other sources. This requirement allows the principle of "pay as you go" to be applied not only to wages subject to withholding but also to other sources of income. The payment of estimated taxes is most commonly required of investors, consultants, lawyers, business owners, and various other professionals who are likely to receive income in a form that is not subject to withholding. Generally, if all of your income is subject to withholding, you probably do not need to make estimated tax payments. Suppose, however, you figure that your estimated tax in the coming year will be $500 or more, while the total amount of income withheld and your credits will be less than the smaller of (1) 90 percent of the tax to be shown on your coming year's income tax return or (2) 100 percent of the tax shown on your prior year's tax return (assuming it covered all 12 months on that year and your current year's income does not increase by more than $40,000 over the prior year's income). In this case you should file a declaration of estimated taxes (Form 1040-ES) and make estimated tax payments. Beginning in 1992, new rules were applied to the payment of estimated taxes by some taxpayers with AGI over $75,000. To avoid penalties, they must pay estimated taxes consistent with the actual income earned in the immediately preceding quarter. Prior to this change, the taxpayer could merely pay either one-fourth of the total *annual* estimated payment or one-fourth of the amount paid in taxes during the immediately preceding year. As a

---

estimated taxes

Quarterly tax payments required on income not subject to withholding.

result taxpayers can no longer "defer" the tax payments on large amounts of income earned early in the year.

The declaration of estimated taxes is normally filed with the tax return. The amount of estimated taxes must be paid in four quarterly installments on April 15, June 15, September 15 of the current year, and January 15 of the following year. Failure to estimate and pay these taxes can result in a penalty levied by the IRS if the total taxes paid through withholdings and estimated payments (paid quarterly) is less than both 90 percent of your actual tax liability and 100 percent of the tax shown on your prior year's tax return when income has *not* increased by more than $40,000 over the prior year. If income has increased by more than $40,000, the 90 percent test is applied and a penalty is levied if it is not met.

April 15: Filing Deadline. At the end of each tax year, those taxpayers who are required to file a return must determine the amount of their *tax liability* — the amount of taxes that they owe as a result of the past year's activities. The tax year corresponds to the calendar year and covers the period January 1 through December 31. Taxpayers are asked to file their returns as soon after the end of the tax year as possible and *must* do so by no later than April 15 of the year immediately following the tax year (or by the first business day after that date if it falls on a weekend or federal holiday). Depending on whether the total of taxes withheld and any estimated tax payments is greater or less than the computed tax liability, the taxpayer will either receive a refund or have to pay additional taxes. As an example, assume that you had $2,000 withheld and paid estimated taxes of $1,200 during the year. After filling out the appropriate tax forms, you find your tax liability amounts to only $2,800. In this case, you have overpaid your taxes by $400 ($2,000 + $1,200 − $2,800) and will receive a $400 refund from the IRS. On the other hand, if your tax liability had amounted to $4,000, you would have a balance due the IRS of $800 ($4,000 − $2,000 − $1,200).

Filing Extensions and Amended Returns. It is possible to receive an extension of time for filing your federal tax return. An automatic four-month **filing extension**, which makes the due date August 15, can be applied for simply by submitting the appropriate form (Form 4868). In filing for an extension, however, the taxpayer must estimate the taxes due and remit that amount with the application. The extension does *not* give taxpayers more time to pay their taxes. Beyond the four-month automatic extension other extensions can be requested, but before granting them the IRS must be convinced that they are justified.

After filing a return, you may discover that you overlooked some income or a major deduction and as a result paid too little or too much in taxes. You can easily correct this simply by filing an **amended return** (Form 1040X), which will show the corrected amount of income or deductions and the amount of taxes that should have been paid along with any tax refund or additional taxes due. If a mistake or oversight has been made, then file an amended return. You generally have three years from the date your original return was filed or two years from the date the taxes were paid, whichever is later. If your amended return is properly prepared and filed and reflects nothing out of the ordinary, it generally will not trigger an audit. By all means, do not "correct" an oversight in one year by "adjusting" next year's tax return — the IRS frowns on that!

AUDITED RETURNS

Since taxpayers themselves provide the key information and fill out the necessary tax forms, the IRS has no proof that taxes have been correctly calculated. Therefore, it more or less randomly selects some returns for a **tax audit** — an examination to validate the return's accuracy. The odds of being audited are actually quite low. About 1.0 to 1.5 percent of all returns are audited annually. However, higher-income earners tend to have a greater chance of audit. For example, those with incomes between $25,000 and $50,000 have less than a 1 percent chance of being audited, but the chance of audit jumps to nearly 5 percent for those with incomes over $100,000. The outcome of an audit is not always owing more taxes to the IRS. In fact, about 5 percent of all audits result in a refund to the taxpayer, and in 15 percent of all audits the returns are found to be correctly prepared.

IRS audits attempt to confirm the validity of filed returns by carefully examining the data reported in them. In the course of an audit, the IRS may deem it necessary to arrange a meeting in which the taxpayer is asked to explain and document some of the deductions taken. Even when the documentation is provided, the IRS examiner may still question the legitimacy of the deductions. If the taxpayer and the IRS examiner cannot informally agree on the disputed items, the taxpayer can meet with the examiner's supervisor to discuss the case further. If there is still disagreement, the taxpayer can appeal through the IRS Appeals Office. Finally, if satisfaction is not obtained from the hearing before the Appeals Office, the case can be brought before the U.S. Tax Court, the U.S. Claims Court, or a U.S. District Court.

It is important to keep satisfactory and thorough tax records, because some day you may be audited by the IRS. Although the IRS does not specify any type of recordkeeping system, you should keep track of the source or use of all cash receipts and cash payments. Notations with respect to the purpose of the expenditures are important, as well as proof that you actually made the expenditures for which you have claimed deductions. Typically, audits question both (1) whether all income received has been properly reported and (2) the amounts and legitimacy of deductions taken. Since the IRS can take as many as three years from the date of filing to audit your return—and in some cases an unlimited period of time—records and receipts used in preparing returns are best kept on hand for several years. Severe financial penalties—even prison sentences—can result from violating tax laws.

In sum, while you should take advantage of all legitimate deductions in order to minimize your tax liability, you must also be sure to properly report all items of income and expenditure as required by the Internal Revenue Code.

TAX PREPARATION SERVICES: GETTING HELP ON YOUR RETURNS

Many people prepare their own tax returns. These "do-it-yourselfers" typically have fairly simple returns that can be prepared without a great deal of difficulty. Of course, some taxpayers with quite complicated financial affairs may also invest their time in preparing their own returns. IRS informational publications that are helpful when preparing your tax return can be ordered directly from the IRS by mail or by calling its toll-free number (1-800-829-3676 or special local numbers in some areas). An excellent (and free) comprehensive tax preparation reference book is IRS Publication 17, *Your Federal Income Tax*. Recently, the IRS added an information service called Tele-Tax that provides recorded phone messages on selected tax topics. The toll-free telephone number for this service is 1-800-829-4477, and special local numbers are available in some areas.

Help from the IRS. The Internal Revenue Service, in addition to issuing various publications for use in preparing tax returns, also provides direct assistance to taxpayers. The IRS will compute taxes for those whose adjusted gross income is not more than $50,000 and who do not itemize deductions. Persons who use this IRS service are required to fill in certain data, sign and date the return, and send it to the IRS on or before April 15 of the year immediately following the tax year. The IRS attempts to calculate taxes so as to result in the "smallest" tax bite. Taxpayers are then sent a refund, if their withholding exceeds their tax liability, or a bill, if their tax liability is greater than the amount of withholding. People who either fail to qualify for or do not want to use this total tax preparation service can still obtain IRS assistance in preparing their returns. The IRS provides a toll-free service through which taxpayers can have questions answered. Consult your telephone directory for the toll-free number of the IRS office closest to you.

---

filing extension
A period of time following the April 15 deadline during which taxpayers may file their returns without incurring penalties.

amended return
A tax return filed to correct errors or adjust for information received after the filing date of the taxpayer's original return.

tax audit
An examination by the IRS to validate the accuracy of a given tax return.

It is important to recognize that the IRS sometimes makes mistakes! It may not always correctly answer your tax questions. In a 1992 survey by *Money* magazine, IRS representatives were correct only 86 percent of the time. To increase your chances of getting correct information, you should use Publication 17 and other resources to research your question before calling, state your question as clearly as you can, and make sure that the IRS representative fully understands your question. Remember: You are liable for any underpayment of taxes, including interest and penalties, that results from incorrect information provided by the IRS over the phone. As an alternative, you may put the question in writing and receive a written response from the IRS. If the written answer is incorrect, and as a result you underpay your taxes, you will have to pay the additional taxes and interest due, but no penalties.

Private Tax Preparers. About 40 percent of all taxpayers prefer to use private *tax preparation services* because (1) they are concerned about accuracy and minimizing their tax liability as much as possible and (2) they believe the complexity of the tax forms makes preparation too difficult and/or time consuming. Taxpayers who do not wish to prepare their returns and have relatively common types of income and expenditures might consider using a *national tax service*, like H&R Block. Many *local tax preparation services* are also available. Caution is recommended when selecting a tax preparation service, however, since differing levels of competence exist. The fees charged by professional tax preparers range from $15 to $25 for very simple returns to $1,000 or more for complicated returns that include many itemized deductions, partnership income or losses, or self-employment income.

Taxpayers with more complex finances often employ an enrolled agent, an attorney with tax training, or a *certified public accountant (CPA)*. These professionals know the various technical points and are able to advise the taxpayer on how to defer income, qualify for deductions, and generally minimize tax liability. *Enrolled agents (EAs)* are individual tax practitioners who have demonstrated their competence in the area of taxation through a grueling, two-day, IRS-administered exam. They are fully qualified to handle tax preparation at various levels of complexity. *Tax attorneys* generally devote most of their attention to counseling taxpayers in the area of tax planning, while CPAs not only provide tax counseling but also are heavily involved with the actual preparation of returns. Since the services provided by EAs, tax attorneys, and CPAs can be expensive, they are usually best used only by those taxpayers whose financial situations are relatively complicated. Taxpayers should check completed returns carefully before signing them, since *the taxpayers themselves must accept primary responsibility for the accuracy of their returns*. The IRS requires professional tax preparers to sign each return as the preparer, enter their own social security number and address, and provide the taxpayers with a copy of the return being filed. In 1988 the IRS began allowing designated tax preparers with the necessary hardware to electronically file their clients' tax returns, thereby permitting eligible taxpayers to more quickly receive refunds.

There is no guarantee that your professional tax preparer will correctly determine your tax liability. In *Money* magazine's annual tax return test for 1992, *none* of the 50 tax preparers — each of whom had five or more years experience — came up with the same tax liability. The tax liability for the hypothetical family in the test ranged from an underpayment of more than $10,000 to an overpayment of nearly $20,000! To reduce the chance of error, you should become familiar with the basic tax principles and regulations, check all documents (such as W-2s and 1099s) for accuracy, maintain good communication with your tax preparer, and request an explanation of any entries on your tax return that you do not understand.

Computer-Based Tax Returns. More and more people are turning to their personal computers for help in preparing their tax returns and doing tax planning. A number of tax software packages are available to save hours of figuring and refiguring all the forms and schedules involved in filing tax returns. These computer programs are not for everyone, however. Very simple returns do not require them. And for very complex returns, there is no substitute for the skill and expertise of an attorney or tax accountant. Those who itemize deductions but do not need tax advice are the ones most likely to find the computer helpful.

Basically there are two kinds of software: tax planning and tax preparation. Programs are available to help you in your tax planning by letting you experiment with different strategies to see their effects on the amount of taxes you must pay. For example, *Managing Your Money*, a financial planning program discussed in Chapter 2, can be used for tax planning. The other category of tax software is designed mainly to help you complete your returns and print them out. Of course, any of these tax preparation programs can be used for tax planning by doing "what if" analysis — changing the values of various income and expense entries and preparing the return to find the tax liability that can be compared to the tax liability associated with other planning alternatives. Popular tax preparation programs for federal tax returns include Andrew Tobias's *Tax-Cut* (available in three versions based on the type of form filed: 1040, *ShortForm*, or *EZ*), *TurboTax*, *Easy Tax*, *MacInTax*, *J. K. Lasser's Your Income Tax Software*, and *Personal Tax Edge*. These software packages are revised annually in accordance with changes in the tax code but, because of this, their final versions may not be available until late February or early March. Most of these programs have separate versions for selected states. The programs vary in ease of use and features, and list prices generally range between $50 and $100. Price discounts are frequently available, and upgrades to the current version at a reduced price are available to those who already own the program.

Tax preparation programs enable you to input income, expenses, and other information required by most or all major tax forms and schedules. Some programs have an interview format that, based on your responses to its questions, guides you to the appropriate forms. These programs make all the necessary tax calculations for you. Many even print out completed forms and schedules that are formatted in a manner acceptable to the IRS, thereby eliminating the need for you to fill in the forms by hand. Of course, because no program can answer all your tax questions, you may want to research the tax laws in order to make sure that you have taken all allowed deductions.

DETERMINING YOUR TAXES ⚡

The amount of taxes you pay depends on the amount of taxable income you have and the rate at which your income is taxed. On average, what percent of every dollar of your income do you pay out in taxes? Try to estimate this percentage before reading on.

Now that we have reviewed the general principles of federal income taxes, we can direct our attention to calculating taxable income and the amount of income taxes due. To do this, we will need to address several key aspects of measuring taxable income and taxes: (1) the tax rates applicable to various types of personal income, (2) the basic tax forms and schedules, and (3) the procedures for determining tax liability.

TAX RATES

As we saw earlier in this chapter, the amount of *taxable income* is found by subtracting itemized deductions (or the standard deduction for nonitemizers) *and* personal exemptions from adjusted gross income. This procedure is used for *both itemizers and nonitemizers* and is a key calculation in determining your tax liability because the amount of income subject to federal income taxes is specified by the amount of taxable income you report. Once you know the amount of your taxable income, you can refer to *tax rate tables* to find the amount of taxes you owe. (When actually filing a tax return, taxpayers with taxable income of more than $50,000 must use the tax rate schedules.)

Tax rates vary not only with the amount of reported taxable income but also with filing status. Thus, there are different tax rate schedules for each filing category, as shown in Exhibit 4.5. The vast majority of taxpayers — perhaps 90 percent or more — fall into the first two brackets and are subject to tax rates of either 15 or 28 percent.

EXHIBIT 4.5

Tax Rate Schedules (1991)

Tax rates levied on personal income vary with the amount of reported taxable income and the taxpayer's filing status.

Single

Taxable Income	Tax Rate	Taxes Due
$0 to $20,350	15%	15% of reported taxable income
$20,351 to $49,300	28%	$3,052.50 *plus* 28% of the amount over $20,350
Over $49,301	31%	$11,158.50 *plus* 31% of the amount over $49,300

Married Filing Jointly or Qualifying Widow(er)

Taxable Income	Tax Rate	Taxes Due
$0 to $34,000	15%	15% of reported taxable income
$34,001 to $82,150	28%	$5,100 *plus* 28% of the amount over $34,000
Over $82,151	31%	$18,582 *plus* 31% of the amount over $82,150

Married Filing Separately

Taxable Income	Tax Rate	Taxes Due
$0 to $17,000	15%	15% of reported taxable income
$17,001 to $41,075	28%	$2,550 *plus* 28% of the amount over $17,000
Over $41,076	31%	$9,291 *plus* 31% of the amount over $41,075

Head of Household

Taxable Income	Tax Rate	Taxes Due
$0 to $27,300	15%	15% of reported taxable income
$27,301 to $70,450	28%	$4,095 *plus* 28% of the amount over $27,300
Over $70,451	31%	$16,177 *plus* 31% of the amount over $70,450

To see how the tax rates in Exhibit 4.5 work, consider two single taxpayers: one has taxable income of $12,500, the other has $29,600 in taxable income. We would calculate their respective tax liabilities as follows:

■ for taxable income of $12,500—

$$\$12,500 \times .15 = \$1,875$$

■ for taxable income of $29,600—

$$\$3,052.50 + [(\$29,600 - \$20,350) \times .28]$$
$$= \$3,052.50 + \$2,590 = \$5,642.50$$

As we can see, the income of $12,500 is taxed at the 15 percent tax rate, and the $29,600 is taxed first at 15 percent and then at 28 percent. Keep in mind that the same procedures would be used whether the taxpayer itemizes or not. In order to show how the amount of tax liability will vary with the level of taxable income, Exhibit 4.6 lists the taxes due on a range of taxable incomes from $500 to $75,000 for both single and married taxpayers.

Recall from our earlier discussions that the *average tax rate* is found by dividing your tax liability by the amount of reported taxable income. Returning to our example involving the taxpayer with an income of $29,600, we see that this individual had an average tax rate of $5,642.50 ÷ $29,600 = 19.1%, which is considerably *less* than the stated tax rate of 28 percent. Actually, the 28 percent represents the taxpayer's **marginal tax rate**—it is the rate at which the next dollar of taxable income is taxed. Notice in our calculations that the 28% tax rate applies only to that portion of the income that exceeds $20,350. Thus, the first $20,350 in income is taxed at 15 percent—only the balance ($29,600 − $20,350 = $9,250) is subject to the marginal tax rate of 28 percent.

Some taxpayers are subject to the *alternative minimum tax (AMT)*, currently a flat rate of 24 percent. A taxpayer's tax liability is the higher of the AMT or the regular tax. The AMT was originally designed to ensure that high-income taxpayers with many deductions pay their fair share of taxes. Prior to its pas-

EXHIBIT 4.6

Taxable Income and the Amount of Income Taxes Due (1991)

Given the progressive tax structure that exists in this country, it follows that the larger your income, the more you can expect to pay in taxes.

	Taxes Due	
Taxable Income	**Individual Returns**	**Joint Returns**
$ 500	$ 75*	$ 75*
1,000	150	150
1,500	225	225
2,000	300	300
2,500	375	375
5,000	750	750
7,500	1,125	1,125
10,000	1,500	1,500
12,500	1,875	1,875
15,000	2,250	2,250
20,000	3,000	3,000
25,000	4,355**	3,750
30,000	5,755	4,500
35,000	7,155	5,380**
40,000	8,555	6,780
50,000	11,376***	9,580
60,000	14,476	12,380
75,000	19,126	16,580
100,000	26,876	24,116***

*Income is taxed at 15%.
**28% tax rate now applies.
***31% tax rate now applies.

sage in 1978, the effective use of tax shelters (investments providing attractive tax write-offs) by many taxpayers allowed them to reduce their taxable incomes to near zero. The AMT includes in taxable income certain types of deductions otherwise allowed, such as state and local income and property taxes, miscellaneous itemized deductions, unreimbursed medical expenses, and depreciation. Therefore, taxpayers with moderate levels of taxable income, including those living in states with high tax rates and self-employed persons with depreciation deductions, may be subject to the AMT.

TAX FORMS AND SCHEDULES

The Internal Revenue Service requires taxpayers to file their returns using certain specified tax forms. As noted earlier, these forms and a variety of instruction booklets on how to prepare them are available to taxpayers free of charge. Generally, all persons who filed tax returns in the previous year are automatically sent a booklet containing tax forms and instructions for preparation of returns for the current year. Inside the booklet is a form that can be used to obtain additional tax forms for filing various tax-related returns and information. Exhibit 4.7 provides a list of some of the more commonly used tax forms.

Variations of Form 1040. All individuals use Form 1040 in one variation or another to file their tax returns. Form 1040EZ is a simple, nearly mistake-proof, one-page form. You qualify to use this form if you are single; under age 65; not blind; do not claim any dependents; have taxable income of less than $50,000 only from wages, salaries, tips, or taxable scholarships or grants; have interest income of less

---

marginal tax rate
The rate at which the next dollar of taxable income is taxed.

EXHIBIT 4.7

Commonly Used Tax Forms

A number of types of 1040 tax return forms are available. If the standard Form 1040 is used, one or more forms (listed below the 1040s) may be included with the tax return, depending on the amount and types of deductions claimed.

1040	Standard tax return, used with itemized deductions
1040A	Short-form tax return
1040EZ	Short-form tax return for single persons with no dependents
1040-ES	Estimated tax payments
1040X	Amended tax return
2106	Employee business expenses
2119	Sale or exchange of principal residence
2441	Credit for child and dependent care expenses
3903	Moving expenses
4562	Depreciation and amortization expenses
4684	Casualties and Thefts
4868	Application for automatic filing extension
8829	Expenses for business use of your home

than $400; and do not itemize deductions or claim any tax credits. Exhibit 4.8 shows the Form 1040EZ filed in 1991 by Mohammed Akbar, a full-time graduate student at Anystate University. His sources of income include a $5,000 scholarship, of which $1,200 was used for room and board, $5,500 earned from part-time and summer jobs, and $75 interest earned on a savings account deposit. Because scholarships used for tuition and fees are not taxed, he must include as income only the portion used for room and board.

To use Form 1040A, a two-page form, your income must be less than $50,000 and derived only from specified sources. Using this form you may deduct certain IRA contributions and claim certain tax credits, but you cannot itemize your deductions. If your income is over $50,000 or you itemize deductions, you must use the standard Form 1040 along with appropriate schedules, briefly described as follows:

Schedule	Description
A	For itemized deductions
B	For interest and dividend income of more than $400 each
C	For profit (or loss) from a personally owned business
D	For capital gains and losses
E	For supplemental income and losses from rents, royalties, partnerships, estates, trusts, etc.
F	For income and expense from farming
R	For credit for the elderly or disabled
SE	For reporting social security self-employment tax

The use of these schedules, which provide detailed guidelines for calculating certain entries on the first two pages of Form 1040, varies among taxpayers depending on the relevance of these entries to their situations. Pages 1 and 2 of Form 1040 summarize all items of income and deduction detailed on the accompanying schedules and are used to determine and report the taxable income and associated tax liability.

THE 1991 TAX RETURN OF TERRY AND EVELYN BECKER

Terry and Evelyn Becker are both 35 years old. They have been married for 11 years and have three children — Tom (age 9), Dick (age 7), and Harriet (age 3). Terry is a staff accountant for a major oil company headquartered in their hometown of Anywhere, Ohio. Evelyn Becker, who has one-and-a-half years of college, works part-time as a sales clerk in a major department store. During 1991, Terry's salary totaled $30,415 while Evelyn earned $3,750. Terry's employer withheld taxes of $3,560 and Evelyn's $550. During the year, the Beckers earned $500 interest on their joint savings account, received $750 in cash dividends on stock they owned jointly, and realized $850 in capital gains on the sale of securities. In addition, Terry kept the books for his brother's car dealership, from which he netted $3,600 during the year. Since no taxes were withheld from any of their

EXHIBIT 4.8

1991 Tax Return for Mohammed Akbar (Form 1040EZ)

Form 1040EZ is very easy to use, and most of the instructions are printed right on the form itself. Mohammed Akbar qualifies to use it because he is single, under age 65, not blind, and meets the income and deduction restrictions.

Form **1040EZ**	Department of the Treasury—Internal Revenue Service **Income Tax Return for Single Filers With No Dependents** (B) **1991**		OMB No. 1545-0675

Name & address

Use the IRS label (see page 10). If you don't have one, please print.

Please print your numbers like this:

9 8 7 6 5 4 3 2 1 0

Mohammed Akbar
Print your name (first, initial, last)

1000 State University Drive   14-A
Home address (number and street). (If you have a P.O. box, see page 11.)   Apt. no.

University City, CA   92000
City, town or post office, state, and ZIP code. (If you have a foreign address, see page 11.)

Your social security number

1 0 0 1 0 1 0 0 1

Please see instructions on the back. Also, see the Form 1040EZ booklet.

Presidential Election Campaign (see page 11)
Do you want $1 to go to this fund?

Note: *Checking "Yes" will not change your tax or reduce your refund.* ▶

Yes No
[X]

Report your income

Attach Copy B of Form(s) W-2 here. Attach tax payment on top of Form(s) W-2.

		Dollars	Cents
1	Total wages, salaries, and tips. This should be shown in Box 10 of your W-2 form(s). (Attach your W-2 form(s).) 1	6,700	00
2	Taxable interest income of $400 or less. If the total is more than $400, you cannot use Form 1040EZ. 2	75	00
3	Add line 1 and line 2. This is your **adjusted gross income.** 3	6,775	00

Note: *You **must** check Yes or No.*

4 Can your parents (or someone else) claim you on their return?
☐ **Yes.** Do worksheet on back; enter amount from line E here.
[X] **No.** Enter 5,550.00. This is the total of your standard deduction and personal exemption.   4 | 5,550 | 00

5 Subtract line 4 from line 3. If line 4 is larger than line 3, enter 0. This is your **taxable income.**   5 | 1,225 | 00

Figure your tax

6 Enter your Federal income tax withheld from Box 9 of your W-2 form(s).   6 | 250 | 00

7 **Tax.** Use the amount on **line 5** to find your tax in the tax table on pages 16-18 of the booklet. Enter the tax from the table on this line.   7 | 186 | 00

Refund or amount you owe

8 If line 6 is larger than line 7, subtract line 7 from line 6. This is your **refund.**   8 | 64 | 00

9 If line 7 is larger than line 6, subtract line 6 from line 7. This is the **amount you owe.** Attach your payment for full amount payable to the "Internal Revenue Service." Write your name, address, social security number, daytime phone number, and "1991 Form 1040EZ" on it.   9

Sign your return

Keep a copy of this form for your records.

I have read this return. Under penalties of perjury, I declare that to the best of my knowledge and belief, the return is true, correct, and complete.

Your signature   X *Mohammed Akbar*

Date **3-12-92**

Your occupation   **Graduate Student**

For IRS Use Only—Please do not write in boxes below.

For Privacy Act and Paperwork Reduction Act Notice, see page 4 in the booklet.   Cat. No. 12615V   Form **1040EZ** (1991)

EXHIBIT 4.9

1991 Tax Return (Form 1040) for the Beckers

Because they itemize deductions, the Beckers use standard Form 1040 to file their tax returns. When filed with the IRS, their return will include not only Form 1040 but also other schedules and forms that provide details on many of the expenses and deductions claimed by the Beckers. *Note:* The 1040 form depicted here is the one used in 1991; it is expected that there will be slight modifications in this form in subsequent years.

Form **1040** Department of the Treasury—Internal Revenue Service
U.S. Individual Income Tax Return **1991** (8)

For the year Jan.–Dec. 31, 1991, or other tax year beginning , 1991, ending , 19   OMB No. 1545-0074

Label
(See instructions on page 11.)
Use the IRS label. Otherwise, please print or type.

Your first name and initial: Terry B.   Last name: Becker
Your social security number: 123 : 45 : 6789

If a joint return, spouse's first name and initial: Evelyn A.   Last name: Becker
Spouse's social security number: 987 : 65 : 4321

Home address (number and street). (If you have a P.O. box, see page 11.): 123 Laughing Lane   Apt. no.

City, town or post office, state, and ZIP code. (If you have a foreign address, see page 11.): Anytown, Ohio 45400

For Privacy Act and Paperwork Reduction Act Notice, see instructions.

Presidential Election Campaign (See page 11.)
Do you want $1 to go to this fund? ...... ✓ Yes □ No
If joint return, does your spouse want $1 to go to this fund? ✓ Yes □ No
Note: *Checking "Yes" will not change your tax or reduce your refund.*

Filing Status
Check only one box.

1 □ Single
2 ✓ Married filing joint return (even if only one had income)
3 □ Married filing separate return. Enter spouse's social security no. above and full name here. ▶
4 □ Head of household (with qualifying person). (See page 12.) If the qualifying person is a child but not your dependent, enter this child's name here. ▶
5 □ Qualifying widow(er) with dependent child (year spouse died ▶ 19). (See page 12.)

Exemptions
(See page 12.)

6a ✓ **Yourself.** If your parent (or someone else) can claim you as a dependent on his or her tax return, do not check box 6a. But be sure to check the box on line 33b on page 2.
b ✓ **Spouse** ...
No. of boxes checked on 6a and 6b: **2**

c **Dependents:**

(1) Name (first, initial, and last name)	(2) Check if under age 1	(3) If age 1 or older, dependent's social security number	(4) Dependent's relationship to you	(5) No. of months lived in your home in 1991
Tom T. Becker		456 : 01 : 2347	son	12
Dick L. Becker		012 : 34 : 5678	son	12
Harriet Z. Becker		234 : 56 : 7890	daughter	12

No. of your children on 6c who:
• lived with you **3**
• didn't live with you due to divorce or separation (see page 14) ___
No. of other dependents on 6c ___

If more than six dependents, see page 13.

d If your child didn't live with you but is claimed as your dependent under a pre-1985 agreement, check here ▶ □
e Total number of exemptions claimed
Add numbers entered on lines above ▶ **5**

Income

Attach Copy B of your Forms W-2, W-2G, and 1099-R here.

If you did not get a W-2, see page 10.

Attach check or money order on top of any Forms W-2, W-2G, or 1099-R.

7	Wages, salaries, tips, etc. (attach Form(s) W-2)	7	34,165 00
8a	Taxable interest income (also attach Schedule B if over $400)	8a	500 00
b	Tax-exempt interest income (see page 16). DON'T include on line 8a [8b]		
9	Dividend income (also attach Schedule B if over $400)	9	750 00
10	Taxable refunds of state and local income taxes, if any, from worksheet on page 16	10	
11	Alimony received	11	
12	Business income or (loss) (attach Schedule C)	12	3,600 00
13	Capital gain or (loss) (attach Schedule D)	13	850 00
14	Capital gain distributions not reported on line 13 (see page 17)	14	
15	Other gains or (losses) (attach Form 4797)	15	
16a	Total IRA distributions . [16a] 16b Taxable amount (see page 17)	16b	
17a	Total pensions and annuities [17a] 17b Taxable amount (see page 17)	17b	
18	Rents, royalties, partnerships, estates, trusts, etc. (attach Schedule E)	18	
19	Farm income or (loss) (attach Schedule F)	19	
20	Unemployment compensation (insurance) (see page 18)	20	
21a	Social security benefits. [21a] 21b Taxable amount (see page 18)	21b	
22	Other income (list type and amount—see page 19)	22	
23	Add the amounts shown in the far right column for lines 7 through 22. This is your **total income** ▶	23	39,865 00

Adjustments to Income
(See page 19.)

24a	Your IRA deduction, from applicable worksheet on page 20 or 21	24a	2,000 00	
b	Spouse's IRA deduction, from applicable worksheet on page 20 or 21	24b		
25	One-half of self-employment tax (see page 21)	25	275 00	
26	Self-employed health insurance deduction, from worksheet on page 22	26		
27	Keogh retirement plan and self-employed SEP deduction	27		
28	Penalty on early withdrawal of savings	28		
29	Alimony paid. Recipient's SSN ▶	29		
30	Add lines 24a through 29. These are your **total adjustments** ▶	30		2,275 00

Adjusted Gross Income

31 Subtract line 30 from line 23. This is your **adjusted gross income.** If this amount is less than $21,250 and a child lived with you, see page 45 to find out if you can claim the "Earned Income Credit" on line 56. ▶ | 31 | 37,590 00 |

Cat. No. 11320B

Form 1040 (1991)   Page **2**

	32	Amount from line 31 (adjusted gross income)	**32**	37,590	00

Tax Compu-tation

33a Check if: ☐ **You** were 65 or older, ☐ Blind; ☐ **Spouse** was 65 or older, ☐ Blind.
Add the number of boxes checked above and enter the total here . . ▶ **33a** ☐

If you want the IRS to figure your tax, see page 24.

b If your parent (or someone else) can claim you as a dependent, check here ▶ **33b** ☐

c If you are married filing a separate return and your spouse itemizes deductions, or you are a dual-status alien, see page 23 and check here . . . . ▶ **33c** ☐

34 Enter the **larger** of your:
{ **Itemized deductions** (from Schedule A, line 26), **OR**
Standard deduction (shown below for your filing status). **Caution:** *If you checked **any** box on line 33a or b, go to page 23 to find your standard deduction. If you checked box 33c, your standard deduction is zero.*
• Single—$3,400   • Head of household—$5,000
• Married filing jointly or Qualifying widow(er)—$5,700
• Married filing separately—$2,850 }

			34	7,138	00
	35	Subtract line 34 from line 32	**35**	30,452	00
	36	If line 32 is $75,000 or less, multiply $2,150 by the total number of exemptions claimed on line 6e. If line 32 is over $75,000, see page 24 for the amount to enter	**36**	10,750	00
	37	**Taxable income.** Subtract line 36 from line 35. (If line 36 is more than line 35, enter -0-.) .	**37**	19,702	00
	38	Enter tax. Check if from **a** ☐ Tax Table, **b** ☒ Tax Rate Schedules, **c** ☐ Schedule D, or **d** ☐ Form 8615 (see page 24). (Amount, if any, from Form(s) 8814 ▶ **e** ___.)	**38**	2,955	00
	39	Additional taxes (see page 24). Check if from **a** ☐ Form 4970 **b** ☐ Form 4972 . .	**39**		
	40	Add lines 38 and 39 . . . . ▶	**40**	2,955	00

Credits
(See page 25.)

	41	Credit for child and dependent care expenses *(attach Form 2441)*	**41**				
	42	Credit for the elderly or the disabled *(attach Schedule R)* .	**42**				
	43	Foreign tax credit *(attach Form 1116)*	**43**				
	44	Other credits (see page 25). Check if from **a** ☐ Form 3800 **b** ☐ Form 8396 **c** ☐ Form 8801 **d** ☐ Form (specify)___	**44**				
	45	Add lines 41 through 44	**45**				
	46	Subtract line 45 from line 40. (If line 45 is more than line 40, enter -0-.) . . . . . ▶	**46**	2,955	00

Other Taxes

	47	Self-employment tax *(attach Schedule SE)*	**47**	551	00
	48	Alternative minimum tax *(attach Form 6251)*	**48**		
	49	Recapture taxes (see page 26). Check if from **a** ☐ Form 4255 **b** ☐ Form 8611 **c** ☐ Form 8828 .	**49**		
	50	Social security and Medicare tax on tip income not reported to employer *(attach Form 4137)*	**50**		
	51	Tax on an IRA or a qualified retirement plan *(attach Form 5329)*	**51**		
	52	Advance earned income credit payments from Form W-2 . . . . ▶	**52**		
	53	Add lines 46 through 52. This is your **total tax** . . . . ▶	**53**	3,506	00

Payments

Attach Forms W-2, W-2G, and 1099-R to front.

	54	Federal income tax withheld (if any is from Form(s) 1099, check ▶ ☐)	**54**	4,110	00		
	55	1991 estimated tax payments and amount applied from 1990 return .	**55**	500	00		
	56	**Earned income credit** *(attach Schedule EIC)*	**56**				
	57	Amount paid with Form 4868 (extension request)	**57**				
	58	Excess social security, Medicare, and RRTA tax withheld (see page 27) .	**58**				
	59	Other payments (see page 27). Check if from **a** ☐ Form 2439 **b** ☐ Form 4136	**59**				
	60	Add lines 54 through 59. These are your **total payments** . . . . . ▶	**60**	4,610	00

Refund or Amount You Owe

	61	If line 60 is more than line 53, subtract line 53 from line 60. This is the amount you **OVERPAID** . ▶	**61**	1,104	00
	62	Amount of line 61 to be **REFUNDED TO YOU** . . . . ▶	**62**	1,104	00
	63	Amount of line 61 to be **APPLIED TO YOUR 1992 ESTIMATED TAX** ▶	**63**		
	64	If line 53 is more than line 60, subtract line 60 from line 53. This is the **AMOUNT YOU OWE.** Attach check or money order for full amount payable to "Internal Revenue Service." Write your name, address, social security number, daytime phone number, and "1991 Form 1040" on it.	**64**		
	65	Estimated tax penalty (see page 28). Also include on line 64.	**65**		

Sign Here

Keep a copy of this return for your records.

Under penalties of perjury, I declare that I have examined this return and accompanying schedules and statements, and to the best of my knowledge and belief, they are true, correct, and complete. Declaration of preparer (other than taxpayer) is based on all information of which preparer has any knowledge.

Your signature	Date	Your occupation
Terry B. Becker	4-1-92	Accountant
Spouse's signature (if joint return, BOTH must sign)	Date	Spouse's occupation
Evelyn A. Becker	4-2-92	Sales Clerk

Paid Preparer's Use Only

Preparer's signature	Date	Check if self-employed ☐	Preparer's social security no.
Firm's name (or yours if self-employed) and address ▶		E.I. No.	
		ZIP code	

outside income, during the year they made estimated tax payments totaling $500. The Beckers' records indicate that they had $8,613 of itemized deductions during the year. Finally, Terry Becker plans to contribute $2,000 to his IRA account, something he's been doing for the past six years. He does this each year without fail, not only to reap immediate tax benefits but also because he strongly feels that such investments are an important part of sound retirement planning.

Finding the Beckers' Tax Liability: Form 1040.

An examination of the Beckers' 1991 tax return will show the basic calculations required in preparing Form 1040. Although the supporting schedules are not included here, the basic calculations they require are illustrated. The Beckers have kept detailed records of their income and expenditures, which they use not only for tax purposes but as an important input into their budgeting process. Using this information, the Beckers intend to prepare their 1991 tax return in a fashion that will allow them to reduce their tax liability as much as possible. A hypothetical 1991 tax return for the Beckers is given in Exhibit 4.9; like most married couples, the Beckers file a *joint return.*

Gross Income. The Beckers' gross income in 1991 amounted to $39,865; this is the amount shown as "Total Income" on line 23 of their tax return. Their income is composed of both *active income* and *portfolio income*, as follows:

Active Income

Terry's earnings	$30,415	
Evelyn's earnings	3,750	
Terry's business income (net)	3,600	
Total Active Income		$37,765

Portfolio Income

Interest from savings account	$ 500	
Stock dividends	750	
Capital gains realized	850	
Total Portfolio Income		2,100
Total Income		$39,865

They have no investment expenses to offset their portfolio income, so they'll be liable for taxes on the full amount of portfolio income. Because they have portfolio income, the Beckers will have to file Schedule B (for their interest and dividend income — each of which is in excess of $400) with the 1040 Form. In addition, Terry will have to file Schedule C, detailing the income earned and expenses incurred in his bookkeeping business, and Schedule D to report capital gains income.

Adjustments to (Gross) Income. The Beckers have only two adjustments to income: Terry's IRA contribution and 50 percent of the self employment on Terry's net business income. Because the Beckers fall below the $40,000 income ceiling (just barely), they can deduct all of their $2,000 contribution to an IRA account even if Terry and/or Evelyn are already covered by a company-approved retirement program. Even though they could put more money into the IRA, they have chosen to stick with Terry's $2,000 contribution (see line 24a). Terry's self-employment tax will be 15.3 percent of his $3,600 net business income, and he will be able to deduct one-half that amount — $275 [(.153 × $3,600)/2] — on line 25.

Adjusted Gross Income. After deducting the $2,000 IRA contribution and the $275 self-employment tax from their gross income, the Beckers are left with an adjusted gross income of $37,590, as reported on lines 31 and 32.

Itemized Deductions or Standard Deduction? The Beckers are filing a joint return and neither is over age 65 or blind, so according to Exhibit 4.4 (married filing jointly with zero boxes checked), they are entitled to a standard deduction of $5,700. However, they want to evaluate their itemized deductions before deciding which type of deduction to take — obviously they'll take the highest deduction, because it will result in the lowest amount of taxable income and keep their tax liability to a minimum. Their preliminary paperwork resulted in the following deductions:

Medical and dental expenses	$723
State income and property taxes paid	960
Mortgage interest	5,193
Charitable contributions	475
Job and other expenses	1,262
Total	$8,613

The taxes, mortgage interest, and charitable contributions are deductible in full; so at the minimum, the Beckers will have itemized deductions that amount to $6,628 ($960 + $5,193 + $475). However, to be deductible, the medical and dental expenses and job and other expenses must exceed stipulated minimum levels of adjusted gross income (AGI) — only that portion which exceeds the specified minimum levels of AGI can be included as part of their itemized deductions. For medical and dental expenses, the minimum is 7.5 percent of AGI and for job and other expenses it is 2 percent of AGI. Since 7.5 percent of the Beckers' AGI is $2,819 (.075 × $37,590), they cannot deduct any medical or dental expense — they fall short of the minimum. In contrast, because 2 percent of the Beckers' AGI is $752 (.02 × $37,590), they can deduct any job and other expenses that exceed that amount, or $1,262 − $752 = $510. Adding the amount of their allowable job and other expenses ($510) to their other allowable deductions ($6,628) results in total itemized deductions of $7,138. Since this amount exceeds the standard deduction by a comfortable margin, the Beckers itemize their deductions. The details of these deductions would be provided on Schedule A and attached to the Beckers' 1040 Form. (The total amount of itemized deductions is listed on line 34 of the 1040 Form.)

Personal Exemptions. The Beckers are entitled to claim two exemptions for themselves and another three exemptions for their three dependent children, so they can claim a total of five exemptions. Since each exemption is worth $2,150, they receive a total personal exemption of $10,750 (5 × $2,150), which is the amount listed on line 36.

The Beckers' Taxable Income and Their Tax Liability. Taxable income is found by subtracting itemized deductions *and* personal exemptions from adjusted gross income. Thus, in the Beckers' case, taxable income amounts to $37,590 − $7,138 − $10,750 = $19,702. This is the amount shown on line 37. Given this information, the Beckers can now refer to the tax rate schedule (like the one in Exhibit 4.5) to find their appropriate tax rate and, ultimately, the amount of taxes they'll have to pay. [Note: Since the Beckers' taxable income is less than $50,000, they should use the *tax tables* (not shown) to find their tax. For clarity and convenience, the schedules are used here.] As we can see, the Beckers' $19,702 in taxable income places them in the lowest (15 percent) tax bracket. Note in the tax rate schedule that joint returns with taxable incomes of up to $34,000 fall into the 15 percent tax bracket. At this point, all the Beckers have to do is multiply their taxable income by 15 percent to find their tax liability: $19,702 × .15 = $2,955; this amount is entered on line 38. (Note: Had the tax tables been used, the tax would have been $2,959.) Since they have no tax credits, they also enter this tax liability on line 46. However, the Beckers do owe self-employment (social security) tax on Terry's $3,600 net business income.

This will increase their tax liability by $551 (.153 × $3,600) and would be reported on Schedule SE and entered on line 47 of Form 1040. (Remember 50 percent of this amount — $275 — was deducted on line 25 as an adjustment to gross income.) The Beckers' total tax liability is $3,506 ($2,955 + $551) and is entered on line 53.

Do They Get a Tax Refund? Because the total amount of taxes withheld of $4,110 ($3,560 from Terry's salary and $550 from Evelyn's wages) shown on line 54 plus estimated tax payments of $500 shown on line 55 total $4,610, the Beckers' total tax payments exceed their tax liability, and, as a result, they are entitled to a refund. The amount of the refund is found by subtracting the tax liability (on line 53) from total tax payments (on line 60): $4,610 − $3,506 = $1,104 in tax refund shown on lines 61 and 62. Instead of paying the IRS, they'll be getting money back. (Generally it takes one to two months after a tax return has been filed to receive a refund check.) All the Beckers have to do now is sign their completed 1040 and send it, along with any supporting forms and schedules, to the nearest IRS district office on or before April 15, 1992. As a final point here, because the Beckers are going to receive such a large tax refund, they might want to stop making estimated tax payments because their combined withholdings more than cover the amount of taxes they owe. Another option is to adjust withholding to reduce the amount withheld. Note that if total tax payments had been less than the Beckers' tax liability, they would have owed the IRS money — the amount due is found by subtracting the tax liability from total tax payments made. A check in this amount would then be included with Form 1040 when they filed their tax return.

OTHER FORMS OF PERSONAL TAXES

In addition to federal income taxes, individuals must pay other types of taxes at the federal, state, and local levels. What other taxes might an employed homeowner have to pay? Spend a few moments answering this question before reading on.

Although the largest tax a person will normally pay is federal income taxes, there are other forms of taxes to contend with. For example, additional federal taxes may be levied on income as well as on specific types of transactions. At the state and local levels, sales transactions, income, property ownership, and licenses may be taxed. Because most individuals have to pay many of these other types of taxes, their impact on one's financial condition must be understood. Thus, a person saving to purchase a new automobile costing $15,000 should realize that the state and local sales taxes, as well as the cost of license plates and registration, may add another $1,300 or so to the total cost of the car.

OTHER FEDERAL TAXES

While income taxes are the single most important source of revenue, the federal government also raises funds through social security, excise, and gift and estate taxes. Next to income taxes, the most common form of tax is social security, which is paid by just about every gainfully employed individual except certain federal employees and some state and local governmental employees. None of the federal taxes described in the following sections, including social security, can be claimed as a deduction for federal income tax purposes.

Social Security Taxes.   People probably pay more in social security taxes than in any other form of federal tax except income taxes. In fact, many families (especially those with incomes of less than $15,000 to $20,000 a year) actually pay more in social security taxes than they do in federal income taxes. As noted earlier in this chapter, social security taxes are paid at a uniform, stipulated rate on a specified maximum amount of income earned from sources such as wages, salaries, bonuses, and commissions. The basis for determining the amount of social security taxes due is the total amount of gross earnings before any adjustments, deductions, or exemptions. In essence, *social security taxes are taken out of the first dollar you earn* and continue to be withdrawn up to a specified maximum amount of taxable income. Once you hit that maximum, your social security taxes stop for the year and begin again on January 1.

In 1991, with a social security tax rate of 7.65 percent and maximum taxable earnings of $53,400, the maximum tax was $4,085 (7.65% × $53,400). An additional 1.45 percent Medicare tax was charged on income between $53,400 and $125,000. The maximum wages to which the social security and Medicare tax apply are adjusted each year in response to changes in the cost of living. Note that an amount equal to the employee's contribution is also paid by the taxpayer's employer. In other words, the total amount of social security taxes paid for every wage earner amounts to twice the amount the employee pays (employers are subject to the same tax rates and taxable maximums as employees). Of course, if you earn less than the maximum taxable income, your social security benefits will also be less than the maximum. The social security tax rate, however, remains the same no matter how much or how little you earn. For example, if you earned only $20,000 in 1991, you would have paid social security taxes of only $1,530 (7.65% × $20,000). Keep in mind that the full amount of social security taxes is paid by each wage earner, regardless of what the spouse or any other household member pays.

On the other hand, if an individual works for more than one employer during the year and earns more than the wage base ($53,900 in 1991), he or she is entitled to a tax credit for the amount of overpayment. This credit can be claimed on your federal income tax return (see line 58 of the 1991 Form 1040).

Excise Taxes.   Taxes levied by the federal government on the purchase of certain luxury items and services—such as jewelry, automobiles, gasoline, telephone services, tobacco products, and liquor—are called **excise taxes**. These taxes are added to the purchase price of the products and services and paid at the time of purchase. In recent years many of these excise taxes have been substantially increased in order to increase government revenues and reduce budget deficits. As an example, new cars with a sales price of over $30,000, jewelry and furs costing over $10,000, boats costing over $100,000, and planes costing over $250,000 are subject to a 10 percent excise tax on the amount paid in excess of these stated limits.

Gift and Estate Taxes. The federal and state governments both tax gifts and estates. *Gift taxes* are levied on a gift, must be paid by the *giver*, and are based on the value of the gift. *Estate taxes* are levied on the value of an estate left upon the death of its owner. These taxes reduce the amount of the inheritance passed on to the heirs. A detailed discussion of these taxes is included in Chapter 16 on estate planning.

Other Taxes. Duties on imports, entrance fees to federal facilities such as parks and museums, and taxes on special types of transactions are still other types of federal taxation.

STATE TAXES

In order to raise revenue needed to finance their operations, state governments levy a variety of taxes. Probably the largest source of state revenue is the sales tax, levied on sales transactions. Other sources are income taxes, property taxes, and licensing fees.

State Sales Tax. All states except for a few apply statewide **sales taxes** to most consumer purchases, though some may exempt food, drugs, and/or services. While sales tax rates vary from state to state, most are in the 3 to 6 percent range.

Sales taxes are applied to the amount of the purchases and are levied by the merchant at the point of sale. The merchant is then responsible for remitting their tax receipts to the appropriate state authorities. Most states allow the merchant to retain a small portion of the receipts as payment for performing the collection function. Because sales taxes are tied to purchases, there is really no practical way to avoid them. When making or budgeting for large purchases, you should recognize that sales taxes will add to their cost.

State Income Taxes. Most states currently have personal income taxes, which may range above 15 percent of reported taxable income. Although numerous states have graduated tax rates that increase with taxable income, many have fixed rates that apply to all levels of income. Nearly all states follow the federal law in defining taxable income, though many provide for varying exclusions and adjust-

ments. As a result, the calculation of state taxes is generally similar to that for federal income taxes, which makes filing of state tax returns relatively easy. Like the federal government, most states operate on a pay-as-you-go basis by withholding a portion of income from each paycheck. Many allow taxpayers to deduct federal taxes from taxable income prior to calculating their state tax liability. (Persons who itemize can deduct state income taxes paid for federal tax purposes.) Nearly all states have personal income taxes, although some states tax only certain types of income, such as interest, dividends, and capital gains.

State Property Taxes, Licensing Fees, and Other Taxes. Although most states obtain the vast majority of their revenues from sales and income taxes, some also tax various forms of property, particularly automobiles and other types of motor vehicles. However, as a principal source of revenue, property taxes are levied primarily by *local governments*. State governments also obtain revenues from the sale of automobile licenses and by licensing certain professions. In addition, the vast majority of states have excise taxes on gasoline, tobacco, liquor, and other luxuries. Most also have gift and estate taxes similar to those levied by the federal government (see Chapter 16). Of these miscellaneous types of state taxes, only property taxes are considered deductible for federal income tax purposes.

LOCAL TAXES

Local governments, which include everything from cities and counties to school districts and stadium authorities, levy taxes in order to obtain the

---

excise taxes
Taxes levied at the point of sale on the purchase of certain luxury items and services, such as jewelry, automobiles, gasoline, and tobacco products.

sales taxes
Taxes levied at the point of sale by state and local governments on most consumer purchases, though food, drugs, and/or services may be exempt.

revenues needed to provide a variety of public services. Although the majority of local revenues come from property taxes, local governments often use income taxes, sales taxes, and licensing fees to add to their coffers.

Local Property Taxes. The primary source of revenues to cities, counties, school districts, and other municipalities is the taxation of real estate and other personal property, such as automobiles and boats. Since the largest source of property ownership for most people is their home, the dominant form of **property taxes** is the *real estate tax*. Property taxes are typically collected by the county and then distributed among other governmental units — the city and school district, for example. The value of the property on which taxes are levied is determined by the governmental unit to which taxes are paid. In general, the more expensive the home, the higher the real estate taxes, and vice versa. If deductions are itemized, these taxes can be deducted when calculating federal income taxes. Further discussion of these taxes is included in Chapter 6 on housing.

Local Income Taxes. Local governments — particularly larger cities in the eastern part of the United States — sometimes levy taxes on the incomes of all those employed within their boundaries. These taxes are similar to federal and state income taxes, but the rates are lower — usually about 1 to 2 percent but sometimes as high as 4 to 5 percent of taxable income (an exception is the District of Columbia, which has an income tax rate that rises to above 10 percent). Most city income taxes are withheld and therefore charged on a pay-as-you-go basis, with final settlement made at the end of the year. These taxes are also a deductible itemized expense for federal income tax purposes.

Local Sales Taxes and Licensing Fees. A large number of cities also have sales taxes, which are collected and remitted to the state government by merchants as part of the *total* sales tax on purchased items. The state government, whose levy makes up the major portion of the tax, then returns to the cities their portion of the collections. *Licensing fees*, such as building permits, also provide local

governments with added revenue. In some states, a portion of the fees collected for automobile and other licenses represents a local licensing fee or property tax.

EFFECTIVE TAX PLANNING

Comprehensive tax planning is aimed at reducing taxes immediately as well as in the long run; it involves several activities that are closely tied to other areas of financial planning. How might you go about preparing your immediate and long-run tax plans? Try to answer this question before reading on.

A key ingredient of personal financial planning is *tax planning*. The overriding objective of effective tax planning is to maximize total after-tax income by reducing, shifting, or deferring taxes to as low a level as is legally possible.

Keep in mind that *avoiding* taxes is one thing, but *evading* them is another matter altogether! By all means, don't confuse tax avoidance with **tax evasion**, which includes illegal activities such as omitting income or overstating deductions. Tax evasion, in effect, involves a failure to fairly and accurately report income and/or expenses and, in extreme cases, a failure to pay taxes altogether. Persons found guilty of tax evasion are subject to severe financial penalties and even prison terms. **Tax avoidance**, in contrast, is concerned with reducing taxes in ways that are legal and compatible with the intent of Congress.

Tax avoidance is an illegal practice that could result in financial penalties and even prison sentences. *Fantasy:* Tax avoidance involves reducing taxes in ways that are legal. Tax evasion is illegal and involves improper reporting of income and/or expenses.

FUNDAMENTAL OBJECTIVES OF TAX PLANNING

Tax planning basically involves the use of various investment vehicles, retirement programs, and estate distribution procedures that have the effect of (1) reducing, (2) shifting, or (3) deferring taxes. You can *reduce* taxes, for instance, by using techniques that create tax deductions or credits, or that receive preferential tax treatment — such as investments that produce depreciation (like real estate) or that generate tax-free income (like municipal bonds). You can *shift* taxes by using gifts or trusts to shift some of your income to other family members who are in lower tax brackets and to whom you intend to provide some level of support anyway, such as a retired, elderly parent.

The idea behind *deferring* taxes is to reduce or eliminate your taxes today by postponing them to some time in the future when you may be in a lower tax bracket. Perhaps more important, *deferring taxes gives you use of the money that would otherwise go to taxes* — which you can invest to make even more money. Deferring taxes is usually done through various types of retirement plans, such as individual retirement accounts, by investing in certain types of annuities, variable life insurance policies, or even Series EE savings bonds.

The fundamentals of tax planning include making sure you take all the deductions to which you are entitled and taking full advantage of the various tax provisions that will minimize your tax liability. Thus, comprehensive tax planning is an ongoing activity with both an immediate and long-term perspective. *It plays a key role in personal financial planning* — in fact, one of the major components of a comprehensive financial plan is a summary of the potential tax impacts of various recommended financial strategies. Tax planning is closely interrelated with many financial planning activities, including investment, retirement, and estate planning.

SOME POPULAR TAX STRATEGIES

Managing your taxes is a year-round activity. Because Congress considers tax law changes throughout the year, you may not know all of the applicable regulations until the middle of the year or later. Like other financial goals, tax strategies require frequent review and adjustment when regulations and personal circumstances change.

Tax planning can become very complex at times and may involve rather sophisticated investment strategies. In such cases, especially those involving large amounts of money, you should seek professional help. Many tax strategies, like those suggested in the *Money in Action* box, are fairly simple and straightforward and can be used by the average middle-income taxpayer. You certainly don't have to be in the top income bracket to enjoy the benefits of many (and perhaps most) of these tax-saving ideas and procedures. For example, the interest income on Series EE (U.S. savings) bonds is free from state income tax, and the holder can elect to delay payment of taxes on the federal level until the earlier of the year the bonds are redeemed for cash or the year in which they finally mature. This feature makes Series EE bonds an excellent vehicle for earning tax-deferred income. Some other popular (and fairly simple) tax strategies follow.

Income Shifting.   One way of reducing income taxes is to use a technique known as **income shifting**. Here the taxpayer shifts a portion of his or her

---

property taxes

Taxes typically levied by local and state governments on the value of real estate and certain other personal property in order to raise revenue needed to finance their operations.

tax evasion

The failure to accurately report income and/or expenses and, in extreme cases, a failure to pay taxes altogether.

tax avoidance

The process of reducing taxes in ways that are legal and compatible with the intent of Congress.

income shifting

A technique used to reduce taxes in which a taxpayer shifts a portion of income to relatives in lower tax brackets.

MONEY IN ACTION

Tax Tips That Pay Off

Paying taxes is no fun. If you are like most taxpayers, you try to forget about taxes for most of the year and don't start looking for ways to reduce taxes until near year end. Or, you might think that only the very rich can benefit from tax avoidance strategies. Actually, nearly all taxpayers can employ some of the following tax planning tips, which can lead to significant tax savings and help avoid problems with the IRS.

1. **Don't ignore the technical details of filing a return.** Check your completed return carefully before mailing it to the IRS. Be sure to include all social security numbers (yourself, your spouse, and any dependents over 1 year of age). Check your filing status and make sure you take all exemptions to which you are entitled. Place all schedules and forms in the designated order (alphabetical for schedules; according to sequence number, *not* the form number, for numbered forms). Check and recheck the arithmetic. Always file joint returns with the same name first. Although these details may seem obvious, errors can be costly. The IRS can fine you for omitting social security numbers or necessary forms. Math errors that result in large underpayments of taxes can result in penalties plus interest (compounded *daily*). These and other mistakes can take considerable time to resolve and may delay refunds.

2. **Consider deferring income until next year.** If you are self-employed, receive bonuses, or have income outside of a regular job (such as consulting), you may be able to postpone receipt of income. Whether this strategy will save you money depends on your current and anticipated level of income and tax bracket. By deferring income, you may be able to avoid either qualifying for deduction and exemption phaseouts or moving into a higher tax bracket.

3. **Time your deductible expenses carefully.** Getting as many deductible expenses into one tax year may allow you to increase the amount of allowable deductible expenses, and possibly itemize rather than take the standard deduction. Accelerating and/or bunching deductions can lower your tax liability. For example, paying your fourth quarter state tax estimate before December 31, rather than waiting until January 15, makes the payment deductible for federal tax

income—and thus taxes—to relatives in lower tax brackets. This can be done by creating trusts or custodial accounts or by making outright gifts of income-producing property to family members. For instance, parents with $125,000 of taxable income (31 percent marginal tax rate) and $18,000 in corporate bonds paying $2,000 in annual interest might give the bonds to their 15-year-old child—with the understanding that such income is to be used ulti-mately for the child's college education. The $2,000 would then belong to the child, who would probably have to pay approximately $218 (.15 × [$2,000 − $550 allowable standard deduction]) in taxes on this income, and at the same time the parents' taxable income would be reduced by $2,000 (along with a reduction in their taxes of $620). Unfortunately, this strategy is not as simple as it might at first appear. The Tax Reform Act of 1986 specifies that the invest-

purposes in the current taxable year. The general strategy is to schedule non-reimbursed elective medical procedures and group job and other expenses so that they fall into one tax year. This can raise them above the required "floor" (7.5 percent of adjusted gross income [AGI] for medical expenses and 2 percent of AGI for miscellaneous expenses) and thereby make them eligible for a deduction. If you think you will be in a lower tax bracket next year, you may want to increase discretionary deductions, such as charitable contributions, this year (or, conversely, postpone them if you expect to be in a higher bracket next year).

4. **Consider the tax implications of investment decisions.** While you should *never allow tax considerations to dictate investment decisions*, you should consider tax consequences whenever you plan to sell securities. A review of your portfolio will allow you to assess whether to sell securities to offset other gains or losses. As an example, assume you are in the 31 percent bracket and in April sold stock that resulted in a long-term capital gain of $4,000. If another stock you bought over a year ago is priced below what you paid for it, and you feel that its outlook isn't too promising, you should consider selling it before the end of the tax year in order to use the loss to offset the capital gain, which would be taxed at 28 percent. You may also wish to delay selling a stock until it qualifies for long-term capital gains treatment or to delay selling it at a profit if you don't have offsetting losses available.

5. **Take advantage of employee benefits that reduce income subject to withholding.** Many companies offer flexible spending accounts (FSAs) for medical and dependent-care expenses. The amounts you allocate to these expenses are not subject to federal, state, or social security taxes (except in New Jersey and Pennsylvania). As a result, you can save 25 to 40 percent or more on FSA expenses.

6. **Make contributions to tax-deferred retirement plans.** Contributions to retirement plans such as employer-sponsored 401(k)s, Keogh and simplified employee pension (SEP) plans for the self-employed, and IRAs have a double benefit. Not only is

(continued)

---

ment income of a minor (under the age of 14) is taxed at the same rate as the parents *to the extent that it exceeds $1,100*. For example, if a 5-year-old girl received $2,400 from a trust set up for her by her parents, the first $1,100 of that income (subject to a minimum $550 standard deduction) would be taxed at the child's rate and the remaining $1,300 would be subject to the parents' (higher) tax rate. These restrictions do not apply to children 14 and over, so it is possible to employ such techniques with older children (and presumably, with other older relatives, like elderly parents).

The reason income shifting is allowed in the first place is because there is a positive side to the practice. It is presumed that income shifting is done not only to reduce taxes, but also to build up a pool of savings for the purpose of meeting some specific future outlay such as a child's college education.

(Continued)

the income generated by your contributions tax-deferred, but contributions to Keogh, SEP, and IRA plans reduce AGI; 401(k) contributions, like FSA expenses, are not reported on W-2 forms. (It is always a good idea to check your W-2 to make sure that the amount of your 401(k) contributions is correctly reported.) Dual-income couples should coordinate their retirement plan contributions. It is usually better for each spouse to contribute to his or her employer's plan, particularly where employers match a portion of 401(k) contributions, rather than to have only one spouse make a large retirement plan contribution. Funding these plans early in the year also pays off by allowing the money to accumulate tax-deferred throughout the year.

7. **Check your withholding and make adjustments as required.** At least once a year you should check to make sure that enough is being withheld from your paycheck to avoid penalties for underwithholding. Use last year's tax return and the worksheet that comes with the W-4 form (available from your employer) to determine the amount of withholding that closely matches your estimated tax liability. Withholding should, at minimum, equal either 90 percent of what you estimate you will owe in the current tax year or 100 percent of the tax shown on your prior year's tax return. Be sure to take all allowed extra allowances for itemized deductions and exemptions and adjust withholding as required. If you usually get a refund, you should seriously consider

reducing your withholding accordingly. Even though a refund seems like "found" money, it reflects an opportunity cost because the government pays no interest on the excess funds withheld. Had those funds not been withheld, they could have been invested to earn interest.

8. **Refinance consumer debt with a home equity loan.** Because interest on consumer loans is not tax-deductible, maintaining credit card balances or similar debt is very expensive. The interest rate charged on credit card debt is typically about 19 percent. Using the proceeds of a home equity loan to refinance consumer debt will allow you to deduct interest on loans (up to the $100,000 limit) used for nonhousing purposes.

According to what is known as the "fruit-of-the-tree" doctrine, individuals cannot give away or place in trust income (fruit) alone. Instead, they must also give away the income-producing property (fruit-bearing tree) as well. Additional tax implications of gifts to dependents are discussed in Chapter 16.

Tax Shelters.   **Tax shelters** are forms of investments that take advantage of certain *tax write-offs*. Some real estate (*income-generating* property) and

natural-resource investments (oil and gas drilling) provide these desirable deductions.

The favorable write-offs come from deductions from gross income that are permitted by the IRS but do not involve an actual outlay of cash by the investor. In accounting terminology, these write-offs are called *depreciation, amortization,* or *depletion.* The presence of these noncash expenditures can lower the amount of taxes paid by taxpayers in certain income brackets. Tax-sheltered investments are generally considered to be *passive* investments; the amount of write-offs that can be taken is limited to the amount of income generated. There are a few exceptions, however. This rule does not apply to income-property investments of taxpayers with adjusted gross income under $100,000 and to certain oil and gas investments. Thus, if your income is under $100,000 a year and you own some rental property in which you actively participate, or you invest in an oil or gas drilling partnership, you may be able to benefit from all or most of the associated tax write-offs. Specifically, if your write-offs from these investments exceed the income they generate, you can use the excess write-offs *to shelter your other income*—the net result will be to reduce your taxable income and, therefore, the amount of taxes you have to pay. For example, you could invest in an apartment project that provided both an actual cash return of $5,000 and a depreciation deduction (from gross income) of $9,000. The net result of this investment would be to completely shelter the $5,000 cash income from taxes; even better, given the fact that you met the income limitations, you would have an additional $4,000 write-off ($9,000 − $5,000) that would reduce both your taxable income and tax liability.

An easy way to earn tax-deferred income is to invest in Series EE savings bonds.
Fact: The interest income from a Series EE savings bond can be tax deferred, since the holder can elect to delay payment of taxes until the earlier of the year the bonds are redeemed for cash or the year in which they finally mature.

With the exceptions noted above, the 1986 Tax Reform Act has pretty much eliminated tax-sheltered investments that rely heavily on tax write-offs as the major (or only) source of income. Indeed, many tax-shelter limited partnerships in the past were structured so that all or more of the return from these investments was derived from nothing more than the tax write-offs (and, therefore, the tax savings) they provided. No longer is this true. Today these investments, too, have to stand on their investment merits. Another noteworthy provision written into the law provides that as much as $25,000 in write-offs from *rental real estate* could be used each year

(to offset income from other sources) by people who "actively participate in the rental activity" and whose adjusted gross income is less than $100,000. This provision is phased out completely for adjusted gross incomes of $150,000 or more.

Tax-Free Income, or Tax Deferred? There are some investments that provide tax-free income; in most cases, however, the tax on the income is only deferred (or delayed) to a later date. Although there aren't many forms of tax-free investments left today, probably the best example would be the *interest* income earned on *municipal bonds*. Such income is free from federal income tax. No matter how much interest income you make, you don't have to pay any taxes on it. (Tax-exempt municipal bonds are discussed in Chapter 12.) Income that is **tax deferred**, in contrast, does not cause taxes to be paid now, but delays their payment to a future date. Until that time occurs, however, the advantage of these vehicles is that they allow you to *accumulate earnings* in a tax-free fashion. A good example of tax-deferred income would be income earned in an *individual retirement account* (IRA). See Chapter 15 for a detailed discussion of this vehicle.

Basically, any wage earner can open an IRA account and contribute up to $2,000 a year to the account. Of course, as noted earlier in this chapter, although any employed person can contribute to an IRA, only those people meeting certain pension and/or income constraints can deduct the annual contributions from their tax returns. If you fail to meet these restrictions, you can still have an IRA but you can't deduct the $2,000 annual contribution from your income. So why have an IRA? *Because all the income you earn in your IRA accumulates tax-free!* Since this is a *tax-deferred* form of investment,

tax shelters
Certain types of investments, such as real estate and natural resources, that provide noncash tax write-offs in the form of depreciation, amortization, or depletion.

tax deferred
Income that is not subject to taxes immediately but which will be subject to taxes at a later date.

you'll eventually have to pay taxes on these earnings, but not until you start drawing down your account. Thus, if you were in, say, the 31 percent tax bracket and could not write off your annual IRA deduction, you'd still be well advised to put $2,000 a year into an IRA to obtain the tax-deferred income feature. That is, if you could earn 12 percent before taxes on your investments, you could put $2,000 a year into fully taxable investments and end up with about $152,000 in 25 years. Or you could put the $2,000 each year into a tax-deferred IRA account and (given the same 12 percent rate of return) end up with approx-

imately *$267,000* at the end of 25 years. You'll eventually have to pay taxes on your earnings when you start drawing down your IRA account, but you can't overlook the fact that the tax-deferred IRA investments results in fully *75 percent more income* (that is, $267,000 with the IRA versus $152,000 without). In addition to IRAs, tax-deferred income can also be obtained from certain types of annuities and pension and retirement plans. See Chapter 15 for more information on these financial products and strategies.

SUMMARY

- Because taxes have an impact on most individuals and families, a basic understanding of them is essential for effective financial planning and intelligent money management.
- The dominant tax in our country today is the federal income tax — a levy that provides the government with most of the funds it needs to cover its operating costs. The administration and enforcement of federal tax laws is the responsibility of the Internal Revenue Service (IRS), a part of the U.S. Department of the Treasury. Because the government operates on a pay-as-you-go basis, employers are required to withhold taxes from their employees' paychecks.
- The amount of taxes you owe depends on your filing status and the amount of *taxable income* you report. To find taxable income, start with your *gross* income (which could be made up of active income, portfolio income, and/or passive income); make allowable adjustments to get *adjusted gross income (AGI)*, and subtract from it the amount of deductions and personal exemptions claimed.
- Personal tax returns are filed on or before April 15 by using one of the following forms: 1040EZ, 1040A, or 1040. Persons who have income not subject to withholding may need to file a declaration

of estimated taxes and make estimated tax payments on a quarterly basis. The IRS audits selected returns to confirm their validity by carefully examining the data reported in them. Assistance in preparing returns is available from the IRS, private tax preparers, and computer programs that can be used both for tax preparation and tax planning.
- In addition to federal income taxes, there are sometimes state and/or local income taxes. Other forms of personal taxes that individuals have to pay at the federal, state, or local level include social security taxes, excise taxes, gift and estate taxes, sales taxes, property taxes, and a few other taxes and fees that may not be obvious.
- Effective tax planning is closely tied to other areas of financial planning. The objectives of tax planning are to reduce, shift, and/or defer taxes in such a way that the taxpayer is able to get maximum use/benefits from the money he or she earns. Some of the more popular tax strategies include shifting income to relatives in lower tax brackets, investing in real estate and other types of tax shelters, investing in tax-exempt municipal bonds, setting up individual retirement accounts, and using annuities and pension and retirement plans to generate tax-deferred income.

QUESTIONS AND PROBLEMS

1. Discuss the following items, and explain their significance with respect to personal taxes: (a) Internal Revenue Code of 1939, (b) the IRS,

(c) federal withholding taxes, and (d) FICA. What was the purpose of the Tax Reform Act of 1986?

2. What does *progressive taxation* mean? What is the economic rationale underlying the notion of progressive income taxes?

3. Mo Huang has an opportunity to earn $2,000 working overtime during the Christmas season. He thinks he will turn it down, however, since the extra income would put him in a higher tax bracket and the government would probably get most of it. Discuss Mo's reasoning.

4. Briefly define the five filing categories available to taxpayers. When might married taxpayers choose to file separately?

5. Distinguish between gross earnings and take-home pay. What does the employer do with the difference?

6. What two factors determine the amount of federal withholding taxes that will be deducted from gross earnings each pay period? Explain.

7. Mary Parker is 24 years old, single, lives in an apartment, and has no dependents. Last year she earned $19,600 as a sales representative for Texas Instruments: $1,800 of her wages were withheld for federal income taxes; in addition, she had interest income of $142. Estimate her taxable income, tax liability, and refund or tax due.

8. Tina Marcelle received the following items and amounts of income during 1992. Help her calculate (a) her gross income and (b) that portion (dollar amount) of her income that is tax exempt.

Salary	$9,500
Dividends	800
Gift from mother	500
Child support from ex-husband	2,400
Interest on savings account	250
Rent	900
Loan from bank	2,000
Interest on state government bonds	300

9. Define and differentiate between gross income and adjusted gross income (AGI).

10. If you itemize your deductions, certain taxes may be included as part of your itemized deductions. Discuss two of these taxes, and indicate their source.

11. Larry Tolle was married on January 15, 1992. His wife, Rebecca, is a full-time student at the university and earns $125 a month working in the library. How many personal exemptions will Larry and Rebecca be able to claim on their joint return? Would it make any difference if Rebecca's parents paid for more than 50 percent of her support? Explain.

12. How does a tax credit differ from an itemized deduction? Demonstrate the differences resulting from a $1,000 tax credit versus a $1,000 deduction for a taxpayer in the 28 percent tax bracket with $35,000 of pretax income.

13. Define what is meant by capital gains and capital losses. If Jenny Perez is in the 31 percent tax bracket, calculate the tax associated with each of the following transactions:

a. She sold stock for $1,200 that she purchased for $1,000 five months earlier.

b. She sold bonds for $4,000 that she purchased for $3,000 three years earlier.

c. She sold stock for $1,000 that she purchased for $1,500 eighteen months earlier.

14. Define estimated taxes, and explain under what conditions such tax payments are required.

15. Briefly discuss the tax preparation services available from (a) the IRS, (b) national or local tax preparation services, (c) an enrolled agent, (d) tax attorneys and CPAs, and (e) tax preparation computer software. When is each of these preferred? Discuss the relative costs.

16. Explain how the following are used in filing a tax return: (a) Form 1040, (b) various schedules that accompany Form 1040, and (c) tax rate schedules.

17. Briefly describe several forms of personal taxes other than federal income taxes.

18. Explain each of the following strategies for reducing current taxes; (a) income shifting, (b) tax shelters, and (c) tax deferral.

19. Identify and briefly discuss at least six specific tax strategies that can be used by individuals to reduce their current taxes.

20. John Otsubo graduated from college in 1992 and began work as a systems analyst in July 1992. He is preparing to file his income tax return for 1992 and has collected the following information:

Tuition scholarships and grants	$4,750
Scholarship, room and board	1,850
Salary	13,650
Interest income	185
Deductible expenses, total	3,000
Income taxes withheld	1,600

a. Prepare John's 1992 tax return, using the standard deduction amount given in Exhibit 4.4, a personal exemption of $2,150, and the tax rates given in Exhibit 4.5. Which tax form should John use, and why?

3,800 —

b. Prepare John's 1992 tax return using the data in part (a) along with the following information:

IRA contribution	$1,000
Cash dividends received	$150

Which tax form should he use in this case? Why?

21. Milo Whitehead is married and has one child. He is currently in the process of putting together some figures so he can prepare their joint 1992 tax return. So far, he's been able to determine the following:

- He can claim three personal exemptions (including himself)
- Total unreimbursed medical expenses incurred: $1,155
- Gross wages and commissions earned: $38,820

- IRA contribution: $2,250
- Mortgage interest paid: $5,200
- Capital gains realized: $1,450
- Income from limited partnership: $200
- Job expenses and other allowable deductions: $875
- Interest paid on credit cards: $380
- Dividend and interest income earned: $610
- Sales taxes paid: $2,470
- Charitable contributions made: $1,200
- Capital losses incurred: $3,475
- Interest paid on a car loan: $570
- Alimony paid by Milo to first wife: $6,000
- Social security taxes paid: $2,750
- Property taxes paid: $700
- State income taxes paid: $1,700

Given the above information, how much taxable income will the Whiteheads have in 1992? (*Note:* Assume Milo is covered by a pension plan where he works, the standard deduction amounts in Exhibit 4.4 are applicable, and each exemption claimed is worth $2,150.)

CONTEMPORARY CASE APPLICATIONS

4.1 The Aggarwals Tackle Their Tax Return

Sabash and Sue Aggarwal are a married couple in their early 20s living in Dallas. Sabash earned $30,000 in 1992 from his job as a sales manager with Carson Corporation. During the year, his employer withheld $2,900 for income tax purposes. In addition, the Aggarwals received interest of $350 on a joint savings account, $750 interest on tax-exempt municipal bonds, and a dividend of $400 on jointly owned stocks. At the end of 1992, the Aggarwals sold two stocks, A and B. Stock A was sold for $700 and had been purchased four months earlier for $800. Stock B was sold for $1,500 and had been purchased three years earlier for $1,100. Their only child, Rohn, age 2, received (as his sole source of income) dividends of $200 on stock of Kraft, Inc.

In spite of the fact that Sabash was covered by his Carson Corporation's pension plan, he planned to contribute $2,000 to an IRA for 1992. Following are the amounts of money paid out during the year by the Aggarwals:

Medical and dental expenses (unreimbursed)	$200
State and local property taxes	831
Interest paid on home mortgage	4,148
Charitable contributions	1,360
Total	$6,539

In addition, Sabash incurred some travel costs (not reimbursed) for an out-of-town business trip as follows:

Airline ticket	$250
Taxis	20
Lodging	60
Meals (as adjusted to 80% of cost)	36
Total	$366

Questions

1. Using the above information, prepare a joint tax return for Sabash and Sue Aggarwal for the year ended December 31, 1992, in a manner that will result in the smallest tax liability — that is, either itemize their deductions or take the standard deduction. (Note: Use Form 1040 and the tax schedule in Exhibit 4.5 to determine the Aggarwals' taxes. Assume the standard deduction amounts in Exhibit 4.4 are applicable and each exemption claimed is worth $2,150.)

2. How much have you saved the Aggarwals as a result of your treatment of their deductions?

3. Discuss whether the Aggarwals need to file a tax return for their son.

4. Suggest some tax strategies that the Aggarwals might use to reduce their tax liability for next year.

◼ 4.2 Joan Cavander: Bartender or Tax Expert?

Joan Cavander, who is single, is a bartender at the Twin Towers Supper Club in Atlanta. During the past year (1992), her gross income was $17,500 made up of wages and tips. She has decided to prepare her own tax return, since she cannot afford the services of a tax expert. After preparing her return, she has come to you for advice. The following is a summary of the figures she has prepared thus far:

Gross income:	Wages	$9,500
	Tips	8,000
Adjusted gross income (AGI)		$17,500
Less: Itemized deductions		2,300
		$15,200
Less: Standard deduction		3,400
	Taxable income	$11,800

Joan believes that if an individual's income falls below $20,350, the federal government considers him or her "poor" and allows both itemized deductions and a standard deduction.

Questions

1. Calculate Joan Cavander's taxable income, being sure to consider her exemption. (Assume the standard deduction amounts in Exhibit 4.4 are applicable and each exemption claimed is worth $2,150.)

2. Discuss with Joan her errors in interpreting the tax laws, and explain the difference between itemized deductions and the standard deduction.

3. Joan has been dating Sam Haley for nearly four years, and they are seriously thinking about getting married. Sam has income and itemized deductions identical to Joan's. How much tax would they pay as a married couple (filing a joint return) versus the total amount the two paid as single persons (filing separate individual returns)? Strictly from a tax perspective, does it make any difference whether Joan and Sam stay single or get married? Explain.

FOR MORE INFORMATION

General Information Articles

Jasen, Georgette. "Marriage Can Tie Knots in Tax Planning." *The Wall Street Journal*, November 5, 1990, p. C1.

McCormally, Kevin. "How to Boost Your Take-Home Pay." *Changing Times*, May 1991, pp. 33–35.

———. "How to Pay Lower Taxes." *Kiplinger's Personal Finance Magazine*, October 1991, pp. 36–40.

———. "Taking the Pain Out of Taxes." *Kiplinger's Personal Finance Magazine*, February 1992, pp. 54–58.

———. "Taxes: Software to the Rescue." *Changing Times*, February 1991, pp. 56–58.

Ratan, Suneel. "Tax Tips for a Tricky Year." *Fortune*, March 9, 1992, pp. 122–124.

Smith, Marguerite T. "How to Avoid 13 Costly Tax Errors." *Money*, March 1991, pp. 84–93.

Tritch, Teresa. "Cut Your Taxes Once and for All." *Money*, August 1991, pp. 83–95.

Tritch, Teresa, and Deborah Lonse. "Taxpayers, Start Worrying!" *Money*, March 1992, pp. 88–96.

Government Documents and Other Publications

Bernstein, Peter, ed. *The Ernst & Young Tax Guide, Annual* (New York: Wiley, annual).

———. *Ernst & Young's Tax-Saving Strategies, Annual* (New York: Wiley, annual).

Esaner, Warren, et al. *Consumer Reports Books Guide to Income Tax Preparation, Annual* (Yonkers, NY: Consumer Reports Books, annual).

J. K. Lasser's Your Income Tax, Annual (New York: Prentice-Hall, annual).

Student's Guide to Federal Income Tax, Internal Revenue Service, Publication 4 (Washington, DC: U.S. Government Printing Office, annual).

Your Federal Income Taxes, Annual, Internal Revenue Service, Publication 17 (Washington, DC: U.S. Government Printing Office, annual).

GETTING A HANDLE ON YOUR FINANCIAL FUTURE

It has been said that nothing is certain except death and taxes. More than likely, unless you take a vow of poverty, you will be faced with a lifetime of coping with various types of taxes. While some would believe that a reasonable financial goal would be to minimize taxes paid, in actuality you should be trying to maximize your after-tax income. You can certainly minimize your tax liability, for example, by working less or investing in lower-yielding tax-free bonds. However, this would also reduce the after-tax income which is available to fund your expenditures and provide money to invest for long-term goals.

The major types of taxes that we must pay include income, sales, social security, and property taxes. By far the most dominant tax that we pay is the federal income tax. The amount and type of income you report and your filing status on your returns have a significant bearing on your tax liability.

Your income tax liability is based on your taxable income, not your gross income. To arrive at taxable income you first have to determine your adjusted gross income (AGI), which is found by reducing gross income by certain allowable deductions such as IRA contributions and alimony payments. To get taxable income, you must reduce your AGI by the amount of your itemized deductions or the standard deduction, whichever is greater, and by an amount based on the number of personal exemptions you claim. This is your taxable income, upon which your tax liability is calculated.

Your actual tax paid could be lower than the calculated liability if you are eligible for certain tax credits that reduce, dollar for dollar, your tax liability. Examples of these credits are for such items as child and dependent care or credit for the elderly or permanently disabled.

In order to achieve the financial goals that you have set, you need to maximize your after-tax income. You can accomplish this by understanding how different sources of income are taxed. You should strive for the optimal combination of the

If You Are Just Starting Out

For most of you just beginning your careers, your taxes are relatively simple. Most, if not all, of your gross income is in the form of wages and salaries, and the standard deduction almost always is greater than itemized deductions. As a result, filling in your income tax return is simply a matter of taking the income information off of the W-2 form (plus any interest and dividend income from Form 1099) to arrive at your gross income. After adjusting for perhaps an IRA contribution, you arrive at your adjusted gross income. Subtracting the standard deduction and the personal exemption gives you taxable income, to which you apply the appropriate tax rate to get your tax liability. To see if any more tax is owed or a refund is due, simply compare the tax liability to what was withheld on your W-2 form.

As simple as this sounds, there are a number of potential problems that could be avoided through good recordkeeping and sound tax planning.

Recordkeeping:

1. You should begin your tax-paying career with a basic understanding of which expenditures are tax deductible so that you can maintain adequate records.

2. If you have a ledger book (or computerized ledger) that you use for your cash budget, as you record your actual expenditures, which you should compare to the budgeted amounts, also record which of the expenditures are tax deductible.

3. Set aside a certain time of day or day of the month to regularly update your records.

4. Keep track of cash contributions to charitable organizations, as these are easily forgotten.

5. Remember that a canceled check is not necessarily proof of payment to the IRS, so keep invoices and receipts as well.

Tax Planning:

1. Review your employee benefits very carefully to determine potential tax savings features.

2. If your employer offers a tax deferred savings plan, such as a 401(k) plan, your participation would reduce your gross income.

3. Where possible pay for health and dependent-care expenditures with pretax dollars through your employer's flexible spending plan.

4. Consider preparing and filing your own tax return, if it is relatively straightforward, or let the IRS compute your tax for you.

5. If income limits allow, set up an IRA account.

types of income that will minimize your taxes by making sure that you have taken advantage of all allowable deductions and exemptions in arriving at your tax liability.

Remember that the tax laws are going to change over time. These changes will be a result of actions that you take, as well as the whims of Congress and state and local governments. Some of the changes will lower your taxes, while others will increase them. As H. L. Mencken said, "No man's life, liberty or property are safe while the legislature is in session."

If You Are Thirtysomething

As time goes by, your tax returns usually become more complex as your marital and family status evolve and you accumulate a wider variety of financial and personal assets. As a result of this complexity, tax planning becomes more important. This involves the use of different investment vehicles, retirement programs, and estate distribution procedures.

In order to minimize your tax burden, you should utilize one of the following strategies: (1) attempt to reduce your taxes through use of deductions, credits, and income subject to preferential tax treatment; (2) shift income to others; or (3) defer taxes. All of these methods require careful consideration on the part of the taxpayer and his or her advisor, as well as increase the need for a formalized record-keeping system to support the decisions if questioned by the IRS.

Recordkeeping:

1. As your marital and family status change, so do the types of expenditures that may favor the use of itemized deductions over the standard deduction, but you must have good records.

2. Keep all records involving expenditures on home improvements because, although they are not deductible, they add to the basis in the house and will reduce taxes due upon sale.

3. If you have children in a day-care center, the expense may be eligible for a child-care credit or could be paid through your employer's flexible spending plan. Regardless of the method of payment, adequate records are essential.

4. Keep good records of interest and dividend income and check them against Form 1099s to ensure correct reporting of investment income.

5. Remember that the IRS can take as long as three years from the date of filing for an audit. Therefore you should keep most of your tax records for at least this long.

Tax Planning:

1. At the end of the year you might want to delay receipt of income and recognize losses in order to reduce your tax liability.

2. You could invest in assets that receive preferential tax treatment such as real estate or tax-free municipal bonds.

3. Income can be shifted to others in lower tax brackets through the use of gifts and trusts.

4. Taxes can be deferred by making pretax contributions to retirement plans or buying Series EE bonds and electing not to claim the interest as current income.

5. Invest in assets with low current income but high growth potential, such as common stocks.

Mark and Ana Williams, who were introduced to you at the end of Chapter 1, would like your help in starting their financial plan. Review the Williams' financial and personal information on pages 36–50 before answering the following questions.

1. Using the January, 1993 asset and liability information, develop a balance sheet for Mark and Ana Williams. Assume they have no unpaid bills.

2. Using the income and expenditure information for 1992, complete an income and expenditure statement for Mark and Ana. Use the "cash flow" concept for this financial statement including all money inflow as income and all outflows as expenditures.

3. Based on their financial statements, calculate the following ratios:

   ■ Savings ratio
   ■ Liquidity ratio
   ■ Solvency ratio
   ■ Debt service ratio

4. Based on the information in the original case and in their financial statements, state at least three positive and three negative aspects of Mark and Ana's current financial position.

After reading Chapter 3, you probably realize that Mark and Ana's financial goals are not defined well enough in the original case to serve as the basis for their financial plan and cash budget. Upon further discussion they have restated their financial goal as follows:

   ■ To buy a $90,000 condominium as soon as possible. Mark's grandmother has promised a $5,000 gift to help with the down payment. They are willing to sell their shares of stock and/or mutual fund to pay for the rest of the down payment and closing costs.
   ■ To have a total of $7,000 accumulated in money market accounts/funds in two years, to be used as their emergency fund.
   ■ To pay off all of their revolving credit debt within the next year.
   ■ To save $3,000 as a buffer account for the birth of their first child in three years.
   ■ To save $15,000 for a down payment and closing costs on a new house in six years. They plan to keep their condo as a rental real estate investment.
   ■ To each contribute $1,000 a year to their respective 401(k) retirement accounts.
   ■ To establish a regular savings program in an amount that will accomplish their stated goals.

5. How much would Mark and Ana have to save this year to be on track in meeting their goals for:

   ■ Their emergency fund (remember they already have $4,025 in their money market account)

   ■ The buffer account for their first child's birth

   ■ A new house (not the condominium)

   ■ Each of their 401(k) retirement accounts?

Use future value calculations for goals that will be achieved over two or more years. Assume Mark and Ana can earn 5 percent after taxes on their savings.

6. Prepare a cash budget for Mark and Ana for 1993 using the income and expenditure data from their original case as well as the figures from Question 5 needed to meet their goals. In addition, Mark and Ana would need to make monthly payments totaling approximately $575 rather than the $354 minimum monthly payments in order to pay off their revolving credit debt within the next year. (It is greater than the $523 a month you get when you divide their revolving debt of $6,275 by 12 because interest would continue to accrue until the debts were paid off.) Assume that income and other expenditures for the upcoming year will be the same as the current year *except* that there will be no sale of securities.

7. Can Mark and Ana achieve all of their stated goals considering their current income and expenditure patterns? If not, what recommendations would you make to help them achieve their goals? If they have trouble agreeing on how their money should be spent, what could they do that might make both of them feel better about their budget?

8. Prepare a 1992 tax return (Form 1040) for Mark and Ana using the financial data in the original case. Do they owe more taxes, or will they receive a refund? How much?

9. Assuming that 1993 will be similar to 1992, should they make any adjustments to their withholding allowances? If the answer is yes, should they increase or decrease the number of withholding allowances claimed?

10. What is Mark and Ana's average tax rate? What is their marginal tax rate?

11. Approximately how much would they save in taxes next year if they did invest $2,000 in their 401(k) retirement accounts? (This move would reduce their taxable income by $2,000.)

12. What tax strategies would you recommend to help Mark and Ana reduce their tax liability?

WILLIAMS *Current Position*

PART two

Managing Basic Assets

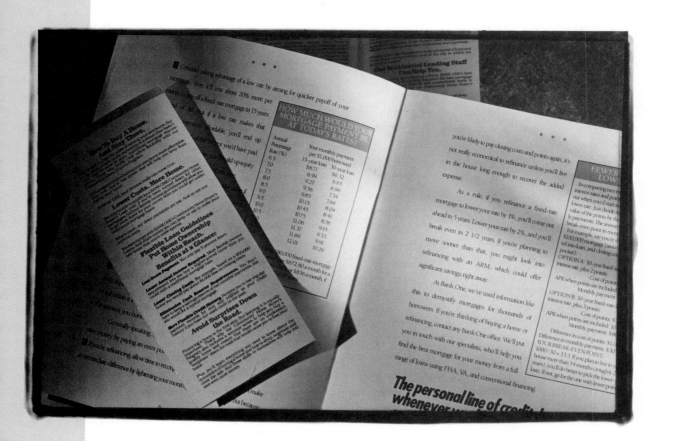

CHAPTER 5 *Managing Your Savings and Other Liquid Assets*

CHAPTER 6 *Making Housing and Other Major Acquisitions*

CHAPTER 5

Managing Your Savings and Other Liquid Assets

How would you like to receive $3,000 a month? Wouldn't be bad, would it? Think of what you could buy and do if you knew you would have $3,000 flowing in month after month. If this sounds farfetched, then stop for a moment and consider the fact that this could very well happen to you in just a few short years. Actually an individual earning $50,000 per year takes home (after taxes) about $3,000 a month. While it's true that most college graduates do not initially earn $50,000 a year, many young, two-income couples do. Unfortunately, those who realize that level of income often spend it on relatively meaningless purchases (which is all too easy to do). Handling it wisely requires establishing financial goals and cash budgets as discussed in Chapter 3. It also requires managing your cash resources efficiently, using one or more financial institutions and checking and savings products. This chapter introduces you to the basics of cash management, describes today's complex financial services marketplace, and discusses the key aspects of savings programs, checking accounts, and other banking services.

THE ROLE OF CASH MANAGEMENT IN PERSONAL FINANCIAL PLANNING

Cash management involves making sure that you have funds available for planned and unplanned expenditures and that your spending patterns are within budgetary limits. What methods do you currently employ in order to make sure that you pay bills promptly and have funds available for unexpected expenditures? Before reading on, spend a few moments answering this question.

This chapter is concerned with **cash management**—an activity that deals with the routine, day-to-day administration of cash and near-cash resources. We identified these resources in Chapter 2 as *liquid assets*. They are considered liquid because they are either held in cash or can be readily converted to cash with little or no loss in value. In addition to cash, there are several other kinds of liquid assets, including checking accounts, savings accounts, money market accounts and funds, and other short-term investment vehicles. Exhibit 5.1 provides a list and brief description of the more popular types of liquid assets and the representative rates of return they earned in early 1992. As a rule, near-term needs are met using cash on hand, and unplanned or future needs are met using some type of savings or short-term investment vehicle.

In personal financial planning, cash management is the way you make sure that funds are available for making household outlays as well as establishing an effective savings program. The success of your financial plans depends on your faithfulness to established cash budgets. An effective way of keeping your spending in line is to make all household transactions (even the allocation of fun money or weekly cash allowances) using a tightly controlled *checking account*. In effect, you should write checks only at certain times of the week or month and, more important, you should avoid carrying your checkbook with you when you might be tempted to write checks for unplanned purchases. If you are going shopping, establish a maximum spending limit beforehand—ideally, an amount consistent with your cash budget. Such a system will not only help you avoid frivolous, impulsive expenditures, but it will also provide valuable documentation on how and where you are spending your money. Then, if your financial outcomes are not consistent with your plans, you can better identify causes and initiate appropriate corrective actions.

Another aspect of cash management, establishing an ongoing savings program, is an important part of personal financial planning. Savings are not only a cushion against financial emergencies but also a vehicle for accumulating funds for meeting future financial goals. You may want to put money aside so you can go back to school in a few years to earn a graduate degree, or to buy a new home, or perhaps to take a luxury vacation—these are all examples of specific financial objectives that can be met through savings. There are many different ways to save; some are better suited to accumulating emergency funds, and others are more appropriate for building reserves for future expenditures. Clearly specifying the objectives of your savings program is a prerequisite to selecting appropriate savings vehicles.

An asset is considered liquid only if it is held in the form of cash.
Fantasy: A liquid asset is one that is held in cash or can be readily converted to cash with little or no loss in value; thus, liquid assets include checking accounts, savings accounts, money market accounts and funds, and other short-term investment vehicles.

THE NEW FINANCIAL MARKETPLACE

Because of deregulation, the financial markets and institutions of today are vastly different (and greatly improved) from what they were five to ten years ago. Many of today's financial institutions provide a full menu of financial products and services. What are some of the financial products and services available from major financial institutions in your area? Spend a few moments listing them before reading on.

EXHIBIT 5.1
Popular Liquid Assets

The wide variety of savings vehicles available makes it possible to meet just about any savings or short-term investment need.

Type	Representative Rates of Return (Early 1992)	Description
Cash	0%	Pocket money — the coin and currency in one's possession.
Checking Account	2.0–3.0%	A substitute for cash. Offered by commercial banks as well as other financial institutions such as savings and loans and credit unions.
Savings Account	3.0–4.0%	Money is available at any time but cannot be withdrawn by check. Offered by banks and other financial institutions.
Money market deposit account (MMDA)	3.5–4.0%	Primarily a savings vehicle that pays market rates of interest. Offers limited check-writing privileges and requires a fairly large (typically $1,000 or more) minimum deposit.
Money market mutual fund (MMMF)	4.3%	Savings vehicle that is actually a mutual fund (not offered by banks, S&Ls, and other depository institutions). Like an MMDA, it also offers check-writing privileges.
Certificate of deposit (CD)	4.0–5.0%	A savings instrument where funds are left on deposit for a stipulated period of time (one week to one year or more); imposes a penalty for withdrawing funds early. Market yields vary by size and maturity; no check-writing privileges.
U.S. Treasury bill (T-bill)	4.0%	Short-term, highly marketable security issued by the U.S. Treasury (originally issued with maturities of 13, 26, and 52 weeks); smallest denomination is $10,000.
U.S. savings bond (EE)	5.6%	Issued by U.S. Treasury: rate of interest is tied to U.S. Treasury securities. Long a popular savings vehicle (widely used with payroll deduction plans). Maturities are approximately five years; sold in denominations of $50 and more.

Prior to the 1970s, there was no real competition in the financial marketplace. The distinctions between various kinds of financial institutions were clear. Commercial banks offered checking accounts and short-term loans. Savings banks offered savings accounts and real estate mortgage loans. Brokerage firms assisted in trading securities. And insurance companies offered life, disability, health, auto, and homeowner's insurance. This segmented market changed in the early 1980s with passage of the *Depository Institutions Deregulation and Monetary Control Act of 1980*. This important law, together with additional legislation passed in 1982, removed many restrictions on banks and savings institutions and allowed them to compete with each other and with nonbank financial institutions.

As a result of deregulation, the differences between financial institutions have blurred considerably. Many now offer the same services and compete directly for your business. For example, at some banks you can make securities transactions and buy insurance, while stockbrokers offer check-writing services and make loans. Today, it is difficult to distinguish between the numerous providers of financial products and services.

From the viewpoint of the individual consumer, today's financial marketplace is far superior to that of just ten years ago. Most noticeable are the wider array of financial products and services, and the more competitive rates of return. The price of these benefits appears to be today's generally higher costs of financial services.

cash management
The routine, day-to-day administration of cash and near-cash resources by an individual or family.

FINANCIAL SUPERMARKETS: ONE-STOP FINANCIAL CENTERS

During the 1980s, an important trend in the financial services industry was the evolution of the large, diversified **financial supermarket** that provided "one-stop shopping" for all financial needs. Customers could obtain a wide array of financial products under one roof, including checking, savings, securities brokerage, insurance, and retirement and estate planning. It was no longer necessary to go one place to do your banking, a second to buy insurance, and a third to trade securities. You could go to the store and, while shopping, look into that renter's insurance policy you were considering or make a deposit into your money market mutual fund.

The development of financial supermarkets was a natural outcome of the growing list of institutional participants that, thanks to deregulation, widened their range of financial products and services. In addition to the traditional banking and savings outlets (commercial banks, S&Ls, savings banks, and credit unions), adopters of the financial supermarket approach included many of the major insurance companies, most of the major national and regional brokerage firms, a number of mutual funds, and other financial companies such as American Express and Household Finance. Also becoming a growing force are the nonfinancial firms such as Sears, General Motors, and General Electric. For instance, Sears, Roebuck and Company's "Sears Financial Network" offered a broad range of financial services, from stock brokerage to insurance, and was widely touted as a model financial supermarket. Other examples of financial supermarkets included American Express (credit card, insurance, investments, and other services) and Prudential Insurance (insurance and investment services).

But in late 1992 Sears began to dismantle its supermarket by selling its Dean Witter Financial Services unit, which included both stock brokerage and Discover card operations, most of its Coldwell Banker real estate holdings, and 20 percent of its Allstate insurance unit. At the same time, a number of other emerging financial supermarkets were rumored to be preparing to dismantle their operations.

Apparently, the break-up of the one-stop financial supermarket resulted from an inability to achieve the expected benefits of combining a number of financial service firms. Although the financial supermarket may be on its way to extinction, specialization within the financial institutions industry continues to decrease as many institutions offer similar services. Consumers can still obtain several types of financial services from a single institution. For example, today it is difficult to tell a savings and loan from a commercial bank, since both offer so many of the same financial products and services; in fact, S&Ls as well as credit unions are now commonly referred to as "banks," much to the chagrin of commercial bankers. And in response to competition from nonfinancial institutions, many banks and S&Ls have begun to offer help with personal financial planning, to take deposits across state lines, sell insurance, and offer discount brokerage services.

Thus, the *financial services* industry as we know it today embraces all institutions that market various kinds of *financial products*, such as checking and savings accounts, credit cards, loans and mortgages, insurance, and mutual funds, and *financial services*, such as financial planning, taxes, real estate, trusts, retirement, and estate planning. In effect, what used to be several distinct (though somewhat related) industries is now, in essence, one industry.

One-stop financial supermarkets will be the dominant source of financial services for consumers during the 1990s.

Fantasy: Large financial supermarkets offer a wide array of services, including checking and savings accounts, credit cards, loans and mortgages, brokerage, mutual funds, insurance, and financial planning. These one-stop financial centers appeared to be gaining in popularity during the late 1980s and early 1990s. However, the trend toward larger, more comprehensive financial services institutions was reversed in late 1992, when Sears Roebuck announced that it was disbanding its Sears Financial Network, and it was expected that several other emerging financial supermarkets would follow suit.

TRADITIONAL FINANCIAL INSTITUTIONS: "BANKS"

In spite of the presence of financial supermarkets and the growing number of firms entering the financial services field, individuals and families continue to make the vast majority of their financial transactions at traditional financial institutions: commercial banks, savings and loan associations, savings banks, and credit unions. Although these are organized and regulated by different agencies, they are frequently referred to as "banks" due to the similarity of their product and service offerings. Compared to their nonbanking counterparts, probably the two biggest advantages these institutions have over their competition is that they are familiar and convenient. Further, while most people have checking and savings accounts, a much smaller number own stocks, bonds, or mutual funds. As a result, most people are not accustomed to dealing with brokerage firms and other types of financial service companies.

Commercial Banks.   To millions of Americans, banking means doing business with a **commercial bank**. Of the four types of traditional financial institutions, commercial banks are by far the largest. In addition to checking accounts, commercial banks offer a full array of financial services, including a variety of savings vehicles, credit cards, several kinds of loans, trust services, and such items as safe-deposit boxes, traveler's checks, and check-cashing privileges. It is little wonder that they are commonly called *full-service banks*.

Commercial banks are the only financial institutions that can offer *noninterest-paying checking accounts* (demand deposits) — a feature that in today's deregulated financial market provides little competitive advantage. Therefore, commercial banks also offer a variety of checking accounts that combine check-writing privileges with features of savings accounts. In addition, they offer several types of pure savings accounts. Most prevalant among these is the *passbook account*, which is a regular savings account on which interest is paid. There is no limit on how much interest a bank can pay on its passbook accounts, so it clearly pays to shop around. However, most passbook accounts still pay low (2 to 4 percent) interest rates. Whereas to many savers, passbook accounts are simply a convenient way of accumulating money, for many others, they represent the only savings or investment vehicle used. Rather than giving each account holder a passbook in which to record all transactions, most banks today issue separate deposit/withdrawal receipts and at the end of the quarter send each depositor a statement itemizing all account transactions during the period.

Commercial banks typically differentiate between their *special savings accounts* on the basis of deposit minimums. For higher minimums they offer a slightly higher rate of interest (.25 to .5 percent) than on accounts requiring lower or no minimum balance. If the account holder does not maintain the required minimum balance, the interest is usually paid on the account as if it were an account requiring no minimum balance.

In addition to offering a variety of special savings accounts, many banks offer *club accounts*. These accounts are established for a special purpose, such as saving money for Christmas shopping. They act as a budgeting device for the customer by requiring specified weekly or monthly deposits toward the particular savings goal — for example, $500 for Christmas shopping. To assist club members in keeping track of scheduled deposits, banks often issue some type of coupon book showing the date and amount of each transaction. Club accounts generally pay less interest than passbook accounts, since the bank must perform additional clerical chores in order to establish and maintain them.

With the variety of products and services and range of fees offered to commercial banks, choosing a bank is no simple matter. Many variables have to be considered.

Savings and Loan Associations.   Savings and loan associations (S&Ls) are found in most parts of the country. One type of S&L is a *mutual association*, in which the depositors actually own

---

financial supermarket
A financial or nonfinancial institution that offers consumers a wide array of financial products and services under one roof.

commercial bank
A financial institution that offers checking and savings accounts and a full range of financial products and services, including several types of consumer loans. It's the only institution that can offer non-interest-paying checking accounts (demand deposits).

savings and loan association (S&L)
A financial institution that channels the savings of its depositors primarily into mortgage loans for purchasing and improving homes. Due to deregulation, however, S&Ls now offer a competitive range of financial products and services.

the institution and the returns they receive technically are called *dividends* rather than *interest*. (Note: In finance, the word *mutual* indicates a type of cooperative ownership arrangement.) Although these payments are called dividends, they are treated as interest for all practical purposes. The other type of S&L is *stockholder owned*: Depositors in this case actually do receive interest on their deposits instead of dividends.

Regardless of their organizational structure, savings and loans are important because they channel people's savings into mortgage loans for purchasing and improving homes. Since deregulation, S&Ls have greatly expanded their product and service offerings. Although they still cannot offer noninterest-paying checking accounts (demand deposits), they do offer many of the same checking, savings, and lending products and services as commercial banks — in fact, it is difficult to differentiate between the two institutions. Typically savings deposits at S&Ls earn about .25 to .5 percent more than those at commercial banks. The availability of products and services at numerous branch offices and their attractive rates of interest contribute to the popularity of savings and loan associations.

Savings Banks. **Savings banks** are a special type of savings institution, similar to savings and loan associations and found primarily in the New England states. In addition to offering a number of different interest-paying checking accounts, they accept a variety of savings deposits on which they pay interest at a rate on par with that paid by savings and loans. Because most savings banks are *mutuals*, depositors are their actual owners. The savings bank accepts deposits and, after deducting the expenses of doing business, distributes the profits to the owners in the form of dividend payments, which are technically equivalent to interest payments. However, instead of distributing all profits, the mutual savings bank typically distributes only enough to provide depositors with a stated return of, say, 3.5 percent. It then reinvests any remaining profits in order to provide greater protection for depositors.

Credit Unions. A **credit union** is a special type of mutual association that provides financial products and services to specific groups of people who belong to a common occupation, religious or fraternal order, or residential area. Credit unions are owned (and, in some cases, operated) by their members. Although credit unions are used by over 50 million people, they are quite small when compared to commercial banks or S&Ls. A person who qualifies for membership in a credit union may buy a share by making a minimum deposit — often $5 or less. One *must* be a member — that is, have money on deposit — in order to borrow from a credit union. Because the credit union is run to benefit the members, the rate of interest it pays on savings is normally .5 to 1.5 percent above that paid by other savings institutions. Being a mutual association in which the savers own shares, credit unions technically pay dividends rather than interest on savings.

Most credit unions, in addition to offering different types of interest-paying checking accounts — called **share draft accounts** — offer a variety of savings accounts to their members. Savers often do not know the dividend rate until the end of the savings period, since the dividends paid in each period depend on the credit union's earnings for that period. Since credit unions not only yield a favorable return on members' savings but also allow them to borrow money at advantageous rates, they are attractive to many people.

THE GROWING MENU OF CHECKING AND SAVINGS PRODUCTS

People basically hold cash and other forms of liquid assets, like checking and savings accounts, for the convenience they offer in (1) making purchases; (2) meeting normal, recurring living expense and purchase requirements; and (3) providing a safety valve (or cushion) for meeting unexpected expenses or taking advantage of unanticipated opportunities. As mentioned before, the competition caused by deregulation has resulted in financial institutions today providing a wide array of products with which to meet every liquid asset need. Let's now take a brief look at the various types of checking and savings accounts. We will look at other short-term investment vehicles later in this chapter.

Checking Accounts. A checking account held at a financial institution is basically a **demand deposit**, meaning that the withdrawal of these funds must be permitted whenever demanded by the account holder. You put money into your checking account by *depositing* funds; you withdraw it by *writing checks*. As long as you have sufficient funds in your account, the bank, when presented with a valid check, must immediately pay the amount indicated. This is done by charging your account for the amount of the check. Money held in checking accounts is liquid and therefore can easily be used to pay bills and make purchases.

Regular checking is the most common type of checking account. It pays no interest, and any service charges that exist can be waived if you maintain a minimum balance (usually about $500 to $1,000). Technically, noninterest-paying regular checking accounts can be offered only by commercial banks. S&Ls, savings banks, and credit unions also offer checking accounts, but these must pay interest and, as such, are known as *NOW accounts* or, in the case of credit unions, *share draft accounts*. Because checks are generally accepted in paying bills and purchasing goods and services, demand deposit balances are considered a common and important type of cash balance. One of the primary advantages of demand deposits is that the use of checks to pay bills provides a convenient record of payment.

Savings Accounts. A savings account is another type of liquid asset that may be kept in commercial banks, savings and loan associations, credit unions, and many other types of financial institutions. Since a passbook is sometimes used to record transactions in these accounts, they are called **passbook accounts**, and their rate of interest is called the *passbook rate*. Savings deposits are referred to as **time deposits**, since they are expected to remain on deposit for a longer period of time than demand deposits. Because generally higher interest rates apply to savings deposits, savings accounts are generally preferable to checking accounts when the depositor's purpose is to accumulate money for a future expenditure or maintain balances for meeting unexpected expenditures. Most banks pay higher interest rates on larger savings account balances. For example, the rates paid by one bank in early 1992 were 3 percent on balances up to $2,500, 3.55 percent on balances between $2,500 and $10,000, and 3.75 percent on balances over $10,000.

While financial institutions generally retain the right to require a savings account holder to wait a certain number of days before receiving payment of a withdrawal, most are willing to pay withdrawals immediately. In addition to withdrawal policies and deposit insurance, the stated interest rate and method of calculating interest paid on savings accounts are important considerations in choosing the financial institution in which to place savings.

Interest-Paying Checking Accounts. As a result of changes that took place in the late 1970s and early 1980s, depositors now have far greater flexibility in choosing how to satisfy their checking and cash balance needs. Beginning with the highly successful money market mutual funds (MMMFs), a variety of new financial products were introduced, including money market deposit accounts (MMDAs) and NOW accounts. These last two are available at virtually every deposit-taking financial institution in the United States and are marketed under various names (Checkmatic Accounts, PrimeChecking, PreferredChecking, Premium Accounts, and so on).

Money market mutual funds. Starting from zero in the mid-1970s, money market mutual funds grew to almost $500 billion in deposits in early 1992, making them the most successful type of mutual fund ever offered. (Mutual funds are discussed in

---

savings bank
A type of savings institution, similar to an S&L and found mainly in the New England states, that is most often a mutual association owned by its depositors.

credit union
A depositor-owned mutual association that offers different types of interest-paying checking (share draft) accounts, savings accounts, and loans to its members.

share draft account
An account offered by credit unions that is similar to interest-paying checking accounts offered by other financial institutions.

demand deposit
An account held at a financial institution from which funds can be withdrawn (in check or cash) upon demand by the account holder; same as a *checking account*.

passbook account
A savings account in which transactions are sometimes recorded in a passbook; it pays the going passbook rate of interest.

time deposit
A savings deposit at a financial institution; so-called because it is expected to remain on deposit for a longer period of time than a demand deposit.

greater detail in Chapter 14.) A **money market mutual fund (MMMF)** pools the funds of many small investors and purchases high-yielding short-term marketable securities offered by the U.S. Treasury, major corporations, large commercial banks, and various government organizations. The portfolio of a typical MMMF contains specialized short-term securities that mature in as little as one day to as long as one year. The securities are all highly liquid and marketable forms of debt that are sold in denominations of at least $10,000 and often as much as $250,000 or more. Because of their lofty minimum denominations, few people are able to buy these securities directly. However, they can do so indirectly through the purchase of MMMFs, many of which have minimum deposits of as little as $500 to $1,000. The interest rate earned on an MMMF depends on returns earned on its investments, which fluctuate with overall credit conditions. MMMFs generally pay interest at rates considerably above (2 to 5 percent) those paid on regular savings accounts, although when short-term interest rates are generally low, as was the case in 1991 and 1992, the gap between them narrows (1 to 2 percent). Moreover, investors have instant access to their funds through check-writing privileges, although the checks often must be written for a stipulated minimum amount (usually $500). These checks look and are treated like any other check drawn on a demand deposit account except that, as with any other interest-bearing checking account, *you continue to earn interest on your money while the checks make their way through the banking system*.

Money market deposit accounts. Money market deposit accounts (MMDAs) were introduced in December 1982 and became extremely popular with depositors almost at once. They were created as a way of giving banks and other depository institutions a vehicle that would compete for deposits with money market mutual funds. MMDAs are popular with some savers and investors due to their convenience and safety because the deposits, unlike those in money funds, are *federally insured*. Most banks require a minimum MMDA balance of $1,000 to $1,500. Depositors can use check-writing privileges or automatic teller machines to access those accounts. A limited number — usually six — of checks and transfers can be made without charge each month, but a fee is charged on additional withdrawals. Although this feature obviously reduces the

flexibility of these accounts, most depositors, who apparently look upon MMDAs as savings rather than convenience accounts, do not consider it a serious obstacle. Moreover, MMDAs pay the highest rate of any bank account on which checks can be written.

Unlike money market mutual funds, money market deposit accounts are federally insured.
Fact: Money market deposit accounts are funds deposited in special, high interest-paying savings accounts at banks, S&Ls, and other depository institutions and thus are federally insured, which is not the case for money market mutual funds.

NOW accounts. Negotiable order of withdrawal (NOW) accounts are checking accounts on which the financial institution can pay whatever rate of interest it deems appropriate. They were first made available on a limited basis in 1972 and were made available to all depository financial institutions beginning in 1980. Since the deregulation of interest rates beginning in January 1986, the NOW account has become widely accepted as an "interest-paying checking account." Today there is no legal minimum balance for a NOW, but many institutions impose their own requirement, often between $500 and $1,000. Some have no minimum, paying interest on any balance in the account. Many institutions pay interest at a higher rate for all balances over a specified amount, such as $2,500. The seemingly high rates of interest, however, can be misleading. As we will see later in this chapter, one of the major problems in the growth of these interest-paying checking accounts has been a rise in monthly bank *charges* that often has virtually wiped out any interest earned on all but the highest account balances. NOW accounts should be viewed primarily as *checking accounts* that can also serve as potentially attractive savings vehicles. In this capacity, they allow individuals and families to earn interest on balances that must be kept for transaction purposes anyway and would otherwise lie idle.

HOW SAFE IS YOUR MONEY?

The 1980s and early 1990s were tumultuous times in the banking industry. The large number of bank failures (discussed later in this section) raised concern about the strength of the deposit insurance system, and many banks merged. As a result, today many depositors remain justifiably concerned about the safety of their deposits. The *Issues in Money Management* box describes how to evaluate the financial condition of your bank and what to expect if your bank is acquired by another bank.

Federal Deposit Insurance. The vast majority of banking institutions — 99 percent of all commercial banks, S&Ls, and savings banks and 90 percent of all credit unions — are *federally insured* by U.S. government agencies. The few that are not are usually insured through either a state-chartered or private insurance agency. Most experts believe that these so-called *privately insured* institutions have less protection against loss than do the federally insured ones. Exhibit 5.2 lists the insuring agencies and maximum insurance amounts provided under the various federal deposit insurance programs.

Deposit insurance protects the funds you have on deposit at banks and other depository institutions against institutional failure. In effect, the insuring agency stands behind the financial institution and guarantees the safety of your deposits up to a specified maximum amount ($100,000 per depositor in the case of federal insurance). Actually, the deposit insurance is provided to each depositor and *not* on the deposit account. Thus, both the checking and the savings accounts of each depositor are insured and, *as long as the maxmum insurable amount is not exceeded*, the depositor can have any number of accounts and still be fully protected. Each account in the financial institution, or any of its branches, will be fully covered regardless of number or type. This is an important feature to keep in mind, since many people mistakenly believe that the maximum insurance applies to *each* of their accounts and *certificates of deposit (CDs)*, which are deposits that earn higher interest rates than passbook accounts because the depositor agrees not to withdraw the funds for a specified period of time. Not so! For instance, an individual with a total of $125,000 in two deposit accounts and one CD at a single commercial bank — for instance, a NOW account with a $15,000 balance at one branch, a MMDA with a $60,000 balance at the main office, and a $50,000 CD — is covered by only $100,000 of deposit insurance. Of course, if either the MMDA or CD were transferred to another bank or financial institution, it would be insured for up to $100,000 and the total amount in all the accounts would then be fully protected.

While $100,000 in deposit insurance is, to say the least, quite a bit, it is possible to increase the amount of coverage if the need arises. Specifically, depositors who carefully follow federal guidelines can increase their coverage by opening accounts in multiple depositor names at the same institution. A married couple, for example, can obtain $500,000 in coverage by setting up *individual* accounts in the name of each spouse (good for $200,000) in coverage), *joint* accounts in both names (good for another $100,000), and *separate trust or IRA* accounts in the name of each spouse (good for an additional $200,000). Note that in this case each depositor is treated as a separate legal entity and as such receives full insurance coverage — the husband alone is considered one legal entity, the wife another, and the man and wife as a couple a third. In addition, the trust and IRA accounts are also viewed as legal entities.

The Banking Industry Crisis. Although deregulation allowed thrift institutions (S&Ls and savings banks) and commercial banks to offer many new products and services, it also placed them in direct competition with other financial institutions. This change created both opportunities and problems.

---

money market mutual fund (MMMF)
A mutual fund that pools the funds of many small investors and purchases high-yielding short-term marketable securities offered by the U.S. Treasury, major corporations, large commercial banks, and various government organizations.

money market deposit account (MMDA)
A savings account that is meant to be competitive with a MMMF, offered by banks and other depository institutions.

negotiable order of withdrawal (NOW) account
A checking account on which the financial institution can pay whatever rate of interest it deems appropriate.

deposit insurance
A type of insurance that protects funds on deposit against failure of the institution. Insuring agencies include the *Federal Deposit Insurance Corporation (FDIC)* and the *National Credit Union Administration (NCUA)*.

Is Your Bank Safe?

With all the publicity about the problems in the banking industry, you may be worried about your bank's financial condition but unsure how to check it out. Even if it is in good financial shape, it could be a candidate for acquisition by another bank. In that case, you need to know how a merger would affect you.

Although most banks are financially sound, you can no longer take bank safety for granted. First, you should verify that your bank is *federally insured* by a unit of the FDIC or NCUA. Then read the financial pages to learn about its reputation in the community and to follow recent developments. Next, periodically evaluate your bank using its most recent annual statement of condition and quarterly call reports (documents that must be filed with the FDIC or OTS). The following three simple questions suggested by Warren Heller, research director at Veribanc, a

Boston-based bank rating firm, will give you a pretty good idea of whether you need to find a new bank. The fourth describes the effects of your bank being acquired by another bank.

1. **Does the bank have enough equity, or capital?** The bank's level of equity should provide a cash cushion to cover significant losses. Find the equity-to-assets ratio by dividing total equity, also called shareholder's equity, by the bank's total assets (both are found on the balance sheet). If the ratio is above 5 percent, the bank's equity, or capital, is considered adequate; lower levels are a warning signal.

2. **How many problem loans does the bank have?** Loans are a major component of a bank's assets. Those that are three or more months past due are

called nonperforming assets, and they are a drain not only to the bank's profits but also to its capital. Lenders must set aside reserves from income to cover these problem loans. Look on Schedules RC-N and RC-C of the call report for the total of all *past due and nonaccrual loans*. Then, compare that amount to the bank's *loan loss reserve balance* on Schedule RI-B, Part II. Heller advises caution when a bank's problem loans are higher than loan loss reserves. If problem loans are greater than equity, the bank may be a candidate for bankruptcy. Another way to assess the level of problem loans is to calculate the ratio of nonperforming loans to total assets. A ratio above 3 percent for thrifts and 4 percent for commercial banks is a sign that trouble

The S&L Crisis. The first crisis hit the S&Ls and was caused primarily by high interest rates, deregulation, and poor economic conditions. Prior to 1980, S&Ls focused on long-term, fixed-rate home mortgage loans. As interest rates rose during the 1970s and early 1980s, in order to attract deposits the S&Ls had to offer higher interest rates on accounts than they were earning on existing loans. About that time Congress deregulated the thrifts, al-

lowing them to make other types of more profitable loans. Many already-troubled thrifts made risky real estate loans and invested in high-risk, high-yield "junk bonds," many of which went into default. As a result of high interest rates, poor management, erosion of real estate values due to the recession, inadequate regulation, and the fraudulent and unethical acts of some major officers, about 2,300 thrifts — *50 percent* of the total — failed. The agency that insured

may lie ahead.

3. Is the bank profitable? This is one of the easiest tests: if a bank is making money, it's probably doing well, says Heller. If a bank is losing money due to high levels of loan loss reserves, it will use up its capital and eventually become insolvent. However, you should also check to see *how* the bank earned its profits. Profitability from operations is key. Profits from extraordinary items — for example, sales of branches, loans, securities, or other assets — temporarily improve the bank's profit picture. If the bank is unprofitable and also flunks one of the other tests, you may want to move your money to another bank.

4. What happens if your bank is acquired by another bank? If your bank is acquired by another bank, you should be aware of how it will affect your banking relationship. Although the merger typically takes several months to a year to complete, the bank will probably begin to communicate the details of the merger and how it will affect customers well before the merger is finalized. Often banks set up special telephone lines to answer customer questions. In today's competitive financial services arena, banks are making every effort to keep their customers despite mergers. In most cases, changes are minor. If your branch is closed because there are two or more within the same area, your account may be transferred and given a new number. You will probably receive new checks, an ATM card with a new personal identification number, and a bank credit card, all with the new bank name. Rates on existing loans usually stay the same, as do interest rates on CDs until maturity (but when a bank acquires a failed institution, it may change the interest rates). Customers with accounts in the same name at both banks in excess of the $100,000 deposit insurance limit will be covered in full during the six months immediately following the effective date of the merger. For CDs, the dual coverage is extended until the first maturity date that occurs beyond the six-month period immediately following the merger.

Sources: Adapted from Robert Hanley, "How Safe Is Your Bank?" *San Diego Union-Tribune*, February 11, 1992, pp. E-1, 3; Georgette Jasen, "Get Set for Changes if Your Bank Merges," *The Wall Street Journal*, August 23, 1991, pp. C1, 17; and Elizabeth M. McDonald, "How Safe Is Your Bank? Give It This Three-Step Test," *Money*, July 1990, pp. 31–32.

S&L deposits, the Federal Savings and Loan Insurance Corporation (FSLIC), ran out of funds in 1988 and was replaced by the Savings Association Insurance Fund (SAIF), which is controlled by the FDIC.

Congress created two new agencies to bail out the S&L industry. The Office of Thrift Supervision (OTS) regulates the industry, while the Resolution Trust Corporation (RTC), a unit of the FDIC, takes over insolvent thrifts, safeguards their deposits, and sells the assets — real estate and loans — of these failed institutions. Through early 1992, the RTC had taken over 700 insolvent institutions, and many more were in danger of insolvency. The cost to taxpayers of the massive S&L bailout has been estimated to be about $500 billion.

Problems in Commercial Banking. By the early 1990s, the commercial banking industry was suffering from many of the same problems as the

EXHIBIT 5.2

Federal Deposit Insurance Programs

If you have your checking and savings accounts at a federally insured institution, you are covered by at least $100,000 of insurance as provided by one of the following federal insurance agencies.

Savings Institution	Insuring Agency	Amount of Insurance
Commercial bank	Federal Deposit Insurance Corporation (FDIC) through the Bank Insurance Fund (BIF)	$100,000/depositor
Savings and loan association	Federal Deposit Insurance Corporation (FDIC) through the Savings Association Insurance Fund (SAIF)	$100,000/depositor
Savings bank	Federal Deposit Insurance Corporation (FDIC) through the BIF	$100,000/depositor
Credit union	National Credit Union Administration (NCUA) through the National Credit Union Share Insurance Fund (NCUSIF)	$100,000/depositor

thrifts. Profits were squeezed because many banks, for competitive reasons, were paying interest on money market accounts at rates that were not much below those they were earning on loans. In addition, the demand for business loans—a major source of bank earnings—dropped as corporations began to use other, lower-cost sources of financing. As a result, banks made higher-risk loans, particularly on commercial real estate and to underdeveloped countries. The recession in the early 1990s severely depressed property values, causing many of the nation's largest banks to be faced with problem real estate loans. Between 1980 and 1991, about 1,340 commercial banks—about 9 percent of the total—failed. In these cases, the FDIC stepped in and either arranged for the acquisition of the failed bank by a stronger bank or liquidation of the bank with the proceeds used to pay depositors directly. In some cases, the FDIC fully reimbursed the depositors, paying more than the $100,000 insurance limit in order to maintain confidence in the banking system and prevent panics at other banks. Mergers among both thrifts and banks increased during this period. Overall, the number of thrift institutions and banks declined 16 percent from 1986 to 1991. Because the large number of bank failures put a strain on the deposit insurance funds, Congress began to explore ways to reform the deposit insurance system.

ESTABLISHING A SAVINGS PROGRAM

To get the most from your savings program, it is important to develop sound savings habits and understand your savings options. Before reading on, spend a few moments describing your savings program, the available savings options, and those that you've chosen to include in your program.

It is estimated that about 75 percent of American households have some money put away in savings. Surveys have shown that while age and income have a lot to do with the amount saved, over half of the people who do save have *more than $10,000* socked away! Clearly, saving money is considered an important activity by many individuals and families. The act of saving is a deliberate, well-thought-out activity designed to preserve the value of money, insure liquidity, and earn a high rate of return. Almost by definition, *smart savers are smart investors*. They regard savings as more than putting loose change into a piggybank; rather, they recognize the importance of savings and know that savings must be managed as astutely as any security. After all, what we normally think of as "savings" is really a form of investment—a short-term, highly liquid, fixed-dollar investment that is subject to minimum risk. Establishing and maintaining an ongoing savings program is a vital element of personal financial planning. To get the most from your savings, however, you must understand your savings options and how different savings vehicles pay interest.

CHOICES INVOLVED IN ESTABLISHING A SAVINGS PROGRAM

Careful financial planning dictates that a portion of your assets be held for the purposes of meeting liquidity needs and as a way of accumulating wealth. While opinions differ as to how much should be held as liquid reserves, the general consensus is that an amount equal to three to six months' after-tax income is best for most families. This means that if you take home $1,500 a month, you should have between $4,500 and $9,000 in liquid reserves. If your employer has a strong salary continuation program during extended periods of illness and/or you have a sizable line of credit available, the lower figure is probably suitable; if you lack one or both of these, however, the larger amount is probably more appropriate.

A specific savings plan is needed with which to accumulate funds. In this regard, saving should be considered as important as any other budget activity rather than an event that occurs only when income happens to exceed expenditures. Some people do this by arranging to withhold savings directly from their paychecks. This has been a common practice for many years with U.S. savings bonds purchase plans and credit union deposits. Today it is also possible to have funds regularly transferred to other financial institutions such as commercial banks, savings and loans, savings banks, and even money market mutual funds. Not only do direct deposit arrangements help your savings effort, they also enable your funds to earn interest sooner. The key to success is to establish a *regular* pattern of savings. You should make it a practice to set aside an amount that you can comfortably afford *each month*, even if it is only $50 to $100. (Keep in mind that earning 5

percent interest, a series of $100 monthly deposits will grow to over $40,000 in 20 years!) The *Smart Money* box suggests several ways you can discipline yourself to achieve your savings goals.

You must also decide which savings products best meet your needs. Many savers prefer to keep their emergency funds in a passbook or money market deposit account at an institution with federal deposit insurance. Although these accounts are safe, convenient, and highly liquid, they tend to pay relatively low rates of interest. Other important considerations include your risk preference, the length of time you can leave your money on deposit, and the level of current and expected interest rates. Suppose one year from now you plan to use $5,000 of your savings to make the down payment on a new car, and you believe that interest rates will drop during that period. You should lock in today's higher rate by purchasing a one-year CD. On the other hand, if you are unsure about when you will actually need the funds or believe that interest rates will rise, you are better off with a MMDA or MMMF because the rates they pay change with market conditions and they allow you to access your funds at any time without penalty.

Because short-term interest rates generally fluctuate more than long-term rates, it is important to monitor interest rate movements, shop around for the best rates, and place your funds in savings vehicles that are consistent with your needs. Short-term interest rates dropped sharply in the late 1980s and early 1990s. For example, over the year ended February 1992, the average interest rate on a three-month CD dropped from 7 percent to 4 percent, rates on MMDAs dropped from 5.6 percent to 3.7 percent, and one-year CDs dropped from 6.6 percent to 4.12 percent. As a result, investors in early 1992 were unable to reinvest their proceeds from maturing CDs at comparable rates. Many of them reevaluated their savings plans and moved their funds into other savings vehicles that paid higher rates of interest, but were also more risky.

Many financial planning experts recommend keeping a minimum of 10 to 25 percent of your investment portfolio in savings-type instruments in addition to the three to six months' holding of liquid reserves noted above. Thus, someone with, say, $50,000 in investments should probably have a minimum of $5,000 to $10,000—and possibly even

Tips for Becoming a Disciplined Saver

To improve your financial health, the obvious thing to do is to save more money—but Americans have a notoriously hard time doing that. Here are 12 tips for mustering financial willpower:

1. **Pay yourself first.** Take your savings out of each paycheck immediately, before paying bills and making purchases. Otherwise, you may have nothing left to save at the end of the month.

2. **Set a realistic goal.** You're more likely to become a successful saver if you establish an objective in league with your budget. Though many financial planners suggest setting aside 10 percent, there's nothing wrong with setting a lesser goal of 5 or even 3 percent. "The basic rule is to save whatever you can, but save something," says Paul Strassels, a Burke, Va., financial consultant.

3. **Remember that savings beget savings.** Leave your nest egg alone and spend only the interest or dividends. If you pump $2,000 a year into a money market mutual fund for five years but spend the interest, you'll still wind up with $10,000. Better yet, let the earnings ride at an average annual yield of, say, 5 percent, and you'll amass $1,050 in interest to go with your $10,000.

4. **Keep it simple.** Stick to just a few basic instruments, such as certificates of deposit (CDs), mutual funds, or perhaps U.S. savings bonds. Stocks, bonds, and more exotic fare such as real estate investment trusts require brokerage fees, research effort—and considerable attention. When picking a mutual fund, remember that the no-load variety does not charge sales commissions and historically has done as well as funds that do.

5. **Hold cash reserves to a minimum.** Your checking account balance should be just big enough to cover monthly expenses. It is recommended that you also keep an amount equal to twice your monthly take-home pay in investments that can be quickly turned to cash—for example, a money-market mutual fund or short-term CDs—to help you cope with any emergencies. The rest of your savings can go to higher-yielding investments, such as long-term CDs or mutual funds that emphasize growth-oriented stocks.

6. **Be yield-conscious.** Banks calculate interest in various ways, so true yields can vary widely on CDs with the same maturity and interest rate. For instance, the annual return on a five-year, 6 percent CD with quarterly compounding is 6.14 percent, but the same CD with daily compounding could yield as much as 6.18

more—in such short-term vehicles as MMDAs, MMMFs, or CDs. Also, at times the amount invested in short-term vehicles could well exceed the recommended minimum and approach 50 percent or more of the portfolio. This generally depends on expected interest rate movements. If interest rates are relatively high and you expect them to fall, you would invest in long-term vehicles in order to lock in the attractive interest rates. On the other hand, if rates are relatively low and you expect them to rise, you might invest in short-term vehicles so that you can more quickly reinvest them when interest rates rise. Clearly, the amount held in savings accounts and short-term vehicles—both for the purpose of maintaining liquid reserves and as a part of an investment portfolio—can be substantial.

percent. Over five years, the difference would amount to $30 on a $10,000 CD. It's not a lot, but why walk away from it?

7. **Don't confuse tax savings with real savings.** People often justify certain big expenses by the fact that they are tax deductible. But the tax law has seriously cramped Uncle Sam's generosity. This year, the maximum tax rate on federal returns is 31 percent. Thus, every dollar you deduct from your income will net no more than 31 cents in tax savings. You'll save more by trimming all your expenses, even the deductible ones.

8. **Enlist a "savings enforcer."** If you lack the discipline to write a check to yourself each month, get somebody else to do it. For example, your bank can regularly transfer a specified sum from your checking account to a savings plan. Better yet, you can arrange for payroll deductions that go to a company credit union or employer-sponsored thrift plan. These can be very sweet deals. Credit unions often pay higher yields on basic savings accounts than commercial banks or savings associations, while many employers will match all or part of your contributions to a thrift plan.

9. **Swap debt for equity.** After you retire an auto loan or another consumer debt, continue to write the same monthly installment checks, but send them to your savings account.

10. **Reward yourself occasionally.** Saving for retirement or your toddler's college education can be hard, since the payoff won't be realized for a long time. So establish a rule that if you exceed your savings goal for a year, you're entitled to spend the extra bucks on something you covet— maybe a new stereo or a trip to the beach.

11. **Try a few gimmicks.** Some people need a little push to put themselves into the savings habit. For example, assess yourself a $10 penalty every time you break your diet and put the money into a savings account. If you're not sure you'll play fair, ask your spouse to be a referee. Some families augment their savings by making a ritual of collecting all the loose change in their pockets, wallets, and drawers once a week or so.

12. **Don't rob the piggy bank.** Diehard spendthrifts should say "No" to mutual funds or savings accounts with check-writing privileges. The temptation is just too great.

Source: Updated and adapted from Patricia M. Scherschel, "A Dozen Painless Ways to Help a Nest Egg Grow," *U.S. News & World Report*, June 8, 1987, pp. 58–60. Copyright, June 8, 1987, U.S. News & World Report.

FINDING INTEREST EARNED ON YOUR MONEY

Interest earned is the reward for putting your money in a savings account or short-term investment vehicle. Because with such accounts or securities there really is no other source of return, it is important for you to understand how interest is earned. Unfortunately, even in the relatively simple world of savings, you will quickly discover that all interest rates are not created equal.

The Matter of Compounding. Basically, interest can be earned in one of two ways. First, some short-term investments are sold on a *discount basis*. This means that the security is sold for a price that is lower than its redemption value, the difference being the amount of interest earned. Treasury bills, for instance, are issued on a discount basis. Another way to earn interest on short-term investments is by *direct payment*, such as what occurs when interest is applied to a passbook savings account. Although this is a simple process, determining the actual rate of return can involve several complications.

The first of these relates to the method used to arrive at the amount and rate of **compound interest** earned annually. You have probably read or seen advertisements by banks or other depository institutions touting the fact that they pay daily, rather than annual, interest. To understand what this means, consider the following example. Assume you invest $1,000 in a savings account advertised as paying annual **simple interest** at a rate of 5 percent. With simple interest, the interest is paid on only the initial amount of the deposit. This means that if the $1,000 is left on deposit for one year, you will earn $50 in interest, and the account balance will total $1,050 at the end of the year. Note that in this case the **nominal (stated) rate of interest** is the same as the effective rate. In contrast, the **effective rate of interest** is the annual rate of return *actually earned* on the transaction. It is found in the following manner:

$$\text{Effective rate of interest} = \frac{\text{Amount of interest earned during the year}}{\text{Amount of money invested or deposited}}$$

In our example, since $50 was earned during the year on an investment of $1,000, the effective rate is $50/$1,000 = 5\%, which is the same as the nominal rate of interest. (Note that in the above formula it is interest earned during the *year* that matters; thus, if you wanted to find the effective return on an account that you had for six months, you would have to double the amount of interest earned.)

But suppose you can invest your funds elsewhere at a 5 percent rate, *compounded semiannually*. Since interest is applied to your account at midyear, this means you will earn *interest on interest* for the last six months of the year, thereby increasing the total interest for the year. The actual dollar earnings are determined as follows:

$$\text{First 6 months' interest} = \$1,000 \times 0.05 \times 6/12 = \$25.00$$

$$\text{Second 6 months' interest} = \$1,025 \times 0.05 \times 6/12 = \underline{25.63}$$

$$\text{Total interest} = \underline{\underline{\$50.63}}$$

Interest is being generated on a larger investment in the second half of the year, since the amount of money on deposit has increased by the amount of interest earned in the first half year ($25). Although the nominal rate on this account is still 5 percent, the effective rate is 5.06 percent ($50.63/$1,000). As you may have guessed, the more frequently interest is compounded, the greater the effective rate for any given nominal rate. These relationships are shown for a sample of interest rates and compounding periods in Exhibit 5.3. Note, for example, that with a 7 percent nominal rate, daily compounding adds one-fourth of a percent to the size of the total return — not a trivial amount.

In all but a few cases, the nominal (stated) interest rate on a savings account is the same as its effective rate of interest.
Fantasy: In only a few cases are the two rates the same. Because the nominal (stated) interest rate paid by a bank or other depository institution typically compounds during the year, the effective rate is greater than the nominal rate.

Compound Interest Equals Future Value.

Compound interest is the same as the *future value* concept introduced in Chapter 3. You can use the procedures described there to find out how much an investment or deposit will grow to equal over time at a compounded rate of interest. For example, using the future value formula and the future value factor from Appendix A, you can determine how much $1,000 will be worth in four years if it is deposited into a savings account that pays 5 percent interest per year compounded annually like this:

$$\text{Future value} = \text{Amount deposited} \times \text{Future value factor}$$

$$= \$1,000 \times 1.216$$

$$= \underline{\$1,216}$$

You can use the same basic procedure to find the future value of an *annuity*, except that you would use the future value annuity factor from Appendix B. For instance, if you put $1,000 a year into a savings account that pays 5 percent per year compounded annually, in four years you will have

$$\text{Future value} = \text{Amount deposited} \times \text{Future value annuity factor}$$

$$= \$1,000 \times 4.310$$

$$= \underline{\$4,310}$$

Measuring the Account Balance Qualified to Earn Interest. Not only are there differences among financial institutions in the way interest is compounded. There may also be differences with respect to how account balances qualify to earn interest — that is, how the size of the account balance is measured. There are four methods in wide use: (1) the minimum balance method, (2) the FIFO method, (3) the LIFO method, and (4) the actual balance method. The minimum balance and actual balance methods are by far the most widely used procedures, but we will look at all four.

The differences in these methods are best illustrated with an example such as the one given in Exhibit 5.4. The depositor here has $10,000 at the beginning of the quarter and adds $2,000 to this balance 30 days later; then, on day 60, the depositor withdraws $6,000, leaving an ending balance of $6,000. While either simple or compound interest could be used, we will assume that the account pays simple interest of 5 percent. In all illustrations, interest earned is computed in the following manner:

$$\text{Interest earned} = \text{Amount invested (or on deposit)} \times \text{Annual interest rate} \times \frac{n}{360}$$

where n equals the number of days the funds are invested (or on deposit). Notice that a 360-day year

is assumed, which is common for many financial calculations. To see how this equation works, consider the sum of $1,000 left on deposit for 30 days at an annual rate of 4.5 percent; the depositor in this case would earn interest of

$$\$1,000 \times .045 \times 30/360 = \underline{\$3.75}$$

Minimum balance method. With this method, interest is paid on the *lowest* balance in the account during the quarter. Because the minimum is $6,000 in our illustration (see Exhibit 5.4), the interest earned amounts to only $75. Since this method places a heavy penalty on withdrawals made late in the period, it is not recommended if substantial withdrawals are anticipated.

FIFO method. FIFO means *first-in, first-out*. It is an assumption that the financial institution makes with respect to when withdrawals are charged. Specifically, it assumes withdrawals are charged against the earlier or opening balances of an account. Thus, the $6,000 withdrawal on day 60 is assumed to reduce the *opening* balance of $10,000, leaving a balance of $4,000. Exhibit 5.4 shows how the interest income of $66.67 is determined. Note that because the $6,000 withdrawal is charged against the opening balance, it is only the remaining amount ($4,000) that earns interest over the full quarter (90

---

compound interest
When interest earned in each subsequent period is determined by applying the nominal (stated) interest rate to the sum of the initial deposit and the interest earned in each prior period.

simple interest
Interest that is paid on only the initial amount of the deposit.

nominal (stated) rate of interest
The promised rate of interest paid on a savings deposit or charged on a loan.

effective rate of interest
The rate of interest that is actually earned (charged) over the period of time funds are held (borrowed).

EXHIBIT 5.3

Nominal and Effective Interest Rates with Different Compounding Periods

The amount of interest that you actually earn from a savings account will exceed the stated nominal rate if interest is compounded more than once a year (as are most savings and interest-paying accounts).

Nominal Rate	Effective Rate				
	Annually	**Semiannually**	**Quarterly**	**Monthly**	**Daily**
4%	4.00%	4.04%	4.06%	4.07%	4.08%
5	5.00	5.06	5.09	5.12	5.13
6	6.00	6.09	6.14	6.17	6.18
7	7.00	7.12	7.19	7.23	7.25
8	8.00	8.16	8.24	8.30	8.33
9	9.00	9.20	9.31	9.38	9.42
10	10.00	10.25	10.38	10.47	10.52
11	11.00	11.30	11.46	11.57	11.62
12	12.00	12.36	12.55	12.68	12.74

days), whereas the deposit ($2,000) earns interest only over the 60 days it was on deposit. For the data given in this illustration, the depositor earns even less with this method than with the minimum balance method, although this is not always the case.

LIFO method. LIFO means *last-in, first-out*. With this method, the bank assumes withdrawals are charged to the most recent deposits or balances. This is to the depositor's advantage, since it means earlier deposits are left untouched and thereby earn interest for the entire period. Thus, the $6,000 withdrawal on day 60 is assumed to first reduce the $2,000 deposit made on day 30, with the remaining $4,000 carried back as an offset against the opening balance of $10,000. This leaves $6,000 ($10,000 − $4,000) against which interest is earned. As it works out in the illustration in Exhibit 5.4, the $75 of interest earned is the same as under the minimum balance method. Although this method is somewhat fairer to the depositor than the FIFO method, it still does not provide interest for the full period over which the money is on deposit.

Actual balance method. This method, sometimes called *day of deposit to day of withdrawal*, is the most accurate and gives depositors the highest interest earnings on their money. It is also considered the fairest procedure, because it gives depositors full credit for all funds on deposit. This procedure is also referred to as *daily interest*, but it should not be confused with the daily *compounding* of interest, which is an entirely different concept. Daily interest does not necessarily mean

daily compounding, although competition among financial institutions has moved most of them in that direction. Before opening a deposit account, a depositor should ask two questions: (1) How often does compounding take place, and (2) what method is used to determine which balances earn interest? (It is the second question we have been addressing here; the first was discussed earlier.) Exhibit 5.4 indicates how the interest of $116.67 is calculated for our example using the actual balance method; you can see that more is earned under this method than with any of the others.

A VARIETY OF WAYS TO SAVE

Over the past decade or so, there has been a tremendous proliferation of savings and short-term investment vehicles, particularly for the individual of modest means. Saving and investing in short-term securities is no longer the easy task it once was, when the decision for most people boiled down to whether funds should be placed in a passbook savings account or in Series E bonds. Today, investors can choose from savings accounts, NOW accounts, money market mutual funds and deposit accounts, certificates of deposit, Treasury bills, Series EE bonds, and central asset accounts. We examined several of these savings vehicles earlier in this chapter, including savings accounts, NOW accounts, MMMFs and MMDAs; accordingly, our attention here will center on the four remaining types of deposits and securities.

EXHIBIT 5.4

Four Methods of Determining Interest (Nominal Rate = 5%)

In addition to the compounding procedures used, the amount of interest you earn will depend on how the financial institution measures the size of your account balance.

A. Quarterly Activity

Day	Transaction	Account Balance
1	Opening balance	$10,000
30	Deposit $2,000	12,000
60	Withdrawal $6,000	6,000
90	Ending balance	6,000

B. Interest Calculations

1. *Minimum balance method:*

$\$ 6,000 \times 0.05 \times 90/360 = \underline{\underline{\$ 75.00}}$

2. *FIFO method:*

$\$ 4,000 \times 0.05 \times 90/360 = \$ 50.00$
$2,000 \times 0.05 \times 60/360 = \underline{16.67}$

Total = $\underline{\underline{\$66.67}}$

3. *LIFO method:*

$\$ 6,000 \times 0.05 \times 90/360 = \underline{\underline{\$ 75.00}}$

4. *Actual balance method:*

$\$10,000 \times 0.05 \times 30/360 = \$ 41.67$
$12,000 \times 0.05 \times 30/360 = 50.00$
$6,000 \times 0.05 \times 30/360 = \underline{25.00}$

Total = $\underline{\underline{\$116.67}}$

Certificates of Deposit. **Certificates of deposit (CDs)** differ from the savings instruments discussed earlier in this chapter in that CD funds must remain on deposit for a specified period of time, which can range from seven days to as long as seven or more years. Although it is possible to withdraw funds prior to maturity, an interest penalty usually makes withdrawal somewhat costly. While the bank or other depository institution is free to charge whatever penalty it likes, most result in a severely reduced rate of interest — typically a rate no greater than that paid on its most basic passbook savings account. Since October of 1983, banks, S&Ls, and other depository institutions have been free to offer any rate and maturity CD they wish. As a result, today a wide variety of CDs are offered by most banks and depository institutions, though as a rule, most pay higher rates for larger deposits and longer periods of time. CDs are convenient to buy and hold because they offer attractive and highly competitive yields plus federal deposit insurance protection.

In addition to purchasing CDs directly from the issuer, they can be purchased from stockbrokers. **Brokered CDs** are simply certificates of deposit sold by stockbrokers. The brokerage house

---

certificate of deposit (CD)

A type of savings certificate that is issued by certain financial institutions in exchange for a deposit; typically requires a minimum deposit and has a maturity ranging from seven days to as long as seven or more years.

brokered CD

A certificate of deposit, typically with a $1,000 minimum denomination, that can be purchased with no commissions from a stockbroker and can be sold without penalty prior to maturity.

searches for the best deal (highest yield) it can get, and then sells these CDs to its customers. In essence, a bank or S&L issues the CDs, and the brokerage house merely sells (or places) them with the investing public. The minimum denomination is usually only $1,000, so they are affordable, and there's no commission to pay since the broker earns it commissions from the issuing bank or S&L. Brokered CDs are attractive for two reasons: First, you can sell them prior to maturity without incurring a penalty, since the brokerage firms maintain active secondary markets; therefore, you can improve your liquidity. But remember, there are no guarantees here. The market always prevails, so if rates go up, the relative value of your CD falls and you don't end up earning the rate you started with. Second, you may be able to get higher yields from brokered CDs than from your local bank or other depository institution. Frequently, you can gain .25 to .75 of a percent by dealing with a broker. But be careful. The broker can always get higher yields by selling CDs issued by troubled financial institutions. Therefore, *buy a brokered CD only from a federally insured institution* — ask your broker, just to be sure.

U.S. Treasury Bills. The **U.S. Treasury bill (T-bill)** is considered the ultimate safe haven for saving and investments. T-bills are obligations of the U.S. Treasury issued as part of its ongoing process of funding the national debt. They are sold on a discount basis in minimum denominations of $10,000 followed by increments of $5,000 and are issued with three-month (13-week), six-month (26-week), and one-year maturities. The one- and six-month bills are auctioned off every Monday and one-year bills roughly every four weeks. They are backed by the full faith and credit of the U.S. government and pay an attractive and safe yield that is free from state and local income taxes.

T-bills are almost as liquid as cash, since they can be sold at any time (in a very active secondary market) without any interest penalty. However, should you have to sell before maturity, you may lose some money on your investment if interest rates have risen, and you will have to pay a boker's fee as well. Treasury bills pay interest on a *discount basis* and as such are different from other savings or short-term investment vehicles — that is, their interest is equal to the difference between the purchase price paid and the worth at maturity. For example, if you paid $9,800 for a bill that will be worth $10,000 at maturity, you will earn $200 in interest ($10,000 − $9,800).

An individual investor may purchase T-bills directly through participation in the weekly Treasury auctions or indirectly through a commercial bank or a security dealer who buys bills for investors on a commission basis. Outstanding Treasury bills can also be purchased in the secondary market through banks or dealers. The biggest advantage to this approach is that the investor has a much wider selection of maturities from which to choose, ranging from less than a week to as long as a year.

It is relatively simple to buy T-bills directly: To participate in the weekly auction, all you need do is submit a "tender" to the nearest Federal Reserve Bank or branch specifying both the amount and maturity desired (tender forms are easy to fill out and readily available from commercial banks). The Treasury tries to accommodate individual investors through its *noncompetitive* bidding system, which most individual investors use because of its simplicity. In essence, all noncompetitive tender offers are awarded T-bills at a price equal to the average of all the accepted competitive bids. Thus, the investor is assured of being able to buy bills in the quantity desired while obtaining the benefit of an open auction system — and without going through the hassle of a competitive bid.

Series EE Bonds. **Series EE bonds** are the well-known savings bonds that have been around for decades. They were first issued in 1941 and used to be called Series E bonds. They are often purchased through payroll deduction plans. Though issued by the U.S. Treasury, they are quite different from T-bills. In fact, perhaps their only similarity is that they are sold on a discount basis and are also free of state and local income taxes. These bonds are *accrual-type securities*, which means that interest is paid when they are cashed, on or before maturity, rather than periodically over their lives. The government does make Series HH bonds available through the exchange of Series E or Series EE bonds; they have a ten-year maturity and come in denominations of $500 to $10,000. Unlike EE bonds, HH bonds are issued at their full face value and pay interest semiannually at the current fixed rate of 6 percent.

Series EE bonds are backed by the full faith and credit of the U.S. government and can be replaced without charge in case of loss, theft, or destruction. They can be purchased at banks or other depository institutions, or through payroll deduction plans. Issued in denominations from $50 through $10,000, their purchase price is a uniform 50 percent of the face amount (thus, a $100 bond will cost $50 and be worth $100 at maturity).

The actual maturity date on EE bonds is unspecified, since the issues pay a variable rate of interest. The higher the rate of interest being earned, the shorter the period of time it takes for the bond to accrue from its discounted purchase price to its maturity value. In an effort to make these securities more attractive to investors, all EE bonds held five years or longer receive interest at the higher of 6 percent or 85 percent of the average return on five-year Treasury securities, as calculated every six months in May and November. The yield, therefore, changes every six months in accordance with prevailing Treasury security yields. Current rates on Series EE bonds can be obtained from your bank or simply by calling 1-800-487-2663. (Note: The rate being quoted for the six-month period ending October 31, 1992 was 5.58 percent.) EE bonds held for less than five years (they can be redeemed any time after the first six months) earn interest according to a fixed, graduated scale beginning at 4.16 percent for bonds held six months and rising gradually to not less than the 6 percent guaranteed minimum rate at five years.

In addition to being exempt from state and local taxes, Series EE bonds provide their holders with an appealing tax twist: *Savers need not report interest earned on federal tax returns until the bonds are redeemed.* Although interest can be reported annually (for example, when the bonds are held in the name of a child who has limited interest income), most investors choose to defer it. In effect, this means the funds are being reinvested at an after-tax rate of no less than the guaranteed minimum rate of 6 percent.

A second attractive tax feature allows partial or complete tax avoidance of EE bond earnings when proceeds are used to pay educational expenses, such as college tuition, for the bond purchaser, a spouse, or other IRS-defined dependent. To qualify, the purchaser must be age 24 or older and have adjusted gross income below $56,950 for single filers and $92,900 for married couples.

U.S. savings bonds are not a very good way to save. *Fantasy:* Investing in Series EE savings bonds is an excellent way to save, because they offer highly competitive rates of return and several attractive tax features.

Central Asset Accounts. With the advent of the new financial marketplace has come a greatly increased number of providers of banking services. No longer are banks and S&Ls the only ones that can provide traditional banking services. Perhaps the best example of this is the **central asset account**. This type of account was first introduced as its *cash management account*, or *CMA*, by the Wall Street brokerage firm of Merrill Lynch in 1977. It is not a separate investment vehicle, but rather a comprehensive deposit account that combines checking, investing, and borrowing activities. Such accounts are offered by banks, other depository institutions, brokerage houses, mutual funds, and insurance companies. Their distinguishing feature is that they automatically "sweep" excess balances into short-term investments. For instance, a bank central asset account might be set up to combine a NOW and a MMDA. At the end of each day, if the NOW account balance exceeds $500, the excess is automatically swept into the higher-yielding MMDA. Thus, Merrill Lynch's CMA automatically sweeps the account holder's funds into its MMMF, and if securities are

---

U.S. Treasury bill (T-bill)
A short-term (three-month to one-year maturity) debt instrument issued by the federal government in the ongoing process of funding the national debt.

Series EE bond
A savings bond issued in various denominations by the U.S. Treasury.

central asset account
A comprehensive deposit account, offered by major financial institutions, that combines checking, investing, and borrowing activities and automatically sweeps excess funds into short-term investments and provides loans when shortages exist.

EXHIBIT 5.5
Some Central Asset Accounts

Most central asset accounts have large minimum investment requirements. If you can meet the minimum, you will find such accounts available at banks, mutual funds, brokerage houses, and even Sears (through its Dean Witter brokerage subsidiary).

Company/Account	Minimum Investment*	Annual Fee	Frequency of Sweep
Charles Schwab (Schwab One Asset Management Account)	$ 5,000	$ 0	All amounts – daily
Citibank (FOCUS Account)	$ 5,000 cash	$125	All amounts – daily
Dean Witter (Active Assets Account)	$10,000	$ 80	All amounts – daily
Fidelity Brokerage Services (Fidelity Ultra Service Account)	$25,000	$ 60	Over $1,000 – daily Under $1,000 – weekly
Kidder Peabody (Premium Account)	$25,000	$ 90	All amounts – daily
Merrill Lynch (Cash Management Account)	$20,000	$100	All amounts – daily
PaineWebber (Resource Management Account)	$15,000	$100	Over $500 – daily Under $500 – weekly
Prudential Securities (Command Account)	$15,000	$ 75	Over $1,000 – daily Under $1,000 – weekly
Shearson Lehman Bros. (Financial Management Account)	$10,000	$100	Over $1,000 – daily Under $1,000 – weekly
Smith Barney (Vantage Account)	$ 5,000	$ 40	Over $1,000 – daily Under $1,000 – weekly

*Unless otherwise indicated, minimum investment can be in the form of either cash or securities.

purchased for an amount greater than the current balance, the needed funds are supplied automatically through a loan. Along with one-stop financial supermarkets, central asset accounts are exceptionally popular with investors. However, stipulated minimum balance requirements ranging from $5,000 to $20,000 — the CMA, for example, requires an initial balance of $20,000 in cash or securities — limit the availability of central asset accounts to those with greater savings. Exhibit 5.5 provides a representative list of some of the institutions offering these accounts, along with recent data on their minimum investment requirements, annual fees, and frequency of sweeps.

MAINTAINING A CHECKING ACCOUNT

Maintaining a checking account is both a safe way to hold money and a convenient way to pay for the goods and services consumed in everyday life. How frequently and for what purposes can you use a checking account? Spend a few moments answering this question before reading on.

Checking account balances are an important component of the money supply. They are a near-perfect substitute for cash and today are viewed by most people as absolutely essential. Checking accounts not only provide a safe and convenient way to hold money but also streamline point-of-sale purchases, debt payments, and other basic transactions. In one form or another (regular or interest-paying checking accounts), they can be maintained at commercial banks, S&Ls, savings banks, credit unions, and even at brokerage houses through central asset accounts. For convenience, we will focus our attention on commercial bank checking accounts, although our discussion applies to checking accounts maintained at other types of financial institutions as well.

OPENING A CHECKING ACCOUNT

The factors that typically influence the choice of where to maintain a checking account are convenience, services provided, and cost. Many people choose a bank solely on the basis of such convenience factors as business hours, location, number of drive-in windows, and/or number and location of branch offices and automatic teller machines (ATMs). Some states permit branch banking throughout communities, while others prohibit branches altogether. Ease of access is obviously an important consideration because most people prefer to bank near their homes or places of employment. Services provided differ from bank to bank. Depending on their size, banks may rent safe-deposit boxes, provide for direct deposits and withdrawals, make loans, offer financial planning, and provide various types of bank card and check-cashing services.

Once you determine the banking services you need, you should evaluate the offerings of conveniently located financial institutions. In addition to convenience and availability of services, you should consider safety (deposit insurance and financial condition, discussed earlier), interest rates, types of accounts (including special accounts that combine features such as credit cards, free checks, and reduced fees), structure and level of fees and charges, and quality of customer service. In today's competitive banking environment, taking the time to investigate several banks can help you obtain the best services at minimum cost.

The Cost of a Checking Account. Free checking used to be fairly common but is not so today. One of the by-products of deregulation and the growth of interest-paying checking accounts has been a sharp increase in bank service charges. Today it is estimated that few, if any, banks and other depository institutions let you write as many checks as you like free of charge. The rest levy monthly and/or per-check fees when your balance drops below a stipulated minimum, and some charge you for checking no matter how large a balance you carry in your account.

Usually you must maintain a minimum balance of $500 to $1,000 or more in order to avoid a service charge. While some banks use the *average* monthly balance in an account to determine whether to charge, the vast majority use the *daily* balance procedure. This means that if your account should happen to fall below the minimum balance just once during the month, you will be hit with the full service charge even if you keep an average balance that is three times the stipulated minimum. Let your balance fall $1 below the minimum on just one day out of the month, and you'll pay! Further, the amount of service charge you will pay will be quite substantial. If the daily balance falls below the minimum, you can expect to get hit in two ways: (1) with a base service charge of, say, $5.00 a month, and (2) with additional charges of, say, 25 cents for each check you write and 10 cents for each automatic funds transfer you make with your ATM card or bank-by-phone service. Using these fees as an illustration, assume you write 20 checks and make 7 ATM transfers in a given month. If your balance falls below the minimum, you will have to pay a service charge of $5.00 + (20 × $.25) + (7 × $.10) = $10.70.

In addition to the service charges levied on checking accounts, banks have increased most other check-related charges and raised the minimum balances required for free checking and waivers of specified fees. The charge on a returned check can be as high as $15 to $20, and stop payment orders may cost $10. Some banks charge fees for ATM transactions, point-of-sale transactions made with an ATM card, or more than a specified number of bank-by-phone transactions. Most also charge for using the ATM of another bank that is a member of the same network.

The size of the required minimum balance and the fee structure vary from bank to bank. Further, the service charges on regular checking acounts are usually much less than on NOW accounts. Thus, if you intend to keep only a small amount in your checking account, you may be better off with a no-frills, regular checking account. All too often individuals find that the service charge they pay on their NOW accounts far exceed any interest they earn and that the net result is a very costly form of checking. It is not surprising, therefore, that many smart consumers today are using cost as the single most important variable in choosing where to set up a checking account.

At most banks and other depository institutions, you will be hit with a hefty service charge if your checking account balance falls just $1 below the stipulated minimum amount for just one day out of the month. **Fact:** Most banks and other depository institutions use the *daily* balance in your account, rather than the *average* monthly balance, to determine whether you must pay a service charge; thus, letting it fall below the minimum even once can have a significant cost.

Single or Joint Account.

Two people wishing to open a checking account may do so in one of three ways: (1) They can each open individual checking accounts (on which the other cannot write checks); (2) they can open a joint account that requires both signatures on all checks; or (3) they can open a joint account that allows either one to write checks (the most common type of joint account). One advantage of the joint account over two single accounts is that it lowers the service charges. In addition, the account has rights of survivorship, which, in the case of a married couple, means that if one spouse dies, the surviving spouse, after fulfilling a specified legal requirement, can draw checks on the account. (If account owners are treated as tenants in common rather than having rights of survivorship,

the survivor gets only his or her share of the account. Thus, when opening a joint account it is important to specify the rights preferred.) It is impossible to say what type of system will be successful for a given couple. One financial expert recommends that couples experiment with different systems until they find the one most comfortable for them.

CHECKING ACCOUNT PROCEDURES

A check should always be written in ink. It should include the name of the person to whom it is made out (the payee), the amount, and the date. The amount of the check should be written both in numerals and in script in order to ensure accuracy; if these amounts do not agree, the *written* amount is considered legally correct. The check should be signed the same way as on the signature card, which was completed when the account was initially opened; otherwise, it may not be accepted by the bank. It is also a good idea to note its purpose directly on the check itself—usually on the line provided in the lower left-hand corner. For example, on the personal check written by James Morrison shown in Exhibit 5.6, he has noted that the $65.17 made out to Gulf Oil Company is payment due on his Gulf credit card. This information can be used for both budgeting and tax purposes at some future date.

The Checkbook Ledger.

Whenever a check is written or a deposit made, a corresponding entry must be made in the **checkbook ledger**, which is provided with the checkbook for purposes of maintaining accurate records of all transactions in the account (see Exhibit 5.6). By subtracting the amount of each check written and adding the amount of each deposit made to the previous balance, the account balance can be kept up to date. Good records of transactions and an accurate balance help avoid overdrawing the account.

Making Deposits.

Deposit slips are normally included in your checkbook and are also readily obtainable from your bank. Filling out a deposit slip is the first step in making a deposit. Separate entries for currency, coins, and checks are typically included on deposit slips (see Exhibit 5.6). Each check deposited is listed separately by its so-called *transit I.D. number*, which is usually printed just to the right of the date. For example, the check in Exhibit 5.6 contains the numbers 11-24/1, which is the transit I.D. number for the bank, Wells Fargo Bank, San Francisco, California. You should use the top group of numbers (here 11-24/1) to identify the checks you are depositing—that is, for each check you deposit, you should list the appropriate transit I.D. number and the amount of the check. If you were depositing James's check in Exhibit 5.6, you would enter the following on your deposit slip: 11-24/1 $65.17.

You should also be sure to properly endorse all checks. Federal regulations require your endorsement to be made in black or blue ink and to be within 1½ inches of the check's trailing edge (left end of the check when viewed from the front) so as not to interfere with endorsements from the bank at which the check is deposited. (If you don't comply, you'll still get your money, but it may take longer.)

To protect against possible loss of endorsed checks, it is common practice to use a special endorsement, such as "Pay to the order of XYZ Bank," or a restrictive endorsement, such as "For deposit only." If the way your name is written on the check differs from the way you signed the signature card, you should sign your correct signature below your endorsement. In order to further ensure that the deposit is properly entered into your account, write your account number below your endorsement.

You can submit your deposit to your bank in several ways: at the bank during normal banking hours; at a remote banking facility, such as a drive-in window; at an **automatic teller machine (ATM)**, a type of remote computer terminal at which transactions can be made 24 hours a day, 7 days a week; in the bank's **night depository**, a protected type of mail slot on the exterior of the bank, in the special envelopes banks usually provide for after-hours deposits; or by mail in the self-addressed, sometimes postage-paid deposit envelopes often provided for this purpose. The use of ATMs, night depositories, and banking by mail is not advised when cash is being deposited because of the risk of an unaccountable loss.

When checks are deposited, a delay in the availability of the funds may result due to the time required for them to clear. In order to avoid overdraw-

ing your account, you should become aware of your bank's "hold" policy on deposits. In 1988, the government established maximum funds availability delays on deposits. It generally takes between one and five business days for funds to become available. For example, on a check drawn on another local bank funds must be made available no later than the second business day after deposit. An out-of-town check, however, may take a maximum of five business days to clear. Longer holds—up to nine business days—can be applied by banks under special circumstances, such as when more than $5,000 is deposited into a given account in one day or when the depositor has repeatedly overdrawn his or her account within the immediately preceding six months.

Endorsing Checks. When you receive a check from someone, you can either cash it, deposit it, or use it to pay someone else (a third party). Regardless of how you use the check, you will have to endorse it on the back in exactly the same way it has been made out on the front. The common forms of endorsement—*blank, special, restrictive,* and *conditional*—are illustrated in Exhibit 5.7. It is important to make sure that all endorsements conform with the federal regulations cited earlier.

Overdrafts. When a check is written for an amount greater than the current account balance,

---

checkbook ledger

A ledger provided with a checkbook for purposes of maintaining accurate records of all transactions in the account.

automatic teller machine (ATM)

A type of remote computer terminal at which customers of a bank or other depository institution can perform basic transactions 24 hours a day, 7 days a week.

night depository

A protected type of mail slot on the exterior of a financial institution that its customers can use to make after-hours deposits.

EXHIBIT 5.6
Checking Account Transactions

Three important parts of a checking account are the checks written, the deposits made, and the checkbook ledger, in which checks written, deposits made, and the latest account balance are recorded.

Check

Checkbook Ledger

Record transactions below: Checks, Express Stop Withdrawals, Express Transfers and Deposits.

CHECK NO.	DATE	TRANSACTIONS	TAX DEDUCT CODES	TRANSACTION AMOUNT	√	DEPOSIT AMOUNT	BALANCE	
							211	47
	2/15	Pay - direct deposit				625 13	836	60
149	2/19	Mastercard		50 00			786	60
150	2/23	Cash		40 00			746	60
	2/25	Deposit - Expenses				78 29	824	89
151	2/28	Gulf Oil Co.		65 17			759	72
152	2/28	Casa Bella Apts - Rent		525 00			234	72
—	3/2	ATM - Cash		40 00			194	72
—	3/3	ATM - Lucky - Groceries		29 47			165	25
—	3/4	ATM - Transfer fr. Savings				200 00	365	25

Deposit Slip

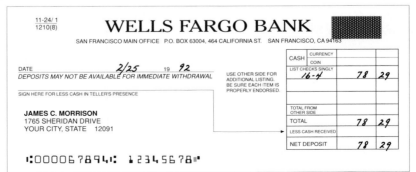

Source: Courtesy of Wells Fargo Bank, San Francisco, California.

EXHIBIT 5.7

Types of Check Endorsement

There are a variety of ways to endorse a check, from a blank endorsement to a highly restrictive one. Regardless of which endorsement is used, technically, it must be made in black or blue ink and be within 1½ inches of the check's trailing edge.

Blank

> *James C. Morrison*

This is the most common form of endorsement. One merely endorses the check by signing his or her name. Once endorsed, the check becomes payable to whoever possesses it.

Special

> Pay to the order of
> John Smith
> *James C. Morrison*

This endorsement includes a notation specifically indicating to whom the check is to be paid. Such an endorsement does not preclude that person from endorsing the check over to yet another person (fourth party).

Restrictive

(1)

> Pay to the order of
> John Smith only
> *James C. Morrison*

(2)

> For deposit only
> *James C. Morrison*

By adding the word "only" after the third party's name, the check cannot be endorsed over to a fourth party. The third party in this case could be either an individual or a bank.

Conditional

> Pay to the order of
> John Smith only
> upon completion
> of car repair
> *James C. Morrison*

This endorsement, although not legally binding, specifies some condition. Its use restricts further negotiation of the check and makes the third party (John Smith) liable to the second party (James C. Morrison) if he or she violates the condition.

the result is an **overdraft**. Poor bookkeeping on the part of the account holder or a delay in the bank's receipt of a deposit can be the cause. If the overdraft is proven to have been intentional, the bank can initiate legal proceedings against the account holder. The action taken by a bank on an overdraft depends on the amount involved and the strength of its relationship with the account holder. In many cases, the bank stamps the overdrawn check with the words "insufficient balance (or funds)" and returns it to the party to whom it was written. The account holder is notified of this action, and a penalty fee of $7 to $20 or more is deducted from his or her checking account. In addition, the depositor of a "bad check" may be charged as much as $10 to $15 by its bank, which explains why merchants typically charge customers who given them bad checks $10 to $20 or more and often refuse to accept future checks from them.

In instances in which a strong relationship has been established between the account holder and the bank or in which arrangements have been made for **overdraft protection**, the bank will go ahead and pay a check that overdraws the account. In cases where overdraft protection has not been prearranged but the bank pays the check, the account holder is usually notified by the bank and charged a penalty fee for the inconvenience. However, the check does not bounce, and the check writer's creditworthiness is not damaged.

There are several ways to arrange overdraft protection. Many banks offer an *overdraft line of credit*, which automatically extends a loan to cover the amount of overdrafts. In most cases, however, the loans are made only in specified increments, such as $50 or $100, and interest (or a fee) is levied against the loan amount, *not* the actual amount of the overdraft. This can be an expensive form of protection, particularly if you do not promptly pay such a loan. For example, if you had a $110 overdraft and the bank made overdraft loans in $100 increments, it would automatically deposit $200 in your account. If the bank charged 12 percent annually (or 1 percent per month) and you repaid the loan within a month, you would incur total interest of $2 [= ($200 × 12%)/12]. But remember you paid interest on $90 ($200 − $110) you didn't need; the annualized rate of interest on this overdraft loan is *21.8 percent*

[($2/$110) × 12]! Another way to cover overdrafts is with an *automatic transfer program*, which automatically transfers funds from your savings to checking account in the event of an overdraft. Under this program, some banks charge both an annual fee and a fee on each transfer. Of course, the best form of overdraft protection is to employ good cash management techniques and regularly balance your checking account.

Stopping Payment. Occasionally it is necessary to **stop payment** on a check that has been issued. This may be due to any of several possible reasons: (1) Checks or a checkbook are either lost or stolen; (2) a good or service paid for by check is found to be faulty (Note: Some states prohibit you from stopping payment on faulty goods or services); or (3) a check is issued as part of a contract that is not carried out. Payment on a check is stopped by notifying the bank. Normally the account holder must fill out a form indicating the check number and date, amount, and the name of the person to whom it was written. Sometimes stop-payment orders can be initiated over the telephone, in which case a written follow-up is normally required. Telephone-initiated stop payments generally remain in effect for fourteen days and written ones for six months.

Once a stop-payment order has been issued, the bank tellers are told to refuse payment on the affected check. At the same time, the stop-payment information is placed in the bank's data processing system so that the check will be rejected if it is presented by another bank in the check-clearing process. Most banks require account holders who wish to stop payment to sign a statement relieving the bank of any liability if payment is erroneously made on the check in question. A fee ranging from $10 to $15 is usually charged for stopping payment on a check.

MONTHLY STATEMENTS

Once each month, your bank will provide a statement that contains an itemized listing of all transactions (checks written and deposits made) within your checking account; also included are any service charges levied and interest earned, such as James Morrison's May 1992 bank statement shown in Exhibit 5.8. Many banks include canceled checks and deposit slips with the bank statement, although they are slowly (but surely) moving away from this practice. Of course, banks that do not return canceled checks and deposit slips will provide photocopies of them upon request, generally for a fee. You can use the monthly statements to verify the accuracy of your account records and to reconcile differences between the statement balance and the balance shown in your checkbook ledger. The monthly statement is also an important source of information for your tax records.

Account Reconciliation. It is advisable to reconcile your bank account as soon as possible after you receive your monthly statement. The **account reconciliation** process (or *balancing the checkbook*, as the process is also known) can uncover errors in recording checks or deposits, in addition or subtraction, and, occasionally, in the bank's processing of the checks. It can also help you avoid overdrafts, since it forces you to periodically verify your account balance. Discrepancies between the account balance reflected in your checkbook ledger and that shown in the bank statement can be attributed to one of four basic factors, assuming neither you nor the bank has made any errors.

1. Checks that you have written, ATM withdrawals, or other automatic payments subtracted from your checkbook balance have not yet been received and deducted by your bank and therefore remain outstanding.
2. Deposits that you have made and added to your checkbook balance have not yet been credited to your account.
3. Any service (activity) charges levied on your account by the bank have not yet been deducted from your checkbook balance.
4. Interest earned on your account (if it is a MMDA or NOW account) has not yet been added to your checkbook balance.

Take the following steps to reconcile your account:

1. Upon receipt of your bank statement, arrange all canceled checks in descending numerical

order based on their sequence numbers or issuance dates. (Note: Skip this step if your bank does not return canceled checks.)
2. Compare each check with the corresponding entry in your checkbook ledger to make sure no recording errors exist. (Note: If your bank does not return canceled checks, you should compare the bank statement information for each check with the corresponding entry in your checkbook ledger.) Place a checkmark in your ledger alongside each entry compared. Also, check off any other withdrawals, such as from ATMs, automatic payments, or point-of-sale debit transactions.
3. List the checks and other deductions (ATM withdrawals) still *outstanding* — that is, those deducted in your checkbook but not returned with your bank statement (see step 2). Total their amount.
4. Compare the deposit slips returned with the statement to deposits shown in your checkbook. Total the amount of deposits still *outstanding* — that is, those shown in your checkbook ledger but not yet received by the bank. Be sure to include all automatic deposits and deposits made at ATMs in your calculations.

---

overdraft
The result of writing a check for an amount greater than the current account balance.

overdraft protection
An arrangement between the depository institution and account holder wherein the institution automatically advances money to cover an overdrawn check.

stop payment
An order made by an account holder asking the depository institution to refuse payment on an already issued check.

account reconciliation
The process of verifying the accuracy of your checking account records in light of the bank's records reflected in the monthly statement, which shows checks written, deposits made, service charges levied, and interest earned during the month.

EXHIBIT 5.8

A Checking Account Statement

Each month you receive a statement from your bank or depository financial institution that summarizes the month's transactions and shows your latest account balance. Similar statements are also sent for savings accounts and interest-paying checking accounts such as NOWs and MMDAs. This sample statement not only shows the checks that have been paid but also lists all ATM transactions, point-of-sale transactions using the ATM card (the Interlink payments at Lucky Stores), and direct deposit of payroll.

```
|   MILLBRAE                                #240
    P.O. BOX 516  MILLBRAE, CA             94030

        JAMES C. MORRISON
        1765 SHERIDAN DRIVE                     N        CALL (415) 375-1181
        YOUR CITY, STATE  12091                21        24 HOURS/DAY, 7 DAYS/WEEK
                                                         FOR ASSISTANCE WITH
                                                         YOUR ACCOUNT.

    PAGE 1 OF 1       THIS STATEMENT COVERS:  4/30/92 THROUGH 5/29/92
```

GOLD ACCOUNT	SUMMARY			
	PREVIOUS BALANCE	473.68	MINIMUM BALANCE	21.78
0123-45678	DEPOSITS	1,302.83+		
	WITHDRAWALS	1,689.02−		
	SERVICE CHANGES	7.50−		
	DIRECT DEPOSIT DISCOUNT	1.00+		
▶	NEW BALANCE	80.99		

CHECKS AND WITHDRAWALS	CHECK	DATE PAID	AMOUNT	CHECK	DATE PAID	AMOUNT
	203	5/01	10.00	213	5/08	40.00
	204	4/30	15.00	214	5/09	9.58
	205	5/10	635.00	215	5/20	66.18
	206	5/08	25.00	216	5/20	64.92
	207	5/07	19.00	217	5/21	25.03
	208	5/07	50.00	218	5/21	37.98
	209	5/08	15.00	219	5/22	35.00
	210	5/10	83.00	220	5/22	105.00
	211	5/10	10.00	222*	5/22	100.00
	212	5/08	70.00	223	5/21	40.00
				224	5/29	40.82

		DATE PAID	AMOUNT
	GOLD ACCOUNT FEE LESS $1.00 DISCOUNT	4/30	6.50
EXPRESS BANKING	INTERLINK PURCHASE #572921 ON 04/30 AT LUCKY STORE NO 043 MILLBRAE CA	5/01	50.00
	WITHDRAWAL #08108 AT 00165A ON 05/04	5/06	20.00
	INTERLINK PURCHASE #807409 ON 05/11 AT LUCKY STORE NO 056 BURLINGAME CA	5/13	12.51
	WITHDRAWAL #01015 AT 00240C ON 05/17	5/17	20.00
	WITHDRAWAL #04792 AT 00167C ON 05/20	5/20	20.00
	WITHDRAWAL #04386 AT 00240D ON 05/21	5/21	40.00
	INTERLINK PURCHASE #880318 ON 05/28 AT LUCKY STORE NO 043 MILLBRAE CA	5/29	30.00

DEPOSITS				DATE POSTED	AMOUNT
	AVS RNT CAR SYST PAYROLL	G2	000000035382	5/03	618.69
	AVS RNT CAR SYST PAYROLL	G2	000000035382	5/17	83.39
	AVS RNT CAR SYST PAYROLL	G2	000000035382	5/17	600.75

EXPRESS STOP LOCATIONS USED		
	00165A:	249 PRIMROSE RD, BURLINGAME, CA
	00240C:	490 BROADWAY, MILLBRAE, CA
	00167C:	1145 BROADWAY, BURLINGAME, CA
	00240D:	490 BROADWAY, MILLBRAE, CA

Source: Courtesy of Wells Fargo Bank, San Francisco, California

5. *Subtract* the total amount of checks outstanding (from step 3) from your bank statement balance, and *add* to this balance the amount of outstanding deposits (from step 4). The resulting amount is your *adjusted bank balance*.

6. Deduct the amount of any service charges levied by the bank from, and add any interest earned to, your checkbook ledger balance. Make sure you include all service charges for the period, including those for returned checks, stop payments, and/or new checks ordered. The resulting amount is your *new checkbook balance*. This amount should equal your *adjusted bank balance* (from step 5). If it does not, you should check all addition and subtraction in your checkbook ledger, since you have probably made an error.

The reverse side of your bank statement usually provides a form for reconciling your account along with step-by-step instructions. Although a number of different approaches to reconciliation exist, the one described here is the most straightforward. Exhibit 5.9 includes an account reconciliation form, following these procedures, that was completed by James Morrison for the month of May 1992. The form can be used to reconcile regular checking accounts or any type of interest-paying checking account (like NOW accounts or MMDAs).

Tax Records. Your monthly bank statement is an important tax record. It can be reviewed along with the checkbook ledger to evaluate past income and expenditures. Although you may maintain accurate records of these items as part of your budgeting process, the statement can be used to provide proof of payment, which you might need if the Internal Revenue Service decides to audit your tax return. At the time a check is written, it is advisable to indicate its purpose both in the checkbook ledger and on the front of the check. Bank statements should be retained for a period of at least five years, since an audit can still be conducted several years after a tax return has been filed.

SPECIAL TYPES OF CHECKS

Because there is no way to be absolutely sure that a check is good, some type of verification is often necessary. This is common for large purchases or when the buyer is not located in the area in which the purchase is being made. The most common instruments used to guarantee payment are *cashier's checks*, *traveler's checks*, and *certified checks*.

Cashier's Check. Anyone can buy a **cashier's check** from a bank. These checks are often used by people who do not have checking accounts. They can be purchased for about $5 and are occasionally issued at no charge to bank customers. In exchange for an appropriate amount of money—the amount of the check plus a service charge—the bank issues a check drawn on itself. In this way, the *bank* is now writing the check, *not* you—which is about the best assurance you can give that the check is good.

Traveler's Check. A number of large financial organizations—such as Citibank, American Express, VISA, and Bank of America—issue **traveler's checks**, which can be purchased at commercial banks and most other financial institutions in denominations ranging from $20 to $100. A fee of about 1.5 percent is charged on their purchase. If properly endorsed, traveler's checks are accepted by most U.S. businesses and can be exchanged for local currencies in most parts of the world. Since these checks are not valid unless properly countersigned by the purchaser, and since they are issued against loss or theft by the issuing agency, they provide a safe, convenient, and popular form of money for travel.

Certified Check. A **certified check** is made out to whoever is to be paid. The bank immediately

---

certified check
A personal check that is guaranteed (for a fee of $10 to $15 or more) by the bank on which it is drawn so that the funds are available for payment.

cashier's check
A check payable to a third party that is drawn by a bank on itself in exchange for the amount specified plus, in most cases, a service fee (of about $5).

traveler's check
A check sold (for a fee of about 1.5 percent) by many large financial institutions, in denominations ranging from $20 to $100, that can be used for making purchases and exchanged for local currencies in most parts of the world.

EXHIBIT 5.9

An Account Reconciliation Form — James Morrison's May 1992 Statement

James Morrison used this form to reconcile his checking account for the month of May 1992. Because line A equals line B, he has fully reconciled the difference between the $80.99 bank statement balance and his $339.44 checkbook balance. Accounts should be reconciled each month — as soon as possible after receipt of the bank statement.

CHECKING ACCOUNT RECONCILIATION

For the Month of ___May___, 19_92_

Accountholder Name(s) ___James Morrison___

Type of Account ___Regular Checking___

1. Ending balance shown on bank statement **$ 80.99**

Add up checks and withdrawals still outstanding:

Check Number or Date	Amount	Check Number or Date	Amount
221	$ 81.55		$
225	196.50		
Lucky - 5/28	25.00		
ATM - 5/29	40.00		
	TOTAL $ 343.05		

2. Deduct total checks/withdrawals still outstanding from bank balance **− $343.05**

Add up deposits still outstanding:

Date	Amount	Date	Amount
5/29	595.00		
	TOTAL $ 595.00		

3. *Add* total deposits still outstanding to bank balance **+ $595.00**

[A] **Adjusted Bank Balance** (1 - 2 + 3) **$ 332.94**

4. Ending balance shown in checkbook **$339.44**

5. *Deduct* any bank service charges for the period _(-7.50 + $1.00)_ **− $ 6.50**

6. *Add* interest earned for the period **+ $ 0**

[B] **New Checkbook Balance** (4 - 5 + 6) **$332.94**

Note: Your account is reconciled when line A equals line B.

deducts the amount of the check from your account and then stamps the check to indicate its certification. There is normally a charge of $10 to $15 or more for this service. In effect, the bank has guaranteed that because the funds are there to cover the check, the check is good. Since the bank has become the guarantor, it usually will not return the canceled check to you but will keep it for its own records.

OTHER BANK SERVICES

Banks and other depository institutions offer their customers a variety of other convenient services. Many of these services rely on the use of current technology to transfer funds electronically. Regulation of electronic funds transfer system services protects consumers in a variety of ways. Safe-deposit boxes are another important bank service.

Electronic Funds Transfer Systems. **Electronic funds transfer systems (EFTS)** use the latest telecommunications and computer technology to electronically transfer funds into or out of your account. For example, your employer may use EFTS to electronically transfer your pay from its bank account directly into your personal bank account at the same or another bank. This eliminates the employer's need to pepare and process checks and the employee's need to deposit them. EFTS include such services as automatic teller machines and debit cards, pre-authorized deposits and payments, bank-by-phone accounts, and computer-based banking-at-home.

Automatic Teller Machines and Debit Cards. Another form of EFTS uses specially coded plastic cards, called **debit cards**, to transfer funds. These cards are used to initiate the transfer of funds from the customer's bank account (a debit) to the recipient's account. Many people who were previously reluctant to use these cards now find them more convenient than cash and checks. Automatic teller machine (ATM) cards are one type of debit card.

The ATM card has become a popular way to make banking transactions. Suppose you need cash at 1:30 a.m. Although no bank is open, you can go to an ATM machine and use your card to withdraw funds from your account. As noted earlier, ATMs are actually remote computer terminals that allow customers to make deposits, withdrawals, and other transactions, such as loan payments or transfers between accounts, 24 hours a day, 7 days a week. Most banks have ATMs outside of their offices, and some locate freestanding ATMs in shopping malls, airports, grocery stores, at colleges and universities, and other high-traffic areas in order to enhance and protect their competitive position. If your bank belongs to an EFTS network, such as Cirrus, Star, or Interlink, you can get cash from the ATM of any bank in the United States that is a member of that network. You can also use your ATM card to make purchases from selected merchants. Many gasoline companies and grocery stores now have terminals that permit payment by ATM card. Most banks charge a per-transaction fee of $3 to $6 for using the ATM of another bank, and some also charge for the use of the ATM card to pay certain merchants.

Other debit cards can be used with *point-of-sale (POS) machines*—electronic machines located at sales outlets—to pay for purchases. These transactions result in the transfer of funds from a customer's bank account directly into the merchant's account. For instance, customers of Von's grocery stores in California can use their VonsCheck debit cards to buy groceries.

Pre-Authorized Deposits and Payments. Two related EFTS services are *pre-authorized deposits and payments*. They allow you to receive automatic deposits or make payments that occur on a regular basis. As an example, you can authorize to have your paycheck or monthly pension or social security benefits deposited directly into your account. Regular, fixed-amount payments, such as mortgage and consumer loan payments or monthly retirement fund contributions, can be pre-authorized to be made automatically from your account. You can also preauthorize payment of regular payments of varying amounts, such as monthly utility bills. In this

---

electronic funds transfer systems (EFTS)

Systems that employ the latest telecommunications and computer technology to electronically transfer funds into and out of customers' accounts.

debit cards

Plastic cards used to withdraw cash or transfer funds from a customer's bank account to the recipient's account in order to pay for goods or services.

case, each month you would specify by phone the amount to be paid. Charges for pre-authorized payments may vary from bank to bank. Typically, customers must maintain a specified minimum deposit balance and pay a per-transaction fee of about 25 cents. Not only does this system better allow the customer to earn interest on deposits used to pay bills, but it also serves as a convenient payment mechanism that eliminates the postage costs incurred when paying bills by mail.

Bank-by-Phone Accounts. EFTS has also made it possible for bank customers to initiate a variety of banking transactions by telephone. There are two types of bank-by-phone services — those under which the customer can call a customer service operator who handles the transaction, or those under which transactions are made electronically with no human intervention using the key pad on a touchtone telephone to instruct the bank's computer. To use electronic phone banking, the customer first punches their secret code into their phone in order to access their accounts. The system then provides step-by-step instructions as to the appropriate codes required to perform various transactions such as learning an account balance, finding out what checks have cleared, transferring funds to other accounts, and dispatching payments to participating merchants. The cost of these services varies depending on the type of service provided and the customer's level of bank balances. Bank-by-phone services typically charge customers who do not maintain adequate bank balances a monthly fee plus a specified amount for each transaction. In order to encourage electronic phone banking, many banks today charge no fee on basic account transactions. Some banks allow customers who do not maintain a minimum account balance to make a limited number of free operator-assisted transactions each month and charge fees only on additional transactions.

Computer-Based Banking-at-Home. A relatively new service that is slowly gaining acceptance is banking at home via computer. With this service, a modem is used to telephonically link your personal computer to your bank's computer. This allows you to execute a number of transactions, such as paying bills electronically and transferring funds from one account to another, from your home at any time of the day or night. In addition, under this system you can request a current statement of your account in order to learn its balance and review recent transactions. Most systems also allow you to automatically dispatch fixed, regular payments, such as monthly mortgage payments or quarterly insurance premiums. While a computer-based bank-at-home system doesn't replace the use of an ATM in order to obtain cash or deposit money, it can save both the time and the postage involved in paying bills.

The cost of most computer-based home-banking services is about $20 to $25 per month, which includes both the bank's fee and the cost of subscribing to an on-line computer information service such as Prodigy. (Note: The on-line service not only provides access to your bank, but also includes numerous other services, such as providing quotes on securities and life insurance rates along with a transaction capability; giving weather reports and news reports; and providing theater and airline ticket purchases as well as catalog purchases.) Such a system can pay for itself by allowing you to monitor and maintain your account balance above the minimum, thereby avoiding service and overdraft fees. However, in order to bank by computer you need a computer costing $500 to $1,000 — a cost that cannot be justified solely by its use for banking! On the other hand, if you already have a computer, home banking can be helpful because it gives you easy access to most of the data needed for budgeting and tax planning.

Regulation of EFTS Services The Federal Electronic Fund Transfer Act of 1978 delineates your rights and responsibilities as an EFTS user. Under this law, you cannot stop payment on a defective or questionable purchase (however, individual banks and state laws have more lenient provisions). In the case of an error, you must notify the bank within 60 days of its occurrence on your periodic statement or terminal receipt. The bank must investigate and tell you the results within 10 days. The bank can then take up to 45 additional days to investigate the error, but it must return the disputed money to your account until the issue is resolved. If you fail to notify the bank within 60 days of the error, the bank has no obligation under federal law to conduct an investigation or return your money. In addition, it is very important that you notify the bank immediately about the theft, loss, or unauthorized use of your EFTS card. Notification within two business days after you discover the card missing limits your loss to

$50. After two business days, you may lose up to $500 (but never more than was actually withdrawn by the thief). Additionally, if you do not report the loss within 60 days after your periodic statement was mailed, you can lose all of the money in your account. When reporting errors or unauthorized transactions, it is best to notify your bank by telephone and *follow up with a letter*. Keep a copy of the letter in your file.

This law also gives you some protection against being forced to use EFTS. Banks cannot require payments via EFTS, although they can encourage you to do so by offering a slightly lower interest rate. If you are required to receive wages or government benefits by EFTS, you must have the right to select the bank where the funds will be sent. Many state regulations offer additional consumer protection regarding your use of EFTS. However, your best protection is to carefully guard the personal identification number (PIN) used to access your accounts by EFTS. Do not write the PIN on your EFTS card, or on anything else for that matter. And be sure to check your periodic statements for possible errors or unauthorized transactions.

Safe-Deposit Boxes. A safe-deposit box is a rented drawer in a bank's vault. The annual rental fee depends on the box size. Small boxes can be rented for about $25 per year, while large ones may cost hundreds of dollars per year. When you rent a box, you receive one key to it, and the bank retains another key. The box can be opened only when both keys are used. This arrangement protects items in the box from theft and makes it an excellent storage place for jewelry, contracts, stock certificates, titles, and other special documents.

SUMMARY

- Cash management plays a vital role in personal financial planning, as it involves the administration and control of liquid assets—cash, checking accounts, savings, and other short-term investment vehicles.

- Financial deregulation has had an enormous impact on the financial institutions and markets of this country, including the creation of financial supermarkets and financial services providers; in a relatively short period of time, the traditional way of doing things has undergone tremendous change.

- In spite of all the change, individuals and families continue to rely heavily on the traditional depository financial institutions for most of their financial services needs—that is, the commercial banks, S&Ls, savings banks, and credit unions, all of which provide a full range of checking accounts, savings accounts, and other financial products and services.

- Most traditional depository institutions are federally insured for up to $100,000 per depositor. However, during the late 1980s and early 1990s, the safety of the banking industry was challenged. The then-prevailing high interest rates, deregulation, and poor economic conditions, resulted in a large number of S&L and bank failures and mergers that put a strain on the deposit insurance system.

- The variety of checking, savings, and other liquid assets that the consumer can choose from has never been greater. Included in this growing menu are not only regular checking and passbook savings accounts, but also money market mutual funds, money market deposit accounts, NOW accounts, certificates of deposit, U.S. Treasury bills, Series EE bonds, and central asset accounts.

- Finding the actual interest earned on your money is often challenging because you have to deal not only with different compounding periods, but also with different ways of measuring qualifying balances.

- The sharp increase in bank service charges that has occurred with deregulation makes it more important than ever to effectively manage one's checking account. It is therefore important to become familiar with checking account procedures and costs, the account reconciliation process, and the special types of checks. In addition, familiarity with other banking services—electronic funds transfer systems and safe-deposit boxes—is helpful in effectively managing your banking activities.

QUESTIONS AND PROBLEMS

1. What is cash management? What are its major functions?

2. Give two broad reasons for holding liquid assets. Identify and briefly describe the popular types of liquid assets.

3. Discuss the effect that deregulation has had on financial markets and institutions. What is a financial supermarket, and how did its emergence affect specialization in the financial services industry?

4. Distinguish among a passbook account, special savings accounts, and a club account.

5. Briefly describe the basic operations and services provided by each of the following traditional banking institutions: (a) commercial bank; (b) savings and loan association; (c) savings bank; and (d) credit union.

6. Define and discuss (a) demand deposits; (b) savings accounts; and (c) interest-paying checking accounts.

7. Briefly describe the key characteristics of each of the following forms of interest-paying checking accounts: (a) money market mutual funds (MMMFs); (b) money market deposit accounts (MMDAs); and (c) NOW accounts.

8. What does "Member FDIC," a sign that is commonly displayed in a bank, mean to a depositor? Do other depository financial institutions provide similar protection? Explain.

9. Would it be possible for an *individual* to have, say, six or seven checking and savings accounts at the same bank and still be fully protected under federal deposit insurance? Explain. Describe how it would be possible for a *married couple* to obtain as much as $500,000 in federal deposit insurance coverage without going to several banks.

10. Briefly discuss the causes of the crisis in the banking industry that resulted in a large number of thrift and commercial bank failures and mergers. What two new agencies were created by Congress to bail out the S&L industry?

11. Bill and Betty Jacobs together earn approximately $42,000 a year after taxes. Through an inheritance and some wise investing, they also have an investment portfolio with a value of almost $90,000.

a. How much of their annual income do you recommend they hold in some form of savings as liquid reserves? Explain.

b. How much of their investment portfolio do you recommend they hold in savings and other short-term investment vehicles? Explain.

c. How much, in total, should they hold in short-term liquid assets?

12. Define and distinguish between the nominal rate of interest and the effective rate of interest. Explain why a savings and loan association that pays 4.5 percent interest, compounded daily, on its savings accounts actually pays an effective rate of 4.60 percent.

13. If you put $5,000 in a savings account that pays interest at the rate of 6 percent, compounded annually, how much will you have in five years? (Hint: Use the *future value* formula.) How much will you earn in interest over the five years? If you put $5,000 *a year* into a savings account that pays interest at the rate of 6 percent a year, how much would you have after five years?

14. Briefly describe the four methods used to measure the deposit account balances that qualify to earn interest. Which approach would you prefer your savings institution to adopt?

15. Briefly describe the basic features of each of the following savings vehicles: (a) certificates of deposit; (b) U.S. Treasury bills; (c) Series EE bonds; and (d) central asset accounts.

16. Describe and differentiate between each of the following forms of check endorsement: (a) blank; (b) special; (c) restrictive; and (d) conditional.

17. Is it possible to bounce a check due to insufficient funds when the checkbook ledger shows a balance available to cover it? Explain what happens when a check bounces. Is it possible to obtain protection against overdrafts?

18. Describe the procedure used to stop payment on a check. Why might one wish to initiate this process?

19. What type of information is found in the monthly bank statement, and how it is used?

Explain the basic steps involved in the account-reconciliation process.

■ **20.** Hun Park has a NOW account at the Third State Bank. His checkbook ledger lists the following checks:

Check Number	Amount
654	$206.05
658	55.22
662	103.00
668	99.00
670	6.10
671	50.25
672	24.90
673	32.45
674	44.50
675	30.00
676	30.00
677	111.23
678	38.04
679	97.99
680	486.70
681	43.50
682	75.00
683	98.50

In addition, he made the following withdrawals and deposits at an ATM near his home:

Date	Amount
11/1	$ 50.00 (withdrawal)
11/2	525.60 (deposit)
11/6	100.00 (deposit)
11/14	75.00 (withdrawal)
11/21	525.60 (deposit)
11/24	150.00 (withdrawal)
11/27	225.00 (withdrawal)
11/30	400.00 (deposit)

Hun's checkbook ledger shows an ending balance of $286.54. He has just received his bank statement for the month of November. It shows an ending balance of $622.44; it also shows that he had interest earned for November of $3.28, had a check service charge of $8 for the month, and had another $12 charge for a returned check. His bank statement indicates the following checks have cleared: 654, 662, 672, 674, 675, 676, 677, 678, 679, and 681. ATM withdrawals on 11/1 and 11/14 and deposits on 11/2 and 11/6 have cleared; no other checks or ATM activities are listed on his statement, so anything remaining should be treated as outstanding. Use a checking account reconciliation form like the one in Exhibit 5.9 to reconcile Hun's checkbook.

21. Briefly describe (a) banking at ATMs using debit cards; (b) pre-authorized deposits and payments; (c) bank-by-phone accounts; and (d) computer-based banking-at-home.

22. Briefly describe your legal rights and responsibilities when using EFTS. Suppose someone stole your ATM card and withdrew $650 from your checking account. State how much money you could lose, according to federal legislation, if you waited the following periods of time before reporting the stolen card to the bank: (a) the day the card was stolen; (b) six days; and (c) 65 days after receiving your periodic statement.

CONTEMPORARY CASE APPLICATIONS

5.1 The Theisens Want to Maximize Their Interest

Anne and Dave Theisen wish to open a savings account and are currently in the process of selecting a savings institution. Having taken courses in personal finance, they know they should inquire with respect to both the effective rate of interest paid on the account and the methods used to determine the balance on which interest will be paid.

Questions

1. Discuss the four basic methods used to measure the size of an account, that is, the amount of money on deposit that is eligible to receive interest for the period.

2. Assume Anne and Dave opened a checking account on September 1; use the following account transaction data to determine *the balances* on which the Theisens will be eligible to receive interest for the month of September 1992 under each of the four methods. (Assume that there are twelve 30-day months in the year.)

3. Assuming the effective rate of interest is 6 percent and using the balance data given, calculate the amount of *interest earned* under each of the four methods for the month ended September 30, 1992.

4. Based on your analysis, which of the four methods would allow the Theisens to maximize their interest earnings? Explain.

Account Transactions for Month of September 1992

Date	Transaction	Amount	Account Balance
1 (initial balance)	—	—	$1,000
3	Deposit	$2,000	3,000
14	Deposit	1,000	4,000
17	Withdrawal	2,500	1,500
24	Withdrawal	1,000	500
25	Deposit	4,000	4,500
30 (ending balance)	—	—	$4,500

◗ 5.2 Reconciling the Pattersons' Checkbook

Nick and Rosalyn Patterson opened their first checking account at The Barclays Bank on September 14, 1992. They have just received their first bank statement for the period ending October 5, 1992. The statement and checkbook ledger are as follows:

Bank Statement

NICK & ROSALYN PATTERSON
2128 E. 51ST ST.
DETROIT, MICHIGAN

THE BARCLAYS BANK
800-231-4567
STATEMENT PERIOD SEPT. 6 to OCT. 5, 1992

	Opening Balance	Total Deposits for Period	Total Checks/Withdrawals for Period	Ending Balance
	$0	$569.25	$473.86	$ 95.39
Date	Withdrawals (Debits)		Deposits (Credits)	Balance
Sept. 14			$360.00	$360.00
Sept. 23			97.00	457.00
Sept. 25	$ 45.20		9.25	421.05
Oct. 1			103.00	524.05
Oct. 1	3.00 BC			521.05
Oct. 2	65.90	$49.76 $45.00		360.39
Oct. 5	265.00			95.39

RT = Returned Checks   DM = Debit Memo   BC = Bank Charges
FC = Finance Charges   CM = Credit Memo

Checkbook Ledger

Check Number	Date 1992	Details	Check Amount	Deposit Amount	Account Balance
—	Sept. 14	Cash — gift from wedding		$360.00	$360.00
—	Sept. 24	Nick's wages from library		97.00	457.00
101	Sept. 24	Kroger — groceries	$ 45.20		411.80
102	Sept. 27	Michigan Bell Telephone bill	28.40		383.40
—	Oct. 1	Nick's wages for library work		103.00	486.40
103	Oct. 1	Univ. book store — college books	65.90		420.50
104	Oct. 1	K mart — sewing material	16.75		403.75
105	Oct. 1	G. Heller — apartment rent	265.00		138.75
106	Oct. 2	Blue Cross — health insurance	17.25		121.50
107	Oct. 3	Kroger — groceries	49.76		71.74
108	Oct. 4	Cash, gas, entertainment, laundry	45.00		26.74
—	Oct. 5	Rosalyn's salary — Universal Corp.		450.00	476.74

Questions

1. From this information, prepare a bank reconciliation for the Pattersons as of October 5, 1992, using a checking account reconciliation form like the one in Exhibit 5.9.

2. Given your answer to Question 1, what, if any, adjustments will the Pattersons need to make in their checkbook ledger? Comment on the procedures used to reconcile their checkbook as well as on your findings.

3. If the Pattersons earned interest on their idle balances as a result of the account being a NOW account, what impact would this have on the reconciliation process? Explain.

FOR MORE INFORMATION

General Information Articles

Davis, Kristin. "Deposit Insurance: Are You Covered?" *Changing Times*, April 1991, pp. 43–44.

———. "The Ups and Downs of Chasing CD Yields." *Kiplinger's Personal Finance Magazine*, April 1992, p. 34.

Giese, William. "Pick the Perfect Money-Market Funds." *Kiplinger's Personal Finance Magazine*, August 1991, pp. 49–51.

Herman, Tom. "Buying Treasurys Without a Middleman," *The Wall Street Journal*, May 1, 1991, pp. C1, 15.

Jasen, Georgette. "Get Set for Changes if Your Bank Merges." *The Wall Street Journal*, August 23, 1991, pp. C1, 9.

Kobliner, Beth. "How to Protect Yourself in the Bank Crisis." *Money*, March 1991, pp. 112–130.

Lavine, Alan. "30 Easy Ways to Make Your Savings Grow." *Consumers Digest*, November/December 1991, pp. 28–33.

Richman, Louis. "Getting America to Save More." *Fortune*, December 16, 1991, pp. 67–76.

Spiro, Leah Nathan. "Accounts That Do It All." *Business Week*, February 3, 1992, pp. 86–87.

———. "Keep Your Cash Safe!" *Money*, February 1991, pp. 68–75.

Government Documents and Other Publications

Basic Information on Treasury Securities—Treasury Direct, U.S. Treasury, Bureau of Public Debt, Washington, DC 20239-0001, phone 202-287-4113. Also available from any local Federal Reserve bank or branch, such as The Federal Reserve Bank of New York, 33 Liberty Street, New York, NY 10045.

Quinn, Jane Bryant. "Saving More Money." *Making the Most of Your Money*. New York: Simon & Schuster, 1991, pp. 156–180.

———. "Your Basic Banking." *Making the Most of Your Money*. New York: Simon & Schuster, 1991, pp. 52–78.

Updegrave, Walter L. *How to Keep Your Savings Safe*. New York: Crown, 1992.

GETTING A HANDLE ON YOUR FINANCIAL FUTURE

The major problem that most people face in implementing a cash management program is selecting the appropriate types of accounts or savings vehicles from a number of providers including commercial banks, savings banks, savings and loan associations, credit unions, mutual funds, and brokerage firms. To do this properly requires some effort on the part of the consumer.

In order to effectively manage your cash you need to have a thorough understanding of your current financial condition and your income and expenditure patterns, as discussed in Chapter 2. This will enable you to determine the amount of funds necessary to meet your normal expenditures as well as the amount that you should have in an easily accessible form for emergencies. Any additional funds can

If You Are Just Starting Out

Everyone needs some type of transactions account to provide a safe and convenient method of paying for goods and services and providing a record of payment to assist you in preparing your tax returns and for monitoring your spending habits. Once this account has been selected, your attention should shift to the selection of a savings account or vehicle to provide you with funds in the event of an emergency. This account should have low risks and high liquidity. Finally you should select a savings account or vehicle in which funds could be accumulated to achieve your financial goals. This would involve balancing the returns available through the various alternatives with the risks associated with each.

Checking:

1. In choosing a transaction account, geographic convenience is usually the first consideration. Determine if your account needs are better suited by a provider close to work, school, or home.

2. Although your initial requirements are usually minimal, you should be aware of all of the services offered by your provider, which you might need in the future.

3. Examine the monthly cash budget you developed in Chapter 3. Decide which and how many items could be paid by check and which could be paid with cash.

4. Determine if there are service charges on the account and how they are applied. Based on your estimated usage and balance in the account, you should compute what the average service charge would be on different accounts at different institutions within your geographic preference for comparison.

5. After setting up your transactions account, be sure to reconcile it every month. The worksheet provided with this chapter is designed to walk you through the steps of this reconciliation.

Savings (Emergency Fund):

1. To determine how large an emergency fund you need, multiply your monthly take-home pay by a minimum of three months and up to six months, depending on what is appropriate for your financial circumstances.

2. Determine how interest is calculated on the account and how often it is credited.

3. Find out if there are any penalties or charges associated on withdrawal of funds from the account.

4. The account should be federally insured or the savings vehicle relatively safe.

Savings Program:

1. Determine how much money is needed for a particular financial goal, such as a down payment on a house, and your timetable for achieving the goal.

2. Based on the amount of funds currently available and the amount to be put aside out of your take-home pay, calculate the rate of return necessary to achieve your financial goal.

3. Select the savings account or vehicle that best meets your return requirements relative to the risk involved.

then be placed in accounts or savings vehicles that are less liquid and earn higher returns to meet future financial goals. Once this basic analysis is performed, you can then begin the process of selecting appropriate cash management vehicles.

The major reasons for holding cash and other forms of liquid assets are (1) to purchase goods and services associated with normal living expenses and (2) to provide a safety net for meeting unexpected expenses or to take advantage of unanticipated opportunities. The use of transaction accounts is appropriate for the first reason, while savings vehicles would be utilized for the second.

There are basically two decisions that have to be made when selecting a transactions account or savings vehicle. The first decision involves choosing the type of account or vehicle. The types of transaction accounts available to the consumer are checking or demand deposit accounts, negotiable orders of withdrawal, and share drafts, while the savings vehicles include passbook and time deposit accounts, money market mutual funds and deposit accounts, and Series EE United States saving bonds. The second decision involves choosing a provider of the service such as a commercial bank, savings and loan, savings bank, credit union, or brokerage firm.

If You Are Thirtysomething

Once you have become established in your career and have accumulated the necessary savings for emergencies, you can begin to concentrate more on your savings program, which is designed to meet your financial goals. As your income increases, you should have more excess funds with which to meet your goals and have a greater ability to accept risks in return for higher expected returns. Also, with greater funds at your disposal you will be faced with an expanded array of savings opportunities that will necessitate more work on your part to make sure your selection of savings vehicles provides you with the best combination of risk and return.

Savings Program:

1. Determine if there are additional savings vehicles that offer better returns and which you could not use in the past because you did not have the minimum amount of funds to open the account.

2. Determine if the returns you are receiving on your existing accounts are consistent with meeting your financial goals.

3. As you accumulate more funds, consider diversifying into other types of savings vehicles.

4. With increased knowledge and experience, your attitude toward risk may change and if so, your savings vehicles should reflect this change.

CHAPTER 6

Making Housing and Other Major Acquisitions

Phillipe and Caron Dominguez just bought their first home after three years of saving money regularly toward that end. The Dominguezes are typical of many young families. They have two incomes, are around 30 years old, and paid about $100,000 for their home, making a down payment of 15 percent ($15,000). Home ownership is an important part of the American way of life. Your home very likely will be the largest purchase you will ever make — spending $100,000 or more for a single item is not an everyday event for most people. To prepare for purchasing a home, you will need to carefully itemize your housing needs and then assess your ability to afford them. Home buying is not all facts and figures, however; it nearly always involves a strong emotional undercurrent. Be aware of this, and try to temper your emotion with rational analysis. Automobiles, furniture, and appliances are other big-ticket acquisitions that, while less costly than a home, can have a substantial effect on the family budget.

A family's housing needs depend on such factors as age, income level, and number of children; these can be met in a variety of ways—from single-family homes to condos and apartments. What are your current as well as planned future housing needs, and what are the key factors shaping each of them? Before reading on, spend a few moments answering these questions.

Everybody's housing needs differ. Some people prefer quiet and privacy; others like the hustle and bustle of big-city life. Some demand to live within walking distance of work, shopping, and restaurants; others do not mind a 45-minute commute. Because you will have your own unique set of likes and dislikes, the best way to start your search for housing is to list your needs and then classify them according to whether their satisfaction is essential, desirable, or merely a "plus." Such a classification is important for three reasons. First, it serves to screen out housing that will not meet your minimum requirements. Second, it helps you recognize that you may have to make trade-offs, since you will seldom find any single home that meets all of your needs. Third, it can help you focus on those needs for which you are willing and able to pay.

ALTERNATIVE FORMS OF HOUSING

Because there are so many different types of residences, it is difficult to describe a "typical" home. We do know a few things, however, about what the "average" American home is like. First, it is getting smaller. Today's new home typically has only about 1,500 square feet. In that space, you'll usually find at least three bedrooms and probably more than one bathroom; in addition, it will have at least a one-car garage or carport, a fireplace, and central heating and air conditioning. We also know something

about home prices. For example, in early 1992 the median price for existing homes was about $103,000. However, as shown in Exhibit 6.1, prices varied widely from one part of the country to another. The stock of housing in America is nearly as diverse as its prices, consisting of not only single-family homes but also manufactured homes, condominiums, cooperative apartments, and numerous types of rental apartments and houses.

Single-Family Homes. The single-family, detached home remains the first choice in housing. Basically, such homes stand alone on their own legally defined lots. Sometimes homes are built side by side so that they share common side walls; these are known as *row houses* and are especially prevalent east of the Mississippi. As a rule, single-family homes offer their buyers privacy, prestige, pride of ownership, and maximum property control. In recent years, however, the cost of single-family residences—and especially residential lots—has increased dramatically. At the same time, the size of the average U.S. household has drastically decreased. These factors have led to much smaller homes; to compensate for their smaller size, other amenities and features have been introduced. For example, so-called *patio homes* are fairly small in size, yet have many luxurious appointments such as cathedral ceilings and jacuzzis; they are built on very small lots, and may even have common walls. Higher costs and changing lifestyles also have led to alternative types of housing; thus, while the single-family, detached home is still the most popular type of residence, its dominant position is declining.

Manufactured Homes. **Manufactured homes** are partially or fully assembled, factory-produced housing units that can be transported to a desired location. They are placed on either a permanent or temporary foundation and then connected to utilities. *Prefabricated homes* are manufactured in partially assembled sections at the factory, with final assembly on the owner's lot. Many of these homes are of excellent quality. Because they are mass-produced, their cost is considerably lower than comparable homes built on-site. Manufactured homes that are fully assembled at the factory are called *mobile homes*, although today they are rarely moved from their installed site. Most mobile home owners lease or purchase sites in mobile home parks specially designed to accommodate these homes. They come in standard sizes and can provide anywhere from 400 to 1,400 square feet of living space, depending on whether they are single- or double-wide units (that is, two units placed side by side to make one larger home). These homes are typically sold with appliances, carpeting, curtains, and sometimes furniture. They cost about half as much as a similar-size home built on-site. Although occasionally used as temporary housing, mobile homes provide *permanent residences* for many families, particularly retired persons. Their prices are low, and as long as it qualifies as a "permanent" structure, loans with low down payments and 10- to 15-year maturities are available. Their low maintenance costs are another attractive feature. Nevertheless, in most parts of the country the market price of mobile homes is likely to decline over time; thus, they are not considered good investments.

Condominiums. The term *condominium* describes a form of ownership rather than a type of building. Condominiums can be apartments, townhouses, or cluster housing. The buyer of a condominium receives title to an individual unit and a joint ownership of any common areas and facilities, such as lobbies, swimming pools, lakes, and tennis courts. Since buyers own their units, they arrange their own mortgages, pay their own taxes, and pay for maintenance and building services. They are typically assessed, on a monthly basis, an amount deemed sufficient to cover their proportionate share of the cost of maintaining common facilities. The owners of condominium units belong to a homeowners' association that elects a board of managers to supervise their building and grounds. The cost of condominiums is generally lower than that of single-family, detached homes, since they tend to be built in a fashion that results in more efficient land use and lower construction costs.

Due to the phenomenal growth in the cost of new homes over the past decade or so, many existing apartment projects have gone through *condo conversions*. In effect, the apartments have been converted from rental to occupant-owned units. The pace of condo conversion began to slow down considerably by the late 1980s as the market became saturated with new units.

Although condominiums traditionally have appealed primarily to retired persons who do not want the responsibilities of maintaining and caring for their property, many younger people now have begun to buy them for similar reasons. Exhibit 6.2 lists some of the key things that should be done before buying a condominium.

Cooperative Apartments. An apartment in a building in which each tenant owns a share of the corporation that owns the building is known as a **cooperative apartment** or **co-op**. Residents lease their units from the corporation and are assessed monthly in proportion to their ownership shares, which are based on the amount of space they occupy. The assessments cover the cost of service, maintenance, taxes, and the mortgage on the entire building. These are subject to change depending on the actual costs of operating the building and the actions of the board of directors, which determine the corporation's policies. Owners of cooperatives may find that the value of their ownership interest increases over time as a result of increased market values and a reduction in the outstanding loan balance. Because cooperative apartments are not

---

manufactured home
A partially or fully assembled, factory-produced housing unit that can be transported to a desired location, placed on either a permanent or temporary foundation, and then connected to utilities and used as a residence.

condominium
A form of direct ownership of an individual unit in a multiunit project in which lobbies, swimming pools, and other common areas and facilities are jointly owned by all property owners in the project.

cooperative apartment (co-op)
An apartment in a building in which each tenant owns a share of the corporation that owns the building.

EXHIBIT 6.1

Housing Prices around the United States (1992)

The price of housing varies widely from one location to another. For example, the median price of an existing home is $91,454 in Birmingham, Alabama, while in Washington, D.C. it is $165,135 and in San Diego, California, $193,083.

Location	Median Price	
	Existing	New
Albuquerque, NM	$ 90,900	$ 90,224
Atlanta, GA	96,582	102,074
Anaheim, CA	243,383	241,573
Baltimore, MD	116,196	122,804
Baton Rouge, LA	72,437	76,556
Birmingham, AL	91,454	96,655
Boston, MA	178,436	189,215
Charlotte, NC	108,372	114,534
Chicago, IL	139,950	192,744
Cincinnati, OH	89,010	122,586
Cleveland, OH	91,744	126,352
Columbia, SC	86,445	91,360
Columbus, OH	88,594	122,013
Dallas, TX	91,260	96,449
Denver, CO	93,861	93,163
Detroit, MI	85,421	117,644
Hartford, CT	151,479	160,630
Honolulu, HI	352,774	350,152
Houston, TX	78,066	82,505
Indianapolis, IN	82,640	113,814
Jacksonville, FL	78,502	82,966
Las Vegas, NV	104,934	104,153
Los Angeles, CA	220,262	218,623
Miami, FL	100,712	106,438
Milwaukee, WI	93,457	128,711
Minneapolis, MN	91,306	125,748
Mobile, AL	65,311	69,025
Nashville, TN	89,743	94,846
Nassau County, NY	161,787	171,561
New Orleans, LA	69,870	73,842
New York, NY	177,941	188,691
Newark, NJ	188,278	199,653
Oklahoma City, OK	61,189	64,669
Orlando, FL	91,598	96,806
Philadelphia, PA	117,885	125,007
Phoenix, AZ	87,256	86,607
Pittsburgh, PA	79,242	84,030
Portland, OR	87,320	86,671
Providence, RI	127,749	135,467
Saint Louis, MO	83,008	114,320
Salt Lake City, UT	74,279	73,727
San Antonio, TX	70,164	74,153
San Diego, CA	193,083	191,648
San Francisco, CA	265,530	263,557
Seattle, WA	147,633	146,536
Tacoma, WA	102,945	102,180
Tucson, AZ	73,788	73,239
Tulsa, OK	67,270	71,095
Washington, DC	165,135	174,525
West Palm Beach, FL	126,483	133,674

Source: Adapted from information in "The Top 100 Markets," *U.S. News & World Report*, April 6, 1992, pp. 85–95.

EXHIBIT 6.2

Things to Do before Buying a Condo

In the long run, it pays to carefully check out the various operating and occupancy features of a condo before you buy.

- Thoroughly investigate the reputation of the developer — through local real estate brokers, banks, or the Better Business Bureau — whether the building is brand new, under construction, or being converted.
- Read the rules of the organization.
- Investigate the condo government association, the restrictions on condo owners, and the quality of the property management.
- Check the construction of the building and its physical condition. If the building is being converted to condos, ask to see an independent inspection firm's report on the building's condition.
- Insist that any future changes in the building be put in writing.
- Query the occupants to see if they are satisfied with the living conditions.
- Determine how many units are rented; generally, owner-occupied units are better maintained.
- Determine if there is sufficient parking space.
- Watch for unusually low maintenance fees that will probably have to be increased soon.
- Consider the resale value (this was especially important in the mid-1980s and early 1990s when many condo units were impossible to sell without sharp price reductions).
- Compare the projected monthly assessment fees with those on similar buildings already in operation.

Source: Adapted from *Your Housing Dollar* (Prospect Heights, IL: Money Management Institute of Household Finance Corporation, 1987), p. 13.

profit-motivated, monthly assessments are likely to be lower than the rent on similar accommodations in a rental unit. Also, the cooperative owner receives the tax benefits resulting from interest and property taxes attributable to his or her proportionate ownership interest.

Rental Apartments and Houses. All of the forms of housing discussed above represent different ways of achieving home ownership. However, for one reason or another, a large number of individuals and families choose to *rent* or *lease* their place of residence rather than own it. They live in apartments and other types of rental units ranging from duplexes, four-plexes, and even single-family homes to large, high-rise apartment complexes containing several hundred units. *Garden apartments* are usually built in groups of four to six units that may be either one or two stories and are separated by landscaped areas. *Efficiency apartments* are generally one-room apartments suitable for single people. *Townhouses* are two- or three-story apartments that usually have the bedrooms upstairs. All of these types of housing are popular and widely available.

The cost and availability of rental units vary from one geographic area to another. Unfurnished units, of course, rent for less than furnished ones. The U.S. Department of Housing and Urban Development (HUD) administers various programs that provide low-rent housing opportunities for people in lower income brackets. Because such a wide variety of rental units are available, people who wish to rent can usually find units that conform to their location, physical, and financial requirements.

The most popular form of single-family housing is the condominium.

Fantasy: The most popular form of single-family housing is the *single-family home* — a detached residence that sits on its own legally defined lot. Condos, in contrast, are built in large, multiunit developments on grounds that are common to all residents.

People buy homes for the emotional and financial payoffs they provide; accompanying these benefits are the costs of buying homes, such as down payments, closing costs, monthly mortgage payments, and homeowner's insurance. What are the typical motives for buying a home, and what purchase and ownership costs must be considered when assessing its affordability? Spend a few moments answering these questions before reading on.

Spending many thousands of dollars to buy a home obviously involves a good deal of careful planning and analysis. Not only must you spend time deciding on the kind of home you want (its location, number of bedrooms, and so on), you must also consider its cost, what kind of mortgage to get, how large a monthly payment you can afford, what kind of homeowner's insurance coverage to have, and so forth. It should be clear that buying a home (or any other major, big-ticket item) touches on many of the elements in personal financial planning. The money you use for a down payment will likely be drawn from your *savings program*; the homeowner's policy you choose is a part of your *insurance planning*; and your monthly mortgage payments undoubtedly will have an enormous impact on your *cash budget*. Sound financial planning dictates caution when buying a home or any other major item. Spending too much for a home or car can have a detrimental effect not only on your budget and lifestyle, but also on your savings and investment plans, and possibly even your retirement plans. Knowing how much housing you can afford will go a long way toward helping you achieve your financial goals.

MOTIVES FOR OWNING A HOME

Whether it is a detached home, a patio home, a manufactured home, or a condominium, home ownership is important to most people. It is preferred over renting for several reasons, the most important of which is probably the basic security and peace of mind derived from living in one's own home — pride of ownership, a feeling of permanence, and a sense of stability. This so-called "psychic reward" is the only reason that many people need to own a home. In addition to the emotional payoff, there's also a financial payoff from home ownership.

The Home as a Tax Shelter. Perhaps the biggest financial payoff from owning a home is the tax shelter it offers. You get a tax break from owning a home because you can deduct both the mortgage interest and the property taxes you pay from your federal and state income taxes. As explained in Chapter 4, mortgage interest (on mortgage loans up to a total of $1,000,000 taken out to buy, build, or improve a principal residence and second home, such as a vacation home, if any), and property taxes can be treated as a tax deduction. Such write-offs reduce your taxable income and thus the amount of taxes you pay. The only requirement is that you itemize your deductions. This tax break is so good that people who have never itemized usually begin doing so after they buy their first house. Also, keep in mind that for the first 15 to 20 years of ownership (assuming a 30-year mortgage) most of your monthly mortgage payment is made up of interest and property taxes — in fact, during the first 5 to 10 years or so, these could well account for *85 to 90 percent of your total payment*. This means you are allowed to write off nearly all of your monthly mortgage payment.

Here is how it works. Suppose you make mortgage payments of $1,000 a month of which $850 is interest and property taxes. That is about $10,000 a year in tax deductions. Assuming you are single with no other itemized deductions, that $10,000 will reduce your taxable income by an additional $6,400 ($10,000 minus your $3,600 standard deduction in 1992). If you are in the 28 percent tax bracket, such a tax deduction will reduce the amount of taxes you pay by an additional $1,792 ($6,400 × .28)!

The Home as an Inflation Hedge. Another financial payoff is the **inflation hedge** allegedly provided by home ownership. An inflation hedge is an investment or asset that appreciates in value at a rate equal to or greater than the rate of inflation. During both the 1970s and the mid-to-late 1980s there were few inflation hedges that could match the performance of home ownership. In fact, a home became one of the best investments you could make, since it generated a far better return than stocks, bonds, mutual funds, and so on. Many people were buying homes simply for their investment value, and in many parts of the country, the local real estate markets became so speculative they took on an almost feverish pitch. The rampant inflation and appreciation in home prices came to a halt in the early 1980s and again in the early 1990s. Although many real estate markets were strong in the late 1980s, housing values fell sharply during the recession of the early 1990s. In many areas of the country, sellers who had owned their homes for a short time were unable to sell them at a profit.

Today, housing prices in most parts of the country are increasing at a rate about equal to or slightly above the rate of inflation. As a result of this, and the fact that the inflation rate has declined dramatically, housing prices in most areas are rising at a much slower pace than in the 1970s and the mid-to-late 1980s. Most experts believe that it will probably be a long time before we again see housing price increases that significantly outstrip the rate of inflation. Housing in the 1990s certainly does not appear to serve as the inflation hedge (or investment) that it once was.

THE COST OF HOME OWNERSHIP

While there definitely are some strong emotional and financial reasons for owning a home, there's still the question of whether or not you can afford to own one. Affordability is a two-edged sword: There is the matter not only of coming up with the down payment and other closing costs but also of meeting the recurring cash-flow requirements associated with monthly mortgage payments and other home maintenance expenses. In particular, there are five items you should consider when evaluating the cost of home ownership and determining how much home you can afford: (1) the down payment, (2) points and closing costs, (3) mortgage payments, (4) property taxes and insurance, and (5) maintenance and operating expenses.

The Down Payment. The first hurdle is the **down payment**. Most buyers finance a major part of the purchase price of the home, but they are also required by lenders to invest money of their own, called *equity*. The actual amount of down payment required varies among lenders, mortgage types, and properties. To determine the amount of down payment that will be required in specific instances, lenders use the **loan-to-value ratio**, which specifies the maximum percentage of the value of a property that the lender is willing to loan. For example, if the loan-to-value ratio is 80 percent, the buyer will have to come up with a down payment equal to the remaining 20 percent. The loan-to-value ratio is normally based on the ~~greater~~ *lower* of the market or appraised value.

A property that is financed with a high loan-to-value ratio involves only a small percentage of borrower equity. For example, a mortgage that equals 90 to 95 percent of a property's purchase price is a high-ratio loan. It involves only 5 to 10 percent equity dollars; thus, if you buy a $100,000 home with a 95 percent loan-to-value ratio, you will need to put down only $5,000 and can finance the other $95,000 through a mortgage.

Generally first-time home buyers must spend a number of years accumulating enough money to afford the down payment and other costs associated with the home purchase transaction. You can best accumulate these funds on a planned basis, using future value techniques (presented in Chapters 5, 12, and 15) to determine the monthly or annual savings (at a given rate of interest) necessary in order to

---

inflation hedge
An investment or asset that appreciates in value at a rate equal to or greater than the rate of inflation.

down payment
A portion of the full purchase price provided by the purchaser at the time of purchase of a house or other major asset; often called *equity*.

loan-to-value ratio
The maximum percentage of the value of a property that the lender is willing to loan.

have a stated amount by a specified future date. While detailed demonstration of this process is included in Chapter 12, for now suffice it to say that a disciplined savings program is the best way to obtain the funds needed to purchase a home or any other big-ticket item requiring a sizable down payment or purchase outlay.

If you do not have enough savings to cover the down payment and closing costs, you can still consider several other sources. You may be able to obtain some funds by withdrawing (subject to legal limitations) your contributions from your company's profit-sharing or thrift plan. Your IRA is another option, although you must pay a 10 percent penalty (prior to age 59½) plus income taxes on any amount you withdraw. However, the higher tax deductions resulting from the mortgage interest will probably offset these costs.

Equity sharing is another down payment source that is becoming popular. It involves finding a partner who will provide all or part of the down payment in exchange for a specified percentage of the equity in the house, usually for a stated number of years. You may be able to arrange an equity sharing deal with a parent or relative in exchange for monthly fair market rent and allowing them to take the tax deductions for their percentage of the depreciation, mortgage interest, and property taxes. Equity sharing consultants can be hired for a fee of about $200 to $500 to match prospective home buyers with an investor. The amount of the down payment, percentage of equity given to the investor, rent paid to the investor, interest payments, and term of the arrangement will vary depending upon the situation. Typically, equity-sharing contracts with nonfamily investors run from three to five years, at the end of which the owner can buy out the investor or extend the agreement. In such cases, the investors do not usually take the tax write offs but rather rely on the expected appreciation in the home's value for their return.

The Federal National Mortgage Association (known as "Fannie Mae") has a special program to assist buyers who haven't saved the 5 percent minimum down payment required on conventional loans. Its "3/2 Option" allows the borrower to obtain up to 2 percent of the 5 percent from a relative or from a public or nonprofit agency. This program is available from local lenders and is limited to home buyers with household incomes below 115 percent of the median amount in their area.

As a rule, when the down payment is less than 20 percent, the lender will require that the loan be made with **mortgage insurance**, which protects the lender from loss in the event the borrower defaults on the loan. Usually the mortgage insurance covers the lender's risk above 80 percent of the price of the house. Thus, with a 10 percent down payment, the mortgage will result in a 90 percent loan, and the mortgage insurance would cover 10 percent of the home's price. You will be charged a one-time fee of about .75 percent of the amount of the loan (paid at closing) plus an annual premium of about .25 to .5 percent (which is included in your monthly payments), until the loan balance is less than 75 or 80 percent of the appraised value of your home.

Mortgage insurance guarantees the lender that the loan will be paid off in the event of the borrower's death.
Fantasy: Mortgage insurance protects the lender from loss in the event the borrower defaults on the loan.

Points and Closing Costs. A second hurdle to home ownership relates to mortgage points and closing costs. **Mortgage points** are fees charged by lenders at the time they grant a mortgage loan. In appearance, points are like interest in that they are a charge for borrowing money. They are related to the lender's supply of loanable funds and the demand for mortgages; the greater the demand relative to supply, the more points you can expect to pay. One point equals 1 percent of the amount borrowed. If you borrow $70,000, and loan fees equal 3 points, the amount of money you will pay in points will be $70,000 × .03 = $2,100.

Lenders typically use points as a way of charging interest on their loans. They can vary the interest rate along with the number of points they charge to create loans with comparable effective rates. For example, a lender might be willing to give you a 10 percent mortgage rather than an 11 percent one if you are willing to pay more points; that is, you take your pick: an 11 percent mortgage rate with 2 points or a 10 percent mortgage with 6½ points. If you choose the 10 percent loan, you will end up paying a lot more *at closing* (though the amount of interest paid *over the life of the mortgage* may be less).

Points increase the *effective rate of interest* on a mortgage. The amount you pay in points and the length of time you hold a mortgage determine the increase in the effective interest rate. For example, on a 9 percent, 30-year, fixed-rate mortgage, each point increases the annual percentage rate by about .11 percent if the loan is held for 30 years, .13 percent if held for 15 years, .20 percent if held 7 years, and .40 percent if held 3 years. You pay the same amount in points regardless of how long you keep your home. Therefore, the longer you hold the mortgage, the longer the time period over which the points are amortized and the smaller the effect of the points on the effective annual interest rate.

According to recent IRS rulings, the points paid on a mortgage at the time a home is originally purchased are usually considered to be tax deductible, though the same points are not considered tax deductible if they are incurred when *refinancing* a mortgage (unless they are paid in connection with the purchase or improvement of a home) — rather, the amount paid in points must be written off (*amortized*) over the life of the new mortgage loan.

Closing costs are all other expenses including mortgage points) that borrowers ordinarily pay at the time a mortgage loan is closed and title to the purchased property is conveyed to them. Closing costs are like down payments: They represent money you must come up with *at the time you buy the house*. Closing costs are made up of such items as (1) loan application fees, (2) loan origination fees, (3) points (if any), (4) title search and insurance, (5) attorneys' fees, (6) appraisal fees, and (7) other miscellaneous fees for things like mortgage taxes, filing fees, inspections, credit reports, and so on.

The loan application and origination fees are charges the lender makes for doing all the paperwork; the other charges are associated primarily with fulfilling the legal and credit requirements necessary to complete the home-purchase transaction. As Exhibit 6.3 shows, these costs can total an amount equal to 50 percent or more of the down payment. For example, with a 10 percent down payment on a $100,000 home, the closing costs, as shown in Exhibit 6.3 can amount to nearly 70 percent of the down payment, or $6,625. A little simple arithmetic

also indicates that this buyer will need nearly $17,000 to buy the house (the $10,000 down payment plus another $6,625 in closing costs).

Many first-time home buyers are shocked to find out how much they must pay in closing costs. In many instances, *sellers*, by custom or contract, will assume the responsibility for some of a buyer's mortgage points and closing costs. Seldom, however, can a buyer escape all — or even most — of the expenses. At best, the seller will probably pick up just a small percentage (perhaps 10 to 15 percent) of the total amount of the closing costs, leaving the buyer to pay the rest.

As a rule, the closing costs on a home are rather insignificant and seldom amount to more than a few hundred dollars.
Fantasy: Closing costs — most of which must be paid by the *buyer* — on most home purchases can amount to several thousand dollars and often total an amount equal to 50 percent or more of the down payment.

Mortgage Payments. The monthly mortgage payment is determined using a fairly complex formula. Each monthly mortgage payment is made up partly of principal repayment on the loan and partly of interest charges. However, as Exhibit 6.4 shows,

---

mortgage insurance
A type of insurance policy that protects the mortgage lender from loss in the event the borrower defaults on the loan.

mortgage points
Fees (each point equals 1 percent of the amount borrowed) charged by lenders at the time they grant a mortgage loan; they are related to the lender's supply of loanable funds and the demand for mortgages.

closing costs
All expenses (including mortgage points) that borrowers ordinarily pay at the time a mortgage loan is closed and title to the purchased property is conveyed to them.

EXHIBIT 6.3

The Hidden Costs of Buying a Home: Closing Costs

The closing costs on a home mortgage loan can be substantial—as much as 5 to 7 percent of the price of the home. Except for the real estate commission (which is generally paid by the seller), the biggest share of the closing costs is charged to the buyer and must be paid—in addition to the down payment—at the time the loan is closed and title to the property is conveyed.

Item	Size of Down Payment	
	20%	10%
Loan application fee	$ 200	$ 200
Loan origination fee	800	900
Points	1,600	2,700
Mortgage insurance	—	675
Title search and insurance	500	550
Attorneys' fees	400	400
Appraisal fees	150	150
Home inspection	250	250
Mortgage tax	575	650
Filing fees	25	25
Credit reports	25	25
Miscellaneous	100	100
Total closing costs	$4,625	$6,625

Note: Typical closing costs for a $100,000 home—2 points charged with 20 percent, 3 points with 10 percent down. Actual amounts will vary by lender and location.

for most of the life of the mortgage the vast majority of each monthly payment goes to *interest*. The loan illustrated in the exhibit is an $80,000, 30-year, 9 percent mortgage with monthly payments of $643.76. Note that it is not until after the 22nd year of this 30-year mortgage that the principal portion of the loan payment exceeds the amount that goes to interest.

In practice, mortgage lenders and realtors use *comprehensive mortgage payment tables* to find monthly payments. These tables contain monthly payments for virtually every combination of loan size, interest rate, and maturity. Exhibit 6.5 provides an excerpt from one such comprehensive mortgage payment table. It lists the *monthly payments* that would be associated with a $10,000 fixed-rate loan for selected maturities of 10 to 30 years and various interest rates ranging from 5 to 13 percent. It can be used to find the monthly payment for any size loan.

Suppose you wish to find the monthly loan payment on an $80,000, 9 percent, 30-year mortgage. To do this, simply divide the amount of the loan ($80,000) by $10,000 and then multiply this factor (8.0) by the payment amount shown in Exhibit 6.5 for a 9 percent, 30-year loan ($80.47):

$$\$80,000/\$10,000 = 8.0 \times \$80.47 \times \underline{\$643.76}$$

The resulting monthly mortgage payment would be $643.76.

Obviously, the key issue with respect to mortgage payments is *affordability*. To ensure that the purchase of a home stays within your budget, you must determine the size of monthly mortgage payment you can afford. This, in turn, will determine how much you can borrow to finance the purchase of a home.

Affordability ratios. In order to obtain a mortgage, a potential borrower must be "qualified"—that is, must demonstrate that he or she has an acceptable credit record and adequate income with which to comfortably make scheduled loan payments. Various federal and private mortgage insurers, as well as institutional mortgage investors, have certain standards they expect borrowers to

EXHIBIT 6.4

Typical Principal and Interest Payment Patterns on a Mortgage Loan

For most of the life of a mortgage loan, the vast majority of each monthly payment goes to interest and only a small portion goes toward principal repayment. Over the 30-year life of the 9 percent, $80,000 mortgage illustrated here, the homeowner will pay more than $150,000 in interest.

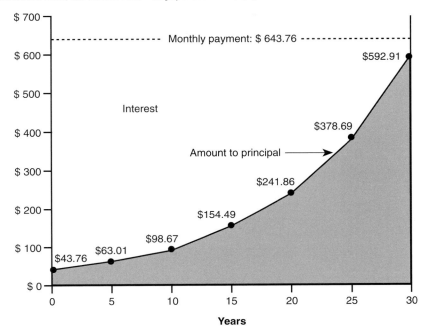

Note: Dollar amounts noted on graph represent the principal amount in the first scheduled payment of the given year.

meet in order to reduce as much as possible the risk of default. Because of the influence these insurers/investors have on the mortgage market, their guidelines tend to be widely followed.

Probably the most important affordability guideline is the one that relates *monthly payments to borrower income*. This is done by relating (1) the size of the monthly mortgage payment and (2) the borrower's total monthly installment loan payments (which would include payments not only on the mortgage, but also on automobile loans, furniture loans, and any other type of consumer installment loan) to monthly income. In this regard, the most widely followed ratios (for a *conventional mortgage*) stipulate that (1) monthly mortgage payments

cannot exceed 25 to 30 percent of the borrower's monthly *gross* (before-tax) income and (2) the borrower's total monthly installment loan payments cannot exceed 33 to 38 percent of monthly gross income. Since both conditions stipulate a range, the lender has some leeway in deciding on the most appropriate ratio for a particular loan applicant.

Here is how these affordability ratios work. Assume you have a monthly income of $3,000. Using the lower end of the ranges (that is, 25 percent and 33 percent) for illustrative purposes, we see that such an income level could support mortgage payments of $750 a month *so long as total monthly installment obligations do not exceed $1,000.* (These values were found as follows: $3,000 × .25 = $750

EXHIBIT 6.5

A Table of Monthly Mortgage Payments
(Monthly Payments Necessary to Repay a $10,000 Loan)

The monthly loan payments on a mortgage vary not only by the amount of the loan, but also by the rate of interest and loan maturity.

Rate of Interest	Loan Maturity				
	10 Years	15 Years	20 Years	25 Years	30 Years
5.0%	$106.07	$ 79.08	$ 66.00	$ 58.46	$ 53.68
5.5%	108.53	81.71	68.79	61.41	56.79
6.0%	111.02	84.39	71.64	64.43	59.96
6.5%	113.55	87.11	74.56	67.52	63.21
7.0%	116.11	89.88	77.53	70.68	66.53
7.5%	118.71	92.71	80.56	73.90	69.93
8.0%	121.33	95.57	83.65	77.19	73.38
8.5%	123.99	98.48	86.79	80.53	76.90
9.0%	126.68	101.43	89.98	83.92	80.47
9.5%	129.40	104.43	93.22	87.37	84.09
10.0%	132.16	107.47	96.51	90.88	87.76
10.5%	134.94	110.54	99.84	94.42	91.48
11.0%	137.76	113.66	103.22	98.02	95.24
11.5%	140.60	116.82	106.65	101.65	99.03
12.0%	143.48	120.02	110.11	105.33	102.86
12.5%	146.38	123.26	113.62	109.04	106.73
13.0%	149.32	126.53	117.16	112.79	110.62

Note: *To use*: (1) Divide amount of the loan by $10,000; (2) Find loan payment amount in table for specific interest rate and maturity; (3) multiply the amount from step 1 by the amount from step 2.
Example: The monthly payment for a $98,000, 9.5 percent, 30-year loan would be: (1) $98,000/$10,000 = 9.8; (2) payment associated with a 9.5 percent, 30-year loan, from table, is *$84.09*; (3) monthly payment required to repay a $98,000, 9.5 percent, 30-year loan is 9.8 × $84.09 = $824.08.

and $3,000 × .33 = $1,000.) Note that if your other monthly installment loan payments exceeded $250 (the difference between $1,000 and $750), your mortgage payment would have to be reduced accordingly. For instance, if you had $350 in other installment payments, your maximum monthly mortgage payment would be $1,000 − $350 = $650.

Determining the largest mortgage for which you qualify is just the first step, however. You also need to consider your lifestyle. Will taking on the responsibility of a mortgage require you to perhaps forgo some luxuries or radically change your spending habits? To see how buying a house affects your cash flow, you should revise your personal budget to include the costs of buying a home—monthly mortgage payments, utilities, maintenance, insurance, and so on. Only you can decide how much of your income you are willing to allocate to a mortgage. Trade-offs are typically involved; you may choose a lower-priced house with a smaller mortgage in order to maintain greater financial flexibility.

The amount of money you earn has a lot to do with the amount of money you can borrow.
Fact: Your monthly income is a key factor in determining how large a mortgage loan you can afford. Also important are your credit record and the level of your total monthly installment loan payments.

Property Taxes and Insurance. Aside from loan costs, mortgage payments often include property tax and insurance payments. When this occurs, the monthly mortgage payment is made up of four parts: (1) part of the loan payment goes to reduce the *principal* amount of the loan; (2) part goes to pay the *interest* on the loan; (3) some of it goes to property *taxes*; and (4) some goes to homeowner's *insurance*. Thus, together, the loan payment consists of *p*rincipal, *i*nterest, *t*axes, and *i*nsurance (or **PITI** for short). Actually, that portion of the loan payment that goes for taxes and insurance is paid into an *escrow account*, where it accumulates over time. Then, once or twice a year, the lending institution draws funds from this account to pay required property taxes and homeowner's insurance premiums. Increases in tax rates and/or insurance premiums are passed on to the home buyer in the form of higher monthly loan payments.

Interestingly, some but not all lenders pay interest — typically at no higher than the passbook rate — on escrow account balances. Generally, though, it is advisable for disciplined borrowers to negotiate with the lender in order to avoid having to pay into an escrow account. Such a strategy, if successful, gives you greater flexibility and an opportunity to earn a higher return on the funds that would otherwise have been held in an escrow account.

Because they are local taxes levied to fund schools, law enforcement, and other local services, the level of **property taxes** differs from one community to another. And within a given community, individual property taxes will vary with the *assessed value* of the property — generally, the more expensive the home, the higher the property taxes, and vice versa. As a rule, annual property taxes vary from less than .5 percent to more than 2 percent of a home's approximate market value. Thus, the property taxes on a $100,000 home could vary from about $500 to more than $2,000 a year, depending on location and geographic area.

The other component of the monthly mortgage payment is **homeowner's insurance**. Its cost varies with such factors as the age of the house, location, materials used in construction, and geographic area. Homeowner's insurance is carried only on the replacement value of the home and its contents and not on the land. Annual insurance costs usually amount to approximately .25 to .5 percent of the home's market value. Thus, the annual cost of insurance for a $100,000 house should range between $250 and $500. The types, characteristics, and features of homeowner's insurance policies are discussed in Chapter 11.

Maintenance and Operating Expenses.
In addition to the monthly mortgage payments, home buyers incur maintenance and operating expenses. Maintenance costs should be anticipated even on new homes. Painting, mechanical repairs, leak repairs, and lawn maintenance, for example, are inescapable facts of homeownership. Such costs are likely to be greater, though, for older, larger homes.

Thus, while a large, established home may have an attractive purchase price, a new, smaller home may be the better buy in view of its lower maintenance and operating costs.

Another point to consider in the selection process is the cost of operating the home, specifically the cost of utilities, such as electricity, gas, water, and sewage. These costs have skyrocketed in the past 10 to 15 years and today represent a sizable component of homeownership costs. Because they are unavoidable and vary with geographic location, type of heating and air conditioning, size of home, amount of insulation, and other factors, operating cost estimates should be obtained when evaluating a particular home-purchase candidate.

PERFORMING HOME AFFORDABILITY ANALYSIS

An estimate of the amount you can afford to spend on a home can be made using the form given in Exhibit 6.6. This analysis determines the maximum home-purchase price using both your monthly income and the amount you have available for a down payment after meeting estimated closing costs. In our example, the Renée and Pierre Goulet family had combined annual income of $48,400 and had $22,500 available for making a down payment and paying closing costs. They estimated monthly taxes and homeowner's insurance of $150 and expected the mortgage lender to use a 28 percent monthly mortgage-payment affordability ratio, to lend at an

---

PITI
Notation used to refer to a mortgage payment that includes stipulated portions of *p*rincipal, *i*nterest, property *t*axes, and homeowner's *i*nsurance.

property taxes
Taxes levied by local governments on the assessed value of real estate for the purpose of funding schools, law enforcement, and other local services.

homeowner's insurance
Insurance required by mortgage lenders that typically covers the replacement value of a home and its contents.

EXHIBIT 6.6

Home Affordability Analysis for the Renée and Pierre Goulet Family

By using the following variables in the home affordability analysis form, the Goulets estimate a maximum home purchase price of about $137,000: their combined annual income of $48,400; the $22,500 available for a down payment; closing costs along with estimated monthly taxes and homeowner's insurance of $150; the lender's 28 percent monthly affordability ratio; an average interest rate of 9 percent and expected loan maturity of 30 years; and a minimum down payment of 10 percent.

HOME AFFORDABILITY ANALYSIS*

Name ___Renée and Peter Goulet___ Date ___December 12, 1992___

Item	Description	Amount
1	Amount of annual income	$ 48,400
2	Monthly income (Item 1 ÷ 12)	$ 4,033
3	Lender's affordabiilty ratio (in decimal form)	.28
4	Maximum monthly mortgage payment (PITI) (Item 2 x Item 3)	$ 1,130
5	Estimated monthly tax and homeowner's insurance payment	$ 150
6	Maximum monthly loan payment	$ 980
7	Approximate average interest rate on loan	9%
8	Planned loan maturity (years)	30
9	Mortgage payment per $10,000 (using Item 7 and Item 8 and Monthly Mortgage Payment Table in Exhibit 6.5)	$ 80.47
10	Maximum loan based on monthly income ($10,000 x Item 6 ÷ Item 9)	$ 121,785
11	Funds available for making a down payment and paying closing costs	$ 22,500
12	Funds available for making a down payment (Item 11 x .67)	$ 15,000
13	Maximum purchase price based on available monthly income (Item 10 + Item 12)	$ 136,785
14	Minimum acceptable down payment (in decimal form)	.10
15	Maximum purchase price based on down payment (Item 12 ÷ Item 14)	$ 150,000
16	Maximum home purchase price (lower of Item 13 and Item 15)	$ 136,785

*Note: This analysis assumes that ⅓ of the funds available for making the down payment and paying closing costs are used to meet closing costs while the remaining ⅔ are available for a down payment. This assumption means that closing costs will represent an amount equal to 50 percent of the down payment.

EXHIBIT 6.7
How Much Mortgage Will Your Payment Buy?

This table provides a quick way to estimate the size of the mortgage you can afford based on the monthly mortgage payment and mortgage interest rate. It assumes a 30-year, fixed-rate loan. Remember that this amount is only for mortgage principal and interest; you must have funds available for paying taxes and insurance as well.

Monthly Mortgage Payment	Mortgage Interest Rate							
	6%	7%	8%	9%	10%	11%	12%	13%
$ 500	$ 83,396	$ 75,154	$ 68,142	$ 62,141	$ 56,975	$ 52,503	$ 48,609	$ 45,200
600	100,075	90,185	81,770	74,569	68,370	63,004	58,331	54,240
700	116,754	105,215	95,398	86,997	79,766	73,504	68,053	63,280
800	133,433	120,246	109,027	99,425	91,161	84,005	77,775	72,320
900	150,112	135,277	122,655	111,854	102,556	94,506	87,497	81,360
1,000	166,792	150,308	136,283	124,282	113,951	105,006	97,218	90,400
1,100	183,471	165,338	149,912	136,710	125,346	115,507	106,940	99,440
1,200	200,150	180,369	163,540	149,138	136,741	126,008	116,662	108,480
1,300	216,829	195,400	177,169	161,566	148,136	136,508	126,384	117,520
1,400	233,508	210,431	190,797	173,995	159,531	147,009	136,106	126,560
1,500	250,187	225,461	204,425	186,423	170,926	157,510	145,828	135,599

Note: *To use:* (1) Find the amount of monthly payment you can afford, to the nearest $100. Then find the current mortgage interest rate, to the nearest percent. The approximate mortgage amount will be at the intersection of the two columns. (2) To estimate the mortgage size if the interest rate ends in .5 percent, add the mortgage amounts for the lower and higher interest rates and divide by 2. (3) To estimate the mortgage size for a payment ending in 50, add the lower and higher mortgage amounts and divide by 2.
Examples: (1) The estimated mortgage size if you have a monthly payment of $900 on a 30-year, 10 percent loan is $102,556. (2) To find the estimated mortgage size if you have a monthly payment of $900 and the market rate is 9.5 percent, add the mortgage sizes for $900 at 9 percent and at 10 percent and divide by 2: [($111,854 + $102,556) ÷ 2] = $214,410 ÷ 2 = $107,205. (3) To find the estimated mortgage size if you have a monthly payment of $950 and the market rate is 9 percent, add the mortgage sizes for $900 and $1,000 at 9 percent and divide by 2: [($111,854 + $124,282) ÷ 2] = $236,136 ÷ 2 = $118,068.

average interest rate of 9 percent on a 30-year mortgage, and to require a 10 percent down payment. The Goulets' analysis showed that they can afford to purchase a home costing about $137,000. Their available monthly income (Item 13) rather than the amount available for down payment (Item 15) was the key determinant of the maximum affordable home-purchase price.

Exhibit 6.7 provides a quick way to estimate the size of the mortgage you can afford, based on different monthly mortgage payment and interest rate assumptions. First, determine the maximum monthly mortgage payment you can handle. Follow that line across to find the approximate size of the mortgage your payment will buy at each interest rate. (This figure assumes a 30-year, fixed-rate loan and does *not* include taxes and insurance.) For example, if you estimate that you have $1,000 available per month and the prevailing mortgage interest rate is 10 percent, you could afford a mortgage of about $114,000. Of course, the price of the home you could

afford to buy also depends on the amount of cash you have available for making the down payment and paying closing costs.

THE OPTION OF RENTING

Many people either cannot afford to buy or choose not to buy their own home. For example, young adults usually rent for one or more of the following reasons: (1) They do not have the funds for a down payment and closing costs; (2) they are unsettled in their job and family status; (3) they do not want the additional responsibilities associated with home-ownership. Monthly rent payments only pay for the use of the property and are not tax deductible. Those who choose to rent should be familiar with rental contracts and know how to compare the costs of renting versus purchasing.

The Rental Contract. When you rent an apartment, duplex, house, or any other type of unit, you

EXHIBIT 6.8
Rent-or-Buy Cost Comparison

Using this procedure to make the rent-or-buy decision, you should *rent* if the total cost of renting is less than the total cost of buying, and *buy* if the total cost of renting is more than the total cost of buying. In this illustration, the rental option requires monthly payments of $650. The purchase option is a $100,000 home, financed with a $15,000 down payment and an $85,000, 9-percent, 30-year mortgage, with additional closing costs of $4,500.

RENT-OR-BUY ANALYSIS			
A. COST OF RENTING			
1. Annual rental costs (12 x monthly rental rate of $ _650_)		$7,800	
2. Renter's insurance		300	
Total cost of renting			$8,100
B. COST OF BUYING			
1. Annual mortgage payments (Terms: $ _$85,000_ , _360_ months, _9_ %) (12 x monthly mortgage payment of $ _684_)	$8,208		
2. Property taxes (_2_ % of price of home)	$2,000		
3. Homeowner's insurance (_.5_ % of price of home)	500		
4. Maintenance (_.8_ % of price of home)	800		
5. After-tax cost of interest lost on down payment and closing costs ($ _19,500_ x _4.5_ % after-tax rate of return)	878		
6. Total costs			$12,386
Less:			
7. Principal reduction in loan balance (see note below)	$ 558		
8. Tax savings due to interest deductions* (Interest portion of mortgage payments $ _7,650_ x tax rate of _28_ %)	2,142		
9. Tax savings due to property tax deductions* (line B.2 x tax rate of _28_ %)	560		
10. Total deductions		$3,260	
11. Annual after-tax cost of home ownership (line B.6 – line B.10.)		$9,126	
12. Less: Estimated annual appreciation in value of home (_3_ % of price of home)		3,000	
Total cost of buying (line B.11 – line B.12.)			$6,126

Note: Find monthly mortgage payments from Exhibit 6.5. An easy way to approximate the portion of the *annual* loan payment that goes to interest (line B.8.) is to multiply the interest rate by the size of the loan (in this case, $85,000 x .09 = $7,650). To find the principal reduction in the loan balance (line B.7.), simply subtract the amount that goes to interest from total annual mortgage payments ($8,208 – $7,650 = $558).

*Tax-shelter items.

normally will be required to sign a **rental contract**, or **lease agreement**. Although oral agreements are generally binding, a written contract is a legal instrument that better protects both the *lessor* (the person who owns the property) and the *lessee* (the person who leases the property). Because the rental contract binds you — the lessee — to various actions, you should make certain that you fully understand it before signing it. As a rule, the contract specifies the *amount* of the monthly payment, the payment *date*, *penalties* for late payment, the *length* of the lease agreement, *deposit* requirements, the distribution of *expenses*, *renewal* options, and any *restrictions*, for example, on children, pets, or the use of facilities.

Most leases have a minimum term of either six months or one year and require payments at the beginning of each month. They initially require a deposit and/or payment of the last month's rent as security against damages and infringement of the lease agreement. In the absence of any serious damage, most of the deposit should be refunded to the lessee shortly after the lease expires; a portion of the deposit is sometimes retained by the lessor to cover the cost of cleaning and minor repairs, regardless of how clean and well-kept the unit is left. Because the landlord has control over the deposit, a written statement describing any damage in evidence *prior* to occupancy may help the lessee avoid losing the entire deposit. Renters should also clarify who bears expenses such as utilities and trash collection and exactly what, if any, restrictions are placed on use of the property. It's also a good idea for renters to check the various renter-landlord laws in their states in order to fully understand their *rights*, as well as responsibilities.

The Rent-or-Buy Decision. During the 1970s, renting a place to live generally was more expensive than buying. This was due, in large part, to three factors: (1) relatively low housing prices and mortgage interest rates; (2) generous tax write-offs for homeowners; and (3) rapid appreciation in home values. However, by 1980 things began to change. Housing prices became out of reach for many families, and interest rates skyrocketed; in addition, housing prices stopped appreciating and even began to decline in many areas. Although interest rates later declined and home prices began to recover in the mid-1980s, the percentage of families living in

rented housing increased slightly and today is about 36 percent. (Conversely, today about 64 percent of all families own their own home.)

Some people are forced to rent rather than buy. They either do not have the money needed to make a down payment and pay closing costs or they do not have adequate income to safely make monthly mortgage payments. Others, however, rent because they prefer to. They have more mobility, they do not have to worry about maintenance and upkeep, or, for them, renting makes more economic sense than buying.

In such a situation, a simple rent-or-buy analysis can be used to choose the least-cost alternative, as illustrated in Exhibit 6.8, which compares the cost of renting with the cost of buying. Note that the procedure assumes that if the residence is purchased, the homeowner will itemize deductions on his or her tax return. If instead the homeowner elects to take the standard deduction, the value of the two tax-shelter entries in Exhibit 6.8 — marked with an asterisk — should be set equal to zero — and in that case, the attractiveness of buying will be greatly diminished.

Assume that you must decide between renting an apartment for $650 a month or buying a $100,000 patio home. Purchasing the home would involve a $15,000 down payment, an $85,000, 9 percent, 30-year mortgage (from Exhibit 6.5, we find monthly mortgage payments would be $684), and $4,500 in closing costs, as well as property taxes, insurance, and maintenance. With renting, the only costs would be the $650 monthly rental payment and an annual renter's insurance premium of $300. Assume that you will itemize deductions if you purchase the home and that you are in the 28 percent tax bracket. Substituting the appropriate values into Exhibit 6.8 and making the required calculations results in the total cost of each alternative. *Buying* is preferred

---

rental contract (lease agreement)
A legal instrument that protects both the lessor and the lessee from an adverse action by the other party; it specifies the amount of the monthly payment, the payment date, penalties for late payment, the length of the lease agreement, deposit requirements, the distribution of expenses, renewal options, and restrictions, for example, on children, pets, or the use of facilities.

over renting, since the total cost of renting is $1,974 ($8,100 − $6,126) a year more than the total cost of buying. Alternatively, of course, you could look for a less expensive apartment. If you could lower the rent by about $165 a month—that is, $1,974/12—renting would be preferred. Renting would also be the preferred course of action if you plan to take the standard deduction (do not plan to itemize) on your tax return, since the values of the entries on lines B.8. and B.9. would then equal zero, thus raising the cost of homeownership by about $2,700 a year.

The rent-or-buy decision cannot be made solely on the basis of the numbers. You should also carefully consider both your personal situation and needs and the general condition of the housing market. If you think you may want to move to a different city in a few years or you are worried about job security, renting may make sense, even if the numbers favor buying. For some people, factors such as the need for privacy, the desire to personalize one's home, and the psychic satisfaction gained from homeownership outweigh the financial considerations. In some housing markets, a relative surplus of rental properties causes the cost of renting to be lower than the cost of owning a comparable house or condominium. It is a good idea to look at the rent-or-buy decision over a time horizon of several years, using different assumptions regarding rent increases, mortgage rates, home appreciation rates in the area, and the rate of return you can earn on the funds you can invest (if you rent) rather than use to make a down payment (if you buy).

BUYING A HOME

Finding the right house at the right price is only part of the home-buying process; other important activities include financing the transaction with the right kind of mortgage and closing the deal. Assuming you are interested in buying a home, how would you identify the "right" house, finance its purchase, and close the deal? Before reading ahead, spend a few moments responding to this question.

Buying a home usually requires a good deal of time, effort, and money. Learning of the available properties and their prices requires a systematic search and careful property analysis. Also, a buyer should have a basic understanding of mortgages, real estate sales contracts, and other documents required to close a deal.

SHOP THE MARKET FIRST

Most people who shop the housing market rely on real estate agents for information, access to properties, and advice. Other sources of information, such as newspaper ads, are also widely used to identify available properties. Occasionally a person seeking to buy or rent property will advertise his or her needs and wait for sellers to initiate contact.

Buying a home involves many factors, both emotional and financial. Frequently, the emotional factors carry the greatest weight. As noted earlier, you must begin by figuring out what *you* require for your particular lifestyle in terms of living space, style, and special features. The location, neighborhood, and school district are usually important considerations as well. You should divide your list into the necessary features, such as the number of bedrooms and baths, and the optional—but desirable—features. And of course, affordability analysis is a critical component of your housing search.

However, once you start looking, you may find that you like a very different house than you thought you originally wanted. For example, you may begin your search by looking for a one-story, contemporary ranch house with a pool, but fall in love with a two-story colonial with wonderful landscaping, no pool, and all the other features you want. It is a good idea to be flexible at first and look at a variety of homes in your price range; this can really help you define your wants and needs more clearly.

It is highly unlikely that you will find the "perfect" home at the "perfect" price. You will have to make some compromises, and the greater your research and advance preparation, the better off you will be. This will also reduce the *buyer remorse* that often accompanies a major purchase. Soon after signing the sales contract, home buyers often question whether they did the right thing: Did I pay too much? Should I have negotiated harder? Is the location as good as I thought? Can I really afford the monthly payments? Can I manage without a pool/playroom/workshop? These feelings are normal and usually decrease once you move in. One way to reduce buyer remorse is to shorten, if possible, the time that elapses between when you sign the sales contract and when you close the deal. The *Smart Money* box provides further advice on how to avoid some common mistakes in the home-buying process.

Using an Agent. Most home buyers rely on real estate agents because they are in daily contact with the housing market. Once you describe your needs to an agent he or she can begin to search for appropriate properties. The agent also will help you negotiate with the seller, assist you in obtaining satisfactory financing, and, although not empowered to give explicit legal advice, help you prepare a real estate sales contract.

Most real estate firms belong to the local **Multiple Listing Service (MLS)**. Basically, MLS compiles a list of properties for sale from information provided by the member firms in a given community or metropolitan area. A brief description of each property and its asking price are included, and the list is updated weekly. As a rule, it is best to deal with a realtor that works for a MLS member firm; otherwise, you might lack access to a large part of the market.

Buyers should remember that *agents typically are employed by the sellers*. Unless you have agreed to pay a fee to the sales agent you are working with, that agent's primary responsibility, by law, is to sell listed properties at the highest possible prices. Further, because agents are paid only if they make a sale, some might pressure you to "sign now or miss the chance of a lifetime." You should avoid that type of agent. Select someone who will listen to your wants and then work to match you with the right property under terms that will benefit both the seller and you. Good agents recognize that their best interests are served when all parties to a transaction are satisfied. Depending on the geographic location, real estate commissions range from 5 to 6 percent for new homes and 6 to 7 percent for previously occupied homes. (It is sometimes possible to negotiate a lower commission with your agent.) However, such commissions are paid only by the seller; the buyer pays the real estate agent nothing.

Of course, since the price of a home is likely to be affected by the size of the real estate commission — indeed, many builders are believed to factor commission costs into the prices of their new homes — the buyer probably absorbs some or even all of the commission paid by the seller.

THE REAL ESTATE SALES CONTRACT

State laws generally specify that in order to be enforceable in court, real estate buy-sell agreements must be in writing and contain certain information, including (1) names of buyer(s) and seller(s), (2) a description of the property sufficient to provide positive identification, (3) specific price and other terms, and (4) usually the signatures of the buyer(s) and seller(s). Real estate sales transactions often take weeks and sometimes months to complete. They involve a fair amount of legal work and therefore require expert assistance in preparation. Contract requirements help keep the facts straight and reduce the chance for misunderstanding, misrepresentation, or fraud.

Although these requirements fulfill the minimums necessary for court enforcement, in practice real estate sales contracts usually contain several other contractual clauses. Among these are provisions relating to earnest money deposits, contingencies, personal property, and closing costs. An **earnest money deposit** is the money you are asked to pledge at the time you make an offer in order to show good faith. If, after you sign a sales contract, you withdraw from the transaction without a valid reason, you forfeit this deposit. A valid reason for withdrawal would be one stated in the contract

---

Multiple Listing Service (MLS)
An organization of real estate companies that compiles and updates weekly a list and brief description, including asking price, of all properties for sale by the member firms in a given community or metropolitan area.

earnest money deposit
Money pledged by a buyer to show good faith when making an offer to buy a home.

Smart Money

Good Advice for Savvy Home Buyers

Buying a home is an experience that can be enjoyable and exciting. Because it is also the largest single purchase you ever make, it can be an intimidating—and even scary—process as well. The following advice will help you avoid some of the most frequent mistakes home buyers make.

1. **Pre-qualify.** Many first-time home buyers and even second- or third-time move-up buyers make the mistake of failing to know how large a mortgage they can obtain. They often overestimate, make a purchase offer on a house that is too expensive, and then lose their good-faith earnest money deposit when they can't obtain financing.

    To avoid this mistake, smart home buyers pre-qualify for a home loan with a mortgage lender. Most lenders welcome pre-qualified borrowers because these buyers are unlikely to shop elsewhere for a mortgage after they find a home

to buy. Although real estate agents and mortgage brokers can give you a general idea of the mortgage amount you can borrow, only a direct lender such as a bank or savings and loan can pre-qualify you—subject to appraisal of the home you decide to buy, of course.

2. **Don't depend completely on your agent.** Your home search can be greatly eased by a competent real estate agent who should phone you at least once a week to inform you of new listings that meet your criteria. When such a new listing comes on the market, make arrangements with your agent to inspect it as quickly as possible.

    But don't become dependent on that agent alone. Read the newspaper classified ads daily and phone your agent when you spot an ad for a home that sounds good. If your agent isn't familiar with the home, he or she can find out

about it and phone you back promptly with the details. However, if your agent doesn't follow up promptly to keep you informed about the local marketplace, don't hesitate to work with more than one agent if the first agent isn't doing a good job.

3. **Take your time.** Out-of-town job transferees are often in a rush to buy a home. As a result they frequently fail to thoroughly check out all aspects of a home in which they will be living many years. If necessary, take several months to make house-hunting trips to thoroughly check out various neighborhoods in your new community.

    Pay special attention to the reputation of the local schools, because school quality influences home market-value appreciation. Leasing a house or apartment is far better than rushing to buy a home that isn't right for your family. Better yet, lease a home with an option to buy. Then if you like the residence, you won't have to move and can merely exercise your purchase option.

4. **Don't buy a "red-ribbon deal."** Most home buyers just want to turn the key in the door of their new home and move in. This can be a very expensive mistake. The reason is that so-called "red ribbon deal" homes in perfect condition sell for top dollar. As a result, it may be a long time before you build any equity in such a home from appreciation in market value, since the seller took most of the profit.

A better idea is to buy a fixer-upper home that needs cosmetic, but not major, repairs; thus you can drive down the price to more than compensate for the needed improvements. After you complete the work, such as painting, carpeting, landscaping, and repairing, you will have forced the value of the home up. This is called "forced inflation" and is the best way to make a profit when buying a home.

If the seller already performed this work and there is nothing left to do but turn the key in the door, the seller (rather than you) earned the profit. However, stay away from houses needing expensive work that doesn't add much value, such as a new roof or foundation repairs.

5. **Negotiate price.** There is no worse feeling than having your first offer accepted by the seller. Then you feel you paid too much. However, the seller may have been desperate to sell and would have accepted virtually any offer. But don't be afraid to negotiate over price and terms because both buyer and seller feel much better after a few counteroffers.

Before making a purchase offer, be sure the real estate agent prepares a written comparative market analysis for you.

6. **Include contingencies in your offer.** Although home sellers and their real estate agents love to receive purchase offers with no contingencies, most home purchase offers include contingency clauses for mortgage financing and professional inspections including termite damage. Some home buyers also insist on making their purchase contingent upon sale of their old home.

7. **Avoid a bidding war.** If another buyer makes a purchase offer at about the same time as yours, unless the seller accepts your offer, it is best to drop out of the bidding. If you continue, the only winner will be the seller because the price gets driven higher. Wait to see what happens with the other bidder's offer before you make another offer.

Source: Adapted from Robert J. Bruss, "Buyers Be Wary of Costly Mistakes in Home Purchase," *The San Diego Union-Tribune*, April 26, 1992, p. F-34, 36. © Tribune Media Services.

as a contingency clause. With a **contingency clause**, you can condition your agreement to buy on such factors as the availability of financing, a termite or other physical inspection of the property, or the advice of a lawyer or real estate expert. Generally speaking, your lawyer should review and approve all agreements before you sign them.

FINANCING THE TRANSACTION

Often the success of a real estate transaction hinges on obtaining a mortgage with favorable terms. Earlier in the chapter, we saw that the mortgage terms can have a dramatic effect on the amount you can afford to spend on a home. A **mortgage loan** is secured by the property in which the lender obtains the legal right to liquidate the property to recover their funds in the event of borrower default. To obtain such a loan, you must be familiar with the available sources of mortgage loans and the types of mortgage contracts.

Sources of Mortgage Loans. The three major sources of home mortgages today are commercial banks, thrift institutions, and mortgage bankers or mortgage brokers. Some *credit unions* also make mortgage loans available to their members. During the past few years, *commercial banks*, formerly viewed primarily as short-term lenders, have become a major force in the residential mortgage market. Commercial banks also are an important source of **interim construction loans** used by persons who are building a home. These loans provide short-term financing during the construction period. After the home is completed, the homeowner obtains *permanent financing* (in the form of a standard, long-term, first mortgage loan) and uses it to repay the construction loan.

Thrift institutions include *savings and loan associations (S&Ls)* and *savings banks*. S&Ls either use customers' deposits to make loans or originate and sell loans to private investors. S&Ls concentrate on first mortgage loans on one-to-four-family houses, although some actively participate in the commercial real estate market as well. While their lending policies are dictated by regulators and mortgage market conditions, their terms are often more attractive than those of other mortgage lenders. Until recently, S&Ls were the largest source of home mortgages. Due to the S&L crisis (discussed in Chapter 5), many homebuyers, concerned about having a long-term loan with an S&L that might not be around in a few years, have turned to other mortgage lenders.

Savings banks, 90 percent of which are located in the Northeast, direct a lot of their mortgage-lending money to their depositors. Because they are most often *mutual* organizations, and therefore depositor-owned, the terms of their mortgage loans tend to be slightly more favorable than those made by commercial banks and S&Ls.

Another way to obtain a mortgage loan is through a **mortgage banker** or **mortgage broker**. Both solicit borrowers, originate loans, and place them with mortgage lenders such as life insurance companies and pension funds. While *mortgage bankers* frequently use their own money to initially fund mortgages that they later resell, *mortgage brokers* take loan applications and then find lenders willing to grant the mortgage loans under the desired terms. Another difference between them is that mortgage bankers deal primarily in government-insured and -guaranteed loans, whereas mortgage brokers concentrate on finding conventional loans for consumers willing to pay their fee.

Using a mortgage broker. The S&L crisis and the increased number and complexity of types of mortgages have caused mortgage brokers to become a more important source of mortgage loans during recent years. Using a mortgage broker can save you the time and inconvenience of talking with a large number of lenders. In addition, brokers typically have computer programs that can be used to help you compare the effective costs of loans with different terms. Most brokers have ongoing relationships with many different types of lenders, thereby increasing your chances of finding a loan for which you qualify. Mortgage brokers frequently find loans for persons who would not qualify for them at a commercial bank or thrift institution. They can often cut through the red tape, act as the borrower's advocate to get more favorable terms, and reduce the amount of time required to close the loan.

For these reasons, a good mortgage broker can make the financing process much easier for homebuyers. However, not all mortgage brokers are competent; some have been known to misrepresent the services they can provide or recommend a loan that might not be best suited to its clients' needs. Before working with a particular mortgage broker, you should carefully investigate the firm and its reputation. Realtors, bankers, and other buyers can provide leads to good brokers. In order to help you get the best rate and terms, the broker should represent ten or more lenders, including some from other parts of the United States. Ask potential brokers how many of their loan applications are actually funded; about 70 percent or more should result in closings. If your state is one of the 30 that license mortgage brokers, be sure to choose one that is licensed and has been in business for several years. Many brokers are certified by the National Association of Mortgage Brokers, although this is not a requirement. You should also request a written estimate of closing costs; most competent brokers will provide this information and justify each cost.

Most mortgage brokers earn their income from commissions and origination fees paid by the lender. These lender costs are typically passed on to the borrower in the points charged on the loan. Borrowers may have to pay application fees of $300 to $500. They must also frequently pay processing and document preparation fees to the lender at closing. If a loan has no points, the buyer may have to pay a fee directly to the broker, which should be paid at closing. A broker that asks for up-front fees and promises to find a loan is one to avoid! Rather than use a mortgage broker, you can shop for a mortgage on your own or with the assistance of your realtor, who is usually a knowledgeable source of information about various lenders and is legally prohibited from collecting fees or kickbacks for helping to arrange financing.

Prequalifying for a mortgage. Before beginning your home search, it may be helpful to meet with one or more mortgage lenders and pre-arrange for a mortgage loan. **Prequalification**, as it is called, can work to your advantage. You will be certain ahead of time that you qualify for a specific mortgage amount (subject, of course, to changes in rates and other terms) and can therefore focus your search on homes within an affordable price range. Prequalification also provides estimates of the required down payment and closing costs for different types of mortgages. It identifies in advance of purchase any problems, such as credit report errors, that might arise as a result of your application, and allows you more time to correct them. Finally, pre-qualification enhances your bargaining power with the seller of a house you want by letting him know

that the deal won't fall through because you can't afford the property or obtain suitable financing, and that the time required to close the sale should be relatively short.

Seller Financing One other increasingly important source of mortgage money is the seller of the property. Known as **seller financing**, this type of loan has long been in use, although it is most popular during periods of generally high interest rates.

---

contingency clause
A clause in a real estate sales contract that makes the agreement conditional on such factors as the availability of financing, property inspections, and obtaining expert advice.

mortgage loan
A loan secured by real property in which the lender obtains the legal right to liquidate the property to recover its funds in the event of borrower default.

interim construction loan
A loan that provides short-term financing while a home is being constructed.

mortgage banker
A firm that solicits borrowers, originates primarily government-insured and -guaranteed loans, and places them with mortgage lenders; frequently uses its own money to initially fund mortgages it later resells.

mortgage broker
A firm that solicits borrowers, originates primarily conventional loans, and places them with mortgage lenders; merely takes loan applications and then finds lenders willing to grant the mortgage loans under the desired terms.

prequalification
The process of arranging with a mortgage lender, in advance of buying a home, to obtain the amount of mortgage financing the lender deems affordable to the home-buyer.

seller financing
A type of loan provided either as a balloon payment by the seller of an older home or as a buy-down by a builder-developer of a new home in order to assist the buyer in purchasing their property; these incentives are commonly offered during periods of generally high interest rates.

Seller financing can take one of two forms: balloon payments or buy-downs.

Balloon payments. If provided by the seller of an older home, seller financing will usually involve a **balloon payment**, which is a single, very large principal payment due at a specified future date. In this case, the seller of the home is a private party—the current occupant, whose primary motivation is to sell the house. The balloon payment will be included in the transaction if the buyer does not have the money required for the down payment and/or does not want to commit to as large a mortgage loan as would otherwise be required. Under such circumstances, the buyer will look to the seller for financing.

Here is how it works. Suppose a potential buyer wants to purchase a $100,000 home that you have offered for sale; she has $15,000 available for a down payment but, because of high interest rates, does not wish to commit to a mortgage of more than $75,000. In order to sell the house, you agree to take a *note*, secured by a second mortgage, in the amount of $10,000. The note is set up so that it will mature (in full) in, say, five years; in addition, it will usually carry an interest rate that is at least a point or two below the market and will require monthly payments of *interest only* over the five-year term of the loan. In this case, the loan has only one, principal (balloon) payment of $10,000, due at maturity. The buyer, of course, is hoping the interest rates drop within the five years so that the balloon payment note can be refinanced at a considerably lower rate.

A word of caution: Such forms of *creative financing* can cause serious problems for both the buyer and seller when interest rates fail to drop as expected or the buyer is simply unable to obtain alternative financing. The net result often is that the seller is left with a balloon-payment note that the buyer is unable to repay at its maturity.

Buy-downs. The other type of seller financing involves new homes and usually takes the form of a **buy-down**. In this case, a builder-developer will arrange with a financial institution (like an S&L) for mortgage financing at interest rates that are well below the market—say, 8 percent financing on his homes at a time when the market rate of interest is around 9 or 9.5 percent. This obviously looks like a good deal, but how is this accomplished? Typically the builder/seller puts his money up front; in effect, he buys a reduced rate of interest by paying a specified number of points. In our example, the builder might have to pay 6 to 10 points to buy down the mortgage. Of course, such an arrangement can be costly and involve thousands of dollars. While the builder is trying to give the buyer the impression that he or she can finance a home bought from him at a special low interest rate, the fact is that the buyer will pay for the reduced interest in the form of a higher home-purchase price.

The intent behind buy-downs is to reduce the monthly mortgage payment—which can be accomplished even with a higher home price. Probably the most popular form of buy-down is the so-called "3–2–1 buy-down," meaning that the builder arranges a discount of 3 percentage points the first year, 2 percentage points the second year, and 1 point the third year. If the prevailing rate of interest is 9.5 percent, in a 3–2–1 buy-down on a 30-year mortgage the builder will arrange financing at 6.5 percent for year 1, 7.5 percent for year 2, 8.5 percent for year 3, and 9.5 percent for the years 4 through 30. Thus, the monthly mortgage payments will start out low but will build up each year until the fourth year, when they will level off. For example, on a $70,000, 30-year mortgage loan, first-year payments would amount to around $442 a month; in the second year, they would jump to about $489; in the third, they would go up to around $536; and in the fourth and following years they would be up to about $583.

Buy-downs have come under a lot of criticism because they tend to encourage homebuyers to overextend themselves and accept a larger mortgage loan than they can afford, especially under 3–2–1 type arrangements. In addition, the homeowner is often in for a big surprise when he has to sell his home after only three or four years. This occurs when the homeowner finds that the market value of his house is actually less than the amount he still owes on the mortgage! The reason, of course, is that the cost of the buy-down not only increased the price of the home, but it also added to the amount of the mortgage. Thus, a homebuyer, should exercise caution when considering a buy-down arrangement, or any other form of creative financing.

TYPES OF MORTGAGE LOANS

Knowing where to look for mortgage money is just the start. You also must choose the type of mortgage that is right for you. The mortgage market today is quite different from what it was 20 years ago. In 1970, for example, just a few basic types of mortgages were available. Today there is a full menu of mortgages; many S&Ls offer more than ten different kinds. Selecting the right mortgage obviously is an important aspect of buying a home.

Fortunately, personal computer programs are available for use in analyzing and comparing loan terms in order to choose those best for you. For example, *Managing Your Money* (see the box on using personal financial planning software in Chapter 2) has a module that performs a rent-or-buy analysis as well as mortgage calculations; you can also purchase this Financial Calculator module separately. Another program, *Mortgage Miser* from Macc-Trac (1-800-444-7071) allows you to compare the total costs of up to 15 loans. In many metropolitan areas you can purchase from a mortgage update service for about $20 a computer printout with the terms of the mortgages offered by lenders in your area. HSH Associates (1-800-UPDATES) is a mortgage information service that covers the whole country. Its reports can be obtained in IBM-compatible disk form, together with software that can be used to compare different options. It is also possible to connect your computer to a network of mortgage lenders; for a fee, a computer program will analyze your loan application and identify the best lenders in light of your individual circumstances.

The cost differentials among different types of mortgages can be substantial. It is not unusual to find differences of 2 full percentage points or more; for example, in early 1992 in a major market the quoted rate on one popular form of mortgage ranged from 5.5 to 7 percent, depending on the lender. Mortgage interest rates have always been a concern to homebuyers—a high interest rate can seriously affect your limits of affordability.

There is no single way to classify mortgages. For our purposes here, we will look at them in two ways: (1) terms of payment and (2) whether they are conventional, insured, or guaranteed. As far as terms of payment are concerned, there are literally dozens of different types of home mortgages from which to choose. For example, there are *graduated payment* and *growing equity* mortgages, in which the amount of the monthly mortgage payment gets progressively larger over time. With a *bi-weekly* mortgage, payments (equal to half of a regular monthly payment) are made every two weeks, rather than once a month. Because you make 26 payments (52 weeks ÷ 2), which is the equivalent of 13 monthly payments, the principal balance declines at a faster rate and you pay less interest over the life of the loan. For example, assume you qualify for a $100,000, 30-year mortgage with a 9 percent interest rate. You can either pay $805 monthly or $402.50 biweekly. The biweekly loan is paid off in the 21st year, saving you almost $62,000 in interest. However, with most 30-year mortgages you can make extra principal payments at any time, without penalty. Such a strategy may be better than committing to the biweekly mortgage, which frequently charges an extra processing fee.

While there are many different types of mortgages, the vast majority of all mortgage loans made today can be categorized as either fixed-rate mortgages or adjustable-rate mortgages. These two types of mortgages account for 90 percent, or more, of all loans made today. Because of their popularity, we now will take a closer look at these mortgages, their features, advantages, and disadvantages.

Fixed-Rate Mortgage. In spite of the fact that since mid-1975 a number of other types of mortgages have been developed, marketed, and popularized, the **fixed-rate mortgage** today still accounts for a large portion of all home mortgages written. It is characterized by the fact that both the rate of interest and the monthly mortgage payment are fixed over the full term of the loan. The most common type by far is the *30-year fixed-rate* loan. Because of the risks that the lender assumes in this type of mortgage, it is usually the most expensive form of home financing.

---

balloon payment
A single, very large mortgage principal payment due at a specified future date.

buy-down
A type of seller financing made available by a builder-developer to a potential new-home buyer at below-market interest rates, often only for the first few years of the mortgage.

fixed-rate mortgage
The traditional type of mortgage, in which both the rate of interest and the monthly mortgage payment are fixed over the full term of the loan.

A variation of this standard fixed-rate loan that is rapidly gaining in popularity is the *15-year fixed-rate* mortgage. Its chief appeal is that it is repaid twice as fast (15 years versus 30) and yet, the monthly payments don't increase significantly. Obviously, to pay off a loan in less time, the homeowner's going to have to pay more each month. But the big (pleasant) surprise comes from the fact that it does not take twice as large a monthly payment to pay off the loan in half the time; rather, the monthly payment on a 15-year loan is generally only about 10 percent larger than the payment on a 30-year loan. (Monthly mortgage payments on fixed-rate loans vary according to interest rates and loan terms, and these can be found by using the mortgage payment table in Exhibit 6.5.)

The basic features of 30- and 15-year fixed-rate mortgages are compared in the following table. In both cases, it is assumed that the purchaser borrows $80,000 at a 9 percent fixed rate of interest:

Type of Loan	Regular Payment	Term of Loan	Total Interest Paid over Life of Loan
Standard 30-year fixed rate	$643.76 per month	30 years	$151,754
15-year fixed rate	$811.44 per month	15 years	$ 66,059

Perhaps the most startling feature is the substantial difference in the total amount of interest paid. In effect, you can save *about $85,000* just by financing your home with a 15-year mortgage rather than a traditional 30-year one — not bad, considering it is only an $80,000 loan. Note that this amount of savings is possible even though monthly payments differ by about $168. In practice this difference would be even less, since 15-year mortgages are usually available at interest rates that are about half a percentage point below comparable 30-year loans. Thus, if the 30-year mortgage carried a 9 percent rate, you would expect the 15-year loan to be priced at, say, 8.5 percent. The monthly payments would then amount to only $788 rather than $811 — a more realistic difference in monthly payments of *less than $150* ($788 − $644)!

While the idea of paying off a mortgage in 15 years instead of 30 may seem like a good idea, it is important to first consider how long you plan to stay in the house. If you plan to sell the house in a few years, paying off the loan faster may not make much sense. In addition, the tax deductibility of mortgage inter-est makes a mortgage one of the least expensive sources of borrowing. You should also determine whether you can earn a higher rate of return on the increase in the monthly payment for a 15-year mortgage than the rate of interest on the loan. If so, you would be better off investing the difference and taking a 30-year loan. You can also make extra principal payments on a regular basis or at times when you have extra funds without committing to the shorter term.

Some lenders also offer other types of fixed-rate loans. The term of a *balloon loan* can be five, seven, or ten years. The interest rate is fixed, typically at .25 to .5 percent below the 30-year fixed rate. The monthly payments are the same as for a 30-year loan at the given rate. Unlike seller-financed balloon loans, which require payments of interest only, the monthly payments on these loans include principal and interest. When the loan matures, the remaining principal balance comes due and must be refinanced. Although the lower rate results in lower monthly payments, these loans have some risk, since it may be difficult to refinance them in the future, particularly if rates have risen.

Similar to the balloon loan but not involving refinancing risk is the *two-step loan*. This loan's initial rate is fixed for five or seven years, typically at .25 to .5 percent below the 30-year fixed rate. At the end of the initial period (the first step), the loan converts to a fixed rate that is about .5 percent higher than the then-prevailing 30-year fixed rate for the remainder of the term (the second step), subject to a maximum rate increase of about 6 percent. If you plan to sell the house before the end of the first period — and most people move every seven years — this loan may be a good option. You can save several thousand dollars in interest during the first step; however, if interest rates are higher when you reach the second step, your monthly payments will rise — often sharply.

Adjustable-Rate Mortgage. Another popular form of home loan is the **adjustable-rate mortgage (ARM)**. Unlike the fixed-rate mortgage, the rate of interest, and therefore the size of the monthly payment, on an ARM is adjusted up and down in line with movements in interest rates. In essence, the rate of interest on the mortgage is linked to a specific *interest rate index* and adjusted at specific intervals (usually once or twice a year) in accordance with changes in the index. When the index moves up, so does the rate of interest on the mortgage and, in turn, the size of the monthly mortgage payment. The new interest rate and monthly mortgage payment will then remain fixed until the next adjustment date, when the adjustment process will repeat itself.

The term of an ARM is set (usually at 30 years but sometimes at 15), while its interest rate and monthly payments are not. Since the size of the monthly payments will vary with interest rates, there is no way for you to tell what your future payments will be. However, because the borrower/homebuyer assumes most or all of the interest rate risk in these mortgages, the *initial* rate of interest on an adjustable-rate mortgage is normally well below—2 to 3 percentage points—the rate on a standard 30-year fixed-rate loan. Of course, whether or not the borrower actually will end up paying less interest depends on the behavior of market interest rates over the term of the loan.

Basic features. There are several basic features of an ARM that a homebuyer should understand. One is the **adjustment period**, which is the period of time between one rate/payment change and the next. Most ARMs have adjustment periods of six months or one year (these are known as *one-year ARMs*), though some have adjustment periods as short as three months and others as long as three or five years. Another feature is the **index rate**, which is meant to capture the movement in interest rates. Many lenders use an index rate that is based on the behavior of *six-month or one-year U.S. Treasury securities*. Others use the index rate based on six-month CDs. Another common index is the average interest paid to depositors in savings institutions, which is commonly measured by the *11th Federal Home Loan Bank District's monthly cost of funds.*

To determine the rate of interest on an ARM, lenders will add to the index a few percentage points called the **margin**, which is usually a fixed amount over the life of the loan. Thus, the rate of interest on an ARM equals the index rate plus the margin. This procedure is used in most cases not only to initially set up the loan but also to periodically adjust interest rates and monthly payments.

Consider a lender who uses an index rate that at inception of the loan equals 5.5 percent; if it charges a 2 percent margin, the loan will be set up initially as a 7.5 percent mortgage (since 5.5 percent + 2 per-

cent = 7.5 percent). Because most ARMs are 30-year loans, the initial monthly payment is found like any other 7.5 percent, 30-year mortgage. For example, for a $65,000 loan, we can use Exhibit 6.5 to find its first-year monthly payments of $454.55. Assuming a one-year adjustment period, if the index rate rises to, say, 7 percent, the interest rate for the second year will be 9 percent; that is, since the margin is fixed at 2 percent, we have 7 percent + 2 percent = 9 percent. The size of the monthly payment for the next 12 months will then be adjusted upward to about $521.90 and the process repeated each year thereafter until the loan matures.

To protect the borrower from extreme increases in interest rates and monthly payments, many adjustable-rate mortgages have **interest rate caps**, which place a limit on the amount the interest rate can increase over a given period. There are two kinds: (1) *periodic caps*, which limit the interest rate increase from one adustment to the next, and (2) *overall caps*, which limit the interest rate increase over the life of the loan. Many ARMs have

---

adjustable-rate mortgage (ARM)

A mortgage on which the rate of interest, and therefore the size of the monthly payment, is adjusted up and down in line with movements in interest rates.

adjustment period

In an adjustable-rate mortgage, the period of time between one rate payment/change and the next.

index rate

An interest rate index that is meant to capture the movement of interest rates; used by mortgage lenders as a base rate for determining the rate of interest to charge on ARMs.

margin

The amount, typically up to a few percentage points, that is added to the basic index rate on an adjustable-rate mortgage loan to determine its prevailing rate of interest; it is usually fixed over the life of the loan.

interest rate cap

A feature of an adjustable-rate mortgage loan that places a limit on the amount that the interest rate can increase each adjustment period (*periodic cap*) as well as over the life of the loan (*overall cap*).

both a periodic and an overall interest rate cap. Typically lenders cap annual rate adjustments at 1 to 2 percentage points and set lifetime interest rate caps at 5 to 6 percentage points. Some ARMs may include *payment caps*, which act to limit the monthly payment increase at the time of each adjustment to a certain amount—usually defined as a percentage of the previous payment. In other words, if your ARM has a 5 percent payment cap, that is the most your monthly payments can increase from one year to the next regardless of what happens to interest rates.

Beware of negative amortization. It is important to recognize that some ARMs are subject to **negative amortization**—an increasing principal balance resulting from the fact that the monthly loan payments are lower than the amount of monthly interest being charged. In other words, with some of these loans you can wind up with a larger mortgage balance on the next anniversary of the loan than on the last. This occurs either when the initial payment is intentionally set below the interest charge or when the ARM has interest rates that adjust monthly, although the actual monthly payment can be adjusted only annually. In this latter case, when rates are rising on these loans the current monthly payment can be less than the interest being charged, and the difference is added to the principal, thereby increasing the size of the loan. For example, assume the monthly payment on a 7.5 percent, $80,000 loan is currently $560 and the loan's next annual adjustment is in ten months. If, as a result of rising interest rates, the applicable interest rate increases to 9 percent (that is, .75 percent per month), the monthly interest owed would be $600 (.75 percent × $80,000). Thus, negative amortization would occur in the amount of $40 per month ($600 interest—$560 monthly payment). If no other interest rate changes were to occur over the ten months remaining until the next annual adjustment, at that time the mortgage balance would be $80,400—the increase of $400 is attributable to the $40 per month negative amortization over the ten months. When considering an ARM, it is important to learn whether or not negative amortization can occur. Generally loans without the potential for negative amortization are available, although they tend to have slightly higher initial rates and interest rate caps.

Convertible ARMs. Since 1987 a majority of large lenders have begun to offer **convertible ARMs**, loans that allow borrowers to convert from an adjustable-rate to a fixed-rate loan, usually at any time from the 13th to the 60th month. While these loans seldom provide the lowest initial rate, they allow the borrower, for a fee, to convert to a fixed-rate loan if interest rates decline. A conversion fee of around $500 is typical, and the fixed rate is normally set at .25 to .5 percent above the going rate on fixed-rate loans at the time you convert. Borrowers who like the generally low initial ARM rates and feel that interest rates will decline during the first 60 months or so of the loan may find the convertible ARM an attractive compromise between a fixed-rate and an adjustable-rate loan.

Choosing an index. When you select an ARM, it is important to understand the differences between the index rates. The index significantly affects the level and stability of your mortgage payments over the term of the loan. The one-year Treasury bill index is one of the most common indexes used by lenders, particularly in the eastern United States. Recently, some lenders have begun to use CD-based indexes. The 11th Federal Home Loan Bank District Cost of Funds is popular in the western United States, although the use of cost of funds indexes is gaining in other parts of the country as well.

The most important difference between the indexes is their volatility. Treasury bill rates are quite volatile because they respond to changes in the financial markets. CD rates also fluctuate considerably, since their issuers can quickly adjust them in response to changing market conditions. The 11th District Cost of Funds index is much less volatile because it represents an average of rates charged on mortgage loans made by S&Ls in the District. It tends to lag T-bill and CD rate movements, both up and down, and exhibits a fairly smooth pattern over time. To more fully understand how one particular index behaves relative to another, you may want to compare the index rates over the past several years.

So what does this mean for the homebuyer considering an ARM? If your mortgage is tied to a T-bill or CD index, you can expect sharper and more frequent upward and downward interest rate movements. On the other hand, cost of funds indexes move more slowly in both directions. To choose which is better for you, consider the annual rate cap on a particular mortgage, the relative level of interest rates, and your future interest rate expectations. If you have a low rate cap of about 1 to 2 percentage points and you think rates are going down, you may be comfortable with a T-bill or CD index.

Some lenders offer special first-year rates, called "teaser" rates, that are set below the index rate on the loan. You should be wary of lenders who advertise very low rates; ask them if the first-year rate is based on the index and then verify the rate for yourself. Be sure you can comfortably make the monthly mortgage payment when the interest rate steps up to the indexed rate.

Monitoring your mortgage payments. You should carefully monitor your mortgage over its life. Always verify the calculation of your loan payment when rate or payment adjustments are made. Recent government reports and consumer surveys estimate that errors may exist in 20 to nearly *80* percent of all ARMs. Most mistakes result from lender carelessness. To verify your payment amount, you need to know the index rate and the margin, and the loan formula used to make the adjustment; all are found in the loan agreement. The interest rates for the most commonly used indexes are readily available in the financial press and are frequently published weekly in the real estate section of most newspapers. The loan formula tells you when the rate is set—for example, 45 days before the adjustment date—and the margin on the loan. You can use a basic financial calculator to calculate the payment once you know the new rate, the number of years until the loan is paid off, and the current principal balance. If you suspect you are being overcharged, call your lender and ask for an explanation of the rate and payment calculations. Special mortgage checking services will review your ARM for a fee of about $70 to $100. These services may be useful if your mortgage is being serviced by a firm that is not the original lender, the lender does not satisfactorily answer your questions about the payment calculation, or your loan formula is particularly complicated.

Adjustable-rate mortgages are relatively complex and place the borrower or homebuyer at the mercy of the market. Their popularity is due not to their simplicity but to their low initial cost. Before using an adjustable-rate mortgage to finance your home purchase, you should take the time to become acquainted with all of the loan's terms and conditions.

In an adjustable-rate mortgage, the size of the monthly mortgage payment will change periodically, along with prevailing mortgage interest rates.

Fact: In this popular form of home mortgage loan, the term of the loan is fixed (usually at 30 years), but the rate of interest, and therefore the size of the monthly mortgage payment, is adjusted up and down in line with movements in interest rates.

Fixed-Rate or Adjustable-Rate? Fixed-rate mortgages are popular with homebuyers who plan to stay in their homes for five to seven years and want to know what their payments will be. Of course, the current level of interest rates and your expectation about future interest rates will significantly impact your choice of a fixed- or adjustable-rate mortgage. In 1984, when the average interest on a 30-year mortgage loan was a relatively high 13.76 percent, many people chose adjustable-rate mortgages in order to avoid being locked in to the then-prevailing high rates. In early to mid-1992, the interest rate on 30-year, fixed-rate loans averaged about 9 percent, its lowest level in many years. Many home buyers chose fixed-rate mortgages, and many homeowners with adjustable-rate mortgages refinanced them with fixed-rate loans in order to lock in the then-prevailing low rates. Even though adjustable rate mortgages were being offered with initial rates as low as about 6.2 percent, the certainty of the fixed-rate loan had great appeal.

Historically, though, adjustable-rate mortgages have been less costly than fixed-rate mortgages; the

---

negative amortization
When the principal balance on a mortgage loan increases due to the fact that the monthly loan payment is lower than the amount of monthly interest being charged; some ARMs are subject to this undesirable situation.

convertible ARM
An adjustable-rate mortgage loan that allows borrowers to convert from an adjustable-rate to a fixed-rate loan, usually at any time from the 13th to the 60th month.

average interest savings during the period from 1981 to 1990 was about 25 percent, due in large part to the overall drop in interest rates during that period. The starting rates for ARMs are set lower to induce borrowers to accept the risk that rates may rise. The future appeal of ARMs largely depends, of course, on future interest rates. Many financial experts recommend monitoring interest rates carefully and being prepared to convert or refinance an ARM to a fixed-rate loan when favorable market conditions exist. Some suggest that the interest rate on an ARM should be at least 2 percentage points below that of a comparable fixed-rate loan in order to adequately compensate you for its greater risk. Again, it is important to consider how long you plan to be in your home; if you expect to move in a few years, the low starting rate on an ARM may allow you to afford a more expensive house.

Conventional, Insured, and Guaranteed Loans.

A **conventional mortgage** is a mortgage offered by a lender who assumes all the risk of loss. To protect themselves on this type of mortgage, lenders usually require a down payment of at least 20 percent of the value of the mortgaged property. Of course, the down payment can be far less than this (sometimes 5 percent or less), but when this happens, the lender usually requires some form of mortgage insurance. Experience has shown that high borrower equity greatly lessens the chance of a mortgage default and a subsequent loss to the lender. However, such a high down payment requirement makes home buying more difficult for many families and individuals.

To promote homeownership, the federal government, through the Federal Housing Administration (FHA), offers lenders mortgage insurance on high loan-to-value ratio loans. The **FHA mortgage insurance** program helps people buy homes even when they have very little money available for a down payment and closing costs. In exchange for a mortgage insurance premium of about 3.8 percent of the loan amount—which is paid by the borrower at closing or included in the mortgage—plus another .5 percent annual charge for five to ten years, the FHA agrees to reimburse lenders in the event of buyer default for their losses up to a specified maximum amount. The minimum required down payment on an FHA loan is 3 percent on the first $25,000 and 5 percent on the amount over $25,000. Buyers

can include 57 percent of closing costs in the mortgage amount. The interest rate on an FHA loan is generally about .5 percent lower than the rate on conventional fixed-rate loans. Affordability ratios are less stringent with FHA loans. In early 1992, the maximum monthly mortgage payment ratio was 29 percent (of monthly *gross* income) and the maximum total monthly installment loan payment ratio was 41 percent (of monthly *gross* income). The maximum mortgage amount that the FHA can insure is based on the national median price of homes. Although the ordinary FHA mortgage limit for single-family homes is $67,500, many areas of the country qualify for higher ceilings—now up to $124,875 where housing costs are especially high. As a result, the FHA program offers little benefit for people buying expensive homes. For those who plan to buy homes equal to or less than the median price, however, an FHA loan might be worth pursuing.

In addition to the FHA, a number of private companies insure low-down-payment mortgage loans for lenders. These plans, called **private mortgage insurance (PMI)** programs, work in a way similar to the FHA program, but their credit standards, insurable loan amounts, and insurance premiums are somewhat different. Their cost depends on the size of your down payment. Put down 10 percent on an $80,000 loan and you'll pay about .5 percent of the amount of the mortgage ($400) at closing and then about $20 per month; put down 5 percent on the same loan and you'll pay 1.25 percent ($1,000) at closing and about $30 per month; generally the monthly payment is made only during the first 7 to 9 years of a 30-year mortgage.

If you would like to buy a house, cooperative, or condominium but have only, say, 5 percent for a down payment, you should ask your real estate agent or mortgage lender whether you might qualify for either an FHA or PMI program. Both types of plans have helped millions of homebuyers.

Guaranteed loans are like insured loans, only better—if you qualify. **VA loan guarantees** are provided by the U.S. Veterans Administration to lenders who make qualified mortgage loans to eligible veterans of the U.S. Armed Forces and their unmarried surviving spouses. This program, however, does not require lenders or veterans to pay a premium for the guarantee. In many instances, an eligible veteran must pay only closing costs; in effect, under such a program, a veteran can buy a home with no down payment. (By the way, this can be done *only once* with a VA loan.) The mortgage loan—subject to a maximum amount—can go up to 100 percent of a purchased property's appraised value. VA loans include a 1.875 percent funding fee (which is lower if the down payment is 5 percent or more) paid by the borrower at closing or included in the mortgage. The maximum interest rate is set by the VA and, like FHA loans, is usually about .5 percent below the rate of conventional fixed-rate loans. The veteran (borrower) can only pay 1 point; the seller must pay for any additional points. The maximum loan currently obtainable with a VA guarantee is $184,000. To qualify, the veteran's total monthly installment loan payment ratio can at maximum equal 41 percent (of monthly *gross* income). The VA loan guarantee is an important fringe benefit available to those who have served in the armed forces.

CLOSING THE DEAL

After your loan has been approved, the closing process begins. There are three important parts to a closing: (1) the RESPA statement, (2) the title check, and (3) the closing statement.

RESPA. Since 1974, closings on owner-occupied houses, condominiums, and apartment buildings of four units or fewer have been governed by the **Real Estate Settlement Procedures Act (RESPA)**. The purpose of this act (and its 1975 amended version) was to spur closing cost reductions primarily by prohibiting kickbacks made in conjunction with closing services and by requiring advance disclosure of closing costs to buyers. Prior to the act, real estate closing costs were believed to be higher than necessary because in many areas real estate agents, attorneys, and others received kickbacks from lenders or title insurance companies in return for steering business to them. Furthermore, because buyers often learned the total amount of closing costs late in the closing process, they did not have time to shop for competing providers of services.

The specific requirements of RESPA are given in a U.S. Department of Housing and Urban Development booklet entitled *Settlement Costs and You: A HUD Guide for Homebuyers*. The law requires lenders to give a copy of this guide to potential borrowers. It can take much of the mystery out of the closing process. Although closing expenses still may

climb into the thousands of dollars, homebuyers often can save significant amounts if they shop for financing, insurance coverages, and other closing items rather than merely accepting the costs quoted by any one lender or other provider of closing services.

Title Check. Numerous legal interests can exist in real estate simultaneously, for example, those of the owner(s), lender(s), lienholders (such as an unpaid roofing contractor), and easement holders. Before you take title to a property, therefore, you should make sure that the title is free of all liens and encumbrances (except those that are specifically referred to in the sales contract) and that the owners who are conveying title to you actually have the legal interest they claim.

Although it is up to you to question the quality of the title to the property you are buying, in most

---

conventional mortgage
A mortgage offered by a lender who assumes all the risk of loss; typically requires a down payment of at least 20 percent of the value of the mortgaged property.

FHA mortgage insurance
A program under which the Federal Housing Administration offers lenders mortgage insurance on loans having a high loan-to-value ratio; its intent is to encourage loans to homebuyers who have very little money available for a down payment and closing costs.

private mortgage insurance (PMI)
An insurance plan offered by a private company that insures low-down-payment mortgage loans for lenders.

VA loan guarantee
A guarantee offered by the U.S. Veterans Administration to lenders who make qualified mortgage loans to eligible veterans of the U.S. Armed Forces and their unmarried surviving spouses.

Real Estate Settlement Procedures Act (RESPA)
A law passed in 1974 that requires mortgage lenders to provide clear, advance disclosure of closing costs to home buyers.

EXHIBIT 6.9

A Simple Closing Statement

At the top in the borrower's (buyer's) statement, his charges, advance payments, reserve deposits with the lender, title charges, and recording fees are added to the $100,000 purchase price, and then the earnest money deposit, principal amount of the loan, and county tax credit are subtracted from the total to find the amount due from the borrower of $12,377.37. In the seller's statement, the total charges, mortgage payoff, and county tax credit to borrower are subtracted from the $100,000 sale price to find the $27,048.32 cash to be paid the seller.

A. Borrower's Statement

Contract Price		$100,000.00
Plus: Charges		
Points (3% × $90,000)	$ 2,700.00	
Appraisal Fee	175.00	
Credit Report	84.00	
Tax Service	32.00	
Total		2,991.00
Plus: Advance Payments		
Interest to End of Month	547.09	
Mortgage Insurance Premium	855.00	
Homeowner's Insurance Premium	347.00	
Total		1,749.09
Plus: Reserves Deposited with Lender		
Homeowner's Insurance (2 mos.)	$ 57.84	
Mortgage Insurance (2 mos.)	56.26	
County Property Taxes (2 mos.)	59.00	
Total		173.10
Plus: Title Charges		
Closing Fee	$ 103.50	
Title Insurance	245.00	
Total		348.50
Plus: Government Recording and Transfer Charges		
Recording Fees		12.00
GROSS DUE FROM BORROWER		$105,273.69
Less: Amounts Paid By or on Behalf of Borrower		
Earnest Money Deposit	$ 3,000.00	
Principal Amount of Loan	90,000.00	
County Tax Credit	(103.68)	
Total		(92,896.32)
AMOUNT DUE FROM BORROWER		$ 12,377.37

B. Seller's Statement

Contract Sales Price		$100,000.00
Less: Charges		
Real Estate Commission	$ 6,000.00	
Closing Fee	103.50	
Title Insurance	535.00	
Affidavit of Value	2.00	
Termite Inspection	25.00	
1 year Home Warranty	315.00	
Total		(6,980.50)
Less: Payoff of Mortgage		(65,867.50)
Less: Credit to Borrower for County Taxes Owed		(103.68)
CASH TO SELLER		$ 27,048.32

cases an attorney or title insurance company performs a **title check**, which consists of the necessary research of legal documents and courthouse records. The customary practices and procedures and the costs involved vary widely throughout the country. Regardless of the specific custom in your area, you should make some form of title check an essential part of your closing process.

Closing Statement. A **closing statement**, provided to both buyer and seller at closing, accounts for the monies that change hands during that procedure. The statement reconciles the borrower's and the seller's costs and shows how much the borrower owes and the seller receives from the transaction. Exhibit 6.9 shows a simplified closing statement for both the borrower (buyer) and seller in a transaction involving sale of a home for $100,000. It can be seen that, in addition to the $100,000 purchase price, the borrower must pay 3 points on the $90,000 mortgage loan with a number of other charges, advance payments, reserve deposits with the lender, title charges, and recording fees — resulting in a gross amount due of $105,273.69. After subtracting the $3,000 earnest money deposit, the $90,000 of loan proceeds, and the county tax credit of $103.68, it can be seen that the borrower will have to pay $12,377.37 at closing. After charges are subtracted, including a $6,000 real estate commission, the seller's mortgage payoff of $65,867.50, and the unpaid county taxes of $103.68 (to be paid by the seller), from the $100,000 sale price, the amount the seller will receive at closing is $27,048.32. Note that frequently the RESPA form developed by the U.S. Department of Housing and Urban Development is used. Before closing a home purchase transaction, you should be given an opportunity to review the closing statement and have your questions answered. Be sure to carefully and critically review the statement in order to make sure that it is accurate and consistent with the contractual terms of the transaction; if not, have the statement corrected before closing the deal.

REFINANCING YOUR MORTGAGE

It sometimes occurs that after you've purchased a home and closed the transaction, interest rates on similar loans will drop. If rates drop by 1 to 2 percent or more, you should consider the economics of refinancing. In the years between 1985 and 1988 and again in 1991 and 1992, many people who obtained mortgage loans during periods of high interest rates found refinancing attractive; loans with fixed rates as high as 13 percent could be refinanced for fixed rates as low as 8.5 percent. The decision to refinance should be made after carefully considering the terms of the old and new mortgages, the anticipated number of years you expect to remain in the home, any prepayment penalty on the old mortgage, and the closing costs associated with the new mortgage.

Exhibit 6.10 presents a form that can be used to analyze a potential refinancing. The data for the Philipatos family's analysis is shown. Their current 5-year-old, 12 percent mortgage with a balance of $80,000 requires monthly payments of $825 per month for 25 more years. If refinanced at the prevailing rate of 9 percent over the remaining 25-year life of the current mortgage, the monthly payment would drop to $670. The Philipatos are very happy with their house and plan to live there for at least five more years. They will not have to pay any penalty for prepaying their current mortgage, and closing and other costs associated with the new mortgage are $2,400 after taxes. Substituting these values into the form in Exhibit 6.10 reveals (in Item 7) that it will take the Philipatos 22 months to break even with the new mortgage. Since 22 months is considerably less than their anticipated five years (60 months) in the home, the economics easily support refinancing their mortgage under the specified terms.

There are two basic reasons to refinance — to reduce the monthly payment or to reduce the total cost over the term of the loan. If a lower monthly payment is the objective, the analysis is relatively

---

title check
The research of legal documents and courthouse records to verify that the title is free of all liens and encumbrances and that the seller conveying title to property actually has the legal interest he or she claims.

closing statement
A statement provided to both buyer and seller at closing that accounts for the monies that change hands during that procedure.

EXHIBIT 6.10

Mortgage Refinancing Analysis for the Philipatos

Using the form below, the Philipatos find that by refinancing their 5-year-old, $80,000, 12-percent, 30-year mortgage (which has no prepayment penalty and requires payments of $825 per month) with an $80,000, 9-percent, 25-year mortgage requiring $670 monthly payments and $2,400 in total after-tax closing costs, it will take 22 months to break even. Since the Philipatos plan to stay in their home for at least 60 more months, the refinancing is easily justified.

MORTGAGE REFINANCING ANALYSIS

Name _____ Demi and Nicholas Philipatos _____   Date _____ September 6, 1992 _____

Item	Description	Amount
1	Current monthly payment (Terms: _____ $80,000, 12%, 30 years _____)	$ 825
2	New monthly payment (Terms: _____ $80,000, 9%, 25 years _____)	670
3	Monthly savings, pretax (Item 1 – Item 2)	$ 155
4	Monthly savings times your tax rate (_28_ %)	43
5	Monthly savings, after-tax (Item 3 – Item 4)	$ 112
6	Costs to refinance:	
	a. Prepayment penalty $ __0__	
	b. Total closing costs (after-tax) __2,400__	
	c. Total refinancing costs (Item 6a + Item 6b)	$ 2,400
7	Months to break even (Item 6c ÷ Item 5)	22

---

simple: determine how long it will take for the monthly savings to equal your closing costs (see Exhibit 6.10). If your objective is instead to reduce the total costs over the life of the loan, the analysis is more complex. The term of the new versus existing loan is a critical input. If you refinance a 30-year loan that has been outstanding five years with another 30-year loan, you are actually extending the total maturity to 35 years; even with a lower interest rate, you may pay more interest. Therefore, you should refinance for a shorter-term loan, one that matures no later than the original loan. (The example in Exhibit 6.10 is prepared on this basis.) Many homeowners want to pay off their loans more quickly to free up funds to pay for their children's college education or for their retirement. By refinancing at a lower rate but continuing to make the same monthly payment, a larger portion of each payment will go toward the principal and the loan will be paid off more quickly.

Alternatively, the borrower can make extra principal payments whenever possible. Paying only an additional $25 per month on a 30-year, 9 percent, $80,000 mortgage reduces the term to about 25 years and saves over $29,000 in interest!

Some people consider the reduced tax deduction associated with a smaller mortgage interest deduction as a disadvantage of refinancing. While the interest tax deduction may indeed be reduced as a result of refinancing, the important concern is the actual after-tax cash payments that must be made. In this regard, refinancing with a lower interest rate mortgage (with all other terms assumed unchanged) will always result in lower after-tax cash outflows, and is therefore economically appealing. Of course, as demonstrated in Exhibit 6.10, the reduction in after-tax cash outflows (that is, monthly savings) needs to be compared to the refinancing costs in order to make the final refinancing decision.

Deciding which type of mortgage — fixed-rate or ARM — is best for you depends on market conditions and the length of time you plan to own your home. Because new mortgage products are offered regularly, you should carefully check out all your options prior to refinancing. Remember that in order to refinance, most lenders require you to have at least 20 percent equity in your home, based on current market appraisal. Be sure to check with your existing lender, because many financial institutions are willing to refinance their existing loans, often charging fewer points and lower closing costs than a new lender would charge.

BUYING AN AUTOMOBILE

Though less expensive than housing, an automobile is a big-ticket purchase that requires careful consideration and deliberation. How would you go about carefully considering, analyzing, and financing the purchase of an automobile? Take a few moments to answer this question before reading on.

As a rule, a car is probably the first major expenditure that most people make. (While pickup trucks, four-wheel drives, and similar vehicles are popular forms of transportation in many parts of the country, in the material that follows we will use the terms *automobile* or *car* to describe these and all other types of passenger vehicles.) An individual typically purchases an automobile every two to five years and pays anywhere from $1,000 to $25,000 (or more) for it, depending on its make, model, and age. The automobile purchase is second only to housing in terms of amount of money spent by the typical consumer. Because you will probably make an automobile-purchase decision many times during your life, a systematic approach to selection and financing can help you realize significant savings.

The automobile plays a major role in our society. It is an important factor in the economy, since the automobile industry provides hundreds of thousands of jobs and is a major consumer of raw materials produced by the steel and other vital industries.

Although the primary motivation for automobile ownership is to provide transportation, automobiles are sometimes viewed as status symbols or purchased as part of a hobby or as an investment. There are a wide variety of models, styles, sizes, and colors. In addition to domestically produced automobiles, imported cars today account for a large share of the American automobile market.

Before you buy a car (or make any major purchase), it is useful to spend some time researching the market and considering your personal needs. Many good sources of information about different types of cars, their prices, features, and reliability are available. Industry resources include manufacturers' brochures and dealer personnel. Car magazines, such as *Car and Driver*, *Motor Trend*, and *Road and Track*, and consumer magazines, such as *Consumer Reports* and *Consumers Digest*, regularly compare and rate cars. In addition, both consumer magazines and *Kiplinger's Personal Finance Magazine* publish annual buying guides that include comparative statistics and ratings on most domestic and foreign autos. *Consumer Reports* includes information on used cars in its guide, and it offers a fee-based service, called Consumer Reports Auto Price Service, that allows you to learn the list price and dealer's cost of a new car and the available options in order to better negotiate with the dealer. You can even use your computer to analyze your options; a program called *Cars, the Intelligent Buyer's Guide* (Lifestyle Software: 1-800-289-1157; updated annually) summarizes the features and costs of about 650 cars and will provide a list of cars that meet the criteria you specify.

For most people, an automobile will be their second largest purchase.
Fact: A car ranks second only to housing with respect to amount of money spent.

PURCHASE CONSIDERATIONS

Affordability. Before you shop for a car, you should determine how much you can afford to spend. This estimate should be stated on a monthly basis in order to be consistent with your budget. The amount you arrive at should result from a careful analysis of your available resources in view of other necessary expenses (including housing) and your transportation requirements. Once you have estimated the monthly amount available, you should evaluate the costs of owning (or leasing) various types of automobiles in order to select the one most suitable for you.

Operating Costs. The monthly out-of-pocket cost of operating an automobile consists of not only car payments, but also insurance, licenses, fuel, oil, tires, and other operating and maintenance outlays. Certain of these costs are *fixed* and remain so regardless of how much you drive; others are *variable* with the number of miles you drive. The biggest fixed cost is likely to be the *installment payments* associated with the loan used to buy the car; the biggest variable cost will probably be fuel. Another cost is **depreciation**, which is the loss in value that occurs from driving the vehicle. In effect, depreciation is the difference between the price you paid for the car and what you can get for it when you sell it. If you paid $15,000 for an automobile that can be sold three years later for $9,000, the car will cost you $6,000 in depreciation. While depreciation costs may not be a recurring out-of-pocket cost, it is nonetheless an important operating expense that should not be overlooked.

Exhibit 6.11 provides an example of what it might cost to operate a motor vehicle. Since the cost of operating an automobile varies with the year and make of the car, its mechanical condition, and even where you live, the figures in the exhibit should be viewed as only *representative* of the kinds of costs you can expect to incur. Note that the biggest cost component is the fixed out-of-pocket costs, followed by depreciation, and finally the variable costs. In total, this particular vehicle costs about $7,000 a year to operate, nearly $5,000 of which is annual out-of-pocket expenses. The figures are shown on an annual, monthly, and cost-per-mile basis. Clearly the more miles you drive each year, the lower the cost per mile. This is due to the fact that the *annual* fixed costs and depreciation (for a reasonable range of annual miles) do not change; thus, on a cost-per-mile basis these expenses go down with increased mileage. You should, of course, make sure that the expected (or actual) out-of-pocket operating costs of owning an automobile remain within budgeted amounts. (Note that for budgetary purposes depreciation can be ignored, since it does not represent an out-of-pocket expense in the normal sense.)

New, Used, or "Nearly New"? One decision you must make is whether to buy a new, used, or "nearly new" car. If you cannot afford to buy a new car, the decision is made for you. Some people always buy used cars, even though they can afford to buy a new car. Others pay more for a used luxury car, such as a Mercedes, than they would to purchase a new car of a less-expensive brand, such as a Chevrolet. The advantages of buying a used car are: (1) it is less expensive than a comparable new car; (2) it will not depreciate in value as quickly as a new car; and (3) because it is less expensive, the purchaser does not have to put down as much money as is required on a new car. Moreover, purchasing a used car less than 18 months old means saving the 10 to 25 percent depreciation in value typically experienced during the first 12 to 18 months of a new car's life.

The main disadvantage of buying a used car is the uncertainty of its mechanical condition. Although it might look good, it could still have some mechanical problems requiring maintenance and repair expenditures in the near future. Even though according to a salesperson the car has low mileage and "has been driven only to and from church by a little old lady," you should have it checked by a reputable mechanic. The money spent on a thorough examination prior to its purchase could save hundreds of dollars and much aggravation later.

Purchasers of used cars have another means of protecting their investment in the *federal odometer disclosure law*. The penalties for violation of this law, which required sellers to give buyers a signed statement attesting to the fact that the mileage shown on the odometer of their used cars is correct, are quite stringent. A seller of a used car should always be asked to provide such a statement.

Prior to purchasing either a new or used car, make certain you know what you want; if you have not done this, a slick auto salesperson may cause you to purchase a car you do not need. If you wish to buy a used car, you may prefer to shop for a car "for sale by owner" in order to avoid paying the added overhead charges of an auto dealer. Classified ads in local or nearby city newspapers provide an excellent source of information on used cars for sale.

EXHIBIT 6.11
Automobile Operating Costs

This car costs nearly $7,000 a year to operate, if it is driven about 12,000 miles a year, the car costs about 57 cents for every mile driven.

	Annual Costs*	Monthly Costs*	Costs per Mile	
			12,000 Miles/Year	25,000 Miles/Year
(1) Fixed Costs				
Installment loan payments	$3,180	$ 265	$ .265	$ .128
Auto insurance	360	30	.030	.014
License plates and taxes	180	15	.015	.007
Total fixed costs	$3,720	$ 310	$ .310	$ .149
(2) Variable Costs				
Fuel	$ 720	$ 60	$ .060	$ .060
Oil and tires	96	8	.008	.008
Repairs and maintenance	264	22	.022	.022
Total variable costs	$1,080	$ 90	$ .090	$ .090
Total out-of-pocket costs [(1) + (2)]	$4,800	$ 400	$ .400	$ .239
(3) Depreciation	$2,000	$ 167	$ .167	$ .080
Total operating costs [(1) + (2) + (3)]	$6,800	$ 567	$ .567	$ .319

*Annual and monthly *variable* costs are based on mileage of 12,000 a year.

However, unlike cars purchased privately, those bought from dealers may have a warranty to protect you.

Another option is the "nearly new" car, usually a car used by the dealer with a few thousand miles on it or a rental car used for about four months or 10,000 miles. These cars may be a good value, come with good warranties, and are typically priced 20 to 40 percent below a comparable new car.

Size, Body Style, and Features. The size, body style, and features selected on a given automobile are largely dependent upon your motive for purchasing it. When considering these items, you should give some thought to their cost and effects, not only on performance, handling, and appearance, but also on fuel economy, reliability, repair problems, and the resale value of the car.

There is a great variety in the size and body style you can choose for your car. A two-passenger compact car may not be appropriate if you need the car for business. When determining size and body style, you should select from only those cars consistent with the primary use of the auto; you should not adapt your needs to fit the car. In most instances, there is also a direct relationship between size and cost: the larger the car, the more expensive it will be to purchase and to operate.

Most cars have certain optional features providing a broad range of conveniences and luxuries for those willing to pay the price. Most cars have at least some optional features. On new cars a window sticker details each optional feature and its price, but on a used car only close observation serves to determine the options. Window stickers quite often list standard features that might be considered optional on some other models, and vice versa. When shopping for a new car, make certain you are comparing comparably equipped models.

depreciation
The loss in the value of an asset such as an automobile that occurs over its period of use.

By listing all options you desire prior to shopping for a new car, you can avoid paying for features you really do not need. There are literally hundreds of options available ranging in price from a few dollars up to $1,000 or more and including automatic transmission, a bigger engine, air conditioning, ABS brakes, radio or cassette or CD player, clock, power windows, power seats, electric door locks, rear window defroster, and special suspension. Other, appearance-related, options are two-tone or metallic paint, vinyl top, electric sunroof, whitewall tires, sport wheels, and various exterior trim packages.

Reliability and Warranties. The *reliability* of a car can be assessed by talking with friends owning similar cars and through objective assessments published in various consumer magazines and buying guides, such as *Consumer Reports*. The *warranty* offered by the manufacturer of new cars should also be studied and compared to that offered by other competing manufacturers. Significant differences may exist. It is important to read the warranty booklet included with a new car and make sure you understand the terms of the warranty. Most warranties are void if the owner has not performed routine maintenance or has somehow abused the car.

On all new cars, manufacturers in effect guarantee the general reliability and quality of construction for a specified period of time in a written warranty that obligates it to repair or replace, at little or no cost to the owner, any defective parts and flaws in workmanship. Today most new car warranties cover a minimum of the first three years of ownership or 36,000 miles, whichever comes first, and some provide coverage for as long as seven years or 70,000 miles. However, most warranties typically have limitations; for example, longer warranty periods may apply to only the engine and drive train. Auto manufacturers and private insurers also sell extended warranties and service contracts, sometimes called "buyer protection plans." Most experts consider these unnecessary and not worth their price given the relatively long initial warranty periods now being offered by most manufacturers.

Old Car: Trade-in or Sell? When buying a new or used car from a dealer in order to replace an old car, the question of a trade-in arises. Although trading-in is convenient, you are generally better off financially selling your old car outright. If you are willing to take the time you can usually sell your car above the wholesale price typically offered by a dealer on a trade-in.

Other Considerations. You should carefully consider fuel economy. When considering a new car, the *EPA (Environmental Protection Agency) mileage ratings* are especially useful. On new vehicles, manufacturers are required to post a sticker indicating the number of miles per gallon each model is expected to get (as determined through EPA tests) for both city and highway driving. The number of *safety features* built into the car should also be considered. These features are likely to be similar in new cars as a result of government regulations, but many features, such as airbags, may not be present in used cars. *Auto insurance costs*, which vary depending upon make, model, safety features, and other factors (and are discussed in detail in Chapter 11), also should be assessed when considering automobile purchase alternatives.

THE PURCHASE TRANSACTION

Once you have determined the amount you can afford to spend and the features you desire, you are ready to begin shopping for a car. If you plan to purchase a new car, visit all dealers who have cars meeting your requirements. Look the cars over and ask questions — but don't make any offers until you have isolated two or three cars with the desired features that are priced within your budget. Comparison shopping is essential, because one dealer selling the same brand as another may give you a better deal. Watch out for the sales technique called "lowballing," where the salesperson quotes a low price for the car in order to get you to make an offer and then negotiates the price upward prior to your signing the sales contract.

Because lowballing, price haggling, and other high-pressure sales tactics often make car buying an unpleasant experience, many dealers during recent years have refocused their sales practices to emphasize customer satisfaction. Some manufacturers are offering firm prices so that if you buy today, you can be sure that no one will get a better deal tomorrow. Saturn, for example, encourages its dealers to adopt this strategy, and in 1992 Ford tested a similar idea on certain Escort models. Some dealers have fully embraced this idea and employ salaried "order takers" rather than commissioned salespeople.

Negotiating Price. The price you pay for a car, whether new or used, can vary widely. Not only must you choose among various makes and models, but there are also numerous options from which to choose; these differences often make comparisons difficult. The "sticker price" posted on a new car represents the manufacturer's *suggested* retail price for that particular car with the listed options. This price really means very little. The key to negotiating a good price is knowing the *dealer's cost* for the car. You can estimate the cost using the sticker price and one of the annual car buying guides. For example, *Consumer Reports* lists a cost factor for each car in its guide; multiplying this factor by the list price results in the approximate dealer's cost. The cost factor for a 1992 Ford Taurus is .86. If the Taurus you wish to buy lists for $16,750, the dealer's cost is about $14,405 (.86 × $16,750). Other sources of cost information include Consumer Reports Auto Price Service and Nationwide Auto Brokers; both sell reports showing the base dealer's price plus the cost of each option for a specified make and model of auto.

Before making an offer, prepare a worksheet with the cost versus the list price for the exact car you want. This will help you avoid high-pressure salesmanship and being pushed to pay for options you don't want or need. Try to negotiate the lowest acceptable markup, push for a firm quote, and make it clear that you are comparison shopping. Don't let the salesperson pressure you into signing a sales contract or leaving a deposit until you are sure that you have negotiated the best deal. Good cost information will improve your bargaining position and possibly allow you to negotiate a price that is only several hundred dollars over the dealer's cost. To research used car prices, you can check one of the popular price guides—the National Automobile Dealers Association (NADA) *Official Used Car Guide*, the *Kelly Blue Book*, or the *Edmund's Used Car Prices*—available at your bank, and the classified ads in your local newspaper.

It is best not to discuss either your plan to finance the purchase or the value of your trade-in until you have settled the question of price. These should be separate issues. Salespeople will typically want to find out how much you can afford monthly and then offer financing deals with payments close to that amount. In the case of trade-ins, the dealer might offer you a good price for your old car and raise the price of the new car in order to compensate, or vice versa. The dealer may offer financing terms that sound attractive, but be sure to compare them to the cost of bank loans. Sometimes the price of the car is increased to make up for a low interest rate, or the attractive financing may apply only to certain models. If you are interested in dealer financing, make sure the monthly payment quoted by the dealer's finance manager is just for the loan. Learn and compare the annual percentage rate (APR) to the rate quoted on a bank loan. Frequently the financing charges include unneeded extras such as credit life insurance, accident insurance, an extended warranty, or service package. Once you understand price, you can negotiate intelligently.

Manufacturers and dealers frequently offer buyers special incentives such as rebates and cut-rate financing, particularly when car sales are slow. (Rebates should be deducted from the dealer's cost when you are negotiating the price.) You may be given a choice between a rebate and low-cost financing. To determine which is the better deal, calculate the difference between the monthly payments on a market-rate bank loan and the special dealer loan for the same term. Multiply the payment difference by the loan maturity, in months, and compare it to the rebate. For example, assume the dealer offers either a $1,000 rebate or a 5 percent interest rate on a $10,000, four-year loan. Your payments would be $230 with dealer financing and $254 on a 10 percent bank loan with similar terms. The payment savings over the life of the loan is $1,152 ($24 per month × 48 months), which is greater than the $1,000 rebate. In this case, you would be better off with the 5 percent loan.

Closing the Deal. Whether you are buying a new or a used car, to make a legally binding offer, you must sign a **sales contract** that specifies the

---

sales contract

An agreement to purchase an automobile that states the offering price and all conditions of the offer; when signed by the buyer and seller, the contract legally binds them to its terms.

EXHIBIT 6.12

Comparing Mary Dixon's Automobile Lease versus Purchase Costs

The form that follows demonstrates Mary Dixon's analysis of whether it is better to lease or purchase a new car costing $13,000. Under the lease, a down payment of $250 and monthly payments of $250 are required over the four-year term of the closed-end lease, while if purchased a $2,600 down payment, sales tax of 5 percent ($650) on the purchase price, and monthly payments of $260 over the four-year term of the loan are required. A 4-percent interest rate on savings and an estimated value for the car at the end of the four years of $6,000 is assumed. Because the total cost of leasing is $12,040 which is greater than the $10,146 total cost of purchasing, the purchase is preferred.

AUTOMOBILE LEASE VERSUS PURCHASE ANALYSIS

Name ___Mary Dixon___ Date ___March 3, 1993___

LEASE

Item	Description		Amount
1	Security deposit required	$	250
2	Term of lease and loan (years)*		4
3	Term of lease and loan (months) (Item 2 x 12)		48
4	Monthly lease payment	$	250
5	Total payments over term of lease (Item 3 x Item 4)	$	12,000
6	Interest rate earned on savings (in decimal form)		.04
7	Opportunity cost of security deposit (Item 1 x Item 2 x Item 6)	$	40
8	Payment/refund for market value adjustment at end of lease ($0 for closed-end leases) and/or estimated end-of-term charges	$	0
9	Total cost of leasing (Item 5 + Item 7 + Item 8)	$	12,040

PURCHASE

Item	Description		Amount
10	Purchase price	$	13,000
11	Down payment	$	2,600
12	Sales tax rate (in decimal form)		.05
13	Sales tax (Item 10 x Item 12)	$	650
14	Monthly loan payment (Terms: $ ___$10,400___ , ___48___ months, _9.5_ %)	$	260
15	Total payments over term of loan (Item 3 x Item 14)	$	12,480
16	Opportunity cost of down payment (Item 2 x Item 6 x Item 11)	$	416
17	Estimated value of car at end of loan	$	6,000
18	Total cost of purchasing (Item 11 + Item 13 + Item 15 + Item 16 – Item 17)	$	10,146

DECISION

If the value of Item 9 is less than the value of Item 18, leasing is preferred; otherwise the purchase alternative is preferred.

*This form is based upon assumed equal terms for the lease and the installment loan, which is assumed to be used to finance the purchase.

offering price and all the conditions of your offer. The sales contract will also specify whether or not the offer includes a trade-in; when it does, the offering price will represent the amount in addition to the trade-in you are willing to pay. Because this agreement contractually binds you to purchase the car at the offering price, if accepted (and signed) by the dealer, you should be certain that you want and can afford the car prior to signing such an agreement. In order to show that you are making an offer in good faith, you may be required to include a deposit of $100 or more with the contract.

Once your offer has been accepted, you will need to complete the purchase transaction and accept delivery of the car. If you are not paying cash for the car, you can arrange financing through the dealer, at your bank, credit union, or a consumer finance company. The key aspects of these types of installment loans, which can be quickly negotiated if your credit is good, are discussed in Chapter 8. Prior to delivery, the dealer is responsible for cleaning up the car and installing any optional equipment. It is a good idea to make sure that all equipment you are paying for has been installed and the car is ready for use before paying the dealer. At the same time you pay, you should also receive the title to the car.

MAINTAINING YOUR AUTOMOBILE

Like any tangible asset, the automobile must be properly maintained and repaired in order to preserve its function, validate its warranty, and enhance its resale value. Maintenance and repairs should be performed by a dealership or independent garage that will stand behind its work and not do unneeded repairs. Performing *preventive maintenance*, which typically involves regularly scheduled changes and checks of various fluids, filters, and other key components, should reduce the frequency, seriousness, and cost of repairs.

LEASING AN AUTOMOBILE

An alternative to purchasing a car is *leasing*, which typically involves receiving the use of a car in exchange for contractually agreeing to make monthly lease payments over a specified period of time, usually two to four years. The size of the lease payments depends on the car's cost, the term of the lease, the number of miles the car is expected to be driven, other financial factors, and the type of lease—closed-end or open-end. Nearly 80 percent of all consumers choose the **closed-end lease**, which is often called the *walk-away lease* because at the end of its term you simply turn in the car, assuming you have neither exceeded the mileage limits nor abused the car. Under the less popular **open-end lease**, the estimated *residual value* of the car at the end of the lease is used to determine lease payments; if the car is actually worth less at the end of the lease, you have to pay the difference.

Leasing has experienced significant growth over the last ten years; in 1992 leased automobiles accounted for over 20 percent of all automobile sales. The appeal of leasing is attributed to its ability to allow a person to obtain use of a car for a smaller down payment and monthly payment than would be required if it were purchased. Of course, the lessee (person who leases) gives up the right to the residual value of the car at the end of the lease. To decide whether it is less costly to lease rather than purchase a car, **lease versus purchase analysis** can be used to estimate the total cost of each alternative over equal periods. Generally in such an analysis the purchase is assumed to be financed with an installment loan with a maturity just equal to the term of the

closed-end lease
The most popular form of automobile lease, often called a *walk-away lease* because at the end of its term the lessee simply turns in the car, assuming the preset mileage limit has not been exceeded and the car hasn't been abused.

open-end lease
An automobile lease under which the estimated residual value of the car is used to determine lease payments; if the car is actually worth less at the end of the lease, the lessee must pay the difference.

lease versus purchase analysis
A procedure used to determine the total cost of leasing and the total cost of purchasing (using an installment loan) a car over equal terms in order to choose the least costly alternative.

MONEY IN ACTION

The Right Way to Lease a Car

Auto leasing has become increasingly popular in recent years and now appeals to a wide range of car buyers. This is due in part to rising new car prices, the cash crunch caused by the recession of the early 1990s, and the elimination of the tax deduction for consumer loan interest. Although it is generally more economical to buy — and own — an asset over the long term, today many buyers lease their cars in order to lower the monthly payment (or to obtain a more expensive car for the same monthly payment) and/or minimize the down payment and preserve their cash. It's easy to focus on the low monthly lease payment and think you've got a great deal. But don't forget that with a lease you aren't paying for the whole car; rather, you're paying only for its use during a specified period. Because leasing is a more complex arrangement than borrowing to buy a car, you need to familiarize yourself with leasing terms and restrictions before signing a lease.

The first step in leasing is the same as in purchasing: research, comparison shop, and find the right car with the desired options at the best price. Visit several dealers and negotiate a price without disclosing whether you plan to lease or buy the car. After you've found the best price, you should ask the dealer about leasing and any financing incentives. In addition to dealers, you should also meet with at least one independent leasing firm. Because a leasing firm is not promoting a particular car, you may find its terms more attractive. Of course, you should always attempt to negotiate lower lease payments; a payment reduction of $20 a month saves nearly $1,000 on a four-year lease.

The lease payment calculation is based on three variables: (1) the cost (purchase price) of the car, (2) the forecast residual (remaining) value of the car at the end of the lease, and (3) the lease rate, which is similar to the interest rate on a loan. The depreciation during the lease term (which is what you are paying for) is defined as cost minus residual value. Dividing the depreciation by the number of months in the lease term and adding the lessor's required return (at the lease rate) results in the monthly payment. It should be clear that the cost and the residual value significantly impact the size of the lease payment. You may want to focus on cars with relatively high residual values in order to lower your payment. Because the residual values quoted by different dealers often vary, it is advisable to check several sources in order to make sure you get the highest residual value on the car you want. Of course, your objective should be to minimize depreciation — the difference between the cost and the residual value.

Closed-end leases, where the residual is guaranteed, are preferred. You may have to pay a considerable amount at the end of an open-end lease if the car's market value is below its forecast residual value. Lease terms typically run two to five years, but longer-term leases typically have lower payments. However, because it may be difficult — and costly — to terminate a lease early, you should be reasonably certain how long you plan to keep the car prior to committing to the lease. Check the lease contract carefully in order to learn how much it will cost you to terminate the lease at various points in time. If you terminate the lease, you could owe the lessor a sum greater than the car's then-prevailing market value. Some leases charge an additional fee on termination prior to the end of the lease term. These early termination clauses also apply to cars that are stolen or totaled in an accident; some leases require "gap insurance" to cover the lost lease payments that would result from early termination caused by one of these events.

Under the terms of most leases, you are responsible for insuring and maintaining the car. At the end of the lease term, you are obligated to pay for any "unreasonable wear and tear." A good lease contract should clearly define what is considered unreasonable. In addition, most leases require the lessee to pay a disposition fee of about $150 to $250 when the car is turned in.

Most auto leases include a purchase option that allows the lessee to buy the car at the end of the lease term. The option may be a fixed amount specified in the lease, the market price at the end of the lease term, or the residual value of the car. The lower the residual, the lower the purchase option price, but the higher the monthly payments. How well you do financially with a lease depends on the relationship between the purchase option price and the market value of the car at the end of the lease term. Experts recommend negotiating a fixed-price purchase option, if possible.

The annual mileage allowance is another important lease consideration. Leases most commonly limit annual mileage during the lease term to about 15,000 miles. The lessee must pay typically between 8 and 15 cents per mile for additional miles. If you expect to exceed the allowable mileage, you should attempt to negotiate up-front a more favorable rate for extra miles.

One of the commonly cited benefits of leasing is the absence of a down payment. However, some leases ask for a "capital cost reduction," which is nothing more than a down payment. You should not be required to pay this, although doing so will lower the depreciation and therefore your monthly lease payments.

Is leasing right for you? If you trade cars at least every four or five years and drive less than 15,000 miles a year, it may be better than purchasing. Use the worksheet in Exhibit 6.12 to find and compare the total cost of leasing to the total cost of purchasing. In addition, consider the factors described here. If you decide to lease, make sure that all terms are set forth in writing and that you understand everything in the lease agreement prior to signing it.

lease. For example, assume that Mary Dixon is considering either leasing or purchasing a new car costing $13,000. If she leases, a $250 security deposit and monthly payments of $250 would be required, over the four-year term of the closed-end lease she is considering. If she purchases the car, she will make a $2,600 down payment and finance the balance with a four-year loan requiring monthly payments of $260; in addition, she will have to pay a 5 percent sales tax ($650) on the purchase, and she expects the car to have a residual value of $6,000 at the end of the four years. Mary can earn 4 percent interest on her savings. After filling in the worksheet shown in Exhibit 6.12, Mary concludes that purchase is best, since its total cost of $10,146 is almost $1,900 less than the $12,040 total leasing cost. Clearly, all else being equal, the least costly alternative is preferred. The *Money in Action* box discusses in greater detail other important factors to consider when making the decision whether to lease or purchase.

FURNITURE AND APPLIANCES

Another group of tangible assets that you will purchase during your lifetime consists of furniture and appliances. Although these assets can be leased, most people purchase them. Since the cost of furniture and appliances can be great, a few comments about purchase and financing are in order here.

PURCHASE CONSIDERATIONS

When buying furniture or appliances, attention should be given to the purchase cost, function, operating and repair expenses, and appearance. By shopping around, you should be able to find pieces that will perform the desired function at the best price. Often, by paying an extra $50 to $100 you can purchase an asset that will provide significantly greater satisfaction. In order to get an indication of the quality and general reliability of a given item of furniture or appliance, it is helpful to consult some type of consumer *buying guide*, such as the monthly magazines *Consumer Reports* (which publishes its *An-*

nual Buying Guide in December), *Kiplinger's Personal Finance Magazine*, and *Consumers Digest*. These are valuable sources of ratings and comparative statistics on furniture, appliances, and many other consumer goods. The operating—including energy—costs and repair costs of items requiring power and/or having moving parts or fabric components should also be considered. In spite of a low purchase price, an item of furniture or an appliance often will have a high total ownership cost if its operating, energy, and repair costs are excessive. Information on these costs can be obtained from consumer publications and friends who have purchased similar items. Many appliances come with an "Energy Guide" rating attached. A final consideration that might enter into your purchase decision is appearance, which may offer a degree of personal satisfaction.

THE PURCHASE TRANSACTION

Once you have selected the basic brands and models that interest you, you should check several stores for the best deal. Many furniture and appliance dealers will negotiate prices. You may be able to pay less than the amount shown on the price tag if you simply ask. You may be able to learn from friends and business associates which dealers have the best prices. Considering the purchase of a floor model or a second-hand item is sometimes worthwhile. Because furniture and appliances have fairly long lives, you may find that the savings resulting from the purchase of used items more than compensates for their slight wear. However, you should know which model you are buying—the preceding year's model or the floor model. Before finalizing your purchase, you should find out who pays for delivery, whether taxes are included in the quoted price, and whether there are any installation costs. If you are able to plan the timing of your purchases, you can often take advantage of sales on furniture in January and August and on appliances in October and November.

FINANCING THE PURCHASE

Because of the relatively high cost of furniture and appliances, borrowing money may be necessary. Of course, before you begin to shop, you should have some idea about whether or not you need financing. Some furniture and appliance dealers offer "90 days same as cash" or "30–60–90–day" financing arrangements, which allow you to pay for the merchandise in three monthly installments without interest. A number of the installment payment plans used to purchase these types of assets are discussed in detail in Chapter 8. If you will need financing on a purchase, you should analyze and compare the costs of financing plans offered by various dealers.

S U M M A R Y

- A family's housing needs can be met in many different ways — in addition to single-family homes, there are manufactured homes, condominiums, cooperative apartments, and numerous types of rental apartments and houses.

- In addition to the emotional rewards, other benefits of homeownership are the tax shelter and inflation hedge it provides.

- Homeownership costs include the down payment, points and closing costs, monthly mortgage payments, property taxes and insurance, and normal home maintenance and operating expenses. Any of these can amount to a considerable sum of money, and all of them should be carefully considered when using home-affordability analysis to estimate how much you can afford to spend on a home.

- Many people rent because they cannot afford to buy a home; others choose to rent because renting is less costly and more convenient for their lifestyle and economic situation. Rent-or-buy analysis can help you choose the least costly alternative.

- Normally, people shopping for a home seek the help of a real estate agent to obtain needed information, access to properties, and advice; the agent earns a 5 to 7 percent commission, paid by the seller, when the transaction is closed. A real estate sales contract is used to confirm in writing all terms of the transaction between the buyer and seller.

- Mortgage loans can be obtained from commercial banks, S&Ls, savings banks, and through a mortgage banker or mortgage broker; in addition, seller financing can be an important source of mortgage money. While there are many types of mortgage loans available, the most widely used are the 15- and 30-year fixed-rate mortgage and the adjustable-rate mortgage (ARM).

- After a mortgage loan is approved, the loan is closed; this involves certain disclosures required by RESPA, a title check, and preparation of a closing statement that shows how much the borrower owes and the seller receives from the transaction. Sometimes interest rates will drop a number of years after closing, and mortgage refinancing will become attractive.

- The purchase of an automobile, usually the second largest expenditure a person will make, should be based on thorough market research and comparative shopping. Important purchase considerations include affordability, operating costs, new versus used car, type of car and its features, and warranties. Knowing the dealer's cost is the key to negotiating a good price, and the economics of leasing versus purchasing the car with an installment loan should be considered once the price is set.

- In addition to your home and car, other tangible assets that you'll likely buy include furniture and appliances — costly budget items that require careful research, comparison shopping, and financial analysis.

Q U E S T I O N S   A N D   P R O B L E M S

1. In addition to single-family homes, what other forms of housing are available in the United States? Differentiate between a condominium and a cooperative apartment.

2. Briefly describe the various motives for owning a home. Which one do you think is most important? Which is least important?

3. What does the *loan-to-value ratio* on a home represent? Is the down payment on a home related to its loan-to-value ratio? Explain. How much would you have to put down on a house costing $100,000 if the house had an appraised value of $105,000 and the lender required an 80 percent loan-to-value ratio?

4. What are *points*? How much would a home buyer have to pay if the lender wanted to charge 2.5 points on an $85,000 mortgage? When would this amount have to be paid? What effect do points have on the mortgage's rate of interest?

5. What are *closing costs*? Who pays these costs, and when? Are points part of closing costs? What items are included in closing costs? How much might a home buyer expect to pay in closing costs on a $95,000 house with a 10 percent down payment? How much *in total* would the home buyer have to pay at the time of closing in the above transaction, taking into account closing costs, down payment, and a loan fee of 3 points?

■ 6. Find the monthly mortgage payments on the following mortgage loans:
   a. $60,000/8.5 percent/30 years
   b. $50,000/10 percent/20 years
   c. $85,000/11.5 percent/15 years

7. What are the most common guidelines used to determine the amount of monthly mortgage payments one can afford? Using the maximum ratios for a conventional mortgage, how big a monthly payment could the Bacon family afford if their gross (before-tax) monthly income amounted to $4,000? Would it make any difference if they were already making monthly installment loan payments of $750 on two car loans?

8. Why is it advisable for the prospective buyer to investigate property taxes, insurance, maintenance, and operating costs when shopping for a home? Explain.

■ 9. Selma and Rodney Jackson wish to estimate the amount they can afford to spend to purchase their first home. They have a combined annual income of $37,500 and have $21,000 available to make a down payment and pay closing costs. The Jacksons estimate that homeowner's insurance and property taxes will be $125 per month. They expect the mortgage lender to use a 30 percent monthly mortgage payment affordability ratio, to lend at an average interest rate of 9 percent on a 30-year mortgage, and to require a 15 percent down payment. Based on this information, use the home affordability analysis form given in Exhibit 6.6 to determine the maximum-priced home the Jacksons can afford.

10. Discuss the relative advantages and disadvantages of renting a home. Does a homeowner have any advantage over a renter with respect to taxes? Explain.

11. Describe some of the steps that homebuyers can take to improve the home-buying process and increase their overall satisfaction with their purchases.

12. What role does a real estate agent play in the purchase of a house? How is the real estate agent compensated, and by whom?

13. What clauses are normally included in a real estate sales contract? What is an earnest money deposit? Explain the purchase negotiation process.

14. Describe the various sources of mortgage loans. What is seller financing? Give two examples of seller financing.

15. Briefly describe the two basic types of mortgage loans. Which has the lowest initial rate of interest? What is *negative amortization*, and which type of mortgage can experience it? Discuss the advantages and disadvantages of each mortgage type.

■ 16. What would the monthly payments be on a $75,000 loan if the mortgage were set up as
   a. A 15-year, 10 percent fixed-rate loan?
   b. A 30-year adjustable-rate mortgage in which the lender added a margin of 2.5 points to the index rate (which presently stands at 5.5 percent)? Find the monthly mortgage payments for the first year only.

17. Latha Yang purchased a condominium four years ago for $70,000. She has been paying $630 per month on her $60,000, 12 percent, 25-year mortgage. Recently interest rates have dropped sharply, causing Latha to consider refinancing the condo at the prevailing 9 percent rate. She expects to remain in the condo for at least four more years and has found a lender

that will make a 9 percent, 21-year loan requiring $530 monthly payments. Although there is no prepayment penalty on her current mortgage, Latha will have to pay $1,500 in closing costs on the new mortgage. She is in the 15 percent tax bracket. Based on this information, use the mortgage refinancing analysis form given in Exhibit 6.10 to determine whether Latha should refinance her mortgage under the specified terms.

18. Briefly discuss how each of the following purchase considerations would affect your purchase of an automobile:
   a. Market research
   b. Operating costs
   c. New, used, or "nearly new" car
   d. Model and feature selection
   e. Reliability and warranty protection

19. Describe the purchase transaction process, including shopping, price negotiation, and closing the deal on a new car.

20. Jack Williamson purchased a new car on January 1, 1993, for $13,000 and plans to keep it for five years. At the end of five years, the car is expected to be worth 25 percent of the original purchase price. How much will the car be worth after five years? Define *depreciation*, and calculate the depreciation cost per year and per month on Jack's new car. What are some of the nonfinancial decisions Jack had to make when selecting his car?

21. Janet Wilhite has an established budget in which she had allotted $500 a month to the out-of-pocket operating costs of a car. She is presently looking at a sporty model with monthly payments of $275; plates and taxes would amount to $360 a year, and car insurance $750 annually. Fuel is expected to cost about $60 for every 1,000 miles driven; because the car is under warranty, repairs, maintenance, tires, and oil are expected to amount to only $20 for each 1,000 miles. The car is expected to depreciate at the rate of about $2,500 a year. Given that Janet drives about 15,000 miles a year, find the total operating costs of this car on both an annual and a cost-per-mile basis (break the cost out by fixed, variable, and depreciation). Will she be able to stay within her budget with this car?

22. Chris Svenson is trying to decide whether to lease or purchase a new car costing $12,000. If he leases, he will have to make a $400 security deposit and agree to make monthly payments of $285 over the 36-month term of the closed-end lease. If, on the other hand, he purchases the car, he will have to make a $1,800 down payment and will finance the balance with a 36-month loan requiring monthly payments of $340; in addition, he will have to pay a 6 percent sales tax ($720) on the purchase price, and he expects the car to have a residual value of $4,300 at the end of three years. Chris can earn 4 percent interest on his savings. Use the automobile lease-versus-purchase analysis form in Exhibit 6.12 to find the total cost of both the lease and the purchase, and recommend the best strategy to Chris.

23. Briefly describe the most important factors to consider when shopping for and financing the purchase of furniture and appliances.

CONTEMPORARY CASE APPLICATIONS

6.1 Evaluating a Mortgage Loan for the Newtons

Farrah and Sam Newton, both in their early 30s, have been married for five years. Sam has an accounting degree and is presently employed as a senior cost accountant at an annual salary of $42,000. The Newtons have two children, ages 2 and 4. At present, they are renting a duplex but wish to buy a home in the suburbs of their rapidly developing city. They have decided that they can afford a $105,000 house and hope to find one with the features they desire in a good neighborhood.

The insurance costs on such a home are expected to be $500 per year, taxes are expected to be $1,000 per year, and annual utility bills are estimated at $1,200—an increase of $500 over those they pay in the duplex. The Newtons are considering financing their home with a fixed-rate, 30-year, 9 percent mortgage; also, the lender charges 2 points on mortgages with 20 percent down and 3 points if less than 20 percent is put down (the commercial bank with which the Newtons will deal requires a minimum of 10 percent down). Other closing costs are estimated at 5 percent on the purchase price of the home. Because of their excellent credit record, the bank will probably be willing to let the Newtons' monthly mortgage payments equal as much as 28 percent of their monthly gross income. Over the last four years, the Newtons have been saving for the purchase of a home and now have $24,000 in their savings account.

Questions

1. How much would the Newtons have to put down if the lender required a minimum 20 percent down payment? Could they afford it?
2. Given the Newtons want to put only $15,000 down, how much would closing costs be? Considering only principal and interest, how much would their monthly mortgage payments be? Would they qualify for a loan using a 28 percent affordability ratio?
3. Using a $15,000 down payment on a $105,000 home, what would the Newtons' loan-to-value ratio be? Calculate the monthly mortgage payments on a PITI basis.
4. What recommendations would you make to the Newtons? Explain.

◼ 6.2 Julie's Rent-or-Buy Decision

Julie Brown is a single career woman in her late 20s. She currently rents an apartment in the fashionable part of town for $900 a month. After considerable deliberation, she is seriously considering the purchase of a luxury condominium for $125,000. She intends to put 20 percent down and expects that closing costs will amount to another $5,000; a commecial bank has agreed to lend her money at the fixed rate of 9 percent on a 15-year mortgage. Julie would have to pay an annual condominium owner's insurance premium of $600 and property taxes of $1,200 a year (she is presently paying renter's insurance of $550 per year). In addition, she estimates that annual maintenance and upkeep expenses will be about .5 percent of the price of the condo (which includes a $30 monthly fee to the property owners' association). Julie's income puts her in the 28 per-

cent tax bracket (she itemizes her deductions on her tax returns), and she earns an after-tax rate of return on her investments of around 4 percent.

Questions

1. Given the information provided above, evaluate and compare Julie's alternatives of remaining in the apartment or purchasing the condo.
2. Working with a friend who is a realtor, Julie has learned that luxury condos like the one she is thinking of buying are appreciating in value at the rate of 3.5 percent a year and are expected to continue doing so. Would such information affect the rent-or-buy decision made in Question 1? Explain.
3. Rework your calculations assuming that Julie does not itemize her deductions on her tax return but instead takes the standard deduction. Would that affect the rent-or-buy decision made in Question 1? Explain.
4. Discuss any nonquantitative factors that should be considered when making a rent-or-buy decision.
5. Which alternative would you recommend for Julie in light of your analysis?

◼ 6.3 The McNeil's New Car Decision: Lease versus Purchase

Jim and Margaret McNeil, a dual-income couple in their late 20s, want to replace their seven-year-old car, which has 80,000 miles on it and needs some expensive repairs. After reviewing their budget, the McNeils conclude that they can afford auto payments of not more than $350 per month and a down payment of $2,000. They enthusiastically decide to visit a local Honda dealer after reading its newspaper ad offering a closed-end lease on a Honda Accord for a monthly payment of $245. After visiting with the dealer, test driving the car, and discussing the lease terms with the salesperson, they remain excited about leasing the car, but decide to wait until the following day to finalize the deal. Later that day the McNeils begin to question their approach to the new-car acquisition process, and they decide to carefully reevaluate their decision.

Questions

1. What are some of the basic purchase considerations the McNeils should take into account when choosing which new car to buy or lease? How can they get the information they need?

2. How would you advise the McNeils to research the lease-versus-purchase decision before visiting the Honda dealer? What are the advantages and disadvantages of each alternative?

3. Assume the McNeils can get the following terms on a lease or a bank loan available for the Honda, which they could buy for $15,000:

Lease: 48 months, $245 monthly payment, one month's payment required as security deposit, $350 end-of-lease charges; residual value of $6,775 is the purchase option price at the end of the lease.

Loan: $2,000 down payment, $13,000 48-month loan at 10 percent interest requiring a monthly payment of $330. They assume the car's value

will be the same as the residual value. Sales tax is 6 percent.

If they choose the lease, they would earn a 4 percent return from investment of the down payment. They expect to drive about the same number of miles per year as they do now.

a. Use the format given in Exhibit 6.12 to determine which deal is better financially for the McNeils.

b. What other costs and terms of the lease option might affect their decision?

c. Based on the available information, should the McNeils lease or purchase the Honda, and why?

FOR MORE INFORMATION

General Information Articles

Dunn, Don. "Smoothing the Way to a Home Mortgage." *Business Week*, December 2, 1991, pp. 148–149.

Gottschalk, Earl C., Jr. "Picking the Wrong Mortgage Broker Can Become a Homeowner's Nightmare." *The Wall Street Journal*, March 26, 1992, pp. C1, 18.

Henry, Ed. "Confessions of a Car Salesman." *Kiplinger's Personal Finance Magazine*, March 1992, pp. 48–53.

————. "How to Buy a Nearly New Car." *Changing Times*, February 1991, pp. 67–70.

Harowitz, Sherry. "The Right Way to Refinance." *Kiplinger's Personal Finance Magazine*, March 1992, pp. 63–64.

McCormally, Kevin. "What to Know When You Lease a Car." *Kiplinger's Personal Finance Magazine*, August 1991, pp. 53–58.

Moreau, Dan. "Love Thy Neighborhood Association." *Kiplinger's Personal Finance Magazine*, May 1992, pp. 91–93.

Smith, Anne Kates. "Revolt of the Homeowners." *U.S. News & World Report*, October 14, 1991, pp. 94–96.

"The 1992 Cars." *Consumer Reports*, April 1992, pp. 210–283. (Annual auto issue published every April.)

"The 1992 Cars." *Kiplinger's Personal Finance Magazine*, December 1991, pp. 43–75. (Annual auto issue published every December.)

"1992 Home Guide." *U.S. News & World Report*, April 6, 1992, pp. 64–95. (Special report published annually.)

Government Documents and Other Publications

Consumer Handbook on Adjustable Rate Mortgages. Prepared by the Federal Reserve Board and the Federal Home Loan Bank Board; available from the Publications Services, MS-138, Board of Governors of the Federal Reserve System, Washington, D.C. 20551, (202) 452-3244.

Gillis, Jack. *The Car Book.* Center for Auto Safety, 20001 S Street NW, Washington, D.C. 20009 (annual).

Miller, Peter G. *The Common-Sense Mortgage*, 1991 Edition. New York: HarperCollins, 1991.

GETTING A HANDLE ON YOUR FINANCIAL FUTURE

Unless you are lucky enough to inherit property, your housing needs will be met by either renting or buying. For most people one of their financial goals is to own their own home. There are a number of reasons for wanting to own a home. Some of the emotional reasons include pride of ownership, a feeling of permanence, and a sense of stability. In addition there are financial considerations such as the deductibility of the interest on the home mortgage, the accumulation of equity, and the inflation hedge normally provided by home ownership.

Your ability to purchase a home is based primarily on the relationship of your monthly income to your monthly payments. The normal requirements are that your mortgage payment should not exceed 25 to 30 percent of your gross income and that total payments should not exceed 33 to 38 percent of gross income. With the knowledge of what lenders in your area require in terms of ratio percentages and minimum down payments, you can calculate the maximum price of a house as illustrated in Exhibit 6.6. This will assist both you and your real estate agent in identifying houses that you can afford.

Once you have selected a house within your price range, you will make an offer (usually less than the asking price) and negotiate the price. If you and the seller agree on terms, you will enter into a sales contract, which will normally require the deposit of ear-

---

If You Are Just Getting Started

A major purchase that you will probably make when you are just starting out is an automobile. You should consider your needs for transportation and the issues of affordability and all operating costs when making this purchase. In today's market you might consider leasing as an alternative. In order to compare the costs of leasing versus purchasing, you should use Exhibit 6.12.

Almost everyone needs furniture and appliances of some kind whether they rent an apartment or own their home. The purchase of these items should involve comparison shopping in regards to price and financing terms. More than likely the store that advertises no money down and "90 days same as cash" has built in the financing charges in the price of the item. You need to analyze your financing options. In addition you may be responsible for delivery and installment or setup charges.

Purchasing an Automobile:

1. Review quality ratings of the different automobiles to help you narrow down your choices.

2. Decide on the amount you can afford to pay before you visit the showroom.

3. Consider purchasing a previously owned automobile that is still under factory warranty.

4. Compare alternative financing options prior to talking with a dealer.

5. Once you have narrowed down your purchases, check with your insurance agent as to the costs of various makes and models. You may be shocked when you hear the difference.

6. Compare leasing to buying.

Purchasing Furniture and Appliances:

1. Decide what you need and the amount you can afford to pay before you begin your comparison shopping.

2. If financing is required to make the purchase, compare financing terms available from sources other than the dealer.

3. Don't be misled by low or no-cost financing advertisements. Nothing is free.

4. Compare warranties from the manufacturer before you buy an "extended" warranty from the dealer.

5. Check to see if the dealer also has a service department and the reliability of the work by asking for references.

6. Ask about the store's policy on the return of items purchased.

nest money and should include for your protection a contingency (escape) clause so that your earnest money can be returned if the sale cannot be consummated because of specified reasons. The actual closing on the sale may take weeks and sometimes months due to the complexity of the transaction.

Selecting the appropriate type of financing for the purchase of your home has become a more difficult decision with the increase in the funding options. The cost differentials among the different types of mortgages can be significant, and you should fully investigate their options before selecting the type of mortgage loan. In addition to the financing decision

at the purchase, you may be faced with a refinancing decision in the future due to a decline in market rates or a need to access your equity in your home. Exhibit 6.9 gives an illustration of the refinancing decision.

In addition to your home, there are other major purchases that you will make in your lifetime. These include automobiles, furnishings and appliances, and perhaps boats and airplanes. You should carefully and systematically evaluate these expenditures in terms of the affordability, operating cost, and financing alternatives to ensure the best use of your funds.

If You Are Thirtysomething

As your income increases during your worklife, there will be an increased temptation to purchase more expensive and exotic consumer goods, automobiles, and homes with special features. You may feel that you have to have the latest HD-TV or newest compact disk player. You may no longer be happy with the family automobile and long for a sports car. You may want a house with a swimming pool or Jacuzzi.

There is nothing necessarily wrong with wanting to have any of these items. It is the purpose of financial planning to assist you in achieving these short-term or long-term goals. However, even if you can afford certain luxuries, you should properly evaluate major purchases with an eye towards the financing and operating costs as if you did not have the resources. Since the same recommendations and suggestions for purchasing an automobile or furniture and appliances for someone just starting out would apply to the more mature individual, this section will focus on home ownership.

Purchasing a Primary Residence:

1. Before you begin to look for a house, decide what your needs are in terms of size and location.

2. Determine the amount that you can pay for a house based on the amount of money you have for a down payment and closing costs as well as your income, as shown in Exhibit 6.6.

3. Carefully consider the additional expenses of home ownership, such as property taxes and insurance.

4. If the house you intend to purchase is not new, ask to

see the utility bills so that this expense can be considered in your cash budget.

5. Make sure you are aware of any restrictive covenants in the deed as well as any easements.

6. Evaluate alternative financing options in light of how long you will be in this house.

7. If possible consider paying bi-weekly instead of monthly on your mortgage.

8. You should consider refinancing your home if market rates decline about 2 percentage points.

Purchasing a Vacation Home:

1. All of the suggestions and recommendations that are mentioned above would apply to a vacation or second home.

2. You must realistically consider how often you would use the house.

3. Based on your usage, you should analyze this decision as a rent-or-buy decision as shown in Exhibit 6.7.

4. Generally, the purchase of a second home requires a larger down payment, higher property taxes, and insurance premiums.

5. If you intend to rent out your second home, you should become familiar with the IRS regulations concerning the treatment of income and expenses so as to properly account for the tax effects of this action.

1. Evaluate the amount of Mark and Ana's liquid assets. According to the general consensus of financial experts, do they currently have enough assets in a highly liquid form? If not, how much should be added to their liquid assets in order to meet the minimum requirements?

2. Using the following information, reconcile Mark and Ana's March bank statement. What adjustments, if any, do Mark and Ana need to make in their checkbook ledger? Their March bank statement for their NOW account, contains the following information:

Ending balance	$1,287.66
Service charge	10.00
Interest earned	4.33

Their checkbook ledger shows a final balance of $1,352.55 and lists the following checks and ATM transactions for the period:

Check #	Amount	Check #	Amount	ATM Transaction	Amount
789	$600.00	806	$ 38.72	Deposit	$1,549.00
790	284.00	807	185.63	Withdrawal – ATM	50.00
791	46.13	808	263.05	Deposit	1,800.00
793	118.00	809	34.16	Withdrawal – ATM	75.00
794	77.00	810	21.34	Withdrawal – ATM	50.00
795	116.00	811	85.17	Withdrawal – ATM	125.00
796	68.00			Withdrawal – ATM	50.00
798	125.00			Withdrawal – ATM	100.00
799	50.00			Withdrawal – ATM	75.00
800	21.00			Deposit – ATM	592.00
801	52.00				
802	163.55				
803	73.98				

The bank statement does not list check numbers 802, 808, and 811, nor does it include the $592.00 ATM deposit; therefore, you should consider them outstanding.

3. Mark and Ana currently maintain their checking account at Mark's place of employment, First Federal Savings. However, Mark would feel more comfortable if the account were at a different financial institution. Mark and Ana are investigating the following two NOW accounts. Both are at institutions that are convenient and are covered by federal deposit insurance. Using the following information, compare the positive and negative aspects of the two accounts Mark and Ana are considering. How much interest would they earn in a month with each account? Which one would you recommend for Mark and Ana?

United Savings and Loan
- no service charge for accounts maintaining a minimum daily balance of $1,000
- monthly service charge of $15 if minimum daily balance falls below $1,000
- 6.5 percent (annual percentage rate) interest is paid monthly on the minimum daily balance
- ATM fee of $1.00 per month
- stop payment fee of $15.00
- insufficient funds fee of $15.00

Milford National Bank
- no service charge for accounts maintaining a minimum daily balance of $1,200
- monthly service charge of $10 plus $.10 a check if minimum daily balance falls below $1,200

- 4.5 percent (annual percentage rate) interest is paid monthly on the average daily balance
- ATM fee of $.25 per deposit and withdrawal transaction
- stop payment fee of $10.00
- insufficient funds fee of $15.00

Mark and Ana report that in an average month they write 25 checks and make 8 ATM transactions. They maintain an average daily balance in their checking account of $1,500, but the minimum daily balance often falls to $1,000. They have never used the stop-payment service, nor have they bounced a check.

4. Mark and Ana want to start a regular savings program to help them achieve several goals. Assuming they want to make monthly contributions, what type of account would you recommend for:

    - their emergency fund
    - the buffer account for their first child's birth

5. If Mark and Ana can afford to contribute a total of $2,000 per year (at $1,000 each) to their respective 401(k) retirement accounts, how much will they have accumulated in 35 years when they want to retire? Assume that Mark's account has no employer contribution and averages 8 percent compounded annually while Ana's employer contributes 50 cents for every $1.00 she contributes and averages 9 percent compounded annually.

One of Mark and Ana's short-term goals is to buy a condominium as soon as possible. They have been condo hunting for several months and have found a home they like that costs $85,000. The lender requires a minimum down payment of 10 percent; however, they plan to make a down payment of $12,750, with Mark's grandmother contributing $5,000 of the $12,750. They have also shopped for home mortgages and narrowed their choices to the following:

30-Year Fixed-Rate Mortgage	30-Year Adjustable Rate Mortgage
8.5% interest with 1 point other closing costs of $2,500 monthly payments	6.5% interest with 1.5 points other closing costs of $3,000 1% annual interest rate cap 6% overall interest rate cap monthly payments

(The closing costs include a 1% loan origination fee.) Mark and Ana expect to have the following costs associated with the purchase and maintenance of the condo:

- Property taxes of 1.2 percent of the value of the condominium
- Homeowners insurance of .5 percent of the value of the condominium for personal property and liability coverage
- Maintenance of 1.5 percent of the value of the condominium (this includes a $75 per month homeowners' association fee)

They expect that the condo will appreciate in value 3.5 percent a year, and that the after-tax cost of interest lost on the front-end costs (down payment, points, and other closing costs) is 4.5 percent.

6. Compare and evaluate the two mortgages for Mark and Ana. What would be the front-end costs and the monthly payments for principal and interest on each of these mortgages? How much could the monthly payments for principal and

interest go up on the adjustable rate mortgage? Keeping in mind their financial situation and risk tolerances, which mortgage would you recommend for Mark and Ana? Why?

7. In addition to an 8.5 percent fixed-rate mortgage with 1 point, the lender has an 8 percent fixed-rate mortgage with 2 points. Compare the difference in monthly payments and front-end costs for these two mortgage options (assuming all else remains the same). How many months would Mark and Ana need to keep the mortgage before it would be wise for them to consider paying the additional point? Which of these mortgages would you recommend for Mark and Ana?

8. Complete a rent-or-buy analysis for Mark and Ana assuming they would buy this condo using the 8.0 percent fixed-rate mortgage with 2 points. Use the rental information from the original case and their marginal tax rate calculated in Part One, Question 10. Include the points paid as part of the closing costs in this analysis. Assume Mark and Ana will be able to itemize deductions if they purchase the condominium. Compare the total cost of renting versus buying.

9. Will Mark and Ana be able to qualify for the 8.0% fixed-rate mortgage if the lender applies the following two affordability ratios:

- Monthly housing costs cannot exceed 28 percent of the borrower's monthly before-tax income.
- Total monthly installment-loan payments (including housing costs) cannot exceed 35 percent of monthly before-tax income?

  In figuring if Mark and Ana will qualify, consider all of their income except the sale of the Maximum Global Mutual Fund Shares. Also use the minimum required payments for the revolving credit ($354) rather than the higher amount needed to pay off this debt within a year. The amount of their monthly housing costs (for the purposes of loan qualification) will be the sum of the following:

- Monthly payment for principal and interest
- One-twelfth of their annual property taxes
- One-twelfth of their homeowner's insurance premium
- Monthly homeowners' association fees

10. Assume that Mark and Ana buy the condo on February 25, 1993, using the 8% fixed-rate mortgage with 2 points. On February 15 they sell their Apple Computer stock for $60.00 a share and their General Motors stock for $35.25 to pay the front-end costs not covered by Mark's grandmother's $5,000 gift. The broker's commissions on the sale are $95 for the Apple stock and $75 for the General Motors stock. The remaining funds are taken from their money market account. Revise the Williams' balance sheet as of March 1, 1993, to reflect the changes in their assets and liabilities. Why did their net worth increase by less than the $5,000 gift?

11. Calculate Mark and Ana's income and expenditure statement for 1993. Remember they were renters for three months and will be homeowners for nine months. Because they sold their Apple Computer and General Motors stocks, they will receive no dividends on those investments in 1993. They expect their interest income on their money market account to be $185, since they had to use money from that account to buy the condo. Also, remember their tax refund from 1992. Assume they have not yet started saving for the goals listed in Part One of this case. How does buying the condo change Mark and Ana's cash flow?

12. Estimate Mark and Ana's 1993 income taxes after the condo purchase. Assume that included in the $2,500 closing costs is a 1 percent loan origination fee. Remember they will be making only nine monthly house payments in 1993. In addition, the commissions for the purchase of the Apple Computer and General Motors stocks are already included in the original cost (basis). How does buying the condominium change Mark and Ana's tax liability (compared to the previous year)?

13. Mark and Ana have now accomplished their first goal—to purchase a condominium. Since their projected budget for 1993 (completed in Part One of this case) indicated they will not be able to accomplish all of their stated goals given their level of income and expenditures, they have decided on the following adjustments:

- Save $105 per month in their money market account for their emergency fund (starting in April)
- Save $1,000 from Ana's December bonus for the buffer account for their first child. They plan on investing this in a certificate of deposit
- Postpone saving for a new house and contributing to their 401(k) accounts
- Pay $475 per month on their revolving credit account (starting in January)
- Reduce their food away from home expenditures to $125 per month, clothing expenditures to $100 per month, and entertainment expenditures to $125 per month (starting in April)
- Reduce their August vacation expenses to $500

Revise Mark and Ana's budget to reflect any changes in income and expenditures caused and/or required by the condo purchase and the above changes in their financial plans. Based on their projected tax refund for 1993, Mark and Ana wish to reduce their income tax withholding to only $725 per month for April through November. How much will need to be withheld in December in order to meet their tax obligations for the year?

PART three

Managing Credit

CHAPTER 7   *Borrowing on Open Account*

CHAPTER 8   *Using Consumer Loans*

CHAPTER 7

Borrowing on Open Account

Just say "Charge it." With those two little words, and a piece of plastic, you can buy gas for your car, have a gourmet meal at an expensive restaurant, or furnish an apartment. It happens more than *200 million times a day* across the United States! Credit, in fact, has become entrenched as a part of our everyday life and we, as consumers, use it in one form or another to purchase just about every type of good or service imaginable. Consider, for example, Georgette Brennan, an environmental resources technician and mother of two; she has a revolving line of credit at her bank that she recently used to buy a new car. Or Peter Thomas, who although only a junior in college, has a bank credit card with a $750 line of credit that he uses on those occasions when he's short of cash. Indeed, because of the ready availability and widespread use of credit, our economy is often called a "credit economy." And for good reason: by year-end 1991, individuals in this country had run up nearly three-quarters of a *trillion* dollars in consumer debt—and that *excludes* home mortgages. There's no doubt that credit is a convenient way to buy things; but when misused, the "buy now—pay later" attitude can lead to some real problems—even bankruptcy! *Consumer credit plays an important role in personal financial planning and using it wisely is the key to successful credit management.*

FINANCIAL *facts* OR *fantasies*

Are the following statements financial facts (true) or fantasies (false)?

One of the benefits of using credit is that it allows you to purchase expensive goods and services by spreading the payments for them over time.

Excluding mortgage payments, most families should have no problem handling their credit so long as they limit their monthly credit payments to 30 percent of their take-home pay.

One of the major differences between bank credit cards and travel and entertainment (T&E) cards is that T&E cards do not come with credit lines.

When you make application for credit, most big lenders will contact the local credit bureau, which decides whether or not you should receive the credit.

The best credit card for someone who does not pay their account balance in full each month is one that has a high interest rate but no annual fees.

You use a check rather than a credit card to obtain funds from an unsecured personal line of credit.

269

THE BASIC CONCEPTS OF CREDIT

Consumer credit is a convenient and effective way to purchase a variety of goods and services. Results can be disastrous, however, if the use of credit is not kept to a manageable level. Stop for a moment to think of the ways you would use consumer credit. What steps would you take to make sure your use of credit doesn't get out of hand?

Consumer credit is important in the personal financial planning process because of the impact that it can have on (1) the attainment of financial goals, and (2) cash budgets. For one thing, various forms of consumer credit can help you reach your financial objectives by enabling you to acquire some of the more expensive items in a systematic fashion, and without throwing your whole budget into disarray. But there's another side to consumer credit: It has to be paid back! And unless it's used intelligently, debt repayment loads can quickly turn an otherwise orderly budget into a budgetary nightmare. So, really, the issue is one of moderation and affordability.

The fact is in our economy today, consumers, businesses, and governments alike rely on the widespread use of credit to make transactions. Without credit, businesses could not supply the goods and services needed to satisfy consumer demand. The availability of credit to businesses also provides for higher levels of employment and helps raise our overall standard of living. Local, state, and federal governments use borrowing to implement various projects and programs that result not only in an increased standard of living but in additional employment opportunities as well. Clearly, borrowing helps fuel our economy and enhance the overall quality of our lives. Consequently, consumers in a credit economy need to know how to establish credit and how to avoid the dangers of using it improperly.

WHY BORROW?

People typically use credit as a way to pay for goods and services that cost more than they can afford to take from their current incomes. This is particularly true for those in the 25-to-44 age group, who simply have not had time to accumulate the liquid assets required to pay cash outright for major purchases and expenditures. As people begin to approach their mid-40s, their savings and investments start to build up, and their debt loads, in turn, tend to decline.

Principal Reasons for Borrowing. Most people do not pay cash for *large outlays*, such as for the purchase of houses and cars. Rather, they borrow a portion of the purchase price and then repay the loan on some scheduled basis. The net result is that by spreading payments over time, big-ticket items become more affordable. This enables consumers to obtain the immediate use of an expensive asset without having to fully pay for it for many years. There is, of course, a cost to borrowing money in this way, but most people tend to view this cost as a small price to pay for the immediate satisfaction they get from owning the house, car, or whatever it happens to be. In essence, people borrow because—in their minds, at least—the benefits of current consumption outweigh the interest costs on the loan. Unfortunately, while the initial euphoria of the purchase tends to wear off over time, the debt service requirements of the loan remain for years to come. Another reason people borrow is to meet a *financial emergency*—for example, to cover living expenses during a period of unemployment, or to purchase plane tickets in order to visit a sick relative. As indicated in Chapter 5, however, use of savings (not credit) is the ideal way to provide for financial emergencies.

An increasingly common motive for borrowing is *convenience*. Merchants as well as banks have made available a variety of charge accounts and credit cards that allow consumers to charge the purchase of all sorts of goods and services. Today just about anything can be charged to a credit card—from gas and oil or clothes and stereos to doctor and dental bills and even college tuition. Further, in a lot of places, it is far easier to use a credit card than to write a check (in restaurants, for instance). And by purchasing with a credit card, the consumer receives a permanent, itemized record of the transaction that can be used for budgetary purposes (to keep track of actual versus budgeted expenditures). Although in many cases no interest is levied on such transactions (at least initially), these credit card purchases are still a form of borrowing, since payment is not made at the time of the transaction. Finally, borrowing is also done for *investment* purposes. As we'll see in Chapters 13 and 14, it's relatively easy for an investor to partially finance the purchase of many different kinds of securities and investment vehicles with borrowed funds.

One of the benefits of using credit is that it allows you to purchase expensive goods and services by spreading the payments for them over time.
Fact: One of the major benefits of buying on credit is that expensive purchases are made more affordable because the consumer is able to pay for them systematically over time.

IMPROPER USES OF CREDIT

Many people use consumer credit to live beyond their means. Overspending is the biggest danger in borrowing, especially because it is so easy to do. Once hooked on "plastic," people may use their credit cards to make even routine purchases and often do not realize they have overextended themselves until it is too late. Overspenders simply won't admit that they're spending way beyond their means. As far as they're concerned, they can afford to buy all those things because, after all, they still have their credit cards and they can still afford to make the *minimum* payments each month. Unfortunately, such spending eventually leads to mounting bills. To avoid the possibility of future repayment shock, you should keep in mind the types of transactions for which it would be *improper* to (routinely, at least) use credit: (1) to meet basic living expenses; (2) to make impulse purchases, especially expensive ones; and (3) to purchase nondurable (short-lived) goods and services. Except in those situations where credit cards are used only occasionally for the sake of con-

venience (such as for gasoline and entertainment) and/or payments on recurring credit purchases are built into the monthly budget, a good rule to remember when considering the use of credit is that *the product purchased on credit should outlive the payments*.

Unfortunately, people who overspend eventually arrive at the point where they must choose to either become delinquent in their payments or sacrifice necessities, such as food and clothing. If payment obligations are not met, the consequences are likely to be a damaged credit rating, lawsuits, or even personal bankruptcy. Exhibit 7.1 lists some common signals that indicate it may be time to stop buying on credit. *Ignoring the telltale signs that you are overspending can only lead to more serious problems.*

ESTABLISHING CREDIT

The willingness of lenders to extend credit depends on their assessment of your creditworthiness — your ability to repay the debt on a timely basis. They look at a number of factors in making this decision, such as your present earnings and net worth. Equally important, they look at your current debt position and your credit history. Thus, it's worth your while to do what you can to build a strong credit rating.

First Steps in Establishing Credit. First, open checking and savings accounts. These signal stability to lenders and also indicate that you handle your financial affairs in a businesslike fashion. Second, use credit — open one or two charge accounts and use them periodically, even if you prefer paying cash. For example, get a Visa card and make a few credit purchases each month (don't overdo it, of course). You might pay an annual fee or interest on some (or all) of your account balances, but in the process, you'll become identified as a reliable credit customer. Third, obtain a small loan, even if you don't need one. If you don't actually need the money, put it in a liquid investment, such as a money market account or certificate of deposit. The interest you earn should offset some of the interest expense on the loan; you can view the difference as a cost of building good credit. (It goes without saying that you should repay the loan promptly, perhaps even a little ahead of schedule, to minimize the difference in interest rates — don't pay off the loan too quickly, though, as lenders like to see how you perform over an extended period of time.) Keep in mind, your ability to obtain a large loan in the future will depend in part on how you managed smaller ones in the past.

Build a Strong Credit History. From a financial perspective, maintaining a strong credit history is just as important as developing a solid employment record! Don't take credit lightly, and don't assume that once you get the loan or receive the credit card the toughest part is over. It's not. Getting the credit is just the first step; servicing it (i.e., making payments) in a prompt and timely fashion — month in and month out — is the really tough part of the consumer credit process. And in many respects, it's the most important element of consumer credit, as it determines your creditworthiness. By using credit wisely and repaying it on time, you're establishing a *credit history* that tells lenders you're a dependable, reliable, and responsible borrower.

The consumer credit industry keeps very close tabs on your credit and your past payment performance (more on this when we discuss *credit bureaus* later in the chapter). So the better job you do in being a responsible borrower, the easier it's going to be for you to get credit when and where you want it. The best way to build up a strong credit history and maintain your creditworthiness is to make payments *on time*, and to do so *consistently*, month after month. Being late occasionally — say, two or three times a year — might label you a "late payer." When you take on credit, you have an *obligation* to live up to the terms of the loan, including how and when the credit will be repaid.

If you foresee difficulty in meeting a monthly payment, let the lender know and usually some sort of arrangements can be made to help you through the situation. This is especially true with installment loans that require fixed monthly payments. If you have one or two of these loans and, for one reason or another, you encounter a month that's going to be really tight, the first thing you should try to do is get an extension on your loan. Don't just skip a payment, because that's going to put your account into a *late status until you make up the missed payment* — in other words, until you make a *double* payment,

your account/loan will remain in a late status, subject to a monthly late penalty. The alternative of trying to work out an extension with your lender obviously makes a lot more sense. Here's what you do: explain the situation to the loan officer and ask for an extension of one (or two) months on your loan. In most cases, so long as this hasn't occurred too often, the extension is almost automatically granted. The maturity of the loan is formally extended for a month (or two) and the extra interest of carrying the loan for another month (or two) is either added to the loan balance or, more commonly, paid at the time the extension is granted (such an extension fee generally amounts to a fraction of the normal monthly payment). Then, in a month (or two), you pick up where you left off and resume your normal monthly payments on the loan. This is the most sensible way of making it through those rough times since it doesn't harm your credit record. Just don't do it too often.

To summarize, here are some ways to build a strong credit history:

- Use credit only when you can afford it and only when the repayment schedule fits comfortably into the family budget — in short, don't overextend yourself.
- Fulfill all the terms of the credit.
- Be *consistent* in making payments *promptly*.
- Consult creditors immediately if you cannot meet payments as agreed.
- Be truthful when applying for credit. Lies are not likely to go undetected.

How Much Credit Can You Stand? Sound financial planning dictates that if you are going to use credit, you should have a good idea of how much you can comfortably tolerate. The easiest way to avoid repayment problems and ensure that your borrowing will not place an undue strain on your monthly budget is to *limit the use of credit to your ability to repay the debt!* In this regard, a useful *credit guideline* (and one that is widely used by lenders) is to make sure your monthly repayment burden does not exceed 20 percent of your monthly *take-home pay*. Most experts, however, regard the 20 percent figure as the *maximum* debt burden and strongly recommend debt ratios closer to 10 to 15

EXHIBIT 7.1

Some Credit Danger Signs

If one or more of these signs exist, you should take them as an indication that it is time to proceed with caution in your credit spending. Revise and update your spending patterns, cut back on the use of credit, and be alert for other signs of overspending.

You may be headed for serious trouble if:

- You regularly use credit cards to buy on impulse.
- You postdate checks to keep them from bouncing.
- You regularly exceed the borrowing limit on your credit cards.
- You never add up all your bills, to avoid facing grim realities.
- You have to borrow just to meet normal living expenses.
- You often use one form of credit — such as a cash advance from a credit card — to make payments on other debt.
- You can barely make the minimum required payments on bills.
- You are using more than 20 percent of your take-home income to pay credit card bills and personal loans (excluding mortgage payments).
- You have no savings.
- You are so far behind on credit payments that collection agencies are after you.

percent. Note that the monthly repayment burden here is *exclusive* of your monthly mortgage obligation.

To illustrate, consider an individual who takes home $1,500 a month. Using a 20 percent ratio, she should have monthly consumer credit payments of no more than $300 — that is, $1,500 × .20 = $300. This is the maximum amount of her monthly disposable income that she should use to pay off both personal loans and other forms of consumer credit (such as credit cards and education loans). This, of course, is not the maximum amount of consumer credit this person can have outstanding — in fact, her total consumer indebtedness can, and likely would, be considerably larger. The key factor is that with her income level, her *payments* on this type of debt should not exceed $300 a month. (Caution: This is not to say that credit terms should be lengthened just to accommodate this guideline; rather, in all cases, it is assumed that standard credit terms apply.)

Exhibit 7.2 provides a summary of low (10 percent), manageable (15 percent), and maximum (20 percent) monthly credit payments for a number of

income levels. Obviously, the closer your total monthly payments are to your desired debt safety ratio, the less future borrowing you can undertake. Conversely, *the lower the debt safety ratio, the better shape you're in, creditwise, and the easier it will be for you to service your outstanding consumer debt.* To find your **debt safety ratio**, simply use the following formula:

$$\text{Debt safety ratio} = \frac{\text{Total monthly consumer credit payments}}{\text{Monthly take-home pay}}$$

debt safety ratio

The proportion of total monthly consumer credit obligations to monthly take-home pay.

EXHIBIT 7.2

Alternative Consumer Credit Guidelines Based on Ability to Repay

Using this credit guideline, the amount of consumer credit you should have outstanding depends on the monthly payment you can afford to make.

Monthly Take-Home Pay	Monthly Consumer Credit Payments		
	Low Debt Safety Ratio (10%)	*Manageable* Debt Safety Ratio (15%)	*Maximum* Debt Safety Ratio (20%)
$ 500	$ 50	$ 75	$100
750	75	112	150
1,000	100	150	200
1,250	125	188	250
1,500	150	225	300
2,000	200	300	400
2,500	250	375	500
3,000	300	450	600

Thus, if you take home $1,360 a month and make total payments of $180 a month on outstanding consumer credit, you will have a debt safety ratio of $180/$1,360 = 13 percent, which is well within the manageable range.

Excluding mortgage payments, most families should have no problem handling their credit so long as they limit their monthly credit payments to 30 percent of their take-home pay.

Fantasy: Most experts suggest that you keep your monthly debt repayment burden, excluding mortgage payments, to 20 percent or less of your take-home pay. Letting it get as high as 30 percent can lead to serious credit problems.

The Special Credit Problems of Women

There used to be a time when a woman stood very little chance of getting credit on her own. In the minds of most lenders, she was just too much of a risk; after all, even if she was gainfully employed, she could always become pregnant and lose her job. Most of these kinds of credit obstacles are gone now, thanks in part to the Equal Credit Opportunity Act, which protects the credit rights of women (the ECOA is more fully discussed later in this chapter).

According to the ECOA, a creditor has no right to check into a woman's marital status or her child-bearing plans. Likewise, with two-income families, creditors must consider the woman's income on the same basis as the man's, even if it's part-time employment. Even with these (and other) protections, however, some women—especially those who are divorced or widowed—still have difficulty getting credit because they do not have a *credit history of their own*. The following steps can help overcome this problem.

First, use your own name when filing a credit application. Do not use a social title, such as Mrs. Thomas Watkins; instead, use your legal name. In marriage, you have your choice of several legal names; for example, if your maiden name is Joan Brown and you take your husband's name of Watkins, you can choose Joan Watkins or Joan Brown Watkins. By selecting a legal name and *using it consistently*, you build your own credit history.

Second, make sure that information reported to the credit bureau is in your name as well as your husband's. This will have been done automatically since June 1977, but account activity prior to that time may be in your husband's name only.

Third, when you marry you may wish to retain a credit file separate from your husband's, particularly if you have already established a good credit rating. You should then notify creditors of your name change and of your intention to maintain your own file.

OBTAINING CREDIT THROUGH AN OPEN ACCOUNT

In open account credit, the consumer obtains a revolving line of credit—which may or may not involve the use of a credit card. What types of open account credit would be most appealing to you? Take a minute to think about this question before reading on.

Open account credit is a form of credit extended to a consumer in advance of any transactions. Typically, a retail outlet or bank agrees to allow the consumer to buy or borrow up to a specified amount on open account. Credit is extended as long as the consumer does not exceed the established **credit limit**, and makes payments in accordance with the specified terms. Open account credit issued by a retail outlet, such as a department store or oil company, is usually applicable only in that establishment or one of its locations. In contrast, open account credit issued by banks, such as *MasterCard* and *Visa* accounts, can be used to make purchases at a wide variety of businesses. In the remainder of this chapter, we will direct our attention to various types and characteristics of open account credit; in Chapter 8, we will look at various forms of single-payment and installment loans.

AN ILLUSTRATION OF OPEN ACCOUNT CREDIT

Having open account credit is a lot like having your own personal line of credit—it's there when you need it. But unlike most other forms of debt, consumers who use open account credit can generally avoid paying interest charges *if they promptly pay*

the full amount of their account balance. For example, assume that in a given month you charge $75.58 worth of purchases on an open account at a department store. Sometime within the next month or so, you will receive a credit statement from the store that summarizes recent transactions on your account. Now, if there are no other charges and the total account balance is $75.58, you can (usually) avoid any finance charges by paying the account in full prior to the next bill date.

A typical **credit statement** is illustrated in Exhibit 7.3. It shows any unpaid balance (which is the amount of credit that was outstanding at the beginning of the month and should not be confused with past-due, or late, payments), along with a list of new charges made during the past month, any finance charges (interest) on the unpaid balance, the preceding period's payment, any other credits (such as those for returns), and the new balance. Notice that in addition to the list of transactions (there was one payment, along with four purchases), the *previous balance* (of $182) is shown toward the bottom of the statement. This represents the *unpaid* account balance at the end of the previous billing period; as such, it also represents the credit balance in the account at the start of the current billing period.

The charges made during the current month are then added to this unpaid balance: Thus, a total of $75.58 in charges incurred during the current period is added to the $182 previous account balance. Also added to the previous balance are any interest

---

open account credit

A form of credit extended to a consumer in advance of any transaction; type of credit that accompanies charge accounts and credit cards.

credit limit

A specified amount beyond which a customer may not borrow or purchase on credit.

credit statement

A monthly statement that summarizes the transactions in a consumer credit account; includes a record of new charges, credits, and payments, any interest charges, and the minimum monthly payment required on the account.

EXHIBIT 7.3

An Open Account Credit Statement

The monthly credit statement provides a summary of the various transactions in an account, including purchases, finance charges (if any), payments, and other credits.

DEPARTMENT NUMBER	DATES MONTH	DATES DAY	TRANSACTION DESCRIPTION	CHARGES	CREDITS
265	10	13	GLOVES	4.98	
64	10	13	SKIRTLINER PT	10.00	
99	10	22	PAYMENT	25.00	
111	11	09	MEN'S SHOES	45.20	
184	11	09	TOILETRIES	15.40	

TO YOUR PREVIOUS BALANCE	WE ADDED YOUR CHARGES	WE ADDED YOUR FINANCE CHARGES	WE DEDUCTED PAYMENTS	WE DEDUCTED OTHER CREDITS	THIS IS YOUR NEW BALANCE
$ 182.00	$ 75.58	$ 2.49	$ 25.00	$	$ 235.07

Account Number	Billing Dates		Finance Charge 1½% (Annual Percentage Rate 18%) Computed On Avg. Daily Balance Of	Minimum Amount To Send
	This Month	Next Month		
	11-10-92	12-10-92	$ 165.87	$ 25.00

*To Avoid Additional Finance Charges, Pay New Balance Before Billing Date Next Month. See Reverse Side For Explanation Of Finance Charges.

EXPLANATION OF FINANCE CHARGES

If the "NEW BALANCE" is received by the "BILLING DATE NEXT MONTH," no additional FINANCE CHARGE is imposed.

If a FINANCE CHARGE is shown, it is computed as follows:
1½% of the AVERAGE DAILY BALANCE as shown on the front hereof; this being an ANNUAL PERCENTAGE RATE OF 18%. When the AVERAGE DAILY BALANCE for a monthly billing period is $33.33, or less, the FINANCE CHARGE for that monthly billing period will be 50¢.

The AVERAGE DAILY BALANCE is determined by dividing the sum of the balances outstanding for each day of the monthly billing period by the number of days in the monthly billing period. The balance outstanding each day of the monthly billing period is determined by subtracting all payments and credits (excepting credits for merchandise purchased and returned within the same monthly billing period) from the previous day's balance, excluding any purchases added to the account during the monthly billing period and excluding any unpaid finance charges.

MINIMUM PAYMENT

A minimum payment of one-tenth (1/10) of the unpaid balance (adjusted to the next highest increment of $5.00) appearing on each monthly billing statement (but not less than $10.00 monthly) PLUS any amount which is past due from previous months must be paid by the "BILLING DATE NEXT MONTH" as shown on the front hereof.

Source: Typical major department store.

charges applicable to the account. In this case, because there's a previous unpaid balance in the account, there was a finance charge of $2.49. (A detailed discussion of how finance charges are determined is presented later in this chapter.) Finally, any payments received and other credits are subtracted from the balance to arrive at the new account balance. The $25 payment is the only deduction shown in Exhibit 7.3. Apparently, no other credits were received during the month. The resulting new balance on the account is $235.07.

Making Minimum Monthly Payments. Most open accounts do not require payment of the entire new balance, but they generally do impose some type of **minimum monthly payment**, usually a specified percentage of the new balance. For example, the statement in Exhibit 7.3 indicates that a minimum payment of $25 is required. The back side of the statement (shown as the bottom half of Exhibit 7.3) explains the method of calculating this minimum payment; here it is figured as 10 percent of the new balance ($235.07) adjusted to the next highest increment of $5 ($25). Of course, any past-due payment will be added to this amount. In our example, as long as the $25 minimum payment is made before next month's billing date (December 10, 1992), the customer's credit privileges will not be jeopardized.

TYPES OF OPEN ACCOUNT CREDIT

Open account credit generally is available from two broadly defined sources: (1) financial institutions and (2) retail stores/merchants. *Financial institutions* issue general-purpose credit cards as well as secured and unsecured revolving lines of credit and overdraft protection lines. Commercial banks have long been a major provider of consumer credit; and since deregulation, so have S&Ls and credit unions. Deregulation has also brought other financial institutions into this market — most notably, major stockbrokerage firms, consumer finance companies, and a growing list of commercial banks that have gone *interstate* to market their credit cards and other consumer credit products. *Retail stores and merchants* make up the other major source of open account

credit. They provide credit chiefly as a way of promoting the sales of their products. Their principal forms of credit include open charge accounts and credit cards.

Of the various *types* of open account credit, the two biggest are retail charge cards and bank credit cards. Together, there are a *billion* of these cards outstanding today. **Retail charge cards** are issued by department stores, oil companies, drug and specialty store chains, hotels, airlines, car rental agencies, and so on. They allow consumers to use prearranged lines of credit to purchase the goods and services sold by the issuing firm. **Bank credit cards**, in contrast, are issued by commercial banks, other financial institutions, and, increasingly, by non-financial institutions like AT&T and GM — Visa and MasterCard are the two dominant types. These cards allow their holders to charge purchases worldwide at literally millions of stores, restaurants, shops, gas stations, and other establishments. In addition, bank credit cards can be used to obtain **cash advances** (loans of money on which interest begins to accrue immediately) without having to make any formal application. While these are the two major types of open account credit — both of which will be examined in more detail later in the chapter — there are several other kinds of credit that you should be

---

minimum monthly payment
In open account credit, a minimum specified percentage of the new account balance that must be paid in order to remain current.

retail charge card
A type of credit card issued by retailers, airlines, and so on, that allows customers to charge goods and services up to a preestablished amount.

bank credit card
A credit card issued by a bank or other financial institution that allows the holder to charge purchases at any establishment that accepts it; can also be used to obtain cash advances.

cash advance
A loan that can be obtained by a bank credit card-holder at any participating bank or financial institution; begins to accrue interest immediately and requires no formal application.

aware of, including 30-day charge accounts, travel and entertainment cards, prestige cards, affinity cards, secured credit cards, and revolving lines of credit.

30-Day Charge Account.   Commonly offered by certain types of businesses for the general convenience of their customers, the **30-day**, or **regular, charge account** requires the customer to pay the full amount billed within 10 to 20 days after the billing date. If payment is made within the specified period, no interest is charged; if received after the due date, however, an interest penalty is usually tacked on to the account balance. These accounts generally do not involve the use of a charge card. They are offered by various types of public utilities (such as gas and electric companies, telephone companies, and so on), as well as some doctors and dentists, drugstores, and repair services.

Travel and Entertainment Cards.   **Travel and entertainment (T&E) cards** are similar to bank credit cards in that they enable holders to charge purchases at a variety of locations. While these cards used to be accepted primarily at travel- and entertainment-related businesses — like hotels, motels, airlines, and restaurants — they have now found their way into all sorts of establishments, from upscale department and clothing stores to gas stations and drugstores. In order to obtain one, the applicant must pay an annual fee of up to $300 just for the privilege of using it. In sharp contrast to retail and bank credit cards, however, most T&E cards do *not* carry an extended line of credit. Instead, the outstanding balances must be *paid in full* each month for the account to remain current. *American Express* is, by far, the biggest issuer of this type of card (with nearly 40 million cardholders worldwide), followed by *Diners Club* (7 million) and *Carte Blanche* (around half a million). However, these numbers are minute compared to the number of bank credit cards outstanding; there are over 250 million Visa cards and another 165 million or so MasterCards in circulation.

Several years ago, American Express added a new twist to this segment of the market by introducing the *Optima* card. Like the regular American Express card, the Optima card is aimed at affluent cardholders who want not only convenience, but also a regular revolving charge account that carries with it a line of credit. Since the Optima card's outstanding balance need not be paid in full each month, it is, for all practical purposes, just another type of *bank credit card!*

One of the major differences between bank credit cards and travel and entertainment (T&E) cards is that T&E cards do not come with credit lines. *Fact:*   T&E cards do not carry extended lines of credit and as such, outstanding balances must be paid in full each month for the account to remain current; in contrast, because regular bank cards come with credit lines, the account balances do not have to be paid in full each month — only a minimum payment must be made and the rest of the amount due can be carried forward on the account.

Prestige Cards.   Not all credit cards are created alike! Some offer many more advantages and features than others. That's precisely what **prestige cards** are; they offer higher credit limits (up to $100,000 or more), worldwide travel services, and other features meant to attract the upscale cardholder. Such cards impose higher credit standards for qualification, along with higher annual fees. MasterCard, Visa, American Express, and Optima all offer prestige cards. MasterCard and Visa have their *Gold* cards, while American Express and American Express Optima each have two prestige cards — the *Gold* card and, the "ultimate" in credit cards, the *Platinum* card, which is available by invitation only.

Exhibit 7.4 compares some of the major features of different bank and T&E cards. Most of these cards are fully interchangeable, since they perform many of the same functions. Together these cards account for about 70 percent of all credit card activity, the balance of the transactions being made with retail charge cards.

Affinity Cards.   Credit cards with a cause. That's the way to describe **affinity cards**. Issued as Visa or MasterCards, an affinity card is nothing more than a standard bank credit card that has been issued in conjunction with a sponsoring group — most commonly, some type of charitable, political, or professional organization. So named because of the bond between the sponsoring group and its members, affinity cards are sponsored by such nonprofit organizations as the American Heart Association, CARE, MADD, Easter Seals, the American Association of Individual Investors, the Sierra Club, and Special Olympics. In addition, they are issued by college and university alumni groups, labor organizations, religious and fraternal groups, professional societies, even airline frequent flyer programs. In many cases, all you have to do is support the cause in order to obtain one of these cards (as in the case of MADD or CARE). In other cases, you'll have to belong to a certain group in order to get one of their cards (for example, you may have to be a graduate of the school, or a member of a particular professional group to qualify).

Why even bother to carry one of these cards? Because, unlike traditional bank cards, affinity cards make money for the group backing the card, as well as for the bank. In short, the sponsoring groups share in the profits. For example, a certain percentage (usually one-half to 1 percent) of retail purchases made with the card go to the sponsoring organization. So, for the credit cardholder, it's a form of "painless philanthropy." But be careful. For while these cards may pull at your heartstrings, they can also tug at your purse strings. Someone has to cover the money that's going to the sponsoring organization, and that someone is usually the cardholder—in the form of higher fees and/or higher interest costs. In spite of this, for some, it may be viewed as a great way to contribute to a worthy cause. Others, however, may feel it makes more sense to use a traditional credit card and then write a check to their favorite charity.

Secured Credit Cards. You may have seen the ad on TV, where the announcer says that no matter how bad your credit, you can still qualify for one of their credit cards. The pitch may sound too good to be true, and in some respects it is. For there's a catch. Namely, the credit is "secured," meaning you have to put up *collateral* in order to get the card! These are so-called **secured**, or **collateralized, credit cards** where the amount of credit is determined by the amount of liquid collateral you're able to put up. These cards are targeted at people with no credit or

bad credit histories, who don't qualify for conventional credit cards. Issued as Visa or MasterCards, except for the collateral, they're like any other credit card. To qualify, a customer must deposit a certain amount (usually $500 or more) in a 12–18 month certificate of deposit, that the issuing bank holds as collateral. The cardholder then gets a credit line equal to the deposit. If the customer defaults, the bank has the CD to cover its losses. By making payments on time, it's hoped that these cardholders will establish (or reestablish) a credit history that may qualify them for a conventional (unsecured) credit card. Even though fully secured, these cards still carry annual fees and finance charges that are equal to, or greater than those of regular credit cards.

30-day (regular) charge account
A charge account that requires customers to pay the full amount billed within 10 to 20 days after the billing date.

travel and entertainment (T&E) card
A credit card, such as American Express, Diners Club, and Carte Blanche that is accepted by travel- and entertainment-related establishments, as well as a growing number of other businesses and stores; these cards require the holder to pay current balances *in full*.

prestige card
A type of bank or T&E card that offers higher credit limits, has stricter requirements for qualification, and generally offers more features than its "regular" counterpart.

affinity cards
A standard bank credit card issued in conjunction with some charitable, political, or other sponsoring nonprofit organization; these cards are a source of revenue to the sponsoring group since they normally earn a small percentage of all retail transactions.

secured credit cards
A type of credit card that's secured with some form of collateral, like a bank CD; with these cards, the amount of credit you get depends on how much collateral you can put up (also known as "collateralized" credit cards).

EXHIBIT 7.4

Major Credit Card Features

There are some important differences among the major credit cards, including the annual fee,
maximum amount of credit available, required minimum monthly payment, and number of outlets
that accept the card.

BANK CARDS	MasterCard[a]	Gold MasterCard[a]	VISA[a]	Premier VISA[a]	Discover Card	American Express Optima
Annual fee	$0–$75, as set by issuing bank	$0–$75, as set by issuing bank	$0–$75, as set by issuing bank	$0–$75, as set by issuing bank	$0	$15
Criteria	Set by issuing bank	Set by issuing bank	Set by issuing bank	Set by issuing bank	Varies by state	Similar to regular American Express Cards
Minimum credit	$300	$5,000	$300	$5,000	$1,000	Determined by credit department
Maximum credit	$10,000	$25,000	$10,000	$25,000	None	Determined by credit department
Minimum payment	Bank sets according to state regulations; expressed as a percentage of amount owed				Percentage of amount owed	Set by state law; expressed as percentage of amount owed
Individual receipts returned	No	No	No	No	No	Yes (photocopies)
Cash machine link	Yes	Yes	Yes	Yes	Yes	Yes
Cash advances available	Yes	Yes	Yes	Yes	Yes	Yes
Number of outlets that accept card	7,800,000 (worldwide)		7,900,000 (worldwide)		1,100,000	3,100,000 (worldwide)

T&E CARDS	American Express (Green)	American Express (Gold)	American Express (Platinum)	Citicorp Diners Club	Citicorp Carte Blanche
Annual fee	$55	$75	$300	$80	$40
Criteria	Minimum income of $15,000	Minimum income of $20,000	Minimum charged by holder must be $10,000 annually	Minimum income of $25,000	Minimum income of $18,000
Minimum credit	None	$10,000	$10,000	None	None
Maximum credit	None	None	None	None	None
Minimum payment	Balance	Balance	Balance	Balance	Balance
Individual receipts returned	Yes (photocopies)	Yes (photocopies)	Yes (photocopies)	Only upon request	Only upon request
Cash machine link	Yes (bank checking)	Yes	Yes	Yes	No
Cash advances available	No	Yes	Yes	Yes	No
Number of outlets that accept card		3,100,000 (worldwide)		N/A	N/A

[a]Data for MasterCard and VISA are meant to reflect the features that are typically found on the vast majority of these cards; unfortunately, more exact
information is not available, as the cards are issued by thousands of financial institutions worldwide, and these institutions are mostly free to set their
own standards.

Revolving Lines of Credit. The last type of open account credit is the **revolving line of credit**, offered by banks, brokerage houses, and other financial institutions. These credit lines normally do not involve the use of credit cards. Rather, they are accessed by simply writing checks on common checking accounts or specially designed credit line accounts. There are basically three types of revolving lines of credit: (1) overdraft protection lines, (2) unsecured personal credit lines, and (3) home equity credit lines. *Overdraft protection* is a revolving line of credit that is added to a regular checking or NOW account and provides protection against overdrawing the account. An *unsecured personal line of credit* lets individuals tap their credit lines whenever the need arises, usually by just writing checks. The *home equity credit line* is a form of credit that is secured by a second mortgage on one's home and operates much like a personal line of credit: Whenever individuals want to draw money from their home equity credit lines, they simply write checks against their credit accounts. These types of open credit lines are discussed in detail later in this chapter under "Other Kinds of Credit Lines."

A Word of Caution. One of the real dangers of credit cards is that they are so easy to use. Too many people tend to overlook the fact that they must eventually pay for the merchandise charged with their cards—but each time they make a transaction this way, they are incurring a liability to the issuer. Indeed, as the accompanying *Money in Action* box illustrates, a growing number of college students are learning this lesson the hard way! The bottom line is, if these cards are used properly, they can go a long way in helping you manage your personal finances; misuse them and you are just asking for trouble.

OPENING AN ACCOUNT

For the sake of convenience, people often maintain a variety of open accounts. Nearly every household, for example, uses 30-day charge accounts to pay their utility bills, phone bills, and so on. In addition, most families have one or more retail charge cards, a couple of bank cards, and possibly a T&E card; some people, in fact, may have as many as 15 to 20 cards, or more! And that's not all—families can also

have one or more revolving credit lines in the form of an overdraft protection, unsecured personal, and/or home equity line. When all these cards and lines are totaled together, a family conceivably can have tens of thousands of dollars of readily available credit. In this light, it is easy to see why consumer credit has become such a popular way of making relatively routine purchases. Although open account credit can increase the risk of budget overload, these accounts can also serve as a useful way of keeping track of expenditures.

Unlike many 30-day charge accounts, retail charge cards, bank credit cards, T&E cards, and revolving lines of credit all require *formal application procedures*. Let's look now at how you'd go about obtaining open account credit, including the normal credit application, investigation, and decision process. We'll couch our discussion in terms of credit cards, but keep in mind that similar procedures apply to other revolving lines of credit as well.

The Credit Application. With over a billion credit cards in the hands of American consumers, one would think that consumer credit is readily available. And it is—but you have to apply for it. Applications are usually available at the store or bank involved. Sometimes they can be found at the businesses that accept these cards or obtained on request from the issuing companies. Exhibit 7.5 provides an example of a bank credit card application. In this case, it is for either Visa or MasterCard. The information requested concerns personal/family matters, housing, employment and income, assets and liabilities, existing charge accounts, and credit references. This information is intended to provide the lender with insight about the applicant's creditworthiness. In essence, the lender is trying to determine whether the applicant has the *character* and

---

revolving line of credit
A type of open account credit offered by banks and other financial institutions that can be accessed by writing checks against demand deposit or specially designated credit line accounts.

MONEY IN ACTION

College Students and Credit Cards: Easy Come—Easy Go

When it comes to credit cards, a lot of college students fail the subject. Bombarded with seductive invitations from banks, department stores and oil companies, many students succumb to the "buy now, pay later" hook—only to find themselves deep in debt when they're barely out of their teens.

Much of the problem stems from the ubiquitous nature of credit cards and their perceived clout, prestige, and convenience. But credit-card issuers, trying to build a loyal following among future big spenders, also have made it easier for students to get cards than it is for many other adults.

While most college-enrolled holders handle their credit cards responsibly, the 4% that card issuers say default create a nightmare for themselves and their families, sometimes derailing college careers as they whittle down a mountain of personal debt built by prodigal spending.

Robert Rodriguez, for example, applied for and got a Master-Card when he was a junior at the University of Houston. Then he added two Visa cards and two department-store cards, as well as some oil-company cards. His credit-card spending was "definitely frivolous," Mr. Rodriguez says. He ate out often, bought clothes, and went to concerts. He even got cash advances from one card to make payments on others. *Within a couple of years he was $7,000 in debt.*

As he fell behind on his payments, Mr. Rodriguez began working double shifts at a parcel delivery company from 8 p.m. to 5 a.m. Soon he was too exhausted to keep up in school. "I couldn't make my 8 o'clock class," says the 25-year-old, "and I couldn't concentrate because I was worrying whether I was working enough hours to make enough money." After his grades slipped, he was suspended. Now

the former economics major is working full time to pay his debts—and trying to save enough money to return to college next year.

Credit counselors and parents say card issuers have made it far too easy for young, financially inexperienced students to qualify for the cards. "The sooner (the card issuers) can get them hooked on spending so much a month, the more money they can make," says Joseph Yura, a professor at the University of Texas, Austin, and a member of the school's financial aid advisory committee. Others say the card issuers lure students because they know parents are likely to pick up the tab if anything goes wrong.

Getting a card *is* simple for many of the nation's 12 million college students. Pre-approved credit card applications arrive by mail; ads and applications plaster school bulletin boards. Often the process

capacity to handle the debt in a prompt and timely manner. When applying for credit, you should provide the information requested as accurately and thoroughly as possible, since it will be verified during the credit investigation process.

The Credit Investigation. Once the credit application has been completed and returned to the establishment issuing the card, it is subject to a **credit investigation**. The purpose is to evaluate

the kind of credit risk you pose to the lender (the party issuing the credit or charge card). So be sure to fill out your credit application in a careful manner. Believe it or not, they really do look at those things. The key items lenders look at are how much money you make, how much debt you presently have outstanding and how well you handle it, and how stable you are (for example, your age, employment history, whether you own or rent a home, and so on). Obviously, the higher your income and the

is about as tough as filling in a magazine subscription form. Filene's department store in Boston, for instance, asks for little more than a student's name, Social Security number and a personal reference. Rarely is a student application denied, says Lori Schlager-Herscott, Filene's credit marketing manager.

On many campuses, American Express uses this siren call to students: "It may never be this easy again." American Express and most other card issuers allow students to get around income and employment requirements by counting other sources of money, such as financial aid and allowances. The card issuers usually don't impose any restrictions — such as lower spending limits — on cards issued to students. The Visa and MasterCard applications that often are distributed in shopping bags at campus bookstores even emphasize the wisdom of building credit his-

tory now for financing later to buy that first car or condominium. The companies say they are eager to sign up students in hopes of latching onto longtime customers.

Card issuers say that students default at about the same rate as other card holders, and some say students are even more responsible than other customer groups. "I think they view (credit cards) as a symbol of adulthood and are reluctant to shirk that responsibility," says Betsy Ludlow, vice president for new accounts at American Express. Such praise, though, is no solace to students faced with runaway debt. Raed Kolaghassi, a 21-year-old architecture major at the University of Houston, has run up a bill of $4,000 on his Visa card in the six months he's had it. Mr. Kolaghassi says he manages to make the minimum monthly payments, but the bills add up faster than what he's able to pay.

Students who use their credit cards improperly can end up ruining their credit ratings — or jeopardizing their college degrees if they have to cut back on school to pay the bills. A huge debt may also limit the careers that students feel they can choose from, requiring them to put big paychecks ahead of other considerations when picking a first job. In the end, many students learn the hard way — as did Mr. Rodriguez, who has since taken a pair of scissors to all but one of his credit cards. Now, he says, besides cash, "the only things in my wallet are photos."

better your credit history, the greater the chances of having your credit application approved.

As a part of the investigation process, the lender will attempt to verify much of the information provided by you on the credit application — for obvious reasons, false or misleading information will almost certainly result in outright rejection of your application. For example, the lender will verify your place of employment, level of income, current debt load and debt service history, and so forth. Often, this can

be done through one or two quick phone calls. If you've lived in the area for a number of years and have established relations with a local bank, a call to

---

credit investigation

An investigation that involves contacting credit references or corresponding with a credit bureau in order to verify information on a credit application.

EXHIBIT 7.5

A Bank Credit Card Application

This credit application, like most, seeks information about the applicant's place of employment, monthly income, place of residence, credit history, and other financial matters that are intended to help the lender decide whether or not to extend credit.

Application for Credit Services

☐ MasterCard   ☐ Visa
☐ Number of cards desired_____   Will non-applicant spouse use account?   ☐ Yes   ☐ No
"Please Approve this application to Valley National Bank's Credit Card and related Personal Indentification Number with the highest credit line for which I/we qualify."
☐ Request credit limit increase to $_____on Credit Card account no._____

Please tell us about Yourself

| Your Name (First, Middle, Last) | Jr. or Sr. | Date of Birth | Social Security No | Your Home Phone. ( ) |
| Co-Applicant's Name (First, Middle, Last) | Jr. or Sr. | Date of Birth | Social Security No. | Your Marital Status ☐ Unmarried ☐ Married ☐ Separated |

| Address (Number and Street) | Apt. # | City | State | Zip | How Long Yrs. Mos. |
| Previous Address (Number and Street) | Apt. # | City | State | Zip | How Long Yrs. Mos. |

Name and Address of Nearest Relative (Not Living with you)   Relationship

Employment and Financial Information

Present Employer	Position	How Long?	Business Phone ( )	Monthly Take Home Pay $
Previous Employer	Position	How Long?		
Co-Applicant's Employer	Position	How Long?	Business Phone ( )	Monthly Take Home Pay $
Source of Other Income				Monthly Other Pay $

Your Income: Income from alimony, child support or maintenance payments need not be revealed if you do not choose to disclose such income in applying for credit. As a creditor we may inquire whether any income stated in an application is derived from such a source.   Total Monthly Take Home Pay

| Name of Your Bank (Check All That Apply) | ☐ Checking | Balance_____ |
| | ☐ Savings (CD, IRA, etc.) | Balance_____ |

Your Existing Accounts - All Existing Accounts Specify Institution or Bank Name

Finance Company	Auto Loans
Bank Credit Cards	☐ Rent ☐ Own Balance Owed _____ Market Value_____
Department Store Cards	Other

Please Answer these Questions

| Have you ever filed Bankruptcy? ☐ Yes ☐ No Year_____ | What are your total monthly payments? (including, mortgage/rent) | What is the total balance owed on all your debts? | What is the make, model and year of your newest auto? |

Signatures

I give the above information for the purpose of obtaining credit and authorize the Bank to obtain information concerning statements made herein. I understand the fees and credit features offered in this application are subject to change without notice.

COMMUNITY PROPERTY DEBT: This application, unless otherwise indicated below, is to be considered as an application for credit extended as a debt of marital community based upon the creditworthiness if that community. Supply all information requested on the application

☐ SOLE AND SEPARATE PROPERTY: This is an application for individual credit as sole and separate debt which will be evaluated without regard to the assets, income or creditworthiness of the applicant's spouse or the applicant's martial community. (The applicant should list only martial status, and no other information should be given regarding the spouse (if any) except name and address. Applicant should also list debts for which he/she is obligated by signing a promise to pay and should also list all sole and separate assets and income.).

_____   _____
Signature of Applicant   Date

_____   _____
Signature of Co-Applicant   Date

_____   _____
Signature of Authorized User (Other)   Date

| Branch # | Employee # |

Source: Reprinted by permission of Valley National Bank of Arizona.

your banker may be all it takes to confirm your creditworthiness. If you haven't established such bank relations — and most young people have not — then the lender is likely to turn to the local credit bureau for a *credit report* on you.

The Credit Bureau.   Basically, a **credit bureau** is a type of reporting agency that gathers and sells information about individual borrowers. If, as is often the case, the lender does not know you personally, it must rely on a cost-effective way of verifying your employment and credit history. It would be far too expensive and time-consuming for individual creditors to confirm your credit application on their own, so they turn to credit bureaus that maintain fairly detailed credit files about you. Information in your file comes from one of three sources: creditors who subscribe to the bureau, other creditors who supply information at your request, and publicly recorded court documents (such as tax liens or bankruptcy records).

Contrary to popular opinion, your credit file does *not* contain everything anyone would ever want to know about you — there's nothing on your lifestyle, friends, habits, religious or political affiliations. Instead, most of the information is pretty dull stuff, and covers such things as:

- Your name, social security number, age, number of dependents, and current and previous addresses
- Your employment record, including current and past employers, and salary data, if available
- Your credit history, including the number of loans and credit lines you have, number of credit cards issued in your name, your payment record, and account balances
- Public records data involving bankruptcies, tax liens, foreclosures, civil suits, and criminal convictions
- Finally, the names of firms and financial institutions that have recently requested copies of your file is also recorded

While one late MasterCard payment probably won't make much of a difference on an otherwise clean credit file, a definite pattern of delinquencies (consistently being 30 to 60 days late with your payments) or a personal bankruptcy certainly will. Unfortunately, poor credit traits will stick with you for a long time, since delinquencies will remain on your credit file for as long as seven years and bankruptcies for ten years. An example of an actual credit bureau report is provided in Exhibit 7.6. It demonstrates the kind of information you can expect to find in one of these reports.

Local credit bureaus (there are more than a thousand of them) are established and mutually owned by local merchants and banks. They collect and store credit information on people living within the community and make it available, for a fee, to members who request it. If the information requested can be transmitted over the phone or by fax, the cost of the inquiry is typically about $5 or $10. On the other hand, if the credit bureau must obtain, either through its own investigation or from another credit bureau, additional information in order to update the applicant's file, the cost of the report will be much higher. Local bureaus are linked together nationally through one of the "big three" national bureaus — Trans-Union, Equifax Credit Information Services, and TRW Credit Data — each of which provides the mechanism for obtaining credit information from almost any place in the United States. It's important to understand that credit bureaus merely collect and provide credit information. They do not analyze it, they do not rate it (or at least they're not supposed to), and they certainly do not make the final credit decision.

Credit bureaus are far from perfect, however, and they do make mistakes. Unfortunately, when they make mistakes, it can mean *BIG* problems for you. That's because a credit report can have an important bearing on whether or not you get credit! Literally millions of Americans have learned the hard way that their credit records are riddled with errors. While consumers do have recourse, the process can be time-consuming and frustrating because, all too often, the credit bureaus themselves seem to have a "care less" attitude about their mistakes — as far as

---

credit bureau

An organization, typically established by local banks and merchants, that collects and stores credit information about individual borrowers and, for a specified fee, supplies it to financial institutions that request it.

EXHIBIT 7.6

An Example of a Credit Bureau Report

Displayed here is an actual credit report from Associated Credit Bureaus, a national trade association of credit bureaus and collection agencies. Notice that in addition to some basic information (like name, address, place of employment, and so on), the report deals strictly with credit information—including payment records, past due status, and types of credit; also reported (on the bottom of the report) is a summary of any relevant public records.

NAME AND ADDRESS OF CREDIT BUREAU MAKING REPORT

☐ SINGLE REFERENCE   ☒ IN FILE REPORT   ☐ TRADE REPORT
☐ FULL REPORT   ☐ EMPLOY & TRADE REPORT   ☐ PREVIOUS RESIDENCE REPORT
☐ OTHER _____

CREDIT BUREAU OF ANYTOWN
1131 MAIN ST.
ANYTOWN, ANYSTATE 12345

CONFIDENTIAL
crediscope® REPORT

Date Received: 4/11/86
Date Mailed: 4/11/86
In File Since: APRIL 1970
Inquired As: JOINT ACCOUNT

Member
Associated Credit Bureaus, Inc.

FOR   FIRST NATIONAL BANK
ANYTOWN, ANYSTATE 12345

REPORT ON: LAST NAME	FIRST NAME	INITIAL	SOCIAL SECURITY NUMBER		SPOUSE'S NAME
CONSUMER	ROBERT	G.	123-45-6789		BETTY R.

ADDRESS:	CITY	STATE:	ZIP CODE	SINCE:	SPOUSE'S SOCIAL SECURITY NO.
1234 ANY ST. ANYTOWN		ANYSTATE	12333	1973	987-65-4321

PRESENT EMPLOYER:	POSITION HELD:	SINCE:	DATE EMPLOY VERIFIED	EST. MONTHLY INCOME
XYZ CORPORATION	ASST. DEPT. MGR.	10/81	12/81	$ 2500

DATE OF BIRTH	NUMBER OF DEPENDENTS INCLUDING SELF:			OTHER: (EXPLAIN)
5/25/50	4	☒ OWNS OR BUYING HOME	☐ RENTS HOME	☐

FORMER ADDRESS:	CITY:	STATE:	FROM:	TO:
4321 FIRST AVE.	ANYTOWN	ANYSTATE	1970	1973

FORMER EMPLOYER:	POSITION HELD:	FROM:	TO:	EST. MONTHLY INCOME
ABC & ASSOCIATES	SALES PERSON	2/80	9/81	$1285

SPOUSE'S EMPLOYER:	POSITION HELD:	SINCE:	DATE EMPLOY VERIFIED	EST. MONTHLY INCOME
BIG CITY DEPT. STORE	CASHIER	4/81	12/81	$1200

WHOSE	KIND OF BUSINESS AND ID CODE	DATE REPORTED AND METHOD OF REPORTING	DATE OPENED	DATE OF LAST PAYMENT	HIGHEST CREDIT OR LAST CONTRACT	PRESENT STATUS BALANCE OWING	PAST DUE AMOUNT	NO. OF PAYMENTS	NO. MONTHS HISTORY REVIEWED	30-59 DAYS ONLY	60-89 DAYS ONLY	90 DAYS AND OVER	TYPE & TERMS (MANNER OF PAYMENT)	REMARKS
2	CONSUMER'S BANK B 12-345	2/6/86 AUTOMTD.	12/85	1/86	1200	1100	-0-	-0-	2	-0-	-0-	-0-	INSTALLMENT $100/MO.	
3	BIG CITY DEPT. STORE D 54-321	2/10/86 MANUAL	4/81	1/86	300	100	-0-	-0-	12	-0-	-0-	-0-	REVOLVING $ 25/MO.	
1	SUPER CREDIT CARD N 01-234	12/12/85 AUTOMATD.	7/82	11/85	200	100	100	1	12	1	-0-	-0-	OPEN 30-DAY	

PUBLIC RECORD: SMALL CLAIMS CT. CASE #SC1001 PLAINTIFF: ANYWHERE APPLIANCES
AMOUNT $225 PAID 4/4/82
ADDITIONAL INFORMATION: REF. SMALL CLAIMS CT. CASE #SC1001--5/30/82 SUBJECT SAYS CLAIM PAID
UNDER PROTEST. APPLIANCE DID NOT OPERATE PROPERLY.

Source: Copyright © and reprinted by permission of the Associated Credit Bureaus, Inc. Washington, D.C.

they're concerned, you're guilty until proven innocent. Obviously, with this kind of track record, you should do what you can to watch out for yourself. Here are some things you can do.

If you plan to take out a big loan — to finance, say, a new car — it might pay to get a copy of your credit report before you do anything. Knowing what kind of information credit agencies have collected on you — and whether or not it's correct — can save you a lot of time later. *It's especially important for young adults and married women to make sure that all accounts for which they are individually or jointly liable are listed in their credit files, as lenders are normally reluctant to consider applicants with little or no credit history.* As for errors, most people don't know there are any in their reports until it's too late. Particularly troubling is *adverse* information about you (i.e., that you're a deadbeat or don't pay your bills on time) that simply isn't true. Common inaccuracies include bad debts of another person with a similar name, tax liens or judgments that have been satisfied, and disputes with merchants that have been resolved.

It's not hard to get a copy of your credit report, and *most consumer advisors recommend you review your file every two or three years.* You can obtain a copy of your credit report by submitting a written request that includes your name, address, date of birth, and Social Security number. The fee varies from $7.50 to $15, unless you've recently been denied credit, in which case you are entitled to a copy of your credit report for free. Most local credit bureaus are listed in the Yellow Pages of the phone book. The addresses and phone numbers of the three national credit bureaus are provided below:

- Equifax Credit Information Services
  P.O. Box 740241
  Atlanta, GA 30374-0241
  (800) 685-1111
- Trans-Union Corporation
  P.O. Box 3307
  Tampa, FL 33601-3307
  (800) 226-6214
- TRW Corporation
  P.O. Box 749029
  Dallas, TX 75374
  (305) 962-5997

When you make application for credit, most big lenders will contact the local credit bureau, which decides whether or not you should receive the credit.

Fantasy: Credit bureaus collect information and maintain credit files about individual borrowers, but they do *not* make the credit decision; that's done by the merchant or financial institution extending the credit.

The Credit Decision. Using the data provided by the credit applicant, along with any information obtained from the credit bureau, the store or bank must decide whether or not to grant credit. Very likely, some type of **credit scoring** scheme will be used to make the credit decision. By assigning values to such factors as your age, annual income, number of years on your present job, whether you rent or own your home and how long you have lived there, age of your car(s), number and type of credit cards you hold, level of your existing debts, whether or not you have savings accounts, whether you have a phone, and general credit references, an overall credit score for you can be developed. There may be 10 or 15 different factors or characteristics that are considered, and each characteristic will receive a score based on some predetermined standard. For example, if you're 24 years old, single, earn $22,000 a year (on a job that you've had for only two years) and rent an apartment, you might receive the following scores:

1.	Age (under 25)	5 points
2.	Marital status (single)	− 2 points
3.	Annual income ($20–25 thousand)	12 points
4.	Length of employment (2 yrs. or less)	4 points
5.	Rent or own a home (rent)	0 points
		19 points

---

credit scoring

A method of evaluating an applicant's creditworthiness by assigning values to factors such as income, existing debts, and credit references.

Based on information obtained from your credit application, similar scores would be assigned to another seven to ten factors.

In all cases, the stronger your personal traits or characteristics, the higher the score you'll receive. For instance, if you had been 44 years old (rather than 24), you might have received 18 points for your age factor, being married rather than single would have given you 9 points, and earning $75,000 a year would obviously have been worth a lot more than earning $22,000! The idea is that the more stable you are *perceived* to be, the more income you make, the better your credit record, and so on the higher the score you should receive. In essence, statistical studies have shown that certain personal and financial traits can be used to determine your creditworthiness. Indeed, the whole credit scoring system is based on extensive statistical studies, which identify the characteristics to look at and the scores to assign. It's all very mechanical: Assign a score to each characteristic, add up the scores, and, based on that total score, determine the credit worthiness of the applicant.

Generally, if your score equals or exceeds a predetermined minimum, you will be given credit; if not, credit will be refused. Sometimes borderline cases are granted credit on a limited basis. For example, a large department store that normally limits the outstanding balance on its revolving charge accounts to $500 might give a customer with a marginal credit score a revolving charge account with a $100 credit limit. Even when a formal credit scoring scheme is used, the credit manager or loan officer is normally empowered to offer credit if such action seems appropriate. Applicants who are granted credit are notified and sent a charge card and/or checks, along with material describing the credit terms and procedures.

IMPORTANT CONSUMER CREDIT LEGISLATION

Just as you have an obligation to service your debt in a prompt and timely fashion, so too do *lenders have certain legal obligations they're expected to fulfill.* Accordingly, when you apply for credit, it's in your best interest to be aware of the legal obligations of the issuing establishment. There is always a possibility that your rights will be violated. Over the past decade or so, several important pieces of consumer legislation have been passed affecting the extension of credit. The major concerns of this legislation have been credit discrimination, disclosure of credit information, errors and complaints, disclosure of finance charges (or so-called *truth in lending*), loss of credit card, recourse on unsatisfactory purchases, protection against collector harassment, and credit card applications and renewal notices.

Credit Discrimination. As of October 1975, the *Equal Credit Opportunity Act (ECOA)* makes it illegal for a creditor to discriminate on the basis of sex or marital status when considering a credit application. The act was passed in order to extend to women the credit rights already held by men. Questions about an applicant's sex, marital status, and childbearing plans are strictly prohibited. Moreover, lenders are required to view the income of women in exactly the same fashion as they do that of men, and they must consider alimony and child support as part of a woman's income. Severe penalties exist for the violation of this law.

On March 23, 1977, ECOA was expanded to prohibit credit discrimination based on race, national origin, religion, age, or the receipt of public assistance. A subsequent extension of the act — effective June 1, 1977 — requires that if a husband and wife open a joint account or cosign a loan, the credit grantor must report the information to the credit bureau in the name of *both* parties. This change was intended to allow a wife to establish a credit history, which would make it easier for her to obtain credit in the event of her husband's death or a divorce.

Disclosure of Credit Information. On April 25, 1971, the *Fair Credit Reporting Act* went into effect. It includes numerous provisions, among which are the following. First, credit bureau reports must contain accurate, relevant, and recent information about the personal and financial situation of credit applicants. Second, only bona fide users of financial information may review credit files. Third, consumers who are refused credit or who find their borrowing costs increased as the result of a credit investigation must be informed of the reasons for such actions as well as the name and address of the reporting credit agency. Perhaps most important, credit reporting agencies must let individuals review their credit files personally and correct any inaccurate information.

Mailing, Error Complaints, and Cash Discounts on Bills.

Because of errors and abuses in credit billing and the poor handling of credit complaints, the *Fair Credit Billing Act* was passed in October 1975. One provision of the act requires creditors to mail bills at least 14 days prior to the payment-due date and to include all credits and refunds on the bill for the period in which they occurred. Another provision requires customers to notify the creditor (in writing), within 60 days of the date they receive the statement, regarding any billing errors. The credit issuer is required to respond within 30 days to customer inquiries concerning a billing error and to resolve the complaint within 90 days of its receipt. During the period in which the complaint is being resolved, the creditor is prohibited from collecting the bill or issuing an unfavorable credit report as a result of the disputed charge. A third provision of the act allows merchants to give cash discounts of any size to customers who pay cash instead of using credit. Since the merchants have to pay credit card companies, such as MasterCard, Visa, and American Express, for the privilege of accepting customers' cards, this act allows them to pass the savings on to those who choose not to use credit cards.

Truth in Lending: Full Disclosure of Finance Charges.

Another major piece of consumer legislation is the *Consumer Credit Protection Act*. Commonly referred to as the **Truth in Lending Act** it initially went into effect July 1, 1969, and has been amended several times since then. The directives for complying with the act are outlined in *Regulation Z*, which was issued by the Federal Reserve Board. Its most significant provision is the requirement that prior to extending credit, all lenders must disclose both the dollar amount of finance charges and the annual percentage rate charged (accurate to the nearest 0.25 percent). This enables credit applicants to make valid comparisons of alternate sources of credit. Such disclosure is included on the reverse side of monthly credit card statements, an example of which was shown earlier in Exhibit 7.3 (see "Explanation of Finance Charges").

The *dollar amount* of finance charges referred to above includes all interest and fees that must be paid in order to receive the loan. The **annual percentage rate (APR)** is the true rate of interest paid over the life of the loan and must be calculated in the manner outlined by the law. Note that on open account credit, creditors cannot specify in advance the dollar amount of interest since they do not know how much will be purchased on the account. The annual percentage rate on these accounts can be stated, however, since there are no fees charged other than interest. Remember: It is your right as a consumer to be told the dollar amount of charges and the APR on any financing you consider.

Loss or Theft of Credit Card.

The Consumer Credit Protection Act requires every credit card to contain some form of user identification — generally a picture or signature — and limits the liability of the credit card owner, in the event the card is lost or stolen, to a maximum of $50 per card. Credit card issuers are also required to send to their account holders a self-addressed form for notification of lost or stolen cards and an explanation of their rights at the time of issue. Some issuers also have toll-free numbers than can be used to report lost or stolen cards. In addition, companies are prohibited from sending unrequested credit cards to potential users (though they can send out unsolicited credit card *applications*).

Truth in Lending Act
A law passed in 1969 that, among other provisions, requires creditors to give customers advance, full disclosure of dollar amounts of finance charges and annual percentage rates.

annual percentage rate (APR)
The actual or true rate of interest paid over the life of a loan.

Recourse on Unsatisfactory Purchases.

One of the provisions of the Fair Credit Billing Act concerns the right of credit cardholders to obtain recourse on unsatisfactory goods or services charged to their accounts. This provision applies mostly to situations in which the credit used to make a purchase was provided by someone other than the seller — through the use of a bank credit card or a travel and entertainment card, for example. This feature protects people who have used credit to purchase goods or services that are subsequently found to be defective or do not perform satisfactorily. If, after good-faith attempts, they cannot satisfactorily work out their disagreement with the seller, they have the right to stop paying the creditor. By placing some of the burden of guaranteeing the value of the purchase on the creditor, this provision has caused creditors to be more concerned with the reputation of the providers of the goods or services being financed.

Protection against Collector Harassment.

Beginning March 20, 1978, the *Fair Debt Collection Practices Act* gave consumers protection against unreasonable collection practices. To begin with, the law requires that within five days of first being contacted by a debt collector, the credit customer must be informed *in writing* as to (1) how much money is owed, (2) to whom, and (3) steps that can be taken if the debt is disputed. If the customer disagrees with the claim, he or she has 30 days in which to send the collector written notification of the dispute. Then, the collector cannot continue collection efforts until the customer has been provided with written verification of the debt. Further, the customer can prevent a collector from communicating with him or her by notifying the collector in writing. Finally, if the collector presses suit for payment, it must be filed in the judicial district in which the customer lives or the contract was signed.

You may have heard stories of unsavory credit collectors gaining access to people's homes by posing as ministers or police officers and, once inside, grabbing a television set or other item on which credit payments were overdue. Frequently violence was threatened, and sometimes used, to collect unpaid bills. All these tactics are now illegal. The act specifically makes it a federal offense for collectors to (1) use abusive language, threaten the customer, or call at inconvenient times or at the place of work; (2) misrepresent themselves; (3) use unfair tactics in an effort to collect the debt; (4) contact anyone else about the customer's debt unless they are trying to locate him or her; and (5) collect an amount greater than the debt or apply payments to another disputed debt.

Unsolicited Credit Card Applications and Renewal Notices.

In 1988, Congress passed the *Fair Credit and Charge Card Disclosure Act*, which spells out the type of information you're entitled to receive in direct-mail credit advertisements. Aimed specifically at credit and charge cards, the law requires card issuers to provide full disclosure of all fees, grace periods, and other financial terms when they mail you an unsolicited invitation to apply for one of their cards. Perhaps more important, the law gives you a chance to shop around for the best deal by making it easier for you to get rid of cards you really don't want, or to switch to cheaper cards. It does that by requiring card issuers to *give you advance notice when your account is about to be renewed* — rather than just slapping the annual fee on your next bill. Face it, most people keep the cards they already have because they simply forget about their anniversary dates, until they get billed for another year. Of course, you can always cancel a card, but that's often a time-consuming process in itself. The renewal notice provision, in effect, gives you the opportunity to dump cards you don't want or need — and to do so without a lot of hassle.

CREDIT CARD FRAUD

Despite all the legislation, an inescapable fact of life is that there are still people out there who are doing their very best to rip you off! And as far as your good credit is concerned, there's no better way to do that than through your credit card. In fact, plastic has become the vehicle of choice among crooks as a way of defrauding and stealing from both you and the merchants that honor credit cards. Stolen account numbers (obtained by dishonest employees or even by thieves going through the trash to find discarded receipts) are the biggest source of credit card fraud. For all a crook needs to order merchandise or services over the phone is your account number. Even worse, a crook who also has your bank account number or home address may be able to get a credit card or open other types of charge accounts — *all in your name!*

Basically, "it's us against them," and the first thing you have to understand is that credit card you're carrying around is a very powerful piece of plastic. Be careful with it. To reduce your chances of being defrauded, here are some suggestions you should follow:

- Never, ever, give your account number to people or organizations *who call you* — no matter how legitimate it sounds, if you didn't initiate the call, don't give out the information!
- It's okay to give your account number over the phone when ordering or purchasing something from a major catalog house, airline, hotel, and so on, but don't do it for any other reason.
- When paying for something *by check*, don't put your credit card account number on the check and don't let the store clerk do it — show the clerk a check guarantee card (if you have one), a driver's license, or some other form of identification.
- Don't put your phone number or address on credit/charge slips, even if the merchant asks for it — they're *not* entitled to it anyway; but if the clerk insists, just scribble down any number you want.
- When using your card to make a purchase, *always keep your eye on it* (so the clerk can't make an extra imprint); and if the clerk makes a mistake and wants to make another imprint, ask for the first imprint, and tear it up on the spot.
- Always draw a line on the credit slip through any blank spaces above the total, so the amount can't be altered.
- *Destroy* all carbons and old credit slips; and when you receive your monthly statement, be sure to *go over it promptly* to make sure there are no errors (if you find a mistake, call or send a letter immediately, detailing the error).
- If you lose a card or it's stolen, *report it to the card issuer immediately* — the most you're ever liable for with a lost or stolen card is $50 (per card), but if you report the loss *before* the card can be used, you won't be liable for any unauthorized charges (the phone number to call is listed on the back of your statement).

CREDIT CARD INSURANCE

Before the passage of the Consumer Credit Protection Act, the liability of credit cardholders for charges made on lost or stolen cards was virtually unlimited. Quite simply, the cardholder was held liable for all charges made prior to the time the issuer received written notice of the card's loss or theft. In order to protect themselves against the consequences of possible loss or theft of their credit cards, many people would purchase **credit card insurance**. *Such insurance really isn't necessary anymore*, since the cardholder's liability, in case of loss or theft, is limited to $50, or the amount charged on the card prior to notification of the issuer, *whichever is less*. Thus, since your liability can't exceed $50, it hardly pays to buy insurance to protect against such a small loss! It does, however, pay to promptly notify the issuer of a lost or stolen card. To do so, keep a list of credit card numbers along with the addresses and phone numbers provided by the card issuers for use in such emergencies.

BANKRUPTCY: PAYING THE ULTIMATE PRICE FOR CREDIT ABUSE

It certainly wouldn't be an overstatement to say that *debt was in* during the decade of the 1980s! In fact, the explosion of debt that occurred in that ten-year period is almost incomprehensible. The national debt tripled, from less than a trillion dollars when the '80s began to nearly $3 trillion when the '90s arrived. Businesses also took on debt at a torrid pace. And, not to be outdone, consumers were using credit like there was no tomorrow. Personal debt, including home mortgages, rose from $1.3 trillion in 1980 to nearly $3.4 trillion in 1990. Debt, in fact, was growing faster than personal income — so much so that by 1990 total consumer debt amounted to a

credit card insurance

A type of insurance that covers charges made on a lost or stolen credit card; no longer necessary because of the Consumer Credit Protection Act's provision limiting cardholder's liability in such instances.

whopping 84 percent of annual personal income. That doesn't leave much room for error. So it shouldn't be too surprising that when you couple this heavy debt load with a serious economic recession (like the one we had in 1990–91), you have all the ingredients of a real financial crisis. And that's just what happened as personal bankruptcies soared—indeed, in 1991 alone, nearly a million people filed for **personal bankruptcy**.

When too many people are too heavily in debt, a recession (or some other economic reversal) can come along and push many of them over the edge. But let's face it, the recession is not the main culprit here, because the only way a recession can push you over the edge is if you're already sitting on it! The real culprit is excess debt. Some people simply abuse credit by taking on more than they can afford. Maybe they're pursuing a lifestyle beyond their means, or an unfortunate event—like the loss of a job—takes place. Whatever the cause, sooner or later, they start missing payments and their credit rating begins to deteriorate. Unless some corrective actions are taken, this is followed by repossession of property and, eventually, even bankruptcy. These people basically have reached the end of a long line of deteriorating financial affairs. Households that cannot resolve serious credit problems on their own need help from the courts. Two legal remedies that are widely used under such circumstances include (1) the Wage Earner Plan and (2) straight bankruptcy.

Wage Earner Plan. The **Wage Earner Plan** (as defined in *Chapter 13* of the U.S. Bankruptcy Code) is a workout procedure that involves some type of debt restructuring—usually by establishing a debt repayment schedule that's more compatible to the person's income. It may be a viable alternative for someone who has a steady source of income and a reasonably good chance of being able to repay the debts in three to five years. The majority of creditors must agree to the plan, and interest charges, along with late-payment penalties, are waived for the repayment period. Creditors usually will go along with this plan because they stand to lose more in a straight bankruptcy. After the plan is approved, the individual makes periodic payments to the court that in turn are used to pay off the creditors.

Throughout the process, the individual retains the use of, and keeps title to, all of his or her assets.

Straight Bankruptcy. Straight bankruptcy, which is allowed under *Chapter 7* of the bankruptcy code, can be viewed as a legal procedure that results in "wiping the slate clean and starting anew." However, straight bankruptcy does not eliminate all of the debtor's obligations, nor does the debtor necessarily lose all of his or her assets. For example, the debtor must keep up alimony and child-support payments but is allowed to retain certain payments from social security, retirement, veterans', and disability benefits. In addition, the debtor may retain equity in a home (up to $7,500), a car (up to $1,200), and other personal assets, such as clothing, books and tools of his or her trade. These are minimums as established by federal regulations; generally, state laws are much more generous with regard to the amount the debtor is allowed to keep.

Other Bankruptcy Options. While most individual bankruptcies involve either straight liquidations or Wage Earner plans, a couple more options have been added recently. To begin with, the U.S. Supreme Court ruled that individuals can now file for reorganization under *Chapter 11* of the bankruptcy code—a type of bankruptcy which had previously been reserved mostly for businesses. Chapter 11 bankruptcy is for higher-income individuals (those with more than $350,000 in secured debt and more than $100,000 in unsecured loans) who don't qualify for Chapter 13 reorganization but who want to try to restructure their debt. For these people, Chapter 11 is really the only alternative to straight bankruptcy. Like the Wage Earner Plan discussed above, Chapter 11 filers can restructure their debts, or a portion of them, to be repaid over time. The big difference is that in Chapter 11 bankruptcy, the creditors vote on—and can possibly block—the restructuring plan. This, of course, means the reorganization process can drag on for years and involve hefty legal fees. The second alternative now available is a so-called *"Chapter 20"* bankruptcy—its labeled as such because it combines parts of both Chapters 7 and 13. Although not actually a part of the bankruptcy code, this procedure allows individuals to wipe out their unsecured debt, as per Chapter 7,

EXHIBIT 7.7
Finding the Average Daily Balance

The average daily balance method is the procedure most widely used by credit card issuers to determine the monthly finance charge on an account.

Number of Days (1)	Balance (2)	Weighted Balance [(1) × (2)] (3)
11	$182	$2,002
20	157	3,140
Total 31		Total $5,140

$$\text{Average daily balance} = \frac{\$5,142}{31 \text{ days}} = \$165.87$$

($182 − $25 payment) and, when the 1.5 percent interest rate is applied to this balance, the resulting charge would amount to $2.36.

Past-Due Balance Method. Merchants occasionally use the **past-due balance method** in order to motivate customers to fully repay their accounts. Under this method, customers who pay their accounts in full within a specified period of time, such as 30 days from the billing date, are relieved of the finance charge that otherwise would be imposed under one of the three preceding methods. If this method were used with the statement in Exhibit 7.3, the customer would have $2.49 in finance charges waived if payment for the full amount of $232.58 ($235.07 − $2.49) were made prior to a specified date, say, December 10, 1992. A comparison of the interest charges resulting from each of these four methods is given in Exhibit 7.8. Because the finance charge varies with the method used to determine the account balance, the wise consumer determines which procedure is used prior to buying on credit.

ADVANTAGES OF RETAIL CHARGE CARDS

The most significant advantage of retail charge cards is that by charging purchases, customers can delay payment until the end of the billing period. Note, however, that because of the high finance charges levied on balances carried from period to period,

there is no real advantage to delaying payment beyond this point. Some of the advantages of using retail charge cards include the following.

Interest-Free Loans. Carrying charge accounts costs merchants money. Since this is an expense the business must absorb, it will be reflected in the price you pay for their goods or services. Therefore, you might as well get the most from your charge card. You can do that by paying your account in full each month, about a week or two after you receive the bill (just be sure you get your payment in before

previous balance method
A method of computing finance charges by calculating interest on the outstanding balance at the beginning of the billing period.

average daily balance method
A method of computing finance charges by applying interest charges to the average daily balance of the account over the billing period, excluding purchases or returns made during that period.

adjusted balance method
A method of computing finance charges by applying interest charges to the balance remaining at the end of the billing period, excluding purchases or returns made during that period.

past-due balance method
A method of computing finance charges in which interest is charged on any account balance that is not paid in full in the current period.

EXHIBIT 7.8
Finance Charges under Alternative Methods of Determining Account Balances

The amount of finance charges that a cardholder pays depends not only on the rate of interest being charged but also on the method used to determine the account balance.

Method of Determining Balance	Balance (1)	Monthly Interest Rate (2)	Finance Charge [(1) × (2)] (3)
Previous balance	$182.00	1.5%	$2.73
Average daily balance	165.87	1.5	2.49
Adjusted balance	157.00	1.5	2.36
Past-due balance	—[a]	1.5	0.0

[a]The finance charge, which does *not* have to be paid if full payment is remitted by a specified date, would be calculated using one of the other three methods.

the end of the billing period). By doing so, you can avoid finance charges and effectively receive an interest-free loan for up to 30 days, or more.

Recordkeeping, Unsatisfactory Purchases, and Credits.
Store charges provide detailed records of transactions in the form of monthly statements. Because there may be errors in these statements, you should save your receipts and check them against the statement entries before paying. It is also easier to resolve any disagreement over goods or services purchased if you have not yet paid for them. If you charge your purchases, you have approximately 30 days in which to ensure that they are satisfactory; if they are not, you can refuse to pay that amount. In addition, when you purchase an item on credit and later wish to return it, you need only have the store credit your account. Some stores credit your account for returns whether the purchase was charged on the store or a bank charge. In this way, the purchase price can be written off the books and no cash need change hands. Some stores issue *due bills* to compensate customers who return items purchased for cash. Due bills can be used only to make purchases within the store and thus are less advantageous than a simple crediting of the account.

Preferred Customer Status.
Customers who have charge accounts in good standing normally receive preferred customer status, which provides such benefits as notification of forthcoming sales, invitations to special shopping events, and check-

cashing privileges. Although these benefits may be rather limited, many people do find them appealing.

Convenience.
Some people find the use of retail charge cards convenient because they eliminate the need to write a check each time a purchase is made. By charging all transactions during the month, the customer need write only one check to pay each monthly bill. This convenience is a particularly important consideration for people who make a large number of transactions at a given store during the month.

Use in Emergencies.
A final advantage of retail charge cards is that they provide a means for purchasing needed items when sufficient cash is not available. With proper planning and budgeting, the consumer should be able to avoid running short of cash; however, charging a needed item because of a cash shortage may be justifiable in some situations. A tendency to run short of cash on a regular basis, however, signals the need to reevaluate one's budget.

DISADVANTAGES OF RETAIL CHARGE CARDS

The use of retail charge cards has two major disadvantages: (1) They offer the temptation to overspend, and (2) their high interest costs add to the price of the purchase.

Tendency to Overspend.
People who don't use budgets tend to forget that what they charge eventu-

ally must be paid for. The credit card gives them a sense of buying power that may not be supported by actual income. One of the consequences of this type of overspending is a tendency to *avoid* paying the full amount of the bill; since consumers who overspend typically don't make enough money to cover their ever-increasing bills, they make only the minimum payments and thus incur costly finance charges. If overspending is not curtailed, the size of the unpaid balance carried from period to period may become so large that it places a real strain on the budget. Essentially, by letting their credit balances build up, these individuals are *mortgaging their future.* Though it may not seem that way at first, when you use credit, you're committing a part of your future income to service—that is, make payments on—your debt. Unfortunately, the more income that has to go just to make payments on your charge cards (and other forms of consumer credit), the less there is available for other purposes.

High Interest Costs on Unpaid Balances.

The rate of interest charged on unpaid credit card balances is usually *quite high!* The typical 1.5 percent per month represents an 18 percent annual rate; and in a number of states, the APR can go as high as 21 percent (1.75 percent per month), or more. To make matters even worse, the interest paid on these charge cards is no longer tax deductible. Thanks to the Tax Reform Act of 1986 (see Chapter 4), the deductibility of interest charges on most forms of consumer loans (including all types of credit cards) has been *totally* eliminated. But you can avoid these high costs by paying your cards in full each month. In fact, as the accompanying *Smart Money* box points out, paying off your credit card debt is an easy way to earn big returns on your money—even if it means using some of your savings to do so!

BANK CREDIT CARDS AND
OPEN LINES OF CREDIT

Banks and other financial institutions offer several different types of open account credit, including bank credit cards, overdraft protection, unsecured personal lines, and home equity credit lines. Before reading on, give some thought to these forms of credit, and how you might be able to use each of them.

Probably the most popular type of open account credit is the *bank credit card.* These cards are accepted at retail stores and banks worldwide, as well as by state and municipal governments, colleges and universities, medical groups, and mail-order houses, among many others. They can be used to pay for just about anything, from college tuition and income taxes to football tickets, airline tickets, and car rentals. *Visa* and *MasterCard* are the leaders in this field. There are literally thousands of banks, S&Ls, credit unions, brokerage houses, and other financial services institutions that issue Visa and MasterCard; each issuer, within reasonable limits, can set its own credit terms and conditions. And in the past few years, several more big-league players have entered the field. Sears introduced its *Discover* card, American Express its *Optima* card; then AT&T jumped in with its *Universal* card (which is actually nothing more than a special Visa or MasterCard), and now GM has a credit card, too. The remainder of this chapter considers the features and basic uses of bank credit cards. In addition, it looks at *debit cards* as well as several other kinds of *revolving lines of credit,* including overdraft protection, unsecured lines of credit, and home equity credit lines—all of which are available from banks and other financial services institutions.

FEATURES OF BANK CREDIT CARDS

Bank credit cards are similar to retail charge cards except that they are issued by a third party and can be used to borrow money as well as buy on credit. Because of their potential for use in thousands of businesses and banks, they can be of great convenience and value to consumers. Individuals who use them, however, should be thoroughly familiar with their basic features.

Line of Credit. The line of credit provided to the holder of a bank credit card is set by the issuer for

Paying Off Your Credit Cards Can Mean Big Returns

Looking for a sure-fire return on your money; say, about 26% before taxes? It's easy: Just pay off your credit-card debt. The fact is, unless you're a very astute investor, you'll probably find it difficult to match the return you can make from paying off your credit cards!

It's all a simple matter of arithmetic: With the national average interest rate on credit cards at 18.94%, every $100 of debt costs $18.94 a year in interest. To get that amount of money, a person in the 28% tax bracket has to earn $26.30 before taxes (i.e., if 28% goes to taxes, you'll be left with only 72% after taxes; so, to end up with $18.94, you'll need to earn

$26.30 — proof: $26.30 × .72 = $18.94). In order to earn that much from a $100 investment, the person would need a pretax yield of 26.30%. Even if you're only in the 15% tax bracket, the numbers are convincing. That is, since the annual cost of credit is the same regardless of your tax bracket, it's still going to cost you $18.94 a year in interest for every $100 in credit card debt. Thus, you'll need to earn a pretax yield of 22.28%, which is still a pretty hefty rate of return! In this case, since you can keep 85% after taxes, you'll need $22.28 to cover the $18.94 in annual interest payments: i.e., $22.28 × .85 = $18.94.

Now, whether its 26% or 22%,

it should be clear that getting anything like that sort of investment return involves a lot of risks. You certainly won't get it from CDs or long-term corporate bonds. Indeed, you'd be hard pressed to get those kinds of returns, year-in, year-out, even from common stocks. Yet the return from paying off your credit card is a fixed, guaranteed rate. There's no risk involved, and as a result, it's often viewed as an investment that's just too good to pass up.

Paying off auto loans and personal loans also means big returns. Indeed, the math is so compelling that some financial advisers urge people to forgo going into hock in the first

---

each card. It is the maximum amount that the cardholder can owe at any point in time. The size of the credit line depends on both the applicant's request and the results of the issuer's investigation of the applicant's credit and financial status. Lines of credit offered by issuers of bank cards can reach $10,000 or more, but for the most part they range from about $500 to $2,500. While the card issuers fully expect you to keep your credit within the specified limits, most won't take any real action unless you extend your account balance a certain percentage beyond the account's stated maximum. For example, if you had a $500 credit limit, you probably wouldn't hear a thing from the card issuer until your outstanding account balance exceeded $600; that is, 20 percent above the $500 line of credit. On the other hand, don't count on getting off scot-free, for an increasing

number of card issuers are beginning to assess so-called *over-the-limit* fees whenever you go over your credit limit (more on this later).

Cash Advances. In addition to purchasing merchandise and services, the holder of a bank credit card can also obtain a *cash advance* from any participating bank. Cash advances are transacted in the same fashion as merchandise purchases except that they take place at a commercial bank or some other financial institution and involve the receipt of cash (or a check) instead of goods and services. You can even use your credit card to draw cash from an ATM, any time of the day or night. Usually, the size of the cash advance from an ATM is limited to some nominal amount (perhaps $300), though the amount that you can obtain from the teller window at a bank is

place. Whenever possible, they say, *pay cash* — even if it means tapping savings or investment funds. A handy rule of thumb to remember is: *The wider the spread between what you're earning on your savings/investments and what you're paying on your consumer debt, the more sense it makes to pay off those debts.* Thus, if you're paying 18 or 19 percent on a credit card and earning only 5 or 6 percent on a savings account, you'd be far better off, financially, to take the cash from your savings and pay off your credit card.

Of course, all this doesn't mean you should use the last dime in your savings account to pay off consumer debts. Most financial professionals recommend that people maintain a cash reserve fund equal to about three to six months' living expenses. But too often, people who do have the wherewithal to get out of debt simply fail to do so. Paul Richard, vice president of the National Center for Financial Education, a San Diego-based education group, says that in almost every workshop he leads on consumer credit, there are participants whose 5.5% savings accounts are much larger than their 18% credit card balances. "They say savings give them a sense of security." And there's the catch! People like the feeling of security that a nice savings account provides. And up to a point, that makes a lot of sense. Everybody should have emergency funds set aside in some type of savings or investment vehicle; and you should never exhaust these funds to pay off your credit cards and the like. But if you do have some excess funds sitting in a low-yielding savings account, you might want to consider paying off some of your consumer debt. The returns can be compelling!

Source: Adapted from: Georgette Jasen, "Paying Off Credit Card Debt Spells a Hefty Return," *The Wall Street Journal*, November 27, 1989, p. C1.

limited only by the unused credit in your account. Thus, if you've only used $1,000 of a $5,000 credit limit, you can take out a cash advance of up to $4,000.

Interest Rates on Bank Card Charges. With very few exceptions, the *annual* rate of interest charged on bank credit cards ranges from about 14 to 21 percent, irrespective of whether the transaction was a purchase or a cash advance; in fact, in the fall of 1991, the national average was nearly 19 percent (18.94% to be exact). However, in some states these rates may be limited by **usury laws** to something more like 12 to 15 percent, and in some areas the interest rate on merchandise purchases may differ from that on cash advances. Generally speaking, *the interest rates on credit cards are higher than any other form of consumer credit!* But there is a small ray of hope, as more and more banks — even the bigger ones — are beginning to offer more competitive rates, especially to their better customers. Moreover, a growing number of banks are willing to negotiate their fees as a way to retain their customers. How long this continues and how much of an impact it has on reducing interest rates and fees remains to be seen, but at least most consumers would agree it is a step in the right direction!

usury laws

State laws governing interest rates on consumer and other types of credit.

The legal requirements with respect to disclosure of interest costs and related information are no different for bank credit cards than for other forms of consumer credit. In the case of purchases of merchandise and services, the specified interest rate is comparable to rates on store charges and, as with store charges, normally applied only to the unpaid balances carried forward from previous periods. Interest on cash advances, however, begins the day the advance is taken out.

Other Fees. In addition to the interest charged on bank credit cards, there are a few other fees you should be aware of. To begin with, many—though not all—bank cards levy *annual fees* just for the "privilege" of being able to use the card. In most cases, the fee is around $15 to $25 a year, though it can amount to much more for prestige cards. Sometimes, this annual fee will be waived in the first year, but you'll be stuck with it for the second and every other year you hold the card. As a rule, the larger the bank or S&L, the more likely it is to charge an annual fee for one of its credit cards. What's more, many issuers also charge a *transaction fee* for each cash advance; this fee usually amounts to about $2 per cash advance *or* 2 percent of the amount obtained in the transaction, whichever is more.

And now, more and more card issuers are coming up with new ways to sock it to you. The newest twist: late-payment fees and over-the-limit charges. If you're a bit late in making your payment, at some banks you'll be hit with a late-payment fee—which is really a redundant charge since you're already paying interest on the unpaid balance anyway. In a similar fashion, if you happen to go over your credit limit, you'll get hit with a charge for that, too (again, this is on top of the interest you're already paying). Critics really dislike this fee because they maintain it's very difficult for cardholders to know when they've hit their credit ceilings. Regardless of when or why any of these fees are levied, the net effect is that *they add to the true cost of using bank credit cards.*

Other Features. Bank credit cards sure aren't what they used to be! The fact is, credit cards today offer a lot more than just a convenient way of getting credit. Because the market has become so competitive, card issuers have had to offer all sorts of services and features (some would call them "gimmicks") in an attempt to get you to use their cards. One popular feature is the so-called *buyer protection plan*, which automatically protects most items of merchandise purchased with your credit card against loss, theft, or damage for up to 90 days. For example, if the purchased item breaks during the 90-day period, the card issuer will see to it that the item is replaced for free. Many of these plans also include an automatic extension of manufacturer's warranties, up to one additional year. Another feature that's growing in popularity gives cardholders a *1 percent rebate* on all purchases (cash advances are *not* included). In effect, use your credit card to buy $10,000 worth of goods and services during the year, and you earn a $100 rebate. In addition, more and more card issuers are offering their own *frequent flyer programs*, where the cardholder earns free frequent flyer miles for each dollar charged on his or her credit card (these frequent flyer miles can then be used with airline-affiliated programs for free first-class upgrades, and so on).

Here's a list of some of the other services offered:

- High-value travel accident insurance
- Full-value auto rental insurance coverage
- 24-hour toll-free travelers' emergency message service
- Lost card registration
- Discounts on long-distance phone calls
- Price protection plans
- 24-hour toll-free customer service lines

While it is not clear just how valuable these services really are, one thing is sure: They do act to keep interest costs on credit cards very high. Make no mistake about it, one way or another, cardholders will end up paying for all these services!

The Statement. If you use a bank credit card, you will receive monthly statements showing all transactions, payments, account balances, finance charges, available credit, and the minimum payment. A sample bank card statement is shown in Exhibit 7.9; as you can see, it is similar in many respects to the monthly statements you would receive with retail charge cards. Although merchandise and cash advance transactions are separated on this statement, the finance charge in each case is calculated at the rate of 1.75 percent per month (21 percent annually). And note that the average daily balance

EXHIBIT 7.9

A Bank Credit Card Monthly Statement

Each month, a bank credit cardholder receives a statement that provides an itemized list of charges and credits, as well as a summary of previous activity and finance charges.

Please detach the above portion and return it with your payment to insure proper credit.

Bank Card Statement

Retain this statement for your records.

MasterCard **VISA**

Account Number	Name(s)	8-24-92	09-21-92
123•XYZ•45678	Mr. and Mrs. Bill A. Bitshort	Statement Date	Payment Due Date

ACCOUNT ACTIVITY		FINANCE CHARGE CALCULATION					
Previous Balance	203.64	Credit Status	Amounts Subject to Finance Charge		This Month's Charge		
Payments −	119.89	Your Credit Limit is:	A. *Average Daily Balance	293.25 =	5.13	ENTIRE BAL. 1.75% 21.00%	
Credits −	.00						
Subtotal	83.75	2000.00	B. *Cash Advance	.00 =	.00	Monthly Periodic Rate	Nominal Annual Rate
New Transaction +	445.93		C. *Loan Advance	.00 =	.00		
Finance Charge +	5.13	Your Available Credit is:			5.13	21.00%	
Late Charge +	.00						
NEW BALANCE	534.81	1465.19	*Finance Charges explained on reverse side		Finance Charge	Annual Percentage Rate	

Mail Billing Inquiries to: Post Office Box 7760, Van Nuys, California, 85258, or call   800/000-0000
For inquiries on Past Due Accounts, Overlimits or Credit Line Increase, call   800/000-0000

Posted Mo./Day	Transaction Description or Merchant Name and Location		Purchase Mo./Day	Bank Reference Number	Purchases/ Advances/Debits	Payments Credits
8-08	AMERICA WEST AIRLINES	LOS ANGELES	07-25	850000008823395192	42.00	
8-13	HACIENDA MOTORS	COSTA MESA	08-05	015400018537022316	166.86	
8-15	RICOS RESTAURANT	PALM SPRG	08-10	114500018856161722	132.47	
8-12	PAYMENT - THANK YOU		08-11	4501000182MD02139		119.89
8-24	RENEES RESTAURANT	NEWPORT	08-13	114500068201632483	104.60	

Notice See reverse side for important information.

					Total Debits	Total Credits
MIN. PAYMENT: 27.00		**NEW BALANCE:** 534.81			445.93	119.89

Source: Typical bank credit card and monthly statement.

---

method is used to compute the finance charge in this statement. The minimum payment required on this account, as noted on the bottom of the statement, is $27, which is equal to 5 percent of the new balance, rounded to the nearest full dollar: $534.81 × .05 = $26.74 = $27.00. If the new balance had been less than $250, the bank would have required a payment of $10 (which is the absolute minimum *dollar* payment), or of the total new balance, if less than $10.

Payments.   Users of bank credit cards can avoid *future* finance charges by paying the total new balance shown on their statement each month. For example, if the $534.81 total new balance shown in Exhibit 7.9 is paid by the due date of September 21, 1992, no additional finance charges will be incurred (the cardholder, however, will still be liable for the $5.13 in finance charges incurred to date). If cardholders cannot pay the total new balance, they can pay any amount that is equal to or greater than the minimum payment specified on the statement. They will, however, incur additional finance charges in the following month. Cardholders who fail to make the minimum payment are considered in default on their account, and the bank issuing the card can take whatever action it deems necessary.

Returning Merchandise. When you return merchandise purchased with a bank credit card, the merchant will issue a *credit* to your account. The credit is transacted in the same fashion as a purchase and will appear on your statement as a *deduction* from the balance. If you purchase an item and have problems with it, you may not have to pay that part of your credit card bill if you have attempted in good faith to resolve the problem with the merchant. This protection is provided by the Fair Credit Billing Act. Of course, if the problem is resolved in the merchant's favor, you will ultimately have to pay.

THE EFFECTIVE USE OF BANK CREDIT CARDS

Much like charge cards, bank credit cards can simplify your life, financially, if they are used properly. They have the same basic advantages and disadvantages as do retail charge cards.

Interest-Free Loans. Like retail charge cards, many bank credit cards provide short-term, interest-free loans on the purchase of goods or services. Known as **grace periods**, they generally cover a 25- to 30-day period of time during which you can pay your bill in full and not incur any interest charges (note that such grace periods do not apply to cash advances). Unfortunately, while most banks still offer grace periods, the trend is to shorten or eliminate such provisions. In addition, a growing number of card issuers are including purchases made during the current period when computing average daily balances. As a rule, bank credit cards should be used primarily to charge merchandise and services, and then monthly statements should be paid in full to

avoid any finance charges. If the card issuer does not offer a grace period, or includes current purchases in the average daily balance, the card should be used only in financial emergencies, since interest would be charged beginning at the time of the transaction. Use of the card for any other purpose (such as for cash advances) signals poor personal financial management.

Shop Around for the Best Deal. They say it pays to shop around, and when it comes to credit cards, that adage certainly applies. With all the fees and high interest costs, it pays to get the best deal possible. So, where do you start? Most credit experts suggest the first thing you should do is step back and take a look at yourself. What kind of "spender" are you, and how do you pay your bills? The fact is, no single credit card is right for everyone. If you pay off your card balance each month, you'll want a card that's different from the one that's best for someone who carries a credit balance from month to month, and may only pay the minimum due.

Regardless of which category you fall into, there are basically three card features to look for:

- Annual fees
- Rate of interest charged on account balance
- Length of the grace period

Now, if you normally pay your account balance in full each month, get a card with *no annual fees and a long grace period*. The rate of interest on the card is really irrelevant, since you don't carry account balances from month to month anyway.

In sharp contrast, if you don't pay your account in full, then look for cards that charge *a low rate of interest on unpaid balances*. The length of the grace period isn't all that important here, but obviously, other things being equal, you're better off with low (or no) annual fees. Sometimes, however, "other things aren't equal," in which case you have to decide between interest rates and annual fees. If you're not a big spender and don't build up big balances on your credit card (i.e., the card balance rarely goes above $400 or $500), then *avoid* cards with annual fees and get one with as *low* a rate of interest as possible. (*Note:* The above situation would probably apply to most college students — or at least it should.) On the other hand, if you do carry big balances (say, $1,000 or more), then you'll probably be better off *paying an annual fee* (even a relatively high one) *to keep the rate of interest on the card as low as possible*. For example, your total yearly finance charges (including annual fees) will likely be *less* with a card that has, say, a $50 annual fee and an interest rate of 15 percent than one which has no annual fee but charges a higher (19 percent) rate of interest.

The bottom line is don't just take the first credit card that comes along. Instead, get the one that's right for you. To do that, call around to the various banks and financial institutions (that is, S&Ls and credit unions) in your area to get information about the credit terms on their cards — be sure to ask about annual fees, grace periods, and interest rates. Also, if the local deals aren't all that great, you might want to consider cards that are offered nationally. Many banks market their cards throughout the United States, and it may pay to check them out. To help you do that, look to publications like *Money* magazine and *The Wall Street Journal*. They regularly publish information about banks and other financial institutions that offer low-cost credit cards nationally, an example of which is provided in Exhibit 7.10.

The best credit card for someone who does not pay their account balance in full each month is one that has a high interest rate but no annual fees.
Fantasy: If you normally carry fairly *small* balances on your account (i.e., the card balance is usually $500, or less), then *avoid* cards with annual fees and get one with a *low* rate of interest; on the other hand, if you normally carry fairly *large* balances (say, $1,000 or more), then you'd probably be better off *paying an annual fee* to keep the rate of interest on the card as *low* as possible.

Consolidated Statement of Expenses.

While bank credit cards offer their users obvious conveniences, probably the most valid reason for using them is to consolidate records of purchases. No matter how many and varied the stores at which bank credit card transactions occur, the consumer receives only one statement that records them all. This greatly simplifies the record-keeping process. And it makes bill paying a lot easier, since only one check needs to be written to pay for all the different transactions.

DEBIT CARDS

It looks like a credit card, it spends like a credit card, it even has the familiar MasterCard and Visa credit card markings. But it's not a *credit* card — rather, it is a *debit* card! Simply put, a **debit card** provides direct access to your checking account and, as such, *works like writing a check*. For example, when you use a debit card to make a purchase, the amount of the transaction is charged directly to your checking account. Thus, using a debit card is not the same thing as buying on credit; it may appear that you are charging, but actually you are paying with cash. Accordingly, there are no finance charges to pay and normally, there are no annual fees.

Debit cards are as convenient as credit cards (they are accepted at any establishment displaying the Visa or MasterCard logo), but they function as an alternative to writing checks. If you use a debit card to make a purchase at a department store or restaurant, the transaction will show up on your next monthly *checking account* statement. Needless to say, to keep your records straight, you should enter debit card transactions directly onto your checkbook ledger as they occur and treat them as withdrawals, or checks, by subtracting them from your checking account balance. Debit cards can also be used to gain access to your account through 24-hour teller machines or ATMs — which is the closest thing to a cash advance that these cards have to offer.

The big disadvantage of a debit card, of course, is that it does not provide a line of credit. In addition, it can cause overdraft problems if you fail to make the proper entries to your checking account or inadvertently use it when you think you are using a credit card. On the plus side, a debit card does not carry with it the potential credit problems and high costs that credit cards do. Further, it is every bit as convenient to use as a credit card — in fact, if convenience

---

grace period
A short period of time, usually 25 to 30 days, during which you can pay your credit card bill in full and not incur any interest charges.

debit card
A card used to make transactions for *cash* rather than credit; replaces the need for cash or checks by initiating charges against one's *checking* account.

EXHIBIT 7.10

Published Information about Bank Credit Card Terms

Information about low-cost credit cards is readily available in the financial media. Here's an example of what you can find in the *Wall Street Journal*. Notice the *Journal* separates the information it reports into three categories: (1) cards offered nationally with the lowest interest rates; (2) cards offered nationally without any annual fees; and (3) the most common credit terms offered by the ten largest issuers (which serves as a handy benchmark for comparing terms).

Bank Credit Card Interest Rates

August 1992

● **Banks or savings institutions with low interest rates offering bank credit cards nationally.** Rates shown are for regular, not premium cards. Though not listed, some cards may be through affiliate or agent banks. Temporary or promotional interest rates are excluded. Grace period (interest free period for cardholders paying purchase balance in full each month) is calculated from the date of billing unless footnoted.

Bank / Location	Int. Rate	Annual Fee	Grace Days
Chas Givens, Altamonte Sp, FL	v7.75%	37.50$	25
Arkansas Federal, Little Rock	v8.00	35.00	z0
Wachovia Bank, Wilmington	v8.90	39.00	25
Oak Brook Bk, Oak Brook, IL	v10.40	20.00	25
Bank of NY, Newark, DE	v11.40	0.00	x0
Union Priv./Bk NY, Washn DC	v11.50	0.00	x0
People's Bk, Bridgeport, CT	c11.50	25.00	25
Bank Montana, Gt Falls, MT	v11.75	19.00	25
Oak Brook Bk, Oak Brook, IL	v11.90	0.00	25
Bank One Cleveland, Cleveland	v12.30	20.00	25
AFBA Industrial, Alexandria, VA	v12.50	0.00	25
Amalgamated Trust, Chicago	v12.50	0.00	25
USAA Fed Savings, Tulsa	v12.50	0.00	25
Bank One Wisconsin, Milwaukee	c13.90	25.00	25
First American, McLean, VA	v14.00	20.00	25
Ohio Savings Bank, Cleveland	14.75	25.00	25
Centurion Bk/Amex, Newark, DE	vc14.75	25.00	25
Oak Brook Bk, Oak Brook, IL	14.90	20.00	25
Fst Natl Omaha, Omaha, NE	v14.90	20.00	25
Wachovia Bank, Wilmington, DE	14.98	25.00	28
Norwest Bank, Minneapolis	v15.00	20.00	25
First Signature, Portsmouth, NH	v15.08	20.00	25
Union Planters, Memphis	v15.25	0.00	z0
Union Planters, Memphis	v15.25	20.00	25
Primerica Bank, Newark, DE	v15.45	15.00	25

● **Banks offering credit cards nationally with no annual fee.**

Bank / Location	Interest Rate Structure	Grace Days
Union Priv/Bk NY, Washington, DC	Prime + 5.0%	x0
Bank of NY, Newark, DE	Prime + 5.4%	x0
Oak Brook Bk, Oak Brook, IL	Prime + 5.9%	25
AFBA Industrial, Alexandria, VA	Prm + 5;12.5% min	25
Amalgamated Trust, Chicago	Prime + 6.0%	25
USAA Fed Savings, Tulsa	26 wk TB + 7%	25
Union Planters, Memphis	Prm + 5.75%; 15.25% min	z0
Wachovia Bank, Wilmington	Prime + 9.9%	25
Abbott Bank, Alliance, NE	T.T.I.A. − 3%	25
Oak Brook Bk, Oak Brook, IL	16.90% fixed	25

● **Interest rates offered by the ten largest U.S. issuers.**

Bank	Int. Rate	Annual Fee Regular	Annual Fee Premium	Grace Days
Citicorp	s19.80%	$20.00	$50.00	. . . .
Grnwood Tr/Dscvr	19.80	0.00	40.00	25
Chase Manhattan	s19.80	20.00	50.00	30
Bank of America	s19.80	18.00	36.00	25
MBNA America	s18.90	20.00	40.00	25
First Chicago	s19.80	20.00	20.00	25
Chemical	s17.80	20.00	45.00	25
Centurion Bk/Opt	vc14.75	15.00	NA	25
Banc One	s19.80	20.00	40.00	25
Household Bank	s18.90	20.00	25.00	25

c-Higher rate charged for cash advances. d-Security deposit required. e-Estimated amount, actual fees not disclosed. r-Relationship required. s-Special lower rate available on some cards. t-Tiered (or lower) rates based on account balance. u-Monthly user fee applies. v-Variable rate. w-Fee waived under special conditions. x-Interest charged from date of purchase. z-Interest charged from date of posting.

CP-High grade commercial paper rate. Prime-Prime rate. QA-Quarterly average. TB-Treasury Bill rate. TTIA-Top Ten Issuers Average.

Source: *Wall Street Journal*, August 10, 1992.

---

is the major reason you use a credit card, you might want to consider switching to a debit card for at least some transactions, especially at outlets such as gas stations that give discounts for cash purchases and consider a debit card to be as good as cash.

OTHER KINDS OF CREDIT LINES

While the use of "plastic" is widespread throughout our economy, there are other forms of revolving credit available to consumers. These are often a far better deal than credit cards, not only because they offer more credit but also because they can be a lot less expensive; and, according to the latest tax laws, there may even be a tax advantage to using one of these other kinds of credit! These lines basically provide their users with ready access to borrowed money (that is, cash advances) through revolving lines of credit. They are every bit as convenient as credit cards, since access is gained by simply writing a check. The three major forms of open (non–credit card) credit are: overdraft protection lines, unsecured personal lines of credit, and home equity credit lines.

Overdraft Protection. An **overdraft protection line** is simply a line of credit linked to a checking account that enables a depositor to overdraw his or her checking account up to a predetermined limit. These lines are usually set up with credit limits of $500 to $1,000, but they can be for as much as $10,000 or more. The consumer taps this line of credit by simply writing a check. If this check happens to overdraw the account, the overdraft protection line will automatically advance funds in an amount necessary to put the account back in the black. In some cases, overdraft protection is provided by *linking the bank's credit card to your checking account*. These arrangements act just like regular overdraft lines, except when the account is overdrawn, the bank automatically taps your credit card line and transfers the money into your checking account. It's treated as a cash advance from your credit card, but the end result is still the same as a regular overdraft protection line: it automatically covers overdrawn checks.

Unfortunately, you never know for sure just how much a given check will overdraw your account (if in fact it does). The reason is that unless you write very few checks, the balance shown on your checkbook ledger will seldom be the same as the amount shown by the bank. The way to handle this is to simply record the check in your checkbook ledger as you normally would, including the new balance after the check is written. If this overdraws your account—at least as far as your checkbook ledger is concerned—this will not be a problem, since you have an overdraft protection line to cover it. If it does in fact overdraw your acount, the bank will notify you of this in a matter of days and inform you that it has advanced funds to your checking account. The amount of the advance will be shown on the notice and should immediately be entered into your checkbook ledger as a *deposit*.

Funds advanced from an overdraft protection line usually carry an interest rate of 12 to 15 percent, though rates as high as 18 to 20 percent are not all that uncommon. Once an advance is made, a monthly repayment schedule is set up for systematically repaying the loan, along with all interest charges—generally with monthly payments being spread out over a period of 18 to 36 months. A statement is sent out each month, along with the monthly check statement, summarizing any activity in the overdraft protection line (new advances, repayments, new balance, and amount of credit still available) and indicating the required monthly payment. Note that since there ordinarily is no limit on the number of times you can overdraw your account, the amount of the monthly payment will change every time the bank advances money to your account.

It should be clear that if you are not careful, you can quickly exhaust this line of credit by writing a lot of overdraft checks. As with any line of credit, there is a limit to how much you can obtain. You should be extremely careful with such a credit line and under no circumstances take it as a license to routinely overdraw your account! If you are doing so on a regular basis, you should take this as a signal that you are probably mismanaging your cash and/or living beyond your budget. It is best to view an overdraft protection line strictly as an *emergency* source of credit—and any funds advanced should be repaid as quickly as possible.

Unsecured Personal Lines. Another form of revolving credit is the **unsecured personal credit line**, which basically makes a line of credit available to an individual on an as-needed basis. In essense, it is a way of borrowing money from a bank, S&L, credit union, savings bank, or brokerage firm any time you wish, without going through all the hassle of setting up a new loan. Here is how it works. Suppose you apply for a personal line of credit at your bank. Of course, you will have to submit a loan application to obtain the credit line, but once you have

---

overdraft protection line
A line of credit linked to a checking account that allows a depositor to overdraw the account up to a specified amount.

unsecured personal credit line
A line of credit that is made available to an individual on an as-needed basis in the form of check-writing privileges against it.

been approved and the credit line established, you will be issued *checks* that you can write against it. Thus, if you need a cash advance, all you need to do is write a check (against your credit line account) and deposit it into your checking account. Alternatively, if you need the money to buy some high-ticket item — say, an expensive stereo system — you can just make the credit line check out to the dealer and, when it clears, it will be charged against your unsecured personal credit line as an advance. (These credit line checks look and "spend" just like regular checks and as such do not have to be channeled through your normal checking account.)

Personal lines of credit are usually set up for minimums of $2,000 to $5,000 and often amount to $25,000 or more. As with an overdraft protection line, once an advance is made, repayment is set up on a monthly installment basis. Depending on the amount outstanding, repayment is normally structured over a period of two to five years; to keep the monthly payments low, larger amounts of debt are usually given longer repayment periods. As a rule, these credit lines are set up with adjustable rates of interest so that the interest charged on advances varies with some benchmark rate, such as the prime rate — normally floating 2 to 4 percentage points above the prime/benchmark rate. Thus, if the *prime rate*, which is the interest rate banks charge to their most creditworthy customers, goes up (or down) by, say, 1 percent, the cost of the credit line will also go up (or down) by the same 1 percent. Monthly statements are sent out that summarize the activity in the credit line and stipulate the required minimum monthly payment.

While these credit lines do offer attractive terms to the consumer, they do not come without their share of problems, perhaps the biggest of which is the ease with which cash advances can be obtained. In addition, these lines normally involve *substantial* credit limits and are about as easy to use as credit cards. This combination can have devastating effects on a family's budget if it leads to overspending or excessive reliance on credit. To be safe, these lines should be used only for emergency purposes or to make *planned credit expenditures*. In addition, systematic repayment on the debt should be built into the budget and every effort should be made to ensure that the use of this kind of credit will not place undue strain on the family finances.

You use a check rather than a credit card to obtain funds from an unsecured personal line of credit. *Fact:* Credit cards are not issued with unsecured personal credit lines; instead, if you want to borrow money through such a line, you do it by simply writing a check directly against it.

Home Equity Credit Lines. Here is a familiar situation. A couple buys a home for $75,000; some 15 years later, it is worth twice that much. The couple now has an asset worth $150,000 on which all they owe is the original mortgage, which may now have a balance of, say $50,000. The couple clearly has built up a substantial amount of equity in their home — $150,000 − $50,000 = $100,000! The problem is how can they tap that equity without having to sell their home? The answer is to obtain a **home equity credit line**. Such lines are much like unsecured personal credit lines except that they are *secured* with a second mortgage on the home. Offered by most banks, S&Ls, major brokerage firms, and a growing number of credit unions, these lines of credit allow you to tap up to 100 percent of the equity in your home by merely writing a check.

While there are banks and financial institutions that do allow their customers to borrow up to 100 percent of the *equity* in their homes, the majority of the lenders set their maximum credit lines at 75 to 80 percent of the *market value* of the home, which sharply reduces the amount of money they'll lend. Here's how these lines work. The above couple has built up an equity of $100,000 in their home — equity against which they can borrow through a home equity credit line. Assuming they have a good credit record and using a 75 percent loan-to-market-value ratio, a bank would be willing to lend up to $112,500; that is, 75 percent of the value of the house is .75 × $150,000 = $112,500. Subtracting the $50,000 still due on the first mortgage, we see that our couple could qualify for a home equity credit line of a whopping $62,500. Note, in this case, that if the bank had been willing to lend the couple *100 percent of the equity* in their home, it would have given them a (much higher) credit line of $100,000, which is the difference between what the house is worth and what they still owe on it. Most lenders don't like to do this because it results in very large credit lines and, perhaps more important, it doesn't provide the lender with any cushion.

Home equity lines also have an interesting tax feature that you should be aware of—the annual interest charges on such lines may be fully deductible for those who itemize. This is the only type of consumer loan that still qualifies for such a tax treatment. In particular, according to the latest provisions of the tax code, a homeowner is allowed to *fully deduct the interest charges on home equity loans of up to $100,000*, regardless of the original cost of the house or use of the proceeds. Indeed, the only restriction is that the amount of total indebtedness on the house cannot exceed its fair market value—which is highly unlikely, since homeowners usually cannot borrow more than 75 to 80 percent of the market value of the house anyway. Thus, in our preceding example, the homeowners could take out the full amount of their credit line ($62,500), and every dime that they paid in interest would be tax deductible. If they paid, say, $7,500 in interest, and if they were in the 28 percent tax bracket, this feature would reduce their tax liability by some $2,100—($7,500 × .28)—given, of course, that they itemize their deductions.

Not only do home equity credit lines offer shelter from taxes, they're also among *the cheapest forms of consumer credit*. That is, while other types of consumer credit may cost 15 to 18 percent, or more, home equity lines can be had for 10 to 12 percent (these were representative rates in early 1992). To see what that can mean to you as a borrower, assume you have $10,000 in consumer debt outstanding. If you had borrowed that money through a standard consumer loan at, say, 16.5 percent, you'd pay interest of $1,650 per year—none of which would be tax deductible. But borrow the same amount through a home equity credit line at, say, 11 percent, and you'll pay only $1,100 in interest. That's all tax deductible though, so if you're in the 28 percent tax bracket, the after-tax cost to you would be $1,100 × (1 −.28) = $792. This is less than half the cost of the other loan. Which would you rather pay for a $10,000 loan, $1,650 or $792? That's really not a tough decision; but it does explain, in large part, why these lines have become so popular and are today the fastest-growing form of consumer credit.

A home equity credit line may involve an extensive credit application process, including an appraisal of the property. In addition, there'll probably be some *closing costs* to pay when the line is set up

(such closing costs are usually much lower than those on first mortgages, but they still can easily amount to $300 or $400, or more). It's not unusual, however, for lenders in highly competitive markets to offer home equity lines with *no fees* whatsoever. In essence, the lenders waive all appraisal fees, title insurance costs, and the like; thus, there are no closing costs on these lines. Once the credit line is set up, the homeowner receives a book of checks that can be used to obtain funds just like the checks used with unsecured personal lines. Repayment terms are flexible, with most lenders charging adjustable rates of interest and giving the borrower 10 to 15 years to repay. Monthly statements are sent out that recap the activity in the account and indicate the size of the monthly payment.

Exhibit 7.11 provides a sample of various home equity credit lines offered by a variety of financial institutions. What is perhaps most startling is the maximum amount of credit available under these lines. Note that $100,000 figures are not at all unusual. And it's precisely because of the enormous amount of money available that this form of credit should be used with caution. *The fact that you have the equity in your home does not mean that you have the cash flow necessary to service the debt that such a credit line imposes.* At the minimum, major expenditures should be made only after you have determined that you can afford the purchase and that the required monthly payments will fit comfortably within your budget. Also, if there are normal closing costs involved, don't even think about setting up a home equity line unless you've decided to actually use it—otherwise, it is too expensive to just have as a form of emergency credit.

Perhaps the biggest problem with this type of credit is the temptation to use the long-term repayment schedule that this type of credit offers to keep payments *artificially* low and, in so doing, purchase items whose lives will be nowhere near as long as that of the associated debt. For example, to use a 15-year second mortgage to buy a car with a 5-year life

---

home equity credit line

A line of credit issued against the existing equity in a home.

EXHIBIT 7.11

Comparative Home Equity Credit Line Terms

Home equity credit lines are offered by a number of different types of financial services institutions, involve relatively large credit limits, and normally have rather generous repayment terms.

Home Equity Credit Line Product	Minimum/ Maximum Credit Line	Maximum Percent of Equity Lent	Interest Rate Formula	Minimum Advances	Repayment Terms	Minimum Monthly Payments
Bank of America Home Equity Credit Line	$10,000/ $150,000	75%	One-month secondary market CD + 4.25%	$300	10 years interest only, then becomes 15-year amortized loan	Interest only
Beneficial Home Equity Credit Line	$12,000/ $50,000	70%	Prime + 4%	None	In full in 15 years	Recalculated on balance
Citibank Equity Source Account	$10,000/ none	75%	Prime + 1.25%, or prime + 2%, or prime + 2.5%, depending on origination fee	None	10 years interest only, then becomes 20-year amortized loan	Interest only for 10 years
Dean Witter Sears Home Equity Line	Varies by state/none	70%	Prime + 2%	None	In full in 5 years	Interest only
First Nationwide Bank Equity Reserve Account	$10,000/ $300,000	80%	Prime + 1.7%	$500	In full in 15 years	Interest only
Merrill Lynch Equity Access	$15,000/ $2 million	80%	Up to $50,000, prime + 2%; more than $100,000, prime + 1.5%	None	In full in 10 years	Interest only
Wells Fargo Bank Equity Line	$10,000/ $2 million	80% if mortgage is with Wells Fargo; 75% if not	One-month CD + 3.6%	None	12 years interest only, then becomes 12-year amortized loan	Interest only

makes absolutely no sense! You will still be paying for the car 10 years after you have sold it. The fact is that if the only way you can afford the car is to buy it with 15 years of payments, you cannot afford it in the first place. Home equity credit lines can be an effective way of tapping the built-up equity in a home, but you should avoid using them to buy items you could not otherwise afford.

SUMMARY

- Families and individuals use credit as a way to pay for relatively expensive purchases and occasionally, to deal with a financial emergency; in addition, consumer credit is being used increasingly simply because it is so convenient. Finally, it is also used to partially finance the purchase of various types of investments.

- Unfortunately, while there are some definite positive aspects to the use of consumer credit, there are also some negatives, the most important being that it can be misused to the point where people live beyond their means by purchasing goods and services they simply can't afford. Such overspending can get so bad that it eventually leads to bankruptcy.

■ Open account credit is one of the most popular forms of consumer credit; it is available from various types of financial institutions, as well as all sorts of retail stores and merchants. The major types of open account credit include 30-day charge accounts, retail charge cards, bank credit cards, travel and entertainment cards, and various forms of revolving lines of credit.

■ Most types of open account credit require formal application, which generally involves an extensive investigation of your credit background and an evaluation of your creditworthiness. You, as a borrower, have certain rights when you apply for and obtain consumer credit; such consumer credit protection is mandated by legislation and covers such things as credit discrimination, full disclosure (truth in lending), loss of credit cards, and your recourse on unsatisfactory purchases.

■ The amount of finance charges, if any, due on consumer credit depends in large part on the technique used to compute the account balance, of which there are four in use today: the previous balance method, the average daily balance method, the adjusted balance method, and the past due balance method.

■ Although credit cards account for a significant portion of consumer transactions, there are some other forms of revolving credit that consumers should be aware of; while you can use credit cards for merchandise transactions and/or cash advances, revolving lines of credit provide their users with ready access to borrowed money (by simply writing checks). Basically, there are three types of revolving credit lines: overdraft protection lines, unsecured personal lines of credit, and home equity credit lines.

QUESTIONS AND PROBLEMS

1. Why do people borrow? What are some of the improper uses of credit? Are there any dangers associated with borrowing? Explain.

2. What steps can you take to establish a good credit rating? What extra steps might be necessary for a woman?

3. Joel Stern has a monthly take-home pay of $1,200; he makes payments of $250 a month on his outstanding consumer credit (excluding the mortgage on his home). How would you characterize Joel's debt burden? What if his take-home pay were $850 a month and he had monthly credit payments of $90?

4. What is open account credit? Explain the workings of (a) a 30-day charge account and (b) a retail charge card.

5. Distinguish between bank credit cards and travel and entertainment cards. Give examples of each. What's a secured credit card and how does it differ from a prestige card?

6. Briefly describe the basic steps involved in opening a charge account; provide your answer from the customer's point of view. Describe credit scoring and explain how it's used (by lenders) in making a credit decision.

7. Describe the basic operations and functions of a credit bureau. What kind of information do they gather about you? Is there anything you can do if the information they have on file is wrong?

8. How does recent consumer credit legislation relate to (a) credit discrimination, (b) disclosure of credit information, (c) disclosure of finance charges, (d) loss of credit card, (e) recourse on unsatisfactory purchases, (f) protection against collector harassment, and (g) credit card renewal notices?

9. What are the provisions of the Fair Credit Billing Act of 1975 with respect to mailing, error complaints, and cash discounts on bills?

10. What's the biggest source of credit card fraud? List at least five things that you can do to reduce your chances of being a victim of credit card fraud.

11. Explain the conditions that might make bankruptcy necessary. Distinguish between a Wage Earner Plan and straight bankruptcy.

12. Describe the four methods used to compute finance charges. Sally Rivera is a student at City Community College, and has a balance of $380 on her retail charge card; if the store levies a finance charge of 21 percent per annum, how much monthly interest will be added to her account?

13. What are the advantages of using retail charge cards? What are the disadvantages?

14. What is a line of credit? Explain. Does a line of credit come with all types of credit cards?

15. Explain how you could use your credit card to obtain a cash advance. Does it make any difference whether you obtain the cash advance from an ATM or the bank's teller window?

16. What's the typical rate of interest charged on bank credit cards, and how are interest charges usually computed? As far as interest charges are concerned, does it make any difference whether you use your credit card to purchase merchandise or obtain a cash advance? What, if any, are the legal requirements with respect to disclosure of interest rates?

17. In addition to interest rates, many bank card issuers also impose different types of fees; briefly describe three of these fees. Do these fees have any impact on the true (effective) cost of using credit cards? Explain.

18. Many bank cards today come with a variety of services and features, like buyer protection plans. List and briefly describe some of the more popular services and features that are now being offered on bank credit cards.

19. One of the key features of bank credit cards is the monthly statement. What does this statement disclose? Why are merchandise and cash-advance transactions often separated?

20. Comment on the following statement: "If used intelligently, bank credit cards can be quite useful."

21. Briefly explain why it pays to shop around for a credit card. What kind of credit terms would you look for if you normally paid off your credit card balance each month? How about if you normally ran a fairly high credit balance (say, $1,000, or more) from month to month? Explain.

22. What is a debit card? How is it similar to a credit card? How does it differ?

23. Mary Maffeo has an overdraft protection line. Explain how she would obtain an advance from this line of credit. Assume that her October 1992 statement showed a latest (new) balance of $862. If the line had a minimum monthly payment requirement of 5 percent of the latest balance (rounded to the nearest $5 figure), what would be the minimum amount she would have to pay on her overdraft protection line?

24. Describe the basic features of a home equity credit line. Don and Judy Summers have a home with an appraised value of $180,000 and a mortgage balance of only $90,000. Given that an S&L is willing to lend money at a loan-to-value ratio of 75 percent, how big a home equity credit line can Don and Judy obtain? How much, if any, of this line would qualify as tax deductible interest if their house originally cost $100,000?

CONTEMPORARY CASE APPLICATIONS

7.1 The Dunnermans Seek Some Credit Card Information

Warren and Patricia Dunnerman are a newly married couple in their mid-20s. Warren is a senior at a state university and will graduate in the summer of 1993. Patricia graduated last spring with a degree in marketing and recently started working as a sales rep for the Alhambra Corporation. She supports both of them on her monthly salary of $1,500 after taxes. At present, the Dunnermans pay all of their expenses by cash or check. They would, however, like to use a bank credit card for some of their transactions. Because neither Warren nor Patricia is familiar with how to go about applying for a credit card, they approach you for help.

Questions

1. Advise the Dunnermans on how they should go about filling out a credit application.

2. Explain to them the procedure that the bank will probably follow in processing their application.

3. Tell them about credit scoring, and how the bank will arrive at a credit decision.

4. What kind of advice would you offer the Dunnermans on the "correct" use of their card? What would you tell them about building a strong credit record?

7.2 Nancy Starts Over after Bankruptcy

A year after declaring bankruptcy, and moving with her daughter back into her parents' home, Nancy Singh is about to get a degree in nursing. As she starts out on a new career, she also wants to start a new life — one built on a solid financial base. Nancy will be starting out as a full-time nurse at a salary of $31,000 a year, and plans to continue working at a second (part-time) nursing job at an annual income of $15,500. She will be paying back $24,000 in bankruptcy debts and wants to be able to move into an apartment within a year, then buy a condo or house in five years.

Nancy will not have to pay rent for the time she lives with her parents. And, she will have child care at no cost, which will continue after she and her daughter are able to move out on their own. While the living arrangement with her parents is great financially, the accommodations are "tight," and Nancy's work hours interferes with her parents' routines. Everyone agrees that one more year of this is about all the family feels it can take. However, before Nancy is able to make a move, even into a rented apartment, she will have to reestablish credit over and above paying off her bankruptcy debts. In order to rent the kind of place she'd like, she will need to have a good credit record for a year. In order to buy a home, she will need to sustain that credit standing for at least three to five years.

Questions

1. In addition to opening checking and savings accounts, what else might Nancy do to begin establishing credit with a bank?
2. While Nancy is unlikely to be able to obtain a major bank credit card for at least a year, how might she begin establishing credit with local merchants?
3. What's one way she might be able to obtain a bank credit card? Explain.
4. How often should Nancy monitor her credit standing with credit reporting services, like TRW?
5. What general advice would you offer with regard to getting Nancy back on track to a new life financially?

FOR MORE INFORMATION

General Information Articles

Bodnar, Janet and Kevin McCormally. "Living Debt-Free." *Kiplinger's Personal Finance Magazine*, May 1992, pp. 38–43.

Davis, Kristin. "Bankruptcy: The 10-Year Mistake." *Kiplinger's Personal Finance Magazine*, October 1991, pp. 89–92.

———. "Credit Bureaus: Will They Get It Right?" *Kiplinger's Personal Finance Magazine*, March 1992, pp. 82–85.

Pae, Peter. "Watch for 'Traps' on Lower Card Rates." *The Wall Street Journal*, February 21, 1992, pp. C1; 10.

Saville, Anita. "The Borrower's Guide to Home Equity Loans." *Investment Vision*, September/October 1989, pp. 22–25.

Tritch, Teresa. "Smart Moves to Make with Your Credit Cards." *Money*, April 1991, pp. 126–135.

Trotsky, Judith. "How to Find the Best Home Equity Loan." *Changing Times*, November 1989, pp. 37–42.

Government Documents and Other Publications

Home Equity Credit Lines. FTC Publications; Federal Trade Commission; Sixth St. and Pennsylvania Ave., N.W.; Washington, D.C. 20580.

Some General Information About Bankruptcy. Administrative Office of the U.S. Courts; Bankruptcy Division; Washington, D.C. 20544.

Understanding Credit Bureaus. Bankcard Holders of America; 460 Spring Park Place, Suite 1000; Herndon, VA 22070.

What Truth in Lending Means to You. FTC Publications; Federal Trade Commission; Sixth St. and Pennsylvania Ave., N.W.; Washington, D.C. 20580.

GETTING A HANDLE ON YOUR FINANCIAL FUTURE

The proper use of consumer credit can provide you with the ability to achieve your financial goals without jeopardizing your cash budget. Among the major reasons for borrowing are (1) to finance purchases requiring large outlay of funds, (2) to provide for funds during a financial emergency, (3) for convenience in transactions, and (4) for investment purposes. The use of debt is not without its disadvantages, however. Easy credit can lead to impulse purchases, high interest charges, and, if payments are not made on time, a poor credit rating. Remember that while credit will increase your purchasing power, it does not increase your ability to pay your bills. Credit is not an increase in income.

Opening a credit account usually involves the following steps. First of all you must submit a credit application that looks at your character, capacity, and capital. Second, the lender will perform a credit investigation on you. Finally, the credit decision will be made based on an analysis of the information provided.

Open accounts are subject to federal laws that provide for equal credit opportunity and fair credit reporting, billing, and collections. In addition, lenders are required to disclose the annual percentage rate (APR) in the credit contract. However, this does not mean that all lenders compute finance charges using the same methods. Some use the pre-

---

If You Are Just Starting Out

One of the most important things you can do when you are just starting out is to establish your credit. This can be accomplished initially by opening a checking and savings account and applying for a retail credit card. You might want to apply for a small loan — even if you don't need the money — in order to establish a payment history. Even while you are in school, you may qualify for a credit card from a financial institution.

In determining how much credit is appropriate, you should consider use of the debt service ratio. You should normally keep your monthly debt repayment to no more than 20 percent (preferably less) of your monthly take-home pay, exclusive of mortgage payments. These payments like others should be included in your cash budget as discussed in Chapter 3.

Establishing Credit:

1. Don't write bad checks. Be sure to reconcile your statement as discussed in Chapter 5.

2. If you are married, establish credit in your own name as well as jointly with your spouse.

3. Read the credit agreement carefully so that you understand all of the terms and conditions. Do not rely on what someone tells you.

4. Avoid using firms that guarantee for a fee that they will get you a credit card regardless of your financial or credit history without thoroughly investigating what it is they are providing.

5. Pay off balances early if possible.

Managing Your Credit:

1. Review your credit report prior to applying for a major loan to give yourself the opportunity to correct any errors.

2. Keep a list of your credit cards and their numbers so that you can report any lost or stolen cards immediately.

3. If you pay the entire balance monthly, shop for a credit card with no annual fee.

4. If you are going to pay over time, shop for a credit card with a low interest rate.

5. Be sure you understand the method of calculating interest on unpaid balances. It does make a difference in the amount of interest you pay.

vious balance method; others the average daily balance, or the adjusted balance methods. Some calculate interest only on the amount past due.

There are many different types of open account credit offered to consumers by financial institutions and retail stores/merchants. All normally specify a credit limit and send you a monthly statement listing all activity in the account along with the minimum monthly payment required. Retail stores and merchants offer credit because it increases customer loyalty and enhances sales, while customers like credit because it offers a convenient way to shop.

Financial institutions issue credit cards to generate interest and fee income, while providing consumers with convenience and the ability to pay for just about anything on credit.

While obtaining credit was relatively easy in the 1980s, those attempting to establish their credit in the early 1990s face a more restrictive environment. Good financial planning will allow you to get the most benefit out of using credit without impairing your credit rating or forcing other action, such as bankruptcy.

If You Are Thirtysomething

Once you have established your good credit, it is essential that you maintain it. You should use credit only when you can afford it and be sure to fulfill all of the terms. This would include paying consistently and promptly. If you have a problem paying your creditors, notify them immediately and be truthful in your explanation of when you will be able to pay.

With your good credit standing, you may fall prey to the temptation of too much credit. Resist the urge to obtain more credit than you need when you receive a notice in the mail that you have been preapproved for a line of credit or new credit card. Having too much access to unused lines of credit could result in your being turned down when you apply for credit that you really want.

You might want to investigate other types of credit at this stage. Some possible examples are overdraft protection on your checking account, unsecured personal lines of credit, and home equity lines of credit.

Maintaining Your Credit:

1. Periodically review your credit file to ensure its accuracy.

2. Monitor your credit balances closely and budget their payments carefully.

3. Watch for warning signs such as paying later each month or only paying the minimum required.

4. If your combined monthly payments become too much to handle, consider a bill consolidation loan coupled with the cancellation of most of your credit accounts until the loan is repaid.

5. Many retail stores will increase your credit limit when you reach your maximum if you are in good standing. This may encourage you to purchase more from that store thereby increasing your debt even more.

Managing Your Credit:

1. Monitor your credit card usage. Consider canceling all credit cards that you have not used in six months.

2. Investigate the use of a home equity line of credit to replace other lines due to lower interest rates and the tax deductibility of interest payments.

3. Where possible, take advantage of the interest-free loan aspects of credit cards by paying the balance in full each month.

4. Determine the due date on your payments and mail your check so that it arrives just in time to be credited on the current statement. This allows you to have use of your money for as long as possible.

5. Note the cutoff dates for the billing cycle and make major purchases after that date to give you an additional billing cycle to pay for the purchase.

Using Consumer Loans

Several months after his graduation from college, Chris Jenkins decided it was time to buy a new car. After a few weeks of careful comparison shopping, he settled on a sporty new Nissan 240SX; with some options added, the car had a price of $17,000 — including plates and taxes. Chris, of course, could not afford to pay cash for the car, so using his old car as a trade-in and some money he had received as a graduation gift, he put $4,000 down and financed the rest with a $13,000, 48-month loan. Fortunately, he held a good-paying job as a film editor for a major West Coast advertising agency and could easily qualify for the loan. At one time or another, most people find themselves in a situation just like the one Chris faced: They need to borrow money in order to finance the purchase of a car or some other expensive item. This is where *consumer loans* come into play, as they provide families and individuals with the financial wherewithal for making expensive purchases. Unlike open account credit, discussed in Chapter 7, these are individually negotiated loans that are made for specific purposes and which end when the loans are paid off.

FINANCIAL *facts* OR *fantasies*

Are the following statements financial facts (true) or fantasies (false)?

Education loans not only carry low, subsidized interest rates, they also have repayment schedules that don't start until the student is out of school.

Consumer loans can be set up with fixed rates of interest or with variable loan rates.

The three biggest lenders in the consumer loan field are commercial banks, S&Ls, and credit unions.

Most single-payment loans are secured with some type of collateral and are usually relatively short in duration (i.e., they generally have maturities of one year or less).

A balloon payment on an installment loan gives the borrower the right to skip monthly payments by deferring them to the very end of the loan.

The Rule of 78s is a regulation that grew out of the Consumer Credit Enhancement Act of 1978 and mandates how installment loans will be set up.

BASIC FEATURES OF CONSUMER LOANS

In addition to open account credit, consumers can also *borrow money* from banks and other financial institutions; these loans can be set up as either single-payment or installment loans, and they can be used to pay for just about any type of big-ticket item. Can you list some reasons why you might want to borrow money through a consumer loan? How important do you think it is that the loan-repayment schedule fit into your monthly budget? Take a few minutes before reading on to think about these questions.

At several points in this book, we have discussed the different types of financial goals that individuals and families can set for themselves. These goals often involve substantial sums of money and may include such things as a college education, or the purchase of a new car. One way to reach these goals is to systematically save the money. Another is to use a loan to at least partially finance the transaction. Consumer loans are important to the personal financial planning process because of the help they provide in reaching certain types of financial goals. Working a major expenditure or purchase into a financial plan can be done just as easily with a consumer loan as it can by saving. The key, of course, is to successfully manage the credit by keeping the amount of debt used and the debt-repayment burden *well within your budget!*

USING CONSUMER LOANS

As we saw in Chapter 7, the use of open account credit can prove helpful to those who plan and live within their personal financial budgets. More important to the long-run achievement of personal financial goals, however, are single-payment and installment consumer loans. These long-term liabilities are widely used to finance goods that are too expensive to buy from current income, to help with a college education, or to pay for certain types of nondurable items, like expensive vacations. Of course, the extent to which this type of borrowing is used must be dictated by personal financial plans and budgets.

These loans differ from open account credit in a number of ways, including the formality of their lending arrangements. That is, while open account credit results from a rather informal process, consumer loans are formal, negotiated contracts that specify both the terms for borrowing and the repayment schedule. In addition, whereas an open account credit line can be used over and over again, consumer loans are one-shot transactions that are made for specific purposes. Because there is no revolving credit with a consumer loan, there is no more credit available (from that particular loan) once it is paid off. Further, there are no credit cards or checks issued with this form of credit. Finally, while open account credit is used chiefly to make repeated purchases of relatively low-cost *goods and services*, consumer loans are used mainly to *borrow money* in order to have the funds to pay for big-ticket items.

DIFFERENT TYPES OF LOANS

While they can be used for just about any purpose imaginable, most consumer loans fall into one of the following categories:

- Auto loans
- Loans for other durable goods
- Education loans
- Personal loans
- Consolidation loans

Getting the financing necessary to buy a new car, truck, or van is the single most important reason for borrowing money through a consumer loan. Indeed, *auto loans* rank ahead of credit cards and account for nearly 40 percent of all consumer credit outstanding! Generally speaking, about 80 to 90 percent of the cost of a new vehicle (somewhat less with used cars) can be financed with credit; the buyer must come up with the rest through a *down payment*. The loan is *secured* with the auto, meaning that the vehicle serves as **collateral** for the loan and can be repossessed by the lender in the event the buyer fails to make payments. These loans generally have maturities that run for 36 to 60 months, perhaps longer.

Consumer loans can also be taken out on other kinds of costly *durable goods*, such as furniture, TVs and home appliances, camper trailers, snowmobiles and other recreational equipment, home computers, and even small airplanes and mobile homes. These loans are also secured, with the item(s) purchased serving as collateral. Some down payment is almost always required with these loans, and their maturities vary with the type of asset purchased: 9- to 12-month loans are common with less costly items, such as TVs and stereos, whereas 7- to 10-year loans are the rule with mobile homes.

Getting a *college education* is another (very important) reason for taking out a consumer loan. Such loans can be used to finance either undergraduate or graduate education, and there are special *government-subsidized loan programs* available to both students and parents—we'll discuss student loans in more detail below. Still another form of consumer loan is the **personal loan**. This type of credit typically is used to make expenditures for nondurables, such as an expensive European vacation or to cover temporary cash shortfalls. Many personal loans are made on an *unsecured* basis— that is, there is no collateral with the loan other than the borrower's good name.

Finally, there are **consolidation loans**, which are used in an attempt to straighten out an unhealthy credit situation. For various reasons, consumers sometimes use credit cards, credit lines, and/or consumer loans to the point where they simply cannot service the debt in a prompt and timely fashion. When this happens, a consolidation loan may help bring this deteriorating credit situation under control. By borrowing money from one source to pay off other forms of credit, they can replace, say, five or six monthly payments that total $400 with one payment amounting to $250. *Consolidation loans are usually pretty expensive, and people who use them must be careful to abstain from using credit cards and other forms of credit until the loans have been fully paid off. Otherwise, they may end up right back where they started.*

Student Loans. Certainly one of the most legitimate reasons for going into debt is to pay for a college education. While there's nothing to prohibit someone from borrowing money for such purposes through normal channels—that is, go into a bank,

take out a regular consumer loan, and use the proceeds to finance an education—there are better ways to go about getting education loans. That's because the federal government (and some state governments) have available several different types of *subsidized educational loan programs*. The four federally sponsored programs are:

- Stafford Loans
- Perkins Loans
- Supplemental Loans for Students (SLS)
- Parent Loans (PLUS)

The Stafford and Perkins loans have the best terms, and act as the foundation to the government's student loan program. SLS and PLUS are *supplemental loans* for students who demonstrate a need but, for one reason or another, do not qualify for Stafford or Perkins loans, or whose total need is not being met by the other types of aid they are receiving. While Stafford, Perkins, and SLS loans are made directly to students, PLUS loans are made to the parents or legal guardians of college students.

To see how student loans work, let's take a look at the Stafford loan program (except where noted, the other three federally subsidized programs have much the same standards and follow the same procedures as discussed here). Stafford loans carry very low, government-subsidized interest rates; most major banks, as well as some of the bigger S&Ls and credit unions participate in the program. Actually, the loans are made directly by one of the participating banks or financial institutions, though the student has no direct contact with the lending institution. Instead, the whole process—and it really is quite simple—begins with a visit to the

---

collateral
An item of value that is used to secure the principal portion of a loan.

personal loan
A type of consumer loan typically used for the purchase of nondurable items or for covering a temporary cash shortfall.

consolidation loan
A loan made from one source to pay off other, existing debts; used to reduce monthly debt-repayment burden.

school's financial aid office, where a financial aid counselor will help you determine your eligibility. To be eligible, you have to demonstrate a *financial need*, where the amount of your financial need is defined as the cost of attending school *LESS* the amount that can be paid by you or your family (in these programs, students are expected to contribute something to their educational expense, regardless of their income). In addition, you have to be making *satisfactory progress in your academic program* and you cannot be in default on any other student loans. In effect, so long as you can demonstrate a financial need, are making satisfactory academic progress, and are not a deadbeat, you'll probably qualify for a Stafford loan.

Now all you have to do to obtain a loan is complete a simple application form, like the one in Exhibit 8.1. The completed application is then submitted to *your school's financial aid office*. You do *not* have to deal with the bank (your school will submit all the necessary papers to the institution actually making the loan), and you will *not* be subject to any credit checks (although with SLS or PLUS loans, you may be subject to a credit judgment by the lender). There are specific loan limits with each of the four programs. For example, with Stafford loans, you can borrow up to $2,625 per academic year for first and second year studies, and $4,000 per academic year thereafter, up to a maximum of $17,250 for undergraduate studies. Graduate students can qualify for up to $7,500 per academic year. Should you require even more money—that is, if your financial need exceeds the maximum amount of a Stafford loan—you can also apply for an SLS loan. There's no limit on the *number* of loans you can have, only on the maximum dollar amount that you can receive annually from each program.

Each year, right on through graduate school, a student can take out a loan from one or more of these government programs. Over time, that can add up to a lot of loans and a substantial amount of debt—all of which has to be repaid. But here's another nice feature: For in addition to carrying low (government-subsidized) interest rates, loan repayment does not begin until after you're out of school (for the Stafford and Perkins programs only—repayment on SLS and PLUS loans normally begins within 60 days of loan disbursement). In addition, interest does *not* begin accruing until you get out of school.

Of course, while you're in school, the lenders will receive interest on their loans, but it's paid by the federal government! Once repayment begins, you start paying interest on the loans, which are amortized with monthly payments over a period of five to ten years. To help you service the debt, if you have a number of student loans outstanding, you can *consolidate* the loans, at a single blended rate, and extend the repayment period out to as far as 20 years. In addition, you can ask for a *graduated repayment schedule* which will give you low payments in the early years and then higher payments later on. But no matter what you do, *take the repayment provisions on these loans seriously, as defaults will be reported to credit bureaus and become a part of your credit file!*

In summary, here are some things about student loans to keep in mind:

- Check with your school's financial aid office to see what programs are available and then apply early.
- Stafford or Perkins loans have the best terms.
- Borrow no more than you need—remember, these loans are eventually going to have to be repaid.
- Consider work-study as an alternative to borrowing.
- Become aware of loan forgiveness programs for selected occupations (military, law enforcement, Peace Corps, and so on).
- Take the loan repayment provisions seriously—defaults aren't taken lightly and can cause serious credit problems for you.
- If you're having problems servicing the loans, contact the lender and see if some arrangements can be worked out (most lenders would rather work with you than have you default).

Education loans not only carry low, subsidized interest rates, they also have repayment schedules that don't start until the student is out of school.
Fact: Getting a loan for an education is one of the major reasons for borrowing money; unlike most other forms of consumer credit, education loans do have some attractive features, including very low interest rates and loan repayment deferrals, all of which are meant to help the student achieve his or her main objective—to get an education.

Single Payment or Installment Payments.

Consumer loans can be broken into categories based on the type of repayment arrangement — single-payment or installment. **Single-payment loans** are made for a specified period of time at the end of which payment in full (principal plus interest) is due. They generally have maturities ranging from 30 days to a year; rarely do these loans run for more than a year. Sometimes single-payment loans are made to finance purchases or pay bills when the cash to be used for repayment is known to be forthcoming in the near future; in this case, they serve as a form of **interim financing**. In other situations, single-payment loans are used by consumers who want to avoid being strapped with monthly installment payments and choose instead to make one large payment at the end of the loan. Often these loans are negotiated on short notice in order to meet some unexpected need.

Installment loans are repaid in a series of fixed, scheduled payments rather than in one lump sum. The payments are almost always set up on a monthly basis, with each installment being made up partly of principal and partly of interest. For example, out of a $75 monthly payment, $60 might be credited to principal and the balance to interest. These loans are typically made to finance the purchase of a good or service for which current resources are inadequate. The repayment period can run from six months to six years, or more.

Installment loans have become a way of life for many consumers. They are popular because they provide a convenient way in which to "buy now and pay later" in fixed monthly installments that can be readily incorporated into a family budget. The process of using installment loans to finance purchases is often referred to as "buying on time."

Fixed or Variable Rate.

The majority of consumer loans are made at fixed rates of interest — that is, the interest rate charged (as well as the monthly payment) remains the same over the life of the obligation. However, variable-rate loans are also being made with increasing frequency, especially on *longer-term installment loans*. As with an adjustable-rate home mortgage, the rate of interest charged on such credit changes every 6 to 12 months in keeping with prevailing market conditions. If market interest rates go up, the rate of interest on the loan goes up accordingly, as does the monthly loan payment. These loans have periodic adjustment dates (6 to 12 months apart), at which time the interest rate and monthly payment are adjusted as necessary. Once an adjustment is made, the new rate remains in effect until the next adjustment date (sometimes the amount of the payments remains the same, but the number of payments changes).

Variable rates can also be used with single-payment loans, but the mechanics are a bit different. That is, the rate charged is usually pegged to the **prime rate**, or some other "base" rate. The prime (or base) rate, in effect, is an administered rate that the bank charges its most creditworthy customers. It's meant to be reflective of the bank's cost of funds and moves in response to fundamental credit conditions in the market. Changes in the prime rate are widely reported in the media because of the widespread impact the prime has on the cost of borrowing.

Here's how it's used to set the interest rate on a single-payment loan. Instead of putting a single, specific rate on a loan, it might be quoted at, say, prime plus 3 points; under these conditions, if prime is 8 percent, the borrower starts with a rate of interest of $8 + 3 = 11$ percent. Then, if the prime rate changes, the rate of interest on the loan changes automatically, except that in this case the adjustment is

---

single-payment loan
A loan made for a specified period of time at the end of which payment in full is due.

interim financing
The use of a single-payment loan to finance a purchase or pay bills in situations where either the funds to be used for repayment are known to be forthcoming in the near future or permanent financing is to be arranged.

installment loan
A loan that is repaid in a series of fixed, scheduled payments rather than a lump sum.

prime rate
The rate of interest a bank charges to its most creditworthy (preferred) customers; it's the lowest rate of interest at which the bank lends money.

EXHIBIT 8.1

The SNAP APP: A Student Loan Application Form

This is a standard application form for Stafford loans, and requests only the most basic information about the student borrower—name, social security number, name of the school, the amount of money being requested, and a few other pieces of information (but nothing about a student's credit history, income level, and so on). The form is so simple, in fact, that the bottom half is the actual promissory note that the student is expected to sign.

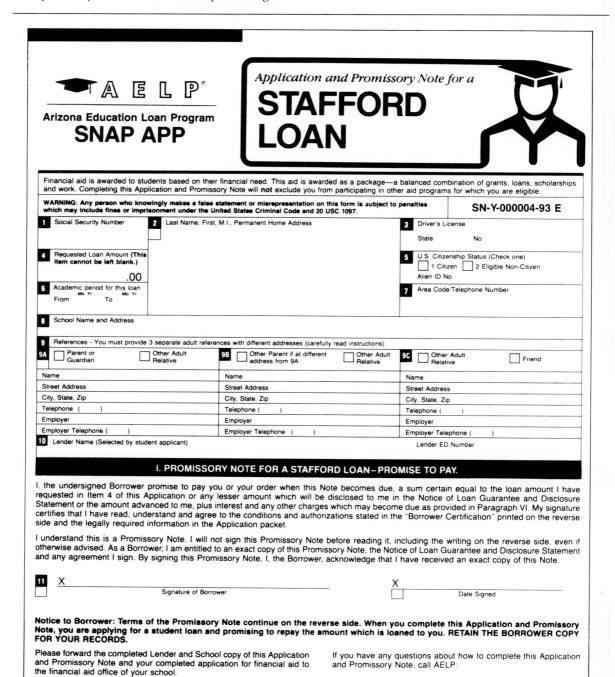

made *immediately* (there are usually no adjustment dates with single-payment, variable-rate loans). The loan will then carry a new rate of interest that will remain in effect until the next change. At maturity, interest charges at the different rates will be totaled and added to the principal to determine the size of the (single) loan payment. Variable-rate loans are desirable *if interest rates are expected to fall* over the course of the loan; in contrast, fixed-rate loans are preferable *if interest rates are expected to rise*.

Regardless of whether the loans are fixed or variable, their cost tends to vary over time with market conditions. Generally, when interest rates move up or down in the market, so will the cost of consumer loans. Inevitably, there are going to be times when *the cost of credit simply becomes too high to justify borrowing* as a way of making major purchases. So when market rates start climbing, you should ask yourself whether the cost is really worth it; financially, you may be far better off delaying the purchase until rates come down.

Consumer loans can be set up with fixed rates of interest or with variable loan rates.
Fact: While fixed-rate loans still dominate the consumer loan market, variable-rate loans are becoming more common, particularly with longer-term debt.

WHERE CAN YOU GET CONSUMER LOANS?

Consumer loans can be obtained from a number of sources, including commercial banks, consumer finance companies, credit unions, savings and loan associations, sales finance companies, life insurance companies, possibly even pawnshops, or friends and relatives. *Commercial banks* dominate the field and provide nearly half of all consumer loans. Behind banks are *consumer finance companies* and then *credit unions;* together these three financial institutions account for fully 80 percent of the consumer loan market! Interestingly, S&Ls are not much of a force in this market, and they're becoming even less so with the passage of time. The selection of a lender often depends on both the rate of interest being charged and the ease with which the loan can be

negotiated. Exhibit 8.2 provides a summary of the types of loans, lending policies, costs, and services offered at the major providers of consumer loans.

The three biggest lenders in the consumer loan field are commercial banks, S&Ls, and credit unions.
Fantasy: While commercial banks are, by far, the biggest providers of consumer loans, S&Ls just are *not* much of a force in this field; instead, the three biggest lenders are commercial banks, consumer finance companies, and credit unions.

Commercial Banks. Because they offer various types of loans at attractive rates of interest, commercial banks are a popular source of consumer loans. One nice thing about commercial banks is that they typically charge lower rates than most other lenders, in large part because they take only the best credit risks and are able to obtain relatively inexpensive funds from their depositors. The demand for their loans is generally high, and they can be selective in making consumer loans. Commercial banks usually lend only to customers with good credit ratings who can readily demonstrate an ability to make repayment in accordance with the specified terms. They also give preference to loan applicants who are account holders. The fact that an applicant is already a good customer of the bank enhances his or her chances of being approved for the requested financing. Although banks prefer to make loans secured by some type of collateral, they also make unsecured loans to their better customers. The interest rate charged on a bank loan may be affected by the loan's size, terms, and whether it is secured by some type of collateral.

Consumer Finance Companies. Sometimes called *small loan companies*, **consumer finance companies** make secured and unsecured (signature) loans to qualified individuals. These companies do not accept deposits but obtain funds from

---

consumer finance company
A firm that makes secured and unsecured personal loans to qualified individuals; also called a *small loan company.*

EXHIBIT 8.2

The Major Sources of Consumer Loans

Banks, finance companies, and other financial institutions provide a full range of consumer credit to their customers. These institutions follow a variety of lending policies and lend money at different rates of interest.

	Commercial Banks	Consumer Finance Companies
Types of Loans	■ Single-payment loans ■ Installment loans ■ Passbook loans ■ Check-credit plans ■ Credit card loans ■ Second mortgages ■ Education loans	■ Installment loans ■ Second mortgages
Lending Policies	■ Seek customers with established credit history ■ Often require collateral or security ■ Prefer to deal in large loans such as auto, home improvement, and modernization, with the exception of credit card and check-credit plans ■ Determine repayment schedules according to purpose of loan ■ Vary credit rates according to the type of credit, time period, customer's credit history, and security offered ■ May require several days to process a new credit application	■ Often lend to consumers without established credit history ■ Often make unsecured loans ■ Often vary rates according to size of loan balance ■ Offer a variety of repayment schedules ■ Make a higher percentage of small loans than other lenders ■ Maximum loan size limited by law ■ Process applications quickly, frequently same day as application is made
Costs	■ Lower than some lenders because they: — Take fewer credit risks — Lend depositors' money, a relatively inexpensive source of funds — Deal primarily in large loans, which yield larger dollar income without raising administration costs	■ Higher than most because they: — Take greater risks — Must borrow and pay interest on money to lend — Deal frequently in small loans, which are costly to make and yield a small income
Services	■ Offer several different types of consumer credit plans ■ May offer financial counseling ■ Handle credit transactions confidentially	■ Provide credit promptly ■ Make loans to pay off accumulated debts willingly ■ Design repayment schedules to fit the borrower's income ■ Usually offer financial counseling ■ Handle credit transactions confidentially

their stockholders and through open market borrowing. Because they do not have the inexpensive sources of funds that banks and other deposit-type institutions do, their interest rates are generally quite high. The actual rates charged by consumer finance companies are regulated by interest rate ceilings (or usury laws) set by the states in which they operate. The maximum allowable interest rate may vary with the size of the loan, and the state regu-

latory authorities may also limit the length of the repayment period. Loans made by consumer finance companies typically are for $5,000 or less and are secured by some type of collateral. Repayment is required on an installment basis, usually over a period of five years or less.

Consumer finance companies generally make small loans to high-risk borrowers. Of course, these loans are quite costly, but they may be the only alter-

Credit Unions	Savings and Loan Associations	Life Insurance Companies
■ Installment loans ■ Share draft credit plans ■ Credit card loans ■ Second mortgages	■ Installment loans ■ Home improvement loans ■ Education loans ■ Savings account loans ■ Second mortgages	■ Single or partial payment loans
■ Lend to members only ■ Make unsecured loans ■ May require collateral or cosigner for loans over a specified amount ■ May require payroll deductions to pay off loan ■ May submit large loan applications to a committee of members for approval ■ Offer a variety of repayment schedules	■ Will lend to all creditworthy individuals ■ Often require collateral ■ Loan rates vary depending on size of loan, length of payment, and security involved ■ As a result of the "S&L Bailout," are becoming less of a force in the consumer loan field	■ Lend on cash value of life insurance policy ■ No date or penalty on repayment ■ Deduct amount owed from value of policy benefit if death or other maturity occurs before repayment

■ Lower than most because they:
  — Take fewer credit risks
  — Lend money deposited by members, which is less expensive than borrowed money
  — Often receive free office space and supplies from sponsoring organization
  — Are managed by members whose services in most cases are donated
  — Enjoy federal income tax exemptions
	■ Lower than some lenders because they:
	  — Lend depositors' money, a relatively inexpensive source of funds
	  — Secure most loans by savings accounts, real estate, or some other asset
		■ Lower than many because they:
		  — Take no risk
		  — Pay no collection costs
		  — Secure loans by cash value of policy

■ Design repayment schedules to fit borrower's income ■ Generally provide credit life insurance without extra charge ■ May offer financial counseling ■ Handle credit transactions confidentially	■ Often offer financial counseling ■ Specialize in mortgages and other housing-related loans ■ Handle credit transactions confidentially	■ Permit repayment at any time ■ Handle credit transactions confidentially

native for people with poor credit ratings. Some people are attracted to consumer finance companies because of the ease with which they can obtain loans. Due to the high rates of interest charged, individuals should consider this source only after exhausting all others.

Credit Unions. Only members can obtain installment and single-payment loans from credit unions.

Because they are nonprofit organizations with minimal operating costs, credit unions charge relatively low rates on their loans.

They make either unsecured or secured loans, depending on the size and type of loan being requested. The maximum allowable size of loans is often set by certain regulatory agencies. In addition, the directors of a credit union frequently set their own in-house loan limits. Generally speaking, membership in a credit union provides the most attractive borrowing opportunities available, since their interest rates and borrowing requirements usually are more favorable than other sources of consumer loans. An added convenience of a credit union loan is that loan payments can often be deducted directly from payroll checks.

Savings and Loan Associations.

Savings and loan associations (as well as savings banks) primarily make mortgage loans. However, they are also permitted to make loans on such consumer durables as automobiles, televisions, refrigerators, and other appliances. In addition, they can make certain types of home improvement and mobile-home loans, as well as some personal and educational loans. Among other things, financial deregulation has enabled S&Ls to enter the consumer loan market. Since 1982, federally chartered S&Ls have been allowed to invest a portion of their assets in consumer loans, although most experts fully expect them to pull back from these loans, as recent "S&L Bailout" legislation mandates that they direct more of their lending to home mortgages. As a rule, the rates of interest on consumer loans at S&Ls are fairly close to the rates charged by commercial banks, though if anything, they tend to be a bit more expensive. Like their banking counterparts, the rates charged on specific loans will, in the final analysis, depend on such factors as the type and purpose of the loan, the duration and type of repayment, and the overall creditworthiness of the borrower.

Sales Finance Companies.

Businesses that sell relatively expensive items—such as automobiles, furniture, and appliances—often provide installment financing to purchasers of their products. Because dealers cannot afford to tie up their funds in installment contracts, they sell them to a **sales finance company** for cash. This procedure is often referred to as "selling paper," since merchants in effect sell their loans to a third party. When the sales finance company purchases these notes, customers are usually notified to make payments directly to it.

The largest sales finance organizations are the **captive finance companies** owned by manufacturers of big-ticket items—automobiles and appliances. General Motors Acceptance Corporation (GMAC) and General Electric Credit Corporation (GECC) are just two examples of captive finance companies that purchase the installment loans made by dealers of their products. Also, most commercial banks act as sales finance companies by buying paper from auto dealers and other businesses. The cost of financing through a sales finance company is generally a little higher than the rates charged by banks and S&Ls, particularly when you let the dealer do all the work in arranging the financing (dealers normally get a cut on the finance income, so it's obviously to their advantage to secure as *high* a rate of interest as possible). However, since the early 1980s, auto makers have been using interest rates on new-car loans as a marketing tool. They do this by dropping the rate of interest on car loans *(for selected models)* to levels that are well below the market—for example, not long ago, Ford and GM were offering 2 percent, two-year financing on some of their cars, and Chrysler was making two-year loans at *zero* interest. In this way the auto manufacturers are able to use these loan rates (along with rebates) to stimulate sales by keeping the cost of buying a new car down. Clearly, cutting the cost of borrowing for a new car can result in big savings!

Life Insurance Companies.

Life insurance policyholders can often obtain loans from their insurance companies. Certain types of policies not only provide death benefits but also have a savings function, in which case they can be used as collateral for loans. (*Be careful with these loans, however, as they could involve a tax penalty if certain conditions are not met.* A detailed discussion of life insurance is presented in Chapter 9.) Life insurance companies are required by law to make loans against the **cash values**—the amount of accumulated savings—of certain types of life insurance policies. The rate of interest on this type of loan is stated on the policy, and it used to be set as low as 5 or 6 percent. The newer policies, however, carry loan rates that aren't set until the loans are made; that usually means borrowing money at or near prevailing market rates. While you will be charged interest for as long as the policy loan is outstanding, these loans do not have repayment dates—in other words, you do not have to pay them back. The reason for this is when you take out a loan against the cash value of your life insurance policy, you are really borrowing from your own money. Therefore, the amount of the loan outstanding, plus any accrued interest, will be deducted from the amount of coverage provided by the policy. The chief danger in life insurance loans is that they do not have a firm maturity date; consequently, borrowers may lack the motivation to repay them.

Friends and Relatives. Sometimes a close friend or relative will be willing to lend you money. In many cases, such loans are attractive because little or no interest is charged. The terms will, of course, vary depending on the financial needs of the borrower, but they should be specified in some type of loan agreement that states the costs, conditions, and maturity date of the loan, as well as the obligations of both borrower and lender. Not only does a written loan agreement reduce opportunities for disagreement and unhappiness, it also protects both borrower and lender should either of them die or other unexpected events occur. Still, *given the potential for disagreement and conflict inherent in this type of arrangement, borrowing from friends or relatives is not advisable*, and should be seriously considered only when there are no other viable alternatives, or perhaps if the terms of credit are so much better than those available from the more traditional sources. Indeed, as the accompanying *Money in Action* box suggests, a loan to or from a friend or family member is far more than a run-of-the-mill banking transaction: the interest is emotional, and the risks are the relationship itself!

As a last resort, you might even want to consider a *pawnshop* — if you have some sort of valuable asset (like a piece of jewelry, a musical instrument, or a CD player) that you can leave as collateral. Such establishments tend to proliferate during economically tough times, as an increasing number of people turn to them as a source of "financing." As long as you have an asset to pawn, you may be able to obtain a short-term, single payment loan from one of these shops. But bear in mind that the amount of money you will receive is likely to be only a small fraction of the perceived resale value of the asset you pawn. Moreover, the rate of interest charged on the loan can be extremely high, and the pawned asset can be sold if you do not repay the loan within the designated period of time.

MANAGING YOUR CREDIT

Borrowing money to make major acquisitions — and, in general, using consumer loans — is a sound and perfectly legitimate way to conduct your financial affairs. Meeting a major financial goal by buying on credit can be worked into your network of financial plans, while servicing the debt can be factored into your monthly cash budget. Doing it this way certainly is far superior to borrowing in a haphazard manner, giving little or no consideration to debt repayment. When borrowing is well thought out in advance and *full consideration is given not only to the need for the asset or item in question but also to the repayment of the ensuing credit*, sound credit management is the result. And sound credit management underlies effective personal financial planning.

From a financial planning perspective, you should ask yourself two questions when considering the use of a consumer loan: (1) Does making this acquisition fit into your financial plans? (2) Does the required debt service on the loan fit into your monthly cash budget? If the expenditure in question will seriously jeopardize your financial plans and/or if the repayment of the loan is likely to place an undue strain on your cash budget, you should definitely reconsider the purchase! Perhaps it can be postponed, or you can liquidate some assets in order to come up with more down payment, or you may even have to alter some other area of your financial plan in order to work the expenditure in. Whatever route you choose, the key point is to make sure that it will

---

sales finance company
A firm that purchases notes drawn up by sellers of certain types of merchandise, typically big-ticket items.

captive finance company
A sales finance company that is owned by a manufacturer of big-ticket merchandise. GMAC is a captive finance company.

cash value (of life insurance)
An accumulation of savings in an insurance policy that can be used as a source of loan collateral.

MONEY IN ACTION

Lending Money to a Relative: How to Say "No"; When to Say "Yes"

Everyone has a story to tell about lending money to family members, but few want to be quoted. With good reason: Not many have endings where lender and borrower walk away hand-in-hand.

"I made every mistake possible when my daughter asked me for a $25,000 loan for a down payment on the home she wanted to buy," says an embarrassed 50-year-old Chicago woman. "It was 10 years since her father and I were divorced, but I was still guilt-ridden about the anguish it had caused her. My financial situation was simple. I had a $40,000-a-year job, a heavily mortgaged house and a $30,000 certificate of deposit. Without telling her of my financial position, I said 'yes'—and cashed in my CD."

The saga gets worse. The daughter added hot tubs, a greenhouse and a stereo system to the house—but didn't repay the loan. The mother resented it—and said something. The daughter became defensive. The relationship soured. It's a familiar story. Tangled in emotions, people frequently say "yes" to a family loan when they want to say "no."

SAYING "NO"

Shy of real need—a debilitating illness, a sum to tide someone over during a few problem months, a life-threatening situation—there are good reasons to say "no" when Cousin Joe asks for a loan.

- *I can't afford it.* Some people find these four words impossible to mouth. They really want to help out, but can't. For these people, Linda Barbanel, a New York City psychotherapist who writes about money matters, suggests a three-step approach to saying "no."

  "Repeat what it is that the borrower wants," she advises. "In case you've misunderstood, you allow Cousin Joe to clarify the situation. Then explain, in general terms, why you can't lend the money. Finally, and most important, suggest joint problem-solving. Perhaps you know people who are in a better position to finance Joe's new business.

Maybe he can use the spare desk in your den as a 'starter office.'" It's a way of providing support without dollars.

- *I think the borrower is irresponsible.* "Any time a person asks you for money, you have a right to know what the money is going to be used for and how it's going to be repaid," says Paul Westbrook, a certified financial planner in Watchung, N.J. "If a person is evasive on either score, I recommend saying 'no.'"
- *I don't like Joe.* Bank lending officers don't assess personalities, but a family lender has every right to. Financial dealings among family members are difficult enough when there's a good relationship built on trust.
- *I don't think it's a good deal.* The nouvelle cuisine restaurant Joe plans to open with a friend he met three months ago is miles out of town. Not only that, all Joe and his friend know about food is that they like to eat. Just because Joe is kin doesn't mean that someone has to finance a failure.

be fully compatible with your financial plans and cash budget *before* the loan is taken out and the money spent.

Shopping for Loans. Once you have decided to use credit, it is equally important that you shop around and evaluate the various costs and terms available. Since truth-in-lending laws require creditors to clearly state all finance charges, it may appear that the only thing you need do to make a sound credit decision is determine which source offers the lowest finance charge. This could not be further

SAYING "YES"

But family *is* family. And more and more, family loans are the source of down payments on first homes, seed money for new businesses and financial first aid when there's a break in earnings. When handled properly, lending money to relatives can be a source of great personal pleasure.

When Cindy Ley, a young Minneapolis attorney, left her apartment for work one morning in July 1987, she found her car in two feet of water. It was ruined. "My insurance company gave me $1800 for it," she says. "I found a wonderful $5000 used car, but I was short $3200. Mom and Dad suggested I borrow the money from them." Cindy admits she was hesitant. "I didn't want to feel like a failure in the real world. I wanted to be financially independent. But they dispelled my fears."

Cindy has never missed a payment. ("I'd make this payment before any others," she says), though her parents aren't concerned. So what makes for a successful transaction?

Here are some suggestions:

- *It's handled in businesslike fashion:*
  1) It needn't be more than a one-page handwritten agreement, but the terms should be explicit and agreed upon by both parties.
  2) Is interest being charged? If so, how much and when is it due — monthly, quarterly or yearly?
  3) When is the loan to be repaid? Whenever the borrower can or at stated intervals? At the end of the loan period?
  4) If the loan can't be paid off as agreed upon, what are the alternative solutions?
  5) If the lender needs the money unexpectedly, what should the borrower be prepared to do?
  6) If the lender dies, what happens to the outstanding loan? Is it terminated? Is it owed to the estate?
- *Both parties understand that this is loan — not a gift.* If this is not clearly spelled out, the loan agreement can fade from the borrower's memory (though the lender rarely has

the same amnesia).
- *The borrower is investing something of himself in the deal.* In Cindy Ley's case, it was her $1800 insurance money. But it doesn't have to be money. It can be time invested in making a new business work or improving a home. Whatever it is, it's important, so that the lender doesn't feel he or she is being taken advantage of.
- *The lender understands the downside if the loan can't be repaid.* When a family loan *can't* be repaid because a business fails or the borrower falls on hard times, chances are the lender will do nothing — no lien will be put on the borrower's home, no salary will be attached. A relative has to be able to accept that — both financially and emotionally.

Source: Adapted from Patricia Schiff Estess, "Shoud You Lend Money to a Relative? When to Say 'Yes' & How to Say 'No,'" *Parade Magazine*, July 24, 1988, pp. 4–5. Reprinted with permission from *Parade* and Patricia Schiff Estess.

from the truth — for as we'll see below, finance charges are just one of the factors to consider when shopping for a loan.

Finance Charges. What's it going to cost me? For a lot of people, that's one of the first things they want to know when taking out a loan. And that's ap-

propriate, because borrowers should know what they're going to have to pay to get the money. Lenders are required by law to clearly state all finance charges and other loan fees. Find out the effective (or true) *rate* of interest you're going to have to pay on the loan, and whether the loan carries a

EXHIBIT 8.3
Tracking Your Consumer Debt

A worksheet like this allows you to keep track of your outstanding credit along with your monthly debt service requirements. Such information is a major component of sound credit management.

AN INVENTORY OF CONSUMER DEBT

Name _____ **Date** _____

Type of Consumer Debt		Current Monthly Payment[a]	Latest Balance Due
Auto loans	1.	$	$
	2.		
	3.		
Education loans	1.		
	2.		
Personal installment loans	1.		
	2.		
Home improvement loan			
Other installment loans	1.		
	2.		
Single-payment loans	1.		
	2.		
Credit cards (retail charge cards, bank cards, T&E cards, etc.)	1.		
	2.		
	3.		
	4.		
	5.		
	6.		
	7.		
Overdraft protection line			
Personal line of credit			
Home equity credit line			
Loan on life insurance			
Margin loan from broker			
Other loans	1.		
	2.		
	3.		
Totals		$	$

$$\text{Debt safety ratio} = \frac{\text{Total monthly payments}}{\text{Monthly take-home pay}} \times 100 = \frac{\$}{\$} \times 100 = \underline{\quad\quad} \%$$

[a] Leave the space blank if there is *no* monthly payment required on a loan (e.g., as with a single-payment or education loan).

fixed or variable rate. Obviously, *so long as every-thing else is equal*, it's in your best interest to secure the least expensive loan. In this regard, ask the lender what the *annual rate of interest* on the loan will be, since it's easier (and far more relevant) to compare percentage rates on alternative borrowing arrangements than the dollar amount of the loan charges. This rate of interest is known as the *APR* (annual percentage rate) and includes not only the basic cost of money, but also any additional fees that might be required on the loan (APR will be more fully discussed later). Also, if it's a variable-rate loan, find out what the interest rate is pegged to, how many "points" are added to the base rate, and how often the loan rate can be changed. Just as impor-tant, how will the lender make the periodic adjust-ments—will the *size* of the monthly payment change, or the *number* of monthly payments? To avoid any future shock, it's best to find these things out before the loan is made.

Loan maturity.   Try to make sure that the size and number of payments will fit comfortably into your spending and savings plans. As a rule, the cost of credit increases with the length of the repayment period. Thus, to lower your cost, you should con-sider shortening the loan maturity—but only to the point where doing so will not place an unnecessary strain on your cash flow. For while a shorter matu-rity may reduce the cost of the loan, it will also in-crease the size of the monthly loan payment. In-deed, finding a monthly loan payment that you will be comfortable with is a critical dimension of sound credit management. Fortunately, the personal com-puter provides an effective way of evaluating differ-ent loan configurations. Altering the loan maturity is just one way of coming up with an affordable monthly payment; with the aid of a personal com-puter, you can quickly run through all sorts of alter-natives to find the one that will best fit your monthly budget.

Total cost of the transaction.   When com-parison shopping for credit, you should always look at both the total cost of the price of the item pur-chased *and* the price of the credit. Retailers often manipulate both sticker prices and interest rates, so you really will not know what kind of deal you are getting until you look at the total cost of the transac-tion. Along this line, comparing *monthly payments* is a good way to get a handle on total cost. It is a

simple matter to compare total costs: Just add the amount put down on the purchase to the total of all the monthly loan payments; other things being equal, the one with the lowest total is the one you should pick.

Collateral.   You should make sure that you know up front what collateral (if any) you will have to pledge on the loan and what you stand to lose in case you default on your payments. Actually, if it makes no difference to you and if it is not too incon-venient, using collateral makes sense, since it may result in *lower* finance charges—perhaps half a per-centage point or so.

Other credit considerations.   In addition to the above guidelines, other questions that you should address include the following: Can you choose *a payment date* that will be compatible with your spending patterns? Can you obtain the loan *promptly and conveniently*? What are the charges for late payments, and are they reasonable? Will you receive a refund on credit charges if you prepay your loan? Taking the time to look around for the best credit deal will pay off not only in reducing the cost of such debt but also in keeping the burden of credit in line with your cash budget and financial plans. In the long run, you are the one who has the most to gain (or lose). Thus, *you should see to it that the consumer debt you undertake does in fact have the desired effects on your financial condition*.

Keeping Track of Your Credit.   In order to stay abreast of your financial condition, it is a good idea to periodically take inventory of the consumer debt you have outstanding. You should do this a mini-mum of once a year, and ideally every three or four months. To take inventory of what you owe, simply prepare a list of all your outstanding consumer debt. Include *everything except your home mortgage*— installment loans, single-payment loans, credit cards, revolving credit lines, overdraft protection lines, and home equity credit lines

You might find a worksheet like the one in Exhibit 8.3 helpful in preparing a list of your debts. To use it, simply list the current monthly payment and the lat-est balance due for each type of consumer credit outstanding; then, total both columns to see how much you are paying each month and how large a debt load you have built up. Hopefully, when all the numbers have been totaled up, you will not be surprised to learn just how much you really do owe.

A way to quickly assess your debt position is to compute your *debt safety ratio* (we looked at this ratio in Chapter 7). You do this by dividing the total monthly payments (from the worksheet) by your monthly take-home pay. If 20 percent or more of your take-home pay is going to monthly credit payments, you are relying too heavily on credit; in contrast, if your debt safety ratio works out to 10 percent or less, you are in a strong credit position. *Keeping track of your credit and holding the amount of outstanding debt to a reasonable level is the surest way to maintain your creditworthiness.*

SINGLE-PAYMENT LOANS

The cost of a single-payment loan depends not only on the stated rate of interest, but also on the type of interest used to calculate finance charges. In addition to the cost of the loan, what other loan provisions — like the need for collateral, the maturity of the loan, and the existence of a prepayment penalty — would be important to you? Stop to think about this question before going on.

A single-payment loan differs from other loans in that it is repaid in full with a single payment on a given due date. The payment usually consists of principal and all interest charges. Sometimes, however, interim interest payments may have to be made (for example, every quarter), in which case the payment at maturity is made up of principal plus any unpaid interest. Single-payment loans can be secured or unsecured and can be taken out for just about any purpose, from buying a new car to paying for a vacation. They are perhaps most useful when the funds needed for a given purchase or transaction are temporarily unavailable but expected to be forthcoming in the near future. By helping you cope with a temporary cash shortfall, these loans can serve as a form of interim financing until more permanent arrangements can be made.

IMPORTANT LOAN FEATURES

The first thing you have to do when applying for either a single-payment or installment loan is submit a **loan application**, an example of which is shown in Exhibit 8.4. Basically, the loan application provides the lending institution with information about the purpose of the loan, whether it will be secured or unsecured, and the financial condition of the borrower. The loan officer uses this document, along with other information (such as a credit report from the local credit bureau), to determine whether or not you should be granted the loan — here again, some type of *credit scoring* (as discussed in Chapter 7) may be used to make the decision. As part of the loan application process, you should also consider the various features of the debt, the three most important of which are loan collateral, loan maturity, and loan repayment.

Loan Collateral. Most single-payment loans are secured by certain specified assets. For *collateral*, lenders prefer to accept only items they feel will be readily marketable at a price sufficiently high to cover the principal portion of the loan — for example, an automobile, jewelry, or stocks and bonds. If a loan is obtained to purchase some personal asset, that asset may be used to secure it. In most cases, lenders do not take physical possession of the collateral but file a **lien**, which is a legal claim that permits them to liquidate the collateral in order to satisfy the loan in the event of borrower default. The lien is filed in the county courthouse and is a matter of public record. If borrowers maintain possession or title to *movable* property — such as cars, TVs, and jewelry — the instrument that gives the lenders title to the property in the event of default is called a **chattel mortgage**. If lenders hold title to the collateral — or actually take possession of it, as in the case of stocks and bonds — the agreement giving them the right to sell these items in case of default is a **collateral note**.

Loan Maturity. As indicated earlier, the maturity, or term, on a single-payment loan usually extends for a period of one year or less and very rarely goes out to two years or longer. When you request a single-payment loan, you should be sure that its term is long enough to allow you to receive the money needed for repayment but not any longer than necessary. Don't stretch the maturity out too far, since the dollar amount of the finance charges paid increases with time. Because the loan is retired in a single payment, the lender must be assured that you will be able to repay it even if certain unexpected events occur in the future. The term of your single-payment loan therefore must be reconciled with your budget, as well as your ability to pay. If the money you plan to use for repayment will be received periodically over the term of the loan, an installment type loan may be more suitable.

Most single-payment loans are secured with some type of collateral and are usually relatively short in duration (i.e., they generally have maturities of one year or less).

Fact: Because these loans require only one payment at maturity, banks and other lenders generally keep them fairly short and usually require some type of collateral.

Loan Repayment. The repayment of a single-payment loan is expected to take place at a single point in time: on its maturity date. Occasionally the funds needed to repay this type of loan will be received prior to maturity. Depending on the lender, the borrower might be able to repay the loan early and thereby reduce the finance charges. Credit unions often permit early repayment of these loans with reduced finance charges. Commercial banks and other single-payment lenders, however, may not accept early repayments; or if they do, they will charge a **prepayment penalty** on them. This penalty normally amounts to a set percentage of the interest that would have been paid over the remaining life of the loan. The Truth in Lending Act requires lenders to disclose in the loan agreement whether or not, and in what amount, prepayment penalties are charged on a single-payment loan. *A borrower should understand this information prior to signing a loan agreement.*

Occasionally an individual will borrow money using a single-payment loan only to discover that he or she is short of money when the loan comes due—after all, making one big loan payment can cause a real strain on one's cash flow. Should this happen to you, don't just let the payment go past due; rather, *inform the lender in advance so that a partial payment, loan extension, or some other arrangement can be made*. Under such circumstances, the lender will often agree to a **loan rollover**, in which case the original loan is paid off by taking out another loan. The lender will usually require that all the interest and at least part of the principal be paid at the time of the rollover. Thus, if you originally borrowed $5,000 for 12 months, the bank might be willing to lend you, say, $3,000 for another 6 to 9 months as part of a loan rollover. In this case, you'll have to "pay down" $2,000 of the original loan, along with all interest due. However, you can expect the interest rate on a rollover loan to go up a bit; that is the price you pay for falling short on the first loan. Also, you should not expect to get more than one, or at the most two, loan rollovers—a bank's patience tends to grow somewhat short after a while!

---

loan application
An application that provides a lender with information about the purpose of the requested loan, whether it will be secured or unsecured, and the applicant's financial condition.

lien
A legal claim that permits the lender, in the event of borrower default, to liquidate the items serving as collateral in order to satisfy the obligation.

chattel mortgage
A mortgage on personal property given as security for the payment of an obligation.

collateral note
A legal note that gives the lender the right to sell collateral in the event of the borrower's default on the obligation.

prepayment penalty
A penalty sometimes charged by a financial institution for advance payment of a loan.

loan rollover
The process of paying off a loan by taking out another, usually with the requirement that all interest and part of the principal on the original loan be paid at the time of rollover.

EXHIBIT 8.4
A Bank Loan Application

The loan application contains information about the person(s) applying for the loan, including source(s) of income, current debt load, and even a short balance sheet.

VALLEY NATIONAL BANK OF ARIZONA

☐ CREDIT CARD ☐ INSTALMENT ☐ CO MAKER ☐ COMMERCIAL
☐ PERSONAL CREDIT LINE

CREDIT CARD REQUEST*

REQUEST ☐ MASTER CARD ☐ VISA ☐ GOLD MASTERCARD

NUMBER OF CARDS DESIRED: _____

WILL NON-APPLICANT SPOUSE USE ACCOUNT? ☐ YES ☐ NO

APPLICATION FOR CREDIT

COMMUNITY PROPERTY DEBT

"This application, unless otherwise marked below, is to be considered as an application for credit extended as a debt of the marital community, based upon the creditworthiness of that community." Supply all information requested on the application.

SOLE AND SEPARATE PROPERTY

☐ This is an application for individual credit as **sole and separate debt**, which will be evaluated without regard to the assets, income or creditworthiness of the applicant's spouse or the applicant's marital community. (The applicant should list only marital status and no other information should be given regarding the spouse (if any) except name and address. Applicant should also list all debts for which he/she is obligated by signing to promise to pay, and should also list all sole and separate assets and income.)

Amount $	Term	Date	Purpose			

Print Full Name	Last	First	Mid. Name	Jr. or Sr.	Social Security No.	Date of Birth

Spouse's Name	Last	First	Mid. Name	Jr. or Sr.	Social Security No.	Date of Birth

Marital Status ☐ MARRIED ☐ UNMARRIED ☐ SEPARATED				No. Dependents

Home Address	City		ZIP Code	Home Phone No.	

Mailing Address	City		State	How Long At Address	Yrs. Mos.

Previous Address	City		State	How Long At Address	Yrs. Mos.

Previous Address	City		State	How Long At Address	Yrs. Mos.

Nearest Relative (Not Living With You)	Address			Relationship

Spouse's Nearest Relative	Address			Relationship

*Income from alimony, child support, or maintenance payments need not be revealed, if you do not choose to disclose such income in applying for credit. As a creditor, we may inquire whether any income stated in an application is derived from such a source.

Present Employer (Type of Business if Self-Employed)				Union and Local No.	Discharge Date

Address	City		ZIP Code	Business Phone

Position	Dept. or Badge No.	How Long	Yrs. Mos.	Net Income (Monthly) $

Spouse's Employer Name and Address	Business Phone	How Long	Yrs. Mos.	Net Income $

Source of Other Income*				*Other Income* $

Previous Employer's Name and Address		How Long	Yrs.	Total Income $

Name of Your Bank	Checking Account No.		Average Balance

Branch Name and Address	Savings Account No.		Average Balance

WHAT I OWN OR AM BUYING	VALUE	WHAT I OWE TO OTHERS	BALANCE DUE	ARE PAYMENTS SUBJECT TO CHANGE? YES/NO MONTHLY PAYMENT
Cash at Valley Bank Which office?	$	Amounts owed to Valley Bank—List office(s): 1. 2. 3.	$	$
Cash in other financial institution(s) Name(s):		Amounts owed to other financial institutions— Names: 1. 2. 3.		
Amounts owed to me				
Stocks and bonds Names — No. Shares 1. 2. 3.		Dept. store charge accts. & credit cards 1. 2. 3. 4. 5.		
Cash value of my life insurance				
Autos—year, make, model 1. 2. 3.		Real estate debt ☐ Rent ☐ Own 1. 2. 3. 4.		
Real Estate at market value 1. 2. 3. 4.		Alimony/child support payments/child care 1. 2.		
Other assets—describe 1. 2.		Other liabilities: (medical, insurance, etc.) 1. 2.		
Total value of my assets	$	Total of my debts	$	

COMMENTS BY APPLICANT

Have you ever filed bankruptcy? ☐ YES ☐ NO When?

*Credit Card Information: There are costs associated with the use of any of our Credit Cards. To obtain information about these costs, call us at 350-7250 in Metro Phoenix, or 1-800-862-2427 outside Metro Phoenix, or write us at P.O. Box 2992, Phoenix, Arizona 85062. THIS FINANCIAL STATEMENT WHICH I CERTIFY AS SETTING FORTH ALL OF MY OBLIGATIONS AND BEING COMPLETE AND ACCURATE, IS MADE WITH THE INTENT THAT THE BANK RELY THEREON IN EXTENDING CREDIT TO ME. THIS APPLICATION SHALL REMAIN PROPERTY OF THE BANK IN ANY EVENT. I AUTHORIZE BANK TO OBTAIN SUCH INFORMATION IT MAY REQUIRE CONCERNING THE STATEMENTS MADE IN THE APPLICATION, AND FURTHER, I AGREE TO GIVE BANK IMMEDIATE WRITTEN NOTICE OF ANY CHANGE IN MY FINANCIAL CONDITION. UNDER THE PENALTY OF PERJURY, I CERTIFY THAT THE ABOVE SOCIAL SECURITY NUMBERS ARE CORRECT FOR IRS REPORTING PURPOSES.

FOR BANK USE ONLY

Vehicle/Collateral Description			
License Plate No.	Tab No.	Exp. Date	Mileage
Officer's Signature and No.			Term
Branch No.	$	Class No.	
Applicant's Signature			
Co-Applicants Signature			

ITEMIZATION: ☐ Refused ☐ Desired
AUTOMATIC IL PAYMENT: ☐ Refused ☐ Desired
CREDIT INSURANCE:
☐ Credit Life on
☐ Life and Disability on
☐ Joint Life
☐ Joint Life and Disability on
☐ Ineligible ☐ Refused
DAYS TO 1ST PAYMENT:
FLOOD INSURANCE: ☐ Required ☐ Not Required
Interviewer   Extension

0-105-0071 Rev. 4/90

Source: Valley National Bank of Arizona.

EXHIBIT 8.5

A Loan Disclosure Statement

The loan disclosure statement informs the borrower of all charges (finance and otherwise) associated with the loan and the annual percentage rate (APR). In addition, it specifies the payment terms as well as the existence of any balloon payments.

FEDERAL TRUTH IN LENDING ACT DISCLOSURES

You have the right to receive at this time an itemization of the Amount Financed.
☐ I want an itemization.   ☐ I do not want an itemization.

ANNUAL PERCENTAGE RATE
The cost of your credit as a yearly rate.
%

Your payment schedule will be:

Number of Payments	Amount of Payments	When Payments Are Due

Insurance: Credit life insurance and credit disability insurance are not required to obtain credit, and will not be provided unless you sign and agree to pay the additional cost.

Type	Premium	Signature
Credit Life		I want credit life insurance ——— SIGNATURE
Credit Life and Disability		I want credit life and disability insurance ——— SIGNATURE
Joint Credit Life		I want joint credit life insurance ——— SIGNATURE
Joint Credit Life and Disability		I want joint credit life and disability insurance ——— SIGNATURE

FINANCE CHARGE
The dollar amount the credit will cost you.
$

Amount Financed
The amount of credit provided to you or on your behalf.
$

You may obtain property insurance from anyone you want that is acceptable to The Valley National Bank of Arizona. If you get the insurance through The Valley National Bank of Arizona, you will pay $ _____ for _____ months of coverage.

Security: You are giving a security interest in the property being purchased.

Total of Payments
The amount you will have paid after you have made all payments scheduled.
$

Filing Fees: $ _____

Late Charge: If a payment is late, you will be charged $10 or 5% of the payment, whichever is less.

Prepayment: If you pay off early, you will not have to pay a penalty.

Assumption: Someone buying your house may, subject to conditions, be allowed to assume the remaining obligation on the original terms.

e means an estimate

See your contract documents for any additional information about nonpayment, default, and any required repayment in full before the scheduled date.

Each undersigned acknowledges receipt of one copy of the above fully completed Disclosure Statement prior to consummation of the proposed transaction. Each undersigned further acknowledges this disclosure statement is not a commitment to extend credit, or to provide or acquire insurance.

DATED _____ , 19 _____   (X) _____
                                                              (DEBTOR'S SIGNATURE)

THE VALLEY NATIONAL BANK OF ARIZONA   (X) _____
                                                              (DEBTOR'S SIGNATURE)

By _____

Source: Valley National Bank of Arizona.

FINANCE CHARGES AND THE ANNUAL PERCENTAGE RATE

As indicated in Chapter 7, the Consumer Credit Protection Act, or Truth in Lending Act, requires lenders to disclose both the dollar amount of finance charges and the annual percentage rate (APR) of interest. A sample **loan disclosure statement** applicable to either a single-payment or installment loan is given in Exhibit 8.5. Note that such a statement discloses not only interest costs but also other fees and expenses that may be tacked on to the loan. Although disclosures like this allow you to compare the various borrowing alternatives, you still need to understand the methods used to compute finance charges, since similar loans with the same *stated* interet rates may have different finance charges and APRs. The two basic procedures used to calculate the finance charges on single-payment loans are the *simple interest method* and the *discount method*.

Simple Interest Method. Interest is charged only on the *actual loan balance oustanding* in the **simple interest method**. This method is commonly used on revolving credit lines by commercial banks, S&Ls, and credit unions. To see how it is applied to a single-payment loan, assume that you borrow $1,000 for two years at a 12 percent annual rate of interest. On a single-payment loan, the actual loan balance outstanding for the two years will be $1,000, since no payments will be made until this period has elapsed. With simple interest, the finance charge, F_s, is obtained by multiplying the *principal* outstanding by the stated annual rate of interest and then multiplying this amount by the term of the loan:

$$F_s = P \times r \times t,$$

where

F_s = finance charge calculated using simple interest method
P = principal amount of loan
r = stated annual rate of interest
t = term of loan, as stated in years (e.g., t would equal 0.5 for a 6-month loan, 1.25 for a 15-month loan, and 2.0 for a two-year loan

Substituting $1,000 for P, .12 for r, and 2 for t in the equation, we see that the finance charge, F_s, on this loan equals some $240 ($1,000 × .12 per year × 2 years). Since the size of the loan payment with this type of credit arrangement is found by adding the finance charges to the principal amount of the loan, you would have to make a loan payment of $1,000 + $240 = $1,240 at maturity to retire this debt.

To calculate the true, or annual, percentage rate (APR) of interest on this loan, the average annual finance charge is divided by the average loan balance outstanding, as follows:

$$APR = \frac{\text{Average annual finance charge}}{\text{Average loan balance outstanding}}$$

The figure for the average annual finance charge is found by dividing the total finance charge by the life of the loan (in years). In our example, the result is $120 ($240/2). Because the loan balance outstanding remains at $1,000 over the life of the loan, the average loan balance outstanding is $1,000. Dividing the $120 average annual finance charge by the $1,000 average loan balance outstanding, we obtain an APR of 12 percent. Thus, the APR and the stated rate of interest are equivalent: They both equal 12 percent. This is always the case when the simple interest method is used to calculate finance charges, *regardless of whether loans are single-payment or installment*.

Discount Method. With the **discount method**, total finance charges are calculated on the principal amount of the loan, and they are then subtracted from the amount of the loan. The difference between the amount of the loan and the finance charge

---

loan disclosure statement

A document that lenders are required to supply borrowers that states both the dollar amount of finance charges and the APR applicable to a loan.

simple interest method

A method of computing finance charges in which interest is charged on the actual loan balance outstanding.

discount method

A method of calculating finance charges in which interest is computed, then subtracted from the principal, and the difference is disbursed to the borrower.

is then disbursed (paid) to the borrower—in other words, finance charges are paid in advance and represent a discount from the principal portion of the loan. The finance charge on a single-payment loan using the discount method, F_d, is calculated in exactly the same way as for a simple interest loan:

$$F_d = F_s = P \times r \times t.$$

Using the above method, the finance charge, F_d, on the $1,000, 12 percent, two-year, single-payment loan is, of course, the same $240 we calculated earlier. However, in sharp contrast to simple interest loans, the loan payment with a discount loan is the original principal amount of the loan, P, since the finance charges on the loan are deducted from the loan proceeds. Thus, for the $1,000 loan above, the borrower will receive $760—which is found by subtracting the interest charges from the loan principal ($1,000 less $240)—and in two years, will be required to pay back $1,000.

To find the APR on this discount loan, substitute the appropriate values into the APR equation cited above. For this two-year loan, the average annual finance charge is $120 ($240/2). However, as explained above, since this is a discount loan, the borrower will receive only $760. And because this is a single-payment loan, the average amount of money outstanding is also $760. When these figures are used in the APR equation we find the true rate for this 12 percent discount loan is more like 15.8 percent ($120/$760). Clearly, the discount method yields a much higher APR on single-payment loans than does the simple interest method. Exhibit 8.6 contrasts the results from both methods for the single-payment loan example discussed here.

INSTALLMENT LOANS ▣

Installment loans are paid off with a series of payments over time; these payments, along with the accompanying finance charges, can be figured using either simple interest or add-on interest. Does it really make much difference which procedure is used? Give some thought to this question before reading on.

Installment loans (known as ILs for short) differ from single-payment loans in that they require the borrower to repay the debt in a series of installment payments (usually on a monthly basis) over the life of the loan. Installment loans are far more popular than single-payment loans—in fact, they rank as one of the most popular forms of consumer credit. Much of this popularity is, of course, due to the convenient way in which the loan repayment is set up; not surprisingly, most people find it easier on their checkbooks to make a series of small payments rather than one big one.

A REAL CONSUMER CREDIT WORK HORSE!

As a financing vehicle, there are few things that installment loans can't do—which explains, in large part, why this form of consumer credit is so widely used. ILs, in fact, account for nearly two-thirds of all consumer debt outstanding (excluding home mortgages). Installment loans can be used to finance just about any type of big-ticket item imaginable. New car loans are, of course, the dominant type of IL, but this form of credit is also used to finance home furnishings, appliances and entertainment centers, camper trailers and other recreation vehicles, even expensive vacations; and, of course, more and more college students are turning to this type of credit as the way to finance their education.

Not only can they be used to finance all sorts of things, they can also be obtained at all sorts of locations. You'll find them at banks and other financial institutions, as well as major department stores and merchants that sell relatively expensive products. Go into a home appliance store to buy a high-priced stereo and chances are you'd be able to arrange for IL financing right there on the spot. These loans can be taken out for just a few hundred dollars, or they can involve thousands of dollars—indeed, ILs of $25,000 or more are really not all that uncommon. What's more, they can be set up with maturities as short as six months to as long as seven to ten years, even fifteen years!

Most installment loans are secured with some kind of collateral—for example, the car or home entertainment center you purchased with the help of an IL will usually end up serving as collateral on the loan. Even personal loans that are used to finance things like expensive vacations can also be se-

EXHIBIT 8.6

Finance Charges and APRs for a Single-Payment Loan ($1,000 Loan for Two Years at 12% Interest)

Sometimes what you see is not what you get—such as when you borrow money through a discount loan and end up paying quite a bit more than the quoted rate.

Method	Stated Rate on Loan	Finance Charges	APR
Simple interest	12%	$240	12.0%
Discount	12	240	15.8

cured—in this case, the collateral could be securities, CDs, or some other type of financial asset. The fastest growing segment of this market is, in fact, ILs secured by second mortgages. These so-called *home equity loans* are similar to home equity credit lines discussed in Chapter 7, except they involve a set amount of money loaned over a set period of time (often as long as 15 years). Thus, if a borrower needs, say, $25,000 to help pay for an expensive new boat, he would simply take out a loan in that amount and secure it with a second mortgage on his home. For all practical purposes, this loan would be like any other IL in the sense that it's for a set amount of money and is to be repaid over a set period of time in monthly installments. In addition to their highly competitive interest rates, a big attraction of these loans is that the interest paid on them can still be used as a tax deduction. So, borrowers get a double whammy of *low interest rates and tax deductibility!* The accompanying *Issues in Money Management* box provides additional information about these home equity loans, along with some caveats that borrowers should keep in mind when using their home for collateral on a loan.

THE INSTALLMENT PURCHASE CONTRACT

All of the information relevant to a transacton that's being financed on an installment loan basis is included in the **installment purchase contract**. This agreement specifies the obligations of both the purchaser (borrower) and the lender. Although its form is likely to vary with the lender, it will probably contain four basic components: a sales contract, a security agreement, a note, and an insurance agree-

ment. A sample installment purchase contract containing all four of these components is presented in Exhibit 8.7.

Security Agreement. The **security agreement** (or **security interest**) indicates whether the lender has control over the item being purchased. Although state laws determine whether or not the borrower retains legal title to the collateral, the lender files a lien on the collateral in order to make the security interest public. In either case, the lender retains legal control over the collateral. If default does occur, the lender can sell the collateral and use the proceeds to satisfy the unpaid balance on the loan and cover any costs incurred in this process. The lender must pay the borrower any excess funds obtained from the liquidation of the collateral. However, if a *deficiency* occurs—that is, if the proceeds from liquidation are *not* sufficient to satisfy the loan—the borrower may or may not be liable for the unsatisfied portion of the debt, depending on state law (in some states, the lender cannot turn to the borrower to make up the deficiency).

---

installment purchase contract

An agreement that specifies the obligations of both the purchaser (borrower) and seller (lender), issued when a purchase transaction is being financed on an installment basis.

security agreement (security interest)

In an installment purchase contract, a legal agreement that indicates whether or not the lender retains control over the item being purchased.

The Ins and Outs of Home-Equity Installment Loans

Want to finance a car, pay college tuition or take an expensive vacation? If you're like a growing number of Americans, you're looking at a home-equity loan. And if you're not, banks are doing their utmost to point you in that direction. Seeing home-equity loans and credit lines as a bright spot in a bleak lending landscape, many banks are offering low teaser rates for the first year; others are waiving closing costs and other fees. "Home-equity loans are our No. 1 strategic consumer lending product," says Donald Grigley, senior vice president of Shawmut Bank, Hartford, Conn., which charges no fees for loans under $50,000.

Indeed, home-equity borrowing (in 1991) is cheaper than it has been in a long time, both because of falling rates and bank competition. That and the fact that interest remains tax deductible makes home-equity loans more attractive than ever. As a result, homeowners are using them for everything from making investments and buying expensive cars to paying education and medical bills. And that worries some in the industry. "You can get a car or a boat or take a vacation on your home," say Keith Gumbinger, spokesman at HSH Associates, a consumer lending information company. But if you get laid off and can't pay off the loan, he says, it's the house you lose, not the car.

Home-equity borrowing comes in two varieties. *Home-equity loans*, the current jargon for traditional second mortgages, let homeowners borrow a given amount for a set period at either a fixed or variable rate. In addition, there are open-ended *home-equity credit lines* (like the ones discussed in Chapter 7) which let people borrow whenever they want, up to a set limit. These typically have variable rates pegged to the prime rate, a benchmark used by banks in setting interest rates on many loans to businesses and individuals.

A major attraction of home-equity borrowing is that Uncle Sam still picks up part of the tab. Interest on borrowings up to $100,000 is still tax deductible. In contrast, interest on credit cards and other types of consumer credit can no longer be written off. Moreover, home-equity borrowing is a lot cheaper than most other types of credit, even without taking the tax deduction into account. For their part, banks like home-equity lending because of the low default rates and affluent borrowers. They can lend more money at one time and the loans are collateralized by

The Note. The formal promise on the part of the borrower to repay the lender is spelled out in the **note**. It states all the legal obligations of both borrower and lender and outlines all details concerning repayment, default, and disposition of collateral. The note is normally secured by the sales contract, or security agreement, which provides the lender with a security interest in the assets being acquired. It is the document that, when signed by both borrower and lender, legally binds the two parties to the terms and conditions stated therein. Although many of the detailed provisions of the note in Exhibit 8.7 are on the reverse side of the contract (not shown), the entire document, once signed, is considered to be the note.

Credit Life Insurance. Sometimes, as a condition of receiving an installment loan, a borrower is required to buy **credit life insurance** and possibly **credit disability insurance**. Credit life (and disability) insurance is tied to a particular IL and basically provides insurance that the loan will be paid off if the borrower dies (or becomes disabled) before the loan matures. In essence, these policies in-people's houses. In addition, lenders like attracting stable, educated consumers who may decide to buy other bank products. Hence, they are going to great lengths to attract borrowers. In Ashtabula, Ohio, People's Savings Bank is promoting its variable-rate home-equity loans by offering a 9.375% rate if payments are automatically made from a borrower's account; and all fees are waived.

Despite the aggressive marketing, lenders are being more conservative about the loans they approve. While some still let people borrow 100% of the equity in their homes, it is more common to see loan-to-equity values of 80%, 75%, or even 70%. A year-end (1990) survey by the Consumer Bankers Association, a trade group, shows that lenders are taking longer to process applications and that borrowers have owned their homes longer, earned more, and had their jobs longer than in 1989. Banks are also charging more fees. Annual fees of $30 or more are showing up at a growing number of banks. And borrowers who take out a line of credit but don't use it may now get socked with inactivity fees of $50 to $150.

There are other caveats that borrowers should be aware of—the most important of which is the fact that the loan is being secured by one of your most valuable assets: your home! If something goes wrong and you default on the loan, you stand to lose your house. That's a terribly expensive price to pay for bad credit. In addition, consumer credit experts caution that people should be careful with loans that charge interest only for a set period. While most lenders then amortize the loan over 10 or 15 years, others call for immediate payment of all principal. Comparison shoppers should also check on the loan's lifetime interest-rate cap, which limits how high variable rates can go over the life of the loan. These caps currently range from as high as 25% to as low as 14.5%, says HSH's Mr. Gumbinger. Such caps are important, he says, noting that the prime rate hit 21.5% in 1980. One final note of caution: While interest from home-equity loans is currently tax deductible, there's no guarantee it will stay that way. Seeing how the government "pulled the rug" on tax shelters in 1986, borrowers should keep in mind that Congress is fully capable of doing that again, by ending the write-offs on home-equity loans!

Source: Adapted from Lynn Asinof, "Banks Are Cutting Costs of Loans to Boost Home-Equity Borrowing," *Wall Street Journal*, June 10, 1991, p. C1.

sure the borrower for an amount sufficient to repay the outstanding loan balance. The seller's (or lender's) ability to dictate the terms of these insurance requirements is restricted by law in some states. If this type of insurance is required as a condition of the loan, its cost must be added in the finance charges and included as part of the APR. From the borrower's perspective, credit life and disability insurance is NOT a very good deal: *it's very costly and really does little more than provide lenders with a very lucrative source of income*. Not surprisingly, because it is so lucrative, some lenders aggressively

note

In an installment purchase contract, the formal promise on the part of the borrower to repay the lender in accordance with the terms specified in the agreement.

credit life (or disability) insurance

A type of life (or disability) insurance sold in conjunction with installment loans in which the coverage decreases at the same rate as the loan balance.

EXHIBIT 8.7
An Installment Purchase Contract

The installment purchase contract contains all the particulars of a given installment loan, including terms of payment, type and amount of credit insurance, financing arrangement, and other pertinent information.

RETAIL INSTALLMENT CONTRACT AND SECURITY AGREEMENT (Goods)

Date _____ , 19 _____

———— SELLER (CALLED "YOU") ————
NAME _____
ADDRESS _____
CITY _____ STATE _____ ZIP _____
SALESMAN _____

———— BUYER (CALLED "I") ————
NAME _____
NAME _____
ADDRESS _____
CITY _____ STATE _____ ZIP _____

ANNUAL PERCENTAGE RATE The cost of my credit as a yearly rate.	FINANCE CHARGE The dollar amount the credit will cost me.	Amount Financed The amount of credit provided to me or on my behalf.	Total of Payments The amount I will have paid after I have made all payments as scheduled.	Total Sale Price The total cost of my purchase on credit, including my downpayment of $_____
%	$	$	$	$

→ Terms

My payment schedule will be:

Number of Payments	Amount of Payments	When Payments Are Due
		.19 _____ and same date of each following month.

→ Security Agreement

Security: I gave you a security interest in the goods or property being purchased.
Late Charge: If I don't pay any payment in 10 days after it's due, I shall also pay 5% of that payment, but not over $5.00.
Prepayment: If I pay off early, I may be entitled to a refund of part of the finance charge.
See the contract document for any additional information about nonpayment, default, any required repayment in full before the scheduled date, and prepayment refunds.

→ Late Charges

DESCRIPTION OF GOODS	MANUFACTURER	MODEL NO.	RETAIL NO.	CASH SALE PRICE
				$
				$

→ Insurance

INSURANCE DISCLOSURE
NO INSURANCE IS REQUIRED FOR THIS SALE. I may buy any insurance from anyone I choose. Only if requested and for cost stated below, you or buyer of this contract will obtain insurance. Charges will be included in the Amount Financed. I understand this is the only insurance you offer and you (or buyer of this contract) expect to profit from its sale. I consent to this. The one Buyer signing this Insurance Disclosure will be insured when coverage begins, unless a different Buyer's name appears here:

(WRITE "YES" OR "NO" AS DESIRED, DATE, AND SIGN. IF NONE DESIRED, SIGN BELOW.)
_____ Credit Life* .... $ _____
_____ Credit Disability* .... $ _____
_____ Property Insurance .... $ _____

DATE _____ SIGNATURE _____
NO INSURANCE DESIRED: _____ SIGNATURE _____

ITEMIZATION OF AMOUNT FINANCED
                                 Sales Tax (if any) $_____
1. Cash Sale Price .... $_____
2. a. Cash Downpayment .... $_____
   b. Trade-in .... $_____
   DESCRIPTION _____
   Total Downpayment (a + b) .... $_____
3. Unpaid Balance of Cash Sale Price (1-2) .... $_____
4. Insurance (for term of credit)
   Credit Life .... $_____
   Credit Disability .... $_____
   Property .... $_____
   Total Insurance Charges .... $_____
5. Amount Financed (3 + 4) .... $_____
6. Finance Charge .... $_____
7. Total of Payments (5 + 6) .... $_____
8. Total Sale Price (1 + 4 + 6) .... $_____
9. Payable in _____ monthly payments of $_____ each beginning _____ and continuing same day of each month until fully paid.

→ Financing

→ Note

PROMISE TO PAY. Instead of the Cash Price, I promise to pay the Total Sale Price and I agree to pay you (or buyer of this contract) a Total of Payments in monthly payments in the amounts and on the dates stated above. I will pay at your business address, or other address given me. If more than one Buyer is named above, you may enforce this contract against all or any Buyers, but not in a combined amount greater than amount owed.

PREPAYMENT. If I fully prepay before the final due date, the amount I owe will be reduced by (a) unearned Finance Charges computed at the Annual Percentage Rate shown above, the unpaid balances of Amount Financed scheduled for the time after prepayment to maturity, (b) unearned credit insurance charges determined by the "Rule of 78ths", and (c) unearned property insurance charges determined by assuming an equal part is carried each month.

→ Prepayment Provision

FAILURE TO PAY. If I don't pay on time, all my payments may become due at once, and without notifying me before bringing suit, you may sue me for the total amount I owe, less the same unearned Finance Charges I would receive if I fully prepaid. You may also repossess the goods described above.
SECURITY. You waive any security interest in my home that could result if the goods are installed.

→ Acceleration Clause

NOTICE
ANY HOLDER OF THIS CONSUMER CREDIT CONTRACT IS SUBJECT TO ALL CLAIMS AND DEFENSES WHICH THE DEBTOR COULD ASSERT AGAINST THE SELLER OF GOODS OR SERVICES OBTAINED PURSUANT HERETO OR WITH THE PROCEEDS HEREOF. RECOVERY HEREUNDER BY THE DEBTOR SHALL NOT EXCEED AMOUNTS PAID BY THE DEBTOR HEREUNDER.
NOTICE TO THE BUYER: 1. Do not sign this agreement before you read it or if it contains any blank spaces. 2. You are entitled to an exact copy of this contract.
I HAVE READ AND RECEIVED A COMPLETED, READABLE, SIGNED COPY OF THIS CONTRACT.

SELLER: _____   BUYER: _____
By: _____   BUYER: _____

push it on unsuspecting borrowers and, in some cases, even require it as a condition for granting a loan. The best advice is to *avoid it*, if at all possible!

Special Features. In addition to the major points discussed above, installment purchase contracts often contain several other features that should be of interest to borrowers. These special features generally are contained in clauses to the sales contract and/or note, and pertain to additional collateral, default, repossession, and balloon payments.

Add-on clause. An **add-on clause** enables the lender to add assets *that are acquired after the contract has been signed* to the collateral on the loan. The lender need not release the security interest in any of these items until the entire loan has been paid off. In the past, this would have allowed lenders to repossess items of merchandise already purchased and paid for if the borrower defaulted on other items purchased under the agreement. The Consumer Credit Protection Act disallowed such practices. It is still advisable, however, to use separate purchase agreements for each item purchased rather than one agreement with an add-on clause.

Acceleration clause. The **acceleration clause** allows the lender to demand immediate repayment of the entire amount of the unpaid debt in the event the purchaser defaults on loan payments. Although this clause is always included in installment loans, the lender is likely to allow a late payment or levy a penalty instead of calling the loan by exercising the acceleration clause.

Recourse clauses. Most installment purchase contracts contain some type of provision that stipulates the type of action the lender can take in case of default. Especially important here are provisions pertaining to wage assignment, garnishment, and repossession.

Some purchase agreements allow the lender to collect a portion of the purchaser's (borrower's) wages if he or she defaults on payments. By signing a purchase agreement with such a **wage assignment** clause, the purchaser agrees to these terms and gives the lender the right to collect part of his or her wages *without obtaining a court order*.

Even if an assignment clause is not enforceable (as is often the case) or not included in the agreement, a lender can still garnish a borrower's wages. **Garnishment** is a legal method of getting an employer to pay a portion of a borrower's wages to the lender. The borrower must, of course, be in default, and a court order must be issued enabling the employer to take such action. The *Federal Garnishment Law* specifically limits the amount of an employee's weekly wages that can be garnished to no more than the smaller of (1) 25 percent of take-home pay or (2) the amount by which weekly take-home pay exceeds 30 times the federal minimum *hourly* wage. Many state laws have completely prohibited garnishing or have placed severe restrictions on this practice.

The act of seizing collateral when the borrower defaults on a loan is termed **repossession**. In many states, the ability of the lender to repossess collateral is limited (and may even require a court order), but in others, collateral can be repossessed without notice and even "stolen," in effect, from the borrower. Quite often there are detailed procedures that the lender must follow when selling repossessed items in order to satisfy unpaid debts. The repossessed item is eventually sold at auction or by some other means, and the amount due the merchant or lender, along with legal and other expenses in connection

---

add-on clause
A clause that permits the lender to add certain assets to the loan's collateral that are acquired after the installment purchase contract has been signed and to keep its security interest in these items until the loan has been paid off in full.

acceleration clause
A clause in an installment loan contract that allows the lender to demand immediate repayment of the entire outstanding loan balance if the purchaser defaults on loan payments.

wage assignment
A type of recourse against borrower default in which the lender is allowed to collect a specified portion of the borrower's wages without obtaining a court order.

garnishment
Court-ordered payment of a portion of a defaulting borrower's wages to a lender.

repossession
The act of seizing collateral when the borrower defaults on an installment loan.

with the repossession, is taken from the sale proceeds. If this amount is not enough to cover the loan, the customer may or may not be liable for the remaining portion.

Balloon clause. Sometimes installment purchase agreements are set up in such a fashion that the final payment is considerably larger than the others. The Truth in Lending Act requires that any **balloon payment**, which is defined as a payment more than twice the normal installment payment, be clearly identified as such. For example, if a loan required payments of $200 per month for 23 months followed by a final payment of $1,000 in the 24th month, the existence of the $1,000 balloon payment would have to be clearly disclosed. Because balloon clauses have been abused by some lenders and can place borrowers in an undesirable position, some states prohibit their use in loans. It is best not to enter into an agreement that includes such a clause, since balloon payments can cause real financial strain when they fall due. Only if you had adequate savings, or are expecting a known sum of money at some future date, could the use of a balloon payment be justified.

A balloon payment on an installment loan gives the borrower the right to skip monthly payments by deferring them to the very end of the loan.
Fantasy: Scheduled monthly payments must always be paid in a prompt and timely fashion, regardless of any other loan provisions. A balloon payment does *not* give borrowers the right to skip payments; rather, a balloon payment is, in fact, a scheduled payment: i.e., it's the final payment on *some* ILs and is called a balloon because it's so much larger than all the others.

FINANCE CHARGES, MONTHLY PAYMENTS, AND APR

Earlier in this chapter, the finance charges and annual percentage rates (APRs) on single-payment loans were discussed. The simple interest and discount methods of determining finance charges were described and illustrated for single-payment loans. In this section, we look at the use of simple and add-on interest to compute finance charges and monthly payments for installment loans (technically, discount interest can also be used with ILs, but because

this is rare, we ignore it here). For purposes of illustration, we will use a 12 percent, $1,000 installment loan that is to be paid off in 12 monthly payments. As in the earlier illustration for single-payment loans, interest is the only component of the finance charge; the presence of any other loan charges (such as credit life insurance, or title and notary fees) is ignored.

Using Simple Interest. When simple interest is used with ILs—and most major banks and S&Ls do use it on their installment loans—interest is charged only on the outstanding balance of the loan. Thus, as the loan principal declines with monthly payments, the amount of interest being charged decreases as well. Because finance charges change each month, the procedure used to find the interest expense is mathematically very complex. Fortunately, this problem is avoided in practice, since the convention in the industry is to use *finance tables*. Essentially, these tables provide the *monthly payment* that would be required to retire an installment loan that carries a given simple rate of interest and has a given term to maturity. Because the tables have interest charges built right into them, the monthly payments cover both principal and interest. Exhibit 8.8 provides an excerpt from such a table for a variety of widely used interest rates and maturities.

The values in the table represent the monthly payments required to retire a $1,000 loan. Even though it's assumed you're borrowing $1,000, the table can be used with any size loan. For example, if you're looking at a $5,000 loan, just multiply the monthly loan payment from the table by 5—that is, $5,000/$1,000 = 5; or if you have, say, a $500 loan, multiply the loan payment by .5 ($500/$1,000 = .5), In many respects, this table is just like the mortgage loan payment schedule introduced in Chapter 6, except we use much shorter loan maturities here than we do with mortgages.

Here's how the table in Exhibit 8.8 is used. Suppose we want to find the monthly payment required on our $1,000, 12 percent, 12-month loan. Looking under the 12-month column and across from the 12 percent rate of interest, we find a value of $88.85; that is the monthly payment it will take to pay off the $1,000 loan in 12 months. When the monthly payments ($88.85) are multiplied by the term of the loan in months (12), the result will be total payments of $88.85 × 12 = $1,066.20. The difference

EXHIBIT 8.8

A Table of Monthly Installment Loan Payments (to Repay a $1,000/Simple Interest Loan)

A table like this can be used to find the monthly payments on a wide variety of simple interest installment loans. While it's set up in reference to a $1,000 loan, with a little modification, it can easily be used with any size loan (the principal can be more or less than $1,000).

Rate of Interest	Loan Maturity						
	6 Months	12 Months	18 Months	24 Months	36 Months	48 Months	60 Months
7.5%	$170.33	$86.76	$58.92	$45.00	$31.11	$24.18	$20.05
8	170.58	86.99	59.15	45.23	31.34	24.42	20.28
8.5	170.82	87.22	59.37	45.46	31.57	24.65	20.52
9	171.07	87.46	59.60	45.69	31.80	24.89	20.76
9.5	171.32	87.69	59.83	45.92	32.04	25.13	21.01
10	171.56	87.92	60.06	46.15	32.27	25.37	21.25
10.5	171.81	88.15	60.29	46.38	32.51	25.61	21.50
11	172.05	88.50	60.64	46.73	32.86	25.97	21.87
11.5	173.30	88.62	60.76	46.85	32.98	26.09	22.00
12	172.50	88.85	60.99	47.08	33.22	26.34	22.25
12.5	172.80	89.09	61.22	47.31	33.46	26.58	22.50
13	173.04	89.32	61.45	47.55	33.70	26.83	22.76
14	173.54	89.79	61.92	48.02	34.18	27.33	23.27
15	174.03	90.26	62.39	48.49	34.67	27.84	23.79
16	174.53	90.74	62.86	48.97	35.16	28.35	24.32
17	175.03	91.21	63.34	49.45	35.66	28.86	24.86
18	175.53	91.68	63.81	49.93	36.16	29.38	25.40

between the total payments on the loan and the principal portion represents the *finance charges on the loan* — in this case, $1,066.20 − $1,000 = interest charges of $66.20.

Now, from each monthly payment, a certain portion goes to interest and the balance is used to reduce the principal. Because the principal balance declines with each payment, the amount that goes to interest also *decreases* while the amount that goes to principal *increases*. Exhibit 8.9 illustrates this pattern. Note that since *monthly* payments are used with the loan, the interest column in Exhibit 8.9 is also based on a *monthly* rate of interest — that is, the annual rate is divided by 12 to obtain a monthly rate (12 percent per year/12 = 1 percent per month). This monthly rate is then applied to the outstanding loan balance to find the monthly interest charges in column 3. Because interest is charged only on the outstanding balance, *the annual percentage rate (APR) on a simple interest IL will always equal the stated rate* — in this case 12 percent.

Add-on Method. A number of installment loans are made using the **add-on method**, which results in a very expensive form of credit. Add-on loans, in

fact, rank as one of the most costly forms of consumer credit, with APRs that are often well above the rates charged even on many credit cards. Unfortunately, the add-on procedure is still widely used, particularly among retail merchants, consumer finance companies, and sales finance companies; it is even used by some banks and S&Ls. With add-on interest, the finance charges are calculated using the *original* balance of the loan, which are then added to the original loan balance. Thus, the amount of finance charges on an add-on loan can be found by using the familiar simple interest formula:

$$F = P \times r \times t.$$

balloon payment
A final payment on an installment loan that is substantially larger than the normal installment payment.

add-on method
A method of calculating interest by computing finance charges on the original loan balance and then adding the interest to that balance.

EXHIBIT 8.9

Monthly Payment Analysis for a Simple Interest Installment Loan (Assumes a $1,000, 12%, 12-Month Loan)

Part of each monthly payment on an installment loan goes to interest and part to principal. As the loan is paid down over time, less and less of each payment goes to interest, and more and more goes to principal.

Month	Outstanding Loan Balance (1)	Monthly Payment (2)	Interest Charges [(1) × 0.01] (3)	Principal [(2) − (3)] (4)
1	$1,000.00	$ 88.85	$10.00	$ 78.85
2	921.15	88.85	9.21	79.64
3	841.51	88.85	8.42	80.43
4	761.08	88.85	7.61	81.24
5	679.84	88.85	6.80	82.05
6	597.79	88.85	5.98	82.87
7	514.92	88.85	5.15	83.70
8	431.22	88.85	4.31	84.54
9	346.68	88.85	3.47	85.38
10	261.30	88.85	2.61	86.24
11	175.06	88.85	1.75	87.10
12	87.96	88.85	0.89	87.96
Total		$1,066.20	$66.20	$1,000.00

Note: Column 1 values for months 2 through 12 are obtained by subtracting the principal payment shown in column 4 for the preceding month from the outstanding loan balance shown in column 1 for the preceding month; thus, $1,000 − $78.85 = $921.15, which is the outstanding loan balance in month 2.

Given the $1,000 loan we have been using for illustrative purposes, the finance charges on a 12 percent, one-year add-on loan would be

$$F = \$1,000 \times .12 \times 1 = \$120.$$

Compared to the finance charges for the same loan on a simple interest basis ($66.20), the add-on loan is a lot more costly, a fact that will also show up in monthly payments and APR. Keep in mind that both of these loans would be quoted as "12 percent" loans; thus, you may think you are getting a 12 percent loan, but looks can be deceiving — especially when you are dealing with add-on interest! So, when taking out an installment loan, make sure you find out whether simple or add-on interest is being used to compute finance charges. And if it's add-on, you might want to consider looking elsewhere for the loan.

To find the monthly payments on an add-on loan, all you need to do is add the finance charge ($120) to the *original* principal amount of the loan ($1,000) and then divide this sum by the number of monthly payments to be made. In the case of our $1,000, one-year loan, this results in monthly payments of $93.33, found as follows:

$$\frac{\text{Monthly}}{\text{payments}} = \frac{\$1,000 + \$120}{12} = \frac{\$1,120}{12} = \$93.33.$$

As expected, these monthly payments are much higher than the ones with the simple interest loan ($88.85).

Because the actual rate of interest with an add-on loan is considerably higher than the stated rate, we must determine the loan's APR. The procedure for finding the mathematically precise APR is highly complex and far beyond the scope of this book. Fortunately, there are several ways to approximate the APR on an add-on loan, the most accurate of which is the so-called **N-ratio method**. The N-ratio actually results in an APR that is remarkably close to the precise figure. This method uses the following formula to find the approximate APR:

$$\text{Approximate APR} = \frac{M(95N + 9)F}{12N(N + 1)(4P + F)},$$

EXHIBIT 8.10

Comparative Finance Charges and APRs (Assumes a $1,000, 12%, 12-Month Installment Loan)

In sharp contrast to simple interest loans, the APR with add-on installment loans is *much higher* than the stated rate.

	Simple Interest	Add-on Interest
Stated rate on loan	12%	12%
Finance charges	$ 66.20	$ 120.00
Monthly payments	$ 88.25	$ 93.33
Total payments made	$1,066.20	$1,120.00
APR	12%	21.4%

where

APR = annual percentage rate of interest
M = number of payments in a year
N = number of loan payments scheduled over life of loan
F = total finance charges
P = principal amount of loan

To see how this formula works, let's return to our $1,000, 12 percent, one-year add-on loan. With this loan, $M = 12, N = 12, F = \$120$, and $P = \$1,000$. *The approximate APR in this case works out to be 21.4%:*

Approximate APR

$$= \frac{(12)[(95)(12) + 9](\$120)}{(12)(12)(12 + 1)[(4)(\$1,000) + \$120]}$$

$$= \frac{(12)(1149)(\$120)}{(12)(12)(13)(\$4,120)}$$

$$= \frac{\$1,654,560}{\$7,712,640} = 21.4\%.$$

As a matter of interest, the precise APR on this loan is 21.36 percent.

When viewed from an APR perspective, this 12 percent add-on loan turns out to be *very expensive*, as it has an actual rate of interest (21.4 percent) that is considerably higher than the quoted rate of 12 percent. (A rough but reasonably accurate rule of thumb is that the APR on an add-on loan is about

twice the stated rate—thus, if the loan is quoted at an add-on rate of 9 percent, you're probably going to end up paying a true rate that's closer to 18 percent.) This is because when add-on interest is applied to an installment loan, the interest included in each payment is charged on the initial principal even though the outstanding loan balance is reduced as installment payments are made. A summary of comparative finance charges and APRs for this example is presented in Exhibit 8.10.

Under the Truth in Lending Act, the exact APR (accurate to the nearest 0.25 percent) must be disclosed to borrowers. Note that not only interest, but also any other fees required to obtain a loan are considered part of the finance charges and should be included in the computation of the APR.

The Rule of 78s. One of the problems in using add-on interest is that it does not account for *monthly* interest charges when installment payments are made. To overcome this deficiency, the

---

N-ratio method

A formula used for estimating the annual percentage rate (APR) on an add-on loan.

finance industry has developed the **Rule of 78s** (or **sum-of-the-digits method**), which is used to determine *monthly interest charges* on add-on ILs. In addition, the Rule of 78s is used to determine monthly premiums on credit life and disability insurance. The object of the Rule of 78s is to derive a monthly factor that can be applied to the loan's *total finance charges* so as to determine interest charges on a monthly basis. (Note that the rule of 78s is *not* used with simple interest loans, since monthly interest charges on such loans are automatically linked to declining loan balances.)

To find the *monthly factors*, the first thing we do is add up all the digits for the number of payments to be made on the loan. For example, with a 12-month loan, we would add up the numbers from 1 to 12 (that is, $1 + 2 + 3 + 4 + \ldots + 10 + 11 + 12$); doing so would result in a total of 78. (Note that while the Rule of 78s gets its name from the sum of the 12 digits in a year, it can be applied to ILs with any maturity.) Instead of computing the sum of the number of payments in a loan—which can become quite a job with long-term loans—the following simple formula can be used:

Sum of the digits = (Number of payments ÷ 2)
  × (Number of payments + 1)

For example, to find the sum of the digits for a 12-month loan, we would have:

Sum of the digits = $(12 \div 2) \times (12 + 1)$
  $= 6 \times 13 = 78.$

The sum of the digits provides the bottom half of the *monthly factor* (that is, its denominator); to complete the factor, we simply use the monthly digits of the loan *in descending order*. Thus, in our example the factor for the first month would be 12/78 (always use the actual *monthly* digits for a given loan, so that if you are working with a two-year loan, the digit for the first month would be 24, for the second 23, and so on down to 1 for the last month). The logic behind this system of declining monthly factors is that the borrower has full (12/12) use of the principal in the first month of a 12-month loan, then, after the first payment is made, only 11/12 in the second month, and so forth. Given that the borrower has use of more money in the early stages of the IL, he or she should pay more in finance charges in the early months of the loan and progressively less with the passage of time. This is exactly what's accomplished with the monthly factors derived from the Rule of 78s.

Applying the monthly factors to the *total finance charges* on the loan results in the appropriate monthly interest charges. With our $1,000, 12 percent, one-year loan as an example, the interest charges for the first month would be (12/78) × $120 = .1538 × $120 = $18.46; for the second month (11/78) × $120 = .1410 × $120 = 16.92; and so on down to the last month (1/78) × $120 = $1.54. Exhibit 8.11 shows how the monthly payments on our $1,000, 12 percent add-on loan are divided between principal and interest, when interest charges are determined according to the Rule of 78s. Principal and interest behave with add-on credit just like the simple interest loan that we saw in Exhibit 8.9, to the extent that the amount that goes to interest decreases with each payment while the amount that goes to principal increases.

Actually most borrowers come in contact with the Rule of 78s only when they pay off an add-on loan prior to maturity. Under such circumstances, the lender is entitled to all *interest* earned to date, while the borrower needs to know how much *principal* is left unpaid on the loan—that is, how much he or she will have to come up with to pay off the loan. To see how this works, let's assume we want to pay off the $1,000, 12 percent, one-year loan after three months. Using the Rule of 78s, the lender would be entitled to 33/78 of the total finance charges—i.e., (12 + 11 + 10)/78; in dollar terms, this amounts to $50.77 [(33/78) × $120]. Because the lender is entitled to $50.77 in interest charges, the borrower should receive the rest of the add-on finance charges as a "refund." This is found by subtracting the amount earned by the lender from the total finance charges on the loan; in this case, it amounts to $120.00 − $50.77 = $69.23. The **loan payoff** can now be found as follows:

Amount of loan, including add-on finance charges	$1,120.00
Less: Interest refunded to borrower	69.23
	$1,050.77
Less: Payments to date (3 × $93.33)	279.99
Loan payoff	770.78

Thus, right after our third payment, we would pay the loan off with another payment of $770.78, which is the amount of the principal we still owe on the loan.

EXHIBIT 8.11

Monthly Payment Analysis for an Add-on Installment Loan (Assumes a $1,000, 12%, 12-Month Loan)

The monthly interest charges on add-on loans are found by using the Rule of 78s. Like simple interest loans, the monthly finance charge declines each month as the outstanding loan balance goes down.

Month	Outstanding Loan Balance (1)	Monthly Payment (2)	Monthly Interest Factor (3)	Interest Charges[a] [(3) × $120] (4)	Principal [(2) − (4)] (5)
1	$1,000.00	$ 93.33	12/78	$ 18.46	$ 74.87
2	925.13	93.33	11/78	16.92	76.41
3	848.72	93.33	10/78	15.39	77.94
4	770.78	93.33	9/78	13.85	79.48
5	691.30	93.33	8/78	12.30	81.03
6	610.27	93.33	7/78	10.77	82.56
7	527.71	93.33	6/78	9.23	84.10
8	443.61	93.33	5/78	7.69	85.64
9	357.97	93.33	4/78	6.15	87.18
10	270.79	93.33	3/78	4.63	88.70
11	182.09	93.33	2/78	3.07	90.26
12	91.83	93.37	1/78	1.54	91.83
Total		$1,120.00		$120.00	$1,000.00

[a]To find monthly interest charges (col. 4), simply convert the monthly *interest factor* (from col. 3) to a *decimal* value and then multiply by the total interest charges on the loan (in this case, $120). For example, in the first month, 12 ÷ 78 = .1538; multiplying this value by $120, we have .1538 × $120 = $18.46.

The Rule of 78s is a regulation that grew out of the Consumer Credit Enhancement Act of 1978 and mandates how installment loans will be set up. **Fantasy:** The Rule of 78s is a procedure that is used to find the monthly finance charges on add-on loans.

BUY ON TIME OR PAY CASH?

Oftentimes, when you buy a big-ticket item, you have little choice but to take out a loan to finance the purchase—the acquisition (perhaps it's a new car) is just so expensive that you cannot afford to pay cash. And even if you do have the money, you may still be better off using something like an IL *if the cash purchase would end up severely depleting your liquid reserves.* But don't just automatically take out a loan. Rather, take the time to find out if, in fact, that's the best thing to do. Such a decision can easily be made by using a worksheet similar to the one in Exhibit 8.12. This worksheet basically considers the cost of the loan relative to the after-tax earnings generated from having your money in some type of short-term investment vehicle. A basic assumption here is that the consumer has an adequate level of liquid reserves, and that these reserves are being held in some type of savings account. (Obviously, if this is not the case, there's little reason to go through the exercise, since you have no choice but to borrow the money.) Essentially, it boils down to this: *If it costs more to borrow the money than you can earn in interest, then draw the money from your savings to pay cash for the purchase; if not, then consider taking out a loan.*

To see how this works, consider the following situation: You're thinking about buying a second car (a nice low-mileage used vehicle) and after the normal down payment, you still need to come up with $9,000. This balance can be taken care of in one of

Rule of 78s (sum-of-the-digits method)
A procedure that is used to determine monthly interest charges on an add-on loan, and to determine the portion of total finance charges that the lender will receive when an add-on loan is paid off prior to its maturity.

loan payoff
The amount required to terminate a loan.

EXHIBIT 8.12

To Borrow or Not to Borrow

Using a worksheet like the one shown here, you can decide whether to buy on time or pay cash by comparing the (after-tax) cost of interest paid on a loan with the after-tax interest income lost by taking the money out of savings and using it to pay cash for the purchase.

BUY ON TIME OR PAY CASH		
Name John E. Jones **Date** February 28, 1992		
■ **Cost of Borrowing**		

1. Terms of the loan
  a. Amount of the loan
  b. Length of loan (in years)
  c. Monthly payment
	$ 9,000.00
	3 yrs.
	$ 298.98	

2. Total loan payments made (monthly loan payment x length of loan in months) $298.98 per month x 36 months		$ 10,763.28
3. Less: Principal amount of the loan		$<9,000.00>
4. Total interest paid over life of loan (line 2 – line 3)		$ 1,763.28

5. Tax considerations:
  • Is this a home-equity loan (where interest expenses
    can be deducted from taxes) .... yes ☐ no ☒
  • Do you itemize deductions on your federal tax returns .... yes ☒ no ☐
  • If you answered yes to BOTH questions, then proceed to *line 6;*
    if you answered no to *either one or both* of the questions, then
    proceed to *line 8* and use *line 4* as the after-tax interest cost of the loan.		

6. What Federal Tax Bracket are you in? (use either 15, 28, or 31%)	— %	
7. Taxes saved due to interest deductions (line 4 x tax rate, from line 6: $ x %)		$ —
8. Total after-tax interest cost on the loan (line 4 – line 7)		$ 1,763.28
■ **Cost of Paying Cash**		
9. Annual interest *earned* on savings (Annual rate of interest earned on savings x amount of loan: 6 % x $9,000.00)		$ 540.00
10. Annual after-tax interest earnings (line 9 x [1 – tax rate] — e.g., 1 – 28% = 72%: $ 540.00 x 72 %)		$ 388.80
11. Total after-tax interest earnings over life of loan (line 10 x line 1-b: $ 388.80 x 3 years)		$ 1,166.40
■ **Net Cost of Borrowing**		
12. Difference in cost of borrowing vs. cost of paying cash (line 8 minus line 11)		$ 596.88
BASIC DECISION RULE: *Pay cash* if line 12 is positive; *borrow the money* if line 12 is negative.		
Note: For simplicity, compounding is ignored in calculating *both* the cost of interest and interest earnings.		

two ways: (1) You can take out a 36-month, 12 percent IL (according to Exhibit 8.8, the *Table of Monthly Loan Payments*, such an IL would have monthly payments of $33.22 × 9 = $298.98); or (2) you can pay cash for the car by drawing the money from a money fund (the fund currently pays 6 percent interest, and that's expected to hold for the foreseeable future). We can now use the worksheet to decide whether to buy on time or pay cash—the complete details of which are provided in Exhibit 8.12. In this case, we assume the loan is a standard IL, where the interest does not qualify as a tax deduction, and that you're in the 28 percent interest bracket. Note in the exhibit that by borrowing the money, you'll end up paying nearly $1,765 in interest (line 8), none of which is tax deductible. In contrast, by leaving your money on deposit in the money fund, you'll receive only $1,166 in interest, after taxes (see line 11). Taken together, we see the net cost of borrowing (line 12) is nearly $600—in essence, you'll be paying over $1,750 to earn less than $1,200, which certainly doesn't make much

sense! Clearly, it's far more cost-effective in this case to *pay cash* for the car, for by doing so, you'll save nearly $600.

While such a figure provides a pretty convincing reason for avoiding a loan, there may be occasions where the actual dollar spread between the cost of borrowing and interest earned is very small, perhaps only $100, or less (actually, if our example above had involved a home equity loan, where interest is tax deductible, the net cost of borrowing [line 12] would have dropped to $103). Being able to deduct the interest on a loan can lead to a relatively small spread, but it can also occur, for example, if the amount being financed is relatively small—say, you want $1,500 or $2,000 for a ski trip to Colorado. Under these circumstances, and so long as the spread stays sufficiently small, you may decide it's still worthwhile to borrow the money in order to maintain a higher level of liquidity. Although this course of action is perfectly legitimate when very small spreads exist, it makes less sense as the gap starts to widen.

SUMMARY

- Single-payment and installment loans are formally negotiated consumer loan arrangements that are used mainly as a way to finance big-ticket items; most of these consumer loans are taken out as auto loans, loans for other durable goods, education loans, personal loans, and consolidation loans.
- Consumer loans can be obtained from a number of sources, including commercial banks (the biggest providers of such credit), consumer finance companies, credit unions, S&Ls, sales finance (and captive finance) companies, life insurance companies, and finally, as a last resort, there are your friends and relatives.
- When shopping for credit, it's in your best interest to seek annual interest rates (APRs), loan maturities, monthly payments, and collateral requirements that are fully compatible to your financial plans and cash budgets.
- In a single-payment loan, the borrower is obligated to make just one principal payment (at the maturity of the loan), though he/she may be required to make one or more interim interest payments. Such loans are usually made for a period

of one year or less, and normally are secured by some type of collateral; a major advantage of the single-payment loan is that it doesn't require monthly payments and as such, won't tie up the borrower's cash flow.
- In an installment loan, the borrower agrees to repay the loan through a series of equal installment payments (usually on a monthly basis) until the obligation is fully repaid; in this way, the borrower can come up with a loan-repayment schedule that fits neatly into his/her financial plans and cash budgets. This highly popular form of consumer credit can be used to finance just about any type of big-ticket asset or expenditure; and many of them are taken out as home equity loans in order to capture tax advantages.
- Most single-payment loans are made with either simple or discount interest, whereas most ILs are made with either simple or add-on interest. So long as simple interest is used, the actual finance charge will always correspond to the stated rate of interest; in contrast, when discount or add-on rates are used, the APR will always be more than the stated rate.

QUESTIONS AND PROBLEMS

1. Define and differentiate between (a) a single-payment loan and (b) an installment loan.

2. List and briefly discuss the five major reasons for borrowlng money through a consumer loan.

3. Identify several different types of federally sponsored student loan programs. Briefly note some of the basic features of these programs and how they differ from regular consumer loans. As a college student, what aspects of these student loan programs appeal to you the most?

4. Compare the consumer lending activities of (a) consumer finance companies and (b) sales finance companies. Describe a captive finance company.

5. Discuss the role of (a) credit unions and (b) savings and loan associations in consumer lending. Point out any similarities or differences in their lending activities. How do they compare to commercial banks?

6. What two questions should be answered before taking out a consumer loan? Explain.
   a. List and briefly discuss the different factors that you should consider when shopping for a loan.
   b. One of the factors to consider is the total cost of the transaction. Explain how this can be done.
   c. Assume you have been shopping for a new car and intend to finance it, in part, through an installment loan. The car you are looking for has a sticker price of $10,000. Big A Autos has offered to sell it to you for $2,500 down and a loan to finance the balance that will require 36 monthly payments of $253.12; Cars-Are-Us will sell you exactly the same vehicle for $3,000 down plus a 48-month loan for the balance, with monthly payments of $177.65. Which is the better deal? Explain.

7. Every six months, Keith Clark takes an inventory of the consumer debts he has outstanding. The latest tally showed the following list: He still owed $4,000 on a home improvement loan (monthly payments of $125); he was mak-ing $85 monthly payments on a personal loan that had a remaining balance of $750; he had a $2,000, secured single-payment loan that is due late next year; he had a $70,000 home mortgage on which he was making $820 monthly payments; he still owed $8,600 on a new-car loan (monthly payments of $205); he had a $960 balance on his Visa card (minimum payment of $40), a $70 balance on his Shell credit card (balance due in 30 days), and a $1,200 balance on a personal line of credit ($60 monthly payments). Use a worksheet like the one in Exhibit 8.3 to prepare an inventory of Keith's consumer debt. Find his debt safety ratio given that he has a take-home pay of $2,500 per month; would you consider this ratio good or bad? Explain.

8. Describe the two methods used to calculate the finance charges on a single-payment loan. As a borrower, which method would you prefer? Explain.

9. Indicate whether the following statements are true or false, and explain your response:
   a. The simple interest method is one in which interest is charged on the average loan balance outstanding.
   b. Under the discount method, the finance charge is calculated and then added to the total amount of the loan.
   c. Most unsecured single-payment loans are made only to the highest-quality borrowers with proven credit reputations.
   d. The instrument giving the lender title to the property in the event of default is called a lien.
   e. A loan rollover is one way to pay off a single-payment loan.

10. Briefly describe and differentiate between (a) a chattel mortgage and (b) a collateral note.

11. Find the finance charges on a 14 percent, 18-month single-payment loan when interest is computed using the simple interest method. Find the finance charges on the same loan when interest is computed using the discount method. Determine the APR in each case.

12. Bill Withers has to borrow $4,000. First State

Bank will lend him the money for 12 months through a single-payment loan at 13.5 percent discount; Home Savings and Loan will make him a $4,000 single-payment, 12-month loan at 15 percent simple. Where should Bill borrow the money? Explain.

13. What is a home equity loan and how are these loans similar to other ILs? Briefly note the basic features of a home equity loan. What are its major advantages and disadvantages?

14. Briefly describe an installment purchase contract, and define the four basic components such a contract is likely to contain.

15. Explain the purpose and describe the general content of the note that is ordinarily included as part of an installment purchase agreement.

16. Why is a borrower often required to purchase credit life and disability insurance as a condition for receiving an installment loan? Explain. Is this a good deal for the borrower?

17. Discuss each of the following features that may be included in an installment purchase agreement: (a) add-on clause, (b) acceleration clause, (c) wage assignment or garnishment, (d) repossession feature, and (e) balloon clause.

18. Define simple interest as it relates to an installment loan. Assuming that interest is the only finance charge, how much interest would be paid on a $500 installment loan to be repaid in six monthly installments of $87.02? If simple interest were charged at the annual rate of 15 percent on the outstanding balance, what would the APR be on this loan? Explain.

19. Return to the opening paragraph of this chapter and take another look at the car loan that Chris Jenkins had to take out in order to buy his new car; recall that after his down payment, Chris still had to borrow some $13,000. Assuming Chris can obtain the money by taking out a 48-month installment loan at a simple interest rate of 12.5 percent, answer the following questions:
   a. What will be the size of his monthly payments? (Use the loan payment table in Exhibit 8.8.)
   b. What will be the total amount of interest Chris pays in the first year of the loan? (Use a monthly payment analysis procedure similar to the one in Exhibit 8.9.)
   c. How much interest will Chris pay over the full (48-month) life of the loan?
   d. What is the APR on this loan?

20. Stan Lee plans to borrow $5,000 and repay it in 36 monthly installments. This loan is being made at an annual add-on interest rate of 11.5 percent.
   a. Assuming that the only component of the finance charge is interest, calculate this charge.
   b. Use your finding in part a to calculate the monthly payment on the loan.
   c. Use the N-ratio method to estimate the APR on the loan.

21. What is the Rule of 78s? Ken Pitowski borrowed $4,000 to be repaid in 36 monthly installments; the loan was made at an add-on interest rate of 9 percent. Using the Rule of 78s, what is the amount the *lender* will receive if Ken repays the loan after six months? Determine the loan payoff at that time.

22. Under what conditions does it make more sense to pay cash for a big-ticket item than to borrow the money to finance the purchase? Are there ever times when borrowing the money is the best course of action?
   a. Consider the following situation: Sherman Jacobs wants to buy a home entertainment center; complete with a big-screen TV, VCR, and sound system, the unit would cost $4,500. Sherman has over $15,000 in a money fund, so he can easily afford to pay cash for the whole thing (the fund is currently paying 5.5 percent interest, and Sherman expects that yield to hold for the foreseeable future). To stimulate sales, the dealer is offering to finance the full cost of the unit with a 36-month installment loan at 9 percent, simple. Use a worksheet like the one in Exhibit 8.12 to determine whether Sherman should pay cash for this home entertainment center or buy it on time. (Note: assume Sherman is in the 28 percent tax bracket and that he itemizes deductions on his tax returns.) Briefly explain your answer.
   b. Rework the above problem assuming Sherman has the option of using a 48-month, 9.5 percent home equity loan to

finance the full cost of this entertainment center. Again, use a worksheet like the one in Exhibit 8.12 to determine if Sherman should pay cash or buy on time. Does your answer change (from the one you came up with in part a, above)? Explain.

CONTEMPORARY CASE APPLICATIONS

■ 8.1 Financing Marilyn's Education

At age 19, Marilyn Bronson is in the middle of her second year of studies at a community college in San Diego. She has done well in her course work; majoring in prebusiness studies, she currently has a 3.75 grade point average. Marilyn currently lives at home and works part-time as a filing clerk for a nearby electronics distributor. Her parents cannot afford to pay her tuition and college expenses — she is virtually on her own as far as college goes. Marilyn hopes to transfer to the University of Texas next year. She has already been accepted and feels that she would get an excellent education there. After talking with her counselor, Marilyn feels that she will not be able to hold down a part-time job and still manage to complete her bachelor's degree program at Texas in two years. Knowing that on her twenty-second birthday she will receive approximately $30,000 from a trust fund left her by her grandmother, Marilyn has decided to borrow against the trust fund in order to support herself during the next two years. She estimates that she will need $20,000 to meet tuition, room and board, books and supplies, travel, personal expenditures, and so on during that period. Unable to qualify for any special loan programs, Marilyn has found two sources of single-payment loans, each requiring a security interest in the trust proceeds as collateral. The terms required by each potential lender are as follows:

  a. California State Bank will lend $25,000 at 10 percent discount interest. The loan principal would be due at the end of two years.

  b. National Bank of San Diego will lend $20,000 under a two-year note. The note would carry a 12 percent simple interest rate and would also be due in a single payment at the end of two years.

Questions

1. How much would Marilyn (a) receive in initial loan proceeds and (b) be required to repay at maturity under the California State Bank loan?

2. Compute (a) the finance charges and (b) the APR on the loan offered by California State Bank.

3. Compute (a) the finance charges and (b) the APR on the loan offered by the National Bank of San Diego. How big a loan payment would be due at the end of two years?

4. Compare your findings in Questions 2 and 3, and recommend one of the loans to Marilyn. Explain your recommendation.

5. What other recommendation might you offer Marilyn relative to the disposition of the loan proceeds?

■ 8.2 Glen Gets His Camaro

Glen Watson, a 27-year-old bachelor living in Charlotte, North Carolina, has been a high school teacher for five years. For the past four months, he has been thinking about buying a Chevrolet Camaro, but feels he is not able to afford a brand-new one. Recently, however, a friend, John McKenzie, has offered to sell him his year-old, fully loaded Camaro Z-28. John wants $12,500 for his car, which has been driven only 8,000 miles and is in very good condition. Glen is eager to buy the car but has only $6,000 in his savings account at Tar Heel Bank. He expects to net $3,000 from the sale of his Chevrolet Vega, but this will still leave him about $3,500 short. He has two alternatives for obtaining the money:

  a. Borrow $3,500 from the First National Bank of Charlotte at a fixed rate of 12 percent per annum, simple interest. The loan would be repaid in equal monthly installments over a three-year (36-month) period.

  b. Obtain a $3,500 installment loan requiring 36 monthly payments from the Charlotte Teacher's Credit Union at a 6½ percent stated rate of interest. The add-on method would be used to calculate the finance charges on this loan.

Questions

1. Using Exhibit 8.8, determine the required monthly payments if the loan is taken out at First National Bank of Charlotte.
2. Compute (a) the finance charges and (b) the APR on the loan offered by First National Bank of Charlotte.
3. Determine the size of the monthly payment required on the loan from the Charlotte Teacher's Credit Union.
4. Compute (a) the finance charges and (b) the APR on the loan offered by the Charlotte Teacher's Credit Union.
5. Compare the two loans and recommend one of them to Glen. Explain your recommendation.

F O R   M O R E   I N F O R M A T I O N

General Information Articles

Davis, Kristin. "Cheap Credit." *Changing Times*, April 1990, pp. 85–89.

Klein, Robert J. "Want Fair Treatment From Lenders? Know Your Rights." *Money,* December 1988, pp. 183–184.

McCormally, Kevin. "When Debt Pays." *Kiplinger's Personal Finance Magazine*, July 1991, pp. 41–43.

Schultz, Ellen E. "Consolidating Debt Can Be a Costly Cure." *The Wall Street Journal*, September 4, 1991, pp. C1, C17.

———. "What You Can Do If You're Facing a Financial Crisis." *The Wall Street Journal*, November 26, 1990, pp. C1, C14.

Sprouse, Mary. "The Pitfalls of Loans from the Heart." *Business Week*, July 29, 1991, pp. 80–81.

Government Documents and Other Publications

The ABC's of Figuring Interest. Public Information Department; Federal Reserve Bank of Chicago; 230 S. LaSalle St.; Chicago, IL 60690.

The Arithmetic of Interest Rates. Consumer Information Center; P.O. Box 100; Pueblo, CO 81002.

Borrowers, Lenders, and Interest Rates. Public Services Department; Federal Reserve Bank of Richmond; P.O. Box 27622; Richmond, VA 23261.

Two Faces of Debt. Division of Consumer and Community Affairs; Board of Governors; Federal Reserve System; Washington, D.C. 20551.

Consumer loans are negotiated for specific purposes and will terminate when the loan is repaid. They are normally used to purchase big-ticket items. The interest rate on consumer loans can be either fixed or variable, and the principal can be repaid in installments or with a single payment. Except for qualifying home-equity loans, the interest paid on consumer debt is not currently tax deductible.

Before you purchase a big-ticket item, you should determine if the acquisition fits into your financial plan. If so and you have the cash to make the acquisition, then you need to determine whether to buy on time or pay cash. This can be accomplished by using a worksheet like the one shown in Exhibit 8.12. Assuming that you are going to finance the purchase, you then need to determine what level of debt service will fit into your cash budget.

There are many sources of consumer loans. Among these are commercial banks, credit unions, finance companies, savings and loans, and life insurance companies. Formal loan documents spell out all the terms and agreements; specifically, the maturity, rate and method of interest calculation, collateral, prepayment penalties, and so on.

In order to compare the total costs of financing your consumer purchase, you may need to consider the cost of the item as well as the financing cost. In the case of captive finance companies (such as GMAC) that help their distributors finance the products they sell, you might find the low rate being

If You Are Just Starting Out

One of your first uses of consumer credit will probably be for the purchase of an automobile. Assuming that the purchase meets your financial goals, you must determine how much of a monthly payment you can afford and then calculate the maximum amount you can finance. However, since this will be dependent on the interest rate charged on the loan, you need to be aware of financing costs prior to going to the dealership.

When you establish your banking relationships, be sure to review all of the types of loans that the institution offers (see Exhibit 8.2 for the major sources of consumer loans) and how competitive they are with others in the market. You might choose an institution with low service charges on checking but with the highest lending rates. If you were to try to borrow money from an institution with which you had no account relationship and you are just starting out in your career, you may not be successful.

Points to Remember:

1. Before you go to borrow money for a major purchase, calculate your expected debt safety ratio to see if you will stay under 20 percent of your monthly take-home pay *with the new loan.*

2. Know the maximum amount you are willing to pay and the maximum length you are willing to finance something before you go shopping.

3. Separate the purchasing decision from the financing decision. Shop for the best price and then choose the best financing package.

4. Even if 100 percent financing is available, consider putting some of your own money into the purchase. This will reduce the payments or allow you to pay off the loan earlier.

5. Avoid financing automobiles for too long a period of time. You may find that when you go to trade for another, the outstanding balance on your existing loan is greater than what the dealer will offer you in trade.

6. If you use single-payment loans, be sure to budget in the principal repayment at the end of the term as well as periodic interest payments, if required.

7. Avoid borrowing from friends and relatives if possible. The quickest way to turn a friend into an enemy is to not repay a debt as promised.

quoted is offset, at least in part, by a higher price on the purchase. In this case it would probably be in your best interest to shop for your financing and then negotiate on the price.

When comparing the interest rate on consumer loans you should be aware of the different methods of calculation. For example, on single-payment loans the finance charge could be determined by the simple interest method, which is the product of the principal multiplied by the interest rate multiplied by time. The APR of a simple interest loan is always equal to the simple interest rate. Another method on single payment loans is the discount method, which subtracts the interest up front from the principal you receive but the interest is based on the entire principal. This increases the APR.

Installment loans may also use the add-on method. As the name implies, the interest over the entire term of the loan is added to the amount to be repaid. This does not assume a declining balance. This results in both a higher APR and a higher balance if the loan were paid off early.

If You Are Thirtysomething

As you get older you will probably accumulate more funds that could be used to make major purchases. You will probably be faced with the decision of whether or not to pay cash or to finance a purchase. The decision hinges on the opportunity cost of your investments and how you would finance the purchase as shown in Exhibit 8.12. Generally, if it costs more to borrow the money than you can earn on your funds, you should pay cash. However, you would not want to deplete all of your liquid assets.

You might want to consider using other sources of financing for your major purchases if you can obtain better rates. Once you have established your credit, you would find it a lot easier to obtain financing from other sources. This, of course, reinforces the importance of establishing and maintaining good credit. If you do not have good credit, you might be looking at borrowing from finance companies at high rates or loan sharks that do not necessarily follow the Fair Credit Collections Act.

Regardless of the sources of credit, you should keep good records of your outstanding loans to ensure that your debt ratio is in line. This can be done by using a form such as shown in Exhibit 8.3.

Points to Remember:

1. All of the points mentioned for those just starting out will also apply here.

2. If you use the purchase as collateral be sure that the lender releases the lien on it after the loan is repaid.

3. Consider using single-payment loans as a source of interim financing when you know where the source of repayment is coming from.

4. You might want to consider using a *home equity installment* loan instead of a consumer loan for some of your major purchases. This may enable you to deduct the interest expense from your income taxes.

5. If you are able to pay off the loan early, do so. However, you should be aware of any prepayment penalties.

6. Be sure you include all relevant information on any loan applications you fill out, as they will be checked for accuracy, especially for the debts you owe.

7. Look for the wage assignment clause in any purchase agreement you sign in conjunction with your financing. In the event of default, this allows the lender to collect part of your wages without a court order.

1. What is Mark and Ana's debt safety ratio? Evaluate their ability to handle this debt.

2. Calculate the minimum monthly payments on each of Mark and Ana's credit cards using the data in the original case.

3. Calculate the finance charges on Mark and Ana's Visa and MasterCard if monthly transactions are as follows:

VISA

Date	Transaction	Amount
6/1	Beginning balance	$1,150
6/7	Purchase	163
6/25	Payment	250

MASTERCARD

Date	Transaction	Amount
6/1	Beginning balance	$2,790
6/5	Purchase	62
6/14	Purchase	208
6/26	Payment	350

4. If all of Mark and Ana's credit cards were stolen, what would their maximum potential liability be according to federal legislation?

5. After paying off all of their revolving credit lines, Mark and Ana plan on keeping only one bank credit card. Compare and evaluate the terms on their Visa and MasterCards, given that all charges will be paid at the end of the billing cycle (that is, they will not allow any charges to revolve). They expect their charges will produce an average daily balance of about $250 a month in a typical month. Recommend the card that would be least expensive for Mark and Ana under these conditions.

6. After moving into their new condominium, Mark and Ana suddenly realize that their old furniture looks pretty shabby. They feel that it would take about $3,000 to buy the furnishings they would like. Upon reviewing their latest balance sheet, they decide they do not want to sell any assets to pay for the furniture, so they investigate the possibility of borrowing $3,000 to buy the furniture. The following loans are available:

First Federal Savings

13% stated interest rate
simple interest loan
24 monthly payments

Acme Furniture Company

9% stated interest rate
add-on interest loan
24 monthly payments

a. Compare the monthly payments, the total finance charges, and the APRs on the two loans. Which would you recommend as the best loan for Mark and Ana? Why?

b. *(For students using the computer disk)* Run the amortization table for the above loan from First Federal Savings. How much interest would be paid in the first year of this loan? During the second year?

c. Before Mark and Ana decide on either of these loans, they decide to take an inventory of their consumer debt. Complete this inventory for them using the information in the original case. Would you recommend their taking on more debt at this time?

PART four

Managing Insurance Needs

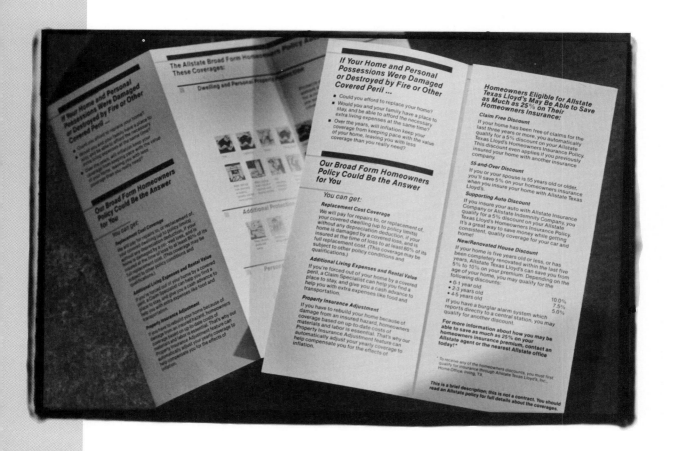

CHAPTER 9 *Insuring Your Life*

CHAPTER 10 *Insuring Your Health*

CHAPTER 11 *Protecting Your Property*

Insuring Your Life

A key ingredient of every successful financial plan is adequate life insurance coverage. The overriding purpose of life insurance is to protect your family from financial loss in the event of your untimely death. In addition, some types of life insurance also possess attractive investment attributes. Place yourself in the following situation: Suppose that through careful financial planning and a lot of hard work, you have acquired a nice home, furnishings, and other assets, along with a comfortable standard of living for your family. Wouldn't you want to protect all this? Most people would, and they do so through various forms of life insurance. In essence, life insurance provides an umbrella for your financial plans. It not only protects that which you have already acquired (like providing funds to pay off the mortgage on your home) but also helps to assure the attainment of unfulfilled financial goals (such as the future education of your children). Being informed about life insurance is clearly just as important to financial planning as being well versed about taxes and investments. As with any other aspect of financial planning, you want to get as much from your insurance dollar as possible. In the case of life insurance, this means not only comparing costs but also buying the proper amount of insurance and picking the right type of policy.

This is the first of three chapters dealing with insurance. After studying life insurance in this chapter, we will look at health insurance in Chapter 10 and at property insurance in Chapter 11. Together these three forms of insurance make up the insurance planning function.

FINANCIAL *facts* OR *fantasies*

Are the following statements financial facts (true) or fantasies (false)?

In a cafeteria-style benefits plan, it is the employee who decides what type of benefits coverage he or she will receive.

About the only way to protect you and your family from the risk of potential economic loss is to buy insurance.

The best way to find out how much life insurance you need is to multiply your annual earnings by 3.

Social security survivor's benefits should be factored into your life insurance plans if you have a dependent spouse and/or minor children.

Term insurance provides nothing more than a stipulated amount of death benefits and, as a result, is considered the purest form of life insurance.

Selecting an insurance company is the first thing you should do when buying life insurance.

BASIC INSURANCE CONCEPTS

Sound insurance planning rests on a basic understanding of your exposure to risk and how insurance can protect you against those risks. Before reading on, give some thought to the different ways that insurance could help protect you personally. Why is it important to have adequate life insurance, and what role should life insurance play in your financial plans?

Over a period of years, the difference between buying life insurance wisely and unwisely can easily add up to thousands of dollars in extra premiums and many times that amount in lost protection. Wide differences exist among the types of life insurance policies that are available, their costs, and the quality of the companies and the agents that sell them. This chapter shows how you can intelligently determine how much life insurance protection you and your family need. In addition, it explains the different types of life insurance policies available today. Although the diversity of market offerings may seem overwhelming, we will show that most policies, despite their different names, are essentially variations of several basic types.

INSURANCE PLANNING

For one reason or another, the financial goals that you've set for yourself may never be reached. A weak economy may result in your earning less income or in realizing a lower return on your investments than expected. Also, unless you plan carefully and with foresight, you may discover that you have embarked on a career that will produce a lower level of earnings than anticipated. Finally, events may occur that cause you to experience substantial financial losses. The fact is, fulfilling your financial goals depends not only on fortitude but also on fate! Everything you have acquired and planned for can all too easily slip away in the face of an unforeseen major emergency. But there are ways to safeguard against such risks—which is where *insurance* comes into the financial planning process. For the basic purpose of insurance is *to protect from loss the things that you have already acquired, and to shield you and your family from an interruption in your expected earnings*. Insurance, in short, lends a degree of certainty to your financial plans.

Auto and homeowners insurance, for example, reimburse you for damage or destruction to existing assets. Life insurance is meant to replace income that would have been earned had premature death not occurred. Disability insurance does the same should you become disabled, while hopsitalization and medical insurance cover the additional expenses that arise from being sick or in an accident. Insurance planning involves trying to anticipate the losses to which your assets and income could be exposed, and considers how you can provide protection against such losses by weaving insurance into your financial plans. To do so, you will have to make decisions about life, health, and property insurance.

EMPLOYEE BENEFITS—YOUR COVERAGE BEGINS AT WORK

If you hold a full-time job, chances are your employer is providing you with certain types of *fringe benefits*. Indeed, every major company in the country today (and many not-so-major ones) provides its employees with a variety of *employee benefits*, ranging from health and life insurance to pension plans. Evolving from the earliest benefit packages that provided little more than "final expense" life insurance, today's greatly expanded benefit plans are what most people rely on for a large part of their financial security. Consider health insurance, for instance. The vast majority of American families rely solely on company-sponsored *group plans* for their health and major medical insurance coverage. And much the same can be said about life insurance and pension plans. Other than social security, most families rely on their employee benefits for a big piece of their life insurance coverage and retirement needs.

Actually, the well-defined employee benefits packages of today cover a full spectrum of benefits, including:

- Health and life insurance
- Disability insurance

- Pension and profit-sharing plans
- Supplemental retirement programs, like 401(k) plans
- Dental and vision care
- Child-care and educational assistance programs
- Subsidized employee food services

Of course, not all companies provide such a complete menu of benefits; some are more generous than others. But even so, these benefits have taken on an increased importance as a form of compensation and presently account for roughly 30 percent of the average employee's total compensation package. Put another way, for every dollar received in wages and salaries, the average employee receives another 40 cents in fringe benefits. All or most of these benefits are paid in full by the employer, though it's not unusual for the employee to pay for at least part of the tab for group health insurance coverage on his or her family, supplemental life insurance, and participation in voluntary retirement programs.

Getting Your Benefits from a Cafeteria.

Traditionally, most group benefit programs were set up in such a way that the employee had little, if any, direct input into the makeup of the fringe benefits package. The types of benefits included and the dollar amount of coverage provided were pretty much set by the company—for example, life insurance coverage was usually defined as a multiple of your annual salary, and medical benefits were the same for everyone. Such benefit packages are still the standard for many companies, but a rapidly growing number of employers today are offering *flexible-benefit*, or **cafeteria-style plans**, in which the employee selects the benefits most desirable to him or her. (Technically, cafeteria-style plans are nothing more than a variation of flexible-benefit programs—you're given just about the same choices with either approach, except that there are some additional tax advantages available with the cafeteria-style plans.)

The growing sentiment in the employee benefits field is that the traditional, rigid programs just are not appropriate with today's diverse group of employees. Financial security needs vary greatly with age, marital status, number of dependent children, level of income, and so forth. Enter the flexible-benefit or cafeteria-style programs in which the employer allocates a certain amount of money to each employee and then lets the employee "spend" that money by selecting the benefits that he or she wants the most. In effect, employees are provided with a "menu" of benefits (usually covering everything from child-care to retirement benefits) to pick and choose from until the allotted money is gone. These plans usually require a minimum amount of life and health insurance coverage, and there are a few limits set on the maximum amount of coverage you can obtain, but within these constraints, you're free to select the benefits that do you the most good. And in some plans, you can even take some of the benefits in the form of more take-home pay or extra vacation time! The accompanying *Smart Money* box provides further discussion about these plans, and offers a few suggestions that should help you get the most from them.

One final point: whether you're covered by a traditional rigid plan or a more flexible careferia-style program, it's a good idea to periodically assess the benefits package you have at work relative to your own individual/family needs, and if you discover a shortfall in coverage, then try to supplement it with your own personal policy. In short, make sure you have the coverage or protection you need, either from your company benefits package and/or your own supplemental coverage. Except perhaps for group medical coverage, *don't rely on your employer as the sole source of financial security*. More often than not, especially when it comes to life insurance and retirement plans, you'll find that such coverage falls short of your total financial needs. Later in this chapter, and in a couple of others, we'll see how you can assess your life insurance, disability insurance, and pension programs to see if they meet your needs and if not, how to bring your coverage up to a desirable standard.

---

cafeteria-style plans

A type of employee benefits plan wherein the *employee*, rather than the employer, picks the type of benefit coverage received from a menu covering everything from child-care to life and health insurance to retirement benefits. (These plans are similar in many respects to so-called flexible-benefit programs.)

Smart Money

Filling Your Tray with Cafeteria-Style Benefits

One decade after the first flexible benefits plan debuted in this country, the idea of letting employees choose their own benefits—from child care to health insurance to extra vacation time—is finally catching on. Once limited because of tax law uncertainties and because the plans made sense for only large companies, flexible—or cafeteria—benefits are now offered by more than 800 major companies, and this year (1989) that number is expected to jump by 25 percent.

"Benefits used to be designed for Ward Cleaver," says Wayne Page, who heads the human resources division of Transamerica Life Companies in Los Angeles. "He supported the family and June stayed home cooking for Wally and the Beav." No longer is that the case. Nancy Oroumieh, 35, has two children and works at Transamerica as a department manager. She used to worry that her benefits packaged didn't include enough life insurance or disability insurance, so when Transamerica introduced its own flex plan in 1986, she promptly upgraded both benefits. "Now I feel confident my family is covered," she says. Oroumieh can also take advantage of a benefits option that lets her set aside money each week, before taxes, to pay for child care.

Flexible benefits plans come in many shapes and sizes, but they typically give employees a number of credits they can use to "buy" benefits. Most plans, for instance, offer a choice among different levels of health and life insurance. Many plans have options to help pay for dependent care or eye and dental benefits, and some even allow employees to trade benefits for more take-home pay or vacation time.

If your company introduces a flex plan, you should keep these basics in mind:

- *Ask questions.* Unlike standard benefits packages of the past, flexible plans force employees to learn how benefits work and know which ones are right for them. Read those company handouts, and if you don't understand something, speak up.
- *Study the options.* If your spouse has a traditional benefits plan, it helps to coordinate your choices. And remember, if your current benefits suit you and you have the option of keeping them, there's no reason to change.
- *Consider tax consequences.* Flexible-benefit "spending accounts," which allow money to be set aside for dependent care before taxes, don't always make sense: Some people are better off spending their take-home pay and then taking a dependent-care tax deduction come April 15.
- *Make sure you're covered.* In times of fat mortgages and shrinking raises, extra cash in the paycheck can be tempting. But beware of swapping basic medical insurance for more pay or vacation.
- *Plan ahead.* By law you can adjust your coverage in cases of birth, death, marriage, divorce, and so on. But if you require elective surgery or your child needs braces and you didn't choose the right coverage, you're out of luck until the next annual enrollment deadline.

Source: Adapted from Ray Alvarez-Torres, "Flexible Benefits Can Stretch Your Coverage," *Savvy*, February 1989, p. 32.

In a cafeteria-style benefits plan, it is the employee who decides what type of benefits coverage he or she will receive.

Fact: In a flexible-benefit or cafeteria-style program, employees pick from a wide-ranging menu of company-sponsored fringe benefits, including health, life and disability insurance, pension plans, dental care, educational assistance programs, child care, and so forth. Working with this menu of benefits and a stipulated amount of money, an employee is free to put together a benefits package that best meets his or her needs.

TRANSFERRING THE RISKS

An insurance policy is a contract between you (the insured) and an insurance company (the insurer) under which the insurance company promises to pay for your losses according to the specified terms. From your perspective, *you are transferring the risk of loss to the insurance company*. The insurance company is willing to accept the risk because it hopes to make a profit by collecting premiums from a large number of insureds, investing the money, and paying out losses and expenses that are less than the premiums collected and investment earnings. Insurers can do this because they are able to combine many insureds into a "pool," for which losses are more predictable than for any one of the insureds individually.

The premiums you pay for insurance usually come out of your current income. Thus, the heart of the insurance decision is the comparison of the premiums you are willing (and able) to take from your current income relative to the need for, and the amount of, protection you will receive from the insurance that you buy. The decision is difficult, because you do not know for sure whether or not losses will occur, but only that you might suffer losses from certain unforeseen events. The following discussion of risk, insurable exposures, and underwriting should help you to better understand the whole concept of insurance and the role that it can play in your financial planning. Later in this chapter we'll also provide some discussion of the factors to consider when making decisions about life insurance coverage.

THE CONCEPT OF RISK

In insurance, *risk* is defined as uncertainty with respect to economic loss. Whenever you and your family have a financial interest in something—whether it be your life, health, home, car, boat, or job—you face risk. You face the chance that your budget will be upset and that your net worth will perhaps be drastically reduced. Because of the devastating effect that losses can have on your financial well-being, you must devise ways to deal with risk. Obviously it makes sense to take steps *before* a loss occurs, as is done in *risk avoidance* and *loss prevention*. However, when losses do occur, you will need an economical way of covering them, which is what you obtain from *risk assumption* and *insurance*.

Risk Avoidance. Perhaps the simplest way to deal with risk is to avoid the act that creates it. As an example, people who are afraid they might lose everything they own because of a lawsuit resulting from an automobile accident could avoid driving. With respect to life and health risks, avid skydivers or bungee jumpers might want to choose another recreational activity!

Although **risk avoidance** can be an effective way to handle some risks, such action is not without its costs. For instance, the people who avoid driving suffer considerable inconvenience, and the retired skydiver may find he or she now suffers *more* stress, which can lead to different types of health risks. Risk avoidance is an attractive way to deal with risk only when the estimated cost of avoidance is less than the estimated cost of handling it in some other way.

Loss Prevention and Control. In a broad sense, **loss prevention** can be defined as any activity that reduces the probability that a loss will

---

risk avoidance
Avoidance of an act that would create a risk.

loss prevention
Any activity that reduces the probability that a loss will occur.

occur (such as driving within the speed limit). **Loss control**, in contrast, is any activity that lessens the severity of loss once it occurs (such as wearing a safety belt or buying a car with air bags). Loss prevention, and loss control should be important parts of the risk management program of every individual and family. In fact insurance provides a reasonable means for handling risk only when people use effective loss prevention and control measures. For example, if everybody drove fast and recklessly, risk avoidance might be the only effective way to deal with the risk of an automobile accident because automobile, life, and health insurance would be too expensive to buy.

Risk Assumption. With **risk assumption**, you choose to accept and bear the risk of loss. Risk assumption can be an effective way to handle many types of potentially small exposures to loss when insurance would be too expensive (for example, the risk of having your *Personal Financial Planning* text stolen). It is also a reasonable approach in the face of very large exposures that you cannot ordinarily prevent, or against which you cannot secure insurance (nuclear holocaust, for instance). Unfortunately, people often assume risks because they are unaware of various exposures to loss or think that their insurance offers adequate protection when in fact it does not. Therefore, one objective of these three chapters on insurance is to help you recognize the loss exposures that you will face and provide you with an understanding of when risk assumption is the preferred manner for handling certain risks.

Insurance. Insurance permits society to reduce financial risks and share losses. Risk or uncertainty can be reduced because insurers are able to combine the loss experiences of large numbers of people and, with certain actuarial data, estimate the chance of loss faced by the insured population. This prediction then allows each person to contribute a relatively small amount (the insurance premium) to an insurance company in exchange for a promise that he or she will be reimbursed for covered losses. Insured individuals gain because they are able to transfer their risk to the insurer. The insurance company, in turn, can realize a gain if the amount of insured losses has been accurately estimated.

About the only way to protect you and your family from the risk of potential economic loss is to buy insurance.

Fantasy: Although insurance is a very effective way to protect you and your family from economic loss, several other methods for handling potential risks should also be considered. These include risk avoidance, loss prevention, loss control, and risk assumption.

CHARACTERISTICS OF AN INSURABLE EXPOSURE

Although insurance can be ideal for handling the risk of economic loss, not all risks are insurable. In order for the insurance mechanism to work well, certain criteria must be met. Several of the more important criteria are the following: (1) there must be a large number of similar exposures to loss; (2) the potential loss must be fortuitous; (3) the cost of the insurance must be reasonably low; and (4) losses must be noncatastrophic.

Large Number of Exposures. Insurers need a large group of similar exposures because they base rate calculations on what may loosely be called "the law of averages." Unless the number is large enough to permit a good estimate of average expected losses, premiums cannot be accurately computed. If rates are set too low, the insurance company may not have enough funds to pay claims; if set too high, people may pay more than is necessary or desirable.

Fortuitous Loss. A **fortuitous loss** is one that happens by chance or accident. Its timing and/or occurrence is for the most part unintentional and unexpected from the standpoint of the insured. If individual losses that were certain or intentional could be insured, insurance companies would be plagued by *adverse selection* — that is, the tendency for those who anticipate losses in the near future to seek insurance more often than the norm.

Reasonable Cost. The cost of an insurance premium should be reasonably low with respect to the potential loss that it covers. Thus, insurance should be used for protection only against large losses that are suffered by a very small percentage of those who buy a given coverage. A company cannot economically insure against a number of small losses, because the expenses of selling and administering such policies could, when coupled with the claims that would be made, total as much as or more than the potential loss covered. Similarly, insurance cannot be economically offered for losses that occur too frequently, because the premiums would exceed the amount that most people are willing to pay.

An excellent example of the application of the reasonable-cost criterion is life insurance for persons over age 70. While insurance companies will issue a new policy to people in this age category, the relatively high probability of loss makes the premiums much larger than most people can afford. Life insurance, of course, is not the only place where high probability of loss can lead to very expensive insurance premiums. For example, in recent years, this phenomenon has played a significant role in increased automobile and professional liability insurance premiums. Insurance works best when in any given year only a relatively few people file claims. In this way, the total amount received in premiums (plus interest earnings) should exceed the total amount paid out for losses and administrative expenses.

Noncatastrophic Loss. The last criterion — **noncatastrophic loss** — means that insurers should not accept risks that have the potential for widespread catastrophe. Foremost for insurance companies is the need to protect their solvency. A company that goes bankrupt is no good to anyone. Thus, such catastrophic occurrences as war, nuclear explosion, and unemployment due to economic conditions generally cannot be adequately insured by private insurance companies.

UNDERWRITING

In all types of insurance, the company must decide whom it can insure and then determine the applicable rates. This function is called **underwriting**. Through underwriting, insurance companies try to guard against adverse selection, which happens when only high-risk clients apply for, and get, insurance coverage. Underwriters design rate-classification schedules so that people pay premiums com-

mensurate with their chance of loss. The success of any insurance company is highly dependent on the quality of the work done here. If the underwriting standards are too high, people will be unjustly denied coverage, and insurance sales will drop. On the other hand, if standards are too low, many insureds will pay less than their fair share, and the insurance company's solvency could be jeopardized.

A basic problem facing underwriters is the choice of appropriate criteria to apply when they select and classify insureds. Since a perfect relationship does not exist between available criteria and loss experience, some people invariably believe that they are being charged more than they should be for their insurance. This situation is most apparent in underwriting automobile insurance. Many young male motorists who have never had an auto accident must pay two or three times the premium that a person age 35 would pay. Similarly, a car owner who has never had a claim but who lives in Manhattan could well pay a considerably higher premium than a small-town driver with a poor driving record.

The primary underwriting factors used in life insurance are age and sex. Health insurance underwriters are principally concerned about the same two factors, plus the occupation of the insured. Some states, however, have passed laws requiring that the same rates and underwriting standards be

---

loss control
Any activity that reduces the severity of loss once the loss occurs.

risk assumption
The choice to bear or accept risk.

fortuitous loss
A loss that is for the most part unintentional and unexpected.

noncatastrophic loss
A loss that is not the result of a catastrophic occurrence, such as war, nuclear explosion, or large-scale flooding.

underwriting
With respect to insurance, the process of deciding who can be insured and determining the applicable rates.

applied to both males and females. Such laws illustrate the conflict between underwriting standards that seem to make sense based upon the insurers' actuarial tables and those that are considered fair by the general public and their elected representatives.

Underwriting is perhaps more of an art than a science. Insurers are always trying to improve their underwriting capabilities in order to set rates that will provide adequate protection against insolvency and yet be reasonable for most policyholders. From your standpoint, though, you should recognize that insurance companies often use very different underwriting standards and rate classification systems. Therefore, you can usually save money by shopping around for a company that has underwriting practices more favorable to your specific characteristics and needs. For instance, some life insurers offer discounts to nonsmokers and to people in better-than-average health. And many companies even offer discounts to those in preferred low-risk occupations, such as professionals and business executives.

HOW MUCH LIFE INSURANCE IS RIGHT FOR YOU? ⍰

While there are many ways to determine the amount of life insurance that's right for you, probably the best is to base the decision on an assessment of your needs. Place yourself in the shoes of a married person with two young children. What kinds of financial needs and obligations would you want to cover with a life insurance policy? Take a moment to think about this question before reading on.

"Life insurance is sold, not bought" is an axiom in the life insurance business. As a rule, people just don't get as strong an urge to buy life insurance as they might to buy a house, car, or new television set. Far too many people simply wait until an agent contacts them and then reluctantly accept "being sold." A partial explanation for this tendency to wait is that life insurance is intangible. Even after you purchase it, you can't see, smell, touch, or taste its benefits. In addition, although most people (especially family breadwinners) recognize they should buy life insurance, many believe it can be delayed another month — or two or three. The need is felt, but it is neither obvious nor pressing. But perhaps as much an explanation as anything else is the fact that the purchase of a life insurance policy is associated with something unpleasant — namely, death. People don't like to talk about death, or the things closely associated with it, so they all too often put off taking care of their life insurance needs. That's unfortunate, because life insurance does have definite benefits to offer, the most important being all the things that a family will still be able to buy after a loss occurs — things they very likely could not otherwise buy.

The point is not to push you to go out and stock up on as much life insurance as you can get, but rather to find out whether or not you do, in fact, need life insurance. If you do, you should give its purchase a high priority. Deciding whether or not, and in what amount, you need life insurance is an important issue. There are two commonly used methods for computing an individual's need for life insurance: the multiple earnings approach and the needs approach, each of which we will discuss below.

MULTIPLE EARNINGS APPROACH

The **multiple earnings approach** gained its popularity on the basis of its simplicity rather than soundness. Using this technique, you calculate the amount of life insurance to buy by simply multiplying your gross annual earnings by some arbitrarily selected number. Multiples of 3, 5, or even 10 times earnings are frequently used to find the amount of life insurance coverage needed.

Exhibit 9.1 illustrates the type of multiples that would be used to estimate life insurance needs with the multiple earnings approach. Note that the multiples in the exhibit are based on replacing 75 percent of lost earnings for a married breadwinner with two children. The multiples would, of course, change if you wanted to replace more or less than that amount. Given the desired replacement rate, the proper multiple to use is based on current gross annual income and the age of the insured. Thus, we can see from the exhibit that, according to this procedure, a married 35-year-old male earning $40,000 a year should use a multiple of 8.7 times if he wants to replace 75 percent of this income. His *total life insurance coverage*, therefore, should amount to $40,000 × 8.7 = $348,000. Now, keep in mind this is *total* life insurance coverage, so from this amount, the individual should subtract the coverage already provided from group and/or personal policies, as well as any pension plan death benefits. For example, if the individual is covered at work by a group life insurance policy in the amount of $50,000, and if he's entitled to another $50,000 in death benefits from the company's pension plan, then his remaining life insurance needs are $248,000 (that is, $348,000 − $50,000 − $50,000). According to the multiple earnings approach, that's the amount of additional life insurance this individual needs to buy to be "adequately" covered.

At best, this procedure should be used only to get a first, very rough approximation of life insurance needs. While it is simple to use, it fails to fully recognize the financial obligations and resources of the individual.

NEEDS APPROACH

Most professional life insurance agents have abandoned the multiple earnings approach in favor of the **needs approach**. This method specifically considers the financial obligations that a person may have and the financial resources that are available, *in addition to life insurance* Essentially, the needs approach involves three steps: (1) estimating the total economic resources needed; (2) determining all financial resources that would be available, including life insurance and pension plan death benefits already in force; and (3) subtracting the amount of resources available from the amount needed in order to determine the amount of *additional* life insurance required to provide for an individual's financial program.

The best way to find out how much life insurance you need is to multiply your annual earnings by 3. *Fantasy:* While the multiple earnings approach is probably the simplest procedure, it suffers from a number of serious shortcomings. A better choice is the *needs approach.*

Economic Needs. The basic question asked in the needs approach is: What financial resources will the survivors need should the income producer die tomorrow? Although life insurance is often used in retirement planning, it primarily protects families from financial loss resulting from the death of an income producer. In this role, life insurance can provide money for the following financial needs: (1) family income, (2) additional expenses, (3) debt liquidation, (4) surviving spouse's income, (5) money for special requirements, such as the children's education, and (6) liquidity. For the well-heeled, the proceeds from a life insurance policy can also be used to pay estate taxes, thereby leaving intact all or most of the family estate. Such tax payments aside, let's look more closely at the six major financial needs of a typical family.

Family income. For most people with dependents, the principal financial need is to protect their families' incomes. If they die, they want to make sure that their families' ability to live comfortably is not seriously impaired. Perhaps the best way to estimate the amount of monthly income necessary to sustain a family is to develop a budget covering all expenses that are likely to be incurred. As discussed in Chapter 3, major items in most family budgets are housing costs; utilities; food; automobile expenses; medical and dental needs; clothing; life, health, property, and liability insurance; property taxes; recreation and travel; and savings.

One important question that you must face in developing a post-death family budget is, "What standard of living do I want my family to have?" While some feel a reduced level of consumption is in order, others want their families to maintain their

---

multiple earnings approach
A method of determining the amount of life insurance coverage needed in which gross annual earnings are multiplied by some largely arbitrarily selected number.

needs approach
A method of determining the amount of life insurance needed that considers the person's available financial resources (including life insurance), along with specific financial obligations.

EXHIBIT 9.1

A Multiple Earnings Table

Some insurance experts suggest that a table like the one below be used to estimate life insurance needs. To do so, first find the factor that corresponds to your age and level of income; then multiply this by your level of income. For example, if you are a married 30-year-old with two children and earn $30,000 a year, you will use a factor of 7.4 to find out how much insurance you need: $30,000 × 7.4 = $222,000.

	Insurance Requirements in Addition to Social Security to Replace 75 Percent of Earnings after Taxes for a Family of Four					
Gross Annual Pay	**Age of Insured**					
	30	**35**	**40**	**45**	**50**	**55**
$ 7,500	5.3	6.2	7.3	8.5	7.9	5.6
9,000	5.1	6.0	7.0	8.1	7.8	5.5
12,000	5.0	5.8	6.7	7.9	7.6	5.4
15,000	4.9	5.7	6.7	7.9	7.4	5.3
20,000	4.9	6.5	7.4	8.1	7.3	5.2
30,000	7.4	8.2	8.4	8.3	7.2	5.1
40,000	8.4	8.7	8.6	8.2	6.9	4.9
60,000	9.0	8.9	8.4	7.8	6.5	4.6

Source: *A Consumer's Guide to Buying Life Insurance* (Des Moines, Iowa: Bankers Life).

present standard of living; still others would like to leave their families with the level of consumption that would have been achieved had the providers continued to live and work.

A final point to keep in mind concerning family income is that many families today depend on two incomes. Emphasis traditionally has been placed on insuring the family against the income loss of the father. But working mothers can also die unexpectedly. Therefore, to the extent that a family (with either one or two incomes) depends on the woman's income to make ends meet, *that income should be counted as part of the family income need*. Equally important, because the death of a working mother can have devastating effects on the family structure as well as the family budget, *her life should also be adequately insured*. In keeping with the growing importance of women in the work force, life insurance sales on the lives of women have increased dramatically in recent years, as seen in Exhibit 9.2. Unfortunately, however, nearly three times as much life insurance is still being written on men than on women. Such a fact indicates that this need is not yet receiving the attention that it de-

serves—and thus family income is often inadequately protected.

Additional expenses. In most households, adult family members are responsible for performing many family and household services. Perhaps the most extreme example of such responsibilities is the homemaker not employed outside the home. Among the valuable services performed by the homemaker are child care, cooking, cleaning, and, of course, family taxi service! If the homemaker were to die, these services would represent new expenses to be paid out of the family's income. Such expenses could stretch the family budget to the breaking point and, thus, should be recognized when estimating insurance needs.

Pay off debts. In the event of their deaths, most breadwinners prefer to leave their families relatively debt-free. Therefore, to accomplish this objective a person must determine the average amount due for outstanding bills. Included in this amount would be the balances on installment loans, credit cards, department store accounts, and other similar obligations, as well as estimated funeral expenses. In addition, some heads of household will want to

EXHIBIT 9.2

Relative Amount of Life Insurance Sold to Men and Women

Even in spite of the surge in two-income families, the vast majority of insurance is still sold on the lives of male wage earners. In 1990, there was nearly three times as much life insurance sold on men as on women.

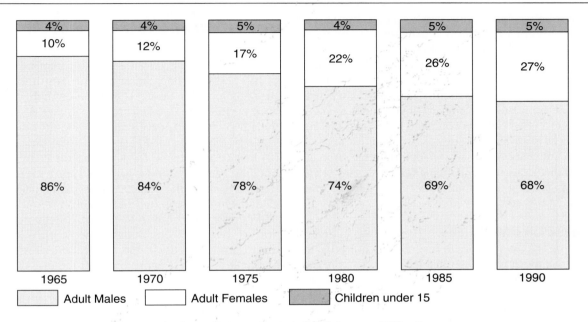

Source: *Life Insurance Fact Book Update* (Washington, D.C.: American Council of Life Insurance, 1991), p. 7.

leave enough money to pay off their home mortgages and will include this amount in their debt-liquidation estimates. The debt-liquidation component of financial needs can be viewed as an estimate of the individual's average liabilities.

Surviving spouse's income. Once children are on their own, the monthly household expenses should decrease substantially. Nevertheless, the surviving spouse may need monthly support for the remainder of his or her life. Therefore, the amount of income needed, as well as the duration of the survivor's life, needs to be estimated.

Special financial needs. In addition to the economic needs that have been discussed, some families would like to have the resources available to meet specific financial requirements, such as a college education fund for the children and/or surviving spouse, an emergency fund for unexpected

pected financial burdens, or, as previously mentioned, a fund for paying off the mortgage.

Liquidity. Often we may have assets but no cash. Real estate investors, for example, are notorious for owning several million dollars' worth of properties but bouncing checks for $100. Similarly, many farmers are land rich and cash poor. People who keep a very high percentage of their wealth in illiquid assets often need life insurance to provide enough cash to avoid estate shrinkage. The life insurance proceeds keep the mortgages paid and assets maintained until they can be sold in an orderly fashion at their fair market value.

Available Resources. After estimating the amount of financial needs that a family must try to satisfy upon the death of an income provider, a list of all available resources for meeting those needs must be prepared. For most families, money from savings and social security survivor's benefits make up the largest non–life insurance financial resources. In addition, there are the proceeds from company-sponsored group life insurance policies and the death benefits payable from accumulated pension plans and profit-sharing programs. Another important source is income that can be earned by the surviving spouse or children. If the surviving spouse is skilled and readily employable, his or her earnings could be a family's largest available resource. Also, many families have real estate (in addition to their home), jewelry, stocks, bonds, and other assets that can be liquidated in order to obtain funds to meet financial needs. After a complete list of available resources is developed, some reasonable estimate of their value should be made. Although this step can be difficult due to the changing values of many of the assets, coming up with a set of reasonably accurate estimates is certainly within reach.

Needs Less Resources. The last step in determining the amount of life insurance required is to subtract the amount of available resources from the total needed to satisfy all of the family's financial objectives. If the amount of available resources exceeds the needs, no (additional) life insurance is required. If, as in most families with children, the resources are less than the needs, that difference is the amount of life insurance necessary to provide the family with its desired standard of living.

Generally, insurance proceeds can be invested, until the money is actually needed, at a rate of return that exceeds taxes and inflation. This after-tax, after-inflation return may be 1 to 2 percent for reasonably conservative investments, and even higher for more risky investments.

By now you can see that insurance planning based on the needs concept can become quite complex. When a family uses a competent financial planner or life insurance agent who understands the process, the planning stage can proceed quite smoothly. Virtually all life insurance companies today have computer programs set up to determine the life insurance requirements of families using the needs approach. Remember, though, that *life insurance needs are not static*. The amount and type of life insurance you need today probably will differ from the amount and type suitable for you five or ten years from now. Life insurance programs should be reviewed and adjusted (as necessary) at least every five years, or after major changes in the family have occurred (for example, the birth of a child or the purchase of a home).

AN ILLUSTRATION OF THE NEEDS APPROACH IN ACTION

To illustrate how the needs approach can be used in insurance planning, consider the hypothetical case of Bill and Joan Benson. At the present time, the Bensons' primary desire is to have enough insurance on Bill's life to take care of Joan (age 35) and their two children (ages 6 and 8) should Bill die. Their priorities are to (1) leave the family debt free, (2) ensure an income for Joan and their children until the youngest child is age 18, (3) provide funds for Joan to make the transition from homemaker to gainful employment, and (4) establish a fund that will permit the children to obtain college educations or begin careers. Because the Bensons know that insurance needs change, they believe a five-year planning horizon is appropriate. At the end of that period, the family's needs and resources will be reevaluated to see if their life insurance program warrants modification. A worksheet like the one in Exhibit 9.3 will be used to calculate the life insurance needs of the Benson family.

Family Economic Needs. Since the Bensons use credit sparsely, their outstanding debts are limited to a mortgage (with a current balance of $65,000), an automobile loan ($4,000), and miscellaneous charge accounts ($1,000). The balances on these debts currently total $70,000. The mortgage is in its early years and will not be reduced significantly during the five-year planning period. Although the existing auto loan will be amortized, a new loan for a replacement vehicle will probably be necessary. Bill therefore believes that $70,000 will be adequate to meet their need for paying off debts. In addition, the Bensons would like to have $15,000 available to pay estate administration expenses, taxes, and funeral costs. (These items are listed on lines 1 and 2 of part A of the worksheet in Exhibit 9.3.)

Bill and Joan have reviewed their budget and feel that the family's monthly living expenses would be

$3,000 while the children are still living at home (12 years). During the period after both children leave home and until Joan retires at age 65 (18 years), the Bensons estimate her monthly living expenses to be $2,300 in current dollars. After Joan's retirement, they anticipate her living expenses to fall to $2,000 a month. The life expectancy of a woman Joan's age is 87 years, so the Bensons calculate that Joan will spend about 22 years in retirement. Because Joan and the children would be eligible for **social security survivor's benefits**, they decide to factor such benefits into their estimate of family income needs. Basically, survivor's benefits are paid to the dependents of deceased workers and are included as part of the social insurance provisions of the social security system. Such benefits are intended to provide basic (minimum) support to families faced with the loss of their principal wage earners. In addition to the elderly and disabled, the principal recipients of social security survivor's benefits include (1) unmarried children under age 18 (or 19 if still in high school), (2) nonworking spouses with children under age 16, and (3) surviving spouses age 60 and over.

Exhibit 9.4 lists some figures showing *approximate* monthly social security benefits available in 1991 to the survivors of qualified wage earners. Note that the level of benefits depends on the wage earner's age at death, earnings history, and the number of survivors. While these benefits used to be notoriously difficult to predict, the Social Security Administration has recently introduced an easy-to-use computer-based estimation system that will provide a fairly accurate estimate of the benefits your *survivors* would be entitled to receive in the event of your death. Such benefit projections are included on a *Personal Earnings and Benefit Estimate Statement* that can be obtained by calling the Social Security toll-free number, 1-800-772-1213, and requesting a short application form to fill out and send back in. (This statement is discussed in more detail in Chapter 15, and an actual sample is reproduced in Exhibit 15.4.)

Bill Benson knew about this program, and several weeks ago, sent the application form in for a statement of his own, which he recently received in the mail. Looking under the "Survivor's" portion of "Estimated Benefits," he learned that, based on his age (35) and recent income (he's close to the "high" level of earnings), his family would receive benefits

of around $2,100 a month. Note that the Bensons would be entitled to the *maximum family benefits* which is paid to a surviving (nonworking) spouse with two or more minor children. However, when their youngest child reaches age 16, the benefits for Joan would cease, and as each child graduates from high school his benefits would also stop. Even so, since the worksheet we are using is an estimate, we will assume they receive $2,100 a month for the full 12 years (a period of time which basically makes up Period 1 of the worksheet).

Knowing what they'd receive from social security, they subtracted that amount from their target income (of $3,000 a month) to arrive at a *net monthly income* (line 3e on the worksheet). This is the amount of income they'll have to come up with from some source other than social security in order to preserve their present standard of living. This is the basic level of income they want to maintain until the children are grown—when the youngest child has reached 18 years of age, a period of 12 years from now. Thus, they estimate that it should take about $129,600 to provide the family with $10,800 a year for 12 years. (All of which is listed under the Period 1 column of the worksheet.) Actually, given that money has a time value, it would take something *less* than the $129,600 to provide the needed income, but this complication can be ignored so long as we also disregard future inflation, which in fact would add to the amount needed. *In essence, since one element (inflation) will have at least a partially offsetting effect on the other (present value), we will ignore both of them in our calculation.* This is, after all, an *estimate* of future needs, so there is really little to be gained by trying to fine-tune with even more estimates of the future rates of inflation and potential rates of return on invested capital!

A similar procedure is used to estimate available income for Period 2, the years after the children leave home and until Joan retires, and then, the years after Joan retires, Period 3. Period 2 is called

---

social security survivor's benefits
Benefits included in the social insurance provision of the social security system that are intended to provide basic support for families who have lost their principal wage earners.

EXHIBIT 9.3

Determining the Need for Life Insurance

A worksheet like this one can be used to determine your life insurance requirements according to the needs approach.

Insured's Name	Bill and Joan Benson	Date	January 1993

A.	**Family Income Needs**				Totals
	1. Debt Liquidation:				
	a. House mortgage	$ 65,000			
	b. Other loans	$ 5,000			
	c. Total debt (a+b)				$ 70,000
	2. Final expenses				$ 15,000
	3. Annual income needs:	Period 1	Period 2	Period 3	
	a. Monthly living expenses	3,000	2,300	2,000	
	b. Less: Social security survivor's benefits	2,100	0	1,000	
	c. Less: Surviving spouse's income	0	2,000	0	
	d. Less: Other pension benefits and income	0	0	700	
	e. Net monthly income needed (a – b – c –d)	900	300	300	
	f. Net yearly income needed (12 x e)	10,800	3,600	3,600	
	g. Number of years in period	12	18	22	
	h. Funding needed each period (f x g)	$ 129,600	$ 64,800	$ 79,200	
	i. Total living needs (add line h for each period)				$ 273,600
	4. Spouse reeducation fund				$ 25,000
	5. Children's opportunity fund				$ 50,000
	6. Other needs				$ 0
	7. TOTAL INCOME NEEDS (add right column)				$ 433,600
B.	**Financial Resources Available**				
	1. Savings and investments	$ 50,000			
	2. Group life insurance	$ 50,000			
	3. Other life insurance	$			
	4. Other resources	$			
	TOTAL RESOURCES AVAILABLE (1 + 2 + 3 + 4)				$ 100,000
C.	**Additional Life Insurance Needed (A – B)** (Note: no additional insurance is needed if number is negative.)				$ 333,600

---

the "Blackout Period," so named because it is a time during which the surviving spouse receives no social security benefits. However, Joan expects to work during this period, and as a result, feels she should be able to make a net monthly income of around $2,000 (in current dollars). That will leave her short about $300 a month, which amounts to a total need of $64,800 during the Blackout Period.

After retirement, the Bensons estimate that Joan's living expenses should drop even more (to around

EXHIBIT 9.4

Approximate Monthly Social Security Survivor's Benefits

These benefits existed in 1991 and applied to the families of qualified wage earners who died in 1990; like other aspects of social security, the amount of monthly benefits depends in large part on the covered worker's level of income.

Worker Age	Salary Level	Monthly Survivor's Benefits		
		One Child Only	Spouse and One Child or Two Children Only	Maximum Family Benefits
25	$10,000	$357	$ 714	$ 717
	$25,000	$651	$1,302	$1,524
	$53,400	$936	$1,872	$2,180
35	$10,000	$346	$ 692	$ 693
	$25,000	$623	$1,246	$1,474
	$53,400	$902	$1,804	$2,101
45	$10,000	$342	$ 684	$ 684
	$25,000	$613	$1,226	$1,457
	$53,400	$848	$1,696	$1,975
55	$10,000	$337	$ 674	$ 674
	$25,000	$614	$1,228	$1,458
	$53,400	$791	$1,582	$1,842

$2,000 a month). Because Joan will have worked for nearly 20 years, they think it is reasonable to assume she will earn retirement benefits of her own. But to be on the safe side, they estimate Joan's retirement benefits should amount to around $700 a month. In addition, once Joan reaches retirement age, she will once again be eligible for monthly social security benefits — which they estimate should amount to around $1,000 a month. Based on this information, Joan will need a total of $79,200 to preserve her standard of living during retirement. Therefore, the Benson's total income needs over Joan's lifetime (Periods 1 through 3) are $273,600, which is listed as the total income needs (line 3i) on the worksheet.

Although Joan is trained as a stockbroker, because she will not go to work until both children are raised, they are concerned that her previous education may be somewhat out of date. Thus, they would like to have enough money to allow Joan to return to college for several years. They believe $25,000 should be sufficient for this purpose. Finally, both Bill and Joan want to guarantee that their children will have the money necessary to take advantage of education or other opportunities that may be available to them when they reach age 18. To do this, they

want to establish an opportunity fund of $50,000. The top part (Section A) of the worksheet in Exhibit 9.3 summarizes the Benson's economic needs. Note that they feel that the total amount necessary to meet their financial goals, should Bill die within the next five years, would be $433,600.

Social security survivor's benefits should be factored into your life insurance plans if you have a dependent spouse and/or minor children.
Fact: Survivor's benefits are paid to the dependents of eligible deceased workers and can be a big factor in helping your family meet their annual income needs.

Available Financial Resources. Bill is employed as an assistant professor at a state university. Although the university has a retirement program, no preretirement survivor's benefits are available, other than social security. However, Bill is covered by an employer-sponsored group life insurance policy in the amount of one year's gross salary ($50,000). Also, the Bensons have roughly $50,000 socked away in a couple of mutual funds and a money market deposit account. These investments were obtained in part from an inheritance and from a $20,000 advance against Bill's textbook royalties.

Other potential resources, such as a promised gift of $20,000 from Joan's Aunt Sarah, a travel accident life insurance policy with a $10,000 face value, and assorted personal property, are ignored in the planning process because of uncertainty as to either their amount or their availability. For example, Aunt Sarah may decide to donate the money to charity, or Bill may die from a cause unrelated to his travel insurance. Overall, then, the resources that the Bensons can count on to help achieve their ecomic objectives total $100,000, as summarized in the lower part (Section B) of Exhibit 9.3.

Additional Life Insurance Needed. As shown in the bottom line of Exhibit 9.3, the difference between the monies available and those that will be required is $333,600. This sum equals the amount of life insurance the Bensons will need to insure Bill's life and meet the family's desired standard of living. Often the amount of the life insurance needed to fulfill a family's desired expenditures will exceed the family's willingness or ability for pay for it. Even after a careful search for the right type of policy at the best price, a family might decide they just cannot afford all of the insurance they would like. In these cases, a priority ranking of needs, coupled with a reassessment of available resources, is necessary. As an example, in the preliminary plans a college education fund might have been included while consideration was not given to income from employment of the surviving spouse or children. The family could decide, however, to let the children work their way through college and have the surviving spouse seek employment. In this manner, ability and willingness to pay for life insurance can be adjusted to meet economic needs.

WHAT KIND OF POLICY IS RIGHT FOR YOU?

Once you have determined how *much* insurance to buy, the next thing you must do is decide on the *kind* of life insurance that's best for you. What factors would you want to consider when deciding on the type of life insurance policy to buy? Would you look for a good investment, or the most life insurance coverage for the money? Stop to think about these questions before going on.

After you have determined the amount of life insurance necessary to meet your family's financial requirements, you must decide on the type of insurance contract that will best fit your needs. Generally speaking, most families can effectively satisfy their insurance needs through the use of one of the three basic types of life insurance: term life, whole life, or universal life insurance. Indeed, these three products account for 90 to 95 percent of all life insurance sales—with whole life being the biggest seller, closely followed by term policies, and universal life being a distant third. Now, there are, of course, other types of life insurance policies available to consumers, but as we'll see, most of these are simply modifications of these three types.

TERM INSURANCE

Under the provisions of a **term life insurance** policy, the insurance company agrees to pay a stipulated amount of money if the insured dies during the policy period. The period of coverage is often five years, with premiums payable annually, semiannually, or quarterly. Many other periods of coverage and payment plans are available. Term insurance is the purest form of life insurance in that it provides a stipulated amount of life insurance (that is, death benefits) and nothing more. There are *no* investment or savings features associated with it. Term insurance can be an economical way to purchase life insurance, on a temporary basis, for protection against financial loss resulting from death, especially in the early years of family formation. A representative premium schedule for five-year renewable term insurance is illustrated in Exhibit 9.5.

Nearly all life insurance companies sell some form of term insurance. In addition, employer-sponsored group life insurance plans and companies that sell directly to the public through the mail or newspaper and magazine advertisements often offer term insurance at low rates. Unfortunately, in the past many families, because of either lack of knowledge or poor advice, did not properly incorporate term life insurance into their insurance programs. As consumers have become more knowledgeable, however, term life insurance sales have increased accordingly. Today, in fact, term policies account for about a third of all (group and individual) life insurance sales.

Term insurance provides nothing more than a stipulated amount of death benefits and, as a result, is considered the purest form of life insurance.
Fact: Term insurance basically provides a given amount of life insurance (that is, death benefits) for a stipulated period of time and nothing more — no investment features or cash value.

Types of Term Insurance. The most common types of term insurance are straight term and decreasing term. With regard to term policies, there are two important provisions that you should be aware of; these pertain to the renewability of the policy, and its convertibility to a whole life policy.

Straight term. Policies written for a given number of years — for example, 1, 5, 10, or 20 years — are called **straight-term** (or **level-term**) **policies**. In such policies, the amount of life insurance coverage remains unchanged throughout the effective period of the policy. In contrast, the *annual premium* on a straight-term policy may increase each year, or every five years. In many cases, however, it will remain level throughout the policy period. Of course, a policy with a premium that increases each year will start off below the level premium amount, subsequently equal it, and finally exceed it.

Decreasing term. Because the death rate increases for each year of life, the premiums on straight-term policies for each successive period of coverage will also increase. As an alternative to such a situation, many companies offer a term policy that *maintains a level premium* throughout all periods of coverage, while *the amount of protection decreases*. Such a policy is called a **decreasing-term policy**, since the amount of protection decreases over its life. Decreasing term can be used when the amount of needed coverage declines over time. For example, decreasing-term policies are popular with homeowners who want a level of life insurance coverage that will decline at about the same rate as the balances on their home mortgages. In addition, these policies are often purchased by families with young children as a way to ensure a sufficient level of family income while the kids are growing up. (As they grow older, the amount of coverage needed decreases until the last child becomes independent and the need expires.)

Renewability. The **renewability** provision allows the insured to renew his or her policy for another term of equal length, without having to show evidence of insurability. Renewal is at the option of the insured, but the premium will increase to offset the greater chance of death at older ages. Generally, term policies may be renewed at the end of each term until the insured attains age 65 or 70. If you buy term insurance, it's a good idea to obtain a *guaranteed renewable provision* in your policy. Otherwise, if you become uninsurable due to accident or illness during the policy period, you will lose your chance to renew your protection. Today, this valuable provision is standard in most term policies at no extra cost. Certainly, you *never* should buy a term policy that does not have guaranteed renewability.

---

term life insurance
Insurance that provides only death benefits, for a specified period (typically five years), and does not provide for the accumulation of any cash values.

straight-term policy
A term insurance policy that is written for a given number of years and whose coverage remains unchanged throughout the effective term; also called level-term policy.

decreasing-term policy
A term insurance policy in which the protection decreases over the policy's life.

renewability
A provision in term policies that allows the insured to renew his or her policy for anther term without proof of insurability. The best type of renewability, from the insured's viewpoint, is the *guaranteed renewable provision*.

EXHIBIT 9.5

A Premium Schedule for Term Life Insurance (Premiums per $1,000 of Level Premium Term Insurance)

When you buy term insurance, you are basically buying a financial product that provides life insurance coverage and nothing more.

Age Nearest Birthday		Five-Year Renewable Term		
Male	Female	Annual	Semiannual	Quarterly
20	25	$ 2.37	$ 1.23	$ .64
21	26	2.40	1.25	.65
22	27	2.44	1.27	.66
23	28	2.50	1.30	.68
24	29	2.55	1.33	.69
25	30	2.58	1.34	.70
26	31	2.62	1.36	.71
27	32	2.67	1.39	.72
28	33	2.73	1.42	.74
29	34	2.78	1.45	.75
30	35	2.88	1.50	.78
31	36	2.97	1.54	.80
32	37	3.11	1.62	.84
33	38	3.27	1.70	.88
34	39	3.49	1.81	.94
35	40	3.73	1.94	1.01
36	41	3.99	2.07	1.08
37	42	4.28	2.23	1.16
38	43	4.59	2.39	1.24
39	44	4.93	2.56	1.33
40	45	5.30	2.76	1.43
41	46	5.69	2.96	1.54
42	47	6.12	3.18	1.65
43	48	6.59	3.43	1.78
44	49	7.08	3.68	1.91
45	50	7.74	4.02	2.09
46	51	8.47	4.40	2.29
47	52	9.25	4.81	2.50
48	53	10.13	5.27	2.74
49	54	11.10	5.77	3.00
50	55	12.16	6.32	3.28
51	56	13.34	6.94	3.60
52	57	14.69	7.64	3.97
53	58	16.14	8.39	4.36
54	59	17.76	9.24	4.80
55	60	18.76	9.76	5.07
56		19.55	10.17	5.28
57		20.56	10.69	5.55
58		22.52	11.71	6.08
59		24.66	12.82	6.66
60		27.03	14.06	7.30

Note: All policies shown are participating, which means that the company will pay policyholders a dividend at the end of the year. Of course, the amount of the dividend cannot be determined beforehand.

Convertibility. The **convertibility** provision allows the insured to convert coverage to a comparable whole life policy (discussed below) without evidence of insurability. The convertibility feature serves as a guarantee to the insureds that (1) they will not lose their insurance protection at the end of the period and (2) upon conversion, they will have lifelong protection (as long as they pay their premiums, of course). The convertibility provision can be useful to persons who need a large amount of death protection at a relatively low cost, but who also want to continue their insurance coverage throughout their entire lives. This way, term coverage can be purchased to provide for a large amount of immediate death protection, and then later, when the insured has more income (and saving for retirement and liquidity for estate taxes become the more dominant issues), it can be converted to whole life. The convertibility option is standard with most of the term policies now marketed.

You should note that many convertible policies place some limitation on when the conversion can take place. For example, a ten-year term policy may stipulate that the conversion has to be made before the end of the eighth year, or a term policy to age 65 may require conversion prior to age 61.

Advantages and Disadvantages of Term.

Since term insurance offers an economical way to purchase a large amount of life insurance protection over a given (relatively short) period of time, it is particularly advantageous during the child-rearing years. And with the guaranteed renewable and convertible options, coverage can be continued throughout the insured's life, although, of course, the cost continually grows due to the increased chance of death. Indeed, this characteristic of increasing cost is the main disadvantage of term insurance, and is a principal reason why people discontinue needed coverage.

Criticizing term insurance on the basis of increasing cost, however, is similar to finding fault with homeowners insurance for not paying for a loss caused by an automobile accident. Clearly, the purpose of homeowners insurance is not to provide automobile coverage, just as the purpose of a term policy is *not* to provide lifelong coverage. The objective of term insurance is to provide a large amount of protection for a limited period of time — something it accomplishes very well!

WHOLE LIFE INSURANCE

Few people ever outlive the need for some type of life insurance. Accordingly, **whole life insurance**, as the name implies, is designed to offer financial protection for the whole life of an individual. In addition to death protection, whole life insurance has a *savings* feature, called **cash value**, which results from the investment earnings on paid-in insurance premiums. Thus, whole life provides not only insurance coverage but also a modest return on your in-

vestment! The idea behind cash value is to provide the insurance buyer with a tangible return while he or she is also receiving insurance coverage — the savings rates on whole life policies are normally *fixed* and *guaranteed* to be more than a certain rate (say, 4 to 6 percent). An illustration of how the cash value in a whole life policy builds up over time is provided in Exhibit 9.6. Obviously, the longer the insured keeps the policy in force, the greater the cash value. Whole life is available through several different payment plans, including continuous-premium, limited-payment, and single-premium. All of these payment plans provide for accumulation of cash values.

Life insurance companies set aside assets (that is, they "accumulate reserves") to pay the claims expected from the policies they issue. As time goes by, the cash value of a policy — the amount of assets allocated for each person insured — increases to reflect the greater chance of death that comes with age. If policyholders decide to cancel their contracts prior to death, that portion of the assets set aside to provide payment for the death claim is available to them. This right to a cash value is termed the policyholder's **nonforfeiture right**. Policyholders, by

---

convertibility
A provision in term policies that allows the insured to convert the policy to a whole life policy providing the same death benefit without proof of insurability.

whole life insurance
Life insurance that is designed to offer financial protection for the entire life of the insured; allows for the accumulation of cash values, along with providing stipulated death benefits.

cash value
The accumulated refundable value of an insurance policy that is based on insurance premiums paid and investment earnings; can be used as a source of loan collateral.

nonforfeiture right
A life insurance option tht gives the policyholder the portion of those assets that had been set aside to provide payment for future death claims. This amount, the **cash value**, is given to the policyholder upon cancellation of the policy by the insured.

EXHIBIT 9.6

Illustration of the Cash Value and Pure Protection in a Whole Life Policy

Here is an example of the projected cash value for an actual $200,000 whole life policy issued by a major life insurer to a male, age 30. For each year of the illustration, the difference between the $200,000 death benefit and the projected cash value represents the *death protection* offered by the insurer.

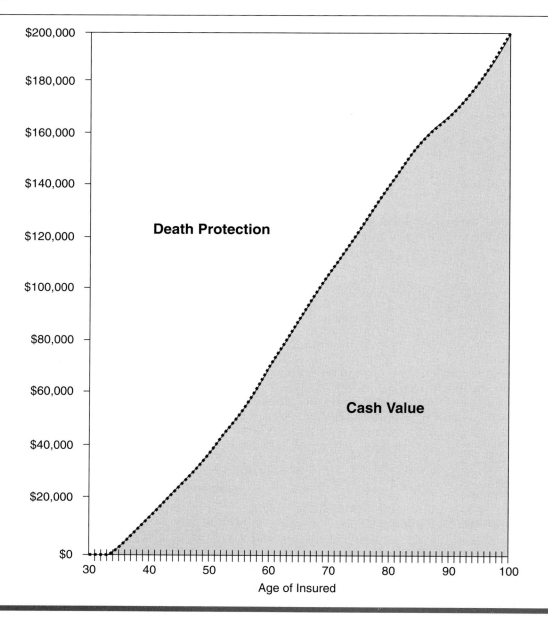

terminating their insurance contracts, forfeit their rights to death benefits. Correspondingly, the company must forfeit its right to keep all of the monies paid by these policyholders for the future death benefit it is no longer required to pay.

Types of Whole Life Policies.   Although a wide variety of whole life policies exists, only the major ones — continuous-premium, limited-payment, and single-premium — are described here. To get a feel for the cost of these policies, a sample premium schedule for several types of whole life policies is illustrated in Exhibit 9.7. By contrasting the premiums in this exhibit with those in Exhibit 9.5, you can readily see how much more expensive whole life is relative to term life. That is the price you pay for the savings/investment feature that comes with whole life.

Continuous-premium.   Under a *continuous-premium whole life* policy, or *straight life*, as it's more commonly called, individuals pay a level premium each year until they die or exercise a nonforfeiture right. The earlier in life the coverage is purchased, the lower the annual premium. This concept is often used as a selling point by some life insurance agents to convince younger persons to buy now. Their argument is that the sooner you buy, the less you pay. What they mean by this is what you pay *annually* rather than the total payments over the life of the policy. Of course, the sooner people purchase whole life, the longer they have coverage in force, but (all other things being equal) the *more* they pay in total.

While good reasons (such as securing needed protection, savings, and insurability) do exist for many young persons to buy whole life, it should seldom be purchased by anyone simply because the annual premium will be less than if it is purchased at a later date. Of the variety of whole life policies available, continuous-premium/straight life offers the greatest amount of permanent death protection and the least amount of savings per dollar of premium paid. Since the emphasis of whole life insurance for most families is *death protection* rather than savings, the continuous-premium policy is usually the wisest choice when filling a permanent life insurance need.

Limited-payment.   The *limited-payment whole life* policy offers coverage for the entire life of the insured but schedules the payments to end after a certain period of time. For example, 20-pay life, 30-pay life, paid-up age 55, and paid-up age 65 are types of frequently sold limited pay whole life policies. Under the 20-pay and 30-pay life contracts, the policyholder makes level premium payments for a period of 20 or 30 years, respectively. Under the premium schedule of paid-up at age 55, 65, or other stipulated-age policies, the policyholder makes premium payments until he or she attains the stated age. Of course, for any individual, the shorter the period of time over which premiums are payable, the larger the amount of the annual premium. Upon completion of the scheduled payments, the insurance remains in force at its face value for the remainder of the insured's life.

Some insurance companies emphasize the sale of limited-pay policies to the detriment of those who purchase them. In the sales presentation, considerable attention is focused on the "large" savings element that will develop and the fact that the policyholder is relieved of having to pay premiums for the entire life of the insured. However, this logic fails on two points. First, for most people, the primary purpose of whole life insurance is permanent protection against financial loss resulting from death — not the accumulation of savings. Second, even if people buy continuous-premium whole life policies, they need pay the premium only as long as they wish to keep the policies in force for their full face value. Policyholders may stop payment of premiums at any time after some nonforfeiture value has been accumulated. Rather than take this benefit in cash, they can convert the policies to ones that are paid up for some amount less than the original face value of the policy. (This is discussed in subsequent sections.)

The preceding discussion is not intended to imply that limited-payment policies are not desirable. Rather, the point is that if lifelong death protection is the primary aim of the life insurance policy, continuous-premium whole life should be purchased instead of a limited-payment policy. Since more continuous-premium whole life insurance can be purchased with the same number of dollars as limited-payment whole life, people who need whole life insurance are probably better off using continuous-premium life insurance so they can make the most of their insurance coverage. Once their insurance needs are reduced, they can convert the policy to a smaller amount of paid-up life insurance. On the other hand, if people have life insurance already

EXHIBIT 9.7

A Premium Schedule for Whole Life Insurance (Premiums per $1,000 of Insurance Coverage)

As with any life insurance product, the older you are, the more expensive it is to buy whole life.
Also, whole life is more costly than term because you are getting an investment/savings account in
addition to life insurance coverage.

Age Nearest Birthday		Straight Life			20-Pay Life			30-Pay Life		
Male	Female	Annual	Semiannual	Quarterly	Annual	Semiannual	Quarterly	Annual	Semiannual	Quarterly
20	25	$10.13	$ 5.27	$ 2.74	$16.44	$ 8.55	$ 4.44	$12.85	$ 6.68	$ 3.47
21	26	10.50	5.46	2.84	16.91	8.79	4.57	13.23	6.88	3.57
22	27	10.86	5.65	2.93	17.40	9.05	4.70	13.61	7.08	3.67
23	28	11.26	5.86	3.04	17.89	9.30	4.83	14.02	7.29	3.79
24	29	11.68	6.07	3.15	18.41	9.57	4.97	14.43	7.50	3.90
25	30	12.07	6.28	3.26	18.87	9.81	5.09	14.82	7.71	4.00
26	31	12.47	6.48	3.37	19.34	10.06	5.22	15.21	7.91	4.11
27	32	12.90	6.71	3.48	19.83	10.31	5.35	15.62	8.12	4.22
28	33	13.34	6.94	3.60	20.34	10.58	5.49	16.05	8.35	4.33
29	34	13.81	7.18	3.73	20.87	10.85	5.63	16.50	8.58	4.46
30	35	14.30	7.44	3.86	21.42	11.14	5.78	16.98	8.83	4.58
31	36	14.82	7.71	4.00	21.99	11.43	5.94	17.46	9.08	4.71
32	37	15.37	7.99	4.15	22.57	11.74	6.09	17.98	9.35	4.85
33	38	15.94	8.29	4.30	23.18	12.05	6.26	18.52	9.63	5.00
34	39	16.54	8.60	4.47	23.83	12.39	6.43	19.09	9.93	5.15
35	40	17.18	8.93	4.64	24.50	12.74	6.62	19.68	10.23	5.31
36	41	17.86	9.29	4.82	25.19	13.10	6.80	20.31	10.56	5.48
37	42	18.58	9.66	5.02	25.90	13.47	6.99	20.96	10.90	5.66
38	43	19.32	10.05	5.22	26.66	13.86	7.20	21.64	11.25	5.84
39	44	20.11	10.46	5.43	27.45	14.27	7.41	22.37	11.63	6.04
40	45	20.94	10.89	5.65	28.27	14.70	7.63	23.13	12.03	6.25
41	46	21.80	11.34	5.89	29.13	15.15	7.87	23.93	12.44	6.46
42	47	22.72	11.81	6.13	30.02	15.61	8.11	24.74	12.86	6.68
43	48	23.69	12.32	6.40	30.95	16.09	8.36	25.63	13.33	6.92
44	49	24.71	12.85	6.67	31.91	16.59	8.62	26.55	13.81	7.17
45	50	25.91	13.47	7.00	33.07	17.20	8.93	27.66	14.38	7.47
46	51	27.17	14.13	7.34	34.30	17.84	9.26	28.84	15.00	7.79
47	52	28.52	14.83	7.70	35.56	18.49	9.80	30.08	15.64	8.12
48	53	29.95	15.57	8.09	36.90	19.19	9.96	31.43	16.34	8.49
49	54	31.47	16.36	8.50	38.34	19.94	10.35	32.84	17.08	8.87
50	55	33.10	17.21	8.94	39.84	20.72	10.76	34.35	17.86	9.27
51	56	34.82	18.11	9.40	41.42	21.54	11.18	35.97	18.70	9.71
52	57	36.65	19.06	9.90	43.10	22.41	11.64	37.71	19.61	10.18
53	58	38.61	20.08	10.42	44.89	23.34	12.12	39.56	20.57	10.68
54	59	40.70	21.16	10.99	46.80	24.34	12.64	41.56	21.61	11.22
55	60	42.79	22.25	11.55	48.34	25.14	13.05	43.43	22.58	11.73
56	61	42.95	22.33	11.60	48.83	25.39	13.18	43.69	22.72	11.80
57	62	45.01	23.41	12.15	50.32	26.17	13.59	45.55	23.69	12.30
58	63	47.36	24.63	12.79	52.40	27.25	14.15	47.82	24.87	12.91
59	64	49.85	25.92	13.46	54.62	28.40	14.75	50.24	26.12	13.56
60	65	52.50	27.30	14.18	56.97	29.62	15.38	52.81	27.46	14.26

Note: All policies shown are participating.

in force that is sufficient to protect against income loss, they can use limited-payment policies as part of their savings or retirement plans.

Single-premium whole life. Continuous-premium and limited-payment whole life policies represent methods of acquiring life insurance on an installment basis. In contrast, a *single-premium whole life* policy is one that is purchased on a cash basis. You make one premium payment at the inception of the contract, and that buys life insurance coverage for the rest of your life. The single-premium policy has only limited usefulness in the life insurance programs of most families. However, because of its investment attributes, single-premium life insurance, or SPLI for short, does hold some appeal for those who are looking for a way to invest in a type of *tax-sheltered investment vehicle*

From an investment perspective, SPLI is attractive because, like any whole life insurance policy, it allows the holder to accumulate interest/investment earnings within the policy on a tax-deferred basis. It also provides some life insurance coverage — usually just enough to qualify under IRS rules — but this amounts to an added bonus. (Of course, the death benefits from an SPLI policy are treated like those from any other life insurance policy in that they pass tax-free to the beneficiaries.) Single-premium policies are purchased with a single payment made right up front, much like you would do when buying a stock, bond, or some other investment vehicle. Minimum premiums usually run around $5,000, though most buyers today put in much more. Once the purchase is made, investment earnings start to build up tax-free!

If all this sounds too good to be true, it's because *there is a catch*! Any cash withdrawals or loans taken against the SPLI cash value before you reach the age of 59½ will receive a double whammy from the IRS. First, the initial withdrawals or loans are likely to be treated as a gain, rather than a return of your premium payment, so they will be subject to income taxes. Second, the IRS will assess an additional 10 percent penalty against the withdrawal or loan. Because of these severe tax limitations, SPLI is ill-suited for young families with moderate incomes. The SPLI product is more appropriate, however, for middle-aged purchasers who want to supplement their retirement plans and also need some additional life insurance protection.

Advantages and Disadvantages of Whole Life. The most noteworthy feature of whole life insurance is that premium payments contribute toward building an estate regardless of how long the insured lives. This feature results because the face value of the policy is paid upon death, or alternatively, because the cash value may be withdrawn when the need for insurance protection has expired. A corresponding benefit of whole life (except single-premium) is that it permits individuals who need insurance for an entire lifetime to budget their premium payments over a relatively long period, thus eliminating the problems of unaffordability and uninsurability often encountered with term insurance in later years.

Some people like whole life because the periodic payments force them to save regularly. And, of course, there's the favorable tax treatment afforded to accumulated earnings — which means that as your earnings build up on a tax-sheltered basis, the underlying cash value of the policy also increases at a much faster rate than it would otherwise. Insurance experts will also point out that the whole life policy offers other potentially valuable options in addition to death protection and cash value. Some of these options include the continuation of coverage after allowing the policy to lapse because premiums were not paid (nonforfeiture option) and the ability to revive an older, favorably priced policy that has lapsed (policy reinstatement). These options, and others, will be discussed in a later section on insurance contract features.

The most frequently cited disadvantages of whole life insurance are that (1) it provides less death protection than term insurance, and (2) it provides lower yields than many other investment vehicles — the fact is that the returns on most whole life insurance policies are just not all that attractive. As with term insurance, the negative aspects of whole life often arise from misuse of the policy. In other words, a whole life policy should not be used to fulfill the objective of obtaining maximum return on investment. However, if a person wishes to combine a given amount of death protection for the entire life of the insured (or until the policy is terminated) with a savings plan that provides a reasonable tax-sheltered rate of return, whole life insurance may be a wise purchase.

One way to keep the cost down is to consider the purchase of *low-load* whole life insurance. Low-load products are sold directly by insurers to consumers, sometimes via a toll-free number, thereby eliminating sales agents from the transaction. With traditional whole life policies sold by an agent, between 100 and 150 percent of the first year's premium, and between 20 and 25 percent of total premiums paid over the life of the policy, are absorbed by sales commissions and marketing expenses. By comparison, only between 5 and 10 percent of low-load policies goes to cover marketing and selling expenses. The end result is that cash values grow much more quickly. In one case, a 50-year-old male was able to purchase a low-load policy with a $500,000 death benefit for an annual premium of $7,500. Within five years, his cash surrender value was projected to be over $36,000, while a comparable, fully loaded policy was projected to produce only a $24,000 cash value.

UNIVERSAL LIFE INSURANCE

The stockbrokerage firm of E. F. Hutton, through its life insurance subsidiary, is generally credited with marketing the first universal life insurance policy in 1979. Today most life companies sell universal life insurance or similar policies. Basically, **universal life insurance** combines term insurance, which provides the death benefits of the policy, with a tax-sheltered savings/investment account that pays interest at *competitive money market rates*. Universal life was a highly successful product in the 1980s, accounting for more than 30 percent of individual life insurance sales in 1988. In the last couple of years, however, sales growth for universal life has slowed dramatically, producing only 15 percent of individual life sales in 1990.

A Type of Whole Life Insurance.
Universal life insurance is like whole life in that it provides both death protection and a savings element, or cash value. The special aspect of a universal life policy is that the death protection (or pure insurance) portion and the savings portion are identified separately in its price. This is referred to as *unbundling*. Traditionally, for whole life insurance, you would pay a premium that would purchase a stated face amount of coverage in a policy with a *fixed cash-value schedule*. Not so with universal life. Here's what happens: When you make a premium payment on a universal life policy, part of that premium is used to pay administrative fees and the remainder is put in the cash value, or savings portion of the policy, where it earns a certain rate of return — this rate of earnings varies with market yields, but is guaranteed to be more than some stipulated minimum rate (say, 4 percent). Then, each month, the price of one month's term insurance is withdrawn from the cash value to purchase the required death protection. So long as there's enough in the savings portion to buy death protection, the policy will stay in force.

Should the cash value grow to an unusually large amount, then the amount of insurance coverage will be increased in order for the policy to retain its favorable tax treatment (tax laws require that the death benefits in a universal life policy *must always exceed the cash value* by a stipulated amount).

The clear separation of the protection and savings elements in the universal policy has raised the question of whether or not this type of insurance is in fact whole life insurance. This question is important, because the accumulation of cash values in whole life policies arises partly from interest credited to them. Under present tax laws, *this accumulation occurs income tax–free as long as the cash value does not exceed the total premiums paid to the insurer*. However, if a whole life policy is surrendered for its cash value, and that cash value exceeds the premiums paid, then *the gain* is taxed. Through an Internal Revenue Service ruling and federal legislation, universal life insurance policies enjoy the same favorable tax treatment as do other forms of whole life insurance — that is, death benefits are income tax–free and, prior to the death of the insured, amounts credited to the cash value, including investment earnings, accumulate on a tax-deferred basis.

Basic Structure.
Insurance companies sell a variety of policies under the heading of universal life. In spite of the different names, the basic structure of these policies is pretty much the same and can be described as follows. The premium you pay for the policy, which is called the *annual contribution* or *annual outlay*, is deposited in a fund, known as an *accumulation account*. The insurer credits interest to the account at a current rate and deducts from it the cost of the death benefits (and other expenses). The size of the deduction for the death protection depends on the amount of term insurance to be purchased and the age of the insured. The crediting of interest and the deductions for expenses and insurance coverage usually occur monthly. Each year the policy is in force, the insurance company will send the insured an annual statement that summarizes all the monthly deductions and credits.

Within the basic structure of a universal life insurance policy, there are two types of death protection. In the first type, known as Option A, a level death benefit is provided. As the cash value increases, the amount of pure insurance protection *decreases*. The second type, Option B, provides a stated amount of insurance plus the accumulated cash value. Thus, the death benefit at any time varies with the rate of earnings on the savings plan and will increase along with the accumulated cash value.

The Flexibility Feature. A characteristic of a universal life insurance policy that is important in your financial planning is its flexible nature. The annual premium you pay can be increased or decreased from year to year. This feature is based on the fact that the cost of the death protection *may be covered from either the annual premium or the accumulation account* (that is, cash value). Thus, as long as the accumulation account is adequate, you can choose to skip an annual premium and cover the cost of the death protection from the accumulation account. In addition, the death benefit can be increased or decreased, and you can change from the level benefit type of policy to the cash value plus a stated amount of insurance. Note, however, that evidence of insurability is usually required if the death benefit is to be increased.

Some Precautions. One of the attractions of a universal life insurance policy is the promise of the cash value being credited with the "current" rate of interest. For example, the current rate of interest may be 10 percent as compared to a guaranteed minimum rate of 4 percent. Make it a point to find out just what current rate of interest is used to credit earnings to your accumulation account. A common rate is that of 90-day Treasury bills. Other rates, however, may be used. Another caution regarding universal life is that you may be attracted to the relatively low interest charge on loans that you take from your cash value. However, the cash value that is equal to the loan is usually then credited with only the *guaranteed interest rate* of 4 to 4.5 percent.

You should also evaluate the charges or fees that the insurance company levies on its universal life policies. Ask the insurance agent about the front-end load or commission you'll have to pay on the first premium, the expense charge on each annual premium, investment expense charged by the insurer in determining the "current" rate of return, and any other charges you may be assessed. Most states require that the insurance company issue an annual disclosure statement that spells out premiums paid, expenses and mortality costs, interest earned, and beginning and ending cash values.

OTHER TYPES OF LIFE INSURANCE

In addition to term, whole life, and universal life, several other types of life insurance policies are available, including variable life insurance, insurance on multiple lives, group life, credit life, mortgage life, industrial life insurance, special purpose policies, and deferred-premium life insurance. These policies serve very different purposes. Some may help you meet specific needs, while others are simply more expensive alternatives to traditional types of life insurance.

Variable Life Insurance. A basic feature of *whole* life insurance is that it combines insurance coverage and a savings account into one package. *Universal* life extends this concept by being a bit more aggressive with the savings component, and thereby offering the potential for slightly higher returns and a quicker build-up of the cash value. *Variable life* goes even further, for it allows the policyholder to decide on how the money in the savings (cash value) component should be invested and as a result, offers the highest and most attractive level of investment returns — but unlike whole or universal life policies, no minimum return is guaranteed. In addition, as the name implies, the amount of insurance coverage provided will vary with the profits (and losses) being generated in the investment account. Thus, in **variable life insurance** policies, the amount of death benefits payable are, for the most part, related to the policies' investment returns.

A variable life policy, in short, combines insurance protection with the ability to spread your money over a variety of different investment accounts, all in one convenient, tax-favored package.

---

universal life insurance
A type of insurance contract that combines term insurance (death benefits) with a tax-deferred savings/investment account that pays competitive money market interest rates.

variable life insurance
Life insurance in which the benefits payable to the insured are related to the returns being generated on the investments that support the policy's payment obligations.

ISSUES IN MONEY MANAGEMENT

Joint Life Insurance: Two Lives, One Policy

Before the surge of two-income families, the insurance industry targeted husbands. Their widows, went the pitch, would need funds for the mortgage and children's education. "But now that both partners are wage-earners, it's important to guard against the loss of either income," says Ted Lietz, at Jackson National Life in Lansing, Mich.

Instead of a husband and wife buying separate policies naming each other as beneficiary, "first-to-die" coverage may be a less costly option. One policy covers both; if either dies, the other collects.

TWO FOR ONE.

The idea works best when each spouse's income is equally vital to maintain the family's lifestyle. First-to-die insurance typically saves 10% to 25% of the cost of separate policies, because premiums are based on a hypothetical "joint equal age."

A typical case: One insurer charges a 55-year-old husband nearly $18,000 a year for his own $1 million whole-life con-

tract. A similar policy for his wife, also 55, costs roughly $11,000. But one first-to-die policy runs about $24,000, a 17% savings. Another insurer will sell two 35-year-olds a $200,000 policy for $255 monthly, vs. $341 for separate policies.

Joint coverage isn't for everyone. An older husband might prefer to buy his own whole-life policy while his younger spouse gets low-cost term coverage. But there are plans to suit different needs. Nationwide sells "joint decreasing term" coverage that lets a couple's surviving member pay off any remaining mortgage sum. The "joint ultimate" policy of Jackson National and "multi-life" plan of Fidelity Union in Dallas let you build up invested funds for retirement if you surrender the policy. Life of Georgia's "joint whole life" plan "isn't only for a couple," says sales support director Carl Saunders. "It's Jim-dandy for buy-sell arrangements where two partners own a business. If one dies, the other has the proceeds to buy his share." Some

policies cover several partners, with payouts pegged to each one's piece of the business.

Many also enable the survivor to do some estate planning. The policy can be converted to one that pays a matching death benefit to the heir of the second-to-die.

The Savings in First-To-Die Insurance

ANNUAL PREMIUMS FOR $1 MILLION OF WHOLE-LIFE INSURANCE

	Separate policies	Multi-life policy
For a couple . . .		
MALE, 55	$17,974	
FEMALE, 50	11,025	
	$28,999	$24,151
For business partners . . .		
MALE, 60	21,567	
MALE, 55	16,027	
MALE, 40	6,193	
	$43,787	$35,179

DATA: FIDELITY UNION LIFE INSURANCE CO.

Source: Don Dunn, "Two Incomes, One Life-Insurance Policy," *Business Week*, July 15, 1991, p. 150.

The investment accounts are set up just like *mutual funds*, and most firms that offer variable life policies let you choose from a full menu of different types of funds, ranging from money market accounts and bond funds to aggressively managed stock funds. As a policyholder, you can specify that your money be placed into any one or more of the funds offered under the policy, and you can also freely move your money from one fund to another as market conditions dictate. Furthermore, like all life insurance products, variable policies offer attractive tax benefits: investment earnings can grow within the policy free of any current taxation; you can switch between funds with no tax consequences; and the policy's death benefit is passed on tax-free to your beneficiaries.

While all these features may sound great, it's important to keep in mind that if you want the benefits of higher investment returns, you must also be willing to assume the risks of reduced insurance coverage — bigger investment profits do, indeed, lead to more death benefits and an accelerated build-up in cash value, but investments can also end up losing money (sometimes in a big way), and that can lead to lower cash values and reduced insurance coverage (though it can never fall below the minimum death benefit stated in the policy). All of which means you should use extreme care when buying variable life insurance.

Insurance on Multiple Lives. Reflecting the rapid growth of two-income families, knowledgeable planners and agents are recommending **joint life insurance**, or "first-to-die" insurance, as it's frequently called. Joint life pays the full death benefit when the *first* spouse dies, and is appropriate where the death of either spouse would result in a loss of income that would jeopardize the family's lifestyle. As demonstrated in the accompany *Issues in Money Management* box, this policy usually is cheaper than buying two policies with the same death benefit — one on each income provider. But what happens if both earners are killed in a common disaster, such as a car accident? This should not be a problem because most joint life policies have a *double indemnity* clause whereby twice the normal death benefit is paid to the beneficiaries.

In contrast, **survivorship insurance**, also known as "last-to-die" insurance, covers two parties, but pays benefits only when the last surviving insured dies. This type of policy normally is used to help pay estate taxes. U.S. tax laws are set up so that estate taxes are minimal when one married partner dies and leaves his or her estate to the surviving spouse. When the surviving spouse dies, however, his or her estate may be subject to federal estate tax rates as high as 55 percent. Survivorship insurance immediately generates the dollars to pay such a tax. Because of certain exclusions allowed by the government, a family generally should not be concerned about estate taxes unless the total estate, including life insurance death benefits, exceeds $600,000.

Group Life Insurance. Under **group life insurance**, one master policy is issued, and each eligible member of the group receives a certificate of insurance. Group life is nearly always term insurance, and the premium is based on the characteristics of the group as a whole, rather than related to any specific individual. Group life insurance is often provided by employers as a fringe benefit for their employees. However, just about any type of group (be it a labor union, professional association, or alumni organization) can secure a group life policy, so long as the insurance is only incidental to the reason for the group.

Accounting for about 30 percent of all life insurance in force in the United States, group life insurance is one of the fastest-growing areas of insurance. Many group life policies now offer coverage for not only the group members but also their dependents. In addition, group life policies generally provide that if individual members leave the group, they may continue the coverage by converting their protection to individually issued whole life policies — such conversion normally does not require evidence of insurability so long as it occurs within a specified period of time. Of course, after exercising the option to convert, these individuals assume all responsibility for the payment of premiums.

As noted earlier in the chapter, the availability of group coverage should be considered when developing a life insurance program. However, because of its potentially temporary nature and relatively low face amount (often equal to about one year's salary), it should fulfill only low-priority insurance needs.

---

joint life insurance
Life insurance on two lives, but which pays only when the first person dies; also known as "first-to-die" insurance.

survivorship life insurance
Life insurance that covers two persons, but only pays when the second one dies; also known as "last-to-die" insurance.

group life insurance
A type of life insurance that provides a master policy for a group and a certificate of insurance for each eligible member.

Only in rare cases should a family rely solely on group life insurance to fulfill its primary income-protection requirements.

Credit Life Insurance. Banks, finance companies, and other lenders generally sell **credit life insurance** in conjunction with installment loans. Usually credit life is a term policy, of less than five years, with a face value that decreases at the same rate as the outstanding balance on the loan. Although liquidating debts upon the death of a family breadwinner is often desirable, the funds for this need should be fulfilled through an individual's term or whole life insurance program. Buying credit life insurance per se is one of the most expensive ways to buy life insurance and should be avoided. Further, contrary to popular belief, a lender cannot legally reject a loan just because the potential borrower chooses not to buy credit life insurance.

Mortgage Life Insurance. **Mortgage life insurance** is a form of term life insurance that's designed to pay off the mortgage balance on a home in the event of the death of the borrower. As in the case of credit life, this need can usually be met less expensively by shopping the market for a suitable decreasing-term policy. Credit life and mortgage life are relatively expensive, because lenders are often influenced by the amount of sales commission they receive in selecting the insurers with whom they place the coverage. Also, as might be expected, an insurer who pays high commissions is frequently one who charges a high premium.

Industrial Life Insurance. **Industrial life insurance**, now called **home service life**, is a type of whole life insurance that is issued in policies with small face amounts, often $1,000 or less. It is sold by agents who call on policyholders weekly or monthly to collect the premiums. The term *industrial* arose because when these policies first became popular, they were sold primarily to low-paid industrial wage earners. Because of high marketing costs, industrial life insurance costs a good deal more per $1,000 of coverage than regular whole life policies. Even so, some insurance authorities believe that industrial life insurance offers the only practical way to deliver coverage to low-income families. Although many of the largest life insurance providers started out in this business, industrial/home service life today accounts for less than 1 percent of the total amount of life insurance in force in the United States.

Special-Purpose Policies. Certain types of policies frequently combine some form of term and whole life insurance for coverage on one or more family members. These policies have often been developed by life insurers because of the highly competitive nature of the life insurance business. You should try to determine whether such a policy truly meets your needs or is primarily a marketing gimmick. Although many of the special-purpose policies are sold under various company trade names, general designations are as follows: family plan policies, family income policies, family maintenance policies, and jumping juveniles.

One appealing feature of certain "family plans" is that they offer the guaranteed insurability of children. For instance, the policy might specify that when the children reach a certain age (say, 21 or 25), they can convert to a specified type of life insurance at a predetermined price regardless of their physical condition. Although special-purpose policies can fill some family needs, more than likely you'll find that these needs can be satisfied at less cost if you simply buy convertible-term or continuous-premium whole life as separate policies.

Deferred-Premium Life Insurance. Several life insurance companies actively market their products to college students. These companies recognize, though, that most college students have little money to spend on life insurance. Their answer is to sign students up for **deferred-premium life insurance**, whereby a modest amount of life insurance is actually *purchased with an interest-bearing debt obligation* that is later paid off through a series of deferred-premium payments. Apart from the fact that many college students do not have enough significant financial responsibilities to justify life insurance, these deferred-payment plans are generally undesirable because they place students in debt. Students who accept this type of payment plan generally are required to sign a legally binding installment loan contract. Although deferred-payment plans have some legitimate business and tax-planning uses, for the majority of college students their purchase is unwise.

ALTERNATIVE LIFE INSURANCE CONTRACT PROVISIONS

Because all life insurance contracts are not alike, it's a good idea to review the various provisions contained in your policy to make sure you're getting just what you want. For example, things like policy loans, dividend participation provisions, settlement options, and so forth, are spelled out in most life insurance policies. What features would you like to see in a life insurance policy? Give some thought to this question before reading on.

All life insurance contracts have various provisions that establish the rights and obligations of the policyholder and the insurance company. Standard or uniform life insurance policies do not exist, and the wording of policy provisions and features varies among companies and according to the state in which the policy is sold. Nevertheless, many elements are common to most life insurance contracts. They can be divided into two groups: (1) life insurance contract features and (2) other policy features. After we review these contract provisions, we'll take a look at the competitive features of life insurance and suggest some guidelines to follow when buying life insurance.

LIFE INSURANCE CONTRACT FEATURES

The key features found in most life insurance contracts are (1) the beneficiary clause, (2) settlement options, (3) policy loans, (4) payment of premiums, (5) grace period, (6) nonforfeiture options, (7) policy reinstatement, and (8) change of policy.

Beneficiary Clause. All life insurance policies should have one or more beneficiaries. The **beneficiary** is the person who will receive the death benefits of the policy if the insured dies. Otherwise, death benefits are paid to the estate of the deceased and are subject to the often lengthy and expensive

legal procedure of going through probate court. An insured person is able to name both a *primary beneficiary* and various *contingent beneficiaries*. The primary beneficiary will receive the entire death benefit if he or she is surviving when the insured dies. If the primary beneficiary does not survive the insured, the insurer will distribute the death benefits to the contingent beneficiary or beneficiaries. If neither primary nor contingent beneficiaries are living at the death of the insured, then the death benefits pass to the estate of the insured and will be distributed by the probate court according to the insured's will or, if no will exists, according to state law.

When naming the beneficiary, the policyholder should make certain the identification is clear. For example, a man could buy a policy and simply designate the beneficiary as "my wife." However, if a subsequent divorce and remarriage were to occur, a controversy could arise as to which "wife" was entitled to the benefits. Similarly, if children are the intended beneficiaries, problems can arise when other children become part of the insured's family.

credit life insurance
A type of term life insurance sold in conjunction with installment loans; the coverage decreases at the same rate as the loan balance.

mortgage life insurance
A term insurance policy on the borrower's life that names the lender as beneficiary, allowing for the mortgage balance to be automatically paid off in the event of the borrower's death.

industrial life insurance (home service life)
A type of whole life insurance that is issued in policies with relatively small face amounts (usually $1,000 or less); formerly was offered to low-paid industrial workers.

deferred-premium life insurance
Life insurance that allows for the deferral of premium payments.

beneficiary
In life insurance, a person who receives the death benefits of an insurance policy upon the insured's death.

For instance, if a man named "my children" as beneficiaries, would proceeds be payable only to his natural and legitimate children, or would his adopted, illegitimate, or stepchildren also share in the proceeds?

What if the insured and the primary beneficiary, such as a husband and wife, were to lose their lives in a common disaster, such as an airplane accident? According to state laws, the contingent beneficiary(ies) normally would receive the death benefits if the deaths are determined to be simultaneous. If the primary beneficiary were determined to have survived the insured, even by a matter of minutes, the death benefits may go to the primary beneficiary's estate, however. This means that the death benefit ultimately would end up in the hands of the primary beneficiary's selected heirs. Imagine what could happen in a common disaster for a married couple where both spouses have children by a previous marriage. The $500,000 death benefit from a deceased wife's insurance policy could wind up in the hands of her husband's children, with her own children receiving nothing, just because her husband survived her by a few minutes! Even for couples with no previous marriages, carefully laid plans to avoid estate taxes could be upset by a common disaster where the deaths were not quite simultaneous.

To combat the common disaster problem, the insured should use a *survival clause* on her or his beneficiary form. For instance, a woman could specify her primary beneficiary as "My husband, Alfred, if he survives me by 60 days." As contingent beneficiaries, she could then name, "My children, Betty and Carl, in equal shares." This simple survival clause should assure that death benefits will go to her children if both she and her husband are fatally injured in a common disaster, even though he might survive her by a short time.

In sum, make sure you have named both a primary and a contingent beneficiary in any life insurance policies you buy and that no mistake can be made in determining who the beneficiaries are. Also be sure to use survival clauses, where appropriate. Note, too, that the person you name as a beneficiary can be changed at any time as long as you did not indicate an *irrevocable beneficiary* when you took out the policy. Thus, if your wishes change, all you need do is notify the insurance company—easy to do but also easy to forget. Therefore, when you write the premium check each year, verify that your policy's named beneficiary is also your desired beneficiary. (Similarly, you should update any prescribed settlement options—discussed next—with desired changes.)

Settlement Options. Insurance companies generally offer several ways of paying death proceeds from a life insurance policy. The decision as to how the funds will be allocated may be permanently established prior to the death of the insured, or the beneficiary may be allowed to select the desired **settlement option** when the policy matures. The most common settlement options besides lump-sum cash payment are (1) interest only, (2) payments for a stated period, (3) payments of a stated amount, and (4) income for life.

Interest only. Under the interest-only settlement option, the policy proceeds are left on deposit with the insurance company for a designated period of time. In exchange, the insurer guarantees to make interest payments to the beneficiary during the time it holds the funds. In some cases, the beneficiary is not permitted to withdraw the proceeds, and upon his or her death the funds are paid to a secondary beneficiary. In other cases, the beneficiary may have the right to fully withdraw policy proceeds at any time. The interest-only option can be useful when there is no current need for the principal amount or when the principal sum is large enough to provide a satisfactory annual income (in the form of interest) to the beneficiary. Typically, however, the rate of interest paid by insurers will be less than that paid by other types of savings medium.

Payments for stated period. With the payments-for-a-stated-period option, the face amount of the policy, along with interest earned, is systematically liquidated over a selected number of years. For example, a beneficiary at age 55 may not be eligible for social security benefits until age 65 but may in need of a monthly income for that ten-year period. Consequently, the option of receiving a monthly income for that duration may be more attractive than taking a lump sum. The amount of the periodic payment is determined by the face amount of the policy and the length of time over which the funds are to be distributed. For any given amount, the shorter the period is, the larger the monthly benefit.

Payments of stated amount. The payments-of-a-stated-amount option is similar to the preceding alternative in that it provides for a systematic liquidation of the policy proceeds. However, it enables you to set the size of the periodic benefit payments rather than the number of years over which income is to be received. Because payments will be made (in the stipulated amount) for as long as the money holds out, it follows that the greater the size of the periodic benefit payment, the quicker the money will run out. Payments of a stated amount offer more flexiblity than payments for a stated period, because beneficiaries usually retain the right to change the amount of income as their needs dictate. Under the stated-period option, the term cannot be modified, except that in some cases total withdrawal is permitted. In essence, the payment-for-a-stated-amount option can be used to accomplish the same objective as the stated-period option. All the beneficiaries need do is estimate the period of time over which they will want to receive payments and determine the amount that will be payable. Then they can select the stated-amount option to provide that amount of income. Should their needs change during the period, they can modify the terms of the settlement agreement.

Life income. Under the life-income option, the insurer guarantees a certain payment amount to the beneficiary for the remainder of his or her life. In contrast to the preceding options, payments under the life-income alternative are related to the age and sex of the beneficiary at the inception of the periodic benefits. The amounts are essentially a function of the face value of the policy, interest rate assumptions, and the life expectancy of the beneficiary. (Technically, mortality rates rather than life expectancy are used in these computations. A *mortality rate* designates the number of deaths per 1,000 that will occur at specified ages each year, whereas *life expectancy* is the mean number of years of life remaining at a given age.)

The life-income option may appeal to people who want to be certain that they will not outlive the income from the policy proceeds and subsequently have to depend on others for support. Under this option, a company usually will agree to guarantee payments for five or ten years to a secondary beneficiary should the original recipient die prior to the passage of that time period. This arrangement is sometimes referred to as a *life-income-with-period-certain* option. Of course, if the life-income-with-period-certain option is selected, monthly benefits will be less than if the option providing for the life of the primary beneficiary only is chosen.

Policy Loans. An advance made by a life insurance company to a policyholder is called a **policy loan**. Such a loan is secured by the cash value of the life insurance policy. A provision in nearly all whole life policies grants this right. Although these loans do *not* have to be repaid, any balance plus interest on the loan remaining at the death of the insured is *subtracted from the proceeds of the policy*. The rate of interest charged on older policies is customarily 5 to 8 percent per annum, and it is stated in the policy. Newer policies, in contrast, offer either a fixed rate loan, with an interest rate normally set at about 8 percent, or a rate that varies with market interest rates on high-quality bonds. Some policies actually give the insured a choice as to whether the loans will be at fixed or variable rates.

Policy loans should be taken out only in unusual circumstances because of the reduction of death proceeds that can occur. One long-time advocate of whole life insurance has decried policy loans as "stealing from your widow." Although not all would agree with this emotional assessment, life insurance is intended to provide basic financial protection for most families, and spending those proceeds prematurely is an unwise practice. On the other hand, because these loans are less expensive than borrowing from other financial institutions, they may appeal to certain persons who wish to keep their borrowing costs low and are not bothered by the accompanying loss of death proceeds if the loans

settlement option
A specified way of paying the death proceeds from a life insurance policy, such as lump-sum cash payment, payments for a stated period, payments of a stated amount, or income for life.

policy loan
An advance made by an insurer to a life insurance policyholder that is secured by the cash value of the policy.

are not repaid. A word of caution: *Be very careful with these loans, because unless certain conditions are met, the IRS may treat them as withdrawals, meaning they could be subject to tax penalties.* If you're in any way unsure, consult your insurance agent or a tax advisor.

Payment of Premiums. All life insurance contracts have a provision that specifies when premiums are due. With most insurers, the policyholder may elect to pay premiums on an annual, semiannual, or monthly basis. Some premium checks are mailed directly to the company; in other instances, a sales agent collects premiums from the policyholder. Another method of payment allows policyholders to pay premiums through an automatic deduction from their bank accounts. In the case of the death of a policyholder who has paid premiums more than one month in advance, many companies refund those premiums along with the policy death proceeds.

Grace Period. The *grace period* permits the policyholder to retain full death protection for a short period of time (usually 31 days) after a premium due date has been missed. In other words, you won't lose your insurance protection just because you're a little late in making the premium payment. If the insured dies during the grace period, the face amount of the policy less the unpaid premium is paid to the beneficiary.

Nonforfeiture Options. As discussed earlier, a nonforfeiture option provides the policyholder with some benefits when a policy is terminated prior to its maturity. State laws require that all permanent whole life policies (and term contracts that extend coverage over a long period) contain a nonforfeiture provision. In addition to cash withdrawal, companies ordinarily offer the following options to the policyholder: (1) a paid-up policy for a reduced amount or (2) a term policy for an extended period. Exhibit 9.8 shows a variety of these options for a $1,000 whole life policy issued to a male age 21.

Paid-up insurance. Under the paid-up insurance option, the policyholder receives a policy exactly like the one that was terminated except that it has a lower face value. In effect, the policyholder has purchased a new policy, with his or her cash value serving as the payment for a single-premium policy.

For example, you can see in Exhibit 9.8 that if this insured canceled the policy after ten years, it would have a cash value of $90.84 per $1,000 of face amount. This $90.84 could also be used to buy $236 of paid-up whole life insurance. Under that option, the $90.84 cash value would continue to grow because of future interest earnings, even though the policyholder is relieved of any further premium payments. This option is useful when a person's income and need for death protection decline, while at the same time some coverage is still desired. Many elect this option on whole life policies when they reach age 60 or 65.

Extended term. Under an extended-term option, the accumulated cash value is used to purchase a term life policy for the same face value as the policy that has lapsed. The period of coverage is determined by the amount of term protection a single-premium payment (equal to the total cash value) will purchase at the present age of the insured. If the insured in Exhibit 9.8 (at the end of 10 years) chose the extended-term option instead of the paid-up insurance, he would receive $1,000 in coverage for a period of 22 years and 29 days. The extended-term option is usually the option that automatically goes into effect if the policyholder quits paying premiums and gives no instructions to the insurer.

Policy Reinstatement. While a policy is under the reduced paid-up option or the extended-term option, the policyholder may reinstate the original policy by paying all back premiums plus interest at a stated rate and providing evidence that he or she can pass a physical examination and meet any other insurability requirements. *Reinstatement* means that the original contractual relationship between the company and the policyholder is revived. Most often the policyholder must reinstate the policy within a specified period (three to five years) after the policy has lapsed. However, before exercising a reinstatement option, a policyholder should make some effort to determine whether buying a new policy (from the same or a different company) might be less costly.

Change of Policy. Many life insurance contracts contain a provision that permits the insured to switch from one policy form to another. For instance, policyholders may decide that they would rather have paid-up age 65 policies as opposed to

EXHIBIT 9.8

Various Nonforfeiture Options (For a 21-year-old Male; Dollar Amount of Benefits for Each $1,000 of Insurance)

Even if the insured stops making premium payments on his whole life policy, he still has certain benefits that he owns in the form of a specified amount of cash value or paid-up (whole life or term) insurance coverage.

End of Policy Year	Cash or Loan Value	Paid-up Insurance	Extended Term Insurance	
			Years	Days
1	$ 0.00	$ 0	0	0
2	0.00	0	0	0
3	4.79	15	1	315
4	16.21	48	6	161
5	27.91	81	11	15
6	39.91	113	14	275
7	52.20	145	17	158
8	64.78	176	19	157
9	77.66	206	20	342
10	90.84	236	22	29
11	104.33	265	22	351
12	118.13	294	23	231
13	132.25	322	24	54
14	146.69	350	24	191
15	161.43	377	24	290
16	176.47	403	24	356
17	191.79	429	25	28
18	207.38	454	25	42
19	223.22	478	25	36
20	239.29	502	25	13
Age 60	563.42	806	17	26
Age 65	608.49	833	15	272

Source: *Principles of Risk Management and Insurance* by George E. Rejda. Copyright © 1992 HarperCollins, p. 407. Reprinted by permission.

their current continuous-premium whole life policies. A change of policy provision would allow this change without penalty. When policyholders change from high- to lower-premium policies, they may need to prove insurability. This requirement reduces the possibility of adverse selection against the company.

OTHER POLICY FEATURES

In addition to the key contractual features described in the preceding section, some other policy features that you should be aware of are (1) a multiple indemnity clause, (2) a disability clause, (3) insurability options, (4) a suicide clause, (5) an incontestability clause, (6) a misstatement of age or sex clause, (7) exclusions, (8) participation, and (9) living benefits.

Multiple Indemnity Clause. **Multiple** (most often double or triple) **indemnity clauses** double or triple the face amount of the policy if the insured dies as a result of an accident. This benefit is usually offered to the policyholder at a small additional cost. Many insurance authorities dismiss the use of a multiple indemnity benefit as irrational. This coverage should be ignored as a source of funds when programming insurance needs, since it provides no protection in the event of death due to illness.

---

multiple indemnity clause

A clause in a life insurance policy that typically doubles or triples the policy's face amount in the event of the insured's accidental death.

Disability Clause. A **disability clause** in a life insurance contract may contain a waiver-of-premium benefit alone or coupled with disability income. A *waiver-of-premium benefit*, excuses the payment of premiums on the life insurance policy if the insured becomes totally and permanently disabled prior to age 60 (or sometimes age 65). Under the *disability income portion*, the insured not only receives a waiver of premium, but also receives a monthly income equal to $5 or $10 per $1,000 of policy face value. Some insurers will continue these payments for the life of the insured, while others will terminate them at age 65. Disability riders that provide waiver-of-premium and disability income protection are relatively inexpensive and can be added to most whole life policies. They are generally not available with term policies.

Insurability Options. The policyholder who has an **insurability option** may purchase additional coverage at stipulated intervals without providing evidence of insurability. This option is frequently offered with the purchase of a whole life policy to buyers under age 40. The increases in coverage usually can be purchased every three, four, or five years in amounts equal to the amount of the original policy or $10,000, whichever is lower. This option should be quite attractive to individuals whose life insurance needs and ability to pay are expected to increase over a 5- to 15-year period.

Suicide Clause. Nearly all life insurance policies have a *suicide clause* that voids the contract if an insured commits suicide within a certain period, normally two years, after its inception. In these cases, the company simply returns the premiums that have been paid. If an insured takes his or her own life after this initial period has elapsed, the policy proceeds are paid without question.

Incontestability Clause. All life insurance policies contain an **incontestability clause** which gives the insurance company one to two years to investigate all information provided by the insured in the application. If during that period a material false statement is discovered, the company can seek a recision of the contract. After the elasped period, the insurer is prohibited from challenging the validity of the policy regardless of whether the insured has died or is still living.

Misstatement of Age or Sex Clause. Notwithstanding incontestability, the insurance company can adjust the payment made under a policy at any time if the insured misstated his or her age or sex in the application. For example, assume that a male age 35 applied for a life insurance policy by mail and stated that he was a female age 35. The incentive for making this misstatement was that for a given amount of coverage, females of the same age as males pay a lower premium because of lower mortality rates. If upon the insured's death ten years later the company discovered the error, it would award a sum equal to the amount of insurance that the premiums paid would have purchased had the insurer known the applicant was a male. Note that technically this is not a violation of the incontestability provision, because the policy has not been voided but simply modified to conform to the facts. However, some observers say that the misstatement of age and sex clause conflicts with the spirit of the incontestability rule and places an undesirable burden on the beneficiaries.

Exclusions. Although all private insurance policies exclude some types of losses, life policies offer very broad protection. In addition to the suicide clause, the only other common exclusions are aviation and war. In avaiation exclusions, the primary types of losses not covered are those occurring when the insured is a relatively inexperienced private pilot or is flying in military aircraft. No restrictions apply to fare-paying passengers of commercial airlines. (Most life insurers accept without premium surcharge the pilots and crews of scheduled airliners.) War exclusions often are inserted in policies in anticipation of or during periods of combat. They typically provide that should the insured die as a result of war, a return of premiums with interest will be made. War exclusions are intended to guard against adverse selection, which could materially disrupt the mortality experience of the company and consequently its solvency. When the potential insured has a hazardous occupation or hobby, the company will either exclude coverage for that activity or charge an additional premium to cover the added risk exposure. Seldom, if ever, would a company be able to modify the premium charged or coverage offered should the insured take up, say, Formula One racing or hang gliding after a policy has been issued.

Participating Policies. Many life insurance companies offer **participating policies**, which means that the policyholder is entitled to receive policy dividends that reflect the difference between the premiums that are charged and the amount of premium necessary to fund the actual mortality experience of the company. When the base premium schedule for participating policies is established, a company estimates what it believes its mortality and investment experience will be and then adds a generous margin of safety to these figures. The premiums charged the policyholder are based on these overly conservative estimates.

When company experience is more favorable than estimated, a return of the overcharge is made to policyholders in the form of **policy dividends**. These policy dividends may be received as cash payments (which, since they are viewed as a return of premium, are not subject to taxation), left with the company to earn interest, used to buy additional paid-up coverage, or applied toward the next premium payment. The dividend option selected is purely a matter of the individual policyholder's preference. Note that it is advantageous to use the dividends to buy paid-up options when more insurance coverage is desired, since these additions are available at their *net* rates, meaning they contain no load for sales expenses and consequently provide an economical way to increase coverage.

Living Benefits. A number of major life insurers, including Aetna, John Hancock, and Prudential, now are offering so-called living benefits options with whole and universal life policies. *Living benefits* allow the insured to receive a percentage of his or her death benefits prior to death. Some insurers actually are offering this option free of charge to established policyholders if the insured suffers a terminal illness expected to result in death within a specified period, such as six months to a year. In one case, an insured dying of cancer was able to receive over $44,000 on a $45,000 whole life policy and to use the money for retiring mortgage and car loans. In this case, the insured died within two months. If the insured had been expected to live longer, he would have received a lower living benefit.

Some insurers are marketing a *living benefit rider*, which allows advances of a policy's death benefit, usually about 2 percent per month, to pay for long-term health care, such as nursing home ex-

penses. This rider can cost an extra 5 to 15 percent of the normal life insurance premium and benefits are capped as a percentage of the death benefit. For example, a living benefit rider may cap benefits at 50 percent of the death benefit, so that an insured with a $100,000 policy could receive a maximum of $2,000 per month for 25 months. The remaining $50,000 death benefit would pass to the beneficiaries upon the death of the insured. While human interest stories have been written about dying persons who receive "peace of mind" because of living benefits, critics say that these options subvert the primary purpose of life insurance, which is to provide adequate cash payments to beneficiaries to cover expenses incurred and income lost because of an insured's death.

COMPETITIVE FEATURES OF LIFE INSURANCE

In addition to the elements that make up the insurance contract and other policy features, the follow-

---

disability clause
A clause in a life insurance contract that may contain either a waiver of premium benefit or a waiver of premium coupled with disability income.

insurability option
An option in a life insurance contract that allows the policyholder the right to purchase additional coverage, at stipulated intervals, without having to provide evidence of insurability.

incontestability clause
A clause in a life insurance contract that gives the insurer one or two years to investigate all information provided on the insured's application and to rescind the contract if false statements are found within this period.

participating policy
A life insurance policy that pays dividends that reflect the difference between the premiums that are charged and the amount of premium necessary to fund the insurer's actual mortality experience.

policy dividends
Payments made to participating policyholders that represent a refund of overcharges which result from the insurance company's overestimation of its mortality experience.

ing competitive features of life insurance require discussion: (1) protection from creditors, (2) medium for savings, and (3) tax benefits.

Protection from Creditors. When an insured dies, all assets and liabilities are totaled, and the heirs receive what is left after all legitimate claims against the estate have been satisfied. However, the purchase of life insurance can be structured so that death benefits will be paid to a named beneficiary rather than the deceased's estate. This way the cash proceeds do not become a part of the estate. Even if the insured had more liabilities than assets, the proceeds would not be used to liquidate them. Similarly, creditors who have successfully secured judgments against persons with substantial accumulations of life insurance cash values often cannot levy any claim on those assets. State laws differ with respect to the rights of creditors to the death benefits or cash values of life insurance policies, but in nearly all cases, both can be better protected than such assets as stocks, bonds, mutual funds, and investment real estate.

Medium for Savings. In addition to protection from creditors, life insurance can be an attractive medium for savings for some people, particularly those who are looking for safety of principal. The financial returns on the savings element in life insurance policies are often contrasted with investments in stocks, bonds, mutual funds, and real estate. Granted, most variable life policies are more investment vehicles than they are life insurance products, and as such, they can legitimately be compared to other investment outlets. For other types of insurance, though, the comparison is inappropriate. Certainly, any time the purchase of life insurance is being considered primarily because of its tax-sheltered investment properties, that transaction should be evaluated relative to what you can earn (on an after-tax basis) from alternative investment vehicles. More often than not, you'll find that *better returns are available from alternative investments*, especially when you factor in load fees, steep surrender charges, and other expenses.

Even though there's been a lot of growth recently in variable life and universal life policies, these products still account for only a small segment of life insurance sales. By far, the biggest share of life insurance is sold for the insurance protection it pro-

vides—without question, that's why most people buy whole or universal life policies. It's the death protection they're after, and the savings feature is just a pleasant by-product. The savings feature is not something to be overlooked, but it's not the principal reason for purchase. In both whole and universal life insurance, the approach to investing the cash-value part of the policy is very much toward the safe, conservative side where stability of income and preservation of capital are the primary concerns of the money managers. Under these conditions, it doesn't make any sense to compare the returns on these accounts to stocks, long-term bonds, and other forms of investing. More appropriately, the returns on whole and universal life insurance cash values should be compared to savings accounts, money funds, U.S. Treasury bills, and the like. When that's done, you're likely to find that the returns on these insurance products stack up very well: indeed, they compare favorably in providing returns ranging from 5 to 8 percent for recently issued policies, especially when you consider these are tax-deferred returns.

Tax Benefits. Life insurance proceeds, as a rule, are not subject to state or federal *income* taxes. Further, if certain requirements are met, policy proceeds can pass to named beneficiaries free of any *estate* taxes. Generally, though, to qualify for this estate tax exemption, the insureds must relinquish various "incidents of ownership" in their policies, including the right to change the beneficiary, to take the policy's cash surrender value, and to choose a settlement option. When the named beneficiary is a spouse, the sacrifice of these rights is unnecessary. In these cases, the life insurance proceeds typically can be excluded from estate taxes as part of the marital deduction.

An equally attractive benefit is that the *investment earnings* in whole, universal, and variable life products build up within the policy on a tax-deferred basis (this is called *inside build-up*). Such a feature means that the cash surrender value will build up much quicker than if you had to pay taxes annually on any investment earnings for the year.

Another tax advantage is that when cash values are withdrawn from an insurer, income taxes are payable only on the amount by which the cash value exceeds the total premiums that have been paid. In practice, this excess seldom results, because part of the premium that is paid is allocated to the death benefit cost incurred by the company during the time the policy is in force. Consequently, it does not become a part of the cash value of the policy. But, here again, *be very careful with cash withdrawals*, because in some cases, unless you're over age 59½, you may be hit with income tax on the withdrawal *plus* a good-sized tax penalty. The IRS rules governing cash withdrawals can get a bit complex (to say the least); and to make matters even worse, Congress has had a tendency lately to change things almost annually. The best course is to check with someone in the know (like a tax accountant) if you're in doubt.

SOME SUGGESTIONS TO FOLLOW WHEN BUYING LIFE INSURANCE

Before buying life insurance, you should (1) estimate the amount of life insurance you need to cover you and your family's financial requirements, (2) consider the types of policies available to meet your needs, and (3) familiarize yourself with the various provisions that life insurance contracts typically include. With this understanding of life insurance in mind, you can then shop the market for the insurance protection best suited for you.

To help you in shopping, the following discussion reviews the needs concept and the types of policies you might want to consider. In addition, it explains several criteria you can use to select life insurance companies and agents that offer the kind of services you'd like.

Selecting an insurance company is the first thing you should do when buying life insurance.
Fantasy: The first thing you should do is determine the *amount* of life insurance you need and then select the type of policy that is best for you. Only after you have taken these steps should you concern yourself with *where* you will buy the insurance.

Review Needs and Coverages. As discussed earlier, life insurance is used in a person's financial program to fill the gap between the resources that will be available after death and those that will be needed. In addition, some life insurance policies can be effectively used as a savings medium. For most young families on limited budgets, though, the need for a large amount of death protection greatly exceeds the need for a savings plan. If you fall into this category, guaranteed renewable and convertible term insurance should account for the largest portion of your insurance protection. Most families also need some amount of permanent insurance and savings, which a continuous-premium whole life policy can satisfy. Limited-payment, variable life, and single-premium policies should be purchased only when the primary need is savings and not protection against financial loss resulting from death. Generally speaking, parents of young children should give highest priority to term life insurance, some attention to continuous-premium whole (or universal) life, and little or no attention to limited-payment or variable life policies.

Selecting a Company. The life insurance company should be selected before the agent is, since in the life insurance business many agents represent only one company. Consequently, before looking for an agent, you might want to develop useful criteria with which to screen out companies. Usually they can be evaluated on the basis of their financial stability, reputation in the community and nation, the liberal/restrictive nature of their policy provisions, and whether they offer participating policies (if this feature is important to you). In addition, you should pay attention to the relative costs and fees of similar policies from competing companies. There is no question that there are substantial differences in policy costs from one company to another. Also, in view of these cost differences, you should be sure that the policies you are comparing *are similar in terms of provisions and amounts*. In other words, you should not compare a $100,000 term policy from one company with a $150,000 universal policy from another. Instead, you should first decide how much and what kind of policy you want and then compare costs.

In shopping around, you might find that one company is preferable for your term protection and another for your whole life needs. Age and size are useful indicators of the financial stability of life insurance companies. Unless a good reason exists to do otherwise, you should probably limit your choice of companies to those that have been doing business for 25 years or more and have annual premium volume in excess of $50 million. Although these criteria will screen out a lot of smaller firms, there'll still be plenty of companies left from which to choose.

Stick with Highly Rated Insurers.

Since 1991, five major life insurers and several dozen smaller ones have collapsed, leaving as many as a million customers dependent on a state-by-state patchwork of guarantee funds that don't hold any money. Indeed, the recent financial difficulties of such large life insurers as Executive Life, First Capital Life, Fidelity Bankers Life, Monarch Life, and Mutual Benefit Life all demonstrate the need to carefully study the financial stability of life insurers offering policies to you. The above noted insurers all invested heavily in high-risk junk bonds and real estate that resulted in large losses in the reserve funds held to pay claims. When policyholders began to demand their cash values earlier than expected, regulators realized that the available funds were inadequate, so they seized the insurers' assets and began the insolvency process, known as *rehabilitation*. As of early 1992, most holders of life insurance policies and annuities issued by the insurers in rehabilitation will receive full benefits, with the exception of Executive Life annuity holders, who can expect to receive only about 70 percent of the promised benefit level. Nevertheless, policyholders of these troubled insurers were forced to deal with the uncertainty of whether they would receive full value on their policies, plus the inability to withdraw their cash values during moratoriums imposed by regulators.

At year-end 1990, life insurers held over $85 billion worth of junk bonds and more than $15 billion worth of distressed mortgages. Certainly, the cautious consumer must wonder at what point his or her policy or annuity is endangered by such holdings. Assuming you are not a trained financial analyst familiar with the subtleties of insurance accounting practices, how can you tell whether your insurer is on firm financial footing? Similarly, how can you compare the financial solvency of competing insurers when deciding which policy or annuity to buy? Fortunately, several private rating agencies are in the business of assessing the financial strength of insurers and can provide the information you need. There are three major rating agencies that study life insurers and assign letter grades for financial

strength. These ratings are available to the public and can be acquired by written request from the rating company (they may even be available in major university or public libraries). These rating agencies include A.M. Best Company (Ambest Road, Oldwick, NJ 08858), Standard & Poor's Corporation (25 Broadway, New York, NY 10004), and Moody's Investor's Service (99 Church Street, New York, NY 10007). Also, at least once a year, Professor Joseph Belth of Indiana University compiles all of these ratings in his monthly publication, *The Insurance Forum* (P.O. Box 245, Ellettsville, IN 47429), which is available by subscription. Although the rating agencies have 19 or more letter grades that they assign, you should only consider insurers in the very top categories. The top three grades for A.M. Best are A + +, A +, and A; for Moody's they are Aaa, Aa1, and Aa2; and for Standard and Poor's they are AAA, AA +, and AA.

At this point, you may wonder how these rating agencies come up with such a letter grade. Generally, the rating agencies examine publicly available financial information and conduct an internal examination of the insurer that ranges from debt structure to pricing practices and management strategies. The purpose of the examination is to assess *the insurer's ability to pay future claims to policyholders*. The insurer pays a fee for this service. The rating agencies then inform the insurer of the assigned rating and, with the exception of Moody's, will *not* publish it if the insurer requests that the rating be withheld. Obviously, an insurer receiving a low rating is more likely to suppress publication, something that should be viewed as a clear signal that here is an insurance company to *avoid*! The consensus of most experts is that you should purchase only from insurers that (1) are assigned ratings by at least two of the major rating agencies, and (2) are consistently rated in the top two or three categories (say, Aaa or Aa1 by Moody's) by each of the major agencies from whom they received ratings. If you do not have access to the ratings, ask your agent how the company is rated by Best's, Moody's and S&P. Or you might want to refer to Exhibit 9.9, which provides a list of life insurance companies that (in 1991) received the *top* rating from all three of the major rating agencies — which truly is a very strong indication of financial strength. It is interesting to note that while there are a lot of household names on this list,

EXHIBIT 9.9

Some Life Insurers with Top Ratings for Financial Strength

These life insurers received the top grade from all three of the leading rating agencies in 1991. These grades are designed to reflect each insurer's long-term ability to pay promised benefits to holders of insurance policies and annuities.

Company	Assigned Rating		
	Best[a]	S&P[b]	Moody's
Connecticut General Life Insurance Company (CT)	A+	AAA	Aaa
Dai-ichi Mutual Life Insurance Company (Japan)	A+	AAA	Aaa
Guardian Life Insurance Company of America (NY)	A+	AAA	Aaa
Legal & General Assurance Society (England)	A+	AAA	Aaa
Meiji Mutual Life Insurance Company (Japan)	A+	AAA	Aaa
Metropolitan Life Insurance Company (NY)	A+	AAA	Aaa
Nationwide Life Insurance Company (OH)	A+	AAA	Aaa
New York Life Insurance & Annuity Corporation (DE)	A+	AAA	Aaa
New York Life Insurance Company (NY)	A+	AAA	Aaa
Northwestern Mutual Life Insurance Company (WI)	A+	AAA	Aaa
Prudential Insurance Company of America (NJ)	A+	AAA	Aaa
State Farm Life Insurance Company (IL)	A+	AAA	Aaa
Sumitomo Life Insurance Company (Japan)	A+	AAA	Aaa
Teachers Insurance & Annuity Association of America (NY)	A+	AAA	Aaa

[a]At the time of this survey, the top rating from A.M. Best was A+. Now it is A++.
[b]S&P indicates Standard and Poor's.
Source: Adapted from Joseph M. Belth, "Financial Strength Ratings of Life Insurance Companies," *The Insurance Forum*, September/October 1991, pp. 227–246.

there are quite a few big name companies—like Travelers, Lincoln National Life, and Equitable, to mention just a few—that did not make the list.

Selecting an Agent. Your selection of a life insurance agent is important because you will be relying on him or her for guidance with respect to some very important financial decisions. Do not assume that just because agents are licensed they are competent and will serve your best interests. Consider an agent's formal and professional level of educational attainment. Does the agent have a college degree with a major in business or insurance? Does the agent have a professional designation, such as Chartered Life Underwriter (CLU), Chartered Financial Consultant (ChFC), or Certified Financial Planner (CFP)? These designations are awarded only to those who meet certain experience requirements and pass comprehensive examinations in such fields as life and health insurance, estate and pension plan-

ning, investments, and federal income tax law. In addition, observe how an agent reacts to your questions. Does he or she use fancy buzzwords and stock answers or instead listen attentively and, after a period of thought, logically answer your questions? These and other personal characteristics should be considered. In most instances, you should talk with several agents before making your decision and give yourself a chance to discuss the pros and cons of each agent with your spouse. Then, when you have decided, call and ask that agent to return for another visit.

When seeking a good life insurance agent, try to obtain recommendations from other professionals who work with agents. For example, bankers in trust departments, attorneys, and accountants who are specialists in estate planning are typically good sources. In contrast, be a bit wary of selecting an agent simply because of the agent's aggressiveness in soliciting your patronage.

SUMMARY

- Adequate life insurance coverage is vital to sound personal financial planning, as it not only protects that which you have already acquired, but also helps to assure the attainment of unfulfilled financial goals.
- The whole notion of insurance is based on the concept of risk and the different methods of handling it: risk avoidance, loss prevention and control, risk assumption, and insurance (a cost-effective procedure that allows families to reduce financial risks by sharing losses).
- There are a number of ways to determine the amount of life insurance that a family should have. Most experts agree that the *needs approach* is the best procedure, since it systematically considers such variables as family income, household expenses, debt liquidation, and liquidity needs, all of which are weighed against the amount of financial resources available to meet these needs.
- The three basic types of life insurance policies are term life, whole life, and universal life; term life insurance basically provides a stipulated amount of death benefits, whereas whole life combines

death benefits coverage with a modest savings program, and universal life packages term insurance with a tax-deferred investment account that pays competitive money market returns. Other types of life insurance include variable life, joint life, survivorship life, group life, credit and mortgage life, industrial life, and deferred-premium life insurance.
- Some important life insurance policy provisions that you should become familiar with are the beneficiary clause, settlement options, policy loans, payment of premiums, grace period, nonforfeiture options, policy reinstatement provisions, and insurability options.
- To get as much coverage as possible from your insurance dollar, it is important that you not only compare costs, but also buy the proper amount of life insurance and pick the right type of insurance policy. Beyond the provisions and cost of the insurance policy, you should also carefully consider the financial stability of the insurer offering the policy, paying special attention to the ratings assigned by major rating agencies.

QUESTIONS AND PROBLEMS

1. Discuss the role that insurance plays in the financial planning process. Why is it important to have enough life insurance?

2. What does the term *employee benefits* mean, and who foots the bill for these benefits? What are *cafeteria-style plans*, and how do they differ from the normal employee benefits packages? Why is it important to assess your own individual needs relative to the benefits package you receive at work?

3. Define (a) risk avoidance, (b) risk assumption, (c) loss prevention, (d) loss control, (e) fortuitous loss, and (f) underwriting. Explain their interrelationships, if any.

4. Discuss the various ways of determining a person's life insurance needs.

5. Name and explain the most common economic needs that must be satisfied after the death of a family breadwinner.

6. What is term insurance? Describe some of the common types of term life insurance policies.

7. What are the advantages and disadvantages of term life insurance?

8. Explain how whole life insurance offers financial protection to an individual throughout his or her entire life.

9. Describe the different types of whole life policies. What are the advantages and disadvantages of whole life insurance?

10. Using the premium schedules provided in Exhibits 9.5 and 9.7, how much in *annual* premiums would a 25-year-old male have to pay

for $150,000 in five-year renewable term versus the same amount of straight life? How much would a 25-year-old woman have to pay for the same coverage? Comment on your findings. Now, consider a 40-year-old male (or female): using annual premiums, how much straight life insurance coverage could he (or she) buy for $3,000 a year? How much term life coverage would that same amount buy? Comment on your findings.

11. What is universal life insurance? Explain how it differs from whole life and from variable life.

12. There are some life insurance contracts that should be avoided. Explain why (a) credit life insurance, (b) mortgage life insurance, (c) industrial or home service life insurance, and (d) deferred-premium life insurance fall into this category.

13. Explain the meaning of group insurance. How is it different from term insurance? Explain what employees stand to gain from group insurance.

14. What is a beneficiary? What is a contingent beneficiary? Explain why it is essential to designate a beneficiary.

15. Explain the basic options that are available for the payment of life insurance proceeds upon a person's death.

16. Explain the following clauses often found in life insurance policies; (a) multiple indemnity clause, (b) disability clause, (c) suicide clause, and (d) incontestability clause.

17. Describe what is meant by a participating life insurance policy, and explain the role of policy dividends in these policies.

18. "Besides the regular policy features, some important competitive features are often found in life insurance policies." Discuss some of these features.

19. Briefly describe the steps one should take when shopping for and buying life insurance.

20. Briefly describe the insurance company ratings as assigned by Best's, Moody's, and S&P. Why is it important to know how a company is rated? What ratings would you look for in a life insurance company? Explain.

CONTEMPORARY CASE APPLICATIONS

9.1 The Parkers' Insurance Decision: Whole Life, Variable Life, or Term?

Charles and Judith Parker are a married couple in their late 30s. They have three children, ages 12, 10, and 4. Charles, who works as a product analyst for Ralston Purina, is considering the purchase of some life insurance (Charles is covered by a group policy at work, but based on some rough calculations, he feels he could use additional protection). David Dustimer, an insurance agent from Siegfried Insurance, has been trying to persuade Charles to buy a $15,000, 25-year limited-payment whole life policy. However, Charles is contemplating buying a variable life policy. To further complicate matters, Judith feels that they should buy term insurance, since it would be more suitable to the needs of their young family. In order to resolve the issue, Charles has decided to consult Zachary Lawrence, a childhood friend who is now a professor of finance and insurance at a nearby private university.

Questions

1. Explain to Charles the differences among (a) a whole life policy, (b) variable life policy, and (c) a term policy.

2. What are the major advantages of each type of policy? What are the major disadvantages of each?

3. In what way(s) is a whole life policy superior to either a variable or term policy? In what way(s) is a variable life policy superior? How about term insurance?

4. Given the limited information in the case, which type of policy would you recommend for the Parkers? Defend and explain your recommendations.

9.2 The Sutters Want to Know When Enough Is Enough

Dave and Karen Sutter are a two-income couple in their early 30s. They have two children, ages 6 and 3.

Dave's monthly take-home pay is $1,800 and Karen's is $2,100. The Sutters feel that because they are a two-income family, they both should have adequate life insurance coverage. Accordingly, they are presently trying to decide how much life insurance *each one of them* should carry.

To begin with, they would like to set up an education fund for their children in the amount of $80,000 (this would guarantee that college funds would be there for both children, as it would provide $10,000 a year — in today's dollars — for four years for each child). Moreover, in the event of either's death, they want the surviving spouse to have the funds for paying off all outstanding debts, including the $110,000 mortgage on their house. They estimate that they have another $15,000 in consumer installment loans and credit cards. They also project that if either of them dies, the other probably will be left with about $10,000 in final estate and burial expenses.

As far as their annual income needs are concerned, Dave and Karen both feel very strongly that each should have enough insurance to replace their respective current income levels until the youngest child turns 18 (a period of 15 years). Though neither Dave nor Karen would be eligible for social security survivor's benefits, because they both intend to continue working, both children would qualify, in the amount of around $1,100 a month. The Sutters have amassed about $75,000 in investments, and they have a declining-term life policy *on each other* in the amount of $85,000, which would be used to partially pay off the mortgage. Further, Dave has a $60,000 group policy at work and Karen a $90,000 group policy.

Questions

1. Assuming that Dave's gross annual income is $30,000 and Karen's $40,000, use the multiple earnings factors in Exhibit 9.1 to find the amount of life insurance each should have if they wanted to replace 75 percent of their lost earnings. Use the age-35 column for Dave and the age-30 column for Karen.

2. Use a worksheet like the one in Exhibit 9.3 to find the additional insurance needed on both Dave's and Karen's lives. (*Note:* Because Dave and Karen hold secure, well-paying jobs, both agree they won't need any additional help once the kids are grown; each also agrees that he/she will have plenty of income from their social security and company pension benefits to take care of themselves in retirement. Thus, when preparing the worksheet, assume "funding needs" of zero in periods 2 and 3.)

3. Is there a difference in your answers to Questions 1 and 2? If so, why? Which number do you think is more indicative of the Sutter's life insurance needs?

4. Using the amounts computed in Question 2 (employing the needs approach), what kind of life insurance policy would you recommend for Dave? For Karen? Briefly explain your answers.

FOR MORE INFORMATION

General Information Articles

Findlay, Steven. "Now, Benefits for the Living." *U.S. News & World Report*, October 8, 1990, pp. 78–79.

Klein, Robert J. "A Shopper's Guide to Buying the Best Term Policy." *Money*, August 1989, pp. 137–138.

Luciano, Lani. "Getting the Most from Your Company Benefits." *Money*, May 1991, pp. 109–120.

Slater, Karen, and Susan Pulliam. "How Healthy Is Your Own Life Insurer? Here Are Tips for Monitoring Vital Signs." *The Wall Street Journal*, April 11, 1991, pp. C1, 14.

Thornton, John H., and Kennes C. Huntley. "A Survey of Life Insurance Policy Provisions." *Journal of the American Society of CLU & ChFC*, May 1990, pp. 72–84.

Government Documents and Other Publications

Belth, Joseph M. *Life Insurance: A Consumer's Handbook*, 2d ed. Bloomington, IN: Indiana University Press, 1985.

Consumer Reports Books with Trudy Lieberman. *Life Insurance: How to Buy the Right Policy from the Right Company at the Right Price*. Mount Vernon, NY: Consumers Union, 1988.

Dorfman, Mark S., and Saul W. Adelman. *Life Insurance: A Financial Planning Approach*, 2d ed. Chicago: Dearborn Financial Publishing, 1992.

The Fundamentals of Employee Benefit Programs, 4th ed. Washington, DC: Employee Benefit Research Institute, 1990.

George E. Rejda. *Principles of Risk Management and Insurance*, 4th ed. New York: HarperCollins, 1992.

For Information on Insurance Company Ratings, See:

A.M. Best Co., Ambest Rd., Oldwick, NJ 08858, (908) 439-2200. Best's Insurance Reports gives performance history of life insurers. Best's Flitcraft Compend is an annual comparative rate manual.

Moody's Investors Service, 99 Church St., New York, NY 10007, (212) 553-0300. Moody's Bank & Finance Manual is an annual report on the financial and operating data of insurance companies.

S&P Insurance Rating Services, 25 Broadway, New York, NY 10004, (212) 208-8000. Publishes S&P Insurance Ratings Book, quarterly; S&P's Insurance Rating Digest; S&P Monthly Insurer Ratings.

Insurance Forum, P.O. Box 245, Ellettsville, Ind. 47429. The Insurance Forum Newsletter is published monthly ($50 per year). The September/October issue includes ratings on life insurance companies and a watch list of insurance companies ($10).

GETTING A HANDLE ON YOUR FINANCIAL FUTURE

The main purpose of life insurance is to protect your family against financial loss in the event of your untimely death. It is also used to provide liquidity for your estate to pay off taxes and other obligations. The major decisions that you have to make concerning the purchase of life insurance involve a determination of the amount needed, the best type of contract, the options to include, and where to purchase it.

In determining your life insurance needs you should be aware that your requirements will change as your marital and family status evolve. Your need for insurance will increase significantly during the early years of a family and remain high until the children leave home. Your life insurance needs will then decrease as you approach retirement. Without a careful analysis of your needs, you may be *under-insured* during your early years and *overinsured* in later life. You should use a worksheet such as the one provided in Exhibit 9.3 to assist you in determining the appropriate amount of life insurance on you and, if you are married, on your spouse.

The analysis involves three steps: (1) estimate your economic needs, (2) determine all financial resources available, and (3) subtract resources available to determine the amount needed. This method most accurately reflects your life insurance needs and will minimize the chances of being overinsured or underinsured.

Once your needs have been determined, you have to select the appropriate type of life insurance. The major types include term life, which provides

If You Are Just Starting Out

If you are single and have no desire to leave anything to anyone, your life insurance needs are probably zero. However, if you are married with no children and a spouse that works, you would probably only need to have enough life insurance to pay off the majority of your debts and provide for funeral expenses upon your death.

Your greatest need for life insurance will occur when you have children. In order to provide for the cost of raising and educating your children in the event of your death, you need to have subtantial amounts of life insurance. Once your children graduate or leave home, your needs will decrease.

In implementing your insurance plan you must pay particular attention to the selection of the right type of policy and a comparison of the costs. Once the plan is in place you need to be aware of changes in your needs as well as changes in the field of insurance that could result in opportunities to maintain your coverage at a lower cost or under better conditions.

Points to Consider:

1. In determining the amount of insurance needed, don't forget to consider social security benefits in your calculations.

2. Review your employee benefits to determine if you have enough coverage through your employer; if you are single or married without children, you may find such coverage is adequate for your needs.

3. Check the benefits associated with the professional organizations to which you belong, or with your credit cards to see if there is any insurance coverage.

4. From your cash budget, you should determine how much money is available for life insurance premiums.

5. Once you have the premium dollars and know your insurance needs, you will be able to shop for the kind of coverage that best fits your budget.

6. In your search, determine whether or not your employer offers a group life policy and compare this to non-group rates.

7. Most young couples, particularly those with children, find they can get the most insurance for their money from *term life insurance* — for someone just starting out, this is the place to look first for life insurance coverage.

8. If you select term insurance, take out a policy that is renewable.

9. Review your coverage frequently to make sure that you are not underinsured.

only death benefits; whole life, which provides a savings feature in addition to a death benefit; universal life, which combines term insurance with a tax-deferred savings/investment account; and variable life, which provides the opportunity for higher investment returns coupled with variable amounts of insurance.

Regardless of the type of policy you select, you need to consider the contract options, such as the method of settlement, selection of beneficiary, policy reinstatement, and others. This will enable you to further tailor your policies to meet your individual needs.

Next you should select the company and then the agent with whom you will deal. Not all companies are competitive in all lines of insurance, so you may best satisfy your life insurance needs by obtaining policies from more than one company. Selection of an agent should be based on his or her reputation and ability to guide you through the insurance maze.

Last but not least, you should continually monitor your insurance needs and periodically review the financial ratings of the company to ensure its safety and soundness.

If You Are Thirtysomething

At the beginning of this stage of the life cycle you are probably at the peak of your life insurance needs. You usually have minor children, a mortgage, car notes, and various other credit obligations. Your estate is increasing in size along with your income.

As when you were just starting out, you must calculate the amount of life insurance you should have based on your needs. However, since your income has probably increased, you might be in a position to convert from term insurance to more permanent insurance to lock in the cost and to use the tax-deferred nature of policies that provide a savings or investment feature.

Careful monitoring is essential during this time to enable you to quickly adjust your coverage to meet your changing needs for life insurance protection. Your attention to detail will result in a wise use of your insurance dollars and adequate coverage in the event of your untimely death.

Points to Consider:

1. All of the points mentioned in the previous section will continue to apply to you regardless of age.

2. If you are vested in your employer's retirement plan, there may be death benefits provided that you should consider when you compare your needs to your coverage.

3. Choose your beneficiary wisely. If your spouse is not good at handling large sums of money or you want to

make sure that the proceeds benefit your minor children, you might want to consider a life insurance trust as beneficiary.

4. If you are buying insurance that has a savings or investment feature, compare the rates of return to other saving and investment alternatives before you commit additional dollars to the premiums.

5. Be sure you read the exclusions on the policy. It may not pay, for example, if you are a pilot or passenger on a noncommercial airline.

6. You might want to consider a disability clause that provides for a waiver of premium in the event you become disabled.

7. You should generally avoid the use of credit life insurance associated with a loan. You can normally buy the coverage, if you need it, at a lower price directly.

8. If you want your home mortgage paid off upon your death, you should obtain a decreasing-term policy that corresponds with your declining balance.

9. Review your coverage periodically to make sure that you are not overinsured.

10. Resist the temptation to continue paying for insurance that is no longer needed. Put the money to use in a savings or investment account.

CHAPTER 10

Insuring Your Health

Probably the next best thing to good health is a good health care insurance plan. Should you ever suffer a serious illness or accident, you may discover that the road to recovery can be painful in more ways than one. In addition to the physical pain that sickness and injury can bring, there is also economic pain. The cost can easily run into the tens of thousands of dollars, because you must deal with not only hospitalization and medical expenses but also the *loss of income* while you are recovering and rehabilitating. Clearly, without adequate health insurance to pay expenses and disability insurance to replace lost income, a person's economic health can suffer long after he or she has recovered physically.

As a case in point, consider the case of Paul Murphy, who fell off a ladder while painting his house. An ambulance was called, and he was taken to the hospital, where he was examined, X-rayed, and assigned to a semiprivate room. Results of the examination revealed that he had a broken leg and a badly sprained back. Treatment included setting the fracture and four days of traction for the back sprain, followed by four weeks of recuperation before Paul could return to work. In all, he spent five days in the hospital and incurred medical and hospitalization costs of over $5,000. In addition, because he could not work for four weeks, he lost $3,000 in pay. Expenses of this magnitude certainly would devastate most family budgets. Fortunately, people can obtain protection from such medical and economic catastrophes through health-care insurance. This chapter looks at health-care insurance programs and their role in your personal financial plans.

FINANCIAL *facts* OR *fantasies*

Are the following statements financial facts (true) or fantasies (false)?

Health-care insurance coverage should be viewed as an essential component of your personal financial plans.

Hospital insurance is the most comprehensive type of medical insurance you can buy.

With health-care insurance that covers the whole family, children may be included in the coverage up to age 24 as long as they are full-time students.

When a person is chronically ill and requires either nursing home care or home health-care services, most of these expenses are absorbed by medicare and private medical expense insurance.

The difference between a health maintenance organization (HMO) and a preferred provider organization (PPO) is that the HMO offers a wider range of choices of physicians, hospitals, and so forth.

The cost of coverage and the quality of the agent and insurance company are two important variables to consider when shopping for health-care insurance.

Health-care insurance coverage is an essential element of the personal financial planning process because of the umbrella of protection it provides for your financial plans. What are your current health-care coverage exposures and needs? Before reading on, take a few moments to list some of the potential health-care needs and costs to which you are exposed.

Assume you have done everything possible to establish and implement fully operational personal financial plans. You have an effective budget, you keep track of expenditures, you have several ongoing investment and retirement plans, and so forth. Imagine what would happen to all of this if a member of your family or you became seriously ill. Without adequate health-care insurance, all of your financial accomplishments and goals could be destroyed. Obviously, health-care insurance coverage should be part of your financial plan. Think of it as not only a way to meet the costs of illness or injury, but more importantly, a vehicle for protecting your existing assets and financial plans.

Health-care insurance coverage should be viewed as an essential component of your personal financial plans.
Fact: Health-care insurance not only helps you meet the costs of illness or injury, but it also protects your existing assets and financial plans.

THE EARLY DAYS

Health insurance policies were first introduced around 1850. At that time the common coverage was the accident policy, which paid a small amount for injuries sustained in specific types of accidents. As more health insurers began writing health coverages, the number of accident perils insured against increased. By 1900, individual accident policies were being written for nearly every type of accident. At about the same time, health insurers began issuing "sickness insurance policies," which offered protection for a small amount of income loss if the insured contracted any of several named diseases. In other words, comprehensive coverage was impossible to obtain, and "extensive" coverage could be achieved only by buying a basketful of policies, each one covering different types of accidents and illnesses.

In the 1930s the modern concept of broadly based health-care insurance was born. At that time, Blue Cross began selling policies that provided families with coverage for hospital and surgical care. Although great strides have been made in the provision of comprehensive health-care plan coverages, amounts of reimbursement provided, and number of persons protected, no standardized all-risk policy has yet been adopted. Needed coverage is often obtained only through a collection of types of health insurance policies. Unfortunately, the heritage of the 1800s and early 1900s is still with us.

MULTIPLE COVERAGE

Despite the extensiveness of various health coverages, many people are covered by more than one policy. Employer-sponsored group plans, social security, worker's compensation, automobile medical payments, veterans' benefits, and individually purchased coverages represent the most popular plans. Yet, even a combination of these programs seldom completely meets the needs of any one person or family. Instead, the result is usually multiple coverage for some risks and gaps in coverage for others.

AN INDUSTRY IN CHANGE

The health-care field is underoing rapid changes today. One such change falls under the heading of *medical entrepreneurism*, which is based on the belief that there is "money to be made in health care." This new philosophy about medicine has led to new ways of delivering it. Only a few years ago, a consumer's basic choices were the doctor's office, a hospital, or a health maintenance organization (HMO). Today, there is also a *neighborhood emergency center (NEC)*, which handles minor emergencies on a walk-in, often 24-hour-a-day basis, an *ambulatory outpatient surgical center* (both usually less costly than comparable in-hospital treatment), an *individual practice association (IPA)*, and a *preferred provider organization (PPO)* for hospital and medical services. These new ways of providing health care are discussed later in the chapter.

Another ongoing change is the rising cost of health care, particularly hospital room charges, and the percentage of personal expenditures devoted to it. Today more than 13 percent of all of our personal expenditures in the United States are made on health care, an increase from less than 11 percent in 1980. Also, the rate of increase substantially exceeds that of the consumer price index (CPI). In 1990, for example, medical-care costs increased by over 9 percent while the *CPI* rose at a 6 percent annual rate. And of the various costs that make up the medical-care portion of the CPI, hospital charges lead the list of price increases. They have nearly doubled since 1980. Rates of $300 per day for a semiprivate room are not uncommon, and when we include ancillary hospital services costs, the average rises to between $500 and $600 per day. Physicians' fees, nurses' salaries, and other product and service costs essential to health care also have increased faster than the CPI, though not as fast as hospital charges.

Several major factors account for this phenomenon, chief among them probably being the aging U.S. population (which needs more health care), the government's medicare and medicaid programs, and the rapid growth in the broad base of private health plans. More than 87 out of every 100 non-institutionalized Americans are now eligible for at least some cost reimbursement for losses resulting from illness or accident. In addition, major acquisitions of expensive new health-care equipment and facilities by hospitals and clinics have pushed costs upward. A poor demand-and-supply distribution of health-care facilities and services may be still another factor. Unfortunately, no immediate relief is foreseen. In light of these spiraling costs, the need for health financing plans and insurance is greater now than it has ever been.

MAKING SENSE OF IT ALL

If we ranked consumer insurance programs on a complexity scale, life insurance would be at the "simple" end and health insurance at the opposite. In all but rare instances, life insurance pays regard-less of the cause of loss. What's more, the loss itself is seldom arguable, and the amount of the loss is the face amount of the policy (or some multiple thereof). In addition, each life insurance policy you own will pay regardless of any other policies you have; there are no deductibles, waiting periods, participation clauses, or chances of cancelation; and differences in policy provisions among leading insurers are relatively slight. In contrast, each of these issues is pertinent to health insurance coverages. Because of these complicating factors, designing the best way to meet your health-care needs requires a truly systematic approach. You need to learn what coverages are available, their various policy provisions, and from whom they can be obtained. Next, you need to inventory your needs and existing coverages. With that task completed, you then can shop the market for the right protection at the best price.

TYPES OF HEALTH CARE COVERAGE

Although many of today's health insurance policies provide much broader coverages than those offered in the past, the wide variety in quality of policies makes caution imperative when shopping among them. Health-care coverage can be separated into four broad categories—medical expense, long-term care, special coverages, and disability income. Within each category, many different versions of policies are available. By understanding the basic uses of each plan, you can make a wiser purchase decision.

MEDICAL EXPENSE PLANS

Today's consumer can choose from a wide variety of medical expense insurance products to obtain precisely the type of protection desired. Are you familiar with any particular types of medical expense policy coverages? Make a list of these coverages and relate them to your health-care needs before reading on.

Frank Payne was a 25-year-old graduate student at Major State University (MSU) when he began to lose feeling in his left hand. Doctors found that the problem was being caused by tumors near his spinal chord. Surgical procedures and treatment costing tens of thousands of dollars were necessary. Frank quickly discovered that his student health insurance plan was woefully inadequate and his parents, who had retired recently, could not help him to any great extent. After countless applications and meetings, Frank received assistance from charitable organizations, who funded many of his medical costs, but he ultimately had to leave MSU to earn the money to pay his remaining bills. Unfortunately, Frank learned the hard way that even young, apparently healthy people should understand and be concerned about their medical expense plans.

TYPES OF MEDICAL EXPENSE PLANS

The major types of medical expense insurance plans include hospital, surgical expense, physicians expense, major medical, comprehensive major medical, and dental plans. You are likely to come across each of these plans as you progress through your career. We will briefly describe each in this section.

Hospital Insurance. *Hospital insurance* policies offer reimbursement plans covering the costs of hospital room (semiprivate) and board and other expenses incidental to hospitalization. In the United States, more people are covered by some type of hospitalization insurance than any other kind of private health insurance. Basically, hospital insurance pays for a portion of (1) the per-day hospital room (semiprivate) and board charges, which typically include floor nursing and other routine services, and (2) ancillary expenses, such as use of an operating room, laboratory tests, X-ray examinations, and medicine received while hospitalized. Although a few hospital insurance policies will pay for an in-hospital private duty nurse, most will not. In some cases, the hospital plan will simply pay a flat daily amount for each day the insured remains in the hospital, regardless of the actual amount of charges levied. Numerous hospital plans now also offer reimbursement for some outpatient and out-of-hospital services, among which might be in-home reha-

bilitation or ambulatory center care, diagnostic and preventive treatment, and preadmission testing.

In most policies, hospital insurance is written to provide daily, semiprivate room and board charges for up to a specified number of days, such as 90, 120, or 360. The maximum reimbursement for ancillary expenses, in contrast, may be a stated dollar amount or sometimes a multiple of the daily room rate. In the first instance, frequently found maximums are $1,000, $2,000, and $5,000, whereas in the second, the multiple might be 15 or 20. Thus, if the room and board rate were $250 per day, applying this multiple would result in an ancillary expense limit of either $3,750 or $5,000.

Surgical Expense Insurance. *Surgical expense insurance* provides coverage for the cost of surgery in or out of the hospital. Most plans provide so-called *service benefits*, which offer reimbursement of surgical expenses that are "reasonable and customary." The insurer determines the level of benefit that is reasonable and customary based upon a survey of surgical costs during the previous year. Most people who have such a policy also have had an experience where the insurer partially reimburses a medical bill because the reasonable and customary rate is less than the physician's actual bill. Nevertheless, service benefits generally cover most of the bill and should rise over time in an era of inflating medical costs.

Some plans still pay *scheduled benefits*, as opposed to service benefits. Under this type of plan the insurer will reimburse you up to a fixed maximum amount for a particular surgical procedure. For example, the policy might state that you would receive no more than $500 for an appendectomy or $700 for arthroscopic surgery on a knee. A sample schedule of benefits for a group, surgical expense plan is shown in Exhibit 10.1. Note that the scheduled benefits shown for this group plan are quite limited and often inadequate when compared with the typical surgical costs provided in Exhibit 10.2.

Surgical expense coverage usually will pay for almost any type of surgery that is required to maintain the health of the insured. In the event that a necessary surgical procedure is not named in the policy, the company will pay the amount listed for a comparable operation. Reimbursement for the cost of anesthetics and their administration is provided in

EXHIBIT 10.1

An Illustrative List of Maximum Benefit Payments for a Group Surgical Expense Policy

This is an example of maximum payments under a scheduled benefit plan. Surgical procedures not listed in the policy will be reimbursed based on comparability to listed procedures.

Aortic valve repair	$700.00
Appendectomy	252.00
Breast, amputation, radical	504.00
Bronchoscopy, diagnostic	91.00
Cataract, removal	427.00
Cholecystectomy	378.00
Circumcision, newborn	21.00
Colon Resection	560.00
Dilation and curetage	84.00
Hemorrhoidectomy, internal	210.00
Hysterectomy, total	420.00
Mastoidectomy, radical, bilateral	588.00
Thyroidectomy, complete	420.00
Tonsillectomy and Adenoidectomy, under age 12	106.00
Tonsillectomy and Adenoidectomy, over age 12	112.00
Varicose veins, cutting operation, one leg	210.00

Source: Group plan offered by a major health insurer.

most surgical expense policies. These benefits may also be covered in an "additional benefits" provision of a hospital insurance policy. Specific surgical expense policies may also allow payment for the nonemergency treatment of tumors and other afflictions using X rays or radium. Some policies provide a limited diagnostic allowance for X rays and lab fees. Surgical expense coverage is typically sold in conjunction with a hospital insurance policy either as an integral part of that policy or as a rider.

Certain surgical procedures may be excluded from reimbursement by the plan. Elective, cosmetic surgery, such as the proverbial "nose job" or "tummy tuck," normally is excluded. Cosmetic surgery following a deforming accident often is reimbursed, however. A more controversial area is exclusion of experimental surgery, especially certain types of organ transplants. If a high mortality rate is associated with such procedures, insurers normally will seek to exclude them. At the current time, many insurers exclude heart-and-lung transplants, as well as mechanical heart implants. As technology improves, however, these procedures may be routinely included in the not-too-distant future.

Physicians Expense Insurance. *Physicians expense insurance*, previously called *regular medical expense*, can cover the cost of such services as

physician fees for nonsurgical care in a hospital, including consultation with a specialist. Also covered are X rays and laboratory tests performed outside of a hospital. Home, clinic, or doctor's office visits normally are not covered except through special provisions. Plans are offered on either a service (customary and reasonable) or scheduled benefit basis. Often, the first few visits with the physician for any single cause will be excluded. This exclusion serves the same purpose as the deductible and waiting period features found in other types of insurance.

Major Medical Insurance. **Major medical plans** are those that provide benefits for nearly all types of medical expenses resulting from either illnesses or accidents. As the name implies, the amounts that can be collected under this coverage are relatively large. Lifetime limits of $100,000, $250,000, $1,000,000, or higher are common, while

---

major medical plan
An insurance plan designed to supplement the basic coverages of hospital, surgical, and physicians expenses; used to finance medical costs of a more catastrophic nature.

some policies have no limits at all. The trend in recent years has been toward the higher benefit levels.

Major medical coverage was first offered in the early 1950s to supplement the basic coverages of hospital, surgical, and physicians expenses discussed earlier. This basic concept still applies today. Because the other three hospital and physicians expense coverages are available to meet the smaller health-care costs, major medical is used to finance medical costs of a more catastrophic nature. Approximately three out of every four Americans are covered by some type of major medical health plan. The popularity of this insurance has grown more since inception than that of any other kind of health insurance in history. To give insureds an incentive to avoid unnecessary medical costs, major medical plans typically are written with provisions that limit payments to less than full reimbursement. These policy provisions are discussed in a subsequent section.

Comprehensive Major Medical Insurance.

A **comprehensive major medical insurance** plan combines the basic hospital, surgical, and physicians expense coverages with major medical protection to form a single policy. Comprehensive major medical insurance is frequently written under a group contract. However, some efforts have been made to make this type of coverage available on an individual basis.

Hospital insurance is the most comprehensive type of medical insurance you can buy.
Fantasy: Major medical or comprehensive major medical provides the most complete coverage, whereas hospital insurance covers only the costs incurred while confined to a hospital.

Dental Insurance. *Dental insurance* covers
necessary dental health care as well as some dental injuries sustained through accidents. (Accidental dental expenses for natural teeth are normally covered under standard surgical expense and major medical policies.) The coverage may provide for oral examinations, including X rays, cleanings, fillings, extractions, inlays, bridgework, dentures, oral surgery, root canal therapy, and orthodontics. Of course, dental policies vary with respect to the number of these items included within the coverage. Some dental plans contain provisions limiting reimbursement (particularly with regard to orthodontics) to a portion of the expenses incurred, and others have "first dollar protection"—they pay for all claims. Most present dental coverage is written through group insurance plans, although some companies do offer individual and family policies. However, since many types of dental insurance function more as budgeting techniques than as true insurance, premiums are often relatively large in light of the dollar amount of coverage obtained.

POLICY PROVISIONS FOR MEDICAL EXPENSE PLANS

To compare the health insurance coverages offered by different insurers, you need to evaluate whether they contain liberal or restrictive provisions. Generally, these provisions can be divided into two classes: terms of payment and terms of coverage.

Terms of Payment. Four provisions govern how much your medical expense plan will pay. These include (1) deductibles, (2) the participation (coinsurance) clause, (3) the internal limits on the policy, and (4) the coordination of benefits clause, if any.

Deductibles. Because major medical plans are designed to supplement the basic hospital, surgical, and physicians expense policies, they frequently have a relatively large **deductible**, typically $500 or $1,000. Comprehensive major medical plans tend to offer lower deductibles, sometimes $100 or less. Most plans currently offer a calendar-year, all-inclusive deductible. In effect, this allows a person to accumulate the deductible from more than one incident of use. Some plans also include a *carryover provision* wherein any part of the deductible that occurs during the final three months of the year (October, November, and December) can be applied to the current year, and can also be included in the following calendar year's deductible. In a few plans, the deductible is on a per-accident or per-illness basis. Thus, if you were covered by a policy with a $1,000 deductible and suffered three separate accidents in the course of a year, each requiring $1,000

EXHIBIT 10.2

Physicians' Fees Vary Widely with Different Types of Surgery

This listing summarizes median fees for some common surgical procedures according to a survey of physicians in 1990.

Specialty	Fees	Specialty	Fees
General Surgery		**Neurosurgery**	
Appendectomy	$ 810	Cranioplasty	$2,801
Cholecystectomy	1,288	Craniotomy	3,276
Inguinal hernia (unilateral)	801	Neuroplasty, median nerve	900
Modified radical mastectomy	1,500	Cervical discectomy (anterior)	3,000
Obstetrics/Gynecology		**Plastic surgery**	
Complete obstetrical care (usual or routine)	1,664	Complete rhinoplasty	2,500
Total hysterectomy	1,836	Facial rhytidectomy	3,000
Dilation and curettage (diagnostic)	486	Suction-assisted lipectomy, trunk	1,501
Dilation and curettage (therapeutic for		Dermabrasion of facial scar	500
abortion)	500	Excision of benign lesion	151
		Blepharoplasty, upper eyelids	1,338
Thoracic surgery		Breast reduction (bilateral)	3,720
Diagnostic flexible bronchoscopy	450		
Lobectomy	2,501	**Orthopedic surgery**	
Esophagoscopy (dilation)	446	Arthrocentesis of knee	55
Thoracentesis	151	Diagnostic knee arthroscopy	706
Abdominal aortic aneurysm repair	3,201	Knee arthroscopy with meniscectomy	1,601
		Closed reduction of Colles' fracture	451
		Total hip arthroplasty	3,522
		Total knee arthroplasty	3,501

Source: *Source Book of Health Insurance Data, 1991* (Washington, D.C.: Health Insurance Association of America, 1991), p. 71.

of medical expenses, you would not be eligible to collect any benefits from the major medical plan.

Participation (Coinsurance).   Another feature of most major medical insurance policies is some type of **participation**, or **coinsurance, clause**. This provision stipulates that the company will pay some portion — say, 80 or 90 percent — of the amount of the covered loss in excess of the deductible rather than the entire amount. The purpose of requiring the insured to participate as "coinsurers" is to reduce the possibility that they will feign illness and to discourage them from incurring unnecessary medical expenses. Although comprehensive major medical plans normally have a participation clause, too, this clause often does not apply to expenses related to basic hospital, surgical, and physicians expense coverage.

Because major medical limits now go up to $1 million or more, many plans have a **stop-loss provision** that places a cap on the amount of partici-

comprehensive major medical insurance

A health insurance plan that combines, into a single policy, basic hospital, surgical, and physicians expense coverages with major medical protection.

deductible

The first amount not covered by an insurance policy, usually determined on a calendar-year or on a per-illness, per-accident basis.

participation (coinsurance) clause

A provision in many health insurance policies stipulating that the insurer will pay some portion — say, 80 or 90 percent — of the amount of the covered loss in excess of the deductible.

stop-loss provision

A cap in a major medical or comprehensive insurance policy that limits the insured's payment under the participation, or coinsurance, clause to a specified amount, such as $10,000.

pation required. Otherwise, a $1 million medical bill could still leave the insured with, say, $200,000 of costs. Often such provisions limit the insured's participation to less than $10,000, and sometimes as little as $2,000.

Internal limits. Most major medical plans are written with internal limits. **Internal limits** place constraints on the amounts that will be paid for certain specified expenses, even if the overall policy limits are not exceeded by the claim. Charges that are commonly subject to internal limits are hospital room and board, surgical fees, mental and nervous conditions, and nursing services. Providing internal or inside limits is similar in purpose to participation, or coinsurance, clauses. The insurer wants to give the insured an incentive not to incur unreasonably high medical expenses and to control costs, thereby keeping premiums down. Therefore, if an insured elects a highly expensive physician or medical facility, he or she will be responsible for paying the portion of the charges that are above a "reasonable and customary" level or beyond a specified maximum amount. The example in the following section illustrates how deductibles, coinsurance, and internal limits constrain the amount a company is obligated to pay under a major medical plan.

Major medical policy: an example. Assume that an insured person has coverage under a major medical insurance policy that specifies a $500,000 lifetime limit of protection, a $1,000 deductible, an 80 percent coinsurance clause, internal limits of $190 per day on hospital room and board, and $1,000 as the maximum payable surgical fee. Assume further that the insured was hospitalized for 14 days at $245 a day and required an operation that cost $900. Other covered medical expenses incurred with the illness totaled $1,800. Therefore, the medical expenses incurred by the insured amount to $6,130, the total of $3,430 for hospital room and board, plus $900 for the surgeon, plus $1,800 for the other medical expenses.

Because of the coinsurance clause in the policy, however, the maximum the company has to pay is 80 percent of the covered loss in excess of the deductible. In the absence of internal limits, the company would pay $4,104 (.80 × [$6,130 − $1,000]). The internal limits further restrict the payment. Even though 80 percent of the $245-per-diem hospital charge is $196, the most the company would have to

pay is $190 per diem. Therefore, the insured becomes liable for $84 ($6 per day × 14 days). The internal limit on the surgery is not exceeded, since after considering coinsurance, the insurer will have to pay $720 (.80 × $900), which is below the $1,000 internal limit. The company's obligation is reduced to $4,020 ($4,104 − $84), while the insured must pay a total of $2,110 ($1,000 deductible + .20 [$6,130 − $1,000) coinsurance + $84 excess hospital charges). The lesson here is that although major medical insurance can offer very large amounts of reimbursement, you may still be left responsible for substantial payments.

Coordination of benefits. In contrast to most property and liability insurance coverages, which are discussed in Chapter 11, health insurance policies are not contracts of *indemnity*. This means that insureds can collect multiple payments for the same accident or illness unless a **coordination of benefits provision** is included in their health insurance contracts. For example, many private health insurance policies have coordination of benefits provisions with medical benefits paid under worker's compensation. In contrast, some companies widely advertise that their policies will pay claims regardless of how much other coverage the policyholder has. Of course, these latter types of insurance contracts are often more expensive per dollar of protection. From the standpoint of insurance planning, use of policies with coordination of benefits clauses can help you prevent coverage overlaps and, ideally, reduce your premiums.

Considering the complexity of medical expense contracts, the various clauses limiting payments, and the coordination of benefits with other plans, one might expect that insurers frequently pay only partial claims and may deny some entirely. If you make a claim and do not receive the payment you expected, do not give up. The accompanying *Money in Action* box provides some guidelines on how you might go about disputing a rejection of a claim by your health insurer.

Terms of Coverage. A number of contractual provisions affect the value of a medical expense insurance contract to you. Some of the more important provisions address (1) the persons and places covered, (2) cancelation, (3) continuation of group coverage, (4) rehabilitation coverage, (5) preexisting conditions, (6) pregnancy and abortion, and (7) mental illness.

Persons and places covered. Some health insurance policies cover only the named insured, while others offer protection to all family members. Of those that offer family coverage, some terminate benefits payable on behalf of children at age 18 and others continue them to age 24 as long as the child remains in school or is single. *If you are in this age group, you or your parents should check to see if you are covered under your parents' policy.* If not, sometimes by paying an additional premium, you can add such coverage. (Note: If a child is over the age stipulated in the policy, and if the additional premium to add the child to the family policy has not been paid, that individual could be without any health-care insurance. If anything should happen to him or her — no matter how severe — the parents and/or child may have to bear the full cost of the accident or illness.) Some policies protect you only while you are in the United States or Canada: others offer worldwide coverage but exclude certain named countries.

Cancelation. Many health insurance policies are written to permit *cancelation* at any time at the option of the insurer. Some policies explicitly state this; others do not. To protect yourself against premature cancelation, you should buy policies that contain a provision that specifically states that the insurer will not cancel coverage as long as premiums are paid.

Continuation of group coverage. At one time, people who lost their jobs or were temporarily laid off could lose their group health insurance coverage in addition to their salary. Because the lack of income and health coverage could place an employee and his family in a precarious position, in 1986 Congress passed the *Consolidated Omnibus Budget Reconciliation Act (COBRA).* Under COBRA an employee who leaves the group voluntarily or involuntarily (except in the case of "gross misconduct") may elect to continue coverage for up to 18 months by paying premiums to his former employer on time (up to 102 percent of the company cost). All benefits previously available — except for disability income coverage — are retained, including hospital, surgical, major medical, dental, and vision coverages.

Similar continuation coverage is available for retirees and their families for up to 18 months or until they become eligible for medicare, whichever occurs first. The dependents of an employee may be covered for up to 36 months under COBRA under special circumstances such as divorce or death of the employee. If the employee worked in a firm of less than 20 employees (minimum COBRA requirements) or after COBRA requirements expire, most states provide for conversion of the group coverage to an individual policy without evidence of insurability. Premium charges and benefits of the converted policy would be determined at the time of conversion. However, the most important aspect of the conversion feature is that group coverage can be changed to individual coverage regardless of the current health of the insured. Clearly, it is important to understand your continuation rights under COBRA as well as the laws of the state in which you are employed.

With health-care insurance that covers the whole family, children may be included in the coverage up to age 24 as long as they are full-time students.

Fact: A child may be covered in a family insurance plan only so long as he or she is a full-time student under 24 years of age. Students 24 and older usually can be added to their parents' plans by paying an additional premium.

Rehabilitation coverage. In the past, health insurance plans focused almost exclusively on reasonable and necessary medical expenses. If an

---

internal limits
A feature commonly found in health insurance policies that places a constraint on the amount that will be paid for certain specified expenses, regardless of whether the overall policy limits are exceeded by a given claim.

coordination of benefits provision
A provision often included in health insurance contracts; it requires that benefit payments be coordinated in the event that the insured is eligible for benefits under more than one policy.

MONEY IN ACTION

How to Get That Insurance Claim Paid

For the average person, "getting a claim processed is a nightmare," says Harvey Matoren, who spent 25 years in the health care field before he and his wife, Carol, a nurse, started Health Claims, a claim-processing service in Jacksonville, Fla. But there are strategies for slaying the demons that haunt insurance claimants.

TAMING THE BUREAUCRACY

File every claim, don't assume you won't be covered, and never take "no" for an answer the first time. Every medical procedure has a code, and sometimes claims are turned down simply because a bored computer operator punches in the wrong numbers. Even omitting your date of birth can be grounds for rejection.

Arm yourself with knowledge of your policy, not always an easy task. Your benefits handbook might state, for example, that physical therapy is covered, but it might neglect to mention that there is a limit on the number of visits or on the total dollar coverage. "We had guidelines and limitations the patient never had access to," says Sharon Stark, who processed claims for health insurance companies in Kansas before writing and publishing her own handbook. Call in advance of your treatment to find out how much your insurer will pay.

TAKING IT TO THE TOP

If you have trouble, go straight to the company's claims supervisor or the home office. Cheryl Gresek was wrangling with Hartford Life and Accident over slow payment of claims when she finally called the office of the company president. The claims were paid almost immediately.

If all else fails, write a letter of complaint to your insurer with a note saying that unless you get a response, you're going to file it with your state insurance department. Be willing to follow through with your threat, although it may not come to that.

MANAGING YOUR OWN CARE

Don't expect so-called managed care to lead you out of the red-tape maze. Managed care is supposed to control overuse of health care services, but it often means more work for the patient.

You can expect to encounter managed care most often in the guise of something called utilization review (UR). You call a toll-free number to get prior approval for hospital admissions or medical procedures, or to find out whether you need a second opinion. If you don't make the call, you can be hit with a penalty of as much as $1,000.

To avoid being penalized, keep careful records. Call your

---

illness or accident left an insured partially or totally disabled, no funds normally would be available to help the person retrain for employment and a more productive life. Now, though, many policies include expense reimbursement for counseling, occupational therapy, and even some educational or job-training programs. With this **rehabilitation coverage**, the goal is not to medicate but to rehabilitate. This is a good feature to look for in disability income and major medical policies.

Preexisting conditions. Most health insurance policies that are sold to individuals (as op-

posed to group/employer-sponsored plans) contain **preexisting condition clauses**. This means that the policy might exclude coverage for any physical or mental problems that you had at the time you bought it. In some policies, the exclusion is permanent; in others, it lasts only for the first year or two that the coverage is in force. Group insurance plans may also have preexisting condition clauses, but these tend to be less restrictive than those in individually written coverages.

Pregnancy and abortion. Many individual and group health insurance plans include special

UR company three to five days in advance of a hospital stay and ask for written confirmation of approval. Jot down the name of the person you talk to. To avoid busy signals, call early in the day and never during lunch.

After you're admitted, your doctor or the hospital should make any necessary follow-up calls, but you still have to stay on top of things. "Ultimately, the consumer is responsible for making sure contact is made," says Fran Hackett, director of group medical insurance at Prudential.

If your UR service is poor, complain to your employer. Companies pay a lot for these services and can write performance standards into their contracts.

PAYING FOR EXPERIMENTAL TREATMENT

Some of the fiercest controversies involve treatments that the UR company deems experimental and therefore not covered by insurance. If you're at odds with the insurance company, file an appeal either by phone or in writing; as a last resort, take your case to court.

BATTLING PREEXISTING CONDITIONS

Medical conditions as serious as a heart ailment or as minor as a headache can haunt you when you sign up for a new policy—even with group coverage. Insurers routinely restrict payment (or require at least a six-month waiting period, before processing claims) for conditions that predate your enrollment.

Restrictions are toughest on individual policies and in group plans with fewer than 25 people. If you have a serious medical condition, a carrier may refuse to cover you at all.

Most states require insurance companies to enroll you if you're a member of a group of about 50 or more. About half the states impose so-called no-gain, no-loss protections, which means that if an employer switches group policies, the new carrier has to cover all employees from day one. However, both state policies still allow insurance companies to impose a waiting period before covering a preexisting condition. If you must switch jobs you can take advantage of your right under federal COBRA legislation to extend insurance from your previous job for up to 18 months at your own expense.

Source: Adapted from Janet Bodnar and Melynda Dovel Wilcox, "When Your Health Insurance Makes Your Sick," *Kiplinger's Personal Finance Magazine*, October 1991, pp. 64–71.

---

clauses that pertain to medical expenses incurred through pregnancy or abortion. The most liberal of these policies pay for all related expenses, including sick-leave pay during the final months of pregnancy. Other, middle-of-the-road policies will pay for medical expenses that result from pregnancy or abortion complications but not for routine procedure expenses. In the most restrictive cases, no coverage for any costs of pregnancy or abortion is granted.

In recent years, the federal government and many states have passed laws that require certain employer-sponsored group health insurance programs

rehabilitation coverage

Insurance that covers the expenses of counseling, occupational therapy, and even some education or job training for persons injured or disabled by illness or accident.

preexisting condition clause

A clause commonly included in most individual health insurance policies that permits permanent or temporary exclusion of coverage for any physical or mental problems that existed at the time the policy was purchased.

to provide more liberal pregnancy and abortion reimbursement plans. Even in the absence of law, though, many employers are expanding their coverage for employees in this area. Because of adverse self-selection problems, individual health insurance will continue to restrict this policy feature.

Mental illness. Mental illness and emotional disorders are perhaps America's most prevalent but least talked about health problems. The high-pressure "get ahead" lives that many people lead often give rise to drug and alcohol abuse, stress-related physical disability, and various forms of psychosis or neurosis. In addition, family problems, economic setbacks, and chemical imbalances within the body all can contribute to poor mental health. Yet, even though mental illness or emotional disorder at some time strikes one out of three families, many of those affected will not admit they need help.

Compounding this problem of denial is the fact that many health insurance coverages omit or offer reduced benefits for treatment of mental disorders. Both hospital insurance and major medical insurance often restrict the duration over which they will reimburse victims. For example, one widely marketed health insurance policy offers hospital benefits that continue to pay as long as you remain hospitalized — except for mental illness. Under this policy, payment for mental illness is restricted to one-half the normally provided payment amounts and for a period not to exceed 30 days. Unfortunately, mental illness is the number one sickness requiring long-term hospital care.

As you can see from this discussion, coverage for mental illness is an important type of insurance protection. Therefore, make sure you check your policies to learn how liberal — or how restrictive — they are with respect to this feature.

COST CONTAINMENT PROVISIONS FOR MEDICAL EXPENSE PLANS

Considering the continued, rapid inflation in medical costs, it's hardly surprising that insurers, along with employers that sponsor medical expense plans, are looking for ways to limit the costs incurred. During the past decade, various cost containment provisions have been added to most medical expense plans. Although the success of such provisions has

been limited, you are likely to find them in your own insurance plan. Among these cost containment provisions are (1) pre-admission certification, (2) continued stay review, (3) second surgical opinions, (4) caseworker assignment, and (5) waiver of coinsurance.

Pre-admission Certification. The pre-admission certification clause requires you to file a form with your insurer prior to entering the hospital for a scheduled stay. You normally will be asked to provide an estimate of the length of expected stay, as well as other details. The insurer must approve your request. Of course, filing such a form is not normally required for emergency stays.

Continued Stay Review. The continued stay review applies when you need to remain in the hospital for a period exceeding that approved by the insurer in your preadmission certification. Once again, the insurer must be informed of your continued stay in advance for you to receive the normal reimbursement.

Second Surgical Opinions. In spite of a physician's opinion, many types of recommended, nonelective surgeries are either unnecessary or can be delayed. Good medical practice may dictate a second surgical opinion in these cases. Most surgical expense plans now provide for full reimbursement of the cost of second opinions. Indeed, many plans *require* second opinions on specific, nonemergency procedures and, in their absence, may reduce the surgical benefits paid.

Caseworker Assignment. For major surgery or extensive stays of a seriously ill person, the family of that person often is not in a position to calmly and rationally discuss hospital and surgical expenses with doctors. Naturally, the family only wants the best for their kin without regard to cost. In these situations, some plans assign a medically trained caseworker to discuss procedures and costs with the physicians involved. This practice gives the insurer some check on the procedures, and resulting costs, prescribed by physicians.

Waiver of Coinsurance. More traditional medical insurance plans provide first-dollar coverage for hospital and surgical expenses incurred during a hospital stay. Outpatient surgery is reimbursed by the major medical plan, which normally means that the insurer only will pay 75 or 80 percent of total costs, thanks to the coinsurance clause. Because insurers can save money on hospital room and board charges by encouraging outpatient surgery, many now agree to waive the coinsurance clause and pay 100 percent of surgical costs for outpatient procedures. A similar waiver sometimes is applied to generic pharmaceuticals, which also are reimbursed via major medical coverage. Under one such plan, a patient had the choice of an 80 percent coinsured payment for a brand-name pharmaceutical that cost $22 or a 100 percent reimbursement for the $7 generic equivalent. Because the patient chose the generic pharmaceutical, both the insurer and insured came out ahead.

> ## LONG-TERM CARE, SPECIAL COVERAGES, AND DISABILITY INCOME INSURANCE

Illnesses or accidents suffered by a member of your family can result in expenses beyond those necessary for immediate medical treatment. Do you know of an elderly family member who has become too ill or too frail to take care of his or her personal needs? If that person required special care at home or needed to enter a nursing home, who paid for these extra expenses? If a breadwinner in a family became too ill to work, how long could that family continue to pay their rent and other monthly bills? List some of the ways a family might pay the bills discussed here and think about the best alternatives for your family before you read on.

If arranged properly, medical expense insurance can help you handle most costs of immediate medical treatment. When a family member loses his or her health, additional losses can result, however. To meet these additional expenses insurers have developed health insurance policies such as (1) long-term care insurance, (2) special health coverages, and (3) disability income insurance. Some of these

plans are particularly complex and some offer only limited protection, so the consumer needs to be especially well informed in these areas.

LONG-TERM CARE INSURANCE

Thanks to ever-improving health care and better knowledge about health risks, such as smoking and poor diet, our population is living longer and will continue to do so in the foreseeable future. Many people are living to very advanced ages. In fact, those aged 85 and above are expected to comprise over 4 percent of the population by the year 2040, up from only 1 percent in 1980. People reaching advanced ages often become too frail to perform basic activities of everyday life, such as eating, bathing, and dressing. You probably know of one or more elderly persons who needed either to enter a nursing home or to hire special care in their own home because they simply could not adequately care for themselves.

Long-term care is the term often used to describe the delivery of medical and personal care, other than hospital care, for persons with chronic medical conditions resulting from either illness or frailty. The cost of such care can be very expensive. For instance, the cost of nursing home care averages between $25,000 and $30,000 per year. By the year 2020, the U.S. Administration on Aging projects that over 2.7 million Americans will be confined to a nursing home. Considering the likelihood of advanced aging in the United States and the costs of adequate long-term care, we must ask ourselves, "Who will pay the price?"

Financing Long-Term Care. Exhibit 10.3 shows how nursing home care, a major component of long-term care, has been financed in the United States in recent years. The primary parties financing nursing home care have been individuals and the medicaid program. Medicaid pays benefits only to

> ✓**long-term care**
> The delivery of medical and personal care, other than hospital care, for persons with chronic medical conditions resulting from either illness or frailty.

the indigent, as classified under the strict eligibility laws of your state. Medicaid benefits are tightly capped by law, and the recent political environment appears to favor continued cutbacks of this program.

Over half of all nursing home costs are paid out-of-pocket by individuals, as shown in Exhibit 10.3. Frequently, the persons receiving care cannot afford this expense, so the younger generation ends up footing the bill. Although the exhibit indicates that private insurance has not been much of a factor in the past, the market for it is developing and expanding rapidly as more people become aware of the costs involved. Major medical insurance plans exclude most of the costs related to long-term care, so a special policy is required. Fortunately, between 1987 and 1990, more than 100 insurers entered the market with new, long-term care insurance policies.

When a person is chronically ill and requires either nursing home care or home health-care services, most of these expenses are absorbed by medicare and private medical expense insurance.

Fantasy: Neither medicare nor private medical expense insurance provide much coverage for extended, nonhospital health care. A special type of health insurance, known as long-term care insurance, is required to assure coverage of these expenses.

Long-Term Care Insurance Provisions and Costs.
Because the market for long-term care insurance is so young, few experts are surprised at the wide range of policy provisions and premiums currently being offered. Because of substantial variation in product offerings, you must be especially careful to evaluate the important policy provisions. These provisions include (1) type of care, (2) eligibility requirements, (3) services covered, (4) daily benefits, (5) benefit duration, (6) waiting period, (7) renewability, (8) preexisting conditions, and (9) inflation protection. Exhibit 10.4 summarizes the benefits typically offered by leading insurers under these, and other, provisions. Of course, policy provisions are important factors in determining the premium for each policy.

Type of care. Some long-term care policies offer benefits only for nursing home care while others

pay only for sevices in the insured's home. Because you cannot easily predict whether or not a person might need to be in a nursing home, most financial planners recommend policies that cover both. Many times these policies focus on nursing home care and any expenses for health care in the insured's home are covered in a rider to the basic policy.

Eligibility requirements. Some very important provisions determine whether or not the insured will receive payment for claims. These are known in the industry as "gatekeeper" provisions. The most liberal policies state that the insured will qualify for benefits so long as his or her physician orders this care. A common and much more restrictive provision restricts payments only for long-term care that is medically necessary for sickness or injury.

One common gatekeeper provision that falls in between the previous two is one that requires the insured's inability to perform a given number of "activities of daily living" (ADLs). The ADLs listed in most policies include walking, eating, dressing, bathing, getting in and out of bed, and using the toilet. Some policies recognize as ADLs certain cognitive disabilities, such as severe short-term memory loss, but many policies do not. In the case of an Alzheimer's patient who remains physically healthy, inclusion of cognitive disabilities as ADLs would be extremely important.

Services covered. The better policies offer to pay for several levels of service, specifically skilled, intermediate, and custodial care. *Skilled care* is required when a patient requires constant attendance by a medical professional, such as a physician or registered nurse. *Intermediate care* occurs when medical attention or supervision is necessary, but not the constant attendance of a medical professional. *Custodial care* provides for assistance in the normal activities of daily living, but the attendance or supervision of a medical professional is not required. A physician or nurse may be on call, however. In the past, some policies restricted services to skilled care only. Such a policy does not cover intermediate and custodial care, which comprise most of the services offered by nursing homes.

Daily benefits. Long-term care policies reimburse the insured for services incurred up to a daily maximum. For nursing home care policies, the daily maximums generally range from $40 to $120 depending upon the amount of premium the insured

EXHIBIT 10.3

Who Pays the Nursing Home Bill?

Because very few people have insurance coverage that will pay for nursing home costs, most of these bills are paid out-of-pocket by patients and their families.

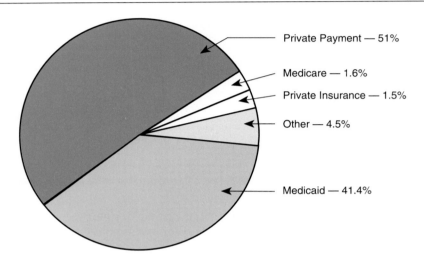

Private Payment — 51%

Medicare — 1.6%

Private Insurance — 1.5%

Other — 4.5%

Medicaid — 41.4%

Note: Based upon total U.S. nursing home expenditures of $38 billion in 1986.
Source: "Long-Term Care: A National Issue," *TIAA-CREF Research Dialogues*, April 1989, p. 5.

is willing to pay. For combination nursing home and home care policies, the maximum home care benefit normally is half the nursing home maximum.

Benefit duration. The maximum duration of benefits ranges from one year to the insured's lifetime. Lifetime coverage is very expensive, however. The consumer should realize that the average stay in a nursing home is about 19 months. Most planners recommend the purchase of a policy with a duration of three to six years in order to give the insured protection for a longer-than-average period of care.

Waiting period. Even if the insured meets the eligibility requirements of his or her policy, he or she must pay out of pocket during the **waiting,** or **elimination, period**. Typical waiting periods are 20 to 100 days. While premiums are much lower for policies with longer waiting periods, the insured must have liquid assets to cover his or her expenses during that period. If the insured still is receiving care after the waiting period expires, he or she will begin to receive benefits for the duration of the policy so long as the eligibility requirements continue to be met.

Renewability. A **guaranteed renewability** provision assures continued coverage for your lifetime so long as you continue to pay the premiums. This clause does not assure a level premium over time, however. Nearly all policies allow the insurer

waiting (elimination) period
The period of time, after the insured meets the eligibility requirements of his or her policy, during which he or she must pay health-care expenses out of pocket; after the waiting period expires, the insured will begin to receive benefits for the duration of the policy so long as the policy's eligibility requirements continue to be met.

guaranteed renewability
Policy provision assuring continued health-care coverage for the insured's lifetime so long as he or she continues to pay the premium. The insurer may raise premiums in the future, however, if the claims experience for the insured's peer group of policyholders is unfavorable.

EXHIBIT 10.4

Typical Coverages Offered in Long-Term Care Insurance Policies

The top 15 insurers issuing long-term care plans provide a wide range of benefits in their policies.

Services covered	Skilled, intermediate, and custodial care
	Home health care
	Adult day care (often)
Daily benefit	$40–$120/day nursing home
	$20–$60/day home health care
Benefit eligibility	Physician certification/medically necessary
Maximum benefit period	5 years, unlimited
Alzheimer's disease coverage	Yes
Deductibility periods	0–20 and 90–100 days
Renewability	Guaranteed
Preexisting condition	6 months
Inflation consideration	Yes
Age limits for purchasing	50–84

Source: Adapted from Ronald D. Hagen, "Long-Term Health Care," *Journal of the American Society of CLU & ChFC*, March 1992, p. 72.

---

to raise premiums if the claims experience for your peer group of policyholders is unfavorable. Watch out for policies with an **optional renewability** clause. These policies are renewable only at the option of the *insurer*!

Preexisting conditions. Many policies include a preexisting conditions clause, similar to those explained earlier, ranging from 6 to 12 months. On the other hand, many policies have no such clause whatsoever, which effectively eliminates one important source of possible claim disputes.

Inflation protection. Many policies offer riders that, for an additional premium, will allow you to increase your benefits over time. Hopefully, this rider would allow an insured to receive benefits roughly matching the rising cost of nursing home and home health care. Most inflation protection riders allow you to increase benefits by a flat amount, often 5 percent, per year. Others offer benefits linked to the rise in the consumer price index. Most policies do not allow increasing benefits for an entire lifetime, but discontinue inflation adjustments after either 10 or 20 years. Inflation protection riders are important, but expensive, adding between 25 and 40 percent to the basic premium for a long-term care policy.

Premium levels. Long-term care insurance is not inexpensive and premiums vary widely across different insurers. For example, *Consumer Reports* found that a 65-year-old desiring an $80 maximum daily benefit for four years on a combination (nursing home plus home care) policy with a 30-day waiting period could pay anywhere from $800 to $3,000 per year. In the current market, the consumer must carefully compare both the key provisions and the premiums quoted on long-term care policies offered by different insurers.

SPECIAL INSURANCE COVERAGES

An examination of every type of health insurance coverage available would fill a book twice the size of this one. However, the types of health insurance plans previously discussed are sufficient to meet the protection needs of most families and individuals. Other popularly available contracts often are simply frills and gimmicks. These plans may be classified as accident policies, sickness policies, and hospital income policies. Sound insurance programming seldom dictates the purchase of these types of policies. Nevertheless, large-scale marketing efforts by some insurers, coupled with public misunderstanding, has brought about their proliferation. Hopefully, the following discussion will help you guard against a potentially unwise purchase.

Accident policies are those that pay a specified sum to an insured who is injured in a certain type of accident. The most common types of accident policies are those relating to travel accidents. These first became widespread with the growing railroad passenger traffic during the 1800s and today include private and for-hire automobiles and commercial aviation. These policies often are sold in conjunction with oil company and travel and entertainment credit cards. Their primary shortcoming is that the amount of the payment is not directly related to the amount of the loss. Also, as noted earlier, since only cerain types of accidents are covered, it becomes impossible to structure a systematic insurance program using these coverages that will not have serious gaps in some places and duplicate coverage in others.

Sickness policies are similar in design and shortcomings to accident policies except that a named disease, as opposed to an accident, conditions the payment. Sickness policies may be written separately or in conjunction with accident policies. *Dread disease policies* are a popular version of sickness insurance. Today's renditions limit health-care coverage to a specific type of disease or illness. Cancer policies appear to be the most common, with some organ transplant policies also being offered. Some states, such as New York, prohibit the sale of single dread disease policies; that is, such coverage can only be sold as part of other hospital, surgical, or accident policies.

Hospital income policies typically guarantee the insured a specified daily, weekly, or monthly amount as long as the insured remains hospitalized. However, they generally exclude illness that could result in extended hospitalization (for example, mental illness or those resulting from health conditions that existed at the time the policies were purchased). Several of these plans have been accused of returning in benefits only 10 to 20 cents of each $1 of premiums collected.

The basic problem with buying policies that cover only a certain type of accident, illness, or financial need is that major gaps in coverage will occur. Clearly, the financial loss can be just as great regardless of whether the insured falls down a flight of stairs or contracts cancer, lung disease, or heart disease. Most limited-peril policies should be used only to supplement a comprehensive insurance program if the coverage is not overlapping. Both dread disease and hospital income policies are frequently offered directly through television and newspaper advertisements.

DISABILITY INCOME INSURANCE

While technically not a form of health insurance, disability income insurance is discussed here since the need for its coverage results from the potentially devastating financial consequences of a health-related disability. **Disability income insurance** is designed to provide families with weekly or monthly payments to replace income when the insured person is unable to work as a result of a covered illness, injury, or disease. Some companies also offer disability income protection for a homemaker–spouse; in that case, the coverage helps pay for the services that the spouse would normally provide.

The need for disability income coverage is great, yet generally ignored by the public. Researchers have found that the need for disability income insurance exceeds that for life insurance by 4 to 14 times, depending upon age. Yet only a little over 20 percent of the public have long-term disability protection while well over 80 percent own some form of life insurance. The first step in considering a disability plan is to determine the dollar amount your family would need (typically on a per-month basis) in the event an earner becomes disabled.

Estimating Your Disability Insurance Needs.   The overriding purpose of disability insurance is to replace all (or most) of the income — that is, earnings — that would be lost in the event you became disabled and physically unable to hold a job. In essence, it should enable you to maintain a standard of living at or near the level you have presently achieved. To help decide how much disability insurance is right for you, you can use the worksheet in Exhibit 10.5 to estimate your monthly disability

---

optional renewability
Contractual clause allowing the insured to continue health-care insurance only at the option of the *insurer*; hence, the insured has no guarantee that insurance protection will be available in the future.

disability income insurance
Insurance that replaces a portion of income when the insured person is unable to work as a result of a covered illness, injury, or disease.

benefit needs (this is a procedure developed and recommended by the Consumer's Union of the United States, publishers of *Consumer Reports*). Here is all you have to do:

1. Disability benefits are generally, but not always, tax-free, so you need replace only your take-home (after-tax) pay. (Note: Be sure to ascertain whether or not, and to what extent, your disability benefits are tax-free.) Estimate take-home pay roughly from your previous year's federal income tax return by subtracting the taxes paid, including social security taxes, from your gross earned income (salary only, since any dividend and interest income you now receive should continue). Divide this total by 12 to get your monthly take-home pay.

2. You may already have disability benefits from government or employer programs. Estimate them as follows:
   a. The local social security office may help you estimate your social security benefits, but you can definitely get an estimate of your benefits by calling 1-800-772-1213 for a *Personal Earnings and Benefit Estimate Statement*. An insurance agent can also often help you make the estimate, since many insurance companies have a computer program that can easily calculate it. As of early 1988, the average social security disability benefit was around $1,100 a month for a wage earner with dependents. To be "disabled" under social security, however, you must be unable to do any job whatever. Benefits are payable only if your disability is expected to last at least a year (or to be fatal). Payments do not begin until you have been disabled for at least five months. The amount paid is a percentage of your previous monthly earnings, with some statistical adjustments. The percentage is higher for people with low earnings. Because the Social Security Administration generally has rejected 40 percent or more of the applicants for disability income coverage, many planners recommend that you assume *no* such benefits for purposes of estimating your need for private insurance coverage.

   b. Other government programs that provide certain disability benefits, if you qualify, include armed services disability benefits, Veterans Administration pension disability benefits, civil service disability benefits, the Federal Employees Compensation Act, and state workers' compensation systems. There are also special programs for railroad workers, longshoremen, and people with black-lung disease.
   c. Ask your company benefits supervisor to help you calculate the company benefits. In a few states (including California, Hawaii, New Jersey, New York, and Rhode Island, plus the Commonwealth of Puerto Rico), employers must provide a certain minimum level of benefits. However, the state-mandated *minimums* tend to be small (up to a maximum of $170 per week in New York, for example), and benefits typically expire after 26 weeks in any 52-week period.

   Ask first about sick pay or wage continuation plans (for all practical purposes, these are disability income insurance). Then ask about any plans formally designated as insurance. For each benefit your employer offers, check on the tax treatment. Some disability income benefits, if funded entirely by an employer, are fully or partially taxable.
   d. Your company may have sponsored a group disability insurance plan. A private insurer provides the coverage, and you pay for it, often through a payroll deduction. A major advantage of a group plan is that it is usually considerably less expensive than individual coverage—sometimes half as much. In addition, enrollment requirements are usually less stringent than for individually purchased policies. A disadvantage is that if you change jobs, you may lose the coverage. The benefits from a group plan in which you pay the premiums are tax-free (unless paid through a flexible spending account).

3. Add up the monthly disability benefits to which you are already entitled.

4. Subtract these from your current monthly take-home pay. The result will show the monthly disability benefits you will need in order to main-

EXHIBIT 10.5
Estimating Disability Insurance Needs

Using a worksheet like this makes the job of estimating disability benefit needs a lot easier.

DISABILITY BENEFIT NEEDS

Name(s) _____ Date _____

1.	Estimate current monthly *take-home* pay		$ _____
2.	Estimate existing benefits:	$ _____	
	a. Social security benefits	_____	
	b. Other government benefits	_____	
	c. Company programs	_____	
	d. Group disability policy benefits	_____	
3.	Total existing disability benefits (2a + 2b + 2c + 2d)		$ _____
4.	Estimated monthly disability benefits needed ([1] − [3])		$ _____

---

tain your present after-tax income. Note that investment income and spousal income (if he or she is presently employed) are ignored, since it is assumed that this income will continue and is necessary to maintain your current standard of living. If your spouse is presently unemployed but would enter the work force in the event you ever became disabled, his or her estimated monthly income (take-home pay) could be subtracted from item 4 of Exhibit 10.5 to determine net monthly disability benefit needs.

Disability Income Insurance Provisions and Costs.
The scope of your disability income coverage, as well as your cost, depends upon a number of contractual provisions. Although disability income insurance policies can be very complex, certain contractual provisions bear very close examination. These provisions include (1) definition of disability, (2) benefit amount and duration, (3) probationary period, (4) waiting period, (5) renewability, and (6) other provisions.

Definition of disability. Disability policies specify the standards that must be met for you to receive benefits. The most liberal definition is one that considers you disabled if you cannot perform at least one primary duty of your own occupation. This is known as the *own occupation* (or "Own Occ")

definition. With this definition, a professor who lost his voice, but still could get paid to write or do research, would receive full benefits because he could not lecture, a primary function of his occupation.

Many policies use a more strict definition based upon whether the insured can perform any occupation for which he or she is reasonably suited on the basis of education, training, or experience. Known as the *any occupation* ("Any Occ") definition, the insurer has more leeway in determining whether or not the insured should receive benefits, so this type of policy is considerably less expensive.

A *presumptive disability* clause often is found in individual disability policies. This provision supersedes the previously discussed definition of disability when certain types of losses occur. Loss of both hands, sight in both eyes, and hearing in both ears are examples where the insured may be *presumed* totally disabled and may receive full benefits even though he or she still can be employed in some capacity.

Benefit amount and duration. Most individual policies pay a flat monthly benefit, which is stated in the policy, while group plans pay a fixed percentage of gross income. In either case, insurers normally will not agree to amounts in excess of 70 percent of the insured's gross income. Insurers will not issue policies for the full amount of gross

ISSUES IN MONEY MANAGEMENT

Make Sure You Have Enough Disability Protection!

Many people worry a lot about whether they've got enough life insurance, but hardly give disability coverage a second thought — especially if their employer has a group disability plan.

But the chance of becoming disabled for more than three months is far greater than the chance of dying before retirement, actuaries say. Accidents, heart attacks, complicated pregnancies, cancer, and even "stress" (which can translate into alcoholism and mental disorders) all take their toll on people's ability to carry on with their normal work lives.

While most employers do provide short-term disability coverage that pays 100 percent of salary, things can get tough after it runs out in three to six months. Many employers' longer-term group disability plans are difficult to qualify for, pay little, and limit benefit payments to only a few years. Social Security and state disability payments don't go very far for formerly well-paid professionals.

The answer may be supplemental coverage. Though these disability contracts are costly and complex, there are ways to make the process easier, and new ways to cut costs significantly.

How Some Policies Compare: A sampling of annual premiums for disability insurance policies

Insurer	Monthly Benefit	Age 35	Age 45	Age 55
		(Elimination Period 1 Year/90 days)[1]		
Adjustable Rate Disability Policies[2]				
General American	$5,000	$803/1,008	$1,363/1,625	$2,517/3,228
	$2,500	$417/519	$731/869	$1,339/1,713
Northwestern Mutual	$5,000	$939/1,123	$1,862/2,229	$3,335/4,212
	$2,500	$491/588	$953/1,143	$1,667/2,106
Level Premium Policies[3]				
Paul Revere	$5,000	$1,487/1,874	$2,349/2,895	$3,274/4,125
	$2,500	$784/966	$1,207/1,499	$1,652/2,077
General American	$5,000	$1,254/1,578	$1,934/2,309	$2,648/3,396
	$2,500	$892/1,077	$1,294/1,496	$1,536/1,898

Note: Premiums are nonsmoker's rates for policies guaranteed renewable and noncancelable until age 65. These policies also include cost-of-living benefit increases, pay benefits (if insured returns to work but suffers a drop in income, give policyholders the right to increase benefits later without a medical exam.
[1]Wait after becoming disabled for benefits to begin
[2]First-year premium
[3]Premium remains flat for life of policy
Source: Individual companies.

The first step is to take a look at your group coverage. Most plans pay 60 percent of base salary while the employee is disabled. But since that doesn't include things like bonuses and profit sharing, the actual benefit may be 40 percent or less of an employee's total compensation. In addition, many group policies don't provide coverage for longer than two to five years and don't provide for cost-of-living increases. Benefits are almost always taxable.

Many group plans also have strict definitions of "disability," which would reduce the chance of qualifying. Typically, employees are considered disabled only if they can't perform the "main functions" of their regular occupations. Some plans are even stricter: After two years, they consider employees disabled only if they can't perform any occupation for which they "may be suited by education or training." The more subjective the criteria, the more control the employer has over payouts.

Even if your group plan seems adequate, it may make sense to look into individual policies anyway. In an environment of mergers and buy-outs, "executives who change jobs, or get smitten with the entrepreneurial bug" need individual policies, says Andrew Reid of R&D Insurance Services in Palo Alto, Calif.

If you decide to buy supplemental coverage, start by looking for policies that aren't cancelable and are guaranteed renewable, which means that the insurance company can't raise the premiums or cancel the coverage. Also, look for those that provide coverage until age 65 or longer.

Next, choose options that tailor the policy to your needs, says Lawrence Mintzer, president of Mintzer Insurance Services, an insurance consulting firm in Newton, Mass. The two most important riders, he says, are a cost-of-living option, which would increase benefits with inflation, and an option to increase coverage as income rises — without a medical examination.

It's also a good idea to select a policy with a "residual benefit" option. This pays a partial benefit that would supplement your income if you could return to work, but were unable to earn as much as you had been making before becoming disabled.

How much supplemental coverage you need depends on several factors, including the other resources you have to fall back on — things like retirement savings plans, investment income and income from a working spouse. Keep in mind that benefits from individual disability policies will go further than those from company-paid plans because they are tax-free.

Insurance agents will work with you to arrive at an appropriate supplemental amount. But insurers make it difficult to get coverage for more than 70 percent of one's salary, since they feel that paying more would encourage malingerers.

FOLLOWING GROUP PLAN'S LIMIT

The first thing they look at is the benefit limit in an employee's group policy. An individual policy combined with the group coverage could significantly increase the total monthly benefit. Peace of mind like that doesn't come cheap, however. Fortunately, there are ways to lower premiums.

Most insurers offer discounts of 10 percent to 15 percent for people who don't smoke. Choosing a longer period before receiving benefits also will save money. If you're coordinating coverage with your group plan, you might choose to wait as long as one to two years.

Some companies now offer "adjustable-rate disability insurance," which costs less than ordinary "level premium" policies in the early years. With adjustable rate policies, the premium increases 8 percent to 10 percent a year until it reaches the level-premium rate in seven years or more. At that time, it can be converted to a level-premium policy.

Saving money also depends on not buying coverage you don't need. One of the most popular options is the "own-occupation" rider. This will pay full benefits if you can't perform your stated occupation, but are still able to work at a related, though lower-paying job. For example, a surgeon who cannot perform surgery could work as a general practitioner and still receive full benefits.

That sounds good, but it may not be worth the extra cost for most white-collar professionals, says Richard Kirtland, director of marketing at General American Life Insurance Co., St. Louis. The residual rider would probably cover the loss of income, he says. The own-occupation rider is "really a marketing-driven thing."

Source: Adapted from Ellen E. Schultz, "Disability Coverage? Well, I Have Some . . . ," *The Wall Street Journal*, April 17, 1990, pp. C1, C23.

income because this would give some people an incentive to fake a disability (for example, "bad back"), thereby allowing them to collect more in insurance benefits than they normally would receive as take-home pay. Monthly benefits can be paid for a few months or for a lifetime. If you are assured of substantial pension, social security, or other benefits at retirement, then you may want a policy that pays benefits until age 65. Most people would not be assured of retirement benefits unless they were able to continue their occupations for many more years, however. Persons in this situation should consider a policy offering lifetime benefits. Many policies offer benefits for periods as short as 2 or 5 years. While these policies may be better than nothing, they do not protect against the major financial losses associated with long-term disabilities.

Probationary period.   Both group and individual policies are likely to contain a probationary period, which is a time delay from the date the policy is issued until benefit privileges are activated. For example, a 30-day probationary period means the policy must be in force for 30 days before any benefits are available. No disability stemming from an illness, injury, or disease that occurs during the probationary period is covered—even if it continues beyond this period. The probationary period often runs from 7 to 30 days. The purpose of this feature is to keep costs down, thereby making these policies more affordable.

Waiting period.   The waiting, or elimination, period provisions are similar to those discussed for long-term care insurance. Typical waiting periods for disability income insurance are one week, two weeks, 30 days, 60 days, 90 days, six months, and one year. Insurers use these to omit coverage for the frequent small loss and to limit further the incentives for insureds to fake disabilities. As long as you have an adequate emergency fund to provide family income during the early months of disability, substantial savings of premium can be realized if you purchase a policy with a relatively long waiting period, as shown in Exhibit 10.6.

With most insurers, you effectively can trade off an increase in the waiting period from, say, 7 days to 90 days for an increase in the duration of benefits from five years to protection to age 65. In fact, as Exhibit 10.6 shows, the premium charged by this insurer for a policy with a one-year term and a seven-day waiting period is about the same as one charged

for benefits payable to age 65 with a 30-day waiting period. Accepting this type of trade-off usually makes sense because the primary purpose of insurance is to protect against a catastrophic loss, rather than smaller losses that are better handled through proper budgeting and saving.

Renewability.   Most individual disability income insurance is either *guaranteed renewable* or *noncancelable*. As with long-term care policies, guaranteed renewability assures that you can renew the policy issued until you reach the age stated in the clause, usually age 65. Premiums can be raised over time if justified by the loss experience of all those in the same class (usually based on age, sex, and occupational category) as you are. Noncancelable policies offer guaranteed renewability, but also guarantee that future premiums will remain the same as those stated in the policy at issuance. Because of this guarantee of future premiums, noncancelable policies generally are more expensive than those with only a guaranteed renewability provision.

Other provisions.   The purchasing power of income from a long-term disability contract that pays, say, $2,000, per month could be severely affected by inflation. In fact, a 6 percent inflation rate would reduce the purchasing power of this $2,000 benefit to only $1,000 in less than 12 years. To counteract such a reduction, many insurers offer a *cost-of-living adjustment (COLA)*. With a COLA provision, the monthly benefit is adjusted upward each year, often in line with the Consumer Price Index, although these annual adjustments frequently are capped at a given rate, say 8 percent.

While the COLA provision only applies once the insured is disabled, the *guaranteed insurability option (GIO)* can allow you to purchase additional disability income insurance in line with inflation increases while you are still healthy. Under the GIO, the price of this additional insurance is fixed at the inception of the contract and you do not have to prove insurability.

A *waiver of premium* is standard in disability income policies. If you are disabled for a minimum period of time, normally 60 or 90 days, the insurer will waive any future premiums that come due while you remain disabled. In essence, the waiver of premium just provides you with additional disability income insurance that just happens to be in the amount of your regular premium payment.

EXHIBIT 10.6
Disability Insurance Premium Costs

The cost of disability income insurance varies with the terms of payment as well as the length of deferral (waiting period).

Waiting Period	Term of Disability Benefits			
	1 Year	3 Years	5 Years	Age 65
7 Days	$30.88	$34.40	$37.30	$53.80
14 Days	24.20	29.10	32.00	47.90
30 Days	14.16	17.60	19.90	31.80
60 Days	9.70	12.75	15.00	26.20
90 Days	—	10.20	12.50	23.50
1 Year	—	—	10.90	19.50

Note: Premiums shown are annual charges per $100 a month of coverage for a 35-year-old male with a desk-type job.

As with other forms of health insurance, the specific policy provisions selected affect the premium cost of a disability income insurance policy. The accompanying *Issues in Money Management* box provides advice from financial planners as to which disability income insurance provisions should be considered as well as some estimates of premium costs.

WHO ARE THE PROVIDERS OF HEALTH-CARE COVERAGE?

Health-care coverage is available from several government agencies, private carriers, and various types of organizations, such as HMOs. From which of these broad groups of providers do you receive health-care coverage? Spend a few moments listing them and the coverages they provide before reading ahead.

There are five traditional sources of financial aid available for losses arising from illness or accidents: (1) social security, (2) worker's compensation, (3) group health insurance, (4) Blue Cross/Blue Shield, and (5) individual health coverage from insurance companies. In addition, health maintenance organizations and similar group providers can help individuals and families meet their health-care needs—in fact, HMOs and the like represent the fastest-growing segment of the health-care delivery industry.

SOCIAL SECURITY

Many people think of social security as merely a retirement system. It can, however, provide a considerable amount of coverage for losses arising from illness and accidents as well as disability. In fact, the official name for what is commonly referred to as social security is *old-age, survivor's, disability, and health insurance (OASDHI)*. Health benefits are provided under two separate programs: (1) medicare and (2) disability income. Although the medicaid program also provides medical benefits under social security, it is not discussed here since it is a public assistance program designed to provide benefits only for those persons who are unable to pay for health care.

Medicare. **Medicare** is a health-care plan that has two primary components: (1) basic hospital insurance and (2) supplementary medical insurance. Although medicare was primarily designed to help

medicare
A health plan administered by the federal government to help persons age 65 and over, and others receiving monthly social security disability benefits, meet their health-care costs.

persons 65 and over meet their health-care costs, it now also covers many persons under age 65 who are current recipients of monthly social security disability benefits.

Basic hospital insurance. Under the basic hospital insurance coverage of medicare (commonly called *Part A*), inpatient hospital services are included for the first 90 days of illness, after a deductible ($628 in 1991) is applied for the first 60 days of illness. Coinsurance provisions, applicable to days 61 through 90 of the hospital stay, can reduce benefits further.

Along with the coverage of hospital room and board, medicare hospital insurance contributes toward the payment of all services normally provided to inpatients, as well as covering stays for limited periods in post-hospital extended-care facilities such as nursing homes providing *skilled care*. (However, the most common types of nursing home care — *intermediate and custodial care* — are not covered under medicare.) Some post-hospital health services, such as intermittent nursing care, therapy, rehabilitation, and home health aid, are also provided. Benefits offered under the basic hospital plan of medicare are subject to deductible provisions and time limits; coinsurance is required on skilled nursing home care. These amounts are revised each year to reflect changes in medical costs. The funds for medicare benefits come from the social security taxes paid by covered workers and their employers.

Supplementary medical insurance (SMI). The **supplementary medical insurance (SMI)** program under medicare (commonly called *Part B*) provides payment for the following items: (1) physicians' and surgeons' services that are provided either at home or in a health-care facility; (2) home health service (visitation by a registered nurse); and (3) medical and health services such as X rays, diagnostics, laboratory tests, rental of necessary durable medical equipment, prosthetic devices, and ambulance trips. Limited psychiatric care is also covered under this part of medicare.

In contrast to the basic hospital plan, this supplementary protection is a voluntary program. Financing is provided by charging premiums to those who participate. These premiums are then matched by funds from general tax revenues of the United States. Unlike private health insurance, SMI assesses no premium differential because of differences in enrollees' ages, health status, or sex. The coverage under SMI is open to nearly anyone age 65 or over as long as he or she is properly enrolled in the program and pays the required monthly premiums. (As a budgeting device, the SMI premium may be subtracted from the social security check the covered worker is receiving.) SMI is similar to many other types of health insurance in that payments are subjected to a deductible in excess of which the insured participates at the rate of 20 percent of costs incurred. However, SMI pays only 80 percent of the *approved charges*, not 80 percent of whatever amount is billed by the physician for the service. As a result, an insured may be covered for substantially less than 80 percent of the total bill. In addition, neither Part A nor Part B of Medicare pays for prescription drugs taken outside of the hospital.

Disability Income under Social Security.

The disability income benefits under social security can be important to families during child-rearing years as well as thereafter. Nearly all families in the United States are covered by social security. The only major exceptions are certain groups of state and local employees who before 1984 elected not to be covered (although they do have the option to voluntarily join) and most employees of the federal government hired before 1984 (who are enrolled in a special system). In order to be eligible for disability income benefits, a covered employee needs 20 quarters (5 years) of coverage out of the 40 quarters (10 years) immediately preceding the date of disability and must have suffered a total disability that has been in effect for at least 5 months and is expected to prevent employment for a minimum of 12 months. After becoming eligible for disability benefits, the worker and his or her family can receive benefits for the duration of the disability, even if it lasts for life. The amount of the monthly family benefit paid on behalf of the disabled worker, say, under age 35 often would range between 40 and 80 percent of his or her predisability monthly earnings. The exact percentage used decreases as a covered worker's average earnings increase.

Eligibility requirements for workers who become disabled before age 31 are more liberal. Benefits may be paid on behalf of young workers if they have coverage in one-half of the quarters elapsing in the period after they attained age 21 up to and including the quarter in which the disability occurred. A minimum of six quarters of coverage is required. Unmarried children 18 or under whose disabled, retired, or deceased parents are covered under social security can draw benefits under the parents' accounts without ever having worked themselves.

A very desirable feature of disability income, as well as the other cash benefit programs of social security, is that all payments are automatically adjusted periodically to reflect increases in the cost of living. Of course, the reason that social security can make this promise is that the financing mechanism is based on the assumption that taxes can always be raised, if needed, to fund the benefits. Another desirable feature of disability income under social security is that it can be paid during periods of rehabilitation even if the recipient may have some type of gainful employment.

WORKER'S COMPENSATION INSURANCE

Worker's compensation insurance statutes have been enacted in every state in the union and by the federal government. These laws generally provide for compensation to workers for job-related illness or injuries. Although the worker's compensation legislation differs in each state, benefits often include medical expenses, rehabilitation, disability income, and scheduled lump-sum amounts for death and certain injuries, such as dismemberment. Wide variations are found among the individual states in benefit amounts and payment periods.

In most instances, covered employees become eligible for worker's compensation benefits when they show that an illness or injury has occured in the course of their employment. Payments are made without question of fault—employee or employer—except in certain cases in which the worker was intoxicated or acted outside the scope of his or her authority. The primary purpose of these laws is to lighten the burden of job-related illness or injury to the worker. The cost of worker's compensation plans in all states is borne directly by employers. However, the amount of premium charged is computed on a merit basis; employers who file the most claims pay the highest rates. Consequently, employers try to reduce accidents and injuries to help keep their premiums low. Employees are not required to make any direct premium payments for this coverage. Self-employed persons who are covered under the law must make contributions for themselves and their employees. The four basic areas of coverage provided by worker's compensation insurance are discussed in the following paragraphs.

Medical and Rehabilitation Expenses. A basic objective of worker's compensation legislation is to help employees recover and reenter the work force as productive members of society. Thus, the laws provide for the payment of hospital, surgical, and other related expenses, including such prosthetic devices as artificial limbs, that may be required to aid in the worker's recovery. In addition, a number of jurisdictions provide compensation for retraining seriously injured victims for new employment.

Disability Income under Worker's Compensation. Disability income benefits are most often paid to covered workers suffering loss due to disease or injury. The amount paid represents a set percentage of their predisability earned wages up to some maximum amount. The duration of disability payments is as short as 50 weeks in some states and as long as a lifetime in others. The maximum weekly benefit payable is seldom more than one-and-a-half times the average weekly wage of workers within the state in which they are employed, and often much less.

supplementary medical insurance (SMI)
A voluntary program under medicare (commonly called *Part B*) that provides payments for extra services, such as physicians' and surgeons' services, home health service, and X-ray and laboratory services, and requires payment of premiums by participants.

worker's compensation insurance
A type of medical and disability insurance, required by state and federal governments, paid for by employers and designed to compensate workers for job-related injuries, illnesses, and disabilities.

EXHIBIT 10.7

Health Insurance Benefits Paid by U.S. Insurance Companies (Millions of Dollars)

Insurance companies pay out billions of dollars annually in health-care benefits, and most of that goes to people covered by group policies.

Year	Total Benefits	Group				Individual and Family Policies		
		Total	Medical Expenses	Dental Expense	Loss of Income	Total	Medical Expense	Loss of Income
1970	$ 9,089	$ 7,476	$ 6,043	$ 140	$1,293	$1,613	$1,090	$ 523
1971	9,498	8,018	6,541	175	1,301	1,480	1,006	474
1972	10,622	8,943	7,315	201	1,427	1,679	1,148	531
1973	11,863	9,764	7,924	262	1,578	2,099	1,462	637
1974	13,636	11,439	9,260	332	1,847	2,197	1,517	680
1975	16,470	14,191	11,607	599	1,985	2,279	1,557	722
1976	20,217	17,795	14,425	1,187	2,183	2,422	1,691	731
1977	22,113	19,479	15,683	1,452	2,344	2,634	1,869	765
1978	26,352	22,868	18,696	1,771	2,401	3,484	2,480	1,004
1979	31,692	27,934	22,159	2,185	3,590	3,758	2,644	1,114
1980	37,002	33,002	25,895	2,795	4,312	4,000	2,970	1,030
1981	41,622	37,691	30,057	3,474	4,160	3,931	2,935	996
1982	49,159	44,202	36,074	3,984	4,144	4,957	3,572	1,385
1983	51,665	46,890	39,853	4,372	3,869	4,775	3,751	1,024
1984	55,980	50,305	42,424	4,913	3,907	5,675	4,422	1,253
1985	59,962	53,669	44,340	5,292	4,037	6,293	4,696	1,597
1986	64,303	58,926	49,640	5,262	4,024	5,377	3,800	1,577
1987	71,000	65,100	54,600	5,900	4,600	5,900	4,100	1,800
1988	80,800	74,200	63,300	6,300	4,600	6,600	4,700	1,800
1989	87,300	80,100	68,600	6,500	5,000	7,200	5,000	2,200

Source: Adapted from *Source Book of Health Insurance Data* (Washington, DC: Health Insurance Association of America, 1991 Edition), pp. 28–29.

Lump-Sum Payments. Worker's compensation legislation also provides for the payment of lump-sum amounts to employees who suffer dismemberment in work-related accidents or to their beneficiaries in the case of death. The lump-sum amounts payable for any specific type of loss are usually listed in a schedule of benefits that applies to all covered workers. These scheduled amounts vary considerably from state to state. In some states, payment for the loss of an arm exceeds the payment for death allowed by other states.

Second-Injury Funds. Second-injury funds are established by the states to operate in conjunction with worker's compensation statutes. Their purpose is to relieve employers of the additional worker's compensation premium burden they might incur if an already handicapped worker sustained further injury on the job. For example, an employer might be reluctant to hire a worker with one eye, because if that individual's other eye were lost, the injury would constitute total disablement under the law. In light of the merit-rating system used in worker's compensation, this would adversely affect the employer's premiums. Established to relieve employers of this burden, second-injury funds are financed in some jurisdictions from state tax revenues and in others from an assessment levied against worker's compensation insurers.

GROUP HEALTH INSURANCE

Group health insurance consists of health-care contracts that are written between a group (usually an employer, union, credit union, college or university, or other organization) and an insurance company. The coverages of each specific plan are subject to negotiation between the group and the insurer. All of the health-care coverages that have been discussed, except disability income and long-term care, are widely provided by group plans. Group insurance accounts for a large majority of all private

EXHIBIT 10.8

Health Insurance Premiums (Millions of Dollars)

The amount of money spent on health insurance premiums has risen dramatically in dollar terms and—more important—as a relative amount of disposable income.

Year	Private Health Insurance Companies	Blue Cross/ Blue Shield and Other Plans	Total Premiums (1)	Disposable Personal Income (2)	Ratio [(1) ÷ (2)] (3)
1970	$11,546	$ 8,439	$ 19,985	$ 715,600	2.79%
1971	12,777	10,058	22,835	776,800	2.94
1972	14,771	11,465	26,236	839,575	3.12
1973	16,104	12,908	29,012	949,775	3.05
1974	17,915	14,533	32,448	1,038,350	3.12
1975	20,795	17,611	36,967	1,142,775	3.23
1976	24,502	21,455	43,468	1,252,625	3.47
1977	28,676	25,333	50,449	1,379,325	3.66
1978	32,713	32,517	63,067	1,551,225	4.07
1979	37,941	37,625	73,930	1,729,275	4.28
1980	43,666	43,674	84,742	1,917,900	4.42
1981	48,998	50,460	95,136	2,127,600	4.47
1982	58,341	57,222	109,472	2,261,425	4.84
1983	63,190	63,188	119,876	2,428,100	4.94
1984	70,440	68,518	127,635	2,668,600	4.78
1985	75,169	78,199	139,525	2,841,100	4.91
1986	75,486	84,122	143,400	3,022,100	4.75
1987	84,100	106,100	167,100	3,205,900	5.52
1988	98,200	122,300	189,900	3,477,800	5.46
1989	108,000	145,100	215,600	3,788,600	5.69

Note: Premiums for the different types of insurers may sum to an amount greater than total premiums because of duplicate counting.

Source: Adapted from *Source Book of Health Insurance Data* (Washington, DC: Health Insurance Association of America, 1991 Edition), p. 29.

health insurance benefits paid in the United States. As Exhibit 10.7 shows, of the $87.3 billion in health insurance *benefits paid* in 1989, over $80 billion was accounted for by group insurance. In addition to private insurance companies, prepaid medical expense plans, including Blue Cross/Blue Shield, provide health-care coverage for groups. In fact, total benefits paid by Blue Cross/Blue Shield and other prepaid plans topped $120 billion in 1989.

Exhibit 10.8 shows how the *premium volume* for both private health insurers and Blue Cross/Blue Shield grew between 1970 and 1989 in relation to disposable personal income. In 1940 (not shown) only .42 percent of disposable personal income went for health-care premiums, while by 1970 this figure had reached 2.79 percent. As of 1989, the figure had risen to 5.69 percent. The proportion of personal disposable income spent on health insurance is expected to continue to increase.

The chances are that if you go to work for an organization of more than just a few employees, you will be covered by some type of group health-care plan. In many group plans, the employer pays the total

second-injury funds
Funds established by states to relieve an employer of the additional worker's compensation premiums it would incur if an already handicapped worker sustained further injury on the job.

group health insurance
A type of health insurance consisting of contracts written between a group (employer, union, and so forth) and an insurance company; typically provides all types of coverage except disability income and long-term care.

premium for basic coverage on employees and their dependents. In others, employees must pay the portions of their premiums that provide protection for their families. Much of the rapid expansion of both benefits and persons covered under group plans has been a direct result of the collective bargaining process involving unions and employers. In recent years, many employee benefit plans have included, in addition to the coverages previously discussed, medical expenses for maternity (in or out of wedlock), abortion, alcoholism, mental and nervous disorders, and drug addiction.

BLUE CROSS/BLUE SHIELD

In a technical sense, **Blue Cross/Blue Shield plans** are not insurance policies but rather can be viewed as nonprofit prepaid hospital expense plans. Blue Cross contracts with hospitals, who in exchange for a specified fee or payment agree to provide specified hospital services to members of groups protected by Blue Cross. Similarly, Blue Shield plans are nonprofit contracts providing for surgical and medical services. These plans serve as intermediaries between groups who want these services and physicians who contractually agree to provide them. Although technically Blue Cross/Blue Shield organizations are nonprofit, they compete for business with private insurance companies (many of which are nonprofit mutual insurance companies) and attempt to retain a portion of their income to finance growth. However, if premium income is substantially larger than necessary to meet all expenses and surplus requirements, benefits are rendered to subscribers in the form of lower premiums and/or expanded coverage.

Currently, about 36 percent of the U.S. population is covered by some type of Blue Cross/Blue Shield protection. Blue Cross/Blue Shield organizations have been formed on a geographic basis and now have more than 70 separate plans in operation. Because they are producer cooperatives, benefit payments are seldom made to the enrollee. Instead, direct payments to the participating hospitals and physicians are the norm. When Blue Cross/Blue Shield first began, premiums were based on a communitywide rating structure. No experience rating or rate adjustment was utilized. However, because of resulting adverse selection, the original rating system was dropped, and premiums are now calculated in much the same way as those for policies from insurance companies.

Historically, Blue Cross/Blue Shield plans have offered very competitive, comprehensive medical expense plans. Recently, some Blue Cross/Blue Shield plans have faced financial difficulties, however. In the worst case thus far, Blue Cross/Blue Shield of West Virginia collapsed in 1990. Although a merger was negotiated by the state insurance commissioner, this insolvency left $53 million in unpaid medical bills. Many individuals insured under the West Virginia plan have been billed directly by hospitals and physicians for these unpaid claims and litigation continues over who will pay. Insolvent Blue Cross/Blue Shield plans are particularly distressing from the consumer's viewpoint because, generally, state guaranty funds that back claims against private insurers are not available to pay Blue Cross/Blue Shield claims. Therefore, before you enter a Blue Cross/Blue Shield plan be sure to check on (1) the financial strength of the Blue Cross/Blue Shield organization *in your geographic area* and (2) whether your Blue Cross/Blue Shield plan will be backed by a state guaranty fund.

INDIVIDUAL HEALTH COVERAGES

All of the coverages discussed previously (including disability income) can be purchased in the open market as *individual health insurance*. Existing group plan coverage can also be converted to an individual plan when a person leaves the group. Since individual insurance policies provide protection directly to policyholders and/or their families, individuals can tailor the coverage to their needs. In contrast, an individual under a group plan is entitled only to the benefits that are available in the master group plan. And although the protection afforded under many group plans is excellent, many families still need to supplement this coverage with an individual health plan. This situation is especially true with respect to the disability income insurance for upper-middle-income wage earners.

In contrast to group life insurance (which is not recommended as a basis for a life insurance plan—

see Chapter 9), group health insurance can serve as the foundation on which a family builds its individual health insurance program.

HEALTH-CARE PROVIDER GROUPS

The health insurance programs discussed previously are used in situations in which the person or organization from which you get the health-care services is separate from the insurer. The insurer pays the provider or reimburses you for expenses. A growing trend in health care is a type of plan under which subscribers/users contract with and make monthly payments to the organization *that provides the health-care service*. Insurance companies may not even be involved. Examples are health maintenance organizations (HMOs), individual practice associations (IPAs), and preferred provider organizations (PPOs).

Health Maintenance Organization. The original **health maintenance organization (HMO)** was started by Kaiser in Los Angeles in 1929. Today over 35 million people in the United States belong to HMOs, which is over 18 times as many members as in the early 1970s. The traditional HMO is often referred to as a *group HMO*, because a group of doctors who are employed by the HMO provide the health-care services from a central facility. These HMOs have developed primarily in larger cities. Usually the doctors and the hospital are in the same complex.

An HMO provides comprehensive health-care services to its members. The plan includes outpatient care, such as minor surgery, doctors' office visits, and X-ray and laboratory services; hospital inpatient care; surgery; maternity care; mental health care; and prescriptions. As a member of an HMO, you pay a monthly fee that varies according to the number of persons in your family. Also, you may pay $2 to $10 each time you use an outpatient service or need a prescribed drug. However, there are no other charges to worry about—there are no doctors' fees, X-ray charges, or other expenses to HMO members who use the facilities for their health-care needs.

The primary purpose of HMOs is to reduce the costs of health care, both by using resources more efficiently and by practicing "preventive medicine"—most HMOs provide physical exams and sponsor pro-health activities such as smoking clinics, exercise programs, and so on. The advantage to members is that they are not faced with exclusions, deductibles, coinsurance, or filing insurance claims. The primary disadvantage is that members are not always able to choose their physicians. Also, because group HMOs practice in central facilities, members should be sure to ask about the benefits provided if they should need care outside the geographic area of their HMOs.

Individual Practice Association. An **individual practice association (IPA)** is often considered to be little more than a variation of a standard HMO, because the financial and service arrangements are similar, with only the physical facility being different. As a member of an IPA, you prepay monthly and are entitled to a wide range of health-care services. However, the services are not provided from a central facility. Physicians operate out of their own offices and from community hospitals that provide services to IPA members as well as others. IPAs appeal to people who would like some choice of physician. They also serve to extend the advantages of an HMO into less populated regions where central facilities are not feasible.

Blue Cross/Blue Shield plans
Nonprofit prepaid expense plans providing for hospital and surgical medical services, rendered to plan participants by member hospitals and physicians, respectively.

health maintenance organization (HMO)
An organization consisting of hospitals, physicians, and other health care personnel who have joined together in a central facility to provide necessary health services to its subscribers.

individual practice association (IPA)
An organization similar to an HMO in financial and service arrangements but whose subscribers receive services from physicians operating out of their own offices and from community hospitals rather than from a central facility.

Preferred Provider Organization. A **preferred provider organization (PPO)** has characteristics of both an IPA and an insurance plan. It offers comprehensive health-care services to its subscribers within a network of physicians and hospitals. In addition, it provides insurance coverage for medical services not provided by the PPO network. You typically would have access to a PPO only through your employer. Your employer would negotiate for services from designated physicians and hospitals at a discount of 10 to 20 percent from usual charges. You will benefit from the lower price if you use those physicians and hospitals. The savings from the lower cost may be passed on to you by your employer in the form of additional benefits or a higher salary. An insurance company is often used in a PPO to negotiate with health-care providers and handle health-care expense payments.

The difference between a health maintenance organization (HMO) and a preferred provider organization (PPO) is that the HMO offers a wider range of choices of physicians, hospitals, and so forth.
Fantasy: One of the drawbacks of an HMO is that you must be treated at its central facility and by its own doctors. In a PPO, on the other hand, you can choose your health-care providers from a network of designated physicians and hospitals.

OTHER SOURCES OF HEALTH-CARE COVERAGE

Supplementing the traditional health payment plans are several other sources of funds or services. As discussed in Chapter 11, both homeowner's and automobile insurance policies contain limited amounts of medical expense protection. Homeowner's policies cover accidents that happen around the home to people who are visiting you (although not to members of the insured household). Automobile policies may cover you if you are involved in an automobile accident regardless of whether you are in a car, on foot, or on a bicycle. Further, if someone negligently injures you, you have legal grounds on which to collect from that person or his or her liability insurer.

In addition to social security, various other government programs help pay for medical expenses. Medical care is provided for people who have served in the armed services and were honorably discharged and for military personnel and their dependents. Public health programs exist to treat communicable diseases, handicapped children, and mental health disorders. In total, federal, state, and local governments now spend well over $300 billion a year on health-care expenses. When people — especially the elderly and low-income — suffer accident or illness, often a government program is available to help out.

A GUIDE TO BUYING HEALTH-CARE INSURANCE

The best way to buy health-care insurance is to match your insurance needs with the various types of coverage available. What types of coverage would best meet your current health-care insurance needs? Before reading on, spend a few moments relating available forms of health-care insurance to your needs.

We have now reached the point where we should address the matter of how to systematically plan your purchases of health-care insurance. In many ways, the approach here is similar to that proposed for life insurance programming in Chapter 9. The primary difference is that with health insurance you generally must consider a variety of both coverages and sources for your protection.

You should list your potential areas of loss; determine what types of coverages and other resources are available to you; and, to spot gaps in your present protection, subtract your coverages and resources from the amount of your potential losses. Once you have identified gaps in protection, you should structure a health-care plan that is best for you.

NEEDS

Most people need protection against two types of losses that can result from accident or injury: (1) expenses for medical bills, rehabilitation counseling, training and education, and, in some cases — such as loss of a homemaker — replacement services and (2) loss of income due to time spent away from work. The amount needed to pay medical expenses cannot be easily estimated, but in cases of long-term, serious illnesses, medical bills and related expenses can run into the hundreds of thousands of dollars. Thus, you should probably figure you face potential hospital, surgical, pharmaceutical, and other charges of at least $250,000 and, with a protracted disability, as high as $1 million. In contrast, the income need is relatively easy to calculate: it is simply a percentage of your (or your spouse's) current monthly earnings — most people believe that 60 or 75 percent is sufficient.

MATCHING NEEDS AND RESOURCES

In the next step of your health insurance purchase planning, you should match your present resources against your needs. Exhibit 10.9 should help you perform this task. It sets forth a checklist for the sources and types of coverages you might already have. Among these resources you should rely most on social security, present group coverages, Blue Cross/Blue Shield, individual coverages, savings, and employer wage continuation plans. The remaining sources of recovery are less significant for planning purposes, since they typically restrict payments to specified types of illnesses or accidents.

After you have identified your present coverages, you should examine them to learn what terms of payments and coverage apply. The key policy provisions that should most concern you will vary with the type of coverage — that is, medical expense, long-term care, or disability income plans. Use the previous discussions of provisions for each type of policy to evaluate your current coverage. If you find gaps for which you do not have adequate coverage or savings, you need to arrange ways in which to meet potential losses.

PREPARING A HEALTH-CARE PLAN

Throughout this chapter, we have emphasized the need for good health insurance protection to cover the costs of illness or accident. However, a good health-care plan encompasses much more than a means of financing medical expenses, replacement services, and lost income. It should also incorporate other means of risk reduction. Accordingly, recall from Chapter 9 that you can deal with risk in four ways: risk avoidance, loss prevention and control, risk assumption, and insurance. Although these four methods apply to all types of risks, each is especially useful in developing health-care plans.

Risk Avoidance. Risk avoidance means avoiding the exposure that creates potential for loss. For example, people who do not stand on the backs of chairs to reach into high places seldom fall off chairs; people who do not take illegal drugs never have to worry about disability from overdose; people who refuse to ride on motorcycles avoid the risk of injury from this relatively dangerous means of transportation; and people who do not smoke in bed will never doze off and start a fire in their house. Looking for ways to avoid exposure to loss is a good starting point for a health care plan.

Loss Prevention and Control. For many instances of illness or accident, risk avoidance is not applicable. This is when you can turn to loss prevention.

Illness. Steven Tiger, senior editor of *Hospital Physician*, has written, "The majority of [poor health] conditions treated by medical doctors are totally — and easily — preventable. The answer [to high health-care costs] is to encourage a wellness-oriented lifestyle, with individuals recognizing and

---

preferred provider organization (PPO)
A hybrid health-care provider that combines the characteristics of an IPA with an insurance plan to provide comprehensive health-care services to its subscribers within a network of physicians and hospitals.

EXHIBIT 10.9

A Checklist of Sources and Types of Coverage

Health-care coverage can be obtained from a variety of providers, each offering various types of coverage.

Social Security

Disability income
Medicare (medical expenses)
Medicaid (medical expenses)

Worker's Compensation

Disability income
Medical expenses
Rehabilitation
Lump sum

Group Health Plans

Hospital expenses
Surgical expenses
Physicians expenses
Major medical
Comprehensive major medical
Pharmaceuticals
Chiropractic, optometry, etc.
Dental
Mental illness
Rehabilitation
Long-term care

Blue Cross/Blue Shield

Hospital expenses
Surgical expenses
Physicians expenses
Other expenses

Existing Individual Resources

Present individual coverages
Family dependency
Savings

Wage Continuation Plan (Employer)

Sick leave
Short-term disability
Long-term disability

Other Plans

Homeowner's medical expenses
Auto medical expenses
Negligence claim
Veterans' medical benefits
Indian health services
Public health clinics (for
   example, communicable
   diseases, maternal and child
   health, migrant health
   expense)

---

accepting responsibility for their own well-being." Mr. Tiger believes that instead of self-reliance, "we slavishly worship high tech medical marvels that cost more and more." These assertions are backed up by life and health insurance company data as well as public health statistics showing that smoking, alcohol, and drug dependency, improper diet, inadequate sleep, and lack of regular, vigorous exercise contribute to more than 60 percent of all diagnosed illnesses. Heart disease, cancer, tuberculosis, and mental disorders all have been positively linked to these forms of self-abuse. In contrast, the odds are overwhelming that if you maintain a basic program for fitness, you will miss fewer days of work, spend less on medical bills, and live a healthier and happier life.

Accidents. The National Safety Council reports that more than one-half of all automobile accidents could be prevented if motorists followed highway safety laws. Topping the list of violations is driving under the influence of alcohol and drugs (DUI). This unnecessary exposure to loss accounts for about half of all automobile fatalities; specifically, alcohol abuse is a leading cause of injury and death among college students and other young persons. (This toll on youth has prompted most states to raise the minimum legal drinking age.)

Further, accident data overwhelmingly document the loss prevention effectiveness of safety belts, shoulder straps, and child passenger seats. Smoke alarms, bathtub safety mats, and proper storage of chemicals, pesticides, cleaning fluids, and prescription drugs also pose easy and effective measures for reducing loss frequency and severity. In sum, regardless of whether you are at home, school, work, or play — or traveling in between — you should integrate accident prevention measures into your health-care plans.

Risk Assumption. The next essential step in preparing a health-care plan involves considering the risks you are willing to retain. Some risks pose relatively small loss potential and therefore can be budgeted for. Of course, this is a primary reason to choose insurance coverages that include deductibles and waiting periods, as it is more economical to pay small losses from savings than to pay higher premiums to insure them. Similarly, although you are wise to buy policies with high limits, few people are willing to pay the premium for 100 percent reimbursement of all losses above the deductible. To increase insurance affordability, most assume part of the risk for large losses through participation or coinsurance, internal limits, and maximum aggregate limits. It is impossible to live in a world in which all of your risks are either avoided, prevented, or insured. Thus, before you buy health-care coverages — or, for that matter, any type of insurance coverage — you should explicitly identify the types and amounts of risk that you are willing and able to bear.

SHOPPING FOR HEALTH INSURANCE

We now return to the focus of this discussion. It is very important for you to recognize that a health-care plan should incorporate methods of risk avoidance, loss prevention and control, and risk assumption. However, our goal throughout this chapter has been to give you a systematic way to decide what health insurance (or other health-care financing plan — Blue Cross/Blue Shield, PPO, and so on) you should buy. To proceed, then, through this step of shopping for health insurance, you need to consider three items: (1) costs of coverage, (2) selecting health insurance as an employee benefit, and (3) quality of agent and company.

Costs of Coverage. In some ways, shopping for health insurance is like shopping for a car. Both are major purchases. It is likely that on a monthly basis, a family would spend as much for their medical insurance as they do on an auto loan payment. In addition, you would not simply compare, say, a major medical coverage from Blue Cross/Blue Shield to that of Prudential any more than you would blindly choose between a Chevrolet and a Ford. In each instance you need to size up competitive offerings on a feature-for-feature basis. (What size engines do the cars have? Does either have air conditioning, antilock brakes, a compact disc system, higher gas mileage, a longer warranty, or better styling?). Similarly, what provisions do available health insurance policies contain? What are their definitions of an accident? What exclusions apply? What persons and places are covered? What are the applicable deductibles, methods of payment, duration of benefits, and participation percentages? Big cost differences exist among health insurance coverages just as they do among different models of Chevrolets and Fords, but you can judge which is the best buy only after you have compared the costs of the coverages in relation to the features they offer.

Selecting Health Insurance as an Employer Benefit. As noted earlier, many people obtain health insurance coverage through their employer group. In some cases, the employer offers only one plan that it may pay entirely or partially. When this is the case, the employee should evaluate the plan's benefits and costs and decide whether to be part of the plan and whether additional private coverage is required to meet his or her needs.

The trend now, however, among medium and large employers is to offer employees a choice in fringe benefits (a cafeteria-style plan as discussed in the previous chapter). Many times the menu of benefits includes more than one health insurance option so the employee can choose among a major medical plan, an HMO, and perhaps an IPA in addition to choosing the amount of life insurance, disability insurance, and other benefits he or she might like. In a typical example, you could be given $350 a month to "spend" on any of the following fringe benefits for you and your family: several forms of health care coverage (major medical: $200 deductible, $425; $500 deductible, $345; HMO, $422; IPA, $480; dental insurance, $55); disability income coverage, $28; several life insurance options for employee only (term life: $75,000, $11; $150,000, $21; accidental death for $500,000, $15). In this case, your benefit dollars from your employer would cover the least expensive health care coverage. The cost of any additional coverage you choose would be deducted from your paycheck.

After reviewing the menu, you see that your employer is giving you enough ($350) to purchase the least expensive health insurance policy for your family. If you want more comprehensive "first-dollar" health care coverage and/or any of the other coverage (dental, disability, and life insurance), they will be paid by you through a deduction from your payroll check. Before making this decision, it is important that you review your insurance needs and carefully evaluate all the coverage being offered. Compare the cost of coverage through your employer with that offered through private policies. Generally health care coverage is much more reasonably priced through group coverage, but disability and life insurance may be less expensive through a private policy (especially for young workers). If your spouse is employed, then you should also evaluate his or her fringe benefit package before making any decisions. Also remember that the purpose of insurance is to protect yourself against the very large possible losses rather than to pay for relatively small expenses. Therefore, if your family depends on your income to live, don't select dental insurance *instead of* life and disability income coverage.

Quality of Agent and Company. As with all types of insurance, you should buy your health-care coverages from an agent who will listen to your needs and answer your questions with well thought out responses — not sales jargon and pressure — and from a company that is rated highly for financial soundness by at least two of the major rating agencies, as discussed in Chapter 9. Also, your health-care insurer should be known to settle claims fairly and promptly. You should avoid companies with narrow and unusual, legalistic claims practices. Friends with claims-settlement experience and the consumer division of your state's department of insurance regulation can help you learn about an insurer's record for service after a loss. You should be just as concerned about the financial soundness and claims service of your group insurance underwriters as you would be when purchasing a private health care policy.

The cost of coverage and the quality of the agent and insurance company are two important variables to consider when shopping for health-care insurance. *Fact:* Even with health-care insurance, it pays to shop around to get the best value for your money. However, you should use a knowledgeable agent that understands your needs and choose a high-rated company with good claims-settlement experience.

SUMMARY

- Health-care insurance coverage is essential because the potential amount of economic loss (from illness or injury) is so great; the rapidly rising health-care delivery costs today make adequate coverage increasingly important.
- The types of health-care coverage available include hospital insurance, surgical expense insurance, physicians' expense insurance (that covers the costs of nonsurgical procedures), and major medical policies (which cover catastrophic medical expenses). Some health insurers offer comprehensive major medical policies that combine basic hospital, surgical, and physicians' expense

coverage with a major medical plan to provide a packaged health-care protection policy, dental insurance, long-term care insurance (that covers out-of-hospital care for those with chronic illnesses), and disability income insurance (designed to replace wages lost due to illness or injury).
- The most important provisions in medical expense insurance policies pertain to terms of payment, terms of coverage, and cost containment.
- Policy provisions that govern how much your medical expense plan will pay include deductibles, coinsurance, internal limits, and coordina-

tion of benefits. The terms of coverage encompass the persons and places covered, cancelation, continuation of group coverage, rehabilitation, preexisting conditions, pregnancy, abortion, and mental illness. Some of the more common cost containment provisions are preadmission certification, continued stay review, second surgical opinion, caseworker assignment, and waiver of coinsurance.

■ Long-term care insurance is necessary to cover nonhospital expenses, such as nursing home care or home health care, that can be caused by chronic illness or frailty. Terms of payment provisions include daily benefits, benefit duration, waiting period, and inflation protection. The availability of coverage depends upon provisions addressing type of care, eligibility requirements, services covered, renewability, and preexisting conditions.

■ The loss of family income caused by the disability of a principal earner can be at least partially replaced by disability income insurance. Provisions pertaining to benefit amount and duration, waiting period, and cost-of-living adjustments represent the terms of payment. Important coverage terms include the definition of disability, probationary period, renewability, waiver of premium, and the guaranteed insurability option.

■ There are several important providers of health-care coverage, including social security (which provides both medical insurance and long-term disability insurance), worker's compensation (for job-related injuries), group health insurance programs, Blue Cross/Blue Shield (with hospital coverage by Blue Cross, and surgical and medical coverage by Blue Shield), and individual health insurance policies (that provide protection directly to policyholders and/or their families).

■ In addition to the traditional health-care insurance programs, a rapidly growing trend is for individuals/families to obtain health-care services directly from specific provider groups. Under these plans the subscribers/users contract with and make monthly payments to the organization that provides the health-care services. The most prevalent examples of these groups are health maintenance organizations (HMOs), individual practice associations (IPAs), and preferred provider organizations (PPOs).

■ From a health-care insurance perspective, most people need protection from two types of losses: (1) the cost of medical bills and other associated expenses and (2) loss of income due to time away from work. The best way to buy health-care insurance is to match your insurance needs with the various types of coverages available; in this respect, when shopping for health-care insurance, you should carefully consider the cost of coverage, as well as the quality of both the agent and the insurer.

QUESTIONS AND PROBLEMS

1. What factors have contributed to today's high costs of health care?
2. Differentiate between hospital and surgical expense insurance. Define and compare *service benefits* and *scheduled benefits* under surgical expense insurance.
3. What is major medical coverage? What are the common features of a major medical policy? What is comprehensive major medical insurance?
4. Briefly describe the key provisions of the Consolidated Omnibus Budget Reconciliation Act (COBRA) as they relate to continuation of group coverage when an employee voluntarily or involuntarily leaves the group.
5. Briefly describe the following policy provisions commonly found in medical expense insurance plans: (a) deductibles, (b) coinsurance, (c) coordination of benefits, and (d) preexisting conditions.
6. Explain the cost containment provisions now frequently found in medical expense policies. Why do insurers use the provision for second surgical opinions to save on medical costs?
7. Why should a consumer consider purchasing a long-term care insurance policy? Describe the

differences between long-term care policies with respect to (a) type of care, (b) eligibility requirements, and (c) services covered.

8. Describe a hospital income insurance plan. How does it differ from medical expense plans that offer hospital insurance?

9. What is disability income insurance? Explain the waiting period provisions found in such policies.

10. Describe the restrictive and liberal definitions used to establish whether or not an insured is disabled. Why is benefit duration an important consideration in shopping for disability income coverage?

11. What is the formal name used for social security? Briefly describe the health-care benefits provided under social security.

12. What is medicare? Explain the eligibility requirements and benefits provided by this plan.

13. What is the objective of worker's compensation insurance statutes? Explain (a) lump-sum payments and (b) second-injury funds as they relate to worker's compensation.

14. What is group health insurance? Differentiate between group health insurance and individual health insurance.

15. Discuss the basics of the Blue Cross/Blue Shield plans.

16. "Health maintenance organizations (HMOs) attempt to reduce the cost of health care to families and individuals through more efficient utilization of health-care personnel and facilities, and by practicing preventive medicine." Explain basically how these organizations work. Contrast HMOs with IPAs and PPOs.

17. Describe the procedures used to evaluate an individual's current health insurance coverages.

18. Briefly discuss the procedures for (a) determining health insurance needs, (b) matching needs and resources, and (c) preparing a health-care plan.

19. Describe the role played in the process of preparing a health-care plan of (a) risk avoidance, (b) loss prevention, and (c) risk assumption.

20. Describe the key considerations that must be addressed when shopping for health insurance relative to (a) costs of coverage and (b) quality of agent and insurance company.

C O N T E M P O R A R Y   C A S E   A P P L I C A T I O N S

10.1 Evaluating John's Health-Care Coverage

John Lannefeld was a self-employed window washer earning approximately $400 per week. One day, while cleaning windows on the eighth floor of the First National Bank Building, he tripped and fell from the scaffolding to the pavement below. He sustained severe multiple injuries but miraculously survived the accident. He was immediately rushed to Mt. Sinai Hospital for surgery. He remained there for 60 days of treatment, after which he was allowed to go home for further recuperation. During his hospital stay, he incurred the following expenses: surgeon, $2,500; physician, $1,000; hospital bill, room and board, $250 per day; nursing services, $1,200; anesthetics, $300; wheelchair rental, $70; ambulance, $60; and drugs, $350. John has a major medical policy with LIC Corporation that has a $3,000 deductible clause, an 80 percent coinsurance clause, internal limits of $180 per day on hospital room and board and $1,500 as a maximum surgical fee. The policy provides no disability income benefits.

Questions

1. Explain the policy provisions as they relate to deductibles, coinsurance, and internal limits.

2. How much should John recover from the insurance company? How much must he pay out of his pocket?

3. Would any other policies have offered John additional protection? What about his inability to work while recovering from his injury?

4. Based upon the information presented, how would you assess John's health insurance coverage? Explain.

10.2 Benito and Teresa Get a Handle on Their Disability Needs

Benito Fernandez and his wife, Teresa, have been married for two years and have a one-year-old son. They live in Detroit, where Benito is a supervisor for Ford Motor Company. He earns $2,200 per month, of which he takes home $1,580. As an employee of Ford, he and his family are entitled to receive the benefits provided by the company's group health insurance policy. In addition to major medical coverage, the policy provides a monthly disability benefit amounting to 20 percent of the employee's average monthly take-home pay for the most recent 12 months prior to incurring the disability. (Note: Benito's average monthly take-home pay for the most recent year is equal to his current monthly take-home pay.) In the instance of complete disability, Benito would also be eligible for social security payments of $700 per month.

Teresa is also employed. She earns $500 per month after taxes working part-time at a nearby grocery store. The store provides her with no benefits other than social security. In the event Benito became disabled, Teresa would continue to work at her part-time job. If she became disabled, social security would provide monthly income of $300. Benito and Teresa spend 90 percent of their combined take-home pay in order to meet their bills and provide for a variety of necessary items. They use the remaining 10 percent to fulfill their entertainment and savings goals.

Questions
1. How much, if any, additional disability income insurance does Benito require in order to insure adequate protection against his becoming completely disabled?
2. Does Teresa need any disability coverage? Explain.
3. What specific recommendations with respect to disability income insurance coverage would you give Benito and Teresa in order to provide adequate protection for themselves as well as their child?

FOR MORE INFORMATION

General Information Articles

"The Crisis in Health Insurance." *Consumer Reports*, August 1990, pp. 533–549, and September 1990, pp. 608–617.

"Gotcha! The Traps in Long-Term Care Insurance." *Consumer Reports*, June 1991, pp. 425–442.

Paulson, Morton C. "What If You Couldn't Work Anymore?" *Changing Times*, August 1990, pp. 53–56.

Schultz, Ellen E. "Disability Coverage? Well, I Have Some. . . ." *The Wall Street Journal*, April 12, 1990, pp. C1, C23.

Zinn, Laura. "Ouch! The Squeeze on Your Health Benefits." *Business Week*, November 20, 1989, pp. 110–122.

Government Documents and Other Publications

Berman, Henry S., and Rose, Louisa. *Choosing the Right Health Care Plan*. Mount Vernon, NY: Consumer's Union, 1990.

The Consumer's Guide to Disability Insurance. Washington, DC: Health Insurance Association of America, September 1991.

The Consumer's Guide to Long-Term Care Insurance. Washington, DC: Health Insurance Association of America, February 1991.

Reynolds, John D., and Bischoff, Robin N. *Health Insurance Answer Book*, 3d ed. (Greenvale, NY: Panel Publishers, 1991.

Williams, Stephen J., and Guerra, Sandra J. *Health Care Services in the 1990s: A Consumer's Guide*. New York: Praeger, 1991.

The rate of increase in health-care costs in the United States is causing employers to implement cost-saving measures in their health insurance plans and in many cases to shift the payment of increased premiums to the employee. As a result of this health-care crisis, there will probably be numerous suggestions for change debated in the halls of Congress during the decade of the 1990s including, but not limited to, some type of national health insurance. Whether you have an individual plan or a group plan, you need to keep up with the changes in health-care terms and provisions to ensure that you do not have duplicate or inadequate coverage.

Health-care coverage in the United Sates is currently provided by government agencies, private carriers, and various types of organizations. Under the Social Security Administration, health benefits are provided under medicare and through a disability income plan. Worker's compensation plans enacted by the various states provide medical, disabil-

If You Are Just Getting Started

As you begin your career, you should look very carefully at your total compensation from your employer. Total compensation includes your salary as well as your fringe benefits. Just because your employer says you are covered by health and disability policies does not mean that the coverage is complete or adequate. It is up to you to determine this.

In analyzing your health-care needs, you should consider your need for protection against two types of losses: (1) medical bills and/or rehabilitation and (2) loss of income. In order to match your needs with your benefits, you should look at the sources of coverage that you already have from Exhibit 10.9 and then analyzing the terms of payment and the terms of coverage of your policies. A checklist of policy features provided in Exhibit 10.5 will help you in this task. If in your review of your coverage you discover that your health insurance program does not have one or more of the features listed, you should arrange for ways to fill these potential gaps.

Remember, just because you may be young and in good health this does not mean you don't need health and disability insurance. Young people are more likely to have an accident resulting in a disability than they are to be killed in an accident or die of an illness.

Health-Care Coverage:

1. In order to lower your health-care premiums (assuming an individual policy), you could increase the deductible, coinsurance percentage, and the waiting period. You would want to use the premium savings to establish an emergency fund to cover this potential cost.

2. Determine how long your policy will pay benefits and how benefit payments are determined. You would want to know whether or not there are specific dollar amounts or payments limited to charges that are "reasonable and customary."

3. In a nonemergency situation, check in advance with your health-care provider to determine whether or not the procedure or treatment will be fully covered by your insurance and if not, how much you will have to pay.

4. You should understand the method of payment on your policy. The service approach method provides the best protection, but frequently has a higher cost.

5. If you leave the country you might not be covered by your health policy. This would mean you might need to purchase a supplemental policy for the duration of your travels.

6. You should choose a health insurance policy that is noncancelable and guaranteed renewable to at least age 65.

Disability Coverage:

1. To determine your need for the amount of disability income insurance, you must first determine your after-tax income (if the premiums are to be paid with after-tax dollars).

2. You should estimate benefits from social security, other government programs, and your employer and then subtract the amount from your income to determine if there is a shortfall. The estimate of disability income requirements can be made using Exhibit 10.5.

3. Be cautious when you consider social security disability benefits in your estimate. Usually benefits are paid if you are disabled for at least one year or you are expected to die.

4. You need to know how disability is defined in your policy. If it says "any occupation," then it might not pay if you can be employed at all. If it says your "own occupation," then you would receive benefits even if you could be employed in another capacity.

5. For planning purposes, you need to know the waiting periods before disability payments will begin and whether or not your employer will keep you on the payroll until this happens.

6. In order to reduce the cost of your private disability insurance, you should consider a longer waiting period and invest the premium savings.

ity income, lump-sum, and rehabilitation payments. In addition to the government programs coverage is provided by both group health and individual plans. A checklist of the sources and types of health-care coverage is provided in Exhibit 10.9.

Health care is essential in order to achieve your financial goals. If you were to have a serious illness or accident while uninsured, the costs could be devastating. Not only would you incur the costs of care, but you would probably experience a loss of income as well. As a result, you should not go without health insurance regardless of your age or current health, and you should have some type of disability income coverage.

There are two main factors that should be considered when you evaluate your health and disability coverage. You should first check for the adequacy of your coverage to determine if there are any gaps that need to be filled with additional insurance. Second, you need to make sure that your coverage is continuous. If you were to change jobs, you need to check the coverage of your new employer to see when it goes into effect. There may be a waiting period. If this is the case you might want to keep your old coverage until the waiting period ends. This is permissable under federal law (COBRA). Once your coverage is in place you should review it on a regular basis or whenever your marital or family status changes to ensure proper coverage. This will prevent any holes in your coverage and also the possibility of duplication of coverage.

If You Are Thirtysomething

Your health-care coverage requirements will normally change with age and your marital and family status. In many cases your employer may provide single coverage at no charge to you, but may require you to pay for family coverage. This sometimes poses a problem of overlapping coverage when the spouse also works. You should analyze the coverage and costs of both plans and, if allowed, opt for the more advantageous one and use the funds to purchase other coverage.

Disability income coverage for both spouses becomes more important as your financial obligations increase with the addition of mortgage payments and funding the education of your children. In analyzing your disability income needs, you should consider not only the cost of taking care of minor children but the possibility of additional costs of caring for a disabled spouse. You may find that just covering lost income is not enough and that you need additional coverage.

As you get older and approach retirement, you should also consider the purchase of long-term care insurance. This would provide you with the funds necessary to cover the costs of a nursing home, if needed. The number of companies offering these policies is increasing and the premiums are becoming more competitive as the companies' experience with these policies increases.

Health Insurance:

1. As your family size increases, you may want to look at the deductibles to see if they apply to each family member or just a total amount per year.

2. Once your children reach a certain age or are no longer full-time students, they may not be covered by your health insurance. Don't let their coverage lapse.

3. Consider adding a dental policy as a substitute for sav-

ings to be used to fund the costs of normal care of children's teeth and other expenses, such as braces.

4. See if your employer has a cafeteria plan with a health-care reimbursement account. This would allow you to pay for health-care expenses with pretax dollars.

5. If you have children in school who are eligible for a group health-care plan, analyze the cost and coverage of this relative to your plan and choose the best.

6. Avoid the purchase of specialty insurance, such as cancer policies, as you may already have adequate coverage in your existing plan.

Disability Insurance:

1. To save on your disability income insurance, you might want to consider a social security rider that lowers the amount the company must pay and, therefore, your costs.

2. Make sure your policy is noncancelable and provides for future insurability so that you can increase your coverage as your income grows.

3. Consider adding a cost-of-living adjustment to your policy to offset the effects of inflation.

4. You might want to increase the waiting period as you get older and accumulate more wealth. This would save on your premiums, which could then be invested.

5. As you approach retirement, you should consider reducing your coverage and eventually canceling it, as many policies will not pay beyond age 65 anyway.

6. If your funds available for insurance are limited, you might want to consider a disability definition of "any occupation," which will offset the payment by the insurance company by your earnings in another occupation.

CHAPTER 11

Protecting Your Property

Suppose a severe storm destroyed your house. Could you afford to replace it? Most people could not. To protect yourself from this and similar types of property loss, you need *property insurance*. Also, every day you face the risk of negligence. For example, you might be distraught over a personal problem and unintentionally run a red light, seriously injuring a pedestrian. Because the consequences of this and other potentially negligent acts can cause financial ruin, appropriate *liability insurance* is essential. Property and liability insurance should be as much a part of your personal financial plans as life and health insurance. Such coverage is needed to protect the assets you have already acquired and to ensure the achievement of your financial goals. In particular, property insurance is used to guard against catastrophic losses of real and personal property caused by perils such as fire, theft, vandalism, wind storms, and many other calamities. Liability insurance, in contrast, offers protection against the financial consequences that may arise from certain types of legal actions.

Although people spend a lot of money for insurance coverage, few really know what they are getting for their premium dollars. Even worse, the vast majority of people are totally unaware of any gaps, over-insurance, and underinsurance in their property and liability insurance programs. Since such inefficient and inadequate insurance protection is completely at odds with the objectives of personal financial planning, you should become familiar with the basics of property and liability insurance.

FINANCIAL *facts* OR *fantasies*

Are the following statements financial facts (true) or fantasies (false)?

Homeowner's insurance provides protection not only on the home itself but also on most of its contents.

If you rent an apartment, you don't need to worry about property insurance since your furniture and other personal belongings are already covered by the landlord's insurance policy.

Uninsured motorists coverage is available as part of most automobile insurance policies.

The type of car you drive really has very little to do with how much you will have to pay for automobile insurance.

As a rule, you must obtain an umbrella personal liability policy if you want liability coverage of $1 million or more.

Filing a property or liability claim is quick and easy to do: Just call your agent, supply a few basic details, and look for your check in a few days.

SOME BASIC INSURANCE PRINCIPLES

The effective use of property and liability insurance requires an understanding of the types of losses to which you are exposed and how to best cover them. Consider your present situation: What kinds of property losses are you exposed to at this point in your life? Do you think your exposure to loss will be any different in 10 or 15 years? Take a minute or two to think about these questions before reading on.

The basic principles of property and liability insurance pertain to types of exposure, criteria for an insurable exposure, the principle of indemnity, and coinsurance. Each of these is discussed in the following sections.

TYPES OF EXPOSURE

Most individuals face two basic types of exposure: physical loss of property and loss through liability.

Exposure to Property Loss. The vast majority of property insurance contracts define the property covered directly in the policy and name the perils (causes of loss) for which insurance proceeds will be available. Some property contracts do offer protection on a comprehensive basis, however, and limit coverage by excluding certain types of property and perils. These contracts impose two obligations on the property owner: (1) developing a complete inventory of the property in need of insurance coverage and (2) identifying the perils against which protection is desired.

Property inventory. Most people neither fully appreciate the value of all the property they own nor do they attempt to itemize their property for insurance purposes. Nevertheless, a *property inventory* should be prepared not only to help you select coverages but also to help you settle a claim if a loss occurs. All property insurance companies require you to show proof of loss when making a claim. Consequently, a prepared schedule of property owned, along with corresponding values at the time of in-

ventory, can serve as evidence to satisfy the company.

Ordinarily, a family has a home, household furnishings, clothing and personal accessories, lawn and garden equipment, and motor vehicles (intended for road use), all of which need to be insured. Fortunately, the majority of automobile and homeowner's insurance policies provide coverage for these types of belongings. Many families also own such items as motorboats and trailers, various types of off-road vehicles, business property and inventories, jewelry, stamp or coin collections, furs, musical instruments, important papers and documents, antiques, paintings, bonds and other securities, and items of special value, such as expensive cameras, golf clubs, electronic recording and playing equipment, or citizen-band radios. Coverage for these types of belongings often must be specially arranged with the insurer. In order to help policyholders prepare inventories, many property insurance companies have easy-to-complete personal property inventory forms available. A partial sample of one such form is shown in Exhibit 11.1. In addition, people can supplement inventory forms with photographs or videotapes of their belongings. For insurance purposes, a picture may truly be worth a thousand words. Regardless of whether the completed inventory forms are supplemented with photographs or videotapes, *every effort should be made to keep these documents in a safe place*, where they can't be destroyed—like a safe-deposit box. As added protection, you might even consider keeping a *duplicate copy* somewhere; for example, with a parent or trusted relative. Remember, you may need these photographs and inventories if something serious does happen and you have to come up with an authenticated list of property losses.

Identifying perils. Many people feel a false sense of security after buying insurance, because they believe that they are safeguarded against all contingencies. The fact is, however, that certain **perils** (defined as a cause of loss) cannot be reasonably insured against. For example, most homeowner's or automobile insurance policies limit or exclude coverage for flood, earthquake, mud slides, mysterious disappearance, war, nuclear radiation, and wear and tear. In addition property insurance contracts routinely limit coverage on the basis of location of the property, time of loss, persons involved, and the types of hazards to which the property is exposed. These limitations are explained further in subsequent sections of this chapter.

Liability Exposures.   Every day you face the risk that you might negligently cause property damage or bodily injury to someone else. For example, when golfing you might become impatient and tee off before the people in front of you are clearly out of range. If your ball struck one of them and you were found legally liable for that injury, a judgment ranging into the thousands, or in some cases millions, of dollars could be levied against you. Of course, a debt that size could force many families into financial ruin and even bankruptcy. Many different liability exposures are encountered every day. Driving a car, entertaining guests at home, and being careless in performing professional duties are some of the more common liability risks. However, even if you were never negligent and always prudent, you still would run the risk that someone might think that you were the cause of a loss and therefore bring a costly lawsuit against you.

Fortunately, *liability insurance* coverage is available to protect against losses resulting from each of these risks, *including the high legal fees required to defend yourself against suits that may or may not have merit*. But before discussing the methods available for insuring against liability exposures, let's look at the ways in which legal liability arises, as well as the defenses available for defeating claims.

Liability based on negligence.   Legal definitions of negligence and liability have evolved over hundreds of years of court decisions and enactments of statutes, and these definitions are expected to continue to be modifed as society's values change. In addition, specific rules of law vary not only over time but also in their interpretations depending on judges, juries, and locations throughout the country. Consequently, only a general overview of these concepts can be presented here.

A person is said to have performed a **negligent action** when his or her behavior has been inconsistent with the **reasonable person doctrine**. This doctrine holds that if a person fails to act in a reasonable manner—as would one with normal intelligence, perceptions, and experiences common to the community—that person is negligent. However, evidence that someone was negligent is only the first step in establishing liability. In addition, the defendant (the person accused of negligence) must be

proven to have had a duty toward the plaintiff (the accuser) and to have caused the plaintiff a compensable loss as a result of a breach of that duty. Further, it must be shown that (physical or financial) injury to a person or damage to property actually occurred. If any of these elements is missing, the defendant is relieved from legal liability. The defendant can also escape payment by the successful use of one of several defenses.

Defenses to a negligence action.   The two most common defenses to a charge of negligence are assumption of risk and contributory negligence. Under the **assumption of risk defense**, the allegation is that some action on the part of the plaintiff relieved the defendant of his or her duty to protect the plaintiff. For example, assume that Bill Putnam voiced his intent to try to cover a 15-mile stretch of highway in less than 10 minutes on his motorcycle. If Janice Morris asked to go with him on this daredevil ride, she may forgo any right to later collect from Bill should an accident occur due to his reckless behavior.

With a **contributory negligence defense**, the defendant maintains that the plaintiff contributed to

---

peril
A cause of loss.

negligent action
An action that is deemed inconsistent with the reasonable person doctrine.

reasonable person doctrine
A doctrine stating that if a person fails to act in a reasonable manner—as would someone with "normal" intelligence, perceptions, and experiences—he or she is guilty of negligence.

assumption of risk defense
A form of defense against a charge of negligence in which it is alleged that some action by the plaintiff relieved the defendant of his or her duty to protect the plaintiff.

contributory negligence defense
A form of defense against a negligence charge in which the defendant maintains that the plaintiff contributed to his or her own loss by personally acting in a negligent manner.

EXHIBIT 11.1

A Personal Property Inventory Form

Using a form like this will help you keep track of your personal property, including date of purchase, original price, and replacement cost. Note that this exhibit is only part of a 19-page homeowner's inventory record; this particular inventory record is put out by the *Personal Insurance Division of the Chubb Insurance Companies*, and includes not only household furnishings, but also clothing, electrical appliances, books and tools, electronic equipment, and various items of exceptional value, like china, antiques, fine art, jewelry, and so forth.

Living Room

Article	Qty.	Date Purchase	Purchase Price	Replacement Cost
Air Conditioners[3] (Window)				
Blinds/Shades				
Bookcases				
Books				
Cabinets				
Carpets/Rugs[1]				
Chairs				
Chests				
Clocks				
Couches/Sofas				
Curtains/Draperies				
Decks				
Fireplace Fixtures				
Hassocks				
Lamps/Lighting Fixtures				
Mirrors				
Musical Instruments				
Pictures/Paintings[1]				
Records/Tapes				
Planters				
Stereo Equipment[2]				
Tables				
Television Sets[2]				
Wall Units				
Other				
Other				
Other				

Living Room

Stereo System

Brand	
Model	
Serial #	Date Purchased
Purchase Price $	Replacement Cost $

Stereo Receiver/Tuner

Brand	
Model	
Serial #	Date Purchased
Purchase Price $	Replacement Cost $

Turntable

Brand	
Model	
Serial #	Date Purchased
Purchase Price $	Replacement Cost $

Cassette Deck

Brand	
Model	
Serial #	Date Purchased
Purchase Price $	Replacement Cost $

Compact Disc Player

Brand	
Model	
Serial #	Date Purchased
Purchase Price $	Replacement Cost $

Source: Homeowner's Inventory, Chubb Insurance Companies, Personal Insurance Division, Warren, NJ 07060.

his or her own loss by also acting in a negligent manner. This defense might be successful, for example, in a case in which motorist A failed to yield the right of way (a negligent act) and was struck by motorist B, who had the right of way but was speeding. If it could be shown that the accident would not have occurred had motorist B been in reasonable control of his or her vehicle, motorist B's claim against motorist A might be defeated. However, because of the potential harshness of the doctrine of contributory negligence, virtually every state in the union has enacted, or is in the process of enacting, **comparative negligence statutes**. Under this legislation, an attempt is made to allocate the loss to each party in proportion to the degree to which each contributed to the accident.

Note that the preceding discussion relates to the legal elements necessary for the successful defense against damages based on a negligent act. In practice, though, juries often make awards on the basis of their sympathy for the plaintiff rather than from the facts pertaining to the case. This is especially apparent when the defendant has substantial ability to pay — or, as plaintiffs' lawyers say, "Look for defendants with deep pockets."

CRITERIA FOR AN INSURABLE EXPOSURE

As noted in Chapter 9, insurance can be an effective way to deal with risk only when the following conditions are met: (1) There are a large number of household units with similar exposures to loss; (2) the loss covered is fortuitous, or accidental; (3) the cost is relatively low and measurable, and (4) losses are noncatastrophic. For certain types of property and liability exposures, such as medical malpractice, product liability, and automobile collision and liability, insurance is becoming less and less able to provide the necessary protection. This undesirable situation is developing because losses in these areas are increasing in both frequency and severity, thereby pushing premiums beyond the levels that many insured persons are willing or able to pay. In fact, over the past few years, property and liability insurers have lost billions of dollars through their underwriting activities. Therefore, unless these losses are reduced to tolerable levels, fewer and fewer types of risks will meet the criteria of an insurable exposure. While some people believe that letting the state or federal government establish insurance operations will solve the problem, such optimism is very likely unjustified. The fact of the matter is, unless losses are reduced, premiums will continue to increase regardless of whether private companies or the government administers the program.

PRINCIPLE OF INDEMNITY

The **principle of indemnity** states that the insured may not be compensated by the insurance company in an amount exceeding the economic loss. Most property and liability insurance contracts are based on this principle. Recall from Chapters 9 and 10 that life and health insurance contracts, in contrast, are *not* specifically contracts of indemnity. Four important concepts that are related to the principle of indemnity are found in property and liability insurance: (1) insurable interest, (2) actual cash value, (3) subrogation, and (4) other insurance.

Insurable Interest. The concept of **insurable interest** means that the individuals who insure property must stand to lose something if that property is subject to loss and that they cannot receive more in payment than their financial interest in the property. For example, assume that John and Mary own equal shares in an apartment house that has a

---

comparative negligence statutes
Laws existing in certain states under which losses to contesting parties in a lawsuit may be allocated to each party in proportion to the degree to which each contributed to the accident or loss in question.

principle of indemnity
An insurance principle stating that an insured may not be compensated by his or her insurer in an amount exceeding the amount of economic loss.

insurable interest
A concept stating that individuals who insure property must stand to lose something if that property is subject to loss and that they cannot receive more in compensation than the extent of their legal interest in the property.

market value of $200,000 (excluding the value of the land, which is uninsurable). If the building is destroyed, the maximum the insurer will pay to each partner is $100,000, since that is the extent of either party's economic interest in the property. If these partners sell the property but forget to cancel their insurance policy, and the property is subsequently destroyed by fire, the insurance company will pay them nothing (since they had no interest in the property at the time of loss).

Ownership, however, is not the only way someone can develop an insurable interest in a property. For instance, an owner of a dry cleaning operation has a legal obligation to return the clothing received in the normal course of business. If a fire damages the clothing, the proprietor may be liable to customers for the value of the damaged clothing. Thus, the proprietor, although not the owner of the clothing, does have a legal obligation to maintain the clothing in good condition and may obtain insurance that will provide protection against this type of loss.

Actual Cash Value. The principle of indemnity also *limits the amount an insured may collect to the actual cash value of the property*. **Actual cash value** is defined as replacement cost less physical depreciation, although some insurers do guarantee replacement cost without taking depreciation into account—for example, most homeowner's policies will settle building losses on a replacement basis if the proper type and amount of insurance is purchased. But since it is common practice in most other situations to deduct depreciation in order to obtain the actual cash value, only that is considered here. If an insured property is damaged, the insurer is obligated to pay no more than what the property would cost new today (its replacement cost) less depreciation from wear and tear. For example, assume that fire destroys two rooms of furniture that have a replacement cost of $5,000. The actual age of the furniture was six years, and it was estimated to have a useful life of ten years. Therefore, at the time of loss the furniture was subject to an assumed physical depreciation of 60 percent (6 years ÷ 10 years)—in this case, $3,000. Since the actual cash value is estimated at $2,000 ($5,000 replacement cost minus $3,000 depreciation), the maximum the insurer would have to pay is $2,000. Note that the original cost of the property has no bearing on the settlement.

Subrogation. After an insurance company pays a claim, its **right of subrogation** allows it to request reimbursement from the person who caused the loss or from that person's insurance company. For example, assume that you are in an automobile accident in which the other party damages your car. You may collect from your insurer or the at-fault party's insurer but not from both (at least not for the same loss). If you receive payment from your insurance company, you must subrogate (transfer) to it your right to sue the other person. Clearly, to collect the full amount from both parties would leave you better off after the loss than before it. Such an action would violate the principle of indemnity. An important by-product of the subrogation clause is that it makes the party who caused the accident (or loss) ultimately responsible for paying the damages. In this way, the *insurance company* can go after the responsible party to collect its loss (the amount it paid out to you); and best of all, it's not your problem.

Other Insurance. Nearly all property and liability insurance contracts have an *other-insurance clause*, which also supports the concept of indemnity. This provision prohibits insured persons from insuring their property with two or more insurance companies and then collecting in full for a loss from all companies. The other-insurance clause normally states that if a person has more than one insurance policy on a property, each company is liable for only a pro rata amount of the loss based on its proportion of the total insurance covering the property. For example, assume that John and Mary in the earlier example purchased two policies of $200,000 each on their $200,000 building. If a total loss occurred, each company would pay 50 percent, because the ratio of the coverage purchased from each company to the total coverage on the property is one-half ($200,000/$400,000). Similarly, if each of *three* companies had issued a $200,000 policy, their individual shares would be one-third ($200,000/$600,000). Without this provision, insured persons could use duplicate property insurance policies to profit from their losses. In liability insurance policies, the other-insurance clause usually provides that if two (or more) policies cover the same exposure, only one of them will provide coverage until its limits are used up, after which the other will provide coverage above that amount up to no more than the amount of the allowable loss.

COINSURANCE

Coinsurance, a provision commonly found in property insurance contracts, requires policyholders to buy insurance in an amount equal to a specified percentage of the replacement value of their property, and, if that's not done, then the *policyholder* is required to pay for a proportional share of the losses. In essence, the coinsurance provision stipulates that if the property isn't properly covered, the property owner will become the "coinsurer" and bear part of the loss. If the stipulated amount of coverage (usually 80 percent of the value of the property) is obtained, then the policyholder will be reimbursed for covered losses dollar for dollar up to the amount of the policy limits. Otherwise, payment will be based on a specified percentage of loss. For example, assume that John and Mary's fire policy on their $200,000 apartment building contained an 80 percent coinsurance clause. This means that the policy limits must equal or exceed 80 percent of the value of their building. Further assume that they had run short of money and decided to save by buying a single $120,000 policy instead of a minimum of $160,000 (80% × $200,000) as required by the coinsurance clause. If a loss of any amount occurred, the company would be obligated to pay only 75 percent ($120,000/$160,000) of it up to the amount of the policy limit. Thus, on damages of $40,000, the insurer would pay only $30,000 (75% × $40,000). Obviously, it is important that you closely evaluate the coinsurance clause of any property insurance policy in order to make sure that you will not have an unexpected additional burden in the event a loss does take place.

HOMEOWNER'S INSURANCE

Because your home is likely to be your biggest (and most expensive) possession, every effort should be taken to make sure that it's adequately insured. What kinds of protection should you look for when insuring a home? Would you want the same protection if you were renting rather than buying a home? Give some thought to these questions before going on.

Although homeowner's insurance is often thought of as a single type of isurance policy, four different forms (HO-1, HO-2, HO-3, and HO-8) are actually available to homeowners, and two other forms (HO-4 and HO-6) are designed to meet the needs of renters and owners of condominiums (see Exhibit 11.2). An HO-4 renter's policy offers essentially the same broad protection as an HO-2 homeowner's policy, except that the coverage does not apply to the rented dwelling unit because tenants usually do not have a financial interest in the real property. All HO forms are divided into two sections. Section I applies to the dwelling, its contents, and accompanying structures; Section II deals with comprehensive coverage for personal liability and for medical payments to others. The forms differ in that the scope of coverage under Section I is least with an HO-1 policy and greatest with an HO-3 policy. HO-8 is a modified coverage policy for older homes. It is used by homeowners to insure houses that have market values well below their costs to rebuild. The coverage in Section II is the same for all forms.

In the following paragraphs, the important features of homeowner's forms HO-2 and HO-3 are emphasized because these are the most frequently sold policies. The coverage offered under these forms is basically the same; the differences lie only in the number of perils against which protection applies.

PERILS COVERED

As mentioned previously, a peril is defined as a cause of loss. Some property and liability insurance agreements, called *comprehensive* policies, cover all

actual cash value
A value assigned to an insured property that is determined by subtracting depreciation from replacement cost.

right of subrogation
The right of an insurer who has paid a claim to request reimbursement from the person who caused the loss or that person's insurer.

coinsurance
In property insurance, a provision that requires a policyholder to buy insurance in an amount equal to a specified percentage of the value of their property, including improvements.

EXHIBIT 11.2

A Guide to Homeowner's Policies

The amount of insurance coverage you receive depends on the type of homeowner's (HO) policy you select. Insurance coverage can also be obtained for those who live in *rental units* (HO-4) or who own units in a *condominium* (HO-6).

Coverage	HO-1 (Basic Form)	HO-2 (Broad Form)	HO-3 (Special Form)
		Section I Coverages	
A. Dwelling	$15,000 minimum	$15,000 minimum	$20,000 minimum
B. Other structures	10% of A	10% of A	10% of A
C. Personal property	50% of A	50% of A	50% of A
D. Loss of use	10% of A	20% of A	20% of A
Covered perils	Fire or lightning Windstorms (including tornados) or hail Explosion Riot or civil commotion Aircraft Vehicles Smoke Vandalism or malicious mischief Theft Breakage of glass or safety glazing material (limit of $100) Volcanic eruption	Fire or lightning Windstorms (including tornados) or hail Explosion Riot or civil commotion Aircraft Vehicles Smoke Vandalism or malicious mischief Theft Breakage of glass or safety glazing material Falling objects Weight of ice, snow, or sleet Accidental discharge or overflow of water or stream Sudden and accidental tearing, cracking, burning, or bulging of a steam, hot water, air conditioning, or automatic fire protective sprinkler system, or appliance for heating water Freezing Sudden and accidental damage for artificially generated electrical current Volcanic eruption	Dwelling and other structures covered against risks of direct physical loss to property except losses specifically excluded Personal property covered by same perils as HO-2 plus damage by glass or safety glazing material, which is part of a building, storm door, or storm window
		Section II Coverages (Minimums)	
E. Personal liability	$100,000	$100,000	$100,000
F. Medical payments to others	$1,000 per person	$1,000 per person	$1,000 per person

perils except those specifically excluded, while others name the perils covered individually. The latter type is called a **named peril policy**.

Section I Perils. The perils against which the home and its contents are insured are shown in Ex-

hibit 11.2. The coverage on household belongings is the same for the HO-2 and HO-3 forms, but coverage on the house and other structures (for example, a detached garage) is comprehensive under HO-3 and named peril in HO-2. Whether homeowners should buy an HO-2 or an HO-3 form depends pri-

HO-4 (Renter's — Contents, Broad Form)	HO-6 (Condominium Unit Owner's)	HO-8 (Older House Form)
Section I Coverages		
Not applicable Not applicable $6,000 minimum 20% of C	$1,000 minimum Not applicable $6,000 minimum 40% of C	Same as HO-1, except losses are paid based on the amount required to repair or replace the property using common construction materials and methods.
Same perils as HO-2 for personal property	Same perils as HO-2 for personal property	Same perils as HO-1, except theft coverage applies only to losses on the residence premises up to a maximum of $1,000; certain other coverage restrictions also apply.
Section II Coverages (Minimums)		
$100,000	$100,000	$100,000
$1,000 per person	$1,000 per person	$1,000 per person

marily on the amount they are willing to spend to secure additional protection. In some states, the premium differential is small, making an HO-3 policy the better buy. In other states, the HO-2 form has a substantially lower premium. Also, the size of the premiums for the HO-2 and HO-3 policies can differ

named peril policy

An insurance policy that names the perils covered individually.

substantially among insurance companies. Because of its more limited coverage, the purchase of an HO-1 is not recommended. (A special note on the HO-8 is presented later.)

Note in Exhibit 11.2 that the types of Section I perils covered includes just about everything from fire and explosions to lightning and wind damage, to theft and vandalism; unfortunately, these are all perils to which any homeowner is exposed. While the list of perils is quite extensive, there are a couple of types that are specifically excluded from most homeowner's contracts — in particular, *most policies (even HO-2 and HO-3 forms) exclude earthquakes and floods.* A major reason for this, of course, is the catastrophic nature of such events — that is, they can, and often do, cause widespread and very costly damage! In addition, many areas of the country simply are not susceptible to earthquakes and/or floods, and as a result, homeowners in those areas shouldn't have to pay for coverage they don't need. But even if you live in an area where the risk of an earthquake or flood is relatively high, you'll find your *standard homeowner's policy does not provide protection against these perils.* Fortunately, as we'll see later in this chapter, coverage for earthquakes and/or floods is available, but it's provided under a separate policy. Thus, if you live in an area where you need such coverage, you'll have to obtain it through some form of a rider or supplemental policy.

Section II Perils. The perils insured against under Section II of the homeowner's contract are the (alleged) negligence of an insured. As discussed earlier in this chapter, negligence is defined as failure to act in a reasonable manner. The coverage is called *comprehensive personal liability coverage,* because it offers protection against nearly any source of liability (major exclusions are noted later) resulting from negligence. It does not insure against other losses for which one may become liable, such as libel, slander, defamation of character, and contractual or intentional wrongdoings. For example, coverage would apply if you carelessly, but unintentionally, knocked someone down your stairs. If you purposely struck and injured another person, however, or harmed someone's reputation either orally or in writing, the homeowner's liability coverage would not protect you. An additional feature of Section II is the limited amount of medical coverage of persons other than the homeowner's family in certain types of minor accidents on or off the insured's premises. The basic purpose of this coverage is to help homeowners meet their moral obligations and also to help deter possible lawsuits. The limited medical payment coverage pays irrespective of negligence or fault.

PROPERTY COVERED

The homeowner's policy offers property protection under Section I for the dwelling unit, accompanying structures, and the personal property of homeowners and their families. Coverage for certain types of losses also applies to lawns, trees, plants, and shrubs. However, structures on the premises used for business purposes (except incidentally) are excluded from coverage, as are animals (pets or otherwise) and motorized vehicles not used in the maintenance of the premises. This latter exclusion means there is no coverage for motorcycles, autos, golf carts, or snowmobiles (an exception is small boats). Further, business inventory (goods held by an insured who is a traveling salesperson or other goods held for sale) is not covered. Even though business inventory is excluded, business property (such as books, typewriters, working materials, and microcomputers) is covered, up to a maximum of $2,500, while it is on the insured premises.

Also, as we will see later in this chapter, there are *limits* to the types and amounts of coverages provided. As a result, your homeowner's policy may offer less protection than is necessary for many expensive items of personal property. To overcome this deficiency, insurers have developed the **personal property floater (PPF) policy**, which provides either blanket or scheduled coverage of such items. Essentially, *a PPF policy extends protection to items that are otherwise slighted in a standard homeowner's policy.*

Homeowner's insurance provides protection not only on the home itself but also on most of its contents.

Fact: Homeowner's insurance covers the home itself and most of the contents in the home, including furniture, stereos and TVs, and clothing. On the other hand, cars, motorcycles, golf carts, and so on usually are not covered under a homeowner's policy.

RENTER'S INSURANCE: DON'T MOVE IN WITHOUT IT

If you live in an apartment (or some other type of rental unit), you should be aware that while the building you live in very likely is fully insured, *your furnishings and other personal belongings are not.* Rather, as a renter (or even as the owner of a condominium unit), you need a special type of HO policy in order to obtain insurance coverage on your possessions. Consider, for example, the predicament of Lois Weaver. She never got around to insuring her personal possessions in the apartment she rented in Denver. One wintry night, a water pipe ruptured, and escaping water damaged her furniture, rugs, and other belongings. When the building owner refused to pay for the loss, Ms. Weaver hauled him into court—and lost. How could she have lost? Simple: *Unless a landlord can be proven negligent*—and this one wasn't—*he or she isn't responsible for a tenant's property.* The moral of this story is clear—once you've accumulated a good deal of personal belongings (from clothing and home furnishings to stereo equipment, VCRs, and TVs), you'd better make sure they are covered by insurance, even if you're only renting a place to live! Otherwise you risk the loss of everything you own. Apparently a lot of tenants don't realize that, as surveys show most of them are without insurance. And that's unfortunate, since insurance for tenants, or renters, is available at very reasonable rates. It's simply a scaled-down version of homeowner's insurance, wherein the contents of a house, apartment or cooperative unit are covered, but not the structure and grounds.

The policy is called Renter's Form HO-4. For owners of condominium units, there's one called HO-6; it's similar but includes a minimum of $1,000 in protection for any building alterations, additions, and decorations paid for by the policyholder. Both the HO-4 and HO-6 policies include liability coverage. Like regular homeowner's insurance, they protect you at home and away. For example, if somebody is injured and sues you, the policy would pay for damages up to a specified limit, generally $100,000, although some insurers go as high as $500,000. A tenant who doesn't want this protection could probably save some money by buying a personal property policy instead.

A standard renter's policy covers furniture, carpets, appliances, clothing, and most other personal items for their cash value at the time of loss. The cost of renter's insurance isn't high: Expect to pay $80 to $100 a year for about $8,000 in coverage, depending on where you live. For maximum protection, you can buy *replacement cost insurance* (discussed again later in this chapter), which pays the actual cost of replacing articles with comparable ones—though some policies limit the payout to four times the cash value. You'll pay more for this, naturally—perhaps as little as another 10 percent, or perhaps much more, depending on the insurer. Also, the standard tenants policy provides only limited coverage of such valuables as jewelry, furs and silverware. Coverage varies, although some insurers now pay up to $1,000 for the loss of watches, gems and furs, and up to $2,500 for silverware. For larger amounts, you need a separate policy or a supplement, called a *personal property floater*, as discussed earlier.

Renter's insurance pays for losses caused by fire or lightning, windstorms, hail, theft, civil commotion, aircraft, vehicles, smoke, vandalism and malicious mischief, falling objects, building collapse, and the weight of ice and snow. Certain damages caused by water, steam, electricity, appliances, and frozen pipes are covered as well. If your residence can't be occupied because of damage from any of those perils, the insurance will pay for any increase in living expenses resulting from, say, staying at a hotel and eating in restaurants. The liability coverage pays for damages and legal costs arising from injuries or damage caused by you, a member of your family or a pet, on or off your premises.

If you rent an apartment, you don't need to worry about property insurance since your furniture and other personal belongings are already covered by the landlord's insurance policy.
Fantasy: If you rent and do not have some sort of insurance coverage on your furniture and other personal property, your possessions are uninsured and could be lost! Your landlord is liable only if you can prove that your loss was due to his or her negligence.

---

personal property floater (PPF) policy
An insurance policy that provides coverage to expensive personal property not otherwise covered in a standard homeowner's policy.

TYPES OF LOSSES COVERED

A person can suffer three different types of property-related losses when misfortune occurs: (1) the direct loss of property, (2) an indirect loss that occurs due to the loss of damaged property, and (3) extra expenses resulting from direct and indirect losses. The homeowner's insurance contract offers compensation for each of these types of loss.

Section I Coverage.   When a house is damaged by an insured peril, the insurance company will pay reasonable living expenses that a family might incur while the home is being repaired. Also, in many instances the insurer will pay for damages caused by perils other than those mentioned in the policy if a named peril is determined to have been the underlying cause of the loss. Assume, for instance, that lightning (a covered peril) strikes a house while a family is away and knocks out all the power, which causes $400 worth of food in the freezer and refrigerator to spoil. The company will pay for the loss even though temperature change (the direct cause) is not mentioned in the policy.

Section II Coverage.   In addition to paying successfully pursued liability claims against an insured, the homeowner's policy includes coverage for (1) the cost of defending the insured, (2) any reasonable expenses incurred by an insured in helping the company's defense, and (3) the payment of court costs. Since these three types of costs apply even in cases in which the liability suit is without merit, coverage in these areas is an added benefit that can save you thousands of dollars in attorney fees.

PERSONS COVERED

The homeowner's policy covers the persons named in the policy and the members of their families who are residents of the household. A person can be a resident of the household even while temporarily living away from home. For example, college students who live at school part of the year and at home during vacations are normally regarded as household residents. As such, their belongings (things like stereo equipment, TVs, personal computers, and microwave ovens) usually are covered by their parents' homeowner's policy, even though they may have them at school. But there could be limits and excep-

tions to the coverage, so check the policy to make sure what is and is not covered (for example, some companies may consider a student living off-campus to be independent and therefore ineligible for coverage under their parents' insurance).

The standard homeowner's contract also extends limited coverage to guests of the insured for property losses that occur at the insured house if the insured wants such coverage to apply. If the insured does not choose to file a claim for the guest's property loss, the guest will be reimbursed only if he or she can prove negligence on the part of the homeowner. If the home is financed, coverage for loss to the house will also apply to the mortgage lender, provided that the lender is named in the insurance policy.

LOCATIONS COVERED

While some insurance contracts have territorial exclusions, homeowner's policies offer coverage worldwide. Consequently, an insured's personal property is *fully covered* regardless of whether it is loaned to the next-door neighbor or kept in a hotel room in Outer Mongolia. The only exception is property left at a second home, such as a beach house or resort condominium — in which case, coverage is reduced to 10 percent of the policy limit, except while the insured is actually residing there. Homeowners and their families have liability protection for their negligent acts wherever they occur. This liability protection, however, does not include negligent acts involving certain types of motorized vehicles (like large boats and aircraft), or arising in the course of employment or professional practice. It does include golf carts (when used for golfing purposes) and recreational vehicles such as snowmobiles and minibikes, provided they are used on the insured premises.

LIMITATION ON PAYMENT

The insurable interest, actual cash value, subrogation, and other insurance features that restrict the amount paid under a property and liability insurance contract have already been described. In addition to these features, replacement cost, policy limits, and deductibles can also influence the amount an insurance company will pay for a loss.

Replacement Cost. The amount necessary to repair, rebuild, or replace an asset at today's prices is the **replacement cost**. The homeowner's coverage on a house and the accompanying structures is based on replacement cost coverage. This means that the insurer will repair or replace damaged items without taking any deductions for depreciation. Here is an illustration of a replacement cost calculation for a 2,400-square-foot home with a two-car garage:

Dwelling: 2,400 sq. ft. at $62 per sq. ft.	$148,800
Extra features: built-in appliances, mahogany cabinets, 3 ceiling fans	8,600
Porches, patios: back screened and trellised patio	2,700
Two-car garage: 900 sq. ft. at $24 per sq. ft.	21,600
Other site improvements: driveway, storage, landscaping	4,700
Total replacement cost	$186,400

The $186,400 represents the amount of money it would take *today* to fully replace the home in question. Keep in mind, however, that *in order for homeowners to be eligible for reimbursement on a replacement-cost basis, they must keep their homes insured for at least 80 percent of the amount it would cost to build them today exclusive of the value of the land*. In periods of inflation, homeowners must either increase their coverage limits on the dwelling unit every year or take a chance on falling below the 80 percent requirement. Alternatively, for a nominal cost, homeowners can purchase an *inflation protection rider*, whereby the amount of coverage is automatically adjusted for the effects of inflation. In essence, such a rider is used to continuously modify the coverage limits (replacement costs) of the home in keeping with prevailing inflation rates. At the same time, an inflation protection rider basically eliminates the chance of a coinsurance penalty. That is, if the 80 percent condition (referred to earlier) is not met, then the coinsurance penalty will kick in, in which case, the maximum compensation allowable for total or partial losses may be determined on an actual cash value basis.

Contrary to popular opinion, actual cash value and replacement cost need not bear any relationship to a home's market value. Because replacement cost and actual cash value relate only to the physical structure and do not consider the influence of location, a home's market value can be in excess of its replacement cost or below its actual cash value. Also, even if a home is in an excellent state of repair, its market value may be lessened because of functional obsolescence within the structure. In fact, the HO-8 homeowner's form was adopted in partial response to this problem. In many older neighborhoods, a 2,200-square-foot home might have a market value, excluding land, of, say, $60,000; the replacement cost, though, might be $160,000. Thus, to get good protection, a homeowner would have to buy a policy with limits of $128,000 (.80 × $160,000). This is expensive to the homeowner and creates moral hazard to the insurer. With the HO-8 policy, however, homeowners generally can get their property repaired in full up to the amount of their loss or up to the property's market value, whichever is less. This reduced limit saves the insured's premiums and reduces the risk that people will burn their houses down to make money on the insurance proceeds.

Although coverage on a house is often on a *replacement-cost basis*, standard coverage on the contents may be on an *actual cash value basis*. Therefore, depreciation is taken into account in calculating the amount of any payments made for losses to furniture, clothing, and other belongings. The depreciation amount is subtracted from the *current replacement cost* of the items—not from what may have been paid for the property several years ago. Thus, it is possible to collect more in insurance than the property's original price if the rate of inflation has exceeded the rate of depreciation.

Recently, many insurers have begun offering, for a slight increase in premium, replacement-cost coverage on contents. It seems likely that in the future the standard coverage on contents will become replacement cost rather than actual cash value. Because the additional premium required to buy replacement-cost coverage is generally small, you should seriously consider this option—as well as an inflation protection rider on the dwelling—when buying homeowner's insurance.

---

replacement cost

The amount necessary to repair, rebuild, or replace an asset at today's prices.

Policy Limits. In Section I of the homeowner's policy, the amount of coverage on the dwelling unit (coverage A) establishes the amounts applicable to the accompanying structures (coverage B), the unscheduled personal property (coverage C), and the temporary living expenses (coverage D). Generally, the limits under coverages B, C, and D are 10, 50, and 10 to 20 percent, respectively, of the amount of coverage under A (see Exhibit 11.2). For example, if the house were insured for $150,000, the limits for coverages B, C, and D would be $15,000, $75,000, and $30,000, respectively (that is, 10% × $150,000; 50% × $150,000; and 20% × $150,000). Each of these limits can be increased if insufficient to cover the exposure. Also, for a small reduction in premium, some companies will permit a homeowner to reduce coverage on unscheduled personal property to 40 percent of the amount on the dwelling unit.

Remember that homeowner's policies usually specify internal limits for certain types of personal property as included under the coverage C category. These coverage limits are within the total dollar amount of coverage C, and they in no way act to increase that total. The limited dollar coverages for each reported loss are as follows:

From any covered peril

1. $200 on money, bank notes, bullion, gold other than goldware, silver other than silverware, platinum, coins, and medals
2. $1,000 on securities, accounts, deeds, evidences of debt, letters of credit, notes other than bank notes, manuscripts, passports, tickets, and stamps
3. $1,000 on watercraft, including their trailers, furnishings, equipment, and outboard motors
4. $1,000 on trailers not used with watercraft
5. $1,000 on grave markers

From theft only

6. $1,000 for loss by theft of jewelry, watches, furs, and precious and semiprecious stones
7. $2,000 for loss by theft of firearms
8. $2,500 for loss by theft of silverware, silver-plated ware, goldware, gold-plated ware, and pewterware; includes flatware, hollowware, tea sets, trays, and trophies made of or including silver, gold, or pewter

In Section II, the standard liability limit (coverage E) is $100,000, and the medical payments portion (coverage F) normally has a limit of $1,000 per person. Additional coverages included in Section II consist of claim expenses such as court costs and attorney fees, first aid and medical expenses, including ambulance costs, and damage to others' property of up to $500 per occurrence.

Although these limits are the ones most commonly sold, most homeowners need additional protection, especially liability coverage. In these days of high damage awards by juries, a $100,000 liability limit may not be adequate—in fact, a greater amount is advisable for persons with higher incomes and net worths. The liability limit with most companies can be increased for only a nominal cost. For example, the annual premium difference between a $100,000 personal liability limit and a $300,000 limit is likely to be only $40 to $50!

Deductibles. Each of the preceding limits on recovery constrains the maximum amount payable under the policy. In contrast, *deductibles* place constraints on what a company must pay for small losses. *Deductibles help reduce insurance premiums*, because they do away with the frequent small loss claims that are proportionately more expensive to administer. The standard deductible in most states is $250 on the physical damage protection provided in Section I. However, deductible amounts of $500 or $1,000 are available on an optional basis. The premium savings on policies with larger deductibles are often significant. For example, in some states an increase in the deductible from $250 to $500 results in an annual premium savings of $40 to $75, depending on the amount of coverage purchased. Homeowners should check with their insurance agents to see whether it is feasible to increase the deductible. Deductibles do not apply to the liability and medical payments coverage, since insurers want to be notified of all claims, no matter how trivial. If companies did not set this procedure, they could in some cases be notified too late to properly investigate and prepare adequate defenses for resulting lawsuits.

HOMEOWNER'S PREMIUMS

Perhaps it might be useful at this point to bring together the previous comments concerning the premiums on homeowner's insurance policies. Generally speaking, a homeowner's contract form is selected by the insured, and it usually provides physical damage coverage on the dwelling up to at least 80 percent of the cost to rebuild at today's prices. With the amount of coverage on the dwelling set, basic amounts of coverage apply to the other structures on the site, personal property, and loss of use. As you will recall, these other coverages are stated as a percentage of the amount of protection placed on the dwelling unit. As a standard provision, each of these property damage coverages is subject to a $250 deductible. Also included in the homeowner's policy are basic amounts of protection for liability losses ($100,000), medical payments to others ($1,000), and additional coverages, such as damage to property of others ($500). For this basic package of protection, an insurer will quote a premium.

As we have discussed, most people need to modify this basic package of coverages. Some will want to add an inflation rider and increase the coverage on their homes to 100 percent of the replacement cost. Also, changing the contents protection from actual cash value to replacement cost and scheduling some items of expensive personal property may be desirable. Most insurance professionals also advise homeowners to increase their liability and medical payments limits. Each of these changes will result in an additional premium charge.

At the same time, you may want to try to *reduce* your total premium by increasing the amount of your deductible, as discussed earlier. Since it is better to budget rather than insure small losses, larger deductibles are becoming more popular. In sum, recognize that although the homeowner's policy is good protection for some people, most homeowners (and tenants) will need to modify the basic coverages offered. Thus, when you compare premiums among insurers, make sure the premiums quoted reflect the same additions to and subtractions from the standard coverages, limits, and deductible.

AUTOMOBILE INSURANCE

Probably no asset involves more exposure to loss than the automobile. Stop for a moment to consider why it's so important to have adequate insurance coverage on your car. What are some of the different types of exposure to loss you face when you get behind the wheel of a car?

Another asset that provides major exposure to loss is the automobile. Damage to this asset as well as negligence in its use can result in significant losses. As can be seen from Exhibit 11.3, U.S. motor vehicle accidents accounted for nearly 46,000 deaths, 1.7 million disabling injuries, and economic loss of some $89 billion in 1990. In addition, indirect monetary losses to society result from police and legal costs, as well as from the lost productive capacity of capital and human resources. Fortunately, from the standpoint of the individual, a big part of these costs can be protected against through insurance.

The major features of automobile insurance are discussed in the next several sections of this chapter. In the first of these sections, the coverages of a typical private passenger automobile policy are discussed. However, a number of states have legislatively provided for the modification of automobile insurance coverages through no-fault insurance. Therefore, following the section on the automobile policy is an explanation of how no-fault laws typically affect reimbursement for losses caused by automobile accidents. Next, auto insurance premiums and financial responsibility laws are discussed.

INSURANCE COVERAGE

For years, individuals and families insured their automobiles by purchasing a *family automobile policy (FAP)*. Many considered the legal terms and other language used in this policy to be too difficult for the typical insurance buyer to understand. As a result, in the late 1970s an "easy-to-read" automobile insurance policy was developed by insurers — the **personal auto policy (PAP)**. An example of the personal nature of this policy is that the named insured is referred to as "you" and "your" and the insurer as "we" and "our." The PAP is made up of six parts; the first four identify the coverages provided in the policy and are as follows:

---

personal auto policy (PAP)

A comprehensive automobile insurance policy developed in the 1970s to be easily understood by the "typical" insurance purchaser (for example, personal pronouns are substituted for legal designations); replaced the family automobile policy (FAP).

- Part A: Liability coverage
- Part B: Medical payments coverage
- Part C: Uninsured motorists coverage
- Part D: Coverage for damage to your vehicle

You are almost sure to purchase liability, medical payments, and uninsured motorists protection. You may, however, choose *not* to buy protection against damage to your automobile if it is "worn" and of relatively little value. On the other hand, if you have a loan against your car, you will probably be *required* to have physical damage coverage — part D — at least equal to the amount of the loan. Let's now take a closer look at the coverage provided by parts A through D.

Part A: Liability Coverage. As part of the liability provisions of PAP, the insurer agrees to (1) pay damages for bodily injury and property damage for which you become legally obligated to pay due to an automobile accident, and (2) settle or defend any claim or suit asking for such damages. This provision for legal defense is quite important. It can mean a savings of thousands of dollars, since even a person who is not at fault in an automobile accident may be compelled to prove his or her innocence in court. Note, though, that the coverage is for a defense in civil cases only. It provides no defense against any criminal charges that may be brought against the insured as a result of an accident (such as a drunk driver who's involved in an accident).

In addition to providing reimbursement for bodily and property damages, the automobile liability portion of your insurance policy stipulates that certain supplemental payments may be made. Examples of supplemental payments include expenses incurred by the insurance company in settling the claim, and other reasonable expenses incurred by the insured at the request of the insurance company (for instance, food and travel expenses). Supplemental payments can also take the form of reimbursement for premiums spent on appeal bonds, bonds to release attachments of the insured's property, and bail bonds required of an insured as a result of an accident. The amount of these supplemental payments is not restricted by the applicable policy limits. In other words, the insurance company does not reduce your policy limits by the amount that it costs to protect you in these ways.

Policy limits. Although the insurance company provides both bodily injury and property damage liability insurance under part A, *there is likely to be a single dollar limit up to which it will pay for damages from any one accident.* Typical limits are $50,000, $100,000, $300,000, and $500,000. You'd probably be well advised to consider nothing less than $300,000 in such coverage in today's legal liability environment. Damage awards are increasing, and the PAP policy provides that the insurer's duty to defend you *ends when the coverage limit has been exhausted*; unfortunately, today it is very easy to "exhaust" $50,000 or $100,000.

Some insurers make so-called *split limits* of liability coverage available. For example, policy limits to protect individuals against claims made for **bodily injury liability losses** may be available in the following combinations: $10,000/$20,000; $25,000/$50,000; $50,000/$100,000; $100,000/$300,000; and $500,000/$1,000,000. The first amount in each combination is a limit per individual and the second a limit per accident. Thus, if you purchased the $50,000/$100,000 policy limits, the maximum amount *any one person* negligently injured in an accident could receive from the insurance company would be $50,000. Further, the total amount that the insurer would pay to *all injured victims* in one accident would not exceed $100,000. If a jury awarded a claimant $80,000, the defendant whose insurance policy limits were $50,000/$100,000 could be required to pay $30,000 out of his or her pocket ($80,000 award − $50,000 paid by insurance). For the defendant, this could mean loss of home, cars, bank accounts, and other assets. In many states, if the value of these assets is too little to satisfy a claim, the defendant's wages may be garnished (taken by the court and used to satisfy the outstanding debt).

The policy limits available to cover **property damage liability losses** are typically $10,000, $25,000, and $50,000. In contrast to bodily injury liability insurance limits, property damage policy limits are stated as a per-accident limit without specifying any limits applicable on a per-item or person basis.

Persons insured. There are two basic sets of definitions in the PAP that determines who is covered under the liability coverage: insured person and covered auto. Essentially, an *insured person* includes you (the named insured) and any family

EXHIBIT 11.3
Travel, Deaths, and Death Rates (1990)

This exhibit shows some grim statistics on motor vehicle accidents in the United States. Motor vehicle accidents result not only in death and injury but in tremendous economic loss as well, which explains why auto insurance premiums are so high.

Deaths	46,300
Disabling injuries	1,700,000
Cost	$89 billion
Motor vehicle mileage	2,150 billion
Death rate per 100 million vehicle miles	2.15
Registered vehicles in the United States	194,502,000
Licensed drivers in the United States	167,655,000

Accident Totals (Rounded)	Number of Accidents	Drivers (Vehicles) Involved
Fatal	41,200	62,200
Disabling injury	1,100,000	2,000,000
Property damage and nondisabling injury	10,400,000	17,700,000
Total	11,500,000	19,800,000

Source: *Accident Facts*, 1991 (Chicago: National Safety Council, 1991), p. 51.

member, any person using a covered auto, and any person or organization that may be held responsible for your actions. The *named insured* is the person named in the declarations page of the policy. The spouse of the person named is considered to be a named insured if he or she resides in the same household. Family members are persons related by blood, marriage, or adoption who are residing in the same household. An unmarried college student living away from home usually would be considered a family member.

The named insured and family members have part A liability coverage regardless of the automobile they are driving. To have the liability coverage, however, other persons must be driving a covered auto and there must be reasonable belief that they are entitled to do so. *Covered autos* are the vehicles shown in the declarations page of your PAP, autos acquired during the policy period, any trailer owned, and any auto or trailer used as a temporary substitute while your auto or trailer is being repaired or serviced. An automobile that you lease for an extended time period can be included as a covered auto.

When a motorist who is involved in an automobile accident is covered under two or more liability insurance contracts, the coverage *on the automobile* is primary and the other coverages secondary. For example, if Dan Slegal, a named insured in his own right, were involved in an accident while driving Deeann Bauer's automobile (with permission), a claim settlement in excess of the limits of Deeann's liability policy would be necessary before Dan's liability insurance would apply. If Deeann's insurance had lapsed, Dan's policy would then offer primary protection (but it would apply to Dan only and not Deeann).

Part B: Medical Payments Coverage.
Medical payments coverage provides for payment to a covered person of an amount no greater than the

---

bodily injury liability losses
A clause in a PAP that protects individuals against losses from bodily injury; may specify coverage as a combination of per-individual and per-accident limits.

property damage liability losses
A provision in a PAP that covers damage to property on a per-accident basis.

policy limits for all reasonable and necessary medical expenses incurred within three years of an automobile accident. It provides for reimbursement even if other sources of recovery, such as health or accident insurance, also make payments. In addition, in most states the insurer reimburses the insured for medical payments even if the insured proves that another person was negligent in the accident and receives compensation from that party's liability insurer.

As with liability and uninsured motorists insurance, a person need not be occupying an automobile when the accidental injury occurs in order to be eligible for benefits. Injuries sustained as a pedestrian or on a bicycle in a traffic accident are covered, too. (Motorcycle accidents normally are not covered.) This insurance also pays on an excess basis. For instance, if you are a passenger in a friend's automobile during an accident and suffer $8,000 in medical expenses, you can collect under your friend's medical payments insurance up to his or her policy limits. Further, you can collect (up to the amount of your policy limits) from your insurer the amount in excess of what the other medical payments provide. Of course, you may also collect from the liability insurance of another person involved in the accident if that person can be shown to have been at fault. In addition, you may also be able to collect from your health insurance policy.

Policy limits. Medical payments insurance usually is available with per-person limits of $1,000, $2,000, $3,000, $5,000 or $10,000. Thus, an insurer conceivably could pay $60,000 or more in medical payments benefits for one accident involving a named insured and five passengers. Most families are advised to buy the $5,000 or $10,000 limit, because even though they may have an ample amount of other health insurance available, they cannot be certain that their passengers are equally well protected. Having automobile medical payments insurance also reduces the probability that a passenger in your auto will sue you and attempt to collect under your liability insurance coverage (in those states that permit it).

Persons insured. Coverage under an automobile medical payments insurance policy applies to the named insured and family members who are injured while occupying an automobile (whether owned by the named insured or not) or while struck by an automobile or trailer of any type. Also, it applies to any other person occupying a covered auto.

Part C: Uninsured Motorists Coverage.

Uninsured motorists coverage is available to meet the needs of "innocent" accident victims negligently injured by uninsured, underinsured, or hit-and-run motorists. Legislation requiring that uninsured motorists insurance be included in each liability insurance policy issued has been enacted in nearly all states. The insured is allowed, however, to reject this coverage in most of these states. In many states, a person may also collect if the negligent motorist's insurance company is insolvent. Under uninsured motorists insurance, an insured is legally entitled to collect an amount equal to the sum that could have been collected from the negligent motorist's liability insurance had such coverage been available, up to a maximum amount equal to the *uninsured motorists limit* stated in the policy.

Three points must be proven in order to receive payment through uninsured motorists insurance: (1) another motorist was at fault; (2) this motorist had no available insurance; and (3) damages were incurred. Property damage is not included in this coverage in most states. Therefore, under uninsured motorists coverage, you generally can collect only for losses arising from bodily injury. If the motorist and insurer cannot agree on the terms of the settlement of a claim under uninsured motorists coverage, the motorist can seek an attorney to negotiate the claim. If a mutually agreeable settlement still cannot be worked out, the insured has the right to have the case arbitrated by a neutral third party. In most cases, the accident victim and the insurer are then bound to accept the decision of the arbitrator. In addition to *uninsured* motorists, for a nominal premium you can also obtain protection for *underinsured* motorists—that is, for coverage when you're involved in an accident where the driver at fault has a liability limit much lower than you're entitled to. Under such coverage, your insurance company makes up the difference and then goes after the negligent driver for any deficiency.

Policy limits. Uninsured motorists insurance is available at minimum cost (usually less than $10 per year). It often is sold with basic limits of $10,000 to $20,000, with additional amounts available for a small increase in the premium. At the least, uninsured motorists insurance should be purchased at the minimum available limits. The cost of this coverage is small relative to the amount of protection it provides.

Persons insured.   The named insured, family members, and any other person occupying a covered auto are covered by the uninsured motorists protection.

Uninsured motorists coverage is available as part of most automobile insurance policies.
Fact: Such insurance is available under standard auto insurance policies and offers protection against uninsured, underinsured, or hit-and-run motorists.

Part D: Coverage for Physical Damage to a Vehicle.   This part of the PAP provides coverage for damage to your auto. There are two basic types of coverage provided: collision and comprehensive (or "other than collision").

Collision insurance.   Collision insurance is first-party property damage coverage that pays for collision damage to an insured automobile *regardless of fault*. The amount of insurance payable is the actual cash value of the loss in excess of a stated deductible. Remember that actual cash value is defined as replacement cost less depreciation. Therefore, if a car is demolished, an insured will be paid an amount equal to the car's depreciated value minus any deductible.

Lenders often require the purchase of collision insurance on cars they finance. In some cases — especially when the auto dealer is handling the financing — the lender will attempt to sell this insurance. Generally, the purchase of collision insurance, or any other type of automobile insurance, from car dealers or finance companies *should be avoided*. Rather, buy such insurance from your regular insurance agent and include it (collision insurance) as part of your full auto insurance policy (PAP). The fact is, a full-time insurance agent is better trained to properly assess and meet a motorist's insurance needs. Moreover, it is likely that the collision provisions of your insurance policy fully protect you even in a *rental car*. Thus, as the accompanying *Smart*

Money box notes, not only is rental car collision insurance expensive — it is probably also unnecessary!

Individuals who purchase collision insurance may select from one of several *deductibles* available — $50, $100, $250, or even $1,000. Significant premium savings often can be obtained by increasing the amount of the deductible. For example, one large automobile insurance company reports that a $50 deductible on a relatively new car can be purchased for an annual premium of $177, whereas the $100 deductible costs $150. Thus, a motorist who buys the $50 deductible is paying $27 for this additional $50 worth of protection.

Comprehensive Automobile Insurance. **Comprehensive automobile insurance** protects against loss to an insured automobile caused by any peril (with a few exceptions) *other than collision*. As one might imagine this coverage offers broad protection and includes, but is not limited to, damage caused by fire, theft, glass breakage, falling objects, malicious mischief, vandalism, riot, and earthquake. Contrary to popular belief, theft of personal property kept or left in the insured automobile normally is not covered under the automobile insurance policy. (It may, however, be covered under the off-premises coverage of the homeowner's policy if the auto was locked at the time the theft occurred.) The maximum compensation provided under this coverage is the actual cash value of the automobile.

---

uninsured motorists coverage
Automobile insurance that is designed to meet the needs of innocent accident victims who are involved in an accident in which an uninsured or underinsured motorist is at fault.

collision insurance
Automobile insurance that pays for collision damage to an insured automobile regardless of who was at fault.

comprehensive automobile insurance
Coverage that provides protection against loss to an insured automobile caused by any peril other than collision.

A Crash Course on Car Rental Insurance

Picture this: You're in the airport. You've been waiting in line for half an hour to pick up your rental car. You get up to the counter, acutely aware of the impatient customers behind you. The person behind the counter hands you a pen and says, "Sign here, then initial here, here and here." Chances are you're not going to take time to decipher the voluminous fine print on the back of the car-rental agreement. So you walk away loaded with rental-car insurance that you may or may not need—*and that may even be worthless*. The only thing you're sure of is that the car you'd reserved for $29.95 a day now costs closer to $45.

Rental-car companies are infamous for offering these price-boosting "insurance options." The one that's come under fiercest attack is the so-called *collision damage waiver*, in which you pay the car-rental company to waive its right to hold you responsible for damages. The collision damage waiver is a trap for the unwary; it's something consumers can pay a lot for and get very little in return. That's the problem with most rental-car insurance, experts say. Either consumers already have the insurance and simply don't know it, or they can get the same insurance free simply by using the right credit card.

For example, personal accident insurance (PAI) pays for any injuries the driver suffers during the time he or she is renting the car (whether or not the injuries are incurred while in the car) and for injuries suffered by passengers while in the car. PAI, in other words, is nothing more than supplemental health insurance. If you already have a health policy, paying for personal accident coverage can be a waste. Or, consider personal effects coverage, which protects you if your rental car is burglarized; the policy pays the cost of replacing possessions. But while the coverage is cheap, deductibles of up to $500 may render it useless. Moreover, most homeowner's insurance policies cover the loss of possessions while away from home anyway.

And then there is the controversial collision damage waiver.

NO-FAULT AUTOMOBILE INSURANCE

The purchase of automobile insurance coverage is relatively widespread in this country. Even so, over the years many accident victims have received inadequate compensation for their losses. Critics of this undercompensation have complained that the existing first-party medical payments portion of the PAP is too low. Further, in order to collect from the automobile policy liability coverage, an injured victim must prove that another motorist was at fault (that is, negligent) in the accident. In addition, even in those cases in which fault is proved, the liability limits of, say, $10,000 or $20,000 may still be too small to pro-vide full reimbursement for a seriously injured victim. Medical costs, lost wages, and funds spent for replacement services have accounted for the bulk of the economic losses that remain undercompensated. At the same time, these critics maintain the liability system pays *too much* for pain and suffering (called *general damages*), especially for minor injuries.

An early critic of the auto liability insurance system has alleged that automobile insurance companies have been selling the wrong product (auto liability insurance) because today the public is more concerned with the compensation of all accident victims rather than just those who can prove another was at fault for the accident. As a consequence, a

Companies are making a bundle off these waivers, according to David Cohen, a Massachusetts state representative. He calculates that at Boston's Logan Airport alone, Avis grosses $2 million a year from the collision damage waiver. So, what happens to this money? Most of it goes to the company's bottom line—that is, it's nearly pure profit! The fact is, the likelihood of damage is so small that the largest companies don't insure individual cars; they simply put the proceeds from the collision damage waiver in their coffers and hope you'll return the car undamaged. What's more, for the majority of consumers, the waiver is unnecessary, since most conventional auto policies already cover the policyholder for damages incurred while driving a rental car. As Cohen puts it, "They are making me pay for something I don't need, and they're using high-pressure tactics. They really have the consumer over the barrel." Demetria Mudar, an Avis spokeswoman, disagrees. "Whenever we get the opportunity, we encourage people to check their policies," she says. "We don't want to encourage people to buy something they don't need."

If you are intent on beating the collision damage waiver, though, beware of certain risks. First, if you decide to rely on your personal policy, make sure you find out what the deductible is and whether there are exclusions—for example, whether the policy covers trips outside U.S. borders. If you plan to charge your rental car on a credit card that offers free collision protection, remember that most programs only provide so-called secondary coverage. Translation: The card companies will pay only the amount not covered by your own auto policy. That means that if you have an accident in your rental car, you will have to file a claim with your own insurance company. As a result, that relaxing vacation may cause your premiums —not to mention your blood pressure—to shoot up.

Source: Adapted from Eric N. Berg, "Crash Course: Read Before You Sign on the Dotted Line," *Savvy*, October 1988, 73–74.

major reform movement began during the mid-1960s to push adoption of no-fault automobile insurance.

The concept of **no-fault automobile insurance** is based on the belief that the liability system should be replaced by a system that reimburses the parties involved in an accident without regard to negligence. The principle is, "My insurance policy should pay the cost of my injuries, and your insurance policy should pay the cost of yours," regardless of who is at fault in an accident. Under the concept of *pure* no-fault insurance, the driver, passengers, and injured pedestrians are reimbursed by the insurer of the car for economic losses stemming from bodily injury. The insurer thus does not have to provide coverage for claims made for losses caused to other motorists. Each insured party is compensated by his or her own company, regardless of which party caused the accident. In return, legal remedies and payments for pain and suffering are restricted.

Unfortunately, the advocates of no-fault forgot that liability insurance was never intended to serve as the primary system for compensating injured parties. Its sole purpose is to protect the assets of the insured,

no-fault automobile insurance
A concept of automobile insurance that favors reimbursement without regard to negligence.

not to pay losses, *per se*. This same concept applies to all liability insurance. The coverages of medical payments, collision, and comprehensive insurance discussed earlier do serve this compensation purpose to a certain extent. In addition, families can and should purchase widely available life, health, and disability protection, which will protect them not only for losses resulting from automobile accidents but also for nearly all other types of economic losses resulting from accident or illness. In fact, the numerous cries that no-fault automobile insurance is needed so that people can be compensated for their losses incurred in automobile accidents have probably had more of a harmful effect on overall insurance planning, since they have detracted from public understanding of the need for full life and health insurance programming. After all, there is no reason to be more concerned about the person who is injured in an automobile accident than for the homeowner who sustains injury while repairing his or her house. Nevertheless, because some valid arguments have been put forth by proponents of no-fault insurance, many states have legislated for modification of the coverages offered by the family automobile policy. *No state has yet adopted a pure no-fault insurance plan*, though.

Basically, the various state laws governing no-fault insurance can be differentiated according to whether or not (1) no-fault and liability insurance is compulsory and/or (2) there are any restrictions on lawsuits. The laws of the separate states vary substantially as to both the amount of no-fault benefits provided and the degree to which the restrictions for legal actions apply. For example, the Virginia statute places no limits on the right to sue for damages for pain and suffering, and requires only that automobile insurers make available modest amounts of medical expense, funeral expense, and wage replacement coverage. At the other extreme is the Michigan law, which eliminates legal action for bodily injury claims for pain and suffering except when the accident victim is killed or incurs serious bodily dysfunction or disfigurement. Michigan is also the only state that restricts the victim's legal recovery of property damage caused by someone else's negligence. For its no-fault benefits, Michigan requires the insured to buy coverage that provides reimbursement for unlimited medical and hospital expenses. In addition, it covers rehabilitation, lost wages, replacement services, and funeral expenses.

In contrast to Michigan, most states provide from $2,000 to $10,000 in first-party benefits (often called *personal injury protection*) and restrict legal recovery for pain and suffering to cases in which medical or economic losses exceed some threshold level, such as $500 or $1,000. In all states, recovery based on negligence is permitted for economic loss in excess of the amount payable by no-fault insurance.

Overall, most of the no-fault laws that have been passed fell short of accomplishing the two objectives fundamental to no-fault insurance — that is, eliminations of liability as a basis for recovery, and provision of adequate compensation for all accident victims. Further, the no-fault concept gained its largest public support because its advocates promised that it would contribute to lower insurance premiums. As might be expected, based on the laws now on the books, that has not always been achieved. In those states with substantive laws, though, some efficiencies have been gained. Still, because only a few states have required first-party benefits of substantial size, most seriously injured accident victims will continue to turn to the liability system or their life and health insurance coverages for large amounts of compensation.

AUTOMOBILE INSURANCE PREMIUMS

What you pay for car insurance depends on many things, including where you live, what kind of car you drive, what kind of coverage you have, the amount of your deductibles, and so forth. One thing is sure, the size of the typical car insurance premium is anything but uniform. The fact is, average auto insurance premiums — for basically the same coverage — vary all over the map. Exhibit 11.4, which lists average insurance premiums for the 50 states and District of Columbia, shows a range from $278 (in Alabama) to $835 (in Massachusetts). And, remember, this is for comparable coverage. If you're fortunate enough to live in one of the low-premium states (say one of the bottom 20), you're probably *relatively* satisfied with the cost of your car insurance; on the other hand, if you're in one of the more expensive states (like New Jersey, California, Arkansas, or Pennsylvania), you may well be feeling the pinch of these high and, in many cases, rapidly increasing auto insurance rates. Indeed, residents in

EXHIBIT 11.4

Comparative Auto Insurance Premiums

Average auto insurance rates vary all over the map; while the national average is about $485 a year, the annual rate in the most expensive state (Massachusetts) is nearly *three times* the cost for the same coverage in the least expensive state (Alabama). You might want to check the list to see where your state stands in the cost of auto insurance.

Rank	State	Average Premium		Rank	State	Average Premium
51	Alabama	$278.33		40	Montana	$406.88
13	Alaska	576.25		43	Nebraska	367.02
12	Arizona	580.47		3	Nevada	681.05
6	Arkansas	613.58		18	New Hampshire	515.16
4	California	673.18		2	New Jersey	733.66
23	Colorado	474.46		34	New Mexico	439.45
14	Connecticut	560.27		10	New York	601.84
11	Delaware	581.46		31*	North Carolina	445.19
7	District of Columbia	606.39		47	North Dakota	343.85
27	Florida	462.66		42	Ohio	376.82
16	Georgia	539.75		31*	Oklahoma	445.19
15	Hawaii	551.59		33	Oregon	444.48
46	Idaho	356.95		5	Pennsylvania	620.33
30	Illinois	448.00		9	Rhode Island	604.28
39	Indiana	414.42		17	South Carolina	526.75
50	Iowa	292.51		49	South Dakota	324.90
41	Kansas	379.89		48	Tennessee	338.48
37	Kentucky	431.73		20	Texas	494.88
22	Louisiana	490.50		35	Utah	436.10
36	Maine	435.20		29	Vermont	452.03
8	Maryland	604.41		26	Virginia	479.54
1	Massachusetts	834.76		28	Washington	455.25
19	Michigan	509.33		21	West Virginia	494.06
25	Minnesota	479.60		38	Wisconsin	422.15
44	Mississippi	360.28		45	Wyoming	359.53
24	Missouri	473.76				

*tie

Source: A.M. Best Co. (March 1990), p. 99.

many of the high-premium states have begun to rally against these rates and are demanding—through their state legislators and/or the ballot box—a return to what they see as more reasonable premiums. This matter is a highly emotional one, because it hits the pocketbooks of so many consumers, and it very likely is an issue that's going to be with us for some time to come. In effect, you have the insurance companies on one side arguing why the rates are necessary and justified, and on the other, you have the consumers arguing that the rates are too high and they're going up too fast.

With this perspective in mind, let's look now at how auto insurance premiums are set. Basically, the starting point for determining them in nearly all states is the *rating territory*. Since more accidents occur in some geographic areas than others, higher rates are applied in those where claims are greatest.

Even an insured who is the pillar of the community and has a perfect driving record will be charged the rates in effect for the territory in which he or she resides regardless of how high they might be. The location in which an automobile is principally garaged usually determines the applicable rating territory. Because insurance rates are influenced by local accident rates and the average cost of resulting claims paid under the various coverages in the area—reflecting auto repair costs, hospital and medical expenses, jury awards, thefts, and vandalism in the locale—where you live can make a big difference in how much you pay for auto insurance. Accordingly, Herbert Dennenburg, former insurance commissioner of Pennsylvania, stated that he had found a magic formula for reducing auto insurance premiums: "I moved from Philadelphia [a high-rate area] to Harrisburg [a low-rate area.]"

Among the other factors that influence automobile insurance rates are (1) the amount of use the automobile receives, (2) the personal characteristics of the drivers, (3) the type of automobile, (4) the insured's driving record, and (5) applicable discounts. Note that while these have been and presently are the determining factors for rates in all but a few states, several jurisdictions prohibit the use of rating territories, age, and/or sex factors. The belief has been that these factors unfairly discriminate against the urban, the young, and the male.

Use of the Automobile.   If an insured has a non-business automobile that is not customarily driven to work — or if an automobile is driven fewer than 3 miles one way to work — it probably will be classified as a pleasure car. This is a favorable rating for the use classification. A motorist who drives more than 3 but fewer than 15 miles to work will pay a slightly higher premium. If an auto is driven more than 15 miles each way to work, an even higher premium will be charged. In addition to the daily drive to work, most insurers also look at total annual miles driven; obviously, the more miles you drive in a year, the more you can expect to pay in auto insurance premiums. Also, higher premiums are charged for automobiles driven for business purposes than for those that qualify for other classifications, and a farm-use designation qualifies for the lowest rates.

Personal Characteristics of Drivers.   Such things as the age, sex, and marital status of the insured affect the premium that is assessed for automobile insurance. As many young people and their parents already know, the rates applicable to youthful motorists can be relatively high. Generally, unmarried females age 24 or under and unmarried males age 29 or under are placed in higher-rate categories than individuals who are older. Married males under age 25 also fall into a relatively high-rate category. Females over 24 and married females of any age are exempt from the youthful operator classification and thus need not pay the higher premiums. Insurance companies believe that such premium differentials based on age are justified because of the great number of accidents that involve youthful operators. For example, drivers in the 20 to 24 age group make up only about 10 percent of the total driving population but are involved in nearly 20 percent of the auto accidents.

Type of Automobile.   Automobiles may be classified as standard performance, intermediate performance, high performance, sports, and rear engine. In some states, even four-door cars are rated differently than two-door models of the same make. As might be expected, if an automobile is not classified as standard performance, higher rates are usually charged. Automobiles that have high horsepower-to-weight ratios and more than three forward gears on the floor frequently are classified in higher-rate categories. Thus, if you are thinking of buying, say, a Corvette or a Nissan 300ZX, you'd better be prepared to handle some pretty hefty insurance rates.

The type of car you drive really has very little to do with how much you will have to pay for automobile insurance.
Fantasy: The type of car you drive is one of the major determinants of auto insurance premiums. You can expect to pay a lot more for insurance on a sporty model than on a more "sedate" one.

Driving Record.   The driving records of the insured and those who live with them play an important part in the determination of premiums. Both traffic violations and traffic accidents are normally considered in assessing driving records. The more severe types of traffic convictions are for driving under the influence of alcohol or drugs (DUI), leaving the scene of an accident, homicide or assault arising out of the operation of a motor vehicle, and driving with a revoked or suspended driver's license. In addition — on a less severe basis — any conviction for a traffic violation that results in the accumulation of points under a state point system may result in higher insurance premiums. Included in this category are such violations as speeding, running a red light, failure to yield the right of way, and illegal passing. Typically, points under a state system are assigned only for moving traffic violations. Therefore, convictions for offenses such as parking violations, improper registration, lack of an operator's license, and lack of a valid safety sticker usually do not result in increased insurance premiums. In most states, a *premium surcharge* is made for traffic offenses and accidents that are determined to be the fault of the insured. Under these plans, designated

EXHIBIT 11.5
Types of Discounts Offered by Ten Leading Auto Insurers

Listed here are ten of the most common types of discounts offered by some of the leading auto insurers in the country. While most of these discounts apply to the total cost of the insurance, some apply to only a certain portion of the coverage (for example, the antitheft discount applies only to the cost of the comprehensive portion of the policy).

Type of Discount	No. of Companies Offering the Discount	Savings Offered
Driver's training	All 10	Range 5–40%; most commonly 10%; not available in all states
Good student	9 of the 10	Range 5–30%; commonly 25%
Student away at school	All 10	Some companies put policyholders in a lower-price bracket; others offer discounts, usually 10–40%
Carpool	All 10	Some companies put policyowners in a lower-price bracket; others offer discounts of 5–25%
Multicar	All 10	Range 10–25%; usually about 15%
Passive restraints	All 10	Range 5–60%; full front airbag discounts range from 40–60%
Antitheft devices	All 10	Range 5–20%; state laws in MI, RI, IL, MA, NY and KY mandate such discounts; however, some companies offer these discounts in other states, too
Mature driver	All 10	Range 5–20%; discounts may start at age 50; driving habits, employment, and retirement affect discount; some companies put policyholder into lower class
Farmer	7 of the 10	Range 10–30%; most commonly 10%; some companies put policyholder into a lower-price bracket
Defensive-driving course	All 10	Range 5–15%; not available in all states; some state laws mandate such a discount

Source: Adapted from George E. Rejda, *Principles of Insurance*, 4th ed. (New York: HarperCollins, 1992), p. 251.

points are charged against the insured. The first point may eliminate the safe driving discount, with each additional point resulting in a certain dollar surcharge being added to the monthly premium. The idea behind surcharge plans is that motorists will exercise safer driving practices to avoid the expense of a surcharge.

Sometimes traffic violations do not directly enter into the premium computations but instead influence whether a motorist will be offered a regular policy or placed in an **automobile insurance plan** (formerly called an *assigned-risk plan*). These plans have been organized in many states to provide automobile insurance to drivers who are refused coverage when they have sought it in a normal manner. Motorists who are placed in an automobile insurance plan generally have less coverage and pay higher premiums. Even with the high premiums, however, insurers lost $2.3 bilion on this type of business in a recent five-year period.

Driving Down the Cost of Car Insurance.

One of the best ways to drive down the cost of car insurance is to take advantage of *discounts*; and, indeed, most auto insurers today offer a variety of them. Taken together, such discounts can knock 5 to 50 percent off your annual premium. A summary of some of the discounts given by the top auto insurance companies is provided in Exhibit 11.5. Some give overall *safe-driving* discounts, and most give youthful operators lower rates if they have had *driver's training*—some states, in fact, have enacted laws that require insurers to offer lower premiums

---

automobile insurance plan

An arrangement that provides automobile insurance to drivers who have been refused coverage under normal procedures; formerly called an *assigned-risk plan*.

EXHIBIT 11.6

Financial Responsibility Requirements by State

Most states have financial responsibility laws that require motorists involved in auto accidents to furnish proof of financial accountability up to certain minimum dollar amounts; as seen here, those financial liability limits vary by state.

State	Liability Limits[a]	State	Liability Limits[a]
Alabama	20/40/10	Montana	25/50/5
Alaska	50/100/25	Nebraska	25/50/25
Arizona	15/30/10	Nevada	15/30/10
Arkansas	25/50/15	New Hampshire	25/50/25
California	15/30/5	New Jersey	15/30/5
Colorado	25/50/15	New Mexico	25/50/10
Connecticut	20/40/10	New York	10/20/5[b]
Delaware	15/30/10	North Carolina	25/50/10
District of Columbia	25/50/10	North Dakota	25/50/25
Florida	10/20/10	Ohio	12.5/25/7.5
Georgia	15/30/10	Oklahoma	10/20/10
Hawaii	35/unlimited/10	Oregon	25/50/10
Idaho	25/50/15	Pennsylvania	15/30/5
Illinois	20/40/15	Rhode Island	25/50/25
Indiana	25/50/10	South Carolina	15/30/5
Iowa	20/40/15	South Dakota	25/50/25
Kansas	25/50/10	Tennessee	20/50/10
Kentucky	25/50/10	Texas	20/40/15
Louisiana	10/20/10	Utah	20/40/10
Maine	20/40/10	Vermont	20/40/10
Maryland	20/40/10	Virginia	25/50/20
Massachusetts	10/20/5	Washington	25/50/10
Michigan	20/40/10	West Virginia	20/40/10
Minnesota	30/60/10	Wisconsin	25/50/10
Mississippi	10/20/5	Wyoming	25/50/20
Missouri	25/50/10		

[a]The first two figures refer to bodily injury liability limits and the third figure to property damage liability. For example, 10/20/5 means coverage up to $20,000 for all persons injured in an accident, subject to a limit of $10,000 for one individual, and $5000 coverage for property damage.

[b]50/100 for wrongful death.

Source: George E. Rejda, *Principles of Insurance*, 4th ed. (New York: HarperCollins, 1992), p. 236.

to *any driver*, young or old, who has taken driver's training. Youthful drivers may also receive *good student* discounts for maintaining a B average or by being on the dean's list at their school. Such student discounts, by the way, apply to both high school and college students. Nearly all insurance companies provide discounts to families with two or more automobiles, if each car is insured by the same company. Most insurers also offer discounts to owners who install *airbags* or *antitheft devices* in their cars. Likewise, *nonsmoker and nondrinker* discounts are offered by a number of insurers. There are even some companies that specialize in insuring certain portions of the population. For example, certain insurers accept only persons who are educators or executives and others only government employees. While not offering discounts in the normal sense,

these companies frequently do have lower premiums because, through more selective underwriting, they are able to reduce losses and operating expenses.

Clearly, it's to your advantage to look for and use as many of these discounts as you can. Another very effective way to drive down the cost of car insurance is to *raise your deductibles* (as discussed earlier in this chapter). This often overlooked tactic can have a dramatic effect on the amount of insurance premium you pay. For example, the difference between a $100 deductible and a $500 deductible may be as much as 30 percent on comprehensive coverage and 25 percent on collision insurance; request a $1,000 deductible and you may save as much as 45 to 50 percent on both comprehensive and collision insurance.

FINANCIAL RESPONSIBILITY LAWS

The annual losses from automobile accidents in the United States run into billions of dollars. For this reason, **financial responsibility laws** have been enacted in most states, whereby motorists are *required* to buy a minimum amount of automobile liability insurance. As the name implies, financial responsibility laws attempt to force motorists to be financially responsible for the damages they cause as a result of automobile accidents. A summary of the financial responsibility requirements in each of the 50 states and the District of Columbia is given in Exhibit 11.6.

Two basic types of laws compel motorists to assume financial responsibility. The first is one in which all automobile owners in a given state are required to show evidence that they have liability insurance coverage prior to obtaining registration for their motor vehicles. Until 1971 only three states had these compulsory liability insurance requirements. Today, more than 40 states have compulsory auto insurance laws whereby motorists are required to show evidence of insurance coverage *before* they can receive their license plates.

Under the second type of financial responsibility legislation, motorists do not have to show evidence of their insurance coverage until after they are involved in an accident. If they then fail to demonstrate compliance with the law, their registrations and/or driver's licenses are suspended. This law has been criticized on the grounds that it allows negligent motorists to have one "free" accident. Even though the motorists who are not financially responsible lose their driving privileges, the losses to their victims may remain uncompensated.

OTHER PROPERTY AND LIABILITY INSURANCE

Besides homeowner's and automobile insurance, there are several other types of property insurance policies that you should be aware of. For example, you can increase your personal liability coverage with a personal liability umbrella policy, you can in-sure certain types of recreational vehicles, and you can even get repair insurance when you buy a car. Do you think there'll ever be a time when you'll find it necessary to use such policies? Take a minute to think about this question before reading on.

While homeowner's and automobile insurance policies represent the basic protection needed by most families, there are still other insurance contracts that some people may find appropriate. Among those discussed here are the personal property floater policy, umbrella personal liability policy, mobile-home insurance, boat insurance, recreational vehicle insurance, automobile repair insurance, earthquake insurance, flood insurance, professional liability insurance, and group plans.

PERSONAL PROPERTY FLOATER (PPF) POLICY

This policy provides comprehensive coverage on a blanket basis for virtually all of the insured's personal property. It is designed for persons who desire the maximum protection available. In fact, the personal property coverage provided by this form of insurance is the same as that found in HO-3 form contracts with special endorsements attached. Because floater coverage is on an all-risk basis, the only property or perils not covered are those listed in the exclusions. Most notably these exclusions are for wear and tear, damage from insects or vermin, nuclear energy, and gradual deterioration.

A personal property floater policy offers protection on a blanket basis that is supplemental to the coverage under a homeowner's policy. In addition, many types of *scheduled* (i.e., itemized) personal property floaters are available to supplement coverage under a homeowner's contract. These coverages are especially useful for the types of property that may not receive adequate protection under the

> **financial responsibility laws**
> Laws that attempt to force motorists to be financially responsible for the damages they become legally obligated to pay as a result of automobile accidents.

homeowner's policy because of limits on amounts payable and perils insured. Coverage under a scheduled personal property floater is extensive and is a good way to guard against loss of or damage to expensive belongings. Some of the more popular policies apply to furs, jewelry, photographic equipment, silverware, fine art and antiques, musical instruments, and stamp and coin collections.

UMBRELLA PERSONAL LIABILITY POLICY

Persons with relatively high levels of income and net worth may find the **umbrella personal liability policy** useful. It provides added liability coverage for both homeowner's and automobile insurance as well as coverage in some areas not provided for in either of these policies. These policies are often sold with limits of $1 million or more. In addition, some provide added amounts of coverage for a family's major medical insurance.

Because upper-income individuals are often viewed as viable targets for liability claims, umbrella protection can provide a desirable, added layer of coverage. In addition, the premiums are usually quite reasonable for the broad coverage afforded ($100 to $300 a year for as much as $1 million in coverage). While the protection is written on a comprehensive basis, it does contain a number of exclusions of which purchasers should be aware. As a rule, in order to purchase a personal liability umbrella policy, the insured party must already have relatively high liability limits on their auto and homeowner's coverage; that is, generally speaking, insurance companies require the insured to have, say, $100,000 in liability limits on their auto and homeowner's policies *before* they'll even consider selling an umbrella policy to that party.

As a rule, you must obtain an umbrella personal liability policy if you want liability coverage of $1 million or more.
Fact: Such policies provide added liability protection for both homeowner's and automobile insurance (simultaneously). They are intended primarily for upper-income families, who are often viewed as prime targets for large liability claims.

MOBILE-HOME INSURANCE

Several hundred thousand mobile homes are sold each year, and several million now serve as homes for young couples, transients (those whose jobs require that they constantly be on the move from one place to another), and retirees. Because of this widespread use, insurers offer special package insurance policies for mobile-home owners just as they do for owners of single-family residences. Coverage on mobile homes may be written to offer protection on a blanket basis against the same perils that are covered on an HO-2 form. In addition, personal property and personal liability coverage is included. Although the coverage offered for mobile-home owners is similar to that available for more permanent structures, rates per $100 of protection are typically higher for mobile homes because they present a greater exposure to wind and fire loss. Total losses on mobile homes occur much more frequently than they do for either wood or brick houses.

BOAT INSURANCE

Most people underinsure their boats. This situation exists partly because homeowner's policies offer limited protection for boat owners, which misleads many into a false sense of security. However, the fact is, only boats less than 26 feet in length (or some other stipulated maximum) or those with motors under 25 horsepower are typically afforded liability coverage under a homeowner's policy. Moreover, the physical damage coverage is usually limited to only a few perils, and in most cases reimbursement cannot exceed $1,000. Consequently, for all but small fishing or sailboats, the coverage provided by the homeowner's policy is totally inadequate. Fortunately, this problem is easily remedied through either a boat and motor endorsement on the homeowner's policy, or a specially designed boat-owner's policy. These endorsements or policies typically contain liability, physical damage and theft, and medical payments coverage. The liability and medical payments protection is similar to that offered in an automobile policy.

The physical damage and theft coverage under boat policies can be either limited or comprehensive, excluding only a few perils such as nuclear explosion, warfare, and government actions. Perils commonly insured against are fire and lightning, collision, overturning of a transporting land conveyance, windstorms, and theft. Other contingencies that can be covered include damage resulting from submersion, vandalism, a motor falling overboard, and burglary from a closed and locked garage or boathouse. Because the physical damage and theft provisions of boat policies are not highly standardized, you should not assume that coverage exists for any given type of loss. Make certain that your insurance agent explains which coverage applies and which losses are not covered.

RECREATIONAL VEHICLE INSURANCE

Although a consistent definition of the term "recreational vehicle" does not exist, the following vehicles generally fall within this classification: all-terrain vehicles, antique automobiles, dune buggies, go-carts, minibikes, trail motorcycles, camping vehicles (both motorized and trailer type), snowmobiles, and customized vans. Complete coverage generally is available for these vehicles, including bodily injury and property damage liability, medical payments, physical damage, and theft. You may have to shop around for the policy that best fits your needs, since not all insurance companies write coverage for recreational vehicles. Among those that do, more restrictions are likely to apply than on, say, a personal automobile policy. Rates will also vary substantially depending on the age of the driver, how the vehicle is used, and the location of the policy owner. As with insuring a boat, when insuring a recreational vehicle you need to discuss with a property insurance agent how best to insure your recreational vehicle, giving particular attention to who and what are covered, and where and when they are covered.

Many types of recreational vehicles — including motorcycles and mopeds — can be insured under the personal auto policy through a *Miscellaneous Type Vehicle Endorsement*. With this endorsement, insureds get the same protection for their recreational vehicles as they do for their private passenger automobiles.

AUTOMOBILE REPAIR INSURANCE

Most automobile dealers today offer plans under which a person buying an automobile can pay an additional fee to warrant the repairs resulting from certain mechanical problems. Generally, this is done to "extend the warranties" on new vehicles from, say, two years to five years; thus, the insured is simply buying another three years of warranty repair coverage on the vehicle. These plans, however, aren't really a form of insurance, but rather an arrangement whereby a fee is paid up front in exchange for future contracted services.

EARTHQUAKE INSURANCE

Although most people think of California when earthquakes are mentioned, areas in other states are also subject to this type of loss. At the present time, very few homeowners buy this coverage even though the premiums are relatively inexpensive. Surprisingly, a great number of Californians were without earthquake coverage when the major San Francisco quake occurred in 1989.

FLOOD INSURANCE

Before 1969, floods were regarded by most private insurers as an uninsurable peril because the risk could not be spread among enough people who were not located in flood-prone areas. But in 1969, the federal government established a subsidized flood insurance program in cooperation with private insurance agents, who can now sell this low-cost coverage to homeowners and tenants *living in communities that have been designated as part of the federal flood program*. In addition, the flood

umbrella personal liability policy
An insurance policy that provides excess liability coverage for both homeowner's and automobile insurance as well as coverage in some areas not provided for in either of those policies.

insurance program is encouraging communities to initiate land-use controls in order to reduce future flood losses.

PROFESSIONAL LIABILITY INSURANCE

Malpractice suits against those in the medical profession have increased substantially in recent years — in fact, liability claims against nearly all types of professionals, including lawyers, architects, financial planners, and engineers, are also rising rapidly. Even worse, this lawsuit mentality is beginning to spread to nonprofessionals as well — for example, sales representatives and agents are increasingly being sued for alleged acts of "errors and omissions." While certain professions and lines of work are more susceptible to malpractice suits than others, each year it seems a wider and wider segment of the work force is becoming exposed to the threat of these suits. Thus, the need for professional liability insurance is rapidly increasing, but the cost of such coverage is simply going out of sight! The courts and juries are giving enormous awards, which in turn simply drives the insurance rates even higher. Thus, professional liability insurance is available, but because of the increasing number of claims, rates are skyrocketing, while stricter underwriting standards are being imposed by insurers.

GROUP PLANS

As a benefit to members of some groups (labor unions, credit unions, fraternal organizations, and various other organizations), group property and liability plans are being introduced. Unlike life and health insurance agreements, these plans are not true group plans because they do not issue a single master policy to the group. Instead, they are arrangements for mass marketing of homeowner's and automobile policies, and the policies are individually sold and issued. The primary benefit of group plans is that the lower marketing expense of the insurance company is passed along to the group members in the form of reduced premiums.

Some groups also have **group legal insurance**. These plans are fee-for-services agreements into which the group enters with a given law firm on behalf of its members. The plans typically cover only basic legal matters such as divorce, writing of wills, small claims settlement, and landlord-tenant problems. In some cases, the group member is entitled to lower charges on other legal services provided by the participating firm.

BUYING INSURANCE AND SETTLING CLAIMS

Buying property and liability insurance requires a decision on what kinds of protection you need. What factors would you consider in making this decision? How about when it comes to filing a claim with an insurance company — do you know what's involved in such a process and how to go about filing a claim? Take some time to think about these questions before going on.

When preparing to buy property and liability insurance, you should first develop an inventory of exposures to loss and arrange them from highest to lowest priority. Losses that lend themselves to insurance protection are those that seldom occur but have the potential for being substantial — for example, damage to a home and its contents or liability arising out of a negligence claim. Less important, but nevertheless desirable, is insurance to cover losses that could be disruptive to the financial plans of a family even though they would not result in insolvency. Such risks include physical damage to automobiles, boats, and other personal property of moderate value. Lowest priority should be given to insuring exposures that can easily be covered by savings or from current income. *Low-dollar deductibles, for instance, usually serve only to increase premiums.* Likewise, personal property of minor value, such as an old auto (one that is not a collectible), normally does not merit coverage. In addition to inventorying exposures and deciding on appropriate coverage and deductibles, you should exercise care in selecting both the property insurance agent and the insurer. Also, a knowledge of the procedures involved in settling property and liability claims can help you obtain maximum benefits from policies when claims do arise.

PROPERTY AND LIABILITY INSURANCE AGENTS

Most property insurance agents can be classified as either captive or independent. A **captive agent** is one who represents only one insurance company and is more or less an employee of that company. Allstate, Nationwide, and State Farm are major insurance companies that market through captive agents. **Independent agents**, in contrast, typically represent between two and ten different insurance companies. These agents may place your coverage with any of the companies with which they have an agency relationship as long as you meet the underwriting standards of that company. Names of companies that may be familiar to you that operate through independent agents include Aetna, Hartford, and Travelers. It is difficult to generalize with respect to the superiority of agents. In some cases an independent agent will provide the best combination of low-cost insurance and good service, while in others the captive agent might be the better choice. Because of wide differences in premiums charged and services rendered, it usually does pay to shop around.

Property insurance agents should be willing to take the time to go over your total property and liability insurance exposures. As you should know by now, there is much more to the purchase of property insurance than simply signing a homeowner's and an automobile insurance application. Decisions must be made about types of property and uses, perils to be covered, limits, deductibles, and floater policies, as well as other items that have been discussed throughout this chapter. An agent should be willing to talk with clients about these items. In the property insurance industry, agents who meet various experiential and education requirements, including passing a series of written examinations, qualify for the **Chartered Property and Casualty Underwriter (CPCU)** designation. Agents who have been awarded CPCUs have proven knowledge and experience in their field.

PROPERTY AND LIABILITY INSURANCE COMPANIES

Although the selection of an agent is probably the most important step in the purchase of property and liability insurance, you should also ask some questions about the company, including its financial soundness, claims-settlement practices, and the geographic extent of its operations (this could be important if you are involved in an accident 1,000 miles from home). The agent should be a good source of information about the technical aspects of a company's operations, whereas friends and acquaintances often can provide insight into its claims-settlement policy.

SETTLING PROPERTY AND LIABILITY CLAIMS

Generally speaking, insurance companies settle claims promptly and fairly, especially for life and health insurance coverages. In settling property and liability claims, though, some chance for claimant-insurer disagreement does exist. The following discussion reviews the claims-settlement process and

group legal insurance
A type of insurance plan consisting of a fee-for-service agreement between a group and a law firm; typically covers only such basic legal matters as divorce, wills, and small claims settlement.

captive agent
An insurance agent who represents only the company that employs him or her.

independent agent
An insurance agent who may place coverage with any company with which he or she has an agency relationship as long as the insured meets that company's underwriting standards.

Chartered Property and Casualty Underwriter (CPCU)
An agent who has met various experiential and educational requirements and passed a series of written examinations in the fields of property and liability insurance.

To File, or Not to File—That Is the Question

Last winter, Gene Robbins was driving just 15 mph, hit an ice patch, and skidded into a tree. His insurer paid the bill: $650, minus a $200 deductible. A few months later, Gene's teenage son backed the same car into a neighbor's empty parked car, denting the door. Again, the insurer paid: $800 net. Then Gene received his new insurance bill—with a 30 percent hike in premiums.

That 30 percent rate rise was a blow, especially since Gene's insurance already cost a bundle, what with a teenage driver in the house. Would he have been better off not making the claims, paying out of his own pocket instead? That's not an uncommon question, but the answer isn't necessarily clear.

On the one hand, too many claims in too short a time or for too much money *can boost your premiums considerably and may jeopardize your cover-*age. On the other hand, not filing might risk serious financial liability later on. Most experts advise that you not take any chances where there's potential liability for serious damage to someone else's property or any damage to a person. But what about the gray areas, such as Gene experienced? He wasn't driving recklessly when he skidded. No one was in the car Gene's son hit, and repair costs were moderate. What would your best move be in a similar situation? The following information can help you make an informed decision. If you have any doubts, check with an attorney as well.

HOW THE INSURERS FIGURE IT

Most insurers work under a concept of "chargeable" accidents, though definitions vary somewhat among companies and states. State Farm, for exam-ple, considers an accident chargeable when the company must pay at least $400 to $600, depending on locale. Exceptions include when your legally parked car is hit, or the other driver gets a moving violation and you don't. Whatever their definition of chargeable, all insurers get nervous when you file more than one claim in a short period—two claims in three years, or three in five, for example.

HOW MUCH WILL PREMIUMS RISE?

Some companies apply simple formulas; for example, an extra 10 percent on your premium for your first accident with a chargeable claim, an additional 20 percent for a second chargeable claim within three years, up to 50 percent more for a third claim. Other companies forgive a first accident if you've been a customer for several

---

the people who participate in it. First, however, let's consider what you should do immediately following an accident.

First Steps Following an Accident. After an accident, the names and addresses of all witnesses, drivers, occupants, and injured parties, along with the license numbers of the automobiles involved, should be recorded. Law enforcement officers as well as your insurance agent should be immediately notified of the accident. You should never admit liability at the scene of an accident or discuss it with anyone other than the police and your insurer. Remember: Prior to the determination of who, if anyone, is legally liable for an accident, the requisites of liability must be established. Also, the duties of the

years, but premiums could take a big leap—at least 40 percent, and as much as 100 percent—for a second incident within three years or some other specified period.

CAN THEY DROP YOUR POLICY?

Companies aren't eager to cancel insurance policies, as long as you can pay ever-higher premiums. Even if you are among the few who are cut, the general rule is that *someone* will insure you, presuming you have a driver's license. The hitch: Your claim record could get you turned down at a new company, or at least cost higher rates. Ultimately, you may have to go to the "assigned risk" pool or a similar plan, often at double the regular cost.

YOUR AGENT IS KEY

Get her or him to explain how your present insurer defines chargeable accidents and how much rates will rise under given circumstances. How long do rate hikes stay in force? What happens if the company finds you have avoided making claims? (Some insurers will cancel.) If you don't like your insurer's rules, shop around with the same questions in hand. You may find a better deal. *Also find out whether your agent is willing after an accident to help you figure whether filing a claim or paying the bill yourself will cost less.*

If you're tempted to settle on your own, whatever your reason, follow the precautions in the section below.

WHAT IF YOU DON'T FILE?

Insurers stress that today's minor accident may turn into next year's personal injury lawsuit. If you don't file a timely claim, they say, you may jeopardize your coverage. Still, it can be tempting not to file under certain circumstances. If so:

- *Always* report to your agent any accident involving another person or someone else's property. Hopefully, the agent will help you decide the smart course to take.
- Try to get a formal release (drawn up by an attorney and witnessed) from the other party, if any, indicating that he or she will not sue. If you pay anything, be sure to get a release saying "paid in full." This isn't guaranteed protection, but it may help.
- If you don't intend to make small claims, *take a large deductible on your policy*. You'll save money.

Source: Adapted from Margaret Daly, "Car Insurance—Is It Ever Smart *Not* to File a Claim?" *Better Homes and Gardens,* September 1987, pp. 91, 93.

---

police are to assess the probability of a law violation and maintain order at the scene of an accident—not to make judgments with respect to liability.

Steps in Claims Settlement. If you're involved in an accident, one of the first things you're going to have to decide is whether or not you even want to file a claim. If it's a minor "fender bender," you may be better off paying for the damages out of your own pocket—particularly if you have a relatively high deductible (of $500 to $1,000). Be careful, however, if there's another party involved—and *never* follow this procedure if there's any kind of bodily injury to any of the parties! Even if you don't file a claim, let your agent know that you've been involved in an accident and discuss the incident with him or her. As the accompanying *Issues in Money Management* box points out, deciding on whether or not to file a claim is not as easy as it sounds — there are a number of factors that have to be considered.

Should you opt to file a claim, it'll probably involve the following steps. First, you must give notice to the company that a loss (or potential for loss) has occurred. Timely notice is extremely important because it leads to the second step, which is the investigation of the claim. To properly investigate a claim, insurance company personnel may have to talk to witnesses or law enforcement officers, gather physical evidence to determine whether the claimed loss is covered by the policy, and check to make sure that the date of the loss falls within the policy period. If you delay filing your claim, you hinder the insurer's ability to check the facts. *All policies specify the time period within which you must give notice.* Failure to report can result in your loss of the right to collect.

Third, you must prove your loss. This step usually requires you to give a sworn statement. When applicable, you must also show medical bills, an inventory and certified value of lost property (for example, a written inventory, photographs, and purchase receipts), an employer statement of lost wages, and, if possible, physical evidence of damage (X rays if you claim a back injury, a broken window or pried door if you claim a break-in and theft at your house). After you have submitted proof of loss, the insurer either (1) pays you the amount you asked for; (2) offers you a lesser amount; or (3) denies that the company has any legal responsibility under the terms of your policy. In the case of a disputed amount — when you are a named insured or covered family member — most policies provide for some form of claims arbitration. You hire a third party, the company hires a third party, and these two arbitrators together select one more person. When any two of the three arbitrators reach agreement, their decision binds you and the company to their solution.

When a company denies responsibility, you do not get the right of arbitration. In such an instance, the company is saying the loss does not fall under the policy coverage. You must then either forget the claim or bring in an attorney or, perhaps, a public adjustor (discussed next).

Filing a property or liability claim is quick and easy to do: Just call your agent, supply a few basic details, and look for your check in a few days.
Fantasy: Filing a property or liability claim is often a detailed and time-consuming process wherein you must prove your loss. The insurance company can offer you an amount less than the loss you claim or deny your claim altogether.

Claims Adjustment. Usually the first person to call when you need to file a claim is your insurance agent. If your loss is relatively minor, the agent can quickly process it. If it is more complex, your company will probably assign a claims adjustor to the case.

Adjustors. The **claims adjustor** works either for the insurance company, as an independent adjustor, or for an adjustment bureau. In any case, the adjustor is primarily looking out for the interests of the company — which might very well be to keep you, its customer, satisfied. However, many claimants think insurance companies have more money than they know what to do with and are out to collect all that is possible. Thus, the adjustor walks a fine line: He or she must diligently question and investigate, while at the same time offering service to minimize settlement delays and financial hardship. To promote your own interest in the claim, you should cooperate with the adjustor and answer inquiries honestly — while keeping in mind that the company writes the adjustor's paycheck.

Public adjustors and attorneys. To this point, we have been referring primarily to the claims that you collect from your own insurance company. In accidents in which a question of fault arises, you may have to file a claim against a negligent party's insurer. In these instances, the insurer will still use an adjustor, but this person will be looking out for the insurer's (and its policyholders') economic interests without any regard to keeping you satisfied. If you are not happy with the offered settlement, you might have to hire an attorney to negotiate the claim for you. Because the attorney will have a better understanding of the law and the legal provisions of your policy than you do, hiring one greatly improves your chances of collecting an amount you're entitled to. Keep in mind, however, that for their services, attorneys will often charge 25 to 50 percent of any amount they get for you (the exact amount of the fee is negotiable). Many times, though, the use of a costly attorney is worthwhile if you are not being treated fairly by the insurance company's adjustor.

> **claims adjustor**
> An insurance specialist, employed by an insurance company, an adjustment bureau, or self-employed, who investigates claims.

S U M M A R Y

- Property and liability insurance protects against the loss of real and personal property that can occur from various types of perils. In addition, such insurance protects against loss from lawsuits based on negligence.
- Most homeowner's insurance contracts are divided into two major sections. Section I covers the dwelling unit, accompanying structures, and the personal property of the insured. Section II pertains mainly to comprehensive coverage for personal liability and medical payments.
- Except for the house and garage, which are covered on a replacement basis, homeowner's insurance normally provides for the payment of *all losses on an actual cash value basis*, subject to applicable deductibles and policy limits. However, for an additional premium, you usually can obtain replacement-cost coverage on personal belongings.
- Automobile insurance policies usually contain provisions that protect the insured from loss due to personal liability, uninsured motorists, medical payments, collision (property damage to the vehicle), and comprehensive coverage (which applies to nearly any other type of noncollision damage your car might suffer, such as theft or vandalism).
- In addition to the major forms of homeowner's and automobile insurance, a variety of property and liability coverages is available, including personal property floater policies, umbrella personal liability policies, mobile-home insurance, boat insurance, recreational vehicle insurance, automobile repair insurance, earthquake insurance, flood insurance, and professional liability insurance.
- Before buying property and liability coverage, you should evaluate your exposure to loss and determine the coverage needed. You should also carefully select both the insurance agent(s) and the insurance company in order to obtain appropriate coverage at a reasonable price; and — equally important — make sure that the agent and company you deal with have reputations for fair claims-settlement practices.

Q U E S T I O N S A N D P R O B L E M S

1. Briefly explain the fundamental concepts related to property and liability insurance.
2. Explain the principle of indemnity. Are there any limits imposed on the amount an insured may collect under this principle?
3. Patricia Murphree's luxurious home in the suburb of Broken Arrow, Oklahoma, was recently gutted in a fire. Her living and dining rooms were completely destroyed, and the damaged personal property had a replacement price of $27,000. The average age of the damaged personal property was 5 years, and its useful life was estimated to be 15 years. What is the maximum amount the insurance company would pay Patricia, assuming it reimburses on an actual cash-value basis?
4. Explain the right of subrogation. How does this feature help lower insurance costs?

5. Describe how the coinsurance feature works. Assume that Clayton Barrow had a property insurance policy of $100,000 on his home. Would a 90 percent coinsurance clause be better than an 80 percent clause in such a policy? Give reasons to support your answer.

6. What are the perils against which most properties are insured under various types of homeowner's policies?

7. What types of property are covered under a homeowner's policy? Are the following included in the coverage: (a) an African parrot, (b) a motorbike, (c) Avon cosmetcs held for sale, and (d) Tupperware for home use?

8. Describe (a) types of losses, (b) persons, (c) locations, and (d) periods that are covered under a homeowner's policy.

9. Describe replacement cost coverage, and compare this coverage to actual cash value. Which is preferable?

10. What are deductibles? Do they apply to either liability or medical payments coverage under the homeowner's policy?

11. Briefly explain the major coverages available under the personal auto policy (PAP). Which persons are insured under (a) uninsured motorists coverage and (b) automobile medical payments insurance?

12. Explain the nature of (a) automobile collision insurance and (b) automobile comprehensive insurance.

13. Define no-fault auto insurance, and discuss its pros and cons.

14. Describe the important factors that influence the availability and cost of auto insurance.

15. Discuss the role of financial responsibility laws, and describe the two basic types of laws currently employed.

16. Briefly describe the following property and liability insurance coverages: (a) personal property floater (PPF) policies, (b) umbrella personal liability policies, (c) mobile-home insurance, (d) boat insurance, (e) earthquake insurance, and (f) flood insurance.

17. What guidelines should be used to distinguish between exposure to high-priority and low-priority risk when buying property and liability insurance?

18. Differentiate between captive and independent insurance agents. What characteristics should you look for when choosing both an insurance agent and an insurance company for purposes of buying property and/or liability insurance?

19. Briefly describe the key aspects of the claims-settlement process, explaining what to do after an accident, the steps in claim settlement, and the role and types of claims adjustors.

CONTEMPORARY CASE APPLICATIONS

11.1 The Salvatis' Homeowner's Insurance Decision

Phil and Anita Salvati, ages 30 and 28, respectively, were recently married in Chicago. Phil is an electrical engineer with Geophysical Century, an oil exploration company. Anita has a master's degree in special education and teaches at a local junior high school. After living in an apartment for six months, the Salvatis have negotiated the purchase of a new home in a rapidly growing Chicago suburb. Republic Savings and Loan Association has approved their loan request for $108,000, which represents 90 percent of the $120,000 purchase price. Prior to closing the loan, the Salvatis must obtain homeowner's insurance for the home. The Salvatis currently have an HO-4 renter's insurance policy, which they purchased from Phil's tennis partner, Kelly Duvall, who is an agent with Kramer's Insurance Company. In order to learn about the types of available homeowner's insurance, Phil has discussed their situation with Kelly, who has offered a variety of homeowner's policies for Phil's and Anita's consideration. He has recommended that the Salvatis purchase an HO-3 policy, since it would provide them with comprehensive coverage.

Questions

1. What forms of homeowner's insurance are available? Which forms should the Salvatis consider?

2. What are the perils against which the home and its contents should be insured?

3. Discuss the types of loss protection provided by the homeowner's policies under consideration.

4. What advice would you give the Salvatis regarding Kelly's suggestion? What coverage should they buy?

11.2 Auto Insurance for the Turners

Marjorie and Rodney Turner of Phoenix, Arizona, are a couple in their late 20s. Rodney is a loan officer at the Frontier National Bank of Arizona, and Marjorie is the merchandising manager at a major department store. At present the Turners own one car, but they have decided to use Rodney's Christmas bonus as a down payment on a second car. One Saturday afternoon in late December, they visited Chuck Thomas's Auto Mall, where they purchased a new, fully equipped Pontiac for $13,500. In order to obtain insurance on the car, Rodney called his agent, Jane Cunningham, who represents Farmers Insurance Company. He explained his auto insurance needs, and Jane said she would investigate the various options for him. Three days later, Rodney and Jane got together to look over the alternative coverages. Jane offered several proposals, including various combinations of the following coverages: (a) basic automobile liability insurance, (b) uninsured motorists coverage, (c) automobile medical payments insurance, (d) automobile collision insurance, and (e) comprehensive automobile insurance.

Questions

1. Describe the key features of these insurance coverages.

2. Are there any limitations on these coverages? Explain.

3. Indicate the persons who would be protected under each of these coverages.

4. What kind of insurance coverages would you recommend the Turners purchase? Explain your recommendation.

F O R   M O R E   I N F O R M A T I O N

General Information Articles

Anthony, Joseph. "Homeowner's Insurance Guide." *Consumers Digest*, May/June 1990, pp. 28–32.

Giese, William. "The Five-Minute Insurance Checkup." *Changing Times*, June 1991, pp. 31–34.

Hannon, Kerry. "How to Save $1,000 on Auto Insurance." *Money*, November 1991, pp. 158–168.

Henry, Ed. "Car Insurance: Dial Up a Better Deal." *Changing Times*, April 1990, pp. 43–48.

———. "10 Ways to Cut the Cost of Car Insurance." *Changing Times*, July 1988, pp. 47–54.

Paulson, Morton C. "The Compelling Case for No-Fault Insurance." *Changing Times*, July 1989, pp. 49–52.

Saunders, Laura. "Disaster Without Relief." *Forbes*, November 27, 1989, pp. 124, 128.

Wiener, Leonard. "Will Your Car Insurance Vanish?" *U.S. News and World Report*, January 9, 1989, p. 62.

Government Documents & Other Publications

Buyer's Guide to Insurance: What the Companies Won't Tell You. National Insurance Consumers Organization: 121 N. Payne St.; Alexandria, VA 22314.

How to Get Your Money's Worth in Home and Auto Insurance. Insurance Information Institute; published by McGraw-Hill (paperback).

Most people are exposed to various forms of property and liability insurance at a relatively early age. When you were a teenager, your parents may have demanded that you take driver's education courses before you got your driver's license in hopes that you would be a safer driver and because it would lower the premiums on your parents' personal automobile policy. Your parents were concerned with protecting against the loss of real and personal property and from losses arising out of lawsuits based on negligence.

Since most individuals are exposed to physical loss of property and loss through liability, it is essen-tial to have adequate coverage to properly protect your assets. In order to select appropriate coverage you must conduct an inventory of your insurable as-sets. You can probably make a list from memory of your major assets such as your home and auto-mobile, but you would more than likely overlook some of your personal property. You should make an inventory of your personal property by writing down the date of purchase, serial number, and origi-nal cost using a form such as the one in Exhibit 11.1. This inventory is invaluable as you must have proof of a loss and it would serve as documentation to sup-port a claim. In addition you might want to take pic-

If You Are Just Starting Out

Whether you are still in school or you have just begun your career, you need to have property and liability insurance. While you probably have some type of automobile insur-ance, it may not be adequate in terms of the policy limits, and if you are renting an apartment, you may not have renter's insurance.

The selection of appropriate insurance policies usually involves a trade-off between the costs of the policy and the amount of coverage. Early in your career you have a lim-ited amount of funds available to pay for your insurance, so you have to make every dollar count. This involves some effort on your part to secure quotes from a number of different insurance agencies and companies on your property and liability coverage. You should try to make sure that you are comparing the same coverage to validate your findings.

If you do have a claim against your insurance company, there are certain steps you should follow. If you are in-volved in an accident, get the names, addresses, and li-cense plate numbers of witnesses and those involved. You should then notify law enforcement officials and your in-surance agent. Remember you should never admit liability or tell anyone of the policy limits on your insurance.

Homeowner's or Renter's Insurance

1. Make an inventory of your personal property.

2. Determine if your coverage on personal property is based on actual cash value or replacement costs.

3. If you live in an apartment or any other type of rental unit, make sure you have renter's insurance — this may ap-ply to you even if you are still in school, as you may *not* be covered by your parents' homeowner's policy (check with their agent to find out).

4. Ask your agent to calculate the change in premium if you raise the deductible.

Automobile Insurance

1. Before you buy an automobile, determine what the in-surance costs would be on various makes and models.

2. Try to pay the premium in full in order to get the best rate. Most insurance companies will charge an additional "service fee" for multiple monthly or quarterly payments.

3. See if you can get a reduced rate if you have both your automobile and homeowner's (renter's) insurance with the same company.

4. Even though the premiums may remain the same, you might want to raise the deductible and increase your pol-icy limits.

Other Insurance

1. If you live in an area prone to earthquakes, you might want to consider taking out earthquake insurance as this is not included under the covered perils in most policies.

2. If you have reasonable policy limits on your auto-mobile and home, you should consider purchasing an umbrella liability insurance policy to protect you against a large judgment in the event of an accident in which you were found at fault.

tures or make a video tape of your personal property and store them in a safe place such as a lockbox.

If you are a homeowner and still have a balance on your mortgage, you are required to have insurance. Even if your home is free and clear, you would be foolish not to have coverage. In selecting the appropriate insurance coverage you should understand that the coverage you receive depends on the type of policy you select. Exhibit 11.2 provides you with a guide to homeowner's (and renter's) policies. Section I of the policy insures the home and its contents while Section II insures against negligence of the insured.

In selecting your automobile policy, you can make a number of choices as to the amount of cover-age you will have. Your personal automobile policy will usually have four parts. Part A will allow you to select the liability coverage you want above some minimum (usually determined by the state in which you reside). Part B provides the limits for medical coverage. You also have the option in part C for coverage of uninsured motorists, while part D covers damage to your auto from collision or other occurrences.

Proper selection and purchase of insurance policies for property loss and liability will provide you with financial piece of mind. As in the case of other expenditures, you should include this in your cash budget and alter the premium payment dates where possible to fit your needs.

If You Are Thirtysomething

As your household expands, you accumulate more personal property. Many times people assume that anything in or around the house is covered by the homeowner's policy. In fact, there are a number of exceptions to this such as the internal limits specified in the policy for certain types of personal property. Structures used on the premises for business purposes are excluded from coverage along with animals, motorcycles, golf carts, ATVs, and so on. In order to cover expensive items of personal property, you should take out a personal property floater for property not covered by your standard property.

Even though your income is probably greater than when you first started out, you still need to exercise good judgment in your purchase of insurance. While you may personally like the agent or company you have been dealing with, you should periodically shop your policies to find out the going rate. You may be surprised how helpful your agent will become in trying to save you on your premiums once she or he finds out that you are comparing rates.

Homeowner's or Renter's Insurance

1. If your policy does not have an inflation adjustment, you need to pay attention to increases in the prices of homes in your neighborhood and make appropriate adjustments in your coverage.

2. Remember that damage to trees and shrubs is usually covered by your policy.

3. If your home is severely damaged, be sure that you take adequate measures to seal off the house and grounds. If you do not and there is an injury or further damage, your policy may not cover the additional loss.

4. Consider the installation of burglar alarms and fire/smoke detectors as a means of lowering your insurance premiums.

Automobile Insurance

1. As your children get older, be sure that they take driver's education courses.

2. Consider canceling your collision and comprehensive coverage if you have a relatively old automobile. Remember, the policy only pays for actual cash value.

3. Review your policy limits on liability to make sure that you have at least $250,000 per person and $500,000 per accident.

4. You should make sure that you have adequate policy limits for coverage of uninsured motorists.

Other Insurance

1. In order to protect yourself in your job, you should check to see if your employer has professional liability coverage for you. If not, you may want to secure this type of insurance. This is not just for physicians anymore. All types of professionals are targets of lawsuits.

2. As your assets grow, you need to review your personal umbrella liability policy to see if your limits need to be increased. Remember, the more assets you have, the more likely you are to be sued in the event of an accident.

■ 1. Use the needs approach to calculate the amount of additional insurance needed on Mark's life. Assume that Mark would like Ana to receive enough money from his life insurance to pay off all of the consumer debt (but not the home mortgage). He would also like to provide an extra $10,000 to add to their emergency fund and $4,000 to cover final expenses. They estimate that Ana's monthly living expenses would be approximately $2,600 while she is working and $2,000 after she retires. Ana's monthly income while working is estimated to be $2,500 and $500 after retirement (assuming she starts funding her 401(k) plan). Investment income should be about $75 a month for the rest of her life. She should also receive about $1,200 a month from social security once she retires. Assuming Ana retires at age 66, she has 42 years of work and about 20 years of retirement to look forward to (given the average life expectancy of a woman her age). Mark and Ana currently have about $7,000 in assets that could be used for Ana's support in addition to the group life policy Mark has through his employer.

■ 2. Use the needs approach to calculate the amount of additional insurance needed on Ana's life. Use the same assumptions as above except that Ana would also like her life insurance proceeds to provide $8,000 for Mark to return to college for his MBA. In addition, Mark's monthly income while working will be only $2,100, but during retirement he will receive $850 a month from his employer pension plan in addition to $1,200 a month from social security. Assuming he retires at age 66, he will be working 41 more years and be retired 18 years. In addition to their assets of $7,000, Ana has a group life policy through her employer to supplement Mark's needs.

3. Evaluate the group term life policies Mark and Ana currently have. Should they keep these policies and/or buy additional life insurance coverage? If so, how much, and what type? Using the examples in this text, calculate the approximate cost of the recommended policies.

4. Recommend appropriate beneficiary and settlement options for Mark and Ana's policies.

5. Calculate Mark's disability income needs. Assume that he does not want to rely on social security or other government programs and that no company programs are available. He has 45 days of paid sick leave accumulated. How much disability coverage does he need? What length of waiting period and duration of benefits would you recommend? Using the examples in this text, calculate the approximate cost of this coverage.

6. Calculate Ana's disability income needs. Use the same assumptions about government and company benefits as in Question 5. Ana has 15 days of paid sick leave accumulated. Disability benefits from her current disability policy would be tax-free, since she pays the premiums on the policy. Does Ana need additional coverage? If so, how much? What terms would you recommend? Approximately how much would it cost?

7. Evaluate Mark's group major medical policy in terms of maximum limit, deductible, participation, and so on. What is the maximum dollar amount of covered expenses Mark would have to pay per year (assuming the insurance benefits remain below the maximum limit)? Is this an acceptable policy for Mark, considering his health and financial conditions?

8. Evaluate Ana's group HMO coverage. What are the potential out-of-pocket costs under this coverage? Is this an acceptable policy for Ana, considering her health and financial conditions?

9. Would you recommend that Ana be covered under Mark's policy or vice versa? Why? If so, how much would it cost?

10. Evaluate Mark and Ana's homeowner's insurance needs. Do they need homeowner's insurance? If so, why, and what HO form is appropriate for them? How much coverage do you recommend for their personal property, personal liability, and so on? Approximately how much will the recommended coverage cost?

11. Evaluate Mark and Ana's auto insurance policy. Is their coverage adequate for their insurance needs? Recommend any needed changes. Approximately how much would the recommended changes cost?

12. Do Mark and Ana need any other types of insurance coverage? If so, what types and why? About how much will the additional insurance cost?

13. Revise Mark and Ana's budget to reflect the change in expenditures caused by all of your insurance recommendations.

WILLIAMS *Insurance Needs*

Managing Investments

Investing in Stocks and Bonds

Have you ever stopped to think about all the different ways there are to invest money? In addition to savings and short-term investment vehicles, you can select from common and preferred stocks, bonds, convertible securities, limited partnerships and annuities, mutual funds, real estate, commodities, financial futures, and puts and calls. Some of these investments are highly conservative and easy to understand; others are very speculative and involve a good deal of risk. With such an extensive menu to choose from, it's easy to understand why a basic knowledge of these securities is so important. For in most cases, the cornerstone of a successful long-term investment program is not luck but *know-how*! The knowledgeable and informed investor understands the world of investing and knows how and when to use the various investment vehicles and strategies to his or her advantage. While knowledge alone will not guarantee success in the uncertain world of investing, it certainly will help you avoid unnecessary exposure to loss. Moreover, a basic understanding of investments is important from a financial planning perspective because *investing is the vehicle through which we reach many of our financial goals*. Alan and Barbara Tracey, for example, regularly invest money as a way to build up a fund for their daughter's college education. In addition, they invest a sizable amount each year as part of their retirement plans and also put away money toward the funds that Barbara feels she will need in the next five to eight years to set up her own law practice. For now, the Traceys confine most of their investing to blue chip stocks, high-grade bonds, and a few highly regarded mutual funds. However, as they learn more about investing, they fully intend to become more aggressive with their capital.

FINANCIAL *facts* OR *fantasies*

Are the following statements financial facts (true) or fantasies (false)?

You would have to save $2,500 a year in order to end up with a $25,000 nest egg in ten years.

Buying American Depositary Receipts is a great way to invest in foreign stocks.

A good investment is one that offers a positive rate of return.

You can get an idea of a stock's price volatility by looking at its beta.

When interest rates go down, bond prices also go down because such securities become less valuable.

Convertible bonds are so named because they can be exchanged for a set number of shares of common stock.

THE OBJECTIVES AND REWARDS OF INVESTING

Getting the most from your investment capital requires not only a clear understanding of your investment objectives, but also a familiarity with the concepts of risk and return. Assume you've just inherited some money and have decided to invest a big chunk of it (say, $40,000). What kind of investment characteristics would you look for when deciding where to put your money? Are dividends and current income important to you? How about capital appreciation? What kind of risk would you be willing to tolerate? These are important questions for an investor — stop to think about them before reading on.

People invest their money for all sorts of reasons. Some do it as a way to accumulate the down payment on a new home; others do it as a way to supplement their income; still others invest in order to build up a nest egg for retirement. Actually, the term "investment" means different things to different people. Millions of people *invest* regularly in such securities as stocks, bonds, and mutual funds; others *speculate* in commodities or options. **Investing** is generally considered to take more of a long-term perspective and is viewed as the process of purchasing securities in which stability of value and level of returns are somewhat predictable. **Speculating**, on the other hand, is viewed as a short-term activity that involves the buying and selling of securities in which future value and expected returns are highly uncertain. Obviously, speculation is considered to be far more risky than investing.

At first, you will probably keep your funds in some form of savings vehicle (as described in Chapter 5). Once you have *sufficient savings* — for emergency and other purposes — you can begin to build up a *pool of investable capital*. This often means making sacrifices and doing what you can to *live within your budget*. Granted, it's far easier to spend money than it is to save it, but if you're really serious about getting into investments, you're going to have

to accumulate the necessary capital! In addition to a savings and capital accumulation program, it's also important to have adequate *insurance coverage* in order to provide protection against the unexpected (we discussed different kinds of insurance in Chapters 9, 10, and 11). For our purposes here, we will assume that you are adequately insured and that the cost of insurance coverage is built into your family's monthly cash budget. Ample insurance and liquidity (cash and savings) with which to meet life's emergencies are two *investment prerequisites* that are absolutely essential for the development of a successful investment program. Once these conditions are met, you are ready to start investing.

BUT HOW DO I GET STARTED?

Contrary to what you may believe, there is really nothing mystical about the topic of investments — in fact, so long as you have the capital to do so, it's really quite easy to get started in investing. The terminology may indeed seem baffling at times and some of the procedures and techniques quite complicated. But don't let that mislead you into thinking there is no room for the small, individual investor. Nothing could be farther from the truth! For as we will see in this and the next two chapters, individual investors have a wide array of securities and investment vehicles to choose from. Further, opening an investment account is no more difficult than opening a checking account.

How, then, do you get started? To begin with, you need some money — not a lot; perhaps $1,000 to $2,000 will do, though $5,000 to $10,000 would be even better (and remember, this is *investment capital* we're talking about here — money you've accumulated above and beyond any basic emergency savings). In addition to money, you need knowledge and know-how. You should never invest in something you are not sure about — that is the quickest way to lose your money. Learn as much as you can about the market, different types of securities, and various trading strategies. This course you're taking on personal finance is a good start, but you may want to do more. You can become a *regular* reader of publications such as *Money, The Wall Street Journal, Barron's,* and *Forbes* (these and other sources of information are reviewed in Chapter 13). Keep up-to-date on developments in the market; start following the stock market, interest rates, and developments in the bond market.

We strongly suggest that, after you have learned a few things about stocks and bonds, you set up a portfolio of securities on paper and make *paper trades* in and out of your portfolio for six months to a year in order to get a feel for what it is like to make (and lose) money in the market. Start out with an imaginary sum of, say, $25,000 (as long as you are going to dream, you might as well make it worthwhile). Then keep track of the stocks and bonds you hold, record the number of shares bought and sold, dividends received, and so on. Throughout this exercise, be sure to use actual prices (as obtained from *The Wall Street Journal* or your local newspaper) and keep it as realistic as possible. If you are going to make mistakes in the market, you are much better off doing so on paper. Also, if your parents, relatives, and/or friends have done a lot of investing, talk to them! Find out what they have to say about investing, pick up some pointers, and possibly even learn from their mistakes. Eventually you will gain a familiarity with the market and become comfortable with the way things are done there. When that happens, you will be ready to take the plunge.

At this point, you need a way to invest — more specifically, you need a broker and some investment vehicle in which to invest. As we will see in the next chapter, the stockbroker is the party through whom you will be buying and selling stocks, bonds, and other securities. If your relatives or friends have a broker they like and trust, have them introduce you to him or her. Alternatively, visit several of the brokerage firms in your community; talk to one of their brokers about your available investment funds and your investment objectives.

As a beginning investor with limited funds, it is probably best to confine your investment activity to the basics. Stick to stocks, bonds, and mutual funds. Avoid getting fancy, and certainly *don't* try to make a killing each and every time you invest — that will only lead to frustration, disappointment, and very possibly, heavy losses. Instead, go for "relatively" high returns; for example, those that comfortably exceed what you can get from a savings account. Further, *be patient!* Don't expect the price of the stock to double overnight, and don't panic when things fail to work out as expected in the short run (after all, security prices do occasionally go down).

Finally, remember that you do not need spectacular returns in order to make a lot of money in the market. Instead, be *consistent* and let the concept of compound interest work for you. Do that and you'll find that just $2,000 a year invested at the fairly conservative rate of 10 percent will grow to well over $100,000 in 20 years! While the type of security in which you invest is a highly personal decision, you might want to give serious consideration to some sort of mutual fund as your first investment (see Chapter 14). Mutual funds provide professional management and diversification that small-time individual investors can rarely obtain on their own.

THE ROLE OF INVESTING IN PERSONAL FINANCIAL PLANNING

Buy a car, build a house, enjoy a comfortable retirement — these are goals that we would all like to attain some day and are, in many cases, the centerpieces of well-developed financial plans. As a rule, a financial goal such as building a house is not something we pay for out of our cash reserves; the cost (even the down payment) is simply too great to allow for that. Instead, we must accumulate the funds over time, which is where investment planning and the act of investing enter into the personal financial planning process. By investing our money, we are letting it work for us.

It all starts with an objective — a particular financial goal that we would like to achieve in a certain period of time. Take the case of the Zacharys. Shortly after the birth of their first child, they decided to start building a college education fund. After performing some rough calculations, they concluded

---

investing
The process of placing money in some medium such as stocks or bonds in the expectation of receiving some future benefit.

speculating
A form of investing in which future value and expected returns are highly uncertain.

they'd need to accumulate about $40,000 over the next 18 years in order to have the money for their daughter's education. Simply by setting that objective, the Zacharys created a well-defined, specific financial goal. The *purpose* is to meet the educational needs of their child, and the *amount* of money involved is $40,000 in 18 years. But how do they reach their goal? The first thing they must decide is where the money will come from. While part of it will come from the return (profit) on their investments, they still have to come up with the *investment capital*.

Coming Up with the Capital. So far, the Zacharys know how much money they want to accumulate, and how long they have to accumulate it. The only other thing they need to determine at this point is the *rate of return* they feel they can earn on their money. Having taken a financial planning course in college, the Zacharys know that the amount of money they'll have to put into their investment program depends in large part on *how much they can earn from their investments* — the higher their rate of return, the less they'll have to put up. Let's say they feel comfortable using a 9 percent rate of return. That's a fairly conservative number, and they're reasonably certain they can reach that level of return, on average, over the long haul. It's important to use some care in coming up with a projected rate of return. Don't saddle yourself with an unreasonably high rate, since that will simply reduce the chance of reaching your targeted financial goal.

Probably the best way of arriving at a reasonable projection is to look at what the market has done over the past three to five years, and then use the average return performance over that period as your estimate — or, if you want to be a bit more conservative, knock a point or two off the market's return. To help you out in that regard, take a look at the following statistics; they show the average annual returns on stocks, bonds, and U.S. Treasury bills over 5-, 10-, and 15-year holding periods:

Notice that unless someone had put just about everything into short-term U.S. Treasury bills, generating an average return of 9 to 10 percent, or even better, was not all that difficult over the past 15 years. Of course, there's no guarantee that these returns will happen again in the next 5 to 10 years, but at least the past does provide us with a basis — or "handle" — for making projections into the future.

Now, returning to our problem at hand, there are two ways of finding the amount of capital needed to reach a targeted sum of money: (1) you can make a lump-sum investment right up front and let that amount grow over time; or (2) you can set up a systematic savings plan and put away a certain amount of money each year. The worksheet in Exhibit 12.1 is designed to help you find the amount of investment capital you'll need to reach a given financial goal. It employs the *compound value* concept discussed in Chapter 3, and is based on a given financial target (line 1), and a projected average rate of return on your investments (line 2). Note that you can use the worksheet to find either a required lump-sum investment (part A), or an amount that will have to be put away each year in a savings plan (part B). For our purposes here, we'll assume the Zacharys have $4,000 to start with (this comes mostly from gifts their daughter received from her grandparents). Since they know they'll need a lot more than that to reach their target, the Zacharys decide to use part B of the worksheet to find out how much they'll have to save annually.

The first thing to do is find the future value of the $4,000 initial investment — the question here is: how much will that initial lump-sum investment grow to? Using the compound value concept and the appropriate "future value factor" (from Appendix A), we see, in line 7, that this deposit will grow to some $18,880. So, that's nearly $19,000 of our targeted $40,000 that we already have covered. Thus, by subtracting the terminal value of the initial investment (line 7) from our target (line 1), we come up with the amount that must be generated from some sort

Holding Periods	Stocks (as measured by the S&P 500)	High-grade Corp. Bonds	Stocks and Bonds Together	U.S. T-Bills	Stocks, Bonds, and T-Bills Combined
5 years: 1987–91	14.48%	10.33%	12.41%	6.38%	10.40%
10 years: 1982–91	17.80	16.22	17.01	7.48	13.83
15 years: 1977–91	12.73	10.08	11.40	8.18	10.33

of annual savings plan—see line 8. (*Note:* if you were starting from scratch, you'd enter a zero in line 5, and the amount in line 8 would be equal to the amount in line 1.) Again, using the appropriate future value factor (this time from Appendix B), we find the Zacharys will have to save $511 a year in order to reach their target of $40,000 in 18 years. That is, the $511 a year will accumulate to $21,120, which when added to the $18,880 that the initial $4,000 will grow to, equals the targeted $40,000. (By the way, they can also reach their target by making a lump-sum investment right up front of $8,475—try working out part A of the worksheet on your own, and see if you can come up with that number.)

You would have to save $2,500 a year in order to end up with a $25,000 nest egg in ten years.
Fantasy: Simply dividing your financial target ($25,000) by the length of time you have to get there (ten years) fails to take into account the fact that your money can earn a positive rate of return over time. Indeed, the amount you'll have to save each year depends on the rate of return you can earn on your money: the more you can earn, the less you'll have to put up each year.

An Investment Plan Provides Direction.

Now that the Zacharys know how much they have to save each year, their next step is to decide how they will save it. Probably the best thing to do in this regard is to follow some type of *systematic routine*—for example, building a set amount of savings each month or quarter into the household budget. But whatever procedure is followed, keep in mind that all we are doing here is accumulating the required investment capital. That money still has to be put to work in some kind of investment program, and that's where an investment plan comes into the picture. Basically, an **investment plan** is nothing more than a simple, preferably written, statement that explains how the accumulated investment capital will be invested for the purpose of reaching the targeted goal. In the example we've been using, the Zacharys' capital accumulation plan calls for a 9 percent rate of return as a target they feel they can achieve. Now they have to come up with a way of obtaining that 9

percent return on their money—meaning they have to specify, in general terms at least, the kinds of investment vehicles they intend to use. *When completed, an investment plan is a way of translating an abstract investment target* (in this case, a 9 percent return) *into a specific investment program.*

WHAT ARE YOUR INVESTMENT OBJECTIVES?

Some people buy securities for the protection they provide from taxes (that's what tax shelters are all about). Others want to have money put aside for that proverbial rainy day or, perhaps, to build up a nice retirement nest egg. Your goals tend to set the tone for your investment program, and they play a major role in determining how conservative (or aggressive) you're likely to be in making investment decisions. In a very real way, they provide a purpose for your investments. Given that you have adequate savings and insurance to cover any emergencies, the most frequent investment objectives are to (1) enhance current income, (2) save for a major purchase, (3) accumulate funds for retirement, and (4) seek shelter from taxes.

Current Income. The idea here is to put your money into investments that will enable you to supplement your income. In other words, it's for people who want to live off their investment income. A secure source of high current income, from dividends or interest, is the principal concern of such investors. Retired people, for example, often choose investments offering high current income—at low risk. Another common reason for seeking supplemental income is that a family member requires extended costly medical care. Even after insurance, such recurring costs can heavily burden a family budget without this vital income supplement.

---

investment plan

a statement, preferably written, that specifies how investment capital will be invested for the purpose of achieving a specified goal.

EXHIBIT 12.1

Finding the Amount of Investment Capital

A worksheet like this one can be used to find out how much money you must come up with in order to reach a given financial goal; note that this worksheet is based on the same future value concept we first introduced in Chapter 3.

<table>
<tr><td colspan="2" align="center">**DETERMINING AMOUNT OF INVESTMENT CAPITAL**</td></tr>
<tr><td colspan="2">Financial goal: <u>*To accumulate $40,000 in 18 years for the purpose of meeting the cost of daughter's college education.*</u></td></tr>
<tr><td>1.   Targeted Financial Goal (see Note 1)</td><td>$ *40,000*</td></tr>
<tr><td>2.   Projected Average Return on Investments</td><td>*9.0%*</td></tr>
<tr><td>**A. Finding a Lump Sum Investment:**</td><td></td></tr>
<tr><td>3.   Future Value Factor, from Appendix A
   ■ based on _____ years to target date and a projected average
     return on investment of _____</td><td></td></tr>
<tr><td>4.   Required Lump Sum Investment
   ■ line 1 ÷ line 3</td><td>$</td></tr>
<tr><td>**B. Making a Series of Investments Over Time:**</td><td></td></tr>
<tr><td>5.   Amount of Initial Investment, if any (see Note 2)</td><td>$ *4,000*</td></tr>
<tr><td>6.   Future Value Factor, from Appendix A
   ■ based on _____*18*_____ years to target date and a projected
     average return on investment of _____*9%*_____</td><td>*4.72*</td></tr>
<tr><td>7.   Terminal Value of Initial Investment
   ■ line 5 x line 6</td><td>$ *18,880*</td></tr>
<tr><td>8.   Balance to Come from Savings Plan
   ■ line 1 – line 7</td><td>$ *21,120*</td></tr>
<tr><td>9.   Future Value <u>Annuity</u> Factor, from Appendix B
   ■ based on _____*18*_____ years to target date and a projected
     average return on investment of _____*9%*_____</td><td>*41.3*</td></tr>
<tr><td>10. Series of Annual Investments Required over Time
   ■ line 8 ÷ line 9</td><td>$ *511*</td></tr>
<tr><td colspan="2">Note 1:   The "targeted financial goal" is the amount of money you want to accumulate by some target date in the future.

Note 2:   If you're starting from scratch—i.e., there is <u>no</u> initial investment—enter a zero in line 5, <u>skip</u> lines 6 and 7, and then use the total targeted financial goal (from line 1) as the amount to be funded from a savings plan; now proceed with the rest of the worksheet.</td></tr>
</table>

Major Expenditures. People often put money aside, sometimes for years, in order to save up enough to make just one major expenditure, the most common ones being:

- Save up for the down payment on a home
- Have the money for a child's college education
- Build up some capital for going into business
- Pay for an expensive (perhaps once-in-a-lifetime) vacation
- Pay for most or all of the purchase of a very special, expensive item
- Accumulate funds for retirement (discussed in the following section)

Whatever your goal, the idea is to set your sights on something and then go about building your capital with that objective in mind. It sure makes the act of investing more pleasurable. Once you have a handle on how much money you're going to need to attain one of these goals (following a procedure/worksheet like the one illustrated in Exhibit 12.1), you can specify the types of investment vehicles you intend to use. For example, you might follow a low-risk approach by making a single lump-sum investment in a bond that matures in the year in which you need the funds; or you could follow a more risky investment plan that calls for investing a set amount of money over time in something like a growth-oriented mutual fund (where there is little or no assurance of what the terminal value of the investment will be). Of course, for some purposes — such as the down payment on a home or a child's education — you will probably want to accept a lot less risk than for others, as the attainment of these goals should not be jeopardized by the types of investment vehicles you choose to employ.

Retirement. Accumulating funds for retirement is *the single most important reason for investing*. Too often, though, retirement planning occupies only a small amount of our time, since we tend to rely very heavily on employers and social security for our retirement needs. As many people learn too late in life, this can be a serious mistake. A much better approach is to review the amounts of income you can *realistically* expect to receive from social security and your employee pension plan, and then decide, based on your retirement goals, *whether or not they will be adequate to meet your needs*. You'll

probably find that you'll have to supplement them through personal investing. Obviously, the earlier in life you make this assessment, the greater your opportunity to accumulate the needed funds. (Retirement plans are discussed in Chapter 15.)

Shelter from Taxes. As Chapter 4 explained, federal income tax law does not treat all sources of income equally. For example, if you own real estate — either directly or through some pooling arrangement — you *may* be able to take depreciation deductions against certain other sources of income, thereby reducing the amount of your final taxable income. This tax write-off feature can make real estate an attractive investment vehicle *for some investors*, even though its pretax rate of return may not appear very high. The goal of sheltering income from taxes was made considerably more difficult with the Tax Reform Act of 1986; even so, such a goal for some investors still goes hand in hand with the goals of saving for a major outlay or for retirement. Clearly, if you can avoid paying taxes on the income from an investment, you will, all other things considered, have more funds available for reinvestment during the period.

DIFFERENT WAYS TO INVEST

Once you have established your investment objectives, there are a variety of investment vehicles from which you can choose in order to fulfill those goals. The various types of investment vehicles are briefly described in the following paragraphs; each will be more fully examined later in this chapter and in Chapters 13 and 14.

Common Stock. *Common stock* is basically a form of *equity* — as an investment, it represents an ownership interest in a corporation. Each share of stock symbolizes a fractional ownership position in a firm; for example, one share of common stock in a corporation that has 10,000 shares outstanding would denote a 1/10,000 ownership interest in the firm. A share of stock entitles the holder to equal participation in the corporation's earnings and dividends, an equal vote, and an equal voice in management. From the investor's perspective, the return to stockholders comes from either dividends and/or appreciation in share price. Common stock has no maturity date and as a result, remains outstanding indefinitely.

Bonds. In contrast to stocks, *bonds* are *liabilities*—they're IOUs of the issuer. The bondholder actually loans money to the issuer. Governments and corporations issue bonds that pay a stated return, called *interest*. When an individual invests in a bond, he or she receives a stipulated interest return, typically paid every six months, plus the return of the principal (face) value of the bond at maturity. For example, if you purchased a $1,000 bond that paid 10 percent interest in semiannual installments, you could expect to receive $50 every six months (that is, 10% × $1,000 × .5 years) and at maturity recover the $1,000 face value of the bond. Of course, a bond can be bought or sold prior to maturity at a price that can differ from its face value since bond prices, like common stock prices, do fluctuate in the marketplace.

Preferreds and Convertibles. These are forms of hybrid securities in that each has the characteristics of both stocks and bonds; in essence, they are a cross between the two. *Preferred securities* are issued as stock and, as such, represent an equity position in a corporation. Unlike common stock, however, preferreds have a stated (fixed) dividend rate, payment of which is given preference over dividends to holders of common stock. Like bonds, preferred stocks are usually purchased for the current income (dividends) they pay. A *convertible security*, in contrast, is a special type of fixed-income obligation (bond or preferred stock) that carries a conversion feature permitting the investor to convert it into a specified number of shares of common stock. Convertible bonds, therefore, provide the fixed-income benefits of a bond (interest) while offering the price appreciation (capital gains) potential of common stock.

Mutual Funds. An organization that invests in and professionally manages a diversified portfolio of securities is called a *mutual fund*. A mutual fund sells shares to investors, who then become part-owners of the fund's securities portfolio. Most mutual funds issue and repurchase shares at a price that reflects the underlying value of the portfolio at the time the transaction is made. Mutual funds have become very popular with individual investors because they offer not only a wide variety of investment opportunities but also a full array of services that many investors find particularly appealing.

Real Estate. Investments in *real estate* can take many forms, ranging from raw land speculation to limited-partnership shares in commercial property. The returns on real estate can come from rents, capital gains, and certain tax benefits. Unfortunately, estimating both risk and return in a real estate venture can be difficult and usually requires expert advice, particularly with respect to income tax implications.

Commodities, Financial Futures, and Options. *Commodities* and *financial futures* are contracts to buy/sell such things as agricultural products and other raw materials, or certain types of financial instruments, at some future date. Because they do not pay interest or dividends, their return depends solely on the change in the price of the underlying commodity or financial instrument. These are very risky investments, because losses can be far greater than the amount invested. In a similar fashion, *options* give the holder the right to buy or sell common stocks (and other financial instruments) at a set price over a specified period of time. Again, to earn a positive return one must correctly anticipate future price movements in the underlying financial asset. In contrast to futures contracts, the price paid for an option is the maximum amount that can be lost; however, options have very short maturities, and consistent losses can quickly exhaust one's investment capital. Futures and options are often referred to as **derivative securities** to the extent that they derive their value from the price behavior of some underlying real or financial asset.

Precious Metals and Collectibles. *Precious metals* and *collectibles* are specialized investments that are sometimes associated with hobbies. While price appreciation for many of these assets has come pretty easily in the past, there is no assurance that it will continue in the future. Before investing in them, one should consider their future salability. Resale markets are very often hard to find, and/or sales agents receive large commissions.

MARKET GLOBALIZATION AND THE ALLURE OF FOREIGN SECURITIES

In addition to all the securities mentioned above, a growing number of American investors are turning to foreign securities as a way to earn attractive returns. Such securities became increasingly popular during the 1980s, and many investment advisors today recommend that investors put at least part of their capital into foreign securities. A good deal of this interest has come about as advances in technology and communications, together with the gradual elimination of political and regulatory barriers, has allowed investors to make cross-border securities transactions with relative ease. As such, not only are more and more Americans beginning to invest in foreign securities, but foreign investors are becoming major players in U.S. markets as well. The net result is a rapidly growing trend toward market globalization, whereby investing is practiced on an international scale rather than confined to a single (domestic) market.

Ironically, as "our world is becoming smaller," our universe of investment opportunities is growing by leaps and bounds. The fact is, all of the investment vehicles noted previously can also be found in every one of the major markets around the world. Stocks, bonds, convertibles, mutual funds, futures and options, even short-term securities like Treasury bills and CDs are actively traded not only in the United States but also in foreign markets. Certainly, these are *not* the exclusive domain of the U.S. securities markets. Twenty years ago (in the early 1970s), our markets dominated the world; the U.S. stock market accounted for fully two-thirds of the world equity markets and our bond market was nearly as big. That's no longer true; by 1991, the U.S. share of the world equity market had plunged to 30 percent, and the U.S. bond market accounted for less than half of the world's supply of debt securities.

Today, the world debt and equity markets are dominated by six countries, which together account for about 80 to 90 percent of the world markets. These six countries are:

STOCKS		BONDS	
Country	Approx. Market Value	Country	Approx. Market Value
U.S.	$4.1 trillion	U.S.	$5.3 trillion
Japan	$3.4 trillion	Japan	$2.2 trillion
U.K.	$850 billion	Germany	$1.1 trillion
Germany	$400 billion	France	$650 billion
France	$360 billion	U.K.	$400 billion
Canada	$250 billion	Canada	$360 billion

Clearly, the United States is still the biggest player, but as these numbers show, there are some very big markets that exist beyond our borders. And keep in mind, these are just the six biggest markets. In addition to these six, there are another half dozen or so markets, like Switzerland, Australia, Italy, and Belgium, that are also regarded as *major world players* — not to mention a number of relatively small, *emerging markets*, like Mexico, South Korea, Denmark, and Norway. Thus, investors who confine all their investing to the U.S. markets are missing out on a big chunk of the worldwide investment opportunities. Not only that, they're missing out on some very attractive returns as well! For over the 15-year period from 1977 through 1991, the U.S. stock and bond markets provided the highest annual returns just *once* — in 1982. Indeed, more often than not, the returns in this country just don't stack up very well to those available in other markets.

So, if you're looking for better returns, you might want to give some thought to investing in foreign securities. There are several different ways of doing that. Without a doubt, from the perspective of an individual investor, the best and easiest way is through *international mutual funds* (we'll discuss such funds in Chapter 14). Mutual funds aside, you could, of course, buy securities directly in the foreign markets. *Investing directly* is not for the uninitiated, however. For while most major U.S. brokerage houses, like Merrill Lynch and Prudential Securities, are set up to accommodate investors interested in buying foreign securities, there are still a lot of *logistical* problems that have to be faced. Fortunately, there is an easier way and that is to buy *foreign securities that are denominated in dollars and traded*

derivative securities
Securities, such as futures and options, whose value is derived from (or linked to) the price behavior of an underlying real or financial asset.

directly on U.S. exchanges. One such investment vehicle is an American Depositary Receipt (ADR). ADRs are just like common stock, except that each ADR represents a specific number of shares in a specific foreign company. Indeed, the shares of more than 800 companies from over 30 foreign countries are traded on U.S. exchanges as ADRs — companies like Sony, Cannon, NEC, Volvo, Unilever, and Cadbury Schweppes. They're a great way to invest in foreign stocks because ADRs are bought and sold, on American markets, just like stocks in U.S. companies — and their prices are quoted in dollars, not British pounds or German marks. Furthermore, all dividends are paid in dollars.

Whereas the temptation to go after higher returns may be compelling, there is one thing to keep in mind when investing in foreign securities — that is, whether investing in foreign securities directly or through something like ADRs, the whole process of investing involves a lot more risk. That's because *the behavior of foreign currency exchange rates plays a vital role in defining returns to U.S. investors.* For as the U.S. dollar becomes weaker (or stronger) relative to the currency in which the foreign security is denominated, the returns to U.S. investors, from investing in foreign securities, will increase (or decrease) accordingly. Currency exchange rates can, in fact, have a dramatic impact on investor returns and quite often can convert mediocre returns, or even losses, into very attractive returns — and vice versa. There's really only one thing that determines whether the impact is going to be positive or negative, and that's the behavior of the U.S. dollar relative to the currency in which the foreign security is denominated. In effect, *a stronger dollar has a negative impact on total returns to U.S. investors, and a weaker dollar has a positive impact.* Thus, other things being equal, the best time to be in foreign securities is when the dollar is *falling,* because that *adds* to returns to U.S. investors.

Buying American Depositary Receipts is a great way to invest in foreign stocks.
Fact: For the typical individual investor, American Depositary Receipts are, indeed, a great way to buy foreign stocks! ADRs are dollar denominated and are just like any other American stock, except that each ADR represents a specific number of shares in a specific foreign company.

THE RISKS OF INVESTING

In selecting investments, you should be sure to consider the possible risks or uncertainties associated with them. Much like foreign securities are exposed to currency exchange risks, just about any type of investment vehicle is subject to one type of risk or another — some more than others. The basic types of investment risk are business risk, financial risk, market risk, purchasing power risk, interest rate risk, liquidity risk, and event risk. Obviously, other things being equal, you'd like to reduce your exposure to these risks as much as possible.

Business Risk. When you invest in a company, you may have to face up to the possibility that the issuing firm will fail, due either to economic or industry factors or, as is more often the case, to poor decisions on the part of management. In a general sense, this is **business risk** and it may be thought of as the degree of uncertainty surrounding the firm's earnings and subsequent ability to meet principal, interest, and dividend payments on time. Companies that are subject to high degrees of business risk generally experience wide fluctuations in sales, have widely erratic earnings, and can, in fact, end the year with substantial operating losses.

Financial Risk. **Financial risk** relates to the amount of debt used to finance the firm. Look to the company's balance sheet to get a handle on a firm's financial risk. As a rule, companies that have little or no long-term debt are fairly low in financial risk. This is particularly so if a company has a healthy earnings picture as well. The problem with debt financing is that it creates principal and interest obligations that have to be met regardless of how much profit the company is generating. As with business risk, financial risk can lead to failure (as in the case of bankruptcy), or a rate of return that is sharply below your expectations.

Market Risk. **Market risk** results from the behavior of investors in the securities markets. The fact is, prices of stocks and bonds will sometimes change even though business and financial risks, and other intrinsic factors, stay about the same. Such changes have little to do with the securities themselves but instead are due to changes in political, economic, and social conditions, and/or in investor tastes and preferences. Essentially, market risk is reflected in the *price volatility* of a security—the more volatile the price of a security, the greater its perceived market risk.

Purchasing Power Risk. Possible changes in price levels within the economy also result in risk. In periods of rising prices (inflation), the purchasing power of the dollar declines. This means that a smaller quantity of goods and services can be purchased with a given number of dollars. In periods of declining price levels, the purchasing power of the dollar increases. An awareness of **purchasing power risk** and changes in purchasing power allows investors to select investments that are best suited for a given price level environment. In general, investments whose values tend to move with general price levels are most profitable during periods of rising prices, whereas those providing fixed returns (like bonds) are preferred during periods of declining price levels or low inflation.

Interest Rate Risk. **Fixed-income securities**, which include preferred stocks and bonds, offer purchasers a fixed periodic return and, as such, are most affected by **interest rate risk**. As interest rates change, the prices of these securities fluctuate, decreasing with increasing interest rates and increasing with decreasing interest rates. For example, the prices of fixed-income securities drop when interest rates increase in order to provide purchasers with a rate of return that is competitive with those available from other, similar securities. Changes in interest rates are the result of fluctuations in the supply of and/or demand for money. These fluctuations are caused by various economic actions of the government or the interactions of business firms, consumers, and financial institutions.

Liquidity Risk. The risk of not being able to liquidate an investment conveniently and at a reasonable price is called **liquidity risk**. The liquidity of a given investment vehicle is important because it provides investors with a safety valve just in case they ever have to get out, for one reason or another. In general, investment vehicles traded in *thin markets*, in which supply and demand are small, tend to be less liquid than those traded in *broad markets*. However, to be liquid, an investment must be easily salable at a reasonable price. One can generally en-

hance the liquidity of an investment merely by cutting its price. For example, a security recently purchased for $1,000 would not be viewed as highly liquid if it could be sold only at a significantly reduced price, such as $500. Vehicles such as mutual funds, or the stocks and bonds of major companies listed on the New York Stock Exchange, are generally highly liquid; others, such as an isolated parcel of raw land in rural Georgia, are not.

Event Risk. More than just a buzz word used by the financial media, **event risk** is real, and it can

business risk
The degree of uncertainty associated with the firm's earnings and consequent ability to pay interest and dividends.

financial risk
A type of investment risk associated with the mix of debt and equity financing used by the issuing firm.

market risk
A type of investment risk associated with factors such as changes in political, economic, and social conditions and in investor tastes and preferences that may cause the market price of a security to change.

purchasing power risk
A type of risk resulting from possible changes in price levels that can have a significant effect on investment returns.

fixed-income securities
Securities such as preferred stocks and bonds that offer purchasers fixed periodic returns.

interest rate risk
A type of risk resulting from changing market interest rates that mainly affects fixed-income securities.

liquidity risk
A type of risk associated with the inability to liquidate an investment conveniently and at a reasonable price.

event risk
The risk that some major, unexpected event will occur, leading to a sudden, substantial change in the financial condition of a firm; for example, a company could go through a leveraged buy-out, or the money manager of a highly successful mutual fund could quit.

have a direct and dramatic impact on investment return. Basically, it occurs when something substantial happens to a company and that event, in itself, has a sudden impact on the company's financial condition. Event risk goes beyond business and financial risk, and it doesn't necessarily mean the company or market is doing poorly. Instead, it involves an event that is largely (or totally) unexpected, and which has a significant and usually immediate effect on the underlying value of an investment. A good example of event risk was the recent action by the Food and Drug Administration to halt the use of silicone breast implants. The share price of Dow Chemical — the dominant producer of this product — was quickly affected (in a negative fashion) as a result of this single event! Event risk can take many forms, though, fortunately, its impact tends to be confined to certain companies, securities, or segments of the market.

THE RETURNS FROM INVESTING

Any investment vehicle — be it a share of stock, a bond, a piece of real estate, or a stock option — has just two basic sources of return: *current income* and/or *capital gains*. Some investments offer only one source of return (for example, options provide only capital gains), but most offer both income and capital gains, which together make up what is called the *total return* from an investment. Of course, where both elements of return are present, the relative importance of each will vary among investments. Whereas current income is more important with bonds, capital gains usually makes up a larger portion of total return in the case of common stocks. Further, in practice, taxes should also be considered in the investment decision, since *taxes determine how much of the current income and capital gains one gets to keep!* As a rule, it is a good idea to use after-tax cash flows or after-tax returns when evaluating investment vehicles.

Current Income. Current income is received with some degree of regularity over the course of a year, and may take the form of dividends on stock, interest from bonds, and rents from real estate. People who invest to obtain income look for investment vehicles that will provide regular and predictable patterns of income. Preferred stocks and bonds, which are expected to pay known amounts at specified times (quarterly or semiannually, for example), are usually good income investments.

Capital Gains. The other type of return available from investments is capital appreciation (or growth), which is reflected in an increase in the market value of the investment vehicle. Capital gains occur when you're able to sell a security for more than you paid for it, or when your security holdings go up in value. Investments that provide greater growth potential through capital appreciation normally have lower levels of current income, since the firm achieves its growth by reinvesting its earnings instead of paying dividends out to the owners. Many common stocks, for example, are acquired for their capital gains potential.

INTEREST-ON-INTEREST: AN IMPORTANT ELEMENT OF RETURN

Question: When does an 8 percent investment end up yielding only 5 percent? Answer: Probably more often than you think! Of course, it can happen when investment performance fails to live up to expectations. But it can also happen even when everything goes right. That is, so long as at least part of the return from an investment involves the periodic receipt of current income (such as dividends or interest payments), that income has to be *reinvested* at a given rate of return in order to achieve the yield you thought you had going into the investment. To see why that's so, consider an investor who buys an 8 percent U.S. Treasury bond and holds it to maturity, a period of 20 years. Each year the bondholder receives $80 in interest, and at maturity, the $1,000 in principal is repaid. There is no loss in capital, no default; everything is paid right on time. Yet this sure-fire investment ends up yielding only 5 percent. Why? Because the investor failed to reinvest the annual interest payments he was receiving. By not plowing back all the investment earnings, the bondholder failed to earn any *interest-on-interest*.

Now take a look at the graph on page 503. It shows the *three* elements of return for our 8 percent, 20-year bond: (1) the recovery of principal, or capital gains if any is earned; (2) periodic interest income;

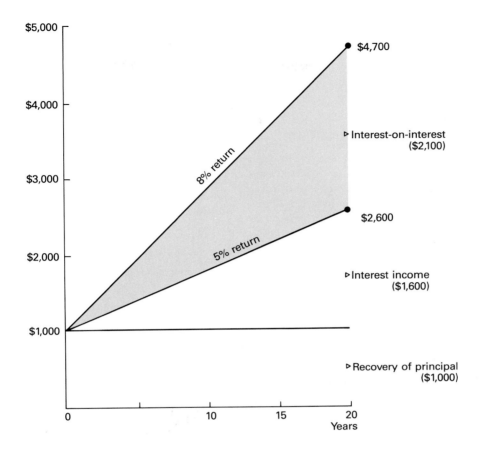

and (3) the interest-on-interest earned from reinvesting the periodic interest payments. Observe that since the bond was originally bought at par ($1,000), you start off with an 8 percent investment. Where you end up depends on what you do with the profits (interest earnings) from this investment; that is, *whereas current income and capital gains make up the profits from an investment, interest-on-interest is a measure of what you do with those profits!* If you don't reinvest the interest income, you'll end up on the 5 percent line.

To move to the 8 percent line, you have to earn interest-on-interest from your investments. Specifically, since you started out with an 8 percent investment, that's the rate of return you have to earn when reinvesting your income. The rate of return you start with, in effect, is the required, or minimum, reinvestment rate. Put your investment profits to work at that rate and you'll earn the rate of return you set out to; fail to do so and your return will decline accord-

ingly. And keep in mind that even though we used a bond in our illustration, *this same principle applies to any type of long-term investment vehicle*. It's just as relevant to common stocks and mutual funds as it is to long-term bond instruments. This notion of earning interest-on-interest is what the market refers to as a *fully compounded rate of return*. It's an important concept because you can't start reaping the full potential from your investments until you start earning a fully compounded return on your money.

So long as periodic investment income is involved, the reinvestment of that income and interest-on-interest are matters you're going to have to deal with. In fact, *interest-on-interest is a particularly important element of return for investment programs that involve a lot of current income*. This is so because, in contrast to capital gains, current income has to be reinvested by the individual investor. (With capital gains, the investment vehicle itself is doing the reinvesting, all automatically.) It follows, therefore, that if your investment program tends to lean toward income-oriented securities, then interest-on-interest — and the continued reinvestment of income — will play an important role in defining the amount of investment success you have.

THE RISK-RETURN TRADE-OFF

The amount of risk associated with a given investment vehicle is directly related to its expected return. This is a *universal* rule of investing and means that if you want a higher level of return from your investment, you will probably have to accept a greater exposure to risk. Thus, investors should *expect* to be compensated for taking higher levels of risk by earning higher rates of return. Since most people are believed to be risk averse — they dislike taking risks — some incentive to taking risks must be offered. If a low-risk investment offered the same return as a high-risk one, investors would naturally opt for the former — or, put another way, investors would choose the investment with the least risk for a given level of return.

The direct relationship between risk and return is shown in Exhibit 12.2, which generalizes the risk-return trade-off for some popular investment vehicles. Note that it is possible to receive a positive return for zero risk, such as at point A; this is sometimes referred to as the **risk-free rate of return**, which is often measured by the return on a short-term government security, such as a 90-day Treasury bill.

WHAT MAKES A GOOD INVESTMENT?

In keeping with the above risk-return discussion, it follows that the value of any investment depends on the amount of return it is expected to provide relative to the amount of perceived risk involved. This basic rule applies to any type of investment vehicle, be it stocks, bonds, convertibles, options, real estate, or commodities. In this respect, they should all be treated the same.

Future Return. In the field of investments, the only return that matters is *the expected future return*. Except to the extent that they can help you get a handle on future income, past returns are of little value to investors — after all, it is not what the security did last year that matters, but rather, what it is expected to do next year.

Earlier, we defined returns as being made up of current income and capital gains. Thus, to get an idea of the future return on an investment, we must formulate expectations of its future current income and future capital appreciation. To illustrate, assume you are thinking of buying some stock in Rose Colored Glasses, Inc. (RCG). By reviewing several financial reports, you have come up with an estimate of the future dividends and price behavior of RCG as follows:

Expected average annual dividends, 1992 – 1994	$ 2.15 a share
Expected market price of the stock, 1994	$75.00 a share

Since the stock is now selling for $60 a share, the difference ($75 − $60) represents the amount of *capital gains* you can expect to receive over the next three years — in this case, $15 a share. Thus, you have estimates of the stock's future *income stream*; what you need now is a way to measure future *return*.

Approximate Yield. Finding the exact rate of return of this (or any) investment involves a highly complex mathematical procedure. However, you can obtain a close estimation of return by computing the investment's *approximate yield*. This measure is widely used by seasoned investors and results in a rate of return (yield) that is remarkably close to the exact figure; and it is relatively easy to use. Best of all, this barometer of return considers not only current income and capital gains, but interest-on-interest as well. As such, *approximate yield provides a measure of the fully compounded rate of return* from an investment and is the preferred way to measure expected return performance.

The method of finding the approximate yield on an investment is shown in Equation 12.1. If you briefly study the formula, you will see that it is really not as formidable as it may at first appear. All it does is relate (1) average current income and (2) average capital gains to the (3) average amount of the investment.

To illustrate, let's use the Rose Colored Glasses example again. Given the average annual dividends

Equation 12.1

$$\text{Approximate yield} = \frac{\text{Average annual current income} + \left[\dfrac{\begin{array}{c}\text{Future price} - \text{Current price}\\\text{of investment} \quad \text{of investment}\end{array}}{\text{Number of years in investment period}}\right]}{\left[\dfrac{\begin{array}{c}\text{Current price} + \text{Future price}\\\text{of investment} \quad \text{of investment}\end{array}}{2}\right]}$$

$$= \frac{CI + \left[\dfrac{FP - CP}{N}\right]}{\left[\dfrac{CP + FP}{2}\right]}$$

where
CI = *average* annual current income (amount you expect to receive annually from dividends, interest, or rent)
FP = expected future price of investment
CP = current market price of investment
N = investment period (length of time, in years, that you expect to hold the investment)

(CI) of $2.15, current stock price (CP) of $60, future stock price ($FP$) of $75, and an investment period (N) of 3 years (you expect to hold the stock through 1995), you can now use Equation 12.1 to find the expected approximate yield of this investment:

$$\text{Approximate yield} = \frac{\$2.15 + \left[\dfrac{\$75 - \$60}{3}\right]}{\left[\dfrac{\$60 + \$75}{2}\right]}$$

$$= \frac{\$2.15 + \left[\dfrac{\$15}{3}\right]}{\left[\dfrac{\$135}{2}\right]}$$

$$= \frac{\$2.15 + \$5.00}{\$67.50} = \frac{\$7.15}{\$67.50}$$

$$= \underline{10.6\%.}$$

In this case, if your forecasts of annual dividends and capital gains hold up, an investment in Rose Colored Glasses should provide a return of around 10.6 percent per year.

Whether or not you should consider RCG a viable investment candidate depends on how this level of expected return stacks up to the amount of risk you must assume. Suppose you have decided that the stock is moderately risky. To determine whether the rate of return on this investment will be satisfactory, you can compare it to some benchmark. One of the

risk-free rate of return
The rate of return on short-term government securities, such as Treasury bills, that have no default risk or maturity premiums.

EXHIBIT 12.2

The Risk-Return Relationship

In the field of investments, there generally is a direct relationship between risk and return: The more risk you face, the greater should be the return you should expect to generate from the investment.

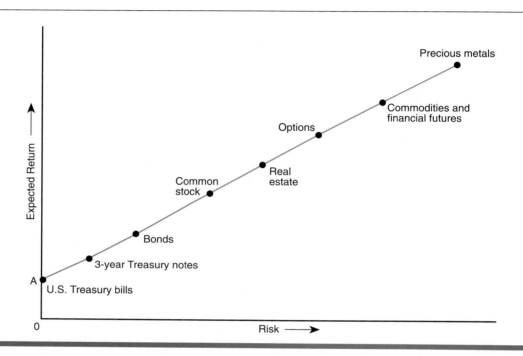

best is the rate of return you can expect from a *risk-free* security such as a *U.S. Treasury bill*. The idea is that the return on a *risky* security should be greater than that available on a *risk-free* security (this is the concept underlying the graph in Exhibit 12.2). If, for example, U.S. T-bills are yielding, say, 4 or 5 percent, then you'd probably want to receive something like 12 to 15 percent for a moderately risky security like RCG. In essence, the 12 to 15 percent is your **desired rate of return** — it is the minimum rate of return you feel you should receive in compensation for the amount of risk you must assume. *An investment should be considered acceptable only if it's expected to generate a rate of return that meets (or exceeds) your desired rate of return.* In the case of RCG, the stock should *not* be considered a viable

investment candidate, since it fails to provide the minimum or desired rate of return. In short, because of the risks involved with the stock, the amount of expected return falls short of the amount you deserve.

A good investment is one that offers a positive rate of return.

Fantasy: A good investment is one that offers an expected return that equals or exceeds the investor's desired rate of return, which is defined relative to the amount of risk imbedded in the investment. Thus, what might be a good return in one case may be totally inadequate in another.

INVESTING IN COMMON STOCK

Remember that money you inherited and decided to invest? Let's say you want to use part of it to buy some common stocks—a popular form of investing that offers attractive returns from both price appreciation and the receipt of dividends. What kinds of stocks (for example, blue chips, growth stock, and so on) would you be most interested in, and how would you decide what price to pay for them? Give some thought to these questions before reading on.

Common stocks appeal to investors for a variety of reasons. To some, investing in stocks is a way to hit it big if the issue shoots up in price; to others, it is the level of current income they offer. In fact, given the size and diversity of the stock market, it is safe to say that no matter what the investment objective, there are common stocks available to fit the bill. Not surprisingly, common stocks are a popular form of investing, used by literally millions of individuals and a variety of financial institutions.

The basic investment attribute of a share of common stock is that it enables the investor to participate in the profits of the firm, which is how it derives its value. Every shareholder is, in effect, a part-owner of the firm and, as such, is entitled to a piece of its profit. However, this claim on income is not without its limitations, for common stockholders are really the **residual owners** of the company, meaning they are entitled to dividend income and a prorated share of the company's earnings only after all the other obligations of the firm have been met. Equally important, as residual owners, *holders of common stock have no guarantee that they will ever receive any return on their investment.*

COMMON STOCK AS A FORM OF INVESTMENT

The stock market can perform beautifully, or it can behave "like a dog." A good example of the former is 1991, when in spite of a war with Iraq and an at-tempted coup in the Soviet Union, the market still went up by some 20 percent (Exhibit 12.3 shows the market's performance for the year). As far as behaving badly, there's probably no better example of that than 1987. Actually, the year started off very nicely as stock prices shot up in the first six months (incredibly, the market had gone up almost 30 percent by midsummer), only to experience a terrible market crash on October 19, when stock prices, as measured by the Dow Jones Industrial Average, fell over 500 points on volume of over 600 million shares. October 19, 1987, was not just another bad day in the market— it was history! As far as the market was concerned, it was like no other day on record and hopefully, it's a situation that won't reoccur any too soon.

Fortunately, the October 19s of this world are the rare exception rather than the rule. And as a result, the stock market is not all risk and wild price volatility. There are also some pretty attractive rewards. Consider the fact that even though the last quarter of 1987 was a wild and woolly one, the market still ended the year on the plus side—if up by only a meager 2 percent. And in 1988, the market went up another 12 percent, followed by an even better 27 percent jump in market prices during 1989. Indeed, if you look at the eight years from August 1982 (which is generally regarded as the beginning of the great bull market of the 1980s) though July 1990 (which is about the time Iraq invaded Kuwait), you'll find the market went up an impressive 280 percent—and that's *after* factoring in the impact of the

desired rate of return
The minimum rate of return that an investor feels should be earned in compensation for the amount of risk assumed.

residual owners
Shareholders of the company, they are entitled to dividend income and shares of the company's profits only after all of the firm's other obligations have been met.

1987 crash and another smaller market plunge that occurred in October 1989. Clearly, it's this kind of resiliency and overall market performance that explains the appeal of common stocks.

Issuers of Common Stock.   Shares of common stock can be issued by any corporation in any line of business. Although all corporations have stockholders, not all have publicly traded shares. The stocks of interest to us in this book are the so-called *publicly traded issues* — the shares that are readily available to the general public and that are bought and sold in the open market. Just about every facet of American industry is represented in the stock market. You can buy shares in public utilities, airlines, mining concerns, manufacturing firms, and retail organizations, or in financial institutions like banks and insurance companies. The number of shares issued depends on the size of the firm and its financial needs.

Aside from the initial distribution of common stock when the corporation is formed, subsequent sales of additional shares may be made through a procedure known as a *public offering*. The corporation, working with its underwriter, simply offers the investing public a certain number of shares of its stock at a certain price. Exhibit 12.4 depicts the announcement for such an offering. Note in this instance that Black & Decker Corp. is offering some 20.7 million shares of stock (in both the United States and abroad) at a price of $23.25 per share. When issued, the new shares will be commingled with the outstanding shares (since they are all the same class of stock), and the net result will be an increase in the number of shares outstanding.

Common stock may also be issued through *rights offerings*. These are used when a firm with a new issue of common stock must, under state law, let the current stockholders purchase new shares in proportion to their existing share ownership; this right is known as a *preemptive right*. In order to efficiently carry out the rights offering, the firm issues *rights* — negotiable instruments allowing the holder to purchase a certain number of shares of the new issue at a specified price — to each shareholder. These rights normally must be exercised within a few weeks. Because the *exercise price* at which the new shares can be purchased is usually below the prevailing market price, *rights have value and may be sold in the market*.

Companies can also use *warrants* to issue additional shares of common stock. Basically, a warrant gives an investor the right to purchase shares of stock at a certain price over some specified period of time. The purchase price of the stock as specified by a warrant is usually higher than the stock's market price at the time of issue. Therefore, warrants become valuable only after the market price of the stock has risen above the purchase price stipulated on the warrants. For instance, suppose a warrant allows the holder to purchase two shares of stock at $30 per share. As long as the warrant is outstanding, this company's stock can be purchased (with the warrant) at $30 a share *no matter how high the market price of the stock goes*. If the current market price of the stock is $45 per share, the warrant will be valuable since the market price of the stock will exceed the $30 price stipulated on the warrant; in effect, even though the current market price of the stock is $45 per share, a warrant holder can still buy the stock at *$30* a share! Warrants, therefore, do have value and, as such, are actively traded in the securities markets. When warrants are exercised, a corporation issues new shares of common stock.

THE PAR VALUE OF A SHARE OF STOCK

A stated value that used to be placed on stock certificates, **par value** was intended to represent not the value of a stock, but the minimum price at which it could be sold without causing the shareholder to assume any liability for the firm's actions. Par value is no longer important; despite its name, it does not reflect value. Many stocks issued today are in fact no-par stocks, which should attest to the insignificance of par value. Occasionally stocks do sell for less than their par value, although in most instances they sell well above their par.

BASIC TAX CONSIDERATIONS

Common stocks provide income in the form of dividends, usually paid quarterly, and/or capital gains, which occurs when the price of the stock goes up

EXHIBIT 12.3

The Stock Market in 1991

1991 was quite a year! It began with the United States about to go to war with Iraq and ended with the collapse of the Soviet Union. But even in spite of all this turmoil, and a recession that just wouldn't go away, the stock market still turned in an impressive performance, as a strong year-end rally helped push the Dow up 20.3 percent.

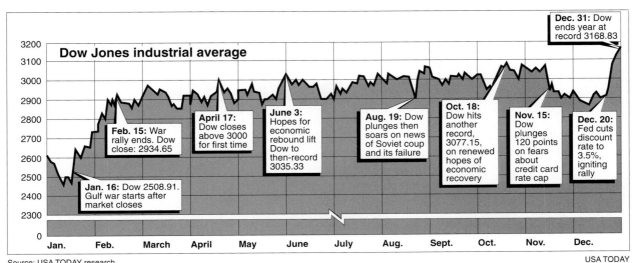

Dec. 31: Dow ends year at record 3168.83

Dow Jones industrial average

Feb. 15: War rally ends. Dow close: 2934.65

April 17: Dow closes above 3000 for first time

June 3: Hopes for economic rebound lift Dow to then-record 3035.33

Aug. 19: Dow plunges then soars on news of Soviet coup and its failure

Oct. 18: Dow hits another record, 3077.15, on renewed hopes of economic recovery

Nov. 15: Dow plunges 120 points on fears about credit card rate cap

Dec. 20: Fed cuts discount rate to 3.5%, igniting rally

Jan. 16: Dow 2508.91. Gulf war starts after market closes

Source: USA TODAY research

USA TODAY

over time. As indicated in Chapter 4, from a tax perspective, it does make a difference (albeit a small one) how the investment income is earned. That is, whereas dividends are fully taxable at regular tax rates (of 15, 28, or 31 percent), capital gains are subject to a maximum tax rate of 28 percent. Thus, capital gains are subject to a little less tax than dividends, but that only applies to taxpayers in the maximum (31 percent) tax bracket. Of course, there is no tax liability on any capital gains until the stock is actually sold (*paper gains* — that is, any price appreciation that occurs on stock that you still own — accumulate tax-free). Taxes are due on any dividends and/or capital gains in the year in which the dividends are received and/or the stock is actually sold. Thus, if you received, say, $125 in dividends in 1992, you would have to include that income on your 1992 tax return.

Here is how it all works: Assume, for example, that you just sold 100 shares of common stock for $30 per share. Also assume that the stock was originally purchased two years ago for $20 per share and that during the current year you received $1.25 per share in cash dividends. For tax purposes, you would have

par value

The stated value placed on stock to reflect the minimum price at which the stock could be sold without causing the shareholder to assume any liability for the firm's actions; carries no significance in the market today.

EXHIBIT 12.4

An Announcement of a New Common Stock Issue

Here the company is issuing nearly 21 million shares of stock at a price of $23.25 a share. For Black & Decker, that'll mean over $480 million in new capital! Note in this case, that in addition to offering the stock in the United States, there's over 4 million shares being offered *outside the country to foreign investors* — which, by the way, is becoming increasingly common as more and more companies are going global in their search for capital.

Number of shares being offered in the United States

Number of shares being offered in foreign markets

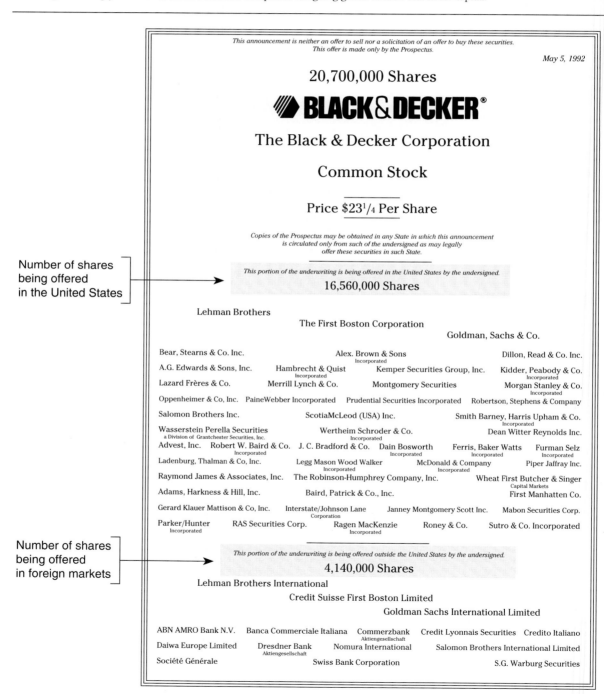

a capital gain of $1,000 ([$30/share − $20/share] × 100 shares) and $125 in dividend income ($1.25/share × 100 shares). If you were in the 31 percent tax bracket, your dividends would be subject to a 31 percent tax rate (that is, $125 × .31 = $38.75 in taxes), but the capital gains you earned would be subject to a tax rate of only 28 percent—that is, $1,000 × .28 = $280 in taxes. Thus, you'd end up paying $318.75 ($38.75 + $280) in taxes. Whatever you are left with would represent your after-tax income—in this case, it would be $1,125 − $318.75 = $806.25.

THE VOTING RIGHTS OF COMMON STOCKHOLDERS

The holders of common stock normally receive *voting rights*, which means that for each share of stock held, they receive one vote. In certain instances, common stock may be designated as nonvoting at the time of its issue, but this is the exception rather than the rule. Although different voting systems exist, the small stockholders need not concern themselves with them since, regardless of the system used, the chance that they will be able to affect corporate control with their votes is quite slim. Corporations have annual stockholders' meetings at which time new directors are elected and special issues are voted on. Since most small stockholders are unable to attend these meetings, they can use a proxy to assign their votes to another person, who will vote their stock for them. A **proxy** is merely a written statement assigning voting rights to another person.

TYPES OF DIVIDENDS

Corporations pay dividends to their common stockholders in the form of cash and/or additional stock. *Cash dividends* are the most common. Since firms can pay dividends from earnings accumulated from previous periods, stockholders may receive dividends *even in periods when the firm shows a loss.* Cash dividends are normally distributed on a quarterly basis in an amount determined by the firm's directors. For example, if the directors declared a

quarterly cash dividend of 50 cents a share, and you owned 200 shares of stock, you would receive a check for $100.

A popular way of assessing the amount of dividends received is to measure the stock's dividend yield. Basically, **dividend yield** is a measure of common stock dividends on a relative (percent), rather than absolute (dollar), basis—that is, the dollar amount of dividends received is related to the market price of the stock. As such, dividend yield is an indication of the rate of current income earned on the investment dollar. It is computed as follows:

$$\text{Dividend yield} = \frac{\text{Annual dividends received per share}}{\text{Market price per share of stock}}$$

Thus, a company that annually pays $2 per share in dividends and whose stock is trading at $50 a share will have a dividend yield of 4 percent ($2/$50 = .04).

Occasionally the directors may declare a stock dividend as a supplement to or in place of cash dividends. **Stock dividends** represent new shares of

proxy
A written statement used to assign a stockholder's voting rights to another person, typically one of the existing directors.

dividend yield
The percentage return provided by the dividends paid on common stock; calculated by dividing the cash dividends paid during the year by the stock's market price.

stock dividends
New shares of stock distributed to existing stockholders as a supplement to or substitute for cash dividends.

stock issued to existing stockholders. Although they often satisfy the needs of some investors, stock dividends really have no value, since they represent the receipt of something already owned. For example, when a firm declares a 10 percent stock dividend, each shareholder receives one-tenth of a share of stock for each share owned — in other words, a stockholder with 100 shares of stock will receive 10 new shares. Since all stockholders receive a 10 percent increase in the *number* of shares they own, their proportion of ownership in the firm remains unchanged. Moreover, the total market value of the shares owned is the same after the stock dividend as before; the reason being that a stock dividend will usually result in a drop in share price. Therefore, in our example, a drop in price will bring the total market value of 110 shares (after the stock dividend) to about the same as the total market value of the 100 shares that existed before the dividend. Clearly, under such circumstances, the investor is right back where he started from: he's received nothing of value. The shareholder who's received a stock dividend can, of course, sell the new shares in order to cash out the dividend. But then the value of the stocks owned by that shareholder will be reduced — granted, he'll then own the same number of shares as before the stock dividend, but they'll be worth less.

SOME KEY MEASURES OF PERFORMANCE

Professional money managers and seasoned investors tend to use a variety of financial ratios and measures when making investment decisions, particularly when common stock is involved. They look at such things as dividend yield (mentioned earlier), book value, return on equity, earnings per share, and price/earning multiples to get a feel for the investment merits of a particular stock. In short, they use these and other ratios to help them decide whether or not to invest in a particular stock. Fortunately, most of the widely followed ratios can be found in published reports (like *S&P Stock Reports* or *Value Line*), so you don't have to compute them yourself. Even so, if you're thinking about buying, or already have a position in common stock, there are a few measures of performance you'll want to keep track of.

Book Value. The amount of stockholders' equity in a firm is measured by **book value**. This is an accounting measure that is determined by subtracting the firm's liabilities and preferred stocks from the value of its assets. Book value indicates the amount of stockholder funds used to finance the firm. For example, assume Rose Colored Glasses (RCG) had assets of $5 million, liabilities of $2 million, and preferred stock valued at $1 million. The book value of the firm's common stock would be $2 million ($5 million − $2 million − $1 million). If the book value is divided by the number of shares outstanding, the result is *book value per share*. If RCG had 100,000 shares of common stock outstanding, its book value per share would be $20 ($2,000,000/100,000 shares). Because of the positive impact it can have on the growth of the firm, you'd like to see book value per share steadily increasing over time; also, *look for stocks whose market prices are comfortably above their book values*.

Net Profit Margin. As a yardstick of profitability, the **net profit margin** is one of the most widely followed measures of corporate performance. Basically, this ratio relates the net profits of the firm to its sales, providing an indication of how well the company is controlling its cost structure. The higher the net profit margin, the more money the company earns. Look for a relatively stable — or even better, an increasing — net profit margin.

Return on Equity. Another very important and widely followed measure, **return on equity** (or ROE, for short) reflects the overall profitability of the firm. It captures, in a single ratio, the amount of success the firm is having in managing its assets, operations, and capital structure. Return on equity is important because it has a direct and significant impact on the profits, growth, and dividends of the firm. The better the ROE, the better the financial condition and competitive position of the firm. Look for a stable or increasing ROE, and watch out for a falling ROE, as that could spell trouble.

Earnings per Share. With stocks, the firm's annual earnings are usually measured and reported in terms of **earnings per share (EPS)**. Basically, EPS translates total corporate profits into profits on a per-share basis and provides a convenient measure of the amount of earnings available to stockholders. Earnings per share is found by using the following simple formula:

$$EPS = \frac{\text{Net profit after taxes} - \text{Preferred dividends paid}}{\text{Number of shares of common stock outstanding}}$$

For example, if RCG reported a net profit of $350,000, paid $100,000 in dividends to preferred stockholders, and had 100,000 shares of common outstanding, it would have an EPS of $2.50 [($350,000 − $100,000)/100,000]. Note that preferred dividends are *subtracted* from profits since they have to be paid before any monies can be made available to common stockholders. The magnitude of earnings per share is considered important by most stockholders because it represents the amount that the firms earned on behalf of each outstanding share of common stock. Here, too, *look for a steady rate of growth in EPS*.

Price/Earnings Ratio. When the prevailing market price per share is divided by the annual earnings per share, the result is the **price/earnings (P/E) ratio**, which is viewed as an indication of investor confidence and expectations. The higher the price/earnings multiple, the more confidence investors are presumed to have in a given security. In the case of RCG, whose shares are currently selling for $30, the price/earnings ratio is 12 ($30 per share/$2.50 per share). This means that RCG stock is selling for 12 times its earnings. P/E ratios are important to investors because they provide a feel for the general expectations of the firm. They reveal how aggressively the stock is being priced in the market. Watch out for very high P/Es, since that could indicate the stock is being overpriced (and thus might be headed for a big drop in price). P/E ratios are not static, but tend to move with the market: when the market's soft, a stock's P/E will be low, and when things heat up in the market, so will the stock's P/E.

Beta. A stock's **beta** is an indication of its *price volatility*; it shows how responsive the stock is to the market. In recent years, the use of betas to measure the *market risk* of common stock has become a widely accepted practice, and as a result, published betas are now available from most brokerage firms and investment services. The beta for a given stock is determined by a statistical technique that relates the stock's historical returns to the market. The market (as measured by something like the S&P index of 500 stocks) is used as a benchmark of performance, and it always has a beta of 1.0. From there, everything is relative: low-beta stocks — those with betas of less than 1.0 — have low price volatility (they're

---

book value
The amount of stockholders' equity in a firm; determined by subtracting the company's liabilities and preferred stock value from the value of its assets.

net profit margin
A key measure of corporate profitability that relates the net profits of a firm to its sales; it shows the rate of return the company is earning on its sales.

return on equity (ROE)
ROE captures the overall profitability of the firm, as it provides a measure of the returns to stockholders; is important because of its impact on the growth, profits, and dividends of the firm.

earnings per share (EPS)
The return earned on behalf of each share of common stock during a given 12-month period; calculated by dividing all earnings remaining after paying preferred dividends by the number of common shares outstanding.

price/earnings (P/E) ratio
A measure of investors' confidence in and expectations for a given security; calculated by dividing the prevailing market price per share by the annual earnings per share.

beta
An index of the price volatility imbedded in a share of common stock; provides a reflection of how the price of a share of stock responds to market forces.

relatively price-stable), while high-beta stocks—those with betas of more than 1.0—are considered to be highly volatile. In short, the higher a stock's beta, the more risky it is considered to be. Stock betas can be either *positive* or *negative*, though the vast majority are positive, meaning that the stocks move in the same general direction as the market (that is, if the market is going up, so does the price of the stock).

Actually, beta is an *index* of price performance and is interpreted as a percentage response to the market. Thus, if RCG has a beta of, say, 0.8, it will rise (or fall) only 80 percent as fast as the market—if the market goes up by 10 percent, RCG will go up only 8 percent (10 percent × .8). In contrast, if the stock had a beta of 1.8, it would go up or down 1.8 times as fast—the price of the stock would rise higher and fall lower than the market. Clearly, if you're looking for a relatively conservative investment, you should stick with low-beta stocks; on the other hand, if it's capital gains and price volatility you're after, then go with high-beta securities.

You can get an idea of a stock's price volatility by looking at its beta.
Fact: Beta shows how responsive a stock is to the market and, as such, is a widely used measure of a stock's price volatility—the higher a stock's beta, the more volatile it is.

PUTTING A VALUE ON STOCK

No matter what kind of investor you are or what your investment objectives happen to be, sooner or later you will have to face one of the most difficult questions in the field of investments: *How much are you willing to pay for the stock?* In order to answer this question, you have to put a value on the stock. Measures such as book value, earnings per share, P/E multiples, and betas are a part of the *fundamental analysis* used to determine the underlying value of a share of stock. Basically, the notion of fundamental analysis is that the value of a stock depends on its expected stream of future earnings. Once you have a handle on the expected stream of future earnings, you can use that information to find the *approximate yield* of an investment (from Equation

12.1). If the expected yield from the investment exceeds your desired or minimum rate of return, you should make the investment—in effect, you should be willing to pay the current or prevailing market price. Put another way, with fundamental analysis you are trying to determine whether or not you should pay the current or prevailing market price of the stock. If the expected yield is less than your desired rate of return, you should not buy the stock (at its current market price), since it is currently "overpriced" and, as such, you will not be able to earn your desired rate of return.

TYPES OF COMMON STOCK

Common stocks are often classified on the basis of their dividends or their rate of growth in EPS. Among the more popular types of common stock are blue-chip, growth, income, speculative, cyclical, and defensive stocks.

Blue-Chip Stocks. These are the cream of the common stock crop; **blue chips** are stocks that are unsurpassed in quality and have a long and stable record of earnings and dividends. They are issued by large, well-established firms that have impeccable financial credentials—firms like GE, Merck, Wal-Mart, and General Mills. The companies hold important, if not leading, positions in their industries and frequently determine the standards by which other firms are measured. Blue chips are particularly attractive to investors who seek quality investment outlets that offer decent dividend yields and respectable growth potential. Many use them for long-term investment purposes, and, because of their relatively low risk exposure, as a way of obtaining modest but dependable rates of return on their investment dollars. They are popular with a large segment of the investing public and, as a result, are often relatively high priced, especially when the market is unsettled and investors become more quality-conscious.

Growth Stocks. Stocks that have experienced, and are expected to continue experiencing, consistently high rates of growth in operations and earnings are known as **growth stocks**. A good growth stock might exhibit a *sustained* rate of growth in earnings of 15 to 20 percent (or more) over a period during which common stocks are averaging only 5 to 6 percent. H&R Block, Newell Company, Stride Rite, GATX Corp., and Shering-Plough are all prime examples of growth stocks. These stocks normally pay little or nothing in dividends, since the firm's rapid growth potential requires that its earnings be retained and reinvested. The high growth expectations for these stocks usually cause them to sell at relatively high P/E ratios, and they typically have betas in excess of 1.0. Because of their potential for dramatic price appreciation, they appeal mostly to investors who are seeking capital gains rather than dividend income.

Income Stocks versus Speculative Stocks.

Stocks whose appeal is based primarily on the dividends they pay out are known as **income stocks**. They have a fairly stable stream of earnings, a large portion of which is distributed in the form of dividends. Income shares have relatively high dividend yields and, as such, are ideally suited for individuals who are seeking a relatively safe and high level of current income from their investment capital. An added (and often overlooked) feature of these stocks is that, unlike bonds and preferred stock, holders of income stock can expect *the amount of dividends paid to increase over time*. Examples of income stock would include Texas Utilities, Wells Fargo, Kimberly-Clark, Duke Power, Texas Utilities, and Brooklyn Union Gas. Because of their low risk, these stocks commonly have betas of less than 1.0.

Rather than basing their investment decisions on a proven record of earnings, investors in **speculative stocks** gamble that some new information, discovery, or production technique will favorably affect the growth of the firm and inflate the price of its stock. For example, a company whose stock is considered speculative may have recently discovered a new drug or located a valuable resource such as oil. The value of speculative stocks and their P/E ratios tend to fluctuate widely as additional information with respect to the firm's future is received. The betas for speculative stocks are nearly always well in excess of 1.0. Investors in speculative stocks should be prepared to experience losses as well as gains,

since *these are high-risk securities*. They include the likes of Amgen, U.S. Bioscience, Flightsafety International, and Archive Corporation.

Cyclical Stocks or Defensive Stocks.

Stocks whose price movements tend to follow the business cycle are called **cyclical stocks**. This means that when the economy is in an expansionary stage (recovery or expansion), the prices of cyclical stocks increase, and during a contractionary stage (recession or depression), they decline. Most cyclical stocks are found in the basic industries—automobiles, steel, and lumber, for example; these are industries sensitive to changes in economic activity. Investors try to purchase cyclical stocks just prior to an expansionary phase and sell just before the contraction occurs. Since they tend to move with the market, these stocks always have positive betas. Caterpillar, Federal Paper & Board, Reynolds Metals, and Worthington Industries are examples of cyclical stocks.

---

blue-chip stock

A stock that is known to provide a safe and stable return; generally issued by companies that are expected to provide an uninterrupted stream of dividends and have good long-term growth prospects.

growth stock

A stock whose earnings and market price have increased over time at a rate that is well above average.

income stock

A stock whose chief appeal is the dividends it pays out; typically offers dividend payments that can be expected to increase over time.

speculative stock

Stock that is purchased in the hope that its price per share will increase.

cyclical stock

Stock whose price movements tend to parallel the various stages of the business cycle.

The prices and returns from **defensive stocks**, unlike those of cyclical stocks, are expected to remain stable during periods of contraction in business activity. For this reason, they are often called *countercyclical*. The shares of consumer goods companies, certain public utilities, and gold mining companies are good examples of defensive stocks. Because they are basically income stocks, their earnings and dividends tend to hold their market prices up during periods of economic decline. Betas on these stocks are quite low and occasionally even negative. Bandag, Loctite, Checkpoint Systems, and Humana are all examples of defensive stocks.

INVESTING IN COMMON

The first step in investing is to know where to put your money; the second is to know when to make your moves. The first question basically involves matching your risk and return objectives with the available investment vehicles. As noted earlier, *a stock (or any investment vehicle for that matter) should be considered a viable investment candidate only so long as it promises to generate a sufficiently attractive rate of return* and, in particular, one that fully compensates you for any risks you have to take. Thus, if you're considering the purchase of a stock, you should expect to earn more than what you can get from T-bills or high-grade corporate bonds. The reason: stocks are riskier than bills or bonds, so you *deserve more return*. Indeed, if you can't get enough return from the security to offset the risk, then you shouldn't invest in the stock!

Selecting a Stock.   Granted, you want an investment that provides an attractive rate of return — one that meets or exceeds your required return. So, how do you go about selecting just such a stock? The answer is by doing a little digging and crunching a few numbers. Here's what you'd want to do: To begin with, find a company that you like and then take a look at how it's performed over the past three to five years. Find out what kind of growth rate (in sales) it has experienced, if it has a strong ROE and has been able to maintain or improve its profit margin, how much it has been paying out to stockholders in the form of dividends, and so forth. This kind of information is readily available in publications like *Value*

Line and *S&P Stock Reports* (which we'll discuss in Chapter 13). The idea is to find stocks that are financially strong, have done well in the past, and continue to be market leaders, or hold prominent positions in a given industry or market segment. Looking at the past is only the beginning, however; for what's really important to stock valuations is the *FUTURE*! That is, as we discussed earlier in this chapter (see the section "What Makes a Good Investment?", *the value of a share of stock at any point in time is a function of future returns, not past performance*.

So, let's turn our attention to the expected future performance of the stock. The idea is to assess the *outlook* for the stock, thereby gaining some insight about the benefits to be derived from investing in it. Of particular concern are future dividends and share price behavior. As a rule, it doesn't make much sense to go out more than two or three years because the accuracy of most forecasts begins to deteriorate rapidly after that point. Thus, using, say, a three-year investment horizon, you'd want to forecast annual dividends per share for each of the next three years, *plus* the future price of the stock at the end of the three-year holding period (obviously, if the price of the stock is projected to go up over time, you'll have some capital gains). You can try to generate these forecasts yourself or, you can look to a publication like *Value Line* and obtain the projections there (*Value Line* projects dividends and share prices five years into the future). Once you have projected dividends and share price, you can use Equation 12.1 to determine the expected return from this investment.

To see how that can be done, consider Merck & Co., a leading producer of health-care products. According to *Value Line*, the company has very strong financials: its sales have been growing at around 15 to 16 percent per year for the past five years, it has a net profit margin of nearly 25 percent, and an ROE of just over 40 percent. Thus, historically, the company has performed very well and is definitely a market leader in its field. In early 1992, the stock was trading for $50 a share, and was paying dividends at the rate of about 90 cents a year. *Value Line* was projecting dividends to go up by about 20 cents a share for each of the next three to five years; also, they were estimating that the price of the stock should rise to about $85 within three years.

Using *Value Line* projections, we'd have dividends per share of 90 cents the first year, $1.10 per share the second year, and $1.30 per share the third year (that is, dividends would grow at the rate of about 20 cents a year); since Equation 12.1 uses "average annual current income" as one of its inputs, we'll use the midpoint of our projected dividends ($1.10 a share) as a proxy for average annual dividends. In addition, given this stock is currently trading at $50 per share, has a projected future price of $85 a share, and we have a three-year investment period, we can use Equation 12.1 to find our expected return as follows:

$$\text{Approx. Yield (Expected Ret.)} = \frac{\$1.10 + \left(\dfrac{\$85 - \$50}{3}\right)}{\left(\dfrac{\$85 + \$50}{2}\right)}$$

$$= \frac{\$1.10 + \$11.67}{\$67.50} = \underline{\underline{18.9\%}}$$

Thus, if Merck stock performs as expected, it should provide us with a return of nearly 19 percent. If that meets or exceeds our required rate of return (and it probably will), then the stock should be considered a viable investment candidate!

Timing Your Investments. Once you find a stock that you think will give you the kind of return you're looking for, you're ready to deal with the matter of timing your investment. So long as the prospects for the market and the economy are positive, the time may be right to invest in stocks. On the other hand, there are a couple of conditions when investing in stocks just doesn't make any sense at all. In particular, *don't* invest in stocks if:

- You feel *very strongly* that the market is headed down in the short run. If you're absolutely certain the market's in for a big fall (or will continue to fall, if it's already doing so), then wait until the market drops, and buy the stock when it's cheaper.
- You feel uncomfortable with the general tone of the market — it lacks direction, or there's way too much price volatility to suit you. This became a problem prior to and after the October 1987

crash, when computer-assisted trading started taking over the market. The result was a stock market that behaved more like a commodities market, with an intolerable amount of price volatility. When this happens, fundamentals go out the window, and the market simply becomes too risky. Do what the pros do, and wait it out on the sidelines.

Why Invest in Stocks? There are three basic reasons for investing in common stock: (1) to use the stock as a warehouse of value, (2) to accumulate capital, and/or (3) to provide a source of income. Storage of value is important to all investors, since nobody likes to lose money. However, some investors are more concerned about it than others and therefore put safety of principal first in their stock selection process. These investors are more quality-conscious and tend to gravitate toward blue chips and other nonspeculative shares. Accumulation of capital generally is an important goal to individuals with long-term investment horizons. These investors use the capital gains and/or dividends that stocks provide to build up their wealth. Some use growth stocks for such purposes; others do it with income shares; still others use a little of both. Finally, some people use stocks as a source of income; to them, a dependable flow of dividends is essential. High-yielding, good-quality income shares are usually their preferred investment vehicle. Now, while these are all good reasons for investing in stocks, the accompanying *Smart Money* box approaches the issue from another angle and discusses why it may be a mistake *not* to invest in stocks.

Advantages and Disadvantages of Stock Ownership. Ownership of common stock has both advantages and disadvantages. Its advantages are threefold. First, the potential returns, in the form

---

defensive stock

Stock that tends to exhibit price movements that are contrary to movements in the business cycle; often called *countercyclical stock*.

Why It's Risky NOT to Invest in Stocks

Americans are investment wimps. Despite the recent (1991–1992) flood of money into stocks and stock mutual funds, individuals still have *only about a fifth of their financial assets in the stock market*, down from 45% in the late 1960s.

Many financial experts contend that investors should be taking far more risk with their money, by owning more stocks. The case for investing in stocks is based not on the market's short-term prospects, but on the superior returns that investors are likely to earn if they hold stocks for five years or longer.

According to Chicago's Ibbotson Associates, stocks have handily outpaced inflation and the tax man—with a pretax total return, which includes rein-vested dividends, of 10.4% a year since 1926. Past returns don't guarantee future results, of course but the historical data are compelling. If you have a 15-year holding period, you can argue that a bond portfolio is much more risky than stocks because of inflation.

So, how much should investors have in stocks? A lot depends on how much risk an investor can tolerate, but many investment advisers say the more people put into stocks, the better. Investing heavily in the stock market can be nerve-wracking for even the most sea-soned investor. But experts say that investors have two weapons they can use to make the stock market's gyrations more bear-able. *One is diversification, and the other is time.*

Diversification is a sort of modern alchemy. If you take highly risky securities and mix them together, you often end up with a portfolio that still gener-ates decent returns, but the portfolio's value doesn't bounce around nearly as much as the price of the portfolio's parts. To achieve the proper kind of di-versification, many experts suggest that you put your money into no less than five or six care-fully selected stocks or stock mutual funds—look for diver-sity in the types of stocks and/or stock funds you select and by all means, consider going interna-tional with at least some of your money. Putting together a well-diversified portfolio of stocks and/or stock mutual funds will certainly help to make owning stocks more bearable, because

of both dividend income and price appreciation, can be quite substantial. The return performance of common stocks over the recent past, as well as over extended periods of time, has been noteworthy, to say the least! Second, many stocks are actively traded (there are literally thousands of such actively traded stocks) and as such they are a highly liquid form of investment—meaning they can be quickly bought and sold. Finally, they don't involve any direct man-agement (or unusual management problems) and market/company information is usually widely pub-lished and easily available.

Risk, the problem of timing purchases and sales, and the uncertainty of dividends are all disadvan-tages of common stock ownership. Although poten-tial common stock returns may be high, the risk and uncertainty associated with the actual receipt of that return is also great. Even though careful selection of stocks may reduce the amount of risk exposure the risk-return trade-off cannot be completely elimi-nated. In other words, high returns on common stock are not guaranteed; they may or may not occur depending on numerous economic, industry, and company factors. The timing of purchases and sales is closely related to risk. Many investors purchase a stock, hold it for a period of time during which the price drops, and then sell it below the original pur-chase price—that is, at a loss. The proper strategy, of

at any one time there will usually be at least one part of your portfolio that is doing well. But for people who are heavily invested in stocks, there is really only one cure for the stock market's volatility, and that is time.

There may have been 20 down years for the stock market since 1926, but the statistics are a lot more appealing if you look at longer time periods. The Ibbotson data, for instance, can be sliced up into 62 rolling five-year periods, beginning with the five years through December 1930, proceeding next to the five years through 1931, and so on, finishing up with the five years through December 1991. *Out of these 62 five-year periods, there have been only seven occasions when stocks have posted a loss.* But even these statistics

may overstate the risk involved in stock market investing. For starters, only two of those seven losing streaks occurred in the post–World War II period. In addition, such statistics are based on the assumption that you unwisely throw all your money into the stock market in one big wad. But imagine instead that you take a more prudent course and use a stock-market entry technique known as dollar-cost averaging. This involves putting equal amounts into the stock market at regular intervals, such as every month or every three months, so that you buy fewer shares when the market is up but more shares when the market is down.

If you put equal amounts into the stock market at the start of every year beginning in 1946,

the only five-year stretch when you would have lost money would have been in the five years through December 1974. And even for these investors, salvation wasn't too far off. Because the stock market rebounded 37.2% in 1975, those who toughed it out for 12 more months would have recouped all of their losses, and then some. The bottom line is if you have time on your side and you're willing to put together a well-diversified portfolio, the stock market can indeed be a rewarding place to be — even in spite of all its risks!

Source: Jonathan Clements, "Why It's Risky Not to Invest More in Stocks," *The Wall Street Journal*, February 11, 1992, pp. C1, 13.

---

course, is to buy low and sell high, but the problem of predicting price movements makes it difficult to implement such a plan.

Be Sure to Plow Back Your Earnings. Unless you're living off the income, the basic investment objective with stocks is the same as it is with any other security: to earn an attractive, fully compounded rate of return. This requires regular reinvestment of dividend income. There is no better way to accomplish such reinvestment than through a **dividend reinvestment plan (DRP)**. The basic investment philosophy at work here is that if the company is good enough to invest in, it's good

enough to reinvest in. In a dividend reinvestment plan, shareholders can sign up to have their cash dividends automatically reinvested in additional shares of the company's common stock — in essence, it's like taking your cash dividends in the form

dividend reinvestment plan (DRP)

A program offered by over 1,000 major corporations whereby stockholders can choose to take their dividends in the form of more shares of the company's stock, rather than cash; it provides a relatively painless way of earning a fully compounded rate of return.

EXHIBIT 12.5

Cash or Reinvested Dividends

Participating in a dividend reinvestment plan is a simple, yet highly effective way of building up
capital over time. Over the long haul, it can prove to be a great way of earning a fully compounded
rate of return on your money.

Situation: Buy 100 shares of stock at $25 a share (total investment $2,500);
stock currently pays $1 a share in annual dividends. Price of the stock increases
at 8 percent per year; dividends grow at 5 percent per year.

Investment Period	Number of Shares Held	Market Value of Stock Holdings	Total Cash Dividends Received
Take Dividends in Cash			
5 years	100	$ 3,672	$ 552
10 years	100	5,397	1,258
15 years	100	7,930	2,158
20 years	100	11,652	3,307
Participate in a DRP			
5 years	115.59	$ 4,245	$0
10 years	135.66	7,322	0
15 years	155.92	12,364	0
20 years	176.00	20,508	0

of more shares of common stock. The idea is to put
your money to work by building up your investment
in the stock. Such an approach can have a tremendous impact on your investment position over time,
as seen in Exhibit 12.5.

Today, over 1,000 companies (including most major corporations) have DRPs in existence, and each
one provides investors with a convenient and inexpensive way to accumulate capital. Stocks in most
DRPs are acquired free of any brokerage commissions, and some plans even sell stocks to their DRP
investors at below-market prices — often at discounts
of 3 to 5 percent. In addition, most plans credit fractional shares to the investor's account. Shareholders
can join these plans simply by sending in a completed authorization form to the company. Once you
are in the plan, the number of shares you hold will
begin to accumulate with each dividend date. There
is a catch, however — that is, even though these dividends take the form of additional shares of stock,
*reinvested dividends are taxable, in the year they're
received*, just as if they had been received in cash.

INVESTING IN BONDS

Bonds are fixed-income securities issued by corporations and various types of governments that provide investors with a high, secure, and regular
source of current income. Stop for a moment and
give some thought to how you might be able to use
bonds in your own investment program. Do you
think you'd want to use them if you were an aggressive investor interested mostly in capital gains? Also,
consider the question of what causes bond prices to
change.

Bonds represent a form of *debt capital*, meaning
that they are borrowed funds. Bonds are often referred to as *fixed-income securities* because the debt

service obligations of the issuer are fixed—that is, the issuing organization agrees to pay a *fixed amount of interest periodically and to repay a fixed amount of principal* at or before maturity. Bonds normally have face values of $1,000 or $5,000, and maturities of 10 to 30 years.

WHY INVEST IN BONDS?

Like many other types of investment vehicles, bonds provide investors with two kinds of income: (1) They provide a generous amount of current income, and (2) they can often be used to generate substantial amounts of capital gains. The current income, of course, is derived from the interest payments received over the life of the issue. Capital gains, in contrast, are earned whenever market interest rates fall. A basic trading rule in the bond market is that interest rates and bond prices move in opposite directions: When interest rates rise, bond prices fall; and when they drop, bond prices rise. Thus, it is possible to buy bonds at one price and, if interest rate conditions are right, to sell them some time later at a higher price. Of course, it is also possible to incur a capital loss should market rates move against the investor. Taken together, the current income and capital gains earned from bonds can lead to attractive and highly competitive investor returns.

In addition to being high-yielding securities, bonds are a versatile investment outlet. They can be used conservatively by those who seek high current income, or aggressively by those who actively go after capital gains. Bonds have long been considered an excellent way of getting high current income, but only since the advent of high and volatile interest rates have they also become recognized as trading vehicles—that is, as a way to earn fat returns from capital gains. Investors found that the number of profitable trading opportunities increased substantially as wider and more frequent swings in interest rates began to occur.

Finally, bond issues, being of generally high quality, can be used for the preservation and long-term accumulation of capital. In fact, many individuals, regularly and over the long haul, commit all or most of their investment funds to bonds because of this single attribute.

BASIC ISSUE CHARACTERISTICS

A bond is a negotiable, long-term debt instrument that carries certain obligations on the part of the issuer. Unlike the holders of common stock, bondholders have no ownership or equity position in the issuing firm or organization. This is so because bonds are debt, and bondholders, in a roundabout way, are only lending money to the issuer.

As a rule, bonds pay interest every six months. The amount of interest paid is a function of the **coupon**, which defines the annual interest that will be paid by the issuer to the bondholder. For instance, a $1,000 bond with an 8 percent coupon would pay $80 in interest every year—generally in the form of two $40 semiannual payments. The principal amount of a bond, also known as *par value*, specifies the amount of capital that must be repaid at maturity—thus, there is $1,000 of principal in a $1,000 bond. To facilitate the marketing of bonds, issues are broken down into standard principal amounts known as *denominations*; for instance, corporate bonds are usually sold in minimum denominations of $1,000. Of course, debt securities regularly trade at market prices that differ from their principal (or par) values. This occurs whenever an issue's coupon differs from the prevailing market rate of interest; in essence, the price of an issue will change until its yield is compatible with prevailing market yields. Such behavior explains why a 7 percent issue will carry a market price of only $825 when the market yield is 9 percent; the drop in price is necessary to raise the yield on this bond from 7 to 9 percent. Issues with market values lower than par are known as *discount bonds* and carry coupons that are less than those on new issues. In contrast, issues with market values in excess of par are called *premium bonds* and have coupons greater than those currently being offered on new issues. (*Note:* We'll discuss the price behavior of bonds in more detail later in this chapter.)

---

coupon

That feature on a bond that defines the annual interest income that the issuer will pay the bondholder.

EXHIBIT 12.6

An Announcement of a New Corporate Bond Issue

The V.F. Corporation, a leading manufacturer of sporting apparel, issued this unsecured bond in 1992; it will not mature until the year 2022. Each year the company will pay more than $9.2 million in interest and, over the full 30-year life of the bond, more than $275 million in interest will be paid.

$100,000,000

V.F. Corporation

9¹⁄₄% Debentures due May 1, 2022

Price 99.796%

Plus accrued interest from May 1, 1992

Upon request, a copy of the Prospectus Supplement and the related Prospectus describing these securities and the business of the Company may be obtained within any State from any Underwriter who may legally distribute it within such State. The securities are offered only by means of the Prospectus Supplement and the related Prospectus, and this announcement is neither an offer to sell nor a solicitation of an offer to buy.

Goldman, Sachs & Co.   J.P. Morgan Securities Inc.

May 12, 1992

Source: *The Wall Street Journal,* May 12, 1992.

Types of Issues. A single issuer may have many different bonds outstanding at a given point in time. In addition to their coupons and maturities, bonds can be differentiated from one another by the type of collateral behind them. In this regard, the issues can be viewed as having either junior or senior standing. *Senior bonds* are *secured* obligations, since they are backed by a legal claim, on some specific property of the issuer, that acts as *collateral* for the bonds. Such issues would include **mortgage bonds**, which are secured by real estate, and **equipment trust certificates**, which are backed by certain types of equipment and are popular with railroads and airlines. *Junior bonds*, on the other hand, are backed only with a promise by the issuer to pay interest and principal on a timely basis. There are several classes of *unsecured* bonds, the most popular of which is known as a **debenture**. Exhibit 12.6 shows the announcement of a 30-year debenture bond issued in 1992. Note that even though there is no collateral backing up the obligation, V.F. Corporation was able to issue $100 million worth of these 30-year bonds.

Sinking Fund. Another provision that's important to investors is the **sinking fund**, which stipulates how a bond will be paid off over time. Not all bonds have these requirements, but for those that do, a sinking fund specifies the annual repayment schedule that will be used to pay off the issue and indicates how much principal will be retired each year. Sinking fund requirements generally begin one to five years after the date of issue and continue annually thereafter until all or most of the issue has been paid off. Any amount not repaid by maturity (which might equal 10 to 25 percent of the issue) is then retired with a single balloon payment.

Call Feature. Every bond has a **call feature**, which stipulates the conditions under which the bond can be retired prior to its maturity date. As a rule, a bond cannot be called until it has been outstanding for five years or more. Call features are used most often to replace an issue with one that carries a lower coupon; in this way, the issuer benefits by being able to realize a reduction in annual interest cost. In an attempt to compensate investors who have their bonds called out from under them, a *call premium* (usually equal to about one year's

interest) is tacked on to the par value of the bond and paid to investors, along with the issue's par value, at the time the bond is called. For example, if a company decides to call its 12 percent bonds some 15 years before they mature, it might have to pay $1,120 (a call premium of one year's interest—$120—would be added to the par value of $1,000) for every $1,000 bond outstanding.

While this might sound like a good deal, it's really not. Indeed, the only party that really benefits from a bond refunding is the issuer. The bondholder loses a source of high current income—for example, the investor may have a 12 percent bond called away at a time when the best she can do in the market is maybe 7 or 8 percent (which is exactly what happened in 1991–1992). To avoid this, stick with bonds that are either *noncallable*, or that have long *call-deferment periods*, meaning they can't be called for refunding (or any other purpose) until the call-deferment period ends.

Registered or Bearer Bonds. Regardless of the type of collateral or kind of issue, a bond may be registered, or many of the older issues could be in

mortgage bond
A bond secured by real estate.

equipment trust certificate
A bond secured by certain types of transportation equipment, like railroad cars and airplanes.

debenture
An unsecured bond that is issued on the general credit of the firm.

sinking fund
A provision in a bond issue that specifies the annual repayment schedule that will be used to pay it off and the amount of principal that will be retired each year.

call feature
A feature often included in bond or preferred stock issues that allows the issuer to retire the security during some specified time period at a predetermined price.

EXHIBIT 12.7

The Reported Results of a Recent Treasury Note Auction

Treasury auctions are closely followed by the financial media; here, the results of a three-year Treasury note auction are reported. These auctions are highly competitive (the amount of bids submitted generally far exceeds the size of the issue) and as a result, the spread between the highest and lowest bid is quite small (here it amounts to just 2 basis points, or 2/100 of 1 percent — 7.09 to 7.07 percent).

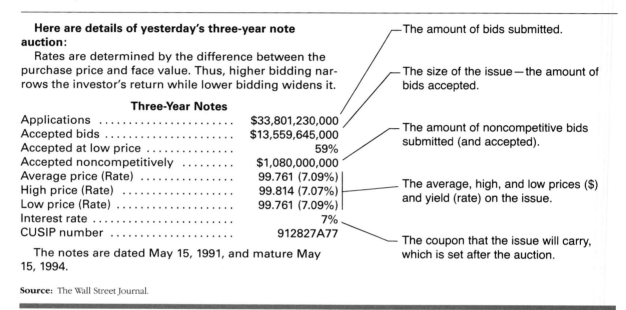

Here are details of yesterday's three-year note auction:

Rates are determined by the difference between the purchase price and face value. Thus, higher bidding narrows the investor's return while lower bidding widens it.

Three-Year Notes

Applications	$33,801,230,000
Accepted bids	$13,559,645,000
Accepted at low price	59%
Accepted noncompetitively	$1,080,000,000
Average price (Rate)	99.761 (7.09%)
High price (Rate)	99.814 (7.07%)
Low price (Rate)	99.761 (7.09%)
Interest rate	7%
CUSIP number	912827A77

The notes are dated May 15, 1991, and mature May 15, 1994.

— The amount of bids submitted.

— The size of the issue — the amount of bids accepted.

— The amount of noncompetitive bids submitted (and accepted).

— The average, high, and low prices ($) and yield (rate) on the issue.

— The coupon that the issue will carry, which is set after the auction.

Source: The Wall Street Journal.

---

bearer form. **Registered bonds** are issued to specific owners and the names of all bondholders formally registered with the issuer, who keeps a running account of ownership and automatically pays interest to the owners by check. In contrast, the holders of **bearer bonds** are considered to be the legal owners, as the issuing organization keeps no record of ownership; bondholders receive interest by "clipping coupons" and sending them in for payment. Bearer bonds once were the most prevalent type of issue but are destined to become a thing of the past, as Congress has mandated that, effective July 1983, all bonds must be issued as *registered* securities.

THE BOND MARKET

Today's bond market offers issues to meet just about any type of investment objective and to suit virtually any type of investor, no matter how conservative or aggressive. As a matter of convenience, the bond market is usually divided into four segments, according to type of issuer: Treasury, agency, municipal, and corporate.

Treasury Bonds. Treasury bonds (sometimes called *Treasuries* or *governments*) are a dominant force in the bond market and, if not the most popular, certainly are the best known. The U.S. Treasury issues bonds, notes, and other types of debt securities (such as the Treasury bills discussed in Chapter 5) as a means of meeting the ever increasing needs of the federal government. All Treasury obligations are of the highest quality (backed by the full faith and credit of the U.S. government), a feature that, along with their liquidity, makes them extremely popular with individual and institutional investors, both here and abroad. Indeed, the market for U.S. Treasury securities is the biggest and most active in the world! Every day, there's more than $100 billion worth of Treasuries that change hands, as these securities are traded in all the major markets of the world, from New York to London to Tokyo. That's half a *trillion* dollars in bond trades — every week; to put that into perspective, in an average week, the New York Stock Exchange trades only about $25 billion worth of stocks.

Treasury notes carry maturities of two to ten years, whereas *Treasury bonds* have maturities of more than ten years — they go out as far as 30 years. Treasury notes and bonds are sold in $1,000 denominations (except two- and three-year notes, which are sold in $5,000 minimums). The Treasury issues its notes and bonds at regularly scheduled auctions, the results of which are widely followed by the financial media (see Exhibit 12.7). Through this auction process, the Treasury establishes the initial yields and coupons on the securities it issues. These auctions are open to the public and as the *Money in Action* box explains, it's an easy and inexpensive way to buy Treasuries. All government notes and bonds today are issued as *noncallable* securities, and while interest income is subject to normal federal income tax, *it is exempt from state and local taxes*.

Agency Bonds. **Agency bonds** are a rapidly growing segment of the U.S. bond market. Though issued by political subdivisions of the U.S. government, *these securities are not obligations of the U.S. Treasury*. They customarily provide yields comfortably above the market rates for Treasuries and therefore, offer investors a way to increase returns with little or no real difference in risk. Some of the more actively traded and widely quoted agency issues include those sold by the Tennessee Valley Authority, the U.S. Postal Service, the Government National Mortgage Association (or "Ginnie Maes," as they are more commonly known), the Federal Land Bank, the Student Loan Marketing Association, and the Federal Home Loan Bank. Although these issues are not the direct obligations of the U.S. government, a number of them actually do carry government guarantees and thus effectively represent the full faith and credit of the U.S. Treasury. Moreover, some have unusual interest-payment provisions (interest is paid monthly in a few instances and yearly in one case), and in many cases, the interest is exempt from state and local taxes.

Municipal Bonds. **Municipal bonds** are the issues of states, counties, cities, and other political subdivisions, such as school districts and water and sewer districts. They are unlike other bonds in that their interest income is usually free from federal income tax (which is why these issues are known as *tax-free bonds*). Any capital gains that might be earned from municipals, however, is subject to the usual federal taxes. The tax-free yield is probably the most important feature of municipal bonds and is certainly a major reason why individuals invest in them. Exhibit 12.8 shows what a taxable bond (like a corporate or Treasury issue) would have no yield in order to equal the take-home yield of a tax-free municipal bond. It demonstrates how the yield attractiveness of municipal bonds varies with an investor's income level; clearly, the higher the individual's tax bracket, the more attractive municipal bonds become.

As a rule, the yields on municipal bonds are substantially lower than the returns available from fully taxable issues. Thus, unless the tax effect is sufficient to raise the yield on a municipal to a level that equals

---

registered bond

A bond that automatically pays interest to the owner, who is formally registered as such with the issuer.

bearer bond

A bond whose owner is not formally registered with the issuer and who receives interest not automatically but by redeeming coupons — whoever *holds* a bearer bond is considered its legal owner.

Treasury bond

A federal government obligation that has a maturity of more than ten years and pays interest semiannually; also called a *government bond*.

agency bond

An obligation of a political subdivision of the U.S. government; typically provides yields above the market rates for Treasury bonds.

municipal bond

A bond issued by state and local governments for the purpose of financing certain projects; interest income is usually exempt from federal taxes.

MONEY IN ACTION

Buying Treasuries at the Auction — A Do-It-Yourself Approach to Investing

The largest issuer of debt securities in the world is the U.S. Treasury. Although the Treasury sells its bills, notes, and bonds primarily to institutional investors, individual investors can also buy from the Treasury through its *Treasury Direct* program. This program gives individual investors the opportunity to buy directly at the auction, without having to pay any fees or brokerage commissions.

Treasury auctions are held on a regular basis throughout the year, with the dollar amount of securities to be sold announced four to six business days before the auction date. Three- and six-month bills are auctioned every Monday; one-year bills, every fourth Thursday; and two-year notes, the last week of each month. Longer maturities, from 3-year notes to 30-year bonds, are auctioned once a quarter on staggered schedules.

The securities are priced at the auction on the basis of competitive bids submitted by large institutional investors. Individual investors can participate in the auction by submitting *noncompetitive bids* (minimum investment requirements are as low as $1,000 to $10,000). Submitting a noncompetitive bid guarantees that you'll get all the securities you want, as *all noncompetitive bids are filled* — at the average of the high and low bids accepted at the auction.

Here's how it works: Suppose the Treasury announces its intention to sell, say, $15 billion worth of ten-year notes at its next auction. At auction, the Treasury may receive $35 to $40 billion in competitive bids (it always receives far more bids than it has securities to sell), and another $1 billion in small noncompetitive bids. The noncompetitive bids are filled first, so that leaves the Treasury with $14 billion worth of securities to be sold through competitive bidding. These bids are filled by accepting the highest price (lowest yield) first, and then accepting successively lower prices (higher yields) until the whole issue is sold — in this illustration, as is typical at most Treasury auctions, there will be a big chunk of the competitive bids that go unfilled. Usually the spread between the highest and lowest bid will be just a few basis points; for example, the competitive bids may range between 6.42 and 6.44 percent. If that's the case, then all noncompetitive bids would be filled at the *average* bid of, say, 6.43 percent. Once the auction is completed, the coupon on the Treasury note or bond will be set at or slightly *under* the range of bids — in this way, the issue price will be equal to or slightly less than par. In our example above, the note would probably come out with a cou-

pon of 6⅜ (or 6.375 percent), which would result in an average purchase price of $99.68.

Suppose you want to purchase $15,000 of these ten-year notes for your personal portfolio. First, you must open a Treasury Direct account with the Federal Reserve by filling out a simple form (available from the nearest Federal Reserve bank or branch). Then you submit a noncompetitive bid using a tender form (like the one shown on the facing page), together with payment for the securities: cash or a personal check for notes and bonds, cash or a cashier's or certified check for Treasury bills. After the auction, your Treasury Direct account will be credited with the purchase and a few days later, you'll receive a statement informing you of the terms of your purchase. The Treasury Direct program, although easy to use and understand, *is best suited for investors who plan to hold their securities to maturity*. Technically, these are "nonmarketable" securities, so to sell them, an investor must first transfer the securities to a bank or other financial institution — a process that might take a week or more.

Source: Adapted from Tom Herman, "Buying Treasurys Without a Middleman," *The Wall Street Journal*, May 1, 1991, pp. C1, 15; Edward Giltenan, "Do-It-Yourself Treasurys," *Forbes*, November 14, 1988, p. 349; and Susan E. Kuhn, "The Tightwad Way to Tank Up on Treasuries," *Fortune*, June 18, 1990, p. 32.

FORM PD F 5174-3
(February 1990)

12–57/R

OMB No. 1535-0069
Expires: 09-30-92

TENDER FOR 5-10 YEAR TREASURY NOTE

TENDER INFORMATION	FOR DEPARTMENT USE

AMOUNT OF TENDER: $ *15,000*

TERM *10-year notes*

BID TYPE (Check One) ☑ NONCOMPETITIVE ☐ COMPETITIVE AT ▪ %

FOR DEPARTMENT USE
TENDER NUMBER
912827
CUSIP
ISSUE DATE
RECEIVED BY
DATE RECEIVED

ACCOUNT NUMBER 5555 - 667 - 8901

INVESTOR INFORMATION

ACCOUNT NAME

LEONARD L. LIPMANN

ADDRESS

1522 ANYWHERE LN.

HOMETOWNSVILLE   USA 1522-2
CITY   STATE   ZIP CODE

EXT REG ☐
FOREIGN ☐
BACKUP ☐
REVIEW ☐

TAXPAYER IDENTIFICATION NUMBER

1ST NAMED OWNER 555 - 66 - 7890 **OR** ▪ - ▪
SOCIAL SECURITY NUMBER   EMPLOYER IDENTIFICATION NUMBER

CLASS ☐

TELEPHONE NUMBERS

WORK (555) 122 - 7890   **HOME** (555) 602 - 5566

PAYMENT ATTACHED

TOTAL PAYMENT: $ 15,000

NUMBERS

CASH (01): $ _____   **CHECKS (02/03): $** 15,000

SECURITIES (05): $** _____   **$ _____

OTHER (06): $** _____   **$ _____

DIRECT DEPOSIT INFORMATION

ROUTING NUMBER 366724003 9

FINANCIAL INSTITUTION NAME SUPERSTRONG BANK & TRUST

ACCOUNT NUMBER 000-05-0067-089

ACCOUNT NAME LEONARD L. LIPMANN

ACCOUNT TYPE (Check One) ☑ CHECKING ☐ SAVINGS

AUTHORIZATION

For the notice required under the Privacy and Paperwork Reduction Acts, see the accompanying instructions.

I submit this tender pursuant to the provisions of Department of the Treasury Circulars, Public Debt Series Nos. 1-86 and 2-86 and the public announcement issued by the Department of the Treasury.

Under penalties of perjury, I certify that the number shown on this form is my correct taxpayer identification number and that I am not subject to backup withholding because (1) I have not been notified that I am subject to backup withholding as a result of a failure to report all interest or dividends, or (2) the Internal Revenue Service has notified me that I am no longer subject to backup withholding. I further certify that all other information provided on this form is true, correct and complete.

Leonard L. Lipmann
SIGNATURE

1-17-93
DATE

SEE INSTRUCTIONS FOR PRIVACY ACT AND PAPERWORK REDUCTION ACT NOTICE

★U.S.GPO:1991-0-282-725/44035

or exceeds the yields on taxable issues, it obviously doesn't make sense to buy municipal bonds. You can determine the return a fully taxable bond would have to provide in order to match the after-tax return on a lower-yielding tax-free issue by computing what is known as a municipal's *fully taxable equivalent yield:*

$$\text{Fully taxable equivalent yield} = \frac{\text{Yield of Municipal bond}}{1 - \text{Tax rate}}$$

For example, if a certain municipal bond offered a yield of 6 percent, an individual in the 31 percent tax bracket would have to find a fully taxable bond with a yield of nearly 8¾ percent in order to reap the same after-tax return: that is, 6% ÷ (1 − .31) = 6% ÷ .69 = 8.70%.

Municipal bonds are generally issued as **serial obligations**, meaning that the issue is broken into a series of smaller bonds, each with its own maturity date and coupon rate. Thus, instead of the bond having just one maturity date 20 years from now, it will have a series of, say, 20 maturity dates over the 20-year time frame. The serial feature of municipal bonds is illustrated in Exhibit 12.9, which contains the announcement of a recently issued municipal bond. Because there is such a diversity of municipal bonds available, investors must also be careful to assess their quality in order to ensure that the issuer will not default. Although it may not seem that municipal issuers would default on either interest or principal payments, it does occur! Investors should be especially cautious when investing in **revenue bonds**, which are municipal bonds that are serviced from the income generated from specific income-producing projects, such as toll roads. Unlike issuers of so-called **general obligation bonds**— which are backed by the full faith and credit of the municipality— the issuer of a revenue bond is obligated to pay principal and interest *only if a sufficient level of revenue* is generated. General obligation municipal bonds, however, are required to be serviced in a prompt and timely fashion regardless of the level of tax income generated by the municipality.

Caution should be used when buying municipal bonds because *some of these issues are tax-exempt and others are not*. One effect of the far-reaching 1986 Tax Reform Act was to change the status of municipal bonds used to finance nonessential projects, so that their interest income is no longer exempt from federal taxes. Such bonds are known as *taxable munies*, and they offer yields that are considerably higher than normal tax-exempt securities. Buy one of these issues and you'll end up holding a bond whose interest income *is fully taxable* by the IRS.

Corporate Bonds. The major nongovernmental issuers of bonds are corporations. The market for **corporate bonds** is customarily subdivided into several segments, which include *industrials* (the most diverse of the group), *public utilities* (the dominant group in terms of volume of new issues), *rail and transportation bonds*, and *financial issues* (banks, finance companies, and so forth). The corporate bond market offers the widest range of issue types. There are *first mortgage bonds, convertible bonds* (discussed in the next section), *debentures, subordinated debentures*, and *income bonds*, to mention just a few. Interest on corporate bonds is paid semiannually, and sinking funds are common. The bonds usually come in $1,000 denominations and are issued on a term basis with a single maturity date. Maturities usually range from 25 to 40 years. Many of the issues—particularly the longer-term bonds—carry call provisions that prohibit prepayment of the issue during the first five to ten years. Corporate issues are popular with individuals because of their relatively high yields.

The Special Appeal of Zero Coupon Bonds and Mortgage-Backed Securities. In addition to the standard bond vehicles described above, investors can also choose from a growing number of *specialty issues*—bonds that, for the most part, have unusual coupon or repayment provisions. Specialty issues are often among the more popular types of bonds on Wall Street. In fact, two of the hottest issues today are securities that are out-of-the-ordinary in one way or another; one is the zero coupon bond and the other is something known as a mortgage-backed bond.

As the name implies, **zero coupon bonds** have no coupons. Rather, they are sold at a deep discount from their par values and then increase in value over time, at a compound rate of return, so that at maturity they are worth much more than their initial investment. Other things being equal, the cheaper the

EXHIBIT 12.8

Table of Taxable Equivalent Yields

Tax-exempt securities generally yield less than fully taxable obligations, and, because of that, you have to be in a sufficiently high tax bracket (28 percent or more) to make up for the yield shortfall.

Tax Bracket	To Match a Tax-Free Yield of:							
	5%	**6%**	**7%**	**8%**	**9%**	**10%**	**12%**	**14%**
	You must earn this yield on a taxable investment:							
15%	5.88	7.06	8.24	9.41	10.59	11.76	14.12	16.47
28	6.94	8.33	9.72	11.11	12.50	13.89	16.67	19.44
31	7.25	8.70	10.15	11.59	13.04	14.49	17.39	20.29

bond, the greater the return one can earn (for example, whereas a 10 percent bond might sell for $239, an issue with a 6 percent yield will cost a lot more — $417). Because they have no coupons, these bonds pay nothing to the investor until they mature. In this regard, zero coupon bonds are like the Series EE savings bonds that we discussed in Chapter 5. Strange as it may seem, this is the main attraction of zero coupon bonds. Since there are no interest payments, investors need not worry about reinvesting coupon income twice a year; instead, the fully compounded rate of return on a zero coupon bond is virtually guaranteed at the rate that existed when the issue was sold. For example, in early 1992 good-grade zero coupon bonds with 20-year maturities were available at yields of around 8 percent; thus, for just a little over $200, investors could buy a bond that would be worth 5 times that amount, or $1,000, when it matures in 20 years. Best of all, they would be *locking in* an eight percent compound rate of return on their investment capital for the full 20-year life of the issue. Because of their unusual tax exposure (even though the bonds do not pay regular yearly interest, the IRS treats the annually accrued interest as taxable income), zeros should be used only in tax-sheltered investments, such as individual retirement accounts (IRAs), or be held by minor children who are likely to be taxed at low rates, if at all.

Zeros are issued by corporations, municipalities, and federal agencies; you can even buy U.S. Treasury notes and bonds in the form of zero coupon securities. Up until about ten years ago, major brokerage houses used to package U.S. Treasury securities as

zeros and sell them to the investing public in the form of investment trusts. These units trusts were marketed under such names as *TIGRS, CATS,* and *LIONS* and became enormously popular with investors. Seeing this, the Treasury decided to eliminate the middleman and "issue" their own form of zero coupon bond, known as *Treasury STRIPS,* or *STRIP-T's,* for short. When that happened, the market for CATS and other felines pretty much dried up. (There are some old issues still out there, but the new issue market for these securities has virtually disappeared.) Actually, the Treasury does not issue zero

serial obligation
An issue, usually a municipal bond, that is broken down into a series of smaller bonds, each with its own maturity date and coupon rate.

revenue bond
A municipal bond that is serviced from the income generated from a specific project.

general obligation bond
A municipal bond that is backed by the full faith and credit of the issuing municipality rather than by the revenue generated from a given project.

corporate bond
A bond issued by a corporation; categories include industrials, public utilities, railroad and transportation bonds, and financial issues.

zero coupon bond
A bond that pays no annual interest but sells at a deep discount to par value.

EXHIBIT 12.9

A Municipal Serial Bond Issue

Like many municipal issues, this bond was sold as a serial obligation. Observe that it has a series of 14 maturity dates running from 1995 to 2013, each with its own coupon rate. Note, for example, that $18.99 million of the issue matures in 1998 and carries a coupon (that is, "interest rate") of 5.60 percent; another $18.99 million matures in 1999 and carries a 5.70 percent coupon; and so forth through the year 2013, when the last part of the issue is retired.

Subject to compliance by the City with certain covenants, in the opinion of Bond Counsel, under present law, interest on the Bonds described below will not be includible in the gross income of the owners thereof for federal income tax purposes, and will not be treated as an item of tax preference in computing the alternative minimum tax for individuals and corporations, but will be taken into account in computing the corporate alternative minimum tax, as more fully discussed under the heading "Tax Exemption" in the Official Statement. Interest on the Bonds will be exempt from present Arizona income taxation.

NEW ISSUE

$237,945,000

City of Phoenix, Arizona

General Obligation Refunding Bonds, Series 1992

Dated: April 1, 1992   **Due: July 1, as shown below**

The General Obligation Refunding Bonds, Series 1992 (the "Bonds") are to be issued by the City of Phoenix, Arizona (the "City") for the purpose of refunding certain of its outstanding general obligation bonded indebtedness as described in the Official Statement. The Bonds are issued only as fully registered bonds without coupons, in denominations of $5,000 or any integral multiple thereof. Principal of, and premium, if any, on the Bonds are payable at the principal office of Citibank, N.A., New York, New York, as Bond Registrar and Paying Agent (the "Bond Registrar"). Interest on the Bonds is payable semiannually on January 1 and July 1 of each year commencing July 1, 1992. Interest on the Bonds is payable by check or draft of the Bond Registrar mailed to the person shown on the bond register of the City maintained by the Bond Registrar as being the registered owner of such Bond as of the fifteenth day of the calendar month immediately preceding such interest payment date, at the address appearing on said bond register or at such other address as is furnished to the Bond Registrar in writing by such registered owner before the fifteenth day of the month prior to such interest payment date.

The Bonds are subject to redemption prior to maturity as described in the Official Statement.

The Bonds are direct and general obligations of the City and are payable as to both principal and interest from ad valorem taxes which may be levied on all taxable property therein without limitation as to rate, but within the limitation as to amount as prescribed by law. (See "THE BONDS – Security and Source Payment" in the Official Statement.)

Amount	Maturity	Interest Rate	Price or Yield	Amount	Maturity	Interest Rate	Price or Yield	Amount	Maturity	Interest Rate	Price or Yield
$10,030,000	1995	6½ %	5.10%	$20,310,000	2000	5.90%	100%	$11,590,000	2004	7½%	6.31%
10,830,000	1996	5.20	100	22,675,000	2001	6.00	100	9,905,000	2005	7½	6.37
17,725,000	1997	5.40	100	17,730,000	2002	6.00	6.10	9,125,000	2006	7½	6.40
18,990,000	1998	5.60	100	17,340,000	2003	6¼	6.20	9,675,000	2007	6¾	6.45
18,980,000	1999	5.70	5.75								

$43,040,000 6⅜% Term Bonds due July 1, 2013 @ 97.75%
(Accrued interest to be added)

Bonds of particular maturities may or may not be available from the undersigned or others at the above prices on and after the date of this announcement.

The Bonds are offered when, as and if issued and received by the Underwriters, and subject to the approving opinion of Chapman and Cutler, Phoenix, Arizona, Bond Counsel, as to validity and tax exemption. Certain legal matters will be passed upon for the Underwriters by Squire, Sanders & Dempsey, Counsel to the Underwriters. The offering of the Bonds is made only by the Official Statement, copies of which may be obtained in any state from such of the undersigned as may lawfully offer these securities in such states.

Goldman, Sachs & Co.

J.P. Morgan Securities Inc.	**Prudential Securities Incorporated**
Rauscher Pierce Refsnes, Inc.	**Smith Barney, Harris Upham & Co.** Incorporated
Alden Capital Markets, Inc.	**Artemis Capital Group, Inc.**
First Interstate Bank of Arizona, N.A.	**Peacock, Hislop, Staley & Given, Inc.**
Pryor, McClendon, Counts & Co., Inc.	**The Valley National Bank of Arizona**

April 8, 1992

Source: *The Wall Street Journal*, April 8, 1992.

coupon bonds, but instead, *they allow government securities dealers to take regular coupon-bearing notes and bonds in stripped form*, which can then be sold to the public as zero coupon securities. Essentially, the coupons are *stripped* from the bond, repackaged, and then sold separately as zero coupon bonds. For example, a 20-year Treasury bond has 40 semiannual coupon payments, plus one principal payment—each of these 41 cash flows can be repackaged and sold as 41 different zero coupon securities, with maturities that range from six months to 20 years.

Another type of specialty issue that appeals to a large segment of the investing public is a **mortgage-backed bond**. Simply put, such securities are debt issues secured by a pool of residential mortgages. Issued primarily by federal agencies like "Ginnie Mae" (the Government National Mortgage Association) or "Freddie Mac" (the Federal Home Loan Mortgage Corporation), these issuers put together a pool of home mortgages and then issue securities to the investing public in the amount of the mortgage pool. These securities, known as *pass-through securities*, or *participation certificates*, are usually sold in minimum denominations of $25,000. Though their maturities can go out as far as 30 years, the average life of one of these issues is generally much shorter (perhaps as short as 8 to 10 years), because so many pooled mortgages are paid off early. As an investor in one of these securities, you hold an undivided interest in the pool of mortgages. Thus, when a homeowner makes a monthly mortgage payment, that payment is essentially passed through to you, the bondholder, to pay off the mortgage-backed bond that you hold. Although these securities come with normal coupons, the interest is paid monthly rather than semiannually. Actually, the monthly payments received by bondholders are, like mortgage payments, made up of *both* principal and interest. Since the principal portion of the payment represents return of capital, it is considered tax free; not so with interest income, however, as it is subject to ordinary state and federal income taxes.

One of the problems with mortgage-backed securities (MBSs) is that they are *self-liquidating*, since a portion of the monthly cash flow to the investor is the principal originally invested in the issue. Thus, the investor is always receiving back part of the original investment capital, so that at maturity there is *no* big principal payment that will be received. (In-stead, the principal has been paid back in little chunks over the life of the bond.) Loan prepayments are another problem with mortgage-backed securities. In fact, it was in part an effort to defuse some of the prepayment uncertainty in standard mortgage-backed securities that led to the creation of **collateralized mortgage obligations (CMOs)**. Normally, as pooled mortgages are prepaid, *all* bondholders receive a prorated share of the prepayments, and as a result the net effect is to sharply reduce the life of the bond. A CMO, in contrast, divides investors into classes (formally called *tranches*, which is French for "slice"), depending on whether they want a short-term, intermediate-term, or long-term investment. Now, while interest is paid to all bondholders, *all principal payments* go first to the shortest class, until it is fully retired; then, the next class (tranche) in the sequence becomes the sole recipient of principal, and so on until the last tranche is retired. Thus, in a CMO, only one class of bond at a time receives principal. Actually, most MBSs today are sold to the public as CMOs—or REMICs (Real Estate Mortgage Investment Conduits), which are just like CMOs except for some differences in the tax treatment accorded the issuers. Generally speaking, with the exception of some highly volatile CMO tranches, mortgage-backed securities are a safe form of investment, and they offer highly competitive, attractive returns. However, these are long-term debt securities and, like any long-term bond, they are subject to wide price swings when interest rates shoot up or down. Just because they're secured with a pool of mortgages doesn't make them immune to price volatility.

mortgage-backed bond
A debt issue secured by a pool of home mortgages; issued primarily by federal agencies.

collateralized mortgage obligation (CMO)
A type of mortgage-backed bond whose holders are divided into classes based on the length of investment desired; then, principal is channeled to short-term investors first, intermediate-term investors next, and long-term investors last.

BOND RATINGS

Bond ratings are like grades: A letter grade assigned to a bond issue designates its investment quality. Ratings are widely used and are an important part of the municipal and corporate bond markets. The two largest and best known rating agencies are Moody's and Standard & Poor's. Every time a large, new issue comes to the market, it is analyzed by a staff of professional bond analysts to determine its default risk exposure and investment quality. The financial records of the issuing organization are thoroughly worked over and its future prospects assessed. The result of all this is the assignment of a bond rating at the time of issue that indicates the ability of the issuing organization to service its debt in a prompt and timely manner. Exhibit 12.10 lists the various ratings assigned to bonds by each of the two major services. Except for slight variations in designations (Aaa versus AAA, for example), the meaning and interpretation are basically the same. Note that the top four ratings (Aaa through Baa; or AAA through BBB) designate *investment-grade* bonds — such ratings are highly coveted by issuers as they indicate financially strong, well-run companies. The next two ratings (Ba/B; or BB/B) are reserved for **junk bonds**; these ratings mean that while the principal and interest payments on the bonds are still being met, the *risk of default* is relatively high, as the issuers generally lack the financial strength found with investment-grade issues. While junk bonds are popular with some investors, it should be understood that these are highly speculative securities. They may offer high rates of return, but they also involve substantial amounts of risks; in particular, there's a very real likelihood that you'll never get your money back!

Once a new issue is rated, the process doesn't stop there. For older, outstanding bonds are also regularly reviewed to ensure that their assigned ratings are still valid. Most issues will carry a single rating to maturity, but it is not uncommon for some to undergo revision. Finally, although it may appear that the firm is receiving the rating, it is actually the individual issue that is being rated. As a result, a firm can have different ratings assigned to its issues; the senior securities, for example, might carry one rating and the junior issues another, lower one. Most bond investors pay careful attention to ratings, since they can affect comparative market yields — specifically, the higher the rating, the lower the yield of an obligation, other things being equal. Thus, whereas an A-rated bond might offer a 9 percent yield, a comparable AAA issue would probably yield something like 8.5 to 8.75 percent.

BOND PRICES AND YIELDS

The price of a bond is a function of its coupon, maturity, and movement of market interest rates. *When interest rates go down, bond prices go up, and vice versa*. The relationship of bond prices to market rates is captured in Exhibit 12.11. Basically, the graph serves to reinforce the *inverse* relationship between bond prices and market interest rates: Note that *lower* rates lead to *higher* bond prices. The exhibit also shows the difference between premium and discount bonds. A **premium bond** is one that sells for more than its par value, which occurs whenever market interest rates drop below the coupon rate on the bond; a **discount bond**, in contrast, sells for less than par, and is the result of market rates being greater than the issue's coupon rate. Thus, the 10 percent bond in our illustration traded as a premium bond when market rates were at 8 percent, but as a discount bond when rates stood at 12 percent.

When a bond is first issued, it is usually sold to the public at a price that equals, or is very close to, its par value. Likewise, when the bond matures — some 15, 20, or 30 years later — it will once again be priced at its par value. But what happens to the price of the bond in between is of considerable concern to most bond investors. In this regard, we know that the extent to which bond prices move depends not only on the *direction* of change in interest rates, but also on the *magnitude* of such changes; for the greater the moves in interest rates, the greater the swings in bond prices. But there's more, for bond prices will also vary according to the coupon and maturity of the issue — that is, bonds with *lower coupons* and/or *longer maturities* will respond more vigorously to changes in market rates and undergo *greater price swings*. It should be obvious, therefore, that if interest rates are moving *up*, the investor should seek high coupon bonds with short maturities, since this will cause minimal price variation and *act to preserve as much capital as possible*. In contrast, if rates are heading *down*, that's the time to be in long-term

EXHIBIT 12.10

Moody's and Standard & Poor's Bond Ratings

Agencies like Moody's and Standard & Poor's rate corporate and municipal bonds; the ratings provide an indication of the bonds' investment quality (particularly with respect to an issue's default risk exposure).

BOND RATINGS*

Moody's	S&P	Description
Aaa	AAA	*Prime-Quality Investment Bonds* — This is the highest rating assigned, denoting extremely strong capacity to pay.
AaA	AA A }	*High-Grade Investment Bonds* — These are also considered very safe bonds, though they're not quite as safe as Aaa/AAA issues; double-A-rated bonds (Aa/AA) are safer (have less risk of default) than single-A-rated issues.
Baa	BBB	*Medium-Grade Investment Bonds* — These are the lowest of the investment-grade issues; they're felt to lack certain protective elements against adverse economic conditions.
Ba B	BB B }	*Junk Bonds* — With little protection against default, these are viewed as highly speculative securities.
Caa Ca C	CCC CC C D }	*Poor-Quality Bonds* — These are either in default or very close to it.

*Some ratings may be modified to show relative standing within a major rating category; for example, Moody's uses numerical modifiers (1, 2, 3), whereas S&P uses plus (+) or minus (−) signs.

bonds — if you're a speculator looking for a lot of capital gains, then go with long-term, *low coupon* bonds, whereas if you're trying to lock in a high level of coupon (interest) income, then stick with long-term, *high coupon* bonds that offer plenty of call protection (which you can get from issues that are noncallable or have extended call-deferment periods).

When interest rates go down, bond prices also go down because such securities become less valuable. *Fantasy:* Bond prices and interest rates move in the opposite direction; as a result, when interest rates go down, bond prices go up.

Current Yield and Yield to Maturity. The

yield on a bond is the rate of return that you would earn if you held the bond for a stated period of time. The two most commonly cited bond yields are current yield and yield to maturity. **Current yield** reflects the amount of annual interest income the

bond provides relative to its current market price. The formula of current yield is

$$\text{Current yield} = \frac{\text{Annual interest income}}{\text{Market price of bond}}.$$

junk bond
Also known as *high-yield* bonds, these are highly speculative securities that have received low ratings from Moody's or Standard & Poor's; the low ratings mean that the issuers could have difficulty meeting interest and principal payments as they come due.

premium bond
A bond that has a market value in excess of par; occurs when interest rates drop below the coupon rate.

discount bond
A bond with a market value lower than par; occurs when market rates are greater than the coupon rate.

EXHIBIT 12.11

Price Behavior of a Bond with a 10 Percent Coupon

A bond will sell at its par value so long as the prevailing market interest rate remains the same as the bond's coupon (for example, when both coupon and market rates equal 10 percent). However, when market rates drop, bond prices rise, and vice versa; moreover, as a bond approaches its maturity, the price of the issue will always move toward its par value, no matter what happens to interest rates.

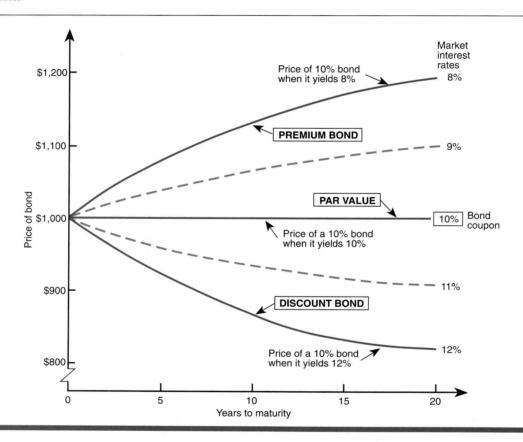

As you can see, the current yield on a bond is basically the same as the dividend yield on a stock. Assume, for example, that a 9 percent bond with a $1,000 face value is currently selling for $910. Since annual interest income would equal $90 (.09 × $1,000) and the current market price of the bond is $910, its current yield would be 9.89 percent ($90/$910). This yield, which is commonly quoted in the financial press, would be of interest to investors seeking current income; other things being equal, the higher the current yield, the more attractive a bond would be to such an investor.

The annual rate of return that a bondholder would receive *if he or she held the issue to its matu-* rity is captured in the bond's **yield to maturity**. This measure captures two types of return; the annual interest income and the recovery of the principal value of the bond at maturity. If a bond is purchased at its face value, its yield to maturity will equal the coupon, or stated, rate of interest. If it is purchased at a discount, its yield to maturity will be greater than the coupon rate because the investor will receive, in addition to annual interest income, the full face value of the bond even though he or she paid something less than par — in effect, the investor will earn some capital gains on the investment. Of course, if the bond is purchased at a premium, the opposite will be true: The yield to maturity on the issue will be less than its coupon rate since the transaction will involve a capital loss — that is, the investor will pay more for the bond than he or she will get back at maturity.

You can find the yield to maturity of a bond by using the *approximate yield* formula introduced earlier in this chapter. In particular, by setting the future price (*FP*) of the investment equal to the bond's face value ($1,000), you can use the following version of the approximate yield equation to find the *approximate yield to maturity of a bond:*

$$\text{Approximate Yield to Maturity} = \frac{CI + \left[\dfrac{\$1,000 - CP}{N}\right]}{\left[\dfrac{CP + \$1,000}{2}\right]}$$

As you will recall, *CI* equals annual current income (or annual interest income, in the case of a bond), *CP* stands for current price (of the bond), and *N* is the investment period (the number of years to maturity). Assume, for example, that you are contemplating the purchase of a $1,000, 9 percent bond with 15 years remaining to maturity, and that the bond currently trades at a price of $910. Given *CI* = $90, *CP* = $910, and *N* = 15 years, the approximate yield to maturity on this bond will be

$$\text{Approximate Yield to Maturity} = \frac{\$90 + \left[\dfrac{\$1,000 - \$910}{\$15}\right]}{\left[\dfrac{\$910 + \$1,000}{2}\right]}$$

$$= \frac{\$90 + \left[\dfrac{\$90}{15}\right]}{\left[\dfrac{\$1,910}{2}\right]} = \underline{\underline{10.05\%}}.$$

This is above both the 9 percent stated rate and the 9.89 percent current yield, since the bond is purchased at a discount from its face value. (Note that had the bond been selling at $1,090, it would have had a current yield of 8.26 percent and an approximate yield to maturity of 8.04 percent — both below the 9 percent coupon rate; such behavior would be due to the fact that the bond was selling at a premium price.)

Yield to maturity measures are used by investors to assess the underlying attractiveness of a bond investment. The higher the yield to maturity, the more attractive the investment, other things being equal. *If a bond provided a yield to maturity that equaled or exceeded an investor's desired rate of return, it would be considered a worthwhile investment candidate*, as it would promise a yield that would adequately compensate the investor for the level of risk involved.

PREFERREDS AND CONVERTIBLES

While stocks and bonds are the most basic of investment vehicles, there are some securities — like preferred stocks and convertible bonds — that combine the features of both equity and debt issues. Can you think of some ways that preferred stocks are like common stocks? In what ways are they like bonds? How about convertibles? in what way are they like bonds? Like stocks? Think about these questions before going on.

Preferred stocks and convertible securities are corporate issues that hold a position senior to common stock. Although preferreds are actually a form of equity ownership, they, along with convertibles, are considered to be fixed-income securities because their level of current income is fixed. Convertible securities, initially issued as bonds or preferred stocks, are subsequently convertible into shares of the issuing firm's common stock. Preferred stocks, in contrast, are issued and remain as equity. They

current yield
The amount of current income a bond provides relative to its current market price.

yield to maturity
The annual rate of return that a bondholder purchasing a bond today would earn if he or she held it to maturity.

derive their name in part from the preferential claim on income they command—that is, all preferred dividends must be paid before any payments can be made to holders of common stock.

PREFERRED STOCKS

Preferred stocks carry a dividend that's usually fixed, and which is paid quarterly and stated either in dollar terms or as a percent of par (or stated) value. They are considered *hybrid securities* because they possess features of both common stocks and corporate bonds. They are like common stocks in that they pay dividends, *which may be passed* when corporate earnings fall below certain levels. Moreover, preferreds represent equity ownership and are issued without stated maturity dates. They are, however, also like bonds in that they provide investors with a prior claim on income and assets, and the level of current income is usually fixed for the life of the issue. Most important, because these securities usually trade on the basis of the yield they offer to investors, they are viewed in the marketplace as fixed-income obligations and, as a result, are treated much like bonds.

Preferred Stock Features. Preferred stocks possess features that not only distinguish them from other types of securities, but also help to differentiate one preferred from another. For example, the amount of dividends that an issue pays is a common way of describing preferred stocks—thus, a company could have a "three dollar" preferred stock outstanding (meaning the issue pays $3 per share in annual dividends) and another issue of preferred that pays $4.75 a share in yearly dividends. These are two separate issues and they would trade at two different prices. A number of preferred stocks are issued with call features, which means they can be retired if the issuing company decides to do so, and some even have sinking fund provisions, indicating how they will be paid off over time (sinking fund preferreds, in effect, have implied maturity dates). In addition to these features, there are two other provisions that preferred stock investors should be aware of: (1) the cumulative-dividends provision, and (2) the dividend-participation feature.

Cumulative versus noncumulative. Most preferred stock is **cumulative**, which means that any dividends passed in previous periods must be

paid in full prior to distributing any dividends to common stockholders—in essence, if the preferred stockholders do not receive any dividends, then neither do the consumers. For example, assume a firm has outstanding a *$4 preferred stock* (which means the stated dividend is $4 per year, or $1 per quarter) and that the last two quarterly dividends have not been paid. Before any dividends can be paid to the common stockholders, the preferred stockholders must be paid the $2 of past dividends *plus the current quarterly dividend of $1*. Had the preferred stock been *noncumulative*, only the current $1 dividend would have had to be paid prior to distributing any earnings to the common stockholders.

Participating versus nonparticipating. As a rule, preferred stocks are issued as *nonparticipating*, which means that the preferred stockholders receive only a specified amount of dividends. Occasionally, a **participating** preferred stock is issued. Such an issue allows the preferred stockholders to share in the distribution of additional dividends once common stockholders have reached a stipulated level of dividends. An example might be a preferred stock in which the preferred stockholders participate equally with the common stockholders on a per-share basis once the latter have received a specified amount of dividends—say, $2 per share.

Investing in Preferreds. Most individuals invest in preferred stocks because of the high current income they provide in the form of annual dividends. Moreover, such dividend income is highly predictable even though it lacks legal backing and can be passed. It is not surprising, therefore, that dividend yield is viewed by many investors as the key ingredient in evaluating the investment appeal of most preferred stocks. *Dividend yield*—which is found by dividing annual dividend income by the market price of the stock—is a reflection of an issue's current yield and, as such, is used to assess preferred stock investment opportunities. Other things being equal, the higher the dividend yield, the more attractive the investment vehicle. For example, suppose a certain preferred stock pays a dividend of $2 per year and is currently priced at $20; this preferred would have a dividend yield of $2/$20 = 10%. Whether or not a 10 percent return from this preferred stock makes for a good investment depends on (1) the amount of risk exposure involved and (2) the kinds of returns you can generate elsewhere — in other words, if you can earn better than 10 percent on other similarly risky investments, then do it!

Once you invest in a preferred, you should keep your eyes on market interest rates, since preferred stock prices are closely related to prevailing market rates; after all, you are investing in a *fixed-income* security whose value is determined chiefly by dividend yield. When the general level of interest rates moves up, the yields on preferreds rise and their prices decline accordingly; in contrast, when rates drift down, the yields on preferreds decrease and their prices rise. Thus, like that of any fixed-income security, the price behavior of most good-grade preferred stocks is inversely related to market interest rates.

CONVERTIBLE SECURITIES

Convertible issues, more popularly known as simply *convertibles*, represent still another type of fixed-income security. Although they possess the features and performance characteristics of both fixed-income and equity securities, *convertibles should be viewed primarily as a form of equity*. Most investors commit their capital to such obligations not because of their attractive yields, but because of the potential price performance that the stock side of the issue offers. In short, convertible securities are popular with individual investors because of the *equity kicker* they provide. Not surprisingly, whenever the stock market is strong, convertibles tend to be strong, and vice versa. Convertible bonds and convertible preferreds are both linked to the firm's equity position and are therefore usually considered interchangeable for investment purposes. Except for a few peculiarities, such as the fact that preferreds pay dividends rather than interest and do so on a quarterly rather than semiannual basis, convertible bonds and convertible preferreds are evaluated in pretty much the same way. The following discussion on convertible bonds, therefore, applies to convertible preferreds as well.

Issue Features. A convertible bond basically is issued as a *debenture* (that is, unsecured debt) but carries the provision that, within a stipulated time period, *it may be converted into a certain number of shares of the issuing company's common stock*. Generally, the investor merely trades in the convert-

ible bond for a stipulated number of shares of common stock. Exhibit 12.12 provides the details of a recently issued convertible bond. Note that this obligation originally came out as a 4½ percent subordinated note but in time, each $1,000 bond can be exchanged for (converted into) Home Depot stock at $77.50 per share. Thus, *regardless of what happens to the market price of the stock*, the convertible bond investor can redeem each $1,000 bond for 12.90 shares of stock: $1,000/$77.50 = 12.90. If at the time of conversion the stocks were trading in the market at $125 a share, then the investor would have just converted a $1,000 bond into $1,612 worth of stocks (that is, 12.90 × $125).

The key element of any convertible issue is its **conversion privilege**, which stipulates the conditions and specific nature of the conversion feature. First, it states exactly when the bond can be converted. Sometimes, there will be an initial waiting period of six months to perhaps two years after the date of issue, during which time the issue cannot be converted. The *conversion period* then begins, after which the issue can be converted at any time. Technically it is the *bondholder* who has the right to convert the bond into the common stock, but more commonly the issuing firm will initiate the conversion by calling the issue. From the investor's point of view, the most important item of information is the **conversion ratio**, which specifies the number of

cumulative (preferred stock)
A preferred stock feature requiring that any passed dividends must be paid prior to distributing any dividends to common stockholders.

participating (preferred stock)
A preferred stock provision that allows the holder to share in the distribution of additional dividends once common stockholders have received their specified dividends.

conversion privilege
The provision in a convertible issue that stipulates the conditions of the conversion feature, such as the conversion period and conversion ratio.

conversion ratio
A ratio that specifies the number of shares of common stock into which a convertible bond can be converted.

EXHIBIT 12.12

A Newly Issued Convertible Bond

Investors who hold this Home Depot bond can convert it, anytime prior to maturity, into the company's common stock at a stated price of $77.50 per share, and in so doing, receive 12.9 shares of stock in exchange for each $1,000 convertible bond they hold. Prior to conversion, the bondholders will receive annual interest income of $45.00 for each bond.

*This announcement is neither an offer to sell nor a solicitation of offers to buy any of these securities.
The offering is made only by the Prospectus.*

<u>NEW ISSUE</u>   January 27, 1992

$805,000,000

The Home Depot, Inc.

4½% Convertible Subordinated Notes Due 1997

The Notes are convertible into Common Stock of the Company at any time on or before February 15, 1997, unless previously redeemed, at a conversion price of $77.50 per share, subject to adjustment in certain events.

Price 100%
plus accrued interest, if any, from February 3, 1992

*Copies of the Prospectus may be obtained in any State in which this announcement is circulated only from such of the undersigned as may legally offer these securities in such State.
These securities are redeemable prior to maturity as set forth in the Prospectus.*

The First Boston Corporation   Invemed Associates, Inc.

Source: *The Wall Street Journal,* January 27, 1992.

shares of common stock that the bond can be converted into. For example, a $1,000 convertible bond might stipulate a conversion ratio of 20, meaning that you can "cash in" one convertible bond for 20 shares of the company's stock.

Convertible bonds are so named because they can be exchanged for a set number of shares of common stock.
Fact: Convertible securities carry the provision that they may, within a stipulated time period, be converted into a certain number of shares of the issuing company's common stock.

Conversion Value.   Given the significance of the price behavior of the underlying common stock to the value of a convertible security, one of the most important measures to a convertible bond investor is conversion value. In essence, **conversion value** is an indication of what a convertible issue would trade for *if it were priced to sell on the basis of its stock value*. Conversion value is easy to find: Simply multiply the conversion ratio of the issue by the current market price of the underlying common stock. For example, a convertible that carried a conversion ratio of 20 would have a conversion value of $1,200 if the firm's stock traded at a current market price of $60 per share (20 × $60 = $1,200). Unfortunately, convertible issues seldom trade precisely at their conversion values; rather, they invariably trade at **conversion premiums**, which means that the convertibles are priced in the market at more than their conversion values. For example, a convertible that traded at $1,400 and had a conversion value equal to $1,200 would have a conversion premium of $200 (i.e., $1,400 − $1,200 = $200).

Investment Merits.   Convertible securities appeal to investors who want *the price potential of a common stock along with the downside risk protection of a corporate bond*. This two-sided feature is critical with convertibles and is virtually impossible to match with straight common or straight debt. As a rule, whenever a convertible trades near or above its par value ($1,000), it will exhibit price behavior that closely matches that of the underlying common stock: If the stock goes up in price, so will the convertible, and vice versa. In fact, the price change of the convertible will *exceed* that of the common, because of the presence of a conversion ratio. For example, if a convertible carries a ratio of, say, 20, then for every point the common stock goes up (or down) in price, the price of the convertible will move in the *same direction by a multiple of 20*. Because of the obvious importance of the underlying common stock, investors should carefully consider this element before investing in convertibles. If the future prospects of a stock are promising, the convertible could turn out to be a good investment.

A final feature of convertible bonds is that the current income from their interest payments normally exceeds the income from the dividends that would be received from a comparable investment in the underlying common stock. For example, a $1,000 convertible with an 8 percent coupon would yield $80 per year to the holder; if the convertible carried a conversion ratio of 20, and each share of stock paid $2.50 in dividends, an investment in 20 shares of the firm's stock would provide only $50 in per year dividend income. Thus, with convertibles it is possible to reap the advantages of common stock (in the form of potential upward price appreciation) and still generate improved current income.

---

conversion value
A measure of what a convertible issue would trade for if it were priced to sell on the basis of its stock value; found by multiplying the conversion ratio by the current market price of the underlying common stock.

conversion premium
The difference between a convertible security's market price and its conversion value.

SUMMARY

- Investing plays an important part in personal financial planning, as it is the vehicle through which many of your financial goals can be reached. Your investment activities should be based on a sound investment plan that is linked to an ongoing savings plan.

- Most people invest their money in order to enhance their current income, accumulate funds for a major expenditure, save for retirement, and/or shelter some of their income from taxes. These objectives can be achieved most effectively when you confine your investment activities to investment vehicles that are expected to provide satisfactory rates of return — that is, rates of return that provide adequate compensation for risk and that meet or exceed desired rates of return.
- While investing offers returns in the form of current income and/or capital gains, it also involves risk; the basic types of investment risk are business risk, financial risk, market risk, purchasing power risk, interest rate risk, liquidity risk, and event risk — all of which combine to affect the level of return from an investment.
- Common stocks are a popular form of investing that can be used to meet just about any investment objective — investors can choose from blue-chip, growth, income, speculative, cyclical, or defensive stocks; and if they're so inclined, they can even buy foreign stocks by investing in ADRs (American Depositary Receipts). Regardless of the type, the value of such stocks is based on measures like net profit margin, ROE, earnings per share; price/earnings (P/E) ratio, beta, and approximate yield.
- Bonds are another popular form of investing; such securities are basically the publicly issued debt of corporations and various levels of government (from the U.S. Treasury and various agencies of the U.S. government to state and local — municipal — governments). Known as fixed-income securities, such obligations can be used to generate either current income or capital gains (as when market interest rates go down).
- Preferred stocks and convertible bonds combine the features of both equity and debt securities, and are also widely used by individual investors. Preferred stocks are like common stocks to the extent that they pay dividends, but they are also like bonds in that they provide investors with a fixed claim on assets and a fixed level of income; in contrast, convertible bonds are issued as debt securities but they carry a provision that allows their holders to convert the bonds into shares of common stock.

QUESTIONS AND PROBLEMS

1. Briefly discuss the relationship between investing and personal financial planning. Do these two activities complement each other?
2. Identify the four major investment objectives. Why are investment objectives important?
3. Describe the various types of risk to which investors are exposed. What is meant by the risk-return trade-off? What is the risk-free rate of return?
4. Beth Kaminski is a young career woman who's presently employed as the managing editor of a well-known financial journal. While she thoroughly enjoys her job and the people she works with, what she would really like to do is open a bookstore of her own. In particular, she would like to open her store in about eight years, and she figures she'd need about $50,000 in capital to do so. Given she thinks she can make about 8 percent on her money, use a worksheet like the one in Exhibit 12.1 to find the following:

   a. How much would she have to invest today, in one lump sum, to end up with $50,000 in eight years?
   b. If she's starting from scratch, how much would she have to put away annually to accumulate the needed capital in eight years?
   c. How about if she already has $12,000 socked away; how much would she have to put away annually to accumulate the required capital in eight years?
   d. Given Beth now has a handle on how much she has to save, briefly explain how she would use an *investment plan* to help her reach her objective.

5. Briefly describe the two basic sources of return to investors. What is interest-on-interest, and why is it such an important element of return?
6. What makes for a good investment? Use the approximate yield formula (Equation 12.1) to rank

the following investments according to their expected returns:

a. Buy a stock for $45 a share, hold it for three years, and sell it for $75 a share (the stock pays annual dividends of $3 a share).

b. Buy a security for $25, hold it for two years, and sell it for $60 (current income on this security is zero).

c. Buy a one-year, 12 percent note for $950 (assume the note has a $1,000 par value and that it will be held to its maturity).

7. What is a derivative security? Give examples of at least two different types of derivative securities and explain why they're considered to be derivatives.

8. What is market globalization, and why should American investors be interested in foreign securities? Identify several different ways of investing in foreign stocks, including ADRs.

9. What are rights? How do they differ from warrants?

10. Define and briefly discuss each of the following common stock measurements: (a) book value, (b) ROE, (c) earnings per share (EPS), (d) price/earnings (P/E) ratio, and (e) beta.

◆ 11. Selected financial information about Engulf and Devour, Inc. is as follows:

Total assets	$20,000,000
Total liabilities	$ 8,000,000
Total preferred stock	$ 3,000,000
Total annual preferred stock dividends	$ 240,000
Net profits after tax	$ 2,500,000
Number of shares of common stock outstanding	500,000 shares
Current market price of common stock	$50.00 per share
Annual common stock dividends	$2.50 a share

Using the above information, compute the following:

a. The stock's dividend yield

b. Book value per share

c. Earnings per share

d. P/E ratio

12. Briefly discuss some of the different types of common stock. Which type(s) would be most appealing to you, and why?

13. Under what conditions would a stock be considered a viable investment candidate? What are dividend reinvestment plans, and how do they fit into a stock investment program?

14. Using the resources available at your campus or public library, select a company from *Value Line* that would be of interest to you. (*HINT:* pick a company that's been publicly traded for at least 10 to 15 years, and *avoid* public utilities, banks and other financial institutions.) Obtain a copy of the latest *Value Line* report on your chosen company. Using the forecasted data reported in *Value Line*, determine the following. (*Note:* Use a three-year holding period throughout this exercise.)

a. What's the latest price of the stock you selected and how much is the stock currently paying in annual dividends?

b. According to *Value Line*, what are the (approximate) projected dividends per share for each of the next three years; also, what's the (approximate) estimated price of the stock at the end of the three-year holding period?

c. Use Equation 12.1 to find the expected return on this stock.

d. If you were investing in this stock, what would you want to earn as a minimum/required rate of return? Briefly explain how you came up with that number.

e. Would you consider this stock to be a worthwhile investment candidate? Explain.

15. What is the difference between a secured bond and an unsecured bond? Give a few examples of each. Briefly describe the following bond features: (a) sinking funds, (b) call features, and (c) coupon.

16. Are junk bonds and zero coupon bonds the same? Explain. What are the basic tax features of a tax-exempt municipal bond? Are there such things as *taxable* municipal bonds? Explain.

17. What is a mortgage-backed bond and why would any investor be interested in such securities? Is there any difference between a mortgage-backed bond and a CMO? Explain.

18. Illustrate why an investor in a high tax bracket would prefer municipal bonds to other investment vehicles.

19. An investor in the 28 percent tax bracket is trying to decide which of two bonds to select: one is a 7.5 percent corporate bond selling at par and the other is a municipal bond with a 5.25

percent coupon, which is also selling at par. Which is these two bonds should the investor select? Why?

20. Explain the system of bond ratings used by Moody's and Standard & Poor's.

21. What effects do current market interest rates have on the price behavior of outstanding bonds?

22. Describe and differentiate between a bond's (a) current yield and (b) yield to maturity. Why are these yield measures important to the bond investor? Explain. Find the approximate yield to maturity of a 20-year, 13 percent, $1,000 par value bond that is trading at a price of $850.

23. Which of the following three bonds offers the highest current yield? Which one has the highest yield to maturity?
   a. A 9.5 percent, 20 year bond quoted at 97¾.
   b. A 16%, 15 year bond quoted at 164⅝.
   c. A 5.25 percent, 18 year bond quoted at 54.

24. What is preferred stock? Distinguish between (a) cumulative and noncumulative preferred stock and (b) participating and nonparticipating preferred stock.

25. What is a convertible bond? Why do investors buy convertible securities?

26. Describe the "conversion privilege" of a convertible security. Explain how the market price of the underlying common stock affects the market price of the convertible bond.

27. Find the conversion value of an issue that carries a conversion ratio of 24, given that the market price of the underlying common stock is $55 a share. Would there be any conversion premium if the convertible bond had a market price of $1,500? If so, how much?

28. Using the resources available at your campus or public library, work the following problems. (Note: Show your work for all your calculations.)
   a. Select any two *common stocks*, and determine the dividend yield, earnings per share, and P/E ratio for each.
   b. Select any two *bonds*, and determine the current yield and approximate yield to maturity of each.
   c. Select any two *preferred* stocks, and determine the current yield of each.
   d. Select any two *convertible debentures*, and determine the conversion ratio, conversion value, and conversion premium for each.

CONTEMPORARY CASE APPLICATIONS

12.1 The Torres Struggle with Two Investment Goals

Like a lot of married couples, Steve and Barbara Torres are trying their best to deal with not one, but two very important investment objectives: (1) building up an *education fund* to put their two children through college; and (2) building up a *retirement nest egg* for themselves. Their children are now 10 and 12 years old, and the oldest will be starting college in six years. Steve and Barbara want to have $40,000 set aside *for each child* by the time each one starts college (so they have six years to go with one child and eight with the other). As far as their retirement plans are concerned, the Torres both hope to retire at age 65, in 20 years. Both Steve and Barbara work, and together, they currently earn about $75,000 a year.

Six years ago, the Torres started a college fund by investing $6,000 a year in short-term CDs. That fund is now worth $45,000 — enough to put one of the kids through any one of the in-state colleges. In addition, they have $50,000, which they received from an inheritance, invested in several mutual funds, and another $20,000 in a tax-sheltered retirement account. Steve and Barbara feel they'll easily be able to continue to put away $6,000 a year for the next 20 years — in fact, Barbara thinks they'll be able to put away even more, particularly after the children are out of school. The Torres are pretty conservative investors and feel they can probably earn about 8 percent on their money. (You can ignore taxes in this exercise.)

Questions

1. Using a worksheet like the one in Exhibit 12.1, determine whether the Torres have enough money *right now* to meet the educational needs of their children. That is, will the $45,000 they've accumulated so far be enough to put their children through school, given they can invest their money at 8 percent? Remember, they want to have $40,000 set aside for *each* child by the time each one starts college.

2. Regarding their retirement nest egg, assuming *no additions* are made to either the $50,000 they now have in mutual funds or the $20,000 in the retirement account, how much would these investments be worth in 20 years, given they can earn 8 percent? (*Hint:* See Appendix A.)

3. Now, if they can invest $6,000 a year for the next 20 years and apply that to their retirement nest egg, how much would they be able to accumulate given their 8 percent rate of return? (*Hint:* See Appendix B.)

4. How do you think the Torres are doing with regard to meeting their twin investment objectives? Explain.

5. What recommendations would you make to them with regard to *where* they should invest their money—what kind of stocks, bonds, or other investment instruments do you think would be right for them?

12.2 Jill Decides to Try Her Hand at Investing

Jill Karras is a 26-year-old management trainee at a large chemical company. She is single and has no plans for marriage. Her annual salary is $34,000 (placing her in the 28 percent tax bracket), and her monthly expenditures come to approximately $1,500. During the past year or so, Jill has managed to save around $8,000, and she expects to continue to save at least that amount each year for the foreseeable future. Her company pays the premium on her $35,000 life insurance policy. Since Jill's entire education was financed by scholarships, she was able to save the money from summer and part-time jobs she held as a student. Altogether, she has a nest egg of nearly $18,000, out of which she would like to invest about $15,000. She will keep the remaining $3,000 in a money market account that pays 4.5 percent interest; she will use this money only in the event of an emergency. Although Jill can afford to take more risks than someone with family obligations, she does not wish to be a speculator; rather, she simply wants to earn an attractive rate of return on her investments.

Questions

1. What options are open to Jill?

2. What chances does she have of earning a satisfactory return on her investments if she invests her $15,000 in (a) blue-chip stocks, (b) growth stocks, (c) speculative stocks, (d) corporate bonds, or (e) municipal bonds?

3. Discuss the factors you would consider when analyzing these alternative investment vehicles.

4. What recommendation would you make to Jill with respect to her available investment alternatives? Explain.

FOR MORE INFORMATION

General Information Articles

Albers, Robert. "What to Expect from a Dividend Reinvestment Plan." *AAII Journal*, April 1991, pp. 17–19.

Barrett, Amy. "Scanning the Globe for High Yields." *Financial World*, September 18, 1990, pp. 48–51.

Fredman, Albert J. "All about Bonds." *Personal Investor*, March 1990, pp. 48–52.

Liscio, John. "Best of All Worlds: Convertibles Never Had It So Good." *Barron's*, August 7, 1989, pp. 16, 25.

Little, Jeffrey B., and Lucien Rhodes. *Understanding Wall Street*. McGraw-Hill/Liberty Hall Press, 1991.

Government Documents & Other Publications

How the Bond Market Works. New York Institute of Finance; 70 Pine St.; New York, NY 10270.

How to Invest. Standard & Poor's Corp.; 25 Broadway; New York, NY 10004.

An Investor's Guide to Tax Exempt Securities. Public Securities Association; 40 Broad Street, 12th floor; New York, NY 10004.

Investors Information Kit; and *The NYSE Fact Book* (Annual). Both available from: New York Stock Exchange; Publications Division; 11 Wall Street; New York, NY 10005.

What Every Investor Should Know. U.S. Securities & Exchange Commission; Publications Section; 450 5th St., NW; Washington, DC 20549.

GETTING A HANDLE ON YOUR FINANCIAL FUTURE

Over your lifetime you will buy securities for a number of objectives. You may need more current income or you are saving for a major purchase. Later in life you may need to accumulate funds for retirement or to shelter your income from taxation. Regardless of the objective, you need to learn as much as possible about the investment opportunities that are available in order to make an informed choice.

Understanding the characteristics of the wide variety of investment options and their proper use is crucial to your achieving your objectives in a timely and cost-effective manner. In order to do this, you must first restate your objectives in terms of financial goals. This would be to determine how much money you will need at some point in time. You also need to decide on an appropriate investment rate of return. Once these factors are determined you need to decide on how to accumulate the funds necessary to achieve this goal either in a lump sum or a series of investments over time. This amount could be determined by using a form such as the one shown in Exhibit 12.1.

To provide you with direction toward achieving your financial goals, you need an investment plan.

If You Are Just Starting Out

In order to accumulate capital for investment purposes, such as the down payment on a house, first of all you need to quantify your financial goals as suggested in Exhibit 12.1. Before you place any money in any investment, you should thoroughly investigate its characteristics in terms of the types of risk involved and the expected return. This requires a commitment on your part to learn as much as you can about an investment before you put your funds at risk. In other words the investment must be suitable for you and your financial goals.

Once the investment is made, you should keep up with its performance. If it is not behaving as anticipated, you want to find out why as soon as possible so you can take appropriate action. However, you must be patient with your investments. A decline in value could only be temporary and does not necessarily mean you have made a bad decision. One of the keys to successful investment performance is consistency. If you feel that your plan is sound, then you would stick with it. You need time to let your plan work, so while you may remember the saying "Fools rush in . . ." you should also be aware that in times of market turbulence such as October 1987 and 1989 that sometimes "Fools rush out."

Setting Financial Goals:

1. Consider the effects of taxes on the investment income in the projected return on investments, unless the funds are placed in a tax-sheltered investment.

2. In selecting the projected rate of return, look at what various investments have returned over an equivalent time period and choose the rates on investment(s) that are consistent with your risk tolerance.

3. Once you have the rate of return, calculate the lump sum necessary to achieve the goal. If sufficient funds are not available, then calculate the series of investments required over time to achieve them.

4. Compare the amount you need to invest periodically with any surplus in your cash budget. If there is no surplus or it is not sufficient to fund this goal, you can either postpone the goal, cut expenses in other areas, or invest to earn a higher rate of return.

Selecting Appropriate Investments:

1. The investment choice in many cases is dependent on the priority of your financial goals. If the goal is extremely important and cannot be delayed, then the investments would probably be relatively low risk, and vice versa.

2. Some investments require minimum dollar amounts to purchase. This may require that a temporary investment vehicle be used until sufficient funds are accumulated. This might result in a rate of return lower than anticipated.

3. Appropriate diversification should be considered when selecting the appropriate investments as will be discussed in the next chapter.

4. After you have investigated the investment options and are now in a position to make a purchase, remember that the ultimate investment decision is yours. Do not be persuaded to purchase something that you have not investigated or that does not seem appropriate just because it is being touted to you by a securities salesperson.

This is generally nothing more than a written statement of how the funds will be invested to achieve the targeted goal. This would involve a selection of appropriate investment vehicles that have the desired characteristics in terms of risk and expected return. Among the investment alternatives are equities (common and preferred stocks), debt (corporate, government, and agency issues, and municipal bonds), derivative securities (options and futures contracts), real estate, and others (precious metals or collectibles). Most of these alternatives can be purchased directly or through investment companies (mutual funds).

In deciding on the appropriate investment you should pay particular attention to the type(s) of risk that the investment has relative to its expected returns. The risks in investment come from factors that are unique to the issuer (business, financial, and event risk) as well as factors that are determined in the marketplace (market, purchasing power, interest rate, and liquidity risk). Returns on your investments come from current income and/or appreciation in value (capital gains). The trade-off between risk and return is shown in Exhibit 12.3.

If You Are Thirtysomething

As you get older, you hopefully will experience the satisfaction of achieving financial goals and setting new ones. You may have accumulated enough money to make the down payment on your home and are now concentrating on setting aside money for your children's education or your retirement.

There are a number of changes that should have occurred since you were just starting out. First, you should have become more knowledgeable about the investment opportunities available, but at the same time somewhat bewildered by the increasing number and complexity of investment options. Second, your attitude toward risk may have changed with your increasing income generating additional investable funds. Third, your time horizon for many of your goals is getting shorter. All of this will necessitate a reevaluation of your financial goals and your investments.

The result of these changes could be that you may be able to achieve the same dollar goal in a shorter period of time or by investing less money by increasing the riskiness of your investments. On the other hand, you may find that many of your goals (being a millionaire by age 35 and retiring) are unattainable.

Investing in Common Stocks:

1. The selection of common stocks as investments to achieve your financial goals revolves around the decisions of where to put the money and when to make moves.

2. Don't buy on a rumor. Even if it is true, by the time you hear it the stock price has probably made most of its adjustment.

3. Carefully analyze the purchase to ensure that it meets your goals. Don't buy a stock just because it has a recognizable name.

4. The release of "favorable" information about a company does not mean that it should be bought. Remember that the price of a share of stock responds to unanticipated information. If the release of the news was to be expected there might not be any change in the stock price.

5. Consider using dividend reinvestment plans as a means of achieving your financial goals. Many allow purchases with no transaction costs and some also provide cash discounts.

Investing in Bonds:

1. If you are trying to increase your return on your fixed-income securities, remember that when interest rates change, the longer the maturity of the bond the greater the price volatility.

2. The lower the coupon on the bond, the greater the price volatility with changes in interest rates. This means that zero coupon bonds have the greatest price risk.

3. Don't be deceived by the term "high yield" investment; this is just another way of describing junk bonds.

4. If you are trying to increase your after-tax income, you should compare the yield on municipal bonds to the after-tax return on corporate bonds and select the higher.

5. When purchasing corporate bonds be sure to look at the bond rating. As a general rule, never invest in any bond with a rating of less than Baa or BBB.

CHAPTER 13

Making Securities Investments

Amy Rosen started investing in the stock market during her junior year in college. It all started when her grandmother left her $25,000. After giving some serious thought to the matter, Amy decided to invest $15,000 of her inheritance and to spend the rest on herself and her education. Though she knew almost nothing about the market, she started dabbling in stocks and mutual funds and, in a relatively short period of time, had invested all of her $15,000. Now would come the fun part: She could sit back and watch her money grow. Much to her dismay, however, she watched her investments steadily go down in price! Finally, after Amy had lost nearly $6,000, she decided to sell out and put what was left of her investment capital into bank CDs — at least until she learned more about securities and the markets. If nothing else, the experience taught Amy a valuable, albeit costly, lesson: that is, *it takes more than money to be a successful investor*. In order to carry out a successful investment program, you must understand the institutions, mechanisms, and procedures involved in making security transactions. We looked at some investment fundamentals, particularly with regard to stocks and bonds, in the preceding chapter. In this chapter, we will examine the different securities markets, sources of investment information, and ways to manage your investment holdings. The overridding theme of this chapter is that *there is no substitute for being an informed investor!*

FINANCIAL *facts* **OR** *fantasies*

Are the following statements financial facts (true) or fantasies (false)?

Stocks listed on the New York Stock Exchange are traded in the over-the-counter market.

If you lose a lot of money because of a lousy investment recommended by your broker, you can recover all or most of your loss by filing a claim with the Securities Investor Protection Corporation.

You short sell a stock when you sell stock that doesn't belong to you.

Because they are so biased, you should pay little attention to annual stockholders' reports.

The MidCap 400 is a relatively new market index that's meant to reflect the market performance of medium-sized companies.

Coming up with a sound asset allocation plan is likely to have more of an impact on long-term return than the specific securities you hold in your portfolio.

SECURITIES MARKETS

Stocks, bonds, and other securities are traded in a highly efficient market network that includes both organized exchanges and over-the-counter (OTC) markets. Would it really make any difference to you, as an investor, if a security is traded on an organized exchange or in the OTC market? How does trading on an exchange differ from that in the OTC market? Take a few moments before reading on to think about these questions.

The term **securities markets** is generally used to describe the place where stocks, bonds, and other financial instruments are traded. The securities markets can be broken into two parts: the capital markets and the money markets. The *capital market* is where long-term securities (those with maturities of more than a year) are traded, while the *money market* is the marketplace for short-term, low-risk credit instruments with maturities of one year or less, like U.S. Treasury bills, commercial paper, negotiable certificates of deposit, and so on. Both types of markets provide a vital mechanism for bringing the buyers and sellers of securities together. Some of the more popular money market securities were discussed in Chapter 5, where we looked at short-term investment vehicles. This chapter considers the capital markets.

PRIMARY OR SECONDARY MARKETS

The securities markets can also be divided into primary and secondary segments. The *primary market* is the market where new securities are sold to the public — where one party to the transaction is always the issuer. The *secondary market*, in contrast, is where old (outstanding) securities are bought and sold — here the securities are "traded" between investors. A security is sold in the primary market just once, when it is originally issued by the corporation or some governmental body, like a state or municipality. Subsequent transactions, wherein securities are sold by one investor to another, take place in the secondary market. As a rule, when people speak of the securities markets, they're referring to the secondary market, since that's where the vast majority of security transactions take place.

Primary Markets.   When a corporation sells a new issue, several financial institutions participate in the transaction. To begin with, the corporation will probably use an *investment banking firm*, which specialized in *underwriting* (selling) new security issues. The investment banker will give the corporation advice on pricing and other aspects of the issue and either will sell the new security itself or arrange for a *selling group* to do so. The selling group is normally made up of a large number of brokerage firms, each of which accepts the responsibility for selling a certain portion of the new issue. On very large issues, the originating investment banker will bring in other underwriting firms as partners and form an *underwriting syndicate* in an attempt to spread the risks associated with underwriting and selling the new securities. Exhibit 13.1 depicts this selling process for a new security issue.

A potential investor in a new issue must be provided with a **prospectus**, which is a document describing the firm and the issue. Certain federal agencies have the responsibility of ensuring that all information included within a prospectus is an accurate representation of the facts. Many times investors have trouble purchasing new security issues because all shares allocated to the stockbrokers have been sold — often prior to the official sale date. Also, if the new shares are sold using *rights* or *warrants* (discussed in Chapter 12), the ability to purchase the new securities will be somewhat restricted, since only the holders of these rights or warrants can buy the stock.

Secondary Markets.   The secondary markets permit investors to execute transactions between themselves — it's the marketplace where an investor can easily sell his or her holdings to someone else. Included among the secondary markets are the various *securities exchanges*, in which the buyers and sellers of securities are brought together. In addition, there is the **over-the-counter (OTC) market**, which is made up of a nationwide network of

EXHIBIT 13.1
The Participants in the Issuance of a New Corporate Security

There are many parties that come into play when a corporation decides to sell its securities to the investing public. This is also the *only* time the issuer is a party to the transaction and, as such, directly benefits from the sale.

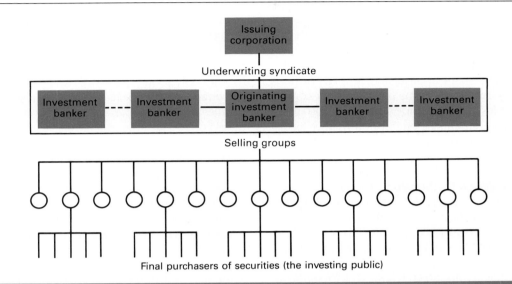

Final purchasers of securities (the investing public)

brokers and dealers who execute transactions in securities that are not listed on one of the exchanges. The **organized securities exchanges** typically handle transactions in the securities of larger, better known companies, and the over-the-counter market handles mostly the smaller, lesser-known firms. The organized exchanges are well-structured institutions that bring together the market forces of supply and demand; the over-the-counter market is basically a mass telecommunications network linking buyers and sellers. Since most transactions of small investors are made in the secondary market, we will focus on it throughout this chapter.

ORGANIZED SECURITIES EXCHANGES

The forces of market supply and demand are brought together in organized securities exchanges. So-called **listed securities** are traded on organized

securities markets
The marketplace in which stocks, bonds, and other financial instruments are traded.

prospectus
A document made available to prospective security purchasers that describes the firm and a new security issue.

over-the-counter (OTC) market
The market in which securities not listed on one of the organized exchanges are traded, usually those of smaller, lesser-known firms.

organized securities exchanges
Exchanges where various types of securities are traded by (exchange) members for their own accounts and the accounts of their customers.

listed security
A security that has met the prerequisites for, and thus is traded on, one of the organized securities exchanges.

exchanges and account for about two-thirds of all shares traded in the stock market. All trading is carried out in one place (such as the New York Stock Exchange on Wall Street) and under a broad set of rules by people who are *members* of the exchange. Members are said to "own a seat" on the exchange, a privilege that is obtained by meeting certain financial requirements. Only the securities of companies that have met certain listing requirements are traded on the exchange, and those firms must comply with established regulations to ensure that they will not make financial or legal misrepresentations to their stockholders. Firms must not only comply with the rules of the specific exchange but also fulfill certain requirements as established by the Securities and Exchange Commission (discussed later).

New York Stock Exchange. *The New York Stock Exchange (NYSE)* is the largest and most prestigious organized securities exchange not only in this country, but in the world. Known as "the big board," there are over *90 billion* shares of stock listed on it that, at year-end 1990, had a market value of over *$3 trillion*. Membership on the NYSE is limited to 1,366 seats. During this century, the cost of a seat has ranged from as little as $17,000 (in 1942) to over $1 million (in 1987); in 1991, seats were going for about $350,000. Most seats are owned by brokerage firms, the largest of which — Merrill Lynch, Pierce, Fenner and Smith, Inc. — owns more than 20.

The NYSE has the most stringent listing requirements of all the organized exchanges. For example, in order to be listed, a firm must have at least 2,000 stockholders, each owning 100 shares or more. It must also have a minimum of 1.1 million shares of publicly held stock outstanding; have demonstrated pretax earning power of $2.5 million at the time of listing and of $2 million for each of the preceding two years; have $18 million in market value of publicly held shares; and must pay a listing fee. Firms that fail to continue to meet listing requirements can be *delisted*. More than 1,700 companies from around the world list their shares on the NYSE. All totaled, more than 2,400 different *stocks* (including a hundred or so *foreign* issues) and nearly 2,900 corporate *bonds* are traded on the NYSE. Some of the NYSE's largest and most actively traded companies are listed in Exhibit 13.2.

American Stock Exchange. The *American Stock Exchange (AMEX)* is the second largest organized stock exchange in terms of the number of listed companies; when it comes to the dollar volume of trading, however, the AMEX is actually smaller than a couple of *regional* exchanges (the Midwest and Pacific). Its organization and procedures are similar to those of the NYSE, though its membership costs and listing requirements are not as stringent. There are approximately 650 seats on the AMEX and over 1,000 listed stocks. The AMEX handles only about 5 percent of the share volume on *organized* security exchanges. In contrast, the NYSE handles around 85 percent of all common shares traded on organized exchanges, so the AMEX is nowhere near the New York exchange in terms of size or stature. Further, whereas the NYSE is home for many of the biggest and best-known companies in the world, firms traded on the AMEX are much smaller and, with few exceptions, would hardly qualify as "household names."

Emerging Company Marketplace. In March of 1992, the American exchange established a separate market for small, emerging companies. Known as the Emerging Company Marketplace (ECM), this market was created for the purpose of listing and trading a select group of small companies (those with total assets of as little as $2 to $4 million) that offer long-term growth potential and investor interest. Initially, there were just 22 companies listed on this market, though the ECM plans to add more over time. Like any listed exchange, companies have to meet certain requirements in order to have their shares listed on the ECM, but those standards are purposely kept fairly low, and are meant to reflect the financial condition and operating results of typical start-up companies.

Regional Stock Exchanges. In addition to the NYSE and AMEX, there are a handful of so-called **regional exchanges**. The number of securities listed on each of these exchanges is typically in the range of 100 to 500 companies. As a group they handle perhaps 10 percent of all shares traded on organized exchanges. The best-known of these are the Midwest, Pacific, Philadelphia, Boston, and Cincinnati exchanges. These exchanges deal primarily in securities with local and regional appeal. Most are mod-

EXHIBIT 13.2

Some NYSE Leaders (1990)

The companies listed here, like others on the NYSE, are some of the largest corporations in the world in terms of both number of shareholders and market value. It's interesting to note that while there are some 1,700 firms on the NYSE, the 25 companies listed here (in the right-hand column) account for about 25 percent of the total market value of all stocks traded on the NYSE!

Most Actively Traded NYSE Stocks		NYSE Stocks with Greatest Market Values	
Company	Share Volume (in millions of shares traded)	Company	Market Value (dollars in millions)
Philip Morris	448.8	Exxon Corp.	$93,808
American Tel. & Tel.	358.2	International Business Machines	64,591
International Business Machines	341.4	General Electric	53,272
General Electric	325.9	Philip Morris	48,403
Citicorp	323.8	Merck & Co.	40,940
Federal National Mortgage	282.3	Coca-Cola Co.	38,947
American Express	274.6	Bristol-Myers Squibb	35,769
Exxon Corporation	246.7	Wal-Mart Stores	34,578
General Motors	243.8	American Tel. & Tel.	32,815
Boeing Company	234.4	Procter & Gamble	31,444
Wal-Mart Stores	227.1	Johnson & Johnson	27,529
Waste Management	221.9	BellSouth Corporation	26,703
Bristol-Myers Squibb	218.1	Amoco Corp.	26,468
Eastman Kodak	208.8	Mobil Corporation	25,401
Chase Manhattan Corp.	204.9	Chevron Corp.	24,846
United Telecommunications	192.4	du Pont de Nemours	24,750
PepsiCo., Inc.	186.4	PepsiCo., Inc.	22,643
BankAmerica Corporation	179.4	General Motors	21,740
Baxter International	178.8	Bell Atlantic	21,423
McDonald's Corporation	177.8	Eli Lilly	20,721
Texas Utilities	177.8	Atlantic Richfield	20,705
du Pont de Nemours	177.2	GTE Corp.	20,600
Ford Motor	172.2	Minnesota Mining & Manufacturing	20,238
Toys "R" Us	171.9	Abbott Laboratories	19,692
Texaco, Inc.	167.1	American Information Technologies (Ameritech)	19,612

Source: New York Stock Exchange, 1991.

eled after the NYSE, but their membership and listing requirements are considerably more lenient. Regional exchanges will often list securities that are also listed on the NYSE or AMEX in order to enhance their trading activity.

THE OVER-THE-COUNTER MARKET

Unlike an organized exchange, the over-the-counter (OTC) market is not a specific institution but, instead, exists as an intangible relationship between the buyers and sellers of securities. Securities traded in this market are sometimes called **unlisted securities**. It is the fastest-growing segment

of the stock market and today trades close to *35,000* issues. The market is linked together by a mass telecommunications network. Unlike those in the organized securities exchanges, the trades in the OTC

regional exchanges

Organized securities exchanges (other than the NYSE and AMEX) that deal primarily in securities having a local or regional appeal.

unlisted security

A security that is traded in the over-the-counter market; such a trade is made directly between the investor and the security dealer.

Pink Sheets: The Hidden Market

Looking for a stock that's not on the New York Stock Exchange or even the NASDAQ bid/ask quotes? Chances are you'll find it in the *pink sheets*. Described by some as "the flea market of Wall Street," the pink sheets are home to about 12,000 thinly traded stocks that, for one reason or another, are unable — or unwilling — to meet the financial reporting requirements of the SEC. Not surprisingly, you'll find a lot of trash here — namely, companies in or near bankruptcy and penny stocks being manipulated by crooked brokers. But you'll also find some tender young growth stocks, as well as a few obscure, yet very solid companies. There are even some well-known companies —

like Rand McNally, Hoffmann-LaRoche, Manischewitz, and Churchill Downs; businesses that you might expect to find on the Big Board but that prefer instead to remain in the pinks because they're closely held or don't want the publicity that comes with active stock trading.

Founded in 1913, the pink sheets market is one of the oldest in the United States. Two Wall Street pioneers, Roger Babson and Arthur Elliott, saw the need to disseminate stock-price information and organized the National Quotation Bureau. Runners were sent to brokerage houses to collect sheets of paper on which traders listed prices for the stocks they were willing to buy or sell.

Babson and Elliott consolidated the information, and in the 1930s started printing it on pink sheets for hand delivery to brokerage offices. That process has changed little in the half century since. Today a desk-thumping 400 pages thick and still printed on pink paper, the pink sheets are hand-carried five days a week to brokerages in the financial districts of major cities, and shipped overnight to trading offices elsewhere.

One concession to the quickly changing nature of securities trading was made in 1986, when a pink sheets data base was offered over the Quotron computer network to which most brokerage firms subscribe. That means some OTC brokers

market represent *direct* transactions between investors and securities dealers — that is, the investors buy from and sell to the securities dealers, whereas on the listed securities exchanges the broker acts as a middleman between buyers and sellers. All municipal bonds, along with most governments and corporate bonds, as well as a numerical majority of common stocks are traded in the OTC market. Dealers make markets in certain securities by offering to either buy or sell them at stated prices.

A part of the OTC market is linked through the *National Association of Securities Dealers Automated Quotation System (NASDAQ)*, which provides up-to-date quotes and bid/ask prices on several thousand securities. (The **bid** and the **ask prices** represent, respectively, the highest price offered to

purchase a given security and the lowest price at which the security is offered for sale. In effect, an investor pays the ask price when *buying* securities and receives the bid price when *selling* them.)

There are about 5,000 different issues traded in the NASDAQ portion of the OTC market, and of these, nearly 2,700 are part of the so-called *National Market System (NMS)*. The national market system is reserved for the biggest and most actively traded stocks; and, in general, for those stocks that have a *national following*. These securities are widely quoted, and the trades are executed about as efficiently here as they are on the floor of the NYSE. A number of large and well-known firms are found on the NASDAQ National Market System, including companies like Apple Computers, Intel, MCI, Lotus,

can look up a pink sheets stock by turning to a desktop terminal. The information your broker sees displayed may be out of date, however. Trades are not reported, and the bid and offering prices on the system are updated only at the request of traders who make the markets in pink sheet stocks.

Most dealing is still done by telephone. If you ask your broker for a quote on a little-known pink, and the firm doesn't happen to own the stock at the time, your broker has to call a market maker — a broker who does hold the issue — to learn the latest price. Change is under way, however. On October 1, 1989, the NASD began publishing information resulting from a new SEC requirement that market makers report significant trading. For the first time, reports will indicate the volume of activity in the non-regulated pink sheets, notes Bob Ferri, a NASD spokesman. There's a chance, too, that a NASD-sponsored electronic bulletin board, for a faster and more complete reporting of pink sheet prices, may be put in operation before too long, Ferri says.

In spite of all these changes, this is still a highly segmented market. Not surprisingly, therefore, bids and offers recorded on the pink sheets should be regarded as nothing more than indications of what the true prices might be. Spreads between them can be surprising. It's not unusual to see a pink sheet bid at 50 cents and offered at $1.50, and there's no such thing as an "inside" market, or best price. While your broker should be willing to sell you a pink sheet stock at $1.50 if that's the offered price, he or she isn't obligated to. "Remember that you enjoy none of the safeguards that come with trading a stock listed on an exchange," notes one analyst.

Source: Adapted from Dan Ruck, "The Hidden Stock Market," *Money Maker*, December/January 1989, pp. 46–48.

Nordstrom, Microsoft, and Seagate Technology, as well as many big banks and insurance companies. Generally speaking, the big-name stocks traded on the NASDAQ/NMS receive about as much national visibility and are about as liquid as those traded on the NYSE. Indeed, because of this, *NASDAQ is now the second biggest market in the United States*, in terms of dollar volume of trading, and the third largest in the world!

The situation is considerably different, however, for OTC stocks that are not part of NASDAQ — which is the case for the vast majority of the firms traded in the OTC market. These include the very small firms that may not even have much of a regional following, let alone a national constituency. These stocks are *thinly traded*, meaning there's not much of a market for them, and they often lack any measurable degree of liquidity. Many of these stocks appear in the so-called *pink sheets*. So named because of the color of paper used, the pink sheets are published daily and are available from brokers. The accompanying *Smart Money* box sheds some light on this little-known and often overlooked segment of the market.

---

bid price
The price at which one can sell a security.

ask price
The price at which one can purchase a security.

Stocks listed on the New York Stock Exchange are traded in the over-the-counter market.

Fantasy: Stocks not listed on organized exchanges (like the NYSE) are traded in the over-the-counter market; listed securities are traded on stock exchanges, which are not part of the OTC market.

FOREIGN SECURITIES MARKETS

In addition to those in the United States, there are organized securities exchanges in more than 30 other countries worldwide. Indeed, actively traded markets can be found not only in the major industrialized nations like Japan, Great Britain, Germany, and Canada, but also in emerging economies such as Mexico, Taiwan, Malaysia, and South Korea. The New York and Tokyo Stock Exchanges are the biggest in the world, while the London Stock Exchange is Europe's largest. Other major exchanges are located in Toronto, Sydney, Frankfurt, Paris, Zurich, Hong Kong, and Singapore. As these and other markets continue to develop, they'll open up opportunities not only for investors in those countries, but also for U.S. investors willing to go off-shore in search of returns. At the same time, it's becoming increasingly clear that the U.S. securities markets can no longer be viewed in isolation, but rather, as a part of a worldwide network of securities markets.

REGULATING THE SECURITIES MARKETS

A number of laws have been enacted to regulate the activities of various participants in the securities markets and to provide for adequate and accurate disclosure of information to potential and existing investors. State laws, which regulate the sale of securities within state borders, typically establish procedures that apply to the sellers of securities doing business within the state. The most important and far reaching securities laws are those enacted by the federal government.

- **Securities Act of 1933.** This act was passed by Congress to ensure full disclosure of information with respect to new security issues and to prevent a stock market collapse similar to that which occurred in 1929–1932. It requires the issuer of a new security to file a registration statement containing information about the new issue with the **Securities and Exchange Commission (SEC)**, an agency of the U.S. government that was established to enforce federal securities laws.

- **Securities Exchange Act of 1934.** This was one of the most important pieces of securities legislation ever passed. It expanded the scope of federal regulation and *formally established the SEC* as the agency in charge of the administration of federal securities laws. The act established the SEC's power to regulate organized securities exchanges and the over-the-counter market by extending disclosure requirements to outstanding securities. It required the stock exchanges as well as the stocks traded on them to be registered with the SEC. In essence, the Securities acts of 1933 and 1934 were aimed at regulating not only securities exchanges and securities markets, but also the disclosure of information on both new and outstanding securities.

- **Investment Company Act of 1940.** This act was passed to protect those purchasing investment company (mutual fund) shares. It established rules and regulations for investment companies and formally authorized the SEC to regulate their practices and procedures. It required the investment companies to register with the SEC and to fulfill certain disclosure requirements. The act was amended in 1970 to prohibit investment companies from paying excessive fees to their advisors as well as charging excessive commissions to purchasers of company shares. From the point of view of the individual investor, this act provides protection against inadequate or inaccurate disclosure of information, and against being charged excessive fees indirectly by the fund's advisors, and directly through the commissions paid to purchase company shares.

- **Other Significant Federal Legislation.** The *Maloney Act of 1938* provided for the establishment of trade associations for the purpose of self-regulation within the securities industry; this act led to the creation of the **National Association of Securities Dealers (NASD)**, which is made up of all brokers and dealers who participate in the OTC market. The NASD is a self-regulatory organization that polices the activities of brokers and dealers in order to ensure that its standards are upheld. The SEC supervises the activities of NASD, thus providing investors with further protection from fraudulent activities. The *Investment Advisors Act of 1940* was passed to protect investors against potential abuses by investment advisors who sell their services to the investing public. The *Securities Investor Protection Act of 1970* created the SIPC (Securities Investor Protection Corp.), an organization that protects investors against the financial failure of brokerage firms, much like the FDIC protects depositors against bank failures (we'll examine the SIPC later in this chapter). The *Insider Trading and Securities Fraud Enforcement Act of 1988* toughened penalties for securities fraud and required brokerage firms to establish written policies to prevent trading abuses by their employees; also made it easier for investors to bring legal action against brokers.

In addition to securities legislation, the *stock exchanges* themselves play important roles in monitoring and regulating the companies, brokerage firms, traders, and other parties that deal in listed securities. Likewise, most *brokerage firms* go to great lengths to prevent trading abuses by aggressively policing their own employees.

BULL MARKET OR BEAR?

The general condition of the market is termed *bullish* or *bearish*, depending on whether security prices are rising or falling over extended periods of time. Changing market conditions generally stem from changing investor attitudes, changes in economic activity, and certain governmental actions aimed at stimulating or slowing down the economy. Prices go *up* in **bull markets**; these favorable markets are normally associated with investor optimism, economic recovery, and governmental stimulus. In contrast, prices go *down* in **bear markets**, which are normally associated with investor pessimism and economic slowdowns. These terms are used to describe conditions in the bond and other securities markets as well as the stock market. For example, the bond market is considered bullish when interest rates fall, causing bond prices to rise; on the other hand, a bear market in bonds exists when bond prices fall (which occurs when rates rise). As a rule, investors are able to earn attractive rates of return during bull markets and only low (or negative) returns during bear markets. Market conditions are difficult to predict and usually cannot be identified until after they exist.

Over the past 50 or so years, the behavior of the stock market has been generally bullish, reflecting the growth and prosperity of the economy. As Exhibit 13.3 shows, there have been five major bull markets since the Second World War, the longest of which lasted *97 months* — from June 1949 to July 1957. The most notorious of the five was surely the latest one, which started in August of 1982 and peaked out in August of 1987. This is the one that's associated with the big market crash of October 19, 1987, when in a *single day*, the market, as measured by the Dow Jones Industrial Average, dropped by a whopping 508 points! Actually, the market had started dropping in late August and by mid-October had already fallen some 400 points. Then came "Black Monday," when the market experienced its biggest and hardest crash in history, not only in absolute numerical terms (508 points), but also in percentage and dollar terms: in one day, the market fell nearly 23 percent and lost roughly half a *trillion* dollars in value.

Securities and Exchange Commission (SEC)

An agency of the federal government that regulates the disclosure of information about securities and generally oversees the operation of the securities exchanges and markets.

National Association of Securities Dealers (NASD)

An agency made up of brokers and dealers in over-the-counter securities that regulates the operations of the OTC market.

bull market

A condition of the market normally associated with investor optimism, economic recovery, and government stimulus; characterized by generally rising securities prices.

bear market

A condition of the market typically associated with investor pessimism, economic slowdown, and government control; characterized by generally falling securities prices.

EXHIBIT 13.3

The Five Biggest Bull Markets since the Second World War (as Measured by Changes in the DJIA)

The prices of most stocks will go up in a bull market. Thus, it is hard to lose money—though not impossible, since not all stocks will appreciate in value during such markets. (Although not shown in this exhibit, the most recent bull market, which started in October 1990, was still going strong in early 1992 and was already up by nearly 40 percent.)

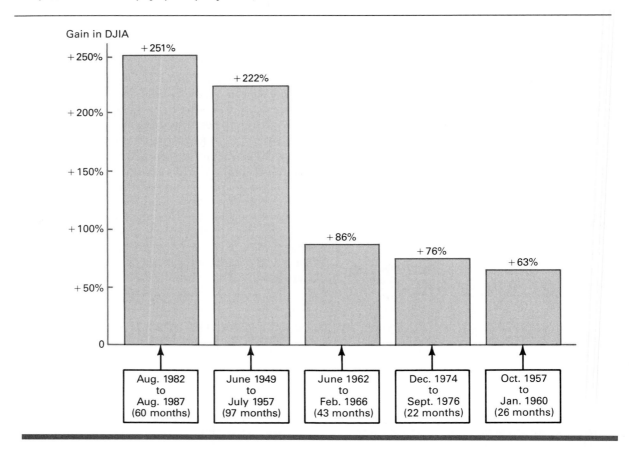

Gain in DJIA

+251%	+222%	+86%	+76%	+63%
Aug. 1982 to Aug. 1987 (60 months)	June 1949 to July 1957 (97 months)	June 1962 to Feb. 1966 (43 months)	Dec. 1974 to Sept. 1976 (22 months)	Oct. 1957 to Jan. 1960 (26 months)

MAKING TRANSACTIONS IN THE SECURITIES MARKETS

Individual investors use the services of stock brokers to buy and sell securities in the marketplace. Stop for a moment to consider the different kinds of services offered by brokers. How great do you suppose the difference would be in the services and cost of a discount broker as opposed to a full-service broker?

In many respects, dealing in the securities markets almost seems like you are operating in another world—one with all kinds of unusual orders and strange-sounding transactions. Actually, making securities transactions is relatively simple once you understand a few of the basics — in fact, you will probably find it is no more difficult than using a checking account! Indeed, while making money in the market isn't all that easy, making transactions is.

STOCKBROKERS

Stockbrokers, or **account executives**, as they're also called, purchase and sell securities for their customers. Although deeply ingrained in our language, the term "stockbroker" is really somewhat of a misnomer, as such an individual assists you in the purchase and sale of not only stocks but also bonds, convertibles, mutual funds, options, and many other types of securities. Brokers must be licensed by the exchanges on which they place orders and must abide by the strict ethical guidelines of the exchanges and the SEC. They work for brokerage firms and in essence are there to execute the orders placed. The largest stockbrokerage firm, Merrill Lynch, Pierce, Fenner and Smith, Inc., has brokerage offices in most major cities. Orders from these offices are transmitted by brokers to the main office of Merrill Lynch and then to the floor of one of the stock exchanges, or to the OTC market, where they are executed. Confirmation that the order has been executed is transmitted back to the original broker and then to the customer. This process is carried out in a matter of minutes with the use of sophisticated telecommunications networks. Although the procedure for executing orders on organized exchanges differs a bit from that in the OTC market, you as an investor would never know the difference, since you would place your order with the broker in exactly the same fashion.

Selecting a Broker. It is important to select a broker *who understands your investment objectives, and who can effectively assist you in pursuing them*. If you choose a broker whose own disposition toward investing is similar to yours, you should be able to avoid conflict and establish a solid working relationship. It is probably best to ask friends, relatives, or business associates to recommend a broker. It is not important — and often even inadvisable — to know your stockbroker personally since most, if not all, of your transactions/orders will probably be placed by phone. In addition, a strict business rela-

tionship eliminates the possibility of social concerns interfering with the achievement of your investment objectives. This does not mean, of course, that your broker's sole interest should be commissions. Indeed, a broker should be far more than just a salesperson; for *a good broker is someone who's more interested in your investments than in commissions*. Should you find you're dealing with someone who's always trying to get you to trade your stocks, or who's pushing new investments on you, then by all means, dump that broker and find a new one!

One of the problems you have to contend with when dealing with a broker is that of properly interpreting some of the jargon he or she may use. Every occupation, it seems, develops its own "jargonese," and certainly the brokerage business is no exception! Buzzwords and nicknames speed transactions while giving insiders warm feelings of belonging to an elite fellowship. Euphemisms often make unpalatable situations seem sweeter and exert subtle pressures. Understanding the lingo of Wall Street will spare beginning investors a lot of confusion and may even save them some money that would otherwise be lost in the fog. The abridged dictionary of "brokerisms" in Exhibit 13.4 hopefully will help you avoid being taken in by "broker babble."

Brokerage Services. In addition to carrying out purchase and sale transactions for commission, stockbrokers offer their clients a variety of other services. Selecting a good brokerage firm is just as important as choosing a good broker, since not all brokerage firms provide the same services. Try to select a broker with whom you can work and who is affiliated with a firm that provides the types of services you are looking for. Many brokerage firms, for example, provide a wide array of free information, ranging from stock and bond guides to research reports on specific securities or industries. Some have a research staff that periodically issues analyses of

---

stockbroker (account executive)

An individual who buys and sells securities on behalf of clients and provides them with investment advice and information.

economic, market, industry, or company behavior and events, and relates them to its recommendations for buying or selling certain securities. As a client of a large brokerage firm, you can expect to receive monthly bulletins discussing market activity and possibly even a recommended investment list. You will also receive an *account statement* describing all of your transactions for the period, commission charges, interest charges, dividends and interest received, and your account balance.

Most brokerage offices have some type of electronic equipment that provides up-to-the-minute stock price quotations and world news. Stock price information can be obtained either from the quotation board (a large screen that electronically displays all NYSE and AMEX security transactions within minutes of their occurrence) or by keying into the telequote system, which relies on a computer terminal to provide a capsulized description of most securities and their prices. World news, which can significantly affect the stock market, is obtained from a news wire service subscribed to by the brokerage office. Most offices also have a reference library available for use by the firm's clients.

Another valuable service offered by most major brokerage firms is the automatic transfer of surplus cash left in a customer's account into one of the firm's money funds, thereby allowing the customer to earn a reasonable rate of return on temporarily idle funds. Brokerage houses will also hold your securities for you, as protection against their loss; the securities kept in this way are said to be held in *street name*. As a client, you are protected against the loss of securities or cash held by your broker by the **Securities Investor Protection Corporation (SIPC)** — a nonprofit corporation, authorized by the Securities Investor Protection Act of 1970 to protect customer accounts against the financial failure of a brokerage firm. Although subject to SEC and congressional oversight, the SIPC is *not* an agency of the U.S. government.

SIPC insurance covers each account for up to $500,000 (of which up to $100,000 may be in cash balances held by the firm). Note, however, that SIPC insurance does not guarantee that the dollar value of the securities will be recovered. It only insures that *the securities themselves will be returned*. So, what happens if your broker gives you bad advice, and as a result, you lose a lot of money on an investment?

SIPC won't help you, as it's not intended to insure you against bad investment advice. Instead, if you have a dispute with your broker, the first thing you should do is discuss the situation with the managing officer at the branch where you do your business. If that doesn't do any good, then write or talk to the firm's compliance officer, and contact the securities office in your home state. If you still don't get any satisfaction, you may have to take the case to **arbitration**, a process whereby you and your broker present the two sides to the argument before an arbitration panel, which then makes a decision about how the case shall be resolved. If it's *binding* arbitration, and it usually is, you have no choice but to accept the decision — you cannot go to court to appeal your case. To make matters worse, many brokerage firms require you to resolve disputes by going to binding arbitration. Thus, before you open an account, check the brokerage agreement to see if it contains a binding arbitration clause.

Now, binding arbitration wouldn't be so bad if the track record were more evenly balanced. But the fact is that until recently, most brokerage firms not only required investors to submit to binding arbitration, but also specified which arbitration panels could be used; not surprisingly, 90 percent of those panels were sponsored by the NASD or the NYSE. There was considerable controversy as to whether the panels, which prior to 1989 were often composed *entirely* of people with strong ties to the securities industry, were fair to investors. As a result of pressure from the SEC, and a July 1990 court decision in New York State, *many investors now have the option of using either securities industry panels or independent arbitration panels, such as those sponsored by the American Arbitration Association (AAA)* — which is considered more sympathetic towards investors. In addition, only one of the three arbitrators on a panel can be connected with the securities industry. Recently, the NASD and other securities organizations began encouraging investors to mediate disputes and voluntarily negotiate a settlement rather than immediately going into arbitration. Although *mediation* is not binding, it can further reduce costs and time for both investors and brokers. But probably the best way of avoiding either mediation or arbitration is to use care when selecting a broker in the first place, and then carefully evaluate the advice he or she offers.

EXHIBIT 13.4
Interpreting "Broker Babble"

Sometimes the slang of Wall Street has hidden meanings. Certainly it behooves you to become better prepared so as to avoid being beleaguered by broker babble.

Alligator spread. Any options transaction in which commissions eat up all potential profit.

Baby bond. A bond sold in denominations of less than $1,000.

Blue-chip performer. This meaningless expression, the Wall Street equivalent of "nice," is used to encourage investors to buy the stock of a company that may or may not have the solid record of a true blue chip.

Bo Dereks. Treasury bonds maturing in the year 2010; also known as Tens.

To cut a melon. To declare a large stock dividend.

Going naked. Selling an option without owning the underlying security.

Indication of interest. Asking a customer for an indication of interest gets a broker's foot in the door. If you decide not to buy a recommended stock, the broker can pressure you through guilt: "Oh, but you asked me to reserve this for you!"

James Bond. A Treasury security due in 2007, hence bearing the same code name as agent 007.

"Let me give you an investment strategy analysis." A broker's way of saying: "Let me talk you into buying something."

Lift your shorts. Commodity jargon for: "Prices are going up, so cover yourself by closing out your short positions." (A short position is a pledge to deliver the underlying commodity at a set price on a future date.)

Promises a greater than average return. Code for: "You could lose your shirt." High potential return is the flip side of high risk.

Shallow river running deep. A stock whose price has moved greatly in response to an unsubstantiated rumor.

Technical correction or technical rally. Translation: "The market just reversed direction and I don't have the vaguest clue why."

"This seems to run contrary to your financial objectives." A broker's way of criticizing a customer's investment idea. Hidden meaning: "You'll never make any money on this."

Transfer your assets. Used most often when an investor has acquired a loser on the broker's recommendation, the expression means: "Cut your losses."

"You're not going to marry this, just take it to the motel." A way of encouraging a reluctant customer to buy a risky stock.

Source: Patricia Dreyfus, "Mastering Broker Babble," *Money,* June 1984, p. 78.

If you lose a lot of money because of a lousy investment recommended by your broker, you can recover all or most of your loss by filing a claim with the Securities Investor Protection Corporation. *Fantasy:* SIPC insurance applies only if you happen to be dealing with a *brokerage firm* that goes out of business; if the brokerage firm fails, you are protected against the loss of securities or cash held by the broker, but that has nothing to do with getting bad advice from a broker (SIPC does not cover such situations).

Odd or Round Lots. Security transactions can be made in either odd or round lots. An **odd lot** consists of fewer than 100 shares of stock, while a **round lot** represents a 100-share unit or multiples thereof. The sale of 400 shares of stock would be considered a round-lot transaction, but the purchase of 75 shares would be an odd-lot transaction; trading 250 shares of stock would involve two round

Securities Investor Protection Corporation (SIPC)

A nonprofit corporation, created by Congress and subject to SEC and congressional oversight, that insures customer accounts against the financial failure of the brokerage firm.

arbitration

A procedure that's used to settle disputes between a brokerage firm and its clients; both sides of the "story" are presented to a board of arbitration, which makes a final and binding decision on the matter.

odd lot

A quantity of fewer than 100 shares of a stock.

round lot

A quantity of 100 shares of stock, or multiples thereof

lots and an odd lot. Because the purchase or sale of odd lots requires additional processing and the assistance of a specialist (an *odd-lot dealer*), an added fee—known as an *odd-lot differential*—is tacked on to the normal commission charge, driving up the costs of these small trades. Indeed, the relatively high cost of an odd-lot trade is why it's best to deal in round lots whenever possible.

Brokerage Fees. Brokerage firms receive commissions for executing buy and sell orders for their clients. Brokerage commissions are said to be *negotiated*, which means that they are not fixed. In practice, however, most firms have *established* fee schedules that they use with small transactions (on larger, institutional trades, negotiation of commissions actually does take place). Although these fees are not really negotiated, they do differ from one brokerage firm to another; thus, it pays to shop around. Also if you're an "active trader," generating a couple thousand dollars (or more) in annual commissions, then by all means try to negotiate a reduced commission schedule with your broker. Chances are, they'll probably cut a deal with you—the fact is, brokers much prefer traders to buy-and-hold investors, since traders generate a lot more commissions.

The suggested fee schedule used by one large brokerage firm to set commissions on *common stock* transactions is given in Exhibit 13.5. Although this schedule does not specifically levy a premium on odd-lot transactions, the fixed-cost fee component does tend to raise their per share cost. (In addition to the fees shown in the schedule, some brokerage firms charge a differential of 12.5 cents per share on odd-lot transactions.) If the fee schedule in Exhibit 13.5 were used to calculate brokerage fees on the purchase of 80 shares of XYZ stock at $30 per share, the total value of the transaction would be $2,400 (80 shares × $30/share) and the brokerage fee would therefore be $16.85 + 1.7% ($2,400) + $.0315 (80 shares) = $16.85 + $40.80 + $2.52 = $60.17; that amounts to about 2.5 percent of the value of the transaction. Generally speaking, brokerage fees on a round lot of common stock will amount to approximately 2 to 3 percent of the transaction value. (As a rule, at full-service brokerage firms, the broker gets to keep about 40 percent of the commission and the brokerage firm gets the rest.)

Brokerage commissions on bond transactions differ from those on stock transactions. Brokerage firms typically charge a minimum fee of $25 to $30, regardless of the number of bonds involved. For multiple bond transactions, the brokerage cost per $1,000 corporate bond typically amounts to around $10 (which is decidedly lower than that on a stock transaction). The commission schedules for other securities, such as mutual funds and options, differ from those used with stocks and bonds (we will look at some of these in the next chapter).

The magnitude of brokerage commissions obviously is an important consideration when making security transactions, since these fees tend to raise the overall cost of purchasing securities and lower the overall proceeds from their sale.

DISCOUNT BROKERS

Security transactions can also be made at **discount brokers**, many of which are now affiliated with major banks. Discount brokers tend to have low overhead operations and offer little or nothing in the way of customer services. Transactions are initiated by calling a toll-free number and placing the desired buy or sell order. The brokerage firm then executes the order at the best possible price and confirms the details of the transaction by mail. In order to discourage small orders, most discounters charge a minimum transaction fee ranging between $30 and $50. Depending on the size of the transaction, *discount brokers can save investors from 30 to 80 percent of the commissions charged by full-service brokers*. The investor who does not need the research and advisory help available from full-service brokers may find discount brokers especially attractive. Listed below are some major discount and full-service brokerage houses:

■ Discount Brokers

Brown & Company*
Charles Schwab
Fidelity Brokerage Services
Muriel Siebert & Company*
Quick & Reilly
Pacific Brokerage Services*

(*Note:* Those firms marked with an * indicate bare-bones, deep-discount brokers.)

■ Full-Service Brokers

Dean Witter Reynolds
Kidder, Peabody
Merrill Lynch
Paine Webber
Prudential Securities
Shearson Lehman

EXHIBIT 13.5

Broker Commissions on Common Stock Transactions

The amount of broker commissions paid on a common stock transaction obviously will vary with the market value of the transaction. You will pay a commission when you buy stocks and again when you sell them.

Value of Transaction	Fees for an Odd or Round Lot	Surcharge
Up to $1,100	Flat fee of $35.00	
$1,100 to $2,500	$16.85 + 1.7% of the value of the transaction	+ 3.15¢/share
$2,500 to $5,000	$29.50 + 1.3% of the value of the transaction	+ 3.15¢/share

Source: A major stockbrokerage firm.

TYPES OF ORDERS

Investors may choose among several different kinds of orders when buying or selling securities. The type of order chosen normally depends on the investor's goals and expectations with respect to the given transaction. The three basic types of orders are the market order, limit order, and stop-loss order.

Market Order. An order to buy or sell a security at the best price available at the time it is placed is a **market order**. It is usually the quickest way to have orders filled, since market orders are executed as soon as they reach the trading floor. These orders are executed through a process that attempts to allow *buy orders* to be filled at the lowest price and *sell orders* at the highest, thereby providing the best possible deal to both the buyers and sellers of a security. Because of the speed with which market orders are transacted, the investor can be sure that the price at which the order is completed will be very close to the market price that existed at the time it was placed.

Limit Order. An order to buy at a specified price (or lower), or sell at (or above) a specified price is known as a **limit order**. When a limit order is placed, the broker transmits it to a *specialist* dealing in the given security on the floor of the exchange. The specialist makes a notation in his or her "book" indicating the limit order and limit price. The order is executed as soon as the specified market price is reached and all other such orders with precedence have been filled. The order can be placed to remain in effect until a certain date or until canceled; such an instruction is called a **good 'til canceled (GTC) order**. For example, assume that you place a limit order to buy 100 shares of a stock at a price of 20, even though the stock is currently selling at 20½. Once the specialist has cleared all similar orders received before yours, and the market price of the stock is still at $20 or less, he or she will execute the order. Although a limit order can be quite effective, it can also cost you money! If, for instance, you wish to buy at 20 or less and the stock price moves from

---

discount broker

A broker with low overhead who charges low commissions and offers little or no services to investors.

market order

An order to buy or sell a security at the best price available at the time it is placed.

limit order

An order to either buy a security at a specified or lower price or to sell a security at or above a specified price.

good 'til canceled (GTC) order

A limit order placed with instructions that it remain in effect indefinitely or until canceled.

its current $20.50 to $32 while you are waiting, your limit order will have caused you to forgo an opportunity to make a profit of $11.50 ($32.00 − $20.50) per share. Had you placed a market order, this profit would have been yours.

Stop-Loss Order. An order to sell a stock when the market price reaches or drops below a specified level is called a **stop-loss**, or **stop order**. Used to protect the investor against rapid declines in stock prices, the stop order is placed on the specialist's book and activated when the stop price is reached. At that point, the stop order becomes a *market order* to sell. This means that the stock is offered for sale at the prevailing market price, which could be *less* than the price at which the order was initiated by the stop. For example, imagine that you own 100 shares of DEF, which is currently selling for $25. Because of the high uncertainty associated with the price movements of the stock, you decide to place a stop order at $21. If the stock price drops to $21, your stop order is activated and the specialist will sell all your DEF stock at the best price available, which may be $18 or $19 a share. Of course, if the market price increases, nothing will have been lost by placing the stop-loss order.

MARGIN TRADES: BUYING SECURITIES ON CREDIT

It is possible to borrow some of the money needed to purchase securities. *Buying on margin*, as it is called, is a common practice that allows investors to use borrowed money to make security transactions. Margin trading is closely regulated and is carried out under strict *margin requirements* set by the Federal Reserve Board. These requirements specify the amount of *equity* an investor must put up when buying stocks, bonds, and other securities. The most recent requirement was 50 percent for common stock, which means that at least 50 percent of each dollar invested must be the investor's own; the remaining 50 percent may be borrowed. For example, with a 50 percent margin requirement, you could purchase $5,000 worth of stock by putting up only $2,500 of your own money and borrowing the remaining $2,500. Other securities besides stocks can be margined, and these have their own margin requirements; Treasury bonds, for example, can be purchased with a margin of as low as 10 percent.

In order to make **margin purchases**, you must open a *margin account* and have a minimum of $2,000 in cash (or *equity* in securities) on deposit with your broker. Once you have met the necessary requirements, the brokerage firm will loan you the needed funds (at competitive interest rates) and retain the securities purchased as collateral. You can also obtain loans for purchasing securities from your commercial bank, but the Fed's margin requirements will still apply even though they may be a bit more difficult to enforce. To see how margin trading works, assume that the margin requirement is 50 percent; also suppose that your brokerage firm charges 9 percent interest on margin loans (brokerage firms usually set the rate on margin loans at 1 to 3 points above prime, or at the prime rate for large accounts). If you want to purchase a round lot (100 shares) of Engulf & Devour, which is currently trading at $50 per share, you can either make the purchase entirely with your own money or borrow a portion of the purchase price. The cost of the transaction will be $5,000 ($50/share × 100 shares.) If you margin, you will have to put up only $2,500 of your own money (50 percent × $5,000); you can then borrow the $2,500 balance. Exhibit 13.6 compares the rates of return you would receive with and without the 50 percent margin. This is done for two cases: (1) a $20 per share increase in the stock price, to $70 per share, and (2) a $20 per share decrease in the stock price, to $30 per share. It is assumed the stock will be held for one year and all broker commissions are ignored.

As indicated in Exhibit 13.6, the use of margin allows you to increase the return on your investment when stock prices increase. Indeed, one of the major attributes of margin trading is that it allows you to *magnify your returns* — that is, you can use margin to reduce your equity in an investment and thereby magnify the returns from invested capital when security prices go up. The return on your investment when the stock price increases from $50 a share to $70 a share is 40 percent without margin and 71 percent with margin. However, when the stock price declines from $50 to $30 per share, the return on your investment will be a negative 40 percent without margin and a whopping 89 percent loss with margin. Clearly, the use of margin magnifies losses as well as profits! If the price of the stock in our example continues to drop, you will eventually reach the point at which your equity in the invest-

EXHIBIT 13.6
The Impact of Margin Trading on Investment Returns

The rate of return that an individual earns on his or her investment is affected by the amount of margin being used; unfortunately, while margin trading can magnify returns, it will also magnify losses.

Transaction	Without Margin	With Margin
The Initial Investment		
Amount invested	$5,000	$2,500
Amount borrowed	0	2,500
Total purchase (100 shares @ $50)	$5,000	$5,000
Price *Increases:* Sell Stock for $70/Share One Year Later		
Gross proceeds (100 shares @ $60)	$7,000	$7,000
Less: Interest @ 9% of amount borrowed	0	225
Net proceeds	$7,000	$6,775
Less: Total investment	5,000	5,000
Net profit (loss)	$2,000	$1,775
Return on your investment (profit ÷ amount invested)	$\frac{\$2,000}{\$5,000} = 40\%$	$\frac{\$1,775}{\$2,500} = 71\%$
Price *Decreases:* Sell Stock for $30/Share One Year Later		
Gross proceeds (100 shares @ $40)	$3,000	$4,000
Less: Interest @ 9% of amount borrowed	0	225
Net proceeds	$3,000	$2,775
Less: Total investment	5,000	5,000
Net profit (loss)	($2,000)	($2,225)
Return on your investment (profit ÷ amount invested)	$\frac{(\$2,000)}{\$5,000} = (40\%)$	$\frac{(\$2,225)}{\$2,500} = (89\%)$

ment will be so low that the brokerage house will require you to either provide more collateral or liquidate the investment. The risks inherent in buying on margin make it imperative that you thoroughly acquaint yourself with the risk-return trade-offs involved *before* using margin in your investment program.

SHORT SALES: THE PRACTICE OF SELLING BORROWED SECURITIES

Most security transactions are *long transactions;* they are made in anticipation of increasing security prices in order to profit by buying low and selling high. A **short sale** transaction, in contrast, is made in anticipation of a decline in the price of a security. Although not as common as long transactions, the short sale is often used by the more sophisticated

investor to profit during a period of declining prices. When used by individual investors, most short sales are made with common stocks. When an investor sells a security short, the broker borrows

stop-loss (stop) order
An order to sell a stock when the market price reaches or drops below a specified level.

margin purchase
The purchase of securities with borrowed funds, the allowable amount of which is limited by the broker and/or the Federal Reserve Board.

short sale
A transaction that involves selling borrowed securities with the expectation that they can be replaced at a lower price at some future date; generally made in anticipation of a decline in the security's price.

the security and then sells it on behalf of the short seller's account — short sellers actually *sell securities they don't own*. The borrowed shares must, of course, be replaced in the future. If the investor can repurchase the shares at a lower price, a profit will result. In effect, the objective of a short sale is to take advantage of a drop in price by first selling high and then buying low (which, of course, is nothing more than the old "buy low, sell high" adage in reverse).

Short selling is perfectly legitimate; there's nothing illegal or unethical about it. Indeed, because the shares sold are *borrowed securities*, numerous rules and regulations are in place to protect the party that lends the securities and, in general, to govern the short-sale process. One regulation, for example, permits stocks to be sold short only when the last change in the market price of the stock has been upward. Another safeguard is the requirement that all proceeds from the short sale of the borrowed securities be held by the brokerage firm — the short seller never sees any of this money! In addition, the short seller must deposit with the broker a certain amount of money (equivalent to the prevailing initial margin requirement) when the transaction is executed — so even a short-sale transaction involves an investment of capital.

A short-sale transaction can be illustrated with a simple example (and one that ignores brokerage fees). Assume that Patrick O'Sullivan wishes to sell short 100 shares of Advanced Buggy-Whips, Inc. at $52.50 per share. After Pat has met the necessary requirements (including making a margin deposit of $52.50 × 100 × 50% = $2,625), his broker borrows the shares and sells them, obtaining proceeds of $5,250 (100 shares × $52.50/share). If the stock price goes down as Pat expects, he will be able to repurchase the shares at the lower price. Now suppose the price drops to $40 per share, and he repurchases the 100 shares. Pat will make a profit, since he will have been able to replace the shares for $4,000 (100 shares × $40/share), which is below the $5,250 received when he sold the stock. His profit will be $1,250 ($5,250 − $4,000). If, on the other hand, the stock price rose to, say, $60 per share, and Pat repurchased the stocks at that price, he would sustain a loss of $750 ($52.50 − $60.00 = − $7.50 × 100 = − $750.00). Because of the high risk involved in short sales, you should thoroughly familiarize yourself with this technique and all its pitfalls *before* attempting to short sell any security.

You short sell a stock when you sell stock that doesn't belong to you.
Fact: As strange as it may sound, that's exactly what you do when you short sell stock, and there's nothing illegal or unethical about it. Basically, short selling involves the sale of borrowed securities and is done as a way to make money when security prices are expected to fall.

BECOMING AN INFORMED INVESTOR

Basing investment decisions on sound information lies at the very heart of most successful investment programs. What do you think it takes to become an informed investor? What kinds of information do you think you should have, and where would you look for such information? Stop to think about these questions before reading on.

Face it: some people are more knowledgeable about investing than others. As a result, they may use certain investment vehicles or tactics that are not even in the vocabulary of others. Investor know-how, in short, defines the playing field. It helps determine how well you'll meet the investment objective you've set for yourself. Being knowledgeable about investments is important since one of the key elements in successful investing is *knowing how to achieve decent rates of return without taking on unnecessary risks*.

There's no substitute for being informed when it comes to making investment decisions. While it can't guarantee success, it can help you avoid unnecessary losses — like the ones that happen all too often when people put their money into investment vehicles they don't fully understand. Such results aren't too surprising, since these investors violate the first rule of investing, which is: *Never start an investment program, or buy an investment vehicle, unless you're thoroughly familiar with what you're getting into!* Indeed, before making any major investment decision, you should thoroughly investigate the security and its merits. Formulate some basic expectations about its future performance, and gain an understanding of the sources of risk and return. This can usually be done simply by being a *regular* reader of the popular financial press and occasionally referring to one of the other basic sources of investment information.

There are four basic types of investment information that you should try to stay abreast of:

- *Economic developments and current events* — to help you evaluate the underlying investment environment.
- *Alternative investment vehicles* — to keep you abreast of market developments.
- *Current interest rates and price quotations* — to enable you to monitor your investments and also stay alert for developing investment opportunities.
- *Personal investment strategies* — to help you hone your skills and stay alert for new techniques as they develop.

In the final analysis, the payoff of such an informed approach to investing is both an improved chance of gain and a reduced chance of loss. While there are many sources of investment information, you, as a beginning investor, should concentrate on the more common ones, such as annual stockholders' reports, the financial press, brokerage reports, advisory services, and investment advisors.

ANNUAL STOCKHOLDERS' REPORTS

Every publicly traded corporation is required to provide its stockholders and other interested parties with **annual stockholders' reports**. These documents provide a wealth of information about companies, including balance sheets, income statements, and other summarized statements for the latest fiscal year, plus a number of prior years. (The balance sheets and income statements for business firms are similar in form to the personal financial statements examined in Chapter 2.) Annual reports usually describe the firm's business activities, recent developments, and future plans and outlook. Financial ratios describing past performance are also included, along with other relevant statistics. In fact, as the *Money in Action* box explains, a great deal of insight into the company's past, present, and future operations can be gained from the stockholders' report. These reports are sent to all stockholders;

other interested parties can obtain them for free directly from the companies, through a brokerage firm, or at most large libraries.

Because they are so biased, you should pay little attention to annual stockholders' reports.
Fantasy: While they do tend to accentuate the positive, annual stockholders' reports are nonetheless an excellent source of information and are widely used by *informed* investors to obtain financial information about specific companies.

THE FINANCIAL PRESS

The most common source of financial news is the local newspaper. The newspapers in many larger cities often devote several pages to business and financial information and, of course, big-city papers, like the *New York Times* and the *Los Angeles Times*, provide investors with an abundance of financial information. Other, more specific sources of financial news include *The Wall Street Journal, Barron's, Investor's Business Daily*, and the "Money" section of *USA Today*. These are all national publications that include articles on the behavior of the economy, the market, various industries, and individual companies. The most comprehensive and up-to-date coverage of financial news is provided Monday through Friday by *The Wall Street Journal. Barron's* concentrates on the week's activities as they relate to the financial markets and individual security prices. Other excellent sources of investment information include magazine-type publications such as *Money, Forbes, Fortune, Business Week, U.S. News and World Report, Smart Money, Worth*, and *Financial World*.

Economic Data. Summaries and analyses of economic events can be found in all of the above sources. Economic data include news items related

---

annual stockholders' report
A report made available to stockholders and other interested parties that includes a variety of financial and descriptive information about a firm's operations during the past year.

MONEY IN ACTION

There's More to an Annual Report Than Meets the Eye

On balance, the annual report of HRE Properties, a real estate investment trust, was upbeat. "Our retail properties generally performed well," it said. Expansion of a regional mall "should produce substantial income increases." Furthermore, chances are good that "we will see opportunities to increase income."

But a careful reader would have found reason for concern. The year had been difficult for the real estate industry, the report noted, "and many markets will be no better next year." Office vacancies were higher than ever. HRE's president said he thought the trust was "very well positioned for the longer term"—a statement that seemed to raise questions about the

short term. More disturbing: Net income had been slipping.

As it turned out, the slippage continued the following year, and HRE cut its dividend by 15 percent. The price of the stock fell proportionately. What does this tell you? That any annual report should be read with care. A dash of skepticism is in order, too. Although they're usually accurate, these presentations always accentuate the positive. Bad news is likely to be downplayed or obscured by majestic prose and flashy graphics.

Yet an annual report should never be ignored. "It's a good way to get a feel for the company, its history and prospects," says John Markese, research director for the American Association of Individual Inves-

tors. From there you can go on to sources that are likely to be more revealing and objective, such as *Value Line Investment Survey*, Standard & Poor's, Moody's and reports of securities analysts.

Here are the most important points to check in any annual report:

■ Look first at the section headed *highlights* or *selected financial data*. It's usually in the front and includes such key information as revenues, net income, assets, earnings per share of common stock, and dividends for the last two years. You'll quickly get a sense of how things have been going. Usually, earnings per share have the greatest impact on a stock's price

to government actions and their effects on the economy, political and international events as they pertain to the economy, and statistics related to price levels, interest rates, the federal budget, and taxes.

Market Data. Usually presented in the form of averages, or indexes, *market data* describe the general behavior of the securities markets. The averages and indexes are based on the price movements of a select group of securities over an extended period of time. They are used to capture the overall performance of the market as a whole. You would want to follow one or more of these measures *to get a feel for how the market is doing over time* and, perhaps,

to get an indication of what lies ahead. The absolute level of the index at a given point in time (or on a given day) is far less important than *what's been happening to that index over a given period of time*. The most frequently cited market measures are those calculated by Dow Jones, Standard & Poor's, the New York Stock Exchange, the American Stock Exchange, and NASDAQ (for the OTC market). These measures are all intended to keep track of the behavior in the stock market, particularly stocks on the NYSE (the Dow, S&P, and NYSE averages all follow stocks on the big board). In addition, there are several averages and indexes that follow the action in other markets, including the bond, commodities, and options

and are the most closely watched figures. A leveling or drop in earnings or in any of the other numbers could be a danger sign, though not necessarily sufficient cause for dumping the stock. Its current price will in most cases reflect any significant change that has occurred.

■ Go next to the *chief executive's message*. Unless the company is obviously in traction, this review and forecast is likely to glow with optimism. Don't be awed by the rhetoric. And watch out for euphemisms: A bad year might be described as a "period of adjustment," a drop in earnings as a "slowing of growth."

■ Check on the year's operations in the section called *management discussion and analysis* or something similar. Details about sales, earnings, debt, inventories, new plants or plant closings, the book value of the stock, pending litigation, and taxes will be found here. Be wary of vagueness or emphasis on projected achievements.

■ Look next at the financial statements. The *income statement, balance sheet,* and *footnotes* may cause your eyes to glaze, but even here you may find clues to the company's health. Are sales improving? Are costs up or down? Has there been a change in the cash position? A significant increase in inven-

tories of new products could mean sales are slowing, and a price drop could diminish income. Any serious shrinkage in net working capital could be a bad enough omen to warrant selling the stock.

■ Go now to the *auditor's report*. This is a statement from independent accountants who examined the figures, and it usually consists of two brief, perfunctory paragraphs when everything appears in order. If there is more, and you see terms such as "except for" or "subject to," the auditors may have spotted problems. Look for an explanation elsewhere in the report.

Source: Adapted from Morton C. Paulson. "'Tis the Season for Annual Reports, and There's More to See Than Meets the Eye," *Changing Times*, December 1988, p. 16.

---

markets and even the markets for mutual funds, real estate, and collectibles. However, because all these other averages and indexes are not followed nearly as much as those of stocks, we will concentrate here on stock market performance measures.

Dow Jones Averages. The granddaddy of them all and the most widely followed measure of stock market performance is the **Dow Jones Industrial Average (DJIA)**. Actually, the Dow Jones averages, which began in 1896, are made up of four parts: (1) an industrial average based on 30 stocks; (2) a transportation average based on 20 stocks; (3) a utility average based on 15 stocks; and (4) a composite average based on all 65 industrial, transportation,

and utility stocks. The makeup of the 30 stocks in the DJIA does change a bit over time as companies go private, are acquired by other firms, or become less of a force in the marketplace; for example, in the past few years, Navistar International, Primerica, and USX Corporation were dropped from the DJIA and replaced with Caterpillar, Disney, and J.P. Morgan.

> **Dow Jones Industrial Average (DJIA)**
> The most widely followed measure of stock market performance; consists of 30 blue-chip stocks listed on the NYSE.

EXHIBIT 13.7

The Dow Jones Industrial Average

The DJIA is made up of 30 of the bluest of blue-chip stocks and has been closely followed by investors for the past 95 years or so.

The 30 Stocks in the DJIA:

Allied Signal	DuPont	Minnesota M&M
Aluminum Co	Eastman Kodak	Morgan, J.P.
Amer Express	Exxon	Philip Morris
Amer T&T	General Electric	Procter & Gamb
Bethlehem Steel	General Motors	Sears Roebuck
Boeing	Goodyear	Texaco
Caterpillar	IBM	Union Carbide
Chevron	Inter Paper	United Technologies
Coca-Cola	McDonalds	Westinghouse El
Disney	Merck	Woolworth

Some Important Dates for the Dow:

May 26, 1896	The Dow Jones Industrial Average makes its debut; originally made up of just 12 stocks (of the 12 stocks that originally made up the DJIA, only GE is still on the list).
January 12, 1906	Closes above 100 for the first time.
October 28, 1929	The infamous "1929 crash"; Dow drops 38.33 points in one day.
October 29, 1929	The Dow drops another 30.57 points — in just *two* days, the market value of stocks drops an incredible 25%; these two days are considered as the start of the Great Depression.
March 12, 1956	Closes above 500 for the first time.
January 18, 1966	Reaches 1000 during the day but closes at 994.20.
November 14, 1972	Closes above 1000 for the first time.
December 6, 1974	Closes at 577.60 to end the worst bear market since the 1930s.
April 27, 1981	Closes at eight-year high of 1024.0.
August 12, 1982	Closes at 776.92, as the market bottoms out and the Great Bull Market of 1982–1987 is born.
December 31, 1982	Closes at 1046.54; DJIA rises 35% in the first three and a half months of the bull market.
December 31, 1985	Closes at 1546.67; in a little over three years, the market has nearly doubled in value.
August 25, 1987	Closes at 2722.42; in the first 8 months of the year, the market rises 44% — this marks the peak of the 1982–1987 bull market; in five years, the DJIA has gone up almost 2,000 points (250%).
October 19, 1987	The market crashes; the DJIA closes at 1738.74, for a record one-day drop of 508 points (23%).
October 21, 1987	Closes at 2027.85, as the market goes up nearly 290 points in the two days following the crash.
December 31, 1987	Closes *the year* at 1938.83, up 2% for the year, even after the crash.
December 31, 1988	Closes at 2168.57, up a very respectable 12% for the year; this marks the first time the market has ended the year above 2000.
April 27, 1989	Market moves to a post-crash high of 2433.10, which totally wipes out the loss of October 19, with about 200 points to spare.
July 16, 1990	Closes just short of 3,000, at 2,999.75; two weeks later, Iraq invades Kuwait and the market goes into a free-fall, tumbling to 2,365.10 by October 11.
April 17, 1991	Closes above 3,000 for the first time.
December 31, 1991	Closes the year at 3,168.83; up nearly 22% for the year.

The stocks are all picked from the NYSE, and while they are intended to represent a cross section of companies, there is a strong bias toward blue chips, which is one of the major criticisms of the Dow Jones Industrial Average. Critics also claim that an average made up of only 30 blue-chip stocks — out of some 2,400 issues — is hardly representative of the market. However, the facts show that as a rule, the behavior of the DJIA closely reflects that of other stock market measures. Exhibit 13.7 lists the 30 stocks in the DJIA, along with some important dates in its life.

Standard & Poor's Indexes. The **Standard & Poor's (S&P) indexes** are similar to the Dow Jones averages to the extent that they both are used to capture the overall performance of the market. However, there are some important differences in the two measures. For one thing, the S&P uses a lot more stocks: the popular S&P 500 composite index is based on 500 different stocks, whereas the DJIA uses only 30 stocks. What's more, the S&P index is made up of all large NYSE stocks, as well as some major AMEX and OTC stocks, so there's not only more issues in the S&P sample, but also a greater breadth of representation. And finally, there are some technical differences in the mathematical procedures used to compute the two measures: the Dow Jones is an *average*, while the S&P is an *index*. In spite of these technical differences, however, the two measures are used in much the same way.

There are six basic indexes: (1) an industrial index based on 400 stocks; (2) a transportation index of 20 stocks; (3) a public utility index of 40 stocks; (4) a financial index of 40 stocks; (5) a composite index for all 500 of the stocks used in the first four indexes; and (6) the newest S&P index, the *MidCap 400*. The MidCap index was launched in June 1991 and is made up of 400 medium-sized companies — those with market values that, for the most part, range from about $200 million to $2 billion, or more (the largest company in the MidCap 400 has a market value of $5 billion). The immediate popularity of this index is testimony to the growing investor interest in the stocks of medium-sized companies.

The S&P 500, like the DJIA, is widely followed by the financial media, and is reported not only in publications like *The Wall Street Journal* and *Barron's*, but also in most of the major newspapers around the country and other market outlets. The S&P has a much lower value than the DJIA — for example, in May 1992, the Dow stood at nearly 3,300, while the S&P index of 500 stocks was around 420. Now this does not mean that the S&P consists of less valuable stocks; rather, the disparity is due solely to the different methods used to compute the measures.

The NYSE, AMEX, and OTC Indexes. The most widely followed exchange-based indexes are those of the New York Stock Exchange (NYSE) and the American Stock Exchange (AMEX), and, for the OTC market, the NASDAQ indexes. The **NYSE index** includes all the stocks listed on the "big board." In addition to the composite index, the NYSE publishes indexes for industrials, utilities, transportation, and finance subgroups.

The **AMEX index** reflects share prices on the American Stock Exchange. Made up of all stocks on the AMEX, it is set up in such a way that it directly captures the actual *percentage change* in share prices. For example, if the price change in AMEX stocks from one day to the next were + 3 percent, the AMEX index would likewise increase by 3 percent over the previous day's value. Like the NYSE indexes, the AMEX index is often cited in the financial news.

Activity in the OTC market is captured by the **NASDAQ indexes**, which are calculated like the S&P and NYSE indexes. The most comprehensive of the NASDAQ indexes is the *OTC composite index*, which is calculated using more than 4,700 stocks traded on the NASDAQ system. The other five NASDAQ indexes are the industrial, insurance, bank, National Market composite, and National Market industrial. Although their degrees of responsiveness may vary, these indexes do tend to move in the same general direction over time. Because the *NASDAQ OTC composite index* is highly reflective of the price behavior of the smaller, more speculative stocks, it tends to be closely followed by investors and speculators interested in the small-stock segment of the market.

In addition to the major indexes described above, another measure of market performance is the

---

Standard & Poor's (S&P) indexes
Indexes compiled by Standard & Poor's Corporation; similar to the DJIA but employ different computational methods and consist of far more stocks.

NYSE index
An index of the performance of all stocks listed on the New York Stock Exchange.

AMEX index
An index of the performance of all stocks listed on the American Stock Exchange.

NASDAQ index
An index, supplied by the National Association of Securities Dealers Automated Quotation, that tracks the performance of stocks traded in the OTC market.

Wilshire 5000 Index. Published by Wilshire Associates, Inc., the Wilshire 5000 is reported daily in *The Wall Street Journal* and in several other major publications. What makes this measure noteworthy is that unlike other major market indexes, the Wilshire 5000 is reflective of the *total market value* of the 5,000 most actively traded stocks. It's estimated that the 5,000 stocks included in this index account for about 98 or 99 percent of the total market value of all publicly traded stocks in this country. Thus, if you want an idea of the size of the U.S. stock market, just look at where the Wilshire 5000 stands; in May 1992, it stood at 4,025. Since this index is in billions of dollars, a measure of 4,025 translates into a total market value of some $4,025 billion — or, a little more than $4 trillion.

The MidCap 400 is a relatively new market index that's meant to reflect the market performance of medium-sized companies.
Fact: The MidCap 400 was launched by Standard & Poor's in June 1991 and is a market index made up of 400 midsize companies; this segment of the market is very popular with investors because it is felt that this is where you'll find the future market leaders.

Industry Data. Local newspapers, *The Wall Street Journal, Barron's*, and various financial publications regularly contain articles and data about different industries. For example, Standard & Poor's *Industry Surveys* provides detailed descriptions and statistics for all the major industries; on a smaller scale, *Business Week* and other magazines regularly include indexes of industry performance and price levels. Other industry-related data can be obtained from industry trade associations, one example of which is the American Petroleum Institute.

Company Data. Articles about the performance and new developments of companies are included in local newspapers, *The Wall Street Journal, Barron's*, and most investment magazines. The prices of the securities of all listed companies and the most active over-the-counter stocks are quoted daily in *The Wall Street Journal, Investor's Business Daily*, and *USA Today*, and weekly in *Barron's*. Many daily newspapers also contain stock price quotations,

though in the smaller ones the listing may be selective; in some cases, only stocks of local interest might be included.

Stock Quotes. To see how price quotations work and what they mean, consider the quotes that appear daily (M–F) in *The Wall Street Journal*. As we'll see, the quotations provide not only current prices, but a great deal of additional information as well. A portion of the NYSE stock quotations from *The Wall Street Journal* is presented in Exhibit 13.8. Let's use the Dial Corporation quotations for purposes of illustration. These quotes were published on Wednesday, May 20, 1992, and are for the trades that occurred on Tuesday, May 19. A glance at the quotations shows that stock prices are quoted in eighths of a dollar, with the factions reduced to their lowest common denominator (²⁄₈, ⁴⁄₈, and ⁶⁄₈ are expressed as ¼, ½, and ¾, respectively). The first two columns, labeled "Hi" and "Lo," contain the highest and lowest price at which the stock sold during the preceding 52 weeks; Dial, for example, traded between 26⅝ and 40⅛ during the 52-week period ending May 19, 1992. Listed to the right of the company's name is its *stock symbol* (Dial goes by the two-letter initial "DL"); these stock symbols are the abbreviations used on the *market tapes* seen in brokerage offices and on CNBC/FNN television to identify specific companies. The figure listed right after the stock symbol is the cash dividend expected to be paid on each share during the year; this is followed by the dividend yield. (Note: Since Dial is expected to pay a cash dividend of $1.12 a share, its dividend yield is 3.1 percent, which is found by dividing $1.12 in dividends by the closing price of $35.75.) The next entry is the P/E ratio, which is the current market price divided by the per share earnings for the most recent 12-month period. Since it is believed to reflect investor expectations concerning the firm's future prospects, the P/E ratio is closely followed by investors as part of the stock-valuation process. Dial's P/E ratio was 12 — which means the stock is trading at 12 times its earnings.

The daily volume follows the P/E ratio. Here, the sales numbers are listed in round lots (of 100 shares); thus the figure 837 for Dial indicates that there were 83,700 shares of Dial stock traded on May 19. The next entries, in the "Hi," "Lo," and "Close" columns, contain the highest, lowest, and last (clos-

EXHIBIT 13.8

Listed Stock Quotes

Common and preferred stocks are listed together and, except for a couple of minor differences, basically follow the same price quotation system.

		52 Weeks Hi	52 Weeks Lo	Stock	Sym	Div	Yld %	PE	Vol 100s	Hi	Lo	Close	Net Chg	
		33¼	27¾	DetEd prB		2.75	8.6	...	5	31⅞	31⅞	31⅞	+ ⅜	
	↑	105	103	DetEd pf		9.72	8.8	...	z100	110	110	110	+10	
		28	24⅞	DetEd pr		2.28	8.6	...	1	26⅜	26⅜	26⅜	+ ¼	
		29	16¾	Diagnstek	DXK		...	36	748	19⅞	19⅝	19¾	+ ⅛	
		53¾	26½	DiagnstPdt	DP	.32	1.0	20	109	31⅛	30⅞	31⅛	+ ¼	
Dial common →		40⅛	26⅝	DialCp	DL	1.12	3.1	12	837	35⅞	35⅜	35¾	+ ⅜	← Common stock quote
		60	50	DialCp pf		4.75	8.3	...	z10	57	57	57	− 1	
		16	9	DialREIT	DR	1.28	12.2	36	43	10¾	10½	10½	− ⅜	
		24⅞	18⅛	DiaSham	DRM	.52	2.4	25	786	21¼	20¼	21¼	+ ¾	
		4⅜	2¼	DiaShamOff	DSP	.31e	9.5	54	159	3¼	3	3¼	+ ¼	
	s	30	12⅜	Diasonic	DIA		...	12	160	14	13¾	14	+ ¼	
		60½	39⅛	Diebold	DBD	1.68	3.4	18	995	50⅛	49¾	50	...	
		23⅝	12⅜	DigitalComm	DCA		...	14	683	19¼	19	19⅛	...	
	↓	71¾	43½	DigitalEqp	DEC		...	...	7065	43¾	42¾	43¼	− ½	
		136¾	110½	DillardStrs	DDS	.24	.2	22	899	123⅝	122⅛	123⅝	+ 1⅛	
		5⅞	2⅜	DimeSvgNY	DME		...	...	476	4⅞	4¾	4⅞	+ ⅛	
		13⅜	8⅝	DiscountNY	DCY	.40	4.1	...	108	10⅛	9⅞	9⅞	− ⅜	
	s ↑	39⅞	25⅞	Disney	DIS		...	32	53063	41⅛	39⅝	40⅞	+ 1¼	
		48	30¾	DoleFood	DOL	.40	1.2	14	632	32¼	31¾	32⅛	...	
	s	39¾	30¾	DominRes	D	2.38	6.1	14	1168	38¾	37¾	38¾	+ ⅞	
		47½	33	Donaldson	DCI	.56	1.2	19	363	47½	46¼	46⅞	+ ⅞	
		57¼	42⅜	Donelley	DNY	1.00	1.8	21	412	56¾	55⅞	56¾	+ ¾	
		43¾	34½	Dover	DOV	.84	2.1	18	960	40	39⅜	39⅝	+ ¼	
		62⅝	47⅝	DowChem	DOW	2.60	4.2	22	3641	61½	59⅞	61½	+ 1¼	
		34¾	21⅝	DowJones	DJ	.76	2.3	40	1319	32¾	32	32¾	+ ¾	
		18⅜	10⅝	DowneySL	DSL	.32	2.2	10	739	14⅞	14¾	14¾	...	
		12¼	5¾	Dravo	DRV		...	...	96	9⅜	9⅛	9⅛	− ¼	
		23⅜	16¼	DresserInd	DI	.60	2.7	23	3810	22⅝	22⅛	22½	− ¼	
		50	31¼	Dreyfus	DRY	.68	1.7	20	642	40	39¼	39⅞	...	
		10	9¼	DreyfStrMunBd	DSM	.71	7.2	...	1902	9⅞	9¾	9⅞	+ ⅛	
		54⅞	42⅛	DuPont	DD	1.76	3.3	20	6661	53¼	52	53⅛	+ ⅜	
DuPont preferred →		65	54¾	DuPont pf		4.50	7.4	...	13	61¼	60½	60⅞	+ ⅛	← Preferred stock quote
	n	21⅝	18	DuffPhelpsCp	DUF		...	17	9	20¼	20⅛	20¼	− ⅛	
		10⅜	8⅝	DuffPhelpsUtil	DNP	.77e	7.8	...	3056	10	9⅞	9⅞	− ⅛	

Source: *The Wall Street Journal*, May 20, 1992.

ing) price, respectively, at which the stock sold on the day in question. Dial closed up ⅜ on May 19, which means that it had closed at 35⅜ the day before.

The same quotation system is used for AMEX and NASDAQ *National Market* stocks. However, a slightly different procedure is used with OTC securities that are not part of the National Market System—that is, for many OTC stocks, only the bid and ask prices are included in the quotes. In particular, the *highest* bid price for the day is listed along with the *lowest* ask price. (Recall that the bid price is what you can *sell* a stock for and the ask price is what you must pay to *buy* the security.)

Preferred stocks are also listed with the common stock quotes. To find a preferred stock, just look for the letters "pf" or "pr" right after the company's name, as shown for the DuPont preferred in Exhibit 13.8. While a company may have any number of preferred issues outstanding (look at the Detroit Edison, DetEd, preferreds), a quote will appear in the

Wilshire 5000 index

An index of the total market value of the 5,000 most actively traded stocks in this country.

paper only if the stock actually traded on the day in question. Thus, whereas DuPont has two preferred issues outstanding, only one of them, *the $4.50 preferreds*, traded on May 19. This particular preferred stock pays $4.50 a year in dividends and based on the closing price for the day (60⅞), it is currently yielding 7.4 percent. Normally, it's the *annual dividend* that separates one preferred stock from another — for example, look at the three Detroit Edison issues: their annual dividends range from $2.28 a share to $9.72 a share. As for the rest of the quotation, you'll notice that preferred quotes are about the same as common stock quotes, except that the P/E ratios are left blank because they are irrelevant in the case of preferred stocks.

Bond Quotes. Exhibit 13.9 contains examples of some NYSE bond quotes; these quotes were also for trades that occurred on May 19, 1992. To understand the system used with listed bonds, look at the Alabama Power (AlaP) issue. The row of numbers immediately following the company name gives the coupon and the year in which the bond matures; the "8¾07" means that this particular bond carries an 8¾ percent annual coupon and will mature sometime in the year 2007. Such information is important, since it lets investors differentiate among the various bonds issued by the same corporation; notice that there were seven different Alabama Power bonds listed on the day of this quote. The next column, labeled "Cur Yld," provides the *current yield* being offered by the issue at its *current market price*. Current yield is found by dividing the bond's annual coupon (here, 8.75%, or $87.50) by the issue's closing price (102⅝, or $1,026.25), which in this case amounts to 8.5 percent. The "Vol" column represents the actual number of bonds traded; there were 16 Alabama Power bonds traded on this day. Price information is contained in the last two columns. Unlike stocks, instead of high, low, and closing prices, bond quotes usually show just the closing price, along with the net change in the closing price from the day before. *All bonds are quoted as a percent of par*, meaning that a quote of 85 translates into a price of 85 percent of the bond's par value. Since corporate bonds typically have par values of $1,000, a bond quote of 85 means that the price is really $850 (85% × $1,000). Corporate bonds are also traded in fractions of ⅛, but each fraction is

worth 1.25 *dollars*. Thus, Alabama Power's closing price for the day was $1,026.25, found by multiplying the quoted price by $1,000, that is, 102⅝ = 102.625% × $1,000 = $1,026.25.

Convertibles are also listed along with other corporate bonds. They are easy to find — just look for the letters "cv" in the current yield column, such as in the case of the Alaska Air (AlskAr) 6⅞ of 07 convertible in Exhibit 13.9. Except for the "cv" in the current yield column, all other aspects of the quote are exactly like that for any other listed bond. Also listed in Exhibit 13.9 are some zero coupon bonds issued by Allied Chemical Corporation (AlldC). Such bonds have the letters "zr" in place of their coupons; for example, with the Allied bonds, the "zr09" means the issue is a zero coupon bond that matures in 2009. Note that on May 19, this particular zero coupon bond traded at 22¾ — in dollars, that means the bond was trading at $227.50. That's what investors were paying in 1992 and, in return, they will receive better than four times that amount ($1,000) sometime in the year 2009.

In addition to corporate bonds, Treasury and agency bond prices are also reported in *The Wall Street Journal* and other major publications. The quotes for these bonds are only slightly different than those for corporates. These issues are also quoted as a percent of par, and the quotes also specify the coupon rates and maturity dates.

BROKERAGE REPORTS

The reports produced by the research staffs of the major (full-service) brokerage firms provides still another important source of investor information. These reports cover a wide variety of topics, from economic and market analyses to industry and company reports, news of special situations, and reports on interest rates and the bond market. Reports on certain industries or securities prepared by the house's backoffice research staff may be issued on a scheduled basis and often contain lists of securities within certain industries classified as to the type of investment return they provide and the type of market behavior they are expected to exhibit. Also, brokerage houses often will issue lists of securities classified as either "buy" or "sell" depending on the research staff's analysis of their anticipated market behavior. Occasionally brokerage houses issue ex-

EXHIBIT 13.9

Listed Corporate Bond Quotes

Bond prices are always quoted as a *percent of par*. Since par for corporate bonds is normally $1,000, each point in a bond quote is worth $10 (and each ⅛ of a point is worth $1.25). Thus, a quote of 89¼ is *not* $89.25, but $892.50 ($1,000 × .8925); likewise, a quote of 115 translates into $1,150 ($1,000 × 1.15).

	Bonds	Cur Yld	Vol	Close	Net Chg.	
	Adien 15s99	21.1	105	71	− 2	
	Advst 9s08	cv	16	91	…	
	AetnLf 8⅛07	8.2	10	98⅞	− ¼	
	AirbF 6¾01	cv	130	81	+ 1	
	AlaP 9s2000	8.7	5	103⅝	…	
	AlaP 7⅞s02	7.9	20	100	+ ¼	
	AlaP 7¾s02	7.8	1	99½	+ ⅝	
	AlaP 8¼s03	8.0	1	102¾	+ ¼	
Alabama Power ⟶	AlaP 8¾07	8.5	16	102⅝	+ ¼	⟵ Corporate bond quote
	AlaP 9¼07	8.8	10	105	+ 2⅜	
	AlaP 9⅝08	9.2	1	104⅞	+ ½	
Alaska Air ⟶	AlskAr 6⅞14	cv	5	82½	− 1½	⟵ Convertible bond quote
	AlskAr zr06	…	260	34	+ ¼	
	AlldC zr98	…	11	60½	…	
	AlldC zr92	…	17	98⁵⁄₁₆	+ ¹⁄₁₆	
	AlldC zr96	…	33	76½	− ⅛	
	AlldC zr95	…	45	81	+ ⅛	
	AlldC zr99	…	10	56⅞	+ ⅞	
Allied Chemical ⟶	AlldC zr09	…	155	22¾	+ ⅞	⟵ Zero coupon bond quote
	AldSig 9⅞97	9.4	127	105⅛	+ ⅛	
	AldSig 9½16	8.7	12	109	+ ½	
	Allwst 7¼14	cv	50	86	+ 2	
	AmStor 01	cv	8	96	…	
	ATT 5⅝95	5.7	54	98⅞	…	
	ATT 6s00	6.6	95	91⅜	+ ⅞	
	ATT 5⅛01	6.1	19	83⅞	+ ⅛	
	ATT 7s01	7.2	434	97¾	+ ⅞	
	ATT 7⅛03	7.4	273	96⅞	+ ⅞	
	ATT 8⅝26	8.5	145	101⅞	+ ¼	
	Amoco 6s98	6.3	10	95⅝	+ ⅛	
	Amoco 7⅞96	7.7	35	102⅞	+ 1⅜	
	Amoco 8⅝16	8.3	287	103¾	− ⅛	
	AmocoCda 7⅜13	6.6	101	111	+ 1	
	Andarko 6¼14	6.5	10	96½	+ ¾	
	Apache 7½00	cv	36	107½	+ ½	
	Arml 13½94	12.8	103	105⅞	+ ⅞	

Source: *The Wall Street Journal*, May 20, 1992.

tensive analyses of specific securities, along with recommendations as to the type of investment returns expected and whether to buy or sell.

ADVISORY SERVICES

A number of subscription advisory services provide information and recommendations on various industries and specific securities. The services normally cost from $50 to several hundred dollars a year. Although these costs may be tax deductible, only the most active investors will find them worthwhile, since you can usually review such materials at your broker's office. Many university as well as public libraries also have these reports available for reference use. Probably the best known financial services are those provided by Standard & Poor's Corporation, Moody's Investors Service, and Value Line Investment Survey. Each of these companies offers an array of subscription services. Both Standard & Poor's and Moody's publish manuals containing historical facts and financial data on thousands of corporations; these are broken down into industry groups. On a monthly basis, Standard & Poor's publishes a stock guide and a bond guide, each of which

EXHIBIT 13.10

An S&P Stock Report

An S&P report like this one provides a wealth of information about the operating results and financial condition of the company and is an invaluable source of information to investors.

Dial Corp

750P

NYSE Symbol DL Options on ASE (Jan-Apr-Jul-Oct) In S&P 500

Price	Range	P–E Ratio	Dividend	Yield	S&P Ranking	Beta
May 5'92	1992					
35	50⅝–33⅜	NM	[5]1.12	[5]3.2%	B+	1.09

Summary

This company makes branded consumer household and food products, operates commercial and institutional foodservice outlets, provides varied consumer and commercial services, and manufactures intercity and transit buses. In March 1992 the company spun off to shareholders its financial segment as GFC Financial Corp. (GFC-NYSE) on the basis of one GFC share for every two Dial common shares held.

Current Outlook

Earnings for 1992 are projected at $3.00 a share, versus 1991's $0.24, which included $2.04 in restructuring charges and excluded a $1.71 charge related to the March 1992 spin-off of financial operations.

Following the March 1992 spin-off, the company expects to pay dividends initially at a $0.28 quarterly rate, down 20% from the $0.35 quarterly rate paid previously.

Earnings for 1992 are expected to benefit from successful new consumer products, regained momentum for the service businesses, and higher sales from the transportation manufacturing division. Earnings should also reflect the absence of 1991's restructuring charges, continued cost cutting efforts, and lower interest costs.

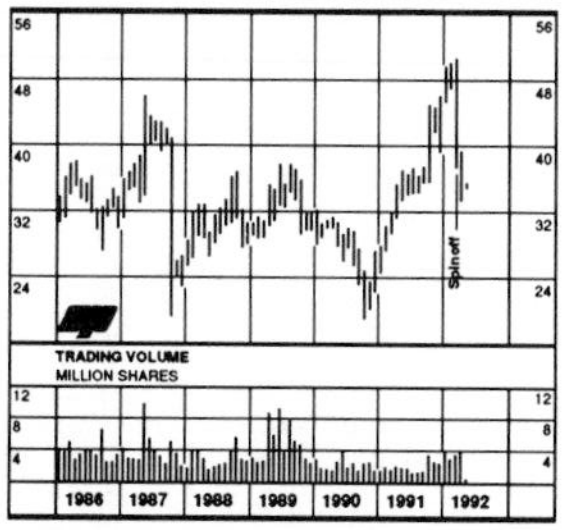

Revenues (Million $)

Quarter:	1992	1991	1990	1989
Mar.	741	839	866	842
Jun.	---	867	912	925
Sep.	---	821	876	906
Dec.	---	783	865	863
	---	3,310	3,519	3,537

Revenues for the three months ended March 31, 1992, were off 12%, year to year, reflecting a 12% decline in consumer products (31% of total sales) and a 43% drop in transportation manufacturing (16%), partially offset by a 5.8% increase in services (53%). Margins widened, despite sharply lower profits in the transportation manufacturing division, and operating profits were down 5.2%. Following lower interest and corporate expenses, pretax income gained 6.1%. After taxes at 37.5%, versus 42.4%, net income rose 15%, to $0.33 a share on 5.5% more shares from $0.30. Results exclude income from discontinued financial operations through the March 18, 1992 spin-off of $0.13 a share against $0.14.

Common Share Earnings ($)

Quarter:	1992	1991	1990	1989
Mar.	0.33	0.30	0.42	0.38
Jun.	E0.92	0.76	0.97	0.92
Sep.	E0.86	0.66	0.80	0.75
Dec.	E0.89	d1.48	0.71	0.70
	E3.00	0.24	2.90	2.75

Important Developments

Mar. '92— On March 18, 1992 Dial spun-off to shareholders its commercial lending and mortgage insurance businesses, including Greyhound Financial Corp., Greyhound European Financial Group, and Verex Corp. The new entity, called GFC Financial Corp., began trading on the NYSE under the ticker symbol GFC. Dial shareholders received one share of GFC for every two Dial common shares held.

Next earnings report expected in mid-July.

Per Share Data ($)

Yr. End Dec. 31	1991	1990	[1]1989	[2]1988	[1]1987	[1]1986	[1]1985	[2]1984	1983	1982
Book Value	[3]22.60	[3]25.30	11.05	10.12	8.44	17.36	17.54	19.35	18.31	17.46
Cash Flow	2.48	5.11	4.93	4.67	3.89	3.60	3.76	3.64	2.50	3.89
Earnings[4]	0.24	2.90	2.75	2.42	2.10	2.08	2.48	2.56	1.47	2.41
Dividends	1.40	1.36	1.32	1.32	1.32	1.32	1.26	1.20	1.20	1.20
Payout Ratio	NM	46%	49%	55%	61%	56%	49%	46%	84%	49%
Prices—High	46⅛	32¼	37¾	36⅞	46	38	34½	26¼	28	19
Low	24⅝	19	28¾	25⅜	19¼	27⅛	23⅞	18⅝	17⅛	12⅝
P/E Ratio—	NM	11–7	14–10	15–10	22–9	18–13	14–10	10–7	19–12	8–5

Data as orig. reptd. 1. Reflects merger or acquisition. 2. Reflects acctg. change. 3. Incl. intangibles. 4. Bef. results of disc. opers. of -1.71 in 1991, -2.52 in 1990, -1.33 in 1987, +2.04 in 1986, +0.44 in 1983 and spec. item(s) of +0.28 in 1988, -0.16 in 1987, +0.31 in 1983, -0.07 in 1982. 5. Rate based on proposed quarterly after Mar. 18, 1992 spin-off. NM-Not Meaningful. d-Deficit. E-Estimated.

Standard NYSE Stock Reports
Vol. 59/No. 93/Sec. 11

May 13, 1992

Standard & Poor's Corp.
25 Broadway, NY, NY 10004

750P

The Dial Corp

Income Data (Million $)

Year Ended Dec. 31	Revs.	Oper. Inc.	% Oper. Inc. of Revs.	Cap. Exp.	Depr.	Int. Exp.	Net Bef. Taxes	Eff. Tax Rate	[6]Net Inc.	% Net Inc. of Revs.	Cash Flow
[1]1991	3,310	318	9.6	135	89.3	67	[5]58	71.8%	11	0.3	99
[1]1990	3,519	535	15.2	108	87.2	249	199	35.8%	116	3.3	202
[2]1989	3,537	521	14.7	107	85.1	251	185	35.0%	109	3.1	193
[3]1988	3,305	495	15.0	121	85.4	254	155	34.1%	93	2.8	178
[4]1987	2,259	225	10.0	115	69.3	61	[5]135	34.5%	83	3.7	151
[4]1986	2,584	152	5.9	157	68.0	69	[5]122	18.0%	[3]94	3.7	161
[2]1985	2,562	191	7.5	125	61.3	49	[5]176	29.0%	120	4.7	180
[3]1984	2,201	189	8.6	88	52.1	20	[5]189	30.9%	125	5.7	176
[1]1983	2,131	142	6.7	85	48.2	38	[5]113	31.6%	70	3.3	117
1982	4,526	197	4.4	143	65.2	50	[5]150	23.7%	106	2.3	171

Balance Sheet Data (Million $)

Dec. 31	Cash	Curr. Assets	Curr. Liab.	Curr. Ratio	Total Assets	Ret. On Assets	Long Term Debt	Common Equity	Total Inv. Capital	% LT Debt of Cap.	% Ret. on Equity
1991	707	1,336	1,755	0.8	3,592	0.2%	504	907	1,505	33.5	1.0
1990	824	NA	1,958	NA	5,431	2.2%	1,939	993	3,123	62.1	11.4
1989	859	NA	1,832	NA	5,205	2.1%	1,797	1,040	3,041	59.1	10.5
1988	695	NA	1,589	NA	5,034	2.2%	1,894	967	3,054	62.9	9.8
1987	634	1,266	1,199	1.1	3,409	2.7%	884	901	1,860	47.5	8.7
1986	578	1,162	982	1.2	2,964	3.5%	607	1,018	1,695	35.8	9.5
1985	503	1,077	942	1.1	2,931	4.6%	605	1,123	1,798	33.7	10.8
1984	427	907	770	1.2	2,347	5.8%	224	1,104	1,397	16.0	11.5
1983	26	522	385	1.4	1,965	3.4%	346	1,063	1,507	23.0	6.6
1982	23	622	437	1.4	2,007	5.5%	422	943	1,478	28.5	11.5

Data as orig. reptd. 1. Excl. disc. opers. 2. Reflects merger or acquisition. 3. Reflects acctg. change. 4. Excl. disc. opers. and reflects merger or acquisition. 5. Incl. equity in earns. of nonconsol. subs. 6. Bef. results of disc. opers in 1991, 1990, 1987, 1986, 1983, and spec. item(s) in 1988, 1987, 1983, 1982. NA-Not Available.

Business Summary

Dial Corp (formerly Greyhound Dial) is a diversified holding company providing varied products and services for consumers and businesses. The financial services segment was spun off in March 1992 and the Greyhound Lines bus operation was divested in 1987. Segment contributions from continuing operations in 1991 (profits in million $):

	Revs.	Profits
Consumer products	31%	$110.6
Services	49%	85.7
Transportation manufacturing	20%	–8.2

Consumer products include Dial, Tone and other soaps, Dial antiperspirants and deodorants, and Breck hair care products; Purex, Trend and Dutch laundry detergents and Brillo soap pads; and food products such as Armour Star and Treet canned meats and Lunch Bucket and Light Balance shelf-stable microwaveable meals. Services provided to consumer markets include Dobbs International Services Inc. in-flight catering, a money order business, travel and tour operations, gift shops, drug stores, restaurants, cruise ships, and duty-free shops. Business market services include contract food services, convention exhibit services, and aircraft ground handling services. Transportation Manufacturing and Service Parts builds and sells intercity and transit buses and after-market replacement parts for both the intercity coach and transit bus markets.

In March 1992, Dial spun off its financial services group as a new entity called GFC Financial Corp., with Dial shareholders receiving one share of GFC for every two common shares of Dial held.

Dividend Data

Dividends have been paid since 1936. A dividend reinvestment plan is available. A "poison pill" stock purchase right was adopted in 1986.

Amt of Divd. $	Date Decl.	Ex–divd. Date	Stock of Record	Payment Date
0.35	May 14	May 24	May 31	Jul. 1'91
0.35	Aug. 15	Aug. 26	Aug. 30	Oct. 1'91
0.35	Nov. 21	Nov. 25	Dec. 2	Jan. 2'92
*Stk	Feb. 5	Mar. 19	Mar. 4	Mar. 18'92
0.35	Feb. 20	Feb. 27	Mar. 4	Apr. 1'92

*0.5 com. sh. of GFC Financial Corp.

Capitalization

Long Term Debt: $582,551,000.

Minority Interest: $53,778,000.

$4.75 Red. Preferred Stock: 400,352 shs. (no par).

Common Stock: 40,718,359 shs. ($1.50 par).
Institutions hold about 58%.
Shareholders of record: 52,151.

Office—Dial Tower, Phoenix, AZ 85077. **Tel**—(602) 207-4000. **Chrmn & Pres**—J. W. Teets. **VP-Fin**—F. E. Lake. **VP-Secy**—F. G. Emerson. **Investor Contact**—Roger Bedier. **Dirs**—J.E. Cunningham, J. T. Ford, D. E. Gill, D. E. Guinn, J. Hay, J. K. Hofer, J. H. Johnson, A. E. Paulson, J. F. Reichert, D. C. Stanfill, R. P. Straetz, J. W. Teets, A. T. Young. **Transfer Agent**—First National Bank of Boston, Boston, Mass. **Incorporated** in Delaware in 1926; reincorporated in Delaware in 1992. **Empl**—31,200.

Information has been obtained from sources believed to be reliable, but its accuracy and completeness are not guaranteed. E.A. Vandeventer

Source: *Standard & Poor's Stock Reports* (New York: Standard & Poor's Corporation, 1992).

summarizes the financial conditions of a few thousand issues; Moody's also publishes stock and bond guides. And a number of reports are also prepared on a weekly basis, like Standard & Poor's *Outlook*.

Separate reports on specific companies are another valuable type of subscription service. An example of one such stock report is given in Exhibit 13.10. This report, prepared by Standard & Poor's, presents a concise summary of a company's financial history, current finances, and future prospects; a similar type of report, with even more emphasis given to the security's investment merits and future prospects, is also available from *Value Line*. Recommended lists of securities, broken down into groups on the basis of investment objectives, constitute still another type of service. In addition to these popular subscription services, numerous *investment letters*, which periodically advise subscribers on the purchase and sale of securities, are available. Finally, by subscribing to weekly chart books, investors may also obtain graphs showing stock prices and volume over extended periods of time.

INVESTMENT ADVISORS

Successful investors often establish themselves as professional investment advisors. In this capacity, they attempt to develop investment plans consistent with the financial objectives of their clients. They may operate their own business, or be associated with large firms that employ research staffs and often publish various subscription materials. Many of the better-known investment advisors limit their practice to a select group of wealthy individuals who have similar investment objectives, while others accept clients with diverse goals. Professional advisors generally do not accept clients with investment assets of less than $50,000, and the more "elite" ones are likely to require considerably larger holdings. Annual fees for advisory services, which may involve the complete management of the client's money, are likely to range from about 1 percent to as much as 2 or 3 percent of assets under management.

There are several different ways you can obtain the services of a professional money manager: (1) you can hire an *independent investment advisor* (but they're usually pretty expensive and prefer to deal with well-heeled clients); (2) you can go to the *trust department of a major bank* (many offer their investment services to the general public at very reasonable costs, and you don't have to die or have a trust account to obtain such services — instead, all you have to do is enter into a simple *agency agreement*); (3) if you deal with a full-service brokerage firm, you can check with your broker to see if they offer fee-based *wrap accounts* (in these portfolio management accounts, your brokerage firm takes over the full-time management of your investments, in return for a flat annual fee — but watch out, that annual fee can get pretty hefty); or (4) you might consider the services of a *financial planner* (preferably a *fee-based* planner who has a strong track record in the field of *investments*). If you're thinking of using a professional money manager, the best thing to do is shop around — look at the kind of returns they've been able to generate (in good markets and bad), and don't overlook the matter of cost — find out right up front how much you'll have to pay and what the fee is based on. Equally important, find out if the advisor has a specialty and if so, make sure it's compatible with your investment objectives; for example, don't go to a financial planner that specializes in high-risk limited partnerships if you're not interested in that kind of investment.

THE PC AS A SOURCE OF INVESTMENT INFORMATION

Any discussion of investment information would be incomplete without mentioning the personal computer. There is no question that one of the greatest technological revolutions taking place in the market today is the widespread introduction of the personal computer to the investment decision-making process. This is occurring not only with professional investors and money managers but also with individual investors. Indeed, a wide variety of software is now available to help the individual investor analyze and evaluate the investment merits of stocks and bonds; in essence, such software provides assistance in the security selection process. In addition, the personal computer can also be used to manage and keep track of *whole portfolios* of securities.

Another significant development has been the introduction of computerized *databases* that literally convert your home computer to an on-line library of investment information. Through these database programs, you can get immediate access to a vast array of historic and up-to-the-minute information on thousands of companies and securities. All sorts of financial information and financial ratios are available, along with equally extensive data on the market performance of stocks, bonds, and other securities — from yields and price/earnings multiples to market prices. For example, if you are thinking about buying a stock, you can have displayed on your computer screen recent news stories about the company, its current financial statements, estimates of its future earnings, and even its current and past stock price and volume data. These computerized databases, in effect, provide everything from quarterly corporate earnings reports to the latest stock prices. You can even *trade securities* with these services, by placing orders in your computer. And the store never closes: You can access the data and/or place orders 24 hours a day, any day of the week (in fact, it is usually cheaper to use the service at night and on weekends and holidays). All you need is a PC that is equipped with a *modem*, which enables computers to communicate with one another over phone lines. To subscribe to one of these services, you must pay a modest, one-time hook-up fee and then a monthly fee based on your usage of the service.

To get an idea of how these computerized databases work, let's look at one of the biggest *CompuServe* (5000 Arlington Centre Blvd., Columbus, OH 43220). *CompuServe* is easy to learn, and requests are filled almost instantaneously. The service functions as a conduit to other resources and, as a result, makes available to subscribers such databases as Value Line and Standard & Poor's (each of which provides extensive financial and market information on a multitude of companies and securities), earnings projections for several thousand companies from the Institutional Brokers' Estimate System, detailed financial statements filed with the Securities and Exchange Commission (SEC) by over 10,000 companies, and more. As a subscriber, you have immediate access to any and all of this information — just indicate what you want to see, and it will show up almost instantaneously on your home computer screen. Subscribers can also trade stocks, bonds, and options electronically through a hookup with a major New York–based discount brokerage firm. Other popular computer-based investor information services include *Dow Jones News/*

Retrieval (P.O. Box 300, Princeton, NJ 08540); and *Trade* Plus* (480 California Ave., Palo Alto, CA 94306). Prices for these databases vary and may include a nominal registration, or start-up, fee and possibly even a minimum monthly service charge. All three of the services noted here have a usage, or connect, fee every time you access the service. (Such fees are charged by the minute or by the hour.)

MANAGING YOUR INVESTMENT HOLDINGS

Developing a portfolio of securities is an important part of investing because a portfolio enables you to diversify your holdings. Why do you suppose diversification is such an important attribute? How would you go about building an investment portfolio? Give some thought to these questions before going on.

Actually, buying and selling securities is not difficult; the hard part is finding securities that will provide the kind of return you're looking for. Like most individual investors, in time you too will be buying, selling, and/or trading securities with ease. Eventually your investment holdings will increase to the point where you are managing a whole portfolio of securities. In essence, a **portfolio** is a collection of investment vehicles assembled to meet a common investment goal. For instance, Bill Hansen's investment portfolio is made up of 150 shares of Merck, 200 shares of Wal-Mart, and 10 Home Depot convertible bonds. But a portfolio is far more than a collection of investments! For a portfolio breathes life into your investment program; *it's an investment philosophy that provides guidelines for carrying out your investment program*. A portfolio, in effect, combines your personal and financial traits with your investment objectives to give some structure to your investments.

Seasoned investors often devote a good deal of attention to constructing diversified portfolios of securities. Such portfolios consist of stocks and bonds selected not only for their returns but also for their combined risk-return behavior. The idea behind **diversification** is that by combining securities with dissimilar risk-return characteristics, you can produce a portfolio of reduced risk and more predictable levels of return. In recent years, investment researchers have shown that you can achieve a measurable reduction in risk simply by diversifying your investment holdings. For the small investor with a moderate amount of money to invest, this means that *investing in a number of securities rather than a single one should be beneficial*. The payoff from diversification comes in the form of reduced risk without a significant impact on return. For example, Joan Rainer, who has $25,000 invested in Stock A, might find that by selling two-thirds of her holdings and using the proceeds to buy equal amounts of Stocks B and C, she will continue to earn the same level of return—say, 10 percent—while greatly decreasing the associated risk. Professional money managers emphasize the point that investors should not put all their eggs in one basket but instead should hold portfolios that are diversified across a broad segment of businesses.

BUILDING A PORTFOLIO OF SECURITIES

Developing a portfolio of investment holdings is predicated on the assumption that diversification is a desirable investment attribute that leads to improved return and/or reduced risk. Again, as emphasized earlier, holding a variety of investments is far more desirable than concentrating all your investments in a single security or industry (for example, a portfolio made up of nothing but auto stocks such as GM, Ford, or Chrysler would hardly be well diversified). Of course, when you first start investing, you will not be able to do much, if any, diversifying because of insufficient investment capital. However, as you build up your investment funds, your opportunities (and need) for diversification will increase dramatically. Certainly, by the time you have $5,000 to $10,000 to invest, you should start to diversify your holdings. To give you an idea of the kind of portfolio diversification employed by individual investors, take a look at the following numbers; they show the types of investments held by *average (small) investors:*

Type of Investment Product	Percent of Portfolio (May 1992)
Stocks and stock funds	34.3%
Bonds and bond funds	24.9
Short-term investments (CDs, money mkt. dep. accts., etc.)	39.5
Other (real estate and gold)	1.3
Total	100.0%

This portfolio, which is regularly up-dated, is used in *Money* magazine's *Small Investor Index*, and reflects the portfolio holdings of a typical individual investor. Whether or not this is what your portfolio should look like depends on a number of factors, including your own needs and objectives.

Investor Characteristics. In order to formulate an effective portfolio strategy, you should begin with an honest evaluation of your own financial condition and family situation. Pay particular attention to such variables as:

■ Level and stability of income
■ Family factors
■ Investment horizon
■ Net worth
■ Investor's experience and age
■ Investor's disposition toward risk

These are the variables that set the tone for your investments. They determine the kinds of investments you should consider and how long you can tie up your money. In order for your portfolio to work, it must be tailored to meet your personal financial needs. Your income, family responsibilities, relative financial security, experience, and age all enter into the delicate equation that yields a sound portfolio strategy. For example, a married investor with young children probably would not be

portfolio
A collection of securities assembled for the purpose of meeting common investment goals.

diversification
The process of choosing securities having dissimilar risk-return characteristics in order to create a portfolio that will provide an acceptable level of return and an acceptable exposure to risk.

interested in high-risk investments until some measure of financial security has been provided for the family. Once that investor has ample savings and insurance protection for the family, he or she may be ready to undertake more risky ventures. On the other hand, a single investor with no family responsibilities would probably be better able to handle risk than one who has such concerns. Simply stated, an *investor's risk exposure should not exceed his or her ability to bear risk.*

The size and certainty of an investor's employment income has a significant bearing on portfolio strategy. An investor with a secure job is more likely to embark on a risk-oriented investment program than one with a less secure position. Income taxes bear on the investment decision as well. The higher an investor's income, the more important the tax ramifications of an investment program become. For example, municipal bonds normally yield about one-third less in annual interest than corporate bonds because the interest income on municipal bonds is tax-free. On an after-tax basis, however, municipal bonds may provide a superior return if an investor is in the 28 or 31 percent tax bracket.

An individual's investment experience also influences the appropriateness of the investment strategy. Normally, investors gradually assume levels of higher investment risk over time. It is best to "get one's feet wet" in the investment market by slipping into it gradually rather than leaping in head first. Investors who make risky initial investments very often suffer heavy losses, damaging the long-run potential of the entire investment program. A cautiously developed investment program will likely provide more favorable long-run results than an impulsive, risky one. Finally, investors should carefully consider risk. High-risk investments not only have high return potential but also a high risk of loss. Remember: By going for the home run (via a high-risk, high-return investment), the odds of striking out are much higher than by going for a base hit (a more conservative investment posture).

Investor Objectives. Once an investor has developed a personal financial profile, the next question is: "What do I want from my portfolio?" This seems like an easy question to answer. We would all like to double our money every year by making low-risk investments. However, the realities of the highly competitive investment environment make this outcome unlikely, so the question must be answered more realistically. There generally is a trade-off between earning a high current income from an investment portfolio and obtaining significant capital appreciation from it. An investor must choose one or the other; it is difficult to have both. The price of having high appreciation potential in the portfolio is low current income potential. One must balance the certainty of high current income and limited price appreciation with the uncertainty of high future price appreciation.

The investor's needs may determine which avenue to choose. For instance, a retired investor whose income depends on his or her portfolio will probably choose a lower-risk, current income-oriented approach out of the need for financial survival. In contrast, a high-income, financially secure investor (a doctor, for instance) may be much more willing to take on risky investments in the hope of improving her net worth. Likewise, a young investor with a secure job may be less concerned about current income and more able to bear risk. This type of investor will likely be more capital gains-oriented and may choose speculative investments. As an investor approaches age 60, the desired level of income likely rises as retirement approaches. The aging investor will be less willing to bear risk and will want to keep what he or she has, because these investments will soon be needed as a source of retirement income.

Asset Allocation and Portfolio Management. A portfolio must be built around an individual's needs, which, in turn, depend on income, family responsibilities, financial resources, age, retirement plans, and ability to bear risk. These needs shape one's financial goals. But to create a portfolio that is geared to those goals, you need to develop an **asset allocation** scheme. Basically, all that asset allocation involves is a decision on how to divide your portfolio among different types of securities. For example, what portion of your portfolio is going to be devoted to short-term securities, longer bonds and/or bond funds, and common stocks and/or equity funds? In asset allocation, emphasis is placed on *preservation of capital*. The idea is to position your assets in such a way that you can protect your portfolio from potential negative developments in the market, while still taking advantage of potential positive developments. Asset allocation is one of the

EXHIBIT 13.11

Four Model Portfolios

The type of portfolio you put together will depend on your financial and family situation as well as on your investment objectives. Clearly, what is right for one family may be totally inappropriate for another.

Family Situation	Portfolio
Newlywed couple:	70% in common stocks, with three quarters in mutual funds aiming for maximum capital gains and the rest in growth funds 30% in a money market fund or other short-term money market securities
Two-income couple:	50% in common stocks, with three quarters of that in blue chips or growth mutual funds and the remainder in more aggressive issues or mutual funds aiming for maximum capital gains 40% in discount Treasury notes whose maturities correspond with the bills for college tuition 10% in money market funds or other short-term money market securities
Divorced mother:	50% in money market funds or other short-term money market securities 50% in growth and income mutual funds
Older couple:	60% in blue-chip common stocks or growth mutual funds 30% in municipal bonds or short- and intermediate-term discount bonds that will mature as they start to need the money to live on 10% in CDs and/or money market funds

most overlooked yet most important aspects of investing. Indeed, there's overwhelming evidence that, over the long run, the total return on a portfolio is influenced more by its assets allocation plan than by specific security selections.

Asset allocation deals in broad categories and *does not tell you which individual securities to buy or sell*. It might look something like this:

Type of Investment	Asset Mix
Short-term securities	10%
Longer bonds (7- to 10-year maturities)	25
Equity funds	65
Total portfolio	100%

As you can see, all you're really doing here is deciding how to cut up the pie. You still have to decide which particular securities to invest in. Once you've decided that you want to put, say, 25 percent of your money into intermediate-term (7- to 10-year) bonds, your next step is to select those specific securities. Security selection and portfolio management are recurring activities that become an almost routine part of your investment program. You receive an interest or dividend check, and you have to find a place to put it; you add new capital to your investment program, or one of the Treasury notes you're holding matures, and you have to decide what to do with the

money. These events occur with considerable regularity, so you're likely to be faced with a series of little (and sometimes not so little) investment decisions over time. This, in short, is portfolio management: the initial construction and ongoing administration of a collection of securities and investments.

Portfolio management involves the buying, selling, and holding of various securities for the purpose of meeting a set of predetermined investment needs and objectives. To give you an idea of portfolio management in action, Exhibit 13.11 provides examples of four different portfolios, each developed with a particular financial situation in mind. Note in each case that the asset allocation schemes and portfolio structures change with the different financial objectives. The first one is the *newlywed couple;* in their late 20s, they earn $45,000 a year and spend just about every cent. They have managed to put away

asset allocation

A plan for dividing a portfolio among different classes of securities in order to preserve capital by protecting the portfolio against negative market development.

EXHIBIT 13.12

A Worksheet for Keeping Tabs on Your Investment Holdings

A worksheet like this one will enable you to keep track of your investment holdings and identify investments that are not performing up to expectations.

AN INVENTORY OF INVESTMENT HOLDINGS

Name(s): John & Mary Maffeo Date: December 1992

Type of Investment	Description of Investment Vehicle	Date Purchased	Amount of Investment (Quote—$ Amount)	Amount of Annual Income from Dividends, Interest, Etc.	Latest Market Value (Quote—$ Amount)	Comments/ Planned Actions
Common stock	200 shares—Dillard Dept. Stores	3/5/85	24½—$4,900	$96	132⅛—$52,850	400 shs.
Common stock	300 shares—Winnebago Inds.	10/12/88	8¾—$2,625	0	5¼—$1,575	SELL?
Common stock	400 shares—Pall Corp.	8/11/84	9½—$3,800	$594	27—$48,600	1,800 shares!
Preferred stock	150 shares—AT&T pf. 3.64	5/20/88	24¼—$3,638	$546	48½—$7,275	
Corporate bond	$5,000—Pacific Telephone 11.35–07	8/19/82	75½—$3,775	$568	103—$5,150	
Corporate bond	$7,000—Texaco 5¾–97	2/27/77	39¼—$2,748	$402	94½—$6,615	
Treasury bond	$6,000—U.S. Treasury 8⅝–94	9/1/87	62—$3,720	$518	99—$5,940	
Mutual fund	500 shares—Fidelity Magellan (growth)	6/16/76	7—$3,500	$3,120	72½—$124,120	1712 shs.
Mutual fund	200 shares—Fidelity high-yield (bond)	1/17/79	6½—$1,300	$246	12¼—$2,450	
Real estate	Four-plex at 1802 N. 75 Ave.	9/16/78	$140,000–$28,000	N/A	(est.) $250,000–$138,000	Time to sell?
Savings	1-year/4% CD at First National Bank	6/10/88	N/A—$10,000	$400	N/A—$10,000	
Savings	Money Fund at Paine Webber	3/13/83	N/A—$7,200	$340	N/A—$7,200	
	TOTALS		$75,206	$6,830	$409,775	

Instructions: List number of shares of *common and preferred stock* purchased as part of the description of securities held; then put the price paid *per share* under the "Quote" column and total amount invested (number of shares x price per share) under the "$ Amount" column. Enter the principal (par) value of all *bonds* held in place of number of shares: "$ Amount" column for bonds = principal value of bonds purchased x quote (for example, $5,000 x .755 = $3,775). List *mutual funds* as you did for stock. For *real estate,* enter total market value of property under "Quote" column and amount actually invested (down payment and closing costs) under "$ Amount." Ignore the "Quote" column for *savings* vehicles. For "Amount of Income" column, list *total* amount received from dividends, interest, and so on (for example, dividends per share x number of shares held). Under "Latest Market Value," enter market price as of the date of this report (for instance, in December 1988, Emory Air Freight was trading at 4½). The latest market value for *real estate* is entered as an *estimate* of what the property would likely sell for (under "Quote") and the *estimated* amount of equity the investor has in the property (under "$ Amount").

some money, however, and are quickly beginning to appreciate the need to develop a savings program. Next there is the *two-income couple;* in their early 40s, they earn $84,000 a year and are concerned about college costs for their children, ages 17 and 12. Next is the *divorced mother;* she is 34, has custody of her children, ages 7 and 4, and receives $28,000 a year in salary and child support. Finally, we have the *older couple;* in their mid-50s, they are planning for retirement in ten years, when the husband will retire from his $70,000-a-year job.

Coming up with a sound asset allocation plan is likely to have more of an impact on long-term return than the specific securities you hold in your portfolio.
Fact: Studies have shown that, over the long run, the total return on a portfolio is influenced more by its asset allocation plan — that is, its mix of assets — than by specific security selections.

KEEPING TRACK OF YOUR INVESTMENTS

Keeping track of your investment holdings is essential to a well-managed securities portfolio. Just as you need investment objectives to provide direction for your portfolio, so you need to *monitor* it by keeping informed of what your investment holdings consist of, how they have performed over time, and whether or not they have lived up to expectations. Sometimes investments fail to perform the way you thought they would. Their return may be well below what you would like, or perhaps you may even have suffered a loss. In either case, it may be time to *sell* the investment(s) and put the money elsewhere. A monitoring system for keeping track of your investments should allow you to identify such securities in your portfolio. In addition, it should enable you to stay on top of the holdings that are performing to your satisfaction. Knowing when to sell and when to

hold can have a significant impact on the amount of return you are able to generate from your investments — certainly it will help you keep your money fully invested.

Exhibit 13.12 provides a simple worksheet that you can use to keep an inventory of your investment holdings. All types of investments can be included on the worksheet — from stocks, bonds, and mutual funds to real estate and savings accounts. To see how it works, consider the investment portfolio that has been built up over the last 15 years or so by John and Mary Maffeo, a two-income couple in their late 40s. As the figures in Exhibit 13.12 reveal, John and Mary hold common and preferred stock in four companies, three bond issues, two mutual funds, some real estate, and two savings accounts. In addition to the type and description of the investment vehicles, the worksheet contains the dates the investments were made (the purchase date is needed for tax purposes), the original amount of the investment, the amount of annual income currently being earned from it, and its latest market value.

Such a report would list all the investments John and Mary held as of December 1992, regardless of when they were purchased. In contrast, any securities/investments sold during the year (1992) would not be included. A report like this should be prepared at least once a year, and preferably every three to six months. When completed, it will provide a quick overview of your investment holdings and enable you to easily identify securities that are performing well and those that are not. Such information is invaluable in effectively managing an investment portfolio, as it lets you know where you stand at a given point in time. Note that the Maffeos earn over $6,800 a year from their investments and that — thanks, in large part, to their investments in a couple of stocks and stock funds — their holdings have grown from $75,000 to over $400,000! In fact, they have only one security that is not doing too well — Winnebego Industries. All the rest are quite profitable.

SUMMARY

■ Stocks, bonds, and other long-term securities are traded in the capital markets; listed securities are traded on organized exchanges, like the New York and American stock exchanges, as well as a number of smaller regional exchanges. In contrast, the over-the-counter (OTC) market handles the thousands of unlisted securities.

▪ Whether your broker is with a full-service or discount brokerage firm, he or she is the one who provides you with access to the securities market — in essence, brokers buy and sell securities for their customers. Investors can buy or sell securities in odd or round lots by simply placing one of several different kinds of orders with their brokers. The three basic types of orders are the market order, limit order, and stop-loss order.

▪ When you buy a security, you can pay cash for it or you can buy it on margin, where part of the cost of the security is paid with borrowed money. The objective of a margin transaction is to obtain magnified returns. It is also possible for an investor to make money when the price of a security drops. This can be done by short selling *borrowed* securities and then repurchasing them after they have dropped in price.

▪ Becoming an informed investor is essential to developing a sound investment program. Vital information about specific companies and industries, the securities markets, the economy, and different investment vehicles and strategies can be obtained from sources such as annual stockholders' reports, brokerage and advisory service reports, and the financial press. In addition, the personal computer is rapidly becoming a popular source of investment information.

▪ Information about daily market performance can be obtained from various averages and indexes, such as the Dow Jones Industrial Average, the Standard & Poor's Indexes, and the NYSE, AMEX, and OTC (or NASDAQ) Indexes. These averages and indexes not only measure performance in the overall market, they also provide standards of performance for specific types of stocks such as transportation issues, banks, insurance companies, and public utilities.

▪ Developing a well-diversified portfolio of investment holdings enables an investor to not only achieve given investment objectives, but also enjoy reduced exposure to risk and a more predictable level of return. A vital ingredient to developing such a portfolio is that full consideration be given to the investor's level and stability of income, family factors, financial condition, experience and age, and disposition toward risk; designing an asset allocation scheme that's based on these personal needs and objectives is also an important part of portfolio management.

QUESTIONS AND PROBLEMS

1. Explain what is meant by the securities markets. Briefly describe the various markets. How does a primary market differ from a secondary market? What is the difference between the money market and the capital market? Give some examples of the types of securities found in the money market; in the capital market.

2. What are organized securities exchanges? What is the difference between the New York Stock Exchange and the American Stock Exchange? What are regional exchanges, and what role do they play? What is the Emerging Company Marketplace (ECM) and why was it established?

3. Describe the operations of the over-the-counter market; compare and contrast it with organized securities exchanges.

4. Explain the difference between a bull market and a bear market. How would you characterize the current state of the stock market? Are we in a bull market or a bear market?

5. What is a stockbroker? Why does the selection of a broker play such an important role in the purchase of securities?

6. "Stockbrokers not only execute buy and sell orders for their clients, they also offer a variety of additional services." Explain what some of these services are.

7. What is SIPC and how does it protect investors? Does the SIPC protect investors against loss? Explain. What is arbitration? Is that the same thing as mediation? Explain.

8. Barbara Moses has just purchased two different stocks. Her first transaction involved 100 shares of Xerox Corporation at $49.50 per share, and the second was 60 shares of Prime Computers at $15 per share. For each transaction, calculate the amount of brokerage commissions Barbara will have to pay, and express

them as a percentage of the total cost of each stock. Use the brokerage fee schedule in Exhibit 13.5.

9. Describe the role that discount brokers play in carrying out security transactions. To whom are their services especially appealing? Explain.

10. Name and describe three basic types of orders. Assume Cecile Higgins places an order to buy 100 shares of Kodak; explain how the order will be processed if it is a market order. Would it have made any difference if it had been a limit order? Explain.

11. What are margin requirements? Helen Emerson wants to buy 300 shares of PepsiCo, which is currently selling in the market for $45 a share. Rather than liquidate all her savings, she decides to borrow through her broker. Assume the margin requirement on common stock is currently 50 percent and the brokerage firm charges 9 percent interest on margin loans. What would be the interest cost on the transaction if Helen sold the stocks at the end of one year? If the stock rises to $60 a share by the end of the year, show the kind of profit (in dollars) and return (in percentages) that Helen would earn if she makes the investment with 50 percent margin; contrast this to what she would make if she uses no margin.

12. Which of the following would offer the best return on investment? Assume you buy $5,000 in stock in all three cases; also, *ignore* interest costs in all your calculations.
    a. Buy a stock at $80 without margin, and sell it at $120 one year later.
    b. Buy a stock at $32 with 50 percent margin, and sell it one year later at $41.
    c. Buy a stock at $50 with 75 percent margin, and sell it in one year at $65.

13. What is a short sale? Explain the logic behind it. How much profit (if any) would Don Summers make if he short sold 300 shares of stock at $75 a share and the price of the stock suddenly tumbled to $60?

14. Identify and briefly discuss the four basic types of information that you, as an investor, should try to stay abreast of. Describe some of the major sources of investment information; briefly note how you can use your PC as a source of investor information.

15. What role do market averages and indexes play in the investment process? Using something like *The Wall Street Journal* or *Barron's*, find the latest values for each of the following market averages and indexes, and indicate how each has performed over the past six months:
    a. DJIA
    b. Dow Jones Utilities
    c. S&P 500
    d. NYSE Composite index
    e. AMEX index
    f. NASDAQ Composite OTC index
    g. MidCap 400
    h. Wilshire 5000

16. Using the stock quotations in Exhibit 13.8, find the 52-week high and low for Dow Chemical. How much does the stock pay annually in dividends, and what is its latest dividend yield? How many shares of Dow Chemical changed hands (were traded), what was the closing price, and at what P/E ratio was the stock trading? According to the information in Exhibit 13.8, which of the Detroit Edison preferred stocks has the best dividend yield?

17. Using the bond quotes in Exhibit 13.9, how much would you have to pay for the following bonds? (Assume all the bonds have $1,000 par values.)
    a. A 7 percent AT&T bond that matures in 2001.
    b. An 8⅝ percent Amoco bond that matures in 2016.
    c. A zero coupon Allied Chemical bond that matures in 1995.
    How much annual interest income will you receive from each of these bonds, and which bond offers the highest current yield? Which has the lowest current yield?

18. Explain why it might be preferable for a person to invest in a portfolio of securities rather than in a single security. Be sure to mention risk and return in your response.

19. Briefly describe the concept of asset allocation and note how it works. Give an example of an asset allocation scheme. Discuss the role that asset allocation plays in the management of a portfolio.

20. What, if anything, is there to be gained from keeping track of your investment holdings?

21. Using the S&P report in Exhibit 13.10, find the

following information as it pertains to Dial Corporation:

a. Amount of revenues (that is, sales) the company generated in 1991.

b. Latest annual dividends per share and dividend yield.

c. Earnings (profit) projections for 1992.

d. Number of common shares outstanding.

e. Book value per share and earnings per share in 1991.

f. Where the stock is traded.

g. Amount of long-term debt the company has.

h. Given its beta, to approximately what price would this stock jump if the market went up by 15 percent over the next 12 months? (Assume the stock is currently priced at 37½.)

CONTEMPORARY CASE APPLICATIONS

13.1 The Gordons' Problem: What to Do with All That Money?

A couple in their early 30s, Allen and Sandra Gordon recently inherited $90,000 from one of their relatives. Allen earns a comfortable income as a sales manager for Smith and Johnson, Inc., and Sandra does equally well as an attorney with a major law firm. Since they have no children and do not need the money, they have decided to invest all of their inheritance in stocks, bonds, and perhaps even some money market instruments. However, they are not very familiar with the market, nor do they know how to go about selecting a broker. As a result, they turn to you for help.

Questions

1. In what markets and on what exchanges do you think most of the Gordons' transactions should take place?

2. What characteristics should the Gordons look for in a stockbroker? Take into consideration brokerage services and brokerage fees.

3. Construct an investment portfolio that you feel would be right for the Gordons; invest the full $90,000. Put *actual* stocks, bonds, preferreds, and/or convertible securities in the portfolio; also, if you like, you may put up to *one-third* of the money into short-term securities like CDs, Treasury bills, money funds, or MMDAs. Select any securities you want, so long as you feel they would be suitable for the Gordons. (Hint: you might want to refer back to Chapters 5 and 12 for some ideas.) Make sure the portfolio consists of *six or more different securities;* use the latest issue of *The Wall Street Journal* to determine the market prices of the securities you select. Show the amount invested in each security, along with the amount of current income (from dividends and/or interest) that will be generated from the investments. Briefly explain why you selected the particular securities for the Gordons' portfolio.

13.2 Steve Takes Stock of His Securities

Steve Harrington is 32 years old, single, and works as a research chemist for a major pharmaceutical firm. He is well paid and over time has built up a sizable portfolio of investments. He considers himself an aggressive investor and, because he has no dependents to worry about, likes to invest in high-risk–high-return securities. His records show the following:

1. In 1990 he bought 100 shares of *Southwest Airlines* (an NYSE stock) at $14 a share; the stock paid a dividend of 10 cents a share in 1990.

2. In 1988 he bought 250 shares of *WD-40 Co.* (an OTC stock quoted on the NASDAQ National Market System) at $28 a share; at the time, the stock was paying annual dividends of $1.63 a share.

3. In 1989, Steve bought 400 shares of *Federal Home Loan Mortgage Corp.* (an NYSE stock) at $50; in 1989 the stock paid annual dividends of $1.60 a share.

4. In early 1991 he bought 200 shares of *Wallace Computer Services* (NYSE) at $21 a share; the stock was expected to pay a dividend of 50 cents a share in 1991.

5. Also in early 1991, Steve bought 300 shares of *Intel* (another OTC-NASDAQ stock quoted on the National Market System) at $40 a share; as of early 1991 this stock had never paid a dividend.

6. He has $8,000 in a 4 percent money market mutual fund.

Every three months or so, Steve prepares a complete, up-to-date inventory of his investment holdings.

Questions

1. Use a form like the one in Exhibit 13.12 to prepare a complete inventory of Steve's investment holdings (Note: Look in the latest issue of *The Wall Street Journal* to find the most recent market value of the five *stocks* in Steve's portfolio.)

2. What is your overall assessment of Steve's investment portfolio? Does it appear that his personal net worth is improving as a result of his investments?

3. Based on the worksheet you prepared in Question 1, do you see any securities that you think Steve should consider selling?

FOR MORE INFORMATION

General Information Articles

Belsky, Gary. "How Your Broker Makes a Buck." *Money*, June 1992, pp. 142–152.

Chandy, P. R., and George Christy. "A History of Bear Markets: How Bad Were They?" *AAII Journal*, October 1989, pp. 15–17.

Coler, Mark. "The Individual Investor's Guide to Selecting a Discount Broker." *AAII Journal*, January 1991, pp. 8–11.

Gottschalk, Earl C. "Psychology of a Scam." *Smart Money*, April 15, 1992, pp. 65–72.

Herman, Tom. "Diversified Portfolios Are More Restful." *The Wall Street Journal*, January 25, 1990, pp. C1, 23.

Jamieson, Dan. "Selling Short: Going Against the Tide." *Personal Investor*, March 1991, pp. 31–34.

Manners, John. "Size Up Your Portfolio Like a Professional." *Money*, May 1992, pp. 88–96.

Government Documents & Other Publications

How the SIPC Protects You. Securities Investors Protection Corp.; 805 Fifteenth St., N.W. — Suite 800; Washington, DC 20005.

How to Proceed with the Arbitration of a Small Claim. U.S. Securities & Exchange Commission; Publications Dept.; 450 - 5th Street, N.W.; Washington, DC 20549.

How to Read a Financial Report. Merrill Lynch, Pierce, Fenner & Smith, Inc.; 111 - 19th Street, N.W.; Washington, DC 20036.

The personal financial planning process revolves around your investment portfolio. It is very important that you understand the sources of financial information, how the financial markets work, and how securities are traded in the markets before you select individual investments to help you achieve your financial goals. In order to obtain the best performance from your investments you must become familiar with current economic developments and events, alternative investment vehicles, current interest rates and price quotations, and personal investment strategies.

Once your goals have been established and you have decided on an investment plan, you are now ready to implement the plan by purchasing and selling securities. You can purchase securities at the time of original issuance in what is referred to as the primary market. Once a security has been sold any subsequent sale is considered to be in the secondary market. The secondary market is further defined by whether or not the securities are listed on an exchange or traded over the counter. These distinctions have an impact on the liquidity of the securities traded as well as transactions costs.

If You Are Just Getting Started

To begin the process of developing an investment portfolio you need to do a critical analysis of yourself in terms of your knowledge of the various types of investment securities and how they will help you achieve your financial goals. You should never start an investment program or buy a security without understanding its characteristics.

Once you have established your financial goals you should select appropriate investments to achieve them. This means that you should spend some time reading about the various markets and securities to aid you in the selection process. You should construct a fictitious portfolio and follow it to see how various assets respond to certain economic events. If done correctly, this will be time well spent before you "put your money where your broker's mouth is."

Since at this stage you probably have very little actual investment experience, you would more than likely select a full-service brokerage firm with access to the major markets and to financial research. This would give you access to investment recommendations to fit your risk and return requirements at the cost of higher commissions.

Selecting a Brokerage Firm:

1. Decide on the services you need to have available to you at this time and make a list so you can begin your evaluation of competing firms.

2. Ask the brokerage house about its research department in comparison with other firms. If you are paying for investment advice, you want to make sure it is good advice most of the time.

3. Look at the firm's commissions on various transactions.

Even though technically commissions are negotiable, most firms have minimum charges on transactions.

4. Determine how the brokerage firm pays interest on cash balances. You want all of your money in an account earning for you.

5. Examine the account agreement form and ask for clarification to any terms or provisions that you do not understand. Don't necessarily take the word of the account executive, as it is the written contract that you have signed that generally prevails in a dispute.

Selecting an Account Executive:

1. Select an account executive like you would any other professional. Ask your friends for references.

2. Arrange to meet in person with the account executive to discuss your goals and objectives. Ask him to describe his investment philosophy to see if it corresponds with yours.

3. If you walk in off the street, you will normally be assigned to whomever is "on duty" that day. This may be the most inexperienced member of the firm.

4. Regardless of how you first meet an account executive, if you do not feel comfortable with him or her, ask the office manager to assign you to someone else and start the interview process over again.

5. If you are still unsure about the account executive, you may want to contact the NASD to see if he or she has had any complaints filed against him or her.

In order to purchase or sell securities, it is generally necessary to enlist the aid of a securities brokerage firm. The selection of the firm will depend on the types of services that you require and the desired level of access to financial markets. If you only want a firm to execute trades for your account and provide no other services, you should consider a discount brokerage firm. However, if you require assistance in your investments in terms of research reports and recommendations, you should consider a full-service brokerage house.

The selection of an account executive to assist you in your investment should be made with care. It is important to select one who understands your financial goals and can assist you in achieving them. You must then decide on the type of account to open. Is it to be a cash account where you pay in full for all purchases, or a margin account where you can increase your purchasing power through the use of borrowed funds?

The proper selection of securities for your portfolio requires a thorough understanding of your personal investment characteristics, your financial goals, and a desired asset mix. Once your portfolio is put together based on these factors you need to monitor your performance by using a form such as the one shown in Exhibit 13.12.

If You Are Thirtysomething

Assuming that you have been involved with investments for some time, you may want to reevaluate the brokerage firm with which you are currently doing business. Since you should have kept track of your investment performance over the years using a form like Exhibit 13.12, determine your rate of actual return relative to what was expected. If you are not achieving these returns, then you may want to consider switching firms.

If you analyze your performance and determine that the selections you made are doing as well or better than the brokerage firm's selections, you might want to consider opening another account with a discount broker. This will enable you to take advantage of both worlds. However, if you do not trade securities in your full-service account, they may assess you with fees.

Regardless of the type of account, as your portfolio grows, it should be monitored periodically to ensure proper performance and diversification of your investments. Studies have shown that the vast majority of your returns will come from being in the right asset class as opposed to the selection of specific securities so you should also review your asset allocation.

Determining Your Asset Allocation:

1. Identify asset classes that are suitable for achieving your financial goals. Examples are debt, equity, cash, and other assets.

2. Determine the weightings of the various asset classes based upon your time horizon and attitude toward risk.

3. Be sure your asset allocation reflects your particular financial objective. This means that you can have a different asset allocation for each goal.

4. Rebalance your portfolios when the allocation in any class exceeds its weight limit.

5. Compare the advantages of rebalancing to the transactions costs. You would normally not rebalance more than once a quarter unless markets are extremely volatile.

Monitoring Your Account:

1. It is not necessary to follow your security prices every day. However, the more active you are in the market the more frequently you should monitor your securities.

2. Compare the change in your security's price to what has happened in the overall market over the same period of time. Try to determine if the change is due to market factors or firm specific factors.

3. To protect against sudden declines in the value of your securities consider using stop-loss orders.

4. Know which securities have gains and losses for year-end tax planning. Using a form like Exhibit 13.12 will assist you in this process.

5. Keep a separate category for commissions paid on transactions and compare this with your profits on your trades. If the commissions equal or exceed your profits, you may be experiencing excessive trades or excessive commissions.

CHAPTER 14

Investing in Mutual Funds, Real Estate, and Derivative Securities

Sound investment planning involves finding investment vehicles that have risk-return characteristics that are consistent with your established financial objectives. In order to realize your full investment potential, you must complement your understanding of the basics of stocks and bonds with a knowledge of the functions and characteristics of other investment vehicles. This chapter looks beyond stocks and bonds as it considers three other investment products that enjoy widespread use among individual investors; they include mutual funds, real estate, and so-called "derivative securities" like commodities and options. Each of these investment outlets offers risk-return opportunities that you may not be able to obtain from stocks or bonds. For example, the investor who is interested in receiving the benefits of professional portfolio management but does not have the funds to purchase a diversified portfolio of securities may find mutual fund shares attractive. Or, some investors may be drawn to real estate because of its perceived return potential or perhaps because of some preferential tax treatment. And there are still other investors who are willing to take higher risks in expectation of higher returns and, as such, they may find commodities, financial futures, or options attractive. Let's now take a closer look at each of these investments, starting with mutual funds.

FINANCIAL *facts* OR *fantasies*

Are the following statements financial facts (true) or fantasies (false)?

Unlike what happened with banks and S&Ls, there's virtually no chance that you'll ever lose any money from the financial failure of a mutual fund.

Phone switching is a service that enables you to move your money from one fund to another, so long as you stay within the same family of funds.

The two principle sources of return to mutual fund investors are dividends and interest income.

A REIT (real estate investment trust) is a popular form of limited partnership that enables individuals to directly invest in income-producing property.

Commodities trading is popular with individual investors because it is so affordable, and with all the safeguards, it's relatively hard to lose a lot of money.

The two basic types of options are puts and calls. Puts give you the right to sell something, and calls give you the right to buy.

Mutual funds are a very popular form of investing — they offer an attractive level of return from a professionally managed, widely diversified portfolio of securities, as well as a variety of investor services. Today there are over 3,200 publicly traded mutual funds available — enough to meet just about any investment need you can think of. Stop for a moment to think about the different types of mutual funds that are available to investors. What kind of fund (or funds) would you be most interested in? What types of investor services would you look for in a mutual fund?

Mutual funds are popular because they offer not only a variety of interesting investment opportunities, but also a wide array of services that many investors find appealing. They provide an easy and convenient way to invest, and are especially suited to beginning investors and those with limited investment capital. A mutual fund is basically a financial services organization that receives money from its shareholders and then invests those funds for them in a diversified portfolio of securities. As such, an investment in a mutual fund represents an ownership position in a professionally managed *portfolio of securities;* when you buy shares in a mutual fund you become a part-owner of that portfolio. This concept underlies the whole mutual fund structure and is depicted in Exhibit 14.1.

THE MUTUAL FUND CONCEPT

The first mutual fund in this country was started in Boston in 1924; by 1940, there were 68 funds with $488 million in assets and nearly 300,000 shareholder accounts. That was only the beginning, however, as the growth in funds really took off in the late 1970s. Indeed, by 1992, assets under management had grown to over $1.3 *trillion*, as more than 63 *million* investors held shares in over 3,200 publicly traded funds. The fact is, we've reached the point where there are more mutual funds today than there are stocks on the NYSE!

Mutual fund investors come from all walks of life and all income levels. And they all share one common view: they've decided, for one reason or another, to turn the problems of security selection and portfolio management over to professional money managers. The fact is, questions of which stock or bond to select, when to buy, and when to sell have plagued investors for about as long as there have been organized securities markets. Such concerns lie at the very heart of the mutual fund concept and, in large part, are behind the growth in funds. A lot of people lack the time, the know-how, or the commitment to manage their own securities. As a result, they turn to others. And more often than not, that means mutual funds.

Basically, a mutual fund is a company that combines the investment capital of many people with similar investment goals and invests it in a wide variety of securities. The individual investor receives shares of stock in the mutual fund and thus is able to enjoy much wider investment diversity than could otherwise be achieved. As the securities held by the fund move up and down in price, the market value of the mutual fund shares moves accordingly. When dividend and interest payments are received by the fund, they are passed on to the mutual fund shareholders and distributed on the basis of prorated ownership. When a security held by the fund is sold for a profit, this too is passed on to fund shareholders. The whole mutual fund idea rests on the concept of pooled diversification and works in much the same way as insurance: individuals pooling their resources for the collective benefit of all contributors.

HOW MUTUAL FUNDS ARE ORGANIZED AND RUN

Although it's tempting to think of a mutual fund as a monolithic entity, that's not really accurate. Various functions — investing, recordkeeping, safekeep-

EXHIBIT 14.1

The Basic Mutual Fund Structure

A mutual fund brings together the funds from numerous individual investors and uses this pool to acquire a diversified portfolio of stocks, bonds, and other securities.

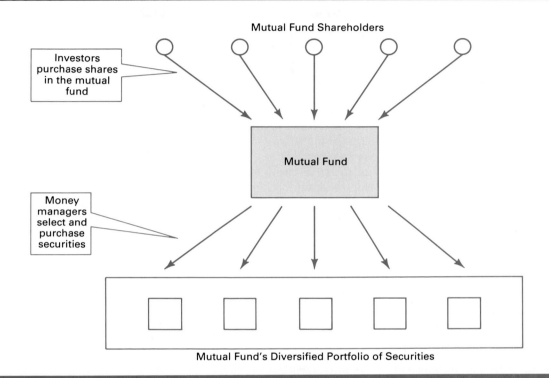

Mutual Fund Shareholders

Investors purchase shares in the mutual fund

Mutual Fund

Money managers select and purchase securities

Mutual Fund's Diversified Portfolio of Securities

ing and others—are split among two or more companies. Besides the fund itself, organized as a separate corporation or trust here are the main players:

- The **management company** runs the fund's daily operations. These are the firms we know as Fidelity, Kemper, IDS, Dreyfus, Oppenheimer, and so forth, and they are the ones that create the funds in the first place. Usually, the management firm also serves as investment adviser to their clients.

- The **investment adviser** buys and sells the stocks or bonds and otherwise oversees the portfolio. Usually, there are three parties that participate in this phase of the operation: the *money manager*, who actually runs the portfolio and makes the buy and sell decisions; *security analysts*, who analyze securities and look for viable investment candidates; and *traders*, who try to buy and sell big blocks of securities at the best possible price.
- The **distributor** sells fund shares, either directly to the public or through certain authorized dealers

Could Your Mutual Fund Go Under?

When historians look back at the 1990s, they'll remember it for traumatizing the nation's financial services industry. Savings and loans were already in trouble for fraud, mismanagement, and simply taking too many risks. The malaise also extended into the banking sector, and even some insurance companies found themselves in hot water, bogged down as they were with junk bond–laden portfolios. One domino that didn't fall, however, was the mutual fund sector. The business remains generally healthy and, more to the point, offers a different set of protections for investors. Obviously, you can lose money if your fund's stock or bond holdings decline in price. But there's little chance of loss stemming from fraud, scandal, or bankruptcy involving the management company itself. That's a key distinction. By trans-

ferring investment risk to shareholders, mutual fund companies have been able to sidestep many of the problems currently plaguing their financial cousins.

In addition, the legal structure and heavy regulation of mutual funds offer key safeguards. Many of these resulted from abuses that infected the fund industry back in the 1920s. At the time, closed-end portfolios were the rage, and managers were often guilty of self-dealing, inadequate disclosure, conflicts of interest, and other practices that are illegal today. Also, many closed-end funds were heavily leveraged. So when the market crashed in 1929, that wiped out a lot of fund shareholders and set the stage for subsequent regulation, including the Investment Company Act of 1940, which governs the fund industry today.

A regular, open-end mutual fund is a separate corporation or trust that's owned by its shareholders, not by the firm that runs it. The only formal link with the management company is through a contract that must be renewed on a regular basis. Consequently, the funds assets—stocks, bonds, and cash in the portfolio—are not kept in the drawers of the management company. Rather, *they're placed in the custody of an independent third party, typically a trust or custodial bank.* "We do not have easy access to our shareholders' money," says Charles J. Tennes, a vice president with the GIT Investment Funds in Arlington, Va. "We have authority to buy and sell securities on their behalf, but the assets are held by someone else."

As another safeguard, each fund features a board of directors or trustees, who are

(such as major brokerage houses and/or commercial banks). When you request a prospectus and sales literature, you deal with the distributor.

- The **custodian** physically safeguards the securities and other assets of a fund, without taking an active role in the investment decisions. To discourage foul play, an independent party (a bank, in most cases), serves in this capacity.
- The **transfer agent** keeps track of purchase and redemption requests from shareholders and maintains other shareholder records.

Each of these parties collects a fee for its services. However, actual ownership of a fund rests with the shareholders. With so many financial institutions wobbling and the economy hung over from a decade-long borrowing binge, one might be tempted to wonder if mutual funds are really all that safe. Well, as the accompanying *Smart Money* box reveals, because of all the safeguards, the chance of your losing any money from a mutual fund collapse is really quite low—almost nonexistent.

charged with keeping tabs on the management company and renewing its contract. If the management firm was facing bankruptcy, the directors would liquidate or merge the fund, or find another outfit to run it. According to federal regulations, at least 40 percent of a fund's board members must be independent of the management company. The directors are elected by shareholders, are paid with shareholder money, and can be sued for ignoring their fiduciary duties. At GIT, for example, the independent board members have their own securities lawyer, who attends all meetings. Many independent directors are themselves shareholders in the fund.

As further protection, the management company and other affiliated parties can't engage in certain types of transactions with a fund. For ex-

ample, the investment adviser can't dump its own stock and bond holdings by selling them to the fund. Nor can an adviser with a brokerage arm charge the fund excessive commissions for conducting trades. These conflict-of-interest provisions are often called the heart of the Investment Company Act of 1940. Bob Pozen, general counsel and managing director of Fidelity Investments in Boston, believes there are some more fundamental reasons besides these structural safeguards for explaining the lack of scandal in the industry. First, he says, funds must stand ready to redeem investor shares upon demand. That forces them to stick with assets for which there's a liquid market. Second, funds must value their holdings every day, a process known as *marking-to-market*. "I feel one of the big problems with insurance com-

panies is that they didn't mark-to-market their assets daily. They were able to go a long time before anybody realized they had a problem," Pozen says. "You can't do that with mutual funds. You know the problems immediately."

In 50 years and $1 trillion in fund assets, there has not been a major crisis or scandal like what has happened in other parts of the financial services industry. Tight regulations and structural firewalls have helped, as has the fact that shareholders bear the investment risks. The best thing you can say about mutual funds is that the federal government never promised to bail them out.

Source: Adopted from Russ Wiles, "Checks and Balances: How Funds Are Organized," *Personal Investor*, September 1991, pp. 28–30.

Unlike what happened with banks and S&Ls, there's virtually no chance that you'll ever lose any money from the financial failure of a mutual fund.

Fact: With all the safeguards in place, there's really very little chance of mutual funds collapsing like banks and S&Ls did in the 1980s; even so, while you don't have to worry about being defrauded (for one thing, mutual funds never take possession of the securities in their portfolios), that doesn't mean you can't lose money by purchasing a fund that does poorly in the market.

OPEN-END VERSUS CLOSED-END

While all mutual funds may be organized in pretty much the same way, there are some major differences that investors should be aware of. One way that funds differ is with respect to how they are structured. That is, funds can be set up either as *open-end companies*, which can sell an unlimited number of ownership shares, or as *closed-end companies*, which can issue only a limited number.

	NAV	Offer Price	NAV Chg.	
Fidelity Selects:				
SlChe r	30.14	31.07	+.12	
SlCmp r	17.16	17.69	+.20	← A load fund with a redemption fee (r)
SlDef r	14.71	15.16	+.08	
SlElec r	11.35	11.70	+.15	
SlEUt r	12.95	13.35	+.03	
SlEng r	15.06	15.53	+.08	
SlEnS r	9.36	9.65	−.11	
SlFnv r	11.99	12.36	+.13	
SlFnS r	37.04	38.19	+.09	
SlFd r	30.87	31.82	+.14	
SlHlth r	86.73	89.41	+.95	
SlInd r	15.12	15.59	+.06	
SlIns r	18.28	18.85	+.13	
SlLesr r	30.18	31.11	+.19	
Financial Funds:				
Dvnm p	10.60	NL	+.17	
USGvt p	7.60	NL	...	
Enrgy	10.46	NL	+.03	
Envirn	9.45	NL	+.19	
Eqty	16.64	NL	+.15	
Europ	11.45	NL	−.04	← A true no-load fund
Flex	16.50	NL	+.07	
IntGov	12.85	NL	−.02	
IntlGr	14.50	NL	...	
Util	10.64	NL	+.04	
TxFre p	15.81	NL	...	
Gold	4.22	NL	...	
HlthSc	45.31	NL	+.39	
HIYld p	6.71	NL	+.04	← A no-load fund that charges a 12(b)-1 fee (p)
Indust p	5.61	NL	+.03	
Indinc p	11.68	NL	+.02	
Leisur	15.98	NL	+.14	
PcBas	12.76	NL	−.01	
Selinc p	6.51	NL	+.02	
Tech	19.90	NL	+.15	
FTAMEq	12.27	12.88	+.04	
FtBosIG	10.21	10.47	−.02	
FstEag r	11.75	11.75	−.01	
FtHawMu	10.62	10.62	...	
Fst Investors:				
BlChp p x	14.54q	15.62	−.04	
Global p	5.40	5.80	−.02	
Govt p	11.85	12.73	−.03	
HighY p	4.61	4.95	+.02	
Inco p	3.70	3.97	+.01	
InvGr p	9.89	10.62	...	← A load fund that also charges a 12(b)-1 fee (p)
NJTF p	12.29	13.20	...	
NYTF p	14.36	15.42	+.01	
SpcBd	11.08	11.95	+.02	
Fortress Invst:				
AdjRt t	10.02	10.02	...	
GlSl r	9.60	9.70	...	
HiQal t	15.57	15.73	+.07	← A fund with a little of everything: a front-end load, back load, and 12(b)-1 fee (t)
Munin t	10.56	10.67	+.01	
TP US r	10.42	10.53	−.02	
Util r	11.93	12.05	+.02	
44 WlEq	6.28	6.28	+.06	
44Wall	2.47	2.47	+.03	
FPA Funds:				
Capit	16.67	17.83	+.18	
NwInc	10.35	10.84	+.01	
Parmt	12.76	13.65	+.10	← A load fund – has a 6.5% front-end load
Peren	21.49	22.98	+.11	
Fairmt	17.20	NL	+.30	

Labels on the left:
- Fidelity Select – Computers → SlCmp r
- Financial Europe → Europ
- Financial High Yield → HIYld p
- First Investors Investment Growth → InvGr p
- Fortress High-Quality Stocks → HiQal t
- FPA Paramount → Parmt

Source: *The Wall Street Journal,* January 6, 1992.

Open-End Investment Companies. The term *mutual fund* is commonly used to denote an open-end investment company. Such organizations are the dominant type of investment company and account for over 90 percent of assets under management. In an **open-end investment company**, investors actually buy their shares from, and sell them back to, the mutual fund itself. When they buy shares in the fund, the fund issues new shares of stock and fills the purchase order with these new shares. There is no limit to the number of shares the fund can issue, other than investor demand. Further, all open-end mutual funds stand behind their shares and buy them back when investors decide to sell. Thus, there is never any trading among individuals.

Both buy and sell transactions in a mutual fund are carried out at prices based on the current value of all the securities held in the fund's portfolio. This is known as the fund's **net asset value (NAV)**; it is calculated at least once a day and represents the underlying value of a share of stock in a particular fund. NAV is found by taking the total market value of all securities held by the fund, subtracting any liabilities, and dividing the result by the number of shares outstanding. For example, if on a given day the market value of all the securities held by the XYZ mutual fund equaled some $10 million, and if XYZ on that day had 500,000 shares outstanding, the fund's net asset value per share would amount to $20 ($10,000,000/500,000 = $20). This figure would then be used to derive the price at which the fund shares could be bought and sold.

Net asset value is included in the fund's quoted price and indicates the price at which an investor can *sell* shares. Consider, for example, *The Wall Street Journal* mutual fund quotations as shown on the opposite page:

The first price column is labeled "NAV." For example, Fidelity Select—Computers has a NAV of $17.16 and an offer price of $17.69; that means the investor can *buy* shares in the fund at an offer price of $17.69 a share or *sell* them at the NAV price of $17.16. The "NAV Chg." column shows the change in the price of the fund; in the case of Fidelity Select—Computers, the NAV went up 20 cents from the day before.

Closed-End Investment Companies. While the term *mutual fund* is supposed to be used only with open-end funds, it is, as a practical matter, regularly used with closed-end investment companies as well. Basically, **closed-end investment companies** operate with a fixed number of shares outstanding and do not regularly issue new ones. In effect, they have a capital structure like any other corporation, except that the corporation's business happens to be that of investing in marketable securities. Closed-end investment company shares are actively traded in the secondary market, just like any other common stock. Most are traded on the New York Stock Exchange, several are on the American Exchange, and a few are traded in the OTC market. Some of the largest closed-end investment companies include Adams Express, ASA Ltd., General American Investors, Korea Fund, and Niagara Share Corporation, all of which are actively traded on the NYSE.

The share prices of closed-end companies are determined not only by their net asset values but also by general supply and demand conditions in the market. As a result, closed-end companies generally trade at a discount or premium to NAV. For example, a fund with a net asset value of $10 per share would be selling at a *discount* of $1 if it were trading at $9

---

open-end investment company
A company that can issue an unlimited number of shares which it buys and sells at a price based on the current value of the securities it owns; also called a *mutual fund.*

net asset value (NAV)
The price at which a mutual fund will buy back its own shares; NAV represents the current market value of all the securities the fund owns.

closed-end investment company
An investment company that issues a fixed number of shares, which are themselves listed and traded on an organized securities exchange or in the OTC market.

and at a *premium* of $1 if it were quoted at a price of $11. Share price discounts can become quite large at times — for example, it is not unusual for discounts to amount to as much as 25 to 30 percent of net asset value. In contrast, price premiums occur less often and seldom exceed 10 to 15 percent.

SOME IMPORTANT COST CONSIDERATIONS

When you buy or sell shares in a closed-end investment company, you pay a commission just as you would with other listed or OTC common stock transaction. This is not so with open-end funds, however. In particular, the cost of investing in an open-end mutual fund depends on the types of fees and load charges that a fund levies on its investors.

Load Funds. Most open-end mutual funds are so-called **load funds**, since they charge a commission when the shares are purchased. Load charges can be fairly substantial, often ranging from 6½ to 8½ percent of the *purchase* price of the shares. Normally there is no charge when you sell your shares. It is easy to find the amount of the load charge — it is part of the price quotation system and is found by taking the difference between the fund's offer price and its NAV. For example, refer back to the quote for the Fidelity Select — Computer fund. The difference between its offer price ($17.69) and NAV ($17.16) represents its load charge of 53 cents a share and is the commission you would pay for each share of Fidelity Select — Computers you bought.

Compared to what it costs to buy and sell common stock, the costs of many load funds are pretty steep, even after taking into account the fact that you normally pay no commission on the sale of most funds! Since 1975, the *maximum* load charge has been set at 8½ percent of the purchase price. However, most mutual funds offer quantity discounts to investors who buy in large blocks (usually 1,000 or more shares). In addition a growing number of so-called **low-load funds** like Fidelity Select — Computers charge commissions of only 1 to 3 percent; on the other hand, there's also an increasing number of **back-end load funds**, which charge a commission — or a so-called *redemption fee* — when you *sell* your shares.

No-Load Funds. Some open-end investment companies charge you nothing to buy their funds; these are known as **no-load funds**. It is easy to spot no-loads — just look for the letters "N.L." under the "Offer Price" column in mutual fund price quotes. For example, the Financial Funds shown in our illustrative quotes on page 594 are no-load funds. This means that the Financial Europe Fund can be bought and sold at its NAV price of $11.45 a share. Actually, there are relatively few pure no-loads left today, charging nothing to buy, sell, or hold their funds! For example, there's nothing to prevent a so-called no-load fund from charging a back-end load when you sell your fund shares; and there are a lot of no-loads that charge something called a 12(b)-1 fee for as long as you hold your shares — see, for example, the Financial High Yield fund.

12(b)-1 Fees. Also known as *hidden loads,* **12(b)-1 fees** have been allowed by the SEC since 1980, and were originally designed to help no-load funds cover their distribution and marketing expenses. Not surprisingly, their popularity spread rapidly among fund distributors, so that they are now used by around 40 percent of all open-end mutual funds. The fees are assessed annually and can amount to as much as 1¼ percent of assets under management. In good markets and bad, they're paid, right off the top. And that can take its toll. Consider, for instance, $10,000 in a fund that charges a 1¼ percent 12(b)-1 fee. That translates into an annual charge of $125, which means $125 a year *less* for you!

Management Fees. The **management fee** is the cost you incur to hire the professional money managers to run the fund's portfolio of investments. These fees are also assessed annually and usually run from about .5 percent to 2 percent of assets under management. All funds — whether they're load or no-load, open- or closed-end — have these fees; and like 12(b)-1 fees, they bear watching, since high management fees will take their toll on performance. As a rule, the size of the management fee is totally unrelated to the performance of the fund — you'll pay the same amount whether it's been a winning year or a real loser.

Keeping Track of Fund Fees and Loads.

Critics of the mutual fund industry have come down hard on the proliferation of fund fees and charges. Indeed, some would argue that all the different kinds of charges and fees are really meant to do one thing—confuse the investor. The fact is, a lot of funds were going to great lengths to make themselves look like something they weren't—they lowered a cost here, but tacked on a fee there and hid a charge somewhere else. These funds all followed the letter of the law in that they did indeed fully disclose all their expenses and fees. Trouble was, the funds were able to neatly hide all but the most conspicuous of their charges in a bunch of legalese. Fortunately, all this is beginning to change as steps are being taken to bring fund fees and loads out into the open.

For one thing, these charges are more fully reported by the financial press. You don't have to look any farther than the mutual fund quotations found in *The Wall Street Journal* and most other major papers. For example, refer back to the quotations on page 594; notice the use of the letters "r," "p," and "t." If you see an "r" behind a fund's name, it means the fund charges some type of *redemption fee* when you sell your shares (this is the case, for example, with Fidelity Select—Computers); use of a "p," in contrast, means the fund levies a *12(b)-1 charge* (which you'll have to pay if you invest in Financial High Yield or First Investors Investment Growth); finally, a "t" will appear with funds that charge both redemption fees and 12(b)-1 fees (notice that's what you get with Fortress Investment's High-Quality Stocks). If you look closely at the quotation, you'll see that Fortress High-Quality not only levies redemption and 12(b)-1 fees, *it also has a front-end load*—as indicated by the difference in its NAV and offer price. The point is: Don't be surprised to find *load* funds that also charge redemption and/or 12(b)-1 fees, and the same goes for no-load funds.

The quotations, of course, only tell you what kinds of fees are charged by the funds; they don't tell you how much is charged. To get the specifics on the amount charged, you'll have to turn to the fund itself. All (open-end) mutual funds are required by the SEC to fully disclose all their expenses in a standardized, easy-to-understand format. Every fund prospectus must contain, right up front, a fairly detailed *fee table;* much like the one illustrated in Ex-

hibit 14.2. Notice that this table has three parts. The first section specifies all *shareholder transaction expenses*. In effect, this tells you what it's going to cost to buy and sell shares in the mutual fund. The next section lists all the *annual operating expenses* of the fund. Showing these expenses as a percentage of average net assets, the fund must break out management fees, those elusive 12(b)-1 fees, and any other expenses. The third section provides a complete rundown of the *total cost over time* of buying, selling, and owning the fund. This part of the table contains both transaction and operating expenses, and it shows what the total costs would be over hypothetical 1-, 3-, 5-, and 10-year holding periods. To assure consistency and comparability, the funds have to follow a rigid set of guidelines when constructing the illustrative costs.

It's obviously in your best interest to pay close attention to the fee table whenever you're considering

---

load fund
A mutual fund on which a transaction cost (associated with the purchase of shares) is levied.

low-load fund
A mutual fund in which commissions charged on purchases of shares range between only 1 and 3 percent of the purchase price.

back-end load fund
A commission charged for redeeming mutual fund shares.

no-load fund
A mutual fund on which no transaction fees are charged.

12(b)-1 fee
A type of fee that's charged annually and which is supposed to be used to offset the promotion and selling expenses of a mutual fund; known as a *hidden load* because it's often used by funds as an indirect way of charging commissions.

management fee
A fee paid to the professionals who administer a mutual fund's portfolio.

an investment in a mutual fund. Other things being equal, look for low initial charges as well as low expense ratios over time. As a rule, the longer you intend to hold a fund, the more willing you should be to trade a higher load charge for lower annual management and 12(b)-1 fees. That will help keep your total holding period costs down. In the final analysis, keep in mind that costs are only one element in the decision. Another very important variable is *performance*. There may be times when higher costs are justified; there may be other times when they're not. Provided below are two guidelines you might want to follow:

- Consider a *more expensive* fund if it has a better performance record (and offers more return potential) than a less expensive fund—it's all a matter of whether you'd rather own a costly performer or a low-cost dog!
- If there's little or no difference in performance records or return potential, go with the *less expensive* fund. In this case, lower expenses will make a difference in comparative returns.

BUYING AND SELLING FUNDS

Buying and selling shares of *closed-end investment companies* is no different from buying shares of common stock. The transactions are executed on listed exchanges or in the OTC market through brokers or dealers who handle the orders in the usual way. They are subject to the normal transaction costs; and because they are treated like any other listed or OTC stock, their shares can even be margined or sold short. The situation is considerably different, however, with *open-end funds*. There are several ways of acquiring such shares, depending on whether the fund is load or no-load. Regardless of type, however, the fund should provide you with a recent prospectus that explains its operations and other pertinent financial matters. Unfortunately, the prospectuses put out by a lot of mutual funds today are not as extensive as they used to be and in many cases, are little more than warmed over sales pitches. So be careful when using such information. Instead of, or in addition to, the fund's prospectus, ask for a copy of its *Statement of Additional Information*, which provides detailed information on the fund's investment objectives, portfolio composition, management, and past performance. Whether it's

the prospectus or the fund's Statement of Additional Information, the bottom line is these publications should be required reading for anybody who's thinking about investing in a mutual fund!

In the case of load funds, investors buy the stocks from a broker or through salespeople employed by the funds—not surprisingly, many of these funds carry the full 8½ percent load charge, or something very close to it. Most brokerage firms are authorized to sell shares in a variety of load funds, and this is the easiest and most convenient way of buying funds for investors who have established brokerage accounts. Sometimes, however, the fund may not be sold through brokerage houses, in which case the investor would deal directly with its commissioned salespeople—individuals who are employed by the mutual fund for the sole purpose of selling its shares. If you happen to be interested in a no-load, or perhaps even a low-load fund, you may be pretty much on your own. You'll have to write or call the mutual fund directly in order to obtain information. You will then receive an order form and instructions on how to buy shares; no salesperson will ever call on you. To complete the transaction, you simply mail your check, along with the completed order form, to the mutual fund or its designated agent. Before you go through all that, however, check with your bank; if it's a major (good-sized) commercial bank, it may be authorized to sell a wide variety of mutual funds. Indeed, during the last five years or so, a lot of big mutual funds have made arrangements to sell their products through major banking and other financial institutions around the country—and at no added cost to you. Thus, you may be able to find just the fund you're looking for right in your local bank.

Selling shares in a fund is also a do-it-yourself affair, whether the fund is load or no-load. Because brokers and salespeople usually don't make anything on fund *sales*, they have little motivation to execute sell orders. As a result, you may find you'll have to redeem your fund shares by directly notifying the mutual fund (by mail) of your intention to sell. The fund then buys the shares back and mails you a check. But before selling your fund shares this way, check to see if the fund offers *phone switching*. This service is available from a number of investment companies, and it enables you to simply pick up the phone to move money from one fund to another—the only constraint is that the funds must be managed by the same investment company. Most

EXHIBIT 14.2

Mutual Fund Expense Disclosure Table

Mutual funds are now required by the SEC to make full disclosure of load charges, redemption fees, and annual expenses in a three-part table like the one shown here; and the table must be conspicuously placed in the front part of the prospectus, not hidden somewhere in the back.

Expenses and Cost of Investing in the Fund

The following information is provided in order to assist investors in understanding the transaction costs and annual expenses associated with investing in the Fund.

A. Shareholder Transaction Costs:

Sales Load on Purchases 2%
Sales Load on Reinvested Dividends......................... None
Redemption Fees or Deferred Sales Charges .... None
Exchange (or Conversion Fees)............................. None

B. Annual Fund Operating Expenses:
(as a percentage of average net assets)

Management Fees 0.40%
12(b)-1 Fees.. None
Other Expenses (estimated)............................... 0.32%

C. Example of Fund Expenses Over Time:

You would pay the following total expenses over time on a $1,000 investment, assuming a 5% annual return, and a complete redemption of the investment at the end of each indicated time period:

1-year	3-years	5-years	10-years
$27	$43	$59	$108

Source: The prospectus of a major mutual fund.

---

companies charge little or nothing for these shifts, although funds that offer free exchange privileges often place a limit on the number of times you can switch each year. (We'll discuss this service in more detail later in the chapter when we cover *conversion privileges.*)

TYPES OF FUNDS

Some mutual funds specialize in stocks and others in bonds; some funds have maximum capital gains as their investment objective, and some seek high income. Some funds thus will appeal to speculators and others primarily to income-oriented investors. Every fund has a particular investment objective, some of the more common ones being capital appreciation, income, tax-exempt income, preservation of investment capital, or a combination thereof. Disclosure of a fund's investment objective is required by the SEC, and each fund is expected to do its best to conform to its stated investment policy and objective. Categorizing funds according to their investment policies and objectives is widely practiced in the mutual fund industry, as it tends to reflect similarities not only in how the funds manage their money, but also in their risk and return characteristics. Some of the more popular types of mutual funds include growth, maximum capital gains, equity-income, balanced, growth-and-income, bond, money market, sector, socially responsible, and international funds.

Growth Funds. The objective of a *growth fund* is simple—capital appreciation. Long-term growth and capital gains are the primary goals of such funds, and as a result they invest principally in common stocks that have above-average growth potential. Because of the uncertain nature of their investment income, growth funds are believed to involve a fair amount of risk exposure. They are usually viewed as long-term investment vehicles that are most suitable for the more aggressive investor who wants to build capital and has little interest in current income.

Maximum Capital Gains Funds. These are the so-called *performance*, or *aggressive growth funds* that tend to increase in popularity when the markets heat up. They are highly speculative funds that seek large profits from capital gains; in many respects, they are really an extension of the growth fund concept. Many are fairly small with portfolios consisting mainly of high-flying common stocks. These aggressive growth funds often buy stocks of small, unseasoned companies, stocks with relatively high price/earnings multiples, and stocks whose prices are highly volatile. Some of these funds even go so far as to use leverage in their portfolios (that is, they buy stocks on margin by borrowing part of the purchase price). All this is designed, of course, to yield big returns. However, maximum capital gains funds are also highly speculative and are perhaps the most volatile of all the fund types. When the markets are good, these funds do well; when the markets are bad, they typically experience substantial losses.

Equity-Income Funds. *Equity-income funds* emphasize current income, which they provide by investing primarily in high-yielding common stocks. Capital preservation is also a goal of these funds, and so is some amount of capital gains, although capital appreciation is not their primary objective. They invest heavily in high-grade common stocks, some convertible securities and preferred stocks, and occasionally even junk bonds or certain types of high-grade foreign bonds. They like securities that generate hefty dividend yields, but also consider potential price appreciation over the longer haul. In general, because of their emphasis on dividends and current income, these funds tend to hold higher-quality securities that are subject to less price volatility than the market as a whole. They're generally viewed as a fairly low-risk way of investing in stocks.

Balanced Funds. *Balanced funds* are so named because they tend to hold a balanced portfolio of both stocks and bonds, and they do so for the purpose of generating a well-balanced return of both current income and long-term capital gains. In many respects, they're a lot like equity-income funds, except that balanced funds usually put much more into fixed-income securities; generally they keep at least 25 percent to 50 percent of their portfolios in bonds, and sometimes more. The bonds are used principally to provide current income, and stocks are selected mainly for their long-term growth potential. The funds can, of course, shift the emphasis in their security holdings one way or the other. Clearly, the more the fund leans toward fixed-income securities, the more income-oriented it will be. For the most part, balanced funds tend to confine their investing to high-grade securities. As such, they're usually considered to be a relatively safe form of investing, one where you can earn a competitive rate of return without having to endure a lot of price volatility.

Growth-and-Income Funds. Like balanced funds, *growth-and-income funds* also seek a balanced return made up of both current income and long-term capital gains, but they place a greater emphasis on growth of capital. Moreover, unlike balanced funds, growth-and-income funds put most of their money into equities—indeed, it's not unusual for these funds to have 80 percent to 90 percent of their capital in common stocks. They tend to confine most of their investing to high-quality issues, so you can expect to find a lot of growth-oriented blue-chip stocks in their portfolios, along with a fair amount of high-quality income stocks. One of the big appeals of these funds is the fairly substantial returns many of them have been able to generate over the long haul. But then, these funds do involve a fair amount of risk, if for no other reason than the emphasis they place on stocks and capital gains. Consequently, growth-and-income funds are most suitable for those investors who can tolerate their risk and price volatility.

Bond Funds. As their name implies, *bond funds* invest exclusively in various kinds and grades of bonds. Income is their primary investment objective, although they do not ignore capital gains. There are three important advantages to buying shares in bond funds rather than investing directly in bonds. First, bond funds generally are more liquid; second, they offer a cost-effective way of achieving a high degree of diversification in an otherwise expensive investment vehicle (most bonds carry minimum denominations of $1,000 to $5,000, or more); and third, bond funds will automatically reinvest interest and other income, thereby allowing the investor to earn fully compounded rates of return.

Although bond funds are usually considered to be a fairly conservative form of investment, they are not totally without risk, since the prices of the bonds held in the funds' portfolios will fluctuate with changing interest rates. Though many of the funds are basically conservative, a growing number are becoming increasingly aggressive—in fact, much of the growth that bond funds have experienced recently can be attributed to this new investment attitude. No matter what your tastes, you'll find there's a full menu of bond funds available, including:

■ *Government bond funds*, which invest in U.S. Treasury and agency securities.
■ *Mortgage-backed bond funds*, which put their money mostly into various types of mortgage-backed securities of the U.S. government (like GNMA issues).
■ *High-grade corporate bond funds*, which invest chiefly in investment-grade securities rated triple-B or better.
■ *High-yield corporate bond funds*, which are risky investments that buy *junk bonds* for the yields they offer.
■ *Municipal bond funds*, which invest in tax-exempt securities, and which are suitable for investors looking for tax-free income. Like their corporate counterparts, municipals can also come out as either high-grade or high-yield funds. A special type of municipal bond fund is the so-called *single-state* fund, which invests in the municipal issues of only one state, thus producing (for residents of that state) interest income that is *fully* exempt from not only federal taxes, but state (and possibly even local/city) taxes as well.
■ *Intermediate-term bond funds*, which invest in bonds with maturities of seven to ten years, or less, and offer not only attractive yields but relatively low price volatility as well; the shorter (two to five year) intermediate-term funds are also used as substitutes for money market investments by investors looking for higher returns on their money, especially when short-term rates are way down (like they were in 1991–1992).

Money Market Mutual Funds. From the introduction of the very first *money fund* in 1972, the concept of investing in a portfolio of short-term money market instruments caught on like wildfire. There actually are several different kinds of money market mutual funds. **General-purpose money funds** essentially invest in any and all types of money market investment vehicles, from Treasury bills to corporate commercial paper and bank certificates of deposit. They invest their money wherever they can find attractive short-term returns. The vast majority of money funds are of this type. The **tax-exempt money fund** limits its investments to tax-exempt municipal securities with very short (30- to 90-day) maturities. Since their income is free from federal income tax, they appeal predominantly to investors in high tax brackets. **Government securities money funds** were established as a way of meeting investors' concern for safety. In essence, these funds eliminate any risk of default by confining their investments to Treasury bills and other short-term securities of the U.S. government or its agencies (such as the Federal National Mortgage Association).

Money funds are highly liquid investment vehicles and are very low in risk, since they are virtually immune to capital loss. However, the interest income they produce tends to follow interest rate conditions, and as such, the returns to shareholders are subject to the ups and downs of market interest rates. (Money funds were discussed more fully in Chapter 5, along with other short-term investment vehicles.)

Sector Funds. One of the hottest products on Wall Street is the so-called *sector fund*—a mutual fund that restricts its investments to a particular sector of the market. In effect, these funds concentrate their investment holdings in the one or more industries that make up the targeted sector. For example,

---

general-purpose money fund
A money market mutual fund that invests in virtually any type of short-term investment vehicle, so long as it offers an attractive rate of return.

tax-exempt money fund
A money market mutual fund that limits investments to tax-exempt municipal securities with short maturities.

government securities money fund
A money market mutual fund that limits its investments to short-term securities of the U.S. government and its agencies, thus eliminating any default risk.

a *health care* sector fund would confine its investments to those industries that make up this segment of the market: drug companies, hospital management firms, medical suppliers, and biotech concerns. Its portfolio would then consist of promising growth stocks from these industries. The underlying investment objective of sector funds is *capital gains*. In many respects, they are similar to growth funds and thus should be considered speculative in nature.

The idea behind the sector fund concept is that the really attractive returns come from small segments of the market. Thus, rather than diversifying the portfolio across wide segments of the market, you should put your money where the action is. This notion may warrant consideration by the more aggressive investor who is willing to take on the added risks that often accompany these funds. Among the more popular sector funds are those that concentrate their investments in the so-called "glamour" industries: energy, financial services, gold and precious metals, leisure and entertainment, natural resources, electronics, chemicals, computers, telecommunications, utilities, and health care.

Socially Responsible Funds. For some, investing is far more than just cranking out some financial ratios. To these investors, the security selection process doesn't end with bottom lines, P/E ratios, growth rates, and betas; rather, it also includes the *active, explicit consideration of moral, ethical, and environmental issues*. The idea is that social concerns should play just as big a role in the investment decision as profits and other financial matters. Not surprisingly, there are a number of funds today that cater to such investors; known as **socially responsible funds**, they actively and directly incorporate morality and ethics into the investment decision. These funds will only consider socially responsible companies for inclusion in their portfolios — if a company doesn't meet certain moral, ethical, and/or environmental tests, they simply won't consider buying the stock, no matter how good the bottom line looks. Generally speaking, these funds abstain from investing in companies that derive revenues from tobacco, alcohol, or gambling; have dealings with South Africa; are weapons contractors; or operate nuclear power plants. In addition, the funds tend to favor firms that produce "responsible" products and/or services, have strong employee relations, have positive environmental records, and are socially responsive to the communities in which they operate. While these screens may seem to eliminate a lot of stocks from consideration, these funds (most of which are fairly small) still have plenty of securities to choose from, so it's not all that difficult for them to keep their portfolios fully invested. As far as performance is concerned, the general perception is that there's a price to pay for socially responsible investing in the form of lower average returns. That's not too surprising, however, for as you add more investment hurdles or screens, you're likely to reduce return potential. But for those who truly believe in socially responsible investing, perhaps they are willing to put their money where their mouths are!

International Funds. In their search for higher yields and better returns, American investors have shown a growing interest in foreign securities. Sensing an opportunity, the mutual fund industry was quick to respond with a proliferation of so-called **international funds** — a type of mutual fund that does all or most of its investing in foreign securities. Just look at the number of international funds around today versus a few years ago. In 1985, there were only about 40 of these funds; by 1992, that number had grown to over 200! The fact is, a lot of people would like to invest in foreign securities but simply don't have the experience or know-how to do so. International funds may be just the vehicle for such investors, *provided they have at least a basic appreciation of international economics*. Since these funds deal with the international economy, balance of trade positions, and currency valuations, investors should have a fundamental understanding of what these issues are and how they can affect fund returns.

Technically, the term *international fund* is used to describe a type of fund that *invests exclusively in foreign securities*, often confining their activities to specific geographical regions (like Mexico, Australia, Europe, or the Pacific Rim). In addition, there's a special class of international funds, known as *global funds*, which invest not only in foreign securities, *but also in U.S. companies* — usually multinational firms. As a rule, global funds provide more diversity and, with access to both foreign and domestic markets, can go where the action is. Regardless of whether they're global or international (from here on out, we'll use the term "international" to apply to both), you'll fund just about any type of fund you could possibly want in the international sector. There are international *stock* funds, international *bond* funds, even international *money market* funds; in addition, there are aggressive growth funds, balanced funds, long-term growth funds, high-grade bond funds, and so forth. Thus, no matter what your investment philosophy or objective, you're likely to find what you're looking for in the international area.

Basically, these funds attempt to take advantage of international economic developments in two ways: (1) by capitalizing on changing foreign market conditions, and (2) by positioning themselves to benefit from devaluation of the dollar. They do so because they can make money not only from rising share prices in a foreign market, but, perhaps just as important, from a falling dollar (which, in itself, produces capital gains to American investors in foreign securities and/or international funds). Many of these funds, however, will attempt to protect their investors from currency exchange risks by using various types of *hedging strategies*. That is, by using foreign currency options and futures (or some other type of derivative product), the fund will try to eliminate (or reduce) the effects of currency exchange rates. Some funds, in fact, do this on a permanent basis — in essence, these funds hedge away exchange risk so they can concentrate on the higher returns that the foreign securities themselves offer. Most others are only occasional users of currency hedges and will employ them only if they feel there's a real chance of a substantial swing in currency values. But even with currency hedging, international funds are still considered to be fairly high-risk investments and should only be used by investors who understand and are able to tolerate such risks.

WHY INVEST IN MUTUAL FUNDS?

Mutual funds can be used by individual investors in a variety of ways. For instance, growth funds can serve as vehicles for capital appreciation, whereas bond funds may be used to provide current income. Regardless of the kind of income a fund provides, individuals tend to use these investment vehicles for one or more of the following reasons: (1) to achieve diversification in their investment holdings; (2) to

obtain the services of professional money managers; (3) to generate an attractive rate of return on their investment capital; and (4) for the convenience they offer.

Diversification. The primary motive for investing in mutual funds is the *ability to diversify* and diminish risk by indirectly investing in a number of different types of securities and/or companies. If you have only $500 to $1,000 to invest, you obviously will not achieve much diversification on your own. However, if you invest that money in a mutual fund, you will end up owning part of a diversified portfolio made up perhaps of 100 or more securities.

Professional Management. Another major appeal of a mutual fund is the professional management it offers. Of course, management is paid a fee from the fund's earnings, but the contributions of a full-time expert manager should be well worth the cost. These pros know where to look for return, and how to avoid unnecessary risk; their decisions should result in better returns than the average investor can achieve.

Financial Returns. While professional managers *may* be able to achieve returns that are better than what small investors can generate, the relatively high purchase fees, coupled with the management and operating costs, tend to reduce the returns actually earned on mutual fund investments. However, the mutual fund industry has not attracted millions of investors because of the substandard returns they generate! Quite the contrary; over the long haul, mutual funds have been able to provide relatively attractive returns. Look at Exhibit 14.3. It shows the average return performance on a variety of different

---

socially responsible fund
A type of mutual fund that puts social concerns on the same level of importance as financial returns, investing only in companies that meet certain moral, ethical, and/or environmental tests.

international fund
A mutual fund that does all or most of its investing in foreign securities; also includes *global funds*, a special type of international fund.

types of mutual funds and is indicative of the kind of return investors were able to achieve during the ten-year period through April 1992. With such return potential, it's easy to see why investors are so anxious to put their money into mutual funds — in many cases, it's probably safe to say that these returns are better than what individual investors could have done on their own.

Convenience. The fact that mutual fund shares can be purchased through a variety of sources is still another reason for their appeal. Mutual funds make it easy to invest, and most do not require a great deal of capital to get started. They are relatively easy to acquire, they handle all the paperwork and recordkeeping, their prices are widely quoted, and it is usually possible to deal in fractional shares. Opening a mutual fund account is nearly as easy as opening a checking account. Just fill in a few blank spaces, send in the minimum amount of money, and you will be in business!

SERVICES OFFERED BY MUTUAL FUNDS

Many people are drawn to mutual funds because of their attractive returns. However, there are other reasons to invest in them, including their automatic investment and reinvestment plans, regular income programs, conversion privileges, and retirement plans. These are all examples of *mutual fund services* that many investors consider valuable — and, in fact, are sometimes the primary reasons for buying these funds.

Automatic Investment Plans. It takes money to make money, and for an investor that means being able to accumulate the capital to put into the market. Unfortunately, that's not always the easiest thing in the world to do. Enter mutual funds, which have come up with a program that makes savings and capital accumulation as painless as possible. The program is the **automatic investment plan** that allows fund shareholders to automatically funnel fixed amounts of money *from their paychecks or bank accounts* into a mutual fund. It's very much like a payroll deduction plan that treats savings a lot like insurance coverage — that is, just as insurance premiums are automatically deducted from your paycheck (or bank account), so too are investments

to your mutual fund. This fund service has become very popular in the past five to ten years, as it allows shareholders to invest without having to think about it. Just about every major fund group offers some kind of automatic investment plan. To enroll, a shareholder simply fills out a form authorizing the fund to siphon a set amount (usually it has to be a minimum of $25 to $100 per period) from your bank account or paycheck at regular intervals — typically monthly or quarterly. Once enrolled, you'll be buying more shares in the fund(s) of your choice every month or quarter (most funds deal in fractional shares); of course, if it's a load fund, you'll still have to pay normal sales charges on your periodic investments. To remain diversified, you can divide your money to as many funds (within a given fund family) as you like; and you can get out of the program anytime you like, without penalty, by simply calling the fund. Although convenience is perhaps the plans' chief advantage, they also make solid investment sense, as one of the best ways of building up a sizable amount of capital is to systematically add funds to your investment program over time. The importance of making regular contributions to your investment program cannot be overstated: it ranks right up there with compound interest!

Automatic Reinvestment Plans. This is one of the real draws of mutual funds, and it's a service that's offered by just about every open-ended mutual fund. Whereas automatic investment plans deal with money shareholders are putting into a fund, automatic *RE*investment plans deal with the disposition of dividends and other distributions that the funds pay to their shareholders. Much like the dividend reinvestment plans we looked at with stocks, the **automatic reinvestment plans** of mutual funds enable you to keep all your capital fully employed. Through this service, dividend and/or capital gains income is *automatically used to buy additional shares in the fund*. Keep in mind, however, that even though you reinvest your dividends and capital gains, the IRS still treats them as cash receipts and taxes them in the year in which they are paid. The funds deal in fractional shares, and these purchases are often commission-free.

The important point is that by plowing back profits (reinvested dividends and capital gains distributions), the investor essentially can put his or her profits to work in generating even more earnings.

EXHIBIT 14.3

The Comparative Performance of Mutual Funds (for the ten-year period through April 1992)

The type of fund you invest in has a lot to do with the kind of return you can expect. For example, had you put $10,000 in a typical equity-income fund in 1982, that investment would have grown to more than $40,000 by 1992; in contrast, if you had invested that same amount of money in a taxable bond fund, it would have been worth some $31,589 in 1992.

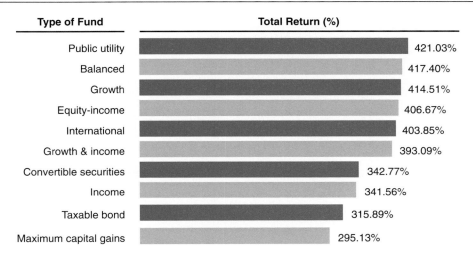

Type of Fund	Total Return (%)
Public utility	421.03%
Balanced	417.40%
Growth	414.51%
Equity-income	406.67%
International	403.85%
Growth & income	393.09%
Convertible securities	342.77%
Income	341.56%
Taxable bond	315.89%
Maximum capital gains	295.13%

*Assumes reinvestment of all dividends and capital gains distributions.
Source: Morningstar's *Mutual Fund Performance Report*, May 1992.

Indeed, the effects of these plans on total accumulated capital over the long haul can be substantial. Exhibit 14.4 shows the long-term impact of one such plan. (These are the actual performance numbers for a *real* mutual fund—the Vanguard Windsor Fund.) In the illustration, we assume the investor starts with $10,000 and, except for the reinvestment of dividends and capital gains, *adds no new capital over time*. Even so, note that the initial investment of $10,000 grew to nearly $360,000 over the 32-year period (which, by the way, amounts to a compound rate of return of 11.8 percent). Clearly, so long as care is taken in selecting an appropriate fund, *attractive benefits can be derived from the systematic accumulation of capital offered by automatic reinvestment plans*, and as such, investors should seriously consider the idea of incorporating these plans into their mutual fund investment programs.

Regular Income. While automatic reinvestment plans are great for the long-term investor, how about

the investor who's looking for a steady stream of income? Once again, mutual funds have a service to meet this kind of need. It's called a **systematic withdrawal plan**, and it's offered by most open-ended funds. Once enrolled in one of these plans,

automatic investment plan
A type of automatic savings program that enables an investor to systematically channel a set amount of money into a given mutual fund; it provides investors with a convenient way to accumulate capital.

automatic reinvestment plan
A plan frequently offered by mutual funds that allows share owners to elect to have dividends and capital gains distributions reinvested in additional fund shares.

systematic withdrawal plan
A plan offered by mutual funds that allows shareholders to be paid specified amounts each period.

EXHIBIT 14.4

The Effects of Reinvesting Income

Reinvesting dividends and/or capital gains can have tremendous effects on one's investment position. This graph shows the results of a hypothetical investor who initially invested $10,000 and for 32 years reinvested all dividends and capital gains distributions in additional fund shares. (No adjustment has been made for any income taxes payable by the shareholder—which would be appropriate so long as the fund was held in an IRA or Keogh account.)

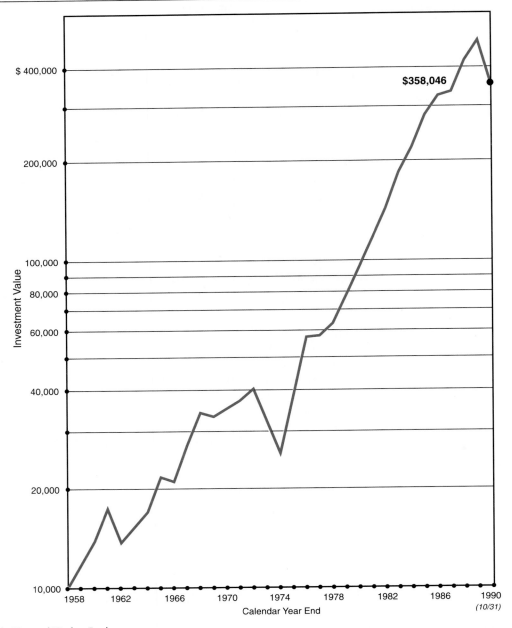

Source: The Vanguard Windsor Fund.

you'll automatically receive a predetermined amount of money every month or quarter.

To participate, shareholders are usually required to have a minimum investment of $5,000 to $10,000, and the size of the withdrawal must usually be $50 or more per month. Depending on how well the fund is doing, the income derived from the fund may actually be greater than the withdrawals, thus allowing the investor to not only receive regular income but also enjoy an automatic accumulation of *additional* shares in the plan. On the other hand, if the fund is not performing well, the withdrawals could eventually deplete the original investment.

Conversion Privileges. Sometimes investors find it necessary to switch out of one fund and into another; for example, their investment objectives may change, or the investment environment itself may have changed. **Conversion** (or **exchange**) **privileges** meet the needs of these investors in a convenient and economical manner. Investment companies that offer a number of different funds to the investing public — these are known as *fund families* — usually provide conversion privileges that enable shareholders to easily move from one fund to another; and as we saw earlier, this is usually done by phone (as in *phone switching*). The only limitation is that the investor must confine the switches within the same *family* of funds. For example, an investor can switch from a Dreyfus growth fund to a Dreyfus money fund, or to its income fund, or to any other fund managed by Dreyfus. With some fund families, the alternatives open to investors seem almost without limit; indeed, some of the larger families offer 20 or 30 funds (or more). One investment company (Fidelity) has over 140 different funds in its family, as it provides everything from high-performance stock funds to bond funds, tax-exempt funds, a couple of dozen sector funds, and half a dozen money funds.

Most fund families, especially the bigger ones, offer investors a full range of investment products, as they all try to provide one-stop mutual fund shopping. Whether you want an equity fund, a bond fund, or a money fund, these fund families have something for you. There are more than a hundred fund families in operation today, every one of which has some type of conversion privilege. Twenty of the largest of these fund families are listed in Exhibit 14.5; note that, together, these 20 families offer nearly 930 different mutual funds to the investing public. Conversion privileges are attractive because they permit investors to manage their holdings more aggressively by allowing them to move in and out of funds as the investment environment changes. Unfortunately, there is one major drawback; even though you never see the cash, the exchange of shares from one fund to another is regarded, for tax purposes, as a sale followed by a subsequent purchase of a new security. As a result, if any capital gains exist at the time of the exchange, the investor is liable for the taxes on that profit.

Phone switching is a service that enables you to move your money from one fund to another, so long as you stay within the same family of funds.
Fact: Phone switching is a type of conversion (or exchange) privilege that allows you to simply pick up the phone to call in an order to sell one fund and buy another, with the only condition being that you confine your switches to the same family of funds.

Retirement Plans. As a result of government legislation, self-employed individuals are permitted to divert a portion of their pretax income into self-directed *retirement plans*. And all working Americans, whether they are self-employed or not, are allowed to establish individual retirement accounts — note that IRAs can still be set up by anyone who is gainfully employed, although, as noted in Chapter 4, the tax deductibility of IRA *contributions* is limited to certain individuals. Today all mutual funds provide a special service that allows individuals to quickly and easily set up tax-deferred retirement programs as either IRA or Keogh accounts. The funds set up the plans and handle all the administrative details in such a way that the shareholders can take full advantage of available tax savings.

conversion (exchange) privileges
A feature offered by many investment companies that allows investors to switch from one mutual fund to another within a specified family of funds.

EXHIBIT 14.5

All in the Family

Here's a list of 20 of the largest fund families, each one of which offers investors a full range of stock, bond, and money funds; these companies do everything they can to keep your money in the family.

Fund Families*	Number of Stock, Bond Funds	Number of Money Funds	Total Number of Funds
American Capital	21	1	22
Colonial Investment Services	26	1	27
Dean Witter Reynolds	29	5	34
Dreyfus Service Corp.	48	16	64
Federated Securities Corp.	15	4	19
Fidelity Distributors Corp.	113	29	142
Franklin Distributors	46	7	53
IDS Financial Services	34	3	37
Kemper Financial Services	36	3	39
Keystone Distributors	28	1	29
Mass. Financial Services	40	2	42
Merrill Lynch Funds	70	22	92
Oppenheimer Fund Mgmt	24	2	26
T. Rowe Price Assocs.	34	3	37
Prudential-Bache	56	13	69
Putnam Financial Services	46	4	50
Shearson Lehman Hutton	47	9	56
SteinRoe	12	3	15
Vanguard Group	48	8	56
Waddell & Reed (United Fds)	17	2	19

*Number of funds in existence in early 1992; all these fund families offer conversion privileges.

GETTING A HANDLE ON MUTUAL FUND PERFORMANCE

If you were to believe all the sales literature, you'd think there was no way you could go wrong by investing in mutual funds. Just put your money into one of these funds and let the good times roll! Unfortunately, the hard facts of life are that *when it comes to investing, performance is never guaranteed*. And that applies just as much to mutual funds as it does to any other form of investing. Perhaps even more so, because with mutual funds, the single variable that drives a fund's market price and return behavior is the performance of the fund's portfolio of securities.

Measuring Fund Performance. If you're thinking about investing in a mutual fund, one of the first things you should do is make sure the fund's investment objectives match your own. In addition, carefully check out the fund's *load charges* and other fees; and if a certain kind of *service* is important to you, then make sure the funds you're looking at offer it. Remember, though, while each of these characteristics is important in the mutual fund selection process, the most essential one is still *investment performance*.

Basically, any mutual fund (or closed-end investment company) has three potential sources of return: (1) dividend income, (2) capital gains distribution, and (3) change in the fund's share price. Depending on the type of fund, some will derive more income from one source than another; for example, we would normally expect income-oriented funds to have higher dividend income than capital gains distributions. Mutual funds regularly publish reports that recap investment performance. One such report is *The Summary of Income and Capital Changes,* an example of which is provided in Exhibit 14.6. This statement, which is found in the fund's prospectus or annual report, gives a brief overview of the fund's investment activities, including expense ratios and portfolio turnover rates. Of interest here is the top part of the report (that runs from *Investment income to NAV at the end of the year* — lines 1 to 9); this is the part that reveals the amount of dividend income and capital gains distributed to the shareholders, along with any change in the fund's net asset value.

Dividend income is the amount derived from the dividend and interest income earned on the security holdings of the mutual fund. When the fund receives dividends or interest payments, it passes these on to shareholders in the form of dividend payments. The fund accumulates all the current income it has received for the period and then pays it out on a pro-rated basis. Capital gains distributions work on the same principle, except that they are derived from the capital gains actually earned by the fund. This capital gains distribution applies only to *realized* capital gains — that is, the case in which the securities holdings were actually sold and the capital gains actually earned. *Unrealized* capital gains (or paper profits) are what make up the third and final element in a mutual fund's return, *for when the fund's securities holdings go up or down in price, its net asset value moves accordingly.*

A simple but effective way of measuring performance is to describe mutual fund returns in terms of the three major sources of return noted above — dividends earned, capital gains distributions received, and change in share price. These payoffs can be converted to a convenient return figure by using the standard *approximate yield* formula that was first introduced in Chapter 12. The calculations necessary for finding such a return measure can be shown by using the 1992 figures from Exhibit 14.6. Referring to the exhibit, we can see that this hypothetical no-load fund paid 55 cents per share in dividends and another $1.75 in capital gains distributions; also, it had a price at the beginning of the year (that is, at year-end 1991) of $24.47 that rose to $29.14 by the end of the year. Putting this data into the familiar approximate yield formula (see Equation 14.1), we see that the hypothetical mutual fund provided an annual rate of return of 26.0 percent. This measure is simple to calculate, yet it captures all the important elements of mutual fund return.

The two principle sources of return to mutual fund investors are dividends and interest income.

Fantasy: Current income (as derived from dividends and interest) is just one source of return; in addition, mutual funds can also generate fairly substantial amounts of capital gains, either in the form of realized capital gains (which is paid out to the shareholders as "capital gains distributions"), or unrealized capital gains (which causes the fund's NAV to go up).

What about Future Performance? There's no question that approximate yield is a handy measure of return. Unfortunately, looking at past performance is one thing, but how about the future? Ideally, we want to evaluate the same three elements of return over the future much like we did for the past. The trouble is, when it comes to the future performance of a mutual fund, it's extremely difficult — if not impossible — to get a handle on what the future holds as far as dividends, capital gains, and NAV are concerned. The reason: a mutual fund's future investment performance is directly linked to the future makeup of its securities portfolio — which is something that is impossible to predict. It's not like evaluating the expected performance of a share of stock, where you're keying in on one company. With mutual funds, investment performance depends on the behavior of many different stocks and bonds.

So, where do you look for insight into the future? Most market observers suggest you do two things. First, give careful consideration to the *future direction of the market as a whole.* This is important because the behavior of a well-diversified mutual fund tends to reflect the general tone of the market. Thus, if the feeling is that the market is going to be generally drifting up, that should bode well for the investment performance of mutual funds.

Second, take a good hard look at the past performance of the mutual fund itself, as that's a good way to get an indication of how successful the fund's

EXHIBIT 14.6

A Summary of Income and Capital Changes

The return on a mutual fund is made up of (1) the (net) investment income the fund earns from dividends and interest, and (2) the realized and unrealized capital gains the fund earns on its security transactions.

PER SHARE INCOME AND CAPITAL CHANGES
(For a share outstanding throughout the year)

	1992	1991	1990
INCOME AND EXPENSES			
1. Investment income	$.76	$.88	$.67
2. Less expenses	.16	.22	.17
3. Net investment income	.60	.66	.50
Dividend Income ⟶ 4. Dividends from net investment income	(.55)	(.64)	(.50)
CAPITAL CHANGES			
5. Net realized and unrealized gains (or losses) on security transactions	6.37	(1.74)	3.79
Capital Gains Distribution ⟶ 6. Distributions from realized gains	(1.75)	(.84)	(1.02)
Change in NAV ⟶ 7. Net increase (decrease) in NAV*	4.67	(2.56)	2.77
8. NAV at beginning of year	24.47	27.03	24.26
9. NAV at end of year	$29.14	$24.47	$27.03
10. Ratio of operating expenses to average net assets	1.04%	.85%	.94%
11. Ratio of net investment income to average net assets	1.47%	2.56%	2.39%
12. Portfolio turnover rate**	85%	144%	74%
13. Shares outstanding at the end of year (000s omitted)	10,568	6,268	4,029

*Note: *Net increase (decrease) in NAV*, line 7 = line 3 − line 4 + line 5 − line 6; for example, the 1992 net increase in NAV was found as $.60 − .55 + 6.37 − 1.75 = $4.67.

**Portfolio turnover rate* relates the number of shares bought and sold by the fund to the total number of shares held in the fund's portfolio; a high turnover rate (for example, in excess of 100 percent) would mean the fund has been doing a lot of trading.

investment managers have been. In essence, the success of a mutual fund rests in large part *on the investment skills of the fund managers.* So when investing in a mutual fund, look for consistently good performance, in up as well as down markets, over extended periods of time (five to seven years, or more). Although past success is certainly no guarantee of future performance, a strong team of money managers can have a significant bearing on the level of fund returns. Put another way, when you buy a mutual fund, you're buying a formula (investment policy + money management team) that has worked in the past, in the expectation that it will work again in the future.

EQUATION 14.1

$$\text{Approximate yield} = \frac{\text{Dividends and capital gains distributions} + \left[\dfrac{\text{Ending price} - \text{Beginning price}}{\text{1-year time period}}\right]}{\left[\dfrac{\text{Ending price} + \text{Beginning price}}{2}\right]}$$

$$= \frac{(\$.55 + \$1.75) + \left[\dfrac{\$29.14 - \$24.47}{1}\right]}{\left[\dfrac{\$29.14 + \$24.47}{2}\right]}$$

$$= \frac{\$2.30 + \$4.67}{\$26.80} = \frac{\$6.97}{\$26.80} = 26.0\%$$

WHERE TO LOOK FOR INFORMATION ABOUT MUTUAL FUNDS

Given the importance of a fund's past performance, where can you find the kind of information you're looking for? A good place to start is with the mutual fund itself. Not too long ago, you would have been putting your financial health in considerable jeopardy if you'd followed such a course of action. But with some recent changes instituted by the SEC, that's no longer so. Along with their load charges and management fees, mutual funds must now report historical return behavior in a standardized format. The funds are *not* required to report such information, but if they do cite performance in their promotional material, they must follow a standardized, full-disclosure manner of presentation. In particular, the funds must disclose the average annual return for the preceding one-, five-, and ten-year periods. The returns must include not only dividends and capital gains distributions, but also any increases or decreases in NAV. In other words, these

are fully compounded, total-return figures, similar to the ones you'd obtain from the approximate yield measure.

In addition, publications like *Barron's, Forbes*, and *Donoghue's Mutual Funds Almanac* provide a wealth of operating and performance information in a convenient and easy-to-read format. What's more, publications like *Money* and *Kiplinger's Personal Finance Magazine* regularly list the top-performing funds. There are also services available that provide background information and assessments for a wide variety of funds. Some of the best in this category include Morningstar's *Mutual Fund Values*, an excerpt from which is shown in Exhibit 14.7, and Wiesenberger's *Investment Companies*. From these sources, you can obtain information on such things as investment objectives, load charges and annual expense rates, portfolio analyses, services offered, historical statistics, and reviews of past performance. And, of course, as in so many other areas of investing, you can use your personal computer to evaluate the past and current performance of mutual funds. A full menu of reasonably priced mutual fund

EXHIBIT 14.7
Mutual Fund Information

Investors who want in-depth information about the operating characteristics, investment holdings, and market performance of mutual funds can usually find what they're looking for in publications like Morningstar's *Mutual Fund Values* (shown here) or Weisenberger's *Investment Companies*.

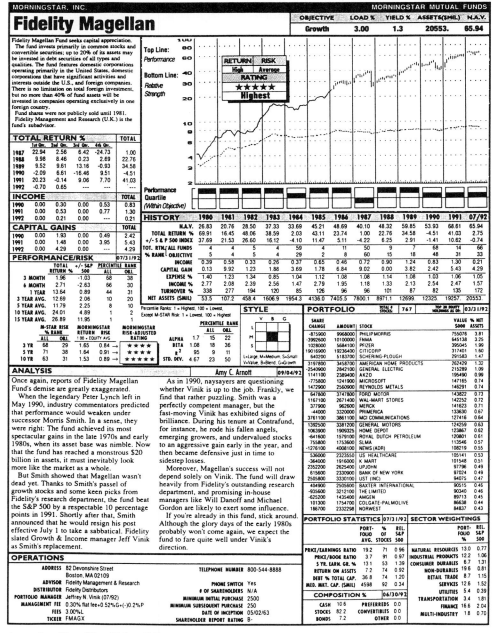

Source: Morningstar, Inc., *Mutual Fund Values*, 1992.

software is available, two of the more popular ones being the *Business Week Mutual Fund Scoreboard* and *Mutual Fund Selector*.

INVESTING IN REAL ESTATE

Investors seeking attractive profit opportunities often turn to real estate. They may speculate in raw land, buy income-producing properties, invest in limited partnerships, or purchase REITs. Which of these vehicles would you use if you wanted to invest in real estate? What kind of return would you want to earn from your investment, and what do you suppose would be the most important source of return—rents or appreciation in value? Take a few minutes before reading on to think about these questions.

Generally speaking, investing in real estate during most of the 1970s and part of the 1980s was quite lucrative! Real estate, it seemed, was one of the few investment vehicles that consistently outperformed the rate of inflation. While inflation was running at 10 to 15 percent a year, a lot of real estate investments were yielding rates of return of 15 to 20 percent, or more. You just couldn't go wrong—*everybody* was making big money in real estate, and according to all the self-proclaimed "experts," there was no end in sight. Unfortunately, the "experts" were wrong, for when inflation dropped to more normal levels, the big real estate boom died—at least in most parts of the country. Granted, there are still some areas where the real estate market is strong, but the record is spotty. In a lot of markets, prices remain "soft," and even some of those areas that were red-hot a couple of years ago are now flat as a pancake. Of course, this doesn't mean that real estate prices are in a nosedive. Far from it. *Prices in most regions are still going up, but at a much slower pace.* And so long as inflation remains in check, you can probably expect more of the same from most real estate investments.

SOME BASIC CONSIDERATIONS

Investing in real estate takes time and should always be based on a careful analysis of the facts. As with any investment, look at the future cash flow you expect to realize from the property, and compare it to the returns obtainable from alternative investment vehicles (like stocks, bonds, mutual funds, and so on). Obviously, don't put your money in real estate if you think you can earn more in some other type of equally risky investment. Current income and capital gains are important sources of return to real estate investors, but measuring such returns involves more than just counting rent receipts. Taxes, cash flow, and the use of leverage are all important in real estate investments. The following material provides a brief description of the basic factors that affect the value of real estate investments, including cash flow and taxes, appreciation in value, risk versus return, and the use of leverage.

Cash Flow and Taxes. The investor's *cash flow*, or annual after-tax earnings, depends not only on the particular piece of property, but also on depreciation and taxes. Certain types of real estate result in large depreciation write-offs that tend to lower the taxable income of certain (*qualified*) investors. Since real estate in general tends to deteriorate over time, **depreciation** provides the property owner with an allowance for this decline in value. Depreciation is basically a bookkeeping entry that is considered an expense for tax purposes even though it involves no outflow of cash. Thus, depreciation can result in lower taxes and, therefore, its existence is viewed as a *tax shelter*. But there's a catch: Depreciation can be used only up to a certain amount and only by investors who meet certain income qualifications.

---

depreciation

In real estate investment, a way of writing off the cost of the investment; it is meant to reflect the decline in the value of real estate property.

First of all, keep in mind that real estate is considered a *passive* investment, no matter how actively involved you are in managing the property. As such, the amount of expenses (*including depreciation*) that can be written off is generally limited to the amount of income generated by this and any other passive investments of the taxpayer/investor. Thus, if you owned some apartments that generated rental income of, say, $25,000 a year, and (in the absence of any other passive investments) if you had mortgage interest and other operating expenses (like property taxes and minor repairs) of, say, $20,000 annually, you may be able to write off no more than $5,000 in depreciation ($25,000 in income − $20,000 in other expenses). However, if your *adjusted gross income* is less than $100,000 a year, you may be able to write off even more depreciation—specifically, as much as $25,000 in losses on *rented real estate* can be used each year to offset the ordinary income of people who "actively participate" in the rental activity of the buildings *and* whose adjusted gross income is less than $100,000 (this provision is phased out at $150,000).

In our example above, if you had, say, $90,000 in adjusted gross income and if there were $15,000 in depreciation expense, then $5,000 of it could be written off against the remaining $5,000 in net rental income, and the other $10,000 could be charged directly against your ordinary income, thereby reducing your taxable income and taxes! Because of its effects on taxes, depreciation is considered an important part of investing in real estate. Since depreciation and taxes are so important in measuring cash flow, an individual investor should employ a tax expert to evaluate proposed real estate investments.

Appreciation in Value. Some types of real estate—especially raw land—have experienced significant growth in value, particularly during certain periods like 1975 to 1980. Other types, such as apartments and duplexes, have also appreciated in value. An investment evaluation of a proposed piece of real estate, therefore, should include not only the recurring cash flows from the property (like rents), but also expected changes in property values (that is, price appreciation). In many cases, such appreciation has a much bigger impact on rate of return than the net annual cash flow from the property! Thus, if

the market price of the real estate is expected to increase by $100,000, that price appreciation should be treated as capital gains and included as part of the return from the investment.

Risk versus Return. If you can earn 6 percent on something like a three-year Treasury note, any money you invest in real estate should promise a considerably higher potential return. For the 6 percent return you receive on the T-note is certain, whereas the returns on a real estate investment are subject to considerable risk. The anticipated level of return on the investment, as well as the stability (or certainty) of those periodic returns, are important in evaluating proposed real estate investments. The risk and return characteristics of such investments should always be judged in light of those available from other investment vehicles.

Use of Leverage. One attraction of investing in real estate is the high degree of financial leverage it permits. Basically, **leverage** involves the use of borrowed money to magnify returns. Because real estate is a tangible asset, investors are able to borrow as much as 75 to 90 percent of its cost. As a result, if the total return on the investment is greater than the cost of borrowing, the net profit on a leveraged investment will be *proportionately greater* than one that does not use leverage. For example, imagine that you're considering a real estate investment that costs $100,000—like the one in Exhibit 14.8. Now let's further assume that you can purchase the property in one of two ways: You can either pay cash for it, or you can put up $10,000 of your own money and borrow the remaining $90,000 at, say, 10 percent annual interest. If the property earns $13,000 per year after all expenses, including property taxes and depreciation, *but before the deduction of interest and income taxes*, the leveraged investment, as shown in Exhibit 14.8, will provide a much better rate of return. Indeed, note that in the no-leverage case, your return on investment will be 9.36 percent, but in the leverage case, you stand to make a return of 28.80 percent.

Because a portion of the leveraged investment is made with borrowed money, the return on investment in Exhibit 14.8 reflects *only your investment in the property*—that is, the amount of money that *you* put up to buy it. Thus, even though the leveraged investment will have provided *less* in earnings after taxes, it will also have had a lower investment, the net result being a *higher return on investment*. In essence, if you leverage your investment, you will get a bigger bang from your investment dollars! Note from this example, however, that when no borrowing is used, there is no risk of default; but in the leverage case, minimum earnings (before interest and taxes) of $9,000 are necessary to avoid default. The risk that comes with leverage therefore must be considered along with the potential benefits — indeed, many people have been driven into bankruptcy as a result of having used too much leverage.

SPECULATING IN RAW LAND

Investing in real estate can take numerous forms. One approach that's popular with many individual investors is to *speculate in raw land*. In this approach, which is usually very risky, investors seek to generate high rates of return by investing in property they hope will undergo dramatic increases in value. The key to such speculation is to isolate areas of potential population growth and/or real estate demand (ideally, before everyone else does) and purchase property in these areas in the hope that the expectations for their development will be realized. Undeveloped acreage with no utilities or improvements is often purchased by land speculators either to hold for future development or to merely sell at a higher price at some later date. Speculation in raw land often occurs near an area in which some type of new development is anticipated. Both residential and commercial developments tend to increase the value of nearby properties. Raw land speculation, because of the high degree of uncertainty involved, should be reserved for real estate investors who recognize and can accept the inherent risks.

INVESTING IN INCOME PROPERTY

Income property is a relatively common type of real estate investment that can provide both attractive returns and *tax shelters* for many investors. The

real estate purchased is leased to tenants in order to generate income in the form of rent receipts. Although the primary purpose in investing in income property is to produce an attractive annual cash flow, certain types of strategically located income properties also offer substantial opportunities for appreciation in value. The two basic types of income property are residential property and commercial property.

Residential Property. Apartments, duplexes, and rental houses are all examples of *residential property* that provide income. This type of income property is available in a variety of sizes, prices, and types, ranging from multifamily apartment complexes to single-family rental homes. First-time investors in real estate usually choose investments of this type. Aside from purchase and financing cost considerations, the major factors influencing the profitability of these investments are the occupancy rates — the percentage of available space rented over the year — and maintenance and management costs.

Commercial Property. Office buildings, stores, strip shopping centers, and warehouses are examples of the variety of investments included in the category of *commercial property*. The risks and returns on commercial property depend more on business conditions and location than do those for residential property. The value of commercial property — especially retail businesses — is enhanced by a location in a high-traffic area. Due to the need for professional management and the magnitude of the expenses involved, investment in commercial types of income property is generally the domain of more seasoned real estate investors.

> **leverage**
> The use of borrowed money to magnify returns.
>
> **income property**
> Real estate purchased to be leased to tenants in order to generate income in the form of rent receipts.

EXHIBIT 14.8

The Use of Leverage in Real Estate Investments

Although earnings after taxes are less with the leveraged investment, the return on investment is considerably higher because the investor puts a lot of his or her own money into the deal.

	No Leverage		Leverage
Owner investment	$100,000		$ 10,000
Borrowed money	0		90,000
Total investment	$100,000		$100,000
Earnings before interest and income taxes*	$ 13,000		$ 13,000
Less: Interest	0	(0.10)($90,000) =	9,000
Earnings before taxes	$ 13,000		$ 4,000
Less: Income taxes (assumed 28% rate)	3,640		1,120
Earnings after taxes	$ 9,360		$ 2,880

$$\text{Return on investment} = \frac{\text{Earnings after taxes}}{\text{Amount of owner investment}} = \frac{\$9,360}{\$100,000} = 9.36\% \qquad \frac{\$2,280}{\$10,000} = 28.80\%$$

*All expenses, including property taxes and depreciation, are assumed to have already been deducted from earnings.

INVESTING IN REAL ESTATE THROUGH LIMITED PARTNERSHIPS

Limited partnerships are professionally managed *syndicates* that invest in, among other things, various types of real estate. The managers assume the role of *general partner*, which means that their liability is unlimited, while the other investors are *limited partners*, meaning they are legally liable for only the amount of their initial investment. Most limited partnerships require a minimum investment of between $2,500 and $10,000. You can invest in limited partnerships directly through ads in the financial press, through stockbrokers or financial planners, or with the assistance of a commercial real estate broker.

Types of Syndicates. There are two basic kinds of real estate limited partnerships: single property and blind pool syndicates. The **single property syndicate** is established to raise money to purchase a specific piece (or pieces) of property. For example, 50 units of a partnership could be sold at $7,500 each to buy a piece of property for $1 million. (Note: A **unit** in a limited partnership is like a share of

stock in a company and represents an ownership position in the partnership.) In this case, a total of $375,000 (50 units × $7,500) would come from the partners and the remaining $625,000 would be borrowed. The **blind pool syndicate**, on the other hand, is formed by a syndicator—often well known—in order to raise a given amount of money to be invested at his or her discretion, though the general partner often has some or all of the properties already picked out. The blind pool syndicator takes a specified percentage of all income generated as a management fee. Large real estate brokerage firms commonly arrange these types of syndicates.

Returns and Risks. Prior to the 1986 Tax Reform Act, much of the appeal of real estate limited partnerships came from the tax-sheltered income that these investments provided. That is no longer the case. Instead, like other forms of real estate, these limited partnerships are considered to be *passive* investments; as such, the amount of write-offs that can be taken on these investments is limited to the amount of income they generate (see Chapter 4). This means that the write-offs from these investments cannot be used to shelter ordinary income from taxes. As a result of major tax reform, limited partnerships lost a good deal of their appeal, but they are still being used, on a much smaller scale, as a vehicle for investing in real estate. The big difference is that rather than emphasizing the tax-sheltered nature of their income, many of the real estate limited partnerships today are less leveraged (some use no debt at all), and are structured to provide attractive current incomes (from rents, etc.) and/or capital gains. An example of this new breed of investment vehicle is the *triple-net limited partnership*, which is discussed in the *Issues in Money Management* box (page 618). The bottom line is that these partnerships, like many others, are now being promoted on the basis of their underlying investment merits and not on the basis of some artificial tax motive. Certainly, for an investor with as little as $1,000 or $5,000 to invest, a carefully selected limited partnership may be a sensible way to invest in real estate.

ments and distributing income. Since they are required to pay out nearly all of their earnings to the owners, they do quite a bit of borrowing to obtain funds for their investments (although, in today's market environment, they do try to keep the amount of leverage they employ at reasonable levels).

A number of insurance companies, mortgage bankers, commercial banks, and real estate investment companies have formed REITs, many of which are traded on the major securities exchanges. Like mutual funds, the income earned by a REIT is not taxed, but the income distributed to the owners is designated and taxed as ordinary income. Although the poor performance of REITs during the 1973 to 1975 recession caused them to fall into disfavor among investors, subsequent restructuring of their portfolios has rekindled a good deal of interest in this form of investing.

REAL ESTATE INVESTMENT TRUSTS

A **real estate investment trust (REIT)** is a type of closed-end investment company that invests money in mortgages and various types of real estate investments. A REIT is like a mutual fund in that it sells shares of stock to the investing public and uses the proceeds, along with borrowed funds, to invest in a portfolio of real estate investments. The investor, therefore, owns a part of the real estate portfolio held by the real estate investment trust. There are three basic types of REITs: those that invest in *properties*, such as shopping centers, hotels, apartments, and office buildings (the so-called *property*, or *equity*, REITs); mortgage REITs — those that invest in mortgages; and *hybrid* REITs, which invest in both properties and mortgages. Mortgage REITs tend to be more income oriented — they emphasize their high current yields (which is to be expected from a security that basically invests in debt). In contrast, while equity REITs may promote their attractive current yields, most of them also offer the potential for earning varying amounts of capital gains (as their property holdings appreciate in value). REITs must abide by the Real Estate Investment Trust Act of 1960, which established requirements for forming a REIT, as well as rules and procedures for making invest-

---

limited partnership

A type of syndicate in which the managers' (general partners') liability is unlimited and the investors' (limited partners') liability is restricted to the amount of their initial investment; used with real estate investments.

single property syndicate

A syndicate established to raise money to purchase a specific piece of real estate.

unit

Represents a share of ownership in a limited partnership deal.

blind pool syndicate

A syndicate formed by a syndicator, who is generally well-known, in order to raise a given amount of money for investment in real estate at the syndicator's discretion.

real estate investment trust (REIT)

A business that accumulates money for investment in real estate ventures by selling shares to investors; like a mutual fund, except REITs confine their investments to real estate and/or mortgages.

ISSUES IN MONEY MANAGEMENT

Hold the Risks: Triple-Net Partnerships Offer Built-in Safety

You may think that risk goes with limited partnerships as fleas go with dogs. But if you pick carefully, one breed of real estate partnership offers the safety of blue-chip stocks plus the generous income of bonds. Called *triple-net lease deals*, these partnerships buy buildings used by major fast-food, day-care, auto parts, and other chains and franchises that don't want to tie up their money in ownership or have mortgage debt on their balance sheets. The partnerships collect rents and pass it along to investors.

They are known as triple net because the rents are net of three costs — insurance, upkeep, and property taxes — *all of which are borne by the tenants*. Many partnerships also reduce their risk by requiring that rent payments be guaranteed, at least for a portion of the lease. Should a Sizzler restaurant fizzle, for example, the chain or an insurance company keeps up the payments for a while.

Limited partners hope, of course, that the tenant's business will be a barn-burner. By putting up a minimum — usually $5,000 — they stand to receive distributions of about 8 to 10 percent on their investment annually, even after a portion is deducted for front-end and other fees. *The partnerships pay cash for the properties*, so distributions tend to be fatter in the early years than those paid by leveraged partnerships, which must siphon off a hefty portion of the rent to pay mortgage interest. Also, since the owners can deduct depreciation, 20 to 25 percent of the income is sheltered from income taxes. When the partnership liquidates, typically in 20 years, the property is sold, and the limited partners get their original investment back, plus a share of any capital appreciation.

Unlike bondholders, however, investors need not content themselves with a fixed payment while they await the hoped-for bonanza. Instead, *many of these partnerships have leases entitling them to higher rents as revenues from the enterprises grow*. Steven Bleier, president of Diversified Financial Management of White Plains, New York, a company that analyzes partnerships, urges investors to make sure theirs has such a "sales override." Says Bleier: "You want an income stream that keeps up with inflation."

Sound good? The growing number of investors buying into triple-net partnerships think so. This doesn't mean there aren't some mutts out there. You don't want a partnership invested in shaky stores on third-rate strip malls, even if the prospective yield is dazzling. "There's a trade-off between income and security," says Bleier. "A high yield means more risk."

Thomas Fendrich, a managing director of Standard & Poor's partnership research service, prefers partnerships that own diversified properties, since they are better hedged in case one of the businesses comes on hard times. He also looks over the pedigree of the sponsor, or general partner. "Rent insurance only covers lost payments for a while," Fendrich says. So if the restaurant folds, "you need a strong sponsor who will quickly get new tenants."

Source: Adapted from Ellen Schultz, "The Built-in Safety of Triple-Net Partnerships," *Fortune*, December 5, 1988, p. 24.

Indeed, in 1992, there were nearly 125 such investment companies. Some of the better known and more actively traded REITs include Federal Realty, Health Care Property Investors, New Plan Realty, Nationwide Health Properties, Washington REIT, and Weingarten Realty Investors. Your stockbroker should be able to give you advice with respect to REITs and help you select those that will be consistent with your investment objectives.

A REIT (real estate investment trust) is a popular form of limited partnership that enables individuals to directly invest in income-producing property. ***Fantasy:*** A REIT is a type of closed-end investment company (it's like a mutual fund) that issues stocks and invests the proceeds in mortgages and various kinds of real estate properties.

INVESTING IN DERIVATIVE SECURITIES

In addition to, or instead of, the more traditional forms of investing, some individuals prefer to put their money into the more esoteric world of commodities, financial futures, and options, all of which are highly specialized investment vehicles that subject investors to considerable amounts of risk. Why do you suppose someone would want to put their money into things like commodities and options? Do you think investor know-how is all that important when investing in these things — or is it all a matter of luck? Stop to give some thought to these questions before reading on.

In addition to the more traditional investment outlets, like stocks, bonds, mutual funds, and real estate, a variety of other investment vehicles are available. Although they may be less commonly used by the small investor (due to their complexity and relatively high risk), a very basic understanding of some of the more popular alternatives should prove useful in developing your portfolio. Accordingly, we will now direct our attention to commodities, financial futures, and options. All three of these are commonly known as derivative securities, since they all derive their value from the price behavior of some underlying real or financial asset. In effect, a derivative security is linked, in one way or another, to the price behavior of some underlying security or asset. Thus, if an option is linked to a particular common stock, as the price of that underlying common stock moves up or down, the market value of the option will move up or down in much the same way. As we'll see, every commodity, financial future, or option has some real or financial asset underlying it, and it's these underlying assets that drive the price/market value of the derivative security.

COMMODITIES

Commodities markets provide a mechanism through which producers of certain goods and products can protect themselves against potential future price declines. Suppliers of commodities, such as cattle, coffee, silver, soybeans, and wheat, who believe that the prices of their products are likely to drop might sell contracts to deliver specified quantities of the commodity at some future date. The buyers of these contracts, in turn, would use them as protection against price increases and to guarantee themselves the future availability of needed raw materials at known prices. Once these contracts are created, *they can be actively traded*. The need (and desire) to trade commodities contracts, not surprisingly, led to the creation of the commodities market. You need not be a producer or user of a commodity in order to buy or sell these contracts; instead, you, as an individual investor, can buy and sell commodities contracts as millions of others do. Generally speaking, commodities contracts are traded by individuals who want to *make money with commodities by speculating on their price swings*. However, investing in commodities involves a considerable amount of speculation and an enormous amount of risk. The payoffs from speculating in commodities can be spectacular; but so can the losses! *These are specialized investment vehicles that require specialized investor skills.*

Because commodities contracts deal with the future delivery of a product, they are also known as *futures contracts*. Today there is an active market for futures contracts — in fact, such trading activity in many ways rivals that of the stock market. It's about as easy to buy and sell commodities as it is stocks and bonds, since all commodities trading is conducted on organized exchanges. The following is a list of the major commodity exchanges in this country:

■ Chicago Board of Trade
■ Chicago Mercantile Exchange
■ Chicago Rice and Cotton Exchange
■ Commodities Exchange of New York
■ Kansas City Board of Trade
■ Mid-America Commodities Exchange
■ Minneapolis Grain Exchange
■ New York Coffee, Sugar and Cocoa Exchange
■ New York Cotton Exchange
■ New York Mercantile Exchange
■ Philadelphia Board of Trade

Each exchange deals in a variety of futures contracts, although some are more limited in their activities than others. Another exchange — the New York Futures Exchange — deals only in financial futures contracts, an investment vehicle that we will review later in this chapter.

Futures Contracts. A **futures contract** is a commitment to deliver a certain amount of a particular item at some specified future date. The seller of the contract agrees to make the specified future delivery, and the buyer agrees to accept it. In essence, the contract creates a legally enforceable obligation on the part of the buyer (or seller) to make (or take) delivery of the underlying asset at some predetermined date in the future. Each exchange establishes its own contract specifications, which include not only the quantity and quality of the item but the delivery procedure and delivery month as well. For example, the Chicago Board of Trade specifies that each of its soybean contracts involve 5,000 bushels of USDA grade No. 2 yellow soybeans; delivery months include January, March, May, July, August, September, and November. The *delivery month* on a futures contract specifies when the commodity or item must be delivered and thus defines the life of

the contract. The maximum life of a futures contract is about one year or less, although some have longer lives.

Exhibit 14.9 lists a number of popular commodities, along with the size of their respective contracts; here we can see that investing in the futures market involves large quantities of the underlying commodity. Note, however, that while the value of a single contract is normally quite large, the amount of investor capital required to deal in these vehicles is actually very small — often no more than a few thousand dollars — since all trading in this market is done on a *margin* basis.

Trading Commodities. Like common stocks and other traditional investment vehicles, futures contracts are bought and sold through local brokerage offices. Except for setting up a special commodities trading account, there is really no difference between trading futures and dealing in stocks or bonds. The same types of orders are used, and the use of margin is a standard way of trading. Any individual can buy or sell any contract, with any delivery month, at any time, so long as it is currently being traded on one of the exchanges. All trades are subject to normal transaction costs, which include **round-trip commissions** of about $50 to $80 for each contract traded (a round-trip commission includes the commission costs on both the buying and selling ends of the transaction). One significant aspect of commodity futures is the very low margin requirements placed on transactions. Investors with commodities trading accounts are required to put up only about 5 to 10 percent of the value of a futures contract at the time of the transaction. If the price of the commodity declines over the holding period, the brokerage firm may require the customer to put up additional money as collateral on the contract. The use of low margin on commodities transactions enhances returns on investments *but also noticeably increases the risks involved*.

To better appreciate the impact of low margins on commodity trading, consider the following example from the silver market. Assume it is January and you purchase a silver contract for delivery in May at a price of, say, $4.25 per troy ounce (there are 5,000 troy ounces in 1 silver contract). If the price of silver increases to, say, $5.50 per troy ounce on or before

EXHIBIT 14.9

Futures Contract Specifications—Selected Commodities

The size and market value of most commodities contracts are quite large. Thus, investors are subject to wide variations in prices—for example, if the price of coffee goes up (or down) by just 25 cents a pound, the value of one coffee futures contract will go up (or down) by a whopping $9,375 (that is, 37,500 × .25)!

Commodity	Size of Contract	Price System	Recent Market Value of a Single Contract*
Corn	5,000 bushels	Cents/bushel	$13,137
Oats	5,000 bushels	Cents/bushel	6,875
Soybeans	5,000 bushels	Cents/bushel	31,075
Wheat	5,000 bushels	Cents/bushel	18,275
Live cattle	40,000 pounds	Cents/pound	29,048
Pork bellies	40,000 pounds	Cents/pound	13,240
Cocoa	10 metric tons	Dollars/ton	8,610
Coffee	37,500 pounds	Cents/pound	23,231
Cotton	50,000 pounds	Cents/pound	29,440
Orange juice	15,000 pounds	Cents/pound	19,687
Copper	25,000 pounds	Cents/pound	25,512
Heating oil	42,000 gallons	Dollars/gallon	25,414
Unleaded gasoline	42,000 gallons	Dollars/gallon	28,266
Lumber	160,000 board feet	Dollars/1,000 board feet	36,688

*Contract values are representative of those that existed in June 1992. The market value of a contract is found by multiplying the size of the contract by its price system.

the maturity date of the contract (May), you will make a profit of $1.25 per ounce, or a total of $6,250 on the contract ($1.25 per troy ounce × 5,000 troy ounces)—all from one contract and all from a mere $1.25 change in the price of the underlying commodity. But there is more good news: Because all commodities trade on margin, you will have been able to earn this profit with a relatively small amount of investment capital. For example, assume the margin deposit on silver is $1,500 per contract; thus, rather than pay full market value for the contract ($4.25 per troy ounce × 5,000 troy ounces = $21,250), you would have to put up only about 7 percent of that amount in your own money. In effect, for $1,500 you would be able to purchase one silver contract with a market value of $21,250! Given the $6,250 profit, you would have made a return on invested capital of a whopping 417 percent ($6,250/ $1,500). Keep in mind, however, that had the price of silver declined by the same amount, you would have lost a lot of money. Although trading commodity futures can provide high potential returns, the risks are also substantial.

Commodities Are Not for Everyone. Most individual investors use commodities for *speculation* as a way of going after the high rates of return that they offer. These vehicles can play an important role in a portfolio so long as the investor understands the risk involved and is well versed in the principles and mechanics of commodities trading. The quickest way to lose money in commodities is to jump in without knowing what you are doing. Because there

futures contract

A contract providing for the delivery of a specified quantity of some commodity or financial instrument at some specified future date; there is an active secondary market for these products.

round-trip commission

A commission on a futures contract that covers both the buying and selling ends of the transaction.

EXHIBIT 14.10
Financial Futures Contract Specs

Financial futures are simply commodities contracts written on a wide assortment of financial assets, including everything from foreign currencies to various debt securities and the stock market. As with most commodities, the size and market value of financial futures contracts can be quite large.

Financial Instrument	Size of Contract	Recent Market Value of a Single Contract*
British pound	62,500 pounds	$113,475
Canadian dollar	$100,000 Canadian	83,220
Japanese yen	12,500,000 yen	97,962
Eurodollar	$1,000,000	959,600
U.S. Treasury bond	$100,000	100,500
U.S. Treasury bills	$1,000,000	962,600
S&P 500 Stock Index	$500 × index	207,100
NYSE Composite Stock Index	$500 × index	114,250
Major Market Index	$500 × index	178,475

*Contract market values are representative of those that existed in May 1992.

is a lot of price volatility in commodities, and because commodities trading is done on very low margin, the potential for loss is enormous. Only a portion of an individual's investment capital should be committed to commodities; the specific amount will, of course, be a function of the investor's aversion to risk and the amount of resources he or she has. An investor must be prepared mentally and should be in a position financially to absorb losses, perhaps a number of them.

Commodities trading is popular with individual investors because it is so affordable, and with all the safeguards, it's relatively hard to lose a lot of money. *Fantasy:* The low margin requirements may make commodities affordable to many investors, but it is *very easy* to lose money in the commodities market — and in a *big* way! It is certainly no place for inexperienced investors.

FINANCIAL FUTURES

In addition to commodities, futures contracts are also available on a wide variety of financial instruments. Known as *financial futures*, these contracts cover everything from foreign currencies to Treasury bonds and the stock market. Exhibit 14.10 lists some of the more actively traded financial futures. Note that financial futures, as a rule, are even bigger than commodities contracts; many have market values that approximate or exceed $100,000 and a few approach $1 million! Financial futures are simply an extension of the commodities concept. They are traded in the same market; their prices behave much like those of commodities; and they have the same low margin requirements. Although financial futures did not come into existence until the early 1970s, they enjoy an active market today — in fact, the best-selling futures contracts today are financial futures, as the level of trading in this segment of the market far surpasses that of the traditional commodities market. For investors who regularly deal in bonds and other forms of fixed-income securities, they offer still another way of speculating on the behavior of interest rates. In addition, they offer a convenient way to speculate in the stock market or in the highly specialized, and often very profitable, foreign currency markets.

From the perspective of the individual investor, probably the most popular type of financial futures are the stock index contracts. **Stock index futures** — like the S&P 500 Stock Index or the NYSE

Composite Index—can be used for purposes of speculating in the stock market. If you think the market is going up, you *buy* stock index futures; if you think it is headed down, you *sell* stock index futures. The key to success is the ability to *correctly predict the future course of the market*. Speculating in this way would prove profitable so long as the investor's expectations about the market actually materialize.

OPTIONS: PUTS AND CALLS ON STOCKS AND OTHER FINANCIAL INSTRUMENTS

An *option* is a type of contract that gives an individual the right to either buy or sell a specific security or some other financial instrument. By far, the most popular form of option with individual investors is the *stock option*. Options are also available on stock market indexes (such as the S&P 500 Index), debt instruments, foreign currencies, commodities, and financial futures. For a variety of reasons, however, these options simply have not caught on with many individual investors; accordingly, we will confine our discussion here to stock options.

Stock Options. A **stock option** is basically a negotiable instrument that gives the holder the right to buy or sell 100 shares of common stock in a given company at a specified price for a designated period of time. The price specified in the option is called the **striking price**; it is the price at which the holder of the option can buy or sell the stock, *regardless of where the stock itself is priced at in the market*. The period of time over which the option can be used is defined by its **expiration date** (at which time the option, if not used, will be totally worthless). Thus, if you held a six-month option on Chrysler Corporation, that option would give you the right to, say, buy 100 shares of Chrysler common stock at a striking price of, say, $20 per share at any time over the next six months. As such, no matter what happens to the market price of Chrysler stock, you can buy 100 shares of it at $20 per share for the next six months. If the price moves up, you stand to make money; if it does not, you will be out the cost of the option. Stock options have relatively short lives—most are written with expiration dates of eight

months or less, meaning that the price of the underlying stock must move within the corresponding life of the option in order for the option holder to make money on the transaction. (While most options do have relatively short lives, a special type of *long-term option* was introduced in 1991—known as *LEAPS*, these options have expiration dates that extend out as far as two years. In early 1992, there were LEAPS available on some 100 different stocks and several stock market indexes.)

Stock options can be bought and sold just like any other security. Today there exists a large and very active market for listed options. Nearly all the trading in options takes place on five listed options exchanges, the largest (and oldest) of which is the **Chicago Board Options Exchange (CBOE)**. In addition, stock options are traded on the AMEX, the NYSE, the Philadelphia Stock Exchange, and the Pacific Stock Exchange. There are over 700 stock options listed on these exchanges, most of which are on big NYSE stocks. There are also options on several dozen OTC stocks, such as Apple Computer,

---

stock index futures
Futures that allow for speculation in the performance of the whole stock market.

stock option
A negotiable instrument that gives the holder the right to buy or sell 100 shares of a particular common stock at a specified price for a designated time period.

striking price
The price at which the holder of a stock option can buy or sell the stock, regardless of the stock's market price.

expiration date
The period of time over which a stock option can be used.

Chicago Board Options Exchange (CBOE)
The dominant exchange on which listed stock options are traded.

Intel, Lotus, and MCI. Exhibit 14.11 provides a short list of some popular and widely traded listed stock options.

Puts and Calls. So far we have discussed options that give the holder the right to either buy or sell stock or some other financial asset. Technically, an option to sell something is a put, and an option to buy is a call. More specifically, a **put** enables the option holder to sell the underlying security at a specified price over a set period of time; a **call**, in contrast, gives the holder the right to buy the securities at a stated price within a certain time period. Puts and calls possess value because they enable the option holder to participate in the price behavior of the underlying financial asset; they also provide attractive leverage opportunities, because they carry prices that are low relative to the market price of the underlying stock.

To illustrate, consider a call that gives the holder the right to buy 100 shares of a $50 stock at a price of, say, $45 a share. The stock would be priced at $50, but (in the absence of any price premium) the call would trade at an effective price of only $5 a share (which is the difference between the market price of the common and the strike price as specified on the call). However, since a single stock option always involves 100 shares of stock, the actual market price of the $5 call would be $5 × 100 shares = $500. Thus, if the price of the underlying stock went up $10 a share, the value of the stock option would go up 100 times that amount, or $1,000!

Puts and calls are unique because instead of being issued by the corporations that issue the underlying stocks, they are *created by investors*. The process works as follows. Suppose an individual wants to sell the right to buy 100 shares of common stock. To do so, that person would *write* a call; the individual (or institution) writing the option is known as the **option maker** or **writer**. The option maker is entitled to receive the price paid for the put or call, less modest commissions and other transaction costs. The put or call option is now a full-fledged financial asset and trades in the open market much like any other security.

Puts and calls are both written and purchased through brokers and dealers and thus can be actively bought and sold in the secondary market. The writer stands behind the option at all times, regardless of how many times the security has been traded or who the current owners are; it is the writer who must buy (or deliver) the stocks according to the terms of the option.

The two basic types of options are puts and calls. Puts give you the right to sell something, and calls give you the right to buy.
Fact: A put gives the holder the right to *sell* a specified amount of a particular stock, or some other financial asset, at a given price for a designated period of time. A call, in contrast, lets the holder *buy* a certain stock, or financial asset, at a stated price for a certain period of time.

How Puts and Calls Work. Using the buyer's point of view, let's now briefly examine how puts and calls work and how they derive their value. To understand the mechanics of puts and calls, it is best to look at their profit-making potential. For example, consider a stock currently priced at $50 a share; assume we can buy a call on the stock for $500 that would enable us to purchase 100 shares of the stock at a fixed price of $50 each. A rise in the price of the underlying common stock is what we are hoping for. What is the profit from this transaction if the price of the stock in fact moves up to, say, $75 by the expiration date on the call? The answer is that we will earn $25 ($75 − $50) on each of the 100 shares of stock in the call, or a total gross profit of some $2,500 — and all from a $500 investment! This is because we own an option (a call) on the stocks, and as such, we can buy 100 shares of stock — from the option writer — at $50 each and immediately turn around and sell them in the market for $75 a share. We could make the same profit by investing directly in the common stock, but because we would have to invest $5,000 (100 shares × $50 per share), our rate of return would be much lower.

We can work out a similar situation for puts. Assume that for the same $50 stock we can pay $500 to buy a put, which gives us the right to sell 100 shares of stock at $50 each. Now we want the price of the stock to drop so that we can use the put as a way to

EXHIBIT 14.11

Selected Stock Options

There are over 700 stock options listed on the various options exchanges. These options are written on large, well-known, actively traded stocks, like those listed here.

Citicorp	Oracle Systems	IBM	Philip Morris
Merck	Hewlett-Packard	United Airlines	Disney
AT&T	Exxon	Upjohn Co.	Digital Equipment
Bristol-Meyers	Chrysler	L.A. Gear	Apple Computers
Syntex	Dow Chemical	American General	USX
NCR Corp.	Ford	General Electric	AMR Corp.
MCI	Avon Products	Eastman Kodak	Union Carbide
Johnson & Johnson	Homestake Mining	Boeing	Procter & Gamble
Norton Co.	Sears	GM	Intel
PepsiCo	BankAmerica	Wal-Mart	Motorola

make money. Assume our expectations are correct and the price of the stock drops to $25 a share. Again we can realize a profit of $25 for each of the 100 shares in the put. We can do this by going to the market and buying 100 shares of the stock at a price of $25 a share, and immediately turning around and selling them to the writer of the put at a price of $50 per share.

Fortunately, put and call investors do not have to exercise these options and make simultaneous buy and sell transactions in order to receive their profits, *since options do have value and can be traded in the secondary market*. The value of both puts and calls is directly linked to the market price of the underlying stock. The value of calls, therefore, increases as the market price of the underlying security rises, whereas the value of puts increases as the stock price declines. Thus, investors can get their money out of an option by selling it in the open market just as they would any other security.

Investing in Options. While there are several ways of investing in options, *buying puts and calls for speculation* is probably the simplest technique and the most popular with individual investors. Basically, it is just like buying stock (buy low and sell high) and, in fact, represents an alternative to investing in stock. For example, if an investor feels the market price of a particular stock is going to move up, one way of capturing that price appreciation is to buy a call on it. In contrast, if the investor feels the stock is about to drop in price, a put could convert the price decline into a profitable situation. In essence, investors buy options rather than stock whenever the options are likely to yield greater returns. The principle here, of course, is to get the largest return from one's investment dollar—something that can often be done with puts and calls because of the desirable leverage they offer.

To illustrate the essentials of speculating with options, consider a situation in which we have found a stock that we feel will move up in price over the next six months. What we would like to find out at this point is: What would happen if we buy a call on this stock rather than invest directly in the stock itself? To find out, let's see what the numbers show.

put

An option to sell a specified financial asset on or before a given future date for a stated striking price.

call

An option to buy a specified financial asset on or before a given future date for a stated striking price.

option maker (writer)

An individual or institution that writes (creates) a put or call option.

EXHIBIT 14.12
How to Read Put and Call Quotes

Note the effect that the expiration date has on options. That is, options that mature in later months characteristically are more expensive than those with near-term expiration dates, because they have more time to move above or below the striking price.

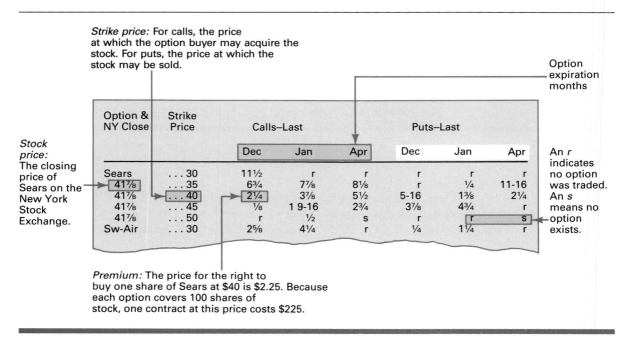

Strike price: For calls, the price at which the option buyer may acquire the stock. For puts, the price at which the stock may be sold.

Option expiration months

Stock price: The closing price of Sears on the New York Stock Exchange.

An *r* indicates no option was traded. An *s* means no option exists.

Premium: The price for the right to buy one share of Sears at $40 is $2.25. Because each option covers 100 shares of stock, one contract at this price costs $225.

Option & NY Close	Strike Price	Calls–Last			Puts–Last		
		Dec	Jan	Apr	Dec	Jan	Apr
Sears	. . . 30	11½	r	r	r	r	r
41⅞	. . . 35	6¾	7⅞	8⅛	r	¼	11-16
41⅞	. . . 40	2¼	3⅞	5½	5-16	1⅜	2¼
41⅞	. . . 45	⅛	1 9-16	2¾	3⅞	4¾	r
41⅞	. . . 50	r	½	s	r	r	s
Sw-Air	. . . 30	2⅝	4¼	r	¼	1¼	r

Assume the price of the stock is now $49, and we anticipate that within six months it will rise to about $65. Thus, if our expectations are correct, it should go up by $16 a share and, in so doing, generate a 33 percent rate of return over the six-month period ($16/$49 = .33). However, there are also some listed options available on this stock, and we want to see how they would do. We will use a six-month call with a $45 striking price as the basis for discussion. In this case, if the stock does indeed move to $65 a share before the option's expiration date, the call itself will be worth $2,000—that is, its value will be equal to the current market price of the underlying stock less the striking price stated on the call, or $65 − $45 = $20 × 100 shares in the call = $2,000. Given that the call could have been purchased for around $400 (the stock's market price of $49 less the

striking price of $45 = $4 × 100 shares in the call), we would earn an incredible 400 percent rate of return in just six months! (Again, the rate of return is found by dividing the profit from the investment— $2,000 − $400 = $1,600—by the amount invested—$400; thus, $1,600/$400 = 400%.)

Note in this example that the profit would be the same for both investments: Buying 100 shares of stock would result in $1,600 in profits, and so would the purchase of one call. Why, then, the big difference in the rate of return? The answer is simple: It takes $4,900 to buy 100 shares of the stock but only $400 to buy one call! This is the concept of leverage at work; with a call, we are able to capture all (or most) of the price appreciation of the underlying stock for a fraction of the cost. The result is a bigger bang from our investment dollar and a much higher rate of return. *There is also less risk on the down side*, since the most we can lose is the cost of the call. If the price of the stock failed to live up to our expectations and instead *dropped* to, say, $40 a share, we would lose $900 if we owned the stock, versus only $400 if we owned the call. Such performance explains why speculating with options is so popular with individual investors. Clearly, it does not take a lot of money to speculate in the market with options, and the payoffs can be substantial.

Making Options Transactions. Your broker can easily make transactions for you in any of the options listed on the CBOE, AMEX, or other options exchanges. The brokerage fees on the purchase or sale of options may differ slightly depending on the exchange on which they are traded or the options dealer through which the transaction is made. As a rule, the fees are similar to those charged on transactions in other listed securities. Information and price data on options can also be obtained from your stockbroker. Price quotations on listed options appear daily in *The Wall Street Journal;* an example and an explanation of how to read stock option quotations is provided in Exhibit 14.12.

Trading in options is not recommended for the beginning investor because of their highly specialized nature. Also, although high potential returns exist, the probability of achieving them is quite low. In most situations, the option doesn't make any sense; it winds up expiring as a worthless piece of paper — which results in a 100 percent loss on the investment in the option. Before attempting to trade in options, you should consult your broker or, better yet, talk to an experienced investor. Above all, you should be fully aware of the risk associated with options trading: They sound a lot safer than they really are!

S U M M A R Y

- Mutual fund shares represent an ownership position in a managed portfolio of securities; since the late 1970s, mutual funds have enjoyed considerable growth in the amount of assets under management, as many investors who lacked the time, know-how, or commitment to manage their own portfolios turned to mutual funds as an investment outlet.

- By investing in one or more of the many types of mutual funds, shareholders benefit from a level of diversification and investment performance they might otherwise find difficult to achieve; moreover, they can establish a sound investment program with a limited amount of capital and obtain a variety of investor services not available elsewhere.

- The investment performance of mutual funds is largely a function of the returns the money managers are able to generate from their securities portfolios; generally speaking, strong markets translate into attractive returns for mutual fund investors. Mutual funds have three basic sources of return: (1) dividends; (2) capital gains distributions; and (3) changes in the fund's NAV (as accruing from unrealized capital gains).

- Real estate has appeal as an investment vehicle due to its attractive cash flow attributes, possible tax benefits, and the general tendency for property to appreciate in value; most real estate transactions involve the use of leverage, which adds risk to the investment but often makes for much higher returns. Investing in real estate can take many forms, including speculating in raw land, buying income-producing residential or commercial property, or investing in limited partnerships or REITs.

- Commodities and financial futures deal in the future delivery of a given product or financial asset; such futures contracts are actively traded, and can be bought and sold just like common stocks. These are highly specialized investment vehicles that involve tremendous exposure to loss — futures contracts control large amounts of the underlying commodity or financial instruments and, as a result, can undergo *very* wide price swings.

- An option provides the investor with the right to buy (a call) or sell (a put) a specified financial asset at a specified price for a specified period of time; while options are available on stock market indexes, various debt instruments, foreign currencies, commodities, and financial futures, the most popular type of option with individuals is the *stock option*. There are listed stock options actively traded on over 700 companies, each giving investors the right to buy or sell 100 shares of common stock in one of these 700 companies.

QUESTIONS AND PROBLEMS

1. Define and discuss investment companies. Distinguish between open-end and closed-end types. Which is more popular?

2. What is a mutual fund? Briefly describe how a mutual fund is organized. Who are the key players in a typical mutual fund organization?

3. Discuss what is meant by the load charge on a mutual fund. Distinguish between a normal load fund and a back-end load fund. What are 12(b)-1 fees? How can you tell what kind of fees and charges a fund has?

4. Look at the mutual fund quotes on page 594. How much would you have to pay to *buy* each of the following funds, and how much would you pay in front-end load charges with each of these funds?
   a. Fidelity Select-Financial Services (SIFnS)
   b. Fairmont Fund (Fairmt)
   c. FPA Capital Fund (Capit)
   d. Financial Fund's Industrial Income (IndInc)

   How much would you receive if you *sold* these funds? Which of the four funds listed here have 12(b)-1 fees? Which ones have redemption fees? Are any of them no-loads?

5. How are mutual funds classified? Briefly describe four different types of mutual funds. How do the objectives of various mutual funds differ?

6. Briefly describe each of the following types of mutual funds:
   a. Aggressive growth fund
   b. Equity-income fund
   c. Growth-and-income fund
   d. Bond fund
   e. Sector fund
   f. International fund
   g. Socially responsible fund

7. For each pair of funds listed below, select the one that would be the *least* risky; briefly explain your answer.
   a. Growth versus growth-and-income
   b. Equity-income versus high-grade corporate bonds
   c. Intermediate-term bonds versus high-yield municipals
   d. International versus balanced

8. What are the most common reasons for purchasing mutual funds? Is financial return important to mutual fund investors? Explain. Identify the three potential sources of return to mutual fund investors.

9. Describe several types of services offered by mutual funds. How do automatic reinvestment plans work? What is phone switching, and why would investors want to use this type of service?

10. How important is the general behavior of the market in affecting the price performance of mutual funds? Why is a fund's *past* performance so important to the mutual fund selection process? Does the *future* behavior of the market matter any in the selection process? Explain.

11. What are fund families? What advantages do these families offer investors? Are there any disadvantages? Using something like *The Wall Street Journal*, or perhaps your local newspaper, find a couple of examples of fund families; list some of the mutual funds they offer.

12. Using a source like *Barron's, Forbes,* or *Money,* select five mutual funds—(a) a growth fund, (b) a balanced fund, (c) a sector fund, (d) an international fund, and (e) a high-yield corporate bond fund—that you feel would make good investments. Briefly explain why you selected each of the funds.

13. About a year ago, Dave Kidwell bought some shares in the Hi-Flyer Mutual Fund. He bought the stock at $24.50 a share, and it now trades at $26.00. Last year the fund paid dividends of 40 cents a share and had capital gains distribu-

tions of $1.83 a share. Using the approximate yield formula (Equation 14.1), what rate of return did Dave earn on his investment? Would he have made a 20 percent rate of return if the stock had risen to $30 a share?

14. A year ago, the Really Big Growth Fund was being quoted at an NAV of $21.50 and an offer price of $23.35; today it's being quoted at $23.04 (NAV) and $25.04 (offer). Using Equation 14.1, find the rate of return on this load fund, given it was purchased a year ago and its dividends and capital gains distributions over the year totaled $1.05 a share.

15. Listed below is the actual per-share performance record of *Fidelity Magellan* for 1990–1991:

	For the Years Ending March 31,	
	1991	**1990**
1. Investment income	$ 1.98	$ 1.90
2. Expenses	.59	.55
3. Investment income — net	1.39	1.35
4. Dividends from investment income — net	(.83)	(1.24)
5. Realized and unrealized gain (loss) on investments — net	8.10	9.39
6. Distributions from realized gain on investments — net	(2.42)	(3.82)
7. Net increase (decrease) in net asset value	6.24	5.68
Net asset value:		
8. Beginning of year	58.60	52.92
9. End of year	$64.84	$58.60

Use the information above to find the rate of return earned on Magellan in 1990 and 1991. What is your assessment of the investment performance of Fidelity Magellan in 1990–91?

16. Define and briefly discuss the role of each of the following in evaluating a proposed real estate investment: (a) cash flow and taxes, (b) appreciation in value, and (c) the use of leverage.

17. How and why is leverage used in real estate? What effect, if any, does leverage have on an investment's rate of return?

18. Describe, compare, and contrast some of the more popular forms of real estate investing.

19. Briefly distinguish between (a) a real estate

limited partnership, and (b) a real estate investment trust (REIT). Briefly note the different types of real estate limited partnerships; do the same for REITs.

20. Patti Arneson is thinking about investing in some residential income property; it can be purchased for $200,000. Patti can either pay cash for the property or put up $50,000 of her own money and borrow $150,000 at 9.5 percent interest. The property is expected to generate $30,000 a year after all expenses but *before* interest and income taxes. Assume that Patti is in the 28 percent tax bracket. Calculate her return on investment assuming that she (a) borrows $150,000 as proposed, and (b) pays the full $200,000 from her own funds.

21. Briefly define, compare, and contrast commodity futures and financial futures. Why are specialized investor skills so important when investing in commodities and financial futures? Explain how the size of a futures contract and the use of margin affect the profit or loss potential of commodities and financial futures.

22. Using the contract specifications in Exhibit 14.9, describe how much profit or loss you would make in the following transactions:
   a. You buy a wheat contract at $2.26 a bushel and sell it at $3.10 a bushel.
   b. The price of soybeans goes up 90 cents a bushel, and you own four soybean contracts.
   c. You recently purchased a coffee contract, and the price drops 27½ cents a pound.
   d. You sell two heating oil contracts at $1.10 a gallon, and the price of heating oil drops 78 cents a gallon.
   e. You hold a lumber contract, and the price of lumber just jumped $2.25 per 1,000 board feet.

23. Mike Jefferson bought three cotton futures contracts when cotton was trading for 68½ cents a pound. Cotton has since risen to 90 cents a pound, and Mike decides to sell his three contracts. What return on investment will Mike make given that he purchased each contract with a margin deposit of $5,000?

24. What are options? What is a put option? How does a put differ from a call? Briefly explain how an investor could make money by buying puts on a stock; by buying calls on a stock.

25. Judy Rothman recently bought a six-month call on a stock with a $65 strike price; she paid $300 for the call. How much profit, and what rate of return, would Judy make if the price of the underlying stock went to $80 a share by the call's expiration date? What would happen to Judy's profits if the stock stayed at $65? How about if the price of the stock dropped to $50 a share?

26. Not long ago, Frank Stevic bought a three-month *put* on a stock — he did this because he thought the stock in question (Roller Aerobics, Inc.) was overpriced and due to take a big fall. The put carried a strike price of $35, and he paid $250 for the option. How much profit, and what rate of return, will Frank make if the price of the underlying stock does, in fact, fall from $35 a share to $22.75 by the expiration date on the put? What will happen to Frank's profits if he's wrong, and the stock continues to go up — to, say, $50 a share?

CONTEMPORARY CASE APPLICATIONS

14.1 Dave's Dilemma: Common Stocks or Mutual Funds?

Dave Brubaker has worked in the management services division of Ace Consultants for the past five years. He currently earns an annual salary of about $45,000. At 33, he is still a bachelor and has accumulated about $25,000 in savings over the past few years. He keeps his savings in a money market account at CitiBank Savings and Loan, where it earns about 4.5 percent interest. Dave is contemplating withdrawing $15,000 from this account and investing it in common stock. He feels that such an investment can easily earn more than 4.5 percent. Marlene Anson, a close friend, suggests that he invest in mutual fund shares. Dave has approached you, his broker, for advice.

Questions

1. Explain to Dave the key reasons for purchasing mutual fund shares.
2. What special fund features might help Dave achieve his investment objectives?
3. What type(s) of mutual fund(s) would you recommend to Dave?
4. What recommendations would you make with respect to Dave's dilemma about whether to go into stocks or mutual funds? Explain.

14.2 Jane Decides to Dabble in Options

Jane Normington, a systems analyst for Butler Products, is interested in buying 100 shares of Xerox. The stock is selling at $52 a share, but because Xerox will soon receive certain large orders from abroad, Jane expects the stock price to increase to $60 per share. If Jane buys the stock at $52 and sells it one year later at $60, she stands to make a profit of $800, or a 15.4 percent gain (ignoring any dividends). Jane recently read an article about options in a magazine published by a brokerage firm and, as a result, has decided to purchase a call option on Xerox rather than buy the stock itself. She pays $300 for the call, which allows her to buy 100 shares of Xerox at $50 per share any time during the next 90 days.

Questions

1. How high must the price of Xerox stock rise in order for Jane to break even on the option transaction?
2. If the price of Xerox rises to $60 per share before the expiration date on the call, what will Jane's net profit be from the option transaction?
3. Based on comparative profit figures, would Jane have been better off by investing directly in the stock? What about in terms of comparative return on investment figures? Explain.

FOR MORE INFORMATION

General Information Articles

Baldwin, William. "Using Funds to Unclutter Your Financial Life." *Forbes*, September 2, 1991, pp. 158–159.

Bosold, Patrick D. "Options: A Walk on the Safe Side." *Personal Investor*, January 1991, pp. 48–53.

Clements, Jonathan. "Taking the First Step in Picking Your Fund." *The Wall Street Journal*, July 22, 1991, pp. C1, 21.

Frailey, Fred W. "Why Fund Expenses Do—and Don't—Matter." *Kiplinger's Personal Finance Magazine*, June 1992, pp. 93–95.

Giese, William. "Brighter Days Ahead for Real Estate?" *Kiplinger's Personal Finance Magazine*, October 1991, pp. 61–63.

Schultz, Ellen E. "A Fund's Past Can Signify Peace or Peril." *The Wall Street Journal*, August 8, 1990, p. C1.

Government Documents & Other Publications

The ABC's of Option Trading. Education Service Bureau; Dow Jones & Co.; Box 300; Princeton, NJ 08540.

The Basic Facts About Commodity Futures Trading. Commodity Futures Trading Commission; Office of Communication and Education; 2033 K Street, N.W.; Washington, DC 20581.

The Investment Company Institute's Guide to Mutual Funds; and *An Investor's Guide to Reading the Mutual Fund Prospectus*. Both available from: Investment Company Institute; 1600 M Street, N.W.; Washington, DC 20036.

Stock Index Futures: A Home Study Course. Chicago Board of Trade; LaSalle at Jackson; Chicago, IL 60604.

GETTING A HANDLE ON YOUR FINANCIAL FUTURE

In order to achieve your financial goals, you must utilize sound investment planning. This involves searching for investments with risk/return characteristics that meet your needs. However, for many investors the task is too time consuming or they do not feel comfortable analyzing financial data necessary to make an appropriate selection of individual stocks and bonds. They would rather someone else do the work for them and then reap the benefits. If this is your approach, then mutual funds are for you.

Mutual funds allow you to have the benefits of owning a diversified portfolio of securities without personally having to make the decisions of what to buy and when to sell. They offer you professional management and the opportunity to earn an attractive rate of return. They offer a convenient means of investing with relatively small amounts of capital. However, as in the case of any investment, you should carefully analyze mutual funds before you place your money in them.

If you are willing to take greater risks with your investment dollars or you have a larger pool of capital to invest, you may want to consider investing in real estate, commodities and financial futures, or

---

If You Are Just Starting Out

The best way to get started in your investment program is through the purchase of shares in a mutual fund. There is a mutual fund for almost any investor's objectives. There are money market funds to meet your needs for short-term, liquid investments. If you want the potential to achieve the highest possible returns from common stocks, you can invest in mutual funds that have as their investment objectives maximum capital gains or specialty funds. Those who would like somewhat lower risks could invest in growth, growth-and-income, or balanced funds.

If bonds are more suited to your risk/return requirements, you can invest according to the type of securities in the fund (corporate, government, or municipal bonds), and/or the maturity of the securities (short-, intermediate-, or long-term).

The purchase of most real estate that is not owner-occupied or the use of futures and options is generally not appropriate when you are just starting out. Once your basic financial goals are met, you can then focus on the more exotic investments.

Choosing a Mutual Fund

1. Decide on your investment objectives and make a list of mutual funds that match your objectives.

2. Screen the funds and eliminate those which do not have the services you require.

3. Review the performance figures of the funds you have selected. Rank them from best performing to worst over the last year, five years, and ten years.

4. Find out if there has been a recent change in the investment manager.

5. Check the prospectus for the transactions costs and the operating expenses. Rank from high to low.

6. Select the fund(s).

Owner-Occupied Real Estate

1. You might want to consider purchasing property that will provide housing for you and income from tenants. This could be accomplished through purchasing a duplex or a home with a basement apartment or a garage apartment.

2. Determine how much you can afford to pay in the same way you would for a single-family home without renting.

3. Review the real estate section of the newspaper or the Multiple Listing Guide in your area to see if appropriately priced properties are available.

4. In addition to your normal review of the property, ask about the rental history on the apartment and the expenses and revise your maximum payment or purchase price accordingly.

5. Determine the length of time that you expect to live there and the annual appreciation rate to help you set the offer price on the property.

6. Make the owner or the agent an offer.

options. Each of these has its own risks and expected returns and capital requirements.

Real estate investment generally requires the largest amount of initial capital and can take the form of speculating on raw land or investing in properties that are income-producing. This can be accomplished by individually purchasing properties or investing through limited partnerships or real estate investment trusts (REITs). Commodities and financial futures offer the opportunity for large returns as well as losses, while the purchase of options offers basically the same profit characteristics with losses limited to the premium paid for the option.

Regardless of the investment vehicle that you choose, you still need to make sure that it fits your requirements in terms of its risk and return characteristics and is best suited to help you achieve your financial goals.

If You Are Thirtysomething

As your financial resources and your investment experience increase, you may begin to experiment with alternative strategies and vehicles. These would include such things as mutual fund switching where you would move your capital among a number of mutual funds in the same family. This is a form of active asset allocation that was discussed in the previous chapter.

You may also consider the use of options and futures as investments with higher risks and higher potential payoffs. Futures contracts require the deposit of a small amount of money called the initial margin. If you are successful in predicting the direction of the price change in the underlying asset, you stand to make a considerable amount of money on your investment. This is due to leverage. However, if the price moves opposite to what you expect, you stand to lose an equal amount. Purchasing options provides the opportunity for large gains, but minimize the downside risk as previously explained.

Real estate investing becomes more attractive as your capital base increases. In addition you may develop skills in collecting works of art, antiques, gemstones, or other collectibles that could offer excellent returns. The keys to success with these investments are knowledge and time.

Investment in Real Estate

1. Decide on the type of real estate investment that suits your financial condition. This would be either a direct purchase or indirect through a partnership or REIT.

2. Select the appropriate type of property. This would be either raw land or income-producing property.

3. If raw land is to be purchased, determine the highest and best use of the property and the time horizon to establish an expected value.

4. Analyze the cash flows of income-producing property and the potential appreciation to determine the return on investment. Be careful not to place too much weight on appreciation in the return calculation.

5. Before purchasing any property make sure that there are no environmental problems. You might want to require the seller to pay for an environmental audit or assessment.

6. Have your attorney check for any restrictions on the use of the property such as zoning or easements that may limit the usefulness of the property.

Other Investments

1. Consider the use of options as a means of increasing the return on your stock portfolio.

2. If you want to participate in an anticipated market move without being in the market, you could purchase a futures contract or option on an index that represents the market.

3. If for tax reasons you don't want to sell securities but want to protect against a downturn in the market, you could purchase put options on your individual securities or on the market.

4. Consider turning your hobbies such as collecting baseball cards or comic books into a profitable business.

5. Be careful that what is meant to be an investment does not turn into something else. For example, investing in rare wines that turn to vinegar or are consumed before they reach their peak.

6. Remember that nothing comes easy, if an investment opportunity seems too good to be true, it probably is.

1. Using the asset values on Mark and Ana's latest balance sheet (after they buy the condo) and the interest rates given in the case, calculate approximately how much interest income they should receive in 1993 from

   ■ their checking account
   ■ their money market account
   ■ their $2,000 certificate of deposit
   ■ their $1,500 certificate of deposit

2. Prepare an inventory of Mark and Ana's savings and investment holdings as of March 1, 1993. Assume that the market value of the Fidelity Mutual Fund has not changed substantially from its value on January 1, 1993, and that the dividends and capital gains distributions from this investment will be the same as in 1992.

3. Approximately how much will Mark and Ana's total annual income from dividends, capital gains distributions, and interest be in 1993? Why will it probably be less than in 1992?

4. What is the current dividend yield on the Fidelity Puritan mutual fund investment?

5. Mark and Ana purchased their Fidelity Puritan shares in December, 1991. What was the approximate yield on this investment from December 1991 to December 1992? Compare the yield on this stock mutual fund to the yield on Mark and Ana's less risky investments. Did the fund provide an adequate yield for the risk taken over that one-year period?

6. Track the net asset value (NAV) of Fidelity Puritan over a two-week period. The needed information can be found in *The Wall Street Journal* and in many daily newspapers.

7. From looking at the mutual fund listings, can you tell whether Fidelity Puritan Fund charges a front-end load, a redemption fee, or a 12(b)-1 fee? If so, what percent?

8. In February 1993, Mark and Ana sold their Apple stock for $60.00 a share and their General Motors stock for $35.25 a share, paying broker's commissions of $170. Of this amount, $95 was for selling the Apple stock and the rest for selling the General Motors stock. Calculate the before-tax capital gain (loss) on the

   ■ Apple stock investment
   ■ General Motors stock investment

9. Given their marginal tax bracket, approximately how much of their capital gain would be paid in federal income taxes in 1993? Or in the case of a net loss, approximately how much would their capital loss save them in federal income taxes in 1993?

10. Mark and Ana's certificates of deposit will mature in June 1993, and they are trying to decide how to reinvest the $3,500 plus interest. They are considering two different stock investments (described below). What is the current dividend yield on each of these investments? What would the approximate total yield be on each given the following assumptions? They plan to keep the investment five years.

	Blue-Chip Stock	Aggressive Growth Stock
Current market value	$41.60	$36.25
Current dividend income	1.58	.37
Average annual dividend income	2.25	.50
Market value in five years	62.00	80.00

11. Mark and Ana are also considering investing this $3,500 plus interest in four corporate bonds that are currently selling at a discount of $892 each. The bonds have a face value of $1,000, mature in five years, and have an A rating from Moody's. They pay annual interest of $65 each. What is the current yield on this bond investment? Calculate the yield-to-maturity on these bonds.

12. An acquaintance of Mark and Ana thought that they should invest in the aggressive growth stock on margin. Would you recommend this strategy for Mark and Ana? Why or why not?

13. What type of savings/investment vehicle would you recommend for Mark and Ana — the blue-chip stock, the aggressive growth stock, the corporate bond, or something else? Remember their goals and their tolerance for risk when making the recommendation. Justify your recommendation.

PART six

Retirement and Estate Planning

CHAPTER 15 *Meeting Retirement Goals*

CHAPTER 16 *Preserving Your Estate*

Meeting Retirement Goals

Do you know your life expectancy? Well, if you're like most college students, and are in your late teens or early 20s, it is very likely that you have another 50 or 60 years to live. While such a prospect can indeed be viewed with delight, it should also bring into focus the need for careful retirement planning. After all, you will not be working all of those 50 or 60 years; rather, you will probably work for only about 40 years—perhaps less—before you retire. If this scenario holds true, you will probably end up spending at least 10 to 20 years in retirement. The challenge, of course, is to do it in style—and that is where retirement planning comes into play! Rudy and Maria Ramirez appreciate the importance of retirement planning. In their mid-30s, they both work. He's a construction superintendent and she's an elementary school principal. Several years ago, they set up a retirement program that they feel will enable them to retire in comfort by the time they are in their late 50s. The Ramirezes strongly believe that if they want to enjoy a comfortable retirement, they must do something about it now. And they're right! For one of the biggest mistakes that people make in retirement planning is *they wait too long to start doing something about it*. It is understandable that when you are young, it is difficult to get excited about an event that will not take place for another 35 to 40 years. But don't wait too long! Because the longer you wait, the harder it will be to reach the kind of retirement income you'd like.

FINANCIAL *facts* **OR** *fantasies*

Are the following statements financial facts (true) or fantasies (false)?

The three biggest mistakes that people make in retirement planning are: they start too late, they try to sock away too much, and they invest their retirement funds too aggressively.

In order to receive maximum social security retirement benefits, a worker must retire before his or her 65th birthday.

Social security retirement benefits should be sufficient to provide retired workers and their spouses with a comfortable standard of living.

Because participation in a company's basic pension plan is mandatory, you're entitled to immediate vesting of all contributions.

Your contributions to an IRA account may or may not be tax deductible, depending in part on your level of income.

Since an annuity is only as good as the insurance company that stands behind it, you should check the company's financial rating before buying an annuity.

AN OVERVIEW OF RETIREMENT PLANNING ▣

Retirement planning is a key element in the financial planning process; to be effective, however, it should begin relatively early in life and involve a strategy of systematically accumulating retirement funds. Stop for a moment and think about how you intend to plan for retirement. At what age do you want to retire? What size nest egg do you want at retirement, and how do you intend to reach that goal?

Like budgets, taxes, and investments, retirement planning is vital to your financial well-being and should be viewed as a critical link in your personal financial plans. Yet it's difficult for most people under the age of 30 to develop a well-defined set of plans for retirement. The reason is that there are just too many years to go until retirement and thus too many uncertainties that have to be dealt with. Uncertainty about inflation, social security, family size, the type of pension to which you will be entitled, and the amount of assets you will have accumulated by the time you are ready to retire all make accurate forecasting extremely difficult. However, contrary to what some people may think, it is just this kind of uncertainty that makes retirement planing so important! To cope with uncertainty, you must plan for a variety of outcomes; and you need to monitor and modify your plans as your hopes, abilities, and personal finances change.

ROLE OF RETIREMENT PLANNING IN PERSONAL FINANCIAL PLANNING

The financial planning process would be incomplete without *retirement planning*. Certainly there is no financial goal more important than achieving a comfortable standard of living in retirement. In many respects, retirement planning captures the very essence of financial planning. It is forward looking (perhaps more so than any other function of financial planning), has an impact on both your current and future standard of living, and, if successful, can be highly rewarding and make a significant contribution to net worth. Okay, it's important; so, where do you start? Well, like most aspects of financial planning, you need a goal or an objective — that is, the first step in retirement planning is to set *retirement goals* for yourself. Take some time to define the things you want to do in retirement, the standard of living you hope to maintain, the level of income you would like to receive, and any special retirement goals you may have (like buying a retirement home in Arizona, or taking an around-the-world cruise). Such goals are important because *they give direction to your retirement planning*. Of course, like all goals, they are subject to change over time as the situations and conditions in your life change. Once you know what you want out of retirement, the next step is to establish the *size of the nest egg* you're going to have to build in order to achieve your retirement goals. In essence, how much money will you need to retire the way you would like?

The final step is to formulate an *investment program* that will enable you to build up your required nest egg. This usually involves creating some type of systematic savings plan (putting away a certain amount each year) and identifying the types of investment vehicles that will best meet your retirement needs. This phase of your retirement program is closely related to two other aspects of financial planning — investment and tax planning. Investments and investment planning (see Chapters 12 through 14) are the vehicles through which retirement funds are built up. They comprise the active, ongoing part of retirement planning in which you manage and invest the funds you have set aside for retirement. It is no coincidence that a major portion of most individual investor portfolios is devoted to building up a pool of funds that can be used in retirement. Indeed, this is just what you'd expect given the vital role that retirement plays in financial planning. Taxes and tax planning (see Chapter 4) are also important, since one of the major objectives of sound retirement planning is to legitimately shield as much income as possible from taxes and, in so doing, maximize the accumulation of retirement funds.

THE THREE BIGGEST PITFALLS TO SOUND RETIREMENT PLANNING

Human nature being what it is, people often get a little carried away with the amount of money they want to build up for retirement. Face it, having a nest egg of $2 or $3 million would be great, but it's beyond the reach of all but a tiny fraction of the population. Besides, you don't need that much to live comfortably in retirement anyway. So, set a more realistic goal. But when you set that goal, remember: It's not going to happen by itself; you have to do something to bring it about. And this is precisely where things start to fall apart. Why? Because when it comes to retirement planning, people tend to make three big mistakes:

- They start too late.
- They put away too little.
- They invest too conservatively.

Many people in their 20s, or even 30s, find it hard to put money away for retirement. More often than not, that's because they have more pressing financial concerns to worry about—like buying a house, retiring a student loan, or paying for child care. The net result is that retirement planning is put off until later in life; in many cases, until they're in their late 30s or 40s. Unfortunately, the longer they put it off, the less they're going to have in retirement. Or, it means they're not going to be able to retire as early as they'd hoped. Even worse, once people start a retirement program, they tend to be too skimpy and put away too little. While this, too, may be due to pressing family needs, all too often it boils down to lifestyle choices. They'd rather spend for today than save for tomorrow. As a result, they end up putting, maybe, $1,000 a year into a retirement plan when, with a little more effective financial planning and family budgeting, they could easily afford to save two or three times that amount!

On top of all this, most people have a tendency to be far too conservative in the way they invest their retirement money. Too often, people fail to achieve the full potential of their retirement programs because they treat them more like savings accounts than investment vehicles! The fact is, they place most, if not all, of their retirement money into *low-yielding*, fixed-income securities, like CDs and Trea-

sury notes. While you should *never speculate* with something as important as your retirement plan, that doesn't mean you have to totally avoid risk. There's nothing wrong with following an investment program that involves a *reasonable* amount of risk, so long as it results in a correspondingly higher level of return. Caution is fine, but being overly cautious can be very costly in the long run. Indeed, a low rate of return can have an enormous effect on the long-term accumulation of capital and, in many cases, may mean the difference between just getting by or enjoying a comfortable retirement.

All three of these pitfalls become even more important when we introduce *compound* interest. Why is that so? Because *compounding essentially magnifies the impact of these mistakes*. To illustrate, consider the first variable—starting too late. If you were to start a retirement program at age 35, by putting away $2,000 a year, it would grow to more than $150,000 by the time you're 65, when invested at an average rate of return of 6 percent. Not a bad deal, considering your total out-of-pocket investment over this 30-year period is only $60,000. But look at what you end up with if you start this investment program ten years earlier, at age 25: That same $2,000 a year will grow to over $300,000 by the time you're 65. Think of it—for another $20,000 ($2,000 a year for an extra ten years), you can double the terminal value of your investment! Of course, it's not the extra $20,000 that's doubling your money; rather, it's *compound* interest that's doing all the work!

And the same holds true for the rate of return you earn on the investments in your retirement account. Take the second situation above—starting a retirement program at 25. Earning 6 percent means a retirement nest egg of over $300,000; increase that rate of return to 10 percent (a reasonable investment objective), and your retirement nest egg will be worth nearly $900,000! You're still putting in the same amount of money, but because your money is working harder, you end up with a much bigger nest egg. Of course, when you seek higher returns (as you would when you go from 6 to 10 percent), that generally means you also have to take on more risks. But that may not be as much of a problem as it appears, because in retirement planning, the one thing you have on your side is time (unless you start your plan very late in life). And the more time you have, the less of a burden risk becomes. That is, the more time you have, the easier it is to recover from those temporary market set backs.

On the other hand, if you simply can't tolerate the higher risks that accompany higher returns (and, certainly, some people cannot), then stay away from the higher-risk investments! Rather, stick to safer, lower-yielding securities and find some other ways to build up your nest egg. For instance, contribute more each year to your plan and/or extend the length of your investment period. The only other option—and not a particularly appealing one—is to accept the fact that you won't be able to build up as big a nest egg as you'd thought and, therefore, will have to accept a lower standard of living in retirement. Finally, all else being the same, it should be clear that the more you sock away each year, the more you're going to have at retirement. That is, put away $4,000 a year, rather than $2,000, and you're going to end up with twice as much money at retirement.

The combined impact of these three variables is seen in Exhibit 15.1. Note that it's really the combination of these three factors that determines the amount you'll have at retirement. Thus, you can offset the effects of earning a lower rate of return on your money by increasing the amount you put in each year and/or by lengthening the period over which you build up your retirement account—meaning you start your program earlier in life (or work longer and retire later in life). In essence, the table shows that *there are several different ways of getting to roughly the same result*; i.e., knowing the kind of nest egg you'd like to end up with, you can pick the combination of variables (period of accumulation, annual contribution, and rate of return) that you're most comfortable with.

The three biggest mistakes that people make in retirement planning are: they start too late, they try to sock away too much, and they invest their retirement funds too aggressively.
Fantasy: While it's true that people do tend to start their retirement programs too late in life, they certainly don't overdo it when it comes to putting money away for retirement—just the opposite is true: They don't put enough away! Moreover, they're far too conservative when it comes to investing their retirement money. While it's true you don't want to take unnecessary risks, being overly conservative can also be very costly.

RETIREMENT GOALS

People have all sorts of retirement goals. Playing more golf, fishing, traveling, or pursuing a favorite hobby are just a few examples. To have the income to realize these goals, people should consider the age at which they will retire and what their financial position is likely to be at that time.

Age at Retirement. Estimating when you are likely to retire is important, because it lets you know how much time you have to save for retirement. Many workers used to elect to retire at age 60, or even 55, several years ago. But the last couple of years have seen a trend toward later retirement. Some people now remain in the work force until age 70 or longer. If you think that a *shorter* working career is for you, then you must take the steps to put more money aside each year for retirement than others who plan to work for as long as they are physically and mentally capable.

Financial Position and Goals. Your financial position at retirement depends not only on your retirement plans but—perhaps even more so—on your choice of career and lifestyle. Remember that the quality of your life and lifestyle goals must be chosen on the basis of projected income and expenditures. Devoting some income toward retirement is essential to economic security in old age. You must be careful, therefore, not to satisfy low-priority, short-run desires at the expense of high-priority, long-run objectives.

ESTIMATING INCOME NEEDS

Retirement planning would be much simpler if we lived in a static economy. Unfortunately (or perhaps fortunately), we don't, and as a result, both your personal budget and the general economy are subject to considerable change over time, making accurate forecasting of retirement needs difficult at best. Even so, it is a *necessary task*, and one that you can handle in one of two ways. One strategy is to plan for retirement over a *series of short run time frames*. A good way to do this is to state your retirement income objectives as a percentage of your present earnings. For example, if you desire a retirement income equal to 80 percent of your final take-home pay, you can determine the amount necessary to fund this need. Then, every three to five years, you can revise and update your plan.

EXHIBIT 15.1

Building Up Your Retirement Nest Egg

The size of your retirement nest egg will depend on when you start your program (period of accumulation), how much you contribute each year, and the rate of return you earn on your investments. As seen in this table, you can combine these variables in a number of different ways to end up with a given amount at retirement.

Accumulation Period*	Amount of Accumulated Capital from							
	Contribution of $2,000/yr. at These Average Rates of Return				Contribution of $5,000/yr. at These Average Rates of Return			
	4%	6%	8%	10%	4%	6%	8%	10%
10 yrs. (55 yrs. old)	$ 24,010	$ 26,360	$ 28,970	$ 31,870	$ 60,030	$ 65,900	$ 72,440	$ 79,690
20 yrs. (45 yrs. old)	59,560	73,570	91,520	114,550	148,890	183,930	228,810	286,370
25 yrs. (40 yrs. old)	83,290	109,720	146,210	196,690	208,230	274,300	365,530	491,730
30 yrs. (35 yrs. old)	112,170	158,110	226,560	328,980	280,420	395,290	566,410	822,460
35 yrs. (30 yrs. old)	147,300	222,860	344,630	542,040	368,260	557,160	861,570	1,355,090
40 yrs. (25 yrs. old)	190,050	309,520	518,100	885,160	475,120	773,790	1,295,260	2,212,900

*Assumes retirement at age 65; parenthetical figure, therefore, is the age at which the person would start his or her retirement program.

Alternatively, you can follow a *long-term* approach in which you actually formulate the level of income you would like to receive in retirement, along with the amount of funds you must amass in order to achieve that desired standard of living. Rather than addressing the problem in a series of short-run plans, this approach goes 20 or 30 years into the future — to the time when you will retire — in order to determine how much saving and investing you must do today to achieve your long-run retirement goals. Of course, if conditions and/or expectations change dramatically, it may be necessary to make corresponding alterations to your long-run retirement goals and strategies.

Determining Future Retirement Needs. To illustrate how future retirement needs and income requirements can be formulated, let's consider the case of Jack and Lois Winter. In their mid-30s, they have two children and an annual income of about $60,000 before taxes. Up to now, Jack and Lois have given only passing thought to their retirement. But even though it's still some 30 years away, they feel it is now time to give some serious consideration to their situation to see if they will be able to pursue a retirement lifestyle that appeals to them. Exhibit 15.2 contains a worksheet that provides the basic

steps to follow in determining retirement needs. This exhibit shows how the Winters have used the worksheet to estimate their retirement income and determine the amount of investment assets they must accumulate to meet their retirement objectives.

Jack and Lois began their calculations by determining what their *household expenditures* will likely be in retirement. They have made their estimate on the basis of being able to maintain a "comfortable" standard of living — one that will not be extravagant yet will allow them to do the things they would like in retirement. A simple yet highly effective way to derive an estimate of expected household expenditures is to base it on the current level of such expenses. Assume the Winter's annual household expenditures (excluding savings) currently run about $42,000 a year — this information can be readily obtained by referring to their most recent income and expenditures statement. Making some obvious adjustments for the different lifestyle they will have in retirement — their children will no longer be living at home, their home will be paid for, and so on — the Winters estimate that they will be able to achieve the standard of living they'd like in retirement at an annual level of household expenditures equal to about 70 percent of the current amount. Thus, *in terms of today's dollars*, their

EXHIBIT 15.2

Estimating Future Retirement Needs

This worksheet will help you define your income requirements in retirement, the size of your retirement nest egg, and the amount that you must save annually to achieve your given retirement goals.

PROJECTING RETIREMENT INCOME AND INVESTMENT NEEDS

Name(s) ___Jack & Lois Winter___   Date ___June, 1993___

I.   Estimated Household Expenditures in Retirement:

A. Approximate number of years to retirement	30
B. *Current* level of annual household expenditures, excluding savings... $	42,000
C. Estimated household expenses in retirement *as a percent* of current expenses	70%
D. Estimated annual household expenditures in retirement (B x C) .... $	29,400

II. Estimated Income in Retirement:

E. Social security, annual income .... $	13,000
F. Company/employer pension plans, annual amounts... $	9,000
G. Other sources, annual amounts .... $	0
H. Total annual income (E + F + G) .... $	22,000
I. Additional required income, or *annual* shortfall (D – H) .... $	7,400

III. Inflation Factor:

J. Expected average annual rate of inflation over the period to retirement	5%
K. Inflation factor (in Appendix A): Based on __30__ years to retirement (A) and an expected average annual rate of inflation (J) of __5%__	4.32
L. Size of inflation-adjusted annual shortfall (I x K) .... $	32,000

IV. Funding the Shortfall:

M. Anticipated return on assets held *after* retirement..	10%
N. Amount of retirement funds required—size of nest egg (L ÷ M)... $	320,000
O. Expected rate of return on investments *prior* to retirement	12%
P. Compound interest factor (in Appendix B): Based on __30__ years to retirement (A) and an expected rate of return on investments of __12%__ (O)	241
Q. Annual savings required to fund retirement nest egg (N ÷ P)... $	1,328

Note: Parts I and II are prepared in terms of current (today's) dollars.

estimated household expenditures in retirement will be $42,000 × .70 = *$29,400*. (This process is summarized in steps A through D in Exhibit 15.2.)

Estimating Retirement Income.

The next question is: Where will they get the money to met their projected household expenses of $29,400 a year? They have addressed this problem by estimating what their *income* will be in retirement — again *in terms of today's dollars.* Their two basic sources of retirement income are social security and employer-sponsored pension plans. Based on today's retirement tables they estimate that they will receive about $13,000 a year from social security (as we'll see later in this chapter, you can now receive an estimate directly from the Social Security Administration of what your future social security benefits are likely to be when you retire) and another $9,000 from their employer pension plans, for a total projected income of *$22,000*. When this is compared to their projected household expenditures, it is clear that the Winters will be facing an annual shortfall of $7,400 (see steps E through I in Exhibit 15.2). This is the amount of retirement income that they must come up with; otherwise, they will have to reduce the standard of living they hope to enjoy in retirement.

At this point, we need to introduce the *inflation factor* to our projections in order to put the annual shortfall of $7,400 in terms of retirement dollars. Here we make the assumption that both income and expenditures will undergo the same average rate of inflation, causing the shortfall to grow by that rate over time. In essence, 30 years from now, the annual shortfall is going to amount to a lot more than $7,400. How large it will grow to will, of course, be a function of what happens to inflation. Assume that the Winters think inflation, on average, over the next 30 years will amount to 5 percent. Using the compound value table from Appendix A, we find that the *inflation factor* for 5 percent and 30 years is 4.32; multiplying this inflation factor by the annual shortfall of $7,400 gives the Winters an idea of what that figure will be by the time they retire: $7,400 × 4.32 = *$31,970*, or nearly $32,000 a year (see steps J to L in Exhibit 15.2). Thus, based on their projections, the shortfall will amount to $32,000 a year when they retire 30 years from now. This is the amount they will have to come up with through their own supplemental retirement program.

Funding the Shortfall.

The final two steps in this estimating process are (1) to determine *how big the retirement nest egg must be* in order to cover the projected annual income shortfall and (2) to determine *how much to save each year* in order to accumulate the required amount by the time the Winters retire. To find out how much money they are going to have to accumulate by retirement, they must estimate the rate of return they think they will be able to earn on their investments *after* they retire. This will tell them how big their nest egg will have to be by retirement in order to eliminate the expected annual shortfall of $32,000. Let's assume this rate of return is estimated at 10 percent, in which case the Winters must accumulate *$320,000* by retirement. This figure is found by *capitalizing* the estimated shortfall of $32,000 at a 10 percent rate of return: $32,000 ÷ .10 = $320,000 (see steps M and N). Given a 10 percent rate of return, such a nest egg will yield $32,000 a year: $320,000 × .10 = $32,000. And so long as the capital ($320,000) remains untouched, it will generate the same amount of annual income for as long as the Winters live and can eventually become a part of their estate.

Now that the Winters know how big their nest egg has to be, the final question is: How are they going to accumulate such an amount by the time they retire? For most people, that means setting up a *systematic savings plan* and putting away a certain amount *each* year. To find out how much must be saved each year to achieve a targeted sum in the future, we can use the table of annuity factors in Appendix B. The appropriate interest factor is a function of the rate of return one can (or expects to) generate and the length of the investment period. In the Winters' case, there are 30 years to go until retirement, meaning the length of their investment period is 30 years. If they feel they will be able to earn an average rate of return of 12 percent on their investments over this 30-year period, they will want to use a 12 percent, 30-year interest factor; from Appendix B, we see that this equals 241. Because the Winters must accumulate $320,000 by the time they retire, *the amount that they will have to save each year* (over the next 30 years) can be found by *dividing* the amount they need to accumulate by the appropriate interest factor, that is, $320,000 ÷ 241 = *$1,328* (see steps O to Q in Exhibit 15.2).

The Winters now know what they must do to achieve the kind of retirement they want: Put away

EXHIBIT 15.3

Sources of Income for Retired Workers (in Percentages of Those Receiving Income from Source)

Nearly all retired workers (and/or their spouses) derive at least part of their income from social
security benefits; in contrast, only about half of the retired population receive income from
employer-sponsored pension plans.

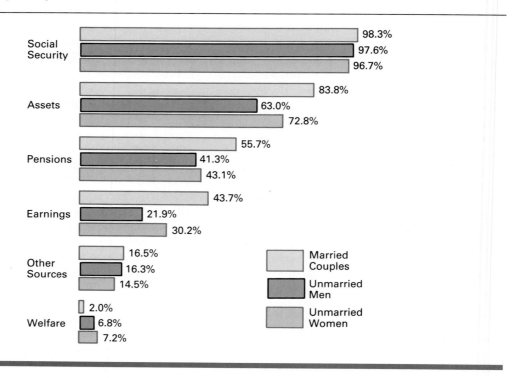

nearly $1,350 a year and invest it at an average an-
nual rate of 12 percent over the next 30 years. If they
can do that, they will have their $320,000 retirement
nest egg in 30 years. How they actually invest their
money so as to achieve the desired 12 percent rate of
return will, of course, be a function of the investment vehicles and strategies they use. All the worksheet tells them is how much money they will need,
not how they will get there; it is at this point that
investment management enters the picture.

The procedure outlined here admittedly is a bit
simplified and does take a few shortcuts, but considering the amount of uncertainty imbedded in the
long-range projections being made, it does provide
a viable estimate of retirement income and investment needs. The procedure certainly is far superior
to the alternative of doing nothing! One important

simplifying assumption in the procedure, though, is
that it ignores the income that can be derived from
the *sale of a house*. The sale of a house not only
offers some special tax features for older people
(see Chapter 4) but can generate a substantial
amount of cash flow as well. Certainly, if inflation
does occur in the future (and it will!), it will very
likely drive up home prices right along with the cost
of everything else. A lot of people sell their homes
around the time they retire and either move into
smaller houses (often in Sun Belt retirement communities) or decide to rent in order to avoid all the
problems of homeownership. Of course, the cash
flow from the sale of a house can have a substantial
effect on the size of the retirement nest egg. However, rather than trying to factor it into the forecast of
retirement income and needs, we suggest that you

recognize the existence of this cash flow source in your retirement planning, and consider it as a cushion against all the uncertainty inherent in retirement planning projections.

COMPUTER-BASED RETIREMENT PLANNING

Most of the fully integrated financial planning software packages contain retirement planning programs that will perform the same basic forecasting functions as those in Exhibit 15.2. In essence, you respond to a few key questions about expected inflation, desired rate of return on investments, and current levels of income and expenditures, and the computer will determine the size of any income shortfall, the amount of retirement funds that must be accumulated over time, and different ways to achieve the desired retirement nest egg. An example of one such program is **Retire ASAP** by Calypso Software. One of the attractive features of these programs is that they allow you to easily run through a series of "what if" exercises. By just punching a few buttons, you can change one or more of the key variables to see their impact on the size of your retirement nest egg and the amount of money you must put away annually. For example, you can find out *what* would happen *if* you failed to achieve the desired rate of return on your investments. In addition to this important retirement planning function, such software will often have routines that allow you to keep track of various retirement accounts. In this way, you can readily see how your performance is stacking up to your retirement goals—whether you are ahead of schedule and, if not, what you can do to get back on track. Thus, modern, computer-based retirement planning assists you not only in establishing retirement goals and plans, but also in keeping track of your progress toward those objectives.

SOURCES OF RETIREMENT INCOME

As Exhibit 15.3 reveals, the three principal sources of income for retired people are social security, assets (income-producing types such as savings, stocks, and bonds), and pension plans. Just about every retired worker receives social security income, about 65 to 85 percent obtain at least some

of their income from savings and/or investment assets, and, surprisingly, only about half (40 to 55 percent) receive benefits from some type of employer-provided pension plan. However, keep in mind these are *sources* of retirement income and not dollar amounts. The *amount* of income retired individuals will receive will, of course, vary from amounts that are barely above the poverty line to six-figure incomes. The amount received in retirement depends on a number of variables, the most important of which is the level of preretirement earnings. Obviously, the more individuals make before they retire, the more they will receive in social security benefits and from company-sponsored pension plans—and, very likely, the greater the amount of income-producing assets they will hold. In this chapter, we will examine social security and various types of pension plans and retirement programs. In addition, we will look briefly at an investment vehicle that is designed especially for retirement income: the *annuity*.

SOCIAL SECURITY

Social security is an important source of income for retired people; however, if it's the *only* source, the retiree is likely to find that his or her standard of living will be considerably less than what had been hoped for. Do you feel social security will be around when you're ready to retire, and, assuming it is, how much do you think you'll receive in monthly benefits? How important will these benefits be to you—that is, what portion of your total retirement income do you think will come from social security benefits? Take a few minutes before reading on to consider these questions.

The Social Security Act of 1935 was a piece of landmark legislation. Not only did it create a basic retirement program for working Americans at all income levels, it also established a number of other social programs, all of which are administered under the auspices of the *Old Age, Survivor's, Disability, and Health Insurance (OASDHI) program*. Some of the other services include supplementary security income (SSI), medicare, unemployment insurance, public assistance, welfare services, and provision for black lung benefits. This chapter gives primary attention to the old age and survivor's portion of the act, since it has a direct bearing on retirement planning. The disability and health/medicare benefits of social security are discussed in Chapter 10.

BASIC CONCEPTS

To fully appreciate the underlying merits of social security as a retirement program, you need to understand (1) its financing, (2) its solvency, and (3) its investment attributes.

Financing. The cash benefits provided by social security are derived from the payroll taxes (FICA) paid by covered employees and their employers. As pointed out in Chapter 4, the tax rate in 1992 was 7.65 percent—this is the amount that was paid by the employee and an equal amount was paid by the employer. Self-employed people are also covered by social security, and in 1992 they had to pay the total rate of 15.3 percent (that is, 7.65% × 2); and of course, since there are no employers to share the burden, self-employed people have to pay the full amount themselves. Regardless of whether the individual is an employee or self-employed, the indicated tax rate stays in effect only until the employee reaches a maximum *wage base*, which increases each year. For 1992, basic social security taxes were paid on the first $55,500 of wages earned, or self-employed income (that wage base is scheduled to increase to $69,000 by 1996). Thus, the maximum social security tax paid by an *employee* in 1992 was $4,246 ($55,500 × .0765) and for the *self-employed*, it was $8,492 ($55,500 × .153). Note that starting in 1991, a second wage base was tacked on in order to cover the rising costs of medicare. In 1992, this so-called *medicare wage base* was $130,200 and it, too, is scheduled to go up each year (to $162,600 in 1996). Now, once the social security wage base is passed, the new, higher medicare wage base kicks in and employees are subject to a tax rate of 1.45 percent (*on all earnings between $55,501 and $130,200*), while the added earnings of the self-employed are taxed at the rate of 2.9 percent.

For years, social security operated on a *pay-as-you-go* approach, collecting roughly enough in pay-

roll taxes each year to cover benefit payments to retirees. But because of some growing problems with this system, Congress passed legislation in the late 1970s and early 1980s that moved social security away from a current funding approach and in the direction of a pension fund, in which resources to at least partially finance future benefits are accumulated well in advance. Because of these changes, the social security system is now running *substantial annual surpluses*, as it's taking in more than it pays out—for example, in 1991 this surplus amounted to nearly $80 billion, and it's growing every year! These surpluses are channeled into social security trust funds, and they're starting to accumulate so fast that by the year 2000—less than eight years from now—it's estimated that there'll be a staggering $1.4 trillion in these trust funds. What this all means is that the current payroll tax system is now collecting enough to not only meet the benefit payments of today's retirees, but also to put money aside for the next generation of retired workers.

Solvency. A lot of people fear that social security will run out of money by the time they are ready to collect their benefits. That's highly unlikely, since surpluses are expected to continue for the next 40 years or so. However, there are some dark clouds lurking on the horizon of this otherwise bright picture. The surpluses won't last forever, and by the year 2050, trillions of dollars in social security reserves will disappear altogether unless steps are taken to replenish them. This is because a larger percentage of our population will be elderly in future years than has been the case in the past. For instance, as shown in Exhibit 15.4, the percentage of persons age 65 or over is expected to increase to 18.4 percent by the year 2030, up from just 5.4 percent in 1930 and 11.3 percent in 1980. This trend means that *retirement benefits will be mushrooming at the very same time that proportionately fewer people will be available in the work force to support those collecting social security*. For example, whereas in 1955 there were seven workers supporting each person on social security, it is estimated that by the year 2000 there will be only *two workers* for each social security beneficiary.

While Congress has long been aware of the existence of this problem, it took action only recently by beginning to slowly raise the retirement age from 65 to 67. As the current legislation stands, by the year

EXHIBIT 15.4
The Growing Importance of the Senior Citizen

As the population grows older, the demands and pressures on the integrity of the social security system will increase accordingly.

Year	Percent of Population 65 and Over	Year	Percent of Population 65 and Over
1930	5.4	1990	12.1
1940	6.8	2000	12.1
1950	8.1	2010	12.6
1960	9.2	2020	15.5
1970	9.8	2030	18.4
1975	10.3	2040	18.1
1980	11.3	2050	17.1

Note: The projected values (2000 and beyond) are based upon the population projections for the central assumptions in the 1977 long-range cost estimates from the *1977 Annual Report of the Board of Trustees of the Federal Old-Age and Survivors Insurance and Disability Trust Funds*.

Source: Adapted from Robert M. Ball, *Social Security* (New York: Columbia University Press, 1978), p. 66, and *Information Please Almanac* (New York: A & W Publishers, 1983), p. 766.

2027 a person will have to wait until age 67 in order to collect full social security benefits. At the same time, the penalty for early retirement (age 62) is being increased substantially. Whereas today an individual can retire at age 62 and collect 80 percent of the full benefits, in the future that person will collect only *70 percent* of the full benefits upon early retirement. This revised penalty structure will be fully phased in by the year 2027.

Investment Attributes. If you are like most people, you probably wonder what social security holds for you. First, you might ask "Will there be any money left when I get to retirement age?" As discussed here, the probability that social security will have funds to pay out benefits is as close to 100 percent as any future economic plan can be — at least for the next 40 or 50 years. As a second concern, you might wonder, "What kind of investment return will I get on my contributions? Wouldn't I be better off to invest the money myself?" This type of question can be answered in terms of (1) social security as an investment and (2) expected rates of return under social security.

To begin with, social security should not be viewed as an investment. It is properly viewed as a social insurance system: an insurance system that insures covered workers and their families against poverty resulting from retirement, death, disability, or health problems. If you die or become disabled at age 30 and have a spouse and two small children, your family could be eligible for monthly social security payments that would total more than $150,000 — even if, up to that point, you had paid less than $10,000 in taxes. Similarly, you might retire and live for another 15, 20, or even 30 years. It makes no difference to social security. You will continue to draw benefits even though they could easily exceed the amount you paid into the system. On the other hand, you might pay social security taxes for 40 years and then die (without dependents) the day you retire — and not collect a penny. An insurance system works only when some participants collect less than they pay in — otherwise no one could collect more. This principle holds regardless of whether we are talking about private life insurance, homeowner's insurance, automobile insurance, or the retirement, life insurance, and disability coverages offered by social security.

Many critics have complained that the investment yields on social security could easily be exceeded through comparable investments in stocks, bonds, or real estate. Even if this claim were true, it would be irrelevant. The fact is that after allowing for all of the cash and noncash (for example, medicare) benefits of social security, the relatively safe nature of the benefits, and a moderate premium for the risk reduction features of the program, *the expected value of most workers' benefits far exceeds the expected value of their tax payments into the system.*

WHO IS COVERED?

Legislation enacted by Congress several years ago extended coverage of social security to just about all gainfully employed workers. There are now only two major classes of employees exempt from *mandatory* participation in the social security system: (1) federal *civilian* employees who were hired before 1984 and are covered under the Civil Service Retirement System; and (2) employees of state and local governments that have chosen not to be covered (though the vast majority of these employees are covered through *voluntary participation* in social security). In addition, certain marginal employment positions, such as newspaper deliverypersons under age 18 and full-time college students working in fraternity and sorority houses, are also exempt. But by far, the largest number of workers in these excluded classes are employees of state and local governments. These groups are not forced to participate because the federal government is not empowered to impose a tax on state and local governments—although once in the program, these employees have to stay in, as they no longer have the option of voting to leave.

WHEN ARE YOU ELIGIBLE FOR BENEFITS?

Social security payments are not paid automatically to eligible individuals (or their dependents). An application for benefits must be filed with the Social Security Administration, which then determines the applicant's eligibility for benefits based on whether he or she has had enough quarters (three-month periods) of participation in the system. In order to qualify for full retirement benefits, nearly all workers today must be employed in a job covered by social security for at least 40 quarters, or ten years. These quarters need not be consecutive. Once this 40-quarter requirement is met, the worker becomes fully insured and remains eligible for retirement payments even if he or she never works again in covered employment. Note, however, that when yearly covered wages are computed,

zeros are inserted for years in which no social security taxes were paid—which substantially reduces the size of future monthly benefit payments.

The surviving spouse and/or dependent children of a *deceased worker* are also eligible for monthly benefits if the worker was fully insured at the time of death or, in some special cases, if certain other requirements are met. Workers may be considered fully insured if they had six quarters of coverage during the three-year-period preceding the date of death.

SOCIAL SECURITY RETIREMENT BENEFITS

Basic social security benefits that are important to retired people and their dependents include (1) old-age benefits and (2) survivor's benefits. Both of these programs provide extended benefits to covered workers and/or their spouses; the major provisions of each of these programs is briefly described in the material that follows.

Old-Age Benefits. Workers who are fully covered (that is, who have worked the required 40 quarters under social security) may receive old-age benefits for life once they reach the age of 65. However, as stated above, the normal retirement age will gradually be increased starting in the year 2000, until it reaches age 67 by the year 2022. In addition, workers may elect to retire early—at age 62—in which case they will receive *reduced benefits*. Currently, a 62-year-old retiree will receive 80 percent of the full benefits; this amount is scheduled to gradually decline, however, so that by the year 2022, the benefits at age 62 will equal only 70 percent of the full amount. If the retiree has a spouse 65 or older, the spouse may be entitled to benefits equal to one-half of the amount received by the retired worker. The spouse may also elect early receipt of reduced benefits at age 62.

In the case of two-income families, both the husband and wife may be eligible for full social security benefits. When they retire, they can choose to receive their benefits in one of two ways: (1) They can each take the full benefits to which each is entitled from his or her account, or (2) they can take the husband and wife benefits of the higher-paid spouse. If each takes his or her own full share, there are no spousal benefits; if they take the husband and wife benefits of the higher-paid spouse, they effectively receive 1.5 shares. Obviously, two-income couples should select the option that provides the greatest amount of benefits (the amount of social security benefits will be described later.)

Survivor's Benefits. If a covered worker dies, the spouse can receive survivor's benefits from social security. These benefits include a small lump-sum payment of several hundred dollars, followed by monthly benefit checks. The lump-sum amount is paid automatically upon application. In order to be eligible for monthly payments, the widowed spouse generally must be at least 60 years of age, or have a dependent and unmarried child of the deceased worker in his or her care. (To qualify for *full* benefits, the surviving spouse must be at least 65 years of age; reduced benefits are payable between ages 60 and 65.) If the children of a deceased worker reach age 16 before the spouse reaches age 60, the monthly benefits cease and do not resume until the spouse turns 60. This period of time during which survivor's benefits are not paid is sometimes called the *widow's gap*. (As seen in Chapter 9, Social Security survivor's benefits play a key role in life insurance planning.)

HOW MUCH ARE MONTHLY SOCIAL SECURITY BENEFITS?

The amount of social security benefits to which an eligible person is entitled is set by law and defined according to a fairly complex formula. Up until recently, it was next to impossible to say with any degree of accuracy what your future benefits might be. All that changed in 1988, however, when the Social Security Administration introduced a computerized benefits estimation service. Under this program, you provide the Social Security Administration with some basic information about yourself and in return, it provides you with something called a *Personal Earnings and Benefit Estimate Statement.* To get one of your own, simply call their toll-free number (1-800-772-1213). You'll then receive a short questionnaire asking for a few basic facts, including your name, social security number, date of birth, previous and current year's earnings, and the age at which you plan to retire. About four to six weeks after you mail the form, you'll receive a personalized

statement just like the one shown in Exhibit 15.5. This report lists the year-by-year social security earnings you've been credited with, and shows (in today's dollars) what benefits you can expect under three scenarios: (1) if you retire at age 62 and receive 80 percent of the full benefit (or less, depending on your age); (2) the full benefit at age 65 to 67 (depending on your year of birth); and (3) the increased benefit (of up to 8 percent per year) that's available if you delay retirement until age 70. The statement also estimates what your children and surviving spouse would get if you die, and how much you'd receive monthly if you became disabled. This statement is a valuable financial planning tool and is something that every working American should obtain — also, it's a good idea to get an updated report every five years or so.

Using information provided by social security, we can describe the *current level of benefits* (for someone who retired in 1991); this is done in Exhibit 15.6. The benefits *as of 1991* are for a retired worker, a retired worker and (nonworking) spouse, and a two-income couple for low, medium, and high career income levels (a *high* income worker is one whose annual earnings equaled or exceeded the maximum social security tax base). Bear in mind the figures listed in the exhibit represent amounts that the beneficiaries will receive in the *first year* of their retirement. Those amounts will, of course, be adjusted upward each year with subsequent increases in the cost of living. For example, between 1988 and 1991, the first-year benefits paid to a retired worker went up by 10 to 15 percent (and that's over a period of just three years). Obviously, if that rate of increase continues, first year benefits in 10 or 20 years could well be 1½ to 2 times what they are today!

Retired social security recipients (aged 65 to 69) had their benefit payments *reduced* if they earned an annual income (in 1991) in excess of $9,720; this same (1991) earnings limitation was $7,080 for retirees between age 62 and 65. (Note that these earnings limitations rise annually with wage inflation.) The applicable rule states that for social security recipients aged 65 to 69, each $3 earned in excess of the stipulated threshold results in a $1 reduction in benefits; and for those under age 65, there's a $1 loss in benefits for each $2 in excess earnings. However, the earnings limitation ceases at age 70; thus, anyone 70 or older will receive full social security benefits regardless of how much they earn. In contrast, *un-*

EXHIBIT 15.5

Personal Earnings and Benefit Estimate Statement

The Social Security Administration keeps a lifetime record of your earnings; when you apply for benefits, it checks your earnings record to see if you've worked long enough to qualify, and then it determines the amount of your monthly benefits. The statement shown on this and the facing page, prepared by the Social Security Administration, is intended to provide an estimate of what one's future benefits are likely to be (*Note:* statement *excludes* record of Medicare credit).

Facts About Your Social Security

The Facts You Gave Us

Your Name ....I. M. Somebody
Your Social Security Number 000-00-0000
Your Date of Birth ....Feb. 32, 1942
1991 Earnings ....Over $53,400
1992 Earnings ....Over $55,500
Your Estimated Future Average Yearly Earnings ....Over $55,500
The Age You Plan To Retire 65

We used these facts and the information already on our records to prepare this statement for you. When we estimated your benefits, we included any 1991 and 1992 earnings you told us about. We also included any future estimated earnings up to the age you told us you plan to retire.

If you did not estimate your future earnings, we did not project any future earnings for you.

Your Social Security Earnings

The chart below shows the earnings on our Social Security record. It also estimates the amount of Social Security taxes you paid each year to finance benefits under Social Security and Medicare. We show earnings only up to the maximum amount of yearly earnings covered by Social Security. These maximum amounts are also shown on the chart. The chart may not include some or all of your earnings from last year because they may not have been posted to your record yet.

Years	Maximum Yearly Earnings Subject To Social Security Tax	Your Social Security Taxed Earnings	Estimated Social Security Taxes You Paid
1937–1950	$ 3,000	$ 0	$ 0
1951	3,600	0	0
1952	3,600	0	0
1953	3,600	0	0
1954	3,600	0	0
1955	4,200	0	0
1956	4,200	18	0
1957	4,200	369	8
1958	4,200	45	1
1959	4,800	1,645	41
1960	4,800	889	26
1961	4,800	259	7
1962	4,800	566	17
1963	4,800	1,840	66
1964	4,800	4,800	174
1965	4,800	4,800	174
1966	6,600	6,600	254
1967	6,600	6,600	257
1968	7,800	0	0
1969	7,800	0	0
1970	7,800	7,053	296
1971	7,800	7,800	358
1972	9,000	9,000	414
1973	10,800	10,800	523
1974	13,200	13,200	653
1975	14,100	14,100	697
1976	15,300	15,300	757
1977	16,500	16,500	816
1978	17,700	17,700	893
1979	22,900	22,900	1,163
1980	25,900	25,900	1,315
1981	29,700	29,700	1,588
1982	32,400	32,400	1,749
1983	35,700	35,700	1,927

Years	Maximum Yearly Earnings Subject To Social Security Tax	Your Social Security Taxed Earnings	Estimated Social Security Taxes You Paid
1984	37,800	37,800	2,041
1985	39,600	39,600	2,257
1986	42,000	42,000	2,394
1987	43,800	43,800	2,496
1988	45,000	45,000	2,727
1989	48,000	48,000	2,908
1990	51,300	51,300	3,180
1991	53,400	0	0

Your Social Security Credits

To qualify for benefits, you need credit for a certain amount of work covered by Social Security. The number of credits you need will vary with the type of benefit. **Under current law, you do not need more than 40 credits to be fully insured for any benefit.** (See "How You Earn Social Security Credits" on the reverse side.)

Our review of your earnings, including any 1991 and 1992 earnings you told us about, shows that you now have **at least 40 Social Security credits.**

Estimated Benefits

Retirement

You must have 40 Social Security credits to be fully insured for retirement benefits. Assuming that you meet all the requirements, here are estimates of your retirement benefits based on your past and any projected earnings. The estimates are in today's dollars, but adjusted to account for average wage growth in the national economy.
If you retire at 65, your monthly benefit in today's dollars will be about $1,270

The earliest age at which you can receive an unreduced retirement benefit is 65 **and 4 months**. We call this your full retirement age. If you work until that age and then retire, your monthly benefit in today's dollars will be about . . .$1,300

If you continue to work and wait until you are 70 to receive benefits, your monthly benefit in today's dollars will be about $1,800

Survivors

If you have a family, you must have 31 Social Security credits for certain family members to receive benefits if you were to die this year. They may also qualify if you earn 6 credits in the 3 years before your death. The number of credits a person needs to be insured for survivors benefits increases each year until age 62, up to a maximum of 40 credits.

Here is an estimate of the benefits your family could receive if you had enough credits to be insured, they qualified for benefits, and you died this year:

Your child could receive a monthly benefit of about $840

If your child and your surviving spouse who is caring for your child both qualify, they could each receive a monthly benefit of about $840

When your surviving spouse reaches full retirement age, he or she could receive a monthly benefit of about $1,120

The total amount that we could pay your family each month is about $1,960

We may also be able to pay your surviving spouse or children a one-time death benefit of $255

Disability

Right now, you must have 31 Social Security credits to be insured for disability benefits. And, **20 of these** credits had to be earned in the **10 year period immediately before you became disabled**. If you are blind or received disability benefits in the past, you may need fewer credits. The number of credits a person needs to be insured for disability benefits increases each year until age 62, up to a maximum of 40 credits.

If you were disabled, had enough credits, and met the other requirements for disability benefits, here is an estimate of the benefits you could receive right now:

Your monthly benefit would be about $1,105
You and your eligible family members could receive up to a monthly total of about $1,655

If You Have Questions

If you have any questions about this statement, please read the information on the reverse side. If you still have questions, please call **1-800-537-7005**.

EXHIBIT 15.6

Selected Monthly Social Security Retirement Benefits

The social security benefits listed here are initial, *first-year benefits*. As time passes, the beneficiary will receive correspondingly higher benefits as the cost of living goes up. For example, the maximum benefit payable to someone who retired in 1980 was $572 a month; by 1991, those benefits had grown to over $900 a month.

I. Latest Benefits (1991)	Career Earnings Level		
	Low	Medium	High
Retired worker, age 65	$488	$ 855	$1,023
Retired worker, age 62	364	620	822
Family benefits:			
Retired worker and spouse, both 65	$732	$1,282	$1,534
Retired worker and spouse, both 62	534	910	1,216
Two-income couple[a]			
Both retire at 65	$976	$1,710	$2,046
Both retire at 62	728	1,240	1,644

[a]*Both* in the same career income category and *both* eligible for normal benefits at their career income levels.

Source: *Social Security Explained: 1991*, Commerce Clearing House.

earned income such as interest, dividends, and rent may be of an unlimited amount without a corresponding benefits reduction. The fact that benefits are subject to reduction with earned income, but not with unearned income, is one of the most criticized features of social security.

In order to receive maximum social security retirement benefits, a worker must retire before his or her 65th birthday.

Fantasy: To qualify for maximum benefits, a worker must be 65 or *older* AND have career earnings (prior to retirement) that were equal to or greater than the maximum social security tax base.

Taxes on Benefits. No longer are social security benefits a source of tax-free income. Not since 1984, anyway, when Congress passed legislation to tax up to half the benefits paid to "upper-income beneficiaries." Specifically, as the law presently stands, *social security retirement benefits are subject to federal income taxes if* the beneficiary's annual income exceeds one of the following base amounts: $25,000 for a single taxpayer, $32,000 for married taxpayers filing jointly, and zero for married taxpayers filing

separately. In determining the amount of income that must be counted, the taxpayer starts with his or her *adjusted gross income* as defined by the present tax law (see Chapter 4) and then adds all nontaxable interest income (such as income from municipal bonds) plus one-half of the social security benefits received. If the resulting amount exceeds one of the qualifying bases (above), the retiree must pay federal income taxes on *up to half* of the amount of social security benefits received—and then only the amount *in excess of the base* is subject to tax.

SOCIAL SECURITY AND RETIREMENT PLANNING

No one can accurately predict the amount of social security benefits that will be paid 30 or 40 years from now. For retirement planning purposes, however, it seems reasonable to expect social security will provide the average retired wage earner (who is married) with perhaps 40 to 60 percent of the wages that he or she was earning in the year before retirement. This, of course, assumes that the retiree has had a full career working in covered employment. Social security should therefore be viewed as *a foundation for your retirement income*. By itself, *it is insufficient to allow a worker and spouse to maintain their preretirement standard of living.* For people who earn in excess of the wage base, a lower percentage of total preretirement wages will be replaced by social security. Consequently, it's essential that average and upper-middle-income families plan to supplement their social security retirement benefits with income from other sources. Two popular sources are pensions and retirement programs, and annuities. These topics are discussed in the next two sections.

Social security retirement benefits should be sufficient to provide retired workers and their spouses with a comfortable standard of living.
Fantasy: Social security is intended to be only a foundation for retirement income; by itself, it will likely permit retirees only a small fraction of their preretirement standard of living.

PENSION PLANS AND RETIREMENT PROGRAMS

There are two basic types of retirement programs: employer-sponsored and self-directed — together, these programs can provide the funds needed for an active and comfortable retirement. If you're covered by a company-sponsored pension plan, why would you need to open a self-directed retirement program? Try to answer this question before going on.

Accompanying the expansion of the social security system has been a corresponding growth in employer-sponsored pension and retirement plans. In 1940, when the social security program was in its infancy, fewer than 25 percent of the work force had the benefit of an employer-sponsored plan. Today, better than 50 percent of all wage and salaried workers (in both the private and public sectors) are covered by some type of employer-sponsored retirement or profit-sharing plan.

WHAT'S BEHIND THE GROWTH?

Although there are many reasons for the widespread development of pension and retirement plans, three stand out the most. Basically, pension plans have been developed by employers to (1) attract and retain quality employees, (2) meet the demands of collective bargaining, and (3) provide benefits to owners and key managers of firms. Many employers stress the advantages of their retirement plans in attracting and keeping valuable employees. In fact, a lot of companies have more or less been forced to implement retirement plans to counteract the effects of other employers competing for the same workers. Of course, few of these firms would go so far as to say that a good retirement plan encourages workers to put forth more effort. Nevertheless, evidence indicates that the lack of a good plan can serve as a job deterrent to prospective employees and may increase labor turnover, especially for employees age 40 and older.

In 1948, the National Labor Relations Board (NLRB) ruled that pensions and other types of insurnace programs are legitimate subjects for collective bargaining. In response, many employers established new pension plans or liberalized the provisions of existing ones to meet or anticipate union demands. Qualified pension plans (discussed later) allow firms to deduct for tax purposes their contributions to employee retirement programs. Nor are these contributions included in employees' taxable income; as a result, the participants are able to build up their own retirement funds on a tax-deferred basis. Eventually, of course, when the funds are paid out as benefits, the employees will have to pay taxes on this income.

Government red tape, however, has slowed things down quite a bit. In particular, the **Employee Retirement Income Security Act** (sometimes referred to as **ERISA** or the *Pension Reform Act*) of

---

Employee Retirement Income Security Act (ERISA)

A law passed in 1974 to ensure that workers eligible for pensions would actually receive such benefits; also permits uncovered workers to establish individual tax-sheltered retirement plans. Also known as the *Pension Reform Act*.

1974, established to protect employees participating in private employer retirement plans, has actually led to a reduction in the number of new retirement plans started among firms, especially the smaller ones. Indeed, the percentage of workers covered by company-sponsored plans has fallen dramatically since the late 1970s. It's estimated that today, *in the private sector*, only about 45 percent of all full-time workers are covered by company-financed plans — even worse, only about 35 percent of the part-time labor force is covered. In addition to ERISA, the widespread availability of Keogh plans, individual retirement accounts (IRAs), and other programs has lessened the urgency of small firms (and bigger ones as well) to offer their own company-financed pension plans.

EMPLOYER-SPONSORED PROGRAMS: BASIC PLANS

Employers can sponsor two types of retirement programs — *basic plans*, in which employees automatically participate after a certain period of employment, and *supplemental plans*, which are mostly voluntary programs that enable employees to increase the amount of funds being set aside for retirement. We will look first at some of the key characteristics of basic plans. Apart from financing, there are certain features of employer-sponsored pension plans that you should become familiar with, including participation requirements, contributory obligations, benefit rights, retirement age, and methods of computing benefits.

Participation Requirements. In most pension plans, employees must meet certain criteria before they become eligible for participation. Most common are requirements relating to years of service, minimum age, level of earnings, and employment classification. Years of service and/or minimum-age requirements are often incorporated into retirement plans in the belief that a much greater labor turnover rate applies to both newly hired and younger employees. Therefore, to reduce the administrative costs of the plans, employees in these categories are often excluded from participation.

What's Your Contribution? Whether or not you, as an employee, have to make payments toward your own pension depends on the type of plan you're in. If you belong to a **noncontributory pension plan**, the employer pays the total cost of the benefits — you don't have to pay a thing. Under a **contributory pension plan**, the cost is shared by both the employer and the employee. While most corporate pension plans today are noncontributory, a growing number of them are rapidly switching to the contributory type. In addition, nearly all plans for employees of federal, state, and local governments require a contribution from the employee. In contributory plans, the employee's share of the costs is frequently between 3 and 10 percent of annual wages and is typically paid through a payroll deduction. Probably the most common arrangement is for the employer to match the employee's contribution such that the employee puts up half the annual contribution and the employer puts up the other half. When employees who have participated in a contributory retirement plan terminate employment prior to retirement they are legally entitled to some benefit, based on the amount of their own contributions. Usually this benefit is a cash lump sum, but in some cases it can be taken as a monthly payment at retirement. Whether departing employees receive any benefit from the *employer's* contributions depends on the plan's benefit rights.

Vested Interest: A Right to the Benefits. Not everyone who participates in a pension plan will earn the right to receive retirement benefits. Pension plans impose certain criteria that must be met before the employee can obtain a nonforfeitable right to a pension. When nonforfeitable rights are secured by employees, they have what are known as **vested rights**. Prior to 1974, employers often required workers to be employed for 25 years or more before vesting would occur. An employee who left before completing this period of employment (and plenty of them did) would lose all of the employer-sponsored pension benefits previously earned. Because of the high mobility of labor and capital, many workers at retirement faced the prospect of having no pension. One of the principal purposes of the Pension Reform Act of 1974 (ERISA) was to eliminate this unfair practice (which indirectly contributed to the social problem of low incomes among the aged). ERISA required covered employers to grant employees vested rights after no more than 10 years of employment (when there was no partial vesting prior to 10 years of service), or alternatively, 15 years, where partial vesting began after five years.

While ERISA was certainly a step in the right direction, even better vesting requirements came in 1986 with the passage of the Tax Reform Act. A provision of that act accelerated the vesting period so that, as it now stands, *full vesting* rights are required after only five to seven years of employment. More specifically, companies must now choose between two vesting schedules. One, the so-called *cliff* vesting, requires full vesting after no more than five years of service—but you obtain no vesting privileges until then. It's sort of a "zero-one" proposition: there are no vesting privileges at all for the first five years, and then all of a sudden you're fully vested. Once vested, you're entitled to everything that's been paid in so far (your contributions *plus* your employer's) and everything that will be contributed in the future. Under the alternative procedure, the so-called *graded* schedule, vesting takes place gradually over the first seven years of employment. At the minimum, after three years you would have a nonforfeiture right to at least 20 percent of the benefits, with an additional 20 percent each year thereafter until you're 100 percent vested after seven years. Note, however, that these are minimum standards, and there's nothing to prohibit employers from granting more favorable vesting terms.

To illustrate the vesting process, assume that a medium-sized firm offers a plan in which full vesting of benefits occurs after five years. The plan is contributory, with employees paying 3 percent of their salaries and the employer paying an amount equal to 6 percent of the salaries. Under this plan, employees cannot withdraw the contributions made by the employer until they reach retirement. The plan provides annual benefits in the amount of $11 per year of service for each $100 of an employee's final monthly earnings—the amount earned during the final month in the employ of the firm. Therefore, an employee who worked a minimum of five years for the firm would be eligible for a retirement benefit from that company even if he or she left the company at, say, age 30. However, because of inflation, the value of the benefit for a worker who left the firm long before retirement age would be very small. Consequently, the employee might be better off simply withdrawing his or her own contributions (which always vest immediately) and terminating participation in the plan at the same time he or she leaves the employer. Of course, any worker who leaves the firm prior to accumulating five years of service would be entitled only to a return of his or her own contributions to the plan (plus nominal investment earnings).

Because participation in a company's basic pension plan is mandatory, you're entitled to immediate vesting of all contributions.
Fantasy: While your employer may offer immediate vesting, that's usually not the case. By law, you're entitled to full vesting rights within a maximum of five to seven years, depending on whether the company is using cliff or graded vesting procedures.

Retirement Age. Nearly all retirement plans specify when an eligible employee is entitled to benefits—in most cases, at age 65. Often pension plans also provide an early retirement age. In these cases, employees may begin receiving benefits prior to the normal retirement age, but the amounts paid out will also be less than normal. Many retirement plans for public employees also give workers the option of retiring after a stated number of years of service (say, 30 or 35) at full benefits, regardless of their age at the time. In the past, the trend in pension plans was toward earlier permissible retirement ages. However, now that many have begun to argue in favor of increasing the age for mandatory retirement (i.e., letting people work longer), it is expected that there'll be little motivation to further reduce the normal retirement age.

---

noncontributory pension plan
A pension plan in which the employer pays the total cost of the benefits.

contributory pension plan
A pension plan in which the employee bears a portion of the cost of the benefits.

vested rights
Employees' nonforfeitable rights to receive benefits in a pension plan based on their own and their employer's contributions.

Defined Contributions or Defined Benefits.

The method used to compute benefits at retirement is spelled out in detail in every retirement plan. The two most commonly used methods are the defined contribution plan and the defined benefits plan. A **defined contribution plan** is one that specifies the amount of contribution that the employer and employee must make. At retirement, the worker is awarded whatever level of monthly benefits those contributions will purchase. While factors such as age, income level, and the amount of contributions made to the plan have a great deal to do with the amount of monthly benefits received at retirement, probably no variable is more important than the level of *investment performance* generated on the contributed funds. A defined contribution plan, in effect, is like a variable annuity—nothing is promised at retirement except the returns that the fund managers have been able to obtain. The only thing that's defined is the amount of contribution that the employee and/or employer have to make (generally stated as a percent of the employee's income). The benefits at retirement depend totally on investment results. Of course, there's a certain standard of care that's followed by the investment managers, so there is some protection provided to the plan participants (indeed, most of the investing is confined to high-quality investment vehicles). But even so, that still leaves a lot of room for variability in returns. There'll be a big difference in retirement benefits for someone who's in a fund that's earned 6 percent versus someone else who's in a fund that's earned 12 percent.

Under a **defined benefits plan**, the formula for computing benefits, not contributions, is stipulated in the plan provisions. These benefits are paid out regardless of how well (or poorly) the retirement funds are invested. If investment performance falls short, the employer has to make up the difference to come up with the benefits agreed to in the plan. This type of plan allows employees to determine before retirement how much their monthly retirement income will be. Often the number of years of service and amount of earnings are prime factors in the formula. For example, a worker might be paid 2.5 percent of his or her final three-year average annual salary for each year of service. Thus, the *annual* benefit to an employee whose final three-year average annual salary was $65,000 and who was with the company for 20 years would be $32,500 (2.5% ×

$65,000 × 20 years). Other types of defined benefits plans may simply pay benefits based on (1) a consideration of earnings excluding years of service, (2) a consideration of years of service excluding earnings, or (3) a flat amount with no consideration given to either earnings or years of service. Many defined benefits plans also increase retirement benefits periodically to help retirees keep up with the cost of living. In periods of high inflation, these increases are essential to maintain retirees' standards of living.

Regardless of the method used to calculate benefit amounts, the employee's basic concern should be with the percent of final take-home pay that the plan is likely to produce at retirement. A pension is usually thought to be good if, when combined with social security, it will result in a monthly income of 70 to 80 percent of preretirement net earnings. To reach this goal, however, today's employee must take some responsibility, because there's a growing trend for *companies to switch from defined benefits plans to defined contributions programs.* Companies don't like the idea of being faced with undefined future pension liabilities—after all, the pension/retirement payments that don't come from investment earnings have to be made up from company earnings, and that means lower profits. So a lot of firms are avoiding these problems by gradually changing over to defined contributions plans—indeed, there are *far more* defined contribution plans in existence today than there are defined benefits plans! And in cases where the firms are sticking with their defined benefits plans, the benefits are often so meager that they don't come close to the desired 70 to 80 percent income target. (Some of the defined contributions plans don't either.) In either case *the employee is being forced to assume more responsibility for assuring the desired level of postretirement income.* The logic from the company's perspective is that if obtaining a comfortable standard of living in retirement is a worthwhile objective, the employee should be willing to help achieve it. That might mean participating in a company-sponsored supplemental retirement plan and/or possibly even setting up your own self-directed program (we'll look at both supplemental and self-directed plans later).

Funding Procedures. Pension plans must provide for the financing of benefits that will be paid out to retired workers. An **unfunded pension**

plan allows the employer to make payments to retirees from current income. One expert has called unfunded pensions "owe as you go" plans. This name really is appropriate, since employers accumulate liabilities throughout the working careers of their employees but do not necessarily put any assets aside to offset them. In the past, only a small minority of employees have been covered under unfunded pension plans; and they have received a good deal of unfavorable publicity as being too risky for employees. Consequently, the Employee Retirement Income Security Act sets forth minimum funding standards for pension plans.

Funded pension plans are those that formally establish charges against current income to allow for pension liabilities as they accrue. The amount of liability that arises under the plan each year is determined by actuarial computations. (An *actuary* is an expert in calculating risks and premiums for insurance.) These computations take into account such factors as mortality rates among workers and retirees, actual and potential investment earnings, labor turnover, normal and early retirement ages, and salary levels. In order for a funded plan to be "actuarially sound," the assumptions concerning the foregoing factors must be realistic. In addition, the method of funding must be sound. Few people would advocate placing pension fund assets in speculative investments such as land development projects or commodity futures. On the other hand, there's growing support for the practice of investing a large percentage of the fund assets in common stocks, corporate bonds and convertible securities, mortgages, and income-producing real estate.

Funding of pension plans represents an attempt to minimize the risk that benefits will not be available to an eligible employee upon retirement. Nonetheless, the unfunded plan of a large, solvent government unit or corporate employer sometimes can offer a better guarantee of payment than the funded plan of a financially weak firm. This may be particularly true when the primary objective of the actuarial assumptions of a funded system shifts from certainty of future payment to minimization of the employer's annual contributions to the plan. Requirements under the Employee Retirement Income Security Act attempt to control the lack of adequate funding in funded plans by requiring that *reasonable actuarial estimates* be used when calculating employer contributions.

Qualified Pension Plans. The Internal Revenue Code permits a corporate employer making contributions to a **qualified pension plan** to deduct from taxable income its contributions to the plan. As a result, the employees on whose behalf the contributions are made do not have to include these payments as part of their taxable income until the benefits are actually received. Further, in contributory plans, *the employee can also shelter his or her contributions from taxes.* In other words, such contributions are not counted as part of taxable income in the year in which they are made, but instead act to reduce the amount of taxable income reported to the IRS, and therefore lead to lower taxes for the employee. Still another tax advantage of these plans is that any and all investment income is allowed to accumulate tax free; as a result, investment capital can build up quicker. Yet, in spite of all these tax benefits, a lot of firms still believe that the costs of regulation exceed any benefits that might result and therefore choose to forgo the procedures required

defined contribution plan
A pension plan that specifies the amount of contributions that both employer and employee must make; it makes no promises concerning the size of the benefits at retirement.

defined benefits plan
A pension plan in which the formula for computing benefits is stipulated in its provisions, thus allowing the employee to determine prior to retirement how much his or her retirement income will be.

unfunded pension plan
A pension plan in which the employer must make payments to retirees from current income, because the plan itself has insufficient assets to cover existing liabilities.

funded pension plan
A pension plan that formally establishes charges against current income to allow for pension liabilities as they accrue in order to minimize the risk that benefits will be unavailable to an eligible employee upon retirement.

qualified pension plan
A pension plan that meets specified criteria established by the Internal Revenue Code.

for having a plan qualified. Probably the biggest disadvantage of nonqualified pension plans from the employee's perspective is that any contributions made to *contributory* plans are fully taxable and as such, are treated just like any other type of income.

EMPLOYER-SPONSORED PROGRAMS: SUPPLEMENTAL PLANS

In addition to basic retirement programs, many employers offer supplemental plans. These plans are often *voluntary* and enable employees to not only increase the amount of funds being held for retirement but also enjoy attractive tax benefits. Essentially, there are three types of supplemental plans: profit-sharing, thrift and savings, and salary reduction plans.

Profit-Sharing Plans. Profit-sharing plans permit employees to participate in the earnings of their employer. A **profit-sharing plan** may be qualified under the IRS and become eligible for essentially the same tax treatment as other types of pension plans. An argument in support of the use of profit-sharing plans is that they encourage employees to work harder because the employees benefit when the firm prospers. Whether these types of plans accomplish this goal is debatable. One advantage of profit-sharing plans from the firm's viewpoint, however, is that they do not impose any specific levels of contribution or benefits on the part of the employer. When profits are low, the employer makes a proportionately smaller contribution to the plan; when profits are high, the firm pays proportionately more.

In order to provide reasonable returns, many employers establish minimum and maximum amounts to be paid as contributions to profit-sharing plans, regardless of how low or high corporate earnings are. Contributions from profit-sharing plans can be invested in certain types of fixed-interest products, stocks and bonds, or, in many cases, securities issued by the employing firm. Employees who receive the firm's securities may actually benefit twice. When profits are good, larger contributions are made to the profit-sharing plan *plus* the price of the shares already owned is likely to increase. A number of big-time, major firms offer voluntary profit-sharing plans that invest heavily in their own stock. It's not unusual in many of these cases for long-term career employees to accumulate several hundred thousand dollars worth of the company's stocks. And we're not talking about highly paid corporate executives here; rather, these are just average employees who had the discipline to consistently divert a portion of their salary to the company's profit-sharing plan. There is a very real and important downside to this practice, however — that is, if the company should hit on hard times not only could you face salary cuts (or even worse, the loss of a job), but the value of your profit-sharing account very likely would take a big tumble as well!

Thrift and Savings Plan. **Thrift and savings plans** were established to supplement pension and other fringe benefits. Most plans require the employer to make contributions to the savings plan in an amount equal to a set proportion of the amount contributed by the employee. For example, an employer might match an employee's contributions at the rate of 50 cents on the dollar up to, say, 6 percent of salary. An employee making $20,000 a year could pay $1,200 into the plan annually, and the employer would kick in another $600. These contributions are then deposited with a trustee, who invests the money in various types of securities, including stocks and bonds of the employing firm. With IRS-qualified thrift and savings plans, the employer's contributions and earnings on the savings are not included in the *employee's* taxable income until he or she withdraws these sums. Unfortunately, this attractive tax feature does not extend to the employee's contributions, and as a result, any money put into one of these savings plans is still considered to be part of the employee's taxable income — subject to regular income taxes.

Thrift and savings plans usually have more liberal vesting and withdrawal privileges than pension and retirement programs. Often the employee's right to the contributions of the employer becomes nonforfeitable immediately upon payment, and the total savings in the plan can be withdrawn by giving proper notice. Those employees who terminate participation in such a plan, however, are frequently prohibited from rejoining it for a specified period, such as one year. An employee who has the option should seriously consider participation in a thrift plan, since the returns are usually pretty favorable — especially when you factor in the added kicker provided by the *employer's* contributions.

Salary Reduction Plans. Another type of supplemental retirement program — and certainly the most popular as judged by employee response — is the **salary reduction plan** or the so-called **401(k) plan** as it's more popularly known. While our discussion here will center on 401(k) plans, similar programs are available for employees of public, nonprofit organizations; known as 403(b) plans, they offer many of the same features and tax shelter provisions as 401(k) plans.

A 401(k) plan basically gives the employee the option to divert a portion of his or her salary to a company-sponsored, tax-sheltered savings account. In this way, the earnings diverted to the savings plan accumulate tax free. Taxes must be paid eventually, but not until the employee starts drawing down the account at retirement, presumably when in a lower tax bracket. In 1992, an individual employee could put as much as $8,728 (depending on his/her salary) into a tax-deferred 401(k) plan — the annual dollar cap increases yearly, as it's indexed to the rate of inflation. (The contribution limits for a 403(b) plan are currently set at a maximum of $9,500 a year, and that amount won't be indexed to inflation until 401(k) contributions attain parity with these plans.) Of course, in order for you to participate in one of these plans, the company you work for must offer it. Fortunately, the vast majority of medium- to large-sized firms have done just that!

To see how such tax-deferred plans work, consider an individual who earned, say, $60,000 in 1992 and would like to contribute the maximum allowable — $8,728 — to the 401(k) plan where she works. Doing so would reduce her taxable income to $51,272 and, assuming she's in the 28 percent tax bracket, lower her federal tax bill by some $2,444 (i.e., $8,728 × .28). Such tax savings will offset a good portion of her contribution to the 401(k) savings plan — specifically, it will fund 28 percent of her contribution. In effect, she will add $8,728 to her retirement program with only $6,284 of her own money; the rest will come from the IRS via a reduced tax bill! Further, all the *earnings* on her savings account will accumulate tax free as well.

These plans are generally viewed as highly attractive *tax shelters* that offer not only substantial tax savings but also a way to save for retirement. As a rule, so long as you can afford to put the money aside, *you should seriously consider joining a 401(k)/403(b) plan if offered at your place of employment.* This is especially true today because the restrictions placed on IRAs by the Tax Reform Act of 1986 mean these plans may be the only avenue you have for setting up a supplemental tax-sheltered retirement program. But there's more: A special attraction of 401(k) plans is that the firms offering them can sweeten the pot by matching all or a part of the employee's contributions. Presently, about 85 percent of the companies that offer 401(k) plans have some type of matching contributions program, often putting up 50 cents (or more) for every dollar contributed by the employee. Such matching plans provide both tax and savings incentives to individuals and clearly enhance the appeal of 401(k) plans.

The GIC in a 401(k). Look inside most 401(k) plans and you'll find something called a **guaranteed investment contract** (or **GIC**, for short). In

---

profit-sharing plan
An arrangement in which the employees of a firm participate in the company's earnings.

thrift and savings plan
A plan established by an employer to supplement pension and other fringe benefits, in which the firm makes contributions in an amount equal to a set proportion of the employee's contribution.

salary reduction, or 401(k), plan
An agreement under which a portion of a covered employee's pay is withheld and invested in an annuity or other qualified form of investment; the taxes on both the contributions and the account earnings are deferred until the funds are withdrawn.

guaranteed investment contract or GIC
An investment product, offered mostly by life insurance companies, that promises to pay a set rate of interest to investors over the life of the contract; found mostly in 401(k) and other company-sponsored retirement plans, the only guarantee they carry is that of the company that sold the contract.

fact, GICs are more widely used in 401(k) plans than any other investment vehicle — in 1992, *about 60 percent of all 401(k) money was invested in GICs!* And yet most people don't have the foggiest idea of what these things are. That's because we usually run into GICs at our place of employment, where they're offered as one of the investment choices in company-sponsored 401(k) plans (they're also available in other company-sponsored retirement programs, especially profit-sharing plans).

Guaranteed investment contracts are sold by insurance companies (and a handful of banks). They're a type of investment product whereby an insurance company accepts a deposit in return for paying a fixed rate of interest over a set period of time (usually from one to five years, and sometimes as long as ten years). In many respects, a GIC looks and acts very much like a bank CD. The big attraction of these fixed-rate investments is twofold: First, they usually pay a fixed rate of interest that's ½ to 1½ points over yields in the Treasury market; and second, the principal is *not* subject to fluctuation, like it is with stocks and bonds. Essentially, the insurance company that issues the GIC invests in all types of securities (ranging from mortgages and real estate to agency bonds — and, yes, even junk bonds). It then pays whatever competitive rate it wants to in order to land the business — that is, in most cases, the GIC is *not* backed by a specific, dedicated portfolio of securities. But what about the "guarantee" in a GIC; doesn't that mean anything? Well, contrary to what most people think, GICs are **NOT** backed by some form of federal insurance or any other type of government guarantee. They're guaranteed by the insurance company that sold the contract — the only *guarantee* in these contracts is that the insurance company promises to pay a fixed rate of interest over the life of the GIC. And that guarantee, of course, is only as good as the insurance company that issued the contract! The bottom line is if you're thinking of putting some of your 401(k) money into a GIC, find out how the issuer is rated by Best's, Standard & Poor's, and/or Moody's.

EVALUATING EMPLOYER-SPONSORED PENSION PLANS

When you participate in a company-sponsored pension plan, you're entitled to certain benefits in return for meeting certain conditions of membership — which may or may not include making contributions to the plan. Whether your participation is limited to the firm's basic plan or includes one or more of the supplemental programs, *it's vital that you take the time to acquaint yourself with the various benefits and provisions* of these retirement plans. And be sure to familiarize yourself not only with the basic plans (even though participation is mandatory, you ought to know what you're getting for your money), but also with any (voluntary) supplemental plans that you may be eligible to join.

So, how should you evaluate these plans? Most experts agree that while there are many aspects that go into a typical company-sponsored pension plan (some of which are a bit complex and difficult to evaluate), you can get a pretty good handle on essential plan provisions and retirement benefits by taking a close look at these features:

- *Eligibility requirements* — precisely what they are, and if you're not already in the plan, when will you be able to participate?
- *Defined benefits* or *contributions* — which are defined? If it's the benefits, exactly what formula is used to define them? Pay particular attention to how social security benefits are treated in the formula. If it's a defined contributions program, do you have any control over how the money is invested? If so, what are your options?
- *Vesting procedures* — does the company use a cliff or graded procedure, and precisely when do you become fully vested?
- *Contributory or noncontributory* — if the plan is contributory, how much comes from you and how much from the company; and what is the total of this contribution, as a percent of your salary? If it is noncontributory, what is the company's contribution, as a percent of your salary?
- *Retirement age* — what is the normal retirement age, and what provisions are there for *early retirement*? What happens if you leave the company before retirement? Are the pension benefits *portable* — that is, can you take them with you if you change jobs?
- *Voluntary supplemental programs* — how much of your salary can you put into one or more of these plans, and what, if anything, is *matched* by the company? Remember, these are like defined contributions plans, so there's nothing guaranteed as far as benefits are concerned. Indeed, as

the *Money in Action* box on pages 664–665 notes, when it comes to defined contributions plans, it's important to find out just who's managing your money — you may be surprised to find that, more often than not, it's *Y-O-U.*

Getting answers to these questions will help you determine where you stand and what, if any, improvements need to be made in your retirement plans. As part of this evaluation process, you should try to work up, as best as you can, *a rough estimation of what your benefits are likely to be at retirement* — you're going to have to make some projections about future income levels, investment returns, and so on, but it's an exercise well worth taking (before you start cranking out the numbers, however, check with the people who handle employee benefits at your place of work; they'll often give you the help you need). Then, using a procedure similar to what we did with the worksheet in Exhibit 15.2, you can estimate what portion of your retirement needs will be met from your company's basic pension plan. If there's a shortfall — *and there likely will be* — it will indicate the extent to which you need to participate in some type of company-sponsored supplemental program, such as a 401(k) plan, or (alternatively) how much you're going to have to rely on your own savings and investments to come up with the kind of standard of living you're looking for in retirement. *Such insights will enable you to more effectively dovetail the investment characteristics and retirement benefits of any company-sponsored retirement plans you're entitled to with the savings and investing that you do on your own.*

SELF-DIRECTED RETIREMENT PROGRAMS

In addition to participating in company-sponsored retirement programs, individuals can also set up their own tax-sheltered retirement plans. There are two basic types of self-directed retirement programs available. *Keogh plans* which are for self-employed individuals, and *individual retirement accounts (IRAs)*, which can be set up by just about anybody.

Keogh Plans. **Keogh plans** go back to 1962, when they were introduced as part of the Self-Employed Individuals Retirement Act, or simply the Keogh Act. Keogh plans allow self-employed individ-

uals to set up tax-deferred retirement plans for themselves and their employees. Like contributions to 401(k) plans, payments to Keogh accounts may be taken as deductions from taxable income. As a result, they reduce the tax bills of self-employed individuals. The maximum contribution to this tax-deferred retirement plan is $30,000 per year or 20 percent of earned income, whichever is less. (Technically, the rules allow 25 percent contributions *based on net income after Keogh contributions* — which works out to 20 percent of earned income. For example, the maximum contribution on $150,000 of earned income is $30,000, which results in a net income after Keogh contributions of $120,000; thus, the $30,000 contribution is equivalent to 25 percent of the $120,000 base, or 20 percent of $150,000.)

Any individual who is self-employed, either full- or part-time, is eligible to set up a Keogh account. Not only can self-employed businesspeople or professionals use Keoghs, they can also be used by individuals who hold full-time jobs and "moonlight" on a part-time basis — for instance, the engineer who has a small consulting business on the side or the accountant who does tax returns in the evenings and on weekends. If the engineer, for example, earns $10,000 a year from his part-time consulting business, he can contribute 20 percent of that income ($2,000) to his Keogh account and, in so doing, reduce both his taxable income and the amount he pays in taxes. Further, he is still eligible to receive full retirement benefits from his full-time job, as well as having his own IRA (though, as we'll see below, contributions to his IRA probably will not qualify for tax shelter). The only catch to Keogh accounts is that the individual must be self-employed — that is, the income must be derived from the net earnings (after all expenses except taxes and retirement contributions) of a self-employed business.

> **Keogh plan**
> An account to which self-employed persons may make payments, up to the lesser of $30,000 or 20 percent of earned income per year, that may be taken as deductions from taxable income; the earnings on such accounts also accrue on a tax-deferred basis.

Who's Managing the Money in Your Plan?

Millions of Americans are trusting their retirement money to inexperienced and confused investment managers — themselves. With more and more companies offering so-called defined contribution plans, workers are calling more of the shots about their retirement investments. And with those decisions go the risk, so investment mistakes made by workers in the new plans come straight out of their pension nest eggs, rather than being made up by companies.

In a defined contribution plan, an employer regularly contributes money to an employee's retirement account, but doesn't promise the size of the payout the employee will get on retirement. Defined contribution plans linked to profit-sharing, stock bonuses and other savings schemes have been around since the 1940s, but they've gotten a big boost in the past decade from expanded tax breaks that shelter contributions and investment

earnings until a worker retires or changes jobs.

A major attraction of many plans is that companies will match half or more of worker contributions to the plan, producing automatic returns of 50% or better on the worker's contribution. But while employees often like the sense of control they get in defined contribution programs, serving as your own money manager is earthshaking to those people who haven't had the responsibility in the past. Furthermore, says financial consultant Jonathan Pond: "Some people are getting hurt along the way that wouldn't have gotten hurt with professionals" managing their retirement accounts.

FASTEST GROWING BENEFIT

So-called defined benefit plans, under which companies shoulder all the investment risk in promising to make specific payouts, still cover millions of workers. But defined contribution plans have become the

fastest growing employee benefit — both as basic employer-sponsored programs and, especially, as supplements to existing pension plans.

Supplemental retirement income has become the focus of greater attention as people increasingly will spend as much time in retirement as they spend working. "Social Security was never meant to be the sole provider of your retirement income, and pension plans were never meant to be the sole provider," says Majorie Neville of pension consulting firm TPF&C. "There has to be a third leg, and that's personal saving."

With so much at stake, many participants in defined contribution plans just run for cover. Far and away the most popular investment choice in defined contribution plans are low-risk, fixed-rate guaranteed investment contracts offered by insurance companies. "Employees do not understand all their alternatives, so they do the safe thing," says Steven G.

Keogh accounts can be opened at banks, insurance companies, brokerage houses, mutual funds, and other financial institutions. Annual contributions must be made at the time the respective tax return is filed or by April 15th of the following calendar year (for example, you have until April 15, 1993, to make the contribution to your Keogh for 1992). While a designated financial institution acts as custodian of all the funds held in a Keogh account, *the actual investments held in the account are under the complete direction of the individual contributor*. These are self-directed retirement programs and, as such, the *individual* decides which investments to buy and sell (subject to a few basic restrictions).

The income earned from the investments must be plowed back to the account and it, too, accrues tax

Vernon of pension consultants Wyatt Co. "They're afraid of the stock market, and they're not aware that over the longer term, the stock market gives them a better rate of return."

For participants, tax benefits and other provisions of individual company plans vary widely, so before you can take advantage of your plan, you need to know its features. Some 89% of defined contribution plans allow tax-deferred employee contributions, according to a Bankers Trust Co. survey.

In other plans, only the company contribution gets a tax shelter, although employees sometimes can make after-tax contributions on which gains accumulate tax-free. Some companies provide no matching funds; others contribute $.50 for each $1 contributed by workers. A handful of companies place no restrictions on where plan assets are invested, while a few others offer no choice on investments, limiting them to company stock, for example. But to-gether, the tax deferral and matching features can add up to produce handsome results.

So, faced with a number of investment decisions, what should an employee with a defined contribution plan do?

DIVERSIFY, DIVERSIFY, DIVERSIFY

Not putting all your eggs in one basket is becoming easier — or more complex, some say — because of the rapid growth in the number of investment options being offered under defined contribution plans. A typical investment menu would include stock, bond and money market mutual funds, a "balanced" fund combining stocks and bonds or perhaps different stock investment styles, and a fixed-rate guaranteed investment contract. Stock index funds, which mimic moves of the Standard & Poor's 500 index, were unheard of in defined contribution plans 10 years ago, but now are increasingly common.

A very basic diversification formula for allocating assets involves dividing investments into thirds — with equal amounts going to stocks, long-term bonds and short-term funds, including guaranteed investment contracts and money market funds. Investors willing to spend time doing their economic homework might make a bigger bet on either stocks or bonds. A 60–40 split in favor of stocks would pay off in a rising economy, and the opposite mix should do better in a declining economy. Whatever investment mix you decide on, force yourself to stick with those choices for at least a couple of years, preferably longer. Don't get caught in the trap of trying to time the market — that truly is a losing proposition. But no matter what you do, don't forget: It's your money!

Source: Adapted from James A. White, "Are You Your Own Pension Manager?" *The Wall Street Journal*, January 16, 1989, C1, p. 13. Reprinted by permission of *The Wall Street Journal* © Dow Jones & Company, Inc. 1989. All Rights Reserved Worldwide.

free. All Keogh contributions and investment earnings must remain in the account until the individual turns 59½, unless he or she becomes seriously ill or disabled — early withdrawals for any other reason are subject to 10 percent tax penalties. However, the individual is *not required* to start withdrawing the funds at age 59½; the funds can stay in the account (and continue to earn tax-free income) until the in-dividual is 70½, at which time he or she has ten years to clean out the account. In fact, so long as the income from self-employment continues, an individual can continue to make tax-deferred contributions to a Keogh account until reaching the maximum age of 70½. Of course, once he or she starts withdrawing funds from a Keogh account (upon or after turning 59½), all such withdrawals are treated as ordinary income and subject to the payment of normal income taxes. Thus, the taxes on all contributions to and earnings from a Keogh account will eventually have to be paid, a characteristic of any tax-*deferred* (as opposed to tax-*free*) program. (*Note:* A program that's similar in many respects to the Keogh account is something called a *Simplified Employee Pension Plan*—or SEP-IRA for short. It's aimed at small-business owners, particularly those with *no employees*, who want a plan that is simple to set up and administer. SEP-IRAs *can be used in place of Keoghs* and while they are simpler to administer and have the same dollar annual contribution cap ($30,000), their contribution rate is less generous; you can put in only 15 percent of earned income for a SEP-IRA, versus 20 percent for a Keogh.)

Individual Retirement Accounts (IRAs).

Some people mistakenly believe that an IRA is a specialized type of investment. It is not. Actually, an **individual retirement account (IRA)** is virtually the same as any other investment account you open with a bank, credit union, stockbroker, mutual fund, or insurance company. The form you complete designates the account as an IRA and makes the institution its trustee. That is all there is to it.

Basically, any gainfully employed individual can have an IRA account, though the *annual contributions* of only certain individuals qualify as tax deductions. Specifically, in order to be able to use your annual IRA contributions as a tax deduction, one of the following two conditions has to be met: (1) Neither you nor your spouse can be covered by a company-sponsored pension plan, or (2) your adjusted gross income has to be less than $40,000 (for married couples) or $25,000 (for singles). Translated, this means your IRA contibutions would fully qualify as a tax deduction if you were covered by a company-sponsored pension plan but your adjusted gross income fell below the specified amounts (of $40,000 for joint filers and $25,000 for singles), *or* if you (or your spouse) weren't covered by a company-sponsored pension plan, no matter how much your adjusted gross income was. (Note that the income ceilings are phased out, so that people with adjusted gross incomes of $40,000 to $50,000 [or $25,000 to $35,000] who are covered by employer pension plans, are still entitled to prorated *partial deductions*.)

The annual contribution limits to IRAs are $2,000 for an individual and $2,250 for an individual and nonworking spouse. If both spouses work, each can contribute up to $2,000 to his or her own IRA. If the contributions qualify as tax deductions (as per the two conditions noted above), then the amount of the IRA contributions can be shown on the tax return as a deduction from taxable income—which, of course, will also reduce the amount of taxes that have to be paid. And understand that even if you don't qualify for a tax deduction, *you can still contribute up to the maximum of $2,000 a year to an IRA account*; the only difference (and it's a big one) is that these nondeductible contributions will have to be made with after-tax income

As with Keoghs and 401(k) programs, the taxes on all the *earnings* from an IRA account are deferred until you start drawing down the funds, and this provision applies regardless of your income or whether you're already covered by a pension plan at your place of employment! You can deposit as much or as little as you want (up to the ceilings), and there are no percentage of income limitations; if your earned income is only, say, $1,800, you can contribute all of it to your IRA.

IRAs are like Keogh plans in that they are both *self-directed accounts*—meaning you are free, within limits, to make whatever investment decisions you want. Actually, as with any investment, an individual can be conservative or aggressive in choosing securities for an IRA (or Keogh), though the nature of these retirement programs generally favors a more conservative approach. In fact, conventional wisdom favors funding your IRA (and Keogh) with *income-producing assets*; this would also suggest that if you are looking for capital gains, it is best to do so *outside* your retirement account. The reasons are twofold: (1) Growth-oriented securities are by nature *more risky*, and (2) you *cannot write off losses* from the sale of securities held in an IRA (or Keogh) account. This does not mean, however, that it would be altogether inappropriate to place a good-quality growth stock or mutual fund in a Keogh or IRA—in fact, many advisors contend that growth investments should always have a place in your retirement account due to their often impressive performance. Such investments may pay off handsomely, since they can appreciate totally free of taxes. In the end, of course, *it is how much you have in your retire-*

ment account that matters rather than how your earnings were made along the way. Also, regardless of what type of investment vehicle you use, keep in mind that once the money's been placed in an IRA, it's meant to stay there for the long haul. For like most tax-sheltered retirement programs, there are severe restrictions on when you can withdraw the funds from an IRA. Specifically, except in the case of permanent disability, any funds withdrawn from an IRA prior to age 59½ are subject to a 10 percent tax penalty, on top of the regular tax paid on the withdrawal. (Note, however, that you can avoid the 10 percent tax penalty and still start withdrawals before age 59½ by setting up a systematic withdrawal program that essentially pays you equal amounts over the rest of your life expectancy; obviously, unless you have a substantial amount of money in your IRA, the annual payments under this program are likely to be pretty small.)

Prior to the Tax Reform Act of 1986, IRAs had become immensely popular. By 1985 over 40 million Americans held IRAs, with an estimated worth of nearly $250 billion! The tax overhaul bill, however, sharply curtailed the tax-shelter feature of IRAs, and as a result, these accounts lost a lot of their appeal. Contributions plunged as most people who no longer qualified for tax-sheltered contributions simply quit putting their money into IRAs. And those who continued to make contributions even though they were nondeductible got hit with horrendous record-keeping requirements and an IRS tax form that is second to none in complexity. In particular, anyone who contributes money that is not tax deductible must now file a *Form 8606* (for "Nondeductible IRA Contributions") with his or her federal tax returns. It's pretty clear that Congress wants to sharply curtail the use of IRAs; and if tax statutes don't do the job, then a bunch of mostly unnecessary red tape will! This is all very unfortunate, since most retirement experts agree that the original IRA concept was a great one.

So, should you contribute to an IRA or not? Obviously, if you qualify for *fully deductible* contributions (as per the two provisions as spelled out above) you should seriously consider making the maximum payments allowable. You do not need to worry about onerous record-keeping requirements or filing a Form 8606 with your taxes. For these individuals, the IRA continues to be an excellent vehicle for sheltering some of their income from taxes. But if your contributions don't qualify for full deductibility, the prevailing sentiment seems to be to avoid nondeductible IRAs; for not only do you have a number of substantial hurdles to overcome, but some equally attractive alternatives are available for sheltering your income. As a starter, find out if the company you work for has a 401(k) — or 403(b) — plan in existence and if so, use it. Or you might want to consider parking your money in a *tax-sheltered annuity* (discussed later in this chapter). It offers basically the same advantages as a nondeductible IRA, with the added kicker that there's no limit as to how much you can put in each year (remember, you can only put $2,000 a year into an IRA).

Your contributions to an IRA account may or may not be tax deductible, depending in part on your level of income.

Fact: Whether or not your IRA contributions are fully deductible depends to a large extent on your adjusted gross income — specifically, the contributions are considered *fully* deductible if your adjusted gross income is less than $40,000, for joint returns ($25,000 for individual returns); if your income is more than this, your IRA contributions would be fully deductible only if you're not already covered by a company-sponsored pension plan.

GOVERNMENT INFLUENCE ON PENSION PLANS

The two major areas of government influence on pension plans are the Internal Revenue Code (IRC) requirements for plan qualification and the rules and regulations established by the Employee Retirement Income Security Act of 1974 (ERISA). The major stipulations of the IRC were discussed earlier in

---

individual retirement account (IRA)

A retirement plan, open to any working American, to which a person may contribute a specified amount each year (up to $2,000 in the case of an individual taxpayer); while annual contributions to IRAs may or may not be tax deductible, the earnings from all IRAs do accrue on a tax-deferred basis.

the chapter. At this point, we will look at the most important features of ERISA. As the name implies, the act's primary objective is to increase the probability that employees who are covered by a retirement plan throughout their working careers will in fact receive benefits upon retirement. ERISA covers nearly all pension and retirement plans created by private employers engaged in interstate commerce. It does not cover plans sponsored by government, charitable organizations, or firms exclusively involved in intrastate commerce. The law regulates only plans that are in existence. It does not require firms to begin a retirement plan for their employees, nor does it prohibit them from discontinuing an existing plan (as many have done to avoid the myriad ERISA rules and regulations). Similarly, ERISA does not force companies to pay any minimum amounts to employees, other than those specified in the plans.

ERISA basically prescribes minimum standards with which covered plans must comply. These standards apply to plan provisions, funding, and administration. Among the major items treated are vesting, eligibility for participation, definition of service, minimum funding requirements, disclosure to participants, and employer fiduciary responsibility. Another important provision establishes the **Pension Benefit Guarantee Corporation (PBGC)**. The purpose of this organization is to guarantee eligible workers that certain benefits will be payable to them even if their employer's plan has insufficient assets to fulfill its commitments. The funding for the PBGC comes from charges that are levied against all employers regulated by ERISA. In essence, the PBGC provides plan termination insurance to covered employees. Although the implementation of ERISA has not been free of problems, most observers agree that this law is a good start in insuring that employees who have earned pensions will receive them.

ANNUITIES

An annuity is a type of investment vehicle that systematically pays out benefits, usually over an extended period of time. They're widely used as a supplemental source of income by people in retirement. When you buy an annuity, you're essentially making a long-term commitment with your money; accordingly, it's important to consider the kind of return you'll get on your investment. You can choose a *fixed-rate* annuity, where your returns are closely linked to yields in the money market, or a *variable-rate* annuity, which allows you to aggressively play the stock and bond markets. What kind of annuity would you find most attractive? What would you see as the advantages and disadvantages of each type? Give some thought to these questions before reading on.

The number of annuity contracts in force with U.S. life insurance companies has grown tremendously in the past 10 to 15 years. Just look at what happened over the decade of the 1980s: In 1980 annuity sales amounted to $35 billion; by 1990, annuity sales had jumped to nearly $60 billion, as insurers competed aggressively with banks, brokerage firms, and mutual funds for consumer savings. Indeed, by 1990, life insurance companies were actually generating more premium income from annuities than they were from the sale of life insurance policies! This growth has resulted primarily from greater public awareness of annuities, as brought about by the increased marketing efforts of life insurance companies. In addition, the surge in retirement programs has contributed to the growth of annuities and so have the tax laws, which treat annuities as tax-sheltered investment vehicles — in fact, the demand for these products has been greatly heightened in recent years as changes in the tax laws have made annuities one of the few tax shelters left to investors. Stripped down, annuities represent little more than an agreement to make contributions now (or in installments) in return for a series of payments later — for a fixed number of years, or for life.

THE ANNUITY PRINCIPLE

An annuity is just the opposite of life insurance. As we pointed out in Chapter 9, life insurance is the systematic accumulation of an estate which is used for protection against financial loss resulting from premature death. In contrast, an **annuity** is the systematic *liquidation* of an estate in such a way that it provides protection against the economic difficulties that could result from outliving personal financial resources. The period during which premiums are paid for the purchase of an annuity is called the **accumulation period**; correspondingly, the period during which annuity payments are made is called the **distribution period**.

Under a pure life annuity contract, a life insurance company will guarantee regular monthly payments to an individual for as long as he or she lives. These benefits are composed of three parts: principal, interest, and survivorship benefits. The *principal* consists of the premium amounts paid in by the *annuitant* (person buying the annuity) during the accumulation period. *Interest* is the amount earned on these funds between the time they are paid and distributed. The interest earnings on an annuity accrue (that is, accumulate) tax-free. The portion of the principal and interest that has not been returned to the annuitant prior to death is the **survivorship benefit**. These funds are available to those members of the annuity group who survive in each subsequent period. By using mortality tables and estimated investment returns, life insurance companies can calculate for a group of annuitants of a given age the amount of monthly payment they can guarantee to each individual without prematurely depleting the total amounts that have accumulated. Consequently, the risk of outliving one's income is eliminated.

CLASSIFICATION OF ANNUITIES

Annuities may be classified according to several key characteristics, including the way the premiums are paid, the disposition of proceeds, inception date of benefits and the method used in calculating benefits. Exhibit 15.7 presents a chart of this classification system.

Single Premium or Installments. There are two ways to pay the premiums when you purchase an annuity contract: you can make a large single (lump-sum) payment right up front or pay the premium in installments. The **single-premium annuity contract** usually requires a minimum investment of anywhere from $2,500 to $10,000, with $5,000 the most common figure. These annuities have become very popular recently, primarily because of the attractive tax features they offer investors. Also, they are often purchased just before re-

tirement as a way of creating a future stream of income. Sometimes the cash value of a life insurance policy will be used at retirement to acquire a single-premium annuity. This is a highly effective use of a life insurance policy: You get the insurance coverage when you need it the most (while you're raising and educating your family) and then a regular stream of income when you can probably use it the most (after you've retired).

While the majority of *group* annuity policies are funded with single premiums, many *individuals* still buy annuities by paying for them in installments. In these so-called **installment-premium annuity contracts**, set payments, starting as low as $100, are made at regular intervals (monthly, quarterly, annually) over an extended period of time. Sometimes, these annuities are set up with a fairly large initial payment (of perhaps several thousand dollars), followed by a series of much smaller installment payments (of, say, $250 a quarter). There are even plans

---

Pension Benefit Guarantee Corporation (PBGC)
An organization established under ERISA that guarantees to eligible workers payability of certain pension benefits regardless of the employer's ability to fulfill its commitments.

annuity
An investment product sold by life insurance companies that provides a series of payments over time.

accumulation period
The period during which premiums are paid for the purchase of an annuity.

distribution period
The period during which annuity payments are made to an annuitant.

survivorship benefit
On an annuity, the portion of premiums and interest that has not been returned to the annuitant prior to his or her death.

single-premium annuity contract
An annuity contract that is purchased with a lump-sum payment.

installment-premium annuity contract
An annuity contract that is purchased through periodic payments made over a given period of time.

EXHIBIT 15.7

Different Types of Annuity Contracts

The different types of annuity contracts vary according to how you pay for the annuity, how the proceeds will be disbursed, how earnings accrue, and when you will receive the benefits.

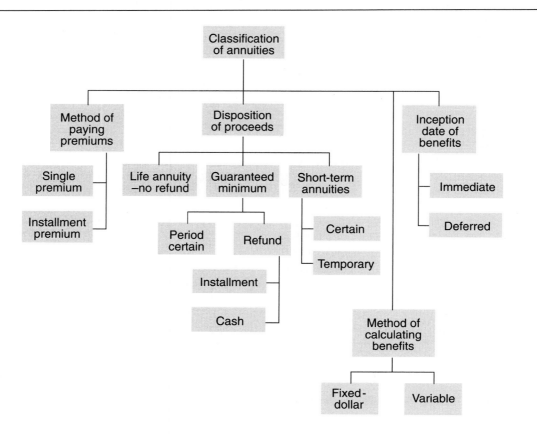

Source: Adapted from Robert I. Mehr, *Life Insurance: Theory and Practice*, rev. ed. (Dallas: Business Publications, 1977).

that combine the features of both single-premium and installment-premium annuities. Known as *flexible plans*, they start out with a sizable initial investment, very much like single-premium annuities, except that the investor can put more money in later, *as desired*. In this type of contract, which is common with variable annuities, the individual is under no obligation to make future set payments at set intervals.

Installment-premium contracts also carry an important *life insurance provision*, which stipulates that if an annuitant dies before the distribution pe-

riod begins, the annuitant's beneficiaries will receive the market value of the contract or the amount invested, whichever is greater (note that single-premium annuities contain similar life insurance provisions, so long as the payout of benefits is deferred to some future date). In addition, the annuitant can terminate an installment-premium contract at any time, or simply stop paying the periodic installments and take a paid-up annuity for a reduced amount. One potential advantage of purchasing an installment-type annuity early is that the scheduled benefits are based on mortality rates in effect when the contract is purchased. Even if the mortality rate improves, as it normally does with the passage of time, the annuitant will not be required to pay the higher premium stipulated in contracts issued later on.

Disposition of Proceeds. All annuities revolve around the basic *pay-now, receive-later* concept. As such, they allow individuals to prepare for future cash needs, like planning for retirement, while obtaining significant tax benefits. When it comes to the distribution of an annuity, you can either take a lump-sum payment, or, as is more often the case, you can *annuitize* the distribution by systematically parceling out the money into regular payments over a defined, or open-ended, period of time. Since most people choose to annuitize their proceeds (which is *conceptually* the way an annuity should be used), let's look at the options that are most widely followed in the distribution of an annuity—these include the life annuity with no refund, the guaranteed minimum annuity, the annuity certain, and the temporary life annuity.

Life annuity with no refund (straight life). Under the **life annuity with no refund (straight life)** option, the annuitant receives a specified amount of income for life, regardless of whether the period over which income is disbursed turns out to be 1 year or 50 years. *No refunds or payments are made to the estate or family when the annuitant dies.* This disposition procedure entitles the annuitant to the largest monthly payments of any of the distribution methods. These larger payments result because when the annuitant dies, the issuer (a life insurance company) does not have to distribute the principal, if any, to the annuitant's heirs.

This is not a particularly popular option and, as such, it's not used by a lot of people. The reason is that most people who purchase annuities are opposed to sacrificing the unused portion of their capital should they die relatively soon after retirement. However, this option often is used under group annuity contracts.

Guaranteed-minimum annuity. The **guaranteed-minimum annuity** was developed to help overcome the emotional and economic objections to the straight life annuity. The two basic types of this annuity are the (1) life annuity, period certain, and (2) refund annuity. With each of these options, the annuitant designates a beneficiary who

also may become eligible for benefits. Under the **life annuity, period certain**, the annuitant is guaranteed a stated amount of monthly income for life. In addition, the insurance company agrees to pay the stipulated monthly benefits for at least a minimum number of years (five or ten, for example) regardless of whether the annuitant survives. Thus, if the annuitant dies soon after the distribution begins, his (or her) beneficiaries will receive the monthly benefits for the balance of the "period certain." A **refund annuity** provides that upon the death of the annuitant, monthly payments will be made to the designated beneficiary *until the total purchase price of the annuity has been refunded*. In place of the monthly payments, the refund may be taken in cash if so specified in the contract.

Annuity certain. A specified amount of monthly income for a specified number of years without consideration of any life contingency is provided by the **annuity certain**. For instance, if an

---

life annuity with no refund (straight life)

An option under which an annuitant receives a specified amount of income for life regardless of the length of the distribution period; in turn, no payments or refunds are made to the person's family or estate upon his or her death.

guaranteed-minimum annuity

An annuity that provides a guaranteed minimum distribution of benefits.

life annuity, period certain

A type of guaranteed-minimum annuity in which the annuitant is guaranteed a stated amount of monthly income for life and the insurer agrees to pay that amount for a minimum number of years regardless of whether or not the annuitant survives.

refund annuity

A type of guaranteed-minimum annuity that provides that upon the annuitant's death, monthly payments will be made to the designated beneficiary until the total purchase price of the annuity has been refunded.

annuity certain

An annuity that provides a specified amount of monthly income for a stated number of years without consideration of any life contingency.

Smart Money

Are Variable Annuities Right for You?

Variable annuities combine the convenience of investing in mutual funds with the tax-deferral of an individual retirement account. But that doesn't mean they are for everybody. Before investing in one, investors should answer the following questions:

■ **Can you lock the money up for at least 10 years?** Most annuity contracts have surrender penalties that can cut off a hefty chunk of principal if money is taken out too soon. For example, take Equitable Life Assurance Society of the U.S.'s EquiVest, one of the largest variable annuities available to individual investors. It takes 6% of the money in the contract if an investor decides to pull out during the first five years, 5% if the withdrawal is made in years six through eight, and 4% in year nine. The penalty phases out by year 12.

Another reason variable annuities are appropriate only for long-term investors is that it takes years for the tax deferral to offset the high contract charges. "An annuity's annual contract charges will offset or exceed the tax-deferral benefits within the first 10 years," says Steven Weinstein, a partner at accounting firm Arthur Andersen & Co. People who will need their money in less than 10 years would be better off in mutual funds, he says.

■ **Will you be at least 59½ years old when you start to make withdrawals?** Annuities, like all tax-deferred retirement vehicles, including IRAs, have restrictions on early withdrawals. Earnings on money taken out before age 59½ are generally subject to a 10% federal tax penalty. There is one exception: If a person under 59½ elects to "annuitize" (that is, agrees to have the money accumulated in the annuity paid out in equal monthly payments for a certain number of years, or until the investor dies), the 10% penalty doesn't apply.

---

annuitant selected a ten-year annuity certain, payments would continue to ten years after that individual retired, regardless of whether he or she lived two or twenty more years. The annuity certain can fill a need for monthly income that will expire after a certain length of time. For example, a widow age 52 could choose a ten-year annuity certain contract to fill the need for income until she reaches age 62, when she plans to apply for social security benefits.

Temporary life annuity. Although similar to the annuity certain, the **temporary life annuity** continues benefits for a specified period only if the annuitant survives. If the above widow had chosen a ten-year temporary life annuity but died at age 60, no further payments would be made under the contract. Since the temporary life annuity provides no survivorship benefit, it provides a larger monthly income than the annuity certain. It's most appropriate for those who have no beneficiaries, or who need the added income. In actuality, annuitants purchase temporary life annuity contracts only infrequently for the same basic reason that they avoid straight life annuities — they do not want a major portion of the purchase price of their annuities to be wasted should they die shortly after payments begin.

Immediate versus Deferred Annuity. An annuitant often has the choice of receiving monthly benefits immediately upon buying an annuity or of deferring receipt for a number of years. Logically, the first type is called an immediate annuity and the

■ *Are lower-cost alternatives available?*

Other vehicles for tax-deferred investing may be more attractive than variable annuities, particularly those that allow you to invest pretax dollars. Among the possibilities: 401(k) retirement plans offered by a growing number of employers, other types of company retirement plans, IRAs for those who can deduct the contribution, and Keogh retirement plans for people with income from self-employment. "These alternatives not only defer taxes on earnings, but they defer taxes on income that's contributed to them," says Mr. Weinstein.

■ *Do you want retirement income?*

People often use variable annuities simply as a tax-deferred investment vehicle. Typically, they liquidate the contract after age 59½, and pay taxes on the earnings. But others use variable annuities to provide a steady stream of income when they retire. Investors who plan to do this need to be especially careful when selecting an annuity to scrutinize the safety of the life insurance company that underwrites the contract.

During the accumulation phase, investors have no exposure to the life insurance company, since the funds are held in separate accounts that aren't subject to general claims by creditors of the life insurance company. But when people annuitize, their money generally goes into the insurance company's pool of assets. While you are getting the company's promise to pay you back, that promise might be jeopardized if the insurer runs into severe financial difficulties and is taken over by regulators — as happened with several insurers in 1991.

Source: Ellen E. Schultz, "Are Annuities the Right Investment for You?" *The Wall Street Journal*, December 11, 1991, pp. C1, 13.

latter a deferred annuity. An **immediate annuity**, purchased with a single premium, is most often used in conjunction with the cash value or death proceeds of a life insurance policy to create a stream of cash receipts needed for retirement or to support a widow and/or dependent children. A **deferred annuity**, in contrast, can be bought with either a single payment or through an installment plan. This contract is quite flexible and can be issued with numerous options for both paying the premiums and receiving the proceeds. The big advantage of a deferred annuity is that your savings can build up over time free of taxes. With no taxes to pay, you have more money working for you and, as such, can build up a bigger retirement nest egg (of course, you'll have to pay taxes on your earnings eventually, but

temporary life annuity

An annuity in which benefits continue for a specified period, only for as long as the annuitant survives.

immediate annuity

An annuity in which the annuitant begins receiving monthly benefits immediately; often purchased with a single premium.

deferred annuity

An annuity in which benefit payments are deferred for a certain number of years; purchased with either a lump-sum payment or in installments.

not until you start receiving payments from your annuity). Most annuities purchased under group contracts are immediate annuities, whereas those purchased by individuals are usually of the *deferred* type. In fact, because of their attractive tax features, a lot of people buy deferred annuities—and especially single-premium deferred annuities—more as a tax-sheltered *investment vehicle* than anything else.

Fixed versus Variable Annuity. When you put your money into an annuity, the premium is invested on your behalf by the insurance company, much like a mutual fund invests the money you put into it. From the time you pay the annuity premium until it is paid back to you as a lump sum or as an annuitized monthly benefit, you'll be earning a rate of return on your investment. How that rate of return is figured determines whether you own a fixed or variable annuity. In a **fixed-rate annuity** the insurance company safeguards your principal and agrees to pay a guaranteed minimum rate of interest over the life of the contract—which often amounts to little more than prevailing money market rates that existed at the time you bought the contract. These are conservative, very low-risk annuity products that essentially promise to return *the original investment plus interest* when the money is paid out to the annuitant (and/or any designated beneficiaries). Unlike bond mutual funds, fixed annuities do not fluctuate in value when interest rates rise or fall; as such, your principal is secure at all times. However, contrary to what many people think, these annuities are *not* backed by a specific, dedicated portfolio of securities (like mutual funds are). Rather, they are backed by the insurance company's "general account," which often consists of a wide variety of investment vehicles; and when it comes to the rate of interest paid on the annuity, *the insurance company can pay whatever they want*, as they are in no way required to pay the rate they earn on their general account! With fixed annuities, once a distribution, or payout, schedule has been selected, the annuitant knows right up front what the (minimum) monthly benefit will be, as that's guaranteed by the annuity contract. These *interest-earning annuities*, as they're also called, are ideally suited for the cautious investor who likes the secure feeling of knowing what his or her monthly cash flow will be.

Imagine an investment vehicle that lets you move between stocks, bonds, and money funds and, at the same time, accumulate profits tax-free. That, in a nutshell, is a variable annuity. With a **variable annuity** contract, the amount that's ultimately paid out to the annuitant varies with the investment results obtained by the insurance company—*nothing* is guaranteed, not even the principal! When you buy a variable annuity, you decide where you want your money invested, based on your investment objectives and tolerance for risk: You can usually choose from stocks, bonds, money market securities or some combination thereof. Insurance companies typically offer five or six stock and bond funds, as well as money market investments for short-term safety; some companies even offer a relatively exotic fleet of alternatives, ranging from zero coupon bonds to real estate and foreign securities. As an annuity holder, you can stay put with a single investment for the long haul, or, as with most variable annuities, you can aggressively play the market by switching from one fund to another. Obviously, when the market goes up, investors in variable annuities do well; but, as many people learned in the market crash of October 1987, the returns on these policies can also go DOWN—and sometimes, in a very big way.

Because the payoff from a variable annuity depends to such an extent on the fate of the markets, the annuitants take a chance that their monthly income will be less than anticipated. Of course, most people who participate in variable annuity plans fully expect to be able to outperform fixed annuities. But that doesn't always happen, as we saw in the 1970s when a sluggish stock market led to variable annuity payments that were well below the amounts paid on corresponding fixed-rate plans. Annuitants, however, do have some control over this type of risk exposure, since they can choose to go with high- or low-risk investment vehicles and in so doing, influence the certainty of return. In effect, if you go with an account that stresses high-risk securities, you should expect a good deal of uncertainty in return—the potential for high return might be there, but so is the chance for loss. If you're uncomfortable with that, then stick to annuities that offer safer investment choices (like zero coupon bonds or Treasury securities). Also, although there's noth-

EXHIBIT 15.8
Lump-Sum Costs Necessary for Funding Payments of $100 a Month

Annuity costs vary not only by the type of annuity and the sex and age of the beneficiary but also by the company selling the contract. Clearly, it pays to shop around: What it would cost a 55-year-old male to buy $100 a month through a life annuity contract from Company 2 would cost nearly 27 percent more if the same type of contract were bought from Company 3.

| | Life Annuity With No Refund | | | | | |
| | Male | | | Female | | |
Company	55	65	75	55	65	75
1	$13,110	$11,170	$8,510	$13,930	$12,280	$9,700
2	11,820	10,250	8,010	12,450	11,140	8,980
3	15,020	11,970	8,420	16,510	13,440	9,580
4	12,900	10,960	8,480	13,660	11,860	9,270

| | Life Annuity — 10 Years Certain | | | | | |
| | Male | | | Female | | |
Company	55	65	75	55	65	75
1	$13,400	$11,840	$10,170	$14,070	$12,660	$10,770
2	12,050	10,800	9,390	12,560	11,440	9,870
3	N/A	N/A	N/A	N/A	N/A	N/A
4	13,190	11,570	9,940	13,790	12,200	10,300

ing to prohibit you from staying with market-sensitive variable annuities during both the accumulation and distribution periods, in most cases you can convert to a fixed annuity at distribution. What you do, in effect, is use the cash value in your variable annuity to buy a paid-up fixed annuity. In this way, you use a *variable annuity during the accumulation period* to build up your capital as much as possible, and then switch to a *fixed annuity for the distribution period* to obtain a certain, well-defined stream of future income. While variable annuities have a lot to offer, they're not for everyone; take a look at the *Smart Money* box (pages 672–673) — it'll help you decide if these annuities are right for you.

SOURCES AND COSTS OF ANNUITIES

Annuities are administered by life insurance companies, and for that reason, it should come as no surprise that they're also the leading sellers of these financial products. In addition, annuities can also be purchased from stock brokers, mutual fund organizations, banks, and financial planners. When you buy an annuity, the cost will vary considerably with the age of the annuitant at issue, the age of the annuitant when payments begin, the method used to distribute benefits, the number of lives covered, and the sex of the annuitant. Exhibit 15.8 presents the lump-sum costs of several leading companies for two types of immediate annuities. Note the substantial differences that exist among the companies' premium. These differences confirm the need to shop

fixed-rate annuity
An annuity in which the insurance company safeguards your principal and agrees to pay a guaranteed rate of interest on your money; in addition, the (minimum) monthly benefit is set by the contract.

variable annuity
An annuity in which the monthly income provided by the policy varies according to the actual investment experience of the insurer.

EXHIBIT 15.9

Life Expectancies of American Men and Women (Latest Available Statistics, 1985)

Life expectancy measures the number of years a person has left to live—for example, on average, a 20-year-old has a little over 56 years remaining. Note, however, that life expectancy varies by age, sex, and race.

		Expectation of Life in Years			
	Total	**White**		**All Other**	
Age	**Persons**	**Male**	**Female**	**Male**	**Female**
0	74.7	71.9	78.7	67.2	75.0
1	74.5	71.6	78.4	67.4	75.1
2	73.6	70.7	77.4	66.5	74.1
3	72.6	69.7	76.5	65.5	73.2
4	71.7	68.7	75.5	64.6	72.2
5	70.7	67.8	74.5	63.6	71.2
6	69.7	66.8	73.5	62.6	70.3
7	68.7	65.8	72.5	61.7	69.3
8	67.7	64.8	71.5	60.7	68.3
9	66.8	63.8	70.6	59.7	67.3
10	65.8	62.9	69.6	58.7	66.3
11	64.8	61.9	68.6	57.7	65.4
12	63.8	60.9	67.6	56.8	64.4
13	62.8	59.9	66.6	55.8	63.4
14	61.8	58.9	65.6	54.8	62.4
15	60.9	58.0	64.6	53.8	61.4
16	59.9	57.0	63.7	52.9	60.4
17	58.9	56.1	62.7	51.9	59.5
18	58.0	55.1	61.7	51.0	58.5
19	57.0	54.2	60.7	50.1	57.5
20	56.1	53.3	59.8	49.1	56.5
21	55.1	52.3	58.8	48.2	55.6
22	54.2	51.4	57.8	47.3	54.6
23	53.3	50.5	56.9	46.4	53.7
24	52.3	49.6	55.9	45.5	52.7
25	51.4	48.7	54.9	44.6	51.7
26	50.4	47.7	53.9	43.7	50.8
27	49.5	46.8	53.0	42.8	49.8
28	48.5	45.9	52.0	42.0	48.9
29	47.6	44.9	51.0	41.1	47.9
30	46.7	44.0	50.1	40.2	47.0
31	45.7	43.1	49.1	39.3	46.0
32	44.8	42.2	48.1	38.4	45.1
33	43.8	41.2	47.1	37.6	44.2
34	42.9	40.3	46.2	36.7	43.2
35	42.0	39.4	45.2	35.8	42.3
36	41.0	38.4	44.3	35.0	41.4
37	40.1	37.5	43.3	34.1	40.4
38	39.2	36.6	42.3	33.3	39.5
39	38.2	35.7	41.4	32.4	38.6
40	37.3	34.7	40.4	31.6	37.7
41	36.4	33.8	39.5	30.8	36.8
42	35.5	32.9	38.5	30.0	35.9

(continued)

around before making an annuity purchase. Note, too, that in every category the cost to females is higher than the cost to males. This is due to the lower mortality rates among women. The differences in mortality rates for males and females can be seen in Exhibit 15.9. Mortality differences not-withstanding, legislation is pending that would exclude sex as a criterion for annuity rate making.

In addition, just like mutual funds, there are some annual fees you should be aware of. In particular, be prepared to pay insurance fees of 1 percent or more—and that's on top of annual management

Expectation of Life in Years *(continued)*

Age	Total Persons	White Male	White Female	All Other Male	All Other Female
43	34.5	32.0	37.6	29.1	35.0
44	33.6	31.1	36.5	28.3	34.1
45	32.7	30.2	35.7	27.5	33.2
46	31.8	29.3	34.8	26.7	32.3
47	31.0	28.4	33.9	26.0	31.5
48	30.1	27.6	32.9	25.2	30.6
49	29.2	26.7	32.0	24.4	29.8
50	28.3	25.8	31.1	23.7	28.9
51	27.5	25.0	30.2	22.9	28.1
52	26.6	24.2	29.4	22.2	27.3
53	25.8	23.3	28.5	21.5	26.4
54	25.0	22.5	27.6	20.8	25.6
55	24.2	21.7	26.7	20.1	24.9
56	23.4	21.0	25.9	19.4	24.1
57	22.6	20.2	25.0	18.8	23.3
58	21.8	19.5	24.2	18.1	22.6
59	21.1	18.7	23.4	17.5	21.8
60	20.3	18.0	22.6	16.9	21.1
61	19.6	17.3	21.8	16.3	20.4
62	18.8	16.6	21.0	15.7	19.7
63	18.1	15.9	20.2	15.1	19.0
64	17.4	15.3	19.4	14.6	18.3
65	16.7	14.6	18.7	14.0	17.6
66	16.1	14.0	17.9	13.5	17.0
67	15.4	13.3	17.2	13.0	16.3
68	14.7	12.7	16.4	12.4	15.7
69	14.1	12.1	15.7	11.9	15.0
70	13.5	11.6	15.0	11.4	14.4
71	12.9	11.0	14.3	10.9	13.8
72	12.3	10.5	13.6	10.5	13.2
73	11.7	9.9	13.0	10.0	12.6
74	11.1	9.4	12.3	9.6	12.1
75	10.6	9.0	11.7	9.2	11.5
76	10.1	8.5	11.1	8.8	11.0
77	9.5	8.0	10.5	8.3	10.4
78	9.0	7.6	9.9	7.9	9.9
79	8.5	7.2	9.3	7.5	9.4
80	8.1	6.8	8.7	7.2	8.9
81	7.6	6.4	8.2	6.8	8.4
82	7.2	6.0	7.7	6.5	8.0
83	6.7	5.7	7.2	6.2	7.6
84	6.4	5.4	6.8	6.0	7.3
85	6.0	5.1	6.4	5.9	7.0

Source: *The 1989 Information Please Almanac* (New York: Houghton Mifflin, 1985), pp. 795–796.

fees of perhaps 1 to 2 percent, which is paid on variable annuities. That's a total of 2 to 3 percent taken right off the top, year after year. And then there's also a *contract charge* (or maintenance fee) that's deducted annually to cover various contract-related expenses; these fees usually run from about $30 to $60 per year. Obviously, these fees can drag down returns and act to reduce the advantage of tax-deferred income. Finally, as we'll see later, most annuities charge hefty penalties for early withdrawal, meaning in order to get out of a poorly performing annuity, you'll have to forfeit a chunk of your money.

EXHIBIT 15.10

The Comparative Returns of Variable Annuities versus Mutual Funds

Variable annuities are structured and operate very much like mutual funds and, as such, you'd expect their performance to be comparable. Unfortunately, as we see here, that's just not the case.

Type of Variable Annuity or Mutual Fund (as Defined by Common Investment Objectives)	Avg. Annual Return* (Over 5-year Period ending 10/31/91)	
	Variable Annuities	Mutual Funds
Aggressive Growth	10.44%	11.33%
Growth	9.98	11.60
Growth and income	9.93	10.54
Avg. Diversified equity	10.03	11.19
Balanced	8.99	9.36
Corporate bond	7.13	8.16
Government bond — general	7.25	7.80
International bond	11.01	8.76
Avg. fixed-income	6.75	8.20

Note: Average returns include reinvestment of all dividends and capital gains, and are net of all contractual and management fees.

Source: Morningstar's *Variable Annuity Performance Report* (December 1991), and Morningstar's *Mutual Fund Performance Report* (December 1991).

THE INVESTMENT AND INCOME PROPERTIES OF ANNUITIES

One of the major attributes of most types of annuities is that they are a source of income that cannot be outlived. While individuals might create a similar arrangement by simply living off the interest or dividends from their investments, they would find it difficult to engage in the systematic liquidation of their principal in a manner that would be timed to closely (or exactly) coincide with their death. Also viewed very positively is the fact that the income earned in an annuity is allowed to accumulate tax-free; thus, it provides a form of *tax-sheltered investment*! Actually, the income from an annuity is *tax-deferred*, meaning that taxes on the earnings will have to be paid when the annuity is liquidated.

While shelter from taxes is an attractive investment attribute, there is a hitch! You may be faced with a big tax penalty if you close out or withdraw money from an annuity before it's time. Specifically, the IRS treats annuity withdrawals like withdrawals from an individual retirement account, meaning that except in cases of serious illness, *anybody who takes money out before reaching 59½ will incur a 10 percent tax penalty*. Thus, if you're under 59½

and in the 28 percent tax bracket, you'll end up paying a 38 percent tax rate on any funds withdrawn from an annuity. (The IRS views withdrawals *entirely as taxable income* until the account balance falls to the amount of original paid-in principal—after which any further withdrawals would be tax-free.) Short of some type of serious illness, about the only way to tap your account penalty-free before you're 59½ is to *annuitize*. Unfortunately, the annuity payments must be spread out over your estimated remaining life span, which means the size of each monthly payment could end up being pretty small. Because of this threat of a tax penalty, the purchase of an annuity should always be considered as a type of long-term investment. Assume it's a part of your retirement program (that's the way the IRS looks at it) and that you're getting in for the long haul, because it's not that easy to get out before you turn 59½.

From an investment perspective, the returns generated from an annuity can, in some cases, prove to be a bit disappointing. For instance, as we discussed above, the returns on *variable annuities* are tied to returns in the money and capital markets, but even so, they are still no better than what you can get from other investment vehicles—and, as you can see in

Exhibit 15.10, more often than not, they're substantially less. Indeed, there was only one category (international bonds) in which variable annuities outperformed mutual funds; in all other categories, the mutual funds provided better—and in some cases far better—five-year returns than comparable annuities. And the differential returns aren't due to tax features, since in both cases returns were measured on a before-tax basis. But the fact is the returns from annuities are tax-sheltered so that makes those lower returns look a lot more attractive. Even so, if you're considering a variable annuity, go over it much the same way you would a traditional mutual fund: Look for superior past performance, proven management talents, moderate expenses, and the availability of attractive investment alternatives that you can switch in and out of.

As far as *fixed-rate annuities* are concerned, while many of them advertise high rates of return, a close look at the fine print reveals that such rates are guaranteed only for the first one to five years, after which time they drop to something closer to money market yields—or less. True, there are minimum guaranteed rates that the annuities have to stand behind, but these are usually so low that they're really not much help. Investors generally have little choice but to accept the going rate or surrender the policy. Surrender can be painful, however, not only because of IRS penalties, but also because of the hefty *surrender fees* that are found on many of these contracts (these fees often amount to 5 to 10 percent of the account balance in the first year and then gradually decline to zero over a seven- to ten-year period).

It's possible to get around a surrender fee if the annuity has a *bailout* clause. Such a provision allows you to withdraw your money, free of any surrender fees, if the rate of return on the annuity falls below a certain level (say, a point or so below the initial rate). But you have to act fairly quickly, since the bailout provision may only exist for a limited period of time. Of course, even if you exercise a bailout provision, you may still have to face a tax penalty for early withdrawal—unless you transfer the funds to another annuity through what is known as a *1035 exchange*.

How Good Is the Insurance Company? One final point, if you're seriously considering buying an annuity, make sure you carefully read the contract and see what the guaranteed rates are, how long the initial rate applies, and if a bailout provision exists. Just as important, since *the annuity is only as good as the insurance company that stands behind it*, check to see how the company is rated by Best, Standard & Poor's, and/or Moody's. As we saw in Chapter 9, the life insurance industry has gone through some rough times lately and, like banks and S&Ls, has been hard hit by problems in the real estate and junk bond markets. Fortunately, the insurance industry's problems have not been as severe as those encountered by banks and S&Ls; but even so, it has caused strain and dozens of insurance companies have gone under, jeopardizing more than 500,000 annuity holders. It's more important now than ever to make sure that the insurance company itself is financially sound before buying one of its annuity products. After all, there is no FDIC or some other federal agency to step in and pick up the pieces. Recall in Chapter 9, we provided a list of some of the stronger life insurance companies; *that same list can be used to check out the issuer of a fixed or variable annuity*. You can also do the checking yourself by referring to Best's, Standard & Poor's, or Moody's. These independent rating agencies provide quality ratings (on hundreds of insurance companies) that are much like those found in the bond market and are meant to reflect the financial strength of the firm. Letter grades are assigned on the principle that the stronger the company, the lower the risk of loss—accordingly, if security is important to you, stick with insurers that carry one of the top ratings (A++ or A+ for Best; AAA or AA for S&P; and Aaa or Aa for Moody's); see Chapter 9 for more discussion on these insurance ratings and how they work.

Since an annuity is only as good as the insurance company that stands behind it, you should check the company's financial rating before buying an annuity. *Fact:* Because it's a life insurance company that guarantees the payout of the policy during the period of distribution, it's a good idea to see how the company's financial strength is rated by Best's, Standard & Poor's, and/or Moody's—and if you're looking for maximum protection, stick with companies that carry one of the top two ratings.

SUMMARY

- Retirement planning plays a vital role in the personal financial planning process. It employs many of the same basic principles and concepts of effective financial planning, including the establishment of financial goals and strategies, the use of savings and investment plans, and the use of certain insurance products, like annuities.

- Rather than address retirement planning in a series of short-run (three- to five-year) plans, the long-term approach goes 20 to 30 years into the future to determine how much saving and investing you must do today to achieve the retirement goals you've set for tomorrow. To implement a long-term retirement plan, certain steps should be followed, including determining future retirement needs, estimating retirement income from known sources (like social security and company pension plans), and deciding on how much to save and invest each year in order to build up a desired nest egg.

- Social security is the basic foundation of the retirement programs of most families; except for a few exempt classes (of mostly government employees), almost all gainfully employed workers are covered by social security. Upon retirement, covered workers are entitled to certain monthly benefits, as determined mainly by the employee's earning history and age at retirement.

- Employer-sponsored pension and retirement plans provide another—and often vital—source of retirement income. Such plans can often spell the difference between enjoying a comfortable standard of living in retirement or a bare subsistence. In addition to *basic* retirement programs, in which all employees participate after a certain period of employment, there are also several forms of *supplemental* employer-sponsored programs, including profit-sharing plans, thrift and savings plans, and perhaps the most popular of all, salary reduction plans (the so-called 401(k) plans).

- In addition to company-sponsored retirement programs, individuals can also set up their own self-directed tax-sheltered retirement plans; it is through such plans that most individuals can build up the nest egg they will need to meet the retirement objectives they have set for themselves. The two basic types of self-directed retirement programs are Keogh plans, which are for self-employed individuals, and IRAs, which can be set up by any salary or wage earner.

- Annuities are also an important source of income to retired people; basically, an annuity is an investment vehicle that provides for the systematic *liquidation (payout)* of all invested capital, and earnings, over an extended period of time. A wide variety of annuities exists, including single-payment and installment-premium, fixed and variable, immediate and deferred.

QUESTIONS AND PROBLEMS

1. Discuss the relationship of retirement planning to financial planning; does investment and/or tax planning have a role in retirement planning? Identify and briefly discuss each of the steps in the retirement planning process.

2. Identify and briefly discuss the three biggest mistakes that people tend to make when setting up retirement programs. Which of these three do you think is most important? Explain. What role does compound interest play in all this?

3. Al and Linda Chung would like to retire while they are still relatively young—in about 20 years. Both have promising careers, and both make good money. As a result, they are willing to put aside whatever is necessary to achieve a comfortable lifestyle in retirement. Their current level of household expenditures (excluding savings) is around $60,000 a year, and they expect to spend even more in retirement; they think they'll need about 125 percent of that amount (note: 125 percent equals a multiplier factor of 1.25). They estimate that their social security benefits will amount to $15,000 a year in today's dollars and they they will receive another $25,000 annually from their company

pension plans. They feel that future inflation will amount to about 3 percent a year; in addition, they think they will be able to earn about 12 percent on their investments prior to retirement and about 8 percent afterward. Use a worksheet like the one in Exhibit 15.2 to find out how big their investment nest egg will have to be and how much they will have to save annually in order to accumulate such an amount within the next 20 years.

4. What benefits are provided under the Social Security Act? Describe the basic operations of the social security system.

5. Many critics of the social security program feel that participants are getting a substandard investment return on their money. Discuss why you agree or disagree with this point of view.

6. Are all employed and self-employed persons covered under the social security program? Explain.

7. Discuss the old-age and survivor's benefits provided to retirees and their dependents under the social security program.

8. Use Exhibit 15.6 to determine the amount of social security retirement benefits that Elwood Cheeseater would receive annually if he had a high level of career earnings, is age 62, and has a dependent wife. If Elwood also receives another $47,500 a year from a company pension and some tax-exempt bonds that he holds, will he be liable for any tax on his social security income? Explain.

9. Does social security coverage relieve you of the need to do some retirement planning on your own? Explain. What is a *Personal Earnings and Benefit Estimate Statement*, and how would such a statement help you in your retirement planning?

10. Which basic features of employer-sponsored pension plans should you be familiar with? Explain.

11. Discuss the distinguishing features of (a) funded, (b) qualified, (c) defined benefit, and (d) contributory pension plans. Under which procedure will you become *fully vested* the quickest — cliff or graded vesting? Explain.

12. What is the difference between a profit-sharing plan and a salary reduction, or 401(k), plan? Are these basic or supplemental plans?

13. What is a guaranteed investment contract and who are the primary issuers of these things? Briefly describe the investment features of a GIC. Where and how does a GIC obtain its guarantee?

14. Why is it important to evaluate the pension plan(s) offered by your employer? What do you stand to gain by becoming familiar with your employer's pension plan provisions and retirement benefits? Identify and briefly discuss at least six different plan provisions that you feel would be important in such an evaluation.

15. Briefly describe the tax provisions of 401(k) plans and IRAs. Would you describe these plans as tax-deferred or tax-free programs? Explain.

16. Describe and differentiate between Keogh plans and individual retirement accounts (IRAs).

17. Describe ERISA, and discuss its influence on pension plans. What does PBGC stand for, and what function does this organization serve?

18. What is an annuity? Briefly explain how an annuity works, and also how it differs from a life insurance policy?

19. Differentiate between a single-premium annuity and an installment-premium annuity.

20. Briefly explain the four procedures that are most widely used in the distribution of annuity proceeds. Which one results in the highest monthly payment?

21. Describe and differentiate among (a) an immediate annuity, (b) a deferred annuity, (c) a straight life annuity, and (d) a refund annuity.

22. What is a fixed-rate annuity, and how does it differ from a variable annuity? Does the type of contract (whether it's fixed or variable) have any bearing on the amount of money you'll receive at the time of distribution? Explain. Which type of contract would probably be most suitable for someone who wants a minimum amount of risk exposure? What's the purpose of a *bailout provision* in a fixed-rate annuity?

23. Explain how the purchase of a variable annuity is much like an investment in a mutual fund. Do you, as a buyer, have any control over the amount of investment risk to which you're exposed in a variable annuity contract? Explain.

24. How do variable annuity returns compare to

mutual fund returns? Can you offer any logical reasons as to why there would be any difference in comparable returns? Explain.

25. Briefly explain why annuities are a type of tax-sheltered investment. Is there anything you have to give up in order to obtain this tax-favored treatment (*Hint:* age 59½)?

a. Why is it important to check the financial ratings of an insurance company when buying an annuity?

b. Why is it important to look at past performance when considering the purchase of a variable annuity?

CONTEMPORARY CASE APPLICATIONS

15.1 Comparing Pension Plan Features: Which Plan Is Best?

Mary Carpenter and Ellen Shoemaker are neighbors in Kansas City. Mary works as a systems engineer for United Foods Corporation, Topeka Foods Division, while Ellen works as an executive assistant for U.S. Steel and Castings. Both are married, have two children, and are well paid. Before Mary and Ellen joined their respective companies, there had been some employee unrest and strikes. To counteract these problems, their firms had developed job enrichment and employee motivation programs. Of particular interest are the portions of these programs that deal with pensions and retirement.

Topeka Foods has a contributory plan under which 5 percent of the employees' annual wages is deducted to meet the cost of the benefits. An amount equal to the employee contribution is also contributed by the company. The plan uses a seven-year graded vesting procedure; it has a normal retirement age of 60 for all employees and the benefits at retirement are paid according to a defined contribution plan.

Although U.S. Steel and Castings has a minimum retirement age of 60, it provides for an extension period of five to six years before compulsory retirement. Employees (full-time, hourly, or salaried) also must meet participation requirements. Further, in contrast to the Topeka plan, the U.S. Steel and Castings program has a noncontributory feature. Annual retirement benefits are computed according to the following formula: 1 percent of the employee's final annual salary for each year of service with the company is paid upon retirement. The plan vests immediately.

Questions

1. Discuss the basic features of the retirement plans offered by Topeka Foods and U.S. Steel and Castings.
2. Which plan do you think is more desirable considering the basic features, retirement age, and benefit computations explained?
3. Explain how you would use each of these plans in developing your own retirement program.
4. What role, if any, could the purchase of annuities play in these retirement programs? Discuss the pros and cons of using annuities as a part of retirement planning.

15.2 Evaluating Tanya Birch's Retirement Prospects

Tanya Birch is 57 years old and has been widowed for 13 years. Never remarried, she has worked full-time since her husband died — in addition to raising her two children, the youngest of which is now finishing college. Forced back to work in her 40s, her first job was in a fast-food restaurant. Eventually, she upgraded her skills sufficiently to obtain a supervisory position in the personnel department of a major corporation, where she is now earning $48,000 a year.

While her financial focus for the past 13 years has, by necessity, been on meeting living expenses and getting her kids through college, she feels she can now turn her attention to her retirement needs. Actually, Tanya hasn't done too bad in that area either. Due to some shrewd investing of the proceeds from her husband's life insurance policy, Tanya has accumulated the following investment assets:

Money market securities,
    stocks, and bonds $48,600
IRA and 401(k) plans $33,500

Other than the mortgage on her condo, the only other debt she has is $7,000 in college loans.

Tanya would like to retire in eight years, and recently hired a financial planner to help her come up with an effective retirement program. He has estimated that in order for her to live comfortably in retirement, she'll need about $30,000 a year (in today's dollars) in retirement income.

Questions

1. Use Exhibit 15.6 to estimate the amount of annual income Tanya can expect from social security.
2. After taking into account the income she'll receive from social security and her company-sponsored pension plan, the financial planner has estimated that Tanya's investment assets will have to provide her with about $12,000 a year in order for her to meet the balance of her retirement income needs. Assuming a 6 percent *after-tax* return on her investments, how big of a nest egg will she need to earn that kind of income?
3. Given she can invest the money market securities, stocks, and bonds (the $48,600) at 5 percent after-taxes, and the amount she's presently accumulated in her tax-sheltered IRA and 401(k)—the $33,500—at 9 percent, how much will her investment assets be worth in eight years, when she retires?
4. Tanya's employer matches her 401(k) contributions dollar for dollar, up to a maximum of $3,000 a year. If she continues to put $3,000 a year into that program, how much more will she have in eight years, given a 9 percent rate of return?
5. What would you advise Tanya about her ability to retire in eight years, as she hopes to?

FOR MORE INFORMATION

General Information Articles

Fierman, Jaclyn. "How Secure Is Your Nest Egg?" *Fortune*, August 12, 1991, pp. 50–54.

Kirkpatrick, David. "Retirement: Save Until It's Painful." *Fortune*, February 25, 1991, pp. 121–126.

Moreau, Dan. "Getting to Know Your G.I.C." *Changing Times*, May 1991, pp. 37–40.

Saunders, Laura. "The IRA Most Folks Can Do Without." *Forbes*, June 25, 1990, pp. 207–208.

Schultz, Ellen E. "How to Safeguard the Nest Egg in a Company Retirement Fund." *The Wall Street Journal*, August 14, 1991, pp. C1, C11.

Updegrave, Walter L. "Getting Past the Hype of Annuities." *Money*, September 1991, pp. 118–128.

Government Documents & Other Publications

Are You Planning on Living the Rest of Your Life? U.S. Government Print Office; Superintendent of Documents; Washington, DC 20402.

Securing Your Retirement Dollars. American Council of Life Insurance; 1850 K Street, NW; Washington, DC 20006.

Social Security Benefits, 1992. Commerce Clearing House; 4025 W. Peterson Ave.; Chicago, IL 60646.

What You Should Know About Your Pension Plan. Labor-Management Services Administration; Pension & Welfare Benefit Programs; U.S. Department of Labor; 200 Constitution Avenue, NW; Washington, DC 20216.

GETTING A HANDLE ON YOUR FINANCIAL FUTURE

"If I'd known I was gonna live this long I'd have taken better care of myself." Like the lyrics from this country and western song, many of you will not have taken adequate steps to take care of yourself financially in retirement. This is usually due to the fact that there appear to be more pressing needs with which you are currently faced and, as such, there is a natural tendency to focus on short-run financial goals. This results in a delay in the implementation of plans to achieve long-term goals, such as retirement planning.

In establishing your retirement plan you must first set your retirement goals. This would include the number of years until your expected retirement and your anticipated lifestyle. The lifestyle that you wish to lead in retirement will dictate the type and level of your expenditures. You then want to estimate your retirement income from all sources and compare this figure with your anticipated expenditures. If these calculations are performed using current dollars, you need to consider the effects of inflation on the difference between income and

---

If You Are Just Getting Started

The earlier you begin setting aside funds, the easier it will be to achieve your financial goals. However, in many cases, younger people have an aversion to planning for retirement. This could be because of the emphasis on youth, a fear of growing old, or the fact that there are too many current concerns to worry about something that will not happen for possibly another 40 years.

Given that your life expectancy is increasing, you should look forward to living many years after your retirement. The question that you have to ask yourself is "How am I going to fund all of my other financial goals and retirement too?" This requires you to utilize all of the financial planning tools that have been previously discussed in Chapter 3. You need to (1) define your goals, (2) develop financial plans and strategies, (3) implement your plans and strategies, and (4) monitor your performance and make changes when necessary.

Reviewing Employer-Sponsored Retirement Plans:

1. Examine your employee benefits package to determine the type of retirement plan it is, such as defined benefit or defined contribution.

2. You need to know the participation requirements to determine when and if you would be eligible.

3. Determine if it is contributory and if so, how much of your money is going into the plan.

4. You need to know the vesting requirements on the plan. Does the plan provide for a seven-year graded vesting or five-year cliff vesting?

5. Determine at what age you can retire.

6. If you leave prior to retirement, can you get your money out of the plan?

7. If your employer offers a 401(k) plan, determine if it provides a matching contribution.

8. If your employer offers a defined contribution plan where you select the investment option, analyze very carefully the performance of the options over time before you make your selection.

Using Other Retirement Programs:

1. Consider opening an IRA account and making monthly contributions instead of waiting until the last minute to make a lump-sum contribution.

2. Remember that you do not have to put in exactly $2,000 in an IRA. You can put in less.

3. If you are considering the purchase of an annuity, investigate the issuer. The annuity's promise to pay is only as good as the financial capability of the issuer.

4. Look at the investment performance of different variable annuities before making a selection.

5. If you are self-employed, consider opening a Keogh plan to provide for a tax-deferred retirement vehicle that would allow you to contribute up to $30,000 a year subject to a limitation of 20 percent of earnings.

6. As an alternative to the Keogh, consider a SEP-IRA, which also allows contributions of up to $30,000 but limited to 15 percent of earnings.

expenditures as shown in Exhibit 15.1. Once these factors are determined, you need to calculate how much money you will need to put aside to achieve this goal and develop an investment plan to assist you in the implementation of your retirement program.

There are a number of different sources of retirement income that may be available to you. Almost all of you will be eligible for social security benefits upon retirement. The amount of the benefit is based upon the length of your working life and the level of your earnings. It does provide very extensive family coverage in the event of your early death or disability but should not be counted on to provide for all of your retirement needs.

Additional sources of retirement income will come from employer-sponsored pension plans, self-directed retirement plans, individual retirement accounts (IRAs), and personal savings and investments. Many of these offer significant tax advantages that should be taken into consideration when establishing your retirement program. To be successful in achieving your retirement goals, remember to start working toward this as soon as possible. With a little bit of luck you may find that you can retire earlier than anticipated and enjoy the fruits of your labor.

If You Are Thirtysomething

You will probably change jobs a number of times during your working life. As such, you may find that your retirement planning will become more complicated. Even if you are vested in your pension plan, most of them are not portable. This means that you would normally have an option to leave the funds with your former employer or take out a lump-sum that would be taxable if you did not roll it over into an IRA. In some cases your new employer will allow you to place the funds in the new plan.

The worst possible situation, however, is when you change jobs so frequently that you never become vested in any retirement plan. This would mean that you would have to take it upon yourself to provide for your retirement and unless you are self-employed, the only tax-deferred retirement options available to you are IRAs and annuities.

Regardless of how you provide funds for your retirement, in most cases you will be faced with making decisions as to how the funds are to be paid in retirement. If you are married, you would have to choose some type of survivor benefit from your employer's plan. On your private plans this is not a requirement.

Evaluating the Impact of Job Changes:

1. When you are young, the decision to change jobs is not usually based on pension benefits but on the salary and opportunity for advancement.

2. Assuming that a change in job will not alter your anticipated retirement date or your expenditures in retirement, you need to estimate the impact of the change on the portion of your retirement income coming from your employer's pension plan. If there is to be a shortfall, you need to increase your personal savings and investment to meet this need.

3. Be sure if you change jobs late in your career that you will be able to work long enough to be vested in the plan. If not, try to negotiate a higher salary or a deferred compensation agreement where payments would be made after retirement.

4. Explore the possibilities with your employer of earning income after retirement in the form of a consulting contract, if you would otherwise not be eligible for retirement benefits.

Selecting Retirement Options and Beneficiaries:

1. If you are single at retirement with no heirs, you would probably choose the straight life payment option that will provide the greatest payment during your life but cease at your death.

2. If you are single and have heirs, you might choose the guaranteed payout option that provides some minimum payout in the event that you died soon after beginning to receive retirement or annuity benefits.

3. If you are married and your spouse also has a retirement benefit you would want to determine how much additional income each would need upon the death of the other and choose the payment option that would maximize current income while providing for the other at the death of one of the spouses.

4. If you do not need all of the retirement income from your various sources at the time of retirement, postpone receiving those funds that have survivorship options such as IRAs and let them increase in value until needed.

1. One of Mark's and Ana's long-term goals is to retire in 35 years when Mark is 60. Their current living expenses are approximately $60,000, but they feel they would be able to live during retirement on about 80 percent of their current living expenses. While future income is difficult to estimate, Mark and Ana expect to receive approximately $1,800 a month from social security and about $850 a month from Mark's company pension plan. The company Ana is employed by does not offer a corporate pension plan. Calculate Mark's and Ana's retirement income and investment needs assuming an average rate of inflation of 5 percent, an 8 percent return on investments after retirement, and an 11 percent rate return on investments prior to retirement.

2. Mark and Ana are uncertain about their ability to invest so much a year for retirement out of their current budget. Calculate their retirement income and investment needs if they decided to retire in 40, rather than 35, years. In this case, they would expect to receive $1,900 a month from social security and $900 a month from Mark's pension plan.

3. As part of Mark's and Ana's restated goals (presented at the end of Part One), they indicated that they wanted to each contribute $1,000 a year to their respective 401(k) retirement accounts. After looking at their retirement needs and reviewing the 401(k) arrangements for each of their employers, recommend an investment strategy for their retirement funds. You might also want to consider an IRA versus the 401(k) accounts.

4. Refer to Mark's and Ana's most recent budget. Can they afford your recommendation? If yes, revise their budget, if needed, to reflect any changes in expenditures resulting from this investment strategy.

CHAPTER 16

Preserving Your Estate

Like it or not, no one lives forever! Although this thought may depress you, its reality certainly warrants your attention. For if you do not give some consideration to the ultimate disposal of your accumulated wealth, chances are that only a part of your estate will be left for your heirs and beneficiaries—the rest will go (often unnecessarily) to taxes and various administrative costs. The importance of developing plans and taking action during your lifetime to ensure that your wealth will be accumulated, preserved, and, upon your death, distributed in the desired fashion cannot be underestimated. This process, which is called *estate planning*, requires knowledge of wills, trusts, and taxes. An understanding of these components and their interrelationships should make it possible for you to minimize the estate shrinkage that will occur after your death while still achieving your lifetime personal financial goals. Also, keep in mind that not only wealthy people but also individuals of modest or moderate means need to plan their estates. Estate planning can be defined as a goal-oriented activity that uses tax-minimization tools and techniques to provide the greatest possible financial security for an individual and his or her heirs or beneficiaries.

PRINCIPLES OF ESTATE PLANNING

The overriding objective of estate planning is to ensure the orderly transfer of as much of one's estate as possible to heirs and/or designated beneficiaries. Do you need estate planning? How about your parents? Before reading on, spend a few moments assessing the importance of estate planning by you and by your parents.

Estate planning is one of the key elements of personal financial planning. It is closely related to both insurance and retirement planning. Certainly the most important reason for buying life insurance is to provide for your family in the event of your premature death. Likewise, one of the principal challenges of effective retirement planning is to achieve a comfortable standard of living in retirement while at the same time *preserving* as much of your accumulated wealth as possible. This not only reduces the chances of you (or your spouse) outliving your financial resources but also leaves money for your estate that can be passed on to your heirs and designated beneficiaries. Another aspect of financial planning that is important to estate planning is *taxes*. As with other parts of financial planning, one of the major objectives of estate planning is to eliminate or minimize tax exposure. Doing so, of course, will increase the amount of your estate that ultimately will be passed on to your heirs and beneficiaries.

Estate planning is very goal-oriented. The goals that usually motivate people to engage in estate planning include securing enough capital to meet college education costs and other special needs; ensuring financial security for family members in the event of the death of the head of household; taking care of oneself and one's family during a long-term disability; and providing for a comfortable retirement.

Planning occurs in every estate. Some planning is controlled by the estate owner and/or his or her professional counselors. Other planning—uncontrolled by the estate owner—is done by the federal and state governments. This *uncontrolled planning* occurs when the estate owner forfeits the right to

arrange for the disposition of assets and the minimization of tax and other estate settlement costs. Individuals who wish to plan their estates must systematically uncover problems in a number of important areas and provide solutions for them. Exhibit 16.1 itemizes the major types of problems along with their associated causes or indicators. These problems can be minimized or eliminated by maximizing the after-tax return on personal and business investments while minimizing the forces of estate impairment, such as taxes and administrative costs. Techniques for accomplishing this objective are discussed in later sections.

Estate planning is one of the key elements of personal financial planning.
Fact: One of the principal objectives of financial planning is to be able to efficiently transfer as much accumulated wealth to your heirs and designated beneficiaries as possible—a goal that is made easier through effective estate planning.

WHO NEEDS ESTATE PLANNING?

Estate planning is indicated when there is a need for either "people planning" or "asset planning."

People Planning. *People planning* means anticipating the psychological and financial needs of those people and organizations you love and providing enough income or capital or both to ensure a continuation of their way of life. People planning also means keeping Mother's cameo brooch in the family and out of the pawnshop or preserving the business that Granddad started in the early 1900s. People planning is especially important to those individuals with (1) children who are minors; (2) children who are exceptionally artistic or intellectually gifted; (3) children or other dependents who are emotionally, mentally, or physically handicapped; and (4) spouses who cannot or do not want to handle money, securities, or a business.

Minor children cannot legally handle large sums of money or deal directly with real estate or securities. Custodial accounts, guardianships, or trusts are necessary for providing administration, security, financial advice, and the legal capacity to act on behalf of minors. Few children are exceptionally artistic or intellectually gifted, but those who are often need—

EXHIBIT 16.1

Potential Estate-Planning Problems and Major Causes or Indicators

A number of problems can arise during the settlement of an estate that could have been prevented through careful estate planning. The first step toward prevention of problems is an awareness and understanding of their major causes or indicators.

Problem	Major Cause or Indicator
■ Excessive transfer costs	Taxes and estate administrative expenses higher than necessary.
■ Lack of liquidity	Insufficient cash. Not enough assets that are quickly and inexpensively convertible to cash within a short period of time to meet tax demands and other costs.
■ Improper disposition of assets	Beneficiaries receive the wrong asset or the proper asset in the wrong manner or at the wrong time.
■ Inadequate income at retirement	Capital insufficient or not readily convertible to income-producing status.
■ Inadequate income, if disabled	High medical costs, capital insufficient or not readily convertible to income-producing status, difficulty in reducing living standards.
■ Inadequate income for family at estate owner's death	Any of the above causes.
■ Insufficient capital	Excessive taxes, inflation, improper investment planning.
■ Special problems	A family member with a serious illness or physical or emotional problem, children of a prior marriage, beneficiaries who have extraordinary medical or financial needs, business problems, or opportunities.

or should have—special (and often expensive) schooling, travel opportunities, or equipment. Emotionally, mentally, or physically handicapped children (and other relatives) may need nursing, medical, or psychiatric care. Clearly, outright gifts of money or property to those who cannot care for themselves are foolishly inappropriate. These individuals may need more (or less) than other children. An individual who gives all of his or her children equal shares may not be giving them equitable shares.

How many of us have handled hundreds of thousands of dollars? Think of the burden we place on others when we expect a spouse who cannot—or does not want to—handle such large sums of money or securities to do so with what may be his or her only assets. The bottom line of "people planning" is that one engages in the process for only one reason—because one cares. Sometimes "spend it" is the best planning under the circumstances.

Asset Planning.   From the standpoint of wealth alone, estate planning is essential for anyone—single, widowed, married, or divorced—with an estate

exceeding $600,000. When a closely held business is involved, estate planning is essential in order to stabilize and maximize the asset- and income-producing value, both during the owner's lifetime and at the owner's death or disability. Likewise, estate planning is essential to avoid the special problems that occur when an estate owner holds title to property in more than one state, such as incurring attorneys' fees in each state or being taxed on the same assets by more than one state.

WHY DOES AN ESTATE BREAK UP?

Quite often, when people die, their estates die with them—not because they have done anything wrong but because they have not done *anything*. There are numerous forces that, if unchecked, tend to shrink an estate, reduce the usefulness of its assets, and frustrate the objectives of the person who built it. These include death-related costs, inflation, improper management, lack of liquidity, incorrect use of vehicles of transfer, and disabilities.

EXHIBIT 16.2

Factual Data Required in Estate Planning

The first step in developing an effective estate plan is to gather comprehensive and accurate data
on all aspects of the family. The types of factual data required by professionals are listed below.

Personal data:
Names, addresses, phone numbers, family consultants
Family birthdates, occupations, health problems, support needs
Citizenship, marital status, marital agreements, wills, trusts, custodianships, trust beneficiary, gifts
or inheritances, social security numbers, education, and military service

Property (except life insurance or business):
Classification, title, indebtedness, basis, date and manner of acquisition, value of marketable
securities, and location

Life insurance:
Insured, kind of policies, amounts, insurance company, agents' names and addresses

Health insurance:
Medical expense insurance: insurance company, policy benefits
Disability income

Business interest:
Name, address, ownership
Valuation factors: desired survivorship control; name, address, and phone number of business
attorney and accountant

Employee benefits

Family income:
Income of client, spouse, dependent children, income tax information

Family finances:
Budget information, investment preferences
Ranking of economic objectives, capital needs, other objectives

Income and capital needs:
Retirement: Age, required amount, potential sources
Disability: Required amount, sources
Death: Expected sources of income

Liabilities:
Classification of liabilities, creditors, amounts, whether insured or secured

Factors affecting plan:
Gift propensity, charitable inclinations, emotional maturity of children, basic desires for estate
distribution

Authorization for information:
Life insurance

Receipt for documents:
Personal and business

Observations from interview

Source: Copyright © 1988 by The American College, Bryn Mawr, PA. Adapted from Confidential Personal and Financial Data form, *Advanced Estate Planning Course.* All rights reserved.

Death-Related Costs. Last-illness and funeral expenses are good examples of **first-level death-related costs**. Most people also die with some current bills unpaid and long-term obligations, such as mortgages, business loans, and installment con-tracts, outstanding. Unpaid income taxes as well as property taxes also constitute debts often payable by the deceased's estate. **Second-level death related costs** consist of the fees of attorneys, appraisers, and accountants and probate expenses—so-called administrative costs, federal estate taxes, and state death taxes (some states have both inheritance and estate taxes).

Inflation.   Death-related costs are only the tip of the estate-impairment iceberg. Less obvious but often more damaging is the profound effect of inflation. Failure to continuously reappraise and rearrange an estate plan so as to counter the effects of inflation can impair the ability of assets — liquid, real and personal property, or investments — to provide steady and adequate levels of financial security.

Improper Management.   Business assets, as well as some commercial real estate properties, require continuous attention; often the estate beneficiaries are unable or unwilling to provide this needed care. The failure to note a change in consumer preferences or product or equipment obsolescence may result in a rapid decline in the value of a decedent's business or of various types of assets included within the estate.

Lack of Liquidity.   Insufficient cash to cover death costs and other estate obligations has always been a major factor in estate impairment. Forced sacrifice sales of assets with substantial income-producing power usually result in a disproportionately large loss of assets and family income. Further, such sales — of the choicest parcel of farmland or a business that has been in the family for generations, for instance — often have undesirable psychological effects on the heirs. The outcome can be a devastating financial and emotional blow.

Incorrect Use of Vehicles of Transfer.   It would be grossly negligent to put a high-powered car in the hands of a child. Yet assets are often put into the hands of beneficiaries who are unwilling or unable to handle them. Because of improper usage of vehicles of transfer, property often passes to unintended beneficiaries or to the proper beneficiaries in an improper manner or at an incorrect time. For example, spendthrift spouses or minors may be left large sums of money outright in the form of life insurance, through joint ownership of a savings account, or as the beneficiaries of an employee fringe benefit plan.

Disabilities.   A prolonged and expensive disability of a family wage earner is often called a *living death*. Loss of income due to disability is frequently coupled with a massive financial drain caused by the illness itself. The financial situation is further complicated by inadequate management of currently owned assets. This not only threatens the family's financial security but also diminishes the value of the estate at an incredible speed.

WHAT IS YOUR ESTATE?

Your *estate* is your property — whatever you own. Your **probate estate** consists of the real and personal property that you own in your own name that can be transferred according to the terms of a will at death or under *intestate* laws if you have no valid will. A distinction must be made between the probate estate (a property law concept that essentially encompasses assets passing by will) and the gross estate (a tax law term that may encompass a considerably larger amount of property). Your **gross estate** includes all the property subject to federal estate tax at your death, both probate and nonprobate. Life insurance, jointly held property with rights of survivorship, and property passing under certain employee benefit plans are common examples of

---

first-level death-related costs
Death-related costs that include last-illness and funeral expenses, unpaid debts, and unpaid income and property taxes.

second-level death-related costs
Administrative death-related costs such as attorneys', appraisers', and accountants' fees, probate expenses, federal estate taxes, and state death taxes.

probate estate
The real and personal property owned by a person that can be transferred at death according to the terms of a will or under intestate laws in the absence of a valid will.

gross estate
All property — both probate and nonprobate — subject to federal estate taxes at a person's death.

nonprobate assets that might be subject to federal (and perhaps state) estate taxes.

In addition, you may provide for property that is not probate property and will not be part of your estate for federal estate tax purposes yet will pass to your family and form part of their financial security program. There are two types of such assets. One is *properly arranged* life insurance. For instance, you could give assets to your daughter to allow her to purchase, pay the premiums for, and be the beneficiary of a policy on your life. At your death, the proceeds would not be included as part of your estate. The other type of financial asset that falls into this category is social security. Payments to a surviving spouse and minor children generally are neither probate assets nor subject to any federal (or state) estate taxes. Because of the freedom from administrative costs and taxes, this category of assets provides unique and substantial estate-planning opportunities.

THE ESTATE-PLANNING PROCESS

The estate-planning process consists of a number of important steps. First, comprehensive and accurate data on all aspects of the family must be gathered. Exhibit 16.2 summarizes the types of factual data required by professionals in order to prepare detailed estate plans. Next, the data gathered must be categorized into general problem areas, and estate transfer costs must be estimated. With this information, the estate plan is then formulated and preparations made for its implementation. The objective of estate plans, of course, is to maximize the usefulness of people's assets during their lives and to achieve their personal objectives after their deaths. The final steps in the estate-planning process involve testing and implementing the proposed plan.

Once the plan has been implemented, it is important to keep in mind that it is good only for as long as it fits the needs, desires, and circumstances of the parties involved. As these elements change, the estate plan must also be modified. Marriage or remarriage, divorce, the birth of a child, a change of job or location, and substantial changes in income, health, or living standards are the types of events that indicate a need for a review. Even if none of these occur,

a review of life insurance needs should automatically be scheduled at least once every two years and a full estate audit made at least once every three to five years (or whenever there has been a major change in the federal or state death tax laws). Because of the general complexity of the laws relating to estate transfer, the assistance of estate planners, life insurance professionals, chartered financial consultants (ChFCs), certified financial planners (CFPs), accountants, and attorneys is often necessary in the planning and evaluation process. Due to the individual nature of estate planning, more specific guidelines cannot be included in this chapter.

WILLS

A will is a legal document that specifies the details of how an individual wishes to dispose of his or her estate. Have you prepared a will? Spend a few moments listing reasons why you have or have not yet prepared a will before reading ahead.

A **will** is a written, legally enforceable expression or declaration of a person's wishes concerning the disposition of his or her property upon death. The importance of a valid will can be illustrated by looking at what happens when a person dies without one.

ABSENCE OF A VALID WILL: INTESTACY

Intestacy describes the situation that exists when a person dies without a valid will. State intestacy laws "draw the will the decedent failed to make" to determine the disposition of the probate property of persons who have died intestate. These statutes enumerate certain preferred classes of survivors. Generally, the decedent's spouse is favored, followed by the children and then other descendants. If the spouse and children or other descendants, such as grandchildren or great-grandchildren, survive, they will divide the estate, and other relatives or charitable organizations will receive nothing. If no spouse, children, or other descendants survive, the deceased's parents, brothers, and sisters will receive a share of the estate.

The disposition of a typical intestate estate can be illustrated with a simple example. Assume an individual died without a valid will. That individual's separately owned property would be distributed as shown in Exhibit 16.3 after deduction of debts, taxes, and state family exemptions. If the deceased left no spouse, child, parent, sibling, grandparent, uncle, aunt, or descendant of any of the above, the state normally would take all of the property. Where property goes to the state due to the absence of a will, the property is said to *escheat to the state*. If a person without relatives dies with a valid will, his or her property will probably go to friends or to charity, rather than to the state. Aside from having lost control of the disposition of the property, the person who dies intestate also forfeits the privileges of naming a personal representative to guide the disposition of the estate, naming a guardian for persons and property, and specifying which beneficiaries would bear certain tax burdens. In addition, estate planning and a valid will may minimize the amount of estate shrinkage through probate expense and transfer taxes. The importance of a valid will — regardless of the size of an estate — must not be overlooked in the personal financial planning process.

PREPARATION OF THE WILL

A will allows a person, called a **testator**, to determine the disposition of property at his or her death. A key characteristic of a will is that it can be changed or revoked at any time prior to the testator's (will owner's) death. Upon the death of the testator, it becomes operative and applies to the situation that exists at that time. Will preparation, or drafting, varies with respect to difficulty and cost depending on individual circumstances. In some cases a two-page will costing $150 may be adequate, while in others a complex document costing $1,500 or more may be necessary. A will must not only effectively accomplish the objectives specified for distribution of assets but also take into consideration income, gift, and estate tax laws. Often a knowledge of the corporate, trust, real estate, and securities laws is required

as well. Note that a will, important as it is, is useless and perhaps even dangerous if it does not consider and coordinate assets passing outside its limits.

Information Requirements. A properly prepared will should (1) provide a plan for distributing the testator's assets in accordance with his or her wishes, the beneficiaries' needs, and federal and state dispositive and tax laws; (2) consider the changes in family circumstances that might occur after its execution; and (3) be unambiguous and complete in describing the testator's desires. By following these general guidelines, the testator generally can develop a satisfactory will.

Use of an Attorney. *Will drafting, no matter how modest the size of the estate, should not be attempted by a layperson.* The complexity and interrelationships of tax, property, domestic relations, and other laws make the homemade will a potentially dangerous document. Nowhere is the old adage, "He who has self for attorney has fool for client," more true, and few things may turn out more disastrous in the long run than the do-it-yourself will.

COMMON FEATURES OF THE WILL

Although there is no absolute format that must be followed in will preparation, most wills contain eight distinct parts: (1) introductory clause, (2) direction of payments, (3) dispositive provisions, (4) appointment clause, (5) tax clause, (6) common disaster clause, (7) execution and attestation clause, and (8) witness clause. Generalized examples of

---

will
A written and legally enforceable document that expresses how a person's assets will be distributed upon his or her death.

intestacy
The condition that exists when a person dies without a valid will.

testator
A person whose will directs the disposition of property at his or her death.

EXHIBIT 16.3

Distribution of a Typical Intestate Estate

If an individual dies intestate — without a valid will — the estate will be distributed according to preestablished state statutes or guidelines.

Decedent Dies Leaving	Distribution*	
Spouse and children or their descendants	Spouse receives one-third	Children receive two-thirds divided equally
Spouse and one child or child's descendants	Spouse receives one-half	Child receives one-half
Spouse but no children or their descendants, and decedent's mother or father survives	Spouse receives $10,000 plus one half of balance	Father and mother or surviving parent (if one is already deceased) receive one-half of balance
Spouse but no children or their descendants, and no parent survives	Spouse receives $10,000 plus one-half of balance	Brothers and sisters receive one-half of balance divided equally
Spouse but no children or their descendants, and no parent, brother, sister, niece, nephew, grandparent, uncle, or aunt survives	Spouse receives all	
Child or children but no spouse		Child or children receive all divided equally
No spouse and no children or their descendants, and decedent's mother or father survives		Mother and father receive all
No spouse and no children or their descendants, and no parent of the decedent survives		Brothers and sisters receive all divided equally

*Because intestate laws vary from state to state, the actual distribution of assets may differ from what is shown here.

Source: Courtesy of Stephen R. Leimberg, Esq., Bryn Mawr, PA.

---

each of these clauses are briefly illustrated and described as follows. *These must be tailored to individual needs and circumstances by an attorney familiar with the testator's own statutory requirements.*

The wealthy are the only ones who have to worry about making out wills.
Fantasy: Nothing could be further from the truth! While the wealthy may have more motivation to do so, anyone who is married or has minor children, and has accumulated an estate — no matter how small — should have a will drawn up that sets out how the estate is to be distributed to beneficiaries and designates guardians for the children.

Introductory Clause. An introductory clause, or preamble, would normally take the following form:

> I, John Steven Fabian, of the city of Chicago, state of Illinois, do, hereby make my last will and revoke all wills and codicils made prior to this will.

The declaration of residence that is included here helps to determine the county that will have legal jurisdiction and be considered the testator's domicile for tax purposes. The portion of the clause related to revocation nullifies old and forgotten wills and *codicils* — legally binding modifications of an existing will.

Direction of Payments. The clause related to directing the estate with respect to certain payments of expenses is typically formulated along the following lines:

> I direct payment out of my estate of all just debts and the expenses of my last illness and funeral.

In many states, the rights of creditors are protected by law and such a clause is largely useless.

Dispositive Provisions. Three examples of dispositive clauses follow:

> I give and bequeath to my wife, Sally Warren Fabian, all my jewelry, automobiles, books, and photography equipment, as well as all other articles of personal and household use.
>
> I give to the Chicago Historical Society the sum of $100,000.
>
> All the rest, residue, and remainder of my estate, real and personal, wherever located, I give in equal one-half shares to my children, Charles Elliot and Lara Sue, their heirs and assigns forever.

The first type of clause disposes of personal effects. A testator may make a detailed and specific list of personal property and carefully identify each item, and to whom it is given, as an informal guide to aid the executor in dividing up the property. Such a list generally should not appear in the will itself, because it is likely to change frequently. The second type of clause, called a **pecuniary legacy**, passes money to a specified party. The correct title of a charity should be ascertained by direct and discreet inquiry. Note that the popular name is seldom the correct or full legal name. The third clause describes the distribution of residual assets after specific gifts have been made. The share of a person who dies before the testator will normally pass to the other residual heirs unless provision is made to the contrary.

Appointment Clause. Examples of appointment clauses, which are typically included to appoint executors (the decedent's personal representatives), guardians, and trustees, as well as their successors, follow:

> I hereby nominate, constitute, and appoint as the Executor of this last Will and Testament my beloved wife, Sally Warren Fabian, but if she is unable or unwilling

to serve then I nominate my brother, Winston James Fabian. In the event both persons named herein predecease me, or for any cause shall cease or fail to act, then I nominate, constitute, and appoint as Executor of my said will in the place and stead of said persons named herein, the Northern Trust Bank of Chicago, Illinois.

> If my wife does not survive me, I appoint my brother, Eugene Lawrence Fabian, Guardian of the person and property of my son, Charles Elliot, during his minority.

The first clause is used to appoint executors and alternates, whose responsibility it is to administer the estate of the deceased. The second clause is used to appoint a guardian. In many states, the surviving parent of an unmarried minor child can appoint a guardian of the person and property of the child. Often, the surviving parent is not allowed to become sole guardian of the property of a minor child.

Tax Clause. An example of a tax clause follows:

> I direct that there shall be paid out of my residuary estate (from that portion which does not qualify for the marital deduction) all estate, inheritance, and similar taxes imposed by a government in respect to property includable in my estate for tax purposes, whether the property passes under this will or otherwise.

In the absence of a specified provision in the will, so-called **apportionment statutes** of the testator's state will allocate the burden of taxes among the beneficiaries. The result may be an inappropriate and unintended reduction of certain beneficiaries' shares or adverse estate tax effects.

---

pecuniary legacy
A type of clause in a will that passes money to a designated party.

apportionment statutes
State laws that allocate the burden of taxes among the beneficiaries of a will in the absence of a specific provision for apportionment therein.

Simultaneous Death Clause. A sample of the type of clause often included within the will to give direction in the event of simultaneous death follows:

> If my wife and I shall die under such circumstances that there is not sufficient evidence to determine the order of our deaths, then it shall be presumed that she survived me. My estate shall be administered and distributed in all respects in accordance with such assumption.

The assumption that the spouse survives is used mainly to permit the marital deduction, which offers a tax advantage. Other types of clauses are similarly designed to avoid double probate of the same assets—duplication of administrative and probate costs. Such clauses require that the survivor live for a certain period, such as 30 or 60 days, in order to be a beneficiary under the will.

Execution and Attestation Clause. An example of the execution and attestation clause follows:

> In witness thereof, I have affixed my signature to this, my last will and testament, which consists of five (5) pages, each of which I have initialed, this 15th day of September, 1993.

John Steven Fabian

Every will should be in writing and signed by the testator at its end as a precaution against fraud. Many attorneys suggest that the testator also initial each page after the last line or sign in a corner of each page.

Witness Clause. The final clause, which helps to affirm that the will in question is really that of the deceased, is similar to the following:

> Signed, sealed, and published by John Steven Fabian, the testator, as his last will, in the presence of us, who, at his request, and in the presence of each other, all being present at the same time, have written our names as witnesses.

One must have the minimum number of witnesses required by the state where the will is being executed (signed). Most states require two witnesses; some require three. The law of most states requires witnesses to sign in the presence of one another, after they witness the signing by the testator. Their addresses should be noted on the will. If the testator is unable to sign his or her name for any reason, most states allow the testator to make a mark and to have another person (properly witnessed) sign for him or her.

Living Will and Durable Power of Attorney for Health Care. Another important aspect of estate planning involves determining the medical care you wish to receive, or *not* to receive, if you become terminally ill. Two documents to achieve this are the *living will* and the *durable power of attorney for health care*. The living will states, in very precise terms, the treatments you want and to what degree you wish them continued. It is essential to be as specific as possible so that your wishes are clear; otherwise, a living will might be put aside because it is too vague. For example, you should define what you mean by "terminal illness." Each state has its own form for a living will, and you can usually complete them yourself.

Many experts prefer the durable power of attorney for health care to the living will; some advise having both to reinforce each other. Through the durable power of attorney for health care you choose an individual to make health-care decisions for you if you are unable to do so. Unlike the living will, it applies in any case where you cannot communicate your wishes, not just when you are terminally ill. You can limit the scope of the durable power of attorney and include specific instructions as to the desired level of medical treatment. You should spend some time making these decisions and then review your ideas and philosophy concerning these matters with your family and the person you designate before signing such a document.

REQUIREMENTS OF A VALID WILL

To be valid, a will must be the product of a person with a sound mind; there must have been no *undue influence* (influence that would remove the testator's freedom of choice); the will itself must have been properly executed; and its execution must be free from fraud.

Mental Capacity. In order to be judged mentally competent, testators must have (1) a full and intelligent knowledge of the act in which they are involved, (2) an understanding of the property they possess, (3) a knowledge of the dispositions they want to make of it, and (4) an appreciation of the objects they desire to be the recipients of their bounty. Generally, such capacity is presumed; clear and convincing proof of mental incapacity is required to set aside a will, and the burden of proof is on the contestant.

Due to recent changes in the law, a person no longer has to be mentally competent in order to draw up a valid will.
Fantasy: A person still must be mentally competent in order to draw up (or have drawn up) a legally enforceable will.

Freedom of Choice. A will is considered invalid if it can be shown that the testator was subject to the undue influence of another person at the time the will was made and executed. Threats, misrepresentations, inordinate flattery, or some physical or mental coercion employed to destroy the testator's freedom of choice are all types of undue influence.

Proper Execution. To be considered properly executed, a will must meet the requirements of the state's wills act or its equivalent. It must also be demonstrable that it is in fact the will of the testator. Most states have statutes that spell out (1) who may make a will—generally any person of sound mind, age 18 or older (age 21 in some states); (2) the form and execution a will must have—most states require a will to be in writing and signed by the testator at the logical end, preferably in black ink; and (3) requirements for witnesses. If at all possible, somebody other than a beneficiary should sign as a witness, since in a few states this could result in the disinheritance of that beneficiary. Many states have now provided for a *self-proving* will. For example, in Pennsylvania, if a testator's signing of the will is witnessed by two individuals who sign in the presence of each other and of a notary, those witnesses do not

have to appear at the probate of the will. This saves time, money, and often a great deal of inconvenience to the executor.

CHANGING OR REVOKING THE WILL: CODICILS

A will is inoperative until the testator's death and therefore can be changed at any time as long as the testator has mental capacity. Wills should be revised periodically for many reasons. Modification is generally in order if there is a significant change in the testator's (or the beneficiaries') health or financial circumstances; if births, deaths, marriages, or divorces have altered the operative circumstances; or if substantial changes in the tax law have occurred. An existing will can be either changed or revoked, although in certain states a so-called *right of election* (explained later) exists.

Changing the Will. In order to change an existing will, a **codicil**, which is a simple and convenient legal means of modifying an existing will, is drawn up. It is used when the will needs only minor modifications and is often a single-page document that reaffirms all the existing provisions in the will except the one to be changed. The codicil should be executed in accordance with the same formalities as a will and should be typed, signed, and witnessed in the same manner. Where substantial changes are required, a new will is usually preferable to a codicil. In addition, if a gift in the original will is removed, it may be best to draw a new will and destroy the old even if substantial changes are not required. This may help to avoid offending the omitted beneficiary. Sometimes, however, the prior will should not be destroyed even after the new will has been made and signed. If the new will fails for some reason (because of the testator's mental incapacity, for example), the prior will may qualify. Also, a prior will

---

codicil
A simple and convenient way of legally modifying an existing will without revoking it.

could help to prove a "continuity of testamentary purpose"—in other words, that the latest will (which may have provided a substantial gift to charity) continued an earlier intent and was not an afterthought or the result of an unduly influenced mind.

Revoking the Will.   A will may be revoked either by the testator or automatically by the law. A testator can revoke a will by (1) making a later will that expressly revokes prior wills; (2) making a codicil that expressly revokes all wills earlier than the one being modified; (3) making a later will that is inconsistent with a former will; and (4) physically mutilating, burning, tearing, or defacing the will with the intention of revoking it. The law automatically modifies a will under certain circumstances, which vary from state to state but generally revolve around (1) divorce, (2) marriage, (3) birth or adoption, and (4) murder. In many states, if a testator becomes divorced after making a will, all provisions in the will relating to the spouse become ineffective. If a testator marries after making a will, the spouse receives that portion of the estate that would have been received had the testator died without a valid will—unless the will gives the spouse a larger share. If a testator did not provide for a child born or adopted after the will was made (unless it appears that such lack of provision was intentional), the child receives that share of the estate not passing to the testator's spouse that would have been given to him or her had the deceased not had a will. Finally, almost all states have some type of *slayer's statute* forbidding a person who participates in a willful and unlawful murder from acquiring property as the result of the deed.

Once a will is drawn up, it is relatively simple to make minor changes to it.
Fact: As long as the changes are minor, a simple and convenient way of legally modifying an existing will is a *codicil*, which is a short, legal document that specifies the changes.

Right of Election.   Many states provide still another way to change a will: through the **right of election** the survivor has a right to "take against the will"—to take a specified portion of the probate estate regardless of what the will provides. Most states give this right only to surviving spouses, while at least one state extends a similar right to the testator's children. One state, for example, allows a surviving spouse to take at least that share that would have been allowed had the deceased died without a valid will. This right is generally forfeited by a spouse who deserted the testator.

SAFEGUARDING THE WILL

In most cases, the original of the will should be kept in a safe and accessible place at home, with copies in a safe-deposit box and with the attorney who drafted it. The original will should *not* be placed in the testator's safe-deposit box because the box would be "frozen" upon his or her death, making it difficult to begin estate administration procedures. Although some authorities and many attorneys recommend leaving the original of a will with the attorney who drafted it, this may make it awkward for the executor to choose his or her own attorney, a right that most states give the executor regardless of who drew the will or what the will states about who should be the estate's counsel. Further, it may discourage the estate owner from changing the will or engaging a new attorney even if he or she moves out of the state in which the will is drawn.

Exhibit 16.4 contains an executor's checklist of documents and information that should be kept in a safe-deposit box. If each spouse has a separate safe-deposit box, the couple may want to keep their wills in each other's boxes. Some states provide for *lodging* of the will, a mechanism for filing and safekeeping it in the office of the probate court (also called *orphan's* or *surrogate's court*). In those states, this procedure satisfies the need to safeguard the will.

LETTER OF LAST INSTRUCTIONS

People frequently have thoughts they want to convey and instructions they wish to have carried out that cannot properly be included in their wills. These suggestions or recommendations should be included in a **letter of last instructions** in the form of an informal memorandum separate from the will. (Note: No bequests in this letter of last instructions should be made, since such documents have no legal standing.) Usually it is best to make several copies of the letter and keep one at home and the others in the hands of the estate's executor or attorney to be mailed or delivered to beneficiaries at the appropriate time.

A letter of last instructions might provide directions with respect to (1) location of the will and other documents; (2) funeral and burial instructions (often a will is not opened until after the funeral); (3) suggestions or recommendations as to the continuation, sale, or liquidation of a business (it is easier to freely suggest a course of action in such a letter than it is in a will); (4) personal matters that the testator might prefer not to be made public in the will, such as statements that might sound unkind or inconsiderate but would prove of great value to the executor (for example, comments about a spendthrift spouse or a reckless son); (5) legal and accounting services (executors are free, however, to choose their own counsel—not even testators can bind them in that selection); and (6) an explanation of the actions taken in the will, which may help avoid litigation (for instance, "I left only $1,000 to my son, Ramon, because . . ." or "I made no provisions for my oldest daughter, Melissa, because . . ."); and (7) suggestions on how to divide up the personal property.

Administration of an Estate When people die, they usually own property and owe debts. Often they will have claims (accounts receivable) against other persons. A process of liquidation called a **probate process**, similar to that which occurs when a corporation is dissolved, must take place. In this process, money owed is collected, creditors (including the tax authorities) are satisfied, and what remains is distributed to the appropriate individuals and organizations. A local court generally supervises the probate process through a person designated as an **executor** in the decedent's will, or if the decedent died intestate (without a valid will), through a court-appointed **administrator**.

An executor or administrator, who is sometimes also referred to as the decedent's personal representative, must collect the assets of the decedent, pay debts or provide for the payment of debts that are not currently due, and distribute any remaining assets to the persons entitled to them by will or by the intestate law of the appropriate state. Estate administration is important for many reasons. One is that bank accounts and other contracts could not be collected without such a formal process because there would be no one who legally could bring suit or be entitled to give a release of liability. Another is that title to real estate could not be made marketable because there would be no insurance against the existence of a creditor with claims against the property. Due to the importance of the estate administration process, executors should be selected who are not only familiar with the testator's affairs but also exhibit good administrative skills.

WHAT ABOUT JOINT OWNERSHIP?

Many people take title to property jointly either through a joint tenancy or as tenants by the entirety. These two forms of joint ownership have the following characteristics:

right of election
The right of a surviving spouse to take a specified portion of the probate estate regardless of what the will provides.

letter of last instructions
An informal memorandum separate from the will and containing suggestions or recommendations for carrying out its provisions.

probate process
The court-supervised process of liquidation that occurs when a person dies, consisting of collecting and/or paying the deceased's debts and distributing the remaining assets to the designated individuals and organizations.

executor
The personal representative of an estate designated in the decedent's will.

administrator
The personal representative of the estate appointed by the court if the decedent died intestate or if the decedent had a will but failed to nominate an executor or the nominated executor cannot or will not serve. In the latter case, the court-appointed personal representative of the estate is called an *administrator with will annexed.*

EXHIBIT 16.4

An Executor's Checklist of Items to Keep in a Safe-Deposit Box

This checklist itemizes the various documents and information that the executor may need to effectively carry out the terms of the will. These items should be kept in a safe-deposit box.

EXECUTOR'S CHECKLIST

Name (Testator) _____   Date _____

_____ 1. Birth Certificates
_____ 2. Marriage Certificates (Including Any Prior Marriages)
_____ 3. Your Will (and Spouse's Will) and Trust Agreements
_____ 4. Listing of Life Insurance Policies or Certificates
_____ 5. Your Social Security Numbers
_____ 6. Military Discharge Papers

_____ 7. Bonds, Stocks, and Securities
_____ 8. Real Estate Deeds
_____ 9. Business (Buy-Sell) Agreements
_____ 10. Automobile Titles and Insurance Policies
_____ 11. Property Insurance Policies
_____ 12. Letter of Last Instructions
_____ 13. Additional Documents

List number of all checking and savings accounts including bank addresses and location of safe deposit boxes:

_____   _____   _____

_____   _____   _____

List name, address, and phone number of property and life insurance agent:

_____   _____   _____

_____   _____   _____

List name, address, and phone number of attorney and accountant:

_____   _____   _____

_____   _____   _____

List name, address, and phone number of (current or past) employer. State date when you retired if applicable. Include employee benefits booklets:

_____   _____   _____

_____   _____   _____

List all debts owed to and owed by you:

_____   _____   _____

_____   _____   _____

List the names, addresses, telephone numbers, and birth dates of your children and other beneficiaries (including charitable beneficiaries):

_____   _____   _____

_____   _____   _____

_____   _____   _____

Source: Stephen R. Leimberg, Herbert Levy, Stephen N. Kandell, Morey S. Rosenbloom, and Ralph Gano Miller, *The Tools and Techniques of Estate Planning*, 7th ed. (Cincinnati: National Underwriter Company, 1989). Reprinted by permission of the publisher.

1. The interest of a decedent passes directly to the surviving joint tenant (that is, to the other joint owner) by operation of the law and is free from the claims of the decedent's creditors, heirs, or personal representatives.
2. A **joint tenancy with right of survivorship** may consist of any number of persons regardless of whether they are related by blood or marriage. A **tenancy by the entirety**, on the other hand, can exist only between husband and wife.
3. In the case of joint tenancy, each joint tenant can unilaterally sever the tenancy. This is not the case with a tenancy by the entirety, which can be severed only by mutual agreement or terminated by divorce or conveyance by both spouses to a third party. In some states a tenancy by the entirety can exist only with respect to real property, while others do not recognize such tenancies at all.
4. The co-owners have equal interests.

The advantage of joint tenancy, the more common form of joint ownership, is that it offers a sense of family security, quick and easy transfer to the spouse at death, exemption of jointly owned property from the claims of the deceased's creditors, and avoidance of delays and publicity in the estate-settlement process. The key disadvantage of joint tenancy is that the jointly owned property cannot be controlled by a will and therefore does not permit the first joint owner to die to control the property's disposition and management upon his or her death. Another disadvantage is that higher potential tax costs are often incurred in both the creation and the severance of a joint tenancy. For example, a father who purchases and pays for property and places it in his own and his daughter's name is making a gift to her. Upon the termination of the tenancy, if the daughter receives the entire proceeds (for example, upon the sale of a jointly owned home), the father is making a second gift to her. In both situations, he will have gratuitously transferred an interest to her that she did not have before. Fortunately, since federal gift tax law does not tax most interspousal transfers, the problem will not arise on a federal level between a married couple (although many states do tax such unintentional gifts). Because most people believe the advantage of joint ownership of major assets,

such as a home or automobile, far outweigh the potential disadvantages, it is commonly utilized by married couples.

Tenancy in Common. A third common form of co-ownership is called **tenancy in common**. There is no right of survivorship, and each co-owner can leave his or her share to whomever he or she desires. Thus, the decedent owner's will controls the disposition of the decedent's partial interest in the asset. If the decedent dies without a will, the intestate succession laws of the state where the property is located will determine who inherits the decedent's interest. Tenancy in common interests can be unequal; a property owned by three co-owners could be apportioned such that their respective shares are 50 percent, 30 percent, and 20 percent of the property.

Community Property. Just as tenancy by the entirety is a special form of marital property co-ownership found only in common law states (that is, states that trace their property law to England), community property is a form of marital property co-ownership based on Roman law and found primarily in the southwestern states which had a Spanish or French influence.

---

joint tenancy with right of survivorship
A type of ownership by two or more parties who share equal rights in and control of the property, with the survivor(s) continuing to hold all such rights on the death of one or more of the tenants. Each joint tenant can unilaterally sever the tenancy.

tenancy by the entirety
A form of ownership by husband and wife recognized in certain states in which the rights of the deceased spouse automatically pass to the survivor. Tenancy can be severed only by mutual agreement or divorce.

tenancy in common
A form of joint ownership under which each co-owner is free to dispose of his or her interest without the consent of other tenants. It is part of the owner's estate if held until death and passes by will or by intestate succession to the owner's heirs.

Community property is all property acquired by the effort of either or both spouses during marriage while they are domiciled in a community property state. For example, wages and commissions earned and assets acquired by either spouse while living in a community property state are automatically owned equally by both spouses, even if only one was directly involved in acquiring the additional wealth. Property acquired before marriage or by gift or inheritance can be maintained as the acquiring spouse's separate property.

By agreement, which typically must be in writing to be enforceable, the couple can change community property into separate property, and vice versa. Each spouse can leave his or her half of the community property to whomever he or she chooses. Thus, there is no right of survivorship inherent in this form of ownership.

TRUSTS

A trust is a legal document that facilitates the transfer of property, and/or the income from that property, to another party or parties. Why do you think trusts are frequently employed in the estate planning process? Before reading ahead, spend a few moments speculating as to the potential estate-planning benefits of trusts.

A **trust** is a relationship created when one party, the **grantor** (also called the *settler* or *creator*) transfers property to a second party, the **trustee**, for the benefit of third parties, the **beneficiaries**, who may or may not include the grantor. The property placed in the trust is called *trust principal* or *res* (pronounced "race"). The trustee holds the legal title to the property in the trust and must use the property and any income it produces solely for the benefit of trust beneficiaries. The trust generally is created by a written document. The grantor spells out the substantive provisions (such as how the property in the trust is to be allocated and how income is to be distributed), as well as certain administrative provisions. A trust may be *living* (created during the grantor's life) or *testamentary* (created in a will). It

may be *revocable* or *irrevocable*. Property placed into a revocable trust can be regained and the terms of the trust altered or amended. Property placed into an irrevocable trust cannot be recovered by the grantor during its term. The establishment of trusts is generally for those with substantial means; however, we will briefly describe the features of trusts as they relate to estate planning.

PURPOSES OF TRUSTS

Trusts are designed for any number of reasons. The most common motives are to (1) attain income and estate tax savings and (2) manage and conserve property.

Income and Estate Tax Savings. Under certain circumstances, the burden of paying taxes on the income produced by securities, real estate, and other investments can be shifted from a high-bracket taxpayer to a trust itself or to its beneficiary, both of whom are typically subject to lower income tax rates than the grantor. However, the Tax Reform Act of 1986 severely limits the ability of a person to shift income in this manner. Specifically, with certain types of trusts, the beneficiary must be over 14 years of age; otherwise the income from the trust will be taxed at the same rate as the beneficiary's parents. In addition to possible income tax benefits, impressive *estate tax* savings are also possible, because the appreciation in property placed into such a trust can be entirely removed from the grantor's estate and possibly benefit several generations of family members without incurring adverse federal estate tax consequences.

Management and Conservation of Property. Minors, spendthrifts, and mental incompetents need asset management for obvious reasons. However, busy executives and others who cannot or do not want to take the countless hours necessary to learn to handle large sums of money and other property often utilize trusts to relieve themselves of those burdens. The trustee assumes the responsibility for managing and conserving the property on behalf of the beneficiaries. The use of independent trustees is frequently employed by members of Congress, presidents, and other government officials to avoid potential conflicts of interest regarding investments. These are often called *blind trusts* because the official will not be informed as to the trust's investments during his or her term of office. In some cases, management by the trustee is held in reserve in case a healthy and vigorous individual is unexpectedly incapacitated and becomes unable or unwilling to manage his or her assets.

SELECTING A TRUSTEE

Five qualities are essential in a trustee. He or she must (1) possess sound business knowledge and judgment, (2) have an intimate knowledge of the beneficiary's needs and financial situation, (3) be skilled in investment and trust management, (4) be available to beneficiaries (specifically, this means the trustee should be young enough to survive the trust term), and (5) be able to make decisions impartially. A corporate trustee, such as a trust company or bank that has been authorized to perform trust duties, may seem best able to meet these requirements. A corporate trustee is likely to have investment experience and will not impose the problems created by death, disability, or absence. Unlike a family member, a corporate trustee can be relied on to be impartial and obedient to the directions of the trust instrument. Such objectivity has added value if there are several beneficiaries. On the other hand, a corporate trustee may charge high fees or be overly conservative in investments, impersonal, or lacking in the familiarity with and understanding of family problems and needs. Often a compromise is suggested: the appointment of one (or more) individual(s) and a corporate trustee as cotrustees.

COMMON TYPES AND CHARACTERISTICS OF TRUSTS

Although there are various types of trusts, the most common are the living trust, the testamentary trust, and the irrevocable life insurance trust, each of which is described below. The *Issues in Money Management* box provides additional information on popular trusts and their uses.

Living Trust. A **living** or **inter vivos trust** is one created during the grantor's lifetime. It can be either revocable or irrevocable and can last for a limited period or continue long after the grantor's death.

Revocable living trust. The grantor reserves the right to revoke the trust and regain the trust

property in a **revocable living trust**. For federal income tax purposes, grantors of these trusts are treated as owners of the property in the trust—in other words, just as if they held the property in their own names. Therefore, they are taxed on any income produced by the trust. Three basic advantages of revocable living trusts are often cited. The first is that management continuity and income flow are assured even after the death of the grantor. No probate is necessary, since the trust continues to operate after the death of the grantor just as it did while he or she was alive. A second advantage is that the burdens of investment decisions and management responsibility are assumed by the trustee. A good example of this can be found in the case of individuals who

---

community property
A form of joint ownership wherein all property acquired by the effort of either or both spouses during marriage while they are domiciled in a community property state is automatically owned equally by both spouses.

trust
A legal document that directs the management and eventual transfer of one person's property and/or the income from that property to a trustee for an extended period of time.

grantor
A party (first party) in a trust relationship who transfers property to a second party for the benefit of third parties, who may or may not include the first party.

trustee
An organization or individual hired by the grantor to manage and conserve her or his property for the benefit of the beneficiaries.

beneficiary
An individual who receives benefits—income or property—from a trust or from the estate of a decedent.

living (inter vivos) trust
A trust created during the grantor's lifetime.

revocable living trust
A trust in which the grantor reserves the right to revoke it and regain the trust property.

Using Trusts to Transfer Assets

Trusts can be used to shift assets (and thus appreciation) out of one's estate and still retain some say in how it will be used in the future. The drawback is that trusts can be cumbersome. They must be drawn up by lawyers, be administered by trustees, file and pay income taxes quarterly, etc. Administrative fees can run from 1 percent to 3 percent annually, unless you can get an hourly rate. For these reasons, says Robert Wagman, a financial planning partner with Price Waterhouse, "do a cost-benefit analysis before you set up trusts. Does the peace of mind and control you will get outweigh the aggravations and costs of setting them up and maintaining them?"

Here are eight of the more important trusts.

CREDIT SHELTER TRUST.

An indispensable tool for couples with assets over $600,000, as it allows full use of each partner's $600,000 estate tax exemption. Assets are divided, and upon death of the first spouse, $600,000 of assets goes to a trust that bypasses the second estate. Typically the second spouse receives rights to the income, and in emergencies the principal, from the trust.

QUALIFIED TERMINABLE INTEREST PROPERTY (QTIP) TRUST.

Useful if one spouse fears the financial consequences of a

remarriage by the other. Usually set up in addition to a credit shelter trust, it receives some or all of the assets in the estate over $600,000. The survivor must receive all income from the property until death, at which point the assets go to a third person. Estate tax on trust assets is postponed until the second spouse dies.

MINOR'S SECTION 2503(c) TRUST.

Set up for a minor, often to receive a tax-free $10,000 or $20,000 gift. Disadvantage is that assets must be distributed by the time the child turns 21.

CRUMMEY TRUST.

Useful for those who want to make $10,000 tax-free gifts to

want to control investment decisions and management policy as long as they are alive and healthy but who set up a trust to provide backup help in case they become unable or unwilling to continue managing their assets. A final advantage of the revocable living trust is that its terms and the amount of assets placed into it do not become public knowledge. Unlike the probate process, the public has no right to know the terms or conditions of a revocable living trust. Disadvantages of such trusts include the fees charged by the trustee for management of the property placed into the trust as well as the legal fees charged for drafting the trust instruments.

Irrevocable living trust. Grantors who establish an **irrevocable living trust** relinquish title to the property they place in it as well as the right to revoke or terminate it. Such trusts have all the advan-

tages of revocable trusts as well as the potential for reducing taxes. Disadvantages of such a trust relate to the fees charged by trustees for management of assets placed in it, the gift taxes on assets put into it, the grantor's complete loss of the trust property and any income it may produce, and the grantor's forfeiture of the right to alter the terms of the trust as circumstances change.

Living trusts and pour-over wills. A will can be written so that it "pours over" designated assets into a previously established revocable or irrevocable living trust. The trust may also be named beneficiary of the grantor's insurance policies. The **pour-over will** generally contains a provision passing the estate—after debts, expenses, taxes, and specific bequests—to the specified trust. The pour-over will assures that the property left out of the living trust,

children, but not directly. The money goes to a trust that, unlike a "minor's trust," does not have to be distributed at age 21. A disadvantage is that the beneficiary has a right to withdraw some interest or principal for a limited time (say, 30 days) each year.

LIFE INSURANCE TRUST.

Receives life insurance proceeds in order to keep them out of an estate. Can be extremely useful for providing liquidity. Disadvantage is that the insured must never have owned the policy—or must outlive a gift of the policy to a trust by three years—and the insured lacks power over the policy, such as the right to borrow against it.

REVOCABLE LIVING (OR INTER VIVOS) TRUST.

Trust into which grantor puts some or all of his assets and which he controls while alive. Does not reduce estate or gift taxes but does provide for secrecy (probate is public) and often for orderly transition if the grantor becomes incapacitated before death.

CHARITABLE LEAD (OR INCOME) TRUST.

Pays some or all of its income to a charity for a period of time (either 20 years or less, or someone's lifetime), after which the property is distributed to noncharitable beneficiaries. Immediate income tax deduction

for grantor relates to expected future payout to charity.

CHARITABLE REMAINDER TRUST.

Similar to a charitable lead trust, except that here the income goes to taxable beneficiaries and the principal to a charity when the trust ends. Both types of trust are complex, although the charitable beneficiary will often help you do the paperwork.

Source: Laura Saunders, "The Bad News about Estate Taxes," *Forbes,* June 26, 1989, pp. 239–240.

---

either inadvertently or deliberately, will make its way into the trust (pour over into it). The trust contains provisions as to how those assets (together with insurance proceeds payable to it) will be administered and distributed. Such an arrangement provides for easily coordinated and well-administered management of estate assets.

Testamentary Trust. A trust created by a deceased's will is called a **testamentary trust**. Such a trust comes into existence only after the will is

In order for a living trust to be legally enforceable, it must be irrevocable.

Fantasy: A legally enforceable living trust, which is created and exists during the lifetime of the person(s) setting it up, may be either revocable (giving the grantor the right to revoke the trust) or irrevocable (beyond the reach of the grantor).

---

irrevocable living trust
A trust in which the grantor relinquishes the title to the property placed in it as well as the right to revoke or terminate it during his or her lifetime.

pour-over will
A provision in a will that provides for the passing of the estate—after debts, expenses, taxes, and specific bequests—to the specified trust.

testamentary trust
A trust created in a decedent's will.

probated. No tax savings are realized by the grantor with this type of trust, since there is no divestiture of property until his or her death.

Irrevocable Life Insurance Trusts. A wealthy individual can establish an **irrevocable life insurance trust** where the major asset of the trust is life insurance on the grantor's life. To avoid having the proceeds of the policy included in the grantor's estate, the policy is usually acquired by the independent trustee. The terms of the trust make it possible for the trustee to use the proceeds to pay the grantor's estate taxes and/or to take care of the grantor's spouse or children.

GIFT TAXES

Sometimes, even when you *give money away*, you may end up having to pay taxes on at least part of the gift. Why do you think a tax may be levied on gifts you make? Try to answer this question before reading ahead.

Federal tax law provides for a **gift tax** on certain gifts made during one's lifetime as well as an **estate tax** on "deathtime" gifts. Both lifetime and deathtime gifts are considered cumulatively and are subjected to the integrated progressive tax rate schedule shown in Exhibit 16.5. The tax on gifts is imposed on the right to transfer property and is measured by the value of the property transferred. The *donor* is primarily liable for the tax; a gift tax return must be filed by the donor and is due when his or her income tax return is filed. The graduated table of rates in Exhibit 16.5 is used for *both* gift and estate tax purposes and is known as the **unified rate schedule**. These rates are applied to all taxable gifts after a number of adjustments and computations have been made.

By unifying the gift and estate taxes in 1976 (for gifts and deaths occurring after December 31, 1976),

Congress sought to tax transfers in basically the same manner, whether occurring during the donor's life, partially during the donor's life and the balance at his or her death, or all at death. Thus, ignoring the annual exclusion for the moment, the following situations would produce the same total transfer taxes, that is, gift taxes plus estate taxes:

1. Fred gives his daughter a $2,000,000 taxable gift and dies in poverty several years later. Gift taxes equal $588,000.
2. Mary gives her son a $1,000,000 taxable gift. She dies several years later and leaves him another $1,000,000. The total transfer taxes are $588,000: gift taxes of $153,000 plus estate taxes of $435,000.
3. Frank dies leaving his daughter a $2,000,000 estate. The estate tax equals $588,000.

TRANSFERS SUBJECT TO GIFT TAX

Almost all property can be the subject of a transfer on which the gift tax must be paid. There is no tax on services that one person performs for another, nor is the rent-free use of property a taxable transfer. A tax may be payable on cash gifts, gifts of personal or real property, and both direct and indirect gifts. For example, if a father makes the mortgage payments on his adult son's home, the payment is an indirect gift from father to son. In fact, almost any shifting of financial advantage in which the recipient does not provide consideration in money or money's worth may be considered a gift. Gifts are generally defined with reference to the *consideration* received: in other words, a transfer for less than adequate and full consideration in money or money's worth is viewed as a partial gift. Where some consideration is received by the transferor, the measure of the gift is found by subtracting the consideration received from the value of the property transferred. For example, suppose your father gave you a summer home having a market value of $75,000 in exchange for $10,000. This type of transaction is referred to as a "bargain sale." The $65,000 excess of the value received over the consideration paid would be treated as a gift. Of course, if you gave no consideration for the property, its market value ($75,000) would represent the amount of the gift.

WHEN IS A GIFT MADE?

The question of when a gift is made is important, because it determines (1) when the gift must be reported and the gift tax, if any, paid and (2) the date at which the value of the gift is measured. Usually a gift is considered to be made when the donor relinquishes dominion and control over the property or property interest transferred. For example, if a mother places cash in a bank account held jointly with her son, no gift is made until the son makes a withdrawal. Until that time, the mother can completely recover the entire amount placed in the account. Therefore, when parents place property into a revocable trust for their children, no gift occurs, since they have not relinquished control over the assets placed in it. However, if they later make the trust irrevocable and thereby relinquish their right to revoke the gift, the transfer will be considered a completed gift.

DETERMINING THE AMOUNT OF A TAXABLE GIFT

All that is transferred by an individual is not necessarily subject to a gift tax. Annual exclusions, gift splitting, charitable deductions, and marital deductions are all means of reducing the total amount for tax purposes.

Annual Exclusions. Almost all gifts are subject to the gift tax, but for reasons of administrative convenience, certain transfers, or gift equivalents, are not counted. The gift tax law eliminates from the computation of taxable gifts transfers by a donor of amounts up to $10,000 per calendar year to each of any number of donees. For example, a person could give gifts of $10,000 each to 30 donees for a total of $300,000 without paying any gift tax. Further, the ability to give tax-free gifts of $10,000 per donee regenerates *annually*. This **annual exclusion** is available only for gifts of a present interest in property—gifts that the donee has the immediate and unrestricted right to use, possess, or enjoy upon receipt. If the donee has to wait to use, possess, or enjoy a gift or if his or her use, possession, or legal right to enjoyment is conditioned in any substantive way, it is then a gift of a future interest in property, and, therefore, the donor will not be allowed the $10,000 annual exclusion.

Gift Splitting. **Gift splitting** is permitted in order to equate the tax treatment of married taxpayers domiciled in common-law states with the tax treatment of married taxpayers domiciled in community-property states. When a spouse earns a dollar in a community-property state, such as California or Texas, half of that dollar is deemed to be owned by the other spouse immediately and automatically. If a gift is made of that dollar, each spouse is considered to have given 50 cents. Similarly, in common-law states, such as Colorado, New York, and Pennsylvania, federal law provides that a married donor, with the consent of his or her spouse, can elect to treat gifts as if they were made one-half by each spouse. Because of this gift-splitting option, if a wife transfers $20,000 to her son and the required consent is given by her husband, for tax computation purposes her gift will be viewed as $10,000 and her husband will be considered to have given the other $10,000. Because of the split, the total amount will be entirely

irrevocable life insurance trust
An irrevocable trust, typically established by a wealthy individual, where the major asset in the trust is life insurance on the grantor's life.

gift tax
A tax levied by federal and/or state governments on the value of certain types of gifts made during the giver's lifetime.

estate tax
A tax levied by federal and/or state governments on the value of certain types of gifts (or an estate) made upon the giver's death.

unified rate schedule
A graduated table of rates applied to all taxable gifts after a number of adjustments and computations; used for both federal gift and estate tax purposes.

annual exclusion
An amount up to $10,000 annually to each donee that is eliminated from the computation of a donor's taxable gift transfers.

gift splitting
A method of reducing gift taxes whereby a gift given by one spouse, with the consent of his or her spouse, can be treated as if each had made one-half of it.

EXHIBIT 16.5

Unified Rate Schedule for Federal Gift and Estate Taxes*

The schedule below defines the amount of federal gift and estate taxes that would have to be paid with gifts/estates of different sizes. Actually, estates of $600,000 or less pay no federal tax, although anything over that amount is currently taxed at 37 to 55 percent.

Amount with Respect to Which the Tentative Tax Is to Be Computed	Tentative Tax
Not over $10,000	18% of such amount
Over $10,000 but not over $20,000	$1,800 plus 20% of the excess of such amount over $10,000
Over $20,000 but not over $40,000	$3,800 plus 22% of the excess of such amount over $20,000
Over $40,000 but not over $60,000	$8,200 plus 24% of the excess of such amount over $40,000
Over $60,000 but not over $80,000	$13,000 plus 26% of the excess of such amount over $60,000
Over $80,000 but not over $100,000	$18,200 plus 28% of the excess of such amount over $80,000
Over $100,000 but not over $150,000	$23,800 plus 30% of the excess of such amount over $100,000
Over $150,000 but not over $250,000	$38,800 plus 32% of the excess of such amount over $150,000
Over $250,000 but not over $500,000	$70,800 plus 34% of the excess of such amount over $250,000
Over $500,000 but not over $750,000	$155,800 plus 37% of the excess of such amount over $500,000
Over $750,000 but not over $1,000,000	$248,300 plus 39% of the excess of such amount over $750,000
Over $1,000,000 but not over $1,250,000	$345,800 plus 41% of the excess of such amount over $1,000,000
Over $1,250,000 but not over $1,500,000	$448,300 plus 43% of the excess of such amount over $1,250,000
Over $1,500,000 but not over $2,000,000	$555,800 plus 45% of the excess of such amount over $1,500,000
Over $2,000,000 but not over $2,500,000	$780,800 plus 49% of the excess of such amount over $2,000,000
Over $2,500,000 but not over $3,000,000	$1,025,800 plus 53% of the excess of such amount over $2,500,000
Over $3,000,000	$1,290,800 plus 55% of the excess of such amount over $3,000,000

*In the case of decedents' dying and gifts made in 1993 and later, the following substitution should be made to the above schedule:
Over $2,500,000 $1,025,800 plus 50% of the excess of such amount over $2,500,000
Source: Copyright © 1988 by The American College. Reprinted from *Advanced Estate Planning Course*. All rights reserved.

gift tax–free, since a $10,000 annual exclusion is allowed to each spouse. The wife could give $20,000 to any number of donees and, by splitting the gift with her husband, avoid the tax on the entire gift. This tax reduction technique is available even if one spouse makes all the gifts and the other spouse gives nothing. It is also available to spouses in community-property states who make gifts of their separately-owned property. Gift splitting is allowed, however, only for gifts from married couples to third parties.

Charitable Deductions. There is no limit on the amount that can be given gift–free to a qualified charity (one to which deductible gifts can be made for income tax purposes). Therefore, people could give their entire estates to charity and receive gift tax deductions for the total amount. There would be no federal gift taxes regardless of the type or amount of assets transferred.

Marital Deductions. Federal law permits an unlimited deduction for gift tax purposes for property given by one spouse to another. An individual conceivably could give the entire estate to his or her spouse during their lifetimes without gift tax cost.

REASONS FOR MAKING LIFETIME GIFTS

There are several tax-oriented reasons why estate planners recommend gift giving.

Gift Exclusion. A single individual can give any number of donees up to $10,000 each year entirely gift tax–free. There are no tax costs to either the donee or the donor for making the transfer. If the donor is married and the donor's spouse consents, the gift tax–free limit will be increased to $20,000 even if the entire gift is made from the donor's assets.

Gift Tax Exclusion. Regardless of the size of a gift — and even if it is made less than three years before the donor's death — it typically will not be treated as part of the donor's gross estate. However, the taxable portion of the gift will have an effect on the estate tax return. The taxable portion of lifetime gifts (technically called an *adjusted taxable gift*) pushes up the rate at which the donor's estate will be taxed. Fortunately, to the extent to which cash or other property qualifies for the annual exclusion, it is not taxable and therefore is both gift and estate tax–free in all respects. The estate tax savings from this type of exclusion can be significant.

Appreciation in Value. One of the most important reasons for making a lifetime gift is that the appreciation on the gift from the time it is made will not be included in the donor's estate. For example, suppose Larry gives his son Steve a gift of stock worth $25,000. At the time of Larry's death two years later, the stock is worth $60,000. The amount subject to transfer taxes will be $15,000, the amount of the gift that exceeded the $10,000 annual exclusion at the time the gift was made. However, under certain conditions, the gift may be includable in the donor's estate. For instance, it would be if the donor retained the right to receive all the dividends for life, in which case the entire value of the gift as of the date of the decedent's death would be brought back into the estate.

Payment Limit. Because of the credit that can be used to offset otherwise taxable gifts, gift taxes do not have to be paid on gifts totaling $600,000 or less. Of course, once this credit is taken, it cannot be used to offset the taxes generated by future lifetime (or deathtime) gifts.

Impact of Marital Deduction. Because of the transfer tax marital deduction, it is possible to give a spouse an unlimited amount of money or other property entirely tax-free without reducing the $600,000 total that can be transferred to others tax-free.

ESTATE TAXES AND PLANNING

Estate taxes may be generated when property is transferred at time of death, so one of the goals of effective estate planning is to minimize the amount of estate taxes paid. Are you aware of any strategies frequently used to plan for estate tax minimization? If so, spend a few moments listing them before reading on.

The federal estate tax is levied on the transfer of property at death. The tax is measured by the value of the property that the deceased transfers (or is deemed to transfer) to others. The parenthetical phrase "deemed to transfer" is important, because the estate tax applies not only to transfers that a deceased actually makes at death but also to certain transfers made during the person's lifetime. In other words, to thwart tax-avoidance schemes, the estate tax is imposed on certain lifetime gifts that in essence are the same as dispositions of property made at death.

While most gifts made during one's life are not part of the decedent's gross estate, there are some exceptions. A major exception pertains to life insurance given away within three years of the owner's death. It will be included in the owner's gross estate at the value as of the date of death. Thus, if the former owner is also insured, the gross estate will include the proceeds (paid out amount) of the policy. For example, two and a half years before his death, Max gives his son Eric a $1 million dollar term insurance policy on Max's life. At the time of the gift, Max was in good health and the actual value of the policy was less than the $10,000 annual exclusion amount for gifts. Therefore, no gift tax return had to be filed. Because Max died within three years of gifting the life insurance policy, the $1 million proceeds amount is included in his gross estate for estate tax purposes. Had Max outlived the transfer by more than three years, the proceeds would not have been included in his gross estate.

COMPUTATION OF THE FEDERAL ESTATE TAX

There are five stages to computing federal estate taxes. The first involves determining the *gross estate*, the total of all property in which the decedent had an interest and that is required to be included in the estate. Second, the *adjusted gross estate* is determined by subtracting from the gross estate any allowable funeral and administrative expenses, debts, certain taxes, and losses incurred during administration. Third, the *taxable estate* is calculated by subtracting any allowable marital deduction or charitable deduction from the adjusted gross estate.

The computation of the *estate tax payable before credits* is the fourth stage. After determining the value of the taxable estate, any "adjusted taxable gifts"—which include certain taxable lifetime transfers not included in the deceased's gross estate—are added to the taxable estate. The unified rate schedule—the same one applicable to gift taxes that was shown in Exhibit 16.5—is then applied to determine a *tentative estate tax*. After this tentative tax is found, any gift taxes the decedent paid on certain gifts are subtracted. The result is the *estate tax payable* before reduction by any available credits.

The final stage involves the determination of the *net federal estate tax payable*. Certain credits are allowed against the estate tax payable, which result in a dollar-for-dollar reduction of the tax: (1) unified tax credit, (2) state death tax credit, (3) credit for tax on prior transfers, and (4) credit for foreign death taxes. After reducing the estate tax payable for any eligible credits, the net federal estate tax is payable by the decedent's executor, generally within nine months of the decedent's death. The worksheet in Exhibit 16.6 can be used to estimate federal estate taxes. The exhibit depicts the computations for a hypothetical situation involving the death in 1992 of a widow who left a gross estate of $1,500,000. This worksheet is useful in following the flow of dollars from the gross estate to the net federal estate tax payable. In 1981 the federal estate tax code was liberalized in a number of ways. Most notably, the max-

imum tax rate on estates was dropped over several years from 70 to 55 percent and is slated to drop to 50 percent in 1993. In addition, the law increased the **unified tax credit**, the amount one may bequeath tax free, between 1981 and 1986 from $47,000 to $192,800, which increased the amount that could pass tax-free from $175,000 to $600,000. Using Exhibit 16.5, you can determine the tentative tax on an estate. For a $600,000 taxable estate, no tax is owed because the unified credit for each estate is $192,800. A taxable estate of $700,000 would pay the estate taxes of $37,000.

The worksheet in Exhibit 16.6 factors this unified credit into the calculation of line 9a. The $192,800 value shown on that line, which is the unified tax credit, represents the amount of tax that *would* be due on the first $600,000 of the estate. It thus reduces the amount of federal estate taxes due. The value shown on line 9a will, of course, be the same for all estates: $192,800. Obviously, if line 9a is equal to or greater than line 8, the estate will owe no federal taxes.

There are no federal taxes on estates of up to $600,000.

Fact: Unless there were taxable lifetime gifts, such estates pass to their heirs and/or beneficiaries free from federal estate taxes. Thus, only larger estates are subject to these taxes.

STATE DEATH TAXES

More individuals are subject to state *death taxes* than are liable for federal estate taxes. This is because (1) federal laws permit certain deductions, such as the marital deduction, that many state laws do not and (2) the amount of property exempted from tax under federal law is larger than that exempted by the laws of most states. The four basic types of state death tax are the state inheritance tax, state estate tax, credit estate tax, and the credit pickup estate tax.

Inheritance Tax. An **inheritance tax**, which is the most common type of state death tax, is a tax on the right to receive a decedent's property. Eighteen states have inheritance taxes. The amount of the tax depends on the value of the property received and

EXHIBIT 16.6

A Worksheet for Computing Net Federal Estate Taxes Payable

This worksheet is useful in determining net federal estate taxes payable. Note that taxes are payable at the marginal tax rate applicable to the total taxable estate (line 5), which is the amount that exists before the tax-free exemption is factored in.

COMPUTING NET FEDERAL ESTATE TAXES PAYABLE

Name __Mary Widow__   Date ____1992____

Line	Computation	Item	Amount	Total Amount
1		Gross estate		$1,500,000
	Subtract sum of:	(a) Funeral expenses	$ 5,000	
		(b) Administrative expenses	30,000	
		(c) Debts	20,000	
		(d) Taxes	5,000	
		(e) Losses	–	
2	Result:	Adjusted gross estate		$1,440,000
	Subtract sum of:	(a) Marital deduction	–	
		(b) Charitable deduction	–	
3	Result:	Taxable estate		$1,440,000
4	Add:	Adjusted taxable gifts		0
5	Result:	Tentative tax base		$1,440,000
6	Compute:	Tentative estate tax[a]	$530,000	
7	Subtract:	Gift taxes payable on post-1976 gifts	–	
8	Result:	Estate tax payable before credits		$ 530,000
9	Subtract sum of:	(a) Unified tax credit	$192,800	
		(b) State death tax credit[b]	60,560	
		(c) Credit for tax on prior transfers	–	
		(d) Credit for foreign death taxes	–	$ 253,360
10	Result:	Net federal estate tax payable		$ 276,640

[a]This value was calculated using the unified rate schedule presented in Exhibit 16.5 as follows:
$448,300 + ($1,440,000 – $1,250,000) x .43 = $448,300 + ($190,000) x .43 = $448,300 + $81,700 = $530,000.

[b]Line 9(b) was determined from Exhibit 16.7 in the same fashion as line 6.

Source: Stephen R. Leimberg, Herbert Levy, Stephen N. Kandell, Morey S. Rosenbloom, and Ralph Gano Miller. *The Tools and Techniques of Estate Planning*, 7th ed. (Cincinnati: National Underwriter Company, 1989). Reprinted by permission of the publisher.

the relationship of the beneficiary to the deceased. In most states, beneficiaries are divided into categories. The lowest rates and largest exemptions are allocated to lineal descendants—that is, those beneficiaries most closely related to the deceased. For example, in Pennsylvania, property left to a child of the deceased is taxed at 6 percent, while the same property left to a cousin is subject to a 15 percent rate. Real property left to a spouse is exempt from state death taxes, while the same property transferred to siblings is subject to a 15 percent tax.

unified tax credit

The credit that can be applied against the tentative gift or estate tax; since 1986 the unified credit has been $192,800, which absorbs all of the tentative tax on taxable transfers up to $600,000.

inheritance tax

A state death tax on the right to receive a decedent's property; the amount is based on the value of the property received and the beneficiary's relationship to the deceased.

Estate Tax. A *state estate tax*, like the federal estate tax, is imposed on the deceased's right to transfer property and is measured by the value of the entire property transferred. Some states impose both an inheritance and an estate tax.

Credit Estate Tax. The **credit**, or **gap**, **estate tax** is designed to bridge the gap between the state's inheritance and estate taxes and the maximum state death tax credit allowed against the federal estate tax (see line 9b of the form for computing the net federal estate tax payable in Exhibit 16.6). The credit tax is best illustrated by a simple example. If a deceased's taxable estate for federal estate tax purposes is $700,000, a credit of up to $18,000 against the federal tax is allowed for taxes paid to the state as death taxes. Exhibit 16.7 gives federal estate tax credits for state death taxes, for the determination of this credit. The amount of any state death taxes paid may be subtracted from the federal tax, provided, however, that the maximum to be subtracted does not exceed the maximum shown in the exhibit. If the state's inheritance tax amounts to only $8,000, an additional tax—a $10,000 credit estate tax—is imposed such that the total state death tax is increased to $18,000, the maximum amount of credit allowed by the federal government for state death taxes.

Credit pickup estate tax. About half of the states have no separate inheritance or estate tax but simply collect the amount that is allowed as the state death tax credit against the federal estate tax (line 9b). This is sometimes referred to as the *pickup tax*. Since the state collects only the federal credit amount (see Exhibit 16.7), which in turn reduces dollar for dollar the federal death taxes, this type of estate tax costs the decedent's estate nothing. It simply shifts money from the federal treasury to that of the state.

Other Factors Affecting Amount of State Death Tax. Other factors that affect the amount of state death tax include (1) state exemptions and deductions, (2) multiple state taxation, and (3) tax rates.

Exemptions and deductions. Not all property is subject to taxation. Generally, states exempt property transferred to the United States, to the state itself, and to certain charitable organizations. Most states exempt property passing to a surviving spouse. Some states either totally or partially exempt life insurance proceeds unless payable to or for the benefit of the estate or its creditors. All states allow deductions for administrative costs, debts, funeral and last-illness expenses, and certain property taxes that are unpaid at the deceased's death.

Multiple taxation. Many individuals have summer and winter homes or land and other property in states other than where they live. Although most estates are taxed by only one state, in certain situations an estate or its beneficiaries may be liable for the taxes of more than one state. The right of a state to impose a death tax depends on the type of property involved. The general treatment of the major types of property is as follows:

- *Real estate.* Land and permanent buildings can be taxed only by the state in which the property is located.
- *Tangible personal property.* Cars, boats, and household goods can be taxed only in the state in which they are situated. A boat, for example, is taxed where it is permanently docked. Its registry and location for insurance purposes are examined in order to determine its legal location.
- *Intangible personal property.* Securities such as stocks, bonds, notes, and mortgages may, in the absence of interstate agreements, be taxed by several states. Generally, intangible personal property is taxed only by the state of the deceased's domicile. Unfortunately, if a deceased has residences in more than one state or does not clearly establish his or her state of domicile, two or more states can impose death taxes on the same intangible personal property.

Tax rates. The rates at which transfers or receipts of property are taxed vary widely from state to state. Some states have graduated rates similar to the federal tax, while others, such as Pennsylvania, have flat rates that do not grow with the size of the estate. In fact, because the impact of state death taxes can be so significant, many individuals go "domicile shopping" at retirement to find a state with favorable rates, exemptions, and deductions.

TOOLS AND TECHNIQUES OF ESTATE PLANNING

The federal and state tax laws described in the preceding paragraphs provide both problems and opportunities for the estate planner. Estate shrinkage

EXHIBIT 16.7
Federal Estate Tax Credit for State Death Taxes

Credit is given on federal estate tax returns for state estate taxes paid up to certain maximum amounts as specified in the table below.

Taxable Estate	Maximum Tax Credit
Not over $150,000	8/10ths of 1% of the amount by which the taxable estate exceeds $100,000
Over $150,000 but not over $200,000	$400 plus 1.6% of the excess over $150,000
Over $200,000 but not over $300,000	$1,200 plus 2.4% of the excess over $200,000
Over $300,000 but not over $500,000	$3,600 plus 3.2% of the excess over $300,000
Over $500,000 but not over $700,000	$10,000 plus 4% of the excess over $500,000
Over $700,000 but not over $900,000	$18,000 plus 4.8% of the excess over $700,000
Over $900,000 but not over $1,100,000	$27,600 plus 5.6% of the excess over $900,000
Over $1,100,000 but not over $1,600,000	$38,800 plus 6.4% of the excess over $1,100,000
Over $1,600,000 but not over $2,100,000	$70,800 plus 7.2% of the excess over $1,600,000
Over $2,100,000 but not over $2,600,000	$106,800 plus 8% of the excess over $2,100,000
Over $2,600,000 but not over $3,100,000	$146,800 plus 8.8% of the excess over $2,600,000
Over $3,100,000 but not over $3,600,000	$190,800 plus 9.6% of the excess over $3,100,000
Over $3,600,000 but not over $4,100,000	$238,800 plus 10.4% of the excess over $3,600,000
Over $4,100,000 but not over $5,100,000	$290,800 plus 11.2% of the excess over $4,100,000
Over $5,100,000 but not over $6,100,000	$402,800 plus 12% of the excess over $5,100,000
Over $6,100,000 but not over $7,100,000	$522,800 plus 12.8% of the excess over $6,100,000
Over $7,100,000 but not over $8,100,000	$650,800 plus 13.6% of the excess over $7,100,000
Over $8,100,000 but not over $9,100,000	$786,800 plus 14.4% of the excess over $8,100,000
Over $9,100,000 but not over $10,100,000	$930,800 plus 15.2% of the excess over $9,100,000
Over $10,100,000	$1,082,800 plus 16% of the excess over $10,100,000

Source: Copyright © 1988 by The American College. Reprinted from *Advanced Estate Planning Course.* All rights reserved.

can be minimized and financial security maximized by judicious use of certain tax-oriented arrangements and maneuvers. It is important to recognize that, as pointed out in the accompanying *Smart Money* box, in addition to preparing your estate plan, you should discuss and possibly advise your parents regarding their estate plans. Techniques of estate planning can be summarized by the three *D*'s: divide, defer, and discount.

Dividing. Each time a new tax-paying entity can be created, income taxes will be saved and estate accumulation stimulated. Some of the more popular techniques are:

1. *Giving income-producing property to children, either outright or in trust.* Since each child can receive a specified amount of unearned income each year, some income tax savings may be realized each year even by persons who are not in high tax brackets.

2. *Establishing a corporation.* Incorporation may permit individuals in high tax brackets, such as doctors or other professionals, to save taxes by accumulating income in a manner subject to relatively lower income tax rates.

3. *Properly qualifying for the federal estate tax marital deduction.* This marital deduction allows an individual to pass — estate tax–free — unlimited amounts to a spouse. It helps obtain the full advantage from both spouses' unified credits. Properly qualifying in some estates may mean something less than fully qualifying. In other words, there are circumstances in which

credit (gap) estate tax
A tax designed to bridge the gap between a state's inheritance and estate taxes and the maximum state death tax credit allowed against the federal estate tax.

Smart Money

Discussing Estate Plans with Your Parents

Mark Edinberg, director of the Center for the Study of Aging of the University of Bridgeport in Connecticut, suggests the key steps for handling the inheritance discussion with your parents.

First, you have to determine why you're bringing up the subject, and then tell your parents your reasons once the discussion begins. Ask yourself, are you merely curious, or do you want to make sure they have a will and have done some financial planning? Are you concerned about whether they have enough money to take care of themselves as they get older? Is there time pressure for the discussion, such as an upcoming hospital stay? Finally, are you really thinking of yourself rather than them? Is your main desire to find out how much money you will receive?

Next consider what their response is likely to be. Children

generally know how their parents deal with sensitive topics. Are they likely to react matter-of-factly or emotionally? If the latter, some of the suggestions offered under the heading "Time and Place for Discussions" in this box may help.

Edinberg suggests children have at least a modest understanding of wills and trusts before the discussion begins. They also should know the names and phone numbers of estate attorneys, financial planners, and accountants that they may recommend.

Think about who should be present for the discussion. In addition to all the immediate family, should there be other family, such as spouses of the children? Most experts believe spouses should take part, inasmuch as openness is preferable to secrecy and suspicion. Any inheritance, however,

probably should go directly to the child, not jointly to the child and his or her spouse.

"The reality, unfortunately, is that divorce is very common, even among couples who've been married for years," says James Podell, executive editor of the *American Journal of Family Law* and an attorney in Milwaukee. "Parents should take the possible divorce of children into consideration to avoid costly litigation for their heirs later on."

Next, Edinberg says, timing should be considered. "The discussion may require three one-hour sessions over the course of a month. Since feelings need time and privacy to unfold, don't plan the meetings to coincide with emotionally demanding family events, such as holiday celebrations, weddings, or big parties."

an advisor may properly recommend passing a lower amount of property than the maximum marital deduction amount, that is, an individual's entire estate to the surviving spouse.

Deferring. Progressive tax rates (rates that increase as the income or size of the estate increases) penalize taxpayers whose maximum earnings (or estates) reach high peaks. This hinders the job of gaining and retaining financial security. There are devices, however, that help minimize the total tax

burden by spreading income over more than one tax year or deferring the tax to a later period so that the taxpayer can invest the tax money for a longer period of time. Examples include:

1. Nonqualified deferred-compensation plans for selected individuals in corporate businesses, as well as private contractors.
2. The making of installment sales instead of cash sales so that the taxable gain can be spread over several years.

The outcome should be a "to do" list that might include drawing a new will, amending an old one, or talking to an accountant about tax planning.

"Talking about inheritance and your parent's deaths is very difficult," says Edinberg, author of *Talking With Your Aging Parents*. "But everyone has a bottom line: the core of what you must say so you don't punish yourself later on and, at the same time, don't damage your current relationship with your parents. You might be tempted to say, 'Dad, how can anyone *not* have a will?' But you probably can live with saying, 'Dad, your not having a will bothers me. It could cause a lot of trouble after you're not here to look after things.'"

TIME AND PLACE FOR DISCUSSIONS

Marc Hankin, a lawyer and estate planner in Beverly Hills,

California says a good time to begin this type of discussion is when the grown children do their own wills and estate planning. "Parents can become a lot more comfortable discussing their finances and plans if 'everyone's' doing it," he says. For example, children can include parents in *their* wills and tell parents of their arrangements. Most parents would be touched by this generosity and may feel less reticent about discussing their own financial plans.

Upon a parent's recovery from an illness is another appropriate juncture, Hankin notes, because at that time there is a greater realization of mortality.

Finally, the death of an elderly relative may prompt discussion. Learning of the deceased's planning — or lack of it — can induce the living to act responsibly.

The place where inheritance is discussed can be as important as timing. The parents' home is a good choice, as it is their "turf" and thus gives them a psychological advantage. Some parents, however, may prefer to have the discussion at their attorney's office, with the attorney present to act as umpire or referee should they feel impartial advice is needed.

Another choice might be a lower-stress locale, such as a hotel where the family is spending a vacation. Or even a long-distance car ride might provide the solitude and intimacy needed to encourage discussion.

Source: Adapted from "Talking to Your Parents About . . . Inheritance," by Allen Evans, copyright © 1988 by Sylvia Porter's Personal Finance Magazine Company. Reprinted by permission of the publisher and may not be reproduced without written permission.

3. Private annuities, which are arrangements whereby one person transfers property to another, usually younger family member. This recipient promises in return to pay an annuity to the original owner for as long as he or she lives. The income tax attributable to such an annuity can thereby be spread over a number of years. Furthermore, the property transferred is not part of the transferor's estate.

4. Qualified pension and profit-sharing plans that allow tax deferral on the income and gains from investments.

5. Government Series EE bonds, since their earnings can be treated as taxable income at maturity rather than yearly as earned.

6. Stocks that pay no or low dividends but provide high price appreciation as a result of investing retained earnings in profitable projects.

7. Life insurance policies in which lifetime growth is not taxed and death values are income tax–free. If the insured survives, earnings inherent in policy values become taxable only as received; thus, the tax on any gain can be deferred over a lifetime.

8. Depreciable real estate that yields high write-offs in years when the estate owner is earning high levels of taxable *passive* income.

9. Installment payment of federal estate taxes applicable to a business interest. Payments can be spread over as many as 14 years with only the interest being paid on the unpaid tax during the first 4 years.

Discounting. Even after everything has been done to accumulate an estate and reduce the income and estate tax burdens on it, there may still be a tax payable. But there are two instruments that make it possible to, in effect, pay estate taxes at a discount: flower bonds and a special type of life insurance policy.

Flower bonds, although no longer issued by the federal government, can be acquired by anyone—even the terminally ill—in the secondary market with the assistance of a stockbroker. They are redeemed by the government at par in payment of the federal estate tax; therefore, whenever they can be purchased at a price substantially below their par value, the result is a "discount" in the estate taxes. Such savings are reduced, however, by inclusion of the bond at par in the gross estate of the deceased and by their low (3.5 to 5 percent) yield.

Life insurance, one of the primary tools of estate planners, can be purchased by a person other than the insured or the insured's spouse, or by a trust, for an annual premium of from 3 to 6 percent of the face (death) value of the policy. If proper arrangements are made, the proceeds of such insurance will pass to the decedent's beneficiaries free of income tax, estate tax, inheritance tax, and probate costs. Such proceeds may be used to pay death taxes, debts, and other probate and administrative costs. Life insurance proceeds can also be used to pay family expenses, special needs (such as college costs), mortgage balances, and other major expenditures. What's more, life insurance acts as an attractive form of loan collateral in the case of whole life and endowment policies. As pointed out in Chapters 8 and 9, some lending institutions and other creditors require borrowers to obtain life insurance in an amount sufficient to repay them in the event borrowers die prior to fully repaying their loans.

SUMMARY

- Estate planning involves the accumulation, preservation, and distribution of an estate in a manner that will most effectively achieve an estate owner's personal goals. The four major steps to estate planning are (1) gathering data, (2) identifying possible problems, (3) formulating a plan and preparing for its implementation, and (4) testing and implementing the plan (subject to periodic reviews and revisions, as necessary).

- Important privileges are forfeited when a person dies without a valid will, including the right to decide how property will be distributed at death, and the opportunity to select who will administer the estate and who will bear the burden of estate taxes and administrative expenses. The will should provide a clear and unambiguous expression of the testator's wishes, be flexible enough to encompass possible changes in family circum-

stances, and give proper regard to minimizing federal and state death taxes.

- A will is valid only if properly executed by a person of sound mind. Once drawn up, wills *can be changed* by codicil or *fully revoked* by a later will. The executor, named in the will, is responsible for collecting the decedent's assets, paying his or her debts and taxes, and distributing any remaining assets to the beneficiaries in a prescribed fashion.

- The trust relationship arises when one party, the grantor, transfers property to a second party, the trustee, for the benefit of a third party, the beneficiary. While there are a variety of different types of trusts, each is designed primarily to accomplish one or more of four purposes: to save income and estate taxes, to provide asset management, to avoid probate, and/or to conserve property.

■ Federal estate taxes are essentially a levy on the transfer of assets at death. They are unified (coordinated) with the gift tax — which imposes a graduated tax on the transfer of property during one's lifetime — so that the rates and credits are the same for both. Once federal estate taxes are computed, certain credits are allowed, and the resulting amount is generally payable in full nine months after the decedent's death.

■ The three *D*'s of estate planning — divide, defer, and discount — are found, to one extent or another, in most well-defined estate plans. *Dividing* involves the creation of new tax entities; *deferring* gives an individual the use of money that would otherwise have been paid in taxes; and *discounting* involves paying expenses with "discounted" dollars.

QUESTIONS AND PROBLEMS

1. Discuss the importance and goals of estate planning. Explain why estates often break up. Distinguish between the probate estate and the gross estate.
2. Briefly describe the steps involved in the estate-planning process.
3. What is a will? Why is it important? Describe the consequences of dying intestate.
4. Describe the basic clauses that are normally included as part of a will.
5. Indicate any requirements that exist with respect to who may make a valid will.
6. How can changes in the provisions of a will be made legally? In what two ways can a will be revoked?
7. Indicate what is meant by each of the following: (a) intestacy, (b) codicil, (c) right of election, (d) lodging of the will, and (e) letter of last instructions.
8. What is meant by the probate process? Who is an executor, and what role does the executor play in estate settlement?
9. Define and differentiate between joint tenancy with right of survivorship and tenancy by the entirety. Discuss the advantages and disadvantages of joint ownership. How does tenancy in common differ from joint tenancy? What is community and separate property?
10. Describe the basic trust arrangement, and discuss purposes for which trusts are typically established. What essential qualities should a trustee possess?

11. What is a living (inter vivos) trust? Distinguish between a revocable living trust and an irrevocable living trust.
12. Explain what is meant by each of the following: (a) grantor, (b) trustee, (c) beneficiary, (d) testamentary trust, (e) pour-over will, and (f) irrevocable life insurance trust.
13. Answer and/or describe the following as they relate to federal gift taxes: (a) what is a gift? (b) when is a gift made? (c) annual exclusion, (d) gift splitting, (e) charitable deduction, (f) marital deduction, (g) application of the tax rate, and (h) payment of the gift tax.
14. Discuss the reasons estate planners cite for making lifetime gifts. How and in what ways might gift giving help reduce estate shrinkage?
15. Explain the following as they relate to federal and/or state estate taxes: (a) general nature of the estate tax, (b) computation of the federal estate tax, (c) state inheritance tax, (d) state estate tax, (e) credit estate tax, (f) credit pickup tax, (g) amount of exemptions and deductions, (h) multiple estate taxation, and (i) rates of state estate taxation.
16. The tools and techniques of estate planning can be summarized by the three *D*'s — divide, defer, and discount. Describe and discuss each of the three *D*'s and their associated strategies.

CONTEMPORARY CASE APPLICATIONS

16.1 A Long Overdue Will for Kris

Kris Pappadopolus, a Greek national, migrated to the United States during the early 1950s. A man of many talents and deep foresight, he has during his stay in the United States built a large fleet of ocean-going oil tankers. Now a wealthy man in his 60s, he resides in Palm Springs, Florida, with his second wife, Veronica, age 35. He has two sons, who are both high school seniors. For quite a while, Kris has considered preparing a will in order to ensure that his estate will be aptly distributed if some unforeseen tragedy or natural cause takes his life. A survey of his estate — all legally owned by him — reveals the following:

Ranch in Amarillo, Texas	$ 500,000
Condominium in San Francisco	200,000
House in Palm Springs	600,000
Franchise in ice cream stores	2,500,000
Stock in Seven Seas International	5,000,000
Shares in Fourth National Bank	1,000,000
Corporate bonds	3,000,000
Other asset	200,000
Total assets	$13,000,000

In addition to $1 million for their education and welfare, he would like to leave each of his sons 20 percent of his estate. He wishes to leave 40 percent of the estate for his wife. The rest of the estate is to be divided among relatives, friends, and charitable institutions. He has scheduled an appointment for drafting his will with his attorney and close friend, Leonard Wiseman. Kris would like to appoint Leonard and his cousin, Plato Jones, as coexecutors of his estate. If one of them predeceases Kris, he would like his bank, Fourth National Bank, to act as coexecutor.

Questions

1. Does Kris really need a will? Explain why or why not? What would happen to his estate if he were to die without a will?
2. Explain to Kris the common features that need to be incorporated into a will.
3. Is a living trust an appropriate part of this estate plan? How would a living trust change the nature of Kris's will?
4. What are the options available to Kris if he de-

cides to change or revoke the will at a later date? Is it more difficult to change a living trust?
5. What duties will Leonard Wiseman and Plato Jones have to perform as coexecutors of Kris's estate?

16.2 Estate Taxes on Philip Colburn's Estate

Philip Colburn of Arlington Heights, Delaware, was 65 and in good health in 1985. He and his wife, Delores, who predeceased him, had been married for 35 years. They had an adult son who had been made sole beneficiary of their estate. When Philip retired as chairman of the Vilanto Corporation in 1985, his net worth (estate) was valued at $1 million. The value had increased 20 percent by 1992. Philip died in 1992. Funeral costs amounted to $10,000, and the cost of administering the estate was $50,000. Miscellaneous debts totaled $10,000. These items were the only applicable deductions from his gross estate. Philip left $75,000 of his estate to his alma mater. Four years prior to his death, he had made adjusted taxable gifts (gifts above the annual exclusion which are not included in his gross estate) of $160,000. No gift taxes were paid or payable on any of these gifts. A state death tax credit was also available to the estate. Assume that current estate tax laws permit an unlimited marital deduction when applicable. Using a worksheet like the one in Exhibit 16.6 as a guide to the calculations, answer each of the following questions.

Questions

1. Compute the value of Philip's gross estate at the time of his death.
2. Determine the total deductions.
3. Determine the taxable estate at Philip's death.
4. Calculate (a) the tentative tax base, (b) the tentative estate tax (using Exhibit 16.5), and (c) the estate tax payable before credits.
5. Determine the value of the net federal estate tax payable on Philip's estate.
6. Comment on the estate shrinkage experienced on his estate. What might have been done to reduce this shrinkage? Explain.

FOR MORE INFORMATION

General Information Articles

Davis, Kristen. "Who Will Raise Your Kids If You Can't?" *Kiplinger's Personal Finance Magazine*, June 1992, pp. 77–81.

Dunn, Dan. "First Things First: Your Last Will and Testament." *Business Week*, December 9, 1991, pp. 108–109.

Faltermayer, Edmund. "The (Financially) Perfect Death." *Fortune*, February 25, 1991, pp. 131–136.

Jasen, Georgette. "Estate Planning Can Mean More for Heirs." *The Wall Street Journal*, March 27, 1990, pp. C1, C23.

————"The Tough Task of Selecting an Executor." *The Wall Street Journal*, July 3, 1990, pp. C1, C17.

Kindel, Stephen. "Triumphs of the Will." *Financial World*, June 25, 1991, pp. 104–108.

Roha, Ronaleen. "Living Trusts: Beyond the Hype." *Kiplinger's Personal Financial Magazine*, October 1991, pp. 97–99.

Saunders, Laura. "In Whom We Trust." *Forbes*, June 24, 1991, pp. 200–202.

Government Documents and Other Publications

Clifford, Denis. *Plan Your Estate*. Berkeley, CA: Nolo Press. 1989.

Esperti, Robert A. and Peterson, Renno L. *The Handbook of Estate Planning*. New York: McGraw-Hill, 1991.

Internal Revenue Service. *Federal Estate and Gift Taxes*, Publication 448. Washington, DC: U.S. Government Printing Office.

Leimberg, Stephan R., et al. *The Tools and Techniques of Estate Planning*, 8th ed. Cincinnati, OH: National Underwriter.

Shenkman, Martin M. *Estate Planning Guide*. New York: John Wiley & Sons, 1991.

What You Ought to Know about Living Trusts. Chicago, IL: Commerce Clearing House, Inc., 1992.

G E T T I N G   A   H A N D L E   O N   Y O U R   F I N A N C I A L   F U T U R E

You have worked very hard over your lifetime to accumulate assets to provide the necessary funds to achieve your financial goals. While you were doing this, you probably had thoughts about what would happen to your family if you were to die prematurely. Your concerns about meeting your family's financial needs probably resulted in the purchase of the necessary amounts and types of insurance. However, having an adequate amount of insurance does not necessarily solve the problem, as it only results in the accumulation of assets and does not address the problem of the disposition of those assets. This is where estate planning comes into play.

Estate planning provides the means to accomplish people planning as well as asset planning. People planning enables you to provide the structure to accommodate the special needs of your family members (such as minor children) or others. Asset planning will provide the means to minimize the tax burden associated with estates greater than $600,000 or when property is owned in more than one state.

There are a number of reasons why an estate will be broken up when people die. Among the most important of the reasons is lack of planning. This usually results in higher costs of settling the estate due to improper management, lack of liquidity, or incorrect vehicles for the transfer of assets. Proper estate planning requires (1) gathering comprehensive and accurate data such as that described in Exhibit 16.2, (2) identifying problem areas, (3) formulating and implementing a plan, and (4) periodically reviewing and updating the plan.

Estate planning is one of the most complex areas of personal financial planning, especially for the wealthy or families with children from previous

If You Are Just Starting Out

Regardless of your age or financial condition, unless you want the state to decide how your assets are distributed upon your death, you need to have a valid will. This involves the services of an attorney to draft the will based upon your plan of distribution. The document itself should have an introductory clause to revoke any previous versions and establish your domicile for tax purposes. The major clauses included in most wills would provide direction for payment of outstanding liabilities and disposition of assets. Other clauses commonly found in a will are the appointment, tax, common disaster, execution and attestation, and witness clauses.

The requirements of a valid will are that the testator be mentally competent and be under no undue influence. In addition, the document must be properly executed. It can be in the testator's own handwriting or typed. Once a will is written, don't worry if you change your mind; you can change or revoke it at any time prior to your death.

Things to Consider when Drafting a Will:

1. After you have made a list of all your assets, you must then decide which assets should go to which of your heirs.

2. Decide on a personal representative to ensure proper administration of your estate. This may or may not be a family member, and your decision would probably depend on the complexity of your estate.

3. You should have only one original copy of the will. Photocopies can be kept by your attorney or other advisor.

4. If you have minor children, you need to name a guardian to raise your children in the event of the death of both spouses.

5. If you don't want your life to be sustained by artificial means, you need to consider using a living will and/or a durable power of attorney to specify under what conditions treatment can be made.

6. Consider leaving letters of instruction attached to your will to give your heirs more personal instructions concerning an explanation of assets, location of documents, or burial instructions.

7. Check on your state law concerning the sealing of lock boxes before you place your will in one for safekeeping.

8. Be sure to provide a checklist for the executor such as the one shown in Exhibit 16.4.

9. If you move to another state, you should have a new will written to reflect the laws of your new state and to establish it as your domicile.

10. Remember that if you die without a will (intestate) you have no control over how your assets will be distributed.

marriages (his, hers, and ours). The ability to achieve your financial goals through managing your estate can be accomplished under normal circumstances through the creation of a trusts, the proper titling of property, the creation of a valid will, and the use of gifts. It should allow you to determine the distribution of your property according to your desires. If properly constructed and implemented, an estate plan should preserve assets by reducing taxation and other expenses associated with the settlement of the estate.

In many instances all you might need is a simple will. However, in some cases more involved estate planning is required and you should seek the assistance of an expert in this field. It may seem to be expensive at the time, but it should save your family from frustration and aggravation at the time of your death.

If You Are Thirtysomething

Many of you will find that your estate-planning needs can no longer be met by a simple will due to changes in your marital and family status and increases in your wealth. A periodic review of your personal balance sheet will provide you with a measure of your adjusted gross estate to see if you are in danger of exceeding the current $600,000 limit.

Over the past few years, as the U.S. Congress has searched for ways to enhance revenues, greater restrictions have been placed on the use of popular tax-reduction techniques. You should be aware of these changes and the potential for future changes. Remember what H. L. Mencken said: "No man's life, liberty or property are safe while the legislature is in session."

There are still a number of techniques and tools that can be used to minimize the shrinkage of your estate and maximize the financial security of your heirs. Among them is creating new tax-paying entities to reduce income taxes and increase the estate. Taking advantage of deductions and deferrals to reduce your tax liability will also increase your estate. The last technique would involve paying for estate taxes at a discount using flower bonds and certain insurance arrangements.

Tools and Techniques of Estate Planning:

1. Consider gifting assets with high-growth potential to children so that further increases in value will occur outside of your estate.

2. If you are a highly paid professional, you might want to incorporate to save on current taxes and provide for growth in your estate.

3. Although the marital deduction allows you to transfer to your surviving spouse all of your estate tax-free, this may not be the best thing to do. You might want to establish a marital trust and a family trust to take advantage of both spouses' $600,000 exclusion.

4. To avoid probate costs and the public disclosure of your assets, consider placing them in a living trust.

5. Remember that while assets that are jointly owned may be transferred without a will, they may not be exempted from inclusion in the taxable estate of the deceased.

6. To take advantage of an income tax deduction as well as estate tax savings, the very wealthy sometimes donate property to charity and continue to receive the benefits of the property until the death of the last beneficiary. This is accomplished through the use of a charitable remainder trust.

7. If you are among the very rich and famous, you might want to protect your estate prior to marriage by having a premarital agreement drawn up and signed.

8. If you inherit property that you do not need or cannot use, consider using a disclaimer. This refusal to accept property will result in its distribution to an alternative beneficiary and could result in estate tax savings.

9. If you have a business interest, the estate taxes can be paid over 14 years to reduce the possibility that the business would have to be sold to pay the federal estate tax.

10. To keep life insurance proceeds out of your taxable estate, you must give up any incidence of ownership.

Mark and Ana own their new condo jointly with right of survivorship (community property in community property states). Assume all other property is owned jointly unless stated differently in the original case.

1. Identify and evaluate the assets that would be included in Mark's gross estate. Would this estate be subject to federal estate taxes? If yes, what steps should be taken to reduce estate taxes?
2. Which of Mark's assets would be probate and which would be nonprobate assets?
3. Identify and evaluate the assets that would be included in Ana's gross estate. Would her estate be subject to federal estate taxes? If yes, what steps should be taken to reduce estate taxes?
4. Which of Ana's assets would be probate and which would be nonprobate assets?
5. Given the Williams' estate planning needs, should Mark and Ana have wills written? If yes, what should be included in these wills?

APPENDIX A

Table of Future Value Factors

Instructions: To use this table, find the future value factor that corresponds to both a given time period (year) and an interest rate. To illustrate, if you want the future value factor for 6 years and 10 percent, move across from year 6 and down from 10 percent to the point at which these two rows intersect: 1.772. Other illustrations: For 3 years and 15 percent, the proper future value factor is 1.521; for 30 years and 8 percent, it is 10.062.

Interest Rate

Year	2%	3%	5%	6%	8%	9%	10%	12%	15%	20%	25%	30%
1	1.020	1.030	1.050	1.060	1.080	1.090	1.100	1.120	1.150	1.120	1.250	1.300
2	1.040	1.060	1.102	1.120	1.166	1.190	1.210	1.254	1.322	1.440	1.562	1.690
3	1.061	1.090	1.158	1.190	1.260	1.290	1.331	1.405	1.521	1.728	1.953	2.197
4	1.082	1.130	1.216	1.260	1.360	1.410	1.464	1.574	1.749	2.074	2.441	2.856
5	1.104	1.160	1.276	1.340	1.469	1.540	1.611	1.762	2.011	2.488	3.052	3.713
6	1.126	1.190	1.340	1.420	1.587	1.670	1.772	1.974	2.313	2.986	3.815	4.827
8	1.172	1.260	1.477	1.590	1.851	1.990	2.144	2.476	3.059	4.300	5.960	8.157
10	1.219	1.340	1.629	1.790	2.159	2.360	2.594	3.106	4.046	6.192	9.313	13.786
12	1.268	1.420	1.796	2.010	2.518	2.810	3.138	3.896	5.350	8.916	14.552	23.298
15	1.346	1.560	2.079	2.390	3.172	3.640	4.177	5.474	8.137	15.407	28.422	51.185
20	1.486	1.810	2.653	3.210	4.661	5.600	6.727	9.646	16.366	38.337	86.736	190.047
25	1.641	2.090	3.386	4.290	6.848	8.620	10.834	17.000	32.918	95.395	264.698	705.627
30	1.811	2.420	4.322	5.740	10.062	13.260	17.449	29.960	66.210	237.373	807.793	2619.936
35	2.000	2.810	5.516	7.690	14.785	20.410	28.102	52.799	133.172	590.657	2465.189	9727.598
40	2.208	3.260	7.040	10.280	21.724	31.410	45.258	93.049	267.856	1469.740	7523.156	36117.754

Note: All factors to nearest 1/1000 as shown to agree with Chapters 3 and 5 of text.

APPENDIX B

Table of Annuity Factors

Instructions: To use this table, find the annuity factor that corresponds to both a given time period (year) and an interest rate. To illustrate, if you want the annuity factor for 6 years and 10 percent, move across from year 6 and down from 10 percent to the point at which these two rows intersect: 7.716. Other illustrations: For 3 years and 15 percent, the proper annuity factor is 3.472; for 30 years and 8 percent, it is 113.282.

							Interest Rate					
Year	**2%**	**3%**	**5%**	**6%**	**8%**	**9%**	**10%**	**12%**	**15%**	**20%**	**25%**	**30%**
1	1.000	1.000	1.000	1.000	1.000	1.000	1.000	1.000	1.000	1.000	1.000	1.000
2	2.020	2.030	2.050	2.060	2.080	2.090	2.100	2.120	2.150	2.200	2.250	2.300
3	3.060	3.090	3.152	3.180	3.246	3.270	3.310	3.374	3.472	3.640	3.813	3.990
4	4.122	4.180	4.310	4.380	4.506	4.570	4.641	4.779	7.993	5.368	5.766	6.187
5	5.204	5.310	5.526	5.630	5.867	5.980	6.105	6.353	6.742	7.442	8.207	9.043
6	6.308	6.460	6.802	6.970	7.336	7.520	7.716	8.115	8.754	9.930	11.259	12.756
8	8.583	8.890	9.549	9.890	10.637	11.030	11.436	12.300	13.727	16.499	19.842	23.858
10	10.950	11.460	12.578	13.180	14.487	15.190	15.937	17.549	20.304	25.959	33.253	42.619
12	13.412	14.190	15.917	16.870	18.977	20.140	21.384	24.133	29.001	39.580	54.208	74.326
15	17.293	18.600	21.578	23.270	27.152	29.360	31.772	37.280	47.580	72.035	109.687	167.285
20	24.297	26.870	33.066	36.780	45.762	51.160	57.274	72.052	102.443	186.687	342.945	630.157
25	32.030	36.460	47.726	54.860	73.105	84.700	98.346	133.333	212.790	471.976	1054.791	2348.765
30	40.567	47.570	66.438	79.060	113.282	136.300	164.491	241.330	434.738	1181.865	3227.172	8729.805
35	49.994	60.460	90.318	111.430	172.314	215.700	271.018	431.658	881.152	2948.294	9856.746	32422.090
40	60.401	75.400	120.797	154.760	259.052	337.870	442.580	767.080	1779.048	7343.715	30088.621	120389.375

Note: All factors to nearest 1/1000 as shown to agree with Chapters 3 and 5 of text.

APPENDIX O

Table of Present Value Factors

Instructions: To use this table, find the present value factor that corresponds to both a given time period (year) and an interest rate. To illustrate, if you want the present value factor for 6 years and 10 percent, move across from year 6 and down from 10 percent to the point at which these two rows intersect: .564. Other illustrations: For 3 years and 15 percent, the proper present value is .658; for 30 years and 8 percent, it is .099.

							Interest Rate					
Period	2%	3%	5%	7%	8%	9%	10%	12%	15%	20%	25%	30%
1	.980	.971	.952	.935	.926	.917	.909	.833	.870	.893	.800	.769
2	.961	.943	.907	.873	.857	.842	.826	.797	.756	.694	.640	.592
3	.942	.915	.864	.816	.794	.772	.751	.712	.658	.579	.512	.455
4	.924	.888	.823	.763	.735	.708	.683	.636	.572	.482	.410	.350
5	.906	.863	.784	.713	.681	.650	.621	.567	.497	.402	.328	.269
6	.888	.837	.746	.666	.630	.596	.564	.507	.432	.335	.262	.207
8	.853	.789	.677	.582	.540	.502	.467	.404	.327	.233	.168	.123
10	.820	.744	.614	.508	.463	.422	.386	.322	.247	.162	.107	.073
12	.789	.701	.557	.444	.397	.356	.319	.257	.187	.112	.069	.043
15	.743	.642	.481	.362	.315	.275	.239	.183	.123	.065	.035	.020
20	.673	.554	.377	.258	.215	.178	.149	.104	.061	.026	.012	.005
25	.610	.478	.295	.184	.146	.116	.092	.059	.030	.010	.004	.001
30	.552	.412	.231	.131	.099	.075	.057	.033	.015	.004	.001	.*
35	.500	.355	.181	.094	.068	.049	.036	.019	.008	.002	.*	.*
40	.453	.307	.142	.067	.046	.032	.022	.011	.004	.001	.*	.*

Note: All factors to nearest 1/1000 as shown to agree with Chapters 3 and 5 of text.

APPENDIX D

Table of Present Value of Annuity Factors

Instructions: To use this table, find the present value of an annuity factor that corresponds to both a given time period (year) and an interest rate. To illustrate, if you want the present value factor for 6 years and 10 percent, move across from year 6 and down from 10 percent to the point at which these two rows intersect: 4.355. Other illustrations: For 3 years and 15 percent, the proper present value is 2.283; for 30 years, and 8 percent, it is 11.258.

Interest Rate

Period	2%	3%	5%	7%	8%	9%	10%	12%	15%	20%	25%	30%
1	.980	.971	.952	.935	.926	.917	.909	.893	.870	.833	.800	.769
2	1.942	1.913	1.859	1.808	1.783	1.759	1.736	1.690	1.626	1.528	1.440	1.361
3	2.884	2.829	2.723	2.624	2.577	2.531	2.487	2.402	2.283	2.106	1.952	1.816
4	3.808	3.717	3.546	3.387	3.312	3.240	3.170	3.037	2.855	2.589	2.362	2.166
5	4.713	4.580	4.329	4.100	3.993	3.890	3.791	3.605	3.352	2.991	2.689	2.436
6	5.601	5.417	5.076	4.767	4.623	4.486	4.355	4.111	3.784	3.326	2.951	2.643
8	7.326	7.020	6.463	5.971	5.747	5.535	5.335	4.968	4.487	3.837	3.329	2.925
10	8.983	8.530	7.722	7.024	6.710	6.418	6.145	5.650	5.019	4.192	3.570	3.092
12	10.575	9.954	8.863	7.943	7.536	7.161	6.814	6.194	5.421	4.439	3.725	3.190
15	12.849	11.938	10.380	9.108	8.560	8.061	7.606	6.811	5.847	4.675	3.859	3.268
20	16.352	14.878	12.462	10.594	9.818	9.129	8.514	7.469	6.259	4.870	3.954	3.316
25	19.524	17.413	14.094	11.654	10.675	9.823	9.077	7.843	6.464	4.948	3.985	3.329
30	22.396	19.601	15.373	12.409	11.258	10.274	9.427	8.055	6.566	4.979	3.995	3.332
35	24.999	21.487	16.378	12.948	11.655	10.567	9.844	8.176	6.617	4.992	3.998	3.333
40	27.356	23.115	17.159	13.332	11.925	10.757	9.779	8.244	6.642	4.997	3.999	3.333

Note: All factors to nearest 1/1000 as shown to agree with Chapters 3 and 5 of text.

INDEX

Note: Running glossary terms and page numbers appear in boldfaced type.